P9-CKZ-671

WITHDRAWN

Hillsboro Public Library
Hillsboro, OR
A member of Washington County
COOPERATIVE LIBRARY SERVICES

CompTIA® A+
220-901 and 220-902
Cert Guide

Mark Edward Soper

00 East 96th Street
ndianapolis, Indiana 46240 USA

CompTIA® A+ 220-901 and 220-902 Cert Guide

Copyright © 2017 by Pearson Education, Inc.

All rights reserved. No part of this book shall be reproduced, stored in a retrieval system, or transmitted by any means, electronic, mechanical, photocopying, recording, or otherwise, without written permission from the publisher. No patent liability is assumed with respect to the use of the information contained herein. Although every precaution has been taken in the preparation of this book, the publisher and author assume no responsibility for errors or omissions. Nor is any liability assumed for damages resulting from the use of the information contained herein.

ISBN-13: 978-0-7897-5652-7
ISBN-10: 0-7897-5652-8

33614081574476

Library of Congress Control Number: 2016945195

Printed in the United States of America

2 17

Trademarks

All terms mentioned in this book that are known to be trademarks or service marks have been appropriately capitalized. Pearson IT Certification cannot attest to the accuracy of this information. Use of a term in this book should not be regarded as affecting the validity of any trademark or service mark.

Warning and Disclaimer

Every effort has been made to make this book as complete and as accurate as possible, but no warranty or fitness is implied. The information provided is on an "as is" basis. The author and the publisher shall have neither liability nor responsibility to any person or entity with respect to any loss or damages arising from the information contained in this book.

Special Sales

For information about buying this title in bulk quantities, or for special sales opportunities (which may include electronic versions; custom cover designs; and content particular to your business, training goals, marketing focus, or branding interests), please contact our corporate sales department at corpsales@pearsoned.com or (800) 382-3419.

For government sales inquiries, please contact governmentsales@pearsoned.com.

For questions about sales outside the U.S., please contact intlcs@pearson.com.

Editor in Chief
Mark Taub

Product Line Manager
Brett Bartow

Acquisitions Editors
Betsy Brown
Michelle Newcomb

Development Editor
Ellie Bru

Managing Editor
Sandra Schroeder

Project Editor
Mandie Frank

Copy Editor
Jeff Riley

Indexer
Ken Johnson

Proofreader
Paula Lowell

Technical Editor
Chris Crayton

Publishing Coordinator
Vanessa Evans

Designer
Chuti Prasertsith

Compositor
Tricia Bronkella

Contents at a Glance

Table of Contents

About the Author

Mark Edward Soper has been working with PCs since the days of the IBM PC/XT and AT as a salesperson, technology advisor, consultant, experimenter, and technology writer and content creator. Since 1992, he has taught thousands of students across the country how to repair, manage, and troubleshoot the hardware, software, operating systems, and firmware inside their PCs. He has created many versions of his experimental computer known as "FrankenPC" for this and previous books. Mark earned his CompTIA A+ Certification in 1999 and has written five other A+ Certification books covering previous versions of the A+ Certification exams for Pearson imprints. Mark is also the creator of *Building and Repairing PCs* (Que Video).

Mark has contributed to many editions of *Upgrading and Repairing PCs*, working on the 11th through 18th and 20th through 22nd editions; co-authored *Upgrading and Repairing Networks*, Fifth Edition; and has written two books about digital photography, *Easy Digital Cameras* and *The Shot Doctor: The Amateur's Guide to Taking Great Digital Photos*.

In addition, Mark has written *Easy Windows 10*, *Easy Windows 8.1*, *Easy Windows 8*, *Easy Microsoft Windows 7*, and *Sams Teach Yourself Microsoft Windows 7 in 10 Minutes*. He also wrote two books about Windows Vista: *Maximum PC Microsoft Windows Vista Exposed* and *Unleashing Microsoft Windows Vista Media Center*.

Mark has also contributed to Que's Special Edition *Using* series on Windows Me, Windows XP, and Windows Vista and to Que's *Windows 7 In Depth*. Mark has also created a number of hardware tutorial videos available from the OnGadgets&Hardware podcast channel at www.quepublishing.com.

Mark has also written many blog entries and articles for MaximumPC.com and *Maximum PC* magazine. He currently teaches Microsoft Office for University of Southern Indiana and Ivy Tech Corporate College in Evansville, Indiana, and also has taught A+ Certification and other technology-related subjects at Ivy Tech Community College. See Mark's website at www.markesoper.com for news and information about upcoming projects.

About the Technical Reviewer

Chris Crayton (MCSE) is an author, technical consultant, and trainer. He has worked as a computer technology and networking instructor, information security director, network administrator, network engineer, and PC specialist. Chris has authored several print and online books on PC repair, CompTIA A+, CompTIA Security+, and Microsoft Windows. He has also served as technical editor and content contributor on numerous technical titles for several of the leading publishing companies. He holds numerous industry certifications, has been recognized with many professional teaching awards, and has served as a state-level SkillsUSA competition judge.

Dedication

For Moses

Acknowledgments

After more than sixteen years as a full-time technology content provider, I realize more than ever how richly I have been blessed by God in my family and in the team of technology experts I get to work with.

Thanks first and foremost to Almighty God, who has given us the ability to create and to receive glimpses of the mysteries of the universe.

Thanks also to my family, PC and Mac users alike, who agree to disagree about the best technology, but work and play well with each other. Thanks especially to Cheryl for her love and patience.

As always, Pearson has put together an outstanding team for this edition, and I especially want to thank Dave Dusthimer for his vision of becoming the leading provider of CompTIA A+ study material. I wish him well in retirement.

A major thank you goes out to Michelle Newcomb, Ellie Bru, Sandra Schroeder, and Mandie Frank for keeping this process rolling along. And a big thank you to Technical Editor Chris Crayton for great suggestions and tips along the way and to Beth Smith for creating thought-provoking questions to test your skills.

Finally, a thank you to Vanessa, Tim, and Gary. We want to see you succeed both in passing your exams and in your IT career. We all wish you the very best.

We Want to Hear from You!

As the reader of this book, you are our most important critic and commentator. We value your opinion and want to know what we're doing right, what we could do better, what areas you'd like to see us publish in, and any other words of wisdom you're willing to pass our way.

We welcome your comments. You can email or write to let us know what you did or didn't like about this book—as well as what we can do to make our books better.

Please note that we cannot help you with technical problems related to the topic of this book.

When you write, please be sure to include this book's title and author as well as your name, email address, and phone number. We will carefully review your comments and share them with the author and editors who worked on the book.

Email: feedback@pearsonitcertification.com
Pearson IT Certification
ATTN: Reader Feedback
800 East 96th Street
Indianapolis, IN 46240 USA

Reader Services

Register your copy of *CompTIA A+ 220-901 and 220-902 Cert Guide* at www.pearsonitcertification.com for convenient access to downloads, updates, and corrections as they become available. To start the registration process, go to www.pearsonitcertification.com/register and log in or create an account*. Enter the product ISBN 9780789756527 and click Submit. When the process is complete, you will find any available bonus content under Registered Products.

*Be sure to check the box that you would like to hear from us to receive exclusive discounts on future editions of this product.

CompTIA.

Becoming a CompTIA Certified IT Professional is Easy

It's also the best way to reach greater professional opportunities and rewards.

Why Get CompTIA Certified?

Growing Demand

Labor estimates predict some technology fields will experience growth of over 20% by the year 2020.* CompTIA certification qualifies the skills required to join this workforce.

Higher Salaries

IT professionals with certifications on their resume command better jobs, earn higher salaries and have more doors open to new multi-industry opportunities.

Verified Strengths

91% of hiring managers indicate CompTIA certifications are valuable in validating IT expertise, making certification the best way to demonstrate your competency and knowledge to employers.**

Universal Skills

CompTIA certifications are vendor neutral—which means that certified professionals can proficiently work with an extensive variety of hardware and software found in most organizations.

 Learn 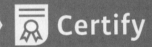 Certify Work

Learn more about what the exam covers by reviewing the following:

- Exam objectives for key study points.

- Sample questions for a general overview of what to expect on the exam and examples of question format.

- Visit online forums, like LinkedIn, to see what other IT professionals say about CompTIA exams.

Purchase a voucher at a Pearson VUE testing center or at CompTIAstore.com.

- Register for your exam at a Pearson VUE testing center:

- Visit pearsonvue.com/CompTIA to find the closest testing center to you.

- Schedule the exam online. You will be required to enter your voucher number or provide payment information at registration.

- Take your certification exam.

Congratulations on your CompTIA certification!

- Make sure to add your certification to your resume.

- Check out the CompTIA Certification Roadmap to plan your next career move.

Learn more: Certification.CompTIA.org/aplus

* Source: CompTIA 9th Annual Information Security Trends study: 500 U.S. IT and Business Executives Responsible for Security
** Source: CompTIA Employer Perceptions of IT Training and Certification

© 2015 CompTIA Properties, LLC, used under license by CompTIA Certifications, LLC. All rights reserved. All certification programs and education related to such programs are operated exclusively by CompTIA Certifications, LLC. CompTIA is a registered trademark of CompTIA Properties, LLC in the U.S. and internationally. Other brands and company names mentioned herein may be trademarks or service marks of CompTIA Properties, LLC or of their respective owners. Reproduction or dissemination prohibited without written consent of CompTIA Properties, LLC. Printed in the U.S. 02190-Nov2015

Introduction

CompTIA A+ Certification is widely recognized as the first certification you should receive in an information technology (IT) career. Whether you are planning to specialize in PC or mobile device hardware, operating systems management, security or network management, the CompTIA A+ Certification exams measure the baseline skills you need to master to begin your journey toward greater responsibilities and achievements in IT.

CompTIA A+ Certification is designed to be a "vendor-neutral" exam that measures your knowledge of industry-standard technology.

Goals and Methods

The number one goal of this book is a simple one: to help you pass the 2016 version of the CompTIA A+ Certification exams 220-901 and 220-902.

Because CompTIA A+ Certification exams now stress problem-solving abilities and reasoning more than memorization of terms and facts, our goal is to help you master and understand the required objectives for each exam.

To aid you in mastering and understanding the A+ Certification objectives, this book uses the following methods:

- The beginning of each chapter defines the topics to be covered in the chapter; it also lists the corresponding CompTIA A+ objective numbers.

- The body of the chapter explains the topics from a hands-on and a theory-based standpoint. This includes in-depth descriptions, tables, and figures that are geared to build your knowledge so that you can pass the exam. The chapters are broken down into several topics each.

- The key topics indicate important figures, tables, and lists of information that you should know for the exam. They are interspersed throughout the chapter and are listed in table format at the end of the chapter.

- You can find memory tables online in Appendix B, "Memory Tables" and Appendix C "Answers to Memory Tables." Use them to help memorize important information.

- Key terms without definitions are listed at the end of each chapter. Write down the definition of each term and check your work against the key terms in the glossary.

What's New?

You'll find plenty that's new and improved in this edition, including:

- Reorganized text to minimize duplication of coverage between objectives
- New coverage of Linux and OS X features and troubleshooting
- New coverage of MacBook features such as Thunderbolt 2
- Updated processor coverage
- Updated BIOS dialogs, including more UEFI BIOS examples
- USB 3.1 and USB-Type C
- mSATA and M.2 SSDs
- Improved photos and illustrations
- Enhanced laptop teardown and subassembly replacement procedures
- Updated memory coverage (DDR4 DIMMs and UniDIMMs)
- Updated coverage of mobile devices including teardown tips
- Enhanced coverage of desktop and laptop upgrades, including Thunderbolt and the miniPCIe card
- Updated coverage of docking stations and video cable adapters
- Updated power supply and cooling system information
- Improved coverage of network hardware and cabling
- Enhanced coverage of device troubleshooting, teardown, and upgrades
- New coverage of dealing with prohibited content/activity
- Enhanced coverage of Windows features
- Enhanced discussion of Windows upgrade paths and methods
- New Windows 8/8.1/10 features
- Enhanced coverage of ESD protection issues
- Enhanced coverage of Windows OS troubleshooting
- Enhanced Control Panel discussion
- Enhanced coverage of iOS and Android devices

- Enhanced coverage of security issues (physical, digital, wireless network, wired network, workgroup and homegroup folders)
- New coverage of network and cloud computing concepts
- Enhanced coverage of security issues
- New coverage of Linux and OS X OS troubleshooting

For a number of years, the CompTIA A+ Certification objectives were divided into a hardware exam and an operating systems exam. Starting with the 2006 exam, the exams were restructured so that knowledge of hardware and operating systems were needed for both exams. The 2012 exams were restructured again, and further restructuring has taken place for the 2016 exams. Exam 220-901 covers hardware, networking, mobile devices, and hardware and network troubleshooting. Exam 220-902 covers Windows operating systems; OS X, Linux, virtualization, cloud and network services; mobile operating systems; security; software troubleshooting for Windows, OS X, Linux, and mobile devices; and operational procedures.

For more information about how the A+ certification can help your career, or to download the latest official objectives, access CompTIA's A+ web page at https://certification.comptia.org/certifications/a.

In this book, we cover the major objectives but combine some of them when necessary to make a topic easier to understand. To make sure you can relate the book's contents to the CompTIA A+ Certification objectives, each chapter contains cross-references to the appropriate objectives as needed, and we provide a master cross-reference list later in this introduction.

Who Should Read This Book?

The CompTIA A+ exams measure the necessary competencies for an entry-level IT professional with the equivalent knowledge of 6 to 12 months of hands-on experience in the lab or field. This book is written for people who have that amount of experience working with desktop PCs, laptops, and mobile devices. Average readers will have attempted in the past to replace a hardware component within a PC or mobile device; they should also understand how to navigate through Windows, access the Internet, and have (or be willing to learn) a basic knowledge of OS X and Linux features.

Readers will range from people who are attempting to attain a position in the IT field to people who want to keep their skills sharp or perhaps retain their job due to a company policy that mandates that they take the new exams.

This book is also aimed at the reader who wants to acquire additional certifications beyond the A+ certification (Network+, Security+, and so on). The book is designed in such a way to offer easy transition to future certification studies.

Strategies for Exam Preparation

Strategies for exam preparation will vary depending on your existing skills, knowledge, and equipment available. Of course, the ideal exam preparation would consist of building a PC from scratch and installing and configuring the operating systems covered.

Chapter 1 contains lists of the tools, software, and operating systems recommended by CompTIA for exam study and preparation and how to track down the best deals. In Chapter 19, in the sidebar "Preparing for the A+ Certification Exam with Virtual Machines," we provide information on how to use popular virtualization programs and operating system trial versions to run Windows and Linux on your existing system. To run OS X as a VM, see http://techsviewer.com/how-to-install-mac-os-x-el-capitan-on-vmware-on-pc/.

This hands-on approach will really help to reinforce the ideas and concepts expressed in the book. However, not everyone has access to this equipment, so the next best step you can take is to read through the chapters in this book, jotting notes down with key concepts or configurations on a separate notepad. Each chapter contains a quiz that you can use to test your knowledge of the chapter's topics. It's located near the end of the chapter.

After you have read through the book, have a look at the current exam objectives for the CompTIA A+ Certification Exams listed at https://certification.comptia.org/certifications/a. If there are any areas shown in the certification exam outline that you would still like to study, find those sections in the book and review them.

When you feel confident in your skills, attempt the practice exam included on the companion website with this book. As you work through the practice exam, note the areas where you lack confidence and review those concepts or configurations in the book. After you have reviewed the areas, work through the practice exam a second time and rate your skills. Keep in mind that the more you work through the practice exam, the more familiar the questions will become.

After you have worked through the practice exam a second time and feel confident with your skills, schedule the real CompTIA A+ 220-901 and 220-902 exams through Pearson Vue (www.vue.com). To prevent the information from evaporating out of your mind, you should typically take the exam within a week of when you consider yourself ready to take the exam.

The CompTIA A+ Certification credential for those passing the certification exams is valid for three years. To renew your certification without retaking the exam, you need to participate in continuing education (CE) activities and pay an annual maintenance fee of $25.00 ($75.00 for three years). See https://certification.comptia.org/continuing-education/how-to-renew/ce-program-fees for fee details. To learn more about the certification renewal policy, see https://certification.comptia.org/continuing-education.

Table I-1 CompTIA A+ Exam Topics

Chapter	Exam Topics	CompTIA A+ Exam Objectives Covered
1	Computer/Device Anatomy 101 Essential tools, equipment, and software for the technician CompTIA six-step troubleshooting theory	220-901 Objectives 1.1, 1.2, 1.3, 1.5, 1.6, 1.7, 1.8, 1.10, 1.11 220-902 5.5
2	Understanding BIOS and UEFI firmware Configuration of BIOS and UEFI firmware Updating BIOS and UEFI firmware Using BIOS and UEFI diagnostics	220-901 Objective 1.1
3	Motherboard form factors Expansion slots Components Power, fan and front-panel connectors Bus speeds Reset button	220-901 Objective 1.2
4	RAM types RAM form factors ECC vs Non-ECC RAM configurations RAM compatibility	220-901 Objective 1.3
5	Expansion card and slot overview Installation and configuration of sound, video, network, USB, and other PC expansion cards Riser cards	220-901 Objective 1.4 220-901 Objective 1.9

Chapter	Exam Topics	CompTIA A+ Exam Objectives Covered
11	Networking	220-901 Objective 2.1
	Cables	220-901 Objective 2.2
	Hardware	220-901 Objective 2.3
	Ports	220-901 Objective 2.4
	TCP/IP	220-901 Objective 2.5
	Routers	220-901 Objective 2.6
	Wireless	220-901 Objective 2.7
		220-901 Objective 2.8
		220-901 Objective 2.9
12	Laptop expansion options	220-901 Objective 3.1
	Replace components	220-901 Objective 3.2
	Laptop display components	220-901 Objective 3.3
	Laptop features	220-901 Objective 3.4
	Tablets, Phablets, Smartphones	220-901 Objective 3.5
	Wearables	
	e-readers	
	Accessories	
13	Troubleshooting motherboards, RAM, power supplies, CPUs	220-901 Objective 4.1
		220-901 Objective 4.2
	Troubleshooting hard drives and RAID arrays	220-901 Objective 4.3
	Troubleshooting video cards and displays	220-901 Objective 4.4
	Troubleshooting networks	220-901 Objective 4.5
	Troubleshooting mobile devices	220-901 Objective 4.6
	Troubleshooting printers	
14	Windows features	220-902 Objective 1.1
	Booting and installing Windows	220-902 Objective 1.2
	Partitions and file systems	
	Installing updates	
	Factory recovery partition	

Chapter	Exam Topics	CompTIA A+ Exam Objectives Covered
15	Using Microsoft Windows command line tools, features, and Control Panel utilities	220-902 Objective 1.3 220-902 Objective 1.4 220-902 Objective 1.5
16	Configuring and managing networks and sharing in Microsoft Windows	220-902 Objective 1.6
17	Safety procedures Environmental controls Addressing prohibited content and activity Software licensing issues Policies and security best practices Communicating methods and professional behavior	220-902 Objective 5.1 220-902 Objective 5.2 220-902 Objective 5.3 220-902 Objective 5.4
18	OS X and Linux common functions Backup Tools Basic Linux commands Features	220-902 Objective 2.1
19	Client-side virtualization SaaS, public cloud, and other cloud computing concepts Roles of network hosts (servers, Internet appliances, legacy/embedded systems)	220-902 Objective 2.2 220-902 Objective 2.3 220-902 Objective 2.4
20	Basic features of Android, iOS, and Windows Mobile operating systems Configuring connectivity and email Mobile device synchronization	220-902 Objective 2.5 220-902 Objective 2.6 220-902 Objective 2.7
21	Security threats and vulnerabilities Prevention methods Windows security settings Security best practices for workstations Securing mobile devices Data destruction and disposal SOHO network security	220-902 Objective 3.1 220-902 Objective 3.2 220-902 Objective 3.3 220-902 Objective 3.4 220-902 Objective 3.5 220-902 Objective 3.6 220-902 Objective 3.7

Chapter	Exam Topics	CompTIA A+ Exam Objectives Covered
22	Troubleshoot Windows, Linux, OS X operating systems	220-902 Objective 4.1
	Troubleshooting iOS and Android devices, applications, security	220-902 Objective 4.2
		220-902 Objective 4.3
		220-902 Objective 4.4

Companion Website

Register this book to get access to the Pearson Test Prep practice test software and other study materials plus additional bonus content. Check this site regularly for new and updated postings written by the author that provide further insight into the more troublesome topics on the exam. Be sure to check the box that you would like to hear from us to receive updates and exclusive discounts on future editions of this product or related products.

To access this companion website, follow these steps:

Step 1. Go to www.pearsonITcertification.com/register and log in or create a new account.

Step 2. Enter the ISBN: 9780789756527.

Step 3. Answer the challenge question as proof of purchase.

Step 4. Click on the Access Bonus Content link in the Registered Products section of your account page to be taken to the page where your download-able content is available.

Please note that many of our companion content files can be very large, especially image and video files.

If you are unable to locate the files for this title by following the steps, please visit www.pearsonITcertification.com/contact and select the "Site Problems/ Comments" option. Our customer service representatives will assist you.

Accessing the Pearson Test Prep Software and Questions

This book comes complete with the Pearson Test Prep practice test software containing several exams. These practice tests are available to you either online or as an offline Windows application. To access the practice exams that were developed with this book, you will need the unique access code printed on the card in the sleeve in the back of your book.

NOTE   The cardboard case in the back of this book includes the paper that lists the activation code for the practice exam associated with this book. Do not lose the activation code. On the opposite side of the paper from the activation code is a unique, one-time-use coupon code for the purchase of the Premium Edition eBook and Practice Test.

Accessing the Pearson Test Prep Software Online

The online version of this software can be used on any device with a browser and connectivity to the Internet including desktop machines, tablets, and smartphones. To start using your practice exams online, simply follow these steps:

1. Go to: HYPERLINK "http://www.pearsontestprep.com/" \t "_blank" http://www.PearsonTestPrep.com.
2. Select **Pearson IT Certification** as your product group.
3. Enter your email/password for your account. If you don't have an account on PearsonITCertification.com or CiscoPress.com, you will need to establish one by going to PearsonITCertification.com/join.
4. In the **My Products** tab, click the **Activate New Product** button.
5. Enter the access code printed on the insert card in the back of your book to activate your product.
6. The product will now be listed in your My Products page. Click the Exams button to launch the exam settings screen and start your exam.

The online version of the Pearson Test Prep software is supported on the following browsers and devices:

Browsers:

- Chrome (Windows and Mac), version 40 and above
- Firefox (Windows and Mac), version 35 and above
- Safari (Mac), version 7
- Internet Explorer 10, 11
- Microsoft Edge
- Opera

Devices:

- Desktop and laptop computers
- Tablets running on Android and iOS
- Smartphones with a minimum screen size of 4.7"

Accessing the Pearson Test Prep Software Offline

If you wish to study offline, you can download and install the Windows version of the Pearson Test Prep software. There is a download link for this software on the book's companion website.

Previous Users: If you have already installed the Pearson Test Prep software from another purchase, you do not need to install it again. Launch the Pearson Test Prep software from your Start menu. Click Activate Exam in the My Products or Tools tab, and enter the activation key found in the sleeve in the back of your book to activate and download the free practice questions for this book.

New Users: You will need to install the Pearson Test Prep software on your Windows desktop. Follow the steps below to download, install, and activate your exams.

1. Click the **Install Pearson Test Prep Desktop Version** link at the bottom of the Practice Test Engine section of the page to download the software
2. Once the software finishes downloading, unzip all the files on your computer
3. Double click the application file to start the installation, and follow the on-screen instructions to complete the registration
4. Once the installation is complete, launch the application and select **Activate Exam** button on the My Products tab
5. Click the **Activate a Product** button in the Activate Product Wizard
6. Enter the unique access code found on the card in the sleeve in the back of your book and click the **Activate** button
7. Click **Next** and then the **Finish** button to download the exam data to your application
8. You can now start using the practice exams by selecting the product and clicking the **Open Exam** button to open the exam settings screen

Desktop Version System requirements

- Windows 10, Windows 8.1, or Windows 7
- Microsoft NET Framework 4.5 Client
- Pentium class 1 GHz processor (or equivalent)
- 512 MB RAM
- 650 MB hard disk space plus 50 MB for each downloaded practice exam
- Access to the Internet to register and download exam databases

Premium Edition eBook and Practice Tests

This book also includes an exclusive offer for 70% off the Premium Edition eBook and Practice Tests edition of this title. Please see the coupon code included with the cardboard sleeve for information on how to purchase the Premium Edition.

This chapter covers the following subjects:

- **The Essential Parts of Any Computer or Mobile Device**—Discover the essential hardware components found in laptops, desktops, all-in-one computers, tablets, and smartphones.

- **Hardware, Software, and Firmware**—Learn how these work together to enable computers and mobile devices to work together.

- **The CompTIA Six-Step Troubleshooting Theory**—Learn this theory, apply it as you study and work, and you're on the road to becoming a successful troubleshooter.

- **Technician Tools and Equipment**—Use this section to evaluate the tools and equipment you already have and to build up your inventory.

- **Important Websites**—Discover the websites the industry relies upon for information about hardware, software, and firmware.

## CHAPTER 1

Technician Essentials and Computer/Device Anatomy 101

Before you start to work on a defective computer or mobile device, it's important to understand the essential parts of these devices. These include the different hardware components found in desktop and laptop computers and mobile devices and the roles played by software and firmware to make hardware function. It's also helpful to be introduced to the most common types of computer failures, how to troubleshoot computer problems, the tools you need to make repairs, and some great websites to use as you prepare for the CompTIA A+ Certification exams.

This chapter introduces the CompTIA A+ 220-901 objectives 1.1, 1.2, 1.3, 1.5, 1.6, 1.7, 1.8, 1.10, 1.11; covers the CompTIA A+ 220-902 objective 5.5; provides a guide to where to find more detailed information elsewhere in this book; and provides CompTIA's recommendations for tools and hardware to prepare for the exams.

Foundation Topics

The Essential Parts of Any Computer or Mobile Device

Introduction to Objectives: 220-901: 1.2, 1.3, 1.5, 1.6, 1.7, 1.8, 1.10, 1.11

What makes a computer a computer? After all, some furniture stores put 3D cardboard facsimile computers on computer desks so you can see that the furniture really will hold a computer. What makes a mobile device a device? Some stores display hollow shells of smartphones and tablets so you can see the size of the screens.

What separates real computers and mobile devices from the stand-ins is what's outside and inside; real computers contain a variety of components and subsystems, including:

- Storage devices
- Motherboards
- Power supplies
- Processors/CPUs
- Memory
- Display devices
- Input, multimedia, and biometric devices
- Adapter cards
- Ports and cables
- Cooling systems

Mobile devices include:

- Display devices
- Memory
- Processors/CPUs

- Input, multimedia, and biometric devices
- Ports
- Integrated cameras
- Cooling systems

The following sections describe the components of a desktop PC and contrasts the features of a desktop with those found in laptops and all-in-one computers and mobile devices.

NOTE What is a subsystem? A subsystem is the combination of hardware, software, and firmware in a computer or mobile device that is used for a particular task. For example, the storage subsystem in a desktop or laptop computer includes mass storage, flash memory storage, card slots, device drivers for storage, chipset drivers for the motherboard, USB and SATA cables and ports, the operating system, and the parts of the BIOS or UEFI firmware that connect them together.

Learn more about hardware, software, and firmware later in this chapter.

Front and Rear Views of a Desktop PC

Many of these components are visible in the front and rear views of a desktop computer. Figure 1-1 shows the front view of a typical desktop computer, and Figure 1-2 shows the rear view of the same computer.

Some components, such as RAM, disk drives, and the CPU, are only visible when you remove part of the cover. Figure 1-3 shows the interior of a typical desktop computer, which, as you can see, is a pretty crowded place.

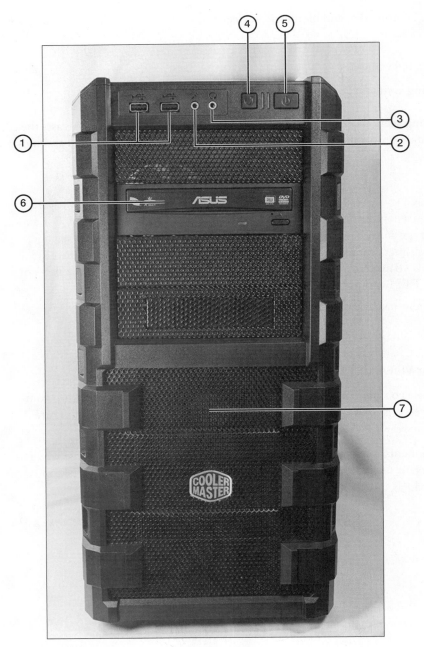

1. USB 2.0 ports
2. microphone jack
3. headphone jack
4. reset button
5. power button
6. rewriteable DVD drive
7. Fan (visible behind front panel)

Figure 1-1   The front of a typical desktop computer.

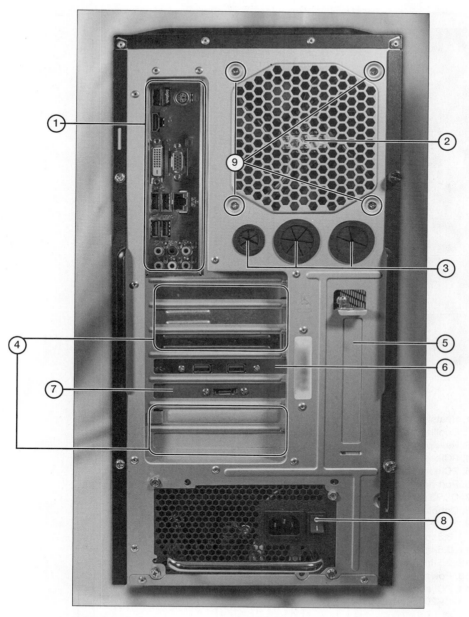

1. Rear port cluster
2. Cooling fan
3. Liquid cooling hose fittings
4. Expansion slot covers
5. Empty card bracket
6. USB 3.0 ports on card bracket
7. eSATA port on card bracket
8. Power supply
9. Fan mounting screws

Figure 1-2 The rear of a typical desktop computer.

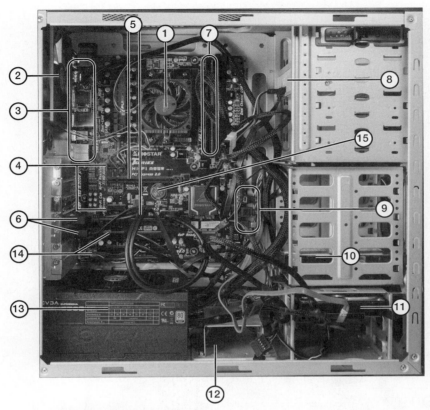

1. Heatsink/fan over processor
2. Cooling fan
3. Rear port cluster
4. PCIe x1 slots
5. PCIe x16 slots
6. Port header cables on card brackets
7. DDR3 DIMMs (under cable)
8. Optical drive in drive bay
9. Front-mounted SATA ports
10. 3.5-inch SATA hard disk
11. 3.5-inch SATA hard disk
12. 2.5-inch drive bays
13. Power supply
14. PCI slots
15. CR2032 CMOS battery

Figure 1-3 The interior of a typical desktop computer.

Systems based on small motherboards, such as the mini-ITX motherboard, may resemble a home theater component, as with the system shown in Figure 1-4.

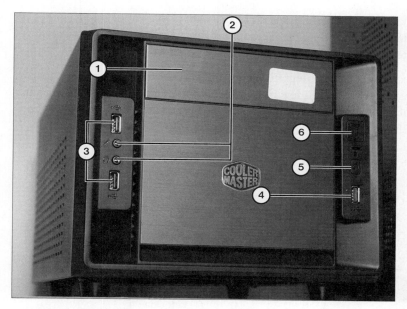

1. Optical drive bay
2. Microphone and headset audio jacks
3. USB 2.0 ports
4. USB 3.0 port
5. Reset button
6. Power button

Figure 1-4   The front view of a typical mini-ITX computer.

All Around a Laptop Computer

Laptop computers use the same types of peripherals, operating systems, and application software as desktop computers. However, laptop computers vary in several ways from desktop computers:

- Most laptop computers feature integrated ports similar to those found in recent desktop computers, such as USB 2.0 or USB 3.0 ports and 10/100/1000 Ethernet network ports. Some also include an ExpressCard slot.

- Some laptop computers support swappable drives, but less-expensive models require a trip to the service bench for a drive upgrade.

- Thin laptop computers (sometimes referred to as Ultrabooks) don't include rewriteable DVD drives.

- Most laptop computers no longer have VGA ports; they use HDMI or mini-DisplayPort or Thunderbolt ports (Apple) for video.

- Laptop computers include single-slot card readers that support SD-family flash memory cards and might also support some other flash memory card form factors.

- Laptop computers have integrated pointing devices built into their keyboards; most use a touchpad, but a few business-oriented models have a pointing stick instead of or in addition to a touchpad (which type is better is a matter of personal preference).

Figures 1-5 and 1-6 illustrate the ports and features of some typical laptop computers.

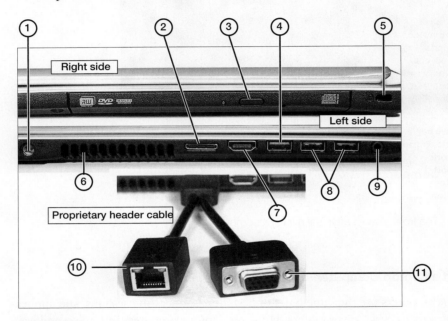

1. Power jack
2. Proprietary header port
3. Eject button for rewriteable DVD drive
4. USB 3.0 port
5. Kensington security lock port
6. Cooling vent
7. HDMI A/V port
8. USB 2.0 ports
9. Headset jack
10. Ethernet port
11. VGA port

Figure 1-5 Right and left sides of an Acer V5-571P laptop computer, which features a proprietary header cable for Ethernet network and VGA video ports.

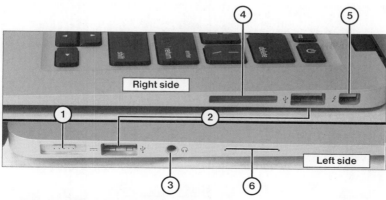

1. Magnetic power connector (MagSafe 2)
2. USB 3.0 ports
3. Headphone jack
4. Flash memory card reader (SDXC, SDHD, SD cards)
5. Thunderbolt 2 I/O and A/V port (compatible with mini-DisplayPort)
6. Microphones

Figure 1-6   Right and left sides of an Apple MacBook Air laptop computer.

All-in-One Computers

All-in-one computers have interiors that resemble laptops. Externally, they look like displays with a separate keyboard and mouse (the processor, RAM, and storage are built into the rear of the display).

Smartphones and Tablets

Smartphones and tablets vary a great deal from each other and from laptops. However, many of them share features in common:

- Recent and current Android models typically use micro-USB (USB-on-the-Go) ports for charging.

- Recent and current Apple models use Lightning ports for charging.

- Many Android-based and Windows models include support for microSD-family cards for expanded storage.

- Almost all smartphones and tablets have forward-facing cameras and rear-facing cameras.

Figures 1-7 through 1-9 illustrate typical devices with these features.

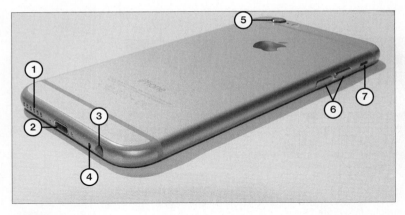

1. Speaker
2. Lightning charging/sync jack
3. Headphone jack
4. Microphone
5. Rear-facing camera
6. Volume controls
7. Toggle for mute and vibrate/ring

Figure 1-7   Rear view of an Apple iPhone 6.

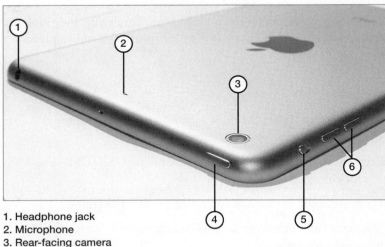

1. Headphone jack
2. Microphone
3. Rear-facing camera
4. Power switch
5. Software-assignable mute/rotation lock switch
6. Volume controls

Figure 1-8   Rear view of an Apple iPad mini 2.

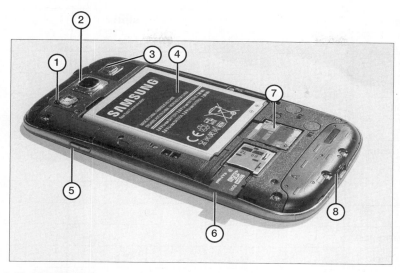

1. Headphone jack
2. Rear-facing camera
3. Microphone for rear-facing camera
4. Battery/NFC chip
5. Power switch
6. MicroSDHC card being inserted into slot
7. SIM card in slot
8. micro-USB (USB-on-the-Go) port

Figure 1-9   Rear view of a Samsung Galaxy (Android) phone with the back removed.

Quick Reference to PC and Mobile Components

Use Table 1-1 to learn more about many of the components and devices shown in Figure 1-1 through Figure 1-9 and more.

Table 1-1   Where to Learn More About PC and Mobile Device Components

Component/Device	Chapter
Audio jacks (microphone, speaker, headphone, and so on)	8
Bluetooth	12
Case fan	9
CMOS battery	3
Drive bay	12
DisplayPort	8

Component/Device	Chapter
DVD drive	6, 12
DVI video port	8
eSATA port	6
Ethernet network port	11
ExpressCard slot	12
Flash memory card reader	6, 12
HDMI port	8
Headphone jack	8
Heatsink fan	9
IEEE-1394 (FireWire) port	6
Kensington security lock	12
Lightning port	12
Liquid cooling	9
Memory module	5
microSD card (SDHC, SDXC)	6
miniHDMI port	8
Motherboard and its components	3
NFC	12
PCIe (PCI Express) x1 slot	3
PCIe (PCI Express) x16 slot	3
PCI slot	3
Power supply	9
PS/2 keyboard and mouse ports	8
SATA hard disk drive and interface	6
S-video port	8
SIM card	12
Sound card	5, 8
Thunderbolt port	5, 8, 12
TV tuner card	5
USB port	8
USB-on-the-Go	12

Component/Device	Chapter
Wi-Fi adapter	11, 12
VGA video port	7
Video card	5

Hardware, Software, and Firmware

The components shown in Figures 1-1 through 1-9 represent the hardware portion of a computer or mobile device. Of these, the processor, or central processing unit (CPU), is king: Other components interact with the processor to create and modify information. However, the CPU relies on other components to receive instructions, store new and updated information, and send information to output or display devices. These essential parts can be broken down into three categories: hardware, software, and firmware. Components in all three categories are necessary to the operation of any computer.

Hardware

Hardware is the part of the computer or mobile device you can pick up, move around, open, and close. Although hardware might represent the glamorous side of computing—whose computer is faster, has a larger hard drive, more memory, and so on—a computer can do nothing without software and firmware to provide instructions. Hardware failures can take place because of loose connections, electrical or physical damage, or incompatible devices.

Software

Software provides the instructions that tell hardware what to do. The same computer system can be used for word processing, gaming, accounting, or Web surfing by installing and using new software. Software comes in various types, including operating systems, application programs, and utility programs.

Operating systems provide standard methods for saving, retrieving, changing, printing, and transmitting information. The current A+ Certification exams focus on recent 32-bit and 64-bit versions of Windows (for example, Windows Vista, Windows 7, and Windows 8/8.1), OS X, Linux, iOS, and Android.

Application programs ("apps"), some of which might be web-based cloud services or Software as a Service (SaaS), are used to create, store, modify, and view information you create, also called data. Because an operating system provides standard methods for using storage, printing, and network devices to work with information, applications must be written to comply with the requirements of an operating system and its associated CPUs. A+ Certification does not require specific knowledge of application programs. However, to provide the best technical support, you should learn the basics of the major applications your company or clients use, such as Microsoft Office, Corel WordPerfect Suite, OpenOffice, Adobe Creative Cloud, and so on.

Certifications are available for major operating systems and applications. Seeking certifications in these areas can further improve your chances of being hired and promoted.

Utility programs are used to keep a computer in good working condition or to set up new devices. In the chapters related to operating systems, you'll learn how to use the major utilities included with Windows, OS X, Linux, iOS, and Android.

Because utilities included in operating systems have limited capabilities, you might also want to invest in other utility programs for use in your day-to-day work, such as disk imaging, file backup, partition management, and others. However, only standard utilities, such as CHKDSK, Disk Management, Defrag, sudo, Time Machine, vi, and others, are covered on the A+ Certification Exams.

Firmware

Firmware represents a middle ground between hardware and software. Like hardware, firmware is physical: a chip or chips attached to devices such as motherboards, optical drives, video cards, mass storage host adapters (RAID, SATA, and SATA Express host adapters and cards), network adapters and cards, modems, and printers. However, firmware is also software: Firmware chips (such as the motherboard **BIOS** and UEFI firmware) contain instructions for hardware testing, hardware configuration, and input/output routines. In essence, **firmware** is "software on a chip," and the software's job is to control the device to which the chip is connected. Because firmware works with both hardware and software, changes in either one can cause firmware to become outdated. Outdated firmware can lead to device or system failure or even data loss. Most firmware today is "flashable," meaning that its contents can be changed through software. You'll learn more about the most common types of firmware, the motherboard's BIOS or UEFI firmware, in Chapter 2, "Configure and Use BIOS/UEFI Tools."

Why Hardware, Software, and Firmware Are Important to Understand

As a computer technician, you will deal on a day-to-day basis with the three major parts of any computing environment. Whether you're working on a computer, printer, or component such as a video card, you must determine whether the problem involves hardware, software, firmware, or a combination of these three.

The CompTIA Six-Step Troubleshooting Theory

220-902 Objective 5.5 Given a scenario, explain the troubleshooting theory.

Because of the complexity of even the simplest computer or mobile device, any given problem could have multiple symptoms and several possible causes. To solve computer and mobile device problems, technicians need a proven and effective troubleshooting theory. CompTIA has included a six-step theory within the current A+ objectives. As Table 1-2 indicates, the steps help you to find the source of a problem, find the solution, and help prevent recurrences.

Table 1-2   The Six-Step CompTIA Troubleshooting Theory

Step	Description
Step 1	Identify the problem.
	–Question the user and identify user changes to computer and perform backups before making changes.
Step 2	Establish a theory of probable cause (question the obvious).
	–If necessary, conduct external or internal research based on symptoms.
Step 3	Test the theory to determine cause.
	–Once theory is confirmed, determine next steps to resolve problem.
	–If theory is not confirmed, re-establish new theory or escalate.
Step 4	Establish a plan of action to resolve the problem and implement the solution.
Step 5	Verify full system functionality and, if applicable, implement preventative measures.
Step 6	Document findings, actions, and outcomes.

As you attempt to troubleshoot computer issues, think in terms of this six-step process. Plug the problem directly into these steps. If you test a theory in Step 3, and the theory is disproven, return to Step 2 and develop another theory. Continue in this manner until you have found a theory that points to the problem. After you solve the problem and verify functionality (Steps 4 and 5), be sure to document what happened (Step 6) so you can more quickly solve a similar problem in the future.

And it is very important to always consider corporate policies, procedures, and impacts before implementing changes.

Technician Tools and Equipment

A technician's best tools are his or her senses and hands. However, a technician needs hardware tools to open a personal computer or mobile device and to install and replace components. Several categories of tools should be a part of every technician's toolkit. The following tools and equipment lists are adapted from the hardware and software list recommended by CompTIA for A+ Certification students and training centers, supplemented with notes based on my years of experience in teaching, building, and tearing down computers and mobile devices.

Basic Tools and Supplies for Assembly/Disassembly of Computers

Use the following tools and supplies when you assemble or disassemble desktop or laptop computers.

- **Phillips and straight-blade screwdrivers**—Used when hex drivers are not compatible; nonmagnetic preferred

- **Torx drivers**—Required for some computers; nonmagnetic preferred

- **Hex drivers**—Used for opening and closing cases and securing and removing cards and motherboards; nonmagnetic preferred

- **3-claw parts retrieval tool**—Used for retrieving loose parts from computer interior; prevents lost parts, which can lead to dead shorts

- **Hemostat clamps**—Replaces tweezers for inserting and removing jumper blocks and cables

- **Needle-nose pliers**—Straightens bent pins

- **Eyebrow tweezers**—Replaces normal tweezers in toolkit for removing and replacing jumpers

- **Penlight**—Illuminates dark cases

- **Magnifier**—Makes small parts and markings easier to read

- **Thermal paste**—Enables safe reinstallation of heatsinks

- **SATA to USB converters**—Enables internal laptop and desktop drives to be connected to USB ports for data transfer, backups, or testing

- **Card brackets**—If you work on small form factor or rack-mounted (U1/U2) systems, have short as well as full-size versions to cover empty expansion slots

- **Storage, case, card, and laptop screw kits**—Use the right-size screws for each job to avoid problems with equipment failure and stripped screw holes

- **Jeweler's screwdriver set**—Enables repairs to devices that use small screws

You can buy toolkits that contain many of these items, but don't hesitate to supplement a kit you already have with additional items from this list or other items you find useful. Figure 1-10 illustrates some important tools.

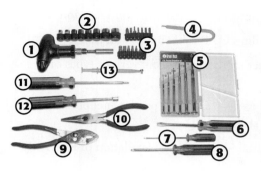

1. Screwdriver with removable tips
   (shown in #2 and #3)
2. Hex driver tips
3. Screw and Torx tips
4. Chip puller (also useful for
   removing keytops)
5. Jeweler's screwdriver set
6. Flat-blade screwdriver
7. Small Phillips-head screwdriver
8. Phillips-head screwdriver
9. Pliers
10. Needle-nose pliers
11. Torx driver
12. Hex driver
13. 3-claw parts retrieval tool

Figure 1-10   Typical tools used by computer technicians.

> **NOTE**   Although some tools in this list also work for opening mobile devices, if you plan to work on smartphones and tablets, you should invest in specific mobile device opening tools. These include spudgers and specialty tweezers to open metal and plastic cases, suction cups to remove glass, and specialized tapes and adhesives for reassembly.

System and Electrical Testing Tools

To help determine whether a component is defective, you should test it. Use the following tools to help test power supplies, cables, and ports on the motherboard or on add-on cards:

- **Multimeter**—Checks AC and DC voltage levels, resistance (Ohms), continuity, amperage, diodes

- **Power supply tester**—Tests power supply operation without the need to install the power supply in a system

- **POST card**—Monitors power-on-self-test and displays checkpoint and diagnostic codes

- **Loopback plugs**—Checks for correct input/output from serial, parallel, network, and USB ports

Network Installation and Configuration Tools

The tools in the following list help you install network cabling and check for correct operation of the physical components in a wired or wireless network:

- **Cable tester**—Checks cable continuity and twisted-pair configuration
- **Punchdown tools**—Used for installing UTP cable into a wall jack
- **Loopback plug**—Checks for correct input/output from various types of Ethernet cables
- **Tone generator and probe**—Used to determine the patch panel port that matches a particular network wall socket
- **Cable/Wire strippers**—Removes cable shielding for installation of RJ-11, RJ-45, or coaxial cable connectors
- **Wi-Fi analyzer**—Displays Wi-Fi channels in use
- **Network cable and connectors**—Use the highest grade in your company or clients' installations, but nothing less than CAT5e.
- **Crimper**—Attaches connectors to cable

> **NOTE** Learn more about using these tools in Chapter 11, "Networking."

Printer Maintenance Tools

To help maintain printers, use the following tools:

- **Maintenance kit**—Most laser printers require the periodic replacement of certain components; contents vary by printer model.
- **Toner vacuum**—Laser printer toner particles are too small to be contained by conventional vacuum cleaner bags; use a toner-rated vacuum cleaner to pick up spilled or leaked toner.
- **Compressed air**—Blows dust and debris out of all types of printers.

> **NOTE** Learn more about these tools in Chapter 10, "Using, Maintaining, and Installing Printers and Multifunction Devices."

Software and Operating Systems

To help restore, protect, and update systems, have the following available in offline installable (no Internet connection required) forms on USB or optical media:

- **Windows, Linux, or OS X operating systems**—Specifics are based on the operating systems your company supports.

- **Antivirus, antimalware**—Installed on bootable media. Full apps as well as specific removal tools for current threats your company or clients face.

- **Driver files**—Download drivers before upgrading to a newer operating system.

- **Virtualization software**—Enables old software to run on newer systems.

Spare Parts and Equipment to Test

Try to locate as many of these items as you can. Check company spare equipment holdings, pawn shops, Craigslist, or eBay for equipment that has relevant features. The more hands-on experience you have, the better.

- Apple tablet / Smartphone
- Android tablet / Smartphone
- Windows tablet / Smartphone
- Windows laptop / Mac laptop / Linux laptop
- Windows desktop / Mac desktop / Linux desktop
- Monitors
- Projectors
- SOHO router/switch
- Access point
- VoIP phone
- Laser printer
- Inkjet printer

  (preferably one or both printers with wireless network support)

- Surge suppressor
- UPS
- Motherboards
- RAM
- Hard drives
- Power supplies
- Video cards

- Sound cards
- Network cards
- Wireless NICs
- Fans/cooling devices/heat sinks
- CPUs
- USB, HDMI, other I/O connectors and cables
- Adapters
- AC adapters
- Optical drives
- Cases
- Mice/keyboards

Important Websites

There are several websites that we will refer to in this book; you will access these websites frequently when working in the field. They include:

- **Microsoft's TechNet**—http://technet.microsoft.com. This site includes highly technical information about all of Microsoft's products.

- **Microsoft Help and Support**—http://support.microsoft.com (previously known as the Microsoft Knowledge Base or MSKB). This site has thousands of instructions and articles that show how to configure Microsoft software and devices and troubleshoot Windows problems such as STOP (BSOD) errors, registry problems, and others.

- **Apple Help and Support**— http://www.apple.com/support/. Apple's official help site for OS X and iOS support.

- **Linux Help**—The major Linux distros each has its own support website; for example, Ubuntu (www.ubuntu.com/support), SuSE (www.suse.com/support), and Fedora (https://ask.fedoraproject.org). There is extensive help for any Linux user at www.Linux.com and http://www.oracle.com/us/technologies/linux/support/overview/index.html.

- **Android Help**—For help with Android OS and devices, visit https://support.google.com/android/?hl=en

- **CompTIA's A+ Web Page**—http://www.comptia.org/certifications/listed/a.aspx. This site describes the A+ certification and provides exam details, sample questions, and has downloadable objectives that show exactly which technology is covered on each exam.

Exam Preparation Tasks

Review Questions

1. Match the components indicated in the following figure to the appropriate component names.

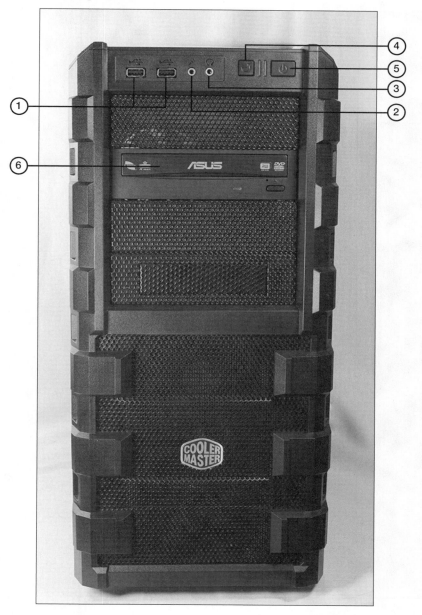

Answer Options:

- **a.** Power button
- **b.** DVD drive
- **c.** Headphone jack
- **d.** Reset button
- **e.** USB 2.0 ports
- **f.** Microphone jack

2. Match the components indicated in the following figure to the appropriate component names.

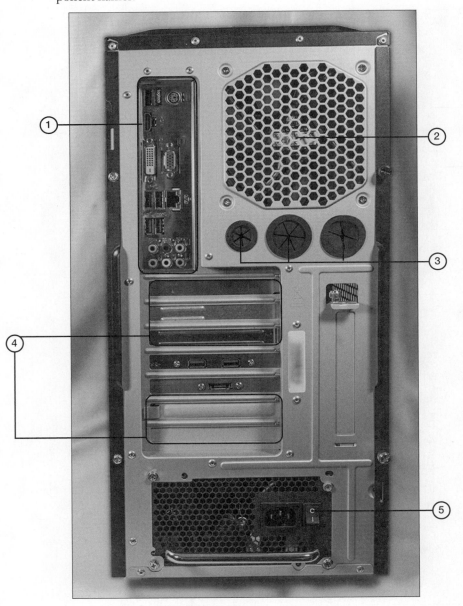

Answer Options:

a. Power supply

b. Cooling fan

c. Rear port cluster

d. Expansion slot covers

e. Liquid cooling hose fittings

3. Which of the following statements best describes firmware?

   a. Firmware is not a solid object; it cannot be picked up and held

   b. Firmware is responsible for allowing a user to surf the Web.

   c. Firmware saves, retrieves, prints, and transmits information.

   d. Firmware is comprised of instructions used by the BIOS or UEFI chip at startup.

4. Use the following blank table to place the six steps of CompTIA's Troubleshooting Theory and the matching descriptions in correct order. Choose from the Names and Descriptions answer options below the blank table.

Step	Name	Description
1		
2		
3		
4		
5		
6		

Names

A. Create a plan of action

B. Verify system functionality

C. Establish theory of probable cause

D. Document actions

E. Identify problem

F. Test theory

Descriptions

a. Write down findings, actions, and outcomes.

b. Verify full system functionality, not just the part you worked on. Implement preventive measures.

c. Test theory to determine cause. Determine next steps.

d. Develop plan to resolve problem and implement solution

e. Question user, identify recent changes to computer, perform backups.

f. Conduct research based on user input and symptoms. Question the obvious.

5. The following figure shows important tools that a technician might use while servicing a computer. Match the tool to its name.

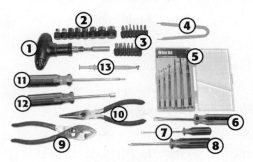

Names (in alphabetical order):

   a. 3-claw parts retrieval tool

   b. Chip puller

   c. Flat-blade screwdriver

   d. Hex driver

   e. Hex driver tips

   f. Jeweler's screwdriver set

   g. Needle-nose pliers

   h. Phillips-head screwdriver

   i. Pliers

   j. Screw and Torx tips

   k. Screwdriver with removable tips

   l. Small Phillips-head screwdriver

   m. Torx driver

6. You suspect a computer has either a bad power supply or incorrect AC line voltage. Which of the following tools is used to check both potential problem areas?

   a. POST card

   b. Power supply tester

   c. Multimeter

   d. Loopback plug

7. You need to test a network port for correct input and output, but there is no network connection available. Which of the following devices can be used to perform these tests?

   a. Loopback plug

   b. Power supply tester

   c. POST card

   d. Multimeter

8. You carry a punchdown tool as part of your network cabling kit. In which of the following situations is the tool used?

   a. When checking for cable continuity and twisted pair configuration

   b. When determining the patch panel port that matches a particular network wall socket

   c. When attaching a connector to a cable

   d. When installing a UTP cable into a wall jack

9. Your client has requested new cabling. Which of the following tasks is the crimper used for?

   a. Installing a UTP cable into a wall jack

   b. Attaching a connector to a cable

   c. Checking for cable continuity and twisted pair configuration

   d. Determining the patch panel port that matches a particular network wall socket

10. Which of the following statements best describes why you should use a special toner vacuum when cleaning a laser printer?

    a. Laser toner particles are too small to be captured by a standard vacuum cleaner bag.

    b. Laser toner particles are toxic and must be held in a special bag for decontamination.

    c. Laser toner particles are heavy and require more suction than a standard vacuum provides.

    d. Laser toner particles are sticky and require more suction than a standard vacuum provides.

Answers and Explanations to Review Questions

1. **A.** 5
   B. 6
   C. 3
   D. 4
   E. 1
   F. 2

2. **A.** 5
   B. 2
   C. 1
   D. 4
   E. 3

3. **D.** Firmware is a combination of hardware and software. Hardware refers to physical objects, like a hard drive or a CPU. Software is programming that tells the hardware what to do. Hardware can't do anything without software and software needs hardware to carry out its instructions. Firmware is programming code that is written onto a ROM chip. The system BIOS or UEFI firmware, for example, is a set of instructions (programming code) that is written onto a ROM memory chip (hardware) and soldered onto the motherboard. Without the system BIOS, the computer would not be able to boot.

4.

Step	Name	
1	E. Identify problem	e. Question user, identify recent changes to computer, perform backups.
2	C. Establish theory of probable cause	f. Conduct research based on user input and symptoms. Question the obvious.
3	F. Test theory	c. Test theory to determine cause. Determine next steps.
4	A. Create plan of action	d. Develop plan to resolve problem and implement solution.
5	B. Verify functionality	b. Test system thoroughly, not just the part you worked on. Implement preventive measures.
6	D. Document actions	a. Write down findings, actions, and outcomes.

This process begins as soon as you communicate with the customer for the first time and isn't finished until the findings, actions, and outcomes are documented.

If you don't formulate a theory or test that theory before beginning your repairs, you might waste your time and your client's money. More than one technician's career and financial well-being has been brought to ruin because he or she failed to perform a backup before starting work.

5. **A.** 13

   B. 4

   C. 6

   D. 12

   E. 2

   F. 5

   G. 10

   H. 8

   I. 9

   J. 3

   K. 1

   L. 7

   M. 11

6. **C.** A multimeter can check AC and DC voltage levels, resistance, continuity, amperage, and diodes.

7. **A.** Loopback plugs are available in versions for serial, parallel, network, and USB ports. Use a network loopback plug for this test.

8. **D.** A punchdown tool is used to install a UTP cable into a wall jack.

9. **B.** A crimper is used to attach a connector to the end of a cable.

10. **A.** Laser toner particles are too small to be captured by a standard vacuum cleaner bag. You should use a vacuum cleaner bag that is especially designed for toner.

This chapter covers the following subjects:

- **Introduction to BIOS/UEFI**—This section explains the motherboard's firmware, known as the BIOS or UEFI.

- **BIOS/UEFI Configuration**—This section demonstrates how to access the BIOS and modify settings; for example, RAM, processor, and video settings.

- **Flash Upgrade BIOS/UEFI**—In this section, you learn how to upgrade the BIOS through a process known as flashing.

- **Using BIOS/UEFI Diagnostics**—In this section, you learn about diagnostic features built into many BIOS/UEFI chips.

## CHAPTER 2

Configure and Use BIOS/UEFI Tools

The **Basic Input/Output System (BIOS)** is an essential component of the motherboard. This boot firmware, also known as System BIOS or, on most recent systems, unified extensible firmware interface (UEFI), is the first code run by a computer when it is booted. It prepares the machine by testing it during bootup and paves the way for the operating system to start. It tests and initializes components such as the processor, RAM, video card, hard drives, optical, and USB drives. If any errors occur, the BIOS/UEFI reports them as part of the testing stage, known as the **power-on self-test (POST)**. The BIOS/UEFI resides on a ROM chip and stores a setup program that you can access when the computer first boots up. From this program, a user can change settings in the BIOS and upgrade the BIOS as well. In this chapter, you find out about how the BIOS/UEFI, **CMOS**, and batteries on the motherboard interact and learn how to configure and upgrade the BIOS.

From this point on, the term *BIOS* refers to both traditional BIOS and UEFI firmware except when they differ in function.

220-901: Objective 1.1 Given a scenario, configure settings and use BIOS/UEFI tools on a PC.

Foundation Topics

BIOS/UEFI Configuration

The system BIOS has default settings provided by the system or motherboard maker, but as a system is built up with storage devices, memory modules, adapter cards, and other components, it is usually necessary to alter the standard settings.

To perform this task, the system assembler must use the BIOS setup program to make changes and save them to the CMOS (complementary metal oxide semiconductor) chip. Originally, the BIOS setup program was run from a bootable floppy disk, but for many years virtually all system BIOS chips have included the setup program.

Accessing the BIOS Setup Program

The BIOS configuration program is stored in the BIOS chip itself. Just press the key or key combination displayed onscreen (or described in the manual) to get started.

Although these keystrokes vary from system to system, the most popular keys on current systems include the escape (Esc) key, the Delete (Del) key, the F1 key, the F2 key, or the F10 key.

Most recent systems display the key(s) necessary to start the BIOS setup program at startup, as shown in Figure 2-1. However, if you don't know which key to press to start your computer's BIOS setup program, check the system or motherboard manual for the correct key(s).

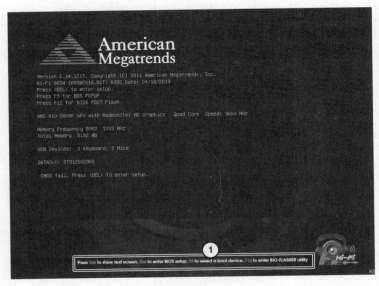

1. Keystrokes for configuration options at startup

Figure 2-1   A typical splash screen displays the keystrokes needed to start the BIOS setup program.

NOTE   Because the settings you make in the BIOS setup program are stored in the nonvolatile CMOS, the settings are often called CMOS settings or BIOS settings. The contents of CMOS are maintained by a battery. See Chapter 3, "Motherboard Components," for typical BIOS chip and CMOS battery locations on current systems.

CAUTION   BIOS configuration programs vary widely, but the screens used in the following sections are representative of the options available on typical recent systems; your system might have similar options but place the settings on different screens than those shown here. Laptops, corporate desktops, and Windows tablets generally offer fewer options than those shown here.

OS X uses operating system menus to make changes to system devices, rather than permitting direct access to the BIOS. See Chapter 18, "OS X and Linux," for details.

Be sure to consult the manual that came with your computer or motherboard before toying with the settings you find here. Fiddling with the settings can improve performance, but it can also wreak havoc on an otherwise healthy device if you don't know what you're doing. Be warned!

UEFI and Traditional BIOS

Most recent desktop and laptop computers (and all desktop and laptop computers from 2014 on) now use a new type of firmware called the Unified Extensible Firmware Initiative (UEFI) to display a mouse-driven GUI or text-based menu for BIOS setup. OS X computers all use UEFI firmware. Compared to a traditional Flash ROM BIOS, UEFI has the following advantages:

- Support for hard drives of 2.2TB and higher capacity. These drives require the use of the GUID Partition Table (GPT) to access full capacity.

- Faster system startup (booting) and other optimizations.

- Larger-size ROM chips used by UEFI make room for additional features, better diagnostics, the ability to open a shell environment for easy flash updates, and the ability to save multiple BIOS configurations for reuse.

UEFI firmware offers similar settings to those used by a traditional BIOS (see Figure 2-2) along with additional options (refer to Figures 2-3 and beyond). Most desktop systems with UEFI firmware use a mouse-driven graphical interface. However, many laptops with UEFI firmware use a text-based interface similar to BIOS.

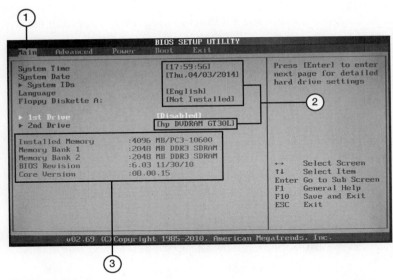

1. Selected menu
2. Editable items
3. Reported by system; not editable

Figure 2-2   This computer uses a traditional BIOS.

To learn more about UEFI, visit http://www.uefi.org/.

> **NOTE**   For more information about BIOS and UEFI functions, beep codes, and up-
> grades, see the BIOS chapter in the 22nd edition of Scott Mueller's Upgrading and
> Repairing PCs.

BIOS Settings Overview

The following sections review the typical setup process using various UEFI firmware versions on systems running Intel Core i3 3227U, Intel Core i5 i6600, AMD
FX-8350, and AMD A10-5800K processors.

Table 2-1 provides a detailed discussion of the most important CMOS/BIOS settings. Use this table as a quick reference to the settings you need to make or verify
in any system. Examples of these and other settings are provided in the following
sections.

Table 2-1 Major CMOS/BIOS/UEFI Settings

Option	Settings	Notes
Boot Sequence	Hard drive, optical (CD/DVD, Blu-ray), USB, network ROM; order as wanted	To boot from bootable OS or diagnostic CDs or DVDs, place the CD or DVD (optical) drive before the hard drive in the boot sequence. To boot from a bootable USB device, place the USB device before the hard drive in the boot sequence. You can enable or disable additional boot devices on some systems.
Memory Configuration	By SPD or Auto (default); manual settings (Frequency, CAS Latency [CL], Fast R-2-R turnaround, and so on) also available	Provides stable operation using the settings stored in memory by the vendor. Use manual settings (frequency, CAS latency, and so on) for overclocking (running memory at faster than normal speeds) or to enable memory of different speeds to be used safely by selecting slower settings.
CPU **Clock** and Frequency	Automatically detected on most recent systems	Faster or higher settings overclock the system but could cause instability (see Chapter 8, "Ports and Interfaces," for details). Some systems default to low values when the system doesn't start properly.
Hardware Monitor	Enable display for all fans plugged in to the motherboard	Also known as PC Health on some systems; can be monitored from within the OS with vendor-supplied or third-party utilities.
Onboard Audio, Modem, or Network	Enable or disable	Enable when you don't use add-on cards for any of these functions; disable each setting before installing a replacement card. Some systems include two network adapters.
USB Legacy	Enable when USB keyboard is used	Enables USB keyboard to work outside the OS.
Serial Ports	Disable unused ports; use default settings for port you use	Also known as COM ports. Most systems no longer have serial ports.
Parallel Port	Disable unused port; use EPP/ECP mode with default IRQ/DMA when parallel port or device is connected	Compatible with almost any parallel printer or device; be sure to use an IEEE-1284-compatible printer cable. Most recent systems no longer include parallel (LPT) ports.
USB Function	Enable	When motherboard supports USB 2.0 (Hi-Speed USB) ports, be sure to enable USB 2.0 function and load USB 2.0 drivers in the OS.

Option	Settings	Notes
USB 3.0 Function	Enable	USB 3.0 ports also support USB 3.1, 2.0, and USB 1.1 devices. Disable when USB 3.0 drivers are not available for operating system.
Keyboard	NumLock, auto-repeat rate/delay	Leave at defaults (NumLock On) unless keyboard has problems.
Plug-and-Play OS	Enable for all except some Linux distributions, Windows NT, MS-DOS	When enabled, Windows configures devices.
Primary VGA BIOS	Varies	Select the primary graphics card type (PCIe or onboard).
Shadowing	Varies	Enable shadowing for video BIOS; leave other shadowing disabled.
Quiet Boot	Varies	Disable to display system configuration information at startup.
Boot-Time Diagnostic Screen	Varies	Enable to display system configuration information at startup.
Virtualization	Varies	Enable to run hardware-based virtualization programs such as Hyper-V or Parallels so that you can run multiple operating systems, each in its own window.
Power Management (Menu)	Enable unless you have problems with devices	Enable CPU fan settings to receive warnings of CPU fan failure.
S1 or S3 standby	Enable S3	Use S1 (which saves minimal power) only when you use devices that do not properly wake up from S3 standby.
AC Pwr Loss Restart	Enable restart or Full on	Prevents the system from staying down when a power failure takes place.
Wake on LAN (WOL)	Enable when you use WOL-compatible network card or modem	WOL-compatible cards use a small cable between the card and the motherboard. Some integrated network ports also support WOL.
User/Power-On Password	Blocks system from starting when password is not known	Enable when physical security settings are needed, but be sure to record the password in a secure place.
Setup Password	Blocks access to setup when password is not known	Both passwords can be cleared on both systems when CMOS RAM is cleared.

Option	Settings	Notes
Write-Protect Boot Sector	Varies	Enable for normal use, but disable when installing drives or using a multiboot system. Helps prevent accidental formatting but might not stop third-party disk prep software from working.
Boot Virus Detection (Antivirus Boot Sector)	Enable	Stops true infections but allows multiboot configuration.
SATA Drives	Varies	Auto-detects drive type and settings at startup time. Select CD/DVD for CD/DVD/Blu-ray drive; select None when drive is not present or to disable an installed drive.
SATA Drive configuration	IDE, AHCI, RAID	IDE setting emulates now-obsolete PATA drives. To take advantage of hot-swapping and Native Command Queuing (NCQ) to improve performance, select AHCI. Use RAID when the drive will be used as part of a RAID array.

Automatic Configuration of BIOS/CMOS Settings

As you can see from Table 2-1, there are many options to select when configuring BIOS settings. Many BIOS firmware versions enable you to automatically configure your system with a choice of these options from the main menu:

- BIOS defaults (also referred to as Original/Fail-Safe on some systems)
- Setup defaults (also referred to as Optimal on some systems)

These options primarily deal with performance configuration settings in the BIOS firmware, such as memory timings, memory cache, and the like. The settings used by each BIOS setup option are customized by the motherboard or system manufacturer.

Use BIOS defaults to troubleshoot the system because these settings are conservative in memory timings and other options. Normally, the setup defaults provide better performance. As you view the setup screens in this chapter, you'll note these options are listed.

CAUTION   If you use automatic setup after you make manual changes, all your manual changes will be overridden. Use Setup Defaults and then make any other changes you want.

With many recent systems, you can select Optimal or Setup defaults, save your changes, and then exit; the system will then work acceptably. However, to configure drive settings, USB settings, or to enable or disable ports, you also need to work with individual BIOS settings, such as the ones shown in the following sections.

TIP On typical systems, you set numerical settings, such as date and time, by scrolling through allowable values with keys such as + and – or page up/page down. However, to select settings with a limited range of options, such as enable/disable or choices from a menu, press Enter or the right-arrow key on the keyboard and then choose the option you want from the available choices.

Main Menu

When you start the BIOS configuration program for your system, you might see a GUI menu similar to the UEFI CMOS Setup Utility menus shown in Figures 2-3 and 2-4. Many laptops and corporate-oriented desktop computers with UEFI BIOS use a text-based menu such as the one shown in Figure 2-5 (later in this chapter).

From this menu, you can go to any menu, select default settings, save changes, or exit setup without saving any changes.

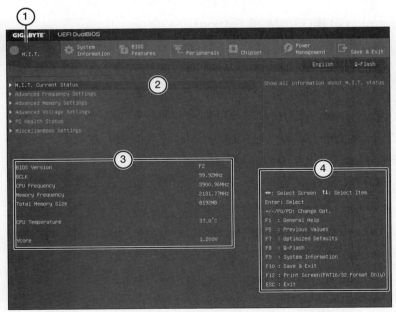

1. Selected menu   3. BIOS, Memory, and CPU information
2. Current submenu   4. Keystroke legend

Figure 2-3 A typical UEFI main setup menu for a desktop system with an Intel processor (UEFI BIOS for Gigabyte Z170XP-SLI).

TIP When you need to quickly find a particular BIOS setting and don't have the manual for the system or the motherboard, visit the system or motherboard vendor's website and download the manual. In most cases, especially with a motherboard-specific manual, the BIOS screens are illustrated. Most vendors provide the manuals in Adobe Reader (PDF) format.

Figure 2-4 A typical UEFI main setup menu for a desktop system with an AMD processor (UEFI BIOS for BIOSTAR Hi-Fi A85W).

Main/Standard Features/Settings

The Main/Standard Features/Settings menus (refer to Figures 2-3 and 2-4) frequently report system features (such as the motherboard model and onboard RAM) and sometimes also configure the system's date and time. To access other settings, use arrow keys or your mouse to highlight the appropriate icon or text menu.

Discovering System Information

Most systems display system information such as processor type, clock speed, cache memory size, installed memory (RAM), and BIOS information from within the

BIOS (see Figure 2-5). Use this information to help determine whether a system needs a processor, memory, or BIOS update.

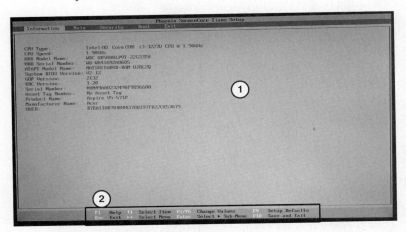

1. Processor and BIOS information
2. Keystroke legend

Figure 2-5   Information dialog on a typical laptop with text-based UEFI firmware.

NOTE   You might need to look at multiple screens to locate all CPU and BIOS information desired, depending upon the system.

Boot Settings and Boot Sequence

Most computers include settings that control how the system boots and the sequence in which drives are checked for bootable operating system files. Depending on the system, these settings might be part of a larger menu, such as an Advanced Settings menu, a BIOS Features menu (see Figure 2-6), or a separate Boot menu (see Figure 2-7).

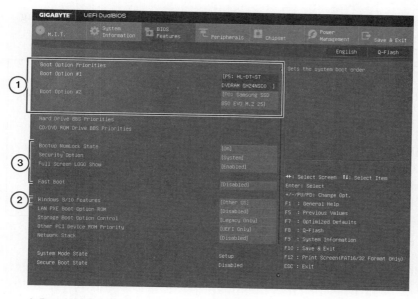

1. **Boot sequence**
2. **Other OS setting [eq] secure boot disabled**
3. **Other boot options**

Figure 2-6   Boot sequence and other boot settings in the BIOS Features menu.

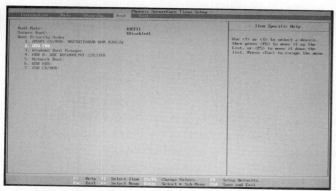

Figure 2-7   A typical Boot menu configured to permit booting from a CD/DVD or USB flash drive before the hard drive.

Enabling Fast Boot skips memory and drive tests to enable faster startup. Enabling Boot Up NumLock turns on the keyboard's NumLock option.

Secure Boot

When enabled, **Secure Boot** (see Figure 2-7)—also known as Windows 8/10 Features in Figure 2-6)—blocks installation of other operating systems and also requires the user to access UEFI setup by restarting the computer in a special Troubleshooting mode from within Windows 8 or later. Secure Boot is enabled by default on systems shipped with Windows 8, 8.1, or 10. Windows 7 users, Linux users, or those who want more flexibility in accessing UEFI BIOS (for example, technicians making changes in UEFI firmware) should disable Secure Boot.

The menus shown in Figures 2-6 and 2-7 are used to adjust the order in which drives are checked for bootable media. For faster booting, set the hard drive with system files as the first boot device. However, when you want to have the option to boot from an optical (CD/DVD/Blu-ray) disk or from a USB flash or hard drive for diagnostics or operating system installations, put those drives before SATA hard drives in the boot order.

NOTE   Even when the first boot drive is set up as CD/DVD, some discs will prompt the user to press a key to boot from the CD/DVD drive when a bootable disc is found. Otherwise, the system checks the next available device for boot files.

Integrated Ports and Peripherals

Typical desktop systems are loaded with onboard ports and features, and the menus shown in Figures 2-8, 2-9, 2-10, and 2-11 are typical of the BIOS menus used to enable, disable, and configure storage, audio, network, and USB ports.

SATA Configuration

Use the SATA configuration options (such as those shown in Figure 2-8) to enable or disable SATA and eSATA ports and to configure SATA host adapters to run in compatible (emulating PATA), native (AHCI), or RAID modes. AHCI supports Native Command Queuing (NCQ) for faster performance and permits hot-swapping of eSATA drives.

To learn more about RAID configuration, see "RAID Types" in Chapter 6, "Storage Devices."

USB Host Adapters and Charging Support

Most systems have separate settings for the USB (2.0) and USB 3.0 (a.k.a. SuperSpeed) controllers (on systems that have USB 3.0 ports). If you don't enable USB 2.0 or USB 3.0 in your system BIOS, all your system's USB ports will run at the next lower speed.

Some USB configuration utilities can also be used to enable a specified USB port to output at a higher amperage than normal to enable faster charging of smartphones. Figure 2-9 illustrates a system with USB 3.0 support enabled and battery charting support being enabled.

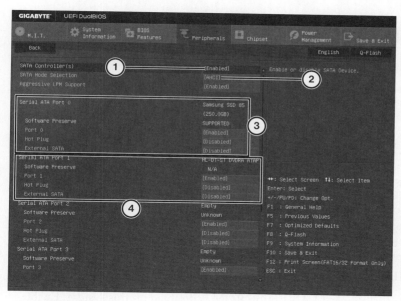

1. SATA ports enabled
2. SATA ports configured to run in AHCI mode
3. Port 0 is connected to a 250GB SSD
4. Port 1 is connected to a DVD optical drive

Figure 2-8   A UEFI configuration dialog for SATA ports.

1. **USB 3.0 host adapter enabled**
2. **Charging option being edited**

Figure 2-9   Configuring a USB host adapter for battery charging.

Audio and Ethernet Ports

Depending upon the system, these and other integrated ports might be configured using a common menu or on separate menus. In Figure 2-10, the HD "Azalia" onboard audio is enabled; if a separate sound card was installed, onboard audio should be disabled. SPDIF audio can be directed through the SPDIF digital audio port (default) or the HDMI AV port (optional) using this menu.

In Figure 2-11, the onboard LAN option ROM is disabled on this system. Enable it when you want to boot from an operating system that is stored on a network drive.

1. HD Audio enabled
2. Change to HDMI to permit HDMI cable to carry audio as well as video signals

Figure 2-10   Configuring onboard HD Audio.

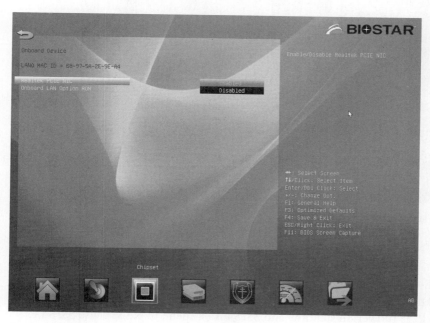

Figure 2-11   Configuring the onboard network adapter.

> **NOTE** Systems with support for legacy ports such as floppy, serial (COM), and parallel (LPT) use a separate BIOS settings menu for configuration. Do not enable these ports unless you use them.

Power Management

Although operating systems include power management features, the BIOS controls how any given system responds to standby or power-out conditions. Figure 2-12 illustrates a typical power management menu.

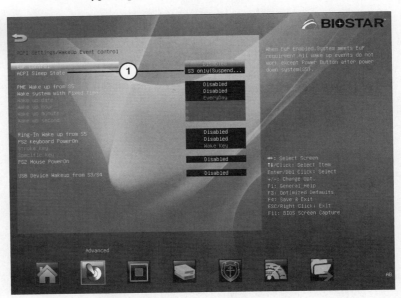

1. ACPI S3 sleep state enabled

Figure 2-12 Typical power management configuration menu.

ACPI is the power management function used in modern systems, replacing the older APM standard; it should be enabled. Most systems offer two ACPI standby states: S1/POS (power on standby) and S3/STR (suspend to RAM). Use S3/STR whenever possible because it uses much less power when the system is idle.

You can also configure your system power button, specify how to restart your system when AC power is lost, and specify how to wake up a system from standby, sleep, or hibernation modes. Some systems display these settings in the same dialog as power management, whereas others use a separate dialog or submenu.

Monitoring

As hot as a small room containing a PC can get, it's a whole lot hotter inside the PC itself. Excessive heat is the enemy of system stability and shortens the life of your hardware. Adding fans can help, but when they fail, you have problems. See Chapter 7, "CPUs," for more information.

The Hardware Monitor BIOS dialog (sometimes referred to as PC Health) is a common feature in most recent desktop systems. It is used to display the following (refer to Figure 2-13):

- Temperature monitoring
- Fan speeds
- Intrusion detection/notification
- **Voltage**

Many systems can also be configured to warn when CPU or system temperatures reach a dangerously high level or when fans stop turning or spin at too low a speed for proper cooling.

Windows-based hardware monitoring programs can also be used to display this information during normal system operation.

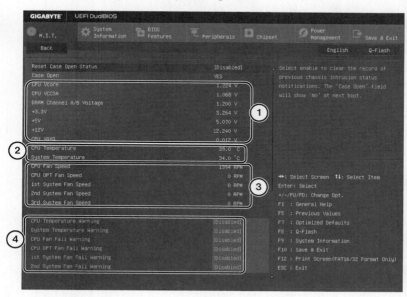

1. Voltage levels
2. Temperature levels
3. Fan speeds
4. Warnings (not configured)

Figure 2-13 Typical PC Health hardware monitoring menu.

Processor and Memory Configuration

To monitor system clock and **bus speed** settings, check the processor and memory configuration dialog typically available on gaming-oriented systems or others designed for overclocking (see Figure 2-14). On these systems, you can disable the normal Auto settings and manually tweak speeds, voltages, and other timing settings.

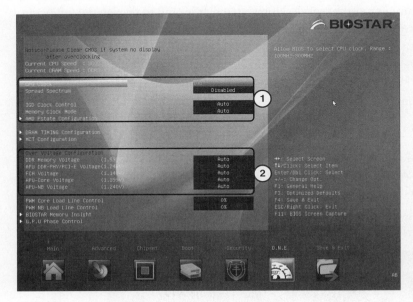

1. Clock adjustment options
2. Voltage adjustments

Figure 2-14   CPU configuration dialog used for viewing and changing clock and bus speeds for overclocking.

Virtualization Support

Virtualization is the capability to run multiple operating systems on a single computer at the same time. Although virtualization does not require processor support, virtualization programs such as Windows Virtual PC and Hyper-V, Oracle VM VirtualBox, and versions of VMware Workstation provide much better performance on systems that have hardware-assisted **virtualization support** enabled.

For a system to support hardware-assisted virtualization, it must include a CPU that supports virtualization and virtualization must be enabled in the system BIOS.

NOTE   Intel processors that include VT-x technology support hardware-assisted virtualization. AMD processors that include AMD-V technology support hardware-assisted virtualization. To determine whether a computer running Windows can support hardware-assisted virtualization, download and run havdetectiontool.exe, which is available from the Microsoft Download Center at www.microsoft.com.

Intel-based systems with VT support might have two entries for virtualization. Intel Virtualization Technology (also known as VT or VT-x) must be enabled for hardware-assisted virtualization to be supported. Intel VT with Directed I/O (VT-d Tech) can also be enabled to help improve I/O performance, although processors that support VT-x vary in their levels of VT-d support. Some systems, such as the one shown in Figure 2-15, have a single entry that enables or disables virtualization. When VT-d is enabled, VT-x is also enabled.

1. Intel virtualization not enabled

Figure 2-15   Virtualization is not enabled on this Intel-based system.

AMD-based systems that support hardware-assisted virtualization feature a single BIOS setting that might be labeled Virtualization, Secure Virtual Machine Mode, or SVM (see Figure 2-16).

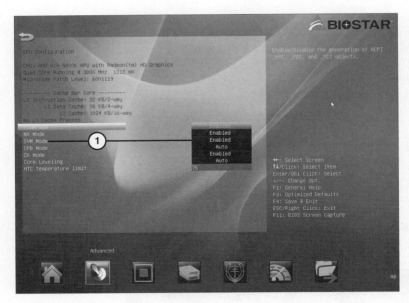

1. AMD virtualization enabled.

Figure 2-16   Virtualization has been enabled on this AMD-based system.

Security Features

Security features of various types are scattered around the typical system BIOS/
UEFI dialogs. Features and their locations vary by system and might include:

- **BIOS password**—BIOS Settings Password or Security dialogs

- **Power-on password**—Configured through the Security dialog

- **Chassis intrusion**—Various locations

- **Boot sector protection**—Advanced BIOS Features dialog

- **Secure Boot**—Boot or other dialogs

- **LoJack for Laptops**—An after-market product embedded in firmware or installed by the end user; not managed with BIOS dialogs

- **TPM (trusted program module)**—Security dialog

Enable the BIOS password feature to permit access to BIOS setup dialogs only for
those with the password. The power-on password option prevents anyone without
the password from starting the system. Note that these options can be defeated by
opening the system and clearing the CMOS memory.

Intrusion detection/notification, also known as Chassis Intrusion, when enabled, displays a warning on startup that the system has been opened.

Boot sector protection, found primarily on older systems, protects the default system drive's boot sector from being changed by viruses or other unwanted programs. Depending on the implementation, this option might need to be disabled before an operating system installation or upgrade.

Secure Boot is a feature that permits only software trusted by the PC manufacturer to be used to boot the system. When Secure Boot is enabled, the UEFI firmware checks for signatures on the boot software, option ROMs, and the operating system. Secure Boot support was first introduced in Windows 8, Windows RT, Windows Server 2012, and is also supported in newer versions.

A **TPM (trusted program module)** is used by Windows editions that support BitLocker full-disk encryption feature to protect the contents of the system hard drive (Vista) or any specified drive (Windows 7/8/8.1/10). Although many corporate laptops include a built-in TPM module, desktop computers and servers might include a connection for an optional TPM. For more information about using BitLocker, see Chapter 21, "Security."

LoJack for Laptops (and other mobile devices) is a popular security feature embedded in the laptop BIOSes of a number of systems and can be added to other systems. It consists of two components: a BIOS-resident component and the Computrace Agent, which is activated by LoJack when a computer is reported as stolen. To learn more about LoJack for laptops, tablets, and smartphones see www.absolute.com/en/lojackforlaptops/home.aspx.

Exiting BIOS and Saving/Discarding Changes

When you exit the BIOS setup program, you can elect to save configuration changes or discard them. Many systems with UEFI firmware permit the user to save multiple BIOS configuration settings (see Figure 2-17).

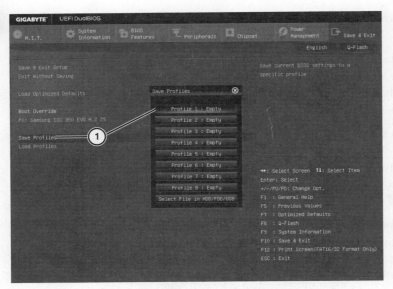

1. Selecting a location for storing the current UEFI firmware settings

Figure 2-17 Preparing to save the current BIOS configuration to a file.

If you made changes you want to keep, choose the option to save changes (see Figure 2-18). If you were "just looking" and did not intend to make any changes, choose the option to discard changes (see Figure 2-19). When you exit the BIOS setup program with either option, the system restarts.

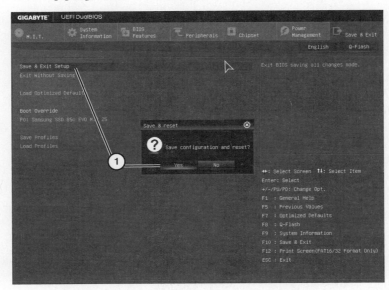

1. Exiting and saving the current UEFI firmware configuration

Figure 2-18 Preparing to save changes and exit the BIOS configuration menu.

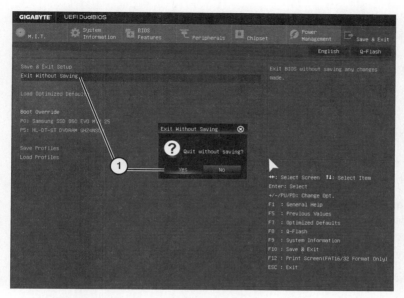

1. Exiting and discarding the current BIOS configuration

Figure 2-19   Preparing to discard changes and exit the BIOS configuration menu.

Flash Upgrade BIOS

The BIOS chip can be regarded as the "glue" that binds the hardware to the operating system. If the BIOS doesn't recognize the operating system or the hardware it communicates with, you're sure to have problems.

Because the BIOS chip bridges hardware to the operating system, you need to update the BIOS whenever your current BIOS version is unable to properly support

- New hardware, such as large SATA hard drives and different types of removable-storage drives

- New CPU models

- Memory modules with different capacities or timings

- New operating systems and features (such as virtualization or power management)

- New BIOS options

BIOS updates can also be used to solve problems with power management or other hardware-related issues.

A computer that is more than one year old or that is a candidate for a new processor might need a BIOS update. In the 1980s into the early 1990s, a BIOS update required a physical chip swap and, sometimes, reprogramming the chip with a device called an Electrically Erasable Programmable Read-Only Memory (EEPROM) burner. If the replacement or reprogrammed BIOS chip was installed incorrectly into the socket, it could be destroyed.

Fortunately, since the mid-1990s, a BIOS update can now be performed with software. The Flash BIOS chips in use on practically every recent system contain a special type of memory that can be changed through a software download from the system or motherboard maker.

Although Flash BIOS updates are easier to perform than the older, replace-the-chip style, you still need to be careful. An incomplete or incorrect BIOS update will prevent your system from being accessed. No BIOS, no boot! Regardless of the method, for maximum safety, follow these initial steps:

Step 1.   Back up important data.

Step 2.   Record the current BIOS configuration, especially hard drive settings as discussed earlier in this chapter.

CAUTION   BIOS configuration information might need to be reentered after a BIOS update, especially if you must install a different chip.

Flash BIOS Update

So you've decided you need a Flash BIOS update. Where do you get it? Don't ask the BIOS manufacturers (Phoenix, Insyde, AMI, and Award/Phoenix). They don't sell BIOS updates because their basic products are modified by motherboard and system vendors. Following are the general steps to locate a Flash BIOS update and install it:

Step 1.   For major brands of computers, go to the vendor's website and look for "downloads" or "tech support" links. The BIOS updates are listed by system model and by version; avoid beta (prerelease) versions.

TIP If your system is a generic system (that is, it came with a mainboard or motherboard manual and other component manuals rather than a full system manual), you need to contact the motherboard maker.

To determine the motherboard's make and model, you can download and run Belarc Advisor (free for personal use) from www.belarc.com/free_download.html.

See the following websites for additional help:

- Wim's BIOS page (www.wimsbios.com)

- eSupport (www.biosagentplus.com)

- American Megatrend's BIOS Support page (www.ami.com/support/bios.cfm)

You can also buy a replacement flash BIOS file from www.eSupport.com if you cannot get an updated BIOS code from your system or motherboard vendor.

Step 2. Locate the correct BIOS update for your system or motherboard. For generic motherboards, Wim's BIOS page also has links to the motherboard vendors' websites.

Step 3. Determine the installation media needed to install the BIOS image. Many recent systems use a Windows-based installer, but some use a bootable CD or USB flash drive.

Step 4. Be sure to download all files needed to install the BIOS image. In most cases, a download contains the appropriate loader program and the BIOS image, but for some motherboards, you might also need to download a separate loader program. If the website has instructions posted, print or save them for reference.

For installation from bootable media, see Steps 5 and 6.

Step 5. If you need to create bootable media, follow the vendor's instructions to create the media and place the loader and BIOS image files on the media.

Step 6. To install from bootable media, make sure the drive is the first item in the BIOS boot sequence. Insert or connect your media and restart the system. If prompted, press a key to start the upgrade process. Some upgrades run automatically, others require you to choose the image from a menu, and still others require the actual filename of the BIOS. The BIOS update might also prompt you to save your current BIOS image. Choose this option if possible so that you have a copy of your current BIOS in case there's a problem. After the process starts, it takes approximately three minutes to rewrite the contents of the BIOS chip with the updated information.

For installation from Windows, see Step 5a and Step 6a.

Step 5a.   Close all Windows programs before starting the update process.

Step 6a.   Navigate to the folder containing the BIOS update and double-click it to start the update process. Follow the prompts onscreen to complete the process. It takes approximately three minutes to rewrite the contents of the BIOS chip with the updated information.

> **CAUTION**   While performing a Flash upgrade, make sure you don't turn off the power to your PC and that you keep children or pets away from the computer to prevent an accidental shutdown. (Read: Your four-year-old decides to unplug the computer.) Wait for a message indicating the BIOS update has been completed before you even think about touching the computer. If the power goes out during the Flash update, the BIOS chip could be rendered useless.

Step 7.   Remove the media and restart the system to use your new BIOS features. Reconfigure the BIOS settings if necessary.

Recovering from a Failed BIOS Update

If the primary system BIOS is damaged, keep in mind that some motherboard vendors offer dual BIOS chips on some products. The secondary BIOS performs the same functions as the primary BIOS so the system can continue to run.

If you use the wrong Flash BIOS file to update your BIOS, or if the update process doesn't finish, your system can't start. You might need to contact the system or motherboard maker for service or purchase a replacement BIOS chip.

Some BIOSes contain a "mini-BIOS" that can be reinstalled from a reserved part of the chip. Systems with this feature have a jumper on the motherboard called the Flash recovery jumper.

To use this feature, download the correct Flash BIOS, make a bootable disc from it, and take it to the computer with the defective BIOS. Set the jumper to Recovery, insert the bootable media, and then rerun the setup process. Because the video won't work, you'll need to listen for beeps and watch for the drive light to run during this process. Turn off the computer, reset the jumper to Normal, and then restart the computer.

If the update can't be installed, your motherboard might have a jumper that write-protects the Flash BIOS. Check the manual to see whether your system has this feature. To update a BIOS on a system with a write-protected jumper, you must follow these steps:

Step 1. Disable the write protection.

Step 2. Perform the update.

Step 3. Re-enable the write-protection to keep unauthorized people from changing the BIOS.

Using BIOS/UEFI Diagnostics

Some system vendors provide UEFI diagnostics programs that can be installed on a bootable USB drive or might be available to run at system startup time. These diagnostic programs can be used to test the motherboard, RAM, displays, drives, fans, and other components. Figure 2-20 illustrates the main menu of the HP Hardware Diagnostics utility.

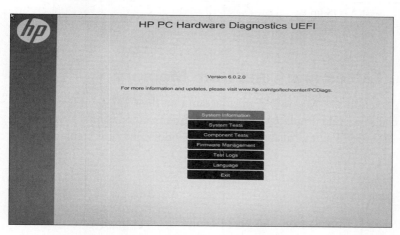

Figure 2-20 Preparing to test a computer with HP PC Hardware Diagnostics UEFI.

Exam Preparation Tasks

Review All the Key Topics

Review the most important topics in the chapter, noted with the Key Topic icon in the outer margin of the page. Table 2-2 lists a reference to these key topics and the page numbers on which each is found.

Table 2-2   Key Topics for Chapter 2

Key Topic Element	Description	Page Number
Text	Common keystrokes used to access BIOS Setup	32
Text	Definition of UEFI firmware	33
Table 2-1	Major CMOS/BIOS/UEFI Settings	35
Figure 2-3	A typical CMOS UEFI Setup main menu	38
Figure 2-4	A typical UEFI main setup menu for a desktop system with an AMD processor (UEFI BIOS for BIOSTAR Hi-Fi A85W).	39
Figure 2-7	A typical Boot Sequence submenu configured to permit booting from a CD/DVD or USB flash drive before the hard disk	41
Figure 2-12	Typical power management configuration menu	46
Figure 2-13	A typical hardware monitor screen	47
Figure 2-17	Typical exit dialog with the option to save changes to a file	52
Text	Flash BIOS update	56

Complete the Tables and Lists from Memory

Print a copy of Appendix C, "Memory Tables" (found on the CD), or at least the section for this chapter, and complete the tables and lists from memory. Appendix D, "Answers to Memory Tables," also on the CD, includes completed tables and lists to check your work.

Define Key Terms

Define the following key terms from this chapter, and check your answers in the glossary.

Basic Input/Output System (BIOS), power-on self-test (POST), CMOS, virtualization support, TPM, LoJack for Laptops, Secure Boot, Intrusion detection/notification, voltage, clock, bus speed

Complete Hands-On Labs

Complete the hands-on labs, and then see the answers and explanations at the end of the chapter.

Lab 2-1: Disable Onboard Audio

Scenario: You are a technician working at a PC repair bench. You need to install a sound card into a system that has onboard audio. Before you can do this, you need to turn off the onboard audio feature in the system BIOS.

Step 1. Review the BIOS screens listed earlier in this chapter. From Figure 2-3, which menu selection would you choose?

Step 2. Review the BIOS screens (see Figures 2-6 through 2-17). Which figure has the correct menu option for disabling onboard audio?

Step 3. What is the menu called?

Step 4. What is the option called?

Step 5. What is the current setting?

Step 6. What is the setting you need to select?

Step 7. What key do you press to exit setup and save changes?

Lab 2-2: Check Fan and Voltage Levels

Scenario: You are a technician working at a PC repair bench. Your client reports that the computer is overheating. You need to check the performance of fans connected to the motherboard and the voltage levels on the motherboard.

Step 1. Review the CMOS (BIOS) setup screens listed earlier in this chapter. From Figure 2-3, which menu selection would you choose?

Step 2. Review the CMOS (BIOS) setup screens (see Figures 2-6 through 2-17). Which figure displays fan speeds and voltage levels?

Step 3. What is the CPU fan speed?

Step 4. What is the CPU voltage called?

Step 5. What is the voltage for the CPU?

Step 6. What key do you press to exit setup without saving changes?

Answer Review Questions

Answer these review questions and then see the answers and explanations at the end of the chapter.

1. Which of the following best describes the BIOS?

   a. Firmware contained on a ROM chip

   b. The first code run when the computer starts up

   c. Volatile and requires a battery to maintain its memory

   d. Program contained in the Master Boot Record (MBR)

2. When the user wants to change the default settings in the BIOS startup program, where are those changes saved and stored?

   a. UEFI

   b. POST

   c. MBR

   d. CMOS

3. Which of the following statements is false?

   a. UEFI does not support traditional Master Boot Record (MBR) hard drive partitioning.

   b. UEFI is capable of working with the GUID Partition Table (GPT).

   c. UEFI enables more efficient use of larger hard drives than traditional BIOS.

   d. Apple OS X uses UEFI.

4. If there were a problem during startup with your computer's memory, where would that problem be reported?

   a. CMOS

   b. POST

   c. MBR

   d. TPM

5. Which of the following steps should be taken before installing a new sound card?

   a. You should disable the onboard audio controller in POST.

   b. You should use POST to configure the new sound card.

   c. You should disable the onboard audio controller in the BIOS settings.

   d. You should configure the new sound card in the MBR.

6. Which of the following statements best describes the function of the Secure Boot setting in UEFI firmware?

   a. It prevents Windows 8 or Windows 10 from booting.

   b. It allows Linux to be used as an operating system.

   c. It enables AHCI mode.

   d. It enables only Windows 8 or Windows 10 to be used as an operating system.

7. In which of the following configuration programs might you navigate the menu screens using a mouse?

   a. UEFI

   b. CMOS

   c. BIOS

   d. POST

8. In the following figure, which of the following actions makes and saves changes to the CMOS chip?

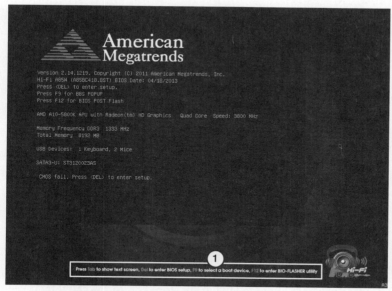

1. Keystrokes for configuration options at startup

   a. Pressing Del

   b. Pressing Tab

   c. Pressing F9

   d. Pressing F12

9. Which of the following information is *not* found in the BIOS/UEFI startup settings?

   a. Time and date

   b. Installed memory

   c. CPU temperature

   d. CPU type and speed

   e. IP address

10. Which of the following statements best describes the effect of enabling Quick Boot in the startup program?

    a. It omits POST.

    b. It does not run the memory and drive tests.

    c. It does not check CMOS settings.

    d. It activates the S3 power saving program.

11. What is the power management system used in modern computers?

    a. APM

    b. SATA

    c. ATAPI

    d. ACPI

12. A friend has just bought a new computer and has given you his old computer. The old computer has a 30 GB IDE hard drive that you want to upgrade to a new 3 TB SATA hard drive, but when you install your new hard drive, you find that you can access only about 2 TB of space. Which of the following statements best describes how to remedy the situation?

    a. You should install new drivers for the new SATA drive.

    b. You should enable the new drive in the CMOS settings.

    c. You should upgrade your current motherboard along with the new hard drive.

    d. You should return the hard disk drive and use a 2 TB hard disk drive instead.

13. In Table 2-3, identify which of the following are stored on ROM chips and which are stored on RAM chips. Also indicate which require(s) an outside source of power to maintain its memory.

Table 2-3   ROM/RAM/POWER

Options	BIOS	UEFI	CMOS
ROM or RAM?			
Requires Battery or No Power Source?			

14. Match the following security features with their definitions.

Features	Definitions
A. TPM	1. Warns when chassis has been opened
B. Secure Boot	2. Limits access to startup screens to users with proper authorization
C. BIOS password	3. Supports BitLocker encryption
D. Power-on password	4. Requires user to provide identification when turning system on
E. Intrusion detection	5. Checks signature of boot software and permits only trusted software to start the system

15. Which of the following best describes to permanently change or upgrade the BIOS program?

   a. Download a new program from the system manufacturer and flash the BIOS.

   b. Make any necessary changes to the CMOS program and save those changes to the BIOS.

   c. Make any necessary changes to the POST program as it is testing and initializing the various components.

   d. After the MBR has been run, save any changes to the BIOS.

Answers and Explanations to Hands-On Labs

Lab 2-1: Disable Onboard Audio

To access the onboard audio screen from Figure 2-3, the most likely menu to go to is the Peripherals menu. However, on other systems, the correct answer might be Advanced or other options.

Figure 2-10 is the figure including the HD Audio setting.

The menu is the Advanced menu.

The option is called HD Audio Azalia Device.

The current setting is Enabled.

The setting to select is Disabled.

The key to save changes and exit varies by BIOS/UEFI firmware. In Figure 2-17, the key is F10 (the most common choice). However, a different BIOS/UEFI firmware dialog shown in Figure 2-16 uses F4.

Lab 2-2: Check Fan and Voltage Levels

The PC Health Status menu is the most likely place to find this information. Figure 2-13 illustrates a typical dialog.

The CPU fan speed is 1394 RPM (rpm). The CPU voltage is listed as two values: CPU Vcore and CPU VCCSA. CPU Vcore is 1.224V, and the CPU VCCSA is 1.068V.

To exit without saving changes, use the Esc key.

Answers and Explanations to Review Questions

1. **A**. During startup, the BIOS program (or the more recent UEFI) is the first program to run and is responsible for starting the computer. The BIOS is stored on a ROM chip and is not volatile. The BIOS is not part of the MBR.

2. **D**. When changes are made to the startup program in either the BIOS or the newer UEFI, those changes are stored on the CMOS chip.

3. **A**. UEFI does support traditional Master Boot Record (MBR) hard drive partitioning and is also capable of working with the GUID Partition Table (GPT) and modern large hard drives. UEFI is also used by OS X.

4. **B**. During startup, the BIOS program runs POST, which tests and initializes components such as memory, CPU, hard drives, optical drives, USB drives, and video cards and then reports any problems found.

5. **C**. Restart the computer and open the startup settings. Disable the onboard audio before installing the new sound card and save the changes to CMOS.

6. **D**. Secure Boot must be disabled when the user wants to install a different operating system.

7. **A**. The UEFI display uses a mouse-driven GUI in addition to the keyboard navigation used by the BIOS.

8. **A.** CMOS is a RAM chip that is used to store changes made to the startup program within the BIOS or UEFI. To edit the startup program, you should check the user's manual or restart the computer and watch the screen for instructions to enter the BIOS setup. In the diagram, pressing Del allows you to enter the startup program. Any changes made here may be saved in CMOS.

9. **E.** The IP address is found in the Network and Sharing Center or through the command-line interface, not in the BIOS or UEFI.

10. **B.** Quick Boot enables faster system startup by skipping the memory and drive tests when booting the computer. POST and CMOS are always involved in the boot process. The S3 power setting does not affect the boot process.

11. **D.** ACPI replaced APM as the power management utility on modern computers. SATA is a type of hard drive. ATAPI is the standard for CDs and DVDs.

12. **C.** An older traditional BIOS can support only a maximum hard drive size of 2.2 TB. To use the new 3 TB hard drive, you need to replace the motherboard with a newer one that supports UEFI (which supports up to 9.4 ZB hard drives).

13.

ROM/RAM/POWER Answers

Options	BIOS	UEFI	CMOS
ROM or RAM?	ROM	ROM	RAM
Requires Battery or No Power Source?	No power source	No power source	Requires battery

BIOS and UEFI are both stored on ROM chips and therefore are permanent and do not require an additional power source. CMOS is stored in RAM, which is volatile and requires a CMOS battery to provide a constant trickle of power to maintain its memory.

14. **A.** 3; B. 5; C. 2; D. 4; E.1. Incorrect definitions: 6, 7.

15. **A.** The BIOS program (or the newer UEFI program) is stored as permanent memory in ROM. To permanently change the programming for either of these chips, you must download a new program from the manufacturer and flash that program onto the BIOS or UEFI. Changes made to the CMOS chip, which is RAM, are temporary and will be lost if power is lost in the CMOS battery. POST and the MBR do not affect the contents of either the BIOS or the UEFI.

This chapter covers the following subjects:

- **ATX, ITX, and Smaller Sizes**—This section compares the sizes and features of ATX and ITX-family motherboards.

- **Expansion Slot Types**—This section discusses PCI and PCIe expansion slots and how they differ.

- **RAM Sockets**—This section introduces the concept of RAM sockets.

- **CPU Sockets**—This section introduces the concept of CPU sockets.

- **Chipsets**—Discover what chipsets do in this section.

- **CMOS Battery**—Learn how to recognize the battery that maintains the CMOS and how to clear its contents in this section.

- **Power Connectors**—This section introduces the most common motherboard power connectors.

- **Fan Connectors**—This section compares CPU and system fan connectors.

- **Front and Top Panel Connectors**—This section discusses how to connect front and top panel cables to the motherboard.

- **Bus Speeds**—This section introduces the concept of bus speeds.

- **Installing Motherboards**—In this section, learn how to remove and install a motherboard.

## CHAPTER 3

Motherboard Components

In this chapter we'll talk about one of the core components of a desktop computer—the guts of the computer—the **motherboard (system board)**. Everything connects to the motherboard, so it stands to reason that proper planning and design of a desktop PC, to a certain degree, starts with this component. Within these pages you learn how to specify and install motherboards and discover some of the considerations to take into account when building the core of a PC.

220-901: Objective 1.2 Explain the importance of motherboard components, their purpose and properties.

Foundation Topics

ATX, ITX, and Smaller Sizes

Although all motherboards have some features in common, their layout and size (also known as the **form factor**) vary a great deal. The most common motherboard designs in current use include ATX (Advanced Technology Integrated), **microATX**, and Mini-ITX. The following sections cover the details of these designs and some other motherboard designs in the same families.

NOTE   You need to know ATX, microATX, and ITX (on which Mini-ITX is based) for the 220-901 exam.

ATX and microATX

The **ATX** family of motherboards has dominated desktop computer designs since the late 1990s. *ATX* stands for Advanced Technology Extended, and it replaced the AT and Baby-AT form factors developed in the mid-1980s for the IBM PC AT and its rivals. ATX motherboards have the following characteristics:

- A rear port cluster for I/O ports
- Expansion slots that run parallel to the short side of the motherboard
- Left-side case opening (as viewed from the front of a tower PC)

NOTE   Port clusters, internal header cables, and other I/O port uses and features are covered in Chapter 8, "Ports and Interfaces."

There are three members of the ATX family, as listed in Table 3-1. In practice, though, the Mini-ATX design is not widely used.

Table 3-1   ATX Motherboard Family Comparison

Motherboard Type	Maximum Width	Maximum Depth	Maximum Number of Expansion Slots	Typical Uses
ATX	12 in.	9.6 in.	Seven	Full tower
Mini-ATX	11.2 in.	8.2 in.	Seven	Full tower
microATX	9.6 in.	9.6 in.	Four	Mini tower

Figure 3-1 illustrates a typical ATX motherboard.

1. PCI slots
2. PCIe x1 slots
3. PCIe x16 slots
4. USB Port headers
5. SATA ports
6. Front-panel cable headers
7. Front-facing SATA ports
8. USB 3.0 header
9. ATX 24-pin power connector
10. DDR3 memory slots (dual-channel)
11. CPU socket
12. EPS12V power connector
13. Port cluster
14. CMOS battery (CR2032)
15. CPU fan header
16. Case fan header

Figure 3-1 A typical late-model ATX motherboard.

Figure 3-2 illustrates a typical microATX (mATX) motherboard.

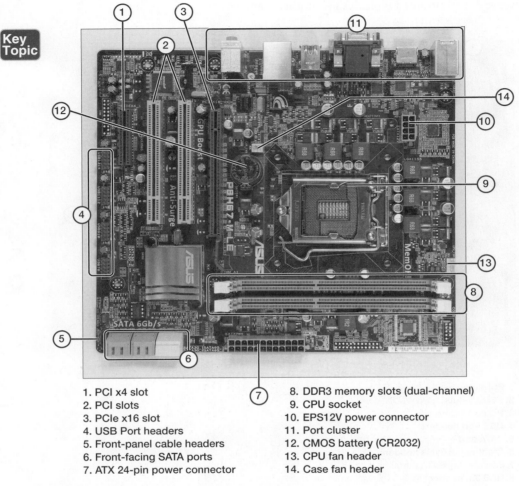

1. PCI x4 slot
2. PCI slots
3. PCIe x16 slot
4. USB Port headers
5. Front-panel cable headers
6. Front-facing SATA ports
7. ATX 24-pin power connector
8. DDR3 memory slots (dual-channel)
9. CPU socket
10. EPS12V power connector
11. Port cluster
12. CMOS battery (CR2032)
13. CPU fan header
14. Case fan header

Figure 3-2 A typical late-model microATX motherboard.

ITX Family

The ITX family of motherboards was originally developed by VIA Technologies in 2001 for use with its low-power x86 C3 processors. The original ITX motherboard form factor was quickly superseded by the smaller Mini-ITX form factor. **Mini-ITX** measures 6.7 × 6.7 inches and has been adopted by many vendors for use with AMD and Intel processors. These processors may be socketed or soldered in place. Original designs featured a single PCI expansion slot, but most recent designs include a PCIe x1 or x16 expansion slot instead. A Mini-ITX motherboard can typically fit into a case made for ATX-family motherboards and uses a similar port cluster; however, Mini-ITX motherboards are used in small form factor PCs and in home theater applications.

Figure 3-3 shows a typical Mini-ITX motherboard optimized for home theater applications. It uses a low-power CPU soldered to the motherboard, a fanless passive heatsink, and SODIMM memory to reduce heat and allow for very quiet operation. It includes a **miniPCIe** slot (normally found in laptops) for use with a Wi-Fi card. Some Mini-ITX motherboards feature socketed processors and a PCIe x16 slot for high-performance 3D video, making them suitable for gaming.

1. Port cluster
2. PCIe x1 slot
3. SATA ports
4. Mini-PCIe slot
5. CMOS battery (CR2032)
6. SO-DIMM DDR3 memory sockets
7. ATX 24-pin power connector
8. Front panel cable headers
9. ATX12V power connector
10. CPU fan header (not used with this processor)
11. USB header
12. Processor heat sink

Figure 3-3 A typical Mini-ITX motherboard optimized for home theater.

Pico-ITX and Nano-ITX motherboards are smaller than Mini-ITX and are used primarily in computing appliances.

Comparing ATX, MicroATX, and Mini-ITX Motherboards

Figure 3-4 compares the general size and layout of Mini-ITX to ATX and micro-ATX motherboards.

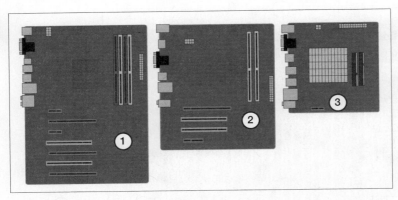

1. ATX motherboard
2. microATX motherboard
3. Mini-ITX motherboard

Figure 3-4   ATX, microATX, and Mini-ITX motherboard component layouts compared.

Expansion Slot Types

Motherboards use **expansion slots** to provide support for additional I/O devices and high-speed video/graphics cards. The most common expansion slots on recent systems include Peripheral Component Interconnect (PCI) and PCI Express (also known as PCIe).

PCI Slots

The **PCI** slot (originally developed in 1992) can be used for many types of add-on cards, including network, video, audio, I/O, and storage host adapters for SATA drives. There are several types of PCI slots, but the one found in desktop computers is the 32-bit slot running at 33MHz (see Figure 3-5 in the next section). PCI slots are also available in 66MHz versions and in 64-bit versions.

NOTE   Early PCI cards used 5V DC power, but virtually all 32-bit PCI cards in use for a number of years use 3.3V DC power.

PCI-X Slots

PCI-X is a faster version of 64-bit PCI, running at speeds of 133MHz. PCI-X slots also support PCI cards. In fact, the PCI-X slot uses the same connectors as 64-bit PCI slot (refer to Figure 3-5). A PCI-X bus supports two PCI-X slots, but if you install a PCI-X card into a PCI-X slot on the same bus as a PCI card, the PCI-X card runs at the same speed as the PCI card. PCI-X slots are typically used in servers and workstations.

PCI-X 2.0 (introduced in 2008) also supports 266MHz and 533MHz speeds; however, like PCI, both types of PCI-X have been replaced by PCIe. Figure 3-5 compares 32-bit and 64-bit PCI and PCI-X slots and card connectors to each other.

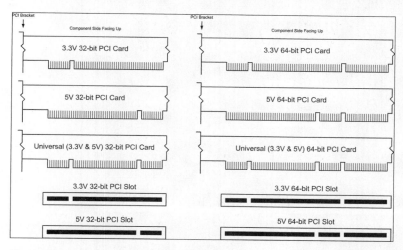

Figure 3-5 32-bit PCI cards and slots (left) compared to 64-bit PCI/PCI-X cards and slots (right). Image courtesy of Wikimedia Commons (see http://en.wikipedia.org/wiki/File:PCI_Keying.png for details).

PCIe (PCI Express) Slots

PCI Express (often abbreviated as **PCIe** or PCIE) began to replace both PCI and AGP slots in system designs starting in 2005. PCIe slots are available in four types:

- x1
- x4
- x8
- x16

Each x refers to an I/O lane. The most common versions include the x1, x4, and x16 designs, as shown in Figure 3-6.

NOTE   PCIe x1 cards can be used in any PCIe slot. PCIe x4 cards can also be used in PCIe x8 and x16 slots. PCIe x8 cards can also be used in x16 slots.

Some motherboards have two or more slots that use the x16 connector. However, the additional slots might actually support only x4 or x8 transfer rates (see Figure 3-7).

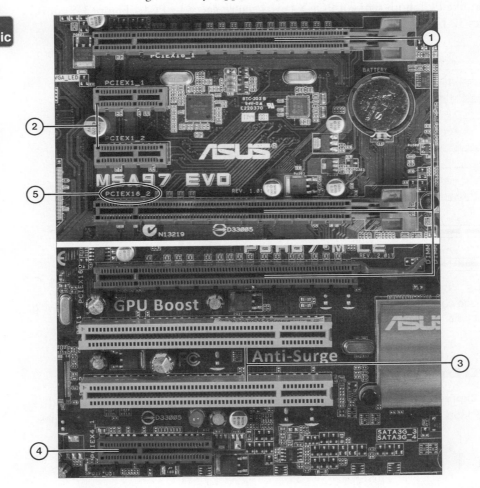

1. PCIe x16 slots
2. PCIex1 slots
3. PCI slots
4. PCIe x4 slot
5. Slot identification

Figure 3-6   PCI Express compared to PCI slots.

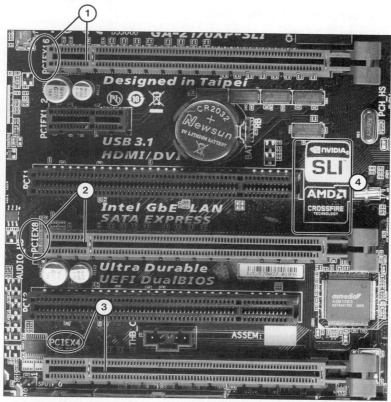

1. PCIe x16 slot

2. PCIe x16 connector, slot supports x8

3. PCIe x16 connector, slot supports x4

4. Multi-GPU (graphics processor) standards supported

Figure 3-7 This motherboard, built for multi-GPU gaming, has three PCIe x16 physical connectors, but only one actually provides x16 speeds.

PCI Express x1 and x4 slots are designed to replace the PCI slot, and x8 and x16 are designed to replace the AGP and PCI-X slots. Table 3-2 compares the performance of PCI, PCI-X, and PCIe.

Table 3-2 Technical Information About Expansion Slot Types

Slot Type	Performance	Suggested Uses
PCI 32-bit, 33MHz	133MBps	Video, network, mass storage (SATA/RAID), sound card
PCI 32-bit, 66MHz	266MBps	Network, mass storage (workstation and server)

Slot Type	Performance	Suggested Uses
PCI 64-bit, 33MHz	266MBps	Network, mass storage (workstation and server)
PCI 64-bit, 66MHz	533MBps	Network, mass storage (workstation and server)
PCI-X 66MHz	533MBps	Network, mass storage (workstation and server)
PCI-X 133MHz	1,066MBps	Network, mass storage (workstation and server)
PCI-X 2.0 266MHz	2,133MBps	Network, mass storage (workstation and server)
PCI-X 2.0 533MHz	4,266MBps	Network, mass storage (workstation and server)
PCIe x1 v1	500MBps*	Network, I/O
PCIe x4 v1	2,000MBps*	Network
PCIe x8 v1	4,000MBps*	Multi-GPU video secondary card
PCIe x16 v1	8,000MBps*	Video primary and secondary cards
PCIe x1 v2	1,000MBps*	Network, I/O
PCIe x4 v2	4,000MBps*	Network
PCIe x8 v2	8,000MBps*	Video secondary card
PCIe x16 v2	16,000MBps*	Video primary and secondary cards
PCIe x1 v3	2,000MBps*	Network, I/O
PCIe x4 v3	8,000MBps*	Network
PCIe x8 v3	16,000MBps*	Video secondary card
PCIe x16 v3	32,000MBps*	Video primary and secondary cards

*Bidirectional data rates (full duplex simultaneous send/receive); unidirectional data rates are one-half of values listed. All versions of PCIe use the same connectors.

GPU = graphics processing unit

NOTE MiniPCI and MiniPCIe are reduced-size versions of the PCI and PCIe standards. They are used in laptop computers. To learn more, see Chapter 12, "Mobile Devices."

To learn more about installing adapter cards, see Chapter 5, "PC Expansion Cards."

RAM Sockets

Most modern motherboards, with the exception of some Mini-ITX and smaller motherboards, include two or more memory slots (refer to Figures 3-1, 3-2, and

3-3). At least one memory slot (also known as RAM slots) must contain a memory module or the system cannot start or function.

Memory slots vary in design according to the type of memory the system supports. Older systems that use SDRAM use three-section memory slots (also known as **RAM slots**) designed for 168-pin memory modules. Systems that use DDR SDRAM use two-section memory slots designed for 184-pin memory modules. Systems that use DDR2 SDRAM use two-section memory slots designed for 240-pin modules. DDR3 SDRAM also uses two-section 240-pin memory slots, but the arrangement of the pins and the keying of the slot are different than in DDR2. DDR2 and DDR3 modules cannot be interchanged.

NOTE   Many systems are now available with DDR4 memory. DDR4 desktop memory uses a 288-pin DIMM and a matching two-section memory slot. DDR4 uses 1.2V DC power and has clock speeds of 1600 to 3200MHz.

To learn more about memory types and slots, see Chapter 4, "RAM Types and Features."

CPU Sockets

ATX, microATX, and some Mini-ITX motherboards use various types of **CPU sockets** according to the CPU brand and family the motherboard and chipset are designed to accommodate. The motherboard shown in Figure 3-1 uses an AMD AM3+ socket, and the motherboard shown in Figure 3-2 uses an Intel LGA 1155 socket. However, some Mini-ITX motherboards, such as the one shown in Figure 3-3, use soldered-in-place processors that cannot be interchanged. Many of these motherboards are intended for embedded systems. For more information about CPUs and CPU sockets, see Chapter 7, "CPUs."

Chipsets

Although the CPU gets most of the attention from casual PC users when evaluating a system, the chipset is just as important. The **chipset** determines which CPUs a system can use, which integrated ports the system can provide without the use of third-party products, and the number and types of expansion slots a motherboard can feature. If the chipset includes the memory controller, it is also responsible for determining what type and speeds of RAM a system can use. As Scott Mueller points out in "Chipsets," in Chapter 4, "RAM Types and Features" of *Upgrading and*

Repairing PCs, 22nd edition: "The chipset is the motherboard." So what exactly is a chipset and what does it do?

Most chipsets include two components:

- **North Bridge (northbridge)**—Also known as the memory controller hub (MCH) or, on Intel systems with chipset integrated graphics, the graphics memory controller hub (GMCH)

- **South Bridge (southbridge)**—Also known as the I/O controller hub (ICH)

The North Bridge chip connects to the CPU and other high-speed components such as memory, PCIe video (either via expansion slots or integrated into the chipset), USB 3.0 ports, and other high-speed components.

The South Bridge chip connects to lower-speed components, such as mass storage interfaces, PCI expansion slots, USB 2.0 ports, audio, and the CMOS.

NOTE   The exact division of tasks between chipset components varies by chipset, and, on some systems, ports such as USB 3.0 are handled by a separate controller chip. See the motherboard, system, and chipset documentation for details.

Unlike the CPU, which is removable and upgradable, the chipset's components are surface mounted to the motherboard. The only way to change the chipset is to replace the motherboard. To protect the chipset's components from damaging heat, chipsets are frequently covered by heat sinks.

Figure 3-8 illustrates the location of the CPU, North Bridge, and South Bridge chips on a typical motherboard and the components they communicate with. On some systems, such as the one shown in Figure 3-8, a separate chip called the Super I/O (or Super IO) chip is also used to control some slower devices. Some recent chipsets have only one chip.

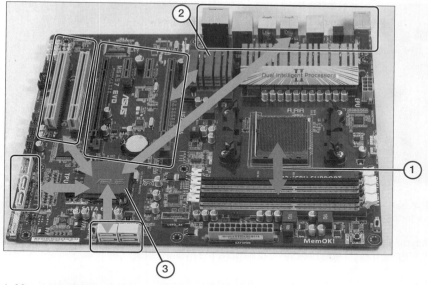

1. Memory controller is built into CPU (not yet installed)
2. North Bridge controls PCIe slots on this system
3. South Bridge controls USB 2.0, Ethernet, and SATA ports on this system

Figure 3-8   CPUs using the AMD AM3+ socket have built-in memory controllers, so the North Bridge chip (hidden under a passive heat sink) controls PCIe expansion slots. Slower devices, such as PCI expansion slots, SATA, USB, and Ethernet ports, are controlled by the South Bridge (also hidden under a passive heat sink).

CMOS Battery

The system BIOS is responsible for configuring the ports and features controlled by the chipset, and the CMOS chip on the motherboard stores the settings. The **CMOS battery** provides power to maintain the contents of the CMOS chip (see Figure 3-9). A **jumper block** placed over two **jumper** pins is how CMOS is cleared on most systems. To learn more about the system BIOS and CMOS, see Chapter 2, "Configure and Use BIOS/UEFI Tools."

NOTE   Some systems feature a port-cluster-mounted push button to clear the CMOS. If you need to clear the CMOS on a particular system, check the documentation for details.

1. CR2032 CMOS battery
2. Jumper block for clearing CMOS memory

Figure 3-9   A typical CMOS battery (CR2032). Put a jumper block over the CLR_CMOS jumper pins to clear CMOS memory if you need to reconfigure the system BIOS settings.

Power Connectors

Motherboards typically feature two power connectors:

- The 24-pin ATX connector provides power to expansion slots and most bus connectors.

- The 8-pin EPS12V connector provides dedicated 12V power for the CPU. The motherboard steps down this voltage to the voltage needed by the installed CPU.

NOTE   Some older motherboards or motherboards designed for low-power CPUs use a four-pin ATX12V connector instead of the EPS12V.

These connectors are illustrated in Figure 3-10.

1. ATX 24-pin main power connector

2. EPS12V power connector

Figure 3-10   24-pin ATX and 8-pin EPS12V power connectors on a typical motherboard.

For more information about these and other power supply connectors, see Chapter 9, "Designing and Building Custom PC Configurations."

Fan Connectors

Almost all motherboards have a **CPU fan connector** and several **system fan connectors** (used for fans connected to the case). Both types of fan connectors have a monitor connection to provide fan speed information to the PC health or system monitor feature built in to the system BIOS. Some motherboards also have a connector to monitor the speed of the fan built in the power supply.

The CPU fan differs from typical system fan connectors by including a fourth pin used for speed control; system fans with speed control also use a four-pin connector. Figure 3-11 shows a typical CPU fan connector and system fan connector before and after connecting the fan leads.

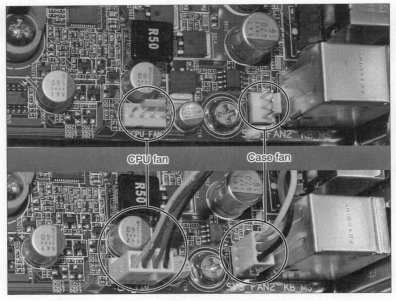

Figure 3-11   CPU (left) and system fan (right) connectors.

Front and Top Panel Connectors

Typical motherboards feature one or more audio connectors designed for different purposes:

- **Front/top-panel audio**—Microphone and headphones; found on almost all motherboards.

- **Music CD playback from optical drives**—This feature is rarely needed because Windows Media Player and other media player programs can play music through the SATA interface and newer optical drives no longer include separate music CD playback connectors.

- **SPDIF header**—Designed to support an optional SPDIF bracket for digital audio playback; the bracket is provided by the motherboard vendor but is not always bundled with compatible motherboards.

Figure 3-12 illustrates these connectors on a typical motherboard.

NOTE   Front-panel audio cables often have two sets of connectors: one for HD audio and one for the older AC'97 audio standard. Use the connector that corresponds to the audio version supported by your motherboard.

ATX and ITX-family motherboards include several **front/top-panel connectors** for the power button, power light, drive activity lights, reset button, USB, and audio case speaker (if present). These connectors are grouped together on or near the front edge of the motherboard (see Figure 3-13).

Because front-panel leads are small and are difficult to install, some motherboard vendors provide a quick-connect extender for easier installation: Connect the leads to the extender, and then connect the extender to the front-panel headers. See Figure 3-14 for a typical example.

Front-panel audio   Connects to SPDIF port

Connects to CD or DVD drive for audio playback

Figure 3-12 Front/top-panel audio, music CD, and SPDIF bracket headers on a typical motherboard.

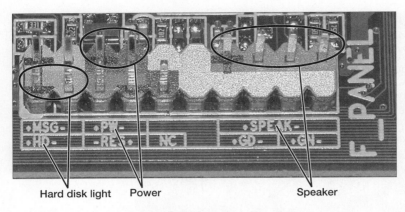

Hard disk light   Power   Speaker

Figure 3-13   A typical two-row front/top-panel connector.

Individual front-panel cables

Extender

Figure 3-14   Individual front-panel cables connected via an extender to the motherboard.

Bus Speeds

Different components of the motherboard, such as the CPU, memory, chipset, expansion slots, storage interfaces, and I/O ports, connect with each other at different speeds. The term **bus speeds** refers to the speeds at which different buses in the motherboard connect to different components.

Some of these speeds, such as the speed of I/O ports and expansion slots (USB, FireWire, and SATA ports; PCI and PCIe slots), are established by the design of the port or by the capabilities of the devices connected to them. However, depending on the motherboard, you might be able to fine-tune the bus speeds used by the processor, the chipset interconnect, and memory. These adjustments, where available, are typically performed through BIOS settings in menus such as Memory, Overclocking, AI Tweaker, and others.

See Chapter 2 for more details.

Installing Motherboards

The current A+ certification exam competencies do not list installing motherboards as an objective. However, if you are called upon to build or upgrade a system, chances are you will need to understand the process.

What keeps a motherboard from sliding around inside the case? When you look at an unmounted motherboard from the top, you can see that motherboards have several holes around the edges and several holes toward the middle of the motherboard. Most ATX-family and ITX-family motherboards are held in place by screws that are fastened to brass spacers threaded into holes in the case or a removable motherboard tray. Holes intended for use with screws are metal-rimmed or metal-reinforced. Holes that are designed for use with plastic spacers are not reinforced.

NOTE   Before you start working with motherboards or other static-sensitive parts such as CPUs and memory, see the section "Component Handling and Storage" in Chapter 17 for precautions you should follow.

Step-by-Step Motherboard Removal

Removing the motherboard is an important task for the computer technician. For safety's sake, you should also remove the motherboard before you install a CPU upgrade.

To remove ATX-family or Mini-ITX motherboards from standard cases, follow these steps:

Step 1.   Turn off the power switch and disconnect the AC power cable from the power supply.

Step 2.   Disconnect all cables (including data and power leads) connected to add-on cards after labeling them for easy reconnection.

Step 3.   Disconnect all cables attached to built-in ports on the motherboard (I/O, storage, and so on) after labeling them for easy reconnection.

Step 4.   Disconnect all cables leading to internal speakers, key locks, speed switches, and other front-panel cables. Most recent systems use clearly marked cables, as shown in Figure 3-15, but if the cables are not marked, mark them before you disconnect them so that you can easily reconnect them later.

Figure 3-15   Front-panel cables attached to a typical motherboard. The cables control system power to the motherboard, case speaker, drive and power lights, and so on.

TIP   You can purchase premade labels for common types of cables, but if these are not available, you can use a label maker or blank address labels to custom-make your own labels.

Step 5.   Remove all add-on cards and place them on an antistatic mat or in (not on top of) antistatic bags.

Step 6.   Disconnect header cables from front- or rear-mounted ports and remove them from the system (see Figures 3-16 and 3-17).

Step 7.   Disconnect the power-supply leads from the motherboard. If the new motherboard uses different power supply connections than the old motherboard, replace the power supply. See Chapter 9 for details about power supply connections.

Step 8.   If possible, remove the heat sink and the processor before you remove the motherboard, and place them on an antistatic mat. Removing these items before you remove the motherboard helps prevent excessive flexing of the motherboard and makes it easier to slip the motherboard out of the case. However, skip this step if removing the heat sink requires a lot of downward pressure and if the motherboard is not well supported around the heat sink/processor area or the heat sink is attached to a metal plate on the bottom of the motherboard, as is common with many high-performance third-party heat sinks.

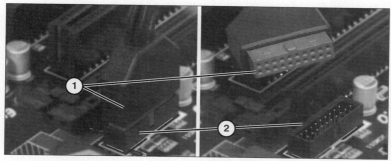

1.USB 3.0 header cable

2.USB 3.0 header

Figure 3-16   Disconnecting a 19-pin dual-port USB 3.0 header cable from a motherboard.

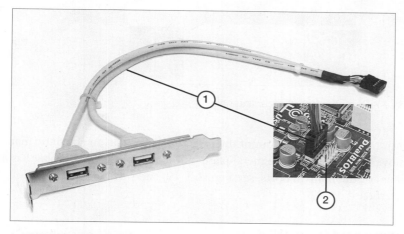

1. USB 2.0 header cable
2. USB 2.0 headers

Figure 3-17   A nine-pin USB 2.0 header cable and motherboard headers.

Step 9.   Remove the motherboard mounting screws (see Figure 3-18 for typical screw locations) and store for reuse; verify that all screws have been removed.

CAUTION   Easy does it with the screwdriver! Whether you're removing screws or putting them back in, skip the electric model and do it the old-fashioned way to avoid damaging the motherboard. If your motherboard is held in place with hex screws, use a hex driver instead of a screwdriver to be even more careful.

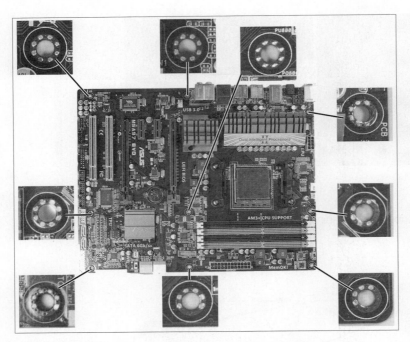

Figure 3-18   Standard ATX motherboard mounting holes.

Step 10.   Remove the motherboard out of the case and place it on an antistatic mat. Remove the I/O shield (the metal plate on the rear of the system that has cutouts for the built-in ports; see Figure 3-19) and store it with the old motherboard.

Preparing the Motherboard for Installation

Before you install the new motherboard into the computer, perform the following steps:

Step 1.   Check the manual supplied with the new motherboard to determine correct sizes of memory supported, processor types supported, and configuration information.

Step 2.   Install the desired amount of memory. See Chapter 5 for details.

Step 3.   Install the CPU and heat sink. See Chapter 7 for details.

1. Port cluster
2. Rear slot covers
3. Port cluster cover plate
4. Motherboard mounting post
5. Matching screw hole
6. Rear case fan

Figure 3-19   An ATX I/O shield and motherboard during installation.

Step-by-Step Motherboard Installation

After you prepare the motherboard for installation, follow these steps to install it:

Step 1.   Determine which mounting holes should be used for brass spacers. You might find it useful to hold the old motherboard over the new motherboard. Matching the motherboards helps you determine whether the new motherboard will fit correctly in the system.

Step 2.   Install or remove brass spacers as needed to accommodate the mounting holes in the motherboard.

Step 3.   Place the I/O shield into the opening at the back of the case. The I/O shield is marked to help you determine the port types on the rear of the motherboard. If the port cutouts on some I/O shields are not completely removed, remove them before you install the shield.

Step 4.   Determine which holes in the motherboard have brass stand-off spacers beneath them and secure the motherboard using the screws removed from the old motherboard (refer to Figure 3-18).

Step 5. Connect the front-panel wires to the speaker, reset switch, drive activity light, and power light connectors on the motherboard.

Step 6. Connect the cables from the SATA drives to the SATA ports on the motherboard. Use SATA port 1 for the first SATA drive, and so on.

Step 7. Connect the power supply connectors to the motherboard.

Step 8. Install the add-on cards you removed from the old motherboard; make sure your existing cards don't duplicate any features found on the new motherboard (such as sound, SATA host adapters, and so on). If they do, and you want to continue to use the card, you must disable the corresponding feature on the motherboard by using the BIOS setup program.

Step 9. Connect header cables that use expansion card slot brackets into empty slots, and connect the header cables to the appropriate ports on the motherboard.

Step 10. Connect any cables used by front-mounted ports, such as USB 2.0, USB 3.0, or IEEE-1394 FireWire ports, to the motherboard and case.

Step 11. Connect power supply leads to drives and add-on cards as needed.

Exam Preparation Tasks

Review All the Key Topics

Review the most important topics in the chapter, noted with the Key Topic icon in the outer margin of the page. Table 3-3 lists a reference of these key topics and the page numbers on which each is found.

Table 3-3 Key Topics for Chapter 3

Key Topic Element	Description	Page Number
Text	Motherboards and their components	68
Text	ATX and microATX	68
Text	Mini-ITX	68
Figures 3-1, 3-2, 3-3, and 3-4	ATX, microATX, and Mini-ITX motherboards	69-72
Text	ITX family	70
Text	PCI slots	72

Key Topic Element	Description	Page Number
Text	PCI-X slots	73
Text	PCIe (PCI Express) slots	73
Figure 3-6	PCIe and PCI slots	74
List	North Bridge and South Bridge	78
Text	CMOS battery	79
Figure 3-9	CMOS battery and CMOS jumper pins	80
List	Power connectors	80
Note	Older motherboard connectors	80
Text	Fan connectors	81
Figure 3-11	CPU and system fan connectors	82
List	Front-panel connectors	82
Text	Bus speeds	84

Complete the Tables and Lists from Memory

Print a copy of Appendix C, "Memory Tables" (found on the CD), or at least the section for this chapter, and complete the tables and lists from memory. Appendix D, "Answers to Memory Tables," also on the CD, includes completed tables and lists to check your work.

Define Key Terms

Define the following key terms from this chapter and check your answers in the glossary.

ATX (Advanced Technology Integrated), bus speeds, chipset, CMOS battery, CPU fan connector, CPU sockets, expansion slots, form factor, front/top-panel connectors, jumper, jumper block, microATX, Mini-ATX, Mini-ITX, miniP-CIe, motherboard, North Bridge, PCI (Peripheral Component Interconnect), PCI Express (PCIe), PCI-X, South Bridge, system fan connectors, RAM slots.

Complete Hands-On Labs

Complete the hands-on labs, and then see the answers and explanations at the end of the chapter.

Lab 3-1: Determine Available USB Ports, Locations, and Types

Scenario: You are a technician on a service call. A client wants to know whether all the available USB ports on the motherboard are accessible.

Equipment needed: System or motherboard documentation and tools to open the case (if needed).

Procedure: Open the system. Use the system or motherboard documentation to determine whether there are any unused USB port headers. To convert a port header into a working USB port, connect a header cable to it.

Lab 3-2: Determine Smallest Form Factor Suitable for a New PC

Scenario: You are a technician tasked with sourcing a new PC. The user's requirements include one PCIe x16 video card, 8GB of RAM, a 1TB hard disk, four USB 3.0 ports, and quiet operation.

Procedure: Check vendors selling Mini-ITX and microATX motherboards to determine whether you can find a suitable system. Design at least one system build using each motherboard if possible. Specify brand and model numbers of major components.

Answer Review Questions

Answer these review questions and then see the answers and explanations at the end of the chapter.

1. Which of the following is the most common motherboard form factor used in desktop computers today?

   a. ATX

   b. microATX

   c. ITX

   d. Mini-ITX

2. Which motherboard form factor is commonly used in a home theater system?

   a. ATX

   b. microATX

   c. ITX

   d. Mini-ITX

3. Match the motherboard figures with the form factor that each represents.

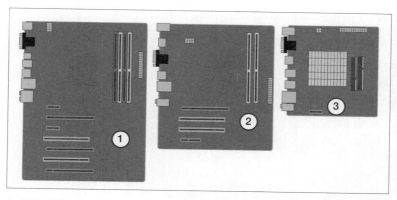

A. Mini-UTX
B. ATX
C. microATX

4. In the following figure, identify the power connectors. (Choose two.)

a. 1	**e.** 5
b. 2	**f.** 6
c. 3	**g.** 7
d. 4	**h.** 8

5. In the following figure, identify the PCI slots. (Choose two.)

6. True or False: DDR2 and DDR3 memory modules are compatible with each other and may be used interchangeably in the same RAM slots on a motherboard.

7. Most motherboards have one connector for the CPU fan and one or more connectors for the system fans that circulate air inside the case. Match the fan connector type to the number of pins. Select the correct answer for the differences.

A Three-pin fan header: Choose all that apply from 1-3

B Four-pin fan header: Choose all that apply from 1-3

1) Monitors fan speed

2) Controls fan speed

3) Provides power to fan

8. Which of the following statements best describes how to make changes to the bus speeds of components such as the processor, chipset interconnect, or memory?

    a. You would make changes to POST and then save those changes on the BIOS/UEFI chip.

    b. You would download the changes you want to make from the manufacturer's website and then save the changes to the BIOS/UEFI chip.

    c. You would make changes to the BIOS settings and then save those changes on the CMOS chip.

    d. You would make all desired changes and save those changes to the South Bridge chipset.

9. Identify the component that uses the connector shown in the following figure.

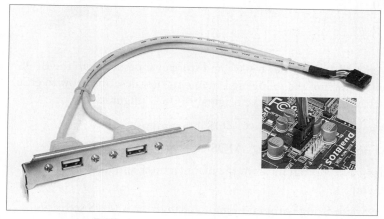

    a. PCIe

    b. PCI-X

    c. USB 2.0

    d. USB 3.0

    e. SATA

10. Identify the component that uses the connector shown in the following figure.

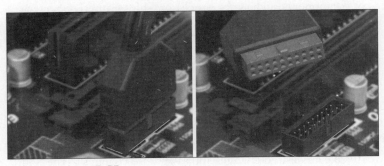

    a. PCIe

    b. PCI-X

    c. USB 2.0

    d. USB 3.0

    e. SATA

11. The CMOS chip allows the user to save and store changes made to the BIOS configurations. Which of the following statements best describes how to clear the CMOS settings and revert to the original BIOS configurations?

    a. Place a jumper block over the CMOS jumper pins.

    b. Write a new program for the CMOS chip.

    c. Download a new program from the manufacturer and flash it to the CMOS chip.

    d. Edit the South Bridge programming to change the CMOS settings.

12. You have noticed that your computer's clock has begun to lose time. You have reset the clock repeatedly, but it still continues to lose time. Which component is most likely at fault?

    a. One of the PCI slots

    b. The CMOS battery

    c. An incorrect entry in the BIOS configurations

    d. An incompatible RAM module

Answers and Explanations to Hands-On Labs

Lab 3-1: Determine Available USB Ports, Locations, and Types

Answers will vary according to the system. Check your work against the system or motherboard documentation.

Lab 3-2: Determine Smallest Form Factor Suitable for a New PC

Answers will vary according to the needs of the system and available components. Check vendor specifications carefully and ensure support for the desired operating system.

Answers and Explanations to Review Questions

1. A. The ATX form factor has been the most frequently used motherboard in desktop computers for the past 15 years.

2. D. Mini-ITX is a small form factor motherboard that is frequently used in home theater systems and gaming computers.

3. 1. B; 2. C; 3. A.

4. E is the 8-pin EPS12V power connector; F is the 24-pin ATX power connector.

5. B, C.

6. False. DDR2 and DDR3 both have 240-pin designs, but the arrangement and keying of the pins are different and thus are not interchangeable.

7. A. 1,3 B. 1, 2, 3 The CPU fan connector usually has four pins and the system fan connectors usually have three pins. The extra pin in the CPU fan connector is used to control fan speed.

8. C. Make any desired changes to the BIOS startup program and then save those changes to the CMOS chip. The BIOS chip is ROM and cannot be edited; the CMOS chip is RAM and may be edited.

9. C. The figure displays a USB 2.0 cable and header.

10. D. The figure displays a USB 3.0 cable and header.

11. A. CMOS is RAM and RAM is volatile. That means that the CMOS chip must have power to maintain its memory. There are two ways to erase the CMOS settings and revert to the default settings in the BIOS. You could remove the CMOS battery or you could place the jumper block over the CMOS jumper pins.

12. B. When the computer's clock begins to lose time, the fault frequently lies in a weak CMOS battery.

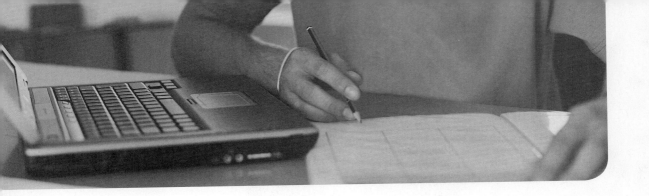

This chapter covers the following subjects:

- **Memory Upgrade Considerations**—This section lists the many different factors you need to take into account when selecting RAM for a particular system.

- **RAM Types**—This section provides the information you need to understand memory chip and module types and how some types of memory are designed to correct memory errors.

- **SO-DIMM vs DIMM**—In this section, you learn the differences between memory modules made for desktop and those made for laptop computers.

- **RAM Configurations**—Discover how multi-channel memory layouts available on many systems can boost performance and how to install the modules.

- **Single-Sided vs Double-Sided**—Learn what these terms mean and how they might affect how much RAM you can install on a particular system.

- **RAM Compatibility**—Learn how to make sure additional memory works with existing memory in this section.

- **Installing Memory**—Laptops and desktops differ in how memory is installed, as you learn in this section.

## CHAPTER 4

RAM Types and Features

RAM is used for programs and data as well as by the operating system for disk caching (using RAM to hold recently accessed information). Thus, installing more RAM improves transfers between the CPU and both RAM and hard drives. If your computer runs short of RAM, the operating system can also use the hard drive as **virtual memory**, a slow substitute for RAM. Although the hard drive can substitute for RAM in a pinch, don't confuse RAM with mass storage devices such as hard disks or SSDs. Although the contents of RAM and mass storage can be changed freely, RAM loses its contents as soon as you shut down the computer, while magnetic storage can hold data for years. Although RAM's contents are temporary, RAM is much faster than magnetic or SSD storage; RAM speed is measured in nanoseconds (billionths of a second), while magnetic and SSD storage is measured in milliseconds (thousandths of a second).

Ever-increasing amounts of RAM are needed as operating systems and applications get more powerful and add more features. Because RAM is one of the most popular upgrades to add to any laptop or desktop system during its lifespan, you need to understand how RAM works, which types of RAM exist, and how to add it to provide the biggest performance boost to the systems you maintain.

220-901: Objective 1.3 Compare and contrast various RAM types and their features.

Foundation Topics

Memory Upgrade Considerations

When you must specify memory for a given system, there are several variables you need to know:

- **Memory module form factor (240-pin DIMM, 184-pin DIMM, 168-pin DIMM, 204-pin SO-DIMM, and so on)**—The form factor your system can use has a great deal to do with the memory upgrade options you have with any given system. Although a few systems can use more than one memory module form factor, in most cases if you want to change to a faster type of memory module, such as from 184-pin DIMM (used by DDR SDRAM) to 240-pin DIMM (such as DDR2 or DDR3 SDRAM), you need to upgrade the motherboard first.

- **Memory chip type used on the module (SDRAM, DDR SDRAM, and so on)**—Today, a particular memory module type uses only one type of memory. However, older memory module types such as early 168-pin DIMMs were available with different types of memory chips. You need to specify the right memory chip type in such cases to avoid conflicts with onboard memory and provide stable performance.

- **Memory module speed (PC3200, PC2-6400, PC3-12800, and so on)**—There are three ways to specify the speed of a memory module: the actual speed in ns (nanoseconds) of the chips on the module (60ns), the clock speed of the data bus (PC800 is 800MHz), or the throughput (in Mbps) of the memory (for example, PC3200 is 3,200Mbps or 3.2Gbps; PC2-2 6400 is 6,400Mbps or 6.4Gbps; and PC3-12800 is 12,800Mbps or 12.8Gbps). The throughput method is used by current memory types.

- **Memory module latency**—Latency is how quickly memory can switch between rows. Modules with the same speed might have different latency values. All of the modules in a bank should have the same latency as well as size and speed.

- **Error checking (parity, non-parity, ECC)**—Most systems don't perform parity checking (to verify the contents of memory or correct errors), but some motherboards and systems support these functions. Although parity-checked memory mainly slows down the system, ECC memory can detect memory errors as well as correct them. If a system is performing critical work (such as high-level mathematics or financial functions or departmental or enterprise-level server tasks), ECC support in the motherboard and ECC memory are worthwhile options to specify. Some systems also support buffered (registered) or nonregistered modules. Buffered (more commonly known as registered) modules are more reliable but are slower because they include a chip that boosts the memory signal.

- **Allowable module sizes and combinations**—Some motherboards insist you use the same speeds and sometimes the same sizes of memory in each memory socket; others are more flexible. To find out which is true about a particular system, check the motherboard or system documentation before you install memory or add more memory.

- **The number of modules needed per bank of memory**—Systems address memory in banks, and the number of modules per bank varies according to the processor and the memory module type installed. If you need more than one module per bank, and only one module is installed, the system will ignore it. Systems that require multiple modules per bank require that modules be the same size and speed.

- **Whether the system requires or supports multi-channel memory (two or more identical memory modules accessed together instead of one at a time)** —Dual-channel memory, triple-channel memory, and quad-channel memory are accessed in an interleaved manner to improve memory latency (the time required between memory accesses). As a result, systems running dual-channel memory offer faster memory performance than systems running single-channel memory. Intel introduced triple-channel memory (which runs even faster than dual-channel memory) with its Core i7 processor. Quad-channel memory, available on some high-performance Intel desktop and server platforms and AMD server platforms, is even faster. Almost all of these systems can run (albeit with reduced performance) if non-identical memory modules are used.

- **The total number of modules that can be installed**—The number of sockets on the motherboard determines the number of modules that can be installed. Very small-footprint systems (such as those that use microATX or Mini-ITX motherboards) often support only one or two modules, but systems that use full-size ATX motherboards often support three or more modules, especially those designed for multi-channel memory (two or more modules accessed as a single logical unit for faster performance).

RAM Types

Virtually all memory modules use some type of dynamic RAM (**DRAM**) chips. DRAM requires frequent recharges of memory to retain its contents.

SRAM

Static random-access memory (SRAM) is RAM that does not need to be periodically refreshed. Memory refreshing is common to other types of RAM and is basically the act of reading information from a specific area of memory and immediately rewriting that information back to the same area without modifying it. Due to SRAM's architecture, it does not require this refresh. You will find SRAM being used as cache memory for CPUs, as buffers within hard drives, and as temporary storage for LCD screens. Normally, SRAM is soldered directly to a printed circuit board (PCB) or integrated directly to a chip. This means that you probably won't be replacing SRAM. SRAM is faster than—and is usually found in smaller quantities than—its distant cousin DRAM.

SDRAM

Synchronous DRAM (SDRAM) was the first type of memory to run in sync with the processor bus (the connection between the processor, or CPU, and other components on the motherboard). Most 168-pin DIMM modules use SDRAM memory. To determine whether a DIMM module contains SDRAM memory, check its speed markings. SDRAM memory is rated by bus speed (PC66 equals 66MHz bus speed; PC100 equals 100MHz bus speed; and PC133 equals 133MHz bus speed). All SDRAM modules have a one-bit prefetch buffer and perform one transfer per clock cycle.

Depending on the specific module and motherboard chipset combination, PC133 modules can sometimes be used on systems that are designed for PC100 modules.

DDR SDRAM

The second generation of systems running synchronous DRAM use double data rate SDRAM (DDR SDRAM). **DDR SDRAM** performs two transfers per clock cycle (instead of one, as with regular SDRAM) and features a two-bit prefetch buffer. 184-pin DIMM memory modules use DDR SDRAM chips.

While DDR SDRAM is sometimes rated inMHz, it is more often rated by throughput (MBps). Common speeds for DDR SDRAM include PC1600 (200MHz/1600Mbps), PC2100 (266MHz/2100Mbps), PC2700 (333MHz/2700Mbps), and PC3200 (400MHz/3200Mbps), but other speeds are available from some vendors.

DDR2 SDRAM

Double data rate 2 SDRAM (DDR2 SDRAM) is the successor to DDR SDRAM. DDR2 SDRAM runs its external data bus at twice the speed of DDR SDRAM and features a four-bit prefetch buffer, enabling faster performance. However, DDR2 SDRAM memory has greater latency than DDR SDRAM memory. Latency is a measure of how long it takes to receive information from memory; the higher the number, the greater the latency. Typical latency values for mainstream DDR2 memory are CL=5 and CL=6, compared to CL=2.5 and CL=3 for DDR memory. 240-pin memory modules use DDR2 SDRAM.

DDR2 SDRAM memory might be referred to by the effective memory speed of the memory chips on the module (the memory clock speed x4 or the I/O bus clock speed x2)—for example, DDR2-533 (133MHz memory clock x4 or 266MHz I/O bus clock x2)=533MHz)—or by module throughput (DDR2-533 is used in PC2-4200 modules, which have a throughput of more than 4200Mbps). PC2- indicates the module uses DDR2 memory; PC- indicates the module uses DDR memory.

Other common speeds for DDR2 SDRAM modules include PC2-3200 (DDR2-400; 3200Mbps throughput); PC2-5300 (DDR2-667); PC2-6400 (DDR2-800); and PC2-8500 (DDR2-1066).

DDR3 SDRAM

Double data rate 3 SDRAM (DDR3 SDRAM) Compared to DDR2, DDR3 runs at lower voltages, has twice the internal banks, and most versions run at faster speeds than DDR2. DDR3 also has an eight-bit prefetch bus. As with DDR2 versus DDR, DDR3 has greater latency than DDR2. Typical latency values for mainstream DDR3 memory are CL7 or CL9, compared to CL5 or CL6 for DDR2. Although DDR3 modules also use 240 pins, their layout and keying are different than DDR2, and they cannot be interchanged.

DDR3 SDRAM memory might be referred to by the effective memory speed of the memory chips on the module (the memory clock speed x4 or the I/O bus clock speed x2); for example, DDR3-1333 (333MHz memory clock x4 or 666MHz I/O bus clock x2)=1333MHz) or by module throughput (DDR3-1333 is used in PC3-10600 modules, which have a throughput of more than 10,600MBps or 10.6GBps). PC3- indicates the module uses DDR3 memory.

Other common speeds for DDR3 SDRAM modules include PC3-8500 (DDR3-1066; 8500MBps throughput); PC3-12800 (DDR3-1600); and PC3-17000 (DDR3-2133).

NOTE Memory modules of the same type with the same speed memory chips can have different CAS latency (CL) values. CL refers to how quickly memory column addresses can be accessed. A lower CL provides faster access than a higher CL. As Figure 4-1 makes clear, CL values increase when comparing different types of memory.

Most, but not all, memory module labels indicate the CL value. For modules that aren't labeled, look up the part number for details.

Figure 4-1 compares DDR, DDR2, DDR3, and DD4 memory modules.

> **NOTE** DDR, DDR2, and DDR3 are the memory types covered on the 900 series exams. However, you might encounter DDR4 memory on the latest desktop and laptop computers. See the following sidebar to learn more.

1. 256MB DDR module, PC3200 (DDR400)
2. CL3 latency
3. 2GB DDR2 module (from matched set), DDR2-667 (PC2-5300)
4. CL5 latency
5. 2GB DDR3 module, PC3-10600 (DDR3-1333)
6. CL9 latency
7. 8GB DDR4 module, DDR4-2133 (PC4-17000)

Figure 4-1 From top to bottom, DDR, DDR2, DDR3, and DDR4 DIMM desktop memory modules.

DDR4 SDRAM: The Next Standard

DDR4 SDRAM, introduced alongside Intel's X99 chipset for Haswell-E Core i-series processors in August 2014, is the fourth generation of DDR memory. Compared to its predecessor, DDR3, DDR4 runs at lower voltage (1.2V) than either DDR3 or lower-voltage DDR3L. DDR4 supports densities up to 16Gb per chip (twice the density of DDR3), twice the memory banks, and uses bank groups to speed up burst accesses to memory, but uses the same eight-bit prefetch as DDR3. Data rates range from 1600Mbps to 3200Mbps, compared to 800Mbps to 2133Mbps for DDR3. To improve memory reliability, DDR4 includes built-in support for CRC and parity, rather than requiring the memory controller to support error-checking (ECC) with parity memory as in DDR3 and earlier designs.

Parity vs Non-Parity

Two methods have been used to protect the reliability of memory:

- Parity checking

- ECC (error-correcting code or error-correction code)

Both methods depend upon the presence of an additional memory chip over the chips required for the data bus of the module. For example, a module that uses eight chips for data would use a ninth chip to support parity or ECC. If the module uses 16 chips for data (two banks of eight), it would use the 17th and 18th chips for parity (refer to Figure 4-2).

Parity checking, which goes back to the original IBM PC, works like this: Whenever memory is accessed, each data bit has a value of 0 or 1. When these values are added to the value in the parity bit, the resulting checksum should be an odd number. This is called odd parity. A memory problem typically causes the data bit values plus the parity bit value to total an even number. This triggers a parity error, and your system halts with a parity error message. Note that parity checking requires parity-enabled memory and support in the motherboard. On modules that support parity checking, there's a parity bit for each group of eight bits.

The method used to fix this type of error varies with the system. On museum-piece systems that use individual memory chips, you must open the system, push all memory chips back into place, and test the memory thoroughly if you have no spares (using memory-testing software). Or you must replace the memory if you have spare memory chips. If the computer uses memory modules, replace one module at a time, test the memory (or at least run the computer for a while) to determine whether the problem has gone away. If the problem recurs, replace the original module, swap out the second module, and repeat.

TIP   Some system error messages tell you the logical location of the error so you can refer to the system documentation to determine which module or modules to replace.

NOTE   Parity checking has always cost more because of the extra chips involved and the additional features required in the motherboard and chipset, and it fell out of fashion for PCs starting in the mid-1990s. Systems that lack parity checking freeze up when a memory problem occurs and do not display any message onscreen.

Because parity checking "protects" you from bad memory by shutting down the computer (which can cause you to lose data), vendors created a better way to use the parity bits to solve memory errors using a method called ECC.

ECC vs non-ECC Memory

For critical applications, network servers have long used a special type of memory called **error-correcting code (ECC)**. This memory enables the system to correct single-bit errors and notify you of larger errors.

Although most desktops do not support ECC, some workstations and most servers do offer ECC support. On systems that offer ECC support, ECC support might be enabled or disabled through the system BIOS or it might be a standard feature. The parity bit in parity memory is used by the ECC feature to determine when the content of memory is corrupt and to fix single-bit errors. Unlike parity checking, which only warns you of memory errors, ECC memory actually corrects errors.

ECC is recommended for maximum data safety, although parity and ECC do provide a small slowdown in performance in return for the extra safety. ECC memory modules use the same types of memory chips used by standard modules, but they use more chips and might have a different internal design to allow ECC operation. ECC modules, like parity-checked modules, have an extra bit for each group of eight data bits.

To determine whether a system supports parity-checked or ECC memory, check the system BIOS memory configuration (typically on the Advanced or Chipset screens). Systems that support parity or ECC memory can use non-parity checked memory when parity checking and ECC are disabled. Another name for ECC is EDAC (Error Detection and Correction).

Buffered (Registered) vs Unbuffered

Most types of desktop memory modules use unbuffered memory. However, many servers and some desktop or workstation computers use a type of memory module called **registered memory** or **buffered memory**: buffered memory is the term used by the 220-901 exam. Buffered (registered) memory modules contain a register chip that enables the system to remain stable with large amounts of memory installed. The register chip acts as a buffer, which slightly slows down memory access.

Buffered (registered) memory modules can be built with or without ECC support. However, most buffered memory modules are used by servers and include ECC support. Figure 4-2 compares a standard (unbuffered) memory module with a buffered (registered) memory module that also supports ECC.

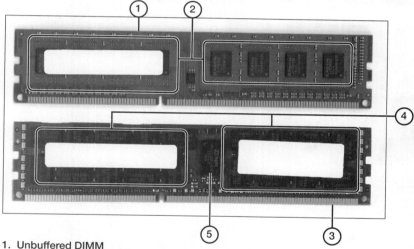

1. Unbuffered DIMM
2. Two groups of four (total eight)memory chips (no parity chip)
3. Buffered (registered) DIMM with ECC
4. Eighteen memory chips (two banks of nine, including parity chip)
5. Buffer chip

Figure 4-2   A standard unbuffered module (top) compared to a buffered (registered) module with ECC (bottom).

SO-DIMM vs DIMM

Most desktop computers use full-sized memory modules known as **DIMMs**. However, laptop computers and some small-footprint mini-ITX motherboards and systems use reduced-size memory modules known as small outline DIMMs (SO-DIMMs or **SODIMMS**).

Figure 4-3 compares common DIMM and SODIMM modules.

Table 4-1 lists common DIMM and SODIMM form factors and their uses.

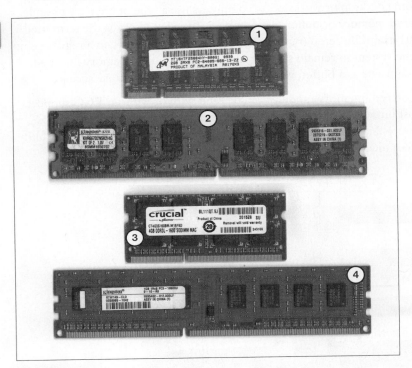

1. DDR2 SO-DIMM
2. DDR2 DIMM
3. DDR3 SO-DIMM
4. DDR3 DIMM

Figure 4-3 DDR2 SODIMM and DIMM modules compared to DDR3 SODIMM and DIMM modules.

Table 4-1 RAM Comparisons

RAM Type	Pins (DIMM)	Pins (SODIMM)	Common Type and Speed	Defining Characteristic
DDR SDRAM	184	200[1]	PC3200 = 400MHz/3200Mbps	Double the transfers per clock cycle compared to regular SDRAM.
DDR2 SDRAM	240[2]	200[1]	DDR2-800 (PC2-6400) = 800MHz/6400Mbps	External data bus speed (I/O bus clock) is 2x faster than DDR SDRAM.

RAM Type	Pins (DIMM)	Pins (SODIMM)	Common Type and Speed	Defining Characteristic
DDR3 SDRAM	240[2]	204	DDR3-1333 (PC3-10600) = 1333MHz/10,600Mbps	External data bus speed (I/O bus clock) is 2x faster than DDR2 SDRAM (4x faster than DDR SDRAM).
DDR4 SDRAM[*]	288	260	DDR4-2400 (PC4-19200)= 2400MHz/19200Mbps	External data bus speed (I/O bus clock) is 2x faster than DDR3 SDRAM (8x faster than DDR SDRAM).
UniDIMM[*3]	—	260	DDR3 or DDR4	Designed for use with Intel Skylake (6th generation Core i-series CPU); memory controller on motherboard/processor must support both DDR3 and DDR4 memory

[1] DDR SODIMM keying is closer to the middle of the motherboard than with SDRAM SODIMM

[2] The keying on DDR3 is offset to one side compared to DDR2

[3] The keying on UniDIMM is different than DDR4 SODIMM

[*] Not an objective on the CompTIA A+ Certification 900-series exams; included for information purposes only

Some less-common SODIMM designs include:

- 214-pin MicroDIMM, used for DDR2 SDRAM
- 244-pin MiniDIMM, used for DDR2 SDRAM

RAM Configurations

Almost all systems can be used with a variety of memory sizes. However, systems that are designed to access two or more identical modules as a single logical unit (multi-channel) provide faster performance than systems that access each module as a unit.

Single-Channel

Originally, all systems that used SDRAM were single-channel systems. Each 64-bit DIMM or SODIMM module was addressed individually.

Dual-Channel

Some systems using DDR and most using DDR2 or newer memory technologies support dual-channel operation. When two identical (same size, speed, and latency) modules are installed in the proper sockets, the memory controller accesses them in interleaved mode for faster access.

Most systems with two pairs of sockets marked in contrasting colors implement dual-channel operation in this way: install the matching modules in the same color sockets (see Figure 4-4). See the instructions for the system or motherboard for exceptions.

1. **Installed DIMM**
2. **Install identical module here for dual-channel operation**
3. **Use a matched pair (same speed and CL value as the first pair) in these sockets for best performance. This pair need not be the same size as the first pair.**

Figure 4-4   To use dual-channel operation on this motherboard, add an identical module to the light-colored memory socket.

Triple-Channel

Some systems using Intel's LGA 1366 chipset support triple-channel addressing. Most of these systems use two sets of three sockets. Populate at least one set with identical memory. Some triple-channel motherboards use four sockets, but for best performance, the last socket should not be used on these systems.

NOTE   To learn more about LGA 1366, see "LGA 1366" in Chapter 7, "CPUs."

Quad-Channel

Some systems using Intel's LGA 2011 chipset support quad-channel addressing. Most of these systems use two sets of four sockets. Populate one or both sets with identical memory.

> **NOTE**   To learn more about LGA 2011, see "LGA 2011" in Chapter 7.

Single-Sided vs Double-Sided

A single-sided (more properly known as single-ranked) module has a single 64-bit wide bank of memory chips. A double-sided (double-ranked) module has two 64-bit banks of memory stacked for higher capacity. Many, but not all, of these modules use both sides of the module for memory. However, the use of smaller memory chips enables "double-sided" modules to have all of the chips on one side. Refer to Figure 4-2. The top module is single-sided (one 64-bit rank) and the bottom module is double-sided (two 64-bit ranks), but all of the memory chips are on the front of the module.

Some systems, primarily older systems using DDR2 or older memory technologies, have different maximum amounts of RAM based on whether single-sided or double-sided modules are used. To determine specifics for a particular system or motherboard, check its documentation or use a memory vendor's compatibility list or system scanner.

RAM Compatibility

When it comes to memory, compatibility is important. The memory module type must fit the motherboard; speed must be compatible and the module storage size/ combination must match your computer system as well.

The labels on the memory modules shown in Figure 4-1 list the manufacturer, module type, size, and speed, and most also list the CAS latency (CL) value. If you want to buy additional modules of the same size, you can use this information to purchase additional modules.

However, to find out exactly which type of memory modules are compatible with your motherboard, visit a memory manufacturer's website and check within its database. Be sure to have the model number of the motherboard or the model of the computer handy.

Some memory vendors, such as Crucial.com, also offer a browser-based utility that checks your system for installed memory and lists recommended memory specific to your system. This type of utility displays installed memory size and speed.

If you are installing memory in a system that uses single-sided modules (8 or 9 chips), don't install double-sided modules (16 or 18 chips) as additional or replacement RAM unless you verify they will work in that system.

Installing Memory

Surprisingly, the CompTIA A+ 220-901 exam lists installing memory in laptops as an objective (220-901 objective 3.1), but it does not list installing memory in desktop computers. Nevertheless, this is an important skill to learn and understand.

Installing Memory Safely

When you install memory, be sure to follow the important safety procedures in exam 220-902 objective 5.1 (see Chapter 17, "Operational Procedures," for details).

Preparations for Installing DIMM Memory

Before working with any memory modules, turn the computer off and unplug it from the AC outlet. Be sure to employ electrostatic discharge (ESD) protection in the form of an ESD strap and ESD mat. Use an antistatic bag to hold the memory modules while you are not working with them. Before actually handling any components, touch an unpainted portion of the case chassis in a further effort to ground yourself. Try not to touch any of the chips, connectors, or circuitry of the memory module; hold them from the sides.

To install a DIMM module, follow these steps:

Step 1.   Line up the modules' connectors with the socket. DIMM modules have connections with different widths, preventing the module from being inserted backwards.

Step 2.   Verify that the locking tabs on the socket are swiveled to the outside (open) position. Some motherboards use a locking tab on only one side of the socket.

Step 3.   After verifying that the module is lined up correctly with the socket, push the module straight down into the socket until the swivel locks on each end of the socket snap into place at the top corners of the module (see Figure 4-5). A fair amount of force is required to engage the locks. Do not touch the metal-plated connectors on the bottom of the module; this can cause corrosion or ESD.

For clarity, the memory module installation pictured in Figure 4-5 was photographed with the motherboard out of the case. However, the tangle of cables and components around and over the DIMM sockets in Figure 4-6 provides a much more realistic view of the challenges you face when you install memory in a working system.

When you install memory on a motherboard inside a working system, use the following tips to help your upgrade go smoothly and the module to work properly:

- If the system is a tower system, consider placing the system on its side to make the upgrade easier. Doing this also helps to prevent tipping the system over by accident when you push on the memory to lock it into the socket.

- Use a digital camera or smartphone set for close-up focusing so you can document the system's interior before you start the upgrade process.

- Move the locking tab on the DIMM sockets to the open position before you try to insert the module (refer to Figure 4-5). The sockets shown in Figure 4-6 have closed tabs.

- If an aftermarket heat sink blocks access to memory sockets, try to remove its fan by unscrewing it from the radiator fin assembly. This is normally easier to do than removing the heat sink from the CPU.

- Move power and drive cables away from the memory sockets so you can access the sockets. Disconnect cables if necessary.

- Use a flashlight to shine light into the interior of the system so you can see the memory sockets and locking tabs clearly; this enables you to determine the proper orientation of the module and to make sure the sockets' locking mechanisms are open.

- Use a flashlight to double-check your memory installation to make sure the module is completely inserted into the slot and locked into place.

- Replace any cables you moved or disconnected during the process before you close the case and restart the system.

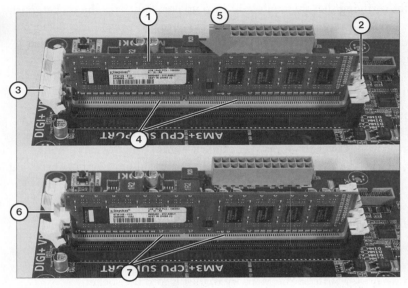

1. **DDR3 module lined up for installation**
2. **Many recent motherboards use fixed guides on one side.**
3. **Motherboards have at least one locking tab per module.**
4. **Connectors visible when module is not fully inserted.**
5. **Push module firmly into place.**
6. **Locking tab holds module in place when fully installed.**
7. **Connectors are no longer visible when module is fully inserted.**

Figure 4-5   A DDR3 DIMM partly inserted (top) and fully inserted (bottom). The memory module must be pressed firmly into place before the locking tab (left) will engage.

TIP   Note the positions of any cables before you remove them to perform an internal upgrade. I like to use self-stick colored dots on a drive and its matching data and power cables. You can purchase sheets of colored dots at most office-supply and discount stores.

1. Memory sockets (some blocked by fan and heat sink)
2. Aftermarket fan and heat sink for CPU
3. Power and data cables

Figure 4-6 DIMM sockets in a typical system are often surrounded and covered up by power and data cables or aftermarket CPU fans and heat sinks, making it difficult to properly install additional memory.

Exam Preparation Tasks

Review All the Key Topics

Review the most important topics in the chapter, noted with the key topics icon in the outer margin of the page. Table 4-2 lists a reference of these key topics and the page numbers on which each is found.

Table 4-2 Key Topics for Chapter 4

Key Topic Element	Description	Page Number
Figure 4-1	Desktop memory modules compared	104
Figure 4-3	DIMM and SO-DIMM modules compared	108
Table 4-1	RAM comparisons	108
Figure 4-5	A DIMM partly inserted (top) and fully inserted (bottom)	114
Figure 4-6	DIMM sockets surrounded by cables	115

Complete the Tables and Lists from Memory

Print a copy of Appendix C, "Memory Tables" (found on the CD), or at least the section for this chapter, and complete the tables and lists from memory. Appendix D, "Answers to Memory Tables," also on the CD, includes completed tables and lists to check your work.

Define Key Terms

Define the following key terms from this chapter, and check your answers in the glossary.

RAM, paging file (virtual memory), SRAM, DRAM, SDRAM, DDR SDRAM, DDR2 SDRAM, DDR3 SDRAM, DDR4 SDRAM, DIMM, SODIMM, ECC, buffered memory, registered memory

Complete Hands-On Lab

Complete the hands-on lab, and then see the answers and explanations at the end of the chapter.

Lab 4-1: Select and Install the Correct RAM

Scenario: You are a technician working at a PC repair bench. You are required to install two sticks of DDR3 RAM into the first channel of the dual channel memory slots in a motherboard. When completed, this should form a "bank" of memory.

Procedure: Select the proper RAM memory modules from the figure and "place" them within the proper memory slots on the motherboard by checking off the correct RAM modules and memory slots in Figures 4-7 and 4-8.

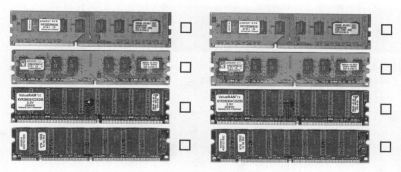

Figure 4-7 Lab 4-1 memory modules.

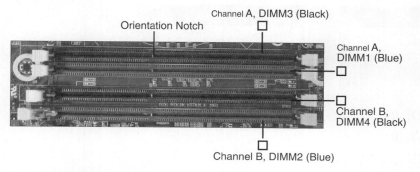

Figure 4-8 Lab 4-1 memory sockets.

Answer Review Questions

Answer these review questions and then see the answers and explanations at the end of the chapter.

1. Which of the following loses its contents when you shut down the computer?

   a. Hard disk drive

   b. USB flash drive

   c. RAM

   d. ROM

2. Identify the type of RAM in the following figure.

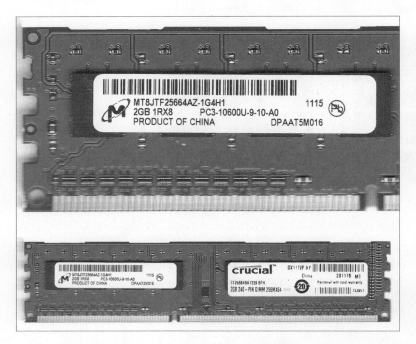

   a. DDR

   b. DDR2

   c. DDR3

   d. DDR4

3. A system that uses matched pairs of memory modules supports which of the following?

   a. ECC

   b. dual-channel

   c. buffered

   d. SDRAM

4. Which two methods are used to protect the reliability of memory? (Select the two best answers.)

   a. Parity checking

   b. System checking

   c. ECC (error-correcting code)

   d. Smart checking

5. Most types of desktop memory modules use which kind of memory?

   a. Unbuffered non-ECC memory

   b. Virtual memory

   c. SODIMM module

   d. ECC memory

6. Critical applications and network servers use a special type of memory. What is it called?

   a. ECC memory

   b. Unbuffered memory

   c. Static memory

   d. Crucial memory

7. Identify the type of memory layout this module uses.

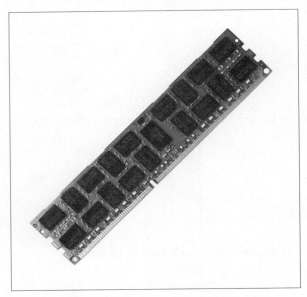

   a. With ECC, with register (or buffer)

   b. With ECC, no register (or buffer)

   c. No ECC, with register (or buffer)

   d. No ECC, no register (or buffer)

8. To correctly install a DIMM module, what should you do? (Choose all that apply.)

   a. Line up the module connectors with the socket.

   b. Verify that the locking tabs on the socket are swiveled to the outside (open) position.

   c. Verify that the module is lined up correctly with the socket. Then push the module straight down until the locks on each end of the socket snap into place at the top corners of the module.

   d. None of these options is correct.

9. You have a dual-channel motherboard. You have two identical 4GB DDR3 modules and two identical 2GB DDR3 modules. In the following diagram, one module of 4GB DDR3 is being installed in the first blue slot. Where should you install the second 4GB DDR3 module for best results?

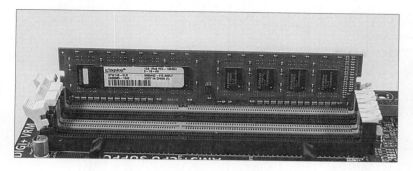

a. Install the second 4GB DDR3 in the second blue slot.

b. Install the second 4GB DDR3 in the first black slot.

c. Install the second 4GB DDR3 in the second black slot.

d. It does not matter as long as all the modules are DDR3.

10. Which of the following types of RAM is also known as PC3-10600?

a. DDR3-800

b. DDR3-1066

c. DDR3-1333

d. DDR3-1600

Answers and Explanations to Hands-On Labs

Lab 4-1: Select and Install the Correct RAM

The first set of RAM (DDR3) should have been selected. Note that DDR3's center notch is to the left of the older DDR2 and DDR center notch. The memory modules should have been installed to the DIMM1 (blue) slot of Channel A and the DIMM2 (blue) slot of Channel B, collectively forming the first bank of RAM. (See Figures 4-12 and 4-13.)

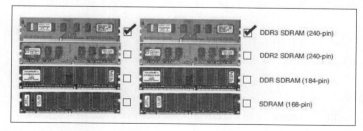

Figure 4-12 Lab 4-1 solution.

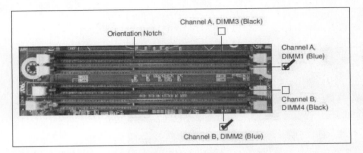

Figure 4-13   Lab 4-1 solution.

The memory notch should be aligned with the slot's corresponding notch, and then placed in the slot and pressed down until the ears lock into place. When installing RAM, try not to touch the chips or connectors. Handle the RAM from the sides and press down on the RAM with your thumbs after it has been placed in the slot.

Answers and Explanations to Review Questions

1. **C.** Random access memory (RAM) loses its contents when the computer shuts down. Hard disk drives, USB flash drives, and Read-Only Memory (ROM) are designed to retain their contents even when they are not receiving power.

2. **C.** DDR3. The label identifies this module as PC3, which indicates that it contains DDR3 type RAM.

3. **B.** Dual-channel support requires that both paired memory slots use memory with identical specifications.

4. **A, C.** Parity memory and ECC have an additional memory chip added for parity. They are both methods used to protect the reliability of memory.

5. **A.** Unbuffered, non-ECC memory is used in most common desktop computers sold in the market. This kind of memory is also used in some servers and workstations.

6. **A.** ECC memory enables the system to correct single-bit errors and notify you of larger errors.

7. **A.** With ECC, with register (buffer). The memory module in the diagram contains 18 memory chips (2 banks of 8 each, plus a parity or ECC chip) and an additional chip that contains the register (or buffer).

8. **A, B, C.** To correctly insert the memory modules, you should follow all the steps listed. You might also have to use a fair amount of pressure to securely lock these modules in place.

9. **A.** For best results, you should always install identical modules in the same channel. The two 4GB modules should be the same size, speed, latency, and so on, and should be installed in the same channel (in this case, in the two blue slots). The same is true for the two 2GB modules, which should be installed in the two blue slots. The slots on this motherboard are color-coded to indicate the channels. Always check your documentation for the correct orientation of the channels and the type of RAM your motherboard will accept.

10. **C.** DDR3-800 is also known as PC3-6400 (6400MBps peak transfer rate). DDR3-1066 is also known as PC3-8500 (8500MBps peak transfer rate). DDR3-1333 is also known as PC3-10600 (10667MBps peak transfer rate). DDR3-1600 is also known as PC3-12800 (12800MBps peak transfer rate).

This chapter covers the following subjects:

- **Expansion Card and Slot Overview**—This section compares PCIe x1, PCIe x16, and PCI 32-bit card and slot designs.

- **Installing Sound Cards**—This section demonstrates how to install and configure sound cards and USB audio devices in Windows, OS X, and Linux.

- **Installing Video Cards**—This section demonstrates how to install and configure video cards.

- **Installing Network Cards**—This section demonstrates how to install and configure network cards and USB network adapters.

- **Installing USB Cards**—In this section, learn how to install a USB 3.0 card to add more USB 3.0 ports.

- **Installing FireWire Cards**—This section demonstrates how to install a FireWire (IEEE 1394) card.

- **Installing Thunderbolt Cards**—This section demonstrates how to install and connect a Thunderbolt card.

- **Installing Storage Cards**—This section demonstrates how to install a storage (flash memory) card.

- **Installing Modem Cards**—Learn how to install a dial-up modem card in this section.

- **Installing Wireless/Cellular Cards**—This section covers installation of both desktop and laptop wireless and cellular cards.

- **Installing TV Tuner Cards**—Learn how to pick up over-the-air TV by installing a TV tuner card.

- **Installing Video Capture Cards**—This section covers what video capture cards do and how to install them.

- **Installing Riser Cards**—Cramped cases might make installing full-height cards or getting access to all audio ports difficult. In this section, you learn how to install riser cards to help out.

## CHAPTER 5

PC Expansion Cards

Although today's desktop computers use motherboards that integrate many components, it is still often necessary to install add-on cards in these systems to

- Replace a defective component
- Improve performance over an onboard port
- Add additional I/O options
- Improve performance by replacing an existing card

This chapter covers the techniques needed for each type of installation or upgrade you might be called upon to perform.

220-901: Objective 1.4 Install and configure PC expansion cards.

Foundation Topics

Expansion Card and Slot Overview

Modern desktop computers primarily use three slot types:

- PCIe x16
- PCIe x1
- PCI 32-bit

These are illustrated in Figure 5-1 along with typical examples of add-on cards that use these slots. Before you select a specific card for a specific computer, be sure the slot and card use the same form factor and that a suitable slot is available.

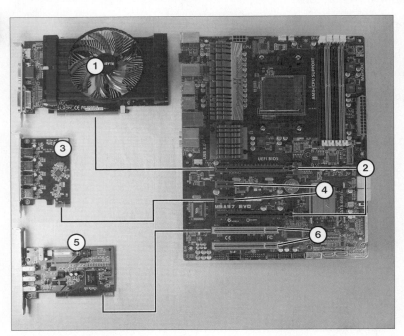

1. PCIe x16 video card
2. PCIe x16 slots
3. PCIe x1 USB 3.0 multi-port card
4. PCIe x1 slots
5. PCI (32-bit) FireWire 400 multi-port card
6. PCI slots

Figure 5-1   PCIe x16, PCIe x1, and PCI 32-bit slots and cards.

Installing Sound Cards

Before installing a **sound card**, be sure to disable onboard audio with the system BIOS setup program and uninstall any proprietary mixer or configuration apps used by onboard audio.

To install a sound card, follow these steps:

Step 1.   Shut down the computer and disconnect it from AC power.

Step 2.   Open the case to gain access to the PC's expansion slots.

Step 3.   Select an empty PCIe or PCI expansion slot as needed for the form factor of sound card to be installed.

Step 4.   Remove the corresponding bracket from the back of the case.

Step 5.   Insert the card into the slot (see Figure 5-2).

1. Front panel audio header
2. Aux in (from optical drive)
3. SPDIF out digital audio header

Figure 5-2   A typical PCIe sound card with 5:1 surround audio after being inserted into an expansion slot.

Step 6.   Secure the card bracket into place, using the screw or locking mechanism you removed or released in Step 4.

Step 7.   Connect any header cables needed (refer to Figure 5-2).

Step 8.   Connect speakers, microphone, line-in and line-out cables as needed to support your audio or home theater subsystem.

Step 9.   Close the system.

Step 10.   Reconnect AC power and restart the system.

Step 11.   Install the **driver** files provided with the sound card or install updated versions provided by the vendor.

Step 12.   If not already installed in Step 11, install the mixer and configuration utilities provided with the new sound card.

NOTE   You can also add surround audio with a USB-based audio device. This is a good solution for laptops and for systems with limited or no expansion slots.

Installing a USB Audio Device

To install a USB audio device, follow these steps:

Step 1.   Turn off your computer.

Step 2.   Connect the USB audio device to your computer's USB 2.0 or USB 3.0 port.

Step 3.   Turn on the computer and then turn on the device.

Step 4.   The computer installs audio drivers automatically.

Step 5.   Install additional or updated drivers downloaded from the vendor's website or provided with the device if needed.

Configuring a Sound Card with Windows

To configure a sound card, onboard audio, or USB audio with Windows:

Step 1.   Open Control Panel

Step 2.   Open the Sound applet.

Step 3.   Select Playback devices and adjust settings with the Playback tab.

Step 4.   Select Recording devices and adjust settings with the Recording tab.

Step 5.   To specify sounds to play during Windows events (startup, shutdown, errors, program events), use the Sounds tab.

Step 6.   Click Apply, and then click OK to accept changes.

If the sound card or onboard audio includes proprietary management or configuration programs, run them from the Start menu.

Configuring a Sound Card with OS X

To configure a sound card, onboard audio, or USB audio with OS X:

Step 1.   Open the Apple menu.

Step 2.   Open System Preferences.

Step 3.   Select the Sound icon.

Step 4.   Select the Output tab.

Step 5.   Select the device to use for sound output.

Step 6.   Adjust balance and volume, and then close the window.

Configuring a Sound Card with Linux

To configure a sound card, onboard audio, or USB audio with Linux (Ubuntu 14.x):

Step 1.   Open System Settings.

Step 2.   Open Sound.

Step 3.   Select the Output tab.

Step 4.   Select the device to use for sound output.

Step 5.   Adjust balance and volume.

Step 6.   Select speaker mode (stereo or surround options).

Step 7.   Click Test Sound to verify proper operation.

Step 8.   Close the window to save the changes.

Installing Video Cards

The installation process for a **video card** includes three phases:

Step 1.   Configuring the BIOS for the video card being installed

Step 2.   Physically installing the video card

Step 3.   Installing drivers for the video card

Figure 5-3 illustrates a typical high-performance video card that uses an AMD GPU.

1. Exhaust panel for fans   4. PCIe 6-pin power connector
2. Cooling fans   5. Connector for CrossFire multi-GPU cable
3. PCIe x16 connector

Figure 5-3   A PCIe x16 video card designed for multi-GPU (CrossFire) support.

BIOS Configuration

Check and adjust the **Primary VGA BIOS** (also known as **Primary Graphics Adapter**) setting as needed:

- Choose PCIE or PCIE->PCI if you use a PCIe video card. On some systems, the term *NB PCIe video slot* is used for PCIe.

- Choose PCI or PCI->PCIE if you use a PCI video card.

- For onboard video (integrated graphics), see the manufacturer's recommendation (onboard video can use PCI or PCI Express buses built into the motherboard). On some recent systems, Auto is the default setting.

Removing Drivers for an Old Video Card or Onboard Video

Although all video cards created since the beginning of the 1990s are based on VGA, virtually all of them use a unique chipset that requires special software drivers to control acceleration features (faster onscreen video), color depth, and resolution. So, whenever you change video cards, you must change video driver software as well. Otherwise, your operating system will drop into a low-resolution mode and might give you an error message because the driver doesn't match the video card.

To delete the old driver in Windows: Open Control Panel > Device Manager, and delete the listing for the current video card. Select Uninstall a program in Control Panel and uninstall driver or configuration apps used by the current video card.

It is not necessary to delete old drivers in OS X or Linux.

Removing the Old Video Card

Follow these steps to remove the old video card (if present):

Step 1. Shut down the computer and disconnect it from AC power.

Step 2. Turn off the display.

Step 3. Disconnect the data cable attached to the video card.

Step 4. Open the case.

Step 5. Disconnect any power cables running to the video card (see Figure 5-4).

1. Push locking tab in   2. Pull power cable away from card

Figure 5-4 Removing the PCIe power cable from a video card.

Step 6.   Remove SLI (NVIDIA) or CrossFire (AMD) cables connected to any card(s) you are removing (see Figure 5-5).

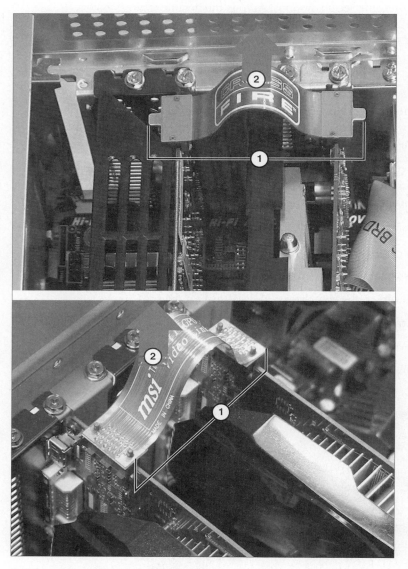

1. **Lift up ends of connector cable to release**
2. **Lift connector cable out of system**

Figure 5-5   SLI and CrossFire cables. Remove these before removing video cards you are replacing.

Step 7.   Remove the old video card(s): remove the screw holding the card bracket in place and release the card-retention mechanism that holds video card in place (see Figure 5-6). Repeat for each video card.

NOTE Card-retention mechanisms vary widely from motherboard to motherboard. In addition to the design shown in Figure 5-6, some use a lever that can be pushed to one side to release the lock; others use a knob that is pulled out to release the lock.

1. **Push down on locking tab**
2. **Pull up on card**
3. **Card connectors now visible**

Figure 5-6   Releasing the card-retention mechanism before removing a PCIe x16 video card.

SLI and CrossFire Multi-GPU Configurations

AMD CrossFire and NVIDIA SLI are competing technologies for using two or more video cards as a single logical unit to improving 3D gaming performance. Although a few systems use the PCIe bus to connect the cards, most configurations use the bridge cables shown in Figure 5-5.

To complete a CrossFire or SLI installation, use the configuration apps supplied with the video card drivers to enable CrossFire or SLI and select specific 3D performance settings. To learn more about SLI, see www.geforce.com/hardware/technology/sli. To learn more about CrossFire, see http://support.amd.com/en-us/kb-articles/Pages/AMD-CrossFireFAQ.aspx.

Video Card Physical Installation

Follow these steps to install the new video card:

Step 1. Insert the new video card into a PCIe x16 slot. If the motherboard has two or more PCIe x16 slots, use the slot closest to the port cluster for the primary (or only) card.

Step 2. Lock the card into position with the card retention mechanism and with the screw for the card bracket.

Step 3. If the card uses power, connect the appropriate PCIe power connector to the card (refer to Figure 5-4).

Step 4. If the card is running in multi-GPU mode and uses SLI or CrossFire, connect the appropriate bridge cable between the new card and a compatible existing (or new) card in the system (refer to Figure 5-5).

Step 5. Reattach the data cable from the display to the new video card.

Driver Installation

Driver installation takes place when the system is restarted:

Step 1. Turn on the display.

Step 2. Reconnect power to the system, turn on the computer.

Step 3. Provide video drivers as requested; you might need to run an installer program for the drivers. If you are installing the card under Linux, check with the card vendor for downloadable Linux drivers for your distribution.

Step 4. If the monitor is not detected as a Plug and Play monitor but as a Default monitor, install a driver for the monitor.

NOTE A driver disc might have been packed with the monitor or you might need to download a driver from the monitor vendor's website. If you do not install a driver for a monitor identified as a Default monitor, you will not be able to choose from the full range of resolutions and refresh rates the monitor actually supports.

Installing Network Cards

Although most computers include a 10/100/1000 Ethernet port or a Wireless Ethernet (Wi-Fi) adapter, you sometimes need to install a **network card** (network interface card or NIC) into a computer you want to add to a network.

To install a Plug and Play (PnP) network card, follow these steps:

Step 1.   Shut down the computer, disconnect it from AC power, and remove the case cover.

Step 2.   Locate an available expansion slot matching the network card's design. (Most use PCIe, but some servers and workstations might use PCI-X and some older desktop systems might use PCI).

Step 3.   Remove the slot cover and insert the card into the slot. Secure the card in the slot.

Step 4.   Reconnect power to the system, restart the system and provide drivers when requested by the system.

Step 5.   If prompted to install network drivers and clients, insert the operating system disc.

Step 6.   Connect the network cable to the card.

Step 7.   Test for connectivity (check LED lights, use a command such as ping, and so on), and then close the computer case.

If there are no available slots, or if you need to add (or upgrade) network connectivity on a laptop, use a USB to Ethernet or USB to wireless adapter.

Although USB network adapters are also PnP devices, you may need to install the drivers provided with the USB network adapter before you attach the adapter to your computer. After the driver software is installed, the device will be recognized as soon as you plug it into a working USB port.

NOTE   If you are using a wireless USB adapter, you can improve signal strength by using an extension cable between the adapter and the USB port on the computer. Using an extension cable enables you to move the adapter as needed to pick up a stronger signal.

Most USB network adapters are bus powered. For best results, they should be attached to a USB port built in to your computer or to a self-powered hub. Most recent adapters support USB 3.0 (5Gbps), which provides support for 100BASE-TX (Fast Ethernet 100Mbps) and 1000BASE-T (gigabit Ethernet 1000Mbps) signal speeds. A USB 2.0 port (480Mbps) is adequate for Fast Ethernet, but does not run fast enough for Gigabit Ethernet.

Installing USB Cards

Adding a **USB** 3.0 card is a quick way to upgrade a system with a spare PCIe slot but no USB 3.0 ports so it can connect to external storage devices at full speed. Here's how:

Step 1.   Shut down the computer, disconnect it from AC power, remove the case cover.

Step 2.   Locate an available PCIe x1 or wider expansion slot.

Step 3.   Remove the slot cover and insert the card into the slot. Secure the card in the slot.

Step 4.   Connect power to the card. Some cards use the Berg connector, while others use the Molex connector (see Figure 5-7).

Step 5.   Reconnect power to the system, restart the system and provide drivers when requested by the system.

Step 6.   Connect a USB device to the card.

Step 7.   After verifying the device works, close the case.

1. Molex power connector   3. USB 3.0 ports
2. Molex power cable   4. PCIe x1 slot

Figure 5-7   Preparing to connect a Molex power connector to a four-port USB 3.0 PCIe card.

Installing FireWire Cards

FireWire cards (see Figure 5-8) enable systems without onboard FireWire ports to connect to DV camcorders and other FireWire-based peripherals.

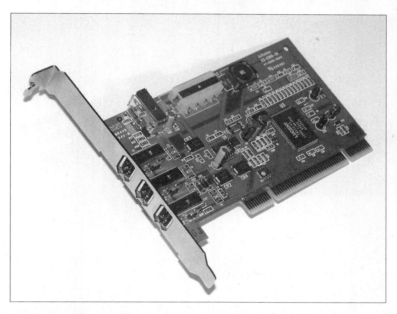

Figure 5-8   A typical FireWire 400 card featuring three external ports and one internal port.

To install and configure a FireWire (IEEE 1394) card, follow these steps:

Step 1.   Turn off the computer, unplug it, and remove the case cover.

Step 2.   Locate an available PCI or PCIe expansion slot.

Step 3.   Remove the slot cover and insert the card into the slot. Secure the card in the slot.

Step 4.   Connect a power lead to the card if necessary (see Figure 5-9).

1. Molex power connector
2. Molex power cable
3. Internal FireWire 400 port
4. PCI 32-bit slots

Figure 5-9   Connecting a Molex power cable to a FireWire card.

Step 5.   Close the system, reattach AC power, restart it, and provide the driver media if requested by the system.

Installing Thunderbolt Cards

Thunderbolt provides a very high-speed connection suitable for both mass storage and the daisy-chaining of multiple displays. Although Thunderbolt cards use the PCIe x4 (or wider) expansion slot that is found on high-performance PC motherboards, Thunderbolt support depends on the Thunderbolt (TB) header's presence on a motherboard. If this header is not present, you cannot install a working Thunderbolt card. If this header is present, you can install a Thunderbolt card designed by the motherboard or system vendor for use with your computer. Figure 5-10 illustrates a typical single-port Thunderbolt card.

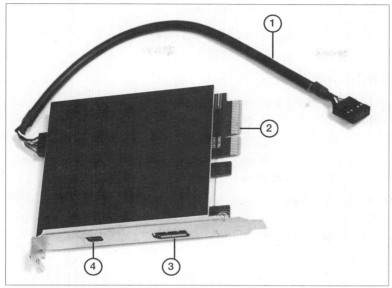

1. Thunderbolt header cable
2. PCIe x4 connector
3. DisplayPort IN connector
4. Thunderbolt port

Figure 5-10   A single-port Thunderbolt card also has a DisplayPort connection to allow Thunderbolt to carry both video and mass storage data.

Here's the procedure for installing it:

Step 1.   Turn off the computer, unplug it, and remove the case cover.

Step 2.   Check the documentation provided with the card for specific recommendations. Locate the recommended slot (must be PCIe 2.0 x4 or wider).

Step 3.   Remove the slot cover and insert the card into the recommended slot. Secure the card in the slot.

Step 4.   Connect the motherboard TB header (typically located on the side or front edge of the motherboard and marked TB_HEADER) to the card with the header cable provided with the card. Some cards have a top-mounted cable header, while others have the cable header along the edge of the card opposite the card bracket. With some motherboards, you might need to use a TB header converter cable.

Step 5.   Connect the DisplayPort IN port on the card to the DisplayPort output on your system's motherboard or video card.

Step 6.   Reconnect power to the system, restart the system and provide drivers when requested by the system.

Step 7.   Connect a Thunderbolt device to the card.

Step 8.   After verifying the device works, close the case.

Installing Storage Cards

Storage cards are flash memory cards, such as SD, which are inserted into internal or external card readers and expand the **storage** of the computer. To install a storage card:

Step 1.   Make sure the card reader is properly connected to a USB port header (internal) or USB port (external).

Step 2.   Check the card reader's documentation to determine which type(s) of cards the reader can handle. For example, very old SD card readers cannot use SDHC or SDXC cards. More recent models might not support SDXC cards.

Step 3.   Insert a compatible card into the appropriate slot on the card reader. The card shows up in your operating system's file manager as an additional drive. Figure 5-11 illustrates Windows 8.1's File Explorer before and after installing a storage card. Windows Vista/7 lists empty card reader slots as empty drives.

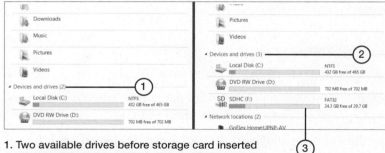

1. Two available drives before storage card inserted
2. Three available drives after storage card inserted
3. Capacity of newly inserted storage card

Figure 5-11   Windows 8.1 File Manager before (left) and after (right) a storage card is installed.

Installing Modem Cards

Modem cards (more often referred to as **internal modems**) most typically use the PCI slot, although a few PCIe versions exist. Single-line modems have two RJ-11 ports (one for line out and one for connection to a standard telephone). Multi-line modems are typically used in fax servers or for dial-up remote access.

To install a modem card (see Figure 5-12):

Step 1. Turn off the computer, unplug it, and remove the case cover.

Step 2. Locate an available PCI or PCIe expansion slot (depending on the card's requirements).

Step 3. Remove the slot cover and insert the card into the slot. Secure the card in the slot.

Step 4. Connect an RJ-11 telephone line from a telephone wall jack to the Line jack.

Step 5. Connect an RJ-11 telephone line from a telephone to the telephone jack on the modem (optional).

Step 6. Close the system, reattach AC power, restart it, and provide the driver media if requested by the system.

Step 7. Configure dial-up networking and call into a remote computer to verify proper operation.

1. Phone line and jack
2. Jack for connection to standard telephone

Figure 5-12   A typical PCI dial-up modem connected to a telephone line.

Installing Wireless/Cellular Cards

Wireless network cards for desktop computers use PCIe x1 slots (older models used PCI slots). External antennas are packaged with the card but must be attached after the card is installed.

To install a wireless card in a desktop computer:

Step 1.   Turn off the computer, unplug it, and remove the case cover.

Step 2.   Locate an available PCI or PCIe expansion slot (depending on the card's requirements).

Step 3.   Remove the slot cover and insert the card into the slot. Secure the card in the slot.

Step 4.   Attach the antenna(s) included with the card. Each antenna screws into a threaded connector on the card bracket (see Figure 5-13).

Step 5.   Close the system, reattach AC power, restart it, and provide the driver media if requested by the system.

Step 6.   Log in to the wireless network to confirm proper operation of the card. Adjust the antenna(s) to improve performance as needed.

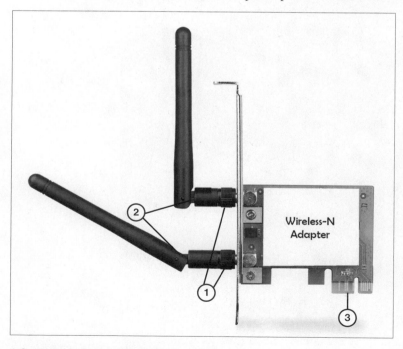

1. Screw each antenna into position
2. Rotate and adjust antenna angles to improve signal strength and performance
3. PCIe x1 connector

Figure 5-13   A typical PCIe x1 wireless network adapter.

Some wireless network cards in laptops also include cellular support; laptops with cellular support also have provision for a SIM card. Older laptops use the mini-PCI card shown in Figure 5-14, while recent and current laptops use the mini-PCIe card shown in Figure 5-15.

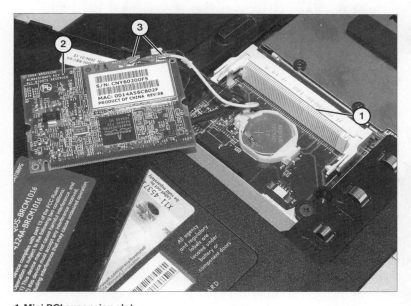

1. Mini-PCI expansion slot
2. Mini-PCI wireless card
3. Antenna wires

Figure 5-14   A typical mini-PCI wireless network card being removed from a laptop.

To replace a wireless network card or **network/cellular card** in a laptop:

Step 1.   Turn off the computer, unplug it, and remove the battery.

Step 2.   Remove the cover over the mini-PCIe network adapter.

Step 3.   Remove mounting screws and flip the adapter out of the laptop (see Figure 5-15).

Step 4.   Detach the antenna wires from the card. Note the order in which the wires connect.

Step 5.   If the wireless card is fastened to a mounting bracket, remove it from the bracket (see Figure 5-16).

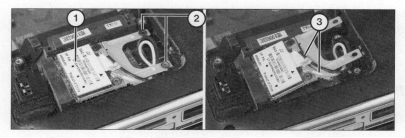

1. Mini-PCIe wireless card
2. Mounting screws
3. Antenna wires

Figure 5-15 Removing a mini-PCIe wireless card from a laptop.

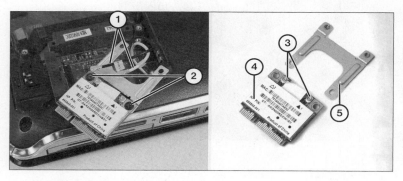

1. Antenna wires detached from card
2. Mounting screws for card
3. Antenna connectors
4. Mini-PCIe card removed from mounting bracket
5. Mounting bracket

Figure 5-16 Removing antenna wires and the mounting bracket from a mini-PCIe wireless card.

Step 6. Connect the replacement wireless card to the mounting bracket (if used) and antenna wires.

Step 7. Reinstall the wireless adapter into the laptop.

Step 8. Replace the cover over the wireless adapter.

Step 9. Replace the battery and/or plug in the laptop.

Step 10. Restart the laptop and install new drivers when prompted.

Step 11.   If you are installing a card with cellular support, install the SIM card provided by the wireless carrier, configure the card for cellular and Wi-Fi connections, and test both types of connections.

Installing TV Tuner Cards

TV tuner cards enable computers to pick up broadcast digital TV and unencrypted cable TV (Clear QAM). TV tuner cards are available in either PCI form factor (see Figure 5-17) or PCIe. TV tuners are also available in USB.

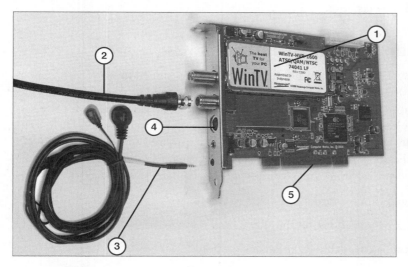

1. TV tuner card
2. Coaxial cable from antenna or cable TV service
3. IR blaster/receiver cable for remote control
4. S-Video in port for video capture
5. PCI 32-bit connector

Figure 5-17   A typical PCI TV tuner card.

TV tuner cards can be used with Windows Media Center (Windows Vista/7/8/8.1) or with TV playback apps bundled with the card or available separately.

To install a TV tuner card in a desktop computer:

Step 1.   Turn off the computer, unplug it, and remove the case cover.

Step 2.   Locate an available PCI or PCIe expansion slot (depending on the card's requirements).

Step 3.   Remove the slot cover and insert the card into the slot. Secure the card in the slot.

Step 4.   Attach the coaxial cable from the antenna or cable TV service to the appropriate port (note: some older cards have a tuner for analog TV; don't use it).

Step 5.   Connect the IR blaster/receiver for remote control.

Step 6.   Close the system, reattach AC power, restart it, and provide the driver media when requested by the system.

Step 7.   If you are not using Windows Media Center, install the TV viewing app bundled with the card (or choose your own app). Set up TV channels, and test reception.

Installing Video Capture Cards

Although many TV tuner cards and USB devices are designed to work with analog video sources (S-Video or composite), they are not designed to work with HD video or high-resolution computer or video game sources. A true **video capture card** (see Figure 5-18) is equipped to receive HDTV or higher-quality signs via HDMI, DVI, or Component. Video capture cards have built-in hardware support for MPEG-4 recording, and can be used to capture video for training, game recording, YouTube, or broadcast purposes. Some video capture devices connect to a USB port.

To install a video capture card:

Step 1.   Turn off the computer, unplug it, and remove the case cover.

Step 2.   Locate an available PCIe expansion slot.

Step 3.   Remove the slot cover and insert the card into the slot. Secure the card in the slot.

Step 4.   Connect the appropriate cable between the video source (computer, video game, and so on) and the video capture card.

Step 5.   Close the system, reattach AC power, restart it, and provide the driver media when requested by the system.

Step 6.   Start the capture utility and capture video or still images from the video source.

1. Video capture card
2. Header for component video capture
3. HDMI port
4 DVI-I port
5 PCIe x1 slot

Figure 5-18   A typical PCIe video capture card.

Installing Riser Cards

Riser cards are used to work around limited space in some systems. Riser cards can make multiple ports available from a single slot bracket or slot, or enable full-size cards to be mounted horizontally in low-profile systems. The two most common uses for riser cards include speakers and video cards ("display devices" on the CompTIA A+ Certification exam).

Speakers

Some of the MSI Big Bang motherboards are bundled with a special PCIe x1 Quantum Wave sound card that provides all audio features. These motherboards do not have audio ports on the rear port cluster. Instead, the bundled audio card includes audio codecs as well as speaker connectors for stereo and surround analog audio and SPDIF digital output to receivers and home theater systems.

Some older systems use a special card bracket or a small riser card to provide additional audio ports. To install a card bracket with additional audio ports:

Step 1.   Turn off the computer, unplug it, and remove the case cover.

Step 2.   Locate an expansion slot of any type that is not in use.

Step 3.   Connect the audio header cable from the card bracket to the appropriate audio header on the motherboard (see Figure 5-19).

Step 4.   Remove the slot cover and insert the audio header card bracket into the slot. Secure the card bracket in the slot.

Step 5.   Connect the appropriate audio cable to the bracket.

Step 6.   Close the system, reattach AC power, restart it, and provide driver media if requested by the system.

Step 7.   Configure the operating system to use the new speaker output. In Windows, use the audio mixer in Control Panel.

Display Devices

Although audio riser brackets and cards are rare today, it's much more common—especially with low-profile and rack-mounted systems—to see riser cards for PCI or PCIe slots. The term *riser card* is used to describe both right-angle brackets and flexible cables. Although riser cards can be used for any type of installed card, it's most common to see them used with video cards.

PCIe x16 video cards are much taller than other types of PCIe cards, so they are often too tall to fit into a low-profile or rack-mount (1U, 2U) chassis. By installing a right-angle riser card, the video card can be mounted horizontally.

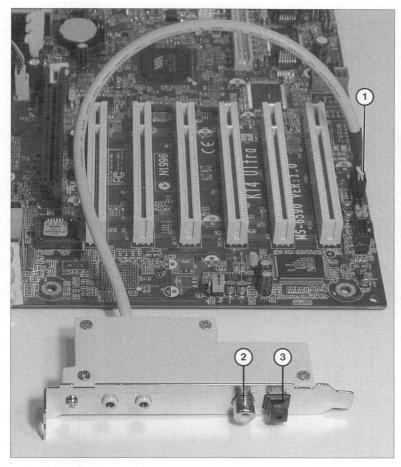

1. Header cable
2. SPDIF coaxial connector
3. SPDIF optical connector and protective plug

Figure 5-19   This special audio header bracket enables SPDIF coaxial or optical output to a home theater system.

Other types of riser cards support PCIe x8, x4, and x1 slots, as well as PCI slots. Some riser cards can convert a single PCIe slot into two or more PCI slots. Some low-profile systems use proprietary riser cards, such as the two-slot Dell model shown in Figure 5-20 for a PCI and a PCIe card. When a rigid riser cart isn't suitable, flexible cables can also be used.

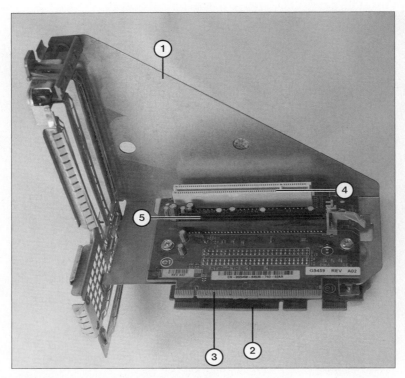

1. **Quick release mounting for riser card**
2. **PCI-X/PCI connector**
3. **PCIe x16 connector**
4. **PCI 32-bit slot**
5. **PCIe x16 slot**

Figure 5-20   A two-slot proprietary riser card and quick-release bracket for use in a low-profile system.

Figure 5-21 illustrates a two-slot (PCIe and PCI) riser card with cards attached.

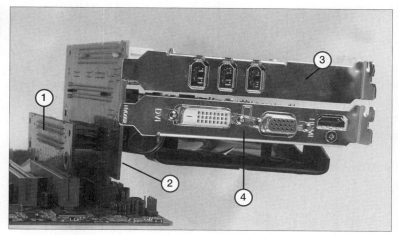

1. PCI portion of riser card
2. PCIe x16 portion of riser card
3. PCI card plugged into riser card
4. PCIe x16 plugged into riser card

Figure 5-21   An example of how a right-angle riser card enables tall cards to fit in a low-profile case (such as a small form factor or 1U/2U rack-mount chassis).

Exam Preparation Tasks

Review All the Key Topics

Review the most important topics in the chapter, noted with the key topics icon in the outer margin of the page. Table 5-1 lists a reference of these key topics and the page numbers on which each is found.

Table 5-1   Key Topics for Chapter 5

Key Topic Element	Description	Page Number
Figure 5-1	PCI, PCIe x1, and PCIe x16 cards and matching slots	126
Figure 5-3	PCIe power connectors and connectors for multi-GPU cables on PCIe x16 video cards	130
Section	Removing Drivers for Old Video Card or Onboard Video	131
Section	Video Card Physical Installation	134
Figure 5-21	Riser card and add-on cards	151

Define Key Terms

Define the following key terms from this chapter and check your answers in the glossary.

sound card, driver, network card, USB, FireWire, Thunderbolt, storage card, modem card, internal modem, wireless network card, network/cellular card, TV tuner card, video capture card, riser card, Primary VGA BIOS, Primary Graphics Adapter, video card, storage

Complete Hands-On Labs

Complete the hands-on labs and then see the answers and explanations at the end of the chapter. In this series of hands-on labs, you are preparing to install cards that will provide missing features to your system.

Lab 5-1: Checking a System for Required I/O Ports

After a discussion with a client, you have determined that the client needs the following:

- Unused USB 3.0 ports for use with 4TB external hard disk drives for video storage.
- An unused FireWire 400 connection to a DV camcorder.

Examine a desktop computer to determine whether one or both of these ports are available.

Lab 5-2: Checking a System for Required Expansion Slots

If one or both of these aforementioned ports are not available, open the system to determine which types and how many of each expansion slot type are available:

Port	Yes/No	Quantity
PCIe x1		
PCIe x4		
PCIe x16		
PCI 32-bit		
Others (specify)		

The client has the following cards available for installation:

- FireWire 400 PCI 32-bit
- FireWire 800 PCIe x1
- USB 3.0 PCIe x1

Which cards can be used in this system? In which slots?

To help you plan the installation (if possible), make a diagram of the motherboard, installed cards, and whether any card slots are blocked by other cards or cables on brackets.

Answer Review Questions

Answer these review questions and then see the answers and explanations at the end of the chapter.

1. When installing an expansion card, what is the first thing that you should do?

   a. Remove the slot cover and insert the card

   b. Install the proper driver

   c. Open the case

   d. Unplug the AC power

2. You are building a computer from existing parts and will be using the video card shown. Which type of slot is used for this card?

    a. PCI

    b. PCIe x1

    c. PCIe x4

    d. PCIe x16

3. You have just bought a new sound card. Before installing it, what should you do first?

    a. Disable onboard audio in the system BIOS

    b. Open the Sound utility in the Control Panel and roll back any existing sound card drivers

    c. Use the Start menu to disable the original Audio configuration settings

    d. In the Control Panel, open the Troubleshooting utility and access Audio

4. Identify the ports, connectors, and slots in the following figure.

A. Molex power connector

B. USB 3.0 port

C. Berg power connector

D. PCIe x1 slot

E. PCI slot

F. FireWire 400 port

5. You plan to install the TV tuner card shown in the following figure into your computer. What kind of cable is used to connect the card to the antenna or the cable TV service?

   a. S-video
   b. Coaxial
   c. SPDIF
   d. HDMI

6. You have just installed a new sound card into your Windows based-computer. How do you configure the recording and playback settings for the card?

   a. Configure recording and playback features in the BIOS.
   b. In the Control Panel, open the Sound utility.
   c. Use toggle switches or jumpers built into the card.
   d. These configurations are set by the manufacturer.

7. Which of the following best describes Thunderbolt technology?

   a. Is a high-performance sound card
   b. Is a high-speed port designed to replace the USB 3.0 port
   c. Is a high-speed port designed to replace FireWire
   d. May be used for mass data storage and for multiple video displays

8. You have been asked to install an internal modem on a fax server. What kind of port/connector does a modem use?

   a. RJ-11
   b. RJ-45
   c. Ethernet
   d. Coaxial

9. Which one of the following contains flash memory?

   a. Thunderbolt

   b. Riser card

   c. SD card

   d. Modem

Answers and Explanations to Hands-On Labs

Lab 5-1: Checking a System for Required I/O Ports

Compare the port clusters on these motherboards as an example of what you might have found in your own research:

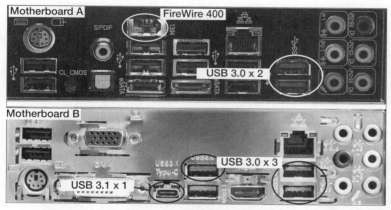

As you can see from this photo, only one of these motherboards, motherboard A, has the potential to have all of the ports needed. It has two USB 3.0 ports and a FireWire 400 (IEEE-1394a) port. However, it turns out that both of the USB 3.0 ports are already in use.

Motherboard B has three USB 3.0 ports plus a USB 3.1 Type C port that could also be used with USB 3.0 devices. Only one of the USB 3.0 ports is already in use. Motherboard B also has a faster processor.

After discussing your findings with your client, you both agree that if there is a suitable expansion slot for a FireWire 400 card on the system using motherboard B that it would be the best choice for this project.

Lab 5-2: Checking a System for Required Expansion Slots

The client has the following cards available for installation:

- FireWire 400 PCI 32-bit

- FireWire 800 PCIe x1

- USB 3.0 PCIe x1

An examination of motherboard B, shown in Lab 5-1, reveals the following slot availability:

Port	Quantity	In Use	Used by	Available
PCIe x1	2	2*	Slot blocked by PCIe x16 video card PCIe x1 video capture card	0
PCIe x4	N/A	N/A		N/A
PCIe x16	3	2	2 – PCIe x16 video cards	1
PCI 32-bit	2	1*		1

The boxes in the following figure indicate the slots that are used up.

E   P

Although one of the FireWire cards will fit into a 32-bit PCI slot (marked P in the figure), the FireWire 800 card (which also supports FireWire 400) will work in a PCIe x16 slot, which is faster. That slot is marked E.

Answers and Explanations to Review Questions

1. D. The first thing you should do before installing any components is to completely remove all power to the computer. Turning off the computer's power switch is not sufficient. You must physically unplug a desktop computer from the wall and remove the battery from a laptop or other mobile device.

2. D. Insert this card into a PCIe x16 slot.

3. A. In the BIOS, be sure to disable the onboard audio that came built into your computer before you install a new audio card.

4. 1. A. (Molex power connector), 2. F. (FireWire 400 port), 3. E. (PCI slot).

5. B. Use the coaxial cable to connect your TV tuner card to the feed from the antenna or cable TV service.

6. B. Recording and playback settings are accessed through the Sound utility in the Control Panel. The BIOS settings are used to disable the onboard audio. There are no audio settings in the Start menu. The Troubleshooting utility is used for troubleshooting problems, not changing configuration settings.

7. D. A single Thunderbolt cable may be used for both high-speed mass data storage and for connecting multiple video displays in a daisy-chain fashion. The Thunderbolt card connects to a PCIe x4 card or higher, but the motherboard must also be designed to accept Thunderbolt.

8. A. RJ-11 connectors are used with cables in telephone and fax systems. RJ-45 connectors are used with Ethernet cables, which are used for network wiring. Coaxial is a type of cable used in cable TV.

9. C. SD cards use flash memory. SD cards are read by inserting them into internal or external card readers.

This chapter covers the following subjects:

- **Optical Drive Features and Capacities**—This section compares CD, DVD, and Blu-ray drives, media, and capacities.

- **Magnetic Hard Disk Drives**—This section compares form factors and discusses performance factors and installation processes.

- **Flash Drives**—This section compares form factors and capacities and the characteristics of card readers.

- **Solid State Drives**—This section discusses drive types that contain solid state memory, including SSD, hybrid, and eMMC

- **Hot-Swappable Drives**—In this section, learn which types of drives can be hot-swapped and how to hot-swap in Windows, Linux, and OS X.

- **RAID Types**—Learn the differences between RAID 0, RAID 1, RAID 10, and RAID 5 and how to create a RAID array.

- **Tape Drive**—Which versions of Windows have built-in support for tape drives? How do you calculate the rated capacity of a tape drive? Which tape drives hold the most data? This section covers all of these topics.

## CHAPTER 6

Storage Devices

Modern desktop and laptop computers feature a variety of built-in and removable storage devices that use three distinct technologies: optical storage, magnetic storage, and flash memory. Tablets use flash memory storage. In this chapter, you learn the characteristics of each type.

220-901: Objective 1.5 Install and configure storage devices and use appropriate media.

Foundation Topics

Optical Drive Features and Capacities

Optical drives fall into three major categories:

- Those based on CD technology, including CD-ROM, CD-R (recordable CD), and CD-RW (rewritable CD)

- Those based on DVD technology, including DVD-ROM, DVD-ROM/ CD-RW combo, DVD-ROM / DVD-RW / DVD-RW DL, DVD-RAM, DVD-R/RW, DVD+R/RW, DVD±R/RW, and DVD±R/RW DL

- Those based on Blu-ray technology, including BD-ROM, Combo BD-ROM/ DVD Super Multi, BD-R, and BD-RE

CD, DVD, and Blu-ray drives store data in a continuous spiral of indentations called pits and lands on the nonlabel side of the media from the middle of the media outward to the edge. All drives use a laser to read data; the difference between the storage capacities of Blu-ray, DVD, and CD is due to the difference in laser wavelength: Blu-ray, which has the highest capacity, uses a blue laser with a shorter wavelength than DVD or CD; DVD uses a red laser with a longer wavelength than Blu-ray but shorter than CD; CD, which has the lowest capacity, uses a near-infrared laser with the longest wavelength. The shorter the wavelength, the smaller the pits and lands, enabling more data to be stored in the same space.

Most CD, DVD, and Blu-ray drives are tray-loading, but a few use a slot-loading design. Slot-loading designs are more common in home and automotive electronics products.

CD-ROM / CD-RW

CD-R and CD-RW drives use special media types and a more powerful laser than that used on CD-ROM drives to write data to the media. CD-R media is a write-once media—the media can be written to during multiple sessions, but older data cannot be deleted. CD-RW media can be rewritten up to 1,000 times. 80-minute CD-R media has a capacity of 700MB, whereas the older 74-minute CD-R media has a capacity of 650MB. CD-RW media capacity is up to 700MB, but is often less, depending on how the media is formatted. CD-RW media is available in four types:

- CD-RW 1x-4x
- High speed CD-RW 4x-12x
- Ultra speed CD-RW 12x-24x
- Ultra speed+ CD-RW 32x

Drives compatible with faster media types can usually work with slower media types, but not vice versa.

DVD Recordable and Rewriteable Standards

DVD-R and DVD+R media is recordable but not erasable, whereas DVD-RW and DVD+RW media uses a phase-change medium similar to CD-RW and can be rewritten up to 1,000 times. DVD-RAM can be rewritten up to 100,000 times, but DVD-RAM drives and media are less compatible with other types of DVD drives and media than the other rewritable DVD types, making DVD-RAM the least popular DVD format.

Here's more about the many members of the DVD family:

- **DVD-RAM**—A rewriteable/erasable media similar to CD-RW but more durable; it can be single-sided (4.7GB) or double-sided (9.4GB).

- **DVD-R**—A single-sided, single-layer, writeable/nonerasable media similar to CD-R; capacity of 4.7GB. Some DVD-RAM and all DVD-RW drives can use DVD-R media. DL (dual-layer) media includes a second recording layer (capacity of 8.4GB).

- **DVD-R DL**—A single-side writeable/nonerasable media similar to CD-R but with a second recording layer; capacity of 8.4GB.

- **DVD-RW**—A single-sided rewriteable/erasable media similar to CD-RW; capacity of 4.7GB. DVD-RW drives can also write to DVD-R media.

- **DVD+RW**—A rewritable/erasable media. Also similar to CD-RW but not interchangeable with DVD-RW or DVD-RAM; capacity of 4.7GB.

- **DVD+R**—A single-side, single-layer writeable/nonerasable media. Also similar to CD-R but not interchangeable with DVD-R; capacity of 4.7GB.

- **DVD+R DL**—A writeable/nonerasable media with a second recording layer. Also similar to CD-R but not interchangeable with DVD-R; capacity of 8.4GB.

So-called SuperMulti DVD drives can read and write all types of DVD media as well as CD media. Sometimes these drives are also referred to as DVD±R/RW. Some early DVD+R/RW and DVD-R/RW drives cannot write to DL media.

NOTE   The CompTIA A+ Certification 220-901/220-902 exam objectives erroneously refer to DVD-RW DL, which is a media type that does not exist. Only recordable DVD media is dual layer.

Blu-ray (BD)

All Blu-ray drives are compatible with BD-ROM (read-only, Blu-ray media), such as the media used for Blu-ray movies. To play back Blu-ray movies, you must have a compatible player app installed. Standard-capacity BD media types include:

- BD-R—Recordable, not erasable; similar to CD-R, DVD+R, DVD-R; 25GB capacity.

- BD-R DL—Dual-layer recordable media; similar to DVD+R DL, DVD-RW DL. 50GB capacity.

- BD-RE—Recordable and rewriteable; similar to CD-RW, DVD-RW, DVD+RW. 25GB capacity.

BDXL

BDXL drives and media represent a large jump in capacity over standard BD drives and media. The BDXL specification was released in April 2010. It supports multi-layer 100GB and 128GB recordable media (BD-R 3.0) and multi-layer 100GB re-writeable media (BD-RE Revision 4.0). Many, but not all, BD-RE compatible drives are compatible with BDXL standards. Check the drive's specifications to determine compatibility.

Drive Speed Ratings

Drive speeds are measured by an X-rating:

- **CD media**—1X equals 150KBps, the data transfer rate used for reading music CDs. Multiply the X-rating by 150 to determine the drive's data rate for reading, writing, or rewriting CD media.

- **DVD media**—1X equals 1.385MBps; this is the data transfer rate used for playing DVD-Video (DVD movies) content. Multiply the X-rating by 1.385 to determine the drive's data rate for reading, writing, or rewriting DVD media.

- **Blu-ray (BD) media**—1X equals 4.5MBps; this is the data transfer rate for playing Blu-ray movies. Multiply the X-rating by 4.5 to determine the drive's data rate for reading, writing, or rewriting Blu-ray media.

Note that Blu-ray drives are also compatible with CD and DVD media. Check the specifications for a particular drive to determine the specific types of media it supports and the maximum read/write/rewrite speeds for each media type.

Recording Files to Optical Discs

You can use the following methods to record files onto optical discs:

- Built-in recording features in Windows or other operating systems
- Third-party disc mastering programs
- Third-party drag-and-drop programs

All optical media must be formatted, but depending on how you write to the media, the formatting process might be incorporated into the writing process or require a separate step.

Creating Optical Discs in Windows

Windows Vista/7/8/8.1/10 can write to recordable and rewriteable Blu-ray discs, DVDs and CDs. Figure 6-1 illustrates burning a disc with the built-in Windows 8.1 disc-writing wizard. Windows Movie Maker (a free download from Microsoft) can be used to create a video file on CD or DVD media. However, you must use a third-party program if you want to create a video file on BD media.

NOTE Windows Vista must be updated to SP1 and have the Windows Feature Pack for Storage 1.0 installed or be updated to SP2 to support Blu-ray (BD-R) disc mastering.

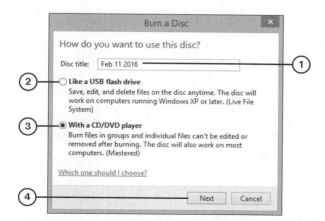

1. The current date is the default for the disc title; click or tap to change it
2. Click to format disc using UDF (Live File System)
3. Click to format disc using CDFS (Mastered)
4. Click or tap to continue

Figure 6-1   Selecting a disc format with Windows 8.1's optical-disc-writing wizard.

When you copy files to a recordable/rewritable CD or DVD drive using Explorer, Send To, or other commands, Windows prompts you to insert a blank disc and prompts you for a disc title. With Windows Vista, click the Show Formatting Options button to choose between mastered (CDFS) or Live File System (UDF) formats. In Windows 7/8/8.1/10, these choices appear by default (refer to Figure 6-1).

Which File System Is Best—and When

The default choice, Live File System, enables drag-and-drop file copying with both recordable and rewritable media, the ability to erase files when used with rewritable media, and support of individual file sizes more than 2GB. (2GB is the limit of the ISO 9660 file system used by the Mastered option.) However, Live File System discs (which use Universal Disc Format version 2.01 file system by default) might not be compatible with older operating systems and aren't suitable for use with CD or DVD drives in consumer and auto electronics systems. You can choose other Live File System (UDF) formats before the format process starts. See http://windows.microsoft. com/en-us/windows/which-cd-dvd-format#1TC=windows-7.

Use the Mastered option (CDFS) if you want to create a disc that can be read by virtually any drive on a PC, consumer electronics, or auto electronics device.

After you select the format desired and continue, Explorer copies the files you want to burn to a temporary folder and opens the drive window. Use the Burn command in the Explorer toolbar (Windows Vista/7) or the Share tab (Windows 8/8.1) to burn the disc. You can select the burn speed and review or change the disk name before continuing.

During the burn process, Explorer displays a progress bar. After the disc is burned, if you use the Live File System, open Explorer, right-click the disc, and select Eject so that the media will be prepared for use on other computers.

NOTE   When you insert a blank disc in Windows, you might have an AutoPlay dialog appear during the process. If you don't want to use any of the options on the AutoPlay menu, or you have already begun a process, close it.

Windows 7/8/8.1/10 include all the CD and DVD writing features of Windows Vista and add the ability to write a CD or DVD from an **ISO image** file (these files usually have the extension .iso) and support for writing to BD-R and BD-RE discs from its initial release. However, you must use a third-party program if you want to create a video file on BD media. Figure 6-2 illustrates the Windows 8.1 Disc Image Burner.

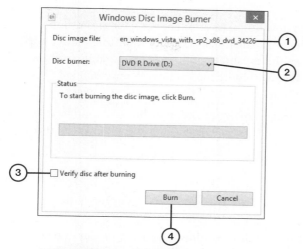

1. Selected disc image (.ISO) file
2. If the system has more than one rewriteable optical drive, open the menu to select the drive desired
3. Check this box to verify the disc after burning
4. Click or tap to burn the disc

Figure 6-2   Burning an ISO image file to DVD with Disc Image Burner.

Using Third-Party Optical Disc Mastering Programs for Windows

For more flexibility and the ability to save file lists for repeated burning at different times, consider a third-party disc-mastering program. Some of the leading programs include Roxio Creator NXT 4 (www.roxio.com), Nero 2016 Platinum (www.nero.com), ImgBurn (www.imgburn.com, freeware), and CDBurnerXP (www.cdburn-erxp.de, freeware). These programs are sometimes bundled with rewriteable DVD and Blu-ray drives or can be purchased or downloaded separately. Typical features include a wizard-based or menu-based burning process that makes it easier than with Windows to select the options needed, a preview option that shows you how much of a particular disc size will be used by your burning task, and options for creating audio discs for playback on a CD player.

Using Third-Party Drag-and-Drop File Copying Programs

Some older versions of third-party disc mastering programs also include a drag-and-drop file copying utility. Examples include Roxio Burn and Nero's InCD. These utilities use the same UDF (Live File System) disc formats supported by Windows but provide more streamlined operation. For example, when you drag files to a disc prepared for drag-and-drop, the files are copied immediately.

CAUTION   Because of differences in how different drag-and-drop programs function and the need to have UDF support installed in a computer that will be used with drag-and-drop media, you should test the capability of different computers to share (read and write) to media before implementing it in a production environment. A utility such as IsoBuster can read UDF media, even if the disc has problems.

Also, media that will be distributed outside an organization or home should be mastered. Mastered media can be read without the need to install a drag-and-drop program.

Burning Discs in OS X

Recent versions of OS X include optical disc burning features in Finder. To get started, insert the blank media you want to burn and select Open Finder when prompted. Drag the files you want to burn to the Untitled disc icon in Finder (see Figure 6-3). After you enter the disc name, select the burn speed and then click Burn (see Figure 6-4).

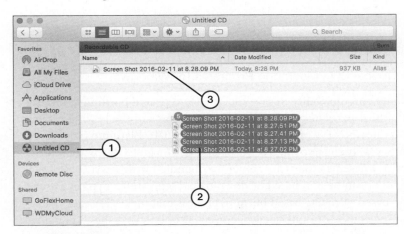

1. **Untitled CD selected**
2. **Files being dragged to the disc for burning**
3. **This file was already dragged to the disc**

Figure 6-3   Dragging files to a blank optical disc with Finder.

Burning Discs in Linux

Linux itself does not include optical disc burning as a standard feature. However, there are many disc-burning apps for Linux, some of which are included or available in popular distributions. Some of the leaders include the following:

- Brasero works with the GNOME desktop—https://wiki.gnome.org/Apps/Brasero/

- K3b works with the K Desktop Environment (KDE)—www.k3b.org

- Xfburn was designed for the Xfce desktop, but works in other Linux GUIs—http://goodies.xfce.org/projects/applications/xfburn

Before downloading a burning app, check the software library included with your distribution for a ready-to-install version.

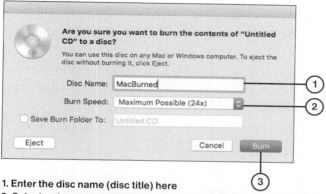

1. Enter the disc name (disc title) here
2. Select a slower speed if the target device can't read discs burned at maximum speed
3. Click to burn the disc

Figure 6-4   Preparing to burn a CD with Finder.

Magnetic Hard Disk Drives

Magnetic hard disk drives are the most important storage device used by a personal computer. Hard disk drives store the operating system (Windows, OS X, Linux, or others) and load it into the computer's memory (RAM) at startup. Hard disk drives also store applications, system configuration files used by applications and the operating system, and data files created by the user.

Traditional hard disk drives use one or more double-sided platters formed from rigid materials such as aluminum or glass. These platters are coated with a durable magnetic surface divided into sectors. Each sector contains 512 bytes of storage along with information about where the sector is located on the disk medium. Sectors are organized in concentric circles from the edge of the media inward toward the middle of the platter. These concentric circles are called tracks.

Hard disk drives are found in almost every PC, with the exception of many mobile computers, which typically use SSDs.

External drives typically include SATA hard disks with a bridge controller for use with USB 2.0 or USB 3.0 ports. Drives made for OS X include USB or FireWire ports, or USB or Thunderbolt ports. Some external drives can also connect to eSATA ports. External drives that use 3.5-inch desktop hard disks require AC power, but most external drives that use 2.5-inch or smaller mobile hard disks can be bus-powered, receiving power from the USB or FireWire port on the host computer.

Form Factors

Internal hard disk drives for desktop computers use 3.5-inch form factors. Their capacities range up to 8TB, but most installed desktop drives in recent systems have capacities ranging from 500GB to 2TB.

Internal hard disk drives or SSDs for laptop computers use 2.5-inch form factors. Their capacity ranges up to 3TB, but most laptop drives in recent systems have capacities ranging from 500GB to 1TB.

Figure 6-5 compares front and rear views of a DVD drive, 3.5-inch desktop hard disk, 2.5-inch laptop hard disk, and 2.5-inch laptop SSD.

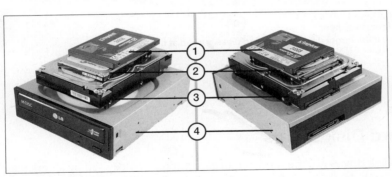

1. 2.5-inch laptop SSD
2. 2.5-inch laptop hard disk
3. 3.5-inch desktop hard disk
4. 5-25-inch DVD rewriteable drive

Figure 6-5   Front (left) and rear (right) internal optical, desktop and mobile internal hard disks, and mobile internal SSD drives.

Spin Rate

The speed at which hard disk media turns, its spin rate, is measured in revolutions per minute (**RPM**). Low-performance or "green" hard disks typically spin at

5,400RPM. Mid-performance drives spin at 7,200RPM. High-performance desktop drives spin at 10,000RPM. Drives designed for use in enterprise computing, such as servers, spin at rates up to 15,000RPM.

Table 6-1 provides a quick-reference table with examples.

Table 6-1   Hard Disk Spin Rate Comparison

Spin Rate (RPM)	Typical Use	Desktop Drive Example	Laptop Drive Example
5400	"Green" power-saving drives	WD Blue	WD Blue
		Seagate 4TB Desktop HDD*	Seagate Laptop HDD
7200	Mid-range performance	WD Black	WD Black
		Seagate Barracuda	Seagate Laptop Thin
10000	High-performance	WD VelociRaptor	(None)

*Actual spindle speed 5900 RPM

Cache Sizes, Areal Density, and Performance

Other than interface type (see Chapter 8, "Ports and Interfaces") and spin rate, another influence on hard disk performance is the drive's cache size. In a hard disk, the cache is used to hold recently read information for reuse. Just as with processor cache memory, which often enables the CPU to read cache memory instead of slower main memory to reuse previously read information, hard disks with larger buffers can re-read recently transferred information more quickly from cache than from the drive's magnetic storage.

In general, high-performance drives have larger caches than lower-performance drives. For example, the current 5400RPM WD Blue desktop drives have caches of 16–64MB, while the 7200RPM WD Black desktop drives have caches of 64MB–128MB, and Seagate 8TB Desktop HDD has a 256MB cache. The larger-capacity drives in any given series typically have larger caches than the smallest-capacity drives in the same drive series.

A fourth factor in hard disk performance is areal density, the amount of information stored on each hard disk platter. Some drive vendors publish specific areal density information. However, if you cannot find a specific value for areal density, keep in mind that the fewer platters used by a hard disk drive for a particular capacity, the greater the areal density. The greater the areal density of a hard disk, the faster the data transfer will be when compared to drives with the same capacity, spin rate, interface type (for example, SATA 6Gbps), and cache size.

Internal Hard Disk Drive, SSD, and Optical Drive Installation

The most common types of internal drives you will install are SATA hard disks. The following sections provide step-by-step installation instructions for these types of drives. You can also use these instructions for other types of SATA drives, such as SSD, optical, tape, or removable-media drives as noted.

Step 1.   Shut down the system and disconnect it from AC power.

Step 2.   Open the system and check for an unused drive bay matching the drive's form factor. The 3.5-inch drive bay is used for hard disks and some tape and removable-media drives. The 5.25-inch drive bay is used for optical drives and can be used for other types of drives as well. The 2.5-inch drive bay is used for SSDs. See Figure 6-6.

1. 2.5-inch drive bays
2. Side-facing 3.5-inch drive bays
3. 3.5-inch hard disk installed in front-facing drive bay

Figure 6-6   2.5-inch and 3.5-inch drive bays in a recent desktop computer chassis.

Step 3a.   For 3.5-inch drives, install the drive into a 3.5-inch drive bay. If a 3.5-inch drive bay is not available but a 5.25-inch drive bay is, attach the appropriate adapter kit and rails as needed, as shown in Figure 6-7. Continue with Step 4.

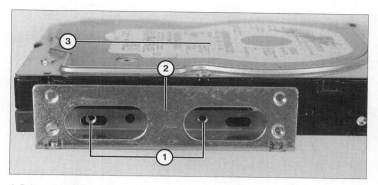

1. **Drive mounting holes**
2. **3.5-inch to 5.25-inch adapter bracket (one on each side of drive)**
3. **3.5-inch hard disk drive**

Figure 6-7   3.5 inch drive with 5.25-inch drive bay adapter

Step 3b.   For 5.25-inch drives or drives adapted to 5.25-inch, if the 5.25-inch drive bays on the system use rails to hold drives in position, attach the appropriate rails. Continue with Step 4.

Step 3c.   For 2.5-inch drives (such as hybrid or SSDs), install the drive into a 2.5-inch drive bay. If one is not available, attach a 2.5-inch to 3.5-inch adapter kit to the drive and install it in a 3.5-inch drive bay. Continue with Step 4.

Step 4.   Install the drive into the appropriate drive bay using screws supplied by the drive vendor. Depending on the chassis layout and the drive type being installed, you might need to remove a cover from the drive bay or remove the drive bay itself. See Figure 6-8.

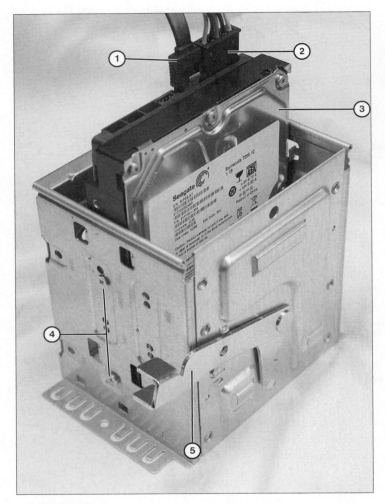

1. SATA data cable
2. SATA power cable
3. 3.5-inch hard disk drive
4. Screws mounting hard disk drive to drive cage
5. Locking lever for securing drive cage to chassis

Figure 6-8   A 3.5-inch hard disk installed in a removable drive cage after connecting power and data cables. The opposite side of each drive is also secured with screws (not shown).

Step 5.   Connect the SATA cable to the drive; it is keyed so that it can be connected in only one direction.

Step 6.   Connect the SATA power lead; if the computer's power supply doesn't have an SATA edge connector, use the adapter provided with the drive or purchased separately to convert a standard Molex connector to the edge connector type used by SATA. See Figure 6-9.

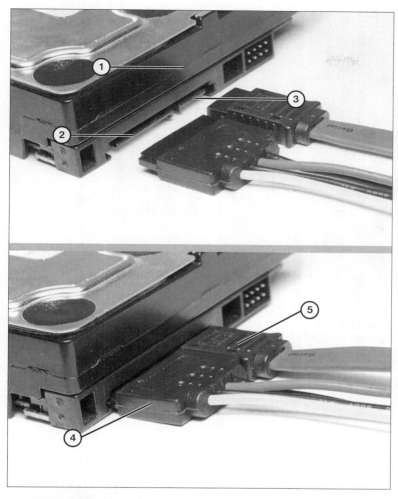

1. SATA hard disk drive
2. SATA power connector
3. SATA data connector
4. SATA power cable
5. SATA data cable

Figure 6-9 A typical SATA hard disk before (top) and after (bottom) installing power and data cables.

Step 7. Connect the SATA data cable to the connector on the motherboard or host adapter card. See Figure 6-10.

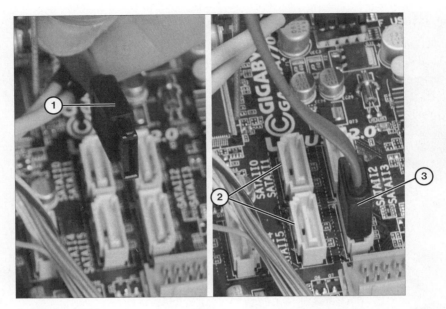

1. SATA data cable
2. SATA host adapters on motherboard
3. SATA data cable after connection to a host adapter

Figure 6-10   Connecting an SATA cable to the SATA header on the motherboard.

NOTE   Some recent motherboards have front-mounted SATA ports. See Chapter 3, "Motherboard Components," for examples.

Step 8.   Reconnect the system to AC power and turn it on.

Step 9.   Start the BIOS configuration program (if the SATA host adapter is built in to the motherboard). Enable the SATA host adapter (if necessary), configure SATA settings, save changes, and restart your system. Install drivers if your new SATA drive is not recognized by the system BIOS.

To learn how to prepare a new hard disk or SSD for use with Windows, see "Diskpart," p.751, " and "Disk Management," p.775 in Chapter 15, "Managing Microsoft Windows."

NOTE   If you need to install an SATA hard disk in a system that lacks an SATA host adapter or you need to install an SATA RAID array in a system that lacks RAID support, you need to install an SATA or SATA RAID host adapter card into a PCI or PCIe (preferred) expansion slot. This type of card has an onboard BIOS (firmware) that is used to set up and configure the drive(s) attached to it.

Installing an eSATA Hard Disk

eSATA host adapters plug in to PCI Express (PCIe) x1 or x4 slots. Some motherboards have built-in eSATA ports. An SATA port can be converted to an eSATA port by connecting a header cable that mounts in an empty expansion slot. Single-port and dual-port cables are available (see Figure 6-11). eSATA cables (see Figure 6-12) are heavier than SATA cables and use a different keying system.

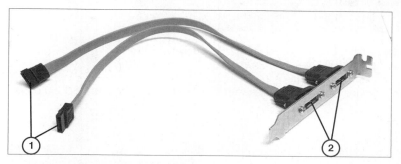

1. SATA cables connect to host adapter
2. eSATA connectors

Figure 6-11   A dual-port eSATA to SATA adapter.

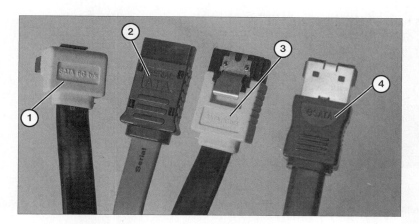

1. Right-angle SATA 6Gbps cable end with locking clip
2. Standard SATA 1.5-3Gbps cable end
3. Straight SATA 6Gbps cable end with locking clip
4. eSATA cable end

Figure 6-12   SATA and eSATA cables compared.

Figure 6-13 illustrates an external hard disk with USB 2.0, eSATA, and dual IEEE-1394a (FireWire 400) ports.

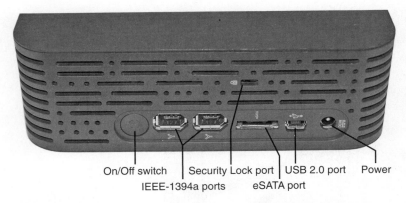

On/Off switch   Security Lock port   USB 2.0 port   Power
        IEEE-1394a ports   eSATA port

Figure 6-13   A multi-interface external hard disk with IEEE-1394a, eSATA, and USB 2.0 ports.

> **NOTE**   If you want to adapt SATA ports on the motherboard to use eSATA ports with a header cable, you should configure the computer's SATA ports to run in AHCI mode. This enables hot-swapping and supports advanced SATA features for better performance.

Some laptops have combo eSATA/USB 2.0 ports, also known as eSATAp, Power over eSATA, or eSATA USB Hybrid Port/EUHP. This type of port can connect to either type of device (see Figure 6-14).

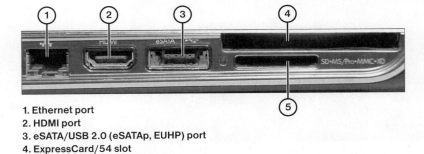

1. **Ethernet port**
2. **HDMI port**
3. **eSATA/USB 2.0 (eSATAp, EUHP) port**
4. **ExpressCard/54 slot**
5. **SD/MemoryStick/MMC card reader slot**

Figure 6-14   A laptop with an eSATA/USB 2.0 port.

Computers with USB 3.0 ports can use third-party adapters to enable USB 3.0 ports to be connected to eSATA drives.

Flash Drives

Flash memory is a type of memory that can retain its contents without electricity. It has no moving parts, so it is very durable. Standard flash memory is used in digital media players, memory cards for cameras and digital media devices, digital camcorders, and USB thumb drives.

Figure 6-15 illustrates the most common types of flash memory cards.

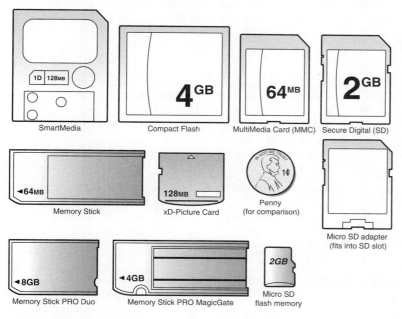

Figure 6-15   Common flash memory card types.

In Table 6-2, the most common types of flash memory are compared to each other.

Table 6-2   Flash Memory Card Capacities and Uses

Media Category	Common Capacity	Common Uses	Notes
SmartMedia (SM)	Up to 128MB	Digital cameras.	Now obsolete. Replaced by xD-Picture Card.
CompactFlash (CF)	Up to 512GB	Professional Digital SLR cameras.	Check manufacturer's speed rating for best performance in burst mode.
MultiMedia Card (MMC)	Up to 4GB	Various devices.	Obsolete. Replaced by SD, SDHC, and SDXC.

Media Category	Common Capacity	Common Uses	Notes
Memory Stick	Up to 128MB	Older Sony point-and-shoot digital cameras and digital media devices; also PlayStation 3 (PS3).	Obsolete. Replaced by SD, SDHC, and SDXC.
Memory Stick PRO MagicGate	Up to 4GB	Older Sony point-and-shoot digital cameras and digital media devices, including PlayStation Portable (PSP) and PS3.	Obsolete. Replaced by SD, SDHC, and SDXC.
Memory Stick PRO Duo	Up to 32GB*	Older Sony point-and-shoot digital cameras and camcorders, and digital media devices, including PSP and PS3 (but not PS4).	Obsolete. Replaced by SD, SDHC, and SDXC.
Secure Digital (SD)	Up to 2GB	Most models of point-and-shoot digital cameras; some digital SLR cameras; many flash memory–based media players.	Has write-protect switch on left side of media. Can also be used in place of SDHC or SDXC memory.
Secure Digital High Capacity (SDHC)	4 to 32GB	Many models of point-and-shoot digital cameras, digital SLR cameras, and flash memory–based media players.	SDHC media has the same physical form factor as SD; however, only devices made for SDHC can use SDHC. These devices are also compatible with SD. Check with device vendor for details.
Secure Digital Extended Capacity (SDXC)	64 to 512GB	Some high-performance digital SLR cameras.	SDXC media has the same physical form factor as SD and SDHC; however, only devices made for SDXC media can use it.
miniSD	2GB	Mobile phones and cameras.	Obsolete. Replaced by MicroSD. Can be used in SD or SDHC slots with an optional adapter.
miniSDHC	32GB	Mobile phones and cameras.	Obsolete. Replaced by MicroSDHC. Can be used in SDHC slots with an optional adapter.

Media Category	Common Capacity	Common Uses	Notes
microSD	2GB	Various portable devices: smartphones, video games, and expandable USB flash memory drives.	Can also be used in place of microSDHC; can be used in SD or SDHC slots with an optional adapter.
microSDHC	32GB	Various portable devices: smartphones, video games, and expandable USB flash memory drives.	Device must support microSDHC; can be used in SDHC slots with an optional adapter.
xD-Picture Card	Up to 512MB (standard) Up to 2GB (Type M, Type M+, Type H)	Older Fujifilm and Olympus digital point-and-shoot cameras	Obsolete. Replaced by SD Card. Some cameras also support SD Card.

*Original version up to 8GB; Mark 2 version up to 32GB

Flash Card Reader

To enable flash memory cards (refer to Figure 6-15 and Table 6-2) to be used with a computer, use a **card reader**. Figure 6-16 shows a typical external multislot card reader, and Figure 6-17 shows a typical internal multislot card reader. Most card readers assign a separate drive letter to each slot.

NOTE Do not confuse flash card readers with smart card readers. Smart card readers are used as part of a security system to read ID cards with embedded security.

1. SDHC card inserted into card reader

Figure 6-16   This multislot card reader supports a wide variety of flash memory cards and connects to a USB 3.0 port.

Figure 6-17   This internal card reader connects to an unused USB 2.0 port header on the motherboard.

> **NOTE**   Some printers and multifunction devices also include card readers. Some card readers built in to printers and multifunction devices are used only for printing, whereas others can be used to transfer files to and from the host computer.

When you insert a flash memory card containing files in Windows Vista/7, Windows might display an AutoPlay dialog providing various programs that can be used to view or use the files on the card (see Figure 6-18).

Figure 6-18   A typical AutoPlay menu displayed by Windows 7 when a flash memory card containing photos is inserted into a card reader.

When you insert a flash memory card containing files in Windows 8, Windows might display a simplified AutoPlay dialog (see Figure 6-19).

If AutoPlay does not appear, open Computer, This PC, Windows Explorer, or File Explorer and navigate to the appropriate drive letter to use the files on the card.

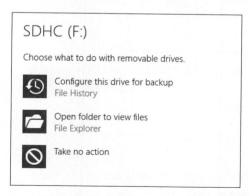

Figure 6-19   A typical AutoPlay menu displayed by Windows 8/8.1 when a flash memory card containing files is inserted into a card reader.

Solid State Drives

Faster and higher-capacity forms of flash memory known as single-level cell (SLC) and multi-level cell (MLC) are used in solid state drives (SSDs), a replacement for conventional hard disk drives.

SSD

A **solid-state drive (SSD)** is a flash memory technology. Unlike conventional flash memory drives, an SSD is designed to emulate a hard disk and you can use it in place of a hard disk in mobile devices as well as for high-performance laptops and desktops. A typical SSD (see Figure 6-20) uses a 2.5-inch form factor, but an optional 2.5-inch to 3.5-inch adapter enables it to be installed in desktop computers that lack 2.5-inch drive bays.

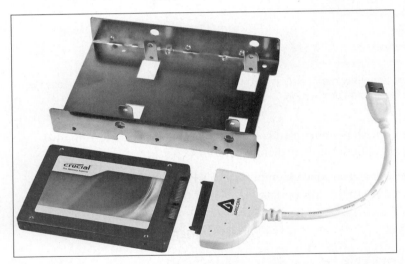

Figure 6-20   An SSD with optional data transfer cable and 2.5-inch to 3.5-inch bay adapter.

SSDs are also available in these form factors:

- mSATA (mini-PCIe form factor)—Used by some high-performance laptops and desktops.

- M.2 (smaller than mini-PCIe)—Faster than mSATA; used in some of the latest high-performance desktops and laptops.

- PCIe card—For high-performance desktops.

Figure 6-21 compares an mSATA to an M.2 card, while Figure 6-22 illustrates an M.2 card installed in a high-performance desktop computer.

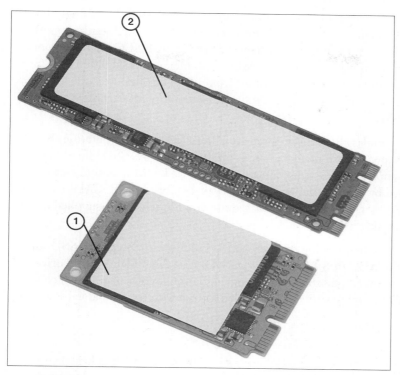

1. mSATA SSD
2. M.2 SSD

Figure 6-21 An M.2 SSD compared to an mSATA SSD.

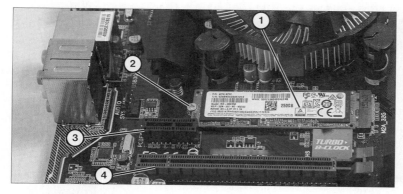

1. M.2 SSD installed in slot
2. Retaining screw for M.2 SSD
3. PCIe x1 slot (for comparison)
4. PCIe x16 slot (for comparison

Figure 6-22 An M.2 SSD installed in a high-performance desktop computer.

SSDs use one of two types of flash memory: multilevel cell (**MLC**) and single-level cell (**SLC**). MLC memory has lower performance than SLC and doesn't support as many write cycles, but it is much less expensive per GB than SLC memory. Almost all SSDs sold in the consumer space use MLC flash memory. The differences in performance for similarly sized drives result from the controller used, the firmware version in use, and whether the drive uses separate memory for caching or uses a portion of the SSD.

Although SSDs emulate hard disks, there are differences in their operation. Because unnecessary writing to flash memory causes premature failure, SSDs should not be defragmented, and newer SSDs use a feature known as TRIM to automatically deallocate space used by deleted files and make it available for reuse. TRIM is supported by Windows 7/8/8.1/10, but older SSDs require you to use vendor-supplied utilities to perform this task.

Windows 7 was the first version of Microsoft Windows with integrated SSD support. When Windows 7/8/8.1/10 detects an SSD, it enables TRIM (if the drive supports this command), disables defragment, and disables other utilities such as SuperFetch and ReadyBoost that are designed for use with traditional hard disks.

Hybrid

Windows 7 was the first version of Windows to support so-called hybrid drives, which combine a standard SATA hard disk with up to 8GB of SLC memory, the same type of memory used in SSDs. SLC memory, just as in SSD disk drives, provides much faster data access than purely mechanical hard disk drives. Consequently, when information needed by the CPU is available in the hybrid drive's SLC memory, it is read from that memory, and this boosts performance. Hybrid hard disk (also known as SSHD) drives are available in both 3.5-inch and 2.5-inch form factors from Seagate (Desktop SSHD, Laptop SSHD) and Western Digital (WD Blue SSHD). Toshiba sells 2.5-inch SSHDs as OEM products.

eMMC

eMMC (embedded multimedia card) is a low-cost, slower alternative to SSDs that is found in many Android tablets and smartphones. Some vendors, such as Samsung, are now using UFS 2.0 (Universal Flash Storage) in their newer tablet and smartphone products. UFS 2.0 has higher capacity, faster performance, and easier integration with the CPU than eMMC.

Hot-Swappable Drives

Hot-swappable drives are drives that can be safely removed from a system or connected to a system without shutting down the system. In Windows, the following drives can be hot-swapped:

- USB drives
- FireWire drives
- eSATA drives*
- SATA drives*
- Flash memory drives

*These drives must be configured as AHCI in the system BIOS/UEFI firmware.

Safely Ejecting a Drive in Windows

To safely eject these drives from a Windows system (see Figure 6-23):

Step 1. Open the Eject/Safely Remove Hardware and Eject Media icon in the notification area. If the icon is not visible, click the up arrow to display hidden icons.

Step 2. Select the drive to eject from the menu.

Step 3. When the Safe to Remove Hardware message is appears, disconnect the drive.

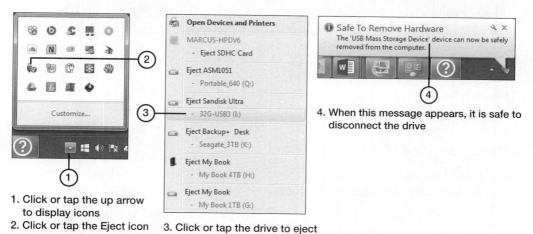

1. Click or tap the up arrow to display icons
2. Click or tap the Eject icon
3. Click or tap the drive to eject
4. When this message appears, it is safe to disconnect the drive

Figure 6-23 Safely ejecting a hot-swappable drive from a system running Windows 7.

If the drive is still in use, a Problem Ejecting *type* Storage Device dialog appears, informing you the drive is in use. Click OK, make sure no apps or processes are using the drive, and then try the process again.

Safely Ejecting a USB Drive in OS X

To safely eject a USB drive in OS X:

Step 1.   Open Finder.

Step 2.   Click the up arrow next to the USB drive icon in the left pane.

Step 3.   When the drive icon is removed from the left pane of Finder, disconnect the drive (see Figure 6-24).

1. Click to open Finder
2. Click to eject USB drive

Figure 6-24   Safely ejecting a hot-swappable drive from a OS X system.

Safely Ejecting a USB Drive in Linux

Some Linux distributions include support for safely ejecting a USB drive. However, the following Terminal commands can also be used:

`df` (lists mounted devices)—If the USB drive is not listed as mounted, it can be removed immediately. If the USB drive is listed as mounted:

`sudo unmount /dev/sdb1` (where *sbd1* is the mounted USB drive)—When the drive access light goes out, disconnect the drive.

RAID Types

RAID (Redundant Array of Inexpensive Disks) is a method for creating a faster or safer single logical hard disk drive from two or more physical drives. The most common RAID levels include:

- **RAID Level 0 (RAID 0)**—Two drives are treated as a single drive, with both drives used to simultaneously store different portions of the same file. This method of data storage is called **striping**. Striping boosts performance, but if either drive fails, all data is lost. Don't use striping for data drives.

- **RAID Level 1 (RAID 1)**—Two drives are treated as mirrors of each other; changes to the contents of one drive are immediately reflected on the other drive. This method of data storage is called **mirroring**. Mirroring provides a built-in backup method and provides faster read performance than a single drive. Suitable for use with program and data drives.

- **RAID Level 5 (RAID 5)**—Three or more drives are treated as a logical array and parity information (used to recover data in the event of a drive failure) is spread across all drives in the array. Suitable for use with program and data drives.

- **RAID Level 1+0 (RAID 10)**—Four drives combine striping plus mirroring for extra speed plus better reliability. Suitable for use with program and data drives. RAID 10 is a stripe of mirrors.

Most PCs with RAID support include support for Levels 0, 1, and 10. Some high-performance desktop systems also support RAID 5. Systems that lack the desired level of RAID support can use a RAID add-on card. Table 6-3 provides a quick comparison of these types of RAID arrays.

Table 6-3   Comparisons of Common RAID Levels

RAID Level	Minimum Number of Drives Required	Data Protection Features	Total Capacity of Array	Major Benefit over Single Drive	Notes
0	2	None.	2 × capacity of either drive (if same size) OR 2 × capacity of smaller drive.	Improved read/write performance	Also called *striping*

RAID Level	Minimum Number of Drives Required	Data Protection Features	Total Capacity of Array	Major Benefit over Single Drive	Notes
1	2	Changes to contents of one drive immediately performed on other drive.	Capacity of one drive (if same size) OR capacity of smaller drive.	Automatic backup; faster read performance	Also called *mirroring*
5	3	Parity information is saved across all drives.	(x-1) Capacity of smallest drive (x equals the number of drives in the array).	Full data redundancy in all drives; hot swap of damaged drive supported in most implementations	
10	4	Changes on one two-drive array are immediately performed on other two-drive array.	Capacity of smallest drive × number of drives / 2.	Improved read/write performance and automatic backup	Also called *striped and mirrored*

Creating an SATA RAID Array

Many recent desktop systems include SATA RAID host adapters on the motherboard. SATA RAID host adapter cards can also be retrofitted to systems lacking onboard RAID support. These types of RAID arrays are also referred to as hardware RAID arrays. RAID arrays can also be created through operating system settings and are sometimes called software RAID arrays. However, software RAID arrays are not as fast as hardware RAID arrays.

NOTE   SATA RAID host adapters might also support non-RAID SATA host adapter functions. Check the system BIOS setup or add-on card host adapter setup for details.

Motherboards that support only two drives in a RAID array support only RAID 0 and RAID 1. Motherboards that support more than two drives can also support RAID Level 1+0 (also known as RAID 10) and some support RAID 5 as well. RAID-enabled host adapters support varying levels of RAID.

NOTE A nonstandard definition of "RAID 10" was created for the Linux MD driver; Linux "RAID 10" can be implemented with as few as two disks. Implementations supporting two disks, such as Linux RAID 10, offer a choice of layouts. Arrays of more than four disks are also possible.

SATA RAID array requires:

- **Two or more drives**—It's best to use identical drives (same capacity, buffer size, and RPMs). However, you can mix and match drives. If some drives are larger than others, the additional capacity will be ignored. You can use standard hard disk drives, hybrid hard disks, or SSDs.

- **A RAID-compatible motherboard or add-on host adapter card**—Both feature firmware (RAID BIOS), which identifies and configures the drives in the array.

NOTE If you have difficulty configuring a RAID array on a system with UEFI firmware (for example, if you are unable to start RAID configuration using the recommended keystrokes for your system), check with the system vendor for a UEFI firmware update for your motherboard or system.

Because RAID arrays typically use off-the-shelf drives, the only difference in the physical installation of drives in a RAID array is where they are connected. They must be connected to a motherboard or add-on card that has RAID support.

NOTE Sometimes RAID connectors are made from a contrasting color of plastic compared to other drive connectors. However, the best way to determine whether your system or motherboard supports SATA RAID arrays is to read the manual for the system or motherboard.

After the drives used to create the array are connected to the RAID array's host adapter, restart the computer. If you are using the motherboard's RAID interface, start the system BIOS setup program, and make sure the RAID function is enabled (see Figure 6-25). Save changes and exit the BIOS setup program.

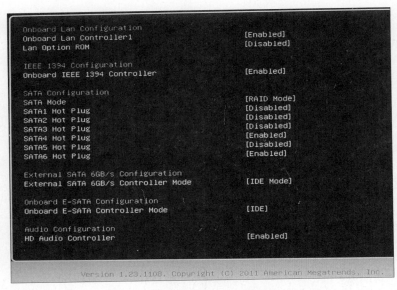

Figure 6-25   Enabling SATA RAID in a typical system BIOS.

When you restart the computer, watch for a prompt from the RAID BIOS to start the configuration process (see Figure 6-26).

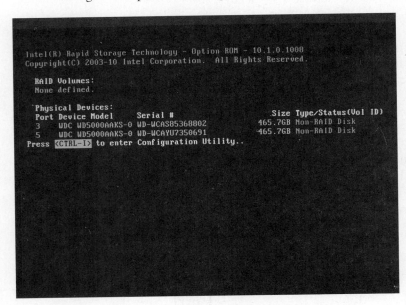

Figure 6-26   A typical prompt to start RAID array setup.

Specify the RAID setting wanted and any optional settings you want to use (see Figure 6-27). After the RAID array is configured, the drives are handled as a single physical drive by the system. If drivers for the array are not already installed, you need to install them when prompted by the computer. For Windows, you can provide driver files on USB or optical discs if necessary.

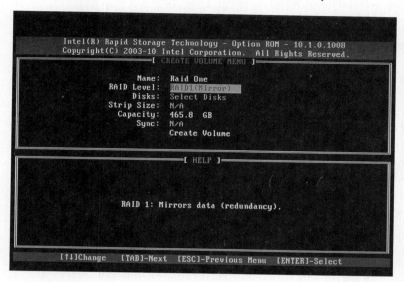

Figure 6-27   Preparing to create a RAID 1 array.

CAUTION   If one or more of the drives to be used in the array already contains data, back up the drives before starting the configuration process! Most RAID array host adapters delete the data on all drives in the array when creating an array, sometimes with little warning.

If you do not have RAID adapters in your system, you can create a software RAID volume, also known as a disk array, by using Windows. To learn how to create a software RAID volume, see "Disk Management" in Chapter 15.

NOTE Some hard disk drive vendors now produce drives especially made for SOHO RAID arrays of eight drives or less. Compared to normal SATA hard disk drives, RAID-optimized drives (also known as NAS drives) typically include features such as vibration reduction, optimization for streaming, disabled head parking, intelligent recovery from errors, and longer warranties.

To learn more about how vendors optimize their drives for RAID, see http://www.anandtech.com/show/6157/western-digital-red-review-are-nasoptimized-hdds-worth-the-premium, http://www.seagate.com/internal-hard-drives/nas-drives/nas-hdd/, and http://www.simply.reviews/hgst-5tb-6tb-nas-drives-review/.

To add a RAID array to a laptop, convertible (2-in-1), or All-in-One PC, use an external RAID drive or drive enclosure that connects to a USB 3.0, Thunderbolt, or eSATA port. External RAID drives contain two hard disks that can be configured as RAID 0 or RAID 1. Enclosures with support for three or more drives can also be configured as RAID 5. Enclosures with support for four drives can be configured as RAID 10. Use the program provided with the drive or enclosure to configure the RAID array.

Tape Drive

Although **tape drives** are primarily used by servers rather than desktops, they are also considered to be removable storage devices. Unlike disk- or flash-based removable storage, tape drives are used only for backup.

Tape drives use various types of magnetic tape. Their capacities are typically listed in two ways:

- Native (uncompressed) capacity
- Compressed capacity, assuming 2:1 compression

For example, a tape drive with a 70GB native capacity would also be described as having a 140GB compressed capacity. However, depending on the data being backed up, you might be able to store more or (more typically) less than the listed capacity when using data compression.

NOTE Windows Vista includes Removable Storage Manager (RSM). RSM supports tape backup drives that do not include drivers for Windows. To enable it, use the Turn Windows Features On and Off setting in Control Panel. Windows 7/8/8.1/10 do not include RSM. To determine whether a particular tape drive is supported by drivers for your version of Windows, check with the tape drive vendor.

Tape Drive Capacities

The highest capacity of each type of tape drive in use is listed in Table 6-4. Maximum capacities listed assume 2:1 data compression.

Table 6-4 Tape Drive Capacities

Tape Drive Family	Version	Maximum Capacity
Travan	Travan 40	40GB
DDS	DAT 320	320GB
SLR	SLR140	140GB
VXA	VXA-3	320GB
AIT	AIT-5	800GB
DLT	DLT-S4	1.6TB
LTO Ultrium	Generation 5	3TB
	Generation 6	6.25TB
	Generation 7	15TB

Most tape drives are designed for use with servers and connect via SCSI interfaces, but some internal drives also connect via SATA interfaces and some external tape drives use USB, FireWire, or Gigabit Ethernet interfaces. Most tape drives are also available in autoloader or tape library forms to permit backup automation, enabling unattended backup of drives that require multiple tapes.

Many vendors that formerly produced tape backup drives are also producing hard disk or SSD-based backup technologies.

Exam Preparation Tasks

Review All the Key Topics

Review the most important topics in the chapter, noted with the Key Topic icon in the outer margin of the page. Table 6-5 lists a reference of these key topics and the page numbers on which each is found.

Table 6-5   Key Topics for Chapter 6

Key Topic Element	Description	Page Number
Section	DVD Recordable and Rewriteable Standards	163
Figure 6-5	Form factors of desktop and laptop hard disks and SSDs	170
Table 6-3	Comparisons of Common RAID Levels	189

Complete the Tables and Lists from Memory

Print a copy of Appendix C, "Memory Tables" (found on the CD), or at least the section for this chapter, and complete the tables and lists from memory. Appendix D, "Answers to Memory Tables," also on the CD, includes completed tables and lists to check your work.

Define Key Terms

Define the following key terms from this chapter, and check your answers in the glossary.

optical drives, magnetic hard disk drives, hot-swappable drives, ISO image, solid-state/flash drives, RAID, RAID 0, RAID 1, RAID 10, RAID 5, revolutions per minute (RPM), card reader, multilevel cell (MLC), single-level cell (SLC), tape drive, striping, mirroring, eMMC.

Complete Hands-On Labs

Complete the hands-on labs, and then see the answers and explanations at the end of the chapter.

Lab 6-1: Researching Optical Drives

Inspect one or more desktop and laptop computers and determine whether optical drives are built in or connected via USB and which type(s) of optical drives are present.

To determine what type(s) of optical drives are installed, check the markings on the drive (see Figure 6.28).

Most optical drives have markings indicating the types of media they support.

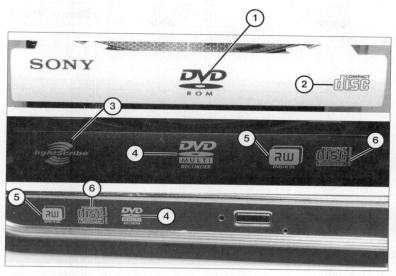

1. Reads DVD media
2. Reads Compact Disc media
3. Supports LightScribe drive-labeled media (see www.lightscribe.com for details)
4. Reads DVD, supports DVD-R, DVD-RW media
5. Supports DVD+R, DVD+R DL, DVD+RW media
6. Reads CD, supports CD-R, CD-RW Ultra speed media

Figure 6.28 Markings on typical optical drives.

Lab 6-2: Checking RAID Support and Creating a RAID Array

Inspect a desktop computer to determine which RAID levels (if any) it supports.

If you have two empty SATA hard drives, create a RAID 1 array.

Answer Review Questions

Answer these review questions and then see the answers and explanations at the end of the chapter.

1. Write the type of storage media (optical, magnetic, or flash) that corresponds to each description.

Description	Storage Media
Records information in tracks and sectors containing 512 bytes	
Stores data in continuous spiral	
Used on memory cards	

Description	Storage Media
Records information in a series of lands and pits	
Uses laser light to read data	
Records information in concentric circles	
Information is recorded from the center outward	
Stores data on double-sided platters	
Information is recorded from the outer edge inward	
Used on solid state drives	

2. Your client is considering purchasing a tablet with eMMC storage. Which one of the following is a correct statement?

   a. The tablet will have faster data access than if it is used in SSD.

   b. eMMC is supplied in Micro-SD cards that can be removed.

   c. The tablet cannot use USB devices.

   d. The tablet will have slower data access than if it is used an SSD.

3. You want to prepare a series of presentations and copy them onto DVDs. You also want to be able to update the presentations as new information becomes available, so you want to choose a medium that can be erased and reused. Which of the following should you choose?

   a. DVD-R

   b. DVD+R

   c. DVD-RW

   d. DVD-DL

4. Your client has requested a hard disk upgrade for a laptop with the following parameters: 1TB, lowest power consumption. Which of the following factors will a matching drive have? (Choose all that apply.)

   a. 3.5-inch form factor

   b. 5,400 rpm

   c. 7,200 rpm

   d. 2.5-inch form factor

5. Match the cables and ports in the following figure with their names.

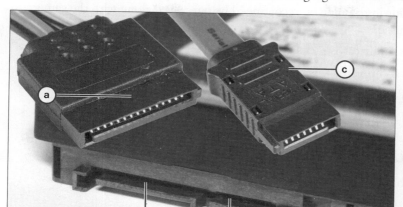

Component	Callout

i. SATA data port

ii. SATA data cable

iii. SATA power port

iv. SATA power cable

6. The user has reported a failure with an eSATA drive. Assuming the drive is configured as AHCI in the system BIOS, which of the following is the correct procedure to replace it?

    a. Shut down the computer before disconnecting it.

    b. Check to see if the drive's Hybrid cache can be disabled.

    c. Eject the drive and disconnect it.

    d. None of the above.

7. A user has requested a RAID array that balances high-performance with data safety. Which of the following would you recommend?

    a. RAID 1

    b. RAID 10

    c. RAID 5

    d. RAID 0

8. A user is replacing a digital camera that uses xD cards with a new one. Which of the following would you recommend be purchased along with the camera so it can be used?

   a. SD-family cards

   b. No additional items; use existing media

   c. Multi-slot card reader

   d. SSD

Answers and Explanations to Hands-On Labs

Here's more about what can happen during these labs.

Lab 6-1: Researching Optical Drives

In most cases, you can determine the types of media (and therefore the drives themselves) from the markings on the drive. However, some drives have no markings or incomplete markings. In those cases, find the drive's brand and model number and check with the manufacturer for this information.

Use Windows Device Manager to find the drive's brand and model number if the drive is built into a system. Note that Windows Device Manager lists all optical drives as CdRom, regardless of actual media support.

For example, when I searched for a drive listed in Device Manager as hp SN-208BB, this is what I learned:

Manufacturer: Samsung

Media types: CD-R, CD-ROM, DVD-RW, CD-RW, DVD+R, DVD+R DL, DVD+RW, DVD-R, DVD-R DL, DVD-RAM, DVD-ROM

Lab 6-2: Checking RAID Support and Creating a RAID Array

To determine if a desktop computer has an onboard RAID host adapter installed and enabled, open the BIOS setup program and look for references to RAID (refer to Chapter 2). The following figure shows a system that can be configured for RAID.

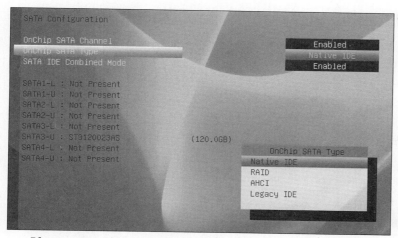

If you can create a RAID 1 array, make sure you determine how motherboard ports are identified in the BIOS. Check documentation if available.

When you connect cables for the drives, make sure you connect a matched pair of empty ports. For example, if front-mounted ports are used, ports stacked on top of each other are a pair as shown in the following figure. In this example, you can use any of the pairs SATA1, SATA2, or SATA4 (the installed hard disk is using one of the SATA3 ports.

Creating a RAID array wipes out the contents of the drives connected to the RAID host adapter. If you are using the RAID host adapter on the motherboard (not a software array in Windows), consider disconnecting the power and data cables to the system drive before you connect and configure the RAID array. You can reconnect the system drive after you are finished.

Answers and Explanations to Review Questions

1. The type of storage media (optical drive, magnetic drive, or flash drive) corresponds to the descriptions as follows:

Description	Storage Media
A. Records information in tracks and sectors containing 512 bytes	Magnetic drive
B. Stores data in continuous spiral	Optical drive
C. Used on memory cards	Flash drive
D. Records information in a series of lands and pits	Optical drive
E. Uses laser light to read data	Optical drive
F. Records information in concentric circles	Magnetic drive
G. Information is recorded from the center outward	Optical drive
H. Stores data on double-sided platters	Magnetic drive
I. Information is recorded from the outer edge inward	Magnetic drive
J. Used on solid state drives	Flash drive

2. D is the only correct answer. eMMC memory is slower than memory used in SSDs. It is built into tablets and therefore not removable. A tablet's ability to use USB devices is a function of whether it has USB ports, not its built-in storage.

3. C. DVD-RW is erasable and rewriteable. –R and +R are writeable but not erasable and rewritable. –DL (dual layer) uses a second recording layer to record more information, but is not erasable.

4. B, D. 5,400 rpm drives are slower but require less energy to run than faster drives. Laptop computers use 2.5-inch or smaller form factor drives.

5.

	Component	Callout
i.	SATA data port	D
ii.	SATA data cable	C
iii.	SATA power port	B
iv.	SATA power cable	A

6. C. An eSATA drive configured as AHCI is hot-swappable, so the power does not need to be shut down to replace it.

7. B. RAID 10. RAID 10 includes striping across two drives for faster performance and mirroring of the striped array for data safety.

8. A, C. A: SD-family cards are used by all current digital cameras. xD cards were formerly used by Olympus and Fujifilm cameras, but are obsolete. C: A multi-slot card reader is not required, but if the user has an old card reader, it might not support SDHC or SDXC media.

This chapter covers the following subjects:

- **Processor Characteristics**—This section examines features such as processor speeds and overclocking, cores, cache size and types, hyperthreading, virtualization support, 32-bit versus 64-bit architecture, integrated GPUs, and Execute Disable Bit.

- **Socket Types**—This section examines the processor sockets and characteristics of AMD and Intel CPUs.

- **Cooling**—Learn about the differences in cooling systems (fan, passive, liquid) used for processors.

- **CPU Installation**—Intel and AMD processors and heat sinks use different installation processes, as you learn in this section.

CPUs

To do well on the 220-901 exam, you must understand the major types of processors available for recent systems, their technologies, and how to install and uninstall them. These topics are covered in this chapter.

220-901: Objective 1.6 Install various types of CPUs and apply the appropriate cooling methods.

Foundation Topics

Processor Characteristics

Intel and **AMD** processors have a variety of characteristics that are useful in determining the most suitable processor for a given task. The following sections explain these characteristics, and later in the chapter, you will learn how these characteristics are incorporated in processor models and families.

Speeds

Different components of the motherboard—such as the CPU, memory, chipset, expansion slots, storage interfaces, and I/O ports—connect with each other at different speeds. The term **bus speeds** refers to the speeds at which different buses in the motherboard connect to different components.

Some of these speeds, such as the speed of I/O ports and expansion slots (USB, FireWire, Thunderbolt, and SATA ports; PCI and PCIe slots), are established by the design of the port or by the capabilities of the devices connected to them. However, depending on the motherboard, you might be able to fine-tune the bus speeds used by the processor, the chipset interconnect, and memory. These adjustments, where available, are typically performed through BIOS/UEFI firmware settings in menus such as Memory, Overclocking, AI Tweaker, and others.

Figure 7-1 is the CPU (processor) overclocking UEFI firmware dialog from a system with an Intel i5 processor. The dialog indicates the current CPU and memory multipliers that can be adjusted.

Figure 7-2 illustrates the memory overclock adjustments dialog on the same system. To change CPU speed, memory timing, or other adjustments, change the Auto setting and enter the wanted values. On this system and others, you can select a CPU overclocking value, and other settings will be adjusted automatically as needed.

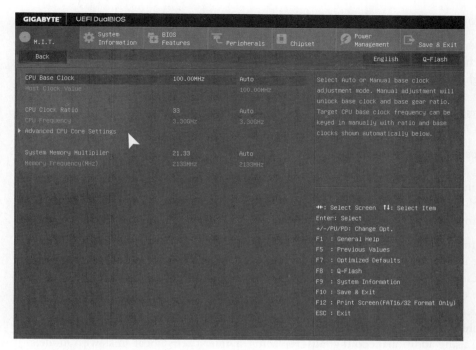

Figure 7-1   CPU and memory speed information on a system that allows speed adjustment.

Figure 7-2   Preparing to overclock memory.

Overclocking

Overclocking refers to the practice of running a processor or other components, such as memory or the video card's graphics processing unit (GPU), at speeds higher than normal. Overclocking methods used for processors include increasing the clock multiplier or running the front side bus (FSB) at speeds faster than normal. These changes are performed by altering the normal settings in the system BIOS setup for the processor's configuration.

Most processors feature locked clock multipliers. That is, the clock multiplier frequency cannot be changed. In such cases, the only way to overclock the processor is to increase the FSB speed, which is the speed at which the processor communicates with system memory. Increasing the FSB speed can lead to greater system instability than changing the clock multipliers.

Some processors from Intel and AMD feature unlocked clock multipliers so that the user can choose the best method for overclocking the system. Intel refers to these processors as Extreme Edition or Extreme Processor or uses the *K* suffix at the end of the model number; AMD uses the term *Black Edition* or uses the *K* suffix. Overclocked processors and other components run hotter than normal, so several techniques are often used to help maintain system stability at faster speeds, including using additional cooling fans, replacing standard active heat sinks with models that feature greater cooling, and adjusting processor voltages.

Intel's Core i7, Core i5, and AMD's FX and A-series processors support automatic overclocking according to processor load. Intel refers to this feature as *Turbo Boost*, whereas AMD's term is *Turbo CORE*.

CAUTION   Overclocking is not recommended for mission-critical systems. However, many gaming-oriented systems have the heavy-duty cooling and extensive BIOS adjustments needed to make overclocking a success.

Cores

Two or more physical processors in a system enable it to perform much faster when multitasking or running multithreaded applications. However, systems with multiple processors are expensive to produce, and some operating systems cannot work with multiple processors. **Multicore** processors, which combine two or more processor cores into a single physical processor, provide virtually all the benefits of multiple physical processors and are lower in cost and work with any operating system that supports traditional single-core processors.

Almost all current desktop processors from Intel and AMD include two or more cores.

Cache Size/Type

Cache memory improves system performance by enabling the processor to reuse recently retrieved memory locations without needing to fetch them from main memory. Differences in cache size and type between processors are some of the major reasons for differences in system performance.

Processors from AMD and Intel feature at least two levels of cache:

- **L1 cache** is built in to the processor core. L1 (Level 1) cache is relatively small (8KB–128KB). When the processor needs to access memory, it checks the contents of L1 cache first.

- **L2 cache** is also built in to the processor core. If the processor does not find the wanted memory locations in L1 cache, it checks L2 (Level 2) cache next.

- **L3 cache** is found on some high-performance processors from Intel (such as the Core i7 series) and on several high-performance and mid-level processors from AMD. L3 (Level 3) is built in to the processor die. On systems with L3 cache, the processor checks L3 cache after checking L1 and L2 caches.

Figure 7-3 shows CPU-Z (CPUID.com) CPU reports from an AMD FX-8350 desktop processor, which features L1, L2, and L3 caches, eight processor cores, and an Intel Core i3 3227U laptop processor, which also features L1, L2, and L3 caches and two processor cores.

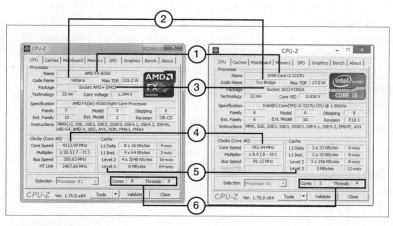

1. CPU model number
2. CPU family
3. Processor socket type
4. Current clock speed
5. Cache types and sizes
6. Processor cores and threads

Figure 7-3   CPU-Z reports of two very different processors with L3 cache.

If cache memory does not contain the needed information, the processor retrieves the needed information from the main memory and stores copies of that information in its cache memory (L1 and L2, or L1, L2, and L3). Processors with larger L2 caches (or L2 and L3 caches) perform most tasks quicker than processors that have smaller L2 caches for two reasons:

- Cache memory is faster than main memory.

- The processor checks cache memory for needed information before checking main memory.

NOTE   Intel's SmartCache is L2 or L3 cache that is accessible by all processor cores. Other types of caches dedicate portions of L2 cache to each processor core, but use shared L3 cache.

Hyper-Threading (HT Technology)

Hyper-Threading (HT Technology) is a technology developed by Intel for processing two execution threads within a single processor core. Essentially, when HT Technology is enabled in the system BIOS and the processor is running a multithreaded application, the processor is emulating two physical processors. The Pentium 4 was the first desktop processor to support HT Technology, which Intel first developed for its Xeon workstation and server processor family. HT Technology is supported by Core i7 and some Core i5 and Core i3 processors, as detailed later in this chapter, to further improve the execution of multithreaded applications. The Core i3 mobile processor shown in Figure 7-3 has HT Technology enabled (two cores, four threads).

Virtualization Support

Most current AMD and Intel processors feature **virtualization support**, also known as **hardware-assisted virtualization**. Virtualization technology enables a host program (known as a hypervisor) or a host operating system to support one or more guest operating systems running at the same time in different windows on the host's desktop. Hardware-assisted virtualization enables virtualized operating systems and applications to run faster and use fewer system resources.

Some of the best-known virtualization programs include Microsoft's Windows Virtual PC and Hyper-V Manager. Major third-party virtualization programs include VMware (www.vmware.com), Oracle VM VirtualBox (www.virtualbox.com), and DOSBox (www.dosbox.com).

Architecture (32-bit vs. 64-bit)

Processors developed before the AMD Athlon 64 were designed only for 32-bit operating systems and applications. 32-bit software cannot access more than 4GB of RAM (32-bit Windows programs can use only 3.25GB of RAM), which makes working with large data files difficult because only a portion of a file larger than the maximum memory size can be loaded into memory at one time.

The Athlon 64 was the first desktop processor to support 64-bit extensions to the 32-bit **x86** architecture. These 64-bit extensions, commonly known as **x64**, enable processors to use more than 4GB of RAM and run 64-bit operating systems but maintain full compatibility with 32-bit operating systems and applications. By supporting more RAM, 64-bit processors can perform tasks much more quickly and handle more complex 3D rendering than 32-bit processors. All recent and current AMD processors are 64-bit.

Late versions of the Pentium 4 began Intel's changeover to 64-bit processing, and all members of the Core i3, Core i5, and Core i7 families (and Celeron and Pentium processors based on these families) are also 64-bit. Today, 32-bit processors, such as the Intel ATOM, are used primarily in low-power notebook and tablet computers.

Integrated GPU

Intel's Core i3, i5, and i7 CPUs and AMD's A-series advanced processing units (APUs) are the first processors to have **integrated GPUs**. By integrating the GPU into the processor, faster video processing, easier access to memory, and lower-cost systems result.

Intel HD Graphics from Clarkdale to Ivy Bridge

Intel uses the term "HD Graphics *xxxx*" to refer to its processor-integrated graphics:

- HD Graphics refers to base-level 3D graphics in any given processor family. Specific features vary by processor family. Clarkdale, low-end Sandy Bridge, and low-end Ivy Bridge use HD Graphics.

- HD Graphics 2000/3000 are included in most Sandy Bridge CPUs and support DirectX 10.1 and OpenGL 3.1. HD Graphics 3000 has more execution units for faster performance.

- HD Graphics 2500 (GT1) and 4000 (GT2) are included in most Ivy Bridge CPUs, features six execution units, and supports DirectX 11.1, OpenGL 4, and OpenCL 1.2. HD Graphics 4000 has 16 execution units for faster performance.

The GPU-Z reporting app from TechPowerUp (www.techpowerup.com) can be used to display information about discrete or integrated GPUs. Figure 7-4 displays information about the HD Graphics 4000 GPU built into an Intel Core i3-2770U processor and the Radeon HD 6520G built into an AMD A6-3420M processor.

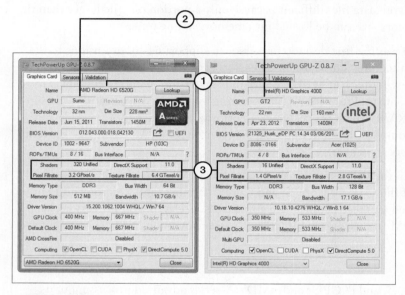

1. **GPU model number**
2. **GPU family**
3. **DirectX version and 3D features**

Figure 7-4 GPU-Z reports on Intel and AMD processors with integrated GPUs.

Intel HD Graphics for Haswell Processors

The GPUs built into Haswell processors are referred to as GTx as well as the marketing names shown in the following list. Each processor family uses a common design for its GPUs, varying them by the number of execution units and clock speed. All support DirectX 12, OpenGL 4.3, and OpenCL 1.2.

- **HD Graphics (GT1)**—12 execution units. Used in Pentium and Celeron.

- **HD Graphics 4400 and 4600 (GT2)**—20 execution units. Used in Core i3, i5, and i7.

- **HD Graphics 5000 and 5100 (GT3)**—40 execution units. Used in Core i3, i5, and i7 mobile processors.

Intel HD Graphics for Broadwell Processors

The GPUs built into Broadwell processors are referred to as GT*x* as well as the marketing names shown in the following list. Each processor family uses a common design for its GPUs, varying them by the number of execution units and clock speed. All support DirectX 12, OpenGL 4.4, and OpenCL 2.0.

- **HD Graphics (GT1)**—12 execution units. Used in Pentium and Celeron mobile processors.

- **HD Graphics 5300, 5500, and 5600 (GT2)**—24 execution units. Used in Core i3, i5, and i7 mobile processors.

- **HD Graphics 6000, 6100 (GT3)**—48 execution units. Used in Core i5 and i7 mobile processors.

- **Iris Pro Graphics 6200 (GT3e)**—48 execution units plus up to 128MB of eDRAM. Used in Core i5 and i7 desktop and mobile processors.

Intel HD Graphics for Skylake Processors

The GPUs built into Skylake processors are referred to as GT*x* as well as the marketing names shown in the following list. Each processor family uses a common design for its GPUs, varying them by the number of execution units and clock speed. All support DirectX 12, OpenGL 4.4, and OpenCL 2.0.

- **HD Graphics 510 (GT1)**—12 execution units. Used in Core i3, i5, and i7 mobile processors.

- **HD Graphics 515, 520, 530 (GT2)**—24 execution units. Used in Pentium, Core, i3, Core i5 and i7 mobile and desktop processors.

- **Iris 540, 550 (GT3e)**—48 execution units plus 64MB of eDRAM. Used in Core i3, i5, and i7 mobile processors.

- **Iris Pro 580 (GT4)**—96 execution units plus 128MB of eDRAM. Used in Core i5 and i7 desktop and mobile processors.

NOTE To learn more about Intel processor graphics, see https://software.intel.com/en-us/articles/quick-reference-guide-to-intel-processor-graphics and http://www.intel.com/content/www/us/en/support/graphics-drivers/000005524.html.

AMD APU Graphics

AMD, which also manufactures Radeon GPUs for video cards, integrates Radeon GPU features into its line of APUs (advanced processing units), which integrate the CPU and GPU:

- APUs in the Llano and Trinity series use Radeon HD 6xxxD, 7xxxD, and 8xxxD graphics using stream processor technology for 3D graphics. These support DirectX 11, OpenGL 4.1 or better, and OpenCL 1.1 or better.

- Radeon R7 graphics, used by current-generation A8/A8 PRO and A10/A10 PRO APUs in the 7000 series, use Compute Cores. Compute Cores permit both CPU and GPU cores to access the same memory. These support DirectX 11.1, OpenGL 4.3, and OpenCL 1.2.

- Radeon R5 graphics, used by current-generation A6/A6 PRO and most A4 PRO APUs in the 7000 series, feature fewer Compute Cores and run more slowly than R7 but are otherwise similar.

NOTE For more information about APU specifications, see http://www.amd.com/en-us/products/processors/desktop/a-series-apu. For more information about Compute Cores, see http://www.amd.com/en-us/innovations/software-technologies/processors-for-business/compute-cores.

Although the fastest CPU integrated graphics are suitable for casual gaming as well as general office use, high-performance graphics cards are still recommended for 3D gaming.

Execute Disable Bit (EDB)

Execute Disable Bit (EDB) is the Intel term for a processor feature that separates memory areas into processor instruction or data storage locations. This helps prevent stack or buffer malware attacks.

EDB was originally developed by AMD as part of its AMD64 instruction set (later adopted by Intel for its 64-bit processors). AMD's term is *NX*. EDB is enabled or disabled through a BIOS/UEFI firmware setting. EDB/NX support in hardware is required on systems that run Windows 8/8.1/10.

NOTE The 220-901 exam might refer to this feature as "Disable Execute Bit."

Socket Types

Although Intel and AMD processors share two common architectures—x86 (used for 32-bit processors and for 64-bit processors running in 32-bit mode) and x64 (an extension of x86 that enables larger files, larger memory sizes, and more complex programs)—these processor families differ in many ways from each other, including:

- Different processor sockets.
- Differences in multicore processor designs. (Two or more processor cores help run multiple programs and programs with multiple execution threads more efficiently.)
- Cache sizes.

Table 7-1 provides a quick reference to Intel and AMD sockets and processor family code names. The following sections provide additional detail.

Table 7-1   CPU Manufacturers, Sockets, and Code Names Quick Reference

CPU Manufacturer	Socket	Compatible Processor Code Name(s)
Intel	LGA 775	Prescott, Presler, Conroe, Wolfdale, Kentsfield, Yorkfield
Intel	LGA 1366	Bloomfield, Gulftown
Intel	LGA 1156	Clarkdale, Lynnfield
Intel	LGA 1155	Sandy Bridge, Ivy Bridge
Intel	LGA 1150	Haswell, Broadwell
Intel	LGA 2011	Sandy Bridge E, Ivy Bridge E
Intel	LGA 2011-v3	Haswell E
AMD	Socket AM3	Thuban, Zosma, Deneb, Propus, Heka, Rana, Callisto, Regor, Sargas
AMD	Socket AM3+	Vishera, Zembezi
AMD	Socket FM1	Llano
AMD	Socket FM2	Trinity, Richland
AMD	Socket FM2+	Kaveri

Intel

Intel has used many processor sockets over the years, but the 220-901 exam specifically cites the following recent and current socket designs:

- LGA 775
- LGA 1155

- LGA 1156
- LGA 1366
- LGA 1150
- LGA 2011

CAUTION   There are two versions of the LGA 2011 socket: the original LGA 2011 supports high-performance second-generation (Sandy Bridge E) and third-generation (Ivy Bridge E) Core i7 processors. LGA 2011-v3 uses the same physical layout, but is compatible only with high-performance, fourth-generation Haswell E) processors. See the Intel ARK website (http://ark.intel.com) for details.

NOTE   The latest Intel desktop platform, Skylake, which uses LGA 1151, uses 100-series chipsets and supports both DDR3 and DD4 memory.

Land Grid Array Sockets

All of the Intel processor sockets listed in the previous sections use the **Land Grid Array (LGA)** design. The LGA design uses spring-loaded lands in the processor socket (see Figure 7-5) that connect to bumps on the backside of the processor (see Figure 7-6).

The number of lands in the processor socket is used for the numeric part of the socket name. For example, LGA 775 has 775 lands in the processor socket.

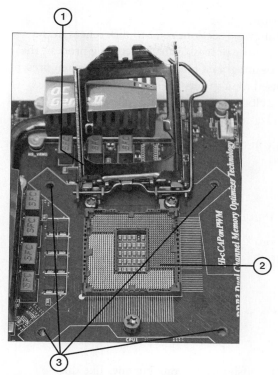

1. CPR retention frame
2. LGA1155 socket
3. Heat sink mounting holes

Figure 7-5   An LGA 1155 socket prepared for processor installation.

1. Processor notch for assuring proper installation
2. Pin 1 triangle marking

Figure 7-6   The front and back side of an LGA processor before installation.

Processor Code Names

The code names referred to in the following sections refer to differences in the processor die design, such as the size of the processor manufacturing process, the location of cache memory, the type of integrated memory controller (when present), and so on. The same code name is used for a variety of processor models, which are distinguished from each other by clock speed, cache size, presence of integrated graphics, and features such as virtualization.

In Socket 775, the ranking is roughly in this order:

- Celeron/Celeron D (slowest)
- Pentium 4
- Pentium D (two Pentium 4 CPUs in the same processor die)
- Pentium 4 EE (Extreme Edition)
- Pentium EE
- Core 2 Duo
- Core 2 Quad
- Core 2 Extreme (fastest)

Starting with the Core i series and its offshoots, the ranking goes like this:

- Celeron (slowest)
- Pentium
- Core i3
- Core i5
- Core i7 (fastest)

See the following sections for more information about multicore processors, cache sizes, and other technical differences.

NOTE   The processor information in the following tables is based on desktop processor series and is extremely simplified. Look up information for specific processor numbers and code names at the Intel ARK website (http://ark.intel.com). To learn how to decode processor model number series, see "About Intel Processor Numbers" at http://www.intel.com/content/www/us/en/processors/processor-numbers.html. Mobile processors with similar model numbers might vary in features.

LGA 775

LGA 775 replaced the older Socket 478 (some Pentium 4 processor models were produced in versions for both sockets) and was the first Intel desktop processor socket to support 64-bit operations. Table 7-2 lists the processor code names and major features used by processors fitting into LGA 775.

Table 7-2   LGA 775 Processor Technologies and Features

Code Name	Processor Family	Cores	Intel 64	L2 Cache	HT Tech	IntelVT-X	FSB Speed
Prescott	Pentium 4 EE	1	Yes	2MB	Yes	No	1066MHz
	Pentium 4	1	Varies	1MB–2MB	Varies	No	533MHz–800MHz
	Celeron D	1	Varies	256KB	No	No	533MHz
Presler	Pentium EE	2	Yes	4MB	Yes	No	1066MHz
	Pentium D	2	Yes	4MB	Varies	Varies	800MHz
Conroe	Core 2 Extreme	2	Yes	4MB	Yes	No	1066MHz
	Core 2 Duo	2	Yes	2MB, 4MB	Varies	Varies	800MHz–1066MHz
	Pentium	2	Yes	1MB	No	No	800MHz
	Celeron	1, 2	Yes	512KB	No	No	533MHz–800MHz
Wolfdale	Core 2 Duo	2	Yes	3MB–6MB	No	Varies	1333MHz–1066MHz
	Pentium	2	Yes	2MB	No	Varies	800MHz
	Celeron	2	Yes	1MB	No	Yes	800MHz
Kentsfield	Core 2 Extreme	4	Yes	8MB	No	Yes	1066MHz–1333MHz
	Core 2 Quad	4	Yes	8MB	No	Yes	1066MHz
Yorkfield	Core 2 Extreme	4	Yes	12MB	No	Yes	1333MHz–1600MHz
	Core 2 Quad	4	Yes	4MB	No	Varies	1333MHz

Processors using LGA 775 range in clock speed from as low as 2.30GHz (Celeron Desktop) to as high as 3.73GHz (Pentium 4 EE, Pentium Desktop EE).

NOTE   Several chipsets have been used with LGA 775 processors; different chipsets support different processors. To determine a particular system compatibility with a particular processor, check the motherboard or system documentation.

LGA 1366

LGA 1366 was used by the Core i7 9xx series Extreme Edition CPUs for desktops and by Xeon processors used for workstations and servers. LGA 1366 uses a newer interconnect method called Quick Path Interconnect (QPI) to connect to the I/O controller hub (North Bridge/northbridge); the memory controller is built in to the CPU and supports triple-channel DDR3 memory. Table 7-3 compares the technologies supported by the Core i7 and Extreme Edition CPUs for desktops. All LGA 1366 processors support Intel 64 (x64).

Table 7-3   LGA 1366 Desktop Processor Technologies and Features

Code Name	Processor Family	Cores	Turbo Boost Version	L2 Cache	HT Tech	IntelVT-X	Bus Speed
Blooomfield	Core i7 EE	4	1.0	8MB	Yes	Yes	6.4GTps
	Core i7	4	1.0	8MB	Yes	Yes	6.4GTps
Gulftown	Core i7 EE	6	1.0	12MB	Yes	Yes	6.4GTps
	Core i7	6	1.0	12MB	Yes	Yes	6.4GTps

EE—Extreme Edition—Very high-performance processor
GT—Gigatransfers

Processors using LGA 1366 range in clock speed from as low as 2.66GHz (Core i7-920) to as high as 3.46GHz (Core i7 Extreme-990X). Turbo Boost maximum Turbo frequency ranges from as low as 2.93GHz (920) to 3.73GHz (990X).

LGA 1156

LGA 1156 was used by the first-generation Core i3 and Core i5 processors and by Core i7 CPUs that did not use LGA 1366. (These processors are listed on the Intel ARK website as "previous-generation" Core i3, i5, and i7 processors.) LGA 1156, like LGA 1366, is designed to connect to a memory controller built in to the CPU. LGA 1156-compatible CPUs support dual-channel DDR3 memory. Some processors that use LGA 1156 also include CPU-integrated video. All LGA 1156 processors support Intel 64 (x64).

Table 7-4 compares the technologies supported by these processors.

Table 7-4   LGA 1156 Processor Technologies and Features

Code Name	Processor Family	Cores	Smart Cache	Turbo Boost Version	HT Tech	Intel VT-x	Bus Speed
Gulftown	Core i7	6	12MB	1.0	Yes	Yes	2.5GTps
Lynnfield	Core i7	4	8MB	1.0	Yes	Yes	2.5GTps
	Core i5	4	8MB	1.0	Yes	Yes	2.5GTps
Clarkdale	Core i5	2	4MB	1.0	Yes	Yes	2.5GTps
	Core i3	2	4MB	No	Yes	Yes	2.5GTps
	Pentium	2	3MB	No	No	Yes	2.5GTps
	Celeron	2	2MB	No	No	No	2.5GTps

Processors using LGA 1156 range in clock speed from as low as 2.26GHz (Celeron G1101) to as high as 3.06GHz (Core i7-880). Turbo Boost maximum Turbo frequency ranges from 3.20GHz (Core i5-750) to 3.86GHz (Core i5-680).

LGA 1155

LGA 1155 is used by the second-generation (Sandy Bridge) and third-generation (Ivy Bridge) architecture Intel CPUs. Compared to the first-generation processors, these processors feature better L1 and L2 caches, CPU integrated video, two load and store operations per CPU cycle, and better performance for advanced mathematical operations. Both of these processor families use integrated memory controllers supporting DDR3.

Compared to Sandy Bridge, Ivy Bridge processors:

- Use a smaller die size using a new 3D Tri-Gate transistor and supporting low-voltage DDR3 (DDR3L) memory to use less power

- Support PCIe version 3.0

- Feature faster 3D graphics

Most motherboards made for Sandy Bridge can support Ivy Bridge after a firmware update. Check with the motherboard or system manufacturer for details.

Table 7-5 compares the technologies used by these processors.

Table 7-5   LGA 1155 Processor Technologies and Features

Code Name	Processor Family	Cores	Smart Cache	Turbo Boost Version	HT Tech	Intel VT-x	Bus Speed
Sandy Bridge	Core i7	4	8MB	2.0	Yes	Yes	5GTps
	Core i5	2, 4	3MB–6MB	2.0	Yes	Yes	5GTps
	Core i3	2	3MB	No	Yes	Yes	5GTps
	Pentium	2	3MB	No	Varies	Yes	5GTps
	Celeron	1, 2	1, 1.5, 2MB	No	Varies	Yes	5GTps
Ivy Bridge	Core i7	4	8MB	2.0	Yes	Yes	5GTps
	Core i5	4	6MB	2.0	Varies	Yes	5GTps
	Core i3	2	3MB	2.0	No	Yes	5GTps
	Pentium	2	3MB	2.0	No	Yes	5GTps
	Celeron	2	2MB	2.0	No	Yes	5GTps

Sandy Bridge processors using LGA 1155 range in clock speed from as low as 1.60GHz (Celeron G440) to as high as 3.40GHz (various Core i5 and i7 models). Turbo Boost 2.0 maximum Turbo frequency ranges from 3.10GHz (Core i5-2300) to 3.90GHz (Core i7-2700K). Sandy Bridge processors support PCIe version 2.0.

Ivy Bridge processors using LGA 1155 range in clock speed from as low as 2.30GHz (Celeron G1610T) to as high as 3.50GHz (Core i7-3770K). Turbo Boost 2.0 maximum Turbo frequency ranges from 3.30GHz (Core i5-33xx series) to 3.90GHz (Core i7-3770 series).

LGA 1150

LGA 1150 is used by fourth-generation (Haswell) and fifth-generation (Broadwell) Intel CPUs. Haswell processors are the first to feature an integrated voltage regulator. Broadwell uses a smaller die size than Haswell for improved power efficiency and allows overclocking of the integrated GPU. All Haswell and Broadwell processors support PCIe version 3.0 along with standard and low-voltage DDR3. Motherboards built for Haswell need a BIOS/UEFI firmware update for Broadwell to assure reliable operation. Table 7-6 compares the major features of processors using LGA 1150.

Table 7-6 LGA 1150 Processor Technologies and Features

Code Name	Processor Family	Cores	Smart Cache	Turbo Boost Version	HT Tech	Intel VT-x	Bus Speed
Haswell	Core i7	4	8MB	2.0	Yes	Yes	5GTps
	Core i5	4	4MB–6MB	2.0	No*	Yes	5GTps
	Core i3	2	3MB–4MB	No	Yes	Yes	5GTps
	Pentium	2	3MB	No	No	Yes	5GTps
	Celeron	2	2MB	No	No	Yes	5GTps
Broadwell	Core i7	4	6MB	2.0	Yes	Yes	5GTps
	Core i5	4	4MB	2.0	No	Yes	5GTps

* Core i5-4570T supports HT Tech

Haswell processors using LGA 1150 range in clock speed from as low as 2.40GHz (Celeron G1820T) to as high as 3.50GHz (various Core i7 models). Turbo Boost 2.0 maximum Turbo frequency ranges from 3.10GHz (Core i5-2300) to 3.90GHz (Core i7-4770 series).

Broadwell processors using LGA 1150 range in clock speed from as low as 3.1GHz (Core i5-5675C) to as high as 3.30GHz (Core i7-5775C). Turbo Boost 2.0 maximum Turbo frequency ranges from 3.60GHz (Core i5-5675C) to 3.70GHz (Core i7-5775C).

LGA 2011

The LGA 2011 socket form factor is actually available in two versions. The original **LGA 2011** supports high-performance Sandy Bridge E and Ivy Bridge E processors. **LGA 2011-v3** supports high-performance Haswell E processors. These sockets and the processors designed for each are *not* interchangeable. None of these processors includes onboard graphics. Table 7-7 lists processor technologies supported by LGA 2011. These processors support DDR3.

Table 7-7 LGA 2011 Processor Technologies and Features

Code Name	Processor Family	Cores	Smart Cache	Turbo Boost Version	HT Tech	Intel VT-x	Bus Speed
Sandy Bridge E	Core i7 Extreme Edition	6	15MB	2.0	Yes	Yes	5GTps
	Core i7	4	10MB–12MB	2.0	Yes	Yes	5GTps

Code Name	Processor Family	Cores	Smart Cache	Turbo Boost Version	HT Tech	Intel VT-x	Bus Speed
Ivy Bridge E	Core i7 Extreme Edition	6	15MB	2.0	Yes	Yes	5GTps
	Core i7	4	10MB–12MB	2.0	Yes	Yes	5GTps

Table 7-8 lists processor technologies supported by LGA 2011-v3. These processors support DDR4.

Table 7-8 LGA 2011-v3 Processor Technologies and Features

Code Name	Processor Family	Cores	Smart Cache	Turbo Boost Version	HT Tech	Intel VT-x	Bus Speed
Haswell E	Core i7 Extreme Edition	8	20MB	2.0	Yes	Yes	5GTps
	Core i7	6	15MB	2.0	Yes	Yes	5GTps

NOTE Intel's latest socket for desktop processors, Socket 1151, supports Intel's Skylake processors. Skylake, the sixth generation of the Core i family, is supported by Intel's 150-series and 170-series chipsets and DDR4 memory. The fastest current Skylake desktop processor is the Core i7-6700K processor with a top speed of 4.2GHz, and the most powerful chipset is the Z170. To learn more about Skylake processors and matching chipsets, visit http://ark.intel.com and search for "Skylake."

AMD

AMD has used many processor sockets over the years, but the 220-901 exam specifically cites the following recent and current socket designs:

- Socket AM3
- Socket AM3+
- Socket FM1
- Socket FM2
- Socket FM2+

All these sockets use the micro pin grid array (mPGA) design. All the AMD processors on the 220-901 exam have integrated memory controllers.

NOTE In the following sections, only processors with thermal design power (TDP) over 25 watts are covered. Processors with 25 watts or less TDP are typically used in laptops or all-in-one units rather than typical desktops.

mPGA Sockets

The **micro pin grid array (mPGA)** design uses pins on the back side of the CPU to connect to pins in the processor socket. To hold the CPU in place, a zero insertion force (ZIF) socket mechanism is used. Open the arm and insert the processor; then close the arm to clamp the CPU pins in place.

The heat sink clips to mounting lugs on two sides of the processor socket. All mPGA sockets listed at the beginning of this section work in the same way.

Socket FM2, which uses mPGA, is shown in Figure 7-7. The back side of a processor designed for Socket FM2 is shown in Figure 7-8.

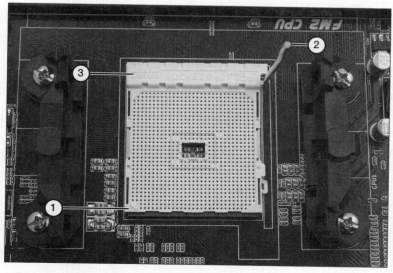

1. Triangle corresponds to pin 1 marking on processor
2. ZIF socket locking lever raised to unlock clamping mechanism
3. Processor socket name embossed here

Figure 7-7   Socket FM2 before processor installation.

1. Pin 1 triangle also visible on top side of processor

Figure 7-8   The back side of an AMD A10 5800K processor made for Socket FM2.

Socket AM3

Socket AM3 supports processors with dual-channel DDR3 or DDR2 memory controllers onboard, including the Phenom II as well as lower-cost processors based on the Phenom II's architecture. See Table 7-9 for the technologies and features supported by AMD desktop processors using Socket AM3.

Table 7-9   Socket AM3 Desktop Processor Technologies and Features

Code Name	Processor Family	# of Cores	AMD 64 (x64)	L2 Cache Size	L3 Cache Size	RAM Type	Turbo CORE	AMD-V	HyperTransport Speed
Thuban	Phenom II X6	6	Yes	3MB	6MB	DDR3	Yes	Yes	8GBps*
Zosma	Phenom II X4	4	Yes	2MB	6MB	DDR3	Yes	Yes	8GBps*
Deneb	Phenom II X4	4	Yes	1.5MB	4MB–6MB (most models)	DDR3	No	Yes	8GBps*

Code Name	Processor Family	# of Cores	AMD 64 (x64)	L2 Cache Size	L3 Cache Size	RAM Type	Turbo CORE	AMD-V	HyperTransport Speed
Propus	Athlon II X4	4	Yes	2MB	None	DDR2, DDR3	No	Yes	8GBps*
Heka	Phenom II X3	3	Yes	1.5MB	6MB	DDR3	No	Yes	8GBps*
Rana	Athlon II X3	3	Yes	1.5MB	None	DDR2, DDR3	No	Yes	8GBps*
Callisto	Phenom II X2	2	Yes	1MB	6MB	DDR3	No	Yes	8GBps*
Regor	Athlon II X2	2	Yes	1MB–2MB	None	DDR2, DDR3	No	Yes	8GBps*
Sargas	Athlon II 1xxu	1	Yes	1MB	None	DDR2	No	Yes	8GBps*
Sargas	Sempron 1xx	1	Yes	1MB	None	DDR2	No	Yes	8GBps*

* 16GBps in HyperTransport 3.0 mode

NOTE Processors built for Socket AM3 can also be used in Socket AM3+.

Desktop processors using Socket AM3 range in speed from as low as 1.8GHz (Athlon II 1xxu) to as high as 3.7GHz (Phenom II X4). Processors built for Socket AM3 can also be used in Socket AM3+.

Socket AM3+

Socket AM3+ supports processors with up to eight cores, such as the FX 9xxx series. Like Socket AM3, it supports processors with dual-channel DDR3 memory controllers onboard. See Table 7-10 for the technologies and features supported by AMD desktop processors using Socket AM3+.

Table 7-10 Socket AM3+ Desktop Processor Technologies and Features

Code Name	Processor Family	# of Cores	AMD 64 (x64)	L2 Cache Size	L3 Cache Size	Turbo CORE	AMD-V	HyperTransport Speed
Vishera	FX 93xx, 95xx*	8	Yes	8MB	8MB	Yes	Yes	8Gbps**
Vishera	FX 83xx	8	Yes	8MB	8MB	Yes	Yes	8Gbps**

Code Name	Processor Family	# of Cores	AMD 64 (x64)	L2 Cache Size	L3 Cache Size	Turbo CORE	AMD-V	HyperTransport Speed
Vishera	FX 93xx, 95xx*	8	Yes	8MB	8MB	Yes	Yes	8Gbps**
Zambezi	FX 81xx	8	Yes	8MB	8MB	Yes	Yes	8GBps**
Vishera	FX 63xx	6	Yes	6MB	8MB	Yes	Yes	8GBps**
Zambezi	FX 61xx, 62xx	6	Yes	6MB	8MB	Yes	Yes	8GBps**
Vishera	FX 43xx	4	Yes	4MB	8MB	No	Yes	8GBps**
Zambezi	FX 41xx	4	Yes	4MB	8MB	No	Yes	8GBps**

* Retail box versions include liquid cooling system

** 16GBps in HyperTransport 3.0 mode

Vishera uses Piledriver architecture (improved version of Bulldozer)

Zambezi uses Bulldozer architecture

Desktop processors using Socket AM3+ range in speed from as low as 3.3GHz (FX 6100) to as high as 4.7GHz (FX 9590). Turbo CORE speeds range from 3.7GHz (FX 4130, FX 8100) to as high as 5.0GHz (FX 9590).

Socket FM1

Socket FM1 supports AMD's first desktop processors with integrated on-chip video, the A-series APUs (Advanced Processing Units), as well as the 6x1 editions of the Athlon II X4 processor (which do not include on-chip video). These processors support dual-channel DDR3 memory (Athlon II X4 also supports dual-channel DDR2 memory). See Table 7-11 for the technologies and features supported by AMD desktop processors using Socket FM1.

Table 7-11   Socket FM1 Desktop Processor Technologies and Features

Code Name	Processor Family	# of Cores	AMD 64 (x64)	L2 Cache Size	Turbo CORE	AMD-V	Radeon Cores on Die
Llano	A8-38xx	4	Yes	4MB	Yes	Yes	400
Llano	A6-36xx	4	Yes	4MB	Yes	Yes	320
Llano	A6-35xx	3	Yes	3MB	Yes	Yes	320
Llano	A4-34xx	2	Yes	1MB	Yes	Yes	160
Llano	A4-33xx	2	Yes	1MB	Yes	Yes	160
Llano	Athlon II X4 6x1	4	Yes	4MB	No	Yes	N/A

Desktop processors using Socket FM1 range in speed from as low as 2.1GHz (A4-3500) to as high as 3.0GHz (A8-3870K). Processors made for Socket FM1 cannot be used with other processor sockets.

Socket FM2

Socket FM2 supports Trinity and Richland A-series APUs as well as some Athlon X4 and X2 processor models (which do not include on-chip video). Processors using Socket FM2 support dual-channel DDR3 memory. Trinity APUs include Radeon HD7xxx graphics, while Richland APUs use the faster Radeon HD8xxx graphics. See Table 7-12 for the technologies and features supported by AMD desktop processors using Socket FM2.

Table 7-12   Socket FM2 Desktop Processor Technologies and Features

Code Name	Processor Family	# of Cores	AMD 64 (x64)	L2 Cache Size	Turbo CORE 3.0	AMD-V	Radeon Cores on Die
Trinity	A10-5xxx	4	Yes	4MB	Yes	Yes	384
Trinity	A8-5xxx	4	Yes	4MB	Yes	Yes	256
Trinity	A6-5xxx	2	Yes	1MB	Yes	Yes	192
Trinity	A4-5xxx	2	Yes	1MB	Yes	Yes	128
Trinity	Athon X4 740	4	Yes	4MB	Yes	Yes	N/A
Trinity	Athlon X2 340	2	Yes	1MB	Yes	Yes	N/A
Richland	A10-6xxx	4	Yes	4MB	Yes	Yes	384
Richland	A8-6xxx	4	Yes	4MB	Yes	Yes	256
Richland	A6-6xxx	2	Yes	1MB	Yes	Yes	192
Richland	A4-6xxx	2	Yes	1MB	Yes	Yes	128
Richland	Athlon X4 750-760 series	2	Yes	1MB	Yes	Yes	N/A
Richland	Athlon X2 350-370 series	2	Yes	1MB	Yes	Yes	N/A

NOTE   All processors using FM2 sockets can also work in FM2+ sockets.

Desktop processors using Socket FM2 range in speed from as low as 3.9GHz (A4-5000) to as high as 4.1GHz (A10-6800K). Turbo Core 3.0 speeds range from as low as 3.2GHz (A4-4000) to as high as 4.4GHz (A10-6800K).

Socket FM2+

Socket FM2+ supports current-generation A-series APUs, as well as the 8xx editions of the Athlon X4 and 4xx versions of the Athlon X2 processor (which do not include on-chip video). Processors using Socket FM2+ support dual-channel DDR3 memory.

See Table 7-13 for the technologies and features supported by AMD desktop processors using Socket FM2+.

Table 7-13   Socket FM2+ Desktop Processor Technologies and Features

Code Name	Processor Family	# of Cores	AMD 64 (x64)	L2 Cache Size	Turbo CORE	AMD-V	Compute Cores (CPU/GPU)
Kaveri	A10-7xxx, PRO 7xxxB	4	Yes	4MB	Enh	Yes	4+8
Kaveri	A8-7xxx, PRO 7xxxB	4	Yes	4MB	Enh	Yes	4+6
Kaveri	A6-7xxx, PRO 7xxxB	2	Yes	1MB	Enh	Yes	2+4
Kaveri	A4 PRO-7350B	2	Yes	1MB	Enh	Yes	2+3
Kaveri	Athlon X4 8xx	4	Yes	4MB	Enh	Yes	N/A
Kaveri	Athlon X2 4xx	2	Yes	1MB	Enh	Yes	N/A

PRO = Processor with enhanced business management features. See http://www.amd.com/en-us/solutions/pro for more information.

Enh = Enhanced Turbo Core with temperature sensing

Desktop processors using Socket FM2+ range in speed from as low as 3.1GHz (Athlon X4 840, A8-7600) to as high as 3.9GHz (A10-7870K). Enhanced Turbo Core speeds range from as low as 3.8GHz (Athlon X4 840) to as high as 4.0GHz (A10-7860K).

Cooling

A CPU is one of the most expensive components found in any computer, so keeping it cool is important. The basic requirements for proper CPU **cooling** include the use of an appropriate active heat sink (which includes a fan) and the application of an appropriate thermal material (grease, paste, or a pre-applied thermal or phase-change compound). Advanced systems might use liquid cooling instead.

Heat Sink

All processors require a **heat sink**. A heat sink is a finned metal device that radiates heat away from the processor. In almost all cases, an **active heat sink** (a heat sink with a fan) is required for adequate cooling, unless the system case (chassis) is specially designed to move air directly over the processor. A fanless **passive heat sink** can be used instead.

Although aluminum has been the most common material used for heat sinks, copper has better thermal transfer properties and many designs mix copper and aluminum components.

Fans

Traditional active heat sinks include a cooling fan that rests on top of the heat sink and pulls air past the heat sink in a vertical direction (see Figure 7-9). However, many aftermarket heat sinks use other designs (see Figure 7-10).

Figure 7-9 Stock (original equipment) active heat sinks made for AMD (left) and Intel (right) processors.

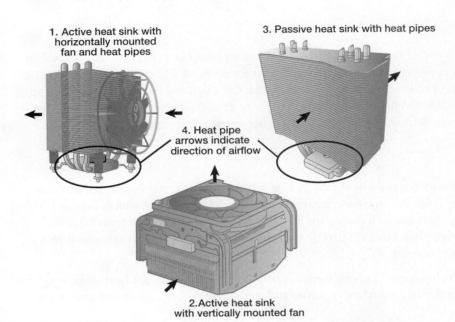

1. Active heat sink with horizontally mounted fan and heat pipes

3. Passive heat sink with heat pipes

4. Heat pipe arrows indicate direction of airflow

2. Active heat sink with vertically mounted fan

Figure 7-10   Typical third-party active and passive heat sinks. The passive heat sink has more fins than the active heat sinks do to help promote better cooling.

Phase-Change Material/Thermal Paste

Before installing a heat sink bundled with a processor, remove the protective cover over the pre-applied thermal material (also known as phase-change material) on the heat sink. When the heat sink is installed on the processor, this material helps ensure good contact between the CPU and the heat sink. Figure 7-11 illustrates pre-applied thermal material on the bottom of typical Intel and AMD active heat sinks.

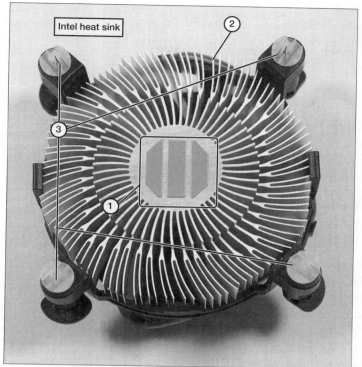

1. Preapplied thermal compound
2. Power cable for fan
3. Locking pins for mounting heat sink to motherboard

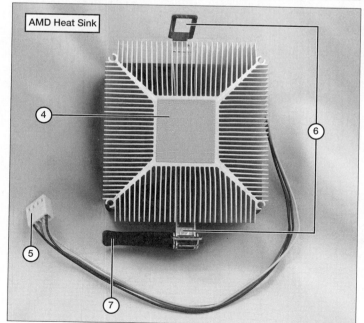

4. Preapplied thermal compound
5. Power connector for fan
6. Clamping mechanism for mounting heat sink to frame
7. Clamping lever

Figure 7-11   Bottom view of OEM (original equipment) active heat sinks made for Intel and AMD processors.

TIP   When you remove a heat sink, keep in mind that the thermal compound acts as an adhesive. Make sure you have loosened the locking mechanism before you remove the heat sink. You may need to exert some force to remove it from the processor.

If you need to remove and reapply a heat sink, be sure to remove all residue from both the processor and heat sink using isopropyl alcohol and apply new **thermal paste** or other thermal transfer material to the top of the CPU.

Liquid-Based Cooling

Liquid-based cooling systems for processors, motherboard chipsets, and GPUs are now available. Some are integrated into a custom case, whereas others can be retrofitted into an existing system that has openings for cooling fans.

Liquid cooling systems attach a liquid cooling unit instead of an active heat sink to the processor and other supported components. A pump moves the liquid (which might be water or a special solution, depending on the cooling system) through the computer to a heat exchanger, which uses a fan to cool the warm liquid before it is sent back to the processor. Liquid cooling systems are designed primarily for high-performance systems, especially overclocked systems. It's essential that only approved cooling liquids and hoses be used in these systems (check with cooling system vendors for details); unauthorized liquids or hoses could leak and corrode system components.

Figure 7-12 illustrates a typical liquid cooling system compared to a typical Intel OEM heat sink.

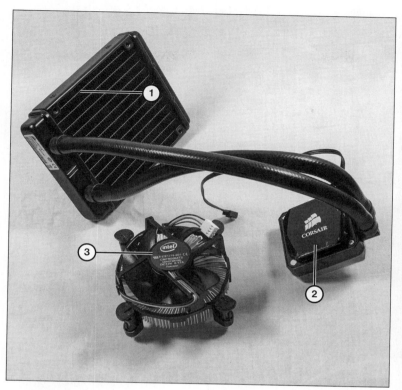

1. Radiator
2. Cooler for processor
3. Intel OEM active heat sink (for comparison)

Figure 7-12 A typical liquid cooling system.

Fanless/Passive Heat Sink

Passive heat sinks do not include a fan, but have more fins than active heat sinks to help dissipate heat. One typical use for fanless heat sinks is on low-power processors that are soldered in place on Mini-ITX or similar small form factor motherboard designs, such as the one shown in Figure 7-13.

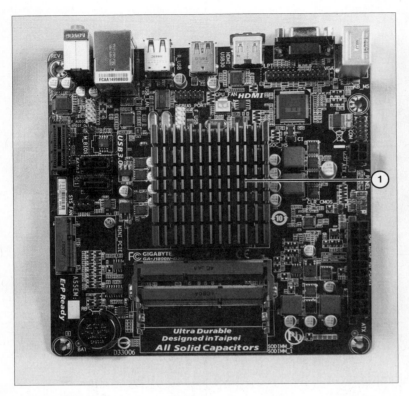

1. Passive heat sink

Figure 7-13   This low-power Mini-ITX motherboard designed for home theater and media streaming uses a soldered-in-place Intel Celeron processor and fanless heat sink.

CPU Installation

Whether a processor is being installed in a new motherboard, as a replacement for a failed unit, or as an upgrade for better performance, it's important to understand how to perform this task safely.

Processors are one of the most expensive components found in any computer. Because a processor can fail, or more likely, need to be replaced with a faster model, knowing how to install and remove processors is important. On the 220-901 exam, you should be prepared to answer questions related to the safe removal and replacement of processors using LGA 775 (Intel) or newer and Socket FM3 and AM1 (AMD) or newer. Be sure to turn off and unplug the system first.

Intel Processors

The following procedures for removal and installation are the same for any of these processors.

Intel Processor Removal

To remove an Intel processor in an LGA socket:

Step 1.   Remove the heat sink: Press down and rotate the locking pins along the outside of the heat sink unit clockwise to release them from the motherboard. Detach the power cable for the heat sink fan from the motherboard (see Figure 7-14). Lift the heat sink away from the motherboard.

1. Locking pins
2. Heat sink fan power cable
3. Heat sink fan header on motherboard
Lock
Release

Figure 7-14   Preparing to remove an Intel heat sink.

Step 2. Unclip and swing the LGA load plate assembly out of the way. To un-click the load plate assembly, move the lever down and to the right, and then swing it up.

Step 3. Remove the old processor.

Step 4. If the old heatsink or processor will be reinstalled, clean off the thermal paste using a soft cloth and isopropyl alcohol.

Step 5. Put the old processor into a static-free package.

Intel Processor Installation

To install an Intel processor in an LGA socket:

Step 1. Unclip and swing the LGA load plate assembly (see Figure 7-15) out of the way. To unclick the load plate assembly, move the lever down and to the right, and then swing it up. Remove the load plate assembly's plastic insert before continuing. Save it for future use.

Figure 7-15 On a new motherboard, an LGA socket is covered by a protective plate before processor installation.

Step 2. Line up the notches in the processor with the key tabs in the processor socket. This assures that the processor's Pin 1 is properly aligned with the socket.

Step 3. Lower the processor into place, making sure the metal heat spreader plate faces up and the gold pads face down (see Figure 7-16). Do not drop the processor, as the lands in the processor socket could be damaged.

Figure 7-16 An LGA socket after a Core i5 processor is installed.

Step 4. Push down the load plate and close the load plate assembly cam lever.

Step 5. Lock the lever in place on the side of the socket.

Step 6. Before attaching the heat sink or fan, determine whether the heat sink has a thermal pad (also called a phase-change pad) or whether you need to apply thermal compound to the processor core (refer to Figure 7-11). Remove the protective tape from the thermal pad or apply thermal paste as needed. You must use some type of thermal material between the processor and the bottom of the heat sink.

Step 7. To attach an OEM heat sink, line up the heat sink's locking pins with the corresponding holes in the motherboard (refer to Figure 7-5). Make sure the power cable from the fan can reach the processor fan header on the motherboard. Push down each of the locking pins and rotate them counterclockwise to secure the heat sink. If you are installing an aftermarket (third-party) heat sink, follow the vendor's directions. In some cases, you might need to attach mounting hardware to the motherboard before you can attach the heat sink.

Step 8.   Plug the fan into the appropriate connector on the motherboard (refer to Figure 7-14).

AMD Processors

On the 220-901 exam, you should be prepared to answer questions related to the safe removal and replacement of processors using the AMD sockets discussed earlier in this chapter.

The following procedures for removal and installation are the same for any of these processors.

AMD Processor Removal

ZIF sockets are used on AMD processors. ZIF sockets have a lever which, when released, loosens a clamp that holds the processor in place. A separate clamping mechanism is used to hold the heat sink in place.

To remove an AMD processor in an mPGA socket:

Step 1.   Remove the heat sink: rotate the heat sink's locking lever 180 degrees to release it. Push the clamp from side to side until the clamp is no longer clipped to the mounting frame. Detach the power cable for the heat sink fan from the motherboard (see Figure 7-17). Lift the heat sink away from the motherboard.

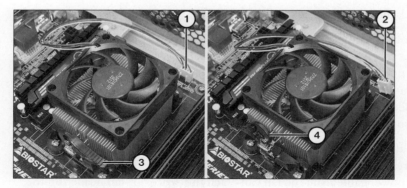

1. Fan connected to motherboard header
2. Fan removed from motherboard header
3. Heat sink clamp locked into place
4. Heat sink clamp unlocked and removed from heat sink mount

Figure 7-17   Preparing to remove a heat sink from an AMD mPGA processor.

Step 2. Release the locking lever on the mPGA socket. Push it slightly to the outside to release it and then rotate it straight up to release the clamping mechanism around the processor pins (see Figure 7-18).

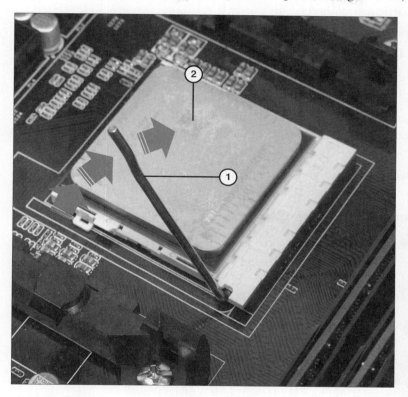

1. Locking lever
2. Thermal compound residue from heat sink

Figure 7-18 Releasing the clamping mechanism from an AMD mPGA processor.

Step 3. Grasp the processor on opposite sides, making sure not to touch the pins, and lift it from the socket.

Step 4. If the old heat sink or processor will be reinstalled, clean off the thermal paste using a soft cloth and isopropyl alcohol.

Step 5. Put the old processor into a static-free package.

AMD Processor Installation

Before installing a new processor, verify that the processor you plan to install is supported by the motherboard. Even though a particular combination of processor and motherboard might use the same socket, issues such as BIOS, voltage, or chipset considerations can prevent some processors from working on particular motherboards. You can destroy a processor or motherboard if you install a processor not suitable for a particular motherboard.

To insert a mPGA-type CPU into a ZIF socket, find the corner of the chip that is marked as pin 1 (triangle). Then follow these steps:

Step 1.   Line up the pin 1 corner with the corner of the socket also indicated as pin 1 (look for an arrow or other marking on the socket).

Step 2.   Make sure the lever on the ZIF socket is vertical (refer to Figure 7-7); insert the CPU into the socket and verify that the pins are fitting into the correct socket holes.

Step 3.   Lower the lever to the horizontal position and snap it into place to secure the CPU (see Figure 7-19).

1. Pin 1 marking on processor
2. Mounting tabs for heat sink clamp
3. Locking lever for mPGA socket

Figure 7-19   An AMD mPGA processor after installation.

Step 4.   Before attaching the heat sink or fan, determine whether the heat sink has a thermal pad (also called a phase-change pad) or whether you need to apply thermal paste to the processor core (refer to Figure 7-10). Remove the protective tape from the thermal pad or apply thermal paste as needed. Attach the heat sink or fan. You must use some type of thermal material between the processor and the bottom of the heat sink.

Step 5. To install an AMD OEM heat sink, line the clips on either side of the heat sink with the mounting tabs on the heat sink mounting frame. Make sure the clips are engaged (see Figure 7-20) before rotating the locking lever 180 degrees to lock the heat sink in place. If you are using a third-party heat sink, see the manufacturer's instructions. In some cases, you might need to attach mounting hardware to the motherboard before you can attach the heat sink.

Step 6. If you are installing an active heat sink (a heat sink with a fan), plug the fan into the appropriate connector on the motherboard.

1. Mounting clip loose
2. Mounting clip around mounting tab
3. Mounting clip around mounting tab on other side of the processor

Figure 7-20 Mounting an AMD heat sink

Exam Preparation Tasks

Review All the Key Topics

Review the most important topics in the chapter, noted with the Key Topic icon in the outer margin of the page. Table 7-14 lists a reference of these key topics and the page numbers on which each is found.

Table 7-14 Key Topics for Chapter 7

Key Topic Element	Description	Page Number
Figure 7-3	CPU cores and caches comparison	209
Table 7-1	CPU Manufacturers, Sockets, and Code Names Quick Reference	215
Section	Land Grid Array Socket	216
Section	mPGA Sockets	225
Section	Phase-Change Material/Thermal Paste	232

Complete the Tables and Lists from Memory

Print a copy of Appendix C, "Memory Tables" (found on the CD), or at least the section for this chapter, and complete the tables and lists from memory. Appendix D, "Answers to Memory Tables," also on the CD, includes completed tables and lists to check your work.

Define Key Terms

Define the following key terms from this chapter, and check your answers in the glossary.

Intel, AMD, bus speeds, overclocking, multicore, Hyper-Threading (HT Technology), virtualization support, hardware-assisted virtualization, Land Grid Array (LGA), micro pin grid array (mPGA), heat sink, active heat sink, passive heat sink, liquid-based cooling, L1 cache, L2 cache, L3 cache, Execute Disable Bit (EDB), x86, x64, LGA 775, LGA 1366, LGA 1156, LGA 1155, LGA 1150, LGA 2011, LGA 2011-v3, Socket AM3, Socket AM3+, Socket FM1, Socket FM2, Socket FM2+, cooling, thermal paste, integrated GPUs

Complete Hands-On Labs

Complete the hands-on labs, and then see the answers and explanations at the end of the chapter.

Lab 7-1: Installed CPUs and Upgrade Options

Examine a computer using a combination of reporting software and physical examination to learn the following:

- The current CPU brand and model; use the System properties sheet.

- Its code name; for Intel processors, look up the processor model at the Intel ARK website. The listing for the processor lists the code name under Related Items ("Products formerly known as *code name*"). For AMD processors, look up the processor model in the tables in this chapter or search online for the processor model to find its code name.

- Other CPUs that could be used as upgrades (faster clock speeds, larger L2/L3 caches, and so on) in this system. This step is determined by the motherboard used in the system. For systems built from standard components, you might need to use the Belarc Advisor (see Chapter 2, "Configure and Use BIOS/UEFI Tools") to learn the motherboard's brand and model number. Read the documentation to learn which processors are suitable upgrades (if any); systems with proprietary motherboards might not have any processor upgrades available. For this exercise, use the system or motherboard documentation to identify two possible upgrades:

  - A cost-is-no-object upgrade for the fastest possible performance

  - A more reasonably priced upgrade that provides a CPU boost of at least 25 percent.

Lab 7-2: Shopping for a CPU Upgrade

Choose a CPU from the list of possible upgrades you discovered in Lab 7-1. Check sources such as Newegg, Amazon.com, and others for a third-party heat sink with fan. Look for one that is designed to support overclocking.

Verify that the heat sink and fan will work on the motherboard by checking clearances around the motherboard.

Shop for the best price for a bare CPU (an OEM CPU without a heat sink/fan) and the heat sink with fan you selected.

Answer Review Questions

1. Your client reports that a system with an Intel i7 Ivy Bridge processor is not running multiple applications as quickly as expected. When you use CPU-Z to check processor specifications, you determine that the number of cores and threads are equal to each other. Which of the following will improve performance?

   a. Installing USB 3 drivers

   b. Enabling virtualization

   c. Enabling Execute Disable Bit

   d. Enabling HT Technology

2. You are building a system that is designed to run office apps at high performance but will not be used for gaming. Which of the following processors will achieve these goals and avoid the expense of a separate video card?

   a. AMD FX-9xxx

   b. Intel Core i7 Haswell

   c. AMD A4-5xxx Richland

   d. Intel Core i3 Ivy Bridge

3. Which of the following statements best describes multicore processing?

   a. Two or more processor cores inside a single physical processor

   b. Two or more physical processors on a single motherboard

   c. Two or more processing threads within a single processing core

   d. Two or more operating systems running on a single processor

4. You are a 3D graphics developer and your computer is too slow. Your computer is capable of accessing a maximum of 4GB of memory, which means that very large files may not be opened in their entirety. Which of the following statements best describes how to improve this situation?

   a. Upgrade your computer from a 32-bit system to a 64-bit system.

   b. Upgrade your memory to DDR4.

   c. Upgrade your memory to quad-channel.

   d. Save your large files as a series of smaller files so they will be easier and faster to use.

5. Select the name and function of the lever shown in the following figure from the following list:

   A. ZIF socket locking lever

   B. ZIF socket pry bar

   C. LGA mounting plateA.

   D. LGA support frame.

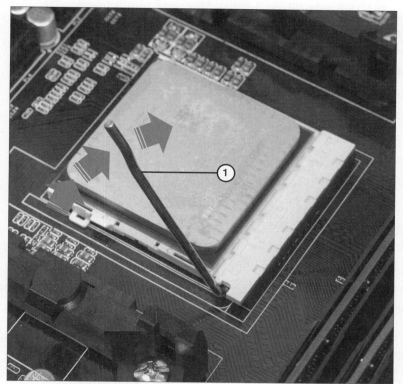

6. You are building a computer for a client from existing components. The motherboard uses Socket 1155. Which of the following processors could be used on this motherboard?

   a. AMD FX 8xxx

   b. Intel Core i7 Haswell

   c. Intel Core i5 Ivy Bridge

   d. AMD A10-5xxx

7. Which of the following is *not* a component of an active heat sink?

   a. Finned metal device to radiate heat away from the processor

   b. Pump for circulating liquid coolant

   c. Cooling fan

   d. Thermal paste

8. After a CPU failure, you have replaced the CPU while retaining the existing third-party heat sink. Which of the following must be done to ensure the system will work properly? (Choose all that apply.)

    i. Remove thermal material residue from old heat sink before reusing it.

    ii. Remove protective cover on new CPU to expose thermal material.

    iii. Reuse thermal paste on old heat sink.

    iv. Install new thermal paste on CPU.

    a. i and iv

    b. iii only

    c. i and ii

    d. ii only

9. Which one of the following statements is true of overclocking your CPU?

    a. The processor's central core will be unable to perform multithreading operations while overclocked.

    b. Overclocking requires a more expensive CPU.

    c. Overclocking requires the CPU to use a faster L1 cache.

    d. The CPU will run at a higher temperature when overclocked.

Answers and Explanations for Hands-On Labs

Complete the hands-on labs, and then see the answers and explanations at the end of the chapter.

Lab 7-1: Installed CPUs and Upgrade Options

To learn a computer's processor brand and model, you can use the System properties sheet.

For an Intel processor:

- For example, if you find out the computer has an Intel Core i5-3340S CPU, you can look up the processor model at the Intel ARK website (http://ark.intel.com).

- Click the listing and look at the "Products formerly labeled *codename*" to determine the code name for this processor family. The processor in this example is code-named Ivy Bridge.

For an AMD processor:

- For example, if you find out the computer has an AMD A8-3820 CPU, you can look up the processor model at the AMD website for desktop processors (http://www.amd.com/en-us/products/processors/desktop). Click the link in the left menu for the type of processor you have.

- You can look up the part number in the tables available in this chapter to determine the processor's code name or you can search the Internet.

To determine what other CPUs could be used as upgrades:

- Look up the documentation for the system or motherboard. The System properties sheet might reveal the name of the system.

- For systems built from standard components, you might need to use the Belarc Advisor (see Chapter 2) to learn the motherboard's brand and model number.

- If you can open the system, this information is sometimes marked on the motherboard instead.

For this exercise, use the system or motherboard documentation to identify two possible upgrades:

- A cost-is-no-object upgrade for the fastest possible performance

---

- A more reasonably priced upgrade that provides a CPU boost of at least 25 percent.

Lab 7-2: Lab 7-2 Shopping for a CPU Upgrade

After identifying a couple of CPU upgrades, look for suitable third-party heat sinks. Note dimensions, performance, and any specific compatibility concerns with your system's motherboard or other components.

Select two models that can be used on the system after a CPU upgrade.

Shop for the best price on the third-party heat sinks and bare CPUs from a reputable vendor in your country.

Answers and Explanations to Review Questions

1. **D. Enable HT Technology.** HT Technology is hyper-threading, which enables a single processor core to run two execution threads at the same time. When multiple apps or a single app with multiple threads are run, the enabling of HT Technology improves performance.

2. **B.** The Intel Core i7 Haswell is the fastest processor listed with an integrated GPU. The AMD FX-9xxx series are also fast processors, but they are not APUs, so they have no onboard graphics.

3. **A.** Multicore processing incorporates two or more processor cores into a single physical processor and provides more computing power and faster speeds. It is similar to having two processors on a single motherboard, but is less expensive.

4. **A.** A 32-bit CPU can only access a maximum of 4GB of memory addresses. A 64-bit CPU can access more than 4GB of RAM, can open larger file sizes, and can support both 64- and 32-bit operating systems and applications.

5. **A.** This is the locking lever on a ZIF socket. When closed, it locks the CPU firmly in place in the micro pin grid array. When opened, the CPU can then be removed.

6. **C.** Intel Core i5 Ivy Bridge is one of two processor families that can use Socket 1155 processors. Sandy Bridge is the other.

7. **B.** A pump is used in a liquid coolant system, not with an active heat sink. An active heat sink uses a finned metal device that radiates heat away from the processor unit, a cooling fan to move the heat away from the processor, and a thermal paste that ensures good contact between the CPU and the heat sink.

8. **A.** The old thermal material must be removed from any component that will be reused and a new layer of thermal material must be applied to the CPU.

9. **D.** Overclocking allows you to increase the bus speed of certain components, which increases the temperature at which those components run. If you plan to overclock your computer, you must also take steps to improve the cooling system for your computer.

This chapter covers the following subjects:

- **Rear Panel Port Clusters**—This section shows you typical rear-panel port clusters and identifies each port.

- **USB**—In this section, you learn about the many flavors of USB and USB connectors, including the latest, USB 3.1 and USB Type C, and how USB can also be adapted to network and legacy devices.

- **FireWire (IEEE 1394)**—This section covers both FireWire 400 and FireWire 800 ports and cables

- **SATA and eSATA**—This section details the cabling and performance of SATA and eSATA's three generations.

- **Thunderbolt**—Intel developed it, Apple embraced it, and it's also showing up on more and more high-performance Windows PCs. Learn about the performance and versatility of Thunderbolt in this section.

- **Video**—As the industry continues to move from analog to digital connectors, this section helps sort out the differences between VGA, DVI, HDMI, DisplayPort, and older standards you might encounter in configuring PCs, HDTVs, and home theater systems.

- **Audio**—Color-coding and SPDIF differences are the focus of this section.

- **PS/2**—The PS/2 port continues to show up on desktop systems, and this section covers the variations you will find on some systems.

## CHAPTER 8

Ports and Interfaces

Although USB is the most versatile of I/O ports, it's scarcely alone on a typical PC. In this chapter, you learn about the home for most connections, the rear port cluster, and the many different types of ports, cables, and uses that enable a PC to work with many different types of peripherals and devices.

220-901: Objective 1.7 Compare and contrast various PC connection interfaces, their characteristics and purpose.

220-901: Objective 1.11 Identify common PC connector types and associated cables.

Foundation Topics

Rear Panel Port Clusters

Most of the external I/O ports discussed in this chapter are located in the port cluster, which is located at the rear of ATX, microATX, and mini-ITX motherboards. Figures 8-1 and 8-2 compare some typical port cluster designs and identify the ports. Use these figures as a reference when you learn more about each port type.

NOTE   The top motherboard shown in Figure 8-2 does not have the faceplate attached.

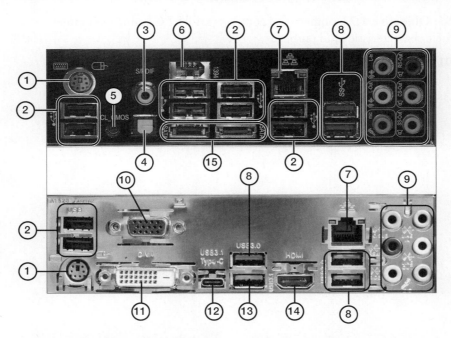

1. Combo PS/2 mouse/keyboard port
2. USB 2.0 ports
3. SPDIF coaxial port
4. SPDIF optical port
5. Clear CMOS button
6. FireWire 400 port
7. Gigabit Ethernet port
8. USB 3.0 ports
9. Surround audio jacks
10. VGA DB15 video port
11. DVI-D video port
12. USB-C port (supports USB 3.1)
13. USB 3.1 Type A port
14. HDMI A/V port
15. eSATA ports

Figure 8-1   ATX motherboard port clusters.

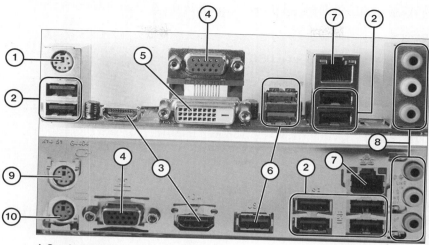

1. Combo PS/2 mouse/keyboard port
2. USB 2.0 ports
3. HDMI A/V port
4. VGA DB15 video port
5. DVI-D video port
6. USB 3.0 ports
7. Gigabit Ethernet ports
8. Stereo audio jacks
9. PS/2 mouse port
10. PS/2 keyboard port

Figure 8-2   Mini-ITX motherboard (top) and Micro-ATX (bottom) port clusters.

USB

Universal Serial Bus (**USB**) ports have almost completely replaced PS/2 (mini-DIN) mouse and keyboard ports on recent systems and can be used for printer, mass storage, and other external I/O devices. Some form of USB port is also used by most mobile devices, game consoles, many network devices, cars and trucks, smart TVs, and other electronics, making it truly "universal."

Most recent desktop systems have at least eight USB ports and many systems support as many as 10 or more front- and rear-mounted USB ports. Laptops typically have three or four USB ports and Windows and Android tablets typically have at least one USB or USB-On-the-Go port. OS X desktop and laptop computers feature two or more USB ports.

USB ports send and receive data digitally.

There are three standards for USB ports included in the A+ Certification exam:

- **USB 1.1**
- **USB 2.0** (also called **Hi-Speed USB**)
- **USB 3.0** (also called **SuperSpeed USB**)

> **NOTE**   A fourth standard, USB 3.1, was introduced in 2015. To learn more about USB 3.1, see "USB 3.1," this chapter, p.260.

USB packaging and device markings frequently use the official logos shown in Figure 8-3 to distinguish the four versions of USB in common use. The industry uses the term Hi-Speed USB for USB 2.0, SuperSpeed USB for USB 3.0, and **SuperSpeed+ USB** for USB 3.1 Gen 2.

Figure 8-3   The USB logo (left) is used for USB 1.1–compatible devices, the Hi-Speed USB logo (second from left) is used for USB 2.0–compatible devices, the SuperSpeed USB logo (second from right) is used for USB 3.0–compatible devices, and the SuperSpeed+ USB logo (right) is used for USB 3.1 Gen 2–compatible devices. Devices bearing these logos have been certified by the USB Implementers Forum, Inc. (USB-IF). Images courtesy of USB-IF.

With any version of USB, a single USB port on an add-on card or motherboard is designed to handle up to 127 devices through the use of multiport hubs and daisy-chaining hubs. USB devices are Plug and Play (PnP) devices that are hot swappable (can be connected and disconnected without turning off the system).

Need more USB ports? You can add USB ports with any of the following methods:

- Motherboard connectors for USB header cables
- Hubs
- Add-on cards

Some motherboards have USB header cable connectors, which enable you to make additional USB ports available on the rear or front of the computer (refer to

Chapter 3, "Motherboard Components"). Some motherboard vendors include these **header cables** with the motherboard, whereas others require you to purchase them separately. Most recent cases also include front-mounted USB ports, which can also be connected to the motherboard. Because of vendor-specific differences in how motherboards implement header cables, the header cable might use separate connectors for each signal instead of the more common single connector for all signals.

USB **generic hubs** are used to connect multiple devices to the same USB port, distribute both USB signals and power via the USB hub to other devices, and increase the distance between the device and the USB port. There are two types of generic hubs:

- Bus-powered

- Self-powered

Bus-powered hubs might be built in to other devices, such as monitors and keyboards, or can be standalone devices. Different USB devices use different amounts of power and some devices require more power than others. A **bus-powered hub** provides no more than 100 milliamps (mA) of power to each device connected to it. Thus, some devices fail when connected to a bus-powered hub.

A **self-powered hub**, on the other hand, has its own power source; it plugs in to an AC wall outlet. A self-powered hub designed for USB 1.1 or USB 2.0 devices provides up to 500mA of power to each device connected to it, whereas a self-powered hub designed for USB 3.0/3.1 devices provides up to 900mA of power to each device. Note that USB hubs are backward compatible to previous USB versions. A self-powered hub supports a wider range of USB devices than a bus-powered hub, and I recommend using it instead of a bus-powered hub whenever possible.

Add-on cards can be used to provide additional USB ports as an alternative to hubs. One advantage of an add-on card is its capability to provide support for more recent USB standards. For example, you can add a USB 3.0 card to a system that has only USB 1.1/2.0 ports to permit use of USB 3.0 hard drives at full performance. Add-on cards for USB 1.1 or USB 2.0 ports connect to PCI slots on desktop computers and CardBus or ExpressCard slots on laptop computers, whereas USB 3.0 cards connect to PCIe x1 or wider slots on desktop computers and ExpressCard slots on laptop computers.

Figure 8-4 illustrates a typical USB 3.0 card, a USB 2.0 self-powered hub, and a USB 2.0 port header cable.

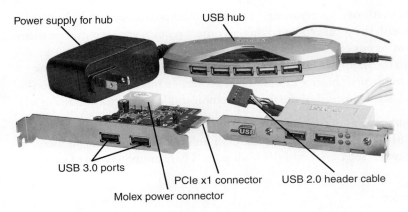

Power supply for hub

USB hub

USB 3.0 ports

PCIe x1 connector

Molex power connector

USB 2.0 header cable

Figure 8-4 USB 2.0 and 3.0 hardware.

Table 8-1 provides an overview of current USB standards.

Table 8-1 USB Standards Overview

Version	Marketing Name	Speeds Supported	Maximum Cable Length**	Notes
1.1	USB	12Mbps 1.5Mbps	3 meters	
2.0	HighSpeed USB	480Mbps	5 meters	Also supports USB 1.1 devices and speeds
3.1 Gen 1 (also known as USB 3.0)	SuperSpeed USB	5Gbps	*	Also supports USB 1.1 and 2.0 devices and speeds
3.1 Gen 2	SuperSpeed+ USB	10Gbps	*	Also supports USB 1.1, 2.0, 3.0/3.1 Gen 1 devices and speeds

* 3 meters is the recommended length, but no maximum cable length has been established for these versions of USB

** To exceed recommended or maximum cable lengths, connect the cable to a USB hub or use an Active USB extension cable

USB 1.1 and 2.0

USB 1.1 and 2.0 standards use the same cable and connector types, which are shown in Figure 8-5.

USB 1.1/2.0 cables use two different types of connectors: Series A (also called **Type A**) and Series B (also called **Type B**). Series A connectors are used on USB root hubs (the USB ports in the computer) and USB external hubs to support USB devices. Type A cables can also connect to USB 3.0 root hubs and external hubs.

Series B connectors are used for devices that employ a removable USB cable, such as a USB printer or a generic (external) hub. Generally, you need a Series A–to–Series B cable to attach most devices to a USB root or external hub. Cables that are Series A–to–Series A or Series B–to–Series B are used to extend standard cables and can cause problems if the combined length of the cables exceeds recommended distances. Adapters are available to convert Series B cables into Mini-B cables, which support the five-pin Mini-B port design (also known as the **USB connector type mini**) used on many recent USB devices.

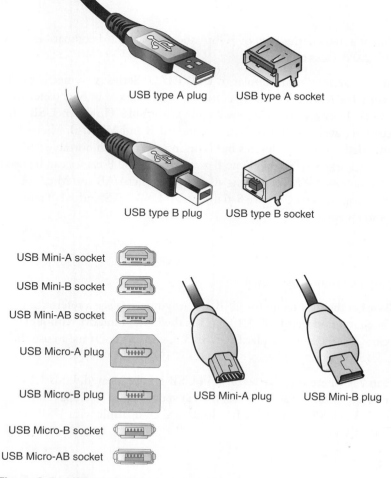

Figure 8-5   USB 1.1/2.0 plugs and sockets.

USB-on-the-Go uses the **USB connector type micro** (micro-B) connector shown in Figure 8-5. USB-on-the-Go is used by most Android smartphones and tablets for charging and file sync.

USB 1.1 ports run at a top speed (full-speed USB) of 12 megabits per second (Mbps); low-speed USB devices, such as a mouse or a keyboard, run at 1.5Mbps; and USB 2.0 (Hi-Speed USB) ports run at a top speed of 480Mbps. USB 2.0 ports are backward compatible with USB 1.1 devices and speeds and manage multiple USB 1.1 devices better than a USB 1.1 port does.

The maximum length for a cable attached to 12Mbps or 480Mbps USB devices is 5 meters, whereas the maximum length for low-speed (1.5Mbps) devices, such as mice and keyboards, is 3 meters.

USB 3.0

USB 3.0 ports run at a maximum speed of 5Gbps and are backward compatible with USB 1.1 and USB 2.0 devices and speeds.

USB 3.0 Standard-A connectors are similar to USB 1.1/2.0 Series A connectors but have additional contacts. Most port cluster connectors are marked in blue (refer to Figures 8-1 and 8-2). They are compatible with any USB cable. However, USB 3.0 Series B connectors are available in two forms: Standard-B and Micro-B. Micro-B was originally intended for mobile devices but is often used by both portable and desktop USB 3.0 hard drives. USB 3.0 Type B and Micro Type B cables can be used only with USB 3.0 devices. USB 3.0 designs also include Micro-AB and Micro-A, but these are not in common use. Figure 8-6 illustrates USB 3.0 Standard-B and Micro-B cables and receptacles.

USB 3.1

USB 3.1 is actually two standards in one:

- **USB 3.1 Gen 1** is the new name for USB 3.0. Anytime you see a reference to USB 3.0, keep in mind that USB 3.1 Gen 1 is the same standard. Although USB 3.1 Gen 1 is the same standard as USB 3.0, vendors continue to use the original USB 3.0 name.

- **USB 3.1 Gen 2** is where the new features in USB 3.1 are located. USB 3.1 Gen 2 (often referred to simply as USB 3.1) runs at speeds up to 10Gbps (2× the speed of USB 3.0/USB 3.1 Gen 1). It is backward compatible with USB 1.1, 2.0, and 3.0/3.1 Gen 1.

Figure 8-6   USB 3.0 Standard-B (left) and Micro-B (right) cables and receptacles.

Both USB 3.1 Gen 1 and Gen 2 use the same cables and connectors as USB 3.0. However, some USB 3.1 Gen 2 ports support a new reversible connector, **USB Type C**, which can be used by both hubs and devices. Some systems, such as the second motherboard shown in Figure 8-1, include both a Type C USB 3.1 port and a standard Type A USB 3.1 Gen 2 port.

NOTE   Although USB Type-C connectors also support older USB standards, it is unlikely that vendors would use it for USB 3.0, USB 2.0, or USB 1.1 ports.

Figure 8-7 illustrates USB 3.0 Type A and Type C cable and USB 3.1 Gen 2 ports.

Other USB standards, such as USB Power Delivery and USB Battery Charging, will take advantage of other features in the USB Type C port. For more information about USB 3.1, USB Type C, USB Power Delivery, or USB Battery Charging, see the official USB website at www.usb.org.

1. USB 3.0/3.1 Type A cable
2. USB 3.0 Type A port
3. USB 3.1 Type A port
4. USB 3.1 Type C port
5. USB 3.1 Type C cable

Figure 8-7   USB 3.0/3.1 Type A and Type C ports and cables.

USB Adapters

USB cable adapter kits enable a single cable with replaceable tips to be used for the following tasks:

- Type A male to female, to extend a short cable.

- Type A female to Type B connectors, to enable a single cable with multiple adapter tips to work with various types of peripherals (see Figure 8-8).

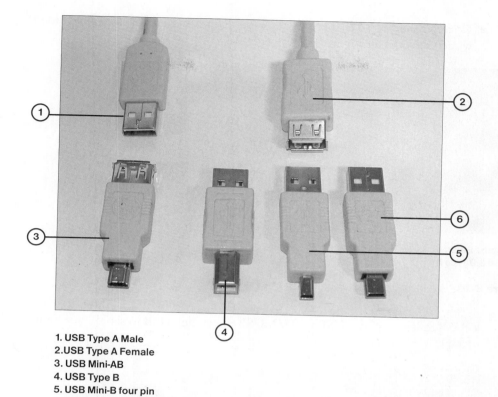

1. USB Type A Male
2. USB Type A Female
3. USB Mini-AB
4. USB Type B
5. USB Mini-B four pin
6. USB Mini-B five-pin

Figure 8-8 USB 2.0 cable kit includes a Type A male/female cable and several B-type connectors.

- Type A female to USB-on-the-Go, for use with tablets or smartphones (see Figure 8-9).

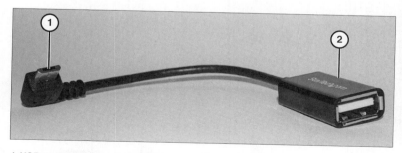

1. USB-on-the-Go
2. USB Type A Female

Figure 8-9 USB-on-the-Go to Type A adapter enables a standard USB cable to work with devices that use the Micro-A connector.

■ USB to Ethernet, to enable a device without an Ethernet port to connect to a wired network (see Figure 8-10).

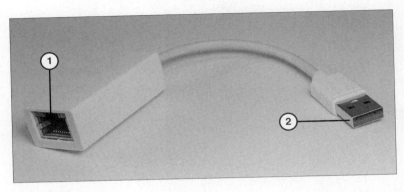

1. Gigabit Ethernet
2. USB 3.0 Type A

Figure 8-10   A typical USB 3.0 to Gigabit Ethernet adapter.

■ USB to legacy ports (USB to PS/2, USB to parallel, USB to serial). See Figure 8-11.

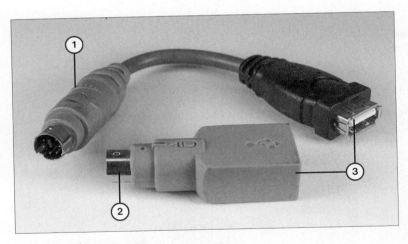

1. PS/2 keyboard connector
2. PS/2 mouse connector
3. USB female port

Figure 8-11   Connect hybrid keyboards and mice to PS/2 ports with these adapters.

NOTE A hybrid keyboard or mouse is one designed to work with either USB or PS/2 ports. Adapters bundled with a mouse or keyboard, such as the ones shown in Figure 8-11, can be used only on mice or keyboards that are designed to work with either type of port. A USB to PS/2 adapter sold at retail stores can also work with PS/2-only devices.

FireWire (IEEE 1394)

FireWire, also known as IEEE 1394, is a family of high-speed, bidirectional, serial transmission ports that can connect digital devices to PCs, or digital devices to each other. FireWire also supported peer-to-peer networking with older versions of Windows, but this feature was discontinued starting with Windows Vista.

The most common version of FireWire is known as FireWire 400 (**Firewire 400**), and is also known as IEEE 1394a. Sony's version is known as i.LINK. FireWire 400 has a maximum speed of 400Mbps and can be implemented either as a built-in port on the motherboard (refer to Figure 8-1) or as part of an add-on card (see Figure 8-12). FireWire 800 (IEEE 1394b or **Firewire 800**) runs at up to 800Mbps but is more often used on systems running OS X than those running Windows.

Up to 16 FireWire devices can be connected to a single IEEE 1394 port through daisy-chaining. By using hubs, up to 63 devices can be connected to a single port. Most external FireWire devices have two ports to enable daisy-chaining.

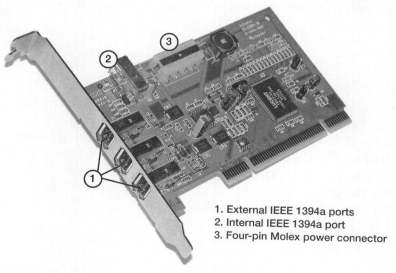

1. External IEEE 1394a ports
2. Internal IEEE 1394a port
3. Four-pin Molex power connector

Figure 8-12 A typical FireWire 400 host adapter card with three external ports and one internal port.

FireWire cards for desktop computers can use PCI or PCI Express buses. (Versions for laptops use ExpressCard or CardBus designs.)

Maximum copper cable length is 4.5 meters; by using active (powered) repeaters or hubs, cables can be daisy-chained up to 72 meters. FireWire carries digital signals.

Table 8-2 compares FireWire 400 and 800 interfaces.

Table 8-2 FireWire 400 and 800 Interfaces Compared

Interface	Interface Speeds	Also Known As	Connection Types	Maximum Cable Length
FireWire 400	100Mbps	IEEE-1394a	Six-pin (Alpha)	4.5 meters
	200Mbps	i.Link	Four-pin (i.Link)	
	400Mbps			
FireWire 800	800Mbps	IEEE-1394b	Nine-pin (Beta)	4.5 meters
			Nine-pin (Bilingual)	

FireWire 400

Standard FireWire 400 ports and cables use a six-pin interface (four pins for data, two for power), but some digital camcorders and all i.LINK ports use the alternative four-pin interface, which supplies data and signals but no power to the device. Six-wire to four-wire cables enable these devices to communicate with each other. Refer to Figure 8.13.

FireWire 800

A faster version of the IEEE 1394 standard, FireWire 800 (also known as IEEE 1394b), runs at 800Mbps. FireWire 800 ports use a nine-pin interface. There are two versions of the FireWire 800 port: The Beta port and cable are used only for FireWire 800 to FireWire 800 connections, whereas the Bilingual cable and port are used for either FireWire 800 to FireWire 800 or FireWire 800 to FireWire 400 connections. Beta cables and ports have a wide notch at the top of the cable and port, whereas Bilingual cables and ports have a narrow notch at the FireWire 800 end and use either the four-pin or six-pin FireWire 400 connection at the other end of the cable. All four cable types are shown in Figure 8-13.

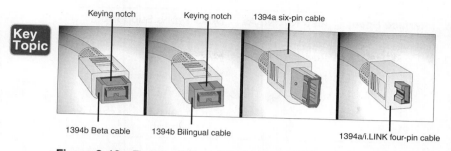

Figure 8-13   FireWire 800 and FireWire 400 cable connectors compared.

SATA and eSATA

The vast majority of desktop and laptop computers in use rely on the Serial ATA (SATA) interface to connect to internal hard disk drives, SSDs, and optical drives. The external version of SATA, eSATA, is not as common, but has been widely used by high-performance Windows and Linux-based desktop computers for external hard disk drives.

Both SATA and eSATA interfaces carry data digitally using high-speed serial transmission, but vary in speeds and connection details. For speed differences, see Table 8-3.

Table 8-3   SATA and eSATA Drive Interface Overview

Interface	Location	Interface Speeds	Also Known As	Drive Types Supported
eSATA	External	1.5Gbps 3Gbps 6Gbps		Hard disk drives, SSD
SATA1	Internal	1.5Gbps	SATA 1.5Gbps SATA Revision 1.0	Hard disk drives, optical (DVD, BD media) drives, RAID arrays, SSD Can be converted to eSATA via header cable
SATA2	Internal	3.0Gbps	SATA 3Gbps SATA Revision 2.0	Hard disk drives, optical (DVD, BD media) drives, RAID arrays, SSD Can be converted to eSATA via header cable

Interface	Location	Interface Speeds	Also Known As	Drive Types Supported
SATA3	Internal	6.0Gbps	SATA 6Gbps Revision 3.0	Hard disk drives, RAID arrays, SSD
				Backward compatible with SATA1, SATA2
				Can be converted to eSATA via header cable

Low-performance and older high-performance desktop motherboards feature top-facing SATA cable headers (see Figure 8-14). However, many recent high-performance motherboards have switched to front-facing SATA cable headers (see Figure 8-15).

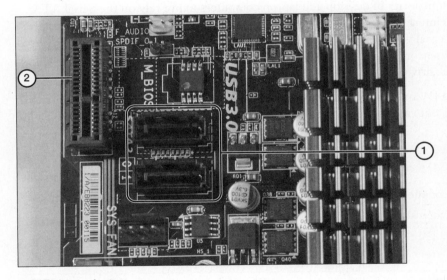

1. SATA host adapters
2. PCIe x1 slot

Figure 8-14   A pair of SATA ports from a mini-ITX motherboard.

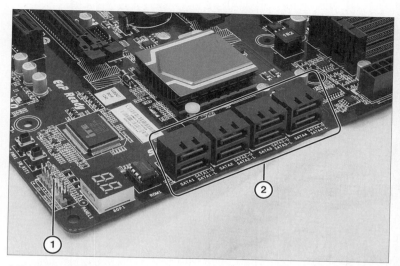

1. Front panel headers
2. SATA host adapters

Figure 8-15   This motherboard features eight front-mounted SATA ports.

SATA Configuration and Cabling

Figure 8-16 compares the power and data connectors and cables used by typical SATA drives.

An SATA drive has a one-to-one connection to the corresponding SATA interface on the motherboard. Drive jumpers on SATA drives, when present, are used to reduce drive interface speed from the default to the next lower speed (from 6.0Gbps to 3.0Gbps or from 3.0Gbps to 1.5Gbps). See the specific drive's documentation for details.

SATA 1.5Gbps (**SATA1**) and 3.0Gbps (**SATA2**) drives and interfaces use the same cabling. However, SATA 6.0Gbps (**SATA3**) drives and interfaces use an improved version with heavier shielding for greater reliability. Cables made for SATA 6.0Gbps are typically marked as such and can also be used with slower SATA drives and interfaces. All SATA data cables use an L-shaped seven-pin connector, and all SATA power cables use a larger L-shaped 15-pin connector as shown in Figure 8-16.

1. SATA power cable
2. SATA power connector on drive
3. SATA data cable
4. SATA data connector on drive

Figure 8-16   The power and data cables and connectors on SATA drives.

NOTE   SATA Express, also known as SATAe or Serial ATA Revision 3.2, was announced in 2014. It uses the PCI Express (PCIe) bus to achieve data transfer rates up to 16Gbps. Although Intel's Z97, H97, and X99 chipsets include support for SATAe, no SATAe drives are currently available. The SATAe host adapter can also be used by two standard SATA 6Gbps or slower drives. For more information about SATAe, see the Serial ATA International Organization website at http://sata-io.org/.

SATA data cables are available with straight-through connectors on both ends or with a right-angle connector on one end for easier connection to SATA drives. Some cables, either straight-through or right-angle, include a metal clip to help lock the drive into place.

eSATA cable headers convert standard SATA headers into eSATA ports available from the rear of the system.

See Figure 8-17 for examples of these cables. For more detail, see Figures 6-11 and 6-12, p.143.

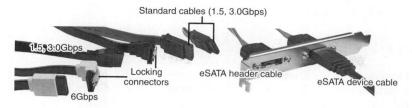

Figure 8-17 SATA and eSATA data cables.

The SATA and eSATA drive interfaces are also designed to support hot-swapping but must be configured for **AHCI** mode (also known as native mode) in the system BIOS or UEFI firmware. If the interface is configured for IDE mode (also known as emulation mode), the drive connected to it cannot be hot-swapped and will also lose access to advanced SATA and eSATA features such as native command queuing (NCQ). RAID mode supports AHCI features along with allowing two or more drives to be used as a logical unit. See Figure 2-8 in Chapter 2, "Configure and Use BIOS/UEFI Tools," for an example of this dialog.

CAUTION If internal SATA hard disks are configured to support hot-swapping (configured as AHCI devices in the system BIOS/UEFI; it might also be necessary to enable hot-swapping as an additional option), they also show up when you open the Safely Remove Hardware and Eject Media dialog in the Notification area of Windows. Do not select these drives for removal.

Thunderbolt

Thunderbolt is a high-speed interface capable of supporting hard disk drives, SSDs, HDTVs up to 4K resolution, and other types of I/O devices. Thunderbolt includes PCIe and DisplayPort digital signals into a compact interface that runs from 2× to 8× faster than USB 3.0, and 2× to 4× faster than USB 3.1 Gen 2. Intel introduced Thunderbolt in 2011. Thunderbolt was initially adopted by Apple, which uses it in the recent and current MacBook product lines. Thunderbolt is also available on some high-end desktop motherboards using Intel chipsets.

Thunderbolt is available in three versions that use two different port types: Thunderbolt 1 and Thunderbolt 2, currently the most common version, use the same physical port as the mini-DisplayPort. The newest version, Thunderbolt 3, uses the same physical connector as USB Type C. All three versions support up to six Thunderbolt devices per port and use daisy chaining to connect devices to each other.

Table 8-4 compares Thunderbolt versions to each other.

Table 8-4   Thunderbolt Interface Overview

Interface Version	Maximum Interface Speeds	Connection Type	Supported Protocols	Maximum Cable Length*
Thunderbolt 1	10Gbps	Thunderbolt 1*	Thunderbolt 1, DisplayPort	3 meters (9.8 feet)
Thunderbolt 2	20Gbps	Thunderbolt 1*	Thunderbolt 1-2, DisplayPort 1.2	3 meters (9.8 feet)
Thunderbolt 3	40Gps	USB Type C	Thunderbolt 1-3, DisplayPort 1.2, PCIe 3, USB 3.0, USB Power Delivery	3 meters (9.8 feet)

* Using copper cable. Some vendors are now shipping optical cable in lengths up to 30 meters.

Figure 8-18 compares a Thunderbolt 2 cable with a USB Type C cable (the cable used by Thunderbolt 3) and a mini-DisplayPort cable, which uses the same physical connector as a Thunderbolt cable.

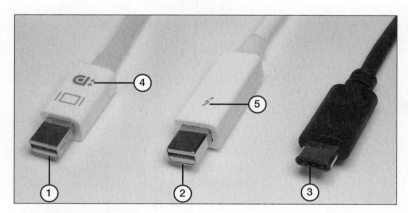

1. Mini-DisplayPort+ cable
2. Thunderbolt 1/Thunderbolt 2 cable
3. USB Type C – Thunderbolt 3 cable
4. DisplayPort++ icon
5. Thunderbolt icon

Figure 8-18   Mini-DisplayPort, Thunderbolt 1-2, and USB Type-C/Thunderbolt 3 cables.

Because of Thunderbolt's high bandwidth, it can be connected to docks that feature multiple port types. Figure 8-19 shows a typical Thunderbolt 2 dock that also provides USB 3.0 ports, an HDMI video port, Gigabit Ethernet port, and audio headphone and microphone jacks.

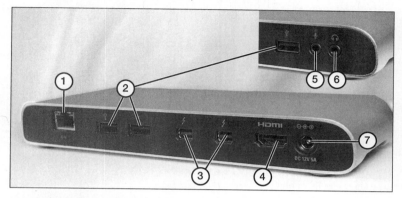

1. Gigabit Ethernet port
2. USB 3.0 ports
3. Thunderbolt 2 ports
4. HDMI port
5. Microphone port
6. Headset port
7. AC power jack

Figure 8-19   A typical Thunderbolt 2 dock.

Video

When selecting a monitor or projector for use with a particular video card or integrated video port, it's helpful to understand the physical and feature differences between different video connector types, such as VGA, DVI, HDMI, DisplayPort Component/RGB, BNC, S-video, and composite. Table 8-5 provides an overview of these connector types.

Table 8-5   Video Connector Types Overview

Connector	Signal Type	Base Resolution	Maximum Resolution (60Hz refresh rate)	HDCP Support	3D Support	Audio
VGA	Analog	640×480 graphics 720×480 text	2048×1536*	No	No	No
HDMI	Digital, Analog	VGA	1920×1200** 4K***	Yes	Yes***	Yes

Connector	Signal Type	Base Resolution	Maximum Resolution (60Hz refresh rate)	HDCP Support	3D Support	Audio
DVI	Digital, Analog@	VGA	1920×1200% 2560×1600#	Varies	No	No
DisplayPort	Digital, Analog	VGA	4K	Yes	Yes	Yes
BNC	Analog	VGA	1080p	No	No	No
Composite	Analog	480i	480i	No	No	No
S-video	Analog	480i	480i	No	No	No
Component	Analog	720p	1080i	No	No	No

* Recommended resolutions lower due to excessive interference

** HDMI 1.0 through 1.3c

***HDMI 1.4b or higher; also known as 4K resolution

@ DVI-D is digital only; DVI-I support analog and digital signals; DVI-A is analog-only

% Single-link

Dual-link

S-video splits luma and chroma signals for a better picture than composite; composite combines these signals

VGA

VGA is an analog display standard. By varying the levels of red, green, or blue per dot (pixel) onscreen, a VGA port and monitor can display an unlimited number of colors. Practical color limits (if you call more than 16 million colors limiting) are based on the video card's memory and the desired screen resolution.

The base resolution (horizontal×vertical dots) of VGA is 640×480. **SVGA** most typically refers to 800×600 VGA resolution.

All VGA cards made for use with standard analog monitors use a DB-15F 15-pin female connector, which plugs into the DB-15M connector used by the VGA cable from the monitor. Figure 8-20 compares these connectors.

DVI

The **DVI** port, a digital video port, is currently used by most LED and LCD displays with sizes under 25-inches diagonal measurement. The DVI port commonly comes in two forms: DVI-D supports only digital signals and is found on digital LCD displays. Most of these displays also support analog video signals through separate VGA ports.

NOTE DVI single-link omits some of the connectors in the DVI interface, limiting the maximum resolution. DVI dual-link uses all of the connectors, enabling higher resolutions than those possible with DVI single-link. See illustrations at https://en.wikipedia.org/wiki/Digital_Visual_Interface.

DB15M VGA cable   DB15F VGA port

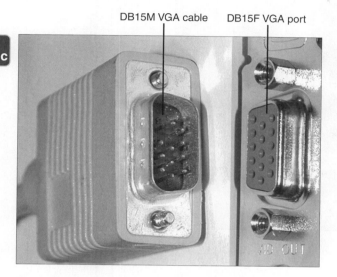

Figure 8-20   DB15M (cable) and DB15F (port) connectors used for VGA video signals.

Most video cards with DVI ports use the DVI-I dual-link version, which provides both digital and analog output and supports the use of a VGA/DVI-I adapter for use with analog displays (refer to Figure 8-28). Figure 8-21 illustrates a DVI-D cable and DVI-I port.

The less-common DVI-A version supports analog signals only. The maximum length for DVI cables is 5 meters.

DVI-D video cable supports digital signals only

DVI-I video port supports
analog and digital signals

Key Topic

Figure 8-21   DVI-I video port and DVI-D video cable.

DVI and Copy Protection

Some integrated and card-based DVI-I and DVI-D connections (as well as some DVI connections in home theater equipment such as HDTVs, projectors, and DVD players) can support High-Bandwidth Digital Content Protection (HDCP). HDCP, a form of digital rights management (DRM), enables playback of DVD or other encrypted content at full resolution. HDCP support is also needed in the display. Some LCD/LED displays with DVI ports do not support HDCP. In such cases, encrypted video will play back at DVD-quality (480p) resolution.

HDMI

Video cards and systems with integrated video that are designed for home theater use support a standard known as **High-Definition Multimedia Interface (HDMI).** HDMI has the capability to support digital audio as well as video through a single cable. HDMI ports are found on most late-model HDTVs as well as home theater hardware such as amplifiers, Blu-ray and DVD players, and many recent laptop and desktop PCs running Windows or Linux. All versions of HDMI support HDCP and DRM.

The most recent HDMI standard, version 1.4b, supports 1080p HDTV and resolutions up to 4096×2160 (also known as 4K×2K), 48-bit color depths, various types of uncompressed and compressed digital audio, 3D over HDMI, and Fast Ethernet support. For more about HDMI specifications, visit www.hdmi.org.

The most common HDMI port is Type A, which has 19 pins. It is used to achieve high-definition resolutions such as 1920 × 1080 (known as 1080p or 1080i). The HDMI 1.3 and later specifications also define a mini-HDMI connector (Type C). It is smaller than the Type A plug but has the same 19-pin configuration. The HDMI 1.4 specification defines a micro-HDMI connector (Type D), which again uses the same 19-pin configuration but in a connector the size of a micro-USB plug.

HDMI hardware, regardless of the version in use, uses cables similar to the ones shown in Figure 8-22 and the ports shown in Figure 8-23. Typical cable lengths range up to 40 feet, but higher-quality copper cables can be longer.

1. DVI-I dual-link
2. DVI-D single-link
3. HDMI
4. Mini-HDMI
5. DisplayPort
6. Mini DisplayPort

Figure 8-22 HDMI cable connectors compared to DVI and DisplayPort cable connectors.

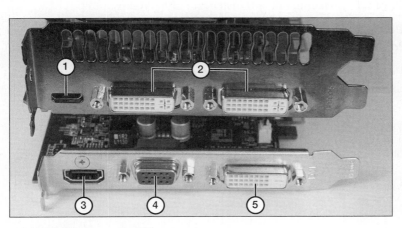

1. Mini HDMI
2. DVI-I Dual-link
3. HDMI
4. VGA
5. DVI-D Dual-link

Figure 8-23 HDMI, DVI, and VGA ports on the rear of two typical PCIe video cards.

DisplayPort

DisplayPort was designed by the Video Electronics Standards Association (VESA) as a royalty-free digital interface to replace DVI and VGA. It offers similar performance to HDMI but is not expected to compete with the HDMI standard.

Unlike HDMI or DVI, which can connect only one display per port, DisplayPort enables multiple displays to be connected via a single DisplayPort connector.

DisplayPort utilizes packet transmission similar to Ethernet and USB. Each packet transmitted has the clock embedded as opposed to DVI and HDMI, which utilize a separate clocking signal.

DisplayPort connectors are not compatible with USB, DVI, or HDMI; however, devices that support Dual-mode DisplayPort (DisplayPort++) technology are capable of sending HDMI or DVI signals with the use of the appropriate adapter. DisplayPort offers a maximum transmission distance of 3 meters over passive cable, and 33 meters over active cable. There are 20 pins in a DisplayPort connector, with pins 19 and 20 being used for 3.3V, 500 mA power on active cables. The mini-DisplayPort cable shown in Figure 8-22 also uses a 20-pin connector.

DisplayPort cables can be up to 15 meters long.

Figure 8-24 illustrates a high-performance video card with a DisplayPort connector.

DisplayPort Versions

DisplayPort is currently available in three versions:

- **DisplayPort 1.1**—maximum data transfer rate of 8.64Gbps.

- **DisplayPort 1.2**—maximum data transfer rate of 17.28Gbps, introduces mini-DisplayPort connector, and support for 3D

- **DisplayPort 1.3**—maximum data transfer rate of 32.4Gbps with support for 4K, 5K, and 8K UHD displays

DisplayPort and Thunderbolt

The Thunderbolt digital I/O interface is backwards-compatible with mini-DisplayPort, so you can connect mini-DisplayPort displays to either a Thunderbolt or mini-DisplayPort connector.

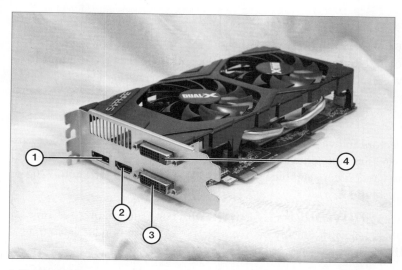

1. DisplayPort
2. HDMI
3. DVI-I dual-link
4. DVI-D dual-link

Figure 8-24   DisplayPort, HDMI, and DVI ports on the rear of a typical PCIe video card.

RCA

The **RCA connector** can be used for both analog video (Composite) and stereo audio. **Composite video** cables use 75 ohm impedance, are usually yellow, and support standard definition video signals up to 480i, but do not support HDCP or other DRM technologies.

The recommended length for composite cables is up to 25 meters.

Refer to Figure 8-25 for a comparison of typical composite, S-video, and component video cables.

S-Video (Mini-DIN 4)

The mini-DIN 4 connector was used by some older video cards, camcorders, and home theater equipment to carry S-video (also known as C/Y) signals. S-video improves on the standard composite signal by splitting luma (brightness) and chroma (color) into separate channels for somewhat better picture quality than that available with composite video.

Like composite, S-video is analog and does not support any form of DRM. It supports up to 480i resolution.

Mini-DIN 6

The **mini-DIN 6 connector**, most commonly used for PS/2 mouse and keyboard connections, is also used to provide power, audio data, and video data connections for surveillance cameras. Cabling is available up to 300 feet in length.

Component

Some data projectors and virtually all HDTVs support a high-resolution type of analog video known as **component video**. Component video uses separate RCA cables and ports to carry red, green, and blue signals (**RGB**), and can support up to 720p or 1080i HDTV resolutions.

The maximum length of component cable varies with construction quality; some high-quality cables can work reliably in excess of 100 feet. Component video does not support HDCP or other types of DRM.

Figure 8-25 compares component, composite, and S-video cables. Figure 8-26 illustrates component, composite, and other connections on the rear of a typical surround-sound home theater receiver with video pass-through.

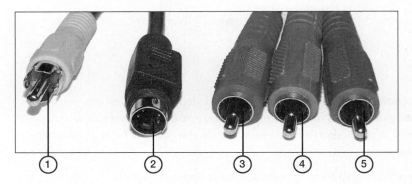

1. Composite cable (yellow)
2. S-video cable
3. Component cable (red)
4. Component cable (green)
5. Component cable (blue)

Figure 8-25   Composite, S-video, and component cables.

1. Component video connectors
2. Composite video connectors
3. HDMI A/V connectors

Figure 8-26   Component, composite, and other A/V connections.

BNC Coaxial

A single-connection **BNC coaxial** cable can be used for composite video.

A 5BNC cable transmits red (red cable/connector), green (green cable/connector), blue (blue cable/connector), horizontal sync (black, gray, or yellow cable/connector), and vertical sync (white cable/connector) signals. A 5BNC cable can be used for component video or, with an adapter, VGA video. Some data projectors use the 5BNC connector.

BNC cables have an impedance of 75Ohms, carry analog signals, and do not support HDCP or other types of DRM. 5BNC cables are available in lengths up to 100 feet, and single-connection BNC cables are available in lengths up to 300 feet.

Figure 8-27 illustrates a typical 5BNC cable adapter to VGA.

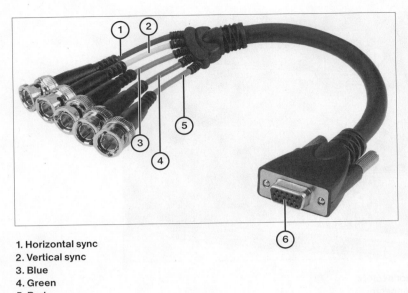

1. Horizontal sync
2. Vertical sync
3. Blue
4. Green
5. Red
6. VGA connector

Figure 8-27   A typical DB15 (VGA) to 5BNC adapter.

Video Adapters and Converters

With so many different types of video connections in use today, it's not always possible to match displays to video card or integrated video connector types. Because different types of physical connectors use the same signaling methods, adapters enable displays and video cards with different connectors to work together.

Thunderbolt to DVI

Because Thunderbolt supports mini-DisplayPort and uses the same physical connector, a mini DisplayPort to DVI adapter, such as the one shown in Figure 8-28, will also work to enable DVI displays to connect to Thunderbolt ports.

HDMI to VGA

As you learned earlier in this chapter, HDMI is a digital video connection, while VGA is an analog video connection. Although some vendors sell simple HDMI to VGA adapter cables, these often do not work due to a lack of power in the HDMI port on some laptops. Look for an adapter that has a USB or AC adapter power source to assure more reliable connections.

DVI to HDMI

Because HDMI uses the same video signals as DVI, DVI to HDMI cables or adapters are widely available.

DVI-I to VGA

DVI-I includes both VGA-compatible analog video and DVI digital video. The DVI-I to VGA adapters shown in Figures 8-28 and 8-29 enable VGA displays to work with DVI-I ports on video cards.

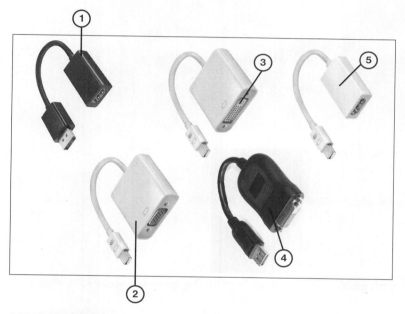

1. DisplayPort to HDMI
2. Mini-DisplayPort to VGA
3. Mini-DisplayPort to DVI-I
4. DisplayPort to DVI-D
5. Mini-DisplayPort to HDMI

Figure 8-28   Adapters for mini-DisplayPort and DisplayPort to other display types.

1. DVI-I dual-link
2. VGA (DB15)
3. DVI-I single-link

Figure 8-29   Single-link and dual-link DVI-I to VGA adapters.

Audio

Motherboards with built-in audio always have analog jacks and some have digital ports as well.

Analog

The 1/8-inch (3.5mm) **audio mini-jack** (also known as the TRS jack) is used by sound cards and motherboard-integrated sound for speakers, microphone, and line-in jacks, as shown in Figures 8-1 and 8-2.

To avoid confusion, most recent systems and sound cards use the PC Design Guide PC 2001 color coding listed as follows:

- **Pink**—Microphone in

- **Light blue**—Line in

- **Lime green**—Stereo/headphone out

- **Brown**—Left-to-right speaker
- **Black**—Rear stereo output
- **Gray**—Side stereo output
- **Orange**—Subwoofer

The recommended maximum length for these cables is 10 meters.

Figure 8-30 illustrates microphone in, line-in, and stereo/headphone out cables and a typical motherboard's integrated audio jacks.

1. Line-in mini-jack
2. Line-in cable
3. Stereo/headset out mini-jack
4. Stereo/headset cable
5. Microphone-in mini-jack
6. Microphone-in cable

Figure 8-30   Typical onboard audio mini-jacks and matching audio cables.

Analog audio can connect to receivers and is used in gaming. However, for digital output (such as from a DVD or Blu-ray), you need digital audio. HDMI carries both digital video and audio, but for situations in which HDMI cannot be used (for example, with a receiver lacking HDMI inputs), you can use SPDIF digital output (refer to Figure 8-1, p.254, for typical examples).

SPDIF (Digital)

Many systems include both analog audio (delivered through 1/8-inch/3.5mm audio mini-jacks) and digital audio (refer to Figures 8-1 and 8-2). Sony/Philips Digital Interconnect Format (**SPDIF**, sometimes spelled S/PDIF) ports output digital audio signals to amplifiers, such as those used in home theater systems, and come in two forms: optical and coaxial.

Optical SPDIF uses a fiber-optic cable, whereas coaxial SPDIF uses a shielded cable with an RCA connector. The cables are shown in Figure 8-31.

> **TIP** By default, systems with both analog and digital output use analog output. To enable digital output, use the Hardware and Sound dialog in Windows Control Panel or the proprietary mixer provided with some sound cards or onboard audio devices.

Figure 8-31   SPDIF optical (top) and coaxial (bottom) cables.

Sound cards might incorporate SPDIF ports into the card (see Figure 8-32) or into drive bay or external extension modules.

SPDIF digital audio ports support compressed and encrypted audio from sources such as DVD and Blu-ray movies.

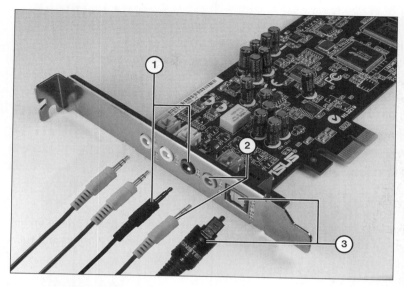

1. Rear audio mini-jack and cable
2. Subwoofer mini-jack and cable
3. SPDIF optical port and cable

Figure 8-32   A PCIe sound card with support for 5.1 analog surround sound and an optical SPDIF output.

PS/2

Although the PS/2 port is identified as a legacy port, it continues to be used for keyboards and mice in many recent systems, as shown previously in Figures 8-1 and 8-2. Unlike USB and FireWire, PS/2 ports do not support hot-swapping: you must shut down the system before connecting or removing a PS/2 device. PS/2 is sometimes referred to as Mini-DIN 6.

PS/2 Keyboard Port

When two PS/2 ports are stacked in a port cluster, the PS/2 keyboard port is the lower port and uses a purple connector.

PS/2 Mouse Port

When two PS/2 ports are stacked in a port cluster, the PS/2 mouse port is the upper port, and uses a green connector.

PS/2 Combo Port

Many systems have only a single PS/2 port, which might function as only a keyboard port, or might be marked half purple and half green, which indicates it can be used for either a mouse or keyboard. Refer to Figures 8-1 and 8-2 for examples of PS/2 keyboard, mouse, and combo ports. Refer to Figure 8-10 for examples of PS/2 connectors incorporated into USB to PS/2 adapters.

Exam Preparation Tasks

Review All the Key Topics

Review the most important topics in the chapter, noted with the Key Topic icon in the outer margin of the page. Table 8-6 lists a reference of these key topics and the page numbers on which each is found.

Table 8-16   Key Topics for Chapter 8

Key Topic Element	Description	Page Number
Figure 8-1	Rear-panel port clusters	254
Table 8-1	USB Standards	258
Figure 8-5	USB 1.1/2.0 plugs and sockets	259
Firewire 400	400Mbps IEEE-1394 interface used for DV camcorders and some high-speed printers and scanners	265
Figure 8-12	A typical FireWire 400 host adapter card with three external ports and one internal port.	265
Figure 8-13	FireWire 400 and 800 cable connections compared	267
Table 8-3	SATA and eSATA Driver Interface Overview	267
Figure 8-20	DB15M/F connectors used for VGA cables and ports	275
Figure 8-21	DVI-I port (supports all DVI types) and DVI-D (digital only) cable	276
Figure 8-23	HDMI, DVI, and DisplayPort Cables	277

Complete the Tables and Lists from Memory

Print a copy of Appendix C, "Memory Tables" (found on the CD), or at least the section for this chapter, and complete the tables and lists from memory. Appendix D, "Answers to Memory Tables," also on the CD, includes completed tables and lists to check your work.

Define Key Terms

Define the following key terms from this chapter, and check your answers in the glossary.

USB 1.1, USB 2.0, USB 3.0, Type A, Type B, USB Type C, USB connector type mini, USB connector type micro, Firewire 400, Firewire 800, SATA1, SATA2, SATA3, eSATA, VGA, High-Definition Multimedia Interface (HDMI) HDMI, DVI, Audio, Analog, Digital (Optical connector), Thunderbolt, Digital, DVI-D, DVI-I, DVI-A, DisplayPort, RCA connector, HD15 (that is, DE15 or DB15), mini-HDMI, mini-Din6 connector, Component video, Composite video, BNC coaxial, SATA, USB, Firewire (IEEE1394), PS/2, SPDIF, Hi-Speed USB, SuperSpeed USB, SuperSpeed+ USB, bus-powered hub, self-powered hub, USB 3.1 Gen 1, USB 3.1 Gen 2, USB-on-the-Go, generic hubs, header cables, AHCI mode, SVGA, RGB, audio mini-jack

Complete Hands-On Labs

Complete the hands-on labs, and then see the answers and explanations at the end of the chapter.

Lab 8-1: Evaluating Port Types and Performance

Examine a computer to learn the following:

- The number of USB 2.0 ports, USB 3.0 ports, and SATA ports.

- Determine whether the SATA ports support SATA 6Gbps, 3Gbps, 1.5Gbps, or if some support the fastest speed, and some a slower maximum speed.

- Determine if the computer supports 5.1 or 7.1 surround audio or digital audio playback.

Use a combination of color-coding and the motherboard or system documentation to identify the ports.

Lab 8-2: Display Connections

Examine a computer to learn the following:

- The number of DVI, HDMI, VGA, and DisplayPort ports. Are the HDMI and DisplayPort ports full-size or are they mini-size?

- Are the ports built into the port cluster or are they on a video card (or cards)?

Assume that you need to connect the computer to the following types of displays:

- A legacy display with a VGA port

- A data projector with an HDMI port

- A display with a DVI-D port

- A display with a DisplayPort port

Determine whether you can connect the computer directly to each port type or if an adapter would be necessary. If an adapter would be necessary, which type of adapter is needed?

Keep in mind that for purposes of this lab we assume that each display has only a single port type. In reality, most displays and projectors have at least two port types that can be selected from an on-screen display.

Answer Review Questions

1. Identify the ports on the ATX motherboard in the following figure. (Note: You may need to use an answer more than one time.)

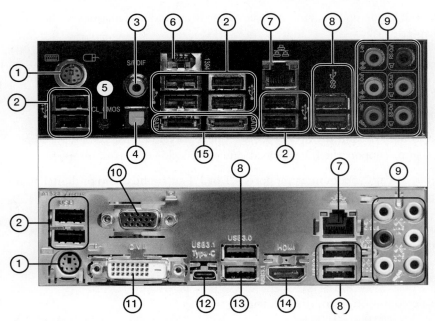

A. FireWire port	**F.** SPDIF coaxial port
B. eSATA ports	**G.** SPDIF optical port
C. Ethernet port	**H.** PS/2 mouse and keyboard ports
D. USB 2.0 ports	**I.** Audio jacks
E. USB 3.0 ports	

2. Which of the following describes a USB 3.0 port? (Choose two.)
   A. Runs at a maximum speed of 365Mbps
   B. Runs at a maximum speed of 480Mbps
   C. Runs at a maximum speed of 3.2Gbps
   D. Runs at a maximum speed of 5Gbps
   E. Usually color-coded blue
   F. Usually color-coded yellow
   G. Usually color-coded pink or red

3. Identify the connectors in the following figure.

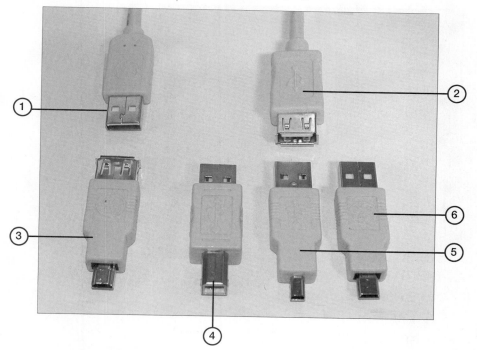

   A. USB Mini-AB
   B. USB Mini-B five-pin
   C. USB Type A Male
   D. USB Type A Female
   E. USB Type B
   F. USB Mini-B four pin.

4. Your client wants to replace an SATA1 hard disk drive with an SATA3 SSD. Which of the following statements are correct?

   A. SATA1 and SATA3 have the same transfer rate.

   B. SATA3 has a 3Gbps transfer rate.

   C. SATA3 has a 6Gbps transfer rate.

   D. SATA3 cables are recommended for all SATA speeds.

   E. SATA3 cables cannot be used with SATA1 or SATA2 drives.

   F. SATA1 has a 1.5Gbps transfer rate.

5. Identify the type of port indicated on the motherboard in the following figure.

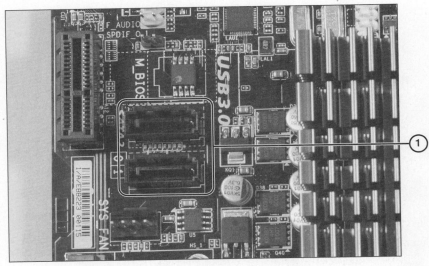

   A. HDMI

   B. SATA

   C. USB 3.0

   D. DVI

6. Which of the following options corresponds to the connector types in the figure?

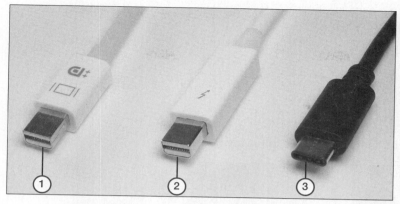

A. HDMI

B. SATA

C. DVI

D. Thunderbolt 1/2

E. Mini-DisplayPort +

F. USB 2.0

G. USB 3.0

H. USB Type-C

7. The following figure shows two typical PCIe video cards with a variety of ports. Which port carries a digital video signal only?

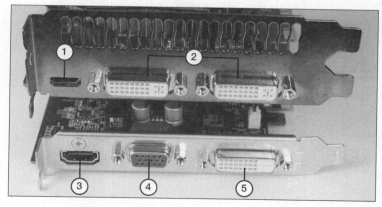

A. 1

B. 2

C. 3

D. 4

E. 5

8. Which of the following transmits both digital video and digital audio signals using a single cable?

   A. DVI-I

   B. VGA

   C. DVI-D

   D. HDMI

9. Identify the connectors in the following figure.

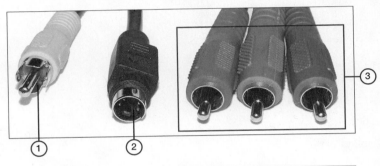

   A. 5BNC

   B. Composite

   C. Component

   D. S-video

10. Which of the following produces the best color?

    A. Component video

    B. Composite video

    C. S-video

11. Identify the adapters in the following figure.

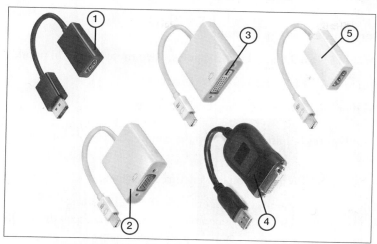

   A. Mini DisplayPort to DVI-I

   B. DisplayPort to HDMI

   C. Mini DisplayPort VGA

   D. Mini DisplayPort HDMI

   E. DisplayPort to DVI-D

12. Identify the connectors and jacks in the following figure.

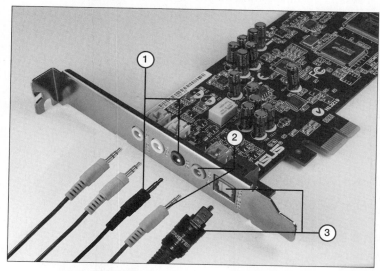

   A. HDMI   **D.** Keyboard

   B. SPDIF coaxial   **E.** SPDIF optical

   C. Microphone   **F.** Headphones

Answers and Explanations for Hands-On Labs

Lab 8-1: Evaluating Port Types and Performance

To answer questions about USB 2.0 and USB 3.0 ports, keep these factors in mind:

- Some older systems might have no USB 3.0 ports at all.
- Recent systems typically have two or four USB 3.0 ports.

Use the illustrations in Figures 8-1 and 8-2 to help determine the answer for the system(s) you examine.

To answer questions about SATA ports, you can try three methods:

- If you can safely open the system, you can examine the SATA ports. Sometimes they are marked with their maximum speed. If not, check the BIOS settings or the motherboard/system manual for this information.
- If you cannot open the system but you can run the BIOS setup program, use the BIOS setup program to identify the number and speeds of the SATA ports on-board. During startup, look for messages about a RAID adapter. Some systems use a separate RAID host adapter chip as well as the built-in SATA support in the chipset.
- If you cannot open the system or run the BIOS setup program, check the motherboard or system documentation for the number and speeds of SATA ports, including RAID ports.

Use Figures 8-14 and 8-15 to identify the SATA ports on a system.

To answer questions about audio ports, remember to check the following:

- Almost all systems have support for stereo audio. Systems with more than three audio mini-jacks support 5.1 or 7.1 surround audio (check the color-coding).
- HDMI ports are A/V ports that carry both digital video and digital audio.
- Some systems have both HDMI ports and SPDIF ports.
- SPDIF ports can be coaxial or optical, and some systems have both types.

Use Figures 8-1, 8-2, 8-23, 8-24, 8-30, 8-31, and 8-32 to determine the type(s) of audio support on your system.

Lab 8-2: Display Connections

As you evaluate systems, count all of the ports in every port type but keep in mind that video cards with two-slot brackets, such as the ones shown in Figures 8-23 and 8-24, typically support one or two displays, even if more ports are available.

Systems with HDMI or DisplayPort ports built into the port cluster usually have full-size HDMI and DisplayPort ports, such as in Figures 8-1 and 8-2. However, some video cards might use mini versions of these ports, such as the video cards shown in Figure 8-23.

Systems with onboard video (such as the ones shown in Figure 8-1 and 8-2) have some video ports built into the port cluster. However, such a system might also have one or more video cards like the ones shown in Figures 8-23 and 8-24. Depending on the video support built into the CPU, it might be possible to use a video card along with one of the built-in video ports for dual-display operations or faster 3D rendering.

Displays using DisplayPort are not as common as displays or projectors using the other port types, but adapters are readily available.

Answers and Explanations to Review Questions

1. **A.** FireWire port (6), **B.** eSATA ports (15), **C.** Ethernet port (7), **D.** USB 2.0 ports (2), **E.** USB 3.0 ports (8), **F.** SPDIF coaxial port (3), **G.** SPDIF optical port (4), **H.** PS/2 mouse and keyboard ports (1), **I.** Audio jacks (9)

2. **D, E.** USB 3.0 runs at a maximum of 5Gbps and is usually color coded blue. USB 2.0 runs at a maximum of 480Mbps. USB 1.1 runs at a maximum of 12Mbps. USB 2.0 and 1.1 are not color coded.

3. **C**; 2. D; 3. B; 4. E; 5. F; 6. A.

4. **C, D,** and **F.** SATA3 runs at 6Gbps. Cables designed for SATA3 also work with slower versions of SATA. SATA1, the original version of SATA, runs at 1.5Gbps.

5. **A.** The ports in the figure are SATA.

6.

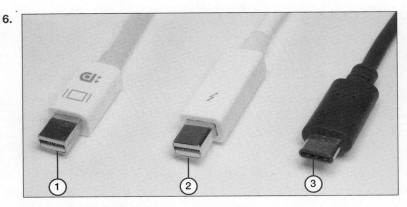

1. E Mini-DisplayPort+ cable
2. H Thunderbolt 1/Thunderbolt 2 cable
3. USB Type C – Thunderbolt 3 cable

7. **E.** Mini-HDMI (1) and HDMI (3) carry digital A/V signals but can be adapted to VGA (analog) video). DVI-I (2) carries digital video signals but can be adapted to VGA (analog) video. VGA (4) carries analog video only. DVI-D (5) carries only digital video only.

8. **D.** HDMI transmits digital audio and digital video signals through the same cable. DVI-I can transmit both digital and analog video signals. DVI-D supports only digital video signals. VGA supports only analog video signals.

9. **A.** 5BNC (4), **B.** Composite (1), **C.** Component (3), **D.** S-video (2)

10. **A.** Component video splits the signal into three channels (red, green and blue), supports some HD signals, and provides the best picture quality of the three.

11. 1. B; 2. C; 3. A; 4. E; 5. D.

12. 1. C; 2. F; 3. E.

This chapter covers the following subjects:

- **Custom PC Configurations**—This section discusses the eight custom configurations in the 220-901 objectives and provides specific product recommendations to help you build them.

- **Evaluating Onboard Components**—Learn how to find out what's "under the hood" of an existing system you're considering as a candidate for customizing or upgrading.

- **Installing Power Supplies**—High-performance systems demand high-performance power supplies, and this section shows you how to evaluate, select, and install power supplies.

- **Installing and Configuring Input, Output, and I/O Devices**—From mice to camcorders, learn how to connect and configure popular devices for computers and home theater systems.

- **Display Types and Features**—Choosing the right display or projector technology is the finishing touch on a custom PC configuration. Discover the options in this section.

- **Video Display Settings and Features**—From resolution to refresh rates, learn how to tweak a display for best appearance, reduce glare, and protect the user's privacy.

## CHAPTER 9

Designing and Building Custom PC Configurations

Either as new builds or as upgrades to existing computers, chances are you'll be working on custom PC configurations for some of your clients. From choosing the right motherboard, CPU, and memory size to selecting the right peripherals, power supply, and display, desktop computers offer an amazing variety of options, and this chapter is devoted to helping you master them.

220-901: Objective 1.8 Install a power supply based on given specifications.

220-901: Objective 1.9 Given a scenario, select the appropriate components for a custom PC configuration to meet customer specifications or needs.

220-901: Objective 1.10 Compare and contrast types of display devices and their features.

220-901: Objective 1.12 Install and configure common peripheral devices

Foundation Topics

Custom PC Configurations

Part of your responsibilities as a PC technician might be to evaluate and select appropriate components for a custom system configuration to better meet the needs or specifications of your client or customer. You might need to custom-build a system or upgrade a system to meet those requirements.

The A+ 220-901 exam objectives provide guidelines for eight configurations for graphics, A/V editing, virtualization, gaming, home theater, thick and thin clients, and home servers. In the following sections, we discuss the specific requirements of each type of system and guidelines for building or upgrading a system to meet them.

Graphic / CAD / CAM Design Workstation

A workstation optimized for graphics or CAD/CAM (computer-aided drafting/computer-aided manufacturing) design needs the maximum performance available at the time of purchase. Because of the heavy demands that 3D CAD rendering or RAW photo editing place on the workstation, there is no place for cost-cutting when equipping this system. Don't be surprised if the total cost of a new workstation optimized for these tasks rivals that of a server. Table 9-1 lists the major features needed for this type of computer along with examples and notes.

Table 9-1   Graphic/CAD/CAM Design Workstation Features

Features	Benefits	Recommendations and Example Products	Notes
Multicore processor	Fast rendering of 3D or 2D graphics	4.0GHz or faster, six cores or more, large cache (8MB or more total cache), 64-bit support	Fastest multicore CPUs available from Intel or AMD.
		Intel Core i7 Extreme Edition, Core i7 "Haswell-E" or "Skylake"	
		AMD FX-9000 series	

Features	Benefits	Recommendations and Example Products	Notes
High-end video	Faster rendering of 3D or 2D graphics on applications that support GPU acceleration (AutoCAD, Photoshop CC, and others)	PCIe CAD/CAM or 3D cards with 2GB or more RAM optimized for OpenGL 4.x, DirectX 11 or 12, support for two or more displays AMD FirePro W-series (CAD, CAM, CGI, Photoshop) AMD Radeon R9 (Photoshop) NVIDIA Quadro M series (CAD, CAM, CGI) NVIDIA GeForce GTX 980 Ti, TITAN Z, TITAN X (Photoshop) NVIDIA Tegra (CAD, CAM, CGI, Photoshop)	Fastest GPUs available from AMD or NVIDIA. More GPU RAM provides faster performance when rendering large 3D objects. FirePro and Quadro cards use drivers optimized for CAD/CAM/CGI.
Maximum RAM	Reduces swapping to disk during editing or rendering	16GB or more DDR3 or DDR4 Use matched memory modules running in multi-channel configurations	System should be running 64-bit version of the operating system

Although the A+ 220-901 exam objectives do not recommend specific motherboard configurations for these custom PC configurations, you should specify systems with adequate support for high-performance memory, processors, and video for the Graphic/CAD/CAM design workstation or Audio/Video editing workstation. A typical high-performance motherboard suitable as a foundation for these configurations is shown in Figure 9-1.

1. M.2 SSD
2. DDR4 memory sockets
3. PCIe video card slots for NVIDIA SLI or AMD CrossFire

Figure 9-1 This high-performance system features a fast SSD using the M.2 form factor, DDR4 memory, and three PCIe video card slots.

Audio/Video Editing Workstation

An audio/video editing workstation has many component features in common with the Graphic/CAD/CAM Design Workstation detailed in the previous section. In fact, the recommendations in Table 9-2 for hard drives and displays are suitable for either type of workstation, and the CPU suggestions in Table 9-1 are also suitable for this type of workstation. Table 9-2 lists the major features needed for this type of computer and why they're important.

Table 9-2 Audio/Video Editing Workstation Features

Features	Benefits	Recommendations	Notes
Multicore processor	Fast rendering of 3D or 2D graphics	4.0GHz or faster, six cores or more, large cache (8MB or more total cache), 64-bit support Intel Core i7 Extreme Edition, Core i7 "Haswell-E" AMD FX-9000 series	Fastest multicore CPUs available from Intel or AMD.

Features	Benefits	Recommendations	Notes
Maximum RAM	Reduces swapping to disk during editing or rendering	16GB or more DDR3 or DDR4 Use matched memory modules running in multi-channel configurations	
Specialized audio card	Higher sampling rates and higher signal-to-noise ratios for better audio quality	24-bit, 192kHz or better audio performance; upgradable Op-amp (operational amplifier,) sockets; PCIe interface Sound Blaster ZxR ASUS Essence STX II, Xonar H6, Essence ST, Essence STX	PCIe interface is preferred because it is faster than PCI. Upgradable Op-amp sockets allow customization of audio characteristics.
Specialized video card	Faster performance when rendering video	AMD FirePro W-series, AMD Radeon R9 NVIDIA Quadro M series, NVIDIA GeForce GTX 980 Ti, TITAN Z (see Figure 9-2), TITAN X, NVIDIA Tegra	Fastest GPUs on market. HDMI, DisplayPort, or DVI interfaces.
Large, fast hard drive	Faster writes during saves, faster retrieval of source material during media editing and creation	Maximum performance: SATA Express or M.2 SSD drive (see Figure 9-1) Good performance: SSD SATA 6Gbps large enough for Windows and applications (128-512GB) and separate SATA 6Gbps or USB 3.0 data drive or SATA hybrid drive 4TB or larger SATA 6Gbps or USB 3.0 drives from Seagate, WD, Toshiba, HGTS	If an SSD is used as the main drive, use a fast hard disk drive or hybrid drive for temporary files.
Dual displays	Editing software menus and playback can be on separate screens Can render and edit while using secondary display for other applications	27-inch or larger from many vendors	HDMI or DisplayPort interfaces recommended; DVI acceptable; avoid VGA-only displays.

1. PCIe x16 slot
2. DVI-I port
3. DVI-D port
4. HDMI port
5. DisplayPort port
6. Dual-slot cooler

Figure 9-2   This high-performance video card uses the NVIDIA TITAN Z GPU and is suitable for video and photo editing and gaming. Photo courtesy Gigabyte.

Virtualization Workstation

A **virtualization** workstation is intended to be a host for two or more operating systems running at the same time in separate virtual machines (VMs). To ensure adequate resources for each VM, this configuration (see Table 9-3) emphasizes RAM and CPU components.

Table 9-3   Virtualization Workstation Features

Features	Benefits	Recommendations	Notes
Maximum RAM	By increasing RAM well above the recommended level for a system running a single operating system, you help ensure sufficient RAM for each VM in use.	16GB or more RAM (64-bit system)	Systems running 32-bit versions of Windows cannot use more than 4GB of RAM.

Features	Benefits	Recommendations	Notes
Maximum CPU cores	Multiple VMs use more execution threads than a single operating system, so a multicore CPU helps VMs perform better.	3.0GHz or faster, six cores or more, large cache (8MB or more total cache), 64-bit support Intel Core i7 Extreme Edition, Core i7 "Haswell-E" AMD FX-9000 series	Fastest and most powerful Intel or AMD CPU. System needs support for hardware-assisted virtualization in processor and BIOS/UEFI for best performance (see Figure 9-3).

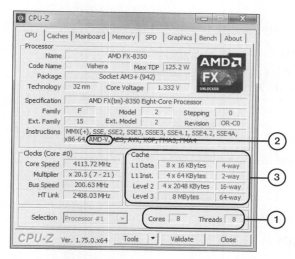

1. Processor cores
2. AMD-V virtualization support
3. Cache sizes

Figure 9-3   The AMD FX-8350 has eight processor cores, supports AMD-V (hardware-assisted virtualization) and has a large amount of L2 and L3 cache as reported by CPU-Z.

Gaming PC

A gaming PC's components are selected with just one objective in mind: provide the user with the computing firepower needed to defeat opponents as quickly as possible. The configuration covered in Table 9-4 is similar to others previously detailed but adds high-end cooling because these systems are frequently overclocked to enhance performance (at a cost in extra heat output).

Table 9-4   Gaming PC Features

Features	Benefits	Recommendations	Notes
Powerful processor	High performance for maximum frame rates, 3D rendering, and audio performance on games where CPU performance is most significant factor	4.0GHz or faster, six cores or more, large cache (8MB or more total cache), 64-bit support Intel Core i7 Extreme Edition, Core i7 "Haswell-E" AMD FX-9000 series	Although multicore CPUs are also the fastest CPUs available from Intel and AMD, many games are not yet optimized for multicore processors.
High-end video/ specialized GPU	High performance for maximum frame rates in 3D rendering where GPU performance is most significant factor	PCIe 3D cards with 2GB or more RAM optimized for OpenGL 4.x, DirectX 11, support for two or more displays with SLI (NVIDIA) or CrossFire (AMD) multi-GPU support AMD Radeon R9 NVIDIA GeForce GTX 980 Ti, TITAN Z, TITAN X	Fastest available GPUs available from AMD and NVIDIA.
Better sound card	5.1 or 7.1 surround audio for realistic, high-performance 3D audio rendering.	24-bit, 96kHz or better audio performance; PCIe interface; hardware acceleration Sound Blaster X-Fi Extreme Gamer Sound Blaster Recon3D series Sound Blaster Fatal1ty series ASUS Xonar DG Azuntech X-Fi Forte	PCIe sound cards provide faster performance than PCI sound cards. Connect to 5.1 or 7.1 surround audio speakers or headsets for 3D audio effects.
High-end cooling	Overclocking is common to reach highest system speeds; overclocked systems can overheat if OEM cooling is not supplemented or replaced by more powerful cooling solutions.	Heat-pipe-based CPU cooler for fan or liquid cooling (see Figure 9-4); heat sinks on RAM (see Figure 9-5); dual-slot video card with high-performance cooler; all optional fan bays on chassis equipped with fans. See www.FrostyTech.com for reviews of numerous heat-pipe CPU cooling products. See www.frozencpu.com for numerous cooling products for CPUs (liquid and heat-pipe), GPUs, and RAM modules.	Be sure to verify compatibility with CPU, clearance around CPU socket, and power requirements for a particular system.

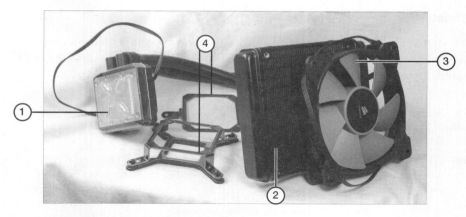

1. CPU water block with thermal material
2. Radiator
3. Cooling fan
4. Water block lockdown mechanisms

Figure 9-4   A high-performance CPU cooling system.

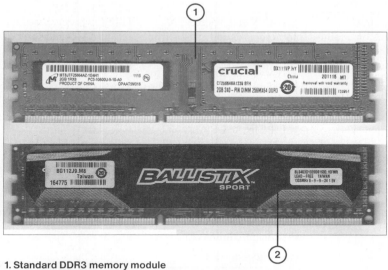

1. Standard DDR3 memory module
2. High-performance DDR3 with heat spreaders over RAM chips

Figure 9-5   A standard DDR3 desktop memory module compared to a high-performance DDR3 memory module with heat spreader.

Home Theater PC

The components in this section (see Table 9-5) emphasize compatibility with common home theater audio and video requirements that fit into the low-profile HTPC chassis designed to complement the rest of the home theater equipment.

Table 9-5   Home Theater PC Features

Features	Benefits	Recommendations	Notes
Surround sound audio	5.1 or 7.1 audio sound from home theater speaker system.	For older home theater amps: coax or optical SPDIF audio output. For home theater amps with HDMI: Verify that onboard or card-based audio can output to HDMI.	Adjust sound mixer settings in Windows to output to SPDIF or HDMI digital audio.
HDMI output	Connect digital A/V output to home theater and HDTV with a single cable.	Look for multiple HDMI ports on an HDTV to make connecting to multiple sources easier.	HDMI version 1.4 supports Ethernet as well as A/V.
HTPC compact form factor	Integrated A/V components on a mini-ITX or MicroATX motherboard form factor enable a small system in a horizontal chassis (see Figure 9-6).	Mini-ITX and MicroATX motherboards and chassis from many vendors. See www.htpc-reviews.com for specialized reviews and product recommendations.	HTPC systems based on recent AMD and Intel CPUs use processor-integrated graphics.
TV tuner	Watch digital broadcast (ATSC) and unencrypted digital cable TV (ClearQAM).	PCI, PCIe, or USB 3.0 or 2.0 (3.0 recommended) with support for digital TV. Major vendors: www.Hauppauge.com www.avermedia-usa.com www.diamondmm.com www.silicondust.com	For connection to encrypted cable TV, choose a TV tuner that supports CableCard.

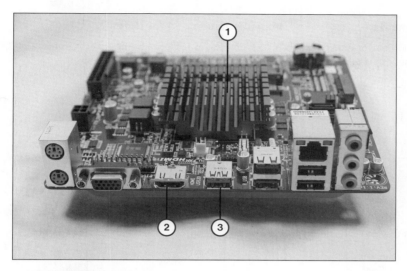

1. Heat sink over Intel processor
2. HDMI port
3. USB 3.0 port

Figure 9-6   This mini-ITX motherboard for home theater systems features an Intel processor with integrated graphics, HDMI A/V output, and a USB 3.0 port.

Standard Thick Client

Unlike the system configurations discussed earlier in this chapter, almost any computer you can purchase at a retail store qualifies as a standard **thick client**. The requirements are simple, as you can see from Table 9-6.

Table 9-6   Standard Thick Client Features

Features	Benefits	Implementation	Notes
Desktop applications	Perform a broad range of office procedures (word processing, spreadsheets, presentations, database, email, and calendaring)	Current versions of Microsoft Office, including PowerPoint and Access Current version of OpenOffice or Corel WordPerfect Office	For maximum compatibility with other office apps and data sources, install office apps with all options enabled.

Features	Benefits	Implementation	Notes
Meets recommended requirements for selected OS	Good performance with basic office tasks	Intel Core i3, i5, or i7, Pentium or AMD FX, A-series, Athlon X4 processors running at 2GHz or faster with 2GB of RAM (32-bit OS) or 4GB of RAM (64-bit OS)	Some older systems might require memory upgrades to meet recommended requirements.

Thin Client

A **thin client** is the most basic type of system configuration, as Table 9-7 indicates.

Table 9-7   Thin Client Features

Features	Benefits	Implementation	Notes
Basic applications	Perform basic office procedures (web browsing, word processing, spreadsheets)	Current version of Internet Explorer, Mozilla Firefox, Google Chrome, or other web browser Current versions of Microsoft Office Word and Excel or OpenOffice or WordPerfect Office	For maximum compatibility with other office apps and data sources, install office apps with all options enabled.
Meets minimum requirements for using selected OS	Runs OS at basic performance levels	Intel ATOM, Celeron or AMD E-series or Sempron processors running at 1GHz or faster with 2GB of RAM (32-bit OS) or 4GB of RAM (64-bit OS)	Some older systems might require memory upgrades to meet minimum requirements for desired OS.
Network connectivity	Fast network connection because server handles most computational tasks	Wired: Gigabit Ethernet or faster Wireless: Wireless-AC	Routers and switches must also support Gigabit Ethernet or Wireless-AC standards.

Home Server PC

A **home server** PC configuration is designed to permit resource sharing, media streaming, and high-speed data retrieval from online or local storage, as detailed in Table 9-8.

Table 9-8 Home Server PC Features

Features	Benefits	Implementation	Notes
Media streaming	Enables media playback on connected systems even if normal file sharing is not enabled	Windows: Configured through Network and Sharing Center Use third-party apps on OS X or Linux	Enable UPnP on routers and devices to enable media streaming.
File sharing	Enables file read or read/write access across the network	Windows: Configured through Share with or Sharing tab on folders; must enable File and Printer sharing through Network and Sharing Center OS X: Configured through Sharing pane in System Preferences using SMB Linux: Install Samba and enable local network sharing with your distribution's file manager	With Windows 7/8/8.1(10), use HomeGroup for easiest configuration if all computers or network have Windows 7 or newer. HomeGroup can coexist with normal file sharing.
Print sharing	Enables printing from any computer on the network	Windows: Configured through Sharing tab on printer properties sheet; must enable File and Printer sharing through Network and Sharing Center; install Samba for sharing with OS X and Linux OS X and Linux: Use Bonjour protocol; use Samba to access Windows printers Linux: Make sure shared printers are published to the system	With Windows 7/8/8.1(10), use HomeGroup for easiest configuration when all computers or network have Windows 7 or newer.

Features	Benefits	Implementation	Notes
Gigabit NIC	Data transfer between computers or computer and router up to 10x faster than with Fast Ethernet NIC	Integrated into many recent systems or available as low-cost add-on card for PCIe x1 or ExpressCard slots; systems with USB 3.0 and USB 3.1 ports can use adapters to connect to Gigabit Ethernet	Router or switch in network must support Gigabit Ethernet.
RAID Array	Faster boot times (RAID 0), protection against failure of one drive (RAID 1), or both (RAID 10)	Use two or four drives with same capacity and configure using BIOS RAID Manager	Install latest storage drivers for motherboard chipset.

Evaluating Onboard Components

From Tables 9-1 to 9-8, you can see that a PC can be customized in many different ways during initial build and setup. However, if you need to upgrade an existing system to optimize it for a particular task, it's important to know what components are already installed. The following methods, Windows features, and third-party utilities can help you find out what's "under the hood" of an existing system.

General System Information

- **BIOS/UEFI setup**—Some systems display information about installed hardware during startup, and you can also find out information such as RAID level, integrated ports, and other information by starting the BIOS setup program and moving through the screens. Be sure to discard changes when exiting.

- **System Information**—A built-in Windows utility (**MSInfo32.exe**) that reports processor type and speed, BIOS/UEFI version and date, operating system information, memory size, components (including multimedia), and software environment. Report can be saved, printed, and searched. Use Run or Instant Desktop Search to start program.

- **Device Manager**—A built-in Windows utility that reports installed hard drives, USB ports, video cards, and other information. Available from System properties.

- **Belarc System Advisor**—A free (for personal use) ActiveX utility that displays hardware, software, and Windows security update information, including motherboard information. Available from www.belarc.com. See Figure 9-7 for a portion of a typical report.

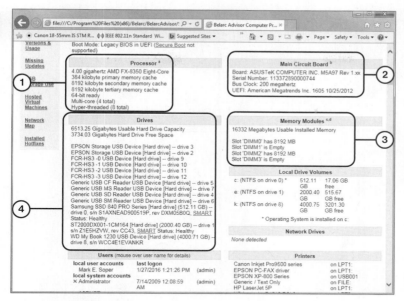

1. Processor information
2. Motherboard information
3. RAM (memory) information
4. Storage information

Figure 9-7   The hardware portion of the Belarc System Advisor report on the author's system provides details about the processor (CPU), motherboard, storage, and installed memory.

■ **SiSoftware Sandra**—Displays extensive information about system hardware including expansion slots, memory, processor details, and much more. Available evaluation and commercial editions from www.sisoftware.net (see Figure 9-8).

NOTE   For the most complete information about a system, use more than one reporting program.

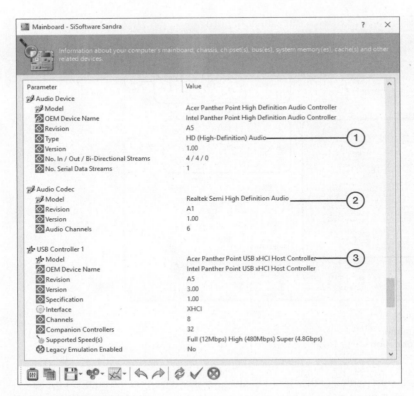

1. System supports HD audio
2. Realtek audio codec
3. USB 3.0 support

Figure 9-8   A portion of the SiSoftware Sandra Lite report on the mainboard (motherboard) displays detailed information about the SuperSpeed USB (USB 3.0) and audio controllers onboard.

Processor Information and Hardware-Assisted Virtualization Readiness

AMD, Intel, Microsoft, and third-party vendors provide various tools to help determine details about a processor, including whether a system supports hardware-assisted virtualization:

- **AMD Virtualization™ Technology and Microsoft® Hyper-V™ System Compatibility Check Utility**—Available from http://support.amd.com

- **CPU-Z**—Available from http://www.cpuid.com/

- **Intel Processor Identification Utility**—Available from www.intel.com

- **Microsoft Windows Hardware-Assisted Virtualization Detection Tool**— Available from the Download Center at www.microsoft.com

- **Gibson Research Corporations SecurAble**—Available from www.grc.com

TIP   Find direct links to these programs and a useful discussion at http://www.tech-norms.com/8208/check-if-processor-supports-virtualization.

For more information about processor virtualization, see "Client-Side Virtualization Overview," p.958, Chapter 19, "Virtualization, Cloud Computing, and Network Services."

Installing Power Supplies

Power supplies vary widely in features and ratings, and when building a custom configuration or updating a system to perform a specific task, the power supply is a critical factor in the success of that system.

The **power supply** is really misnamed: It is actually a power converter that changes high-voltage alternating current (**AC**) to low-voltage direct current (**DC**). There are lots of wire coils and other components inside the power supply that do the work, and during the conversion process, a great deal of heat is produced. Most power supplies include one or two fans to dissipate the heat created by the operation of the power supply; however, a few power supplies designed for silent operation use passive heat sink technology instead of fans. On power supplies that include fans, fans also help to cool the rest of the computer. Figure 9-9 shows a typical desktop computer's power supply.

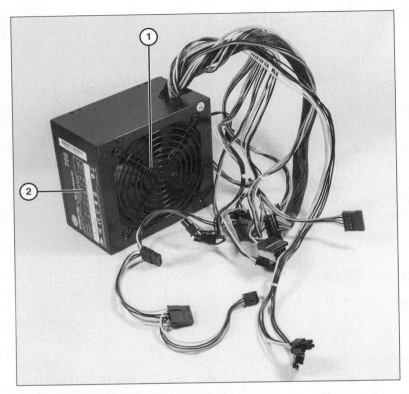

1. Power supply intake fan (faces into system)
2. Specification and safety information label

Figure 9-9   A typical ATX power supply.

Power Supply Ratings

Power supply capacity is rated in watts, and the more watts a power supply provides, the more devices it can safely power.

You can use the label attached to the power supply, shown in Figure 9-10, to determine its wattage rating and see important safety reminders.

A power supply with two separate +12V rails is a **dual rail** design. Some high-performance power supplies feature more than two +12V outputs, such as the 650-watt model shown in Figure 9-10. Another term for two or more +12V outputs is split rail.

NOTE   Power supplies with two or more separate +12V power sources are common today to provide adequate power for CPUs (which use voltage regulators on the motherboard or in the CPU itself to reduce +12V power to the power level needed) and other devices such as PCIe video cards, fans, and drives). Add the values of each +12V rail together to get the total +12V output in amps.

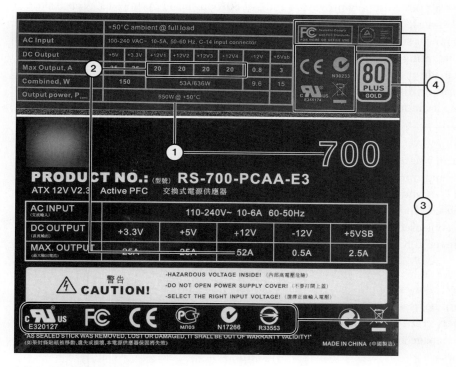

1. Rated maximum output (watts)
2. +12V amperage
3. Safety approvals
4. 80 PLUS Gold rating

Figure 9-10   Typical power supply labels. Many, but not all, power supplies now include some level of 80 PLUS certification.

Typically, power supplies in recent tower-case (upright case) machines use 500-watt or larger power supplies, reflecting the greater number of drives and cards that can be installed in these computers. Power supplies used in slimline desktop computers have typical ratings of around 220-300 watts. The power supply rating is found on the top or side of the power supply, along with safety rating information and amperage levels produced by the power supply's different DC outputs.

Wattage Versus Amperage

The power supply label shown at the top of Figure 9-10 is rated at 650 watts, while the power supply label shown at the bottom of Figure 9-10 is rated at 700 watts. Take a closer look at the amperage ratings, though, and it becomes clear that the 650-watt power supply provides much more of the +12V power needed by processors and motors.

The 650-watt power supply provides a total of 80A on the +12V lines (20A each on four +12V lines). The 700-watt power supply provides only 52A on its +12V line. The 700-watt power supply provides no information about the temperature or load factor at which its rating is calculated, while the 650-watt power supply indicates its calculations are made at 50 degrees Celsius (about 122 degrees Fahrenheit) at full load. Despite the rating difference, it's clear that the 650-watt power supply shown in Figure 9-10 provides more useful power than the 700-watt power supply in the same figure.

How can you tell whether a power supply meets minimum safety standards? Look for the appropriate safety certification mark for your country or locale. For example, in the U.S. and Canada, the backward UR logo is used to indicate the power supply has the UL and UL Canada safety certifications as a component (the familiar circled UL logo is used for finished products only). Both power supplies shown in Figure 9-10 meet U.S. and other nations' safety standards.

CAUTION Power supplies that do not bear the UL or other certification marks should not be used, as their safety is unknown. For a visual guide to electrical and other safety certification marks in use around the world, visit the Standard Certification Marks page at www.technick.net/public/code/cp_dpage.php?aiocp_dp=guide_safetymarks.

Use the following methods to determine the **wattage** rating needed for a replacement power supply:

- Whip out your calculator and add up the wattage ratings for everything connected to your computer that uses the power supply, including the motherboard, processor, memory, cards, drives, and bus-powered USB devices. If the total wattage used exceeds 70 percent of the wattage rating of your power supply, you should upgrade to a larger power supply. Check the vendor spec sheets for wattage ratings.

- If you have amperage ratings instead of wattage ratings, multiply the amperage by the volts to determine wattage and then start adding. If a device uses two or three different voltage levels, be sure to carry out this calculation for each voltage level and add up the figures to determine the wattage requirement for the device. Review Figure 9-10 and the "Wattage Versus Amperage" sidebar earlier in this chapter for a reminder of the importance of +12V amperage.

- Use an interactive power supply sizing tool, such as the calculators provided by eXtreme Outervision (www.extreme.outervision.com) or MSI (https://us.msi.com/power-supply-calculator/).

Table 9-9 provides calculations for typical compact desktop and high-performance desktop systems, based on the eXtreme Outervision online calculator.

Table 9-9 Calculating Power Supply Requirements

Components	MicroATX System with Integrated Video	Full-Size ATX System with SLI (Dual Graphics Cards)
CPU	AMD A8-7650K (4 core, 3.3GHz with 4MB cache)	Intel Core i7-5930K (6 core, 3.7GHz with 15MB cache)
RAM Size/Type	2 x 4GB DDR3	2 x 8GB DDR4
Rewritable DVD drive	Yes	Yes
Blu-ray	No	Yes
SATA hard disk	5400 RPM	7200 RPM
SSD	No	M.2
Case fans	2 x 120mm	2 x 140mm
Liquid cooling	No	Corsair Hydro H75
GPU	Integrated into CPU	NVIDIA GeForce GTX TITAN Z SLI
PCIe card	0	High-end sound card TV Tuner (cable) card
USB 2.0 device	1	2
Estimated wattage	224 Watts	1239 Watts
Recommended power supply size (80 percent efficiency assumed)	400 Watts	1600 Watts

NOTE The 80 PLUS certification standard is an industry standard for evaluating power supply efficiency. 80 PLUS certified power supplies achieve 80 percent efficiency at up to 100 percent of rated load. The use of power supplies with 80 PLUS certification is assumed in Table 9-9. Higher standards (80 PLUS Bronze, Silver, Gold, and Platinum) achieve up to 89 percent efficiency at 100 percent of rated load on 115V power and up to 91 percent on 230V power. For more information, see the Ecova Plug Load Solutions website at http://www.plugloadsolutions.com/. For non-80 PLUS power supplies, assume 70 percent efficiency.

Multivoltage Power Supplies

Most power supplies are designed to handle two different voltage ranges:

- 110–120V/60Hz
- 220–240V/50Hz

Power supplies that support these ranges are known as **dual voltage** power supplies. Standard North American power is now 115–120V/60Hz-cycle AC (the previous standard was 110V). The power used in European and Asian countries is typically 230–240V/50Hz AC (previously 220V).

Some older power supplies have a slider switch with two markings: 115 (for North American 110–120V/60HzAC) and 230 (for European and Asian 220–240V/50Hz AC). Figure 9-11 shows a slider switch set for correct North American voltage. If a power supply is set to the wrong input voltage, the system will not work. Setting a power supply for 230V with 110–120V current is harmless; however, feeding 220–240V into a power supply set for 115V will destroy the power supply and possibly other onboard hardware.

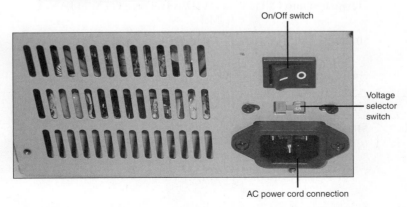

Figure 9-11 An older power supply's sliding voltage switch set for correct North American voltage (115V). Slide it to 230V for use in Europe and Asia.

NOTE   Note that most recent power supplies for desktop and notebook computers can automatically determine the correct voltage level and cycle rate. These are referred to as autoswitching power supplies and lack the voltage/cycle selection switch shown in Figure 9-11.

The on/off switch shown in Figure 9-11 controls the flow of current into the power supply. It is not the system power switch, which is located on the front or top of desktop systems and is connected to the motherboard. When you press the system power switch, the motherboard signals the power supply to provide power.

CAUTION   Unless the power supply is disconnected from AC current or is turned off, a small amount of power can still be flowing through the system even when it is not running. Do not install or remove components or perform other types of service to the inside of a PC unless you disconnect the AC power cord or turn off the power supply. Wait a few seconds afterward to ensure that the power is completely off. Some desktop motherboards have indicator lights that turn off when the power has completely drained from the system.

Power Supply Form Factors and Connectors

When you shop for a power supply, you also need to make sure it can connect to your motherboard. There are two major types of power connectors on motherboards:

- **20-pin**, used by older motherboards in the ATX family

- **24-pin**, used by recent **ATX/microATX**/mini-ITX motherboards requiring the ATX12V 2.2 power supply standard

Some high-wattage power supplies with 20-pin connectors might also include a 20-pin to 24-pin adapter. Some 24-pin power supplies include a split connector to support either 24-pin or 20-pin motherboard power connectors (refer to Figure 9-13).

Most motherboards use power supplies that feature several additional connectors to supply added power, as follows (see Figure 9-12):

- The four-wire square ATX12V connector provides additional 12V power to the motherboard; this connector is sometimes referred to as a "P4" or "Pentium 4" connector.

- Most recent power supplies use the **4/8 pin +12V** (EPS12V) connector (see Figure 9-14) instead of the ATX12V power connector. The EPS12V lead is split into two four-wire square connectors to be compatible with motherboards that use either ATX12V or EPS12V power leads.

- Some very old motherboards use a six-wire AUX connector to provide additional power.

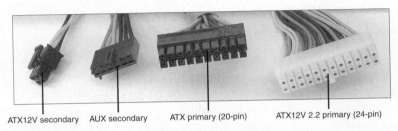

ATX12V secondary   AUX secondary   ATX primary (20-pin)   ATX12V 2.2 primary (24-pin)

Figure 9-12   20-pin ATX and 24-pin ATX power connectors compared to four-pin ATX12V and six-wire AUX power connectors.

Figure 9-13 shows both sides of a convertible 24-pin/20-pin ATX power supply connector. For a complete pinout, see Figure 13-12.

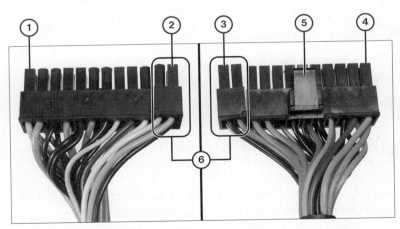

1. Pin 1 (+3.3V, orange wire)
2. Pin 12 (+3.3V, orange wire)
3. Pin 24 (ground wire, black)
4. Pin 13 (+3.3V, orange wire)
5. Retaining clip
6. Used only on motherboards that use a 24-pin ATX power supply

Figure 9-13   Both sides of a 24-pin ATX power supply cable (also compatible with 20-pin motherboards)

The power supply also powers various peripherals, such as the following:

- Older (PATA and early SATA) hard disks, CD and DVD optical drives, and case fans that do not plug into the motherboard use a 4-pin **Molex** power connector.

- 3.5-inch floppy drives use a 4-pin Berg power connector.

- Serial ATA (SATA) hard disks use an L-shaped 15-pin thinline power connector.

- High-performance PCI Express x16 video cards that require additional 12V power use a PCI Express 6-pin or 8-pin power cable (**PCIe 6/8-pin**).

Figure 9-14 illustrates these power connectors as well as the EPS12V motherboard power connector.

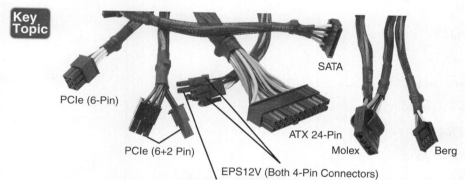

Figure 9-14   Power supply connectors for peripherals and modern motherboards.

Table 9-10 lists the power levels carried by each connector type.

Table 9-10   Power Levels by Connector Type

Connector	+5V	+12V	+3.3V	Notes
Molex	Y	Y	N	Used today primarily for case fans that do not connect to the motherboard or can be adapted to SATA drives
Berg	Y	Y	N	Used for floppy drives; some add-on cards use this connector for power
SATA	Y	Y	Opt	Use Molex to SATA power connector if power supply lacks adequate SATA connectors
PCIe 6-pin	N	Y	N	Mid-range PCIe video cards

Connector	+5V	+12V	+3.3V	Notes
PCIe 8-pin	N	Y	N	High-performance PCIe video cards
ATX12V	N	Y	N	Most recent and current motherboards except those using EPS12V
EPS12V	N	Y	N	Split into two ATX12V-compatible sections

If your power supply doesn't have enough connectors, you can add Y-splitters to divide one power lead into two, but these can short out and can also reduce your power supply's efficiency. You can also convert a standard Molex connector into an SATA or Berg floppy drive power connector with the appropriate adapter.

Standard power supply wires are color-coded thus:

Red: +5V

Yellow: +12V

Orange: +3.3V

Black: Ground (earth)

Purple: +5V (standby)

Green: PS-On

Gray: Power good

White: No connection (24-pin); -5V (20-pin)

Blue: -12V

Some power supplies (see Figure 9-15) use modular connections so that you can customize the power supply connections needed for your hardware.

CAUTION Many recent and older Dell desktop computers use proprietary versions of the 20-pin or 24-pin ATX power supply connectors. Dell's versions use a different pinout that routes voltages to different wires than in standard power supplies. Consequently, if you plug a standard power supply into a Dell PC that uses the proprietary version, or use a regular motherboard as an upgrade for a model that has the proprietary power supply, stand by for smoke and fire! You can look up your Dell computer model or power supply number at www.atxpowersupplies.com/power-supply-cross-reference.php to see whether you can use a standard or proprietary-pinout power supply.

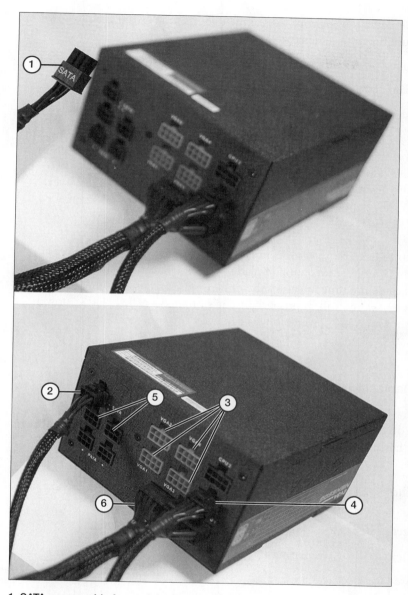

1. SATA power cable for modular power supply
2. SATA power cable after connection
3. PCIe power ports
4. EPS12V power cable
5. Additional SATA power ports
6. Motherboard main power cable

Figure 9-15   A modular power supply includes cables you can attach to customize support for your system's needs.

If your wattage calculations or your tests agree that it's time to replace the power supply, make sure the replacement meets the following criteria:

- Has the same power supply connectors and the same pinout as the original.

- Has the same form factor (shape, size, and switch location).

- Has the same or higher wattage rating; a higher wattage rating is highly desirable.

- Supports any special features required by your CPU, video card, and motherboard, such as SLI support (support for PCIe connectors to power two or more high-performance PCIe video cards), high levels of +12V power (ATX12V v2.2 4-pin or EPS12V 8-pin power connectors), and so on.

TIP   To ensure form factor connector compatibility, consider removing the old power supply and taking it with you if you plan to buy a replacement at retail. If you are buying a replacement online, measure the dimensions of your existing power supply to ensure that a new one will fit properly in the system. So-called "EPX" power supplies are longer than ATX power supplies, and won't fit into smaller cases.

Removing and Replacing the Power Supply

Installing a new power supply is one of the easier repairs to make. You don't need to fiddle with driver CDs or Windows Update to get the new one working. But, you do need to be fairly handy with a screwdriver or nut driver.

NOTE   Follow these recommendations to make power supply replacement as safe as possible:

- Disconnect power before repairing PC

- Remove jewelry before repairing PC

- Be prepared for electrical fires

- Wear safety goggles

NOTE   To learn more about these precautions, see "Personal Safety," p.891, Chapter 17, "Operational Procedures."

Typical power supplies are held in place by several screws that attach the power supply to the rear panel of the computer. The power supply also is supported by a shelf inside the case and screws can secure the power supply to that shelf. To remove a power supply, follow these steps:

Step 1.   Power down the computer. If the power supply has an on/off switch, turn it off as well.

Step 2.   Disconnect the AC power cord from the computer.

Step 3.   Open the case to expose the power supply, which might be as simple as removing the cover on a desktop unit, or as involved as removing both side panels, front bezel, and case lid on a tower PC. Consult the documentation that came with your computer to determine how to expose the power supply for removal.

Step 4.   Disconnect the existing power supply from the motherboard (see Figure 9-16). The catch securing the power supply connector must be released to permit the connector to be removed.

Step 5.   Disconnect all other power supply leads to the motherboard (fan monitors, ATX12V, EPS12V, AUX).

1. Push in until clip releases
2. Pull cable upwards
3. Clip
4. Empty socket

Figure 9-16 Disconnecting the power supply from the motherboard.

Step 6.   Disconnect the power supply from all drives and add-on cards (see Figure 9-17).

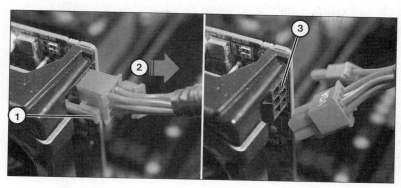

1. Press to release clip
2. Pull cable from PCIe power connector
3. Empty PCIe power connector

Figure 9-17   Disconnecting the power supply from a PCIe video card.

Step 7.   Disconnect the power supply from all fans.

Step 8.   Remove the power supply screws from the rear of the computer case (see Figure 9-18).

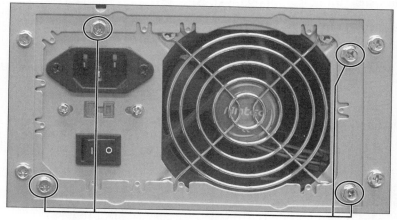

Mounting screws

Figure 9-18   Preparing to remove the mounting screws from a typical power supply.

Step 9.   Remove any screws holding the power supply in place inside the case. (Your PC might not use these additional screws.)

Step 10.   Lift or slide the power supply out of the case.

Before installing the replacement power supply, compare it to the original, making sure the form factor, motherboard power connectors, and switch position match the original. If the new power supply has a fan on top (as well as the typical rear-mounted fan), make sure the fan faces the inside of the case.

To install the replacement power supply, follow these steps:

Step 1.   Lift or slide the power supply into the case.

Step 2.   Attach the power supply to the shelf with screws (if required).

Step 3.   Slide the power supply to the rear of the computer case; line up the holes in the unit carefully with the holes in the outside of the case.

Step 4.   Connect the power supply to all fans, drives, add-on cards, and motherboard.

Step 5.   Check the voltage setting on the power supply. Change it to the correct voltage for your location if necessary.

Step 6.   Connect the AC power cord to the new power supply. Turn on the power supply

Step 7.   Start the computer.

Step 8.   Start the system normally to verify correct operation, and then run the normal shutdown procedure for the operating system. If necessary, turn off the system with the front power switch only.

Step 9.   Close the case and secure it.

Installing and Configuring Input, Output, and I/O Devices

Custom PC configurations might also require the installation of input, output, and I/O devices. The following sections discuss the installation processes for these devices.

NOTE   Printer installation is covered in Chapter 10. Video card installation is covered in Chapter 5. Video card connections to displays are covered in Chapter 8.

Mouse

Windows, OS X, and Linux include **mouse** (pointing device) drivers. To install a USB mouse, simply plug it in, and the operating system installs the drivers needed. Mice are part of the human interface device (HID) device category, and Windows installs HID drivers after the mouse is connected.

To install a wireless mouse, plug the receiver into a USB port and follow the directions to pair up the mouse and receiver. Receivers that can control multiple devices, such as Logitech's Unifying receiver, might require you to install additional software to enable pairing of multiple devices with a single receiver.

Mouse alternatives, such as touchscreens, trackballs, or touch pads, are considered mouse devices because they install and are configured the same way.

If a mouse has special buttons for gaming, install drivers for the mouse from the vendor. These can be installed after the mouse has been connected.

NOTE   Some systems running Windows and Linux have PS/2 mouse and/or keyboard ports. To install a PS/2 mouse or keyboard, be sure to shut down the system and remove power before connecting the mouse or keyboard. PS/2 devices, unlike USB devices, are not hot-swappable devices.

If the mouse uses Bluetooth, it needs to be paired with the computer's Bluetooth receiver.

Pairing a Bluetooth Mouse (Windows)

To pair a Bluetooth mouse computer from the desktop:

Step 1.   Click the **Bluetooth** icon in the taskbar.

Step 2.   Click or tap **Open Settings**.

Step 3.   Enable **Discovery**.

Step 4.   Enable **Allow Bluetooth Devices to Connect to This Computer** (see Figure 9-19).

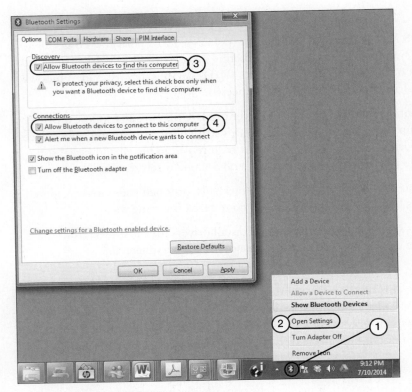

1. Click Bluetooth icon to start pairing process
2. Click to open Settings dialog.
3. Must be enabled to allow a new Bluetooth device to find this computer
4. Must be enabled to enable Bluetooth devices to connect to this computer

Figure 9-19   Enabling discovery and connections to Bluetooth devices.

Step 5.   Open the **Bluetooth** icon in the Taskbar and click or tap **Add a Device**.

Step 6.   Press the **Connect** button on the mouse.

Step 7.   Select the mouse from the list of Bluetooth devices and click **Next** (see Figure 9-20).

Step 8.   After the mouse is detected and the drivers have been installed, click **Close**.

Step 9.   To prevent connections from unauthorized Bluetooth devices, disable discovery until the next time you want to add a Bluetooth device.

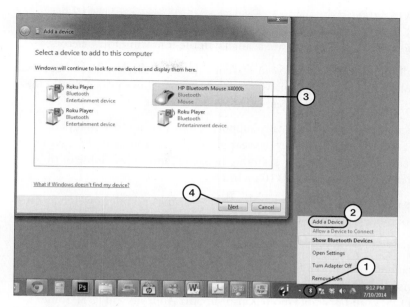

1. Click Bluetooth icon to continue pairing process.
2. Click to add a device.
3. Click the device to pair with the computer.
4. Click Next

Figure 9-20   Selecting a device to pair.

Keyboard

Windows, OS X, and Linux include **keyboard** drivers. To install a USB keyboard, simply plug it in, and the operating system installs the drivers needed. Keyboards are part of the human interface device (HID) device category and Windows installs HID drivers after the keyboard is connected.

To install a wireless keyboard, plug the receiver into a USB port, and follow the directions to pair up the keyboard and receiver.

If a keyboard has special buttons for multimedia or gaming, install drivers for the keyboard from the vendor. These can be installed after the keyboard has been connected.

If the keyboard uses Bluetooth, it needs to be paired with the computer's Bluetooth receiver. The instructions for pairing a Bluetooth keyboard are similar to those for pairing a mouse, except that the user is prompted to enter a code on the keyboard during the pairing process.

Scanner

Scanners for documents and photos are available in the following form factors:

- Almost all multifunction print/scan/fax/copy devices include a flatbed **scanner** with resolutions up to 2400 dpi. Most of these also include a sheet feeder for easier scanning of multiple pages.

- Scanners made for photos typically support resolutions up to 4800 dpi or greater. Some include a diffuser or clear glass lid light source with negative or transparency holders for use in scanning negatives and slides. Some of these can scan negatives as large as 8×10 inches.

- Scanners made for travel scan a single sheet at a time and might weigh as little as one pound (about a half-kilogram). These typically have resolutions up to 600 dpi.

All of these scanners plug into a USB port (some can also use Wi-Fi). Drivers are typically installed before the scanner is connected. Drivers are available for Windows and OS X, and portable models also support Android and iOS. Some scanner vendors also provide Linux drivers.

Software included with a scanner varies, but scanners for Windows and OS X typically include page-recognition software and some type of photo editing or organizing app.

Barcode Reader

Barcode (bar code) **readers** are used in a variety of point-of-sale retail, library, industrial, medical, and other environments to track inventory.

Barcode readers use one of the following technologies:

- Pen-based readers use a pen-shaped device that includes a light source and photo diode in the tip. The point of the pen is dragged across the bar code to read the varying thicknesses and positions of the bars in the bar code and translate them into a digitized code that is transmitted to the point-of-sale (POS) or inventory system.

- Laser scanners are commonly used in grocery and mass-market stores. They use a horizontal-mounted or vertical-mounted prism or mirror and laser beam protected by a transparent glass cover to read bar codes.

- CCD or CMOS readers use a hand-held gun-shaped device to hold an array of light sensors mounted in a row. The reader emits light that is reflected off the bar code and is detected by the light sensors.

- Camera-based readers contain many rows of CCD sensors that generate an image of the sensor that is processed to decode the barcode information.

Wired bar code readers typically interface through the USB port. See the documentation for the reader to determine whether you install the driver before or after connecting the reader. Many bar code readers use Bluetooth to make a wireless connection between the reader and the computer or other data-acquisition device. In such cases, you need a Bluetooth receiver in your PC and the device needs to be paired with the computer or POS system.

Biometric Devices

Biometric devices measure a bodily characteristic to identify a trusted user. The most common biometric device for PCs is a fingerprint reader. Some laptops have fingerprint readers, but one can be added via the USB port if needed.

When a fingerprint reader is attached to the USB port on a Windows computer, drivers are installed automatically. However, a fingerprint reader app must also be installed and the user's fingerprints must be read and added to the authentication modes used by the operating system before a user can log in by using fingerprints.

Some computers running OS X have built-in (embedded) fingerprint readers, but current versions of OS X do not support third-party fingerprint readers.

To use a fingerprint reader (USB or embedded) with a Linux computer, be sure to check compatibility. The Fprint utility is designed to help Linux use fingerprint readers. For more information, see https://wiki.archlinux.org/index.php/Fprint. To see how to install specific readers in a specific Linux distribution, search for the distribution version and specify fingerprint reader in the search.

Iris-based readers are being used for access control, banking, and other applications where positive identification is needed. These devices often use Power over Ethernet to enable use at some distance from the server hosting the identification databases.

Game Pads and Joysticks

Game pads and joysticks are popular game control devices that plug into a computer's USB port. In most cases, Windows installs compatible drivers automatically as soon as a **game pad** or **joystick** is plugged in. However, if the controller does not work, it might be necessary to manually select the correct driver from the controller's properties sheet in Device Manager. If the controller uses Bluetooth, pair it with the receiver in your system.

OS X has varied support for game pads and joysticks. With some controllers, you can install vendor-supplied OS X drivers. If the controller uses Bluetooth, pair it with your system. Otherwise, use a driver package such as Joystick Mapper (http://joystickmapper.com/), Tattiebogle driver (Xbox controllers; see http://tattiebogle.net/index.php/ProjectRoot/Xbox360Controller), GamePad Companion (Apple App Store), USB Overdrive, DarwinRemote (Wii controller—https://sourceforge.net/projects/darwiin-remote/) and Wjoy driver (Wii controller: https://github.com/alxn1/wjoy). For more information, see http://www.cnet.com/how-to/how-to-connect-game-controllers-to-your-mac/.

Game pads and joysticks on Linux are supported by the "Joystick" interface and the newer "evdev" interface. If a specific driver is not available, go to https://wiki.archlinux.org/index.php/Gamepad to learn how to configure your controller.

Digitizer

A **digitizer** translates touch into a command recognized by a computing device. Digitizers can be retrofitted to a PC in two ways:

- Drawing tablets from companies such as Wacom and Turcom plug into the USB port and include a pressure-sensitive pen. After installing drivers, you can draw with your finger or the pen in graphics programs such as Adobe Photoshop or any app that accepts mouse input. Without drivers, touch pads emulate mice.

- Touch screens, which include a digitizer layer to register touch, have long been available for use in industry and POS systems, but are now common in all-in-one computers, laptops, and as displays for use with non-touch consumer PCs. For details, see "Touch Screen," later in this chapter.

Motion Sensor

A **motion sensor** connected to a computer is typically used for gaming, computer control, and video chatting. Some representative products include:

- Leap Motion sensor (www.leapmotion.com)—uses a sensor that is placed in front of the computer to detect motion and depth; also supports virtual reality (VR) headsets.

- Microsoft Kinect (www.xbox.com/en-US/xbox-one/accessories/kinect-for-xbox-one)—uses a motion and depth-detection camera.

- Creative Senz3D (http://us.creative.com/p/web-cameras/creative-senz3d)—combines depth and gesture recognition with a 720p webcam.

To install a USB-based motion sensor:

Step 1.   Connect the sensor to the recommended USB port. With some sensors being used with VR apps, you might need to use USB 3.0 ports because of their much greater speed.

Step 2.   Turn on the unit.

Step 3.   Install software from the vendor.

Step 4.   Download apps compatible with the device.

Touch Pads

Touch pads (also known as touchpads, trackpads, or track pads) are built into almost all laptops and the keyboards on many tablets. Touch pads are also available as standalone devices or integrated into keyboards. Touch pads and keyboards that include touch pads plug in through the USB port, and are recognized as mice by Windows' built-in drivers.

If the touch pad or keyboard with integrated touch pad is wireless, it is normally recognized automatically. If the touch pad or keyboard has additional keys or buttons, it might be necessary to install proprietary drivers to enable the additional keys or buttons. Proprietary drivers are also necessary to enable multi-touch gestures (using two or more fingers).

Smart Card Readers

A smart card reader plugs into a USB port. Once a smart card reader has been installed, it works the same as a built-in smart card reader for controlling access to corporate networks or other restricted resources.

Smart card readers are supported by Windows, OS X, and popular Linux distributions. Drivers are typically installed automatically when the smart card reader is connected.

Digital Cameras

Digital cameras have almost completely replaced film cameras for both amateur and professional photography. They use CMOS or CCD image sensors to record images onto internal or card-based flash memory form factors. For casual snapshots and sharing on social media such as Facebook, Twitter, and Instagram, the integrated cameras in smartphones have largely replaced point-and-shoot cameras.

Digital cameras and smartphones transfer images to computers for emailing, printing, or storage via either flash memory card readers, direct USB port connections, or through wireless connections.

Installing a Digital Camera

To connect a digital camera to your PC, follow these steps:

Step 1.   Connect the USB cable provided with the camera to the camera's USB port and the computer's USB port.

Step 2.   Turn on the camera.

Step 3.   If the camera is not recognized after a few seconds, select the picture playback option on the camera. If the camera is still not recognized, install drivers for the camera.

Depending on the version of Windows and the camera's capabilities, the camera might be assigned a drive letter, show up as an imaging device, or display a menu with options for working with photos (see Figure 9-21). The contents of a Windows AutoPlay menu vary according to the photo-handling apps installed.

With OS X, open Image Capture and select the camera, then select the pictures to import. For details, see https://support.apple.com/kb/PH17894.

With Linux, the photo import options vary by distribution. Some popular choices include digiKam (for KDE), gThumb (for GNOME), and Rapid Photo Downloader (http://www.damonlynch.net/rapid/).

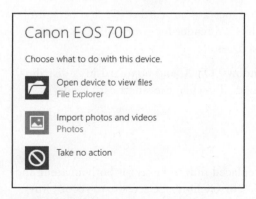

Figure 9-21   Windows 8.1 displays an AutoPlay menu including Photos (Windows 8/8.1/10 Modern UI) and File Explorer when a digital camera is connected.

NOTE   If you are configuring a computer running Windows Vista or 7 to work with RAW photos, you might need to add the appropriate RAW codec (coder-decoder) program to the computer so image thumbnails are visible in Windows Explorer. RAW codecs are available from the camera vendor, from Microsoft, or from third-party vendors. The Microsoft Camera Codec Pack for 32-bit and 64-bit versions of Windows Vista and Windows 7 is available from the Microsoft Download Center. Commercial codecs for use with Windows are available from fastpicturereviewer.com, Ardfry.com, and others.

Windows 8/8.1/10 include RAW codec support via Windows Update. OS X also includes RAW codec support. Some photo import apps for Linux, such as digiKam, also support RAW photos.

Microphone

A **microphone** plugs into the 1/8-inch (3.5mm) mini-jack microphone jack on a sound card or integrated motherboard audio. The most common microphones used on PCs include those built in to headsets or those that use a stand.

In Windows, microphone volume is controlled by the Windows Sound applet's mixer control. Open the Recording tab to adjust volume, to mute or unmute the microphone, or to adjust microphone boost.

In OS X, open **System Preferences > Sound > Input** to find the microphone volume control. In Linux, open **System Settings > Sound >Input** to find the microphone volume control.

NOTE   The microphone jack is monaural, whereas the line-in jack supports stereo. Be sure to use the line-in jack to record from a stereo audio source.

Installing and Configuring a Microphone

To install a microphone on a PC with a sound card or integrated audio, follow this procedure:

Step 1.   Connect the microphone into the microphone jack, which is marked with a pink ring or a microphone icon.

Step 2.   Audio hardware that supports **AC'97 version 2.3 audio** or **HD Audio** standards might pop up a dialog that asks you to confirm the device you have plugged into the microphone jack. Select **Microphone** from the list of devices.

Step 3. If the microphone has an on-off switch, make sure the microphone is turned on.

To verify that the microphone is working in Windows:

Step 1. Open the **Sounds** icon in Control Panel.

Step 2. Click the **Recording** tab.

Step 3. Make sure the microphone you installed is enabled and selected as the default device.

Step 4. Click **Configure**.

Step 5. From the Speech Recognition menu that opens, click **Set Up Microphone**.

Step 6. Select the microphone type and click **Next**.

Step 7. Adjust the microphone position and click **Next**.

Step 8. Read the onscreen text when prompted and click **Next** when finished.

Step 9. Click **Finish**. Close the Speech Recognition dialog to return to the Sounds dialog.

> **TIP** If the volume displayed in Step 8 is too low or too high, click Properties from the Sounds dialog. Click the Levels tab, adjust Microphone boost to the midpoint (10.0db), and retry Steps 4-9. If the volume is still too low or too high, adjust the volume on the Levels tab.

Webcam

A **webcam** is a simple digital camera capable of taking video or still images for transmission over the Internet. Unlike digital cameras, webcams don't include storage capabilities.

Virtually all webcams plug into a USB port or use wireless technology. Webcams are generally used in live chat situations, such as with Skype, AOL Instant Messenger, or other IM clients. They offer resolutions ranging from sub-VGA to full 1080p HD. Some offer autofocus and zoom features for better image clarity, and most have built-in microphones.

Installing and Configuring a Webcam

Before connecting the webcam, you typically need to install driver and configuration software. Obtain the most up-to-date drivers from the vendor's website.

After the webcam is installed, use its setup menu to adjust white balance, exposure, gain, and other options (see Figure 9-22). If you plan to use the webcam's microphone, disable other microphones in your computer's audio mixer application.

Before using the webcam for IM or phone calls, make sure the application is configured to use the webcam.

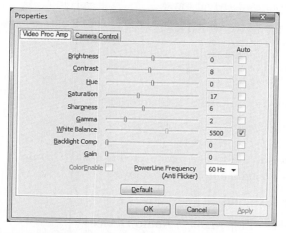

Figure 9-22   A typical webcam properties sheet being used to configure the camera's video processor.

Camcorder

A **camcorder** is used to record video. When a camcorder is connected via the USB port on a computer running Windows 8/8.1/10, Windows displays an AutoPlay app with options for importing or viewing the video files. Files stored in an HD Camcorder's onboard or flash card memory can be imported directly without conversion. With Windows 7, it might be necessary to install Windows Live Essentials to import video (get it from http://windows.microsoft.com/en-us/windows/essentials).

With older DV camcorders (these used tape for video storage), selecting the Import Video option from AutoPlay brings up these choices: create an Audio Video Interleaved (single file), also known as an AVI file; create a Windows Media Video File (single file) or Windows Media Video (one file per scene). See http://windows.microsoft.com/en-US/windows-vista/Import-live-video-from-a-DV-camera for details.

With OS X, use iMovie to import your video. See https://support.apple.com/en-us/HT201734 for details.

With Linux, use an app such as Shotcut (www.shotcut.org, for many popular distros, also available from OS X 64-bit and Windows 64-bit), Kdenlive (www.kdenlive.org, for GNU/Linux), and others (see https://www.linux.com/news/top-3-linux-video-editors for additional choices).

Speakers

You can connect **speakers** to a computer in several ways:

- 3.5mm speaker mini-jack (see Figures 8-30 and 8-32, Chapter 8)
- SPDIF digital audio port (see Figure 8-1 and 8-31, Chapter 8)
- Proprietary sound card header cable
- HDMI digital A/V port (see Figures 8-1 and 8-2, Chapter 8)
- USB surround audio external device

The default setting for audio mixers is to use speakers connected to analog 3.5mm audio jacks. To use a digital speaker or audio output in Windows:

Step 1.   Click or tap **Hardware and Sound**.

Step 2.   In the Sound category, click or tap **Manage Audio Devices**.

Step 3.   Click or tap a playback device on the Playback tab (see Figure 9-23).

Step 4.   To make the selected device your default, click or tap Set Default.

Step 5.   Click **Apply** and then click **OK** to use your new selection.

To make changes in OS X or Linux audio output, see "Configuring a Sound Card with OS X," p. 129, Chapter 5, and "Configuring a Sound Card with Linux," p. 129, Chapter 5.

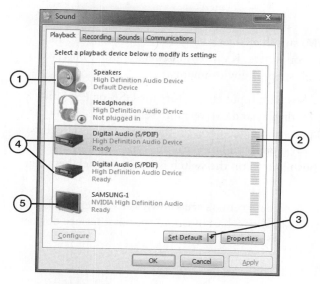

1. Current default
2. Selected device
3. Click or tap to set selected device as default
4. Two SPDIF outputs (coaxial and optical)
5. HDMI A/V connection to HDTV

Figure 9-23 Selecting a digital audio output (SPDIF) on a PC.

Touch Screen

Touch screen displays are now available as upgrades to non-touch displays on Windows PCs. They differ from standard displays by incorporating a touch-sensitive digitizer layer that connects to the PC through a USB port, while the display functions connect to the PC's video ports.

Touch screen displays are available from vendors such as Planar, ViewSonic, ASUS, Dell, Acer, HP, and others. For best compatibility with Windows 10, look for displays that support 10-point multitouch.

Linux has included multitouch display support for several years. See http://stack-overflow.com/questions/16976512/does-linux-support-multi-touch-screen for details. OS X supports multitouch in its touch pads, but display support is spotty.

NOTE Multitouch refers to the use of two or more fingers on a touch screen or touch pad. 10-point multitouch is the most desirable, because it supports all fingers on both hands.

KVM

A keyboard-video-mouse (**KVM**) switch enables a single keyboard, display, and mouse to support two or more computers. KVM switches are popular in server rooms and are also useful in tech support environments.

The simplest KVM switch is a box with input connectors for USB or PS/2 mouse and keyboard and VGA or other display and two or more sets of cables leading to the corresponding I/O ports and video ports on the computers that will be hosted. Some KVM switches also support audio. With this type of KVM switch, a special key combination or a push button on the switch is used to switch between computers.

KVM switches for server rooms and data centers are known as local remote KVM and typically use CAT5 or higher-quality cables to run to special interface devices on each server.

To install a KVM switch:

Step 1.   Shut down the computers and display.

Step 2.   Connect the keyboard and mouse and other shared connectors (such as speakers) to the KVM switch.

Step 3.   Connect the KVM switch to the computers.

Step 4.   Start the computers.

Step 5.   Install drivers if necessary.

Be sure to use the correct key combinations to switch between computers and to emulate other keyboards (for example, if a Windows keyboard is used with an OS X computer). In some situations, a firmware upgrade for the switch might be needed. Follow the instructions provided with the switch to perform a successful upgrade.

Smart TV

A **smart TV** combines a standard HDTV with support for streaming channels such as Amazon Prime, Netflix, YouTube, and others. After connecting a smart TV to power and to a cable or antenna source, you need to do the following to complete setup:

- Configure the Internet connection type (wired or wireless).

- Obtain an IP address from the DHCP server on the network.

- Install any firmware updates available for the smart TV.

- Select the streaming services the client wants to use.

- For some streaming services, the client might need to sign up for a subscription or obtain an unlock code.

After completing these tasks, test the smart TV by pressing the button(s) on the remote to switch to the streaming service desired.

Set-Top Box

The term **set-top box** refers to any device that enables a TV (HDTV, standard, or smart TV) to watch more types of programs or media. The most common set-top boxes today include:

- TV boxes (cable, satellite, fiber) used to unencrypt TV channels for viewing and recording TV. Some of these boxes include a PVR (personal video recorder).

- Streaming media devices such as Roku, Amazon Fire TV, Apple TV, and so on.

- Blu-ray and DVD players.

To connect a TV box directly to the TV:

Step 1.   Connect the cable from the TV provider to the TV box.

Step 2.   Connect the video output cable from the TV box to the TV. Use the highest-quality signal supported by both the TV and the TV box. (The best signal quality is HDMI, component is the next best.)

Step 3.   Note the input used by the connection at the TV (Input 1, Input 2, and so on). To watch TV, this is the input the viewer must select.

Step 4.   Turn on the TV, switch to the correct input on the TV, and verify proper operation.

To connect a streaming media device directly to the TV:

Step 1.   Connect the cable from the streaming media device to the TV or to the receiver. Use the highest-quality signal supported by both the TV and the TV box. (The best signal quality is HDMI, component is the next best).

Step 2.   Note the input used by the connection from the streaming media device or at the TV (Input 1, Input 2, and so on). To watch TV, this is the input the viewer must select.

Step 3.   Turn on the TV, switch to the correct input on the TV, and set up the streaming media device. Select the correct network connection, select and install channels, and then set up any subscriptions.

Step 4.   Verify proper operation.

To connect a Blu-ray or DVD player directly to the TV:

Step 1.   Connect the cable from the streaming media device to the TV. Use the highest-quality signal supported by both the TV and the TV box. (The best signal quality is HDMI, component is the next best.)

Step 2.   Note the input used by the connection from the Blu-ray or DVD player or receiver to the TV (Input 1, Input 2, and so on). To watch TV, this is the input the viewer must select.

Step 3.   Turn on the TV and select the correct input.

Step 4.   Turn on the player and insert a disc.

Step 5.   Play the disc.

TIP   If a home theater receiver is being used, the cabling setup differs:

- If the receiver is an audio-only receiver (doesn't distribute video signals), connect audio leads from the TV box, streaming media device, or Blu-ray/DVD drive to the receiver. Be sure to select the appropriate input and output on the receiver to hear audio.

- If the receiver also distributes video signals, connect audio and video leads from the TV box, streaming media device, or Blu-ray/DVD drive to the receiver. Connect a video lead from the receiver's output jack to the TV. Be sure to select the appropriate input and output on the receiver and input on the TV to see video and play audio.

Installing a MIDI-Enabled Device

Although sounds cards and onboard audio can play MIDI files, **MIDI** interfacing must be available if you need to connect a MIDI-enabled device to a PC (a MIDI port is a five-pin DIN port). Some older sound cards had provision for a MIDI port adapter to be connected via the sound card's joystick port. Newer sound cards use breakout boxes for MIDI ports, or you can attach a self-contained MIDI port via the USB port.

After ensuring that a MIDI port is available on a system, you can install a MIDI-enabled device. When connecting a MIDI-enabled device:

- Connect MIDI Out on the device to MIDI In on your PC's MIDI interface.

- Connect MIDI Out on your PC's MIDI interface to MIDI In on the device.

Display Types

A customized system configuration often requires selection of a display of a particular type, size, and resolution. There are five types of displays you need to understand for the A+ Certification exams:

- LCD (CCFL) displays

- LED (LCD-LED) displays

- Plasma

- Data projectors

- OLED

The following sections help you understand the common and unique features of each.

LCD Display Types

LCD displays use liquid crystal cells to polarize light passing through the display to create the image shown on the monitor. In color LCD displays, liquid crystal cells are grouped into three cells for each pixel: one each for red, green, and blue light.

LCD displays typically use one of two types of designs:

- Twisted nematic (TN)

- In-plane switching (IPS)

TN vs IPS

A **TN** display provides short response time (gray to gray [GTG] response time as fast as 2ms) and high brightness (especially when used with an LED backlight), making them highly suitable for gaming. They also draw less power and are less expensive than IPS displays. However, TN displays tend to lose contrast and display less accurate colors as the viewing angle increases.

An **IPS** display has a slower response time (5ms) and uses as much as 50% more power than a TN display with comparable resolution and screen size. However, an IPS display has a wider viewing angle without distorted colors or loss of contrast —up to 170 degrees or wider horizontally and vertically. IPS displays are better choices for presentations, graphics, or video editing.

Fluorescent vs. LED Backlighting

LCD displays can use one of two types of backlighting:

- **Fluorescent backlighting** (CCFL)

- **LED backlighting**

LCD-CCFL displays use a cold cathode fluorescent lamp (CCFL) as the lighting source. The CCFL develops ultraviolet light by discharging mercury into the lamp. The lamp's inner fluorescent coating then allows for the emitting of visible light, which is sent to the actual display panel.

LCD-LED are frequently called LED displays because the CCFL has been replaced by one or more strips of LEDs along the edges of the display.

Plasma

Plasma displays are rarely found in computer monitors but are often found in televisions. Nowadays, computers can use many types of HDTVs as their display, including plasma, as long as the computer has the correct type of video port. Plasma displays use small cells that contain electrically charged ionized gases; effectively, these are fluorescent lamps. Plasma screens are known for brightness and low-luminance black level in comparison to LCD screens. This makes the plasma screen a higher energy consumer than LCD. It also prompted the LCD community to re-lease LED-backlit LCD displays that were mentioned previously.

Data Projector

A data **projector** can be used in place of a primary display or can be used as a clone of the primary display to permit computer information and graphics to be displayed on a projection screen or a wall.

Data projectors use one of the following technologies:

- Liquid crystal display (LCD)

- Digital light processing (DLP)

LCD Projectors

LCD projectors use separate LCD panels for red, green, and blue light, and combine the separate images into a single RGB image for projection, using dichroic mirrors. A dichroic mirror reflects light in some wavelengths, while permitting light in other wavelengths to pass through. In Figure 9-24, red and blue dichroic mirrors are used to split the image into red, blue, and green wavelengths. After passing through the appropriate LCD, a dichroic combiner cube recombines the separate red, green, and blue images into a single RGB image for projection.

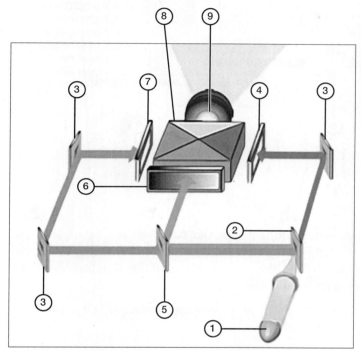

1. Projection lamp
2. Dichroic mirror (passes red)
3. Mirror
4. Red LCD
5. Dichroic mirror (passes blue)
6. Green LCD
7. Blue LCD
8. Dichroic combiner cube
9. Projection lamp

Figure 9-24 How a typical three-LCD data projector works.

LCD projectors use a relatively hot projection lamp, so LCD projectors include cooling fans that run both during projector operation and after the projector is turned off to cool down the lamp.

DLP Projectors

All types of DLP displays, including projectors, use an array of tiny mirrors known as a digital micromirror device (DMD). Each tiny mirror in the DMD corresponds to a pixel, and the mirrors reflect light toward or away from the projector optics. DLP devices differ in the light source used. DLP devices such as HDTVs and digital theater projectors sometimes use a spinning wheel with red, green, and blue sections to add color data to light before it reaches the DMD. However, DLP data projectors use three different LED light sources (red, green, and blue) along with dichroic mirrors to provide color (see Figure 9-25). DLP technology dominates the ultra-compact pico and larger pocket projector categories.

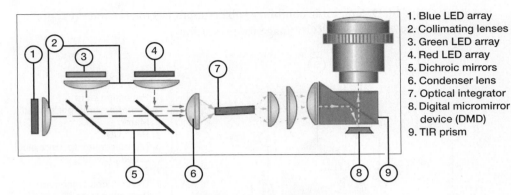

1. Blue LED array
2. Collimating lenses
3. Green LED array
4. Red LED array
5. Dichroic mirrors
6. Condenser lens
7. Optical integrator
8. Digital micromirror device (DMD)
9. TIR prism

Figure 9-25   How a typical DLP projector works.

OLED

OLED stands for organic light emitting diodes. **OLED** displays use organic semiconductor material usually in the form of polymers. Organic colored molecules are held in place between electrodes. A conductive layer made up of plastic molecules allows the organic colored molecules to emit light.

OLED display panels are currently used in some laptop displays as well as large screen HDTVs.

Video Display Settings and Features

Once a display is connected to your computer, it might need to be properly configured. The following sections discuss display settings issues and feature questions you might encounter in A+ Certification exams.

> **NOTE**   Be sure you know where various tools and settings are located within the operating systems that are specified in the CompTIA A+ Exam objectives. For example, a performance-based question may ask you to change screen resolution settings in Windows.

Resolution

Display **resolution** is described as the amount of pixels (picture elements) on a screen. It is measured horizontally by vertically (HxV). The word *resolution* is somewhat of a misnomer and can also be referred to as pixel dimensions. Table 9-11 shows some of the typical resolutions used in Windows, Linux, and OS X. The more commonly used resolutions are in bold.

An LCD display has only one **native resolution** (the resolution it was designed to display); it must scale lower resolutions to fit the panel or, depending on the options configured in the video card driver, might use only a portion of the display when a lower resolution is selected. When a lower resolution is scaled, the display is less sharp than when the native resolution is used.

Some LCD displays use the standard **4:3 aspect ratio** (1.33:1), but most use one of the widescreen aspect ratios: **16:9 aspect ratio** (1.78:1) is the aspect ratio used by 720p and 1080i/1080p HDTVs; **16:10 aspect ratio** (1.6:1) provides additional vertical pixels, making it better for productivity applications. LCD displays are currently available in sizes from 14 inches (diagonal measure) to 30 inches or larger.

Table 9-11 List of Typical Resolutions

Pixel Dimensions	Aspect Ratio	Resolution Type	Full Name	Notes
640×480	4:3	VGA*	Video Graphics Array	
800×600	4:3	SVGA*	Super Video Graphics Array	
1024×640	16:10	WSVGA	Wide Super VGA	Used by MacBook Air
1024×768	4:3	XGA	eXtended Graphics Array	
1152×720	16:10			Used by MacBook Air
1280×720	16:9	720p	HD (High Definition)	
1366×768	16:9	WXGA (HD)	Widescreen eXtended Graphics Array (High Definition)	Typical native resolution of many 15.6-in laptop displays
1440×900	16:10	WSXGA	Widescreen Super eXtended Graphics Array	Native resolution of MacBook Air 13.3-in
1600×900	16:9			
1600×1200	4:3	UXGA	Ultra XGA	
1920×1200	16:10	WUXGA	Widescreen Ultra eXtended Graphics Array	

Pixel Dimensions	Aspect Ratio	Resolution Type	Full Name	Notes
1920×1080	16:9	1080P and 1080i	Full High Definition	Native resolution of Microsoft Surface Pro, Pro 2
2048×1152	16:9	QWXGA	Quad Wide XGA	
2160×1440	3:2	2K		Native resolution of Microsoft Surface Pro 3
2560×1440	16:9	WQHD	Wide Quad HD	
2560×1600	16:10	WQXGA	Wide Quad XGA	
2736×1824	3:2			Native resolution of Microsoft Surface Pro 4
3840×2160	16:9	4K	4K Ultra HD	

*VGA and SVGA modes are usually only seen if you attempt to boot the system into Safe Mode or another advanced boot mode, or if the driver has failed.

To modify screen resolution do the following:

- **In Windows 7/8/8.1/10**—Right-click the desktop and select Screen Resolution. Use the Resolution vertical slider to select the desired pixel dimensions (see Figure 9-26). Click **Apply**, then **Keep Changes** on the confirmation dialog to keep the new resolution (otherwise, Windows reverts to the old one). Click **OK** when finished.

- **In Windows Vista**—Right-click the desktop and select **Personalize**. Then click the **Display Settings** link. Toward the bottom left of the window is a box called Resolution. Use the slider to select the desired resolution.

- In **Linux**—If you are using a GUI, open **System Settings > Displays** to select the desired resolution. After selecting a resolution, click **Apply** to use it. Figure 9-27 shows resolution options available in Ubuntu. If you are managing Linux from Terminal, use the `xrandr` command to see and select from available resolutions. See http://www.ubuntugeek.com/how-change-display-resolution-settings-using-xrandr.html for details.

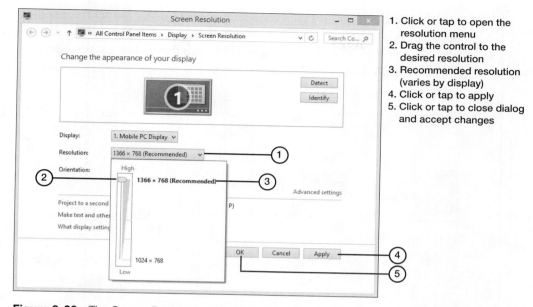

Figure 9-26   The Screen Resolution window in Windows 8.1 controls display resolution, can detect monitors, and offers multiple monitor support.

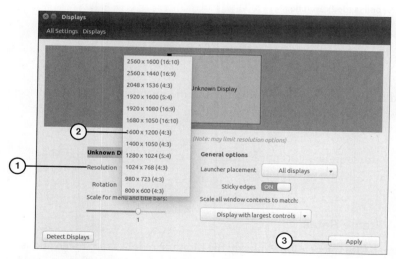

1. Click to open the resolution menu
2. Click the desired resolution
3. Click to apply

Figure 9-27   The Displays window in Ubuntu 14 workstation controls display resolution and offers multiple monitor support.

■ In **OS X**—Open **System Properties** > **Displays** to select the desired resolution. To choose the native resolution for the display, click **Default for display**. To choose a different resolution, click **Scaled** and click the resolution desired (Figure 9-28).

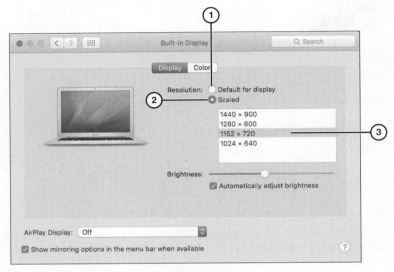

1. **Click to choose native (recommended)resolution**
2. **Click to choose a different resolution**
3. **Click the resolution desired**

Figure 9-28   Selecting a scaled resolution with OS X.

Unless you need to select a lower resolution for specific purposes, you should select an LCD monitor's native (recommended) resolution.

NOTE   To learn about configuring multiple displays, see "Multiple Monitor Misalignment/Orientation," p.1098, Chapter 22.

Refresh Rates and Frame Rates

The vertical **refresh rate** refers to how quickly the monitor redraws the screen and is measured in hertz (Hz), or times per second. The refresh rate usually defaults to 60Hz.

Some displays offer an adjustable refresh rate. The vertical refresh in Windows 7/8/8.1/10 can be adjusted by accessing the Screen Resolution dialog, clicking Advanced Settings and then opening the Screen Refresh Rate menu. In Windows Vista, open the Display Properties sheet, click the Advanced button, and open the Screen Refresh Rate dialog.

NOTE If your monitor is listed as Default monitor rather than Plug and Play monitor or as a specific monitor model, you will not be able to choose flicker-free refresh rates. Install a driver provided by the vendor.

CAUTION Selecting a refresh rate that exceeds the monitor's specifications can damage the monitor or cause the monitor to display a blank screen or a "signal out of range" error. If you select a refresh rate that exceeds the monitor's specifications, press the ESC (Escape) key on the keyboard to return to the previous setting.

In the context of display devices, **frame rate** refers to the frames per second (fps) speed of 3D rendering during games. The higher the frame rate the better, but any frame rate below 30fps makes a 3D game essentially unplayable. To improve frame rate, adjust the following, either with in-game menus or by using the 3D settings available for your GPU in its control center app:

- Quality setting—The lower the quality, the faster the frame rate. Depending on the driver settings or game options, you might be able to select which settings to reduce in quality, such as sampling, anti-aliasing, anisotropic filtering, and others.

- Display resolution—The lower the resolution, the faster the frame rate.

Some games feature an option to display frame rate during game play. Otherwise, I recommend Fraps (fraps.com). Fraps can benchmark games, capture screens, or perform real-time video capture on both DirectX and OpenGL games played on Windows.

NOTE For more information about adjusting 3D gaming settings, see Chapter 13, "Fixing Slow 3D Gaming," in my book The PC and Gadget Help Desk (http://www.quepublishing.com/store/pc-and-gadget-help-desk-a-do-it-yourself-guide-to-troubleshooting-9780789753458).

Analog versus Digital Displays

Although most desktop computers continue to include a VGA port, this **analog display** connector, introduced in 1987, is definitely a legacy port. When shopping for a display, you should consider displays that support one or more of the following **digital display** connectors:

- DVI-D
- HDMI
- DisplayPort

Many LCD displays and projectors also include a VGA port, but using an analog display connector requires a digital-to-analog conversion in the computer and an analog-to-digital conversion at the display or projector, which can introduce display quality problems, limits resolution, and prevents the playback of protected digital content (Blu-ray, premium movie channels, and so on) at full resolution. To make sure you can play back protected digital content with your computer, make sure the video card and display/projector support HDCP (high-bandwidth digital copy protection).

To learn more about video cards and ports, see "Video," p.273, Chapter 8.

Brightness/Lumens

The brightness of an LCD display is measured in candelas per square meter (cd/m^2), sometimes referred to as "nits." The higher this value, the brighter the display. Typical values for LCD panels range from 250 cd/m^2 to 350 cd/m^2.

The brightness of a projector is measured in **lumens**. The higher the value, the brighter the output. To use a projector in a normally lit room, look for a projector with a rating of 3000 lumens or higher, as in most portable and conference room projectors). Pico and pocket projectors have lumen ratings of 700 to as little as 15 lumens. These require a very dark room to be usable.

Privacy and Antiglare Filters

Glossy screen finishes have become very common with the rise of streaming TV and movie playback on computer displays. Unfortunately, glossy screens can cause eyestrain and headaches due to glare. Some display vendors sell **antiglare filters**, and they are also available from third-party sources such as 3M, Kantek, Accurate Films, and others.

A **privacy filter** narrows viewing angles to prevent onlookers from seeing information on your computer screen. As a side benefit, it also reduces glare. Privacy filters are available from third-party sources such as 3M, Kensington, Akamai, and others.

Exam Preparation Tasks

Review All the Key Topics

Review the most important topics in the chapter, noted with the key topics icon in the outer margin of the page. Table 9-12 lists a reference of these key topics and the page numbers on which each is found.

Table 9-12 Key Topics for Chapter 9

Key Topic Element	Description	Page Number
Table 9-1	Graphic/CAD/CAM Design Workstation Features	302
Table 9-2	Audio/Video Editing Workstation Features	304
Section	Gaming PC	307
Table 9-4	Gaming PC Features	308
Section	Home Theater PC	310
Section	Standard Thick Client	311
Section	Thin Client	312
Table 9-8	Home Server PC Features	313
Figure 9-7	Using the Belarc System Advisor for determining onboard hardware and software	315
Section	Processor Information and Hardware-Assisted Virtualization Readiness	316
Section	Installing Power Supplies	317
Section	Power Supply Ratings	318
Table 9-9	Calculating Power Supply Requirements	321
Section	Power Supply Form Factors and Connectors	323
Table 9-10	Power Levels by Connector Type	325
Figure 9-14	Power supply connectors for peripherals and modern motherboards.	325
Section	Removing and Replacing a Power Supply	328
Section	Display Types	349
Section	Pairing a Bluetooth Mouse (Windows)	333
Table 9-11	List of Typical Resolutions	353

Define Key Terms

Define the following key terms from this chapter, and check your answers in the glossary.

Belarc System Advisor, Device Manager, MSInfo32.exe, SiSoftware Sandra, CPU-Z, power supply, Molex, 4/8-pin 12v, PCIe 6/8-pin, 20-pin, 24-pin, wattage, AC, DC, dual rail, dual voltage, multicore processor, virtualization, surround sound audio, HDMI, HTPC, TV tuner, thick client, thin client, home server, media streaming, file sharing, print sharing, gigabit NIC, RAID array, mouse, keyboard, scanner, barcode reader, biometric devices, game pads, joysticks, digitizer, motion sensor, touch pads, smart card readers, digital cameras, AC'97 version 2.3 audio, HD Audio, microphone, webcam, camcorder, speakers, touch screen, KVM, smart TV, set-top box, MIDI, LCD, TN, IPS, fluorescent backlighting (CCFL), LED backlighting, plasma, projector, OLED, refresh rate, frame rate, resolution, native resolution, lumens, analog display, digital display, privacy filter, antiglare filter, 16:9 aspect ratio, 16:10 aspect ratio, 4:3 aspect ratio.

Complete the Tables and Lists from Memory

Print a copy of Appendix C, "Memory Tables" (found on the CD), or at least the section for this chapter, and complete the tables and lists from memory. Appendix D, "Answers to Memory Tables" also on the CD, includes completed tables and lists to check your work.

Complete Hands-On Labs

Complete the hands-on labs, and then see the answers and explanations at the end of the chapter.

Lab 9-1: Investigating a Power Supply

After disconnecting all power, open a desktop computer and determine the number and types of power connectors it has.

Connector	Number
Molex	
Berg	
SATA	
PCIe six-pin	
PCIe eight-pin	
ATX12V	
EPS12V	

Examine the power supply label to determine the following:

Wattage rating _____

Total 12V Amps _____

Number of 12V rails _____

Lab 9-2: Adding I/O Devices

If you have a Linux or OS X computer available, set up a game pad or joystick.

Connect a digital camera to two computers running Windows and compare how each computer reacts. For example, are the same apps offered in the AutoPlay menu?

Set up or check the configuration for a microphone and speakers.

Answer Review Questions

1. When designing and building a new customized PC to be used for graphic design, audiovisual editing, 3D game development, virtualization, or home theater, which of the following will probably need to be upgraded?

   A. CPU

   B. RAM

   C. Sound and display

   D. Cooling system

   E. All of the above

2. When building a home theater system, which of the following will probably not be selected?

   A. HDMI

   B. A high-end cooling system to counter the heat generated by overclocking

   C. Surround sound

   D. A compact form factor

3. The System Information utility contains hardware and software configuration information. Which of the following commands starts System Information?

   A. chkdsk

   B. msinfo32

   C. msconfig

   D. dxdiag

4. Which of the following statements best describes the function of the computer's power supply?

   A. The function of the computer's power supply is to provide DC power from the wall outlet to the computer.

   B. The function of the computer's power supply is to convert DC power to AC power.

   C. The function of the computer's power supply is to convert AC power to DC power.

   D. The function of the computer's power supply is to provide AC power from the wall outlet to the computer.

5. Refer to the following figure to answer the following questions and complete the chart.

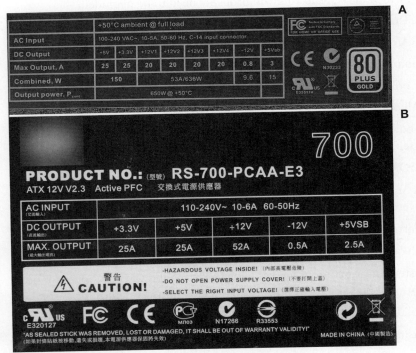

What is the rating for each power supply in watts?

How many +12V rails does each power supply have?

How many total amps does each power supply produce?

Which power supply provides more power to the computer components? _____

	Total Watts (W)	Number of +12V Rails (R)	Amp Output from +12V Rails (Amp)
Power Supply A			
Power Supply B			

6. Identify the port and connector shown in the following display. Choose from the following options:

   A. ATX power supply cable and connector

   B. ATX12V power supply cable and connector

   C. EPS12V power supply cable and connector

   D. USB 3.0 cable and connector

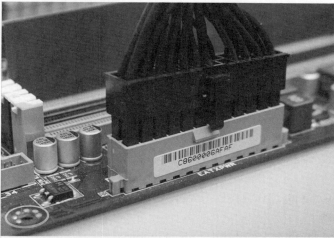

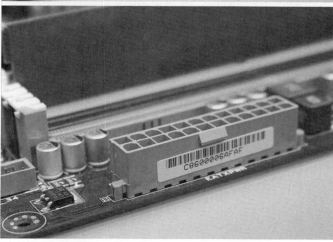

7. Your client has just connected a computer to a receiver for better music playback, but there is no audio coming from the receiver. After checking the SPDIF cable connection and the output setting on the receiver and verifying that audio is not muted on the computer, which of the following is the most likely cause?

   A. SPDIF audio is not selected as the default output.

   B. The VGA cable is loose.

   C. The microphone is disconnected.

   D. There is interference from the smart card reader.

8. Which one of the following USB devices needs additional drivers installed in order to operate?

   A. A keyboard

   B. A mouse

   C. A touch pad

   D. A scanner

9. Your client has just started shooting digital photos in RAW format. Windows 8.1's File Explorer displays thumbnails, but when the photos are viewed on a Windows 7 computer in Windows Explorer, the files are displayed as icons. Which of the following statements describes the best solution?

   A. Your client must upgrade to Windows 8.1 or later to view thumbnails of RAW photos.

   B. Your client must shoot RAW+JPEG and rely on the JPEG version for viewing.

   C. Your client must install a RAW codec for Windows 7.

   D. RAW photos are incompatible with Windows 7.

10. Your client has just upgraded to a touch screen display for a desktop computer running Windows 8.1. The display functions work fine, but the touch functions have not worked since the display was set up. Which of the following should be performed first?

    A. Disconnecting the mouse to see if it is interfering with the touch screen

    B. Rebooting the computer

    C. Making sure the USB cable from the display is plugged in

    D. Connecting all USB devices to a USB hub

11. Your client wants to upgrade to a display capable of displaying Full HD video content. Which of the following resolutions must the display and video card support to make this possible?

   A. 1280×720

   B. 1920×1080

   C. 1600×1200

   D. 1366×768

Answers and Explanations for Hands-On Labs

Lab 9-1: Investigating a Power Supply

With recent power supplies, you are likely to find three or four Molex and three or four SATA power connectors. A power supply designed to support SLI (NVIDIA multi-GPU) or CrossFire (AMD multi-GPU) will have two or more PCIe six-pin or eight pin (six+two) power connectors. Most recent power supplies have only one Berg connector at most.

If you are planning to upgrade a system by installing a new motherboard or new PCIe video cards, be sure to review the power supply connectors and power levels provided by the power supply. It might be necessary to replace the power supply as well.

Lab 9-2: Adding I/O Devices

Which method(s) or apps were successful in setting up a game pad or joystick on your Linux or OS X computer? Which distribution of Linux was used? With a different distribution, the answer might be different.

Which apps were the same in the AutoPlay menu when connecting a digital camera? Which were different?

When you set up the microphone or speakers, did you test the setup? If not, go back and test it to assure your changes are working.

Answers and Explanations to Review Questions

1. **E.** In a high-end customized system, one or all of these components must be upgraded. The CPU will need as many cores as possible for the fastest processing. More and faster RAM, high-end sound cards, multiple displays, and HDMI might be required for peak performance in some systems. In a gaming computer where overclocking is used, you might choose to use a liquid cooling system. A customized system will probably be comparable in cost to a new system.

2. **B.** High-end cooling systems are usually found in gaming computers that use overclocking and not in home theater systems.

    A home theater system usually uses HDMI to connect a computer to a big screen HD tuner. Most home theater systems also have surround-sound speakers to provide a more theatrical experience. They also use a space-saving compact form factor such as mini-ITX.

3. **B.** The System Information utility is accessed by typing **msinfo32.exe** at the command line. Chkdsk is the Windows utility for checking drives for errors. Msconfig is used to change Windows startup behavior. Dxdiag is used to view and test DirectX drivers.

4. **C.** The computer's power supply is really a power converter. It converts AC power from the wall outlet to DC power that the computer can use.

5.

	Total Watts (W)	Number of +12V Rails (R)	Amp Output from +12V Rails (Amp)
Power Supply A	650	4	80
Power Supply B	700	1	52

Power Supply #1 produces 650 watts of power and uses four +12V rails that produce 20 amps each for a total of 80 amps. Power Supply #2 produces 700 watts, but it has a single +12V rail that produces only 52 amps. Power Supply #1 has more usable amperage available to components, so it is the better value. Notice also that Power Supply #1 was tested at 50 degrees C (122 degrees F) at full load. Power Supply #2 does not tell you how it was tested.

6. **A.** The ATX 24-pin power cable and connector provides primary power to the motherboard and connected devices.

7. **A.** SPDIF audio not selected as default output. Computers use analog speakers as the default output. You must select SPDIF as the output if you are now connecting to a receiver via the SPDIF (digital audio) port. VGA and microphone cables have no effect on audio output. Smart card readers do not cause interference.

8. **D.** The keyboard, mouse, and touch pad options are incorrect because all use standard input device drivers incorporated into the operating system. A scanner driver is not included in the operating system.

9. **C.** Your client must install a RAW codec for Windows 7. Newer versions of Windows install RAW codecs with Windows Update, but Windows 7 does not. Once an appropriate RAW codec is installed, Windows 7 can view both JPEG and RAW photos as thumbnails in Windows Explorer.

10. **C.** Make sure the USB cable from the display is plugged in. The touch screen digitizer must connect to a USB port or it will not work. Rebooting the computer could help if the touch screen had been working but then had stopped. However, in this example, it had never worked. The mouse will not interfere with the touch screen. A USB hub is necessary when there are more USB devices than ports, but that is not the issue here.

11. **B.** 1920×1080, also known as 1080p, is full HD resolution. 1280×720, also known as 720p, is the minimum HD resolution. 1600×1200 isn't wide enough to support 1080p resolution. 1366×768 can display 720p, but not 1080p.

This chapter covers the following subjects:

- **Laser Printers**—Detailed review of laser printers, the seven-step laser imaging process, and maintenance guidelines are in this section.

- **Inkjet Printers**—This section includes a detailed look at how inkjet printers work and how to maintain them.

- **Thermal Printers**—Thermal transfer, direct thermal, and dye-sublimation printers and maintenance guidelines are the focus of this section.

- **Impact Printers**—This section covers printheads, ribbons, paper feed types, and maintenance for this venerable but still useful printer type.

- **Virtual Printers**—The "printers" in the Printer menu that create documents instead of printouts are covered in this section.

- **Installing Your Printer or Multifunction Device**—Installation processes for Windows, OS X, Linux, iOS, and Android are the focus of this section.

- **Configuring Your Printer or Multifunction Device**—From collation to paper type, this section discusses how to set print options in Windows, OS X, Linux, iOS, and Android.

- **Device Sharing Options**—In this section, learn how to share a printer with an Ethernet network.

- **Wireless Device Sharing Options**—In this section, learn how Bluetooth as well as Wi-Fi can be used for printer sharing.

- **Cloud and Remote Printing**—Discover what vendors and services exist to make these types of printing a reality.

- **Configuring Your Operating System to Share a Printer or Device**—In this section, discover the services that Windows, OS X, and Linux use to share printers.

- **Maintaining Data Privacy**—In this section, discover methods for making printing more secure.

## CHAPTER 10

Using, Maintaining, and Installing Printers and Multifunction Devices

Whether standalone devices or multifunction devices that also incorporate copy, scan, and fax features, printers are important output devices—second only to video displays. They output hard-copy versions of files stored on the computer, such as documents, spreadsheets, photos, and web pages, using laser, inkjet, thermal, impact, and virtual (software) technologies.

Printers and multifunction devices can connect to a computer's USB or parallel port via Bluetooth, Wi-Fi, cellular wireless networks, or directly to a wired network. This chapter focuses on laser, inkjet, thermal, and impact printers. Virtual printing techniques such as printing to a file, PDF, XPS, or image are also covered.

Generally, Windows Vista/7/8/8.1/10 behave the same when it comes to printers. So whenever Windows is mentioned in this chapter, the information applies to modern Windows versions unless otherwise stated. This chapter also deals with printer issues for OS X, Linux, iOS, and Android operating systems.

220-901: Objective 1.14 Compare and contrast differences between the various print technologies and the associated imaging process.

220-901: Objective 1.15 Given a scenario, perform appropriate printer maintenance.

Foundation Topics

Laser Printers

A **laser printer** is a page printer that stores the entire contents of the page to be printed in its memory before printing it. By contrast, inkjet, thermal, and impact printers print the page as a series of narrow bands.

Laser Components

The major components of a laser printer include:

- **Imaging drum**—Applies the page image to the transfer belt or roller; frequently combined with the toner supply in a toner cartridge

- **Developer**—pulls toner from the toner supply and sends it to the imaging drum

- **Fuser assembly**—Fuses the page image to the paper

- **Transfer belt** or **transfer roller**—Transfers the page image from the drum to the page

- **Pickup rollers**—Picks up paper

- **Paper separation pad** (**separate pad**)—Enables pickup rollers to pick up only one sheet of paper at a time

- **Duplexing assembly** (optional)—An assembly that switches paper from the front to the back side so that the printer can print on both sides of the paper

Here's a closer look at how these and other components work together to make printing possible.

Toner Cartridges

Most monochrome laser printers use **toner cartridges** that combine the imaging drum and the developer along with a supply of black toner. This provides you with an efficient and easy way to replace the laser printer items with the greatest potential to wear out.

Depending on the model, a new toner cartridge might also require that you change a wiper used to remove excess toner during the fusing cycle. This is normally packaged with the toner cartridge.

NOTE   Recycled toner cartridges are controversial in some circles, but many firms have used new and rebuilt toner cartridges for years without problems. Major manufacturers (such as Apple, HP, and Canon) place a postage-paid return label in cartridge boxes to encourage you to recycle your toner cartridges.

Reputable toner cartridge rebuilders can save you as much as 30 percent off the price of a new toner cartridge.

When you install the toner cartridge, be sure to follow the directions for cleaning areas near the toner cartridge. Depending on the make and model of the laser printer, this can involve cleaning the mirror that reflects the laser beam, cleaning up stray toner, or cleaning the charging corona wire or conditioning rollers inside the printer. If you need to clean the charging corona wire (also called the *primary corona wire* on some models), the laser printer will contain a special tool for this purpose. The printer instruction manual will show you how to clean the item.

Keep the cartridge closed; it is sensitive to light, and leaving it out of the printer in room light can damage the enclosed imaging drum's surface.

CAUTION   When you change a toner cartridge, take care to avoid getting toner on your face, hands, or clothing. It can leave a messy residue that's hard to clean. For information about cleaning up toner spills and taking precautions against inhaling toner, see Chapter 17, "Operational Procedures."

Laser Imaging Process

A laser printer is an example of a page printer. A page printer does not start printing until the entire page is received. At that point, the page is transferred to the print mechanism, which pulls the paper through the printer as the page is transferred from the printer to the paper.

TIP   To master this section, make sure you

- Memorize the seven steps involved in laser printer imaging.

- Master the details of each step and their sequence.

- Be prepared to answer troubleshooting questions based on these steps.

The laser printing process often is referred to as the **electrophotographic (EP) process.**

Before the seven-step laser printing process can take place, the following events must occur:

- Laser printers are page-based; they must receive the entire page before they can start printing.

- After the page has been received, the printer pulls a sheet of paper into the printer with its feed rollers.

After the paper has been fed into the print mechanism, a series of seven steps takes place, which results in a printed page: processing, charging, exposing (also known as writing), developing, transferring, fusing, and cleaning.

The following section describes this process in more detail. Steps 1–7 are identified in Figure 10-1.

TIP   Make sure you know this exact order for the exam:

1. Processing
2. Charging
3. Exposing
4. Developing
5. Transferring
6. Fusing
7. Cleaning

Also, make sure you know the parts that make up a laser printer:

- imaging drum
- developer
- fuser assembly
- transfer belt
- transfer roller
- pickup rollers
- separate pads
- duplexing assembly

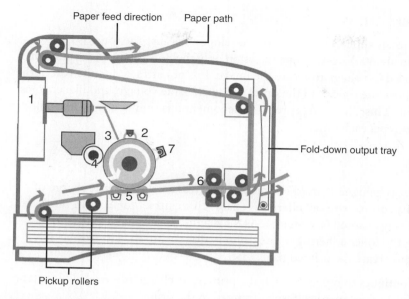

Figure 10-1   A conceptual drawing of a typical laser print process.

Step 1: Processing

The printer's raster image processing engine receives the page, font, text, and graphics data from the printer driver, creates a page image, and stores it in memory. Depending on the amount of information on the page compared to the amount of memory in the printer, the printer might need to compress the page image to store it. If there is not enough memory to store the page image, a memory error is triggered.

Step 2: Charging

The cylinder-shaped imaging drum receives an electrostatic charge of –600Vdc (DC voltage) from a conditioning roller. (Older printers used a primary corona wire.) The smooth surface of the drum retains this charge uniformly over its entire surface. The drum is photosensitive and will retain this charge only while kept in darkness.

Step 3: Exposing

A moving mirror moves the laser beam across the surface of the drum. As it moves, the laser beam temporarily records the image of the page to be printed on the surface of the drum by reducing the voltage of the charge applied by the charger corona to –100Vdc. Instead of using a laser beam, an LED printer activates its LED array to record the image on the page.

Step 4: Developing

The drum has toner applied to it from the developer; because the toner is electro-static and is also at –600Vdc, the toner stays on only the portions of the drum that have been reduced in voltage to create the image. It is not attracted to the rest of the drum because both the toner and the drum are at the same voltage, and like charges repel each other. This "like charges repel" phenomenon is similar to two like poles of magnets that repel each other.

Step 5: Transferring

While the sheet is being fed into the printer, it receives an electrostatic charge of +600Vdc from a corona wire or roller; this enables it to attract toner from the drum, which is negatively charged (see Step 3). As the drum's surface moves close to the charged paper, the toner adhering to the drum is attracted to the electrostatically charged paper to create the printed page.

As the paper continues to move through the printer, its charge is canceled by a static eliminator strip, so the paper itself isn't attracted to the drum.

Step 6: Fusing

The printed sheet of paper is pulled through fuser rollers, using high temperatures (approximately 350°F) to heat the toner and press it into the paper. The printed im-age is slightly raised above the surface of the paper.

The paper is ejected into the paper tray, and the drum must be prepared for another page.

Step 7: Cleaning

To prepare the drum for a new page, the image of the preceding page placed on the drum by the laser or LED array (see Step 3) is removed by a discharge lamp. Toner that is not adhering to the surface of the drum is scraped from the drum's surface for reuse.

Color Laser Printing Differences

Color laser printers differ from monochrome laser printers in two important ways: They include four different colors of toner (cyan, magenta, yellow, and black) and the imaging drum is separate from the toner. Thus, instead of waste toner being reused as in a monochrome laser printer that has a toner cartridge with an inte-grated imaging drum, waste toner in a color printer is sent to a separate waste toner container.

Color laser printers use the same basic process as monochrome lasers, but some use a transfer belt instead of an imaging drum. The use of a transfer belt enables all four colors (cyan, magenta, yellow, and black) to be placed on the paper at the same time, enabling color print speeds comparable to monochrome print speeds. When a transfer belt is used, the conditioning and transferring processes are performed on the transfer belt. See Figure 10-2.

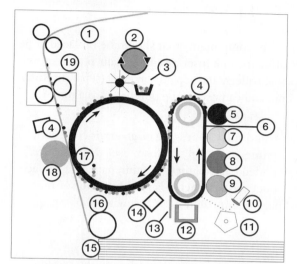

1. Paper path
2. Cleaning unit
3. Waste toner
4. Toner particles
5. Black toner
6. OPC belt
7. Yellow toner
8. Magenta toner
9. Cyan toner
10. Laser
11. Laser mirror
12. Charger
13. Cleaning blade
14. Erase lamp
15. Paper in paper tray
16. Paper pickup
17. Imaging drum
18. Transfer roller
19. Fusing rollers

Figure 10-2 The printing process in a typical color laser that uses a transfer belt.

Laser Media Types

Laser printers use standard smooth-finish printer or copier paper. Use labels and transparency media especially designed for laser printers, as other types of media might jam the printer or become distorted because of the high heat used in the laser printing process.

Labels made for copiers are not suitable for laser printers because they can come off the backing and stick to the printer's internal components.

Laser Maintenance

The major elements in laser printer maintenance include: Replacing toner, applying maintenance kit, calibration (color lasers only), and cleaning.

Replacing Toner Cartridges

If the laser printer's toner cartridge also includes the imaging drum, replacing the toner cartridge also replaces the imaging drum. Because the imaging drum's surface can become damaged, leaving marks on print output, changing the toner cartridge is helpful in improving print quality.

Installing Maintenance Kits

Many HP and other laser printers feature components that should be replaced at periodic intervals. These components often include fuser assemblies, air filters, transfer rollers, pickup rollers, other types of rollers, and separation pads (separate pads). These components wear out over time, and can usually be purchased as a **maintenance kit** as well as separately.

A printer that uses a maintenance kit will display a message or an error code with a meaning such as "Perform printer maintenance" or "Perform user maintenance" when the printer reaches the recommended page count for maintenance kit replacement. Depending upon the printer model and whether it is used for color or monochrome printing, the recommended page count could be at as few as 50,000 pages or as much as 300,000 pages or more.

NOTE   Sources for maintenance kits can also provide useful installation instructions. Sources for HP and Lexmark printers include PrinterTechs.com, Inc. (http://www.printertechs.com/maintenance-kits.php) and Depot International (http://www.depot-america.com) among others.

Resetting Paper Counts

After a fuser assembly or full maintenance kit is installed in a laser printer, the page count must be reset; otherwise, you will not know when to perform recommended maintenance again. Typically, the page count is reset by pressing a specified combination of buttons on the printer's control panel.

NOTE   If the printer is under service contract or being charged on a per-page (or per-click) basis, it is not recommended to reset the paper count after servicing. However, most laser printers print the page count when you perform a self-test.

Calibration

Color laser printers should be calibrated if print quality declines. The **printer calibration** process on a color laser printer adjusts image density settings to make up for changes caused by environmental differences or aging print cartridges.

Some color laser printers perform automatic calibration, but you can also force the printer to perform calibration on an as-needed basis. See the instruction manual for your printer for details.

NOTE **Print quality** is affected by many factors, such as the print resolution for graphics (the higher the dpi, the sharper and better), while using an economy printing mode that uses less toner reduces print quality. A damaged imaging drum or dirty rollers leaves marks on the paper that detract from print quality. If a color laser printer requires four passes to print in color and the colors are not properly lined up (a process known as color registration), print quality is affected.

Cleaning

Because laser printers use fine-grain powdered toner, keeping the inside of a laser printer clean is an important step in periodic maintenance. If you want to use a vacuum cleaner to pick up loose toner, be sure to use a vacuum cleaner that is designed to pick up toner, as toner particles are so small they will pass through conventional bags and filters. If you prefer to use a damp cloth, be sure to turn off the laser printer and disconnect it from power first.

To keep the paper path and rollers clean, use cleaning sheets made for laser printers, as follows:

Step 1. Insert the sheet into the manual feed tray on the laser printer.

Step 2. Create a short document with Notepad, WordPad, or some other text editor and then print it on the sheet.

As the sheet passes through the printer, it cleans the rollers. If a specialized cleaning sheet is not available, you can also use transparency film designed for laser printers. Some laser printers use a special software program to print a cleaning pattern onto plain paper.

NOTE Be sure to know how to maintain a laser printer for the 220-901 exam: Replacing toner, applying a maintenance kit, calibration, and cleaning.

CAUTION   Never use transparency media not designed for laser printers in a laser printer. Copier or inkjet media isn't designed to handle the high heat of a laser printer and can melt or warp and possibly damage the printer.

Inkjet Printers

Inkjet printers represent the most popular type of printer in small-office/home-office (SOHO) use today and are also popular in large offices. Their print quality can rival laser printers and virtually all inkjet printers in use today are able to print both color and black text and photographs.

From a tightly spaced group of nozzles, inkjet printers spray controlled dots of ink onto the paper to form characters and graphics. On a typical 5,760×1,440 dots per inch (dpi) printer, the number of nozzles can be as high as 180 for black ink and more than 50 per color (cyan, magenta, yellow). The tiny ink droplet size and high nozzle density enables inkjet printers to perform the seemingly impossible at resolutions as high as 1,200dpi or higher: fully formed characters from what is actually a high-resolution, non-impact, dot-matrix technology.

Inkjet printers are character/line printers. They print one line at a time of single characters or graphics up to the limit of the print head matrix. Inkjet printers are functionally fully formed character printers because their inkjet matrix of small droplets forming the image is so carefully controlled that individual dots are not visible.

Larger characters are created by printing a portion of the characters across the page, advancing the page to allow the print head to print another portion of the characters, and so on until the entire line of characters is printed. Thus, an inkjet printer is both a character and a line printer because it must connect lines of printing to build large characters. Some inkjet printers require realignment after each ink cartridge/print head change to make sure that vertical lines formed by multiple print head passes stay straight (this may be automatic or require the user to start the process); with other models, alignment can be performed through a utility provided as part of the printer driver when print quality declines due to misalignment.

Inkjet Components

The essential components in the inkjet printing process include: ink cartridges, print head, roller, paper **feeder**, duplexing assembly, carriage, and belt.

NOTE   Make sure you know this list of components for the 220-901 exam.

Some inkjet printers use external ink tanks for longer ink life between refills. Figure 10-3 shows how many of these components look in a typical printer.

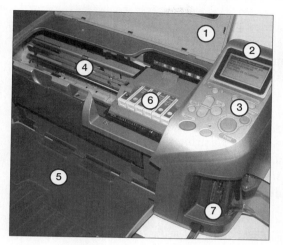

1. Dust cover
2. LCD instruction panel
3. Control panel
4. Printhead drive belt
5. Output tray
6. Ink cartridges
7. Flash memory card reader

Figure 10-3   A typical inkjet printer with its cover open.

Inkjet Printing Process

Inkjet printers use ink cartridges filled with liquid ink for printing. Some older inkjet printers use a large tank of black ink and a second tank with separate compartments for each color (typically cyan, magenta, and yellow; some models feature light versions of some of these colors for better photo-printing quality). However, almost all inkjet printers produced for a number of years use a separate cartridge for each color. This improves print economy for the user because only one color at a time needs to be replaced. With a multicolor cartridge, the entire cartridge needs to be replaced, even when only one of the colors runs out.

NOTE   Inkjet printers are sometimes referred to as CMYK devices because of the four ink colors used on most models: cyan, magenta, yellow, and black.

The **carriage and belt** mechanism move the **print head** back and forth to place ink droplets as the paper passes under the printer. Depending on the printer, the print head might be incorporated into the ink tank; be a separate, user-replaceable item; or be built into the printer.

Some inkjet printers feature an extra-wide (more nozzles) print head or a dual print head for very speedy black printing. Some models enable the user to replace either the **ink cartridge** only or an assembly comprising the print head and a replaceable ink cartridge.

NOTE   On an inkjet printer, print quality settings are typically good, better, best or text, text and image, photo, and best photo and are selected in the printer settings dialog. However, clogged nozzles (leading to ink dropouts), mismatch of paper type setting to actual paper used, and dirty rollers reduce actual print quality.

An inkjet printer is only as good as its print head and ink cartridges. Clogged or damaged print heads or ink cartridges render the printer useless. If an inkjet printer fails after its warranty expires, you should check service costs carefully before repairing the unit. Failed inkjet printers are often "throwaway" models and can be replaced, rather than repaired, even during the warranty period.

CAUTION   Inkjet printers should never be turned off with the power switch on a surge protector; doing so prevents the printer from self-capping its ink cartridges, which is a major cause of service calls and printer failures. Cleaning the print head, either with the printer's own cleaning feature, a cleaning utility built into the printer driver, or with a moistened cleaning sheet, will restore most printers to service.

Always use the printer's own power switch, which enables the printer to protect the ink cartridges and perform other periodic tasks (such as self-cleaning) properly.

Two major methods are used by inkjet printers to create the ink dots that make up the page. Most inkjet printers heat the ink to boiling, creating a tiny bubble of ink that is allowed to escape through the print head onto the paper. This is the origin of the name BubbleJet for the Canon line of inkjet printers. Printers using this method feature either ink cartridges that include the print head, or print heads with removable ink cartridge inserts. In case of a severely clogged print head, you can simply replace the ink cartridge if the ink cartridge incorporates the print head.

Another popular method uses a piezo-electric crystal to distribute the ink through the print head. This method makes achieving high resolutions easier; the Epson printers using this method were the first to achieve 5,760×1,440 dpi resolutions. This method also provides a longer print head life because the ink is not heated and cooled. However, the print heads are built into the printer, making a severely clogged print head harder to clean. Both types of inkjet printers are sometimes referred to as drop-on-demand printers.

During the inkjet print process:

Step 1.   The paper or media in a feed tray is pulled into position by a roller mechanism.

Step 2.   The print head is suspended on a carriage over the paper, and is moved across the paper by a belt. As the print head moves across the paper, it places black and color ink droplets as directed by the printer driver.

Step 3.   At the end of the line, the paper or media is advanced, and the print head either reverses direction and continues to print (often referred to as Hi-Speed mode) or returns to the left margin before printing continues.

Step 4.   After the page is completed, the media is ejected.

Inkjet Media Types

Inkjet printers can use the same types of paper and labels that laser printers can use. However, inkjet printers can also use special matte or glossy-coated paper and business card stock for presentation or photo-realistic images. Transparency stock must be designed specifically for inkjet use. Because of improvements in media and print design, old inkjet photo paper should be recycled rather than used, as older paper types have very slow drying times compared to recent types.

When printing, it's important to select the correct media type in the printer driver to avoid banding, overuse of ink, and other poor-quality results.

Inkjet Maintenance

Ink cartridge replacement, calibration, nozzle check, and head cleaning, and clearing jams are the major elements in maintaining an inkjet printer.

NOTE   Make sure you know ink cartridge replacement, calibration, nozzle check, and head cleaning, and clearing jams for the 220-901 exam.

Replacing Ink Cartridges

Use the printing preferences or printer properties dialog (varies by printer and operating system) to determine when it's time to purchase additional ink or replace the ink cartridges (see Figure 10-4).

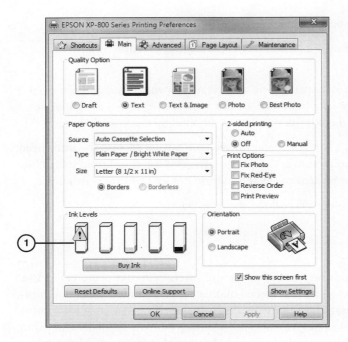

1. Warning of critically low ink level

Figure 10-4   All of the ink levels in this printer are low, but the ink cartridge marked with an ! is about to run out.

> **NOTE**   Most inkjet printers stop printing when one color runs out, even if that color is not being used in the current print job. Some printers offer to use a mixture of photo black and colors if the normal black ink runs low during a print job.

Some printers run automatic nozzle cleaning or calibration routines when you change ink cartridges. If the ink cartridge includes a print head, whenever you change the ink cartridge you also change the print head. Consequently, replacing ink cartridges is the single best maintenance item you can perform on an inkjet printer.

Calibration

Inkjet printers might require or recommend some type of printer calibration, most typically print head alignment. This process involves printing one or more sheets of paper and selecting the print setting that produces straight lines. Some printers perform this step automatically, while others might require user intervention to determine the best setting.

Some inkjet printers can use two printing methods: unidirectional, in which the printer prints only when the print head is moving from left to right, and bidirectional, in which the printer prints when the print head is moving in either direction (left to right or right to left). If the print head is misaligned, bidirectional printing (sometimes referred to as high-speed printing) will have much poorer print quality than unidirectional printing.

Be sure to align the print head as needed, using the calibration or alignment utility provided in the printer driver (see Figure 10-5A), to permit successful use of bidirectional printing.

To enable bidirectional printing, select this option (when it's offered) in the Print Preferences menu (see Figure 10-5B).

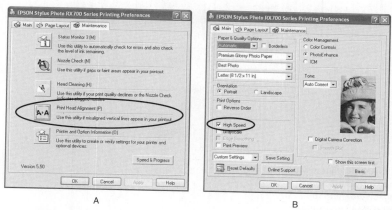

A   B

Figure 10-5   Aligning the print head (a) helps produce better-quality high-speed (bidirectional) printing (b).

NOTE   With some printers, it might be necessary to realign the print head each time after changing ink cartridges (some of these printers perform this task automatically). However, with others, it might be an optional utility that you can run on an as-needed basis.

Nozzle Check and Head Cleaning

Periodically, especially if a printer has not been used for a while or has been used only for monochrome printing, it's a good idea to use the **nozzle check** routine to verify that all the print heads' nozzles are working correctly.

The nozzle check or pattern check routine prints a pattern that uses all of the nozzles in all of the print heads and displays the pattern's correct appearance. Compare the printout to the on-screen display, and if you see gaps or missing colors, activate the head cleaning routine (see Figure 10-6). Repeat these steps until the nozzle check printout matches the screen display. Keep in mind that using nozzle check uses ink.

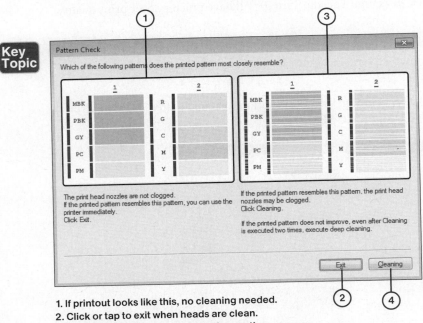

1. If printout looks like this, no cleaning needed.
2. Click or tap to exit when heads are clean.
3. If printout has streaks, run cleaning routine.
4. Click or tap to start head cleaning routine.

Figure 10-6   The Pattern Check (nozzle check) dialog from a Canon inkjet printer driver's maintenance tab.

Depending on the printer, these options might be located in the printer preferences' Maintenance tab, a toolbox dialog, or other places, such as the printer's onboard menu. See your printer's documentation for details.

CAUTION   If you use a Windows-provided printer driver, these options might not be available. Install a driver from your printer vendor.

Thermal Printers

A **thermal printer** uses heat transfer to create text and graphics on the paper. Thermal printers are used in point-of-sale and retail environments as well as for some types of portable printing.

Thermal printers are available using three different technologies:

- Thermal transfer
- Direct thermal
- Dye sublimation

Thermal Feed Assembly and Heating Element

Thermal printers can use a dot-matrix print mechanism or a dye-sublimation technology to transfer images. Direct thermal printers use heat-sensitive paper (**special thermal paper**), while thermal transfer printers use a wax, resin, or dye **ribbon** to create the image. Some printers can use either heat-sensitive media or a ribbon.

The **feed assembly** on a typical thermal receipt or point-of-sale printer pulls paper from a roll wound around a center plastic spool or spindle. The feed assembly on a typical desktop thermal barcode printer uses notched rollers and spring-loaded sprockets to advance roll paper. Larger thermal barcode printers might also use fanfold media as well as roll media.

The **heating element** in the print head is used to heat thermal paper or ribbons to make the image. Printers that use ribbons are thermal transfer printers, and printers that use thermal paper are known as direct thermal printers.

Thermal Printer Ribbons

Thermal transfer printers use wax or resin-based ribbons, which are often bundled with paper made especially for the printer. Dye-sublimation (dye-sub) printers use dye-based film ribbons technology to print continuous-tone photographs. Examples of consumer-grade dye-sublimation printers include Kodak printer docks and Canon's Selphy CP series; these printers print 4×6-inch photos. Many vendors also sell larger-format dye-sublimation printers for use in photo labs and professional photography studios.

Figure 10-7 illustrates a typical dye-sublimation ribbon for a Canon Selphy CP printer.

Figure 10-7   A dye-sublimation ribbon for a 4x6-inch photo printer (Canon Selphy CP).

Thermal Print Process

Although thermal transfer, direct thermal printing, and dye sublimation all involve heating the elements in a print head to a particular temperature to transfer the image, there are some differences in operation. The basic process of thermal printing works like this:

Step 1.   The print head has a matrix of dots that can be heated in various combinations to create text and graphics.

Step 2.   The print head transfers text and graphics directly to heat-sensitive thermal paper in direct thermal printing, or to a ribbon that melts onto the paper in thermal transfer printing.

Step 3.   If a multicolor ribbon is used on a thermal transfer or dye-sublimation printer, each ribbon is moved past the print head to print the appropriate color. In the case of dye-sublimation printers, the paper is moved back into position to enable the next color to be printed.

Step 4.   Once all colors have been printed, the paper is ejected.

Figure 10-8 compares direct thermal and thermal transfer printing technologies.

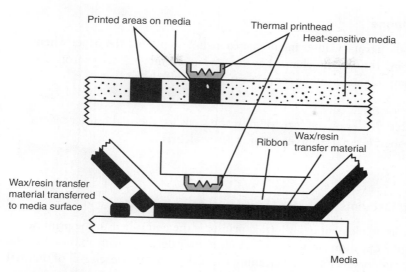

Figure 10-8   Direct thermal (top) and thermal transfer (bottom) printing technologies.

Thermal Paper and Media

Direct thermal printers use special thermal (heat-sensitized) paper, while thermal transfer printers might use either standard copy paper or glossy photo paper, depending on their intended use.

If the printer uses direct thermal printing, heat-sensitive paper with characteristics matching the printer's design specifications must be used. For portable printers using direct thermal printing such as the Brother PocketJet series, the usual source for such paper is the printer vendor or its authorized resellers. If the direct thermal printer is used for bar codes or point-of-sale transactions, you can get suitable paper or label stock from bar code or POS equipment suppliers and resellers.

Thermal transfer ribbons are available in three categories: wax (for paper; smooth paper produces the best results), wax/resin (synthetics), and resin (glossy hard films such as polyester). Choose the appropriate ribbon type for the material you will be printing on.

Dye-sublimation photo printers in the consumer space use special media kits that include both a ribbon and suitable photo paper stocks. Larger format dye-sublimation printers are designed to print on standard-size and special-format roll and sheet dye-sublimation paper stocks available separately from the ink or ribbon.

Thermal Maintenance

The elements of thermal printer maintenance include replacing the paper when it runs out, cleaning the heating element as directed and removing debris from the heating element, rollers, or other components as needed.

NOTE   For the 220-901 exam, be sure to know the steps for thermal printer maintenance: Replace paper, clean heating element, remove debris.

Cleaning Heating Elements

Because the heating element in a thermal printer is the equivalent to the print head in impact or inkjet printers, it must be kept clean in order to provide maximum print quality. Many vendors recommend cleaning the print head after each roll of thermal transfer ribbon.

Some thermal transfer ribbons for POS and warehouse printers include special cleaning materials at the beginning of the roll. Some thermal printer vendors also supply special cleaning film you can use to remove dust, debris, and coating residue from print heads.

You can also use isopropyl alcohol to clean print heads. It is available in wipes, pens, pads, and swabs from various vendors. The ribbon must be removed before using isopropyl alcohol. When isopropyl alcohol is used in cleaning, it is essential to wait until the printer dries out before reinstalling the ribbon.

Removing Debris

Debris from torn paper, solid ink flakes, and label coatings can build up on rollers and other components as well as the print head. Use isopropyl alcohol wipes or other cleaning materials as recommended by the printer supplies to clean up debris for better print quality and longer print life.

Impact Printers

An **impact printer** is so named because it uses a mechanical print head that presses against an inked ribbon to print characters and graphics. Impact printers are the oldest printer technology, and are primarily used today in industrial and point-of-sale applications.

Dot-matrix printers, the most common form of impact printers, are so named because they create the appearance of fully formed characters from dots placed on the page.

NOTE For the 220-901 exam, be sure to know the basic elements of impact printing: print head, ribbon, tractor feed, and impact paper.

Impact Components and Print Process

Impact dot-matrix printers have the following parts moving in coordination with each other during the printing process:

Step 1.   The paper is moved past the print head vertically by pull or push tractors or by a platen.

Step 2.   The print head moves across the paper horizontally, propelled along the print head carriage by a drive belt, printing as it moves from left to right. Bidirectional printing prints in both directions but is often disabled for high-quality printing because it can be difficult to align the printing precisely.

Step 3.   As the print head moves, the pins in the print head are moving in and out against an inked **printer ribbon** as the print head travels across the paper to form the text or create graphics.

Step 4.   The ribbon is also moving to reduce wear during the printing process.

Steps 1–4 are repeated for each line until the page is printed. Figure 10-9 illustrates a typical impact dot-matrix printer.

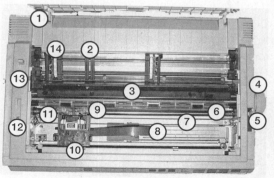

1. Rear cover (top cover removed, not shown)
2. Paper supports for tractor-feed paper path
3. Platen for using single sheets of paper
4. Manual paper advance knob
5. Paper bail lifter
6. Paper bail
7. Timing/drive belt
8. Printhead signal control cable
9. Printhead with heat sink
10. Ribbon holder
11. Printhead support rod
12. Head gap adjustment
13. Tractor/friction-feed selector lever
14. Tractor feed

Figure 10-9   Components of a typical impact dot-matrix printer. The model pictured is a wide-carriage version, but its features are typical of models using either standard or wide-carriage paper.

Impact Dot-Matrix Print Heads

The most common types of print heads include 9-pin, 18-pin (two columns of nine pins), and 24-pin (which produces Near Letter Quality or NLQ quality printing when used in best quality mode).

Figure 10-10 shows actual print samples from a typical 9-pin printer's draft mode, a typical 24-pin printer's draft mode, and the Near Letter Quality (NLQ) mode of the same 24-pin printer.

```
RN_clients.html.Z ───────── 9-pin printer draft mode
RN_loc_cal.html.Z
RN_loc_doc.html.Z
RN_loc_uucp.html.Z

This is a test of switching ── 24-pin printer draft mode

Congratulations! ───────── 24-pin printer NLQ mode

If you can read this inform
Panasonic KX-P1624.

The information below descr
```

Figure 10-10 Actual print samples illustrating the differences in 24-pin and 9-pin impact dot-matrix printers.

NOTE The print samples shown in Figure 10-10 are taken from printers that use 8.5 ×11-inch or wider paper sizes. The print head design and print quality vary greatly on printers that use smaller paper sizes in point-of-sale applications.

Impact Printer Ribbons

Printer ribbons for impact printers use various types of cartridge designs. Some span the entire width of the paper, and others snap over the print head. Figure 10-11 compares various types of ribbons for impact printers.

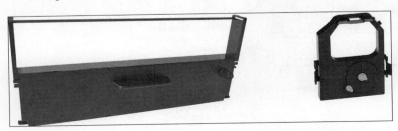

Figure 10-11 Some typical ribbons for impact dot-matrix printers.

Impact Printer Paper Types

Impact printers use plain uncoated paper or labels in various widths and sizes. Impact printers designed for point-of-sale receipt printing might use roll paper or larger sizes of paper. When larger sizes of paper are used, these printers typically use a **tractor feed** mechanism to pull or push the paper past the print head. Paper and labels used with tractor-fed printers has fixed or removable sprocket holes on both sides of the paper. This type of media is often called "**impact paper**," "dot matrix," "continuous feed," or "pin-feed" paper or labels. Media with standard perforations can be difficult to separate from the paper edge after printing, but are less likely to separate prior to use than micro-perforated media.

Multi-part forms are frequently used with impact printers used in point-of-sale (POS) systems. Be sure to adjust the head gap appropriately to avoid print head or ribbon damage.

Impact Printer Maintenance

The keys to successful maintenance of an impact printer include: replacing the ribbon, replacing the print head, and replacing the paper.

NOTE   For the 220-901 exam, be sure to know the basic elements of impact printer maintenance: replace ribbon, replace print head, and replace paper.

Replacing the Ribbon

When the ribbon is worn, the quality of printing goes down. But what you might not realize is that the ribbon on an impact dot-matrix printer also lubricates the pins in the print head and protects the print head from impact damage.

In addition to replacing the ribbon when print quality is no longer acceptable, be sure to immediately discard a ribbon that develops cuts or snags, as these can snag a print head pin and break or bend the pin.

Replacing the Print Head

If you replace ribbons when needed, you minimize the chances of needing to replace the print head. However, if a print head suffers damage to one or more pins, you must replace it. Damaged pins might snag the ribbon, and if a pin breaks, it will leave a gap in the characters output by the printer.

Instead of purchasing a new print head, consider having the old print head reconditioned or rebuilt.

TIP   If you need a replacement quickly, some vendors offer advance exchange programs, which enable you to obtain a remanufactured or refurbished print head on a cross-shipped basis rather than waiting until they receive your old print head.

Replacing Paper

When you replace paper, be sure to check continuous-feed (tractor-fed) paper for problems with torn sprocket holes, separated tear-offs, and damaged sheets. Tear off any problem pages and use only good paper from the stack in your printer.

Be sure tractor feeders are properly adjusted, and if the printer can be run as either a push tractor (allows zero-tear paper feed) or a pull tractor, be sure the printer is properly configured for the feed type.

Check the head gap carefully: be sure to adjust it if you need to run multi-part forms, thick labels, or envelopes. An incorrect head gap can lead to ribbon and print head damage.

Virtual Printers

The term "**virtual printer**" applies to any utility that is used as a printer by an app, but creates a file instead of a printout. There are three major categories of virtual printers:

- Print to file
- Print to PDF or XPS
- Print to image

Print to File

Print to file is used to create a file that can be copied to a specific printer for output. This type of file contains not only the text and graphics but also specific printer control sequences and font references for the targeted printer.

CAUTION   To avoid problems with print output, make sure you use fonts in your document that are also available to the target printer. If the printer doesn't have the same fonts as the system used to create the file, font substitutions will take place.

To use print to file in Microsoft Windows:

Step 1.   Open the print dialog.

Step 2.   Select the printer.

Step 3.   Check the **Print to file** box.

Step 4.   Click **Print**.

Step 5.   You are typically prompted for a file location. If not, check your Documents folder to locate the file after printing. The file is stored with the PRN file extension (.prn).

Print to file is intended for use primarily with printers using the parallel (LPT) port and is not available with all apps. The printer that will be used to output the PRN file must be configured as the default port. However, by sharing a USB printer, it is possible to copy a print file to a USB printer.

> **NOTE**   For more information about printing to a file, see http://filext.com/faq/print_from_prn_file.php

As an alternative, use Print to PDF or XPS. With these options, it is not necessary to be concerned about font matching.

With OS X, use the Print dialog and select PostScript for output to a PostScript printer. For PDF options, see "Print to PDF or XPS," coming up next.

Linux can print text, PostScript, PDF, and image files using the lpr command or CUPS (Common Unix Printing System). For more information about CUPS, see www.cups.org.

Print to PDF or XPS

Some recent Windows apps can save files directly to **PDF** (Adobe Acrobat/Adobe Reader) format. For apps that don't support direct save to PDF, you can install a print to PDF virtual printer. Some versions of Windows include this capability or it can be added by installing Adobe Acrobat or most third-party PDF reading or editing apps.

Print to PDF or XPS in Windows

When you print to PDF using a Windows app, you are prompted to specify the destination for the file. However, most other PDF options (compression, metadata support, and others) are not available. Use the Save to PDF option, when offered, to control these settings.

Current versions of Windows include the Microsoft XPS Document Writer virtual printer. Select this printer if you want to create an **XPS** (XML Paper Specification) document. When you select this option, you can optionally enable the opening of your XPS file after it is saved.

Print to PDF in OS X

With OS X, use the Print dialog and open the PDF menu to select the type and destination for the PDF file:

- **Save as PDF**—With this option, you can add Title, Author, Subject, and Keywords metadata. Use the Security Options button to set up password restrictions for opening, copying content, or printing the document.

- **Fax PDF**—Sends the PDF to your fax device

- **Mail PDF**—Creates a new email message and attaches your PDF.

- **Save as PDF-X**—Creates a PDF-X file (used by professional print shops).

- **Save PDF to iPhoto**—Imports your PDF into iPhoto.

- **Save PDF to Web Receipts**—Saves your PDF to your Web Receipts folder.

Print to PDF in Linux

To print to PDF in Linux, install CUPS-PDF (the CUPS printer driver for PDF). Restart your system (if necessary) and PDF will show up in your list of printers.

Print to Image

Some virtual printer apps are designed to convert documents directly into common bitmap graphics formats such as TIFF, JPEG, BMP, and others. Some of these apps can also create PDF files.

Print to Image for Windows

Some of the apps available for Windows include:

- Image Printer Pro—https://code-industry.net

- Print&Share—www.printandshare.info

- Raster Image Printer and TIFF Image Printer—www.peernet.com

- Universal Document Converter—www.print-driver.com
- Zan Image Printer—www.zan1011.com

Print to Image for OS X

The print subsystem in OS X can be used to create many types of bitmap images. A freeware app that makes this easy is Spool Pilot for Mac: www.colorpilot.com/spool.html.

Ghostscript (Linux, OS X, and Windows)

Ghostscript is an open-source command-line utility that can output to PDF, PostScript, EPS, text, and most current and legacy bitmap formats (PSD, PCX, TIFF, JPG, PNG, and others). For more information, see www.ghostscript.com.

Installing Your Printer or Multifunction Device

Printers and multifunction devices cannot function without operating system support. Depending on the printer or multifunction device and operating system, the printer or device might be recognized automatically and the drivers installed, or it might be necessary to download and install drivers manually.

Printer/Multifunction Device Installation for Windows

Windows offers a variety of methods for installing a printer or multifunction device. Choose the appropriate method based on your version of Windows and the source of your driver file.

Using Add Printer (Windows 7/8/8.1)

The Add Printer option can be used if Windows includes a suitable driver and the enhanced features that might be provided by a vendor-supplied driver are not necessary. Add Printer is run from the Devices and Printers Control Panel applet in Windows 7 and 8/8.1/10; Windows 8/8.1/10 can also run Add Printer from the Devices dialog in PC Settings. Local printers are automatically detected when connected to a USB port and turned on, or you can manually specify a local port, network share, wireless network, or Bluetooth network connection.

After selecting the printer brand and model, Windows installs the printer. You can also specify the option to use Windows Update to locate a suitable driver or select Have Disk to use the printer vendor's driver disc or file (see Figure 10-12).

After the printer is installed, specify whether or not to share the printer, whether the new printer is the default printer, and (optionally) print a test page. The printer is added to your list of printers and multifunction devices.

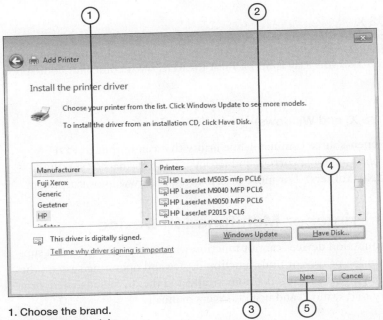

1. Choose the brand.
2. Choose the model.
3. Can't find your printer? Click or tap to run Windows Update to locate a driver (option not available in Windows 8/8.1/10).
4. Have a driver disk or extracted driver file? Click or tap to use it.
5. After your printer is selected, click or tap to continue.

Figure 10-12   Installing a printer using Add Printer in Windows 7.

Installing a Printer with a Vendor-Supplied Driver

Whether you use a vendor-supplied install disc or a downloaded file, the installation process is quite different from the Add printer method. After opening the disc or the downloaded driver file, connect your printer to the USB (or FireWire) port as needed but don't turn it on. Select your device, then turn on the printer or device when prompted. After the installation process is complete, you might be prompted to restart your system.

Printer/Multifunction Device Installation for OS X

To install a printer or multifunction device, open the Printers & Scanners dialog in System Preferences. Click the plus (+) sign at the bottom of the left-hand pane to add a printer (refer to Figure 10-14).

Local and network printers and multifunction devices are listed (see Figure 10-13). Select the desired printer or device and the driver file is downloaded from the Apple website.

At the end of the process, the printer or device is listed in the Printers & Scanners menu (see Figure 10-14). Click the plus (+) sign in the left pane to install another printer when necessary.

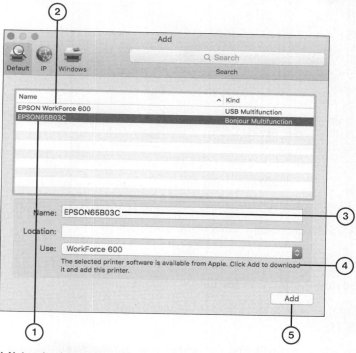

1. Network printer (selected)
2. Local (USB) printer
3. Printer name (change as desired)
4. Driver available from Apple
5. Click to download driver

Figure 10-13   Selecting a printer with OS X 10.11.

If you need to install a driver manually, download a driver made for your printer and OS X version and install it before connecting your printer and turning it on.

1. Click to add another printer
2. Information about selected printer

Figure 10-14   The Printers & Scanners dialog in OS X 10.11.

Printer/Multifunction Device Installation for Linux

Use the Printers dialog (found in System Settings in many Linux distros) to install a printer (see Figure 10-15).

If you need to install a driver manually, use the printer configuration tool included with most distros to:

- Select the correct printer driver (or one for a similar model that will work with your printer) from the database of printers provided.

- Install a PPD (Postscript Printer Description) file or download a driver.

NOTE   See the Printer Driver List at www.openprinting.org/drivers/ for driver links and sources supporting many brands and models of inkjet and laser printers. Be sure to choose the correct driver type for your distro (Debian or RPM).

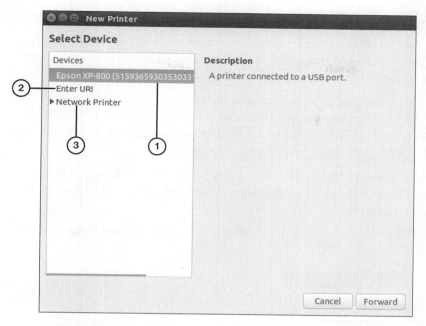

1. Selected printer
2. Click to enter the uniform resource indicator (URI) for the printer
3. Click to view network printers

Figure 10-15   The New Printer—Select a Device dialog in Ubuntu 14.

When the printer or multifunction device is installed, it is displayed in the list of installed printers (see Figure 10-16).

1. Check mark indicates printer is default

Figure 10-16   A local multifunction device after installation in Ubuntu 14.

Printer/Multifunction Device Installation for iOS and Android

Android and iOS users can connect to wireless printers and multifunction devices by installing drivers available through each device's app store. These drivers are released by the printer/device vendor.

Connect to the same wireless network that is used by your printer or device. Some printers and devices can also be configured to use **Ad-Hoc** (local, routerless) Wi-Fi connections for direct wireless connection between devices. If your printer or device supports Bluetooth, you might prefer to use it for printing.

Verify that the printer or device has its own IP address (Wi-Fi). After you visit your mobile device's app store and download the printer software, use it to locate your printer on the network.

Figure 10-17 illustrates a typical Android printing app, Epson iPrint. Similar apps are available for iOS.

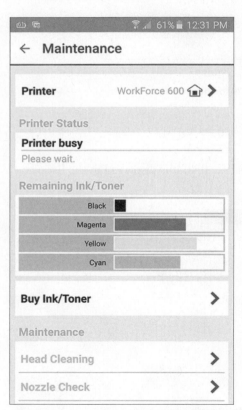

Figure 10-17   Epson iPrint's Maintenance menu shows the ink levels on the remote printer.

Configuring Your Printer or Multifunction Device

Typical configuration options for printers or multifunction devices include:

- **Duplex** (double-sided) printing—This option may be available on single-sided printers as well as true duplex (both-side of paper) printers. With a single-side printer, the duplex setting is used to determine how to position the paper for printing the second side.

- Collating—The **collate** setting is used when printing two or more copies of a document with two or more pages. When enabled, each copy of page 1 is printed before printing page 2, and so on. Useful when creating print jobs for binding, stapling, or punching, but is slower than uncollated print jobs.

- **Orientation**—Portrait (long side up) or landscape (short side up) may be selected automatically in some printer drivers by the orientation of the document to be printed. If not selected automatically, choose the correct orientation. Use print preview to help determine the setting needed.

- Print quality (laser)—With laser printers and multifunction devices, you might be able to select the desired resolution (dots per inch [DPI]). Higher DPI levels produce smoother text output and more finely detailed graphics, but require more printer RAM. As an alternative, some drivers have options to enable smoother text printing or adjust page compression.

- Print quality (inkjet)—Instead of specific resolutions, inkjet printers use quality settings such as High, Standard, Fast (Canon); Draft, Text, Text and Image, Photo, and Best Photo (Epson); Draft, Normal, Best (HP). Each setting optimizes the size of the ink droplet and paper coverage for the best results with the specified paper.

- Paper type (inkjet)—In addition to specifying the print quality desired, it is critical to select the actual paper type in use. The default is plain paper, but if matte presentation, semi-gloss, or glossy paper is used with the plain paper setting, the resulting printouts will be of very poor quality.

Configuring Printer Settings in Windows

To configure these and other printer settings in Windows, right-click the printer or multifunction device in Devices and Printers and select Printing Preferences.

NOTE   Printing Preferences is used to set options such as print quality, resolution, scaling, and maintenance features. The location of options on tabs and the names of the tabs vary from printer to printer. Use Printer Properties to configure printer/multifunction device sharing, color management, security, and other less-frequently-used settings.

Figure 10-18 illustrates the Paper/Quality dialog for an HP LaserJet Pro M402 printer as print resolution is being selected.

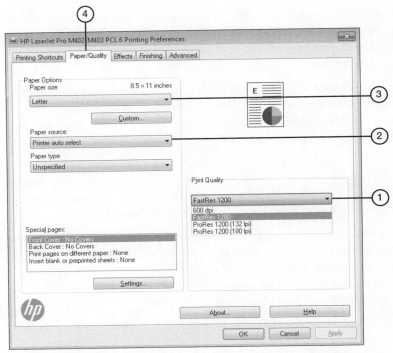

1. Click or tap to select resolution
2. Click or tap to select paper tray
3. Click or tap to select paper size
4. Selected tab

Figure 10-18   Selecting print resolution with an HP LaserJet Pro.

Figure 10-19 illustrates the Page Setup menu for a Canon inkjet printer on Windows 8.1. This dialog includes settings for page size, orientation, page layout, duplex printing, copies, and collation.

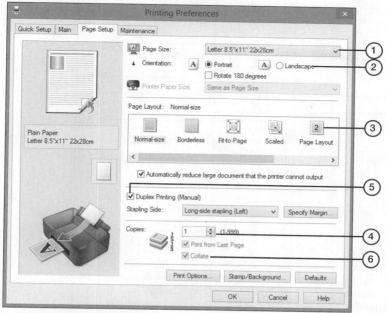

1. Click or tap to select paper size
2. Click or tap correct page orientation
3. Click or tap desired page layout
4. Click, tap, or enter number of copies
5. Click to print on both sides of paper (manual page flipping needed)
6. Collating already selected on app's main Print menu

Figure 10-19   Selecting page settings with a Canon Pixma Pro series printer.

Configuring Printer Settings in OS X

Although a few settings can be configured through the Printers & Scanners menu, most printer configuration is performed through the File/Print menu in an app. Select the printer, and you can configure the number of prints, paper size, and orientation from the main menu (see Figure 10-20). Open the submenus to select media type, print quality, and other settings.

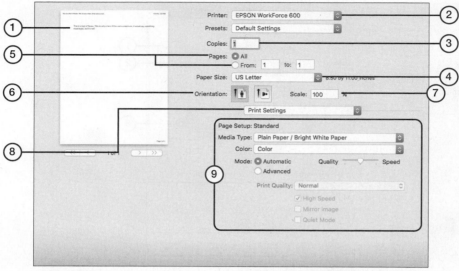

1. Print preview
2. Click to select printer
3. Click to enter number of copies
4. Click to select paper size
5. Click to select pages to print

6. Click to select page orientation
7. Click to adjust scaling
8. Click to select different submenus
9. Items in selected submenu

Figure 10-20   Basic print settings for a document being printed from Notes.

If you print a photo, you are also prompted to choose the size and layout of the photo on a page (see Figure 10-21).

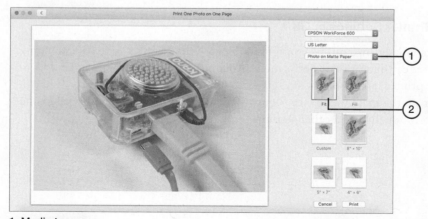

1. Media type
2. Print layout

Figure 10-21   Selecting paper size and type and picture layout in Photos.

Use the Paper Handling submenu to specify collation, pages to print, and scaling. Use the Print Settings menu and submenus (shown in Figure 10-20) to specify print quality and media type.

Use the Presets menu to save your settings for reuse.

Configuring Printer Settings in Linux

Use the Printer Properties dialog (a submenu of Printers) to configure print settings. In Figure 10-22, you see paper and quality settings for an Epson inkjet printer being used to print on glossy photo paper.

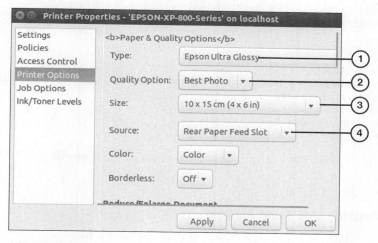

1. Media type
2. Print quality
3. Paper size
4. Paper source (paper tray)

Figure 10-22   Using the Ubuntu 14 Printer Properties dialog to configure an inkjet printer for 4x6-inch glossy photos.

Figure 10-23 shows job options (copies, orientation, and image options) in Ubuntu 14. For additional settings such as resolution, click or tap the **More** button.

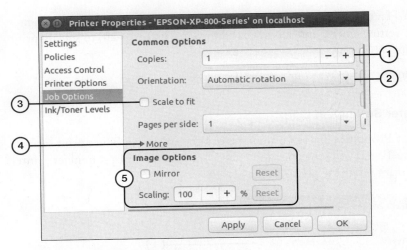

1. Click to change number of copies
2. Automatic rotation changes printer orientation to match document; you can also select orientation manually
3. Click to scale print job to paper
4. Click to see additional print settings
5. Additional settings

Figure 10-23   A portion of the Job Options page in Ubuntu 14's Printer Properties dialog.

Configuring Printer Settings in iOS and Android

The exact features in a Print Settings menu for an iOS or Android printer app vary by printer and app, but Figure 10-24 shows a typical example (Epson app for Android).

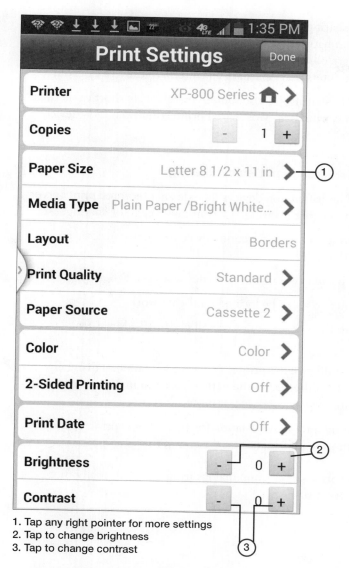

Figure 10-24   Configuring a printer with the Epson iPrint app for Android.

1. Tap any right pointer for more settings
2. Tap to change brightness
3. Tap to change contrast

Device Sharing Options

Printer and multifunction devices can be shared between two or more computers by using one of the following wired sharing methods: USB, Serial, or Ethernet.

Serial (RS-232) and USB sharing use switchboxes that can be manually switched between devices or can automatically detect print jobs and switch to the active computer. Serial switchboxes are obsolete for most tasks, and USB switchboxes are limited by the number of computers that can share a printer: typically two or four.

Both serial and USB printer sharing are also limited by relatively short cable runs and a lack of management capabilities. Most wired printer/multifunction device sharing now uses Ethernet.

Integrated Ethernet Print/Multifunction Device Sharing

Many recent printers and multifunction devices include an **integrated print server** with support for Ethernet network printing. To configure them for sharing:

Step 1.   Connect the printer or multifunction device to the network via an Ethernet (RJ-45) cable.

Step 2.   Configure the printer or multifunction device to use Ethernet.

Step 3.   Name the printer so it can be located on the network.

Step 4.   Specify whether the printer or device will get an IP address from a DHCP router.

Step 5.   If you need to configure the printer or device's IP address manually, determine which IP addresses on the network are not in use and manually assign the printer or device to one of those addresses.

Step 6.   Record the configuration information for reuse. Some printers and devices might print the information at the end of the setup process.

Figure 10-25 shows some print server setup dialogs from a typical small office printer with wireless Ethernet support.

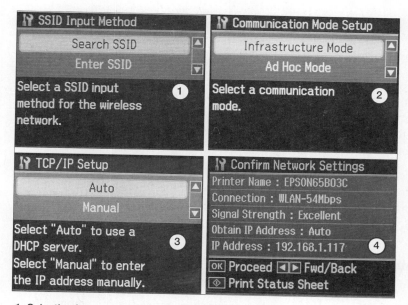

1. Selecting how to locate the SSID for wireless print serving
2. Selecting the network mode for the wireless print server
3. Specifying where to get an IP address (wired/wireless)
4. Confirming network settings

Figure 10-25   Configuring a printer as an Ethernet or wireless Ethernet print server.

Adding Ethernet Print/Multifunction Device Sharing

To add support for Ethernet local area networking to a printer that does not have a built-in Ethernet port, connect it to an Ethernet print server. Print servers enable the printer to be accessed via the print server's IP address. Figure 10-26 illustrates a typical Ethernet print server for USB printers.

Figure 10-26   Front and rear views of an Ethernet print server that supports USB printers.

NOTE   Some laser printers can be upgraded with an internal Ethernet print server card.

When a printer includes its own Ethernet port, it is assigned an IP address on a TCP/IP network; similarly, a print server is also assigned an IP address on a TCP/IP network. Print servers are configured and managed via your computer's web browser, and some also support configuration via FTP.

To print to a network printer or device, you might need to install a network printer driver instead of the normal printer driver on the computer that will use the printer or multifunction device. To learn more about TCP/IP, see Chapter 11, "Networking."

Wireless Device Sharing Options

The two major network protocols used for wireless device sharing include Bluetooth and 802.11 (Wi-Fi). Bluetooth is suitable for very short-range sharing among a few devices, while 802.11-based print sharing supports a much larger number of guest devices at much longer ranges.

Bluetooth

Most printers with built-in Bluetooth support are portable or receipt printers.

Printers lacking Bluetooth support can use special Bluetooth adapters to enable them to connect with computers or mobile devices that use Bluetooth. Check with the printer device vendor for models compatible with a specific printer.

Before a computer or mobile device can connect to a printer or multifunction device using Bluetooth, both the computer/mobile device and the printer/multifunction device must have Bluetooth transceivers. Bluetooth support is common among laptop and mobile devices, and can be added with a USB dongle to computers lacking Bluetooth support.

After enabling Bluetooth on the printer and computer, you must configure both for pairing and pair them before print jobs can be sent. For details, see Chapter 11.

802.11(a,b,g,n,ac)

Many recent printers and multifunction devices now include some level of 802.11 (Wi-Fi) support. The configuration process is typically similar to that used for wired Ethernet, with the added step of specifying the wireless network's SSID and encryption key (if used). Refer to Figure 10-25.

To add support for 802.11 Wireless Ethernet local area networking to a printer, connect it to a Wireless Ethernet (Wi-Fi) print server. As with their Ethernet siblings, Wi-Fi print servers are managed via browser interfaces.

NOTE   Most Wireless Ethernet print servers also include Ethernet support.

Infrastructure vs. Ad Hoc

If you want to use wireless Ethernet (Wi-Fi) printers or multifunction devices but don't use Wi-Fi networking with a wireless router, configure the printers/devices to work in Ad-Hoc (adhoc) mode. In Ad-Hoc mode, each device is connected directly to other devices: no router is used.

Infrastructure mode supports WPA2 encryption, while Ad-Hoc mode supports only WEP encryption, making it unsuitable for secure networking.

Ad-Hoc Wireless Network Support in Windows

Ad-hoc wireless networking is supported in Windows 7 through the Network and Sharing Center. It is also available in Windows 8/8.1 from the command line using Netsh, but it has been removed in Windows 10.

Ad-Hoc Wireless Network Support in OS X

OS X supports Ad-Hoc wireless networking through the Wi-Fi Status icon on the Finder menu. OS X refers to this feature as "computer-to-computer" networking. When you enable this feature, your computer cannot connect to other Wi-Fi networks at the same time. Figure 10-27 illustrates the dialog.

1. Select the least-used wireless channel
2. Click to create network

Figure 10-27   Creating a computer-to-computer (Ad-Hoc) wireless network with OS X 10.11.

Ad Hoc Wireless Networking Support in Linux

Ad Hoc wireless networking in Linux is sometimes referred to as an IBSS (independent basic service set) network. Depending on the distro, this can be done by turning on the Wireless Hotspot service in Network settings or by using command-line utilities iw and ip. NetworkManager (https://wiki.gnome.org/Projects/NetworkManager) can be installed on distros that lack easy network management.

Wireless Hosted Networking

As a replacement for Ad Hoc mode, Windows 7 introduced Wireless Hosted Networking, which is also available in Windows 8/8.1/10. With Wireless Hosted Networking, you can create a Wi-Fi network that is detectable and usable by Wi-Fi-enabled printers and other computers and devices.

To create an unsecured wireless hosted network, open a command prompt and enter this command:

```
netsh wlan start hostednetwork
```

(replace "hostednetwork" with the name of your network).

Set up your printer or multifunction device to use the same network name. To print, have each user connect to that network. A printer or multifunction device can only use one network at a time, but computers can connect to this network and to other networks (including wireless) at the same time.

NOTE   For more information on Windows 7 and older Windows versions' Ad-Hoc support, see http://www.cryptoman.com/storage/Pubs/en/ntwk_guide/d0e744.html.

For a good introduction to Windows Hosted Networking, see http://www.aztcs.org/meeting_notes/winhardsig/WiFi-peer-to-peer/wirelessHostedNetwork.pdf. See also https://msdn.microsoft.com/en-us/library/windows/desktop/dd815243(v=vs.85).aspx.

For more about creating a computer-to-computer (Ad-Hoc) network on OS X, see http://www.macobserver.com/tmo/article/how-to-create-and-use-an-ad-hoc-network-on-your-mac.

Cloud and Remote Printing

With **cloud printing**, you no longer need to be at your office or home office to make a printout. With **remote printing**, you can print a document stored on your host with your remote printer.

Cloud and remote printing require the following:

- A printer or multifunction device that can be accessed from the cloud or remotely via the Web.

- An app that supports remote or cloud printing.

Using Public and Shared Devices

Public cloud printing devices are available in some hotels, hospitals, libraries, print and copy businesses, schools, and airport lounges. Depending upon the specific device and service in use, print jobs can be submitted via email, web interfacing, mobile apps, or special print drivers. Thus, public cloud printing is available to any type of computer or device with Internet access.

To receive the print job from the printer, provide the credentials needed (such as a retrieval or account code). By using public cloud printing services, it is no longer necessary to have a printer you might only use occasionally.

Some of the major vendors of cloud printing include Google (Google Cloud Print, www.google.com/cloudprint/learn/), HP Connected (formerly HP ePrint, www.hpconnected.com), PrinterOn Hosted (www.printeron.com), and Ricoh (HotSpot, www.ricoh-usa.com/services_and_solutions/hotspot/MobilePrintingOfferings.aspx).

Using Apps

Smartphones and tablets running Android or Apple iOS operating systems typically install apps from their respective app stores to make cloud or remote printing possible.

Connect older printers and multifunction devices that do not have built-in Google Cloud Print support to a computer running Google Chrome and enable its Google Cloud Print feature to enable cloud printing. The Google Print Connector can be used to enable multiple printers in businesses or schools to be used with Google Cloud Print.

Remote access apps such as LogMeIn and GoToMyPC enable remote users to print host documents directly to their remote printers.

Configuring Your Operating System to Share a Printer or Device

Windows, MacOS, and Linux offer a variety of ways to make a local printer available on the network. For Windows computers, File and Print sharing is used. OS X can use Bonjour Print Services or AirPrint. Linux computers can use Bonjour or the distro's own Print server settings.

Windows Print Sharing

Printer sharing in Windows 7 and 8/8.1/10 is enabled through the Network and Sharing Center. Printers shared with Network and Sharing are available to any Windows computers on the same workgroup.

To restrict printer usage to specified computers using Windows 7 or later, create a homegroup from the Network and Sharing Center. Each computer on the workgroup can share or disallow sharing of printers and folders with other computers, and a single password is used to protect the homegroup.

To enable OS X or Linux computers to use a shared Windows printer, install LDP Print Services from Programs and Features in Control Panel, then share the printer using the Printer Properties tab for the printer in Devices and Printers. Make sure that the OS X or Linux and Windows computers are on the same network and the same workgroup.

TCP/IP

When a printer or multifunction device connects directly to a wired or wireless network, it can be discovered and used through TCP/IP by browsing to it using Windows, OS X, or Linux.

When you set up a printer as a network printer in Windows, you have the option of searching for the printer by the printer or host device's IP address or specifying the correct IP address.

Bonjour

Bonjour is a zero-configuration print sharing service originally designed for OS X. Bonjour is included in OS X, and it is also distributed as part of iTunes for Windows. When you install iTunes for Windows, you install the appropriate version of Bonjour for your operating system (32-bit or 64-bit). You can also extract the MSI (.msi) installation file manually from the iTunes archive with third-party archive tools such as 7-Zip (www.7-zip.org).

When Bonjour is running on a Windows computer, an OS X computer on the same network can detect and use printers hosted on the Windows computer. Likewise, a Windows computer running Bonjour can detect and use printers hosted on the OS X computer. Linux includes support for Bonjour.

CAUTION   When a printer is hosted on OS X or Linux and a Windows computer connects with it using Bonjour, Bonjour might not install the best possible driver for your printer. For example, instead of a driver for a specific Epson printer, Bonjour running on OS X installed the Epson ESC/P-R driver on a Windows PC. This driver lacks support for maintenance and most other printer functions.

Rather than using the driver provided by Bonjour, install a model-specific driver from the manufacturer, set up the printer as a network printer, and search for the printer by the host's IP address.

AirPrint

AirPrint enables iOS and OS X devices to print wirelessly to AirPrint-compatible printers without installing printer drivers. Linux computers that use CUPS printer drivers also support AirPrint. Microsoft Windows computers can also provide AirPrint services with legacy printers. For details, see http://jaxov.com/2010/11/install-airprint-for-windows-the-easy-way/.

For a list of AirPrint-compatible printers, see https://support.apple.com/en-us/HT201311.

Maintaining Data Privacy

When a document is sent to a printer, a special print file is created by the print spooler. To prevent unauthorized users from opening the print file and extracting information from it, two methods can be used: user authentication and hard drive caching.

Using User Authentication

User authentication (which matches print jobs to the IP address of the computer or device requesting the print job) can be enabled at the printer itself or by security settings used on Active Directory-enabled networks.

When user authentication is enabled in the printer (a common feature on enterprise-level print or multifunction devices), the user must provide the appropriate identification during the print process. On an OS X system, this can be done through the Job Log portion of the printer submenu (the same menu that includes sections for Layout, Print Settings, and so on). On a Windows system, the printer driver or the network might prompt for this information.

Using Hard Drive Caching

On a system running Windows, print spool files are normally stored on the system hard drive at `C:\Windows\system32\spool\PRINTERS`. If a different location is desired, make sure the location is not shared on the network to avoid access from unauthorized users.

The default location of the print spool files can be changed by selecting the printer or multifunction device in Devices and Printers, opening the Print Server properties dialog, clicking Advanced, clicking Change Advanced Settings, and specifying a different location.

Exam Preparation Tasks

Review All the Key Topics

Review the most important topics in the chapter, noted with the key topics icon in the outer margin of the page. Table 10-1 provides a reference to these key topics and the page numbers on which each is found.

Table 10-1   Key Topics for Chapter 10

Key Topic Element	Description	Page Number
List	The major components of a laser printer	370
Tip and Figure 10-1 and seven steps of laser printing	How a laser printer works (steps are numbered in Figure 10-1)	372-373
Figure 10-6	Checking inkjet printer nozzles for clogs	384
Section	Printer/Multifunction Device Installation in Windows	395
Section	Configuring Your Printer or Multifunction Device	401

Complete the Tables and Lists from Memory

Print a copy of Appendix C, "Memory Tables" (found on the CD), or at least the section for this chapter, and complete the tables and lists from memory. Appendix D, "Answers to Memory Tables," also on the CD, includes completed tables and lists to check your work.

Define Key Terms

Define the following key terms from this chapter, and check your answers in the glossary.

Ad-Hoc, AirPrint, Bonjour, carriage and belt, cloud printing, collate, developer, duplex, duplexing assembly, electrophotographic (EP) process, feed assembly, feeder, fuser assembly, heating element, imaging drum, impact paper, impact printer, infrastructure , ink cartridge, inkjet printer, integrated print server , laser printer, maintenance kit, nozzle check , orientation, paper separation pads, PDF, pickup rollers, print head, print quality, printer calibration, printer ribbon, remote printing, ribbon, separate pad, special thermal paper, thermal printer, toner cartridges, tractor feed, transfer belt, transfer roller, virtual printer, XPS

Complete Hands-On Labs

Complete the hands-on lab, and then see the answers and explanations at the end of the chapter.

Lab 10-1: Printer Maintenance

Open the access panels on a laser printer and observe the position and appearance of the toner cartridge or imaging drum, fuser assembly, and paper trays. Clean the fuser if it appears dirty.

Check the page count on the laser printer and compare the count to the maintenance interval for installing a maintenance kit.

Check the ink levels in an inkjet printer. Run a nozzle check. If some nozzles are clogged, run the cleaning routine. Run the calibration utility.

Check the heating element on a thermal printer for debris and clean it if necessary.

Check the ribbon on an impact printer and change it if it appears faint or worn.

Lab 10-2: Printer Properties and Sharing

Review the printer properties and print preference dialogs for the printers you or your client uses. Note any settings that might cause sub-par print quality.

Use a virtual printer to create a PDF file.

Check the network settings for a printer being shared via Ethernet or Wi-Fi.

Set up a Windows Hosted Network connection for wireless print sharing.

Answer Review Questions

1. Place the steps in the laser printing imaging process in the correct order.

    Charging

    Cleaning

    Developing

    Exposing

    Fusing

    Processing

    Transferring

2. True or False: During the charging step in the laser printing imaging process, the drum receives an electrostatic charge of -600 volts. Because the drum is photosensitive, it will retain its charge only if it is kept in the dark.

3. In Devices and Printers, which of the following graphics indicates the default printer?

    A. A red square outlines the default printer.

    B. A white checkmark on a green background indicates the default printer.

    C. The two heads in the box indicate the default printer.

    D. The red exclamation mark indicates the default printer.

4. A laser printer uses which of the following processes?

    A. Line-by-line printing

    B. Impact plus heat transfer

    C. Impact against an inked ribbon

    D. Whole page printing

5. You are attempting to print a large document to a laser printer. Each time you try to print, the printer stops at the same page in the document and generates a memory overflow error. Which of the following solutions does *not* solve this printing problem?

    A. Adding more memory to your printer

    B. Adding more memory to your computer

    C. Removing graphics from the page where the error occurred

    D. Printing the document at a lower resolution

6. How do inkjet printers create characters and graphics?

   A. By spraying tiny dots of ink onto the page

   B. By fusing fine grains of toner into the page

   C. By using a thermal transfer ribbon

   D. By using an ink impregnated ribbon

7. Which acronym refers to the colors used by an inkjet printer?

   A. CMYB

   B. CMYK

   C. RBG

   D. RBGY

8. In the following figure, which kind of problem does the right half of the screen demonstrate?

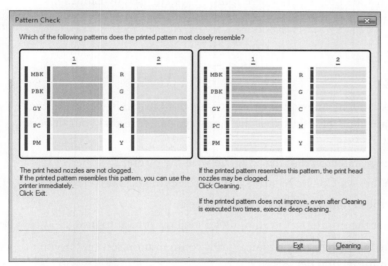

   A. The drum of a laser printer has old toner clinging to it and needs cleaning.

   B. The ribbon on an impact printer is old and is wearing out.

   C. The heating mechanism of a thermal printer is not getting hot enough.

   D. The print heads on an inkjet printer are clogged or faulty.

9. Thermal printers use which of the following?

    A. A non-impact matrix of dots that can be heated and used in various combinations to create an image.

    B. Toner to create an image and heated rollers to fix the toner to the paper.

    C. Closely grouped nozzles of heated ink to produce an image.

    D. An ink impregnated ribbon to create an image, followed by heated rollers to set the image.

10. Which type of printer typically uses multi-part forms?

    A. Laser printer

    B. Impact printer

    C. Inkjet printer

    D. Thermal printer

11. What is the name of the open-source printing system used by Linux?

    A. PRT

    B. LPT

    C. XPS

    D. CUPS

12. You have just bought a new printer and are about to install it. Which of the following statements best describes the best way to be sure that your drivers are up to date?

    A. Use the installation disc that shipped with the printer.

    B. Use Windows Update to automatically select the best drivers.

    C. Go to the vendor's website to select drivers.

    D. Connect the printer to the computer and allow it to auto install.

13. Which of the following is not a typical print configuration setting for your printer or multifunction device?

    A. Selecting duplex printing

    B. Configuring collating

    C. Choosing a cover page

    D. Changing the orientation of the page

14. Which type of encryption is supported by a printer in Ad-Hoc mode?

    A. WEP

    B. WPA

    C. WPA2

    D. NIC

Answers and Explanations for Hands-On Labs

Lab 10-1: Printer Maintenance

The diagrams shown in Chapter 10 may vary from some actual models. Note any differences you might see.

If you discovered that the page count on a laser printer is beyond the maintenance interval, check with management to see if the printer has had a maintenance kit installed. The page count might not have been reset.

If you find that there are clogs in an inkjet print head but the printer has one or more colors almost empty, keep in mind that the cleaning process uses ink. Make sure replacement ink cartridges are available before cleaning. I recommend labeling ink cartridges and laser printer toner cartridges with the date of installation to help determine how long a typical cartridge lasts in use.

Lab 10-2: Printer Properties and Sharing

Some settings that could cause sub-par printing would be a mismatch of paper type settings and actual paper used on an inkjet printer or the use of economy print settings for final drafts. Call the users' attention to issues of this type.

Most printers with built-in network ports can create a printout of the network settings. Make a printout for information or to have a way to recreate the settings in case of a problem with the printer.

Answers and Explanations to Review Questions

1. Step 1: Processing

   Step 2: Charging

   Step 3: Exposing

   Step 4: Developing

   Step 5: Transferring

   Step 6: Fusing

   Step 7: Cleaning

2. **True.** As long as the drum is kept in the dark, it will retain its charge. During the exposing phase, when the laser writes an image onto the drum, the areas where the laser strikes the drum lose their strong negative charge and become charged at only -100 volts. This lesser charge allows the toner—also charged at -600 volts—to stick to only the lower voltage areas, which contain the image to be printed.

3. **B.** A white checkmark on a green background indicates the default printer.

4. **D.** A laser printer stores an entire page in its memory and then prints the entire page at one time. An inkjet printer prints one line at a time. Thermal printers do not use impact printing. A dot matrix printer is an impact printer. It creates characters by pressing each character onto an inked ribbon and then onto the paper.

5. **B.** Because a laser printer is a page printer, it will not print any part of a page until the entire page has been loaded into the printer's memory. Increasing the computer's memory will not improve the printer's ability to receive and store the pages of the document. Increasing the printer's memory will enable it to store more information. Also, removing graphics and lowering the resolution will decrease the amount of information stored on a single page and will therefore decrease the amount of memory required to store the page in the printer's memory.

6. **A.** Inkjet printers use closely grouped nozzles of ink to spray tiny dots of color onto the paper to form letters, numbers and graphics.

7. **B.** CMYK refers to cyan, magenta, yellow, black.

8. **D.** The diagram shows the result of a nozzle check for an inkjet printer. If the print head nozzles are clean and are working properly, the test pattern should look like the left half of the screen. If they are clogged and are in need of cleaning, the pattern may look similar to the right side of the screen.

9. **A.** Thermal printers use either dot matrix or dye sublimation. The dot-matrix mechanism has a print head that uses a series of raised dots that can be used to create an image. These dots are heated and used in conjunction with special heat-sensitive paper or ribbon to transfer the image to the paper.

10. **B.** Multi-part forms require an impact printer to transfer the image through multiple layers of paper. Laser, inkjet and thermal printers will only print on the top layer of the multi-part form.

11. **D.** CUPS is the open-source printing system used by Linux.

12. **C.** The vendor's website will have the most updated drivers available. The disc that ships with the printer will contain the vendor's drivers, but they might not be the most updated versions. The drivers included in Windows might not support recent printers and Windows Update in version 8/8.1/10 does not update printer drivers.

13. **C.** Choosing a cover page is a function of the current application (such as a word processor), not the printing process.

14. **A.** Ad-Hoc mode supports only WEP encryption. This type of encryption is not as secure as WPA or WPA2 and is not generally recommended for secure networking. The NIC is a network interface card, not a type of encryption.

This chapter covers the following subjects:

- **Network Cable and Connector Types and Characteristics**—This section defines twisted pair cable, coaxial, fiber-optic, and the different connectors each cable uses.

- **TCP/IP**—In this section, you learn the basics about the Transmission Control Protocol/Internet Protocol (TCP/IP) suite and common protocols, the differences between IPv4 and IPv6, static vs. dynamic IP addressing, client-side DNS, and much more.

- **TCP and UDP Ports, Protocols, and Purposes**—This section covers the concepts behind TCP and UDP ports, typical port numbers, and the protocols and features they support.

- **WiFi (Wi-Fi) Network and Encryption Standards**—Learn the characteristics of Wi-Fi standards from 802.11b to 802.11ac, MIMO antennas, and encryption types.

- **Configure SOHO Wired or Wireless Router**—Discover how to select the best channels, use port forwarding and DMZ, control the DHCP address range, use basic QoS and UPnP for better media playback, and improve your router with vendor-supplied and third-party firmware updates.

- **Internet Connection Types**—This section covers the essential features of Internet connections from cable, DSL, and dial-up to fiber, satellite, ISDN, and line-of-sight wireless.

- **Network Types**—A brief review of network types.

- **Network Architecture Devices**—This section covers the building blocks of networks from hubs and switches to routers and repeaters.

- **Using Networking Tools**—Learn how to choose and use the tools you need for the network types you support.

## CHAPTER 11

Networking

Network support is universal in computers and mobile devices of all types. There are many hardware and software components involved in connecting computers and mobile devices to each other, from cabling, connectors, and Wi-Fi radios to routers, TCP ports, and DHCP servers. This chapter helps you understand the fundamentals of wired and wireless networking.

220-901: Objective 2.1 Identify the various types of network cables and connectors.

220-901: Objective 2.2 Compare and contrast the characteristics of connectors and cabling.

220-901: Objective 2.3 Explain the properties and characteristics of TCP/IP.

220-901: Objective 2.4 Explain common TCP and UDP ports, protocols, and their purpose.

220-901: Objective 2.5 Compare and contrast various WiFi networking standards and encryption types.

220-901: Objective 2.6 Given a scenario, install and configure SOHO wireless/wired router and apply appropriate settings.

220-901: Objective 2.7 Compare and contrast Internet connection types, network types and their features.

220-901: Objective 2.8 Compare and contrast network architecture devices, their functions and features.

220-901: Objective 2.9 Given a scenario, use appropriate networking tools.

Foundation Topics

Network Cable and Connector Types and Characteristics

There are three major types of network cables:

- Fiber
- Twisted-pair (UTP)
- Coaxial

Network cards are designed to interface with one or more types of network cables, each of which is discussed in the following sections.

Fiber

Fiber-optic cabling transmits signals with light rather than with electrical signals, which makes it immune to electrical interference. It is used primarily as a backbone between networks. Fiber-optic cable comes in two major types:

- **Single-mode fiber**—Has a thin core (between 8 and 10 microns) designed to carry a single light ray long distances (up to 60Km or further). Single-mode cable uses a laser diode as a light source. Typical uses: cable TV and telephone companies.

- **Multi-mode fiber**—Has a thicker core (62.5 microns) than single-mode; carries multiple light rays for short distances (up to 10Km). Multi-mode cable uses an LED light source. Typical uses: local and metropolitan area networks (LANs, MANs).

Fiber-optic cabling can be purchased prebuilt, but if you need a custom length, it should be built and installed by experienced cable installers because of the expense and risk of damage. Some network adapters built for servers are designed to use fiber-optic cable. Otherwise, media converters are used to interconnect fiber-optic to conventional cables on networks.

Fiber-optic devices and cables use one of several connector types. The most common include:

- **SC**—Uses square connectors
- **LC**—Uses square connectors
- **ST**—Uses round connectors

These connectors can be used singly or in pairs, depending upon the implementation. Figure 11-1 illustrates duplex (paired) SC, LC, and ST multimode cables.

NOTE If you need to interconnect devices that use two different connector types, use adapter cables that are designed to match the connector types and other characteristics of the cable and device.

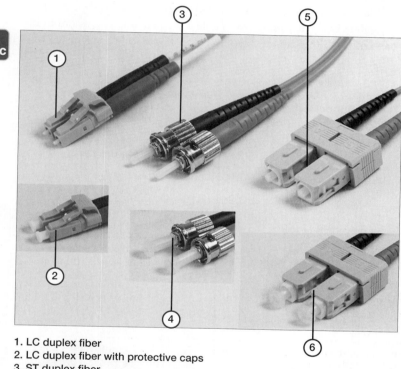

1. LC duplex fiber
2. LC duplex fiber with protective caps
3. ST duplex fiber
4. ST duplex fiber with protective caps
5. SC duplex fiber
6. SC duplex fiber with protective caps

Figure 11-1   SC, LC, and ST fiber-optic cable connectors compared.

Twisted-Pair

Twisted-pair (TP) cabling is the most common of the major cabling types. The name refers to its physical construction: four twisted-pairs of wire surrounded by a flexible jacket (unshielded TP or **UTP**) or various types of metal foil or braid (shielded TP or **STP**).

TP Cable Grades

TP cable comes in various grades, of which Category 5e (**CAT5e**), Category 6 (**CAT6**), and Category 6a (**CAT6a**) are the most common of the standard cabling grades. These are suitable for use with both standard 10BASE-T and Fast Ethernet networking and can also be used for Gigabit Ethernet networks if it passes compliance testing. CAT6, CAT6a, and Category 7 (**CAT7**) are capable of supporting 10GBASE-T (10 Gigabit) Ethernet networks. Table 11-1 provides the essential information about each of the TP cable types you need to know for the exam.

Table 11-1   Categories and Uses for TP Cabling

Category	Network Type(s) Supported	Supported Speeds	Cable Type, Notes
3	10BASE-T Ethernet	Up to 10Mbps	Also supports Token Ring networks at up to 16Mbps
5	10BASE-T, 100BASE-T (Fast Ethernet)	Up to 100Mbps	Uses 24 gauge wires
5e	10BASE-T, 100BASE-T, 1000BASE-T (Gigabit Ethernet)	Up to 1000Mbps	Enhanced version of CAT5
6	10BASE-T, 100BASE-T, 1000BASE-T (Gigabit Ethernet)	Up to 1000Mbps (1Gbps)	Often uses 22 gauge or 20 gauge wire pairs (both are thicker than 24 gauge)
6a*	10BASE-T, 100BASE-T, 1000BASE-T, 10GBASE-T (10Gb Ethernet)	Up to 10Gbps	Enhanced version of CAT6
7	10BASE-T, 100BASE-T, 1000BASE-T, 10GBASE-T (10Gb Ethernet)	Up to 10Gbps	Uses 12-connector GG45 connector (backward-compatible with RJ-45)

* Some vendors sold a so-called "CAT6e" cable, an enhanced version of CAT6, before the release of CAT6a. "CAT6e" is not an official standard.

Shielded Twisted-Pair (STP) versus Unshielded Twisted-Pair (UTP)

STP uses the same RJ-45 connector as UTP but includes a metal shield for electrical insulation between the wire pairs and the outer jacket. It's stiffer and more durable, but also more expensive and harder to loop through tight spaces than UTP. It is used where electromagnetic interference (EMI) prevents the use of UTP cable.

Figure 11-2 compares the construction of STP and UTP cables.

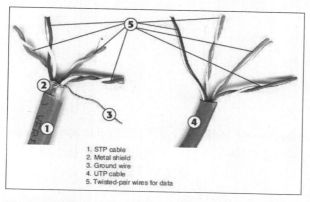

1. STP cable
2. Metal shield
3. Ground wire
4. UTP cable
5. Twisted-pair wires for data

Figure 11-2   An STP cable (left) includes a metal shield and ground wire for protection against interference, while a UTP cable (right) does not.

UTP and STP cable can be purchased in prebuilt assemblies or can be built from bulk cable and connectors.

T568B (EIA-568B) and T568A (EIA-568A) Standards

The *de facto* wire pair standard for all types of Ethernet UTP cables is known as **T568B** (also known as EIA-568B). The wire order from left to right when looking at the top of the connector is:

> Pin 1—Orange/white stripe
>
> Pin 2—Orange
>
> Pin 3—Green/white stripe
>
> Pin 4—Blue
>
> Pin 5—Blue/white stripe
>
> Pin 6—Green
>
> Pin 7—Brown/white stripe
>
> Pin 8—Brown

The **T568A** (EIA-568A) standard swaps the position of the orange and green wires used in T568B. The wire order from left to right when looking at the top of the connector is:

> Pin 1—Green/white stripe
>
> Pin 2—Green

Pin 3—Orange/white stripe

Pin 4—Blue

Pin 5—Blue/white stripe

Pin 6—Orange

Pin 7—Brown/white stripe

Pin 8—Brown

Figure 11-3 illustrates cable pairings for a T568B cable, a T568B cable with connector, and the cable pairings for a T568A cable.

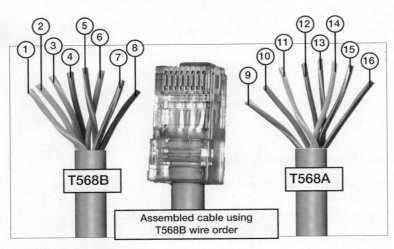

Assembled cable using
T568B wire order

1. Pin 1 – Orange/white stripe
2. Pin 2 – Orange
3. Pin 3 – Green/white stripe
4. Pin 4 – Blue
5. Pin 5 – Blue/white stripe
6. Pin 6 – Green
7. Pin 7 – Brown/white stripe
8. Pin 8 – Brown
9. Pin 1 – Green/white stripe
10. Pin 2 – Green
11. Pin 3 – Orange/white stripe
12. Pin 4 – Blue
13. Pin 5 – Blue/white stripe
14. Pin 6 – Orange
15. Pin 7 – Brown/white stripe
16. Pin 8 – Brown

Figure 11-3   T568B (left) and T568A (right) wire pairs. In the center is an assembled T568B cable.

NOTE   You can create a crossover cable by building one end to the T568B standard and the other end to the T568A standard.

RJ-45 Versus RJ-11

The connector used by Ethernet cards that use UTP or STP cable is commonly known as an RJ-45 connector. *RJ* stands for registered jack; the **RJ-45** has eight contacts that accept eight wires, also known as *pins*. It resembles a larger version of the **RJ-11** connector used for telephone cabling. TP cabling runs between a computer on the network and a hub or switch carrying signals between the two. The hub or switch then sends signals to other computers (servers or workstations) on the network. When a computer is connected to a hub or switch, a straight-through cable is used. This means that both ends of the cable are wired the same way. When a computer needs to be connected directly to another computer, a crossover cable, which has a different pin configuration on one end, is used. Keep in mind that between the computer and the hub or switch, other wiring equipment might be involved, for example, RJ-45 jacks, patch panels, and so on. TP cable can be purchased in prebuilt form or as bulk cable with connectors, so you can build the cable to the length you need. Figure 11-4 compares RJ-11 and RJ-45 cables.

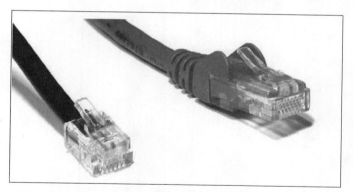

Figure 11-4   RJ-11 cable (left) compared to RJ-45 cable (right).

NOTE   Although RJ-45 is the common name for the TP Ethernet connector, this is a misnomer; the proper name is 8P8C (8 position, 8 contact). Don't confuse it with the RJ-45S connector, an eight-position connector used for telephone rather than computer data. An RJ-45S jack has a slightly different shape than the connector.

Figure 11-5 compares RJ-11 and RJ-45 ports.

10BASE-T, 100BASE-T, and 1000BASE-T Ethernet cards using copper wire all use the RJ-45 connector shown in Figure 11-5, as do some ISDN and most cable Internet devices. DSL devices often use the RJ-11 connector shown in Figure 11-5, as do dial-up modems.

To attach a cable using RJ-11 or RJ-45 connectors to a network card or other device, plug it into the connector so that the plastic locking clip snaps into place; the cable and connector will fit together only one way. To remove the cable, squeeze the locking clip toward the connector and pull the connector out of the jack. Some cables use a snagless connector; squeeze the guard over the locking clip to open the clip to remove the cable.

1. RJ-45 port locking tab position
2. RJ-11 port locking tab position

Figure 11-5   RJ-45 port (left) compared to RJ-11 ports (right).

Coaxial

Coaxial cabling is the oldest type of network cabling; its data wires are surrounded by a wire mesh for insulation. Coaxial cables, which resemble cable TV connections, are not popular for network use today because they must be run from one station directly to another rather than to or from a hub/switch. However, coaxial cabling is used for most cable TV, cable Internet, and satellite TV installations as well as CCTV cameras used for security.

Legacy 10Mbps Ethernet Coaxial Cable Standards

Coaxial cabling creates a bus topology; each end of the bus must be terminated, and if any part of the bus fails, the entire network fails.

The oldest Ethernet standard, 10BASE5, uses a very thick coaxial cable (RG-8) attached to a NIC through an AUI transceiver that uses a so-called "vampire tap" to connect the transceiver to the cable. This type of coaxial cable is also referred to as Thick Ethernet or Thicknet.

Thin Ethernet, also referred to as Thinnet, Cheapernet, or 10BASE2 Ethernet was used for low-cost Ethernet networks before the advent of UTP cable. The coaxial cable used with 10BASE2 is referred to as RG-58. This type of coaxial cable connects to network cards through a T-connector that bayonet-mounts to the rear of the network card using a BNC connector. The arms of the *T* are used to connect two cables, each running to another computer in the network.

If the workstation is at the end of a network, a terminating resistor is connected to one arm of the *T* to indicate the end of the network. If a resistor is removed, the network fails; if a station on the network fails, the network fails.

Both of these connection types are shown in Figure 11-6. Note that some 10Mbps Ethernet cards are combo cards that might feature both legacy connector types as well as, on some models, an RJ-45 jack.

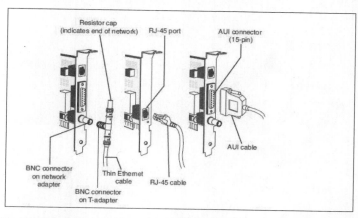

Figure 11-6   Combo UTP/BNC/AUI Ethernet network cards (left and right) compared with a UTP/STP-only Ethernet card (center) and cables.

RG-59 and RG-6 Coaxial Cable

Two other types of coaxial cable are common in cable Internet, satellite Internet, and fixed wireless Internet installations:

- **RG-59**—Used in older cable TV or satellite TV installations as well as in CCTV security installations; 75-ohm resistance. RG-59 uses a 22-gauge (AWG) center conductor and a single outer shield. It is designed for signals up to 50MHz.

- **RG-6**—Uses same connectors as RG-59 but has a larger diameter with dual shielding; used in cable TV/Internet, satellite TV/Internet, fixed wireless Internet/TV service, and closed-circuit (security) TV; 75-ohm resistance. RG-6 uses an 18-gauge (AWG) center conductor, which can carry a signal further than RG-59. RG-6 is also available in quad-shielded versions. RG-6 can carry signals up to 1.5GHz, making it much better for HDTV signals.

BNC connectors are used for CCTV cameras and for some types of video projectors. BNC connectors are crimped to the coaxial cable and use a positive locking bayonet mount.

The **F-connector** is used for cable, satellite, and fixed wireless Internet and TV service. F-connectors can be crimped or attached via compression to the coaxial cable. High-quality cables use a threaded connector. However, some F-connector cables use a push-on connector, which is not as secure and can lead to a poor-quality connection. Figure 11-7 compares BNC and F-connectors on an RG-6 coaxial cable.

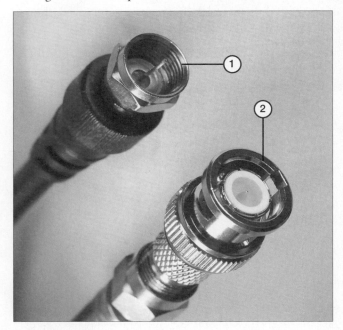

1. F-connector
2. BNC connector

Figure 11-7   F-connector and BNC connectors on RG-6 cables.

A two-way splitter such as the one shown in Figure 11-8 reduces signal strength by 50 percent (3.5dB) on each connection. If you split the signal only once with a high-quality signal and cables, you will usually not have issues with your TV or Internet signal. However, if you do, contact your TV or Internet provider for a splitter or ask what type of booster is recommended for your installation.

Figure 11-8   A two-way coaxial splitter.

NOTE   Many antennas used for over-the-air digital TV now include a small in-line booster that is powered by a 500mA USB connection or a small AC adapter. The booster helps improve range and bring in more stations.

Plenum and PVC

There are three categories of TP and coaxial cable in terms of fire rating:

- Standard cable suitable for patch cables between a NIC and a network jack or in a patch panel. This type of cable typically uses a PVC jacket, which can create a lot of smoke when burned.

- Riser cable is stiffer and is designed for vertical cable runs. Riser cable is also suitable for use in horizontal runs such as patch cables and patch panels. In fact, some cable vendors sell only riser and plenum cables.

- **Plenum** cable is designed for use in plenum space (space used for HVAC air exchange), such as ventilator shafts, under floors, or between suspended ceilings and the permanent ceiling. Plenum cable produces less smoke when burned, a lower level of toxic chemicals when burned, and is typically self-extinguishing. Plenum cable jackets might be made from Teflon or from a modified version of PVC that produces less smoke when burned than standard PVC.

TCP/IP

TCP/IP is short for Transport Control Protocol/Internet Protocol. It is a multiplatform protocol used for both Internet access and local area networks. Though there are other networking protocols, TCP/IP is by far the most common and is used by all major operating systems including Windows, OS X, Linux, Android, and iOS.

TCP/IP actually is a suite of protocols used on the Internet for routing and transporting information. The following sections discuss some of the application protocols that are part of the TCP/IP suite, as well as some of the services and technologies that relate to TCP/IP.

The TCP/IPv4 protocol, although it was originally used for Internet connectivity, is the main network protocol for LANs as well as larger networks; in networks today, TCP/IP v4 and v6 are used side by side. To connect with the rest of a TCP/IP-based network, each computer or other device must have a unique IP address. If the network connects with the Internet, additional settings are required.

IPv4

An **IPv4** address consists of a group of four numbers that each range from 0 to 255, for example: 192.168.1.1. IP addresses are divided into two sections: the network portion, which is the number of the network the computer is on, and the host portion, which is the individual number of the computer. Using the IP address we just mentioned as an example, the 192.168.1 portion would typically be the network number, and .1 would be the host number. A subnet mask is used to distinguish between the network portion of the IP address and the host portion. For example, a typical subnet mask for the IP address we just used would be 255.255.255.0. The 255s correspond to the network portion of the IP address. The 0s correspond to the host portion, as shown in
Table 11-2.

Table 11-2 An IPv4 Address and Corresponding Subnet Mask

IP Address/Subnet Mask	Network Portion	Host Portion
192.168.1.1	192.168.1	1
255.255.255.0	255.255.255	0

The subnet mask is also used to define subnetworks, if subnetworking is being implemented.

Both computers and other networked devices, such as routers and network printers, can have IP addresses, and some devices can have more than one IP address. For example, a router typically has two IP addresses—one to connect the router to a LAN and the other that connects it to the Internet, enabling it to route traffic from the LAN to the Internet and back.

Class A, B, and C IP Address Ranges

Traditionally, IP addresses were divided into three major categories: Class A, Class B, and Class C, which define ranges of IP addresses. Class A is designated for large corporations, ISPs, and government. Class B is designated for midsized corporations and ISPs. Class C is designated for small offices and home offices. Each class of IP address uses a default **subnet mask**, as shown in Table 11-3.

Table 11-3 Internet Protocol v4 Classification System

Class	First Octet Range	Starting IP	Ending IP	Default Subnet Mask	Maximum Number of Hosts
Class A	1–126	1.0.0.0	126.255.255.255	255.0.0.0	16,777,214
Class B	128–191	128.0.0.0	191.255.255.255	255.255.0.0	65,534
Class C	192–223	192.0.0.0	223.255.255.255	255.255.255.0	254

NOTE The 127 network is reserved for testing. This is known as the IPv4 loopback address (for example, 127.0.0.1). The usable starting IP for Class A is actually 1.0.0.0.

In any given network, the first and last addresses are reserved and cannot be assigned to computers or other hosts. For example, in the 192.168.1.0 network, 192.168.1.1 through 192.168.1.254 can be assigned, but 192.168.1.0 is reserved for the network number, and 192.168.1.255 is reserved for something called the broadcast.

Each number in an IP address is called an *octet*. An octet is an eight-bit byte. This means that in the binary numbering system the number can range from 00000000–11111111. For example, 255 is actually 11111111 when converted to the binary numbering system. Another example: 192 equals 11000000. Because there are four octets in an IPv4 address, it is a 32-bit address. IPv4 supports up to 4.3 billion addresses (4.3×10^9).

NOTE   To convert numbers from decimal to binary and vice versa use the Windows calculator. Press Windows+R to bring up the Run prompt; then type calc. This runs the Windows Calculator. From there, click View on the menu bar and select Scientific (Vista) or Programmer (7/8/8.1/10). Now you will notice radio buttons on the upper left (Vista) or left (7/8/8.1/10) that allow you to change between numbering systems. Simply type any number, and then select the numbering system you want to convert it to.

In a Class A network, the first octet is the network portion of the IP address, and the three remaining octets identify the host portion of the IP address. Class B networks use the first and second octets as the network portion and the third and fourth octets as the host portion. Class C networks use the first three octets as the network portion and the last octet as the host portion of the IP address. Table 11-4 gives one example IP address and subnet mask for each class.

Table 11-4   Internet Protocol v4/Subnet Mask Examples for Classes A, B, and C

Class	IP Address/Subnet Mask	Network Portion	Host Portion
Class A	10.0.0.1	10	0.0.1
	255.0.0.0	255	0.0.0
Class B	172.16.0.1	172.16	0.1
	255.255.0.0	255.255	0.0
Class C	192.168.1.100	192.168.1	100
	255.255.255.0	255.255.255	0

See a pattern? The size of the network portion increases in octets, and the host portion decreases as you ascend through the classes.

Using Subnetting

By changing the subnet mask from the default value, you enable a network to be subdivided into smaller networks. When you change the subnet mask, you borrow bits from the network portion and add them to the host address portion.

For example, a Class C network starting with 192.168.1.1 has a default subnet mask of 255.255.255.0, which does not subnet the network.

In binary, 255.255.255.0 is represented as 00000000 (eight zeros).

Some of the allowable subnetting values for Class C networks include:

255.255.255.128 (binary 10000000, two subnets)

255.255.255.192 (binary 11000000, four subnets)

255.255.255.224 (binary 11100000, eight subnets)

NOTE   For an excellent guide to subnetting, see the TCP/IP Guide's IP Subnet Addressing ("Subnetting" Concepts) at http://www.tcpipguide.com/free/t_IPSubnetAddressingSubnettingConcepts.htm

Using CIDR

Even with subnetting enabling a single larger network to be subdivided for easier management and security, class-based IPv4 networks can still have problems with unused IP address space and problems with connecting networks with other networks. To solve these problems, classless interdomain routing (**CIDR**) was developed.

Instead of using subnet masks, CIDR lists networks by a prefix consisting of the starting IP address and the number of mask bits set to 1 (binary). For example, a CIDR value such as 172.168.0.1/18 represents a range of IP addresses from 172.168.0.0 to 172.168.63.255 using a subnet mask of 255.255.192.0. This translates to 16,256 addresses (equivalent to 64 Class C networks).

Decimal: 255. 255. 192. 0

Binary: 11111111   11111111   11000000   00000000

If CIDR was not used, each of the 64 networks in this address range would need to be advertised separately. By using the CIDR address prefix, only one prefix needs to be advertised, making routing between networks easier and faster.

NOTE   The term advertising in TCP/IP refers to routing tables that provide information about the hosts that can be reached from a particular IP address. CIDR enables fewer entries in the routing table for better performance.

Public and Private IP Addresses

A **public IP address** is one that faces the Internet and can be seen by any computers that connect to the Internet. For example, for google.com to have a properly functioning web server, the web server needs to have a public IP address. If it didn't, no one would be able to connect to it. Private IP addresses are hidden from sight; usually they are behind a firewall. If your computer has an IP address on the 192.168.0 or 192.168.1 networks, it is a **private IP address**, and you most likely have a router that is protecting your IP from the Internet. Each IPv4 class has its own range of private IP addresses:

- **Class A**—Uses the entire 10 network, from 10.0.0.0 to 10.255.255.255

- **Class B**—Uses the range 172.16.0.0 through 172.31.255.255

- **Class C**—Uses the range 192.168.0.0 through 192.168.255.255

Computers on a LAN normally are given private IPs, whereas servers on the Internet use public IPs.

NOTE   In some cases, you might need to determine the public IP address for a device on a private network. You can use a service such as IPLocation (www.iplocation.net) to find this information.

APIPA IP Addresses

Most IP networks use addresses provided automatically by dynamic host configuration protocol (DHCP). However, in the event that the DHCP server becomes unavailable and an alternate IP address has not been set up, devices on the network assign themselves **APIPA/link-local** addresses. These addresses are in the IPv4 address range of 169.254.0.1 to 169.254.255.254 (subnet mask of 255.255.0.0); the IPv6 version is called a link-local address with the FE80::/64 prefix. A device with an APIPA address cannot connect to the Internet.

To resolve the problem, users should check the device's network connection and try using ipconfig/release and ipconfig/renew to obtain a new IP address from the

DHCP server. If these actions don't solve the problem, the DHCP server (often located in the router on a SOHO network) should be checked and restarted if necessary.

APIPA was originally developed by Microsoft, but it is now a standard (RFC 3927) that is also supported by OS X and Linux.

IPv6

IP version 6 enables a huge increase in the number of available IP addresses for computers, smartphones, and other mobile devices. **IPv6** uses 128-bit source and destination IP addresses (compared to 32-bit for IPv4), enabling up to 340 undecillion addresses (3.4×1038). IPv6 also features built-in security, and provides better support for Quality of Service (QoS) routing, which is important to achieve high-quality streaming audio and video traffic. Windows, OS X, and Linux all support IPv6.

IPv6 Addressing

IPv6 addresses start out as 128-bit addresses that are then divided into eight 16-bit blocks. The blocks are converted into hexadecimal, and each block is separated from the following block by a colon. Leading zeros are typically suppressed, but each block must contain at least one digit.

Here is a typical IPv6 address:

> 21DA:D3:0:2F3B:2AA:FF:FE28:9C5A

A contiguous sequence of 16-bit blocks set to zero can be represented by :: (double colon). This technique is also known as *zero compression*. To determine the number of zero bits represented by the double colon, count the number of blocks in the compressed address, subtract the result from 8, and multiply the result by 16. An address can include only one zero-compressed block.

Here is an IPv6 address that does use the double colon:

> FF02::2.

There are two blocks (FF02 and 2). So, how many zero bits are represented by the double colon? Subtract 2 from 8 (8–2=6, then multiply 6 by 16 (6 × 16=96). This address includes a block of 96 zero bits.

The loopback address on an IPv6 system is 0:0:0:0:0:0:0:1, which is abbreviated as ::1. Thus, if you want to test your network interface in Windows where IPv6 is enabled by default, you can type **ping ::1**.

IPv6 Address Types

IPv6 supports three types of addresses: unicast, multicast, and anycast. There are five types of unicast addresses:

- Global unicast addresses are used in the same way as IPv4 public addresses. The first three bits are set to 001, followed by 45 bits used for the global routing prefix; these 48 bits are collectively known as the public topology. The subnet ID uses the next 16 bits, and the interface ID uses the remaining 64 bits.

- Link-local addresses correspond to the Automatic Private IP address (APIPA) address scheme used by IPv4 (addresses that start with 169.254). The first 10 bits are set to FE80 hex, followed by 54 zero bits, and 64 bits for the Interface ID. Using zero compression, the prefix would thus be FE80::/64. As with APIPA, link local addresses are not forwarded beyond the link.

- Site-local addresses correspond to IPv4 private address spaces (10.0.0.0/8, 172.16.0.0/12, and 192.168.0.0/16).

- Special addresses include unspecified addresses (0:0:0:0:0:0:0:0 or ::), which are equivalent to IPv4's 0.0.0.0 and indicate the absence of an IP address; a loopback address (0:0:0:0:0:0:0:1 or ::1) is equivalent to the IPv4 loopback address of 127.0.0.1.

- Compatibility addresses are used in situations in which IPv4 and IPv6 are both in use. In the following examples, w.x.y.z are replaced by the actual IPv4 address. An IPv4-compatible address (0:0:0:0:0:0:w.x.y.z or ::w.x.y.z) is used by nodes that support IPv4 and IPv6 communicating over IPv6. An IPv4-mapped address (0:0:0:0:0:FFFF:w.x.y.z or ::FFFF:w.x.y.z) represents an IPv4-only node to an IPv6 node. A 6to4 address is used when two nodes running both IPv4 and IPv6 connect over an IPv4 routing. The address combines the prefix 2002::/16 with the IPv4 public address of the node. ISATAP can also be used for the connection; it uses a locally administered ID of ::0:5EFE:w.x.y.z (w.x.y.z could be any unicast IPv4 address, either public or private); Teredo addresses are used for tunneling IPv6 over UDP through Network Address Translation (NAT); they use the prefix 3FFE:831F::/32.

Both IPv4 and IPv6 support multicasting, which enables one-to-many distribution of content such as Internet TV or other types of streaming media. IPv6 multicast addresses begin with FF.

Anycast addressing sends information to a group of potential receivers that are identified by the same destination address. This is also known as one-to-one-to-many association. Anycast addressing can be used for distributed services, such as DNS or other situations in which automatic failover is desirable. IPv6 uses anycast addresses as destination addresses that are assigned only to routers. Anycast addresses are assigned from the unicast address space.

Viewing IP Address Information

To see the IPv4 and IPv6 addresses assigned to a Windows device using both IPv4 and IPv6, use the command-line ipconfig utility. Here's an example of the output from a system using a wireless Ethernet adapter:

```
Wireless LAN adapter Wireless Network Connection:
 Connection-specific DNS Suffix . :
 Link-local IPv6 Address . . . . . : fe80::5cf1:2f98:7351:b3a3%12
 IPv4 Address. . . . . . . . . . . : 192.168.1.155
 Subnet Mask . . . . . . . . . . . : 255.255.255.0
 Default Gateway . . . . . . . . . : 192.168.1.1
```

For more information, see http://technet.microsoft.com/en-us/library/dd392266(WS.10).aspx.

OS X provides this information through the TCP/IP tab of the Network utility (see Figure 11-9).

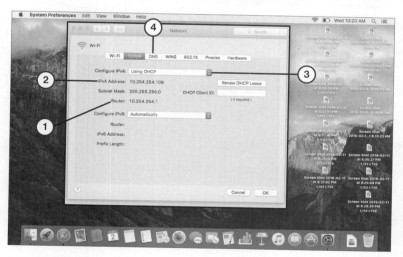

1. IPv4 address
2. Router (gateway) address
3. Open this menu to configure IP address manually
4. Click DNS tab to view or edit DNS addresses

Figure 11-9 OS X's TCP/IP tab.

Many Linux distros include a GUI-based network utility similar to the one used in OS X, but with any Linux distro (as well as with OS X), you can open Terminal and use the command `ifconfig -a` to view this information. Figure 11-10 shows a portion of the output for a wireless connection.

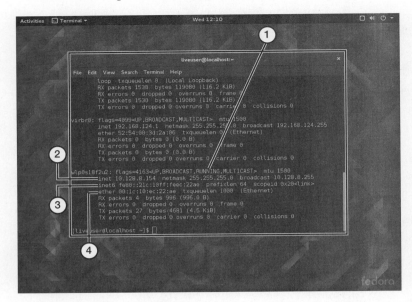

1. RUNNING = active connection
2. inet = IPv4 address information
3. inet6 = IPv6 address information
4. ether = MAC (physical) address

Figure 11-10   Linux `ifconfig` output for a wireless connection.

Dynamic versus Static IP Addresses

There are two ways to configure a computer's TCP/IP settings:

- Dynamic (DHCP server-assigned) IP address
- **Static IP address**

Table 11-5 compares the differences in these configurations.

Table 11-5   Static Versus Dynamic IP Addressing

Setting	What It Does	Static IP Address	Dynamic IP Address
IP address	Identifies computer on the network; unique value for each device	Entered manually on the device	Automatically assigned by DHCP server

Setting	What It Does	Static IP Address	Dynamic IP Address
DNS configuration	Identifies domain name system servers	IP addresses of one or more DNS servers, host name, and domain name must be entered	Automatically assigned by DHCP server
Gateway	Identifies IP address of device that connects computer to Internet or other network; same values for all devices on network	IP address for gateway must be entered	Automatically assigned by DHCP server

Windows, OS X, and Linux default to using a **dynamic IP address**. As Table 11-5 makes clear, this is the preferable method for configuring a TCP/IP network. Use a manually assigned IP address if a Dynamic Host Configuration Protocol (DHCP) server (which provides IP addresses automatically) is not available on the network—or if you need to configure a firewall or router to provide different levels of access to some systems and you must specify those systems' IP addresses.

NOTE   Routers, wireless gateways, and computers that host an Internet connection shared with Windows's Internet Connection Sharing or a third-party sharing program all provide DHCP services to other computers on the network.

To configure TCP/IP in Windows, access the Internet Protocol Properties window; this window contains several dialogs used to make changes to TCP/IP. To open the General tab of the Internet Protocol Properties window, open Network Connections, right-click the network connection, select Properties, click Internet Protocol v4 (TCP/IPv4) or TCP/IPv6 in the list of protocols and features, and click Properties.

TCP/IP configuration in Linux is performed by editing the /etc/network interfaces file. If you use a GUI that features a Network configuration panel, you can use it to make changes for you.

To configure TCP/IP in OS X, go to System Preferences, open the Network panel, and select the appropriate tab (refer to Figure 11-9).

Client-Side DHCP Settings

Client-side DHCP settings are used to configure a workstation to receive its IP address from a DHCP server. Figure 11-11 shows the Windows 8.1 TCP/IPv4 properties General tab as it appears when a DHCP server is used.

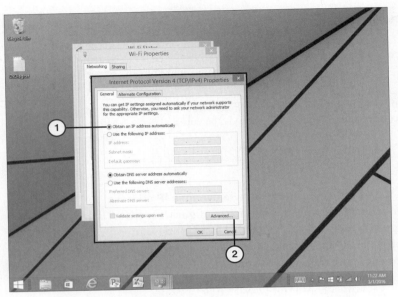

1. DHCP (server-assigned addressing) is default
2. Click to open Advanced dialog

Figure 11-11   The General tab is configured to obtain IP and DNS server information automatically when a DHCP server is used on the network.

NOTE   To determine the IP address, default gateway, and DNS servers used by a system using DHCP addressing, open a command prompt and enter the `ipconfig /all` command.

TCP/IP Alternate Configuration

The Alternate Configuration tab shown in Figure 11-12 is used to set up a different TCP/IPv4 configuration for use when a DHCP server is not available or when a different set of user-configured settings is needed, as when a laptop is being used at a secondary location. By default, automatic private IP addressing (APIPA) is used when no DHCP server is in use. As mentioned earlier in the chapter, APIPA assigns each system a unique IP address in the 169.254.x.x range. APIPA enables a network to perform LAN connections when the DHCP server is not available. However, systems with APIPA addresses cannot connect to the Internet. Linux and OS X refer to this type of connection as IPv4 link-local.

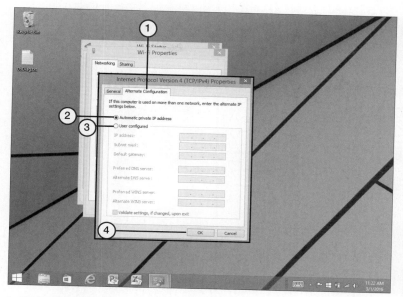

1. Click or tap to view Alternate Configuration
2. Default setting is APIPA (link-local)
3. Click or tap if you want to enter IP address, subnet, gateway, DNS, and WINS server addresses manually
4. Click or tap OK when finished

Figure 11-12   The Alternate Configuration tab is used to set up a different IP configuration for use on another network or when no DHCP server is available.

You can also use the Alternate Configuration tab to specify the IP address, subnet mask, default gateway, DNS servers, and WINS servers. This option is useful if this system is moved to another network that uses different IP addresses for these servers.

NOTE   In IPv6, all devices are assigned a link-local address using the prefix fe80::/64, even if a DHCP server is running or a manual IPv6 address has been assigned.

Client-Side IP and DNS Addresses

When a DHCP server is not used for a Windows device, the General tab is used to set up the IP address, subnet mask, default gateway, and DNS servers used by the network client. (The information shown in Figure 11-13 is fictitious.)

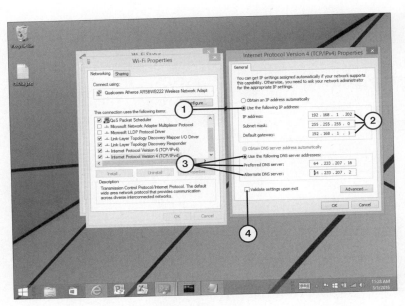

1. Click or tap to configure IP address manually
2. Enter IP address, subnet mask, and default gateway
3. When manual IP address is selected, DNS servers must be added manually
4. Click or tap this checkbox to have these settings validated when you exit the dialog

Figure 11-13   Configuring a Windows 8.1 client with manually entered IP and DNS addresses.

With OS X, use the TCP/IP tab (refer to Figure 11-9) to configure IPv4 or IPv6 address information. OS X uses the term *router* to refer to the default gateway. Use the DNS tab to configure DNS server information.

With Linux, you can use the network configuration tool provided in the GUI, or edit the network configuration scripts from Terminal using the distro's text editor if no GUI-based network configuration program is available. There are two scripts that need to be edited:

- `ifcfg-connection name` is used to identify IP addresses for IPv4 and IPv6 and the default gateway as well as other IP settings. It is located in the /etc/sysconfig/network-scripts/ folder. The loopback script is called ifcfg-lo. There is a separate ifcfg file for each connection (wired, wireless, and so on).

- The file resolv.conf is used to identify DNS servers. It is located in the /etc/ folder.

For syntax, see the documentation for the distribution in use.

TIP For the 220-901 exam be sure you understand the difference between static and dynamic IP addressing and where to go within a given operating system to set or change client-side DHCP, DNS, subnet mask, and default gateway settings.

Client-Side DNS Configuration

The Internet uses the domain name service (DNS) to map domain names, such as www.microsoft.com, to their corresponding IP address or addresses. A computer using the Internet must use at least one DNS server to provide this translation service. Use the **client-side DNS** Configuration tab to set up the computer's host name, domain name, and DNS servers (refer to Figure 11-13) if the computer doesn't use DHCP to obtain an IP address.

NOTE Most ISPs and networks have at least two DNS name servers to provide backup in case one fails. Be sure to enter the IP addresses of all DNS servers available to your network. In Windows, these are referred to as preferred and alternate DNS servers.

CAUTION Can't access the site you're looking for? Got the wrong site? You might have made one of these common mistakes:

- Don't assume that all domain names end in .com—Other popular domain name extensions include .net, .org, .gov, .us, .cc, and various national domains such as .uk (United Kingdom), .ca (Canada), and many others.
- Don't forget to use the entire domain name in the browser—Some browsers add the www. prefix used on most domain names, but others do not. For best results, spell out the complete domain name.

If you want a unique domain name for either a website or e-mail, the ISP that you use to provide your e-mail or web hosting service often provides a registration wizard you can use to access the domain name registration services provided by various companies such as Verisign.

A domain name has three major sections, from the end of the name to the start:

- The top-level domain (.com, .org, .net, and so on).
- The name of the site.
- The server type; www indicates a web server, ftp indicates an FTP server, mail indicates a mail server, and search indicates a search server.

For example, Microsoft.com is located in the .com domain, typically used for commercial companies. Microsoft is the domain name. The Microsoft.com domain has the following servers:

- www.microsoft.com hosts web content, such as product information.

- support.microsoft.com hosts the Microsoft.com support website, where users can search for Knowledge Base (KB) and other support documents.

- ftp.microsoft.com hosts the File Transfer Protocol server of Microsoft.com; this portion of the Microsoft.com domain can be accessed by either a web browser or an FTP client.

Many companies have only WWW servers, or only WWW and FTP servers.

NOTE Some small websites use a folder under a domain hosted by an ISP: www.isp-name.com/~smallsitename.

TCP/IP User-Configured Advanced Settings

In Windows, click the Advanced button shown in Figure 11-13 to bring up a multi-tabbed dialog for adding, editing, or removing gateways (IP Settings), DNS server addresses (DNS), and adjusting WINS resolution settings (WINS). These options can be used whether DHCP addressing is enabled or not. Figure 11-14 shows these tabs.

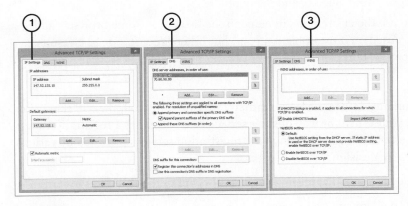

1. IP settings tab
2. DNS servers tab
3. WINS tab

Figure 11-14 The tabs used for Advanced TCP/IP Settings.

Gateway

A **gateway** is a computer or device (such as a router) that provides a connection between a LAN and a wide area network (WAN) or the Internet. OS X uses the term *router* to refer to the default gateway.

Computers that use a LAN connection to connect to the Internet need to enter the IP address of the default gateway on this tab if the computer doesn't use DHCP to obtain an IP address.

If a computer on a LAN cannot reach the Internet, it is likely the default gateway is down or the default gateway address is misconfigured in the TCP/IP properties on the client-side.

TCP and UDP Ports, Protocols, and Purposes

For two computers to communicate, they must both use the same protocol. For an application to send or receive data, it must use a particular protocol designed for that application and open up a port on the network adapter to make a connection to another computer. For example, let's say you want to visit www.google.com. You would open a browser and type http://www.bing.com. The protocol being used is HTTP, short for Hypertext Transfer Protocol, which makes the connection to the web server: google.com. The HTTP protocol would select an unused port on your computer (known as an outbound port) to send and receive data to and from google.com. On the other end, bing.com's web server will have a specific port open at all times ready to accept sessions. In most cases the web server's port is 80, which corresponds to the HTTP protocol. This is known as an *inbound port*.

Transmission Control Protocol (**TCP**) sessions are known as connection-oriented sessions. This means that every packet that is sent is checked for delivery. If the receiving computer doesn't receive a packet, it cannot assemble the message and will ask the sending computer to transmit the packet again. No one packet is left behind.

User Datagram Protocol (**UDP**) sessions are known as *connectionless sessions*. UDP is used in streaming media sessions, Voice over IP (VoIP), for protocols that use a simple query and response such as DNS, and gaming. In these cases if a packet is dropped, it is not asked for again. Let's say you were listening to some streaming music and you heard a break in the song or a blip of some kind. That indicates some missing packets, but you wouldn't want those packets back because by the time you get them you would be listening to a totally different part of the music stream.

It's expected to lose packets in UDP streams, but not when making TCP connections. Both TCP and UDP utilize ports to make connections. Remember, it's the inbound ports that you are concerned with. For example, an FTP server that stores files for customers needs to have inbound port 21 open by default. Table 11-6 displays some common protocols and their default corresponding inbound ports. Most use the same TCP and UDP port numbers, but Table 11-6 lists exceptions.

Table 11-6 Common Protocols and Their Ports

Port Number(s)	Protocol	Port Type
21	FTP	TCP, UDP
22	SSH	TCP, UDP
23	Telnet	TCP, UDP
25	SMTP	TCP, UDP
53	DNS	TCP, UDP
80	HTTP	TCP, UDP
110	POP3	TCP, UDP
143	IMAP	TCP
443	HTTPS	TCP, UDP
3389	RDP	TCP, UDP
137–139*	NetBIOS/NetBT	TCP, UDP
445	SMB/CIFS	TCP
427**	SLP	TCP, UDP
548	AFP	TCP

* See also 445

** Can also be used for AFP

TIP Know these protocols and their corresponding port numbers for the exam.

In the following sections, you learn more about each of these protocols.

FTP

File Transfer Protocol (**FTP**) is a protocol used by both web browsers and specialized FTP programs to access dedicated file transfer servers for file downloads and uploads. When you access an FTP site, the site uses the prefix ftp://.

Windows and Linux contain a command-line FTP program; type FTP, press Enter, and then type **help** at the FTP prompt to see the commands you can use. See http://linux.about.com/od/commands/l/blcmdl1_ftp.htm.

For OS X, see http://osxdaily.com/2011/02/07/ftp-from-mac/ or use ftp from the command line.

FTP sites with downloads available to any user support anonymous FTP; if any credentials are required, it's typically the user's e-mail address as a password (the username is preset to anonymous). Some FTP sites require the user to log in with a specified username and password. FTP is not considered secure because FTP users can authenticate in clear-text sign-ins. FTP is often secured with SSL/TLS (FTPS) or use SSH File Transfer Protocol (SFTP) instead. FTP uses port 21.

TIP Although you can use an operating system's built-in FTP client for file uploads and downloads with both secured and unsecured FTP sites, you should consider using third-party FTP products such as FileZilla (http://filezilla-project.org/). These programs enable you to create a customized setup for each FTP site you visit and will store passwords, server types, and other necessary information. They also enable faster downloads than typical web browsers running in ftp:// mode.

SSH

Secure Shell (**SSH**) allows data to be exchanged between computers on a secured channel. This protocol offers a more secure replacement to FTP and Telnet. The Secure Shell server housing the data you want to access would have port 22 open (SSH uses port 22). Several other protocols use SSH as a way of making a secure connection. One of these is Secure FTP (SFTP) as previously mentioned. Regular FTP can be insecure. SFTP combats this by providing file access over a reliable data stream, generated and protected by SSH.

Telnet

Telnet enables a user to make a text-based connection to a remote computer or networking device and use it as if he were a regular user sitting in front of it, rather than simply downloading pages and files as he would with an http:// or ftp:// connection.

Windows and Linux contain a command-line Telnet program. To open a connection to a remote computer, open a command prompt (Windows) or terminal session (Linux) and type telnet and press the Enter key. This command opens the Telnet command prompt. For help with commands, type help and press the Enter key.

OS X includes a menu-driven Telnet program available from Terminal. See http://www.wikihow.com/Use-Telnet-on-OS-X.

NOTE   The remote computer must be configured to accept a Telnet login. Typically, TCP port 23 on the remote computer must be open before a login can take place.

SMTP

The Simple Mail Transfer Protocol **(SMTP)** is used to send e-mail from a client system to an e-mail server, which also uses SMTP to relay the message to the receiving e-mail server. SMTP uses port 25.

NOTE   When configuring e-mail settings on a client, you need to know the server type(s) used (SMTP, POP3 or IMAP); the ports used (default values may be changed by some ISPs); the user name and password for the e-mail service; the security settings (for example, whether SSH is used). Check with the ISP or organization that provides Internet access for the correct values.

DNS

The domain name service (**DNS**) is the name for the network of servers on the Internet that translate **domain names**, such as www.informit.com, and individual host names into their matching IP addresses. If you manually configure an IP address, you typically provide the IP addresses of one or more DNS servers as part of the configuration process. DNS uses port 53.

HTTP/HTTPS

Hypertext Transfer Protocol (**HTTP**) is the protocol used by web browsers, such as Internet Explorer, Microsoft Edge, Firefox, and Chrome, to access websites and content. Normal (unsecured) sites use the prefix http:// when accessed in a web browser. Sites (**HTTPS**) that are secured with various encryption schemes are identified with the prefix https://. HTTP uses port 80 and HTTPS uses port 443.

NOTE   Most browsers connecting with a secured site will also display a closed padlock symbol onscreen.

POP3

The Post Office Protocol version 3 (**POP3**) is the more popular of two leading methods for receiving e-mail (IMAP is the other). In an e-mail system based on

POP3, e-mail is downloaded from the mail server to folders on a local system. POP3 is not a suitable e-mail protocol for users who frequently switch between computers because e-mail might wind up on multiple computers. The POP3 version is the latest current standard. Users that utilize POP3 servers to retrieve e-mail typically use SMTP to send messages. POP3 uses port 110.

> **TIP**   For users who must use POP3-based e-mail and use multiple computers, a remote access solution, such as Windows Remote Desktop Connection or a service such as GoToMyPC, is recommended. A remote access solution enables a user to remotely access the system that connects to the POP3 mail server so she can download and read e-mail messages, no matter where she is working.

IMAP

The Internet Message Access Protocol **(IMAP)** is an e-mail protocol that enables messages to remain on the e-mail server so they can be retrieved from any location. Compare it to POP3, which downloads messages to the mail client. IMAP also supports folders, so users can organize their messages as desired. IMAP4 is the current version of IMAP.

To configure an IMAP-based e-mail account, you must select IMAP as the e-mail server type and specify the name of the server, your username and password, and whether the server uses SSL. IMAP uses port 143.

SMB/CIFS

Server Message Block **(SMB)** provides access to shared items such as files and printers. They are actual packets that authenticate remote computers through what are known as *interprocess communication mechanisms*. SMB uses ports 137–139 for SMB traffic using NetBIOS over TCP (NBT), and 445 (SMB hosted on TCP).

Port 445 is also used by the Common Internet File System **(CIFS)**. CIFS was widely used after its introduction as a standard method for sharing files across corporate intranets and the Internet. CIFS is an enhanced version of Microsoft SMB, which is an open, cross-platform protocol. CIFS has now been widely replaced by updated versions of SMB (SMB 2.0 and 3.0).

> **NOTE**   If traffic on ports 137–139 is blocked, you must use the device's IP address to access shared files or printers. When these ports are open, you can use the name of the device to access its shared files or printers.

AFP

Apple Filing Protocol (**AFP**) was previously known as AppleTalk Filing Protocol. AFP uses TCP/IP for transport, and is used by OS X 10.9 (Mavericks) and newer versions to connect to devices running older Mac OS and OS X versions, and for Apple's Time Machine backup app.

Starting with OS X 10.9, OS X uses SMB2 to connect between OS X devices, Linux devices, or with Windows devices.

Remote Desktop Protocol

The RDP port, 3389, is used by Remote Desktop Services (RDS), which is the Windows Server-based companion of Remote Desktop Connection. To learn more about Remote Desktop Connection, see "Remote Desktop Connection," p.791, Chapter 15.

SSL

Secure Socket Layers (SSL) is an encryption technology used by secured (https://) websites. To access a secured website, the web browser must support the same encryption level used by the secured website (normally 128-bit encryption) and the same version(s) of SSL used by the website (normally SSL version 2.0 or 3.0). Sites secured with SSL display a padlock in the browser's URL and often a green address bar if secured by a certificate.

TLS

Transport Layer Security (**TLS**) is the successor to SSL. SSL3 was somewhat of a prototype to TLS and was not fully standardized. TLS was ratified by the IETF in 1999. However, many people and companies might still refer to it as SSL.

HTML

Hypertext Markup Language (**HTML**) is the language used by web pages. An HTML page is a specially formatted text page that uses tags (commands contained in angle brackets) to change text appearance, insert links to other pages, display pictures, incorporate scripting languages, and provide other features. Web browsers, such as Microsoft Internet Explorer, Microsoft Edge, Google Chrome, and Firefox, are used to view and interpret the contents of web pages, which have typical file extensions such as .htm, .html, .asp (Active Server pages generated by a database), and others.

You can see the HTML code used to create the web page in a browser by using the View Source or View Page Source menu option provided by your browser. Figure 11-15 compares what you see in a typical web page (main window) with the HTML tags used to set text features and the underlined hyperlink (inset window). The figure uses a different text size and shading to distinguish tags from text, and so do most commercial web-editing programs used to make web pages.

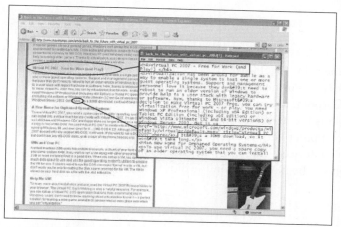

Figure 11-15   A section of an HTML document as seen by a typical browser uses the HTML tags shown in Notepad for paragraphs (<P>) titles (<H4>, </H4>), and hyperlinks (<A HREF>, </A>).

Tags such as <P> are used by themselves and other tags are used in pairs. For example, <A HREF...> is used to indicate the start of a hyperlink (which will display another page or site in your browser window), and </A> indicates the end of a hyperlink.

NOTE   The World Wide Web Consortium (http://www.w3c.org) sets the official standards for HTML tags and syntax.

DHCP

The Dynamic Host Configuration Protocol (**DHCP**) is used to automatically assign IP addresses to hosts. These hosts could be computers, printers, servers, routers, and so on. In most SOHO networks a router uses DHCP to assign IP addresses to the client computers. However, your ISP also uses DHCP to assign an IP address to you; usually your router gets this. The DHCP service makes life easier for the network administrator by automatically assigning IP addresses, subnet masks, gateway addresses, DNS servers, and so on. If you get your address from a DHCP server, you are getting your address assigned dynamically, and it could change periodically. However, some computers require a static address, one that is assigned by the network administrator manually. It is better in many situations for servers and printers to use static addresses, so you know exactly what the address is, and so it won't change.

SNMP

Simple Network Management Protocol (**SNMP**) is used as the standard for managing and monitoring devices on your network. It manages routers, switches, and computers and is often incorporated in software known as a network management system or NMS. The NMS is the main software that controls everything SNMP-based; it is installed on a computer known as a manager. The devices to be monitored are known as managed devices. The NMS installs a small piece of software known as an agent that allows the NMS to monitor those managed devices.

LDAP

Lightweight Directory Access Protocol (**LDAP**) is used to access and maintain distributed directories of information such as the kind involved with Microsoft domains. Microsoft refers to this as *directory services*.

WiFi (Wi-Fi) Network and Encryption Standards

Wireless Ethernet, also known as IEEE 802.11, is the collective name for a group of wireless technologies compatible with wired Ethernet; these are referred to as wireless LAN (WLAN) standards. Wireless Ethernet is also known as Wi-Fi, after the Wireless Fidelity (Wi-Fi) Alliance (www.wi-fi.org), a trade group that promotes interoperability between different brands of Wireless Ethernet hardware.

Wi-Fi Standards

There are five different Wi-Fi standards:

- **802.11b** has a maximum speed of 11Mbps and can fall back to 5.5Mbps or slower if necessary. It uses the 2.4GHz frequency band with 20MHz-wide **channels**.

- **802.11a** has a maximum speed of 54Mbps and supports slower speeds from 6–48Mbps as needed and uses the 5GHz frequency band.

- **802.11g** has a maximum speed of 54Mbps and supports slower speeds from 6–48Mbps as needed. Unlike 802.11a, 802.11g uses the 2.4GHz frequency band, so it is backward-compatible with 802.11b.

- **802.11n** has a maximum speed of 150Mbps when using a single 20MHz channel, or up to 300Mbps when using channel bonding (40MHz channel). All 802.11n devices use the 2.4GHz frequency by default, but 802.11n can optionally support 5GHz frequencies as well. 802.11n supports MIMO (multiple in, multiple out) antennas to improve performance and range, although not all devices include multiple antennas.

- **802.11ac** uses only the 5GHz band and supports up to 80MHz wide channels, compared to 20MHz with 802.11b/g and 40MHz with 802.11n using channel bonding. It supports Multi-user MIMO (MU-MIMO). The speed of 802.11ac is up to 433Mbps per stream when 80MHz wide channels are used.

Table 11-7 compares different types of Wireless Ethernet to each other.

Table 11-7   Wireless Ethernet Standards

Wireless Ethernet Type	Frequency	Maximum Speed	MIMO Support	Estimated Range Indoors/ Outdoors	Channel Width/ Number of Channels	Interoperable With
802.11a	5GHz	54Mbps	No	35m / 120m	20MHz / 12*	Requires dual-mode (802.11a/b or 802.11a/g) hardware; 802.11n networks supporting 5GHz frequency
802.11b	2.4GHz	11Mbps	No	32m / 140m	20MHz / 3**	802.11g
802.11g	2.4GHz	54Mbps	No	32m / 140m	20MHz / 3**	802.11b, 802.11n
802.11n	2.4GHz	72Mbps per stream (20MHz channel)	Yes^	70m / 250m	20MHz / 3**	802.11b, 802.11g (802.11a on networks also supporting 5GHz frequency)
802.11n (optional)	5GHz	150Mbps per stream (40MHz channel)	Yes^	70m / 250m	20MHz / 40MHz / 12*	802.11a (20MHz wide channels only)

Wireless Ethernet Type	Frequency	Maximum Speed	MIMO Support	Estimated Range Indoors/ Outdoors	Channel Width/ Number of Channels	Interoperable With
802.11ac	5GHz	433Mbps per stream (80MHz channel)	Yes^	70m 250m	20MHz 40MHz 80MHz	802.11a, 802.11n (5GHz). 802.11ac routers also support previous standards.

^ Up to four streams supported. Most devices have up to three antennas but can receive/transmit only two streams at a time.

* Non-overlapping channels; exact number varies by country

** Non-overlapping channels

NOTE Wi-Fi–certified hardware is 802.11-family Wireless Ethernet hardware that has passed tests established by the Wi-Fi Alliance. Most, but not all, 802.11-family Wireless Ethernet hardware is Wi-Fi–certified.

Understanding MIMO

The number of antennas supported by the router and the adapters (either built-in or add-on devices) is one of the reasons for different performance levels in a given 802.11n or 802.11ac device:

- 1x1—one transmit, one receive antenna
- 2x2—two transmit, two receive antennas
- 2x3—two transmit, three receive antennas
- 3x2—three transmit, two receive antennas
- 3x3—three transmit, three receive antennas

The number of transmit antennas generally corresponds to the number of spatial streams (data streams) the device can support. In the case of a router that supports both 2.4GHz and 5GHz signals, the specifications include this information for each band.

NOTE When a device has a different number of receiving and sending antennas, the device might be identified by the number of spatial (data) streams it can send and receive. For example, a device with a 2x3 antenna configuration can also be identified as having a 2x3:2 configuration (two send antennas, three receive antennas, and two spatial [data] streams send/receive support). Some smartphones and tablets simply use the term MIMO (multiple input, multiple output) if they support two or more 802.11n or 802.11ac streams.

Wi-Fi Encryption Types

Although many public Wi-Fi hot spots are not encrypted, encryption is a necessity for both SOHO and larger business wireless networks to preserve privacy and to prevent criminals from borrowing your network. However, there are several types of encryption.

WEP (Wired Equivalent Privacy)

WEP is the oldest and weakest Wi-Fi encryption standard. All network devices must use the same WEP key and encryption strength if WEP is enabled.

Use the highest setting supported by both WEP and adapters for best security. Small-office or home-office hardware might use 64-bit encryption with a 40-bit key (10 hexadecimal characters or 5 ASCII characters); business-market hardware often uses 128-bit encryption with a 104-bit key (26 hexadecimal characters or 13 ASCII characters). WEP cannot use punctuation marks in its encryption keys.

WEP can be configured using a pre-shared key (PSK) or Open System authentication. PSK is easier to break than Open System, but either form is easy to break and should not be used unless some network devices don't support superior WPA or WPA2 encryption. 802.11n and 802.11ac do not support WEP.

WPA (Wi-Fi Protected Access)

WPA uses a variable-length encryption key (up to 63 ASCII characters including punctuation marks) and temporal key integrity protocol (**TKIP**) 128-bit encryption, making it much more secure than WEP.

WPA can use PSK or a RADIUS authentication server to generate unique keys (used in enterprise and government Wi-Fi networks).

WPA has been largely replaced by WPA2, but some routers can be configured to support both WPA and WPA2 clients on the same network.

WPA2 (Wi-Fi Protected Access 2)

Unlike most sequels, this sequel is better (in the sense of being more secure) than the original. **WPA2** replaces TKIP with advanced encryption standard (**AES**), a 128–256-bit encryption protocol used in several technologies such as hard drive encryption as well as networking. It can be used exclusively or in conjunction with TKIP and is the recommended option. Some router configurations use the term *WPA-AES* to refer to WPA2. If you use a mixture of WPA and WPA2 devices and can't update the firmware on the older devices to support AES, use the WPAs-TKIP-AES setting on your router.

WPS (Wi-Fi Protected Setup)

WPS is simply an easier way to configure a wireless network than entering the router's IP address on each device connecting to it. Routers that support WPS typically have the default WPS key on the bottom of the device. To use WPS, use the setup software provided with the router on each computer and follow the directions on devices such as printers or multifunction. Note that WPS should not be used unless all devices on a wireless network support it.

There are two ways to use WPS: the default PIN method (in which the PIN on the router is used to set up clients) and a pushbutton method, in which a physical or software button is pushed on the router and clients to set up the network. In December 2011, researchers announced that the PIN and the pre-shared key could be compromised by a brute-force attack. Since that time, users have been encouraged to use the pushbutton method or to forgo using WPS for configuration.

Table 11-8 compares WEP, WPA, and WPA2 to each other.

Table 11-8   Wireless Ethernet Encryption Types

Setting	Encryption Type	Encryption Key Length	Encryption Key Rules	Strength
Open	None	N/A	N/A	None
Wired Equivalent Privacy (WEP)	RC4	10 hex/5 ASCII characters (64-bit)	ASCII: alphanumeric (no punctuation)	Very weak
		26 hex/13 ASCII characters (128-bit)		
Wi-Fi Protected Access (WPA)	TKIP (128-bit)	Up to 63 ASCII characters	Punctuation is OK; some devices can't use a full-length encryption key	Strong

Setting	Encryption Type	Encryption Key Length	Encryption Key Rules	Strength
Wi-Fi Protected Access 2 (WPA2)	AES (128-bit)	Up to 63 ASCII characters	Punctuation is OK; some devices can't use a full-length encryption key	Very Strong

Configure SOHO Wired or Wireless Router

A small-office home-office (SOHO) wired or wireless router can provide a secure way for users to access the Internet and local network resources or become a magnet for attack. The difference is in how it is configured. In the following sections, we look at how to configure SOHO routers to meet typical network requirements.

Channels

When installing a 2.4GHz wireless network, avoiding overlapping channels and selecting a channel with little or no traffic can be challenging. Only channels 1, 6, and 11 do not overlap with other channels. Use one of these channels.

Some routers feature an Auto setting that will use the least-active channel, but if you prefer (or must) select a channel manually, use a Wi-Fi diagnostic utility (discussed later in this chapter) to find the least-used channel.

To change the channel used by your wireless network:

Step 1.   Log in to your router.

Step 2.   Navigate to the Wireless Configuration dialog.

Step 3.   Select a different channel (when using 2.4GHz networking, channels 1, 6, and 11 have less interference than others).

Step 4.   Save your changes and exit the router configuration dialog.

Figure 11-16 illustrates a typical wireless channel configuration dialog on a dual-frequency (2.4 and 5.0GHz) Wireless-N router from Western Digital.

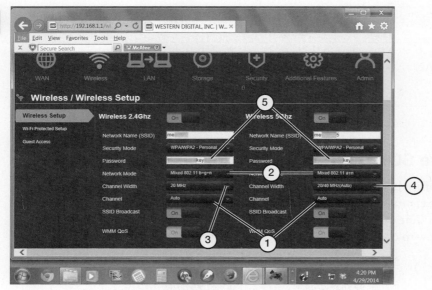

1. Auto channel selection lets router decide which channel works best
2. Mixed mode supports older network devices
3. Default channel width supported by all 2.4GHz devices
4. Auto channel width uses 40MHz channels with Wireless-N or AC clients and 20MHz channels with Wireless-A clients
5. Pre-shared key (blanked out for security)

Figure 11-16 Configuring wireless frequencies and channels.

NAT

Network address translation (**NAT**) is the process of modifying IP addresses as information crosses a router. Generally, this functionality is built into a router. It hides an entire IP address space on the LAN; for example, 192.168.0.1 through 192.168.0.255. Whenever an IP address on the LAN wants to communicate with the Internet, the IP is converted to the public IP of the router; for example, 68.54.127.95. This way, it appears that the router is the only device making the connection to remote computers on the Internet, providing safety for the computers on the LAN. It also allows a single IP to do the work for many IP addresses in the LAN.

SOHO routers perform NAT automatically when connected to an IPv4 network. NAT is not necessary on an IPv6 network because IPv6 is much more secure and has no shortage of IP addresses.

Port Forwarding, Port Triggering, and DNAT

Port forwarding is used to forward external visitors through the router to a specific computer. Instead of opening up the entire LAN, port forwarding directs particular traffic where you want it to go. A basic example would be if you were to set up an FTP server internally on your LAN. The FTP server might have the IP address 192.168.0.250 and have port 21 open ready to accept file transactions, or you could use a different inbound port if you want. Clients on the Internet that want to connect to your FTP server would have to know the IP address of your router, so for example the clients would connect with an FTP client using the IP 68.54.127.95 and port 21. Once you create the appropriate port-forwarding rule, the router would then see these packets and forward them to 192.168.0.250:21, or whatever port you choose. Now, many ISPs block this type of activity, but it becomes a common and important method in larger networks.

Figure 11-17 illustrates port forwarding for an incoming VPN that uses PPTP. PPTP uses two non-contiguous ports and thus needs two rules, one for each port.

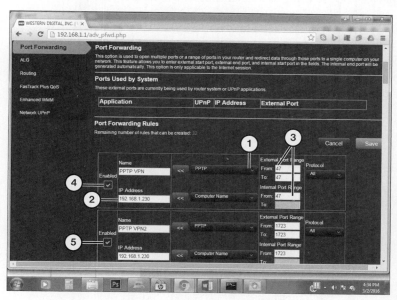

1. Select the protocol needed
2. Enter the IP address for the device receiving the traffic
3. Enter the port range
4. Enable the setting
5. Add additional ranges or additional protocols as needed

Figure 11-17   Configuring port forwarding to permit incoming VPN connections

Port triggering, which is available on some routers, opens an outgoing port or range of ports on demand by a particular service, such as internet relay chat (IRC). Port triggering can be used without tying it to a specific IP address.

Another name for port forwarding is destination network address translation (**DNAT**) DNAT is sometimes also used to refer to DMZ.

DMZ

A demilitarized zone **(DMZ)** allows outside traffic through to a particular IP address on your LAN. In a SOHO router, any device assigned to the DMZ receives traffic that is not specified for a particular device. Using a DMZ host makes sense for gaming or other types of traffic where you cannot specify in advance the ports needed. However, it's important that the DMZ host has its own firewall, because DMZ hosts are not protected by the router firewall.

Figure 11-18 illustrates a typical DMZ configuration. After DMZ is enabled, the IP address for the device you are using as a DMZ host must be specified.

TIP   Use static IP addresses for any devices that use port forwarding or DMZ to assure that the correct device is being specified. Dynamic IP (server-assigned DHCP) addresses can change according to the number of devices on the network and whether some devices leave the network and then return to it.

1. DMZ enabled
2. IP address for computer in DMZ

Figure 11-18   Configuring DMZ.

DHCP

By default, SOHO routers have the **DHCP** service turned on, enabling them to provide IP addresses to any wired or wireless device that connects. Most routers enable you to specify the range and number of IP addresses available via DHCP. If a router does not have sufficient IP addresses for the devices that need to connect to it, devices arriving after the pool of addresses is used up will not receive an IP address and will switch to APIPA, the non-routable IP address range (169.254.x.x). Figure 11-19 illustrates a router with DHCP enabled and a range of IP addresses the DHCP server can assign.

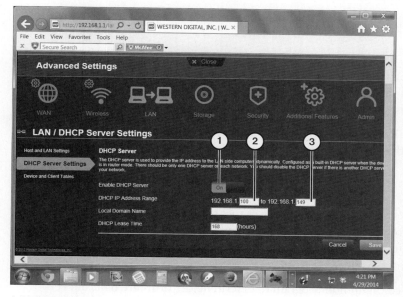

1. DHCP enabled
2. Starting IP address for DHCP assignment
3. Ending IP address for DHCP assignment

Figure 11-19   Configuring DHCP to provide a range of 50 IP addresses.

TIP   When you need to use static IP addresses, make sure you don't assign all possible IP addresses to the DHCP server, and use addresses beyond the DHCP range for those devices. For example, in the network illustrated in Figure 11-19, IP addresses below 100 and above 149 in the 192.168.1.x network could be used for devices needing static IP addresses.

Basic QoS

Quality of service (QoS) is an important feature to enable on any network that provides streaming media, gaming, or VoIP services. QoS prioritizes real-time and streaming traffic. Depending on the router, QoS can simply be turned on and off (**Basic QoS**) or it can be tweaked by specifying services to prioritize, whether to optimize for gaming, and uplink/downlink speeds to use.

QoS can be configured by your ISP or by your router. If your ISP is already performing QoS optimization, any changes you make on your router will not improve your traffic.

UPnP

Universal plug and play (**UPnP**) is a router feature that enables devices on your network to add themselves to your network without the need to reconfigure your router. UPnP is widely used for media streaming across a network.

However, UPnP can be vulnerable to attacks. If you don't use media streaming or other services that use UPnP, you can disable it.

Firmware

Routers are specialized computing devices that are controlled by **firmware**. When you log into a router to view or change its configuration, the options you can choose are limited by its firmware. Buggy firmware can cause network problems or make your network more vulnerable to attack.

Use a router's configuration program to determine the firmware date and version it uses. If the router is using an older version of firmware, check the vendor's website for an update. Before downloading the update, read the technical notes to see what issues the firmware affects and if any other problems are caused by the update. Download the update and follow the vendor's instructions for installing the firmware.

If you want more features than the vendor-provided firmware includes, check for third-party firmware. DD-WRT is the most popular replacement firmware for routers, and some vendors now use it in their high-end routers.

To determine if a router can use DD-WRT firmware, visit the router database at the DD-WRT website (www.dd-wrt.com) and look up the router. You need to know the brand, model number, and revision. Figure 11-20 illustrates a portion of the System Information dialog from a Netgear router running DD-WRT firmware.

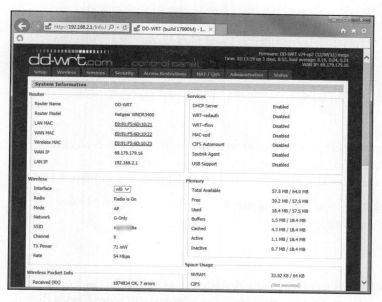

Figure 11-20 DD-WRT firmware on a Netgear router.

Internet Connection Types

One of the best reasons to create a network of any size is to provide access to the Internet. The many types of connectivity technologies that can be used for Internet access are discussed in the following sections.

> **NOTE** As you review the following sections, try to determine which type of Internet connections you use at home and at your workplace. If you are shopping for Internet service, the Broadband Now website (www.broadbandnow.com) is a useful way to find all types of broadband Internet access available in a specified zip code.

Cable

Cable Internet service is provided by a cable TV company. Virtually all cable Internet service today is built upon the fiber-optic and coaxial network used for digital cable and music services provided by most cable TV vendors. In most cases today, separate coaxial cables are used for TV and for Internet service into home or office.

Cable Internet can reach download speeds anywhere from 3Mbps up to 300Mbps or faster. Upload speeds are typically about 10–20 percent of upload speeds, but vary by vendor.

NOTE You can have cable Internet service without having cable TV.

Most cable modems connect to a computer or a router via an RJ-45 cable, but some use USB. When a cable provider also provides telephone service, a special modem is used that also includes a backup battery. A typical model is shown in Figure 11-21.

A cable Internet connection can be configured through the standard Network properties sheet in the operating system.

DSL

DSL (digital subscriber line) was originally designed to work on the same telephone line used by your telephone and fax machine if the telephone line can carry a digital signal. For home use, DSL is designed strictly for Internet access. But for business use, DSL can be used for additional services and can be used in site-to-site scenarios between organizations.

While telephone line–based DSL is still available, it is much slower than cable Internet. Newer types of DSL use the same signaling methods, but use fiber to provide speed comparable to high-performance cable.

There are two major types of DSL that use telephone lines: **ADSL (Asynchronous DSL)** and **SDSL (Synchronous DSL)**. Two newer types of DSL, VDSL (very high bit-rate digital subscriber line) and VDSL2, use fiber for at least part of the signal path.

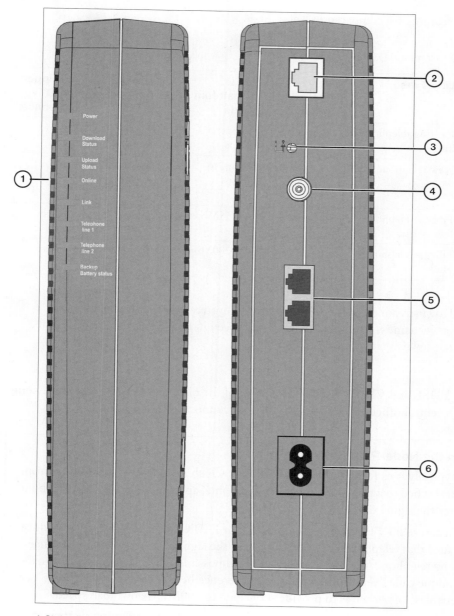

1. Status lights (front of unit)
2. Connection to router (rear of unit)
3. Reset button
4. Coaxial cable connection to Internet cable
5. Phone jacks
6. Power cable jack

Figure 11-21   A typical cable/telephone (VoIP) modem.

Their features are compared in Table 11-9.

Table 11-9   Common DSL Services Compared

Service Type	Line Type	User Installation Option	Typical Downstream Speeds	Typical Upstream Speeds	Supports HDTV Service
ADSL	Existing telephone line	Yes	384Kbps to 24Mbps	128Kbps to 3.3Mbps	No
SDSL	New telephone line	No	384Kbps to 2.0Mbps	Same as downstream speed	No
VDSL	Fiber + telephone line	No	Up to 55Mbps	15Mbps	Yes
VDLS2	Fiber + telephone line	No	Up to 200Mbps	Up to 100Mbps	Yes

NOTE   Downstream refers to download speed; upstream refers to upload speed. SDSL gets its name from providing the same speed in both directions; ADSL is always faster downstream than upstream.

Both VDSL and VDSL2 use fiber for most of the distance from the telephone company's central office (where all DSL services connect to the Internet).

Fiber to the Node-Premises-Curb

VDSL typically uses fiber to the node (FTTN), which carries the VDSL signal from the central office to a node in the vicinity of a home, apartment, or office. Telephone lines carry the signal the rest of the way.

VDSL2 can use FTTP (fiber to the premises) or FTTC (fiber to the curb) to reduce the distance that telephone line is used to carry the signal. The smaller the distance covered by telephone line, the greater the speed possible. VDSL2 uses a new signaling technique called vectoring to reduce interference between copper wire pairs. Vectoring enables copper wires to provide service up to 100Mbps download speed.

A device known as a *DSL modem* is used to connect your computer to DSL service. DSL modems connect to your PC through the RJ-45 (Ethernet) port or the USB port. The rear of a typical DSL modem that uses an Ethernet (RJ-45) connection is shown in Figure 11-22.

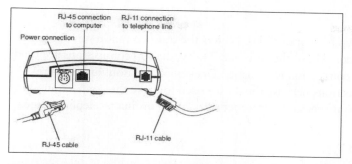

Figure 11-22 The rear of a typical ADSL modem with a power port (top left), RJ-45 data port to the PC (top center), and an RJ-11 telephone line port (top right). The RJ-45 cable is shown at bottom left, and the RJ-11 cable is shown at bottom right.

Many companies offering ADSL, VDSL, or VDSL2 services now provide a wireless router with DSL support and an integrated Gigabit Ethernet switch. Some of these devices also support HPNA, which uses coaxial wiring in the home as a network, or connections to a cable modem.

As Figure 11-23 indicates, DSL uses the same telephone lines as ordinary telephone equipment. However, your telephone can interfere with the DSL connection. To prevent this, in some cases a separate DSL line is run from the outside service box to the computer with the DSL modem. However, if your DSL provider supports the self-installation option, small devices called *microfilters* are installed between telephones, answering machines, fax machines, and other devices on the same circuit with the DSL modem. Microfilters can be built in to special wall plates but are more often external devices that plug into existing phone jacks, as shown in Figure 11-23.

Some DSL connections are configured as an always-on connection similar to a network connection to the Internet. However, many vendors now configure the DSL connection as a PPPoE (point-to-point protocol over Ethernet) connection instead. A PPPoE connection requires the user to make a connection with a username and password. PPPoE connections are supported in Windows, OS X, and Linux.

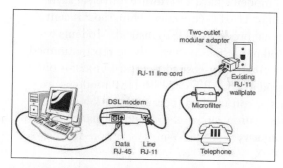

Figure 11-23 A typical self-installed DSL setup. The DSL vendor supplies the DSL modem (center) and microfilters that attach between telephones and other devices and the wall outlet (right).

Dial-up

Until the late '90s, **dial-up** networking (DUN) was the most common way for home and small businesses to connect to the Internet. Today, dial-up connections are used when no other Internet connection is available. Dial-up connections are often referred to as *analog* connections because the device used to make the connection is an analog modem, which connects to the Internet through an ordinary telephone line.

Modem Technologies and Types

A modem sending data modulates digital computer data into analog data suitable for transmission over telephone lines to the receiving modem, which demodulates the analog data back into computer form.

> **NOTE**   Properly used, the term modem (modulator-demodulator) refers only to a device that connects to the telephone line and performs digital-to-analog or analog-to-digital conversions. However, other types of Internet connections such as satellite, wireless, DSL, fiber and cable Internet also use the term modem, although they work with purely digital data. When used by itself in this book, however, modem refers only to dial-up (telephone) modems.

Modems come in many form factors, the most common of which include:

- **Add-on card**—Add-on card modems for desktop computers fit into a PCI expansion slot. See Figure 5-12 on page 141, Chapter 5, for a typical example.

- **External**—External modems plug into a serial or USB port.

- **Mini-PCI card**—Some older-model computers that appear to have built-in modems actually use modems that use the mini-PCI form factor and can be removed and replaced with another unit.

Although some high-end add-on card modems have a hardware universal asynchronous receiver transmitter (UART) or UART-equivalent chip, most recent models use a programmable digital signal processor (DSP) instead. Modems with a DSP perform similarly to UART-based modems but can easily be reprogrammed with firmware and driver updates as needed. Low-cost add-on card modems often use host signal processing (HSP) instead of a UART or DSP. HSP modems are sometimes referred to as Winmodems or soft modems because Windows and the computer's processor perform the modulation, slowing down performance. HSP modems might not work with some older versions of Windows or non-Windows operating systems such as Linux or OS X.

External modems must be connected to a serial or USB port. Serial port versions require an external power source (USB modems are usually powered by the USB port or hub), but the portability and front-panel status lights of either type of external modem make them better for business use.

There have been various standards for analog modems used to make dial-up connections. Before the advent of so-called "56K" standards, the fastest dial-up connection possible was 33.6Kbps. Virtually all modems in more recent systems or available for purchase support either the ITU v.90 or v.92 standards.

NOTE Although v.90 and v.92 modems are all designed to perform downloading at up to 56Kbps, FCC (Federal Communications Commission) regulations limit actual download speed to 53Kbps. Speeds greater than 33.6Kbps apply only to downloads from Internet service providers (ISPs) and their special modems. If you make a direct connection between two PCs, the fastest speed you can have in either direction is just 33.6Kbps (if both modems can run at least that fast).

NOTE You can drive yourself crazy trying to make a connection with your modem if you plug the RJ-11 telephone cord into the wrong jack. There are actually three ways to make this mistake:

- Plugging in the RJ-11 cord to the phone jack instead of the line or telco jack on the modem

- Plugging in the RJ-11 cord to the slightly larger RJ-45 jack used for 10/100/1000 Ethernet networking

- Plugging in the RJ-11 cord to a HomePNA network card (which also has two RJ-11 jacks) instead of the modem

Requirements for a Dial-Up Internet Connection

All dial-up ISPs must provide the following information to enable you to connect to the Internet:

- TCP/IP configuration information

- Dial-up access telephone numbers

- Modem types supported (33.6Kbps, 56Kbps, v.90, v.92)

- The username and initial password (which should be changed immediately after first login)

Even if the client software provided by the ISP configures the connection for you, you should record the following information in case it is needed to manually configure or reconfigure the connection:

- **The dial-up access telephone number**—Dialing prefix, area code, and phone number are needed.

- **The username and password**—Windows often saves this during the setup of a DUN connection, but it should be recorded in case the system must be reconfigured or replaced.

- **The TCP/IP configuration**—This is set individually for each dial-up connection through its properties sheet.

To determine this information, right-click the icon for the connection and select **Properties**.

Creating a Dial-Up Connection

Windows creates dial-up networking (DUN) connections within the Network and Sharing Center window. To create a dial-up connection:

Step 1.   Click **Connect to a network**.

Step 2.   Choose **Set up a dial-up connection**.

Step 3.   If your modem is not connected, click **Set up a connection anyway** to continue. Your settings will be saved.

Step 4.   Enter the phone number, the user name (usually your e-mail address) and password assigned by the ISP, and name the connection. If you need to set dialing rules (such as numbers to reach an outside line), click the **Dialing Rules** link.

Step 5.   Click **Create** or **Connect** (see Figure 11-24).

If the dial-up connection is the only network connection, it appears when you open your browser. If you have other connections, you can select the connection to use from the Internet Options dialog's Connections tab.

To create a dial-up connection with OS X:

Step 1.   Open the Network dialog.

Step 2.   Select the modem from the list of network devices.

Step 3.   Enter the phone number, the user name (usually your e-mail address) and password assigned by the ISP.

Step 4.   To see the modem status in the menu bar, select the checkbox.

Step 5.   Click **Apply**.

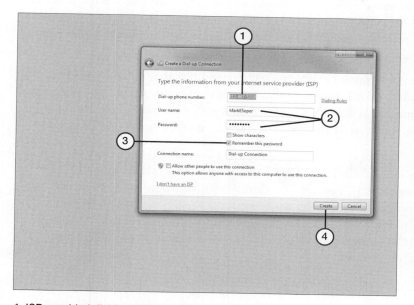

1. ISP-provided dial-in phone number
2. ISP-provided user name and password
3. After you change your password, click the empty checkbox to remember it
4. Click or tap Create to create the connection or Connect to start the connection

Figure 11-24   Creating a dial-up network connection with Windows 7.

In Linux, you can create a dial-up connection using the Network configuration features in the GUI or by using the **wvdial** and **wvdialconf** programs and editing the wvdial.conf configuration file to specify the phone number, username, and password assigned by your ISP. For details, see http://www.tldp.org/HOWTO/PPP-HOWTO/x314.html.

Fiber

Instead of using a copper connection to the home or business the way dial-up, ADSL/SDSL, or cable Internet do, many companies offer **fiber** (fiber-optic cable) connections to the home (FTTH, also known as fiber to the premises or FTTP) at their highest service levels. Fiber network download speeds can reach up to 2Gbps, and some vendors provide the same upload speed. DSL vendors such as Verizon, AT&T, and CenturyLink offer fiber connections in some service areas, as does

Google Fiber. Contact your ISP to determine if fiber connections are available or coming to your area.

The conversion between the fiber connection entering the home and the Ethernet or coaxial WAN connection used to connect a router or gateway is performed by an optical network terminal (ONT), which is supplied by the fiber provider and installed in the home.

Fiber users rent the router or gateway, which resembles the router or gateway included with cable or DSL Internet service, from the fiber provider. The fiber router or gateway connects to the ONT. Some vendors offer a network box that incorporates a wireless router as an alternative to a separate ONT and router or gateway.

NOTE   To learn more about FTTH/FTTP service in the USA, see Google Fiber (https://fiber.google.com/); Verizon Fios (http://www.verizon.com/home/fios/); AT&T U-verse with Gigapower (https://www.att.com/shop/u-verse/gigapower.html); or CenturyLink Fiber (https://www.centurylink.com/fiber/). Additional regional provider information is available at https://en.wikipedia.org/wiki/Fiber_to_the_premises_in_the_United_States.

Satellite

Satellite Internet providers, such as HughesNet (previously known as DirecWAY, and before that as DirecPC), StarBand, and WildBlue use dish antennas similar to satellite TV antennas to receive and transmit signals between geosynchronous satellites and computers. Separate antennas are needed for satellite Internet and TV services.

NOTE   Geosynchronous satellites orbit the Earth's equator at a distance of more than 22,000 miles (approximately 35,000 kilometers). Because of their orbits and altitudes, they remain in the same location in the sky at all times. In the Northern Hemisphere, you need an unobstructed view of the southern sky to make a connection. In the Southern Hemisphere, you need an unobstructed view of the northern sky to make a connection.

Satellite Internet services use external devices often called *satellite modems* to connect the computer to the satellite dish. They connect to the USB or Ethernet (RJ-45) port in a fashion similar to that used by DSL or cable modems.

The FCC requires professional installation for satellite Internet service because an incorrectly aligned satellite dish with uplink capabilities could cause a service outage on the satellite it's aimed at. Setup software supplied by the satellite vendor is used to complete the process.

NOTE   Satellite connections can also be made between buildings to allow for the high-speed exchange of data. In this scenario, a satellite dish would need to be installed on each building, and they would need to be in direct line of sight of each other. Internet access can also be offered in this manner.

ISDN

ISDN (Integrated Services Digital Network) was originally developed to provide an all-digital method for connecting multiple telephone and telephony-type devices, such as fax machines, to a single telephone line and to provide a faster connection for teleconferencing for remote computer users. A home/small office-based connection can also provide an all-digital Internet connection at speeds up to 128Kbps. Line quality is a critical factor in determining whether any particular location can use ISDN service. If an all-digital connection cannot be established between the customer's location and the telephone company's central switch, ISDN service is not available or a new telephone line must be run (at extra cost to you!).

NOTE   The telephone network was originally designed to support analog signaling only, which is why an analog (dial-up) modem that sends data to other computers converts digital signals to analog for transmission through the telephone network. The receiving analog modem converts analog data back to digital data.

ISDN Hardware

To make an ISDN connection, your PC (and any other devices that share the ISDN connection) needs a device called an ISDN terminal adapter (TA). A TA resembles a conventional analog modem. Internal models plug into the same PCIe or PCI slot used by analog modems, and external models use USB or serial ports.

Setting Up an ISDN Connection

ISDN connections (where available) are provided through the local telephone company. There are two types of ISDN connections:

- **Primary Rate Interface (PRI)**—A PRI connection provides 1.536Mbps of bandwidth, whereas a BRI interface provides 64Kbps (single-channel) or 128Kbps (dual-channel) of bandwidth.

- **Basic Rate Interface (BRI)**—BRI is sold to small businesses and home offices; PRI is sold to large organizations.

Both types of connections enable you to use the Internet and talk or fax data through the phone line at the same time.

A direct individual ISDN connection is configured through the network features of the operating system with the same types of settings used for an analog modem connection. Configuring a network-based ISDN connection is done through the network adapter's TCP/IP properties window.

NOTE   Most telephone companies have largely phased out ISDN in favor of DSL, which is much faster and less expensive for Internet connections.

Line of Sight Wireless

Line of sight wireless, sometimes referred to as terrestrial wireless, uses small antennas to connect users to Internet service transmitted from microwave towers. As the name states, a clear line of sight must be available from the transmission tower to the customer site. In some cases, this means that the customer antenna must be placed on the roof or on its own stand, or trees must be trimmed to provide adequate signal quality.

To bring the network signal into the premises, coaxial cable connects from the antenna to a line of sight wireless modem (similar to a cable modem). Connect the modem to a router to provide multiple devices with Internet access.

Typical download speeds range from 256Kbps up to 10Mbps. To find information about a wireless Internet Service Provider (WISP) in your area, visit wispdirectory.com.

Network Types

A network is a group of computers, peripherals, and software that are connected to each other and can be used together. Special software and hardware are required to make networks work.

LAN

A **LAN** (local area network) is a group of computers and other devices usually located in a small area: a house, a small office, or a single building. The computers all connect to one or more switches, and a router allows the computers access to the Internet.

WAN

A **WAN** (wide area network) is a group of one or more LANs over a large geographic area. Let's say a company had two LANs, one in New York and one in Los Angeles. Connecting the two would result in a WAN. However, to do this would require the help of a telecommunications company. This company would create the high-speed connection required for the two LANs to communicate quickly. Each LAN would require a router to connect to each other.

MAN

A smaller version of a WAN is known as a **MAN** (metropolitan area network), also known as a municipal area network. This is when a company has two offices in the same city and wants to make a high-speed connection between them. It's different from a WAN in that it is not a large geographic area, but it is similar to a WAN in that a telecommunications company is needed for the high-speed link.

PAN

A **PAN** (personal area network) is a smaller computer network used for communication by smartphones, tablets, and other small personal computing devices, typically using Bluetooth.

Network Architecture Devices

To create, update, repair, or manage a network effectively, you must understand the hardware building blocks used in networking. The following sections cover these components, their functions, and their features.

Hub

A **hub** is the simplest device used on an Ethernet network for connecting devices to each other. Hubs feature multiple RJ-45 ports, a power supply and signal lights to indicate network activity. Stackable hubs can be connected together to provide more ports.

Hubs have been almost completely replaced by switches because hubs split the bandwidth of the connection among all the computers connected to it. For example, a five-port 10/100 Ethernet hub divides the 100Mbps speed of Fast Ethernet among the five ports, providing only 20Mbps of bandwidth to each port for Fast Ethernet and 10/100 adapters. A hub also broadcasts data to all computers connected to it.

Switch

A **switch** is similar to the hub in appearance, but when it comes to sending data it works differently. Each port on a switch works independently, allowing more than one concurrent session. The switch makes a direct connection between the sending and receiving device by identifying the MAC address of each device. In today's networks, the switch is king and is common in 100Mbps, 1000Mbps, and 10Gbps networks. Switches, like hubs, are stackable.

A switch resembles a hub but creates a dedicated full-speed connection between the two computers that are communicating with each other. A five-port 10/100/1000 switch, for example, provides the full 100Mbps bandwidth to each port connected to a Fast Ethernet or 10/100 card. If the network adapters are configured to run in full-duplex mode (send and receive data simultaneously) and the switch supports full-duplex (most modern switches do), the Fast Ethernet bandwidth on the network is doubled to 200Mbps and Gigabit Ethernet (1000Mbps) bandwidth is doubled to 2Gbps. Switches can be daisy-chained in a manner similar to stackable hubs, and there is no limit to the number of switches possible in a network.

Low-cost switches used in **SOHO** networks (see Figure 11-25) are unmanaged. Managed switches, common in corporate and enterprise networks, also support simple network management protocol (SNMP) for diagnostics and performance measurement, support for Virtual LANs (VLANs) to enable multiple workgroups to use the same physical switch but keep their traffic separate, and redundancy.

1. **100Mbps connection**
2. **Unused RJ-45 port**
3. **Ethernet cable**

Figure 11-25   An unmanaged Fast Ethernet (10/100) five-port switch.

Router

The **router** connects one network to another. For example, a router connected to a cable or DSL modem enables multiple devices on a LAN to share a single broadband connection.

Most routers sold for SOHO configurations are Wi-Fi (802.11-family) wireless routers with integrated Fast or Gigabit Ethernet switches. Both wired and wireless devices can be on the same network and share folders and printers as well as Internet access.

Figure 11-26 shows the rear of a typical 802.11ac router for cable Internet from ASUS.

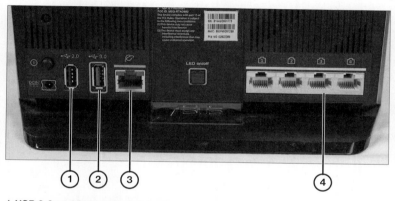

1. USB 2.0 port for external storage
2. USB 3.0 port for external storage
3. WAN (Internet) port to cable modem
4. Gigabit Ethernet switch for LAN

Figure 11-26 Many wireless routers can now be used as hosts for USB drives for shared network storage.

A router used for DSL is similar in appearance, but features a DSL port. The switches built into routers are also stackable. If a router needs more ports, add a switch.

Wireless Access Point

While hubs and switches deal with wired networks, the **wireless access point (WAP)** deals with wireless connections. It is also based on Ethernet, but now we are talking about the IEEE 802.11 group of standards, which define wireless LANs (WLANs). Wireless access points act as a central connecting point for computers equipped with wireless network adapters; like switches, the WAP identifies each computer by its MAC address.

To turn a wireless router into a WAP (which would then need to connect to a separate router), check the configuration options available for the router.

Bridge

The **bridge** is a device that can either connect two LANs together or separate them into two sections. There are wired and wireless bridges that are more commonly used today to increase the size of networks.

Modem

Now, let's move outside the LAN and talk about Internet and wide area network connectivity. The term **modem** is a conjunction of the words *modulate* and *demodulate*. Originally, the term *modem* was used only for analog (dial-up modems). It is a device that allows a computer (or in rare cases multiple computers) access to the Internet by changing the digital signals of the computer to analog signals used by a typical land-based phone line. These are slow devices and are usually used only if no other Internet option is available. However, they might be used in server rooms as a point of remote administration as well.

Today, any device that connects to the Internet is sometimes referred to as a modem.

Firewall

A **firewall** is any hardware appliance or software application that protects a computer from unwanted intrusion. In the networking world we are more concerned with hardware-based devices that protect an entire group of computers such as a LAN. When it comes to small offices and home offices, firewall functionality is usually built into the router. In larger organizations it is a separate device. The firewall stops unwanted connections from the outside and can block basic networking attacks.

Patch Panel

A **patch panel** is a box designed as a junction point for coaxial, TP, or fiber cable used in networks. Patch panels are typically built into wiring closets or added to equipment racks in a 1U or taller form factor. Patch panels can also be incorporated into homes or offices that have network or telephone wiring in the walls.

For a patch panel for TP cable, the patch panel must match the fastest cable grade in your network (CAT5e, CAT6, and so on). After removing any connector on the cable, each wire in the TP cable must be untwisted before being punched into the appropriate connection on the back of the panel. Use the same T568B or T568A color-coding that matches the rest of your network.

The front of the patch panel uses RJ-45 connectors for short standard network cables.

Repeaters/Extenders

Wireless network signals can be blocked by masonry, steel, or concrete walls and weaken over distance. By using a signal repeater or extender, areas of weak or no signals can also take advantage of a wireless network.

A wireless **repeater** (see Figure 11-27) resembles a wireless router and might sometimes include a switch, but instead of connecting to a cable or DSL modem, it connects wirelessly to your wireless router.

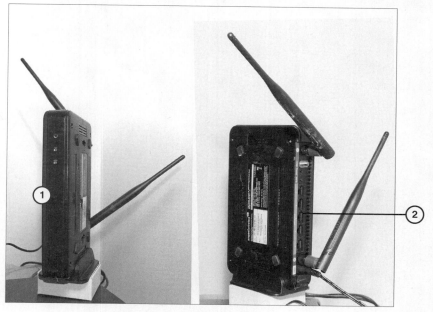

1. Front view
2. Gigabit Ethernet switch on rear of unit

Figure 11-27   A wireless repeater. Adjust the antennas to improve connections to the wireless router elsewhere in the building.

A powerline **extender** kit can be used to extend wired or wireless Internet connections. Powerline adapters are sold in pairs: one unit plugs into an AC wall socket near the router and is connected to the router via a switch. The other unit plugs into an AC wall socket in the room or area that needs network/Internet access. The AC wiring in the home or office (as long as it's on the same circuit) carries network signals between units. With a wired extender, plug a computer or switch into the Ethernet port. With a wireless extender, log into the network via the wireless extender's SSID.

Figure 11-28 illustrates a typical wired powerline extender.

1. Ethernet cable
2. Reset button
3. Activity lights

Figure 11-28   A powerline extender.

Power Over Ethernet

Power over Ethernet (**PoE**) uses CAT5 or better grades of TP cable to carry up to 25.5 watts of power on the unused TP pairs (pins 4-5, 7-8) in 10BASE-T or 100BASE-T Ethernet (PoE Mode B) or by using all four wire pairs (PoE Mode A), enabling it to be used with Gigabit Ethernet. PoE enables wireless access points, IP security cameras, VoIP phones, routers, and other Ethernet devices to be usable away from traditional power sources.

A PoE endspan device is a switch that supports PoE. A PoE midspan, also known as **a power over Ethernet injector**, is installed between a standard Ethernet switch and a PoE device to provide power only.

Using Networking Tools

If you plan on building a physical network, you need to stock up on some key networking tools. These tools aid you when running, terminating, and testing cable. For this short section, let's imagine a scenario where you are the network installer and are required to install a wired network for 12 computers.

To start, you should check with your local municipality for any rules and regulations for running networking cable. Some municipalities require a person to have an electrician's license. But most only require an exemption of some sort that anyone can apply for at the town or county seat. Due to the low-voltage nature of network wiring (for most applications), some municipalities have no rules regarding this. But in urban areas you need to apply for a permit and have at least one inspection done when you are finished with the installation.

Permits and regulations aside, let's say that in this scenario you have been cleared to install 12 wired connections to computers (known as drops) and have diagrammed where the cables will be run and where they will terminate. All cables will come out of a wiring closet where you will terminate them to a small patch panel. On the other end, they will terminate at in-wall RJ-45 jacks near each of the computers. Let's discuss each of the tools that you will use to complete this job.

Cutting Tool

The first tool you should have is a good, sharp cutting tool. You need to make a clean cut on the end of the network cable; scissors will not do. Either cut pliers or other cable cutting tools will be necessary. Klein Tools (www.kleintools.com) is an excellent manufacturer of these types of tools.

Cable Stripper

The second tool is a **cable stripper**. This tool is used to strip a portion of the plastic jacket off of the cable exposing the individual wires. At this point you can separate the wires and get ready to terminate them. Figure 11-29 illustrates a typical cable stripper.

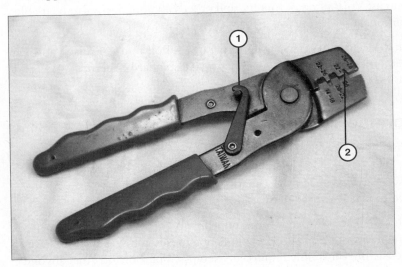

1. Release this clip to use the tool
2. Select the appropriate wire thickness based on the cable type

Figure 11-29   A cable (wire) stripper

Crimper

A **crimper** attaches a connector to the end of raw TP or coaxial cable. There are two types of crimpers you might need. If you are working with TP, you need an RJ-45 crimping tool (some also work with RJ-11 telephone cable). After untwisting the wire pairs and aligning them according to the appropriate standard (typically T568B), insert them into an RJ-45 connector and push the cable and connector assembly into the crimper. Line up the crimper jaw with the recessed area of the connector, and squeeze (see Figure 11-30).

If you are working with coaxial using F-connectors, a compression-crimping tool is recommended. It produces a better, more water-resistant connection than a hex-type crimper.

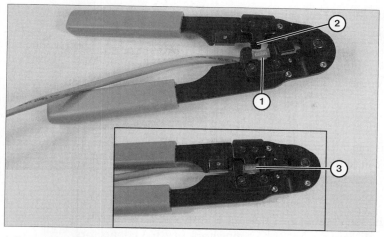

1. Connector and cable assembly inserted into crimper
2. Crimping jaw lined up and ready to crimp
3. Squeeze handles to complete crimp

Figure 11-30   Crimping an Ethernet cable.

Punchdown Tool

A **punchdown tool** (see Figure 11-31) punches the individual wires down into the 110 IDC clips of an RJ-45 jack and the patch panel. This "punching down" of the wires is the actual termination. The patch cables connect the various ports of the patch panel to a switch and the RJ-45 jacks to the computers.

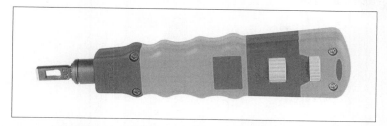

Figure 11-31   A typical punchdown tool.

Multimeter

A **multimeter** is a very flexible tool. It can be used for testing both coaxial and TP cabling as well as AC and DC voltage (see "Multimeter," p.588, Chapter 13). However, it is easier to test cables with specially made cable testers.

Tone Generator and Probe

The **tone generator and probe** kit consists of two parts: a tone device, which connects to one end of the network cable and when turned on, sends a tone along the length of the cable; and a probing device, also known as an inductive amplifier, that can pick up the tone anywhere along the cable length and at the termination point. This tool is not as good as a proper network cable tester because it only tests one of the pairs of the wires. However, it is an excellent tool for finding individual phone lines and is more commonly used for that.

Cable Tester

The best option is a proper network **cable tester**. This device includes a LAN testing unit that you can plug in to a port on the patch panel and a terminator that you plug in to the other end of the cable in the corresponding RJ-45 jack. This tool tests each wire in the cable and makes sure that everyone is wired properly.

Some cable testers, such as the one shown in Figure 11-32, can also be used to test coaxial cable using F-connectors, BNC connectors, or RCA connectors.

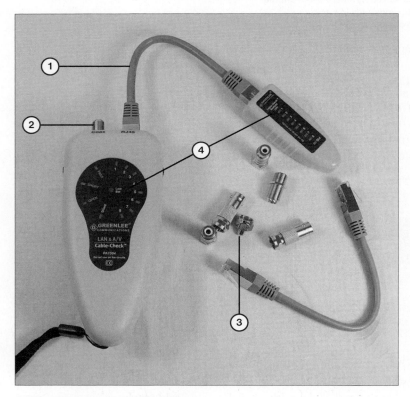

1. STP cable for testing patch panels
2. Threaded connector for testing coaxial cable
3. Adapters for various types of coaxial cable
4. Lights on remote and main unit light up as each line is tested

Figure 11-32   A typical cable tester equipped for testing RJ-45 and coaxial cable.

Loopback Plug

A **loopback plug** connects directly to the RJ-45 port of a PC's network adapter. By using it with a network diagnostic program, it simulates a network and tests whether the network adapter and TCP/IP are functioning properly.

Wi-Fi Analyzer

A **Wi-Fi analyzer** provides an easy-to-use view of both 2.4 and 5.0GHz wireless networks in your area. You can use a standalone device, a program for your desktop computer, or an app for your Android smartphone.

The InSSIDer Wi-Fi analyzer program for Windows and Mac (www.metageek. com) is a commercial product as of version 4 ($19.95), but free downloads of the previous 3.x version are still available from some download sites, such as MajorGeeks (www.majorgeeks.com) and Softpedia (www.softpedia.com). In Figure 11-33, InSSIDer v3 is displaying both 2.4GHz and 5GHz wireless networks in an office building. Most 2.4GHz networks in this example are using channels 1 or 11, making channel 6 (the only other non-overlapping channel) the best one to use for the selected network. InSSIDer also lists which networks are secure and the MAC address of each router.

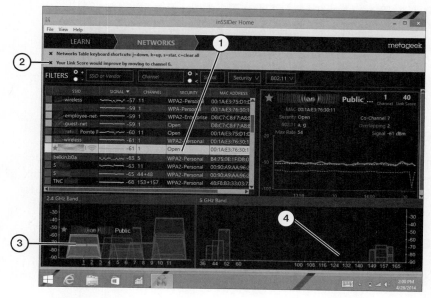

1. Selected network
2. Recommendation to use Channel 6
3. Lots of interference on Channel 1
4. Hardly any usage of 5GHz band with many more channels available

Figure 11-33   Using InSSIDer v3 to view wireless networks in an office building.

You can also use smartphone apps such as WiFi Analyzer (from farproc, on Google Play), the built-in Wireless Diagnostics feature in OS X, and the `iwlist` command in Linux to learn about the channels used by wireless networks in your vicinity.

Exam Preparation Tasks

Review All the Key Topics

Review the most important topics in the chapter, noted with the Key Topic icon in the outer margin of the page. Table 11-10 lists a reference of these key topics and the page numbers on which each is found.

Table 11-10   Key Topics for Chapter 11

Key Topic Element	Description	Page Number
Figure 11-1	Types of fiber-optic cables	427
Figure 11-3	T568B versus T568A TP cables	430
IPv6 Address Types	IPv6 Address Types and How They Compare to IPv4 Addresses	442
Table 11-7	Wireless Ethernet standards	459
Figure 11-16	Configuring wireless frequencies and channels	464

Complete the Tables and Lists from Memory

Print a copy of Appendix C, "Memory Tables" (found on the CD), or at least the section for this chapter, and complete the tables and lists from memory. Appendix D, "Answers to Memory Tables," also on the CD, includes completed tables and lists to check your work.

Define Key Terms

Define the following key terms from this chapter, and check your answers in the glossary.

SC, ST, LC, RJ-11, RJ-45, T568A, T568B, fiber, BNC, F-connector, single-mode fiber, multi-mode fiber, STP, UTP, CAT3, CAT5, CAT5e, CAT6, CAT6e, CAT7, coaxial, plenum, PVC, RG-6, RG-59, IPv4, IPv6, public IP address, private IP address, APIPA/link local, static IP address, dynamic IP address, client-side DNS, client-side DHCP, subnet mask, CIDR, gateway, DHCP, DNS, LDAP, CIFS, SSH, AFP, TCPUDP, 802.11a, 802.11b, 802.11g, 802.11n, 802.11ac, POP3, HTTP, HTTPS, IMAP, SMB, Secure Sockets Layer (SSL), TLS, WEP, WPA, WPA2, TKIP, AES, channels, port forwarding, port triggering, DMZ, SNMP, NAT/DNAT, basic QoS, firmware, UPnP, cable, DSL, dial-up, satellite, ISDN, LAN, WAN, PAN, MAN, hub, switch, router, wireless access point (WAP), bridge, modem, firewall, patch panel, repeater, extender, PoE, power over Ethernet injector, crimper, cable stripper, multimeter, tone generator and probe, cable tester, loopback plug, punchdown tool, Wi-Fi analyzer, SOHO, TCP/IP, FTP, SMTP, domain name, HTML, ADSL (Asynchronous DSL), SDSL (Synchronous DSL), wvdial, wvdialconf.

Complete Hands-On Labs

Complete the hands-on labs, and then see the answers and explanations at the end of the chapter.

Lab 11-1: Exploring Wired and Wireless Network Hardware

Examine the physical network in your home, SOHO, or office and determine as much of the following as you can:

- TP cable type (5, 5e, 6, and so on). Most cables have the type marked on the protective jacket.

- If you have cable Internet service, determine the coaxial cable type.

- Does your wireless network use a separate router or is the router built into the cable or DSL modem or fiber gateway?

- What is the maximum speed of your wired network? Note: it is the fastest speed supported by all devices. For example, a network with 10/100/1000 (Gigabit) adapters with a 10/100 (Fast Ethernet) switch (or router) runs at Fast Ethernet speeds.

- Which wireless standard(s) are supported by your wireless network router? By your wireless adapters?

Lab 11-2: Exploring TCP/IP and Wi-Fi Configuration

Examine the TCP/IP settings in your network and determine as much of the following as you can:

- Is your network configured to use DHCP addresses or are some or all devices configured with manual IP addresses?

- Do any of your devices use WPS wireless configuration?

- Do any of your devices that use DHCP addresses have manual IP addresses set up as alternate addresses?

- If you use a wireless network, which type of encryption is used on your network?

- If you use WEP encryption, which devices do not support WPA/WPA2 encryption? If you determine that some devices don't support WPA/WPA2 encryption, determine whether they can be replaced by devices that support WPA/WPA2 encryption to make the wireless network more secure.

Answer Review Questions

1. Complete the following chart with the information provided below.

Cable Type	Size	Distance	Light Source	Typical Uses
Single-mode				
Multi-mode				

Answer options:

8-10 microns   LED

62.5 microns   laser diode

10 Km   cable TV, telephone company

60 Km   LAN, MAN

2. Which of the following is true of fiber-optic cable as it is compared to twisted-pair or coaxial? (Choose all that apply.)

   A. Fiber-optic cable uses light to transmit information.

   B. Fiber-optic cable uses high-conductivity copper wire.

   C. Fiber-optic cable does not experience crosstalk.

   D. Fiber-optic cable is more expensive.

   E. Fiber-optic cable is easily installed.

3. Identify the connectors in the following figure.

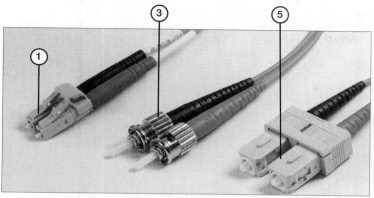

    A. SC duplex fiber

    B. ST duplex fiber

    C. LC duplex fiber

4. Match the callouts to the terms below to identify these cables and their components;

    A. UTP jacket

    B. ground wire

    C. TP wire pairs

    D. TP jacket

    E. Metal shield

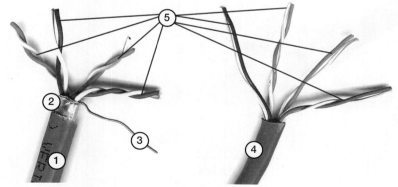

5. Under which of the following circumstances is a crossover cable used?

    A. When connecting one computer to another computer

    B. When connecting a computer to a hub

    C. When connecting a computer to a patch panel

    D. When connecting a computer to a switch

6. Identify the connectors in the following figures.

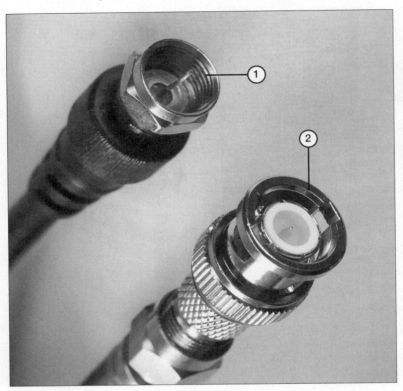

A. ST

B. RJ-11

C. F-connector

D. AUI

E. BNC

F. LC

G. RJ-45

7. If you need to run network cables through ceiling spaces or air vents, which type of cable should be used?

    A. Plenum cable

    B. PVC cable

    C. Duplex cable

    D. Crossover cable

8. Which protocol is used to access the Internet and is used by all major operating systems, including Windows, OS X, Linux, Android, and iOS?

    A. APIPA

    B. DHCP

    C. Telnet

    D. TCP/IP

9. 192.168.28.10 is an example of which type of IP address?

    A. Class A

    B. Class B

    C. Class C

    D. APIPA

10. Given the IP address of 192.168.28.10, which is the network portion of the address and which is the host portion?

    A. 192.=network, 168.28.10=host

    B. 192.168. =network, 28.10=host

    C. 192.168.28. =network, 10=host

11. Which of the following is the subnet mask for a 192.168.28.10 IP address?

    A. 255.255.255.255

    B. 255.255.255.0

    C. 255.255.0.0

    D. 255.0.0.0

12. 127.0.0.1 and ::1 are both IP addresses. Which of the following statements are true? (Choose all that apply.)

    A. 127.0.0.1 is a Class A address.

    B. ::1 is an IPv6 address.

    C. 127.0.0.1 is a Class C address.

    D. ::1 is a CIPS address.

    E. Both addresses are loopback addresses.

13. 10.0.0.1 is which type of IP address?

   A. Public

   B. Private

   C. APIPA

   D. Loopback

14. 169.254.0.1 is which type of IP address?

   A. Loopback

   B. Subnet mask

   C. DHCP

   D. APIPA

15. Which of the following statements best describes an advantage of IPv6 over IPv4?

   A. IPv6 is less complicated and easier to use.

   B. IPv6 automatically assigns IP addresses on a network.

   C. IPv6 translates domain names into IP addresses.

   D. IPv6 provides a dramatic increase in the number of available IP addresses.

16. Which of the following protocols is used to automatically assign IP addresses on a network?

   A. APIPA

   B. DHCP

   C. TCP/IP

   D. DNS

17. In the address *www.mycompany.com/locations*, which of the following is the top-level domain name?

   A. www.

   B. .mycompany

   C. .com

   D. /locations

18. As an IT technician, it is important for you to be familiar with the protocols and ports used by various applications to send and receive information across a network. Complete the following chart by adding the port numbers associated with each of the protocols listed.

Protocol	IMAP	FTP	HTTP	HTTPS	SMTP	DNS	SSH	POP3
Port								

19. Which of the following statements best describes SMTP?

    A. SMTP is a protocol for sending e-mail from your computer to a server.

    B. SMTP is a naming system that links your computer's name with its IP address.

    C. SMTP is a method for automatically assigning IP addresses to computers on a network.

    D. SMTP is a protocol used to access the Internet.

20. Which of the following is the family of IEEE standards used by Wi-Fi networks?

    A. 802.5

    B. 802.11

    C. 802.9

    D. 802.3

21. Which of the following Wi-Fi encryption methods is the strongest?

    A. WPA

    B. WPA2

    C. WEP

22. Which of the following statements best describes the function of NAT?

    A. NAT changes a private IP address for use inside a LAN into a public IP address for use outside a LAN.

    B. NAT automatically assigns IP addresses to computers on a LAN.

    C. NAT automatically assigns a 169.254.x.x address to a computer on a LAN.

    D. NAT is a secure wireless encryption standard.

23. Match the following devices with their definitions.

Device	Definition
Bridge	
Router	
Switch	
Modem	
Firewall	
Hub	
Patch panel	

Converts digital signals to analog and analog signals to digital

Uses a MAC address to direct data to a specific computer

Junction point for network cabling

Allows networks to communicate with each other

Broadcasts data to all attached computers

Connects two LANs

Prevents unwanted intrusion from outside the network

24. Identify the tool in the following figure.

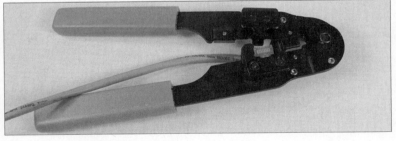

A. Cable tester

B. Crimper

C. Punchdown tool

D. Cable stripper

Answers and Explanations for Hands-On Labs

Complete the hands-on labs, and then see the answers and explanations at the end of the chapter.

Lab 11-1: Exploring Wired and Wireless Network Hardware

When you examine a TP network cable, you might see markings similar to the following:

CAT5E PATCH CABLE

In this example, the cable type is CAT5e (cable markings are usually uppercase).

A coaxial cable might have markings similar to the following:

RG-59/U

RG-6QS

QS = quad shielded (improved shielding to protect the signal quality of HDTV services)

Many vendors who provide Internet and voice service over the same connection include a wireless router in the cable or DSL modem. However, these devices are not as fast and typically have shorter range than mid-range or high-end 802.11ac wireless routers. You can ask the provider to disable the built-in wireless router and provide your own.

To determine the speed of a wired network, you can check the signal lights on each switch port that is connected to a cable. With a Gigabit Ethernet switch, one signal light indicates a connection and the other indicates 1000Mbps (Gigabit) connections. It might use different colors to indicate Gigabit or Fast connections.

Check the label on the wireless router to determine the standards it supports. Check Device Manager in Windows or the comparable utilities on OS X or Linux to determine what wireless network standard(s) their adapters support.

Lab 11-2: Exploring TCP/IP and Wi-Fi Configuration

Devices that have manual IP addresses will not lose their addresses if the DHCP server stops working. However, if the DHCP server is built into the router and the router is shut down or fails, there won't be any Internet access for any users until it is restored.

WPS wireless configuration should be used for either all devices or no devices. If the network is not already using WPS, don't use it going forward.

The safest encryption type to use on a wireless network is WPA2 (also known as WPA/AES). Some of the devices that don't support WPA/WPA2 include some wireless printers and older video game systems with wireless support. If it is not feasible to replace these devices, consider using a separate network for these devices if possible. Then put computers and other devices with sensitive data (tablets, smartphones) on a secure network. Some routers support multiple networks, such as a Guest network.

Answers and Explanations to Review Questions

1.

Cable Type	Size	Distance	Light Source	Typical Uses
Single-mode	8-10 microns	60 Km	laser diode	cable TV, telephone company
Multi-mode	62.5 microns	10 Km	LED	LAN, MAN

Single-mode uses a smaller core to carry less information longer distances while multi-mode uses a larger core to carry more information shorter distances.

2. **A, C, D.** Fiber-optic cables use light instead of electrical signals to transmit information. Because of this, they do not experience electrical interference known as crosstalk and are not susceptible to wire taps and other breaches in security. Fiber-optic cables are also more expensive than twisted-pair or co-axial cables and are more difficult to install.

3. **1–C; 2–B; 3–A.** Here is a shortcut to help you remember the names for these connectors. The LC connector has a locking mechanism that clicks the connector into place (LC = lock and click). You stick the ST connector into the port and twist it into position (ST = stick and twist). You stick the SC connector into the port and click it into position (SC = stick and click).

4. **A. 4** (UTP jacket); **B. 3** (ground wire); **C. 5** (TP wire pairs); **D. 1** (STP jacket); **E. 2** (metal shield).

5. **A.** Use a crossover cable when connecting two computers to each other. Use a straight-through cable when connecting a computer to a hub, switch, or patch panel.

6. **1–C:** F-connector used with cable TV. **2–E:** BNC connector used with coaxial cables. **3–B:** RJ-11 connector used with CAT 3 telephone cables. **4–G:** RJ-45 connector used with Ethernet network cables. Answers A, D, and F were not used.

7. **A.** Normal network cable is encased in a PVC jacket, which, in case of fire, creates a poisonous thick smoke. Cables that run through ceiling spaces or air vents should be plenum grade, which is more expensive but less toxic if burned.

8. **D.** TCP/IP is a suite of protocols used for managing traffic on the Internet and is the accepted standard used by all major operating systems.

9. **C.** 192 is in the Class C range of IP addresses. That means that the first three octets identify the network portion of the address and the fourth octet is the host portion.

10. **C.** 192 is in the Class C range of IP addresses. That means that the first three octets identify the network portion of the address and the fourth octet is the host portion.

11. **B.** 255.255.255.0 is the subnet mask for a Class C IP address.

12. **B, E.** 127.0.0.1 is a diagnostic tool known as the IPv4 loopback address, which is used to test connectivity between a computer and its network. ::1 is the IPv6 counterpart.

13. **B.** This is an example of a Class A private IP address.

14. **D.** APIPA addresses are automatically assigned in the event the DHCP system is unable to provide IP addresses. As a technician, any time you see an IP address that begins with 169.254.x.x, you should look for problems with DHCP. APIPA is supported by Microsoft, OS X, and Linux.

15. **D.** Every device that accesses the Internet (every PC, laptop, notebook, tablet, smartphone, and so on) must have its own IP address—and no two addresses may be the same. In our modern society, a single family might need a dozen addresses; the world is simply running out of IPv4 addresses. IPv6 provides a huge increase in the number of available IP addresses.

16. **B.** DHCP automatically assigns IP addresses to computers on a network.

17. **C.** In this example, .com is the top-level domain name. Other examples of top-level domains are .net, .org, and .us.

18.

Protocol	IMAP	FTP	HTTP	HTTPS	SMTP	DNS	SSH	POP3
Port	143	21	80	443	25	53	22	110

As an IT technician, you might be called upon to configure ports for a network. The ports in this chart are only a few of the ones you might need to know.

19. **A.** SMTP is an acronym for Simple Mail Transport Protocol. It is used to send e-mail.

20. **B.** 802.11 includes 802.11a, 802.11b, 802.11g, 802.11n, and 802.11ac wireless network standards.

21. **B.** WPA2 uses stronger encryption than WPA. Both WPA and WPA2 have stronger encryption, use longer passphrases, and have other security improvements compared to WEP.

22. **A.** NAT is a protocol used by a router to change a computer's private IP address used inside a LAN to a public IP address when communicating outside the network. NAT allows the computers on a LAN to remain hidden from the outside world.

23.

Device	Definition
Bridge	Connects two LANs
Router	Allows networks to communicate with each other
Switch	Uses a MAC address to direct data to a specific computer
Modem	Converts digital signals to analog and analog signals to digital
Firewall	Prevents unwanted intrusion from outside the network
Hub	Broadcasts data to all attached computers
Patch panel	Junction point for network cabling

24. **B.** A crimper is used to attach an RJ-45 or RJ-11 connector to a TP cable.

This chapter covers the following subjects:

- **Install and Configure Laptop Hardware and Components**—From ExpressCard to USB, this section shows you how to use the special features of laptops to increase their versatility.

- **Replace Laptop Components**—From a broken screen to memory that's too small, use this section to learn how to replace laptop components.

- **Laptop Display Components**—Use this section to master terminology and to determine which components to look for in a new laptop display panel.

- **Using Laptop Features**—Discover the Fn key, learn about docking stations, and how devices with rotatable/removable screens bridge the gap between tablet and laptop.

- **Characteristics of Other Mobile Devices**—Get up to speed on phablets, learn why there's still a place for GPS devices, and discover the features of other mobile devices.

- **Accessories and Ports Used by Other Mobile Devices**—In this section, discover what NFC can do, the most common sync/charge cables used on smartphones and tablets, the wide variety of accessories available for point-of-sale applications, recharging batteries away from an AC outlet, and more.

## CHAPTER 12

Mobile Devices

The mobile device category includes laptops, tablets, convertible 2-in-1 devices, and smartphones. Thanks to different operating systems, form factors, port types, and capabilities, supporting these devices is a bigger challenge than ever before.

Use this feature to learn how to configure, use, and upgrade all types of mobile devices.

220-901: Objective 3.1 Install and configure laptop hardware and components.

220-901: Objective 3.2 Explain the function of components within the display of a laptop.

220-901: Objective 3.3 Given a scenario, use appropriate laptop features.

220-901: Objective 3.4 Explain the characteristics of various types of other mobile devices.

220-901: Objective 3.5 Compare and contrast accessories and ports of other mobile devices.

Foundation Topics

Install and Configure Laptop Hardware and Components

Although laptops have many of the same components as desktop computers, they differ in two significant ways:

- How they are expanded
- How internal components are upgraded, replaced, or serviced

For the A+ 220-901 exam, you must know the unique components of a laptop, how to safely remove and reinstall laptop hardware, the ports built in to a typical laptop, and how to troubleshoot laptops.

NOTE   As you study, pay particular attention to the following expansion options: ExpressCard/34, ExpressCard/54, SODIMM, and flash memory.

ExpressCard

Many business and gaming laptops use the **ExpressCard** high-speed bus for internal expansion. ExpressCard can use one of two methods to communicate with the system chipset: PCI Express or USB.

ExpressCard uses a 26-contact connector and is available in two forms:

- ExpressCard/34 is 34mm wide.
- ExpressCard/54 is 54mm wide; ExpressCard/54 slots can use either ExpressCard/54 or ExpressCard/34 devices and are sometimes referred to as Universal slots.

Both types of ExpressCard modules are 75mm long and 5mm high. Figure 12-1 compares ExpressCard/34 and ExpressCard/54.

NOTE   Some vendors supply ExpressCard/34 cards with removable adapters that permit cards to be inserted more securely into ExpressCard/54 slots.

To insert an ExpressCard, just push it into the slot until it stops. Then, attach any cables or dongles needed for operation.

To remove an ExpressCard from a Windows laptop, follow these steps:

Step 1. Remove any cables or dongles from the card.

Step 2. Click the **Safely Remove Hardware and Eject Media** icon in the Windows taskbar and select the card you want to remove from the list of cards.

Step 3. Stop and wait for the system to acknowledge the card can be removed.

Step 4. Click **OK** to close the message.

Step 5. Push in the card to release it. Pull the ExpressCard the rest of the way out of the slot, and store it in its original case or an antistatic bag.

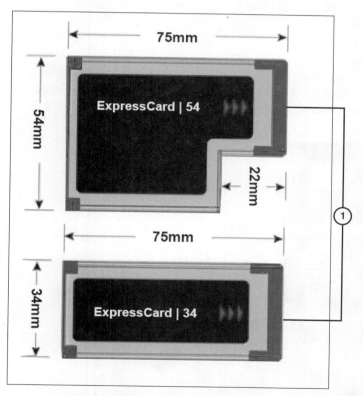

1. Card connection to laptop

Figure 12-1 ExpressCard/34 and ExpressCard/54 cards.

NOTE   Some systems with ExpressCard slots use the slot to store a media remote control. If a media remote control is stored in the ExpressCard slot, go directly to Step 5 to remove it.

To remove an ExpressCard from an OS X laptop, follow these steps:

Step 1.   Remove any cables or dongles from the card.

Step 2.   Drag the card's icon to the Trash.

Step 3.   Push in the card to release it. Pull the ExpressCard the rest of the way out of the slot, and store it in its original case or an antistatic bag.

NOTE   If the ExpressCard is a cellular modem, use the card's own management software to stop and power down the card before following the removal process.

SODIMM Memory

Generally, laptops have two connectors for memory, typically using small outline DIMMs (SODIMMs), which are reduced-size versions of DIMM modules. Figure 12-2 compares a typical DDR3 **SODIMM** with a DDR2 SODIMM and a DDR3 DIMM.

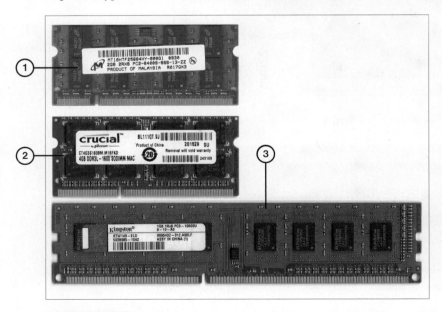

1. DDR2 SODIMM
2. DDR3L (low voltage) SODIMM
3. DDR3 DIMM

Figure 12-2   Comparison of SODIMMs to a DIMM.

Table 12-1 compares the major features of SODIMMs (also known as SO-DIMMs).

 Table 12-1   SODIMM Features

Memory Type	Number of Pins	Notch Location	Notes
DDR	200	After pin 20	67.6mm long – 30mm high
			Notch closer to short end* than with DDR2
DDR2	200	After pin 20	Notch closer to long end* than with DDR
DDR3	204	After pin 36	Same dimensions as DDR, DDR2
DDR4	260	After pin 72	69.7mm long 30mm high

* short end = left side (20 pins); long end = right side (80 pins) front view

NOTE   A variation on DDR4 SODIMM known as UniDIMM has been proposed by some memory vendors to support Intel Skylake processors. Skylake processors integrate memory controllers for DDR3 and DDR4, so UniDIMM is designed for either type of RAM. UniDIMM is the same length as DDR SODIMM, but is only 20mm high. UniDIMM is not a JEDEC standard, and no actual products use this form factor as this book went to press.

TIP   The best memory upgrade for a portable system is to add the largest-capacity memory modules that can be installed in the system. Use matched sets on systems that support multichannel memory to improve performance.

Flash Memory

Most recent laptops include a single-slot **flash memory** card reader that is compatible with the most common memory card standards, such as SD, SDHC, and SDXC. Consult the manual for your laptop to determine whether all SD standards are supported and if other types (Sony Memory Stick/Pro, Olympus/Fujifilm xD-Picture Card) are supported.

The flash card memory slot might be located on the front or the left side of a typical laptop.

Ports and Adapters

Because laptops are available from many vendors, with different sizes and chipsets, onboard hardware, and the need to add additional features via USB, vary a great deal.

> **NOTE**   For the 220-901 exam, be sure to keep in mind these **ports** and **adapters** for expansion:
>
> - Thunderbolt
> - DisplayPort
> - USB to RJ-45 dongle
> - USB to Wi-Fi dongle
> - USB to Bluetooth
> - USB Optical Drive

Laptops based on OS X typically feature the following ports:

- **Thunderbolt** (advanced I/O for storage, displays, and docking stations)
- **DisplayPort** (digital A/V for displays and audio; usually a miniDisplayPort that uses the same connector as Thunderbolt 1-2)
- USB 2.0 or 3.0; some MacBooks include a USB 3.0 Type C (USB-C) port that supports USB Power Delivery.

Some ports are shown in Figure 12-3.

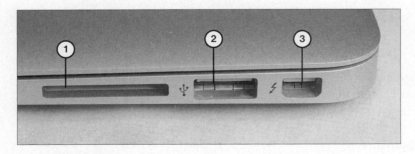

1. Flash memory card reader slot
2. USB 3.0 port
3. Thunderbolt port

Figure 12-3   Flash memory card reader slot, USB 3.0 port, and Thunderbolt port on a MacBook Air.

Laptops based on Windows or Linux typically feature the following ports:

- HDMI (digital A/V for displays and audio)
- USB 2.0, 3.0, or 3.1 (Type A and/or Type C)

> **NOTE** Some laptops with USB 3.1 Gen 2 Type C ports also support Thunderbolt 3.
> For example, see http://www.acer.com/ac/en/US/content/series/aspirer13 and http://
> www.dell.com/us/p/xps-13-9350-laptop/pd.

Some of these ports are shown in Figure 12-4. For an example of USB 3.1 Gen
2 Type A and Type C ports, see Figure 8-1 on page 201. USB 3.0 and 3.1 Gen 2
Type C ports look identical.

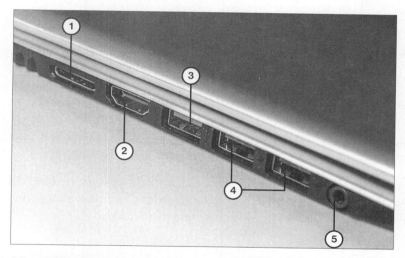

1. **Proprietary connector for VGA/Ethernet header cable**
2. **HDMI port**
3. **USB 3.0 port**
4. **USB 2.0 ports**
5. **Headset jack**

Figure 12-4 I/O ports on an Acer laptop

For laptops that do not include RJ-45 (Ethernet) ports, a suitable Wi-Fi (wireless
Ethernet) network adapter, a Bluetooth adapter, or an optical drive, the USB port
can be used.

Figure 12-5 illustrates a typical **USB to RJ-45 dongle** and a **USB to Wi-Fi dongle**.

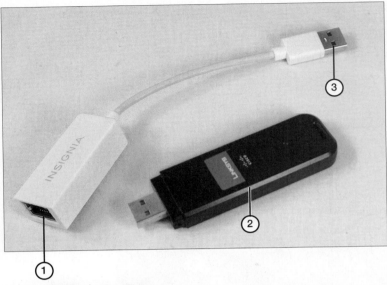

1. Gigabit Ethernet RJ-45 port
2. USB 3.0 connector
3. Wi-Fi adapter with USB 2.0 connector

Figure 12-5   USB adapters for Wi-Fi and Gigabit Ethernet networking.

USB to Bluetooth dongles vary widely in size. A **USB optical drive** typically supports recordable and rewriteable DVD and CD media.

Some of these devices include driver media, while others might be supported by drivers built into the operating system. Check the instructions for installation to determine if you need to install drivers before connecting these devices.

Replace Laptop Components

Because a laptop integrates its display, keyboard, and network hardware and uses specialized or proprietary components for hard drive, optical drive, system board, CPU, and other components, replacing these devices involves much different procedures than on a desktop computer.

NOTE   Be sure to focus on the following topics as you study the hardware replacement process:

- Keyboard
- Hard Drive: SSD vs. Hybrid vs. Magnetic disk; 1.8in vs. 2.5in
- Memory
- Smart card reader
- Optical drive
- Wireless card
- Mini-PCIe
- Screen
- DC jack
- Battery
- Touchpad
- Plastics/frames
- Speaker
- System board
- CPU

Some of the general differences include

- **Component sources**—Replacement components such as display, keyboard, wireless network card, and system board are available only as OEM parts. Other components, such as optical drives and hard drives, memory, and the CPU, can be purchased from third-party sources but differ greatly from their desktop counterparts.

- **Power sources**—A laptop is powered by an internal battery and an AC adapter that also charges the battery. As with other laptop components, the original vendor is the most typical source for replacements, although some third-party vendors sell so-called "universal" replacement AC adapters.

- **Components unique to laptops**—Laptops include several components typically not included on desktop computers, including integrated wireless networking implemented via an antenna in the display connecting to a mini-PCIe card, a keyboard with an integrated touchpad or pointing stick, a touch screen or non-touchscreen display, and integrated speakers.

516 CompTIA A+ 220-901 and 220-902 Cert Guide

These differences, along with the extensive use of plastics and the use of tiny screws, make servicing a laptop a major challenge, even if you are experienced with servicing a desktop computer.

Laptop Repair Best Practices

Whether you need to disassemble a laptop to upgrade internal hardware or to replace a defective component, there are several best practices you should use to make the reassembly process as easy as possible:

- **Refer to manufacturer documentation**—Documentation helps you properly identify screw types, screw lengths, number of screws (some laptops have more than 100), cable and component locations, and other information needed. Most vendors offer this information online.

- **Use appropriate hand tools for case disassembly and component removal**—Using recommended tool types and sizes helps prevent problems such as damaging screw heads by using too large a Phillips-head screwdriver. Repair documentation typically lists the recommended tools for each procedure.

- **Document and label cable and screw locations**—Laptops typically use a mixture of screw lengths and sometimes screw types. Mix them up, and you could damage components or not secure them properly.

- **Organize parts**—Consider using a multiple-compartment parts tray with a lid (available at hardware stores) for parts sorting and storage. A magnetic dish also helps prevent loss of parts.

NOTE The Laptop Repair Help website (www.laptoprepair101.com) provides many useful resources, including links to major vendors' laptop service manuals, illustrated step-by-step procedures for the removal of many components, and links to parts sources.

CAUTION Laptops contain proprietary parts. If you break an internal optical drive or an integrated keyboard, you can't run to your favorite electronics superstore for a replacement. You have been warned.

If you need to replace the battery, mass storage (hard disk, SSD, SSHD, or optical drive), SODIMM RAM, or wireless adapter on a typical laptop, access to these components is from the bottom of the laptop. Figure 12-6 shows the underside of a typical laptop and its access panels. Figure 12-7 shows the same laptop after access panels have been removed for component upgrades or replacements.

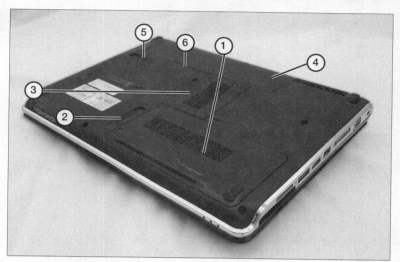

1. Access panel for hard disk or SSHD and wireless card
2. Optical drive ejector switch
3. Access panel for SODIMM RAM
4. Battery
5. Battery ejector switch
6. Access panel for CMOS battery

Figure 12-6 The underside of a typical laptop has one or more removable panels for access to storage, RAM, and other components.

NOTE Some laptops use a single cover for all upgradeable components, rather than multiple covers. Some laptops require disassembly to access the hard disk drive or SSD mass storage. Check system documentation for details.

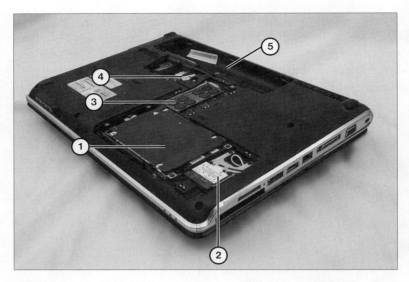

1. Hard disk
2. Wireless card
3. SODIMM RAM
4. CMOS battery
5. Main battery compartment after battery removal

Figure 12-7   The same laptop after opening access panels to permit component replacements or upgrades.

Battery

A laptop **battery** is a rechargeable power source. Before performing any replacement of internal components, the system must be removed from all power sources. Follow this procedure:

Step 1.   Turn off the computer.

Step 2.   Disconnect the AC adapter or line cord from the computer.

Step 3.   Open the battery compartment in the unit; it might be secured by a sliding lock or by screws.

Step 4.   If the battery is under a removable cover, remove the battery compartment cover.

Step 5.   Open the lock that holds the battery in place.

Step 6.   Slide out or lift out the battery (see Figure 12-8). If the battery is a flat assembly, it might be held in place by a clip; push the clip to one side to release the battery.

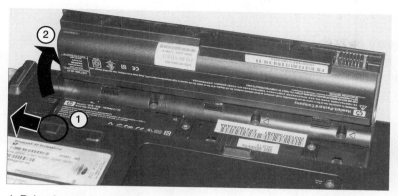

1. Releasing the battery catch
2. Rotating the battery up and out of the battery compartment

Figure 12-8   Removing a battery from a typical laptop computer.

Step 7.   Examine the battery contacts inside the computer for dirt or corrosion, and clean dirty contacts with a soft cloth.

To replace the battery, follow these steps:

Step 1.   Line up the replacement battery with the contacts inside the battery compartment. Make sure you insert the battery so that the positive and negative terminals are in the right directions.

Step 2.   Slide in or clip the battery into place.

Step 3.   Replace any cover over the battery compartment.

Step 4.   If the battery must be charged before use, plug in the line cord or AC adapter to both the computer and wall outlet. Check the computer's manual for the proper charge time for a new battery.

CAUTION   Take precautions against ESD when you change the battery. Discharge any static electricity in your body by touching a metal object before you open the battery compartment and don't touch the contacts on the battery or the contacts in the battery compartment with your hands.

If you need to purchase a replacement battery for a laptop, consider a larger-capacity battery. Relative battery capacity is measured in cells. For example, a nine-cell battery will have a longer run time than a six-cell battery. Keep in mind that larger-capacity batteries are bulkier.

Keyboard

If a laptop **keyboard** or its **pointing device** device (touchpad or pointing stick) fails, you must replace the unit. Laptops with touchpads have separate keyboards and touchpads, whereas laptops with pointing sticks integrate the pointing stick with the keyboard. Some laptops have both types of pointing devices (see Figure 12-9).

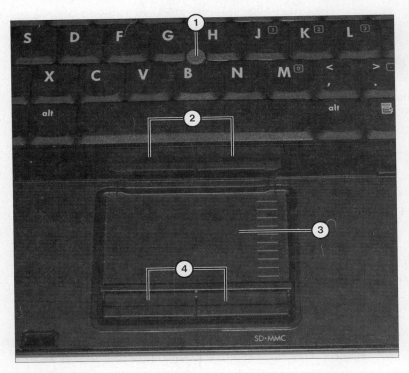

1. Pointing stick
2. Buttons for pointing stick
3. Touchpad
4. Buttons for touchpad

Figure 12-9   A business-class laptop with a pointing stick and touchpad.

> **NOTE**   Touchpads are generally located in the palm rest (which extends below the keyboard), while pointing sticks, such as the IBM/Lenovo TrackPoint and Toshiba AccuPoint, are located in the middle of the keyboard (the buttons are located in the palm rest).

To replace a keyboard, including keyboards with pointing sticks, follow this basic procedure:

Step 1.   After disconnecting all power sources, turn over the laptop so the bottom of the unit faces upward.

Step 2.   Remove the screws that hold the keyboard in place.

Step 3.   Turn the laptop upright.

Step 4.   Open the screen so that the keyboard is visible.

Step 5.   If necessary, remove the bezel that holds the keyboard in place.

Step 6.   Lift up the keyboard to expose the keyboard cable.

Step 7.   Remove any hold-down devices used to hold the keyboard cable in place.

Step 8.   Disconnect the keyboard cable from the system board (see Figure 12-10).

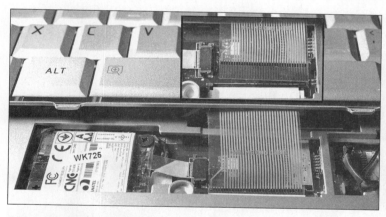

Figure 12-10   Removing the keyboard cable.

Step 9.   Remove the keyboard.

To install the replacement, reverse these steps.

NOTE   On some laptops, you must remove the display assembly first before you can remove the keyboard.

Storage (HDD) and Optical Drives

Most laptop computers use one **2.5-in. drive** (hard disk, SSD, or SSHD hybrid drives: magnetic hard disk plus SSD in a single unit). The larger **3.5-in. drive** form factor is used in desktop drive enclosures or in desktop computers. However, some Ultrabooks use the **1.8-in. drive** form factor (hard disks or SSD).

Although a few laptop computers require you to remove the keyboard to access the hard drive, most laptops feature storage devices that can be accessed from the bottom of the system. Follow this procedure to remove and replace a storage device (hard disk, SSD, or SSHD) accessible from the bottom:

Step 1.   After disconnecting all power sources, turn over the laptop so that the bottom of the laptop faces upward.

Step 2.   Loosen or remove the screw or screws used to hold the drive cover in place.

Step 3.   Slide the cover away from the retaining lug or clips and remove it.

Step 4.   Remove the screws holding the drive to the chassis.

Step 5.   Slide the drive away from the retaining screw holes, and lift it out of the chassis.

1. Retaining screw holes
2. Drive mounting frame tabs
3. Remove/attach bolts through tabs into screw holes
4. Protective cover over hard disk circuit board

Figure 12-11   Removing a laptop hard disk after removing the retaining screws.

Step 6.   If the computer uses an interposer (a proprietary connector) between the drive's SATA connector and the drive bay, remove it and save it for reuse.

Step 7.   Remove the screws fastening the drive to the drive frame.

Step 8.   Remove the drive from the drive frame (see Figure 12-12).

1. Mounting tabs
2. Mounting holes for drive
3. Matching screw holes in drive
4. SATA data and power connectors

Figure 12-12   A laptop hard disk after being removed from its mounting frame (compare to Figure 12-11).

Step 9.   Insert the new hard drive into the drive frame.

Reverse these steps to install the new hard drive.

After the system is restarted, start the computer and enter the BIOS or UEFI setup program to verify that the new hard drive has been properly recognized by the system.

Although fewer laptops these days come with built-in optical drives, some laptops feature modular optical drives designed for swapping. However, if the optical drive is not designed for swapping, follow this procedure to remove it:

Step 1.   After disconnecting all power sources, turn the laptop over so that the bottom faces upward.

Step 2.   Locate the latch that holds the drive in place, or locate the mounting screw that holds the drive in place and unscrew it. It might be located inside the access panel for another component.

Step 3.   Slide open the latch or remove the mounting screw.

Step 4.   Slide the drive out of the system. See Figure 12-13 for a typical example.

To reinstall the drive, reverse the preceding steps. If a range of drives are available for a laptop, you can use this method to upgrade to a better drive.

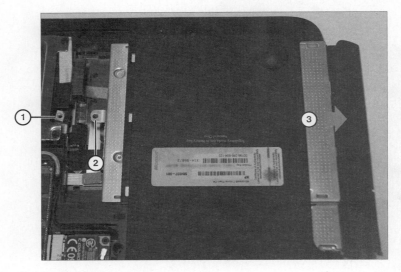

1. Screw hole for mounting bolt
2. Retaining lug on optical drive
3. Pull drive from drive bay

Figure 12-13   Removing an optical drive from a typical laptop.

Memory

You need to know the following information before you can select the right memory upgrade for a laptop:

- **Form factor**—Most laptops in service use DDR2, DDR3, or DDR4 SODIMMs.

- **Memory speed**—If you plan to add a module, make sure it is the same speed as the existing module. If you plan to replace the modules, buy a matched set of modules in the fastest speed supported by the system.

- **Memory timing**—The most common way to refer to memory timing is by its column address strobe (CAS) value. If you install memory modules that use different CAS values, the laptop could become unstable and crash or lock up.

To determine the correct memory to use for a memory upgrade, use one of the following methods:

- **Use the interactive memory upgrade tools available from major third-party memory vendors' websites**—These tools list the memory modules suitable for particular laptops, and some use an ActiveX web control to detect the currently installed memory. Crucial System Scanner is a very useful tool for showing what's currently installed and what is compatible. For more information, visit https://www.crucial.com/usa/en/systemscanner.

- **Check the vendor's memory specifications**—You can determine part numbers using this method, but this method is best if memory must be purchased from the laptop vendor rather than from a memory vendor.

Follow these steps to perform a typical memory upgrade:

Step 1. After disconnecting all power sources, remove the cover over the memory upgrade socket on the bottom of the system.

Step 2. Remove any screws or hold-down devices.

Step 3. Remove the old memory module(s) if necessary. To remove a memory module, pull back the clips on both sides and swing the memory up and out.

Step 4. Insert the new memory upgrade, making sure the contacts on the edge of the module make a firm connection with the connector.

Step 5. Push the top of the module down until the latches lock into place (see Figure 12-14).

1. Push the SODIMM into the connector at the appropriate angle
2. Push the SODIMM down until the latches lock into place
3. The latches hold the SODIMM in place

Figure 12-14 Installing an SODIMM module on a typical laptop.

Step 6.   If the memory socket uses screws to secure the memory in place, install them.

Step 7.   Close the cover and secure it to complete the upgrade.

Step 8.   Test the upgrade by starting the system and running a memory diagnostic tool (Windows includes memory testing software, or you can download a memory testing program).

Smart Card Reader

A **smart card reader** is typically used on corporate laptops for access control (do not confuse it with a flash memory card reader).

To remove a smart card reader (see Figure 12-15):

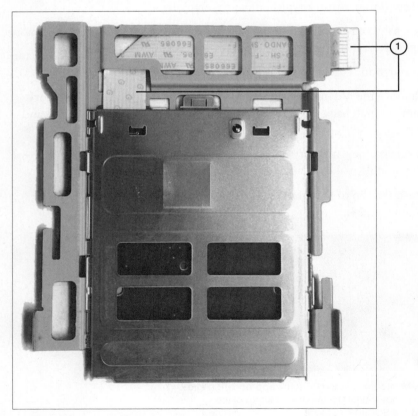

1. Ribbon cable connector to motherboard

Figure 12-15   A typical smart card reader from a Dell laptop.

Step 1.   Disconnect the laptop from AC power and remove the battery.

Step 2.   Remove the bottom cover.

Step 3.   Locate the ribbon cable connecting the reader to the motherboard.

Step 4.   Disconnect the ribbon cable.

Step 5.   Remove the screws holding the reader in place.

Step 6.   Remove the reader from the system.

To replace the smart card reader, reverse the following steps.

Wireless Card

Laptops with Wi-Fi support typically use either a **miniPCIe** or, on units built in 2015 or later, an M.2 card to provide wireless network support. The M.2 card form factor (also called NGFF for next generation form factor) is also used for SSD and other I/O devices. Note that an M.2 card slot made for SSD cannot be used for Wi-Fi or Bluetooth cards.

Whichever **wireless card** a laptop uses, two antennas lead from the Wi-Fi antennas built into the display panel connect to the card.

To remove a wireless card, follow this basic procedure:

Step 1.   Verify the location of the card. Some laptops have the card under the keyboard, whereas others have the card located under a removable cover on the bottom of the computer.

Step 2.   After disconnecting all power sources, place the computer appropriately for access to the card.

Step 3a.   If the card is located under the keyboard, remove the keyboard.

Step 3b.   If the card is located under an access panel, remove the screws holding the access panel in place.

Step 4.   Disconnect any wires connected to the adapter. They might be screwed into place or snapped into place. Note their positions.

Step 5.   Unscrew any bolts holding the card in place. MiniPCIe cards (refer to Figure 12-16) use two bolts, while M.2 cards (refer to Figure 12-17) use a single bolt.

Step 6.   Rotate the card upwards at a slight angle and remove it from the slot.

Step 7.   If the card is attached to a bracket, remove it from the bracket.

To reinstall the card or replace it with a different card, reverse these steps.

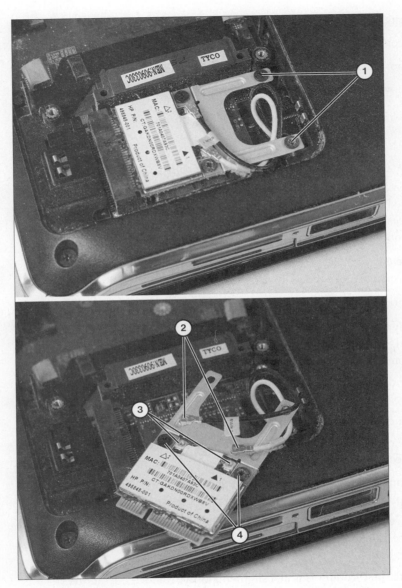

1. Unscrew mounting bolts
2. Antenna wires
3. Antenna wire attachment points
4. Unscrew mounting bolts to remove card from bracket

Figure 12-16 Removing a miniPCIe wireless card.

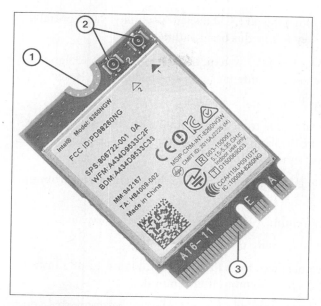

1. Mounting screw fits here
2. Antenna connectors
3. M.2 connector

Figure 12-17 A typical M.2 wireless adapter.

Screen

Screen replacement on laptops can be complex, especially if you need to replace the LCD display panel or the backlight, or if the screen assembly includes the Wi-Fi antenna, as on most recent models. LCD display panels built in to portable computers are customized for each model of portable computer and require the disassembly of the computer for removal and replacement. You can get replacements from either the vendor or an authorized repair parts depot. Many vendors require that you be an authorized technician before you remove or replace LCD display panels in portable computers. However, the process of replacing the entire LCD display assembly is simpler and might be possible for you to perform in the field.

CAUTION Should you do your own LCD display panel replacement? Vendors are of two minds about this. Some vendors provide online documentation that guides you through the entire process of reducing an intact portable into a pile of parts and rebuilding it. However, this information is primarily intended for professional computer service staff.

The details of the process for removing an LCD display assembly from a portable computer vary by model, but they follow this basic outline:

Step 1. After removing power from the system, if the system has an integrated wireless card, disconnect the antenna leads attached to the adapter.

Step 2. Remove the keyboard frame and keyboard.

Step 3. Disconnect the display cable from the system board; this cable transmits power and data to the display assembly. On touchscreen-equipped models, this cable also carries touchscreen data.

Step 4. If the system has integrated wireless, remove the antenna leads from the clips in the top cover.

Step 5. Rotate the display assembly to a 90-degree angle to the base unit.

Step 6. Remove the screws that secure the display assembly.

Step 7. Pull the display assembly free from the base unit. Figure 12-18 illustrates a typical 15.6-inch display assembly after removal.

Step 8. Be sure to save all screws, ground springs, and other hardware that you removed during the disassembly process.

NOTE If you need to replace the inverter, the backlight, or the webcam, further disassembly is necessary.

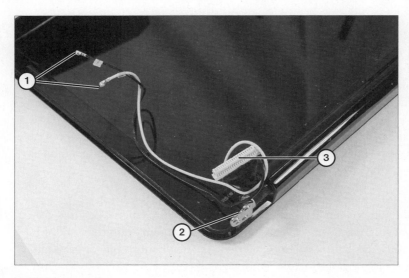

1. Wi-Fi antenna wires
2. Display hinge mount
3. Display connector

Figure 12-18 Detail from a typical laptop LCD panel after removal.

Many vendors offer replacement LCD display assemblies that can be installed by following the previous steps in reverse order. Although you can also purchase components of the assembly, such as the LCD display panel or backlight, this type of repair is difficult and time-consuming and should be performed at a repair depot.

Although you can't get a panel with a different resolution, you might be able to swap a glossy LCD panel optimized for video playback for a low-reflectivity matte panel that's preferred by some for working with documents.

DC Jack

The **DC jack** (also referred to as the power adapter port) receives DC power from the AC/DC power adapter and passes it to the battery. If the DC jack fails, the laptop's battery cannot be charged and the laptop cannot run on external power either. To replace the DC jack on a typical laptop:

Step 1.   After removing power from the laptop, remove components that block access to the DC jack and cable. These might include mass storage, WLAN card, service cover, optical drive, keyboard, palm rest, memory modules, display assembly, other ports, and bottom cover (see Figure 12-19).

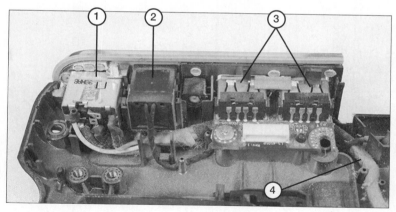

1. DC jack
2. RJ-11 modem port
3. USB 2.0 ports
4. DC jack power cable

Figure 12-19   Access to the DC jack may be blocked by other ports that must be removed first.

Step 2.   Unplug the DC jack power cord from the system board.

Step 3.   Remove the DC jack power cord from the guides holding it in place on the system board.

Step 4.   Remove the screw or clip that holds the DC jack in place.

Step 5.   Lift out the DC jack (see Figure 12-20).

To replace the DC jack, reverse these steps.

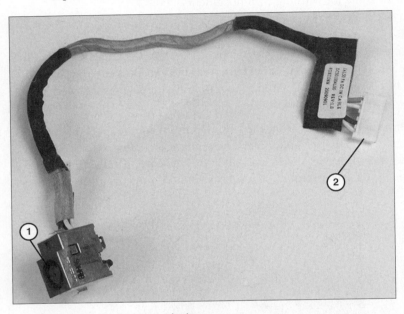

1. DC jack connection to power adapter
2. Motherboard power connector

Figure 12-20   The DC jack after successful removal from a laptop.

Touchpad

If you need to replace the **touchpad**, you must partially disassemble the portable computer. Details vary from unit to unit (check with your vendor for details), but the basic procedure is described here. To remove the touchpad, follow these steps:

Step 1.   Check service documents to determine whether the touchpad is a separate component or is built in to the top cover.

Step 2.   Remove all power from the laptop.

Step 3a.   If the touchpad is built in to the top cover, remove the top cover.

Step 3b. If the touchpad is a separate component, remove components that block access to the screws that hold the touchpad in place. These might include the storage devices, wireless adapter, optical drive, keyboard, keyboard cover, display assembly, and top cover.

Step 4. Place the system so the bottom of the system faces up.

Step 5. Disconnect the cable from the pointing devices to the motherboard.

Step 6. Remove the clips or screws holding the touchpad in (see Figure 12-21).

Step 7. Remove the touchpad assembly.

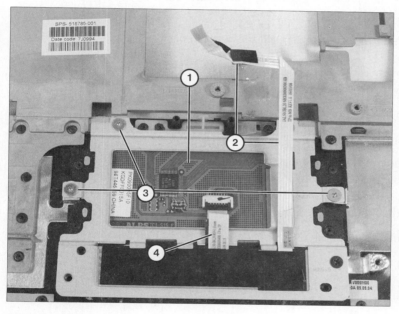

1. Touchpad
2. Ribbon cable to motherboard
3. Mounting screws to remove
4. Ribbon cable for touchpad buttons

Figure 12-21 This touchpad is secured to the top cover of the laptop with several screws.

To replace the touchpad, reverse these steps.

Plastics/Frames

Most laptops use plastic bezels, case covers, and frames (sometimes referred to collectively as **plastics/frames**). These can be cracked during normal use or during replacement or upgrades to internal components.

To replace a service cover on the bottom of the laptop, such as the cover over mass storage, the wireless adapter, or SODIMMs:

Step 1. Loosen the screws that hold the cover in place or use the unlocking latch (varies by system).

Step 2. Lift the cover by the edge(s) recommended in the service manual. It might need to be unsnapped from the base enclosure by careful use of a straight-blade screwdriver or pry tool.

Step 3. When the cover comes off, set it aside.

Step 4. Place the new service cover in place of the old one. It might snap down or swing into position.

Step 5. Tighten the screws that hold the cover in place.

The base enclosure is the part of the case that covers the bottom of the computer. The service cover snaps and screws into it.

To remove the base enclosure:

Step 1. Remove the service cover.

Step 2. Remove any components that cover up screws that must be removed to enable the base enclosure to be removed. These might include mass storage, optical drives, SODIMMs, or Wi-Fi adapters. See the service manual for the laptop for details.

Step 4. Remove the rubber feet if they are used to conceal mounting screws.

Step 5. Remove the screws holding the base enclosure in position.

Step 6. Lift the base enclosure from the computer frame.

Reverse these steps to install a replacement base enclosure.

To remove the display bezel:

Step 1. Remove the display assembly from the computer.

Step 2. The display bezel might be held in place by screws or be snapped into place. If the bezel uses screws, remove any screw covers and remove the screws. If the bezel snaps into place, pry up the display bezel from the inner edges.

Step 3. Lift the display bezel away from the display assembly.

Reverse these steps to install a replacement display bezel.

Speaker

To remove a laptop **speaker** or speakers, follow this basic procedure:

Step 1. After removing power from the laptop, remove components that block access to the speakers. These might include the hard drive, WLAN cover, optical drive, keyboard, keyboard cover, display assembly, and top cover.

Step 2. If necessary, turn the laptop over.

Step 3. Disconnect the Num Lock cable or other cables as directed.

Step 4. Remove the screws holding the speakers in place.

Step 5. Lift out the speakers.

To replace the speakers, reverse these steps.

System Board

To remove a typical **system board** (motherboard), follow these basic instructions:

Step 1. Remove all mass storage devices (hard disk, SSD, SSHD, optical drive).

Step 2. Remove the base enclosure. Disconnect the fan from the motherboard if it is part of the base assembly.

Step 3. Remove the display assembly.

Step 4. Disconnect all cables from the system board. These might include fingerprint reader, power connector, display panel, webcam and microphone cables, wireless antenna cables, connector board cables, speaker cables, touchpad and keyboard cables, fan connector, and power button board cable. Some of these are round cables, while others are flat ribbon cables.

Step 5. Remove all screws holding the top cover in place. Remove the top cover and turn it upside down so the motherboard is visible.

Step 6. Remove any additional screws holding the motherboard to the top cover (see Figure 12-22).

Step 7. Remove the system board from the bottom plate. This might require you to lift one end of the board at an angle and slide it out.

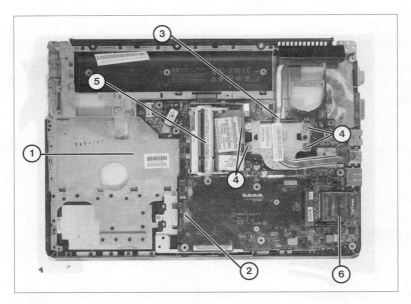

1. Top cover
2. Motherboard
3. Heat sink assembly
4. Mounting screws for heat sink
5. SODIMM memory sockets
6. Flash memory card reader (built into motherboard)

Figure 12-22   Preparing to remove the motherboard after removing all mounting screws.

Figure 12-23 illustrates a typical motherboard after being removed from a laptop.

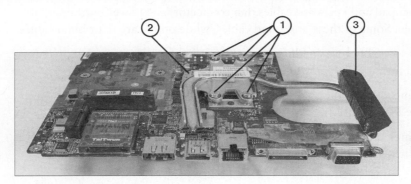

1. Mounting screws for heat sink
2. Retaining assembly for heat sink pipe
3. Fan exhaust/heat exchanger for heat sink

Figure 12-23   A typical laptop motherboard after removal.

After removing the system board, remove any components you plan to use on the new system board, such as the heat sink, CPU, and memory.

After attaching the heat sink and CPU to the new system board and installing the memory, reverse the preceding steps to replace the system board.

CPU and Heat Sink

Before replacing the CPU in a laptop, you must determine which models are supported by the installed motherboard. Laptop motherboards are customized for a narrow range of CPUs. A BIOS update might enable additional CPUs to be used successfully. Install any required BIOS update before disassembling the laptop.

The CPU cannot be replaced without removing the heat sink module. Laptop heat sinks are typically one-piece or two-piece units that pull heat away from the chipset and the processor. Some units incorporate the fan. To remove the heat sink (refer to Figures 12-22 and 12-23), follow these steps:

Step 1.   Remove the screws holding the heat sink in place.

Step 2.   If the heat sink incorporates a fan, disconnect the fan power lead from the motherboard.

Step 3.   Lift up on the heat sink to remove it. (Move it from side to side if necessary to loosen the thermal material.) Retain it for reuse.

Figure 12-24 shows what a typical heat sink looks like after removal from a working system.

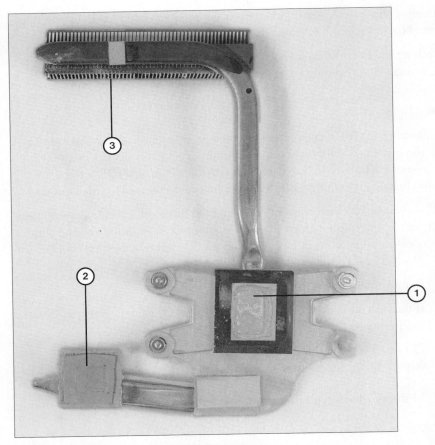

1. Remove thermal compound from CPU heat sink
2. Phase-change thermal material on chipset heat sink can be reused
3. Use compressed air to clean fan exhaust/heat exchanger before
   reusing heat sink

Figure 12-24   A heat sink after removal.

To remove the CPU, follow these steps:

Step 1.   Loosen the processor locking screw. Note the markings on the CPU and the socket. The CPU must be aligned in the same position when installed.

Step 2.   Remove the CPU from the socket. Retain it for possible reuse. See Figure 12-25.

If you are using a factory CPU assembly, use the new CPU and heat sink in the re-assembly process. Before doing so, be sure to remove the old thermal material from the fan and other motherboard components that use the heat sink. The new heat sink includes thermal material (thermal pads and/or paste). Use 70% or higher isopropyl alcohol for cleaning these components.

NOTE   Laptop processors use different sockets than desktop processors. They are not interchangeable.

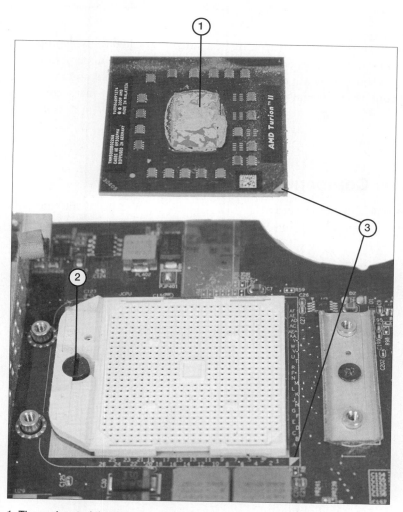

1. Thermal material residue on CPU must be removed before reuse
2. Clamping mechanism for CPU socket
3. Pin 1 markings for correct orientation of processor in socket

Figure 12-25   A typical laptop processor and its socket.

If you are reinstalling the same processor and heat sink, or if you are using a heat sink and processor from a vendor other than your laptop vendor, you typically need to supply your own thermal material. Be sure to clean old thermal material from the fan, processor, heat sink, and other motherboard components before applying new material.

Install the processor first, followed by the heat sink, fan (if not built in to the heat sink), and the remainder of the components you removed.

Cooling Fans

The cooling fan in a laptop might be part of the heat sink or attached to the laptop's enclosure. If you plan to reuse a fan, be sure to clean it. However, if you are performing a disassembly of a laptop that will enable you to replace the fan, we recommend replacing it. If the cooling fan in a laptop fails, it can damage or destroy many components.

Laptop Display Components

Laptop displays typically include an LCD or OLED display, a webcam and microphone, a digitizer (touch screen), and Wi-Fi antennas. Some also include a removable inverter.

NOTE   Be sure to focus on these key terms for the 220-901 exam:

Display Types: LCD (TN vs. IPS); fluorescent vs. LED backlighting; OLED

Display components: Wi-Fi antenna connector/placement, webcam, microphone, inverter, digitizer

---

LCD

Laptops use active-matrix liquid crystal displays. Active-matrix refers to screens that use a transistor for every dot seen onscreen: for example, a 1,600 × 900 active-matrix LCD screen has 1,440,000 transistors.

Fluorescent versus LED Backlighting

Older laptops use a fluorescent backlight and an inverter. These are sometimes referred to as LCD-**CCFL** (cold cathode fluorescent lamp) displays. As with any fluorescent light source, the backlight contains poisonous mercury. LCD-CCFL displays must be treated as toxic waste and disposed of in compliance with local government regulations, such as by recycling the unit through an approved electronic recycler. Fluorescent backlights often produce uneven screen brightness and make precise color control difficult.

A so-called **LED display** panel actually uses an LCD display, but has replaced the fluorescent backlight and its inverter power source with LED backlighting. LED backlighting is more reliable, provides better color rendition than CCFL backlighting, and is less toxic when disposed of.

What's different about an LED panel? The difference starts at the rear. Instead of an inverter, an LED-backlit panel has an LED driver module. The module drives one or more strips of LEDs located at one or more edges of the display. To provide even lighting, a light guide plate is sandwiched between two diffusers. At the front of the display is the LCD display layer and, on touchscreens, a digitizing layer.

IPS versus TN Panels

Laptop displays typically use LCD panels with some form of in-plane switching (**IPS**), which enables wider horizontal and vertical viewing angles than the older twisted nematic (**TN**) LCD panels. TN panels are sometimes found on inexpensive laptops and tablets.

OLED

Organic LED (**OLED**) displays use a layer of organic compounds between two electrodes to emit light. As a consequence, the brightness of each OLED pixel can be individually controlled. OLED displays have been developed in two forms, passive matrix (PMOLED) and active matrix (AMOLED), which supports larger sizes and higher resolutions. OLED screens are much thinner than LCD screens, making them a good choice for tablets and convertible (2-in-1) units that switch between laptop and tablet modes. OLED displays are now being incorporated into high-end 2-in-1 units, HDTVs, and smartphones. A defective OLED display should be swapped out.

Wi-Fi Antenna Connector/Placement

Although the mini-PCIe card that contains the Wi-Fi radio is located in the base of the laptop, the **Wi-Fi antenna** is usually part of the screen assembly (refer to Figure 12-25). If a laptop screen is damaged, the Wi-Fi antennas might also be damaged. In a LED display, the inverter is not present, but the rest of the components are in the same locations.

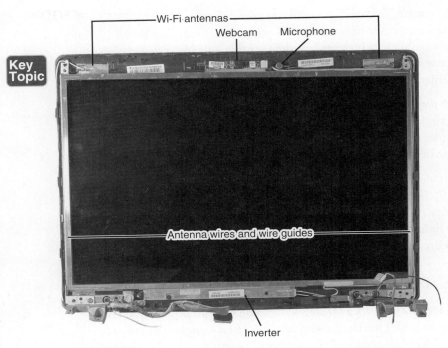

Figure 12-26 Wi-Fi antennas, wires, CCFL inverter, webcam, and microphone in a typical LCD-CCFL display.

Webcam

Almost all laptop display assemblies include a **webcam** at the top center edge of the display assembly (refer to Figure 12-25). If the webcam fails, it can be replaced after performing a partial tear down of the laptop assembly. However, if you need a higher-resolution webcam, you can use an external webcam that plugs into a USB port.

Microphone

A **microphone** is also part of the display assembly. It is used by the webcam or for other recording purposes as needed (refer to Figure 12-26). If the microphone fails, it can be replaced after performing a partial tear down of the laptop assembly. However, if you need a higher-quality microphone, you can use a microphone as part of a headset that plugs into an audio port or a USB port.

Inverter

An LCD-CCFL laptop display is easy to read because of two components: the inverter and the backlight. If either fails, the laptop display becomes so dim that it is almost impossible to use.

The **inverter** (refer to Figure 12-26) is a power converter, changing low-voltage DC power into higher-voltage AC power needed to power a CCFL backlight. If the inverter fails, there is no power to run the backlight. Inverter failure is the most common cause of LCD display failure. However, inverter replacement is relatively inexpensive, and inverters can be purchased for do-it-yourself (DIY) replacement.

A CCFL backlight failure is far less common than an inverter failure. If the CCFL backlight fails, a complete disassembly of the display down to individual component level is required. If a CCFL backlight failure occurs, swapping the screen assembly for a known-working replacement often makes more sense than attempting a repair unless you are experienced with screen disassembly.

NOTE   Some vendors offer kits that can be used to convert laptop LCD or other types of CCFL displays to use LED backlights instead. To learn more, see www.lcd-parts.net.

Digitizer

A touchscreen display differs from a standard laptop display by having a **digitizer** layer on top of the display panel. The digitizer detects and transmits touches to the laptop processor. Digitizers are also used on touchscreen smartphones, tablets, fitness monitors, smart watches, phablets, e-readers, and smart cameras.

If the digitizer layer is damaged, but the display panel is intact, the digitizer layer can be replaced separately.

NOTE   For examples of pricing and availability of digitizers, see these websites: http://touchscreendigitizer.net/ and http://screensurgeons.mybigcommerce.com/.

Using Laptop Features

Because laptop computers incorporate multimedia and networking components, they include special function keys on the keyboard and special controls for displays, wireless, volume, screen brightness, Bluetooth networking, and (in some cases) keyboard backlighting.

Laptops also have special provisions for expansion, such as docking stations, and provision for physical security through locking mechanisms.

NOTE   Be sure to make special note of features such as docking stations, physical laptop locks and cable locks, and rotating/removable screens for the 220-901 exam.

Learn more in the following sections.

Special Function Keys

To save space, laptops use keyboards with fewer keys than desktop computers have. However, laptop computers also need to control screen displays and other options not needed on desktop computers.

NOTE   Be sure to make special note of what Fn keys can do (varying by device): dual displays, wireless (on/off), cellular (on/off), volume settings, screen brightness, Bluetooth (on/off), keyboard backlight, touchpad (on/off), screen orientation, media options (fast forward/rewind), GPS (on/off), and airplane mode.

To enable reduced-size keyboards to perform all the functions needed, laptop and portable keyboards use Fn keys. While the **Fn key** is held down, pressing any key with an additional Fn function performs the Fn function; when the Fn key is released, the key reverts to its normal operation. Fn functions are usually printed below or beside the normal key legend and sometimes in a contrasting color.

NOTE   On some laptops, the special functions are the default. On such systems, to use the function keys for normal operating system functions (for example, refresh Windows Explorer/File Explorer view in Windows), hold down the Fn key and press the function key (for example, F5 to refresh).

Typical Fn + key or other special function key features include:

- Dual displays (secondary monitor or projector)
- Screen brightness and/or contrast

- Bluetooth
- Wi-Fi (on/off)
- Backlit keyboard (on/off)
- Embedded keypad (on/off)
- Cellular (on/off)
- Touch pad (on/off)
- Screen orientation
- Media options (fast forward/rewind)
- Volume settings
- GPS (on/off)
- Airplane mode

Figure 12-27 illustrates some of these keys on a MacBook Air laptop (top) and a Samsung ATIV-500 convertible tablet (bottom).

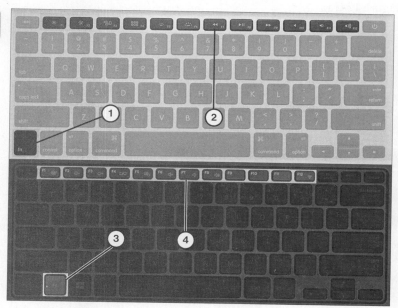

1. Fn key on MacBook Air
2. Special keys that work with Fn key
3. Fn key on Samsung ATIV-500 (Windows)
4. Special keys that work with Fn key

Figure 12-27 Examples of Fn keys.

To determine exactly which features are controlled through the Fn key, check the documentation for your mobile device.

Docking Station

A **docking station** expands the capability of a portable computer by adding features such as

- One or more expansion slots
- Additional I/O ports, such as ExpressCard, Ethernet, display output (HDMI or DisplayPort), Thunderbolt ports, USB ports (USB 2.0, 3.0, USB 3.1 Type C), and others
- Power connection for the laptop
- Connectors for a standard keyboard and mouse

Most docking stations are produced by portable computer vendors, although some third-party products are also available. Business-class laptops that support docking stations might feature a proprietary expansion bus on the rear or bottom of the computer (see Figure 12-28).

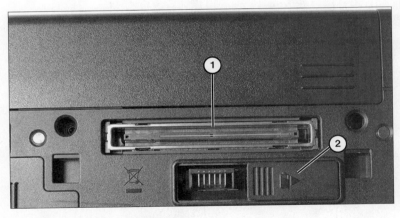

1. Laptop connection to docking station
2. Open door to permit battery charging by docking station

Figure 12-28   A typical proprietary bus for a docking station on a business-class laptop.

However, docking stations made for tablets or thin and light laptops might connect via a high-speed bus such as Thunderbolt or USB 3.0/3.1 or via a proprietary charging/data cable (see Figure 12-29).

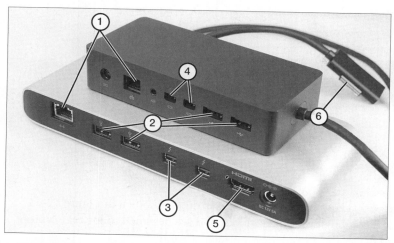

1. Ethernet
2. USB
3. Thunderbolt
4. Mini DisplayPort
5. HDMI
6. Proprietary charging/docking cable

Figure 12-29   Microsoft Dock for Surface Pro 3 and 4 (top) and a third-party dock for MacBook Air and Pro with Thunderbolt ports (bottom).

Wireless docking stations are now available for mobile systems running fifth-generation or newer Intel Core vPro (business-class) processors with the Intel Tri-Band Wireless-AC 17265 adapter. For an example, see http://accessories.dell.com/sna/productdetail.aspx?sku=452-BBUX.

Regardless of how a docking station connects to a portable computer, the user can leave desktop-type peripherals connected to the docking station and can access them by connecting the portable computer to the docking station.

NOTE   So-called "mobile docking stations" used in vehicles (police, insurance, EMS, and other industries) are not used for additional ports. Instead, they securely hold a laptop or tablet in place. Thus, the term "vehicle mounts" is more appropriate.

Laptop and Cable Locks

Most laptops as well as other mobile devices such as projectors and docking stations feature a security slot. On a laptop, the slot is typically located near a rear corner (see Figure 12-30).

1. Security slot

Figure 12-30   A security slot on a laptop.

This slot is used with a laptop **cable lock** such as the one shown in Figure 12-31. Laptop locks use a combination or keyed lock and are designed to lock the laptop (or other secured device) to a fixed location such as a table.

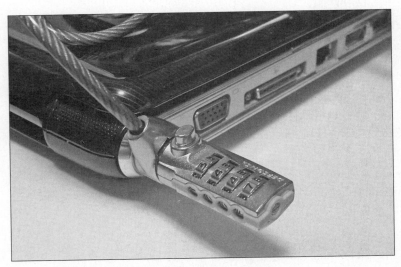

Figure 12-31   A combination laptop security lock.

Stopping Data Theft with Hardware and Software

To prevent data theft from occurring, you should also use the password-lock function in your operating system to require a password whenever the keyboard is locked. In Windows, press Windows+L. For maximum protection, use some type of full-disk encryption such as Windows BitLocker, OS X FileVault, or a third-party solution such as PGP (http://www.pgpi.org/products/pgp/versions/commercial/) or Symantec Endpoint Encryption (http://www.symantec.com/endpoint-encryption/).

Rotating/Removable Screens

One of the fastest growing types of mobile devices are those with **rotating/removable screens**. Bridging the gap between tablet and laptop, this category includes all performance levels from low-end 32-bit processors with 32GB storage and 2MB RAM to systems running high-performance multi-core 64-bit processors.

Devices with removable keyboards (see Figure 12-32) typically feature screen sizes under 12 inches. When used without the keyboard, the device functions as a large tablet. Many models feature additional ports built into the keyboard.

1. Push button to detach keyboard from tablet
2. Tablet
3. Keyboard includes charging jack
4. Keyboard includes two USB ports (only one visible here)

Figure 12-32   A Samsung ATIV-500 Windows tablet with a removable keyboard.

Devices with rotating screens feature larger displays, more ports, and have more powerful processors. Although the display size and port availability rival conventional laptops, these devices are not intended for easy upgrading. Memory, storage, and wireless upgrades typically require a major disassembly process.

Characteristics of Other Mobile Devices

Mobile devices have become major players in business IT and personal electronics usage. With the vast range of available products you might need to use or support, it's more important than ever to understand their basic functions.

Tablets

Tablets, which use a touch screen instead of a mouse or keyboard for user input, are available in a wide variety of types and sizes. However, non-Windows tablets typically share the following features:

- Use of iOS or Android mobile operating systems

- Keyboard and other device interfacing uses Bluetooth

- Port and storage expansion options are limited or non-existent

- Apps installed or updated through the operating system's app store

- Operating system updates often require the device be plugged into AC power or have most of its battery life remaining

Windows tablets with screens larger than 8 inches typically run standard editions of Windows 8.1 or Windows 10. Smaller Windows tablets typically use the latest edition of Windows Mobile.

Smartphones

Smartphones (smart phones), also use typically either Android or iOS operating systems, although a few use Windows Mobile. App store, charging, and Bluetooth interfacing are similar.

Some differences between tablets and smartphones include:

- Operating system updates are provided by the wireless carrier for Android phones.

- Wireless carriers provide network-specific updates for iPhones (iOS) but Apple provides OS updates.

Wearable Technology Devices

Wearable technology devices such as Fitbit (**fitness monitor**), Apple Watch (fitness monitor, **smart watch**), Pebble Watch (fitness monitor, smart watch), **glasses and headsets** such as Google Glass (computer built into a pair of glasses), and Oculus Rift and Gear VR (VR headsets used with smartphones) have expanded the definition of personal technology and computing.

These devices connect to your smartphone via Bluetooth and can be charged in as little as 15 minutes.

When selecting wearable technology, it's important to verify compatibility with your device's operating system and the device's features.

If Bluetooth is not enabled in your smartphone, it must be turned on before a wearable technology device can connect with it.

Phablets

Phablets are smartphones with screen sizes of 5.5-inches or larger. Most feature QHD or HD resolution panels, and some include dedicated styluses. Although smaller smartphones typically don't include flash memory storage, some phablets do.

E-Readers

E-readers such as Amazon Kindle, B&N Nook, and others are optimized for text reading. Because these devices are similar in size to a paperback, they are widely used for recreational reading.

However, e-readers with monochrome screens do not display graphic designs well, which limits their suitability for reading graphic novels or technical documents. Some users have also complained of poor formatting and a lack of indexing with some e-reader books.

E-readers that support ePub or PDF formats are more suitable for graphically rich books. E-readers from Kobo (kobobooks.com), Amazon Kindle Fire, and others (as well as the Google Books app) support ePub.

Smart Camera

The term "**smart camera**" in the mobile device world refers to cameras that use a mobile operating system (typically Android). Smart cameras can integrate a full range of social connectivity, NFC (Near field communication) photo sharing, onboard editing, and GPS support with traditional camera features.

Samsung's Galaxy Camera 2 (www.samsung.com) is a typical example.

GPS

Standalone **GPS** devices such as TomTom Go and Garmin provide turn-by-turn navigation. Although smartphone mapping apps such as MapQuest and Google Maps also provide these features, standalone GPS units are still useful because they can:

- Provide navigation without draining a phone battery
- Feature larger screens
- Have an easier user interface

One potential drawback to standalone GPS usage is the need to keep maps updated. Many of these units do not include map updates in the purchase price, so these must be purchased separately.

If you manage standalone GPS units, you should familiarize yourself with the devices' map update cycles and with subscription renewal information. Whether a standalone GPS or a smartphone as GPS will be used in a vehicle, a suitable mount and 12V power adapter should be made available.

Accessories and Ports Used by Other Mobile Devices

Many different types of connections, ports, and accessories are available for mobile devices. In the following sections, you can review the essential features of each.

NFC

Near field communication (**NFC**) is a feature included in many mobile devices such as tablets for data transfer and shopping. When NFC is enabled and a suitable payment system (such as Apple Pay or Android Pay) is installed on a mobile device, it can be used for payment at any retailer that supports NFC payments.

NFC can also be used to automatically turn on Bluetooth and transfer files between devices (a feature sometimes referred to as "tap and go"). This feature is referred to as Android Beam on Android devices. It can be enabled separately from NFC for payments.

Apple does not currently permit its devices with NFC to work for file transfers except with iTunes purchasing and Apple Pay.

Proprietary Vendor-Specific Ports (Communication/Power)

Until recently, every smartphone and tablet used its own proprietary connection for charging and file sync. Older Android tablets and smartphones uses various proprietary chargers. To support these, multiple-head AC or 12V DC chargers were sold as well as dedicated devices.

Lightning for Apple iOS

Older iOS devices (up through the iPhone 4 series, third-generation iPad) used the 30-pin connector. However, starting in 2012, Apple standardized on the eight-pin reversible **Lightning** connector for iPhones, iPads, iPods, and other mobile devices.

MicroUSB/MiniUSB for Android, Windows

For a brief period, the 5-pin **miniUSB** port was used for Android smartphones. Most recently, the USB-on-the-Go connector has become the de facto standard for both Android smartphones and tablets. However, some recent Android tablets use the reversible USB Type C connector.

Most Windows tablets and smartphones use the USB-on-the-Go (microUSB) connector or the USB Type C connector (varies by model).

Figure 12-33 compares 30-pin, Lightning, 5-pin miniUSB, and **microUSB** cables. All of these cables have the standard USB Type A connector on the other end.

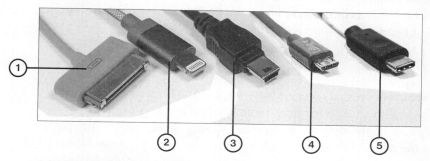

1. 30-pin power/sync cable (iOS)
2. Lightning power/sync cable (iOS)
3. 5-pin miniUSBpower/sync cable (Android)
4. microUSB(USB-on-the-Go) power/sync cable (Android smartphones and tablets, Windows tablets)
5. USB Type C power/sync cable (latest Windows smartphones)

Figure 12-33   The most common mobile power/sync cables.

Bluetooth

Bluetooth is a feature of almost every mobile device, enabling wireless connections to headsets, mice and keyboards, printers, and other types of devices. When you enable Bluetooth, you can specify whether to make your device discoverable and which devices you can pair with.

To learn more about the pairing process, see Chapter 20, "Mobile Operating Systems and Devices."

IR

Some recent and current-model smartphones and phablets include built-in **IR** (infra-red) capabilities. However, this feature is designed for use with TV and home theater remote control apps rather than for data transfer as with older mobile devices. If your smartphone can be used to control your TV, it has an IR blaster onboard.

Hotspot/Tethering

Most smartphones can share a cellular data connection by using **hotspot/tethering**. For details, see Chapter 20, "Mobile Operating Systems and Devices."

Headsets

For music listening, mobile devices feature the same 3.5mm mini-jack available on computers for headsets or earbuds. However, for hands-free telephone use, you can pair wireless **headsets** via Bluetooth with your smartphone.

Speakers

Portable **speakers** use rechargeable batteries, and the USB cable on portable speakers is used only for recharging. Some low-cost speakers use a 3.5mm mini-jack speaker cable, but most use Bluetooth. By using Bluetooth, you can place the speaker in the midst of the action while keeping your smartphone or tablet out of harm's way.

Game Pads

Game pads with Bluetooth connections can be used with smartphones or tablets for game play. For example, the Android Gamepad Games website (http://androidgamepadgames.com/) has an extensive list of Android games that are compatible with game pad controllers. On iOS, games that support the MFi controller standard (introduced with iOS 7) will work on MFi-compatible games. Some iOS controllers connect via Lightning rather than with Bluetooth.

NOTE   The Apple MFi Program ("Made for iPhone/iPod/iPad") is a licensing program for developers of hardware and software peripherals that work with Apple's iPod, iPad, and iPhone, the so-called iDevices. The name is a shortened version of the original long-form Made For iPod. To learn more, see https://mfi.apple.com/MFiWeb/getFAQ.action.

Tablet/Smartphone Docking Stations

Docking stations for tablets and smartphones are designed to charge these devices and many also provide additional features such as stereo speakers and clock radio support.

It's important to verify compatibility with your device, because there are still many docking stations on the market for the old 30-pin iOS devices. Some docking stations support wireless charging with compatible smartphones.

Extra Battery Packs/Battery Chargers

Although a few smartphones and tablets have user-replaceable batteries, a much more convenient solution is a portable battery charger, also known as a portable power bank. This type of device has a battery onboard and a USB connection, so it can be used to charge a smartphone or tablet by using its normal USB charging cable.

These devices differ in the following ways:

- **mAh (milli-ampere-hour) rating**: The higher the rating, the more charges the device can supply before it needs to be recharged.

- **Amperage output**: An output rating of 2.1A or higher is needed to charge an iPad or Android tablet.

- **Number of USB charging ports**: If more than one mobile device needs to be charged at the same time, two or more USB charging ports is a useful feature to specify.

Protective Covers/Waterproofing

Protective covers/waterproofing are two ways to protect a smartphone or tablet from damage.

Without a protective cover, a smartphone or tablet is very vulnerable to impact damage. Although broken screens are the most common problem, damage to the case can cause failures to other systems.

A rubberized protective cover with raised edges to protect the screen is a good investment for any tablet or smartphone. For better protection against dampness, look for a cover that has good weather sealing.

The IP (ingress protection) rating scale, developed to measure dust and dirt-protection of an electronic enclosure, is a convenient way to rate the dust and water protection features of a smartphone. The maximum level of protection, IP68, has been achieved by a few smartphones. To learn more, see www.dsmt.com/resources/ip-rating-chart/.

Credit Card Readers

Credit card readers for smartphones and tablets enable credit card transactions almost anywhere. Readers plug into the 3.5mm headset jack, and are available in versions for magnetic strip cards, chip cards, and NFC (contactless) payment devices.

Some systems are designed to work as commercial grade point-of-sale systems with support for cash drawers and receipt printer. Before selecting a system, check the following:

- Operating system support
- Optional hardware support
- Swipe fees

Memory/MicroSD

Although the amount of onboard storage in smartphones and tablets has increased in recent years, users who download a lot of media or take a lot of photos can always use more storage.

Some Android-based and Windows-based tablets and smartphones have **microSD** card slots, but iOS devices do not have upgradeable storage. Depending on the operating system a device uses, it might be possible to store some apps on the memory card.

Exam Preparation Tasks

Review All the Key Topics

Review the most important topics in the chapter, noted with the key topics icon in the outer margin of the page. Table 12-2 lists a reference of these key topics and the page numbers on which each is found.

Table 12-2   Key Topics for Chapter 12

Key Topic Element	Description	Page Number
Table 12-1	SODIMM Features	511
Section	Ports and Adapters	512
Figure 12-6	Removable panels for access to upgradeable parts (hard disk drive, RAM, wireless card)	517
Figure 12-26	Wi-Fi antennas, webcam, and microphone locations in a typical laptop	542
Figure 12-27	Examples of Fn keys from OS X and Windows devices	545

Memory Table

Print a copy of Appendix C, "Memory Tables" (found on the CD), or at least the section for this chapter, and complete the tables and lists from memory. Appendix D, "Answers to Memory Tables," also on the CD, includes completed tables and lists to check your work.

Define Key Terms

Define the following key terms from this chapter, and check your answers in the glossary.

ExpressCard, SODIMM, flash memory, ports, adapters, Thunderbolt, DisplayPort, USB to RJ-45 dongle, USB to Wi-Fi dongle, USB to Bluetooth, USB optical drive, keyboard, pointing device, 1.8-in drive, 2.5-in drive, smart card reader, wireless card, miniPCIe, screen, DC jack, battery, touchpad, plastics/frames, speaker, system board, TN, IPS, CCFL, LED display, OLED, Wi-Fi antenna, webcam, microphone, inverter, digitizer, Fn key, docking station, cable lock, rotating/removable screens, tablets, smartphones, wearable technology devices, smart watches, fitness monitors, glasses and headsets, phablets, e-readers, smart camera, GPS, NFC, microUSB, miniUSB, Lightning, Bluetooth, IR, hotspot/tethering, headsets, speakers, game pads, protective covers/water proofing, credit card readers, MicroSD

Complete Hands-On Labs

Complete the hands-on labs, and then see the answers and explanations at the end of the chapter. In this series of hands-on labs, you are preparing to install devices that will provide missing features to your system.

Lab 12-1: Laptop Features and Upgrade Options

Examine a laptop computer and determine as many of the following facts as possible:

How many USB 3.0 ports?

How many USB 2.0 ports?

Are there any other USB ports (USB Type C, USB 3.1, charging ports) Which type? How many?

Are there any ExpressCard slots?

Is there a flash memory card reader?

Which Fn keys are included? Describe the function of each key.

What is the maximum amount of RAM for the laptop?

How much RAM is installed now?

Which of the following can be accessed from the bottom of the computer?

Hard disk or SSD

RAM

Battery

Wireless card

Other components (specify)

Search for memory and drive upgrades for this system and list possible sources (three maximum).

Lab 12-2: Mobile Device Features

Examine iOS or Android tablets and smartphones and determine which of the following features are available. You might need to use the device's settings menu to answer some questions.

Device Name

Operating system and version

NFC support? Enabled?

Expandable storage? Card installed?

Type of charge/sync cable

Is this device used with any of the following?

Wearable tech (glasses, smart watch, activity tracker, etc).

External portable battery charger

Does the device have cellular service (some tablets do)?

Answer Review Questions

1. Which type of object is shown in the following figure?

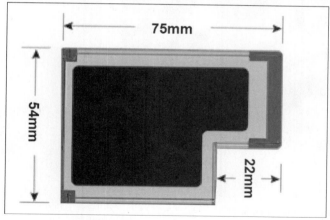

A. SODIMM

B. ExpressCard/54

C. Smart card

D. Flash memory

2. Your client has requested a memory upgrade for a laptop that uses DDR4 RAM. Which of the following pin counts matches this type of RAM?

   A. 100

   B. 200

   C. 240

   D. 260

3. Which of the following ports on an OS X device is a flash memory card reader?

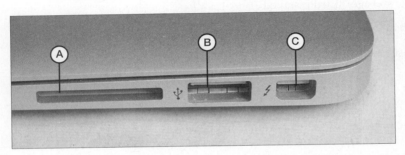

4. Identify the ports on this laptop. (You may use an answer more than once.)

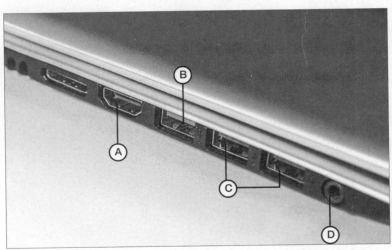

Answer Options (in alphabetical order):

   1. HDMI

   2. Headset jack

   3. USB 2.0

   4. USB 3.0

5. Several key laptop components are available for replacement through compartments in the bottom of the laptop case. Identify the locations of these key components in the following figure.

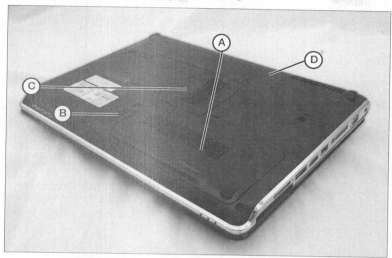

Answer Options (in alphabetical order):

1. Hard drive

2. Laptop battery

3. Optical drive release

4. SODIMM memory

6. After installing a new hard drive, which of the following steps should be performed next?

   A. You should verify that the new drive has been recognized in the BIOS.

   B. You should check the Device Manager to be sure that the new hard drive is listed.

   C. You should check the Device Manager to be sure that the new hard drive has an "!".

   D. You should verify that the new hard drive is recognized in the System Information utility.

7. Which of the following best describes the function of a smart card reader on a laptop computer?

   A. It reads the contents of an ExpressCard.

   B. It is used on smartphones for point of sale transactions.

   C. It reads the contents of flash memory modules.

   D. It is used for access control.

8. Where is the Wi-Fi antenna located on a laptop computer?

   A. The back of the computer has a telescoping antenna that can be collapsed when not needed.

   B. Each side of the laptop case has an antenna (two antennas total) that can be rotated up or down as needed.

   C. The antenna is built into the display screen.

   D. The antenna is housed under the keyboard.

9. Which of the following statements best describes a DC jack?

   A. It is a port for receiving DC power for a laptop.

   B. It is a microphone adapter that changes an analog signal to a digital signal.

   C. It is a digital controller used by high-end sound cards to amplify an audio signal.

   D. It is a dynamic power converter for a Wi-Fi system.

10. You are preparing to reinstall a laptop processor. Review the following figure and specify which processor is properly oriented for installation. What else needs to be done before the heatsink can be reattached? Place the steps listed in the correct order:

    A. Reapply thermal compound to the processor.

    B. Lock the processor into the socket.

    C. Clean off the thermal compound residue from the processor and heatsink.

11. Which of the following display types—although it might be more expensive—is generally considered to be the best choice for high-end tablets and 2-in-1 mobile devices?

    A. CRT

    B. Plasma

    C. OLED

    D. LCD

12. Which of the following best describes the difference between a touchscreen display and a standard display?

    A. A touchscreen adds an inverter to the display.

    B. A touchscreen adds a digitizer layer on top of the display.

    C. A touchscreen adds a backlight to the display.

    D. A touchscreen adds a plasma layer to the display.

13. The Fn key on a laptop computer does which of the following?

   A. It allows a single key to perform more than one action.

   B. It creates faster access to the Internet.

   C. It opens a special function menu.

   D. It automatically sets the computer to function in airplane mode.

14. Your client uses the same laptop at the office and home. Which of the following would make it easier to connect to USB and external display devices at the office and at home?

   A. A laptop lock

   B. A docking station

   C. Fn key actuation

   D. An ExpressCard slot

15. Which of the following operating systems are most commonly used for mobile devices such as tablets and smartphones? (Choose two.)

   A. Windows

   B. Linux

   C. iOS

   D. Android

   E. OS X

16. Your client reports that the company president's Fitbit is not communicating with the smartphone. Both devices are charged. Which of the following needs to be running on the smartphone?

   A. Bluetooth

   B. Wi-Fi

   C. GPS

   D. IR

17. Your client wants to make purchases at retail locations by using a smartphone. Which of the following features must be enabled?

   A. GPS

   B. NFC

   C. Bluetooth

   D. Fn key combination

Answers and Explanations to Hands-On Labs

Lab 12-1: Laptop Features and Upgrade Options

USB 2.0 ports are normally color-coded black and USB 3.0 ports are normally color-coded blue. Vendors use various colors for USB ports that can be used for device charging at higher amperages than normal.

Fn key definitions vary according to laptop model.

To determine the amount of RAM in a laptop, use the System Properties sheet in Windows or the Memory pane in OS X. On a Windows system, use the Crucial. com memory scanner to see the memory modules already installed and what the expansion options are for a system.

Most laptops with user-replaceable components use icons on the bottom of the system to indicate which access panels are used for particular devices. Tablets and tablet-like systems such as the MacBook Air will not have access panels.

Memory and drive updates can be ordered from the system vendor or from third-party websites. Check both sources.

Lab 12-2: Mobile Device Features

Use the checklist you create by answering the questions in this lab to help you determine what your current smartphone or tablet can do. It can be helpful when you are shopping for an upgrade.

Answers and Explanations to Review Questions

1. **B.** This is an ExpressCard/54. The ExpressCard is an expansion card with a 26-wire connector that communicates with the motherboard's chipset through either PCI Express or USB.

2. **D.** A DDR4 SODIMM has 260 pins. DDR and DDR2 SODIMMS have 200 pins. A DDR3 SODIMM has 204 pins.

3. A is the flash memory card reader.

4.
   - **A.** 1 (HDMI)
   - **B.** 4 (USB 3.0)
   - **C.** 3 (USB 2.0)
   - **D.** 2 (Headset jack)

5.
   A. 1 (Hard disk)

   B. 3 (Optical drive release)

   C. 4 (SODIMM)

   D. 2 (Battery)

6. **A.** The new hard drive must be recognized in the BIOS before it can be used by the operating system.

7. **D.** A smart card reader reads smarts cards. A smart card is generally about the size of a credit card and may contain security authentication information or other identifying information about the owner.

8. **C.** A laptop antenna is usually installed around the edges of the display housing.

9. **A.** AC power from the wall outlet in your home or office must be converted to DC power before it can be used by your computer. The DC jack is the port on your laptop that receives the DC power from the converter.

10. Choose processor 2 because it is correctly oriented with the socket. The correct order is B. Clean off the thermal compound residue from the processor and heatsink. C. Clean off the thermal compound residue from the processor and heatsink.

    A. Reapply thermal compound to the processor.

    B. Lock the processor into the socket.

    C. Clean off the thermal compound residue from the processor and heatsink.

11. **C.** OLEDs are thinner and lighter than other screen types, making them an excellent choice for handheld devices. OLEDs are designed with a layer of organic compounds sandwiched between two light-emitting electrodes. CRT monitors are big, bulky, and use a cathode ray tube. Plasma displays, popular in home big-screen TV systems, are made of small cells of ionized gas and provide excellent contrast ratio. LCDs use liquid crystal displays and are frequently used in laptop computers.

12. **B.** A touchscreen adds a digitizer layer to the display. The digitizer detects the pressure of a touch. Inverters and backlights are found on LCD screens in laptops. Plasma displays, popular in home big-screen TV systems, are made of small cells of ionized gas.

13. **A.** Laptop keyboards are smaller than standard PC keyboards and they have fewer keys, yet they need to perform more functions than standard keyboards. To solve this dilemma, laptop keyboards have a special Fn or function key that allows a single key to perform a second task.

14. **B.** A mobile docking station is used to create a mobile office environment. It provides a stable work platform, plus it provides the user with additional I/O ports (such as ExpressCard, Ethernet, HDMI, DisplayPort, Thunderbolt, USB 2.0 or 3.0), additional expansion slots, and a power connection to re-charge the battery.

15. **C, D.** iOS (closed source, used by Apple devices), and Android (open source) are commonly used for mobile devices such as tablets and smartphones. Windows, Linux, and OS X are operating systems for laptops and desktops. Windows Mobile is used for smartphones and small tablets, but it is not nearly as popular as iOS and Android.

16. **A.** Fitbit connects to mobile phones, laptops, or PCs via a Bluetooth connection.

17. **B.** NFC is a smartphone feature that is be used to transfer data and can be used at retailers to pay for purchases.

This chapter covers the following subjects:

- **Troubleshooting Motherboard, RAM, CPU, and Power Issues**—This section covers how to troubleshoot the core components of a PC.

- **Recommended Tools**—Learn what the essential tools for system troubleshooting are and how to use them.

- **Troubleshooting Hard Drives and RAID Arrays**—Storage is crucial to computer operation, and in this section, you learn how to keep them running.

- **Troubleshooting Video, Projector, and Display Issues**—Display problems are big problems with desktops, laptops, and mobile devices, and this section helps you get them working again.

- **Network Troubleshooting**—With many different components in even a simple network, there are plenty of possible points of failure. This section discusses wired and wireless problems and solutions.

- **Overview of Network Command-Line Tools**—Use this section to find the Windows command-line tool needed to find or fix a problem with networked systems running Windows.

- **Mobile Device Troubleshooting**—Learn how to troubleshoot GPS, display, Bluetooth, and other common mobile device issues in this section.

- **Mobile Device Disassembly Process**—Organization is the key to successful disassembly (and reassembly), and this section teaches you how.

- **Printer Troubleshooting**—From paper jams to toner that falls off the paper, learn how to troubleshoot all types of printers in this section.

## CHAPTER 13

Hardware and Network Troubleshooting

In Chapter 1, you learned the CompTIA A+ certification six-step troubleshooting theory. In Chapters 2-12, you've learned about the many hardware components that make up computers and their peripherals, printers, networks, and mobile devices. In this chapter, you learn specific troubleshooting methods for computers, peripherals, printers, mobile devices, and networks.

Before performing the diagnostic tests in this chapter, be sure to read and follow the precautions against ESD covered in Chapter 17, "Operational Procedures." If you need to remove or install internal components in a device, make sure AC power is disconnected. Remove the battery from a laptop.

220-901: Objective 4.1 Given a scenario, troubleshoot common problems related to motherboards, RAM, CPU, and power with appropriate tools.

220-901: Objective 4.2 Given a scenario, troubleshoot hard drives and RAID arrays with appropriate tools.

220-901: Objective 4.3 Given a scenario, troubleshoot common video, projector and display issues.

220-901: Objective 4.4 Given a scenario, troubleshoot wired and wireless networks with appropriate tools.

220-901: Objective 4.5 Given a scenario, troubleshoot and repair common mobile device issues while adhering to the appropriate procedures.

220-901: Objective 4.6 Given a scenario, troubleshoot printers with appropriate tools.

Foundation Topics

Troubleshooting Motherboard, RAM, CPU, and Power Issues

Many system problems are caused by bad motherboards, RAM, CPUs, and power. In the following sections, you learn about common symptoms for these problems and the most likely causes. Use this information as you track down real-life issues your company's and clients' systems might have.

Unexpected Shutdowns

Typical causes for unexpected shutdowns include:

- Dead short caused by loose screws, slot covers, or cards—Shut down system and secure all metal components.

- CPU overheating—Check fan speed for CPU heatsink; clean fan if it dirty; replace fan if it has failed or turning too slowly; check power management settings and CPU drivers in the operating system to make sure that thermal throttling is working.

- Power supply **overheating**—Check power supply fan and clean it if possible; replace power supply with higher wattage–rated unit if problem persists.

- Power supply failure—Test power supply to verify proper operation.

System Lockups

System lockups are typically caused by the corruption of memory contents. Follow these steps to diagnose system lockups:

Step 1.   Shut down the system, remove and reinstall memory, and remove dust from the modules, the sockets, cooling vents, and fans. If the problem persists, memory might be overheating.

Step 2.   Check the specifications for memory; the memory installed might not be the correct type for the motherboard and processor. If memory is incorrect for the CPU or motherboard, replace it with correct-specification memory. On some systems, you can see memory specifications in the system BIOS (see Figure 13-1), or you can run diagnostic apps such as SiSoftware Sandra or the Crucial.com memory advisor. If two or more modules are installed, they should have matching clock speed and timing specifications.

Step 3. If memory has been overclocked, reset the memory to factory specifications by using the Auto or by SPD options in the system BIOS setup.

Step 4. Add additional system cooling.

NOTE All references to BIOS in this chapter apply to both traditional BIOS and UEFI firmware, except where noted otherwise.

If you run the processor or memory at speeds faster than those recommended, a process called *overclocking*, you could cause components to overheat and the system to crash. If your system crashes after overclocking, return the settings to standard values and restart the system. If the system is now stable, don't overclock it until you can add adequate cooling to the system. Overclocking is not recommended for business uses or for beginners.

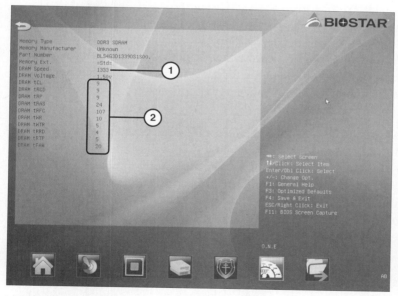

1. Memory speed (frequency)
2. Memory timings. The first four values shown can be written as 9-9-9-24.

Figure 13-1 Viewing memory speed and timings for a selected module in a typical UEFI BIOS.

CAUTION Overclocking generates excess heat, which alone can cause damage to components. To make matters worse, one of the favorite ways that overclockers have to improve system stability is to slightly increase the voltage going to the processor core (Vcore) or to the memory modules, which further increases heat.

Don't even think about overclocking unless you study overclocking-oriented websites such as www.overclockers.com or publications such as MaximumPC/PCGamer (www.pcgamer.com/hardware). A careful perusal of these and other resources will tell you that successful overclocking requires a lot of time, a fair amount of cash, a lot of tolerance for damaged components, frequent rebooting, crashes, voided warranties, and so on.

NOTE   Some motherboards come with a basic type of overclocking that only increases CPU frequency by 10 percent maximum. An example of this is Intel's Turbo-Boost and AMD's Turbo Core technologies. While built-in overclocking is relatively safe, it should still be approached with caution.

POST Code Beeps

POST code beeps are used by many BIOS versions to indicate either a fatal error or a serious error. Beep codes vary by the BIOS maker. Although some vendors create their own BIOS chips and firmware, most major brands of computers and virtually all "clones" use a **BIOS** made by one of the following vendors: American Megatrends (AMI), Phoenix Technologies, IBM, Award Software (now owned by Phoenix Technologies), and Insyde Software.

As you might expect, the beep codes and philosophies used by these companies vary a great deal. AMI, for example, uses beep codes for more than 10 fatal errors. It also uses eight beeps to indicate a defective or missing video card. Phoenix uses beep codes for both defects and normal procedures (but has no beep code for a video problem), and the Award BIOS has only a single beep code (one long, two short), indicating a problem with video. Insyde BIOS uses beep codes for errors, but these codes vary widely from model to model.

NOTE   Some vendors have switched from beep codes to blink codes with the advent of UEFI BIOS firmware. An example of blink codes for some HP laptops is available at http://h20564.www2.hp.com/hpsc/doc/public/display?docId=emr_na-c01732674. Check the documentation for your system or motherboard to determine if beep, blink, or other reporting methods are used to indicate POST problems.

Because beep codes do not report all possible problems during the startup process, you can't rely exclusively on beep codes to help you detect and solve system problems. Also, beep codes can be heard only on systems with built-in speakers.

TIP   To add a speaker to a desktop computer, plug it into the speaker wires in the front-panel header pins.

The most common beep codes you're likely to encounter are listed in Table 13-1.

Table 13-1   Common System Errors and Their Beep Codes

Problem	Phoenix BIOS	Award BIOS	AMI BIOS	IBM BIOS
Memory	Beep sequences: 1-3-4-1 1-3-4-3 1-4-1-1	Beeping (other than 2 long, 1 short)	1 or 3 or 11 beeps 1 long, 3 short beeps	(None)
Video	(None)	2 long, 1 short beep	8 beeps 1 long, 8 short beeps	1 long, 3 short beeps, or 1 beep
Processor or motherboard	Beep sequence: 1-2-2-3	High-frequency beeps Repeating high-low beeps	5 beeps or 9 beeps	1 long, 1 short beep

For additional beep codes, see the following resources:

- **AMI BIOS**—www.ami.com/support/bios.cfm
- **Phoenix BIOS**—www.phoenix.com/
- **IBM, Dell, Acer, other brands**—www.bioscentral.com; http://wimsbios.com

NOTE   Don't mix up your boops and beeps! Many systems play a single short boop (usually a bit different in tone than a beep) when the system boots successfully. This is normal.

POST Error Messages

Most BIOS versions do an excellent job of displaying POST error messages indicating what the problem with the system is. These messages can indicate problems with memory, keyboards, hard drives, and other components. For example, if the CMOS memory used to store system setup information is corrupt (possibly because of a battery failure or because the CMOS memory has been cleared), systems display a message such as the following:

- System CMOS Checksum Bad - Run Setup—Phoenix BIOS

- CMOS Checksum Invalid—AMI BIOS

- CMOS CHECKSUM INVALID - RUN SCU—Insyde BIOS

- CMOS Checksum Error - Defaults Loaded—Award BIOS

Some systems document these messages in their manuals, or you can go to the BIOS vendors' websites or the third-party sites listed earlier in this chapter for more information.

NOTE   Keep in mind that the system almost always stops after the first error, so if a system has more than one serious or fatal error, the first problem might stop the boot process before the video card has been initialized to display error messages.

Blank Screen on Bootup

A **blank screen on bootup** can be caused by a variety of video configurations or cabling problems, some of which can be caused by motherboard issues:

- If you have only one display, plugging the video cable in to an inactive video port on a system will cause a blank screen. For example, some systems deactivate onboard video when you install a video card. If onboard video offers DVI and HDMI ports, typically only one can be selected (usually with motherboard jumpers).

- If a display with two or more inputs (for example, DVI and HDMI or DVI and VGA) is not configured to use the correct cable, the display will be blank. Use the display's push button controls to select the correct signal input.

- If a DVI or VGA cable is not tightly attached to the video port or display, the screen might be blank. Secure the cable.

- If an HDMI, miniHDMI, DisplayPort, or miniDisplayPort cable is not completely plugged into the video port or display, the screen might be blank. Completely insert the cable into the port.

- If input cables and display input settings check out OK, but the screen is still blank, shine a flashlight on the screen to see if any text or graphics are visible. If you can see text or graphics with the flashlight, the backlight on the display has failed. On an LCD-CCFL, check the inverter first. Inverter failures are much more common than backlight failures and are relatively easy to replace. On an LED display, check the LED driver board first. Keep in mind that LCD and LED display modules for laptops or complete displays for desktops are far less expensive today than previously, and it might make sense to replace the entire display assembly.

Figure 13-2 shows a typical inverter for an LCD-CCFL display in an all-in-one computer.

1. LCD-CCFL inverter
2. SODIMM memory modules
3. 2.5-inch hard disk in removable drive cage

Figure 13-2   An all-in-one computer with the back open for servicing.

BIOS Time and Settings Resets

Problems with BIOS time and settings resets are typically caused by a problem with either the CMOS battery on the motherboard or the CMOS chip itself.

If date and time settings or other BIOS settings reset to system defaults or display CMOS corrupted error, replace the CMOS battery and reset the BIOS settings to correct values. A CMOS battery (usually a CR2032 on recent systems) will work properly for about three years before it needs to be replaced. Figure 13-3 illustrates a typical CR2032 CMOS battery on a recent motherboard.

If replacing the battery does not solve the problem, the CMOS chip on the motherboard might be damaged. This is a surface-mounted chip that cannot be replaced, so the motherboard itself must be replaced.

If other settings, such as BIOS passwords, have been lost or corrupted, the CMOS contents can be cleared by using a jumper on the motherboard. Depending upon the motherboard, the jumper might be labeled as JBAT (as in Figure 13-3), CLRTC, or CLR_CMOS. See motherboard/system documentation for details. Turn off the system, move the jumper block, leave it in place for a few seconds, then move it back to the normal position. The jumper is often, but not always, near the CMOS battery.

1. CR2032 battery for maintaining CMOS contents
2. JBAT jumper for clearing CMOS contents

Figure 13-3   It might be necessary to remove cards or cables to access the CMOS battery on some systems.

Attempts to Boot to Incorrect Device

The boot sequence listed in BIOS settings determine which drives can be used to start the computer and in what order. If a non-bootable drive is in the boot sequence, the system will not start. For example, if a USB drive is listed first and a non-bootable USB drive is plugged in, the system will not start.

Change the boot order to list the location where the operating system is installed (such as the system hard drive), then restart the computer.

Continuous Reboots

Continuous reboots can be caused by problems with the power supply or by a Windows or other operating system configuration setting:

- **Power Good voltage is too high or too low**—When the Power Good line to the motherboard carries too high or too low a voltage, the processor resets, shutting down the system and rebooting it. Test the power supply voltage levels; replace the power supply if Power Good tests out of specifications. See "Multimeter" later in this chapter for details.

- Windows configuration setting for dealing with STOP error (Blue Screen of Death, or BSOD)—If Windows is configured to reboot when a STOP error occurs, the system will continuously reboot until the error is resolved. To leave a STOP error message onscreen until you decide to restart the system, clear the Automatically Restart check box in the System Failure setting in the Startup and Recovery section of Advanced System Properties.

No Power

No power when you turn on the system can be caused by several issues.

Power Supply Failure

A power supply that has stopped working prevents the system from starting. Use a multimeter or a power supply tester to determine if a power supply has failed. For more details, see the "Multimeter" section on page 588 in this chapter and the "Power Supply Tester" section on page 592 in this chapter.

Incorrect Front Panel Wiring Connections to the Motherboard

The power switch is wired to the motherboard, which in turn signals the power supply to start. If the power lead is plugged in to the wrong pins on the motherboard, or has been disconnected from the motherboard, the system will not start and you will not see an error message.

Check the markings on the front panel connectors, the motherboard, or the motherboard/system manual to determine the correct pinouts and installation.

Loose or Missing Power Leads from Power Supply

Make sure both the ATX and ATX12V or EPS12V power leads from the power supply are connected firmly to the motherboard. The connectors lock into place.

Surge Suppressor or UPS Failure

If the surge suppressor or UPS unit connected to the computer has failed, the computer cannot start. Replace the defective surge suppressor or UPS unit, or replace the battery in the UPS unit.

Overheating

Got an overheated power supply? Not sure? If you touch the power supply case and it's too hot to touch, it's overheated. Overheated power supplies can cause system failure and possible component damage, due to any of the following causes:

- Overloading
- Fan failure
- Inadequate airflow outside the system
- Inadequate airflow inside the system
- Dirt and dust

Use the following sections to figure out the possible effects of these problems in any given situation.

Overloading

An overloaded power supply is caused by connecting devices that draw more power (in watts) than the power supply is designed to handle. As you add more card-based devices to expansion slots, use more bus-powered USB, Thunderbolt, and FireWire drives and devices, and install more internal drives in a system, the odds of having an overloaded power supply increase.

If a power supply fails or overheats, check the causes listed in the following sections before determining whether you should replace the power supply. If you determine that you should replace the power supply, purchase a unit that has a higher wattage rating and a higher +12V rating.

Fan Failure

The fan(s) inside the power supply cool it and are partly responsible for cooling the rest of the computer. If they fail, the power supply and the entire computer are at risk of damage. Fans also might stop turning as a symptom of other power problems.

A fan that stops immediately after the power comes on usually indicates incorrect input voltage or a short circuit. If you turn off the system and turn it back on again under these conditions, the fan will stop each time.

To determine whether a fan has failed, listen to the unit; it should make less noise if the fan has failed. You can also see the fan blades spinning rapidly on a power supply fan that is working correctly. If the blades aren't turning or are turning very slowly, the fan has failed or is too clogged with dust to operate correctly.

To determine whether case fans have failed, look at them through the front or rear of the system, or, if they are connected to the motherboard, use the system monitoring feature in the system BIOS to check fan speed. Figure 13-4 illustrates a typical example.

NOTE   If a fan has failed because of a short circuit or incorrect input voltage, you will not see any picture onscreen because the system cannot operate.

If the system starts normally but the fan stops turning later, this indicates a true fan failure instead of a power problem.

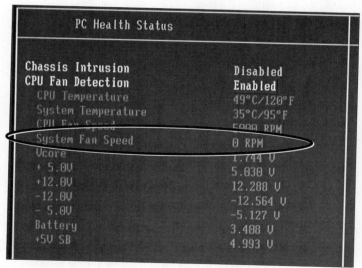

Figure 13-4   The system fan (case fan) has either failed or was never connected to the motherboard power/monitor header.

Inadequate Airflow Outside the System

The power supply's capability to cool the system depends in part on free airflow space outside the system. If the computer is kept in a confined area (such as a closet or security cabinet) without adequate ventilation, power supply failures due to over-heating are likely.

Even systems in ordinary office environments can have airflow problems; make sure that several inches of free air space exist behind the fan outputs for any computer.

Inadequate Airflow Inside the System

As you have seen in previous chapters, the interior of the typical computer is a messy place. Data cables (particularly wide ribbon cables on older systems), drive power cables, header cables, and expansion cards can create small air dams that block air-flow between the heat sources—such as the motherboard, CPU, drives, and memory modules—and the fans in the power supply and the case. Figure 13-5 illustrates a typical system with a lot of cable clutter that can interfere with airflow.

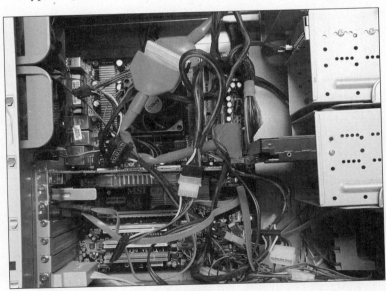

Figure 13-5   A cluttered system with plenty of unsecured cables to block airflow.

Although the use of SATA drives and the elimination of internal floppy drives have eliminated the wide ribbon cables used on the old PATA and floppy drives, disor-ganized systems can still cause overheating. You can do the following to improve airflow inside the computer:

- Use cable ties to secure excess ribbon cable and power connectors out of the way of the fans and the power supply.
- Replace any missing slot covers.
- Make sure that case fans and CPU fans are working correctly.

Figure 13-6 illustrates a different system that uses cable management (cable ties, bundling cables between the drive bays and outer case wall, and routing behind the motherboard) to improve airflow.

Figure 13-6   A system with good airflow due to intelligent cable management.

Dirt and Dust

Most power supplies, except for a few of the early ATX power supplies, use a cooling technique called *negative pressure*; in other words, the power supply fan works like a weak vacuum cleaner, pulling air through vents in the case, past the components, and out through the fan. Vacuum cleaners are used to remove dust, dirt, cat hairs, and so on from living rooms and offices, and even the power supply's weak impression of a vacuum cleaner works the same way.

When you open a system for any kind of maintenance, look for the following:

- Dirt, dust, hair, and gunk clogging the case vents
- A thin layer of dust on the motherboard and expansion slots
- Dirt and dust on the power supply vent and fans

For the most thorough check, be sure to remove the computer's front panel. You never know what you'll find inside a PC that hasn't been cleaned out for a year or two. As you can see from Figure 13-7, you might discover a system with almost completely clogged air vents. A system in this condition could fail catastrophically at almost any time.

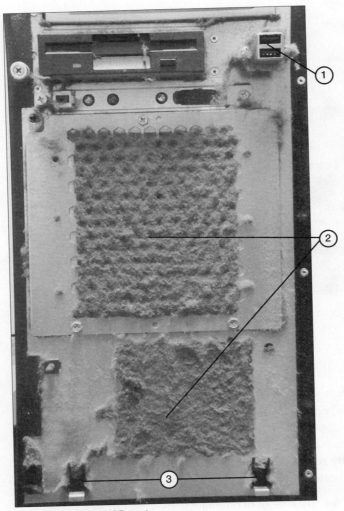

1. Front-mounted USB ports
2. Clogged air intakes
3. Retaining clips for the front of the case

Figure 13-7 A system with extremely dirty air vents.

So how can you get rid of the dust and gunk? You can use a vacuum cleaner specially designed for computer use or compressed air to remove dirt and dust from inside the system. If you use compressed air, be sure to spread newspapers around the system to catch the dirt and dust. If possible, remove the computer from the computer room so the dust is not spread to other equipment.

Installing/Replacing Case Fans

If an overheating system has failed fans or empty fan bays, replace the failed fans or add new ones. Here's how:

Step 1. After removing all power to the system and opening the case, locate any failed fans. (Refer to Figures 1-1 and 1-2 in Chapter 1 for typical fans on the rear of a case.)

Step 2. Disconnect the fan from the motherboard or the power supply.

Step 3. Remove the fan from the case. Fans are held in place by four screws inserted from the outside of the case.

Step 4. (Start here to add a new fan). Determine the size of fan needed (typical sizes are 120mm, 140mm, and 200mm) and hold the fan inside the case as you attach screws to the fan from the outside.

Step 5. Connect the fan to a system fan header (use the same one as before if you are replacing a fan) on the motherboard. If you don't have an available system fan header, use a Molex power supply connector (you can use a splitter if you don't have an unused Molex connector.

Loud Noise

Computers usually run quietly, but if you hear a **loud noise** coming from the power supply, it's a sure sign of problems. A whirring, screeching, rattling, or thumping noise while the system is on usually indicates a fan failure. If a fan built in to a component such as a heat sink or power supply is failing, replace the component immediately.

CAUTION Should you try to replace a standard power supply fan? No. Because the power supply is a sealed unit, you would need to remove the cover from most power supplies to gain access to the fan. The capacitors inside a power supply retain potentially lethal electrical charges. Instead, scrap the power supply and replace it with a higher-rated unit. Refer to the "Removing and Replacing the Power Supply" section on page 328 in Chapter 9.

A power supply that makes a loud bang, followed by a system crash, has had an onboard capacitor blow up.

Intermittent Device Failure

Intermittent failures of USB bus-powered devices (mice, keyboard, USB flash drives, portable USB hard drives) usually happen because these devices draw power from the system's power supply via the USB port. These types of failures, especially for devices with low power draws such as mice and keyboards, can be an early sign of an overloaded power supply. Replace the power supply with a higher-rated unit.

Intermittent failures of other USB external devices or of internal devices can be caused by damaged data cables, power supplies or connectors, or ports.

To troubleshoot these problems:

Step 1. Shut down the device (and computer if the device is internal) and replace the data cable with a known-working replacement. If a USB device is plugged into a front-mounted USB port or a USB port on a card bracket, check the USB header cable connections to the motherboard.

Step 2. Turn on the device or computer.

Step 3. Test the device over time. If the device works correctly, the problem is solved.

Step 4. If Step 3 didn't resolve the problem, use the original data cable and try plugging it into a different internal or external port. Repeat Steps 2-3.

Step 5. Try Steps 1-4 again, but this time use a replacement power connector or AC adapter.

Step 6. When you find the defective component, the problem stops. If the problem is not resolved with different data cables, connectors, or power supplies/AC adapters, the device itself needs to be replaced.

Fans Spin—No Power to Other Devices

Fans connected directly to the power supply will run as soon as the system is turned on, but if the computer never displays any startup messages, this could indicate a variety of problems. Check the following:

- Make sure the main ATX and 12V ATX or EPS power leads are securely connected to the appropriate sockets.
- Make sure the CPU and memory modules are securely installed in the appropriate sockets.

Indicator Lights

Indicator lights on the front or top of most desktop computers display power and hard drive activity. If these lights go out but the system is otherwise working properly, check the motherboard connection for the indicator lights. See Chapter 3, Figures 3-13 and 3-14.

Smoke or Burning Smells

If you can see smoke or smell a burning odor with a chemical overtone to it coming from the power supply's outside vent, your power supply has died. This odor can linger for weeks. Sadly, when a power supply blows up like this, it can also destroy the motherboard, bus-powered USB devices connected to the computer, and other components.

Smoke or a burning smell inside the system can also be caused by failing capacitors. The capacitors are cylindrical components near the CPU socket on the motherboard or inside the power supply. If capacitors fail or other components burn up, replace the component.

Step-by-Step Power Supply Troubleshooting

Use the procedure outlined next to find the actual cause of a dead system. If one of the test procedures in the following list corrects the problem, the item that was changed is the cause of the problem. Power supplies have a built-in safety feature that shuts down the unit immediately in case of short circuit.

The following steps are designed to determine whether the power problem is caused by a short circuit or another problem:

Step 1.   Smell the power supply's outside vent. If you can detect a burnt odor, the power supply has failed. Replace it.

Step 2.   Check the AC power to the system; a loose or disconnected power cord, a disconnected surge protector, a surge protector that has been turned off, or a dead AC wall socket will prevent a system from receiving power. If the wall socket has no power, reset the circuit breaker in the electrical service box for the location.

Step 3.   Check the AC voltage switch on the power supply; it should be set to 115V for North America. Turn off the power, reset the switch, and restart the system if the switch was set to 230V. Note that many desktop computer power supplies no longer require a switch selection because they are autoswitching.

> **CAUTION**   If your area uses 230V and the power supply is set to 115V, you need a new power supply and possibly other components, because they've been damaged or destroyed by 100 percent overvoltage.

Step 4.   If the system uses a PS/2 mouse or keyboard, check the connectors; a loose keyboard connector could cause a short circuit.

Step 5.   Turn off the system, disconnect power, and open the system. Verify that the power leads are properly connected to the motherboard. Connect loose power leads, reconnect power, and restart the computer.

Step 6.   Check for loose screws or other components such as loose slot covers, modem speakers, or other metal items that can cause a short circuit. Correct them and retest.

Step 7.   Remove all expansion cards and disconnect power to all drives; restart the system and use a power supply tester or a multimeter to test power to the motherboard. For more details, see the "Multimeter" section on page 588 of this chapter.

Step 8.   If the power tests within accepted limits with all peripherals disconnected, reinstall one card at a time and check the power. If the power tests within accepted limits, reattach one drive at a time and check the power.

Step 9.   If a defective card or drive has a dead short, reattaching the defective card or drive should stop the system immediately upon power-up. Replace the card or drive and retest.

Step 10.   Check the Power Good line at the power supply motherboard connector with a multimeter or a power supply tester.

It's a long list, but chances are you will track down the offending component before you reach the end of it.

Distended Capacitors

Capacitors, sometimes referred to as "caps," are used as part of the voltage step-down circuits that provide power to the processor. From 2002-2007, many motherboards were built using faulty capacitors that became distended and leaked, causing system failure and sometimes physical damage to the motherboard.

Figure 13-8 illustrates a motherboard with **distended capacitors**.

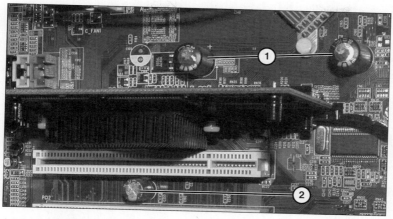

1. Distended, leaking capacitors
2. Capacitor in good working order

Figure 13-8   This system has at least two faulty capacitors.

Some of these systems might still be in service, and the faulty capacitors can be replaced.

NOTE   For a detailed step-by-step tutorial on replacing bad capacitors, visit www. itsacon.net/computers/hardware/replacing-bad-motherboard-capacitors/.

Newer systems typically use solid capacitors (see Figure 13-9). These capacitors are much more reliable.

1. Solid capacitors

Figure 13-9   A typical recent motherboard with solid capacitors.

Proprietary Crash Screens (BSOD/Pin wheel)

Proprietary crash screens such as the Windows STOP error ("blue screen of death" or BSOD) or the OS X pin wheel can be caused by hardware problems as well as software problems.

For coverage of crash screens in Windows, Linux, and OS X, see Chapter 22.

Recommended Tools

To diagnose problems with these components, use the following tools:

- Multimeter
- Power supply tester
- Loopback plugs
- POST Card / USB

Multimeter

A **multimeter** is one of the most flexible test devices available. When set for DC voltage, it can be used to test computer power supplies and AC adapters. When set for continuity (CONT), it can be used as a cable tester. It can also be used to test ohm (resistance) and ampere (amp, current) levels.

Multimeters are designed to perform many different types of electrical tests, including the following:

- DC voltage and polarity
- AC voltage and polarity
- Resistance (Ohms)
- Diodes
- Continuity
- Amperage

All multimeters are equipped with red and black test leads. When used for voltage tests, the red is attached to the power source to be measured and the black is attached to ground.

Multimeters use two different readout styles: digital and analog. Digital multimeters are usually *autoranging*, which means they automatically adjust to the correct range for the test selected and the voltage present. Analog multimeters, or non–autoranging digital meters, must be set manually to the correct range and can be damaged more easily by overvoltage. Figure 13-10 compares typical analog and digital multimeters.

Figure 13-10 Typical analog (left) and digital (right) multimeters. Photos courtesy of Colacino Industries, Newark, NJ.

Table 13-2 summarizes the tests you can perform with a multimeter.

Table 13-2 Using a Multimeter

Test to Perform	Multimeter Setting	Probe Positions	Procedure
AC voltage (wall outlet)	AC	Red to hot, black to ground.	Read voltage from meter; should be near 115V in North America.
DC voltage (power supply outputs to motherboard, drives, batteries)	DC	Red to hot, black to ground.	Read voltage from meter; compare to default values.

Test to Perform	Multimeter Setting	Probe Positions	Procedure
Continuity (cables, fuses)	CONT	Red to lead at one end of cable; black to corresponding lead at other end.	No CONT signal indicates bad cable or bad fuse.
		For a straight-through cable, check the same pin at each end. For other types of cables, consult a cable pinout to select the correct leads.	Double-check leads and retest to be sure.
Resistance (Ohms)	Ohms	Connect one lead to each end of resistor.	Check reading; compare to rating for resistor.
			A fuse should have no resistance.
Amperage (Ammeter)	Ammeter	Red probe to positive lead of circuit (power disconnected!); black lead to negative lead running through component to be tested.	Check reading; compare to rating for component tested.

You can use a multimeter to find out whether a power supply is properly converting AC power to DC power. Here's how: Measure the DC power going from the power supply to the motherboard. A power supply that does not meet the measurement standards listed in Table 13-3 should be replaced.

Table 13-3   Acceptable Voltage Levels

Rated DC Volts	Acceptable Range
+5.0	+4.8–5.2
-5.0	-4.8–5.2
-12.0	-11.4–12.6
+12.0	+11.4–12.6
+3.3	+3.14–3.5
Power Good	+3.0–6.0

If the system monitor functions in the system BIOS do not display voltage levels (refer to Figure 13-4 for an example of a system that does display voltage levels in the BIOS) or a display is not available, you can take the voltage measurements directly from the power supply connection to the motherboard after the computer is turned on. Both 20-pin and 24-pin (ATX) power connectors are designed to be back-probed as shown in Figure 13-11; you can run the red probe through the top of the power connector to take a reading (the black probe uses the power supply enclosure or metal case frame for ground).

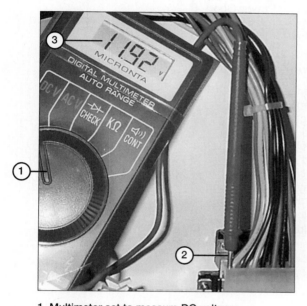

1. Multimeter set to measure DC voltage
2. Red probe inserted into +12V DC (yellow power line) connector
3. DC voltage readout

Figure 13-11   Testing the +12V line on an ATX power supply. The voltage level indicated (+11.92V) is well within limits.

Use the power supply pinouts in Figure 13-12 to determine which lines to check.

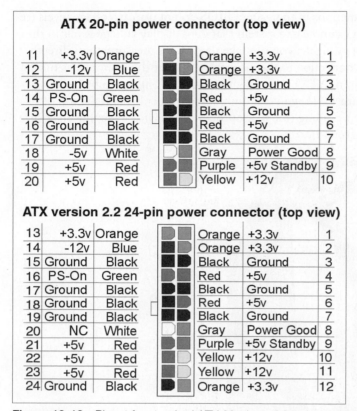

Figure 13-12   Pinout for standard ATX 20-pin and 24-pin power connectors.

Some motherboards bring these same voltage levels to a more convenient location on the motherboard for testing.

If a power supply fails any of these measurements, replace it and retest the new unit.

Power Supply Tester

You can also use a **power supply tester** to determine if a power supply is working. The power supply does not need to be removed from the computer for testing. However the 24-pin (or, on older systems, 20-pin) ATX power supply cable and the four-pin ATX12V or eight-pin EPS12V connectors must be disconnected from the motherboard for testing. The power supply must also be plugged into a working AC outlet or surge suppressor.

Figure 13-13 illustrates two types of power supply testers. One tester is a simple go-no-go tester. When you plug it into a power supply's 20-pin or 24-pin motherboard connector, the power supply starts if it is working, and the green LED turns on. If the power supply doesn't work, the green LED stays off.

The second tester has its own power switch, and checks the major voltage levels, including Power Good, when you turn it on. The display turns a light blue if the power supply tests OK. However, if any voltage level is out of range, the display turns red, as in Figure 13-13.

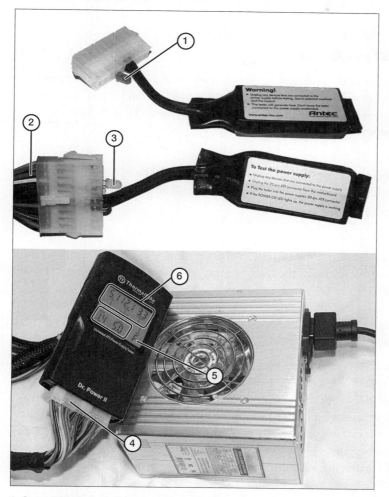

1. Green LED turns on if the power supply works
2. Power supply connected to tester
3. Power supply works – green LED is on
4. Power supply plugged into Dr. Power II tester
5. The power good line has failed, so the power supply is defective
6. All other voltage levels are OK

Figure 13-13   A simple power supply tester (top) compared to a deluxe model that tests voltages and can also test other components.

Loopback Plugs

If you use parallel (LPT) or serial (COM) ports, you can attach **loopback plugs** to these ports and run diagnostic programs to make sure that the port receives the same characters it sent. Loopback plugs and diagnostic tests are also available for USB ports.

POST Card and POST Hex Codes

As you learned earlier in this chapter, beep codes and text messages can inform you of problems with a computer. There's also a third way a PC can let you know it needs help: by transmitting hexadecimal codes to an I/O port address (usually 80h) that indicate the progress of testing and booting.

> **NOTE**   In 80h, h=hexadecimal. The codes displayed by a POST card or device are also displayed in two-digit hexadecimal code. Hexadecimal code uses the characters A-F and 0-9.

The hexadecimal codes output by the BIOS change rapidly during a normal startup process as different milestones in the boot process are reached. These codes provide vital clues about what has gone wrong when your system won't boot and you don't have a beep code or onscreen message to help you. It would be handy if systems included some way to view these codes, but only a few systems have an LED display on the motherboard to display these codes.

To monitor these codes on most systems, you need a POST card such as the one shown in Figure 13-14, available from a variety of vendors, including Elston Systems (www.elstonsystems.com), Sintech (www.sintech.cn), Ultra-X (www.ultra-x.com), and many others. The POST card shown in Figure 13-12 plugs into PCI slots, but other versions are available for use in PCIe slots, laptop mini-PCI and mini-PCIe slots (see Figure 13-15), the long-obsolete ISA slot, and LPT (printer) ports. Some POST cards use a USB port for power; these are sometimes referred to as **POST card/USB** testers.

The POST card shown in Figure 13-15 is designed for use in the mini-PCIe slot found in most recent laptops or the mini-PCI slot found in older laptops. To use it, remove the wireless network card that normally uses this slot and insert the test card in its place.

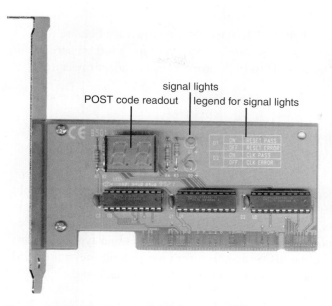

Figure 13-14   This POST card plugs in to a PCI slot.

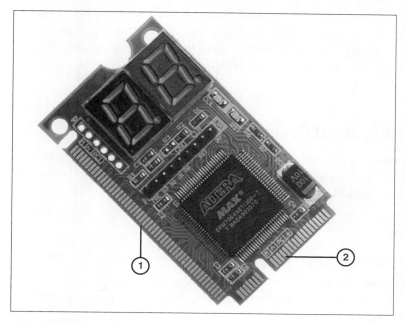

1. Mini-PCI connector
2. Mini-PCIe connector

Figure 13-15   This POST card plugs in to a mini-PCIe or mini-PCI slot.

NOTE   POST cards made especially for PCIe slots are very expensive because they perform active testing. If you want to use a simple POST card in a motherboard with only PCIe slots, you can use a mini-PCIe to PCIe adapter card to adapt the laptop POST card to desktop use.

The simplest POST cards have a two-digit LED area that displays the hex codes, whereas more complicated (and expensive) models display the code's meaning, and some also perform additional built-in tests.

The same hex code has different meanings to different BIOS versions. For example, POST code 31h (displayed as 31 on the card) means "display (video) memory read/ write test" on an AMI BIOS, but it means "test base and extended memory" on the Award BIOS, and it is not used on Phoenix BIOS. As with other types of error messages, check your manual, the BIOS manufacturer's website, or one of the third-party resources earlier in this chapter for the meaning of any given code.

TIP   The worst time to learn how to interpret a POST card is when your system is sick. On the other hand, the best way to learn to use a POST card is to plug it into a healthy system and watch the codes change during a normal system startup. Typically, the codes change quickly until the final code (often FF) is reached and the system starts. On a defective system, the codes will pause or stop when a defective item on the system is tested. The cards don't need to be left in systems routinely.

Troubleshooting Hard Drives and RAID Arrays

Problems with mass storage devices are among the most frightening to a business or individual. Use the tips and techniques in this section to help solve problems and make data recovery possible.

Read/Write Failure

Read/write failures can take place for a number of reasons, including

- **Physical damage to the drive**—Dropping any magnetic storage drive can cause damage to read/write heads and platters. The drive may start to make noise or might not spin up at all.

- **Damaged cables**—SATA cables are often included with new motherboards and are inexpensive to purchase. Swapping cables is an easy first step that often solves the problem.

- **Damaged SATA host adapter on motherboard**—Most late-model motherboards have several SATA ports; if swapping an SATA cable doesn't solve the problem, use the original cable in a different SATA port on the motherboard.

- **Overheated hard disk**—The faster a hard disk turns (higher RPM), the more likely overheating can take place, especially if airflow is restricted. To prevent overheating, install a cooling fan in front of the 3.5-inch drive bays used for your hard disk(s) and make sure it pulls air into your PC. If you have two or more drives stacked on top of each other with limited airflow, move drives to other drive bays to improve airflow.

- **Overheated CPU or chipset**—Overheated CPU, chipset, or other components can cause read/write failures. Double-check case fans, the power supply fan, and the CPU and chipset's heat sinks. Remove dust and dirt from air intakes and fans. Remove loose or failed heat sinks, remove old thermal grease, and reassemble them with properly applied thermal grease.

Slow Performance

Although SATA drives can manifest slow performance, the causes and solutions for each type of drive vary widely.

To improve slow performance with SATA hard disks, look for these problems:

- **Reduced-performance configuration of 3Gbps or 6Gbps drives**—Some 3Gbps and 6Gbps SATA drives are jumpered to run at the next slower rate to enable compatibility with older host adapters. Remove the speed-reduction jumper when it is not needed; see drive documentation for details. Figure 13-14 illustrates a jumper on a 3Gbps drive that limits its performance to 1.5Gbps.

- **Using a 3Gbps cable with a 6Gbps drive and host adapter**—SATA cables made for 6Gbps drives can also be used with slower speeds.

- **SATA host adapter configured for IDE or emulation mode**—SATA host adapters can be configured by the system BIOS (conventional or UEFI) to run in IDE (emulation) mode, RAID mode, or AHCI mode. Use AHCI mode to enable full performance because this mode supports native command queuing (NCQ) and other advanced features.

- **SATA host adapter configured to run at reduced speed**—SATA host adapters on some systems can be configured to run at different speeds, such as 6.0Gbps, 3.0Gbps, or Auto. Select **6.0Gbps** when using a 6.0Gbps drive and cabling. To enable the drive and host adapter to auto-negotiate the correct speed, select **Auto**.

1. Drive is jumpered to run at 1.5Gbps
2. Configuration pins for other settings

Figure 13-16   To run this drive at its designed 3.0Gbps interface speed, remove the jumper.

NOTE   Some SATA drives use a configuration jumper to permit power up in standby (PUIS) mode. Before removing a jumper block from an SATA hard disk, check the drive's documentation at the vendor's website. Some drives are marked with incorrect jumper block legends.

To improve slow performance with SSDs, look for the following issues:

- **Connecting the drive to a slow SATA host adapter**—Early SSDs were designed for 3Gbps SATA interfaces, but most recent models support the faster 6Gbps interface. When using an SSD on a system with a mixture of 3Gbps and 6Gbps SATA ports, be sure to use the 6Gbps ports.

- **The partition may be misaligned**—Windows automatically creates the first partition on an SSD so that it is on a page boundary to provide maximum performance. However, if you do not use the entire SSD for a single partition, additional partitions might be misaligned (starting in the middle of a page rather than on a page boundary). Misaligned partitions cause slow read/write/reallocate performance. Instead of using Disk Management to create additional partitions, use the command-line program DISKPART and specify Align=1024 as part of the Create partition command. See http://support.microsoft.com/kb/300415 for the complete syntax.

TIP   Intel's white paper, "Partition Alignment of Intel SSDs for Achieving Maximum Performance and Endurance," available at http://www.intel.ph/content/dam/www/public/us/en/documents/technology-briefs/ssd-partition-alignment-tech-brief.pdf, provides methods for detecting partition misalignment and for realignment for SSDs on systems running Windows and Linux. The information is useful for any brand of SSD.

- **The TRIM command is not enabled for the drive**—If the drive does not support TRIM, you must periodically run a utility provided by the drive vendor to reallocate deleted drive sectors. If the drive supports TRIM and you are using it with Windows 7/8/8.1/10, Windows needs to be optimized for use with SSDs.

- **Not optimizing the operating system for use with SSDs**—Although Windows 7/8/8.1/10 are designed to disable SuperFetch, defragment, and other services that can slow down SSD performance, Windows does not always detect an SSD as an SSD. Use the SSD Tweaker Utility (www.elpamsoft.com) to configure Windows for maximum performance with SSDs.

TIP Rather than enabling TRIM in real time, Linux users should run the command fstrim periodically and use the Ext4 file system. For details, see https://wiki.archlinux.org/index.php/Solid_State_Drives.

Loud Clicking Noise

Magnetic hard disk drives are generally quiet. Loud noises coming from a drive can have at least two causes:

- **A loud clicking noise is typically caused by repeated re-reads of defective disk surfaces by the hard disk drive heads**—This is typically a sign of a failing drive. Replace the hard disk immediately after making a backup copy.

- **Humming noises can be caused by rapid head movement on a normally functioning hard disk**—This noise can be reduced or eliminated by enabling Automatic Acoustic Management (AAM), a feature of most recent hard disks. Some vendors provide a downloadable acoustic management tool. These reduce head speed to reduce noise, and may reduce drive performance as a result.

NOTE A softer clicking noise is typical of hard disks when the system is in sleep mode. By changing the hard disk drive's power management settings, this noise can be eliminated. To learn more, see http://disablehddapm.blogspot.com/2011/12/disabling-hard-disk-drive-advanced.html

Failure to Boot

The primary hard drive is almost always the boot drive. **Failure to boot** can be caused by:

- **Boot sequence does not specify system hard disk, or lists system hard disk after other drives with nonbootable media**—Use the Boot Sequence dialog in the system BIOS to configure the hard disk as either the first boot device or as the second boot device after the optical drive or USB. If a USB flash drive is listed as the first boot device and the system is started with a nonbootable USB flash drive connected, the system boot process will stop and display a boot error.

- **CMOS settings have been corrupted and system cannot find a bootable drive**—Reconfigure the CMOS settings, specify the system drive as a boot drive, and restart the system. Replace the battery if the settings continue to be corrupted.

- **The BCD (boot configuration data) store used by Windows to control disk booting has been corrupted**—To learn how to fix this problem, see "Failure to Boot," p.1082, Chapter 22.

Drive Not Recognized

A **drive not recognized** issue can involve problems with cabling, power, BIOS settings, or hard disk failure. If the hard disk is running (you can usually hear faint sounds from a working hard disk), check the following:

- **Bus-powered USB hard disk not recognized**—A bus-powered USB 2.0 or USB 3.0/3.1 hard disk needs 500mA of power to run (and some temporarily use more power to spin up). Some computers don't provide enough power in their root hubs (built-in USB ports) to support a bus-powered hard disk, and bus-powered hubs can provide only 100mA of power per port. Connect the drive to another port on a different root hub (each pair of USB ports is a root hub) or a self-powered USB hub, or use a Y-cable to pull power from two USB ports. Figure 13-17 illustrates a USB 3.0/3.1 Y-cable.

- **USB, FireWire, or Thunderbolt drive not recognized**—If the data cable between the drive and the port is loose, the drive will not be recognized. Reconnect the cable to both the drive and the port and the drive should be recognized. If the drive is connected to a front-mounted port, make sure the port header is securely connected to the motherboard.

- **SATA Hard Disk or SSD drive not recognized**—Loose or missing power or data cables causes this problem. Shut down the computer, disconnect it from AC power, and reconnect power and data cables. If you use Y-splitters or

converters to provide power to some drives, keep in mind that these can fail.
See Figure 13-18.

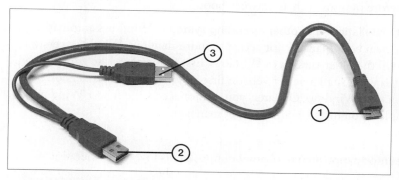

1. mini-USB 3.0 connector to drive
2. USB 3.0 connector (data and power)
3. USB 3.0 Y-connector (power only)

Figure 13-17 USB 3.0/3.1 Y-cable provides bus power from two USB ports.

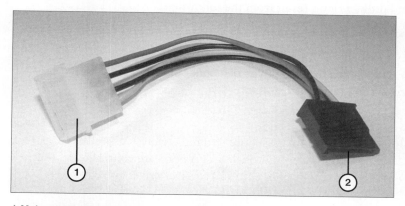

1. Molex power connector
2. SATA power connector

Figure 13-18 A Molex to SATA power converter cable is a potential point of failure.

OS Not Found

An **OS not found** (operating system not found) error during boot can be caused by:

- **Nonbootable disk in USB Drive**—If a USB drive is listed before the hard disk in the boot sequence and it contains a nonbootable disk, the computer displays an error message that it couldn't find the operating system. Remove the USB flash drive and restart.

- **Boot sequence doesn't list hard disk**—Restart the computer, start the BIOS setup procedure, and make sure the hard disk is listed as a bootable drive and is listed before options such as network boot.

- **Incorrect installation of another operating system**—Windows automatically sets up its own boot manager for access to more than one Windows version if you install the older version of Windows first followed by the later version. However, if you install a newer version first and install an older version later or install a non-Windows OS later, you cannot access the newer Windows version unless you install a custom boot manager.

NOTE   For more information about solving boot problems involving operating system issues, see Chapter 22.

RAID Not Found

RAID not found problems can result from the following:

- **RAID function disabled in system BIOS**—Reconfigure SATA ports used for RAID as RAID and restart the system.

- **Power or data cables to RAID drives disconnected**—Reconnect cables to RAID drive(s) and restart the system.

NOTE   Some motherboards offer RAID support from the chipset as well as a separate RAID controller chip. Be sure to identify which SATA ports are controlled by the chipset versus a separate RAID controller chip and connect drives accordingly.

RAID Stops Working

A RAID failure is caused by the failure of one or more of the disk drives in the RAID array. Take the following steps if a single drive failure occurs:

- **RAID 0**—Determine which drive has failed. Replace it and follow the vendor's recommendations to re-create the array. Restore the latest backup. Any data that has not been backed up is lost.

- **RAID 1, RAID 10, and RAID 5**—Determine which drive has failed. Replace it. Follow the procedures provided by the RAID vendor to rebuild the array.

If both drives have failed in a RAID 0 or RAID 1 array, you must rebuild the array with new drives and restore the latest backup. Any data that has not been backed up is lost.

If two or more drives have failed in a RAID 10 or RAID 5 array, your recovery options might vary according to the exact configuration of the array. See the RAID vendor's procedures for details and recovery options.

Proprietary Crash Screens (BSOD/PinWheel)

> **NOTE**   For information about solving system crashes involving operating system issues, see Chapter 22.

S.M.A.R.T. Errors

Both Serial ATA (SATA) hard disks and older Parallel ATA (PATA or ATA/IDE) hard disk support a detect-warning feature known as Self-Monitoring, Analysis, and Reporting Technology, or S.M.A.R.T. (also referred to as SMART). S.M.A.R.T. monitors internal hard disks and warns of impending failure. Typical items monitored include:

- Drive temperature
- Read retries
- Slow spin up
- Too many bad sectors.

Typical **S.M.A.R.T.** warnings include:

- Hard disk failure is imminent
- A hard drive in your system reports that it may fail
- Smart failure imminent, back up your data

When S.M.A.R.T. errors are displayed, back up the system immediately. Then, to determine if the drive is actually bad or if the message was a false positive, download and run the disk testing software provided by your system or drive vendor. The long or complete tests detect surface problems and might also swap defective sectors for good sectors. For more details, see the "Using Hard Disk Diagnostics" section on page 611 of this chapter.

When Should You Check SMART Attributes?

Under normal operating conditions, you should test your hard disks every month using a program such as CHKDSK (included in Windows) or a vendor-supplied hard disk utility and review their SMART attributes for errors. On a portable or laptop hard disk, I recommend checking twice a month, because these drives are in greater danger of being physically damaged or overheating.

Although third-party S.M.A.R.T. attribute testing apps are available from many sources, drive manufacturers recommend using their own apps, as they are more reliable in interpreting test results and warning of immediate problems.

Recommended Hardware and Software Tools

If read/write errors or other problems that could lead to data loss occur, become familiar with the following tools and techniques you can use to recover data and restore an ailing drive to health.

Screwdriver

A **screwdriver** with interchangeable tips is extremely useful for removing drives from laptop or desktop computers. Keep in mind that laptop computers use 2.5-inch or smaller drives and tiny screws, so jeweler's Phillips-head screwdrivers in sizes 1, 0, and 00 are a must-have.

Drive Enclosures

The easiest way to retrieve data from a drive you believe is working but is installed in a failed system is to move the drive into a drive **enclosure**. Drive enclosures include a PATA or SATA interface internally and a USB 2.0, USB 3.0, eSATA, or FireWire interface externally. A bridge component converts one type of signal to the other. Figure 13-19 illustrates a typical drive enclosure designed for SATA hard disks.

When connected, a hard disk in an drive enclosure is detected like any other external drive. Assuming the drive is working properly, the data on the drive can be copied to a different computer.

As an alternative to a drive enclosure, you can use an external drive dock. It has a slot on one side to allow an SATA hard disk (or a PATA hard disk in older dock models) to be plugged in for temporary access (see Figure 13-20). Because laptop and desktop SATA drives use exactly the same power and data connectors, most docks, including this example, have a cutout for laptop drives.

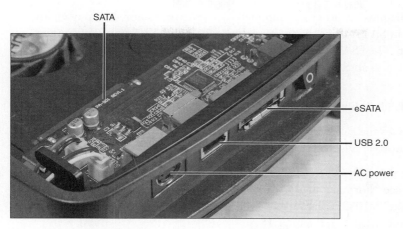

Figure 13-19   A typical external drive enclosure for SATA drives; this example connects to eSATA and USB ports.

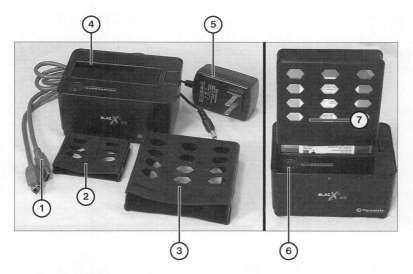

1. **USB 3.0 Type B cable**
2. **2.5-inch hard disk protective sleeve**
3. **3.5-inch hard disk protective sleeve**
4. **Drive dock cutout for 2.5-inch drive**
5. **AC adapter**
6. **On/off switch for drive dock**
7. **3.5-inch drive in protective sleeve**

Figure 13-20   A typical USB 3.0 external drive enclosure for SATA drives.

One limitation of drive enclosures and docks, especially when connected to USB ports, is that the SATA (or PATA)/USB bridge prevents low-level access to the drive for disk diagnostics programs supplied by the drive vendor. If you need low-level access to an SATA drive, use a drive dock with an eSATA port and connect to an eSATA port. The eSATA port can be on the port cluster or can be an eSATA header connected to an SATA port header on the motherboard.

Windows-Based Disk Tools

Windows includes the following disk tools: CHKDSK (error-checking), FORMAT, Recycle Bin, Bootrec, Diskpart, and defragmentation.

To learn more about Diskpart, see "Diskpart," p.751, Chapter 15. To learn more about Format, see "Format," p.745, Chapter 15. To learn more about Bootrec, see "Failure to Boot," p.1082, Chapter 22. To learn more about Disk Management, see "Disk Management," p.775, Chapter 15.

Recycle Bin

Recycle Bin holds files and folders that have been removed from Computer/ Windows Explorer/File Explorer/This PC. When you select an item and press the Delete key, Windows asks if you want to move the item to Recycle Bin. Answering **Yes** moves the file to Recycle Bin. Once in Recycle Bin, the item can be retrieved until the bin runs out of space, forcing the discarding of the item.

However, if you hold down the Shift key while pressing the Delete key, answering **Yes** to the deletion question bypasses the Recycle Bin. You must use third-party data recovery software to restore the items(s) you deleted.

Figure 13-21 compares the deletion prompts.

To retrieve an item from the Recycle Bin:

Step 1.   Open the Recycle Bin from the Windows desktop.

Step 2.   Select an item to retrieve.

Step 3.   Click or tap **Restore This Item**.

To empty the Recycle Bin:

Step 1.   Open the Recycle Bin from the Windows desktop.

Step 2.   Click or tap **Empty the Recycle Bin**.

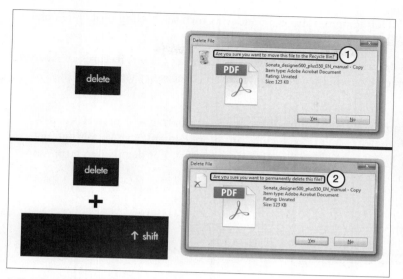

1. Delete key moves file to Recycle Bin
2. Shift+Delete deletes file

Figure 13-21 Preparing to move files to the Recycle Bin with Delete versus discarding them with Shift+Delete.

Defragmentation

Over time, a hard disk becomes fragmented as temporary and data files are created and deleted, particularly when the full capacity of the hard disk is used.

When a file can no longer be stored in a contiguous group of allocation units, Windows stores the files in as many groups of allocation units as necessary and reassembles the file when it is next accessed. The extra time needed to save and read the file reduces system performance. Windows includes a disk **defragmentation tool** to help regain lost read/write performance.

CAUTION Do not run defragmentation on a flash memory drive or an SSD.

Defragment can be run in the following ways:

- From the Accessories menu's System Tools submenu (Disk Defragmenter; Windows Vista/7)
- From a drive's properties sheet's Tools tab (Defragment Now)
- From the command line: **defrag** (type **defrag /?** for options)

Windows' Disk Defragmenter utility includes its own scheduling tool. The default schedule is weekly.

The Windows defragmenter in Windows 7 and newer versions features an Analyze button that determines whether defragmentation is necessary (see Figure 13-22).

NOTE There is no Analyze button in Vista; however, Defrag will analyze the disk automatically before defragmenting. If you want more control over Vista's defragment feature, use Vista's command-line defrag.exe utility. For details, see http://support.microsoft.com/kb/942092.

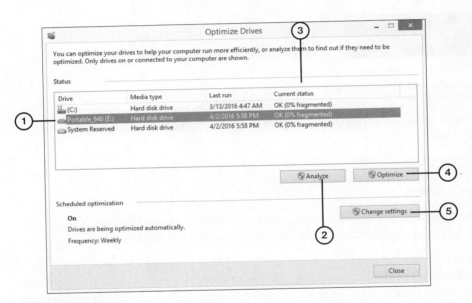

1. Selected drive
2. Click or tap to analyze
3. Analysis results
4. Click or tap to optimize now
5. Click or tap to change optimization settings

Figure 13-22 Disk Defragmenter's analysis indicates these drives have no fragmentation (Windows 8.1 shown).

Small hard disks with many changes to their contents are the most likely to need defragmentation, especially if they use a FAT-based file system. Linux and OS X drives hardly ever need defragmentation because their file systems work differently than Windows file systems do.

Linux and OS X users with hard disk drives (not SSDs) can achieve the effects of defragging by copying the disk contents to a different disk, erasing the original disk, and transferring the files back to the original disk.

> **NOTE**   A good comparison of Windows and Linux file systems, along with tips for defragmenting or copying/recopying files for Linux, is available at https://www.ma-ketecheasier.com/defragment-linux/. Copy/recopy techniques for OS X are available at https://discussions.apple.com/docs/DOC-4032.

CHKDSK (Error-Checking)

Windows includes the **CHKDSK** program to check disk drives for errors. It can be run from the Windows GUI (where it is known as Error-Checking) or from the command line.

Windows 8/8.1's version (see Figure 13-23) is able to test and repair the system drive without rebooting the system.

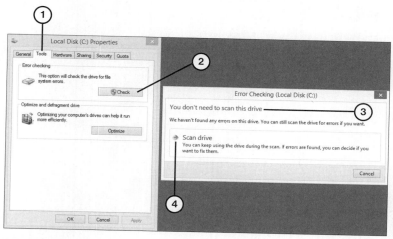

1. Tools tab
2. Click or tap to check drive
3. Drive status
4. Click or tap to scan drive

Figure 13-23   Windows C: Properties Sheet and Error Checking dialogs after the Check now button has been clicked (Windows 8.1).

TIP   It's no coincidence that error-checking (Check now) is listed before Defragmentation (Optimize) in the Windows disk Tools menu. You should check the drive for errors first before you perform a defrag operation.

Windows Vista/7's version (see Figure 13-24) provides options to automatically fix file system errors and attempt the recovery of bad sectors with CHKDSK. If you select the option to automatically fix file system errors on the system drive, CHKDSK will be scheduled to run at the next restart. This is necessary because CHKDSK requires exclusive access to the drive. CHKDSK performs a three-phase test of the drive after the system is rebooted but before the Windows desktop appears. The results are reported after the Windows desktop appears.

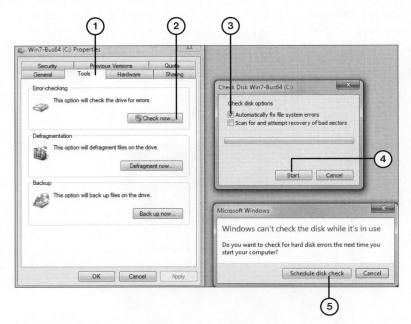

1. Tools tab
2. Click to start process
3. To check drive without making changes, clear this checkbox
4. Click to continue
5. Click to schedule check with file system error repair on next reboot

Figure 13-24   Scheduling a disk check after reboot with Windows 7's error-checking.

If a non-system drive is tested with Windows Vista/7 with the file system error check enabled, the check happens immediately, and the results are posted immediately. A post-check report like the one shown in Figure 13-25 is displayed if any errors are detected on either a system or non-system disk. To view details as in Figure 13-25, click the Show details down arrow.

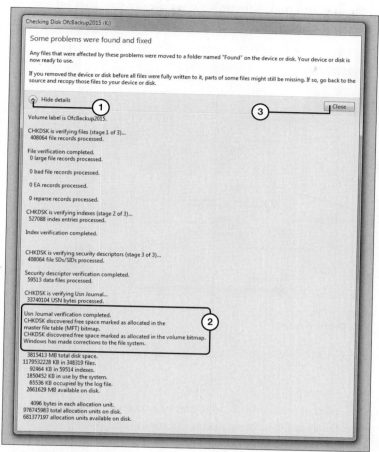

1. Toggle to show/hide details
2. Repairs performed
3. Click to close report

Figure 13-25   Details of repairs to a disk performed with Windows 7's error-checking.

You can also run CHKDSK from the command prompt in elevated mode. For options, type **CHKDSK /?** from the command prompt.

Using Hard Disk Diagnostics

Most hard disk vendors provide diagnostic programs that can be used to test drives for errors. The latest versions of these programs can be obtained from the drive vendors' websites.

Typically, these programs offer a quick and a long test option. To determine whether a hard disk is functioning, run the quick test first (see Figure 13-26). If the drive passes, use the long test to determine whether the drive is working within specifications.

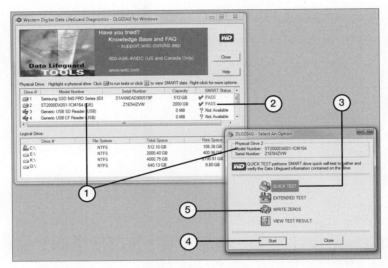

1. Selected drive
2. Current SMART status
3. Selected test
4. Click to start test
5. Overwrites data

Figure 13-26 Performing a quick test on a Western Digital hard disk with vendor-supplied diagnostic software.

During the long test, defective areas on the drive can be replaced by spare capacity built in to the drive. Because defective areas on the disk might not be able to be moved to another location, drive vendors often recommend you perform a full backup before testing a hard disk.

Using Data Recovery Software

If you cannot restore a hard disk to health but do not have up-to-date backups of the data it contains, you might need to use **data recovery software** to attempt to locate and rescue your data.

CAUTION To avoid data loss, never install a data recovery program on a drive that you are attempting to recover data from. And make sure you select a program that copies the data located to another drive. Because the need for data recovery is often caused by a failing drive, it's essential to make sure the data is safe after it is recovered.

There are three levels of data recovery software to consider:

- Do-it-yourself data recovery
- Commercial data recovery software
- Data recovery services

By booting with a Linux Live CD or Live USB distribution (distro) that supports Windows file systems (most systems use NTFS), you can often recover your data by copying it to a different drive. The KNOPPIX Linux Live CD and Live USB (http://www.knoppix.org/) and Parted Magic (https://partedmagic.com/) distros are often used for this purpose.

Many vendors offer data recovery software, and most provide trial versions that you can use to preview your results. These programs work by bypassing normal disk structures, such as partitions and root directories, to access the disk contents directly.

If you cannot retrieve data with a bootable disc, USB drive, or with data recovery software, your last alternative is to use a data recovery service. These services can cost hundreds or thousands of dollars, but if you need to recover large amounts of customer data, accounting data, or line-of-business information, these services might be worth the money. These services can be performed remotely on drives that don't have physical damage to circuit boards or read-write heads, but some recovery services also use clean rooms that enable the safe dismantling of damaged drives so that defective read-write heads or other components can be replaced.

Troubleshooting Video, Projector, and Display Issues

Desktop, laptop, and mobile users alike need displays that work properly. Use the following sections to learn how to diagnose and fix problems with displays.

VGA Mode

A Windows system starts in **VGA mode** if **Low-resolution mode** or **Safe Mode** has been selected at startup (see Chapter 22 for details) or if the correct drivers are not available. Check the following:

- Make sure correct chipset (motherboard/system) drivers have been installed—Many business desktops and most laptops use CPU-integrated graphics. Until chipset drivers are installed, these are used as ordinary VGA GPUs. Download the latest system or motherboard drivers from the vendor.

- If the system is being upgraded from integrated graphics to a separate video card, be sure to install the new drivers after the card is installed—Download the latest graphics from the card vendor or GPU vendor: www.amd.com (Radeon, Fire GL) or www.nvidia.com (GeForce, Quadro).

■ If the system is being upgraded by replacing an existing video card with a new video card with a different manufacturer's chipset, be sure to uninstall the current video card drivers and support apps from Device Manager and Programs—Install the new drivers after the new card is installed.

Until the new card's drivers are installed, the card will function as a VGA card (no 3D acceleration, limited video modes).

No Image on Screen

The possible causes and solutions for no image on screen vary according to the computer and display type.

Laptop/Tablet/Convertible 2-1

With a laptop or tablet, the most likely cause for no image on the built-in screen is a failure of the LCD-CCFL, LCD-LED, or OLED display, particularly if there is no external display plugged in.

If an external display is plugged in, the computer might be configured to use the external display only. To quickly determine if the built-in display is working, turn off the external display, shut down the computer, and unplug the display from the computer's video port. Turn the computer back on and see if the built-in display now works. If it does, then configure the built-in display as primary and the external display as a mirror or as an extended desktop. Note that OS X is not designed to use an external display only unless it is being run in keyboard-closed mode.

Desktop Computer

If an external display has no image on screen when it is the only display, check power, display cables, and input setting on the display. If these check out, use a flashlight to determine if there is any image on-screen. If you see one, the LCD-CCFL backlight has failed. If you don't see any image, the display has failed.

If a secondary or additional display or projector has no image, set the display properties for extended desktop or mirror as desired.

Projector

Check the lens cap or shutter and make sure it is open. Check the image source selection. Make sure the computer source is configured to use the projector as an extended desktop or mirror of the primary display. Check power and video cables.

Overheat Shutdown

Projectors shut down when they overheat. To avoid overheat shutdown, check the following:

- Clean or replace filters when recommended. Projectors with filters usually display a message on-screen when it is time to clean or replace the filter.

- Make sure the projector has adequate ventilation.

- Check air intakes and exhaust ports for dust and dirt and clean as necessary.

- Use lower brightness setting on projectors to reduce heat.

- Be sure to allow the projector to cool down completely before removing it from power.

A video card (GPU) that overheats will usually display screen artifacts before shutting down.

Dead Pixels

Dead pixels (black pixels) typically result from manufacturing defects in an LCD screen. Check with the manufacturer of the panel or laptop to determine the number of dead pixels that are needed to qualify for screen replacement.

Some "dead" pixels are actually stuck on (bright) or off (dark). There are a variety of ways to solve this problem. They include:

- Navigate to the JScreenFix website (www.jscreenfix.com) and start the pixel fixer app. Drag the app window to the area of your screen with the pixel problem and leave it over the area for up to 10 minutes. JScreenFix uses HTML5 and JavaScript controls in the web browser to work. Works with any LCD or OLED device including mobile devices.

- Gently massage the stuck pixel with a stylus or other objects with a blunt, narrow end. See http://www.wikihow.com/Fix-a-Stuck-Pixel-on-an-LCD-Monitor for illustrations.

- For Windows systems, download and run the UDPixel utility (http://ud-pix.free.fr/index.php). Requires .NET Framework 2.0, which can be added to Windows 7/8/8.1/10 through Control Panel's Add/Remove Windows Features.

Artifacts

Display or screen **artifacts** (distorted shapes, colors, pixelated images, scrambled text, lines through an image) can be caused by an overheated GPU, projector, overclocked GPU, overcompressed graphics, overcompressed video, and enlarging a low-resolution video or image to a higher-resolution display.

To solve overheating problems with a projector, see "Overheat Shutdowns." To solve overheating problems with a GPU (video card):

- Check the card's cooling fan
- Check the CPU heatsink/fan with CPU-integrated video
- Disable overclocking and return the card/system to normal clock speeds

To solve problems with video or graphics compression and sizing:

- Capture or shoot videos and photos in high resolution, best quality and reduce to needed size.
- Use H.264 compression for MPEG-4 video to obtain high video quality at a reasonable size.
- Save JPEG at Adobe Photoshop quality settings of 8 or higher (maximum quality is 12) or 75 percent or higher quality (other photo editors) to obtain high photo quality at a reasonable size.
- Always work from an original image for conversions and editing. Editing and converting a compressed version leads to loss of image quality over time.

Incorrect Color Patterns

Incorrect color patterns on a projector can have several causes:

- Check the signal type in the projector menu and change it if incorrect.
- If one LCD panel (red, green, or blue) is failing in an LCD projector, replace the panel. Blue panels often fail before others due to ultraviolet light.
- On a DLP projector, check the LED light sources (red, green, or blue) or dichroic mirrors.
- Clean the projector LCD panels if odd-colored specks are visible.
- If a laptop has been serviced or upgraded, the LCD ribbon connector to the motherboard might have been damaged. If an external display works correctly, check the LCD ribbon cable inside the laptop.
- Check a VGA cable for bent or broken pins (some pins are not present by default). Check all video cables for cracked outer casings and loose or damaged connectors.

Dim Image

A **dim image** can be caused by settings issues or by equipment failure. Check the following:

- Check screen brightness control on the displays or projector.

- If a display management program is being run (Intel, NVIDIA, AMD install these as part of their 3D GPU driver), check its settings.

- On a laptop, tablet, or mobile device, check the built-in screen brightness setting.

- On a projector, check the projector bulb. Some of them become milky, which reduces light output, near the end of their service life.

- On a device that uses a CCFL backlight, check the inverter. A failing inverter can cause a dim display before it fails. The inverter can be replaced separately from the LCD panel or backlight.

Flickering Image

A **flickering image** can have many causes:

- Before looking at hardware replacements, be sure to try updating the GPU (video card) or chipset drivers.

- On displays using an LCD-CCFL backlight, flickering could be caused by a failing inverter or a failing backlight—Inverters are relatively inexpensive and can sometimes be replaced without a complete teardown. Backlights cost more and it may make more sense to buy a replacement LCD screen or retire the computer or display.

- On any type of LCD display (CCFL or LED backlight), loose internal cables can cause flickering. Some 2-in-1 convertible devices (tablet/laptop) have hinge problems that can lead to flicker.

- On desktop computers, check the power connector to the PCIe card (if it uses a separate power cable) and the power supply itself—If the problem happens after the computer's been running for a while, it could indicate a heat-related problem.

Distorted Image

A **distorted image** can have several causes and solutions, including the following:

- If image tearing or distortion occurs in 3D games only, change video drivers—In most cases, the newest video driver is recommended, but in a few cases with certain games, the best short-term fix might be to install an older driver. Check driver versions with Device Manager's properties sheet or the proprietary app installed by your GPU or video card maker.

- Distortion with DisplayPort connections can be caused by problems with the way some DisplayPort cables and connectors are manufactured—If you can use a different connection (DVI or HDMI) between a system and a display and the problem is no longer present, replace the DisplayPort cable.

Distorted Geometry

Distorted geometry (pincushion, barrel, and others) common with CRT displays are not present on LCD or LED displays. However, other factors can cause issues:

- If a projector lens is tilted upward or downward toward the screen, keystoning (non-parallel sides on the projected image) is the result (see Figure 13-27). Most projectors have keystone correction options in their display menus or control panels.

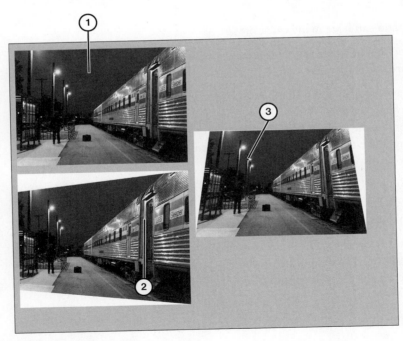

1. Normal projected image
2. Horizontal distortion (right side of screen closer to projector)
3. Keystone distortion (bottom of screen closer to projector)

Figure 13-27 Simulations of normal, keystoning, and horizontal distortions with projectors.

- If a projector is not at a 90-degree angle to the projection screen, the image will be larger on one side than the other (see Figure 13-27). Some projectors have adjustments for this problem. If not, adjust the projector or screen position until the image is the same size across the screen.

- When the projector is tilted or is not at a 90-degree angle to the screen, parts of the picture might also be out of focus.

- Curved screen HDTVs have subtle geometric distortions that increase at greater off-axis viewing angles. Place seating closer to the middle of the display.

- When viewing 4:3 aspect ratio content on a widescreen display (16:9 or similar), using the zoom option on the HDTV to fill the screen can distort the edges of the image. Try different zoom options or advise the user that the best picture is at the original aspect ratio.

Burn-In

Burn-in, the persistent display of a "ghost" image on-screen that was displayed previously, even after the current screen contents have changed, can affect both LCD and plasma displays.

LCD Displays

With LCD displays, stuck pixels are the usual cause. Programs that run constantly changing patterns across the area, such as JScreenFix or UDPixel, can be used to fix the problem.

Another solution is to create an all-white image using a graphics program, set it as the screen saver, and turn down the display brightness. Leave the screen saver running about as long as the original image was on-screen.

To avoid image persistence with IPS displays (the most common type of LCD display in use, offering wide viewing angles), Apple recommends using display sleep to turn off the display when idle. To eliminate a persistent image, enable the screen saver to come on before display sleep and run it as long as the persistent image was originally on-screen. For more information, see https://support.apple.com/en-us/HT202580.

Plasma Displays

Plasma displays use phosphors, which can wear unevenly over time. This was also the cause of burn-in on CRT displays. To avoid either temporary or permanent image persistence, try the following:

- For customers who watch mainly 4:3 ratio TV or movie content, advise periodically switching to full-screen (zoomed) mode to avoid black bar persistence on the sides of the image.

- Use the screen clean (screen washing) option available on some plasma HDTVs—This puts a constantly changing display across the entire screen.

TIP For plasma and LCD display/HDTV users, there are many YouTube videos that can be played to help fix image retention. To play these on an HDTV, use the HDTV's Smart TV feature or a set-top box such as a Roku or Amazon Fire TV to go to the YouTube channel. To find these videos, use the search "image retention fix."

Oversized Images and Icons

Oversized images and icons in Windows can be caused by the following issues:

- Booting in Limited resolution ("VGA" mode)—On Windows Vista/7, selecting this mode from the special startup (F8) options menu sets the display for 640×480 resolution. Many apps cannot be used at this resolution, and menus and icons are enormous (see Figure 13-28). To fix, restart the system and select normal resolutions from the Display properties sheet in Control Panel.

NOTE In Windows 8/8.1/10, the Limited resolution option chooses the lowest resolution available on the display's Resolution slider in Control Panel.

- Using the Change the Size of All Items option in Display > Resolution > Make Text Larger or Smaller—100 percent is the default setting. If too large a custom size is selected (such as 200 percent; see Figure 13-29), the effect is the same as if a very low resolution was selected. To fix, select Smaller (see Figure 13-30), log off the user, and log the user back in again.

Tip For users who need larger text, use the Change only the text size dialog on this menu.

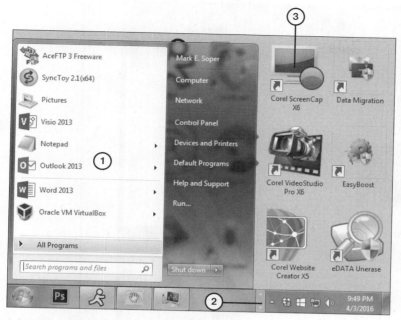

1. Start menu occupies more than half the screen
2. To see all running apps, use the vertical scroll on the taskbar
3. Enormous icons

Figure 13-28   Windows 7 after starting in Limited Resolution (640×480) mode.

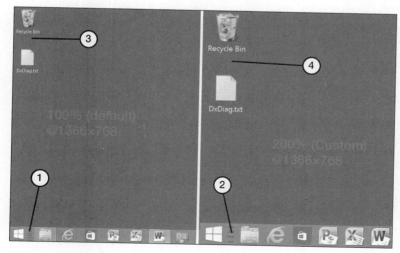

1. Normal taskbar
2. Enlarged taskbar
3. Normal icon size
4. Enlarged icon size

Figure 13-29   Windows 8.1 desktop at normal (left) and 200 percent (right) magnifications.

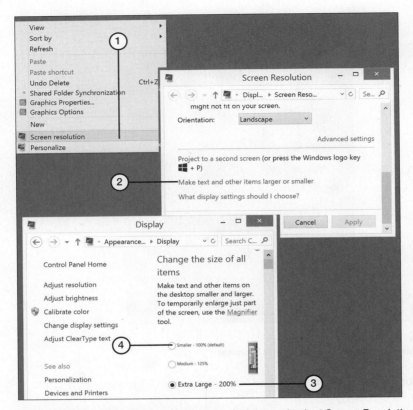

1. Step 1. Right-click or press and hold on desktop and select Screen Resolution
2. Step 2. Click or tap Make text and other items larger or smaller
3. Current percentage
4. Select 100%. Log out and log back in again to finish.

Figure 13-30   Resetting a custom item size setting (Windows 8.1 shown).

Network Troubleshooting

Keeping a network running smoothly can be challenging because a single problem could have multiple causes and solutions. Understand the problems and solutions in the following sections are not just for the 220-901 exam but to aid in your ongoing work.

No Connectivity

No connectivity errors can have several causes:

- Check the power supply going to the hub, switch, wireless access point, or router. Reset the device.

- If only the users connected to a new switch that is connected to an existing switch lose their network connection, check the connection between the existing switch and the new one. Most switches have an uplink port that is used to connect an additional switch. You can either use the uplink port or the regular port next to the uplink port, but not both. Connect the computer using the port next to the uplink port to another port to make the uplink port available for connecting the new hub or switch.

- If the uplink port appears to be connected properly, check the cable. Uplink ports perform the crossover for the user, enabling you to use an ordinary network cable to add a hub or switch.

TIP   If you use a crossover cable, you must connect the new hub or switch through a regular port, not the uplink port.

APIPA/Link-Local Address

An **APIPA/Link-Local address** (IPv4 169.254.x.x range) is assigned to a computer if the DHCP server (which assigns IP addresses) cannot be reached. This is one cause of limited connectivity.

Check the device that provides DHCP service (usually a router on a SOHO network). If that device is working properly, restart the computer and check the IP address after the computer restarts. If the problem persists, check for a bad cable or inability to connect to a wireless network.

Limited Connectivity/Local Connectivity

The yellow ! symbol next to the network icon in the Windows taskbar (see Figure 13-31) indicates the network has **limited connectivity** (the Internet cannot be reached), also called **local connectivity**.

1. Click up arrow to see hidden notifications
2. Wired network connection has limited connectivity

Figure 13-31   Connection problem (Windows 7).

Before following the next steps, check connectivity on other devices on the network. If all devices can't connect:

- To diagnose this problem with Windows Vista/7, open the Network and Sharing Center and click the red X in the Internet connection dialog. This launches an Internet troubleshooter. Follow the troubleshooter's recommendations.

- With Windows 8/8.1/10, use Search to locate and start the Internet trouble-shooter. Follow the troubleshooter's recommendations.

- For connection problems with any OS, turn off the broadband modem or access device, wait about a minute, and then turn it on. Then, turn off the router, wait about a minute, and turn it on again. If the problem was with the broadband modem/access device, this should solve the problem. If not, contact the ISP as the problem might be on their network.

- If only one device is affected, disconnect from a wireless network and recon-nect to it. For a wired network, restart the computer.

Local Connectivity

See "Limited Connectivity" earlier for details.

Intermittent Connectivity

Intermittent connectivity can be caused by:

- Dead spots (poor signal) on a wireless network—Relocate the wireless router.

- Too many networks using same channel—Use a wireless network scanning device or app to see local wireless networks and their channels. Reconfigure network to use a channel with less traffic.

- EMI or RFI interference with wired network— Alarm systems, elevators, fluorescent lights, and motors can interfere with networks running UTP. Switch to STP cable or relocate cables away from interference.

- Defective network cable, such as cracked outer jacket or broken locking tab—Replace cable.

- Problems with ISP's Internet service—Contact ISP after troubleshooting local network if problem persists.

IP Conflict

An **IP conflict** results if two devices on a network have the same IP address. A common cause is if a DHCP server assigns the same address that has been assigned manually to a device on the network. Configure devices with manual IP addresses to use a different range of addresses than those used by the DHCP server.

Slow Transfer Speeds

Significant drops in network performance and slow transfer speeds can be traced to a variety of causes, including

- Damage to cables, connectors, hubs, switches, and routers—Check cables for damage.

- Connecting high-speed NICs to low-speed switches— When using Gigabit Ethernet switches and routers, confirm that all devices on the network (switches, router, cables, and NICs) meet Gigabit Ethernet standards (CAT 5e or 6, 6a, 7 cable) and are configured to use Gigabit Ethernet.

- Fast local connections but sluggish Internet connections can be caused by too much demand for the Internet connection (may be due to multiple downloads or streaming services) or Internet congestion outside the home or office.

- RFI/EMI interference with wireless networks—Check wireless phones and microwave ovens to see if their use interferes with the network. Move router away from interference sources. Switch to a wireless 802.11ac router and NICs and use 5GHz band to avoid most of this type of interference.

Low RF Signal

A **low RF signal** on a wireless network can be caused by:

- Interference from other wireless networks—Use a wireless network analyzer to determine the least-used channels for your network and switch to one of those channels.

- Concrete or masonry walls in the building—If it is not possible to relocate the router, add repeaters. In residential construction, consider using powerline repeaters.

- Improper antenna positioning on the router or NICs with adjustable antennas—Follow manufacturer's recommendations.

- The router or NICs do not support MIMO—MIMO (multiple in, multiple out) antennas are characteristic of higher-speed Wireless-N (300Mbp or faster-rated hardware) and all Wireless-AC equipment. Upgrade the router to the best Wireless-AC model in the clients' price range, even if clients are using Wireless-N, as it will improve performance at a given distance. Upgrading clients to Wireless-AC as well will improve performance even more.

NOTE Some Wireless-AC routers now support multi-user MIMO (MU-MIMO). MU-MIMO enables a router to make MIMO connections to multiple users at the same time. MU-MIMO requires routers and client device support, but it can be implemented on client devices that have only a single antenna. As firmware and drivers updates become available to enable MU-MIMO on routers and client devices, MU-MIMO will become more common. To learn more, see www.techhive.com/article/2928725/how-mu-mimo-wi-fi-works.html.

SSID Not Found

If the SSID is configured not to broadcast its name, users can still connect to it. It is listed as a Hidden network in the list of wireless networks in Windows. Users must supply the SSID as well as an encryption key to make the connection.

If an SSID not found error is displayed (either by name or as Hidden network), reboot the router. If rebooting the router does not help, open its configuration web page from your router (most SOHO routers use the IP address 192.168.1.1) and verify that it is configured as a router. Change and save configuration, and try the connection again.

Quick Reference to Network Hardware Tools

The following network hardware tools are useful for troubleshooting wired or wireless networks:

- **Cable tester**—Checks cables for proper connectivity.

- **Loopback plug**—Returns sent signals for comparison by a network card/cable testing program.

- **Punchdown tools**—Use to create or repair wired connections to a patch panel.

- **Tone generator and probe**—Use to test network cable for problems.

- **Wire strippers**—Use to prepare network cable for assembly.

- **Crimper**—Use to attach coaxial or TP connectors to a cable.

- **Wireless locator**—Displays available wireless networks and their channels. Use to locate a wireless network or to find an unused channel.

To learn more about using these hardware tools for troubleshooting a network, see the "Using Networking Tools" section in Chapter 11.

Overview of Network Command-Line Tools

Windows contains several command-line tools for troubleshooting and configuring the network. These include the following:

- **NET**—Displays and uses network resources

- **PING**—Tests TCP/IP and Internet connections

- **TRACERT**—Traces the route between a specified website or IP address and your PC. The equivalent command in OS X and Linux is Traceroute.

- **NSLOOKUP**—Displays detailed information about DNS

- **IPCONFIG**—Displays detailed TCP/IP configuration about your Windows system

- **NETSTAT**—Displays protocol statistics and current TCP/IP network connections

- **NBTSTAT**—Displays protocol statistics and current TCP/IP connections using NBT (NetBIOS over TCP/IP)

- **NETDOM**—Administers Active Directory domains and trust relationships. Installed as part of Windows Server, but can be downloaded for use with Windows desktop OS versions.

> **NOTE** The comparable command to ipconfig in Linux and OS X is IFCONFIG.

Commands can be entered in uppercase, lowercase, or mixed case.

The following sections describe these tools, including ifconfig.

PING

Windows can use the **PING** command to test TCP/IP, check for connectivity to other hosts on the network, and check the Internet connection for proper operation. PING is a more reliable way to check an Internet connection than opening your browser because a misconfigured browser could cause you to think that your TCP/IP configuration is incorrect.

To use PING to check connectivity with another host on the network, follow this procedure:

Step 1.   Open a command-prompt window.

Step 2.   Type **PING *IPaddress*** or **PING *servername*** to ping another host on the network; then press Enter. For example, to ping a router on a SOHO network, typical syntax would be PING 192.168.1.1.

To use PING to check your Internet connection, follow this procedure:

Step 1.   Start your Internet connection. If you use a LAN to connect to the Internet, you might have an always-on connection.

Step 2.   Open a command-prompt window.

Step 3.   Type **PING *IPaddress*** or **PING *servername*** and press Enter. For example, to ping a web server called www.erewhon.net, type **PING www.erewhon.net**.

By default, PING sends four data packets from your computer to any IP address or servername you specify. If your TCP/IP connection is working properly, you should see a reply from each ping you sent out indicating how quickly the signals traveled back from the target and the IP address or URL of the target. Note that some websites and servers are configured to ignore pings as a security measure. The replies indicate that the host is alive. Any other message would indicate a problem; for example, the "Request timed out" or "Destination host unreachable" messages would require further troubleshooting. Keep in mind that if the local computer is configured incorrectly, you might not be able to "ping" anything! Also watch for the amount of time the ping took to reply back. A longer latency time could indicate network congestion. Conversely, the lower the time in milliseconds (ms), the faster your connection. Connection speeds vary a great deal due to various factors, such as Internet network congestion, server speed, and the number of relays needed to transfer your request from your computer to the specified server. To check relay information, use the TRACERT command.

IPCONFIG

The **IPCONFIG** command-line utility is used to display the computer's current IP address, subnet mask, and default gateway (see Figure 13-32). Ipconfig combined with the /all switch will show more information including the DNS server address and MAC address, which is the hexadecimal address that is burned into the ROM of the network adapter.

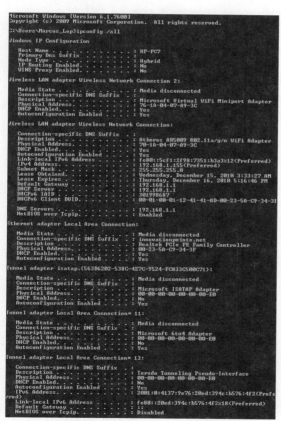

Figure 13-32 IPCONFIG /all displays complete information about your TCP/IP configuration.

TIP   If you're having problems seeing other computers on the network or connecting to the Internet on a network that uses server-assigned IPv4 addresses, type ipconfig /release and press Enter; then type ipconfig /renew and press Enter to obtain a new IP address from the DHCP server on your network. The comparable commands for releasing/renewing an IPv6 address are ipconfig /release6 and ipconfig /renew6.

IFCONFIG

The **IFCONFIG** command is used by Linux and OS X (see Figure 13-33) to display detailed information about the computer's current IP configuration. Linux and OS X refer to an IPv4 address as "inet," and an IPv6 address as "inet6."

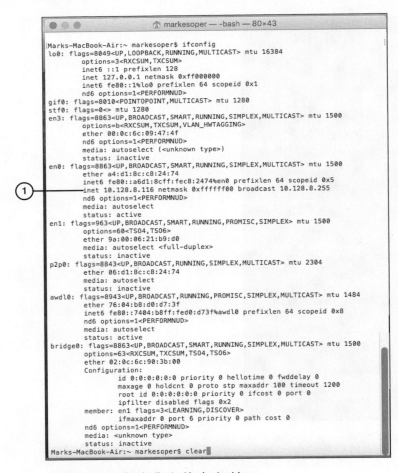

1. **Active connection indicated by inet address**

Figure 13-33   Ifconfig on OS X El Capitan.

TRACERT

The **TRACERT** command is used by Windows to trace the route taken by data traveling from your computer to an IP address or website you specify. By default, TRACERT checks up to 30 hops between your computer and the specified website or IP address. To use TRACERT to check the routing, follow this procedure:

Step 1. Start your Internet connection. If you use a LAN to connect to the Internet, you might have an always-on connection.

Step 2. Open a command-prompt window.

Step 3. Type **TRACERT** *IP address* or **TRACERT** *servername* and press **Enter**. For example, to trace the route to a web server called www.ere-whon.tv, typing **TRACERT www.erewhon.tv**. TRACERT displays the IP addresses and URLs of each server used to relay the information to the specified location, as well as the time required.

To see help for the TRACERT command, type **TRACERT** without any options and press the **Enter** key.

NETSTAT

Most commonly **NETSTAT** is used to show the current connections to a remote computer. Let's say you connected to google.com, opened a command prompt, and typed **NETSTAT**. You would get several results, one of which would look similar to this:

```
TCP   192.168.0.5:49732   google.com:80    Established
```

The NETSTAT command shows only TCP connections. If you were interested in seeing both TCP and UDP connections, you could use the command **NETSTAT –a**. And to see the information in numerical format, use **NETSTAT –n**. This displays IP addresses instead of domain names as shown here:

```
TCP   92.168.0.5:49732   74.125.113.106:80    Established
```

NETSTAT can also be used to show the network adapter's Ethernet statistics with the **NETSTAT –e** command. Check out the other various switches by typing **NETSTAT /?**.

NBTSTAT

NBTSTAT can be used to show the services running on the local computer or a remote computer. It calls this the name table. For example, you could find out what services are running, what the computer's name is, and what network it is a part of by typing **NBTSTAT –a 192.168.0.5** (or whatever your local IP is). The results would be similar to the following:

```
Computer1        <00>   Unique      Registered
Workgroup        <00>   Group       Registered
Computer1        <20>   Unique      Registered
```

The computer and network names are easy to see: Computer1 and Workgroup. But also notice that there are numbers in alligators such as <00> and <20>. These are the services mentioned previously. <00> is the workstation service, the service that allows your computer to redirect out to other systems to view shared resources. <20> is the server service that allows your computer to share resources with other systems. Check out the other various switches by typing **NBTSTAT /?**.

NET

Windows includes the **NET** command for use in displaying and using network resources from the command prompt. Some of the NET commands you can use include

- **Net Help**—Displays help for a Net option; for example, use Net Help View for help with the Net View command.

- **Net Use**—Maps a network drive to a shared resource on the network; for example, **Net Use Q: \\Tiger1\shared**. In this example, Q: will behave just like any other drive letter such as C:, D:, and so on. The only difference is that it will redirect to another computer on the network.

- **Net View**—Displays other hosts on the network.

- **Net Helpmsg errorcode#**—Displays the meaning of any Microsoft error code.

To display a complete list of Net commands, type **Net /? |More** from the command prompt.

NETDOM

The **NETDOM** command is used to manage Active Directory. To install it on a Windows desktop computer, download and install Remote Server Administration Tools (RSAT) from the Microsoft website. To run Netdom, open an elevated command prompt.

Netcom commands include:

- **Netdom add**—Adds a workstation or server account to the domain.

- **Netdom computername**—Manages the primary and alternate names for a computer. This command can safely rename Active Directory domain controllers as well as member servers.

- **Netdom join**—Joins a workstation or member server to a domain. The act of joining a computer to a domain creates an account for the computer on the domain, if it does not already exist.

- **Netdom move**—Moves a workstation or member server to a new domain. The act of moving a computer to a new domain creates an account for the computer on the domain, if it does not already exist.

- **Netdom query**—Queries the domain for information such as membership and trust.

- **Netdom remove**—Removes a workstation or server from the domain.

- **Netdom renamecomputer**—Renames a domain computer and its corresponding domain account. Use this command to rename domain workstations and member servers only. To rename domain controllers, use the netdom computername command.

- **Netdom reset**—Resets the secure connection between a workstation and a domain controller.

- **Netdom resetpwd**—Resets the computer account password for a domain controller.

- **Netdom trust**—Establishes, verifies, or resets a trust relationship between domains.

- **Netdom verify**—Verifies the secure connection between a workstation and a domain controller.

For more information about Netdom, see https://technet.microsoft.com/en-us/library/cc772217.aspx.

NSLOOKUP

NSLOOKUP is a command-line tool used to determine information about the DNS. When NSLookup is run without options, it displays the name and IP address of the default DNS server before displaying a DNS prompt. Enter the name of a website or server to determine its IP address; enter the IP address of a website or server to determine its name. Enter a question mark (?) at the prompt to see more options; type **exit**, and then press **Enter** to exit the program.

Mobile Device Troubleshooting

With more organizations than ever using laptops, tablets, and smartphones, it's important to know how to troubleshoot devices on the go. You need to understand the following concepts for the 220-901 exam and to improve your technical skills.

No Display

On a laptop, no display can be caused by the failure of the LCD inverter or back-light, a damaged cable leading to or from an LCD inverter, the failure of the LED control board, the failure of the display panel, the failure of the onboard display circuit, or by toggling the laptop to use an external display only with an Fn-key.

First, try toggling the laptop to use the internal display. If this doesn't help, connect it to a monitor or projector. If the external display works, the problem might be with the cable to the LCD inverter or the LCD inverter or the LCD-CCFL back-light on an LED display, or the problem could be with the cable to the LED control board, the LED control board, or the LED backlight. If the external display doesn't work, the motherboard needs to be repaired or replaced.

On a tablet or smartphone, the usual cause is that the unit is out of power. Connect it to a suitable charging connection, wait about ten minutes and try to power it up. If there's still no display, have the unit serviced.

Dim Display

On any device, the first step in dealing with a **dim display** is to check the brightness settings first. Smartphones and tablets typically use auto brightness. Disable it and try adjusting the brightness manually. Also, check the charge level. Many devices set the screen to a very dim setting right before shutting down in a last-ditch attempt to stretch battery life. If the screen doesn't return to normal brightness after being connected to AC power, service it.

If a laptop has a dim display not caused by user settings, the most likely cause is the failure of the fluorescent backlight inverter. If the screen flashes for a moment and then becomes dim at startup, the inverter is almost always the cause. Replace it.

If a smartphone or tablet has a dim display that won't respond to user settings, try performing a hard reset (power down, wait a few moments, than power up again. Also, make sure the ambient light sensor is working and is not being blocked by the case.

If the display dims after the device has been turned on for several minutes and left unattended, the most typical cause is a power management setting. Adjust power management settings as desired.

Flickering Display

On a laptop with an LCD-CCFL backlight, a **flickering display** is almost always caused by a dying backlight. You can replace it, but it's easier to swap the complete screen assembly for a remanufactured unit. If the unit has been opened, the problem could also be a damaged LCD ribbon cable to the motherboard.

On an Android smartphone running Jelly Bean or newer editions, you can use the Turn off hardware overlays setting or the Disable hardware overlays setting available in the Developer options menu. To enable developer options:

Step 1.   Choose **Settings > More > About Device**.

Step 2.   Tap **Build number** until the device says "You are now a developer."

Step 3.   Choose **Home > Settings > More > Developer options**.

Step 4.   Choose the hardware overlays setting used by your device.

See http://www.problogbooster.com/2014/06/on-screen-display-flickering-error-android-xda.html for more information.

On an iOS 9 iPhone 6s Plus or 6 Plus, the flickering is usually caused by dropped frames during graphically intense calculations. To fix it:

Step 1.   Choose **Settings > General > Accessibility > Increase Contrast > Reduce Transparency**.

Step 2.   Turn on **Reduced Transparency**.

Some apps will have less appealing backgrounds when this option is enabled. Learn more at http://www.idigitaltimes.com/iphone-6s-plus-screen-flickering-problems-how-fix-frame-drop-issue-486761.

Sticking Keys

Sticking keys on a laptop or tablet usually indicate a problem with the keyboard. It is not always necessary to replace the entire keyboard. Several online vendors offer individual key replacements for laptops. If more than one or two keys are sticking, it may be most cost-effective to replace the entire keyboard.

If the tablet uses a removable keyboard, the keyboard can be replaced if keys are not available.

NOTE   Some laptop models might use two or more key styles. Use the illustrations available on some sites to determine exactly which key style you need.

Intermittent Wireless

Some tablets and smartphones may have intermittent wireless if the Wi-Fi signal is very weak. Switch to a cellular data connection (if available) until a stronger Wi-Fi signal is available.

Change the angle of your laptop or 2-in-1 device screen or turn the entire unit to help improve Wi-Fi reception, as these units have their antennas in the screen.

Use the signal strength indicator to find the strongest wireless signal that can be used. In a public setting, there might be two or more open networks to choose from.

Battery Not Charging

Battery not charging issues on a tablet or smartphone may be caused by:

- Make sure the charger is rated for the tablet or smartphone. Chargers are rated in amperage (1A = 1000mA). A minimum of 500mA is needed to charge a smartphone (1A is much faster), and a minimum of 2.1A is needed to charge a tablet.
- If the charger has a toggle for iOS and non-iOS devices, choose the correct setting for your device.
- If you use a USB port on a laptop or desktop computer, enable USB fast charging if it is available on the computer, and be sure to use that port.
- You can't charge a smartphone from an unpowered USB hub; it has only 100mA available per port.
- Ordinary USB ports cannot charge a device when the computer is asleep.

If you have checked these issues with no success, replace the cable. If a known-working cable doesn't help, replace the battery or have the unit serviced.

On a laptop, if the system works when plugged in to AC power, but not on battery power, check the following:

- Make sure the battery is installed properly.
- Wipe off any corrosion or dirt on the battery and laptop battery contacts.
- Determine whether the battery can hold a charge. Make sure the battery is properly installed and the AC adapter has proper DC voltage output levels. Leave the system plugged in for the recommended amount of time needed to charge the battery; then try to run the system on battery power. If the battery cannot run the system, or the system runs out of battery power in less than 1 hour, replace the battery. If replacing the battery does not solve the problem, the laptop needs to be serviced or replaced.
- If the battery is hot after being charged or has a warped exterior, replace it.

Ghost Cursor/Pointer Drift

A **ghost cursor** is usually caused by mouse movement too fast for screen refresh rate. To make the mouse pointer easier to see, adjust the mouse properties to slow down mouse acceleration, use a larger mouse pointer, or enable visibility options (pointer trails, or press the Ctrl key to display mouse location).

Pointer drift can be caused by accidentally swiping or pressing on the device's touchpad or by a problem with the device's integrated pointing stick. If you use a mouse, disable the touchpad or change its sensitivity settings to ignore accidental touches.

No Power

If the laptop has no power when plugged in to an AC outlet, verify that the battery is not the problem. Remove it.

- Make sure the laptop is plugged in to a working AC outlet. Check the outlet with an outlet tester. Use a voltmeter or a multimeter set to AC voltage to determine whether the output is within acceptable limits.

- Make sure the AC power cord running from the AC outlet to the external AC adapter "power brick" is plugged in completely to the outlet and the adapter. If the power cord or plug is damaged, replace the cord.

- To determine whether the adapter is outputting the correct DC voltage, use a voltmeter or multimeter set to DC voltage to test the voltage coming from the adapter and compare it to the nominal output values marked on the adapter. As Figure 13-34 illustrates, it might be necessary to use a bent paperclip to enable an accurate voltage reading. A value of +/– 5 percent is acceptable.

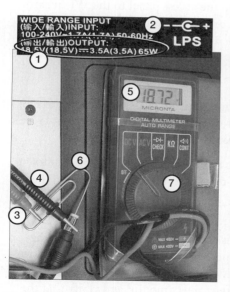

1. Nominal output voltage
2. AC adapter tip polarity
3. Positive (red) lead from multimeter
4. Negative (black) lead from multimeter
5. Measured DC voltage output
6. Bent paperclip inserted into adapter tip
7. Multimeter mode selector

Figure 13-34   Checking the output voltage from a laptop's AC adapter.

Num Lock Indicator Lights

Some laptops with embedded keypads don't start up with the keypad enabled (Num Lock on). Check the BIOS to see if this option can be enabled.

If **Num Lock indicator lights** will not come on, there might be a problem with the keyboard.

No Wireless Connectivity

Most laptops have a push button, pressure-sensitive touch button, or Fn-key combination to enable or disable Wi-Fi networking. If there is no wireless connectivity, press the button or Fn-key combination to enable the connection. Most laptops display an indicator light when the connection is enabled.

Late-model laptops, tablets, and smartphones have an airplane mode that disables all onboard radios (Wi-Fi, Bluetooth, and cellular) when enabled. Turn off airport mode and try the connection again. Wi-Fi can also be disabled separately from airplane mode. Check the Settings menu and enable Wi-Fi if necessary.

If the connection fails, check the Wi-Fi connection dialog in the notification area. You might need to reconnect manually. If there is no Wi-Fi connection dialog, open the Device Manager and check the Network Adapters category. If the Wi-Fi adapter is not listed, rescan for hardware changes.

If the Wi-Fi adapter cannot be located by Device Manager, shut down the system, disconnect it from all power sources, and open the access panel to the Wi-Fi card. If the card is loose, reconnect it and retry the connection after restoring power and restarting the computer. If the Wi-Fi antenna wires are loose, tighten them.

No Bluetooth Connectivity

Most laptops with built-in Bluetooth have a push button, pressure-sensitive touch button, or a Fn-key combination to enable or disable Bluetooth networking. Here's how to diagnose problems with no Bluetooth connectivity:

Step 1.   If there is no connection, press the button or Fn-key combination to enable the connection. Most laptops display an indicator light when the connection is enabled.

Step 2.   If the connection fails, verify that a Bluetooth adapter is installed and enabled. If the Bluetooth adapter is accessible from the outside of the unit, you can physically verify proper connection. Also Check Windows Device Manager, Linux Hardware, or OS X System Information. If the Bluetooth adapter is not listed, restart the computer and verify that the Bluetooth adapter is enabled in system BIOS setup.

Step 3. If the Bluetooth adapter is installed, use the Bluetooth configuration utility provided by the computer vendor (or device vendor, in the case of a USB Bluetooth adapter) to set up the adapter to connect to other devices.

Step 4. If the adapter is already set up to connect to other devices, check the Bluetooth settings on those devices.

On a tablet or smartphone, also check airplane mode (see the "No Wireless Connectivity" section for details).

Cannot Display to External Monitor

To display to an external monitor or projector, use the appropriate keyboard Fn-key combination after connecting the display or projector (see documentation for your device for details). If the system **cannot display to external monitor**:

- Check cabling between the computer and external display.

- Make sure the display is set to the correct input.

- Try a different display to determine if the problem is the mobile device or the external monitor.

Touchscreen Non-Responsive

The most common reason for a touchscreen non-responsive problem is dust, dirt, and grease on the surface. Use an antistatic wipe or spray designed for touchscreens to clean it.

Dry hands may not work well with touchscreens. Gloves without special fingertips can't use a touchscreen.

To determine if the touchscreen has failed, try a stylus made for the touchscreen. Reset the device and retry. If the touchscreen is still not responsive, have the unit serviced.

Apps Not Loading

To solve problems with apps not loading, check the following:

- Check available storage space—If your system is almost out of space, apps can't run. Uninstall apps you never use.

- If you have adequate free storage space, the device might not have enough free RAM—Close some apps.

- For a web-enabled app, make sure the device has a good Internet connection.

Slow Performance

Slow performance can be caused by:

- Device overheating—Remove the case, close apps to help cool the unit.

- Check power management settings—If a laptop is plugged into AC power, I recommend using the High Performance power setting in Windows.

- Close apps that are running but not in use.

- Don't charge the phone while running a bunch of apps.

Unable to Decrypt Email

Mobile devices that receive messages from Outlook 2010 might be unable to decrypt email. Outlook 2010 changed how it used the Cryptographic Message Service (CMS). Make sure Outlook 2010 is updated to SP1 to solve this problem (which does not exist in Outlook 2013).

Missing or out-of-date security certificates on devices can also cause problems with decrypting email. Update security certificates to solve this problem.

Extremely Short Battery Life

Although Li-Ion batteries do not have the memory effect that plagued old Ni-Cd batteries, various factors can still cause extremely short battery life. Check the following:

- Don't overcharge a device's battery

- For best results, don't wait until a device is almost out of power to charge it.

- Adjust screen brightness to the lowest level that is comfortable to use.

- On iOS devices, turn off background app refresh.

- Upgrade to the latest OS or OS updates available for your device.

- Use a phone battery helper app to manage charging, but don't run other apps while the device is charging.

- Close apps from the iOS App Switcher.

- Shut down an iOS device weekly with the slider switch.

- On devices that use AMOLED displays, switch to black wallpaper (theme) to save power.

Overheating

Mobile device **overheating** can have several causes:

- On a laptop, make sure the intake and exhaust fan ports aren't being blocked during use. Despite the name, a lap is not a suitable place for a computer because clothing can block airflow.

- Adjust power settings, especially when on battery power.

- Make sure CPU power management drivers are installed (check Device Manager under System devices).

- On a tablet or smartphone, shut down unnecessary apps, and keep in mind that HD video playback can stress the processor. Some protective cases can cause smartphones to overheat.

Frozen System

A **frozen system** is usually caused by a malfunctioning app. Sometimes, going to the lock screen for a few seconds helps a mobile app to start responding. If that doesn't work, shut down the system, wait a minute, and then restart it. Check for updates for the app and device.

No Sound from Speakers

No sound from speakers can have several causes:

- With wired speakers, keep in mind that the case might prevent 3.5mm mini-jack connector from making a good connection. It may be necessary to remove the case to make a good connection.

- With Bluetooth speakers, make sure Bluetooth is turned on. Check device pairing.

- Check the volume or mute controls on the mobile device. Apple iPhones have a sliding switch to mute them as well as software controls. The side button on iPads can be configured to lock screen or mute speaker output. Check the volume control on the keyboard or OS on OS X and Windows devices.

GPS Not Functioning

Check the following if the GPS not functioning:

If Airplane mode is on, the **GPS** is shut down as well. Turn off Airplane mode and the GPS may come back on. If not, turn on the GPS in the Settings > Location menu.

Swollen Battery

A swollen battery is most likely due to overcharging. In addition to replacing the battery, check the AC adapter to make sure it is putting out the correct voltage.

Mobile Device Disassembly Process

Mobile devices, even for experienced technicians, can be a challenge to disassemble. Follow these guidelines to ensure a successful disassembly and reassembly when you upgrade or service a laptop, convertible 2-in-1, tablet, or smartphone.

Document and Label Cable and Screw Locations

A typical laptop may have as many as 100 or more screws of varying sizes. A smartphone could have a dozen or more. Be sure to document and label cable and screw locations: as each screw is removed, note its location and size.

A digital camera or smartphone camera is a good tool, as you can use it to photograph the device and the screws as they are removed.

Figure 13-35 shows a few of the different screws removed from a typical laptop.

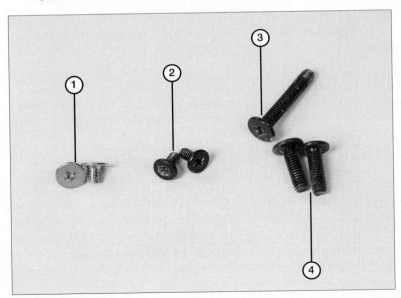

1. Hard disk mounting screws
2. Subassembly mounting screws
3. Keyboard mounting screw
4. Case cover screws

Figure 13-35 Typical laptop screws and their uses.

TIP   If you have a service manual for the device, note the screw sizes and positions listed for each component. Use it to create a checklist as you disassemble a device.

Organize Parts

There are many ways to organize parts:

- Use a plastic divided-compartment lidded tray from a hardware store to keep screws and bolts organized. As you put each set of screws into a compartment, add a label to indicate which subassembly they go to.

- Place static-sensitive materials (CPU, RAM, etc.) in anti-static bags.

- Use anti-static bubble wrap for larger components such as motherboards.

- Use boxes to protect case and trim components.

TIP   If you have a service manual for the device, label components by the subassembly and page number in the manual.

Refer to Manufacturer Resources

Before you start to disassemble a device, make sure you have the information you need to refer to **manufacturer resources**.

- Get the manufacturer's service manual if it is available.

- For the easiest time in searching, check the underside of a laptop or tablet to discover the actual service number or catalog number (not the marketing model number).

Most manufacturers make this information readily available. Some third-party websites also have service manuals, but don't use these resources unless you can't download the service manual directly from the website.

CAUTION   YouTube has many videos on tablet, smartphone, and laptop disassembly. Also, there are many unofficial teardown documents online. They can be helpful in the absence of manufacturer-supplied documentation, but be careful! Some might advocate potentially dangerous methods for disassembling a device.

Use Appropriate Hand Tools

For an easier time in disassembling mobile devices, use appropriate hand tools. They are smaller and differ in other ways from those needed for a desktop computer. For example, Apple now uses the five-point Pentalobe screw for external screws in its smartphones, although some models use the standard Phillips head for internal screws.

Although some users advocate guitar picks or even playing cards for opening tight enclosures on smartphones, special tools work better. Figure 13-36 illustrates one of many specialty toolkits on the market for working on mobile devices.

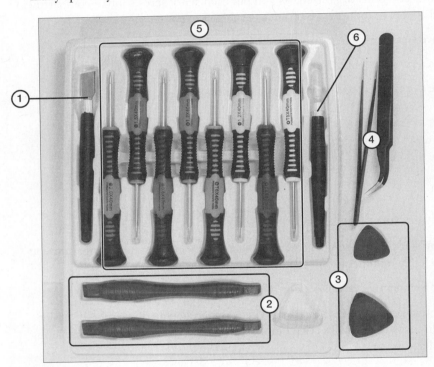

1. Scraper
2. Pry bars
3. Triangle paddles
4. Tweezers
5. Screwdrivers (Phillips, straight-blade, Torx, and 5-point/Pentalobe)
6. Precision cutting knife

Figure 13-36   A typical mobile device toolkit.

Printer Troubleshooting

For the 220-901 exam, be sure you understand how to deal with the symptoms and how to use the tools listed in the following sections.

Streaks

Streaks and smudges can have many causes, depending on the type of printer in use.

Laser Printer

Randomized streaks in printed output, such as uneven printing or blank spots, are usually caused by low toner. As a temporary workaround, remove the toner cartridge and gently shake it to redistribute the toner. Install a new toner cartridge as quickly as possible.

Long vertical streaks that repeat on each page are usually caused by damage to the imaging drum. Replace the drum or toner cartridge if it includes the drum.

Inkjet Printer

Smudged print output from an inkjet printer can be caused by dirty printheads or paper rollers, incorrect head gap settings, and incorrect resolution and media settings.

If you see smudges only when printing on heavy paper stock, card stock, labels, or envelopes, check the head gap setting; use the default setting for paper up to 24 lb. rating; and use the wider gap for labels, card stock, and envelopes.

Clean the printhead. If the cleaning process doesn't result in acceptable results, remove the printhead (if possible) and clean it. If the printhead is built in to the printer or if the paper-feed rollers or platen have ink smudges, use a cleaning sheet to clean the paper-feed rollers, platen, and printhead.

Check the Printer Properties setting in the operating system to ensure that the correct resolution and paper options are set for the paper in use. Horizontal streaks in inkjet output are usually caused by trying to print on glossy photo paper using plain paper setting.

Unlike laser output—which can be handled as soon as the page is ejected—inkjet output, particularly from older printers, printed to old paper stocks made for older printers, or output on transparencies or glossy photo paper, often requires time to dry. For best results, use paper specially designed for inkjet printers. Paper should be stored in a cool, dry environment; damp paper also will result in smudged printing.

Thermal Printers

Streaky output in thermal transfer printers can have several causes, including media and print head problems.

If the coating on the media is poor quality, replace the media. If preprinted ink on the media is sticking to the printhead, replace the media with media printed using heat-resistant ink.

If the heating element is dirty, clean the heating element.

Smeared output (primarily when printing bar codes) can be caused by incorrect print head energy settings, too high a print speed, and using a 90-degree or 270-degree orientation.

With direct thermal printers, check for improperly stored paper or an incorrect setting in the printer driver. If the printer can be used in either direct or thermal transfer modes, an incorrect driver setting can cause print quality problems of various types.

Impact Printers

Streaky output in dot-matrix impact printers is usually caused by a dried-out ribbon. If the ribbon has an auxiliary ink reservoir, activate it. Otherwise, replace the ribbon.

Faded Prints

Faded prints also have many possible causes, depending on the printer.

Laser Printers

If the printing is even, the printer might be set for Economode or a similar mode that uses less toner. Adjust the printer properties to use normal print modes for final drafts.

For a color laser printer, also check the toner levels or the operation of the toner belt.

Inkjet Printers

The print nozzles might be clogged or some colors may be out of ink. Clean the nozzles, and use the nozzle check utility to verify proper operation. Replace any cartridges that are out of ink.

Thermal Printers

A faded image can result from installing a thermal transfer ribbon backward. Remove, verify proper loading, and reinstall.

If the ribbon is installed correctly, the ribbon might not be compatible with the media. Check the media settings in the printer configuration to verify.

Impact Printers

If the print is evenly faded, the ribbon is dried out. Replace the ribbon to achieve better print quality and protect the printhead. If the print appears more faded on the top of each line than on the bottom, the head gap is set too wide for the paper type in use. Adjust the head gap to the correct width to improve printing and protect the printhead from damage.

Ghost Images

Laser printers that display **ghost images** of part or all of the previous page on a new printout might have problems with the toner cartridge, imaging drum wiper blade, or fusing unit. To determine the cause of the ghosting, measure the distance between the top of the page and the ghost image and consult the service manual for the printer. Clean or replace the defective component.

Toner Not Fused to the Paper

The fuser in a laser printer is supposed to heat the paper to fuse the toner to the paper; fuser failure results in **toner** not fused to the paper. If the printed output from a laser printer can be wiped or blown off the paper after the printout emerges from the laser printer, the fuser needs to be repaired or replaced.

Creased Paper

Creased paper is usually caused by incorrect adjustment of the paper guides for feeding pages. If the paper guide is not set to the actual paper width, the paper might move horizontally during the feed process and become creased. Adjust the paper guides to the correct width for the paper or media in use.

Paper Not Feeding

The causes of paper not feeding can vary by printer type:

- With an inkjet, laser, or impact printer running single-sheet paper, check the paper's positioning in the paper tray. Remove the paper, fan it, and replace it.

If the problem continues, check for paper jams. If there are no paper jams, the pickup rollers might be worn out.

■ With a printer that uses continuous-feed paper (impact or thermal), check the tension of the feeder rollers or the position and operation of the tractor-feed mechanism.

Paper Jam

A **paper jam** can have a variety of causes, depending on the printer type. Use the following sections to solve paper jams.

Paper Path Issues

The more turns the paper must pass through during the printing process, the greater the chance of paper jams. Curved paper paths are typical of some inkjet and many laser printers as well as dot-matrix printers using push tractors: The paper is pulled from the front of the printer, pulled through and around a series of rollers inside the printer during the print process, and then ejected through the front or top of the printer onto a paper tray. Because the cross-section of this paper path resembles a *C*, this is sometimes referred to as a C-shaped paper path.

Some printers, especially those with bottom-mounted paper trays, have more complex paper paths that resemble an *S*.

A straight-through paper path is a typical option on laser printers with a curved paper path. Printers with this feature have a rear paper output tray that can be lowered for use, which overrides the normal top paper output tray. Some also have a front paper tray. Use both front and rear trays for a true straight-through path; this is recommended for printing on envelopes, labels, or card stock. Inkjet printers with input paper trays at the rear of the printer and an output tray at the front also use this method or a variation in which the paper path resembles a flattened V.

Paper Loading, Paper Type, and Media Thickness Issues

Paper jams can be caused by incorrect paper-loading procedures, overloading the input tray, or using paper or card stock that is thicker than the recommended types for the printer. If the printer jams, open the exit cover or front cover or remove the paper tray(s) as needed to clear the jam.

Media Caught Inside the Printer

If paper, labels, envelopes, or transparencies come apart or tear inside the printer, you must remove all debris to avoid additional paper jams. Don't try to use creased media because it increases the likelihood of a paper jam. However, if paper jams continue to happen, check the paper feed or paper tray operation.

Avoid using paper with damaged edges or damp paper; this can cause paper jams and lead to poor-quality printing.

> **TIP**   When you insert a stack of sheet paper into any type of printer, be sure to fan the pages before you insert the paper into the tray to prevent sticking.

No Connectivity

A loose printer or network cable can cause **no connectivity**, as can a router or switch failure. If the shared printer is connected to a computer, determine whether the computer can connect to the network. If not, the problem is network-related. If it can, the problem is related to the printer, printer port, or printer cable.

If the printer has an integrated network connection or connects to a print-sharing device on the network, check the network settings on the printer or device.

If the printer uses wireless networking, check the settings for SSID or ad-hoc networking. Move the printer closer to the router. Add a wireless repeater. Replace Wireless-N or Wireless-G routers with Wireless-AC routers to boost network connection reliability to G, N, and AC devices and printers.

Garbled Characters on Paper

Garbled characters on paper (gibberish printing) can occur for several reasons. Check the printer driver first: If the printer driver files are corrupted or the incorrect printer driver has been selected for a printer, gibberish printing is a likely result.

If you can use a printer in an emulation mode or change it to use a different printer language with a personality module or DIMM (for example, a special Postscript DIMM can be used in some PCL-language laser printers), be sure you have correctly configured the printer and the printer driver or installed a new printer driver.

A parallel printer cable that fails can also cause this type of problem.

Vertical Lines on Page

Vertical lines on page printed with a laser printer can be caused by debris stuck to the imaging drum, surface damage to the imaging drum, or dirty components in the printer (fuser, paper rollers, charging rollers, and so on). To determine which component is the cause, compare the distance between marks on the paper with the circumference of each component. The printer's manual will provide this information. Replace the imaging drum (part of the toner cartridge on many printer models) if the drum is at fault. Clean other components if they're at fault, and retest.

Vertical lines on a page printed with an inkjet printer are usually caused by ink on a feed roller. Clean the feed rollers, and if the problem persists, there might be a problem with a leaky ink cartridge.

Vertical lines in thermal printer output can be caused by a dirty heating element or by the failure of part of the heating element. Angled streaks can be caused by a creased ribbon. To solve this problem, adjust the ribbon feed mechanism.

Vertical lines on impact printer output usually indicate dirt on the paper. Replace the paper.

Backed-Up Print Queue

The Windows print spooler switches to offline mode if the printer goes offline, is turned off, or has stopped for some other reason (such as a paper jam or loss of connection to the network). Print jobs are sent to the **print queue**, but a backed-up print queue fills up until the print jobs are dealt with. After the printer goes online, you can release the print jobs. You can also kill all print jobs or kill selected print jobs.

To access the print queue, open the Printer icon in the notification area, or go to Printers, or Devices and Printers and open the printer icon.

Releasing a Print Queue

To release print jobs stored in the queue in offline mode after the printer is available, use one of these methods:

Step 1.   Open the print queue.

Step 2.   Open the **Printer** menu.

Step 3.   Click **Use Printer Offline** (it's a toggle) and the print jobs will go to the printer.

Clearing Select Print Jobs or All Print Jobs in a Queue

You might need to clear a print queue for a variety of reasons:

- The wrong options are selected for the installed paper.

- Gibberish printing occurs because of a problem with the printer driver, cable, or port.

- You decide not to print the queued documents.

You can clear selected print jobs or all print jobs in a queue. To discard a print job in the print queue, follow these steps:

Step 1.   Open the print queue.

Step 2.   Right-click the print job you want to discard.

Step 3.   Select **Cancel Print** and the print job will be discarded.

To discard all print jobs in the queue, follow these steps:

Step 1.   Open the print queue.

Step 2.   Right-click **Printer**.

Step 3.   Click **Cancel All Documents** (varies by Windows version) to discard all print jobs.

Low-Memory Errors

If you send a page to a laser printer that requires more memory than the laser printer contains, the laser printer tries to print the page but stops after the printer's memory is full. The printer displays **low-memory errors** (either with an error message or by blinking error status lights), at which point you must manually eject the page. Only a portion of the page is printed.

If the page requires an amount of memory close to the maximum in the laser printer, most laser printers have techniques for compressing the data going to the printer. Although this technique means that more pages can be printed successfully, compressing the data can slow down the print process.

You can use three options if the pages you need to print require too much memory:

- Reduce the resolution of the print job. Most laser printers today have a standard resolution of 600dpi or 1,200dpi. Reducing the graphics resolution to the next lower figure (from 1,200 to 600dpi or from 600dpi to 300dpi) will reduce the memory requirement for printing the page by a factor of four. The option, when present, could be located on various tabs of the printer's properties sheet. See Figure 13-37 for a typical example.

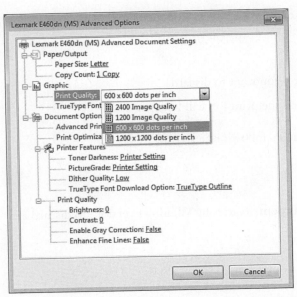

Figure 13-37   The Layout – Advanced – Graphics – Print Quality dialog in Windows 7 for a Lexmark laser printer enables you to adjust the graphics resolution; text quality is not affected by this option.

- Eliminate or reduce the size of graphics on the page.
- Convert color photos to black-and-white photos before placing in a desktop publishing document or printing them directly from the file. This can actually enhance the output quality from a monochrome laser printer as well as reduce the memory requirement for pages with photos.

These options are temporary workarounds that might be unsatisfactory for permanent use. The best solution to out-of-memory problems with a printer, as with the computer, is to add more RAM.

NOTE   If you reduce the graphics resolution, text resolution stays the same, so a document that is not designed for reproduction or mass distribution will still have acceptable quality. However, graphics resolutions of 600 dots per inch (dpi) or less produce poor-quality photo output.

Access Denied

If you get an **Access Denied** message when trying to print to a network printer, make sure your account has been granted access to the printer or to the computer hosting the networked printer.

Printer Will Not Print

Some of the reasons a printer will not print include:

- If a laser printer produces a blank page immediately after the toner cartridge has been changed, remove the toner cartridge, and make sure the tape that holds the toner in place has been removed; without toner, the printer can't print.

- If the printer produces a blank page after printing thousands of pages, the toner probably is exhausted. Replace the toner cartridge.

- If you send a print job to a printer that has specified hours of activity, the print job will not be released to the printer until the printer is ready for it.

- If you set up a printer manually and the wrong printer port is specified, the printer won't print.

- Check the cable connecting the printer to the device (USB) or network (Ethernet). Check wireless or wired network connections.

- To print from a mobile device, install the print app for the printer brand/model from the device's app store.

Color Prints in Wrong Print Color

If color prints in wrong print color take place, the most likely cause on a color ink-jet printer is a clogged printhead. On a color laser, check for low color toner or an empty color toner cartridge.

For Epson inkjet printers on Windows systems, use the Maintenance tab of the printing preferences sheet (see Figure 13-38) to check ink levels, clean and align print heads, and check nozzles for clogs.

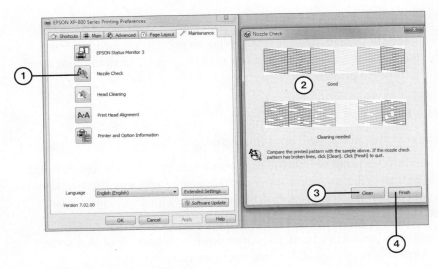

1. Click to start Nozzle Check
2. Compare printout with these examples
3. Click to clean printheads
4. Click when Nozzle Check results are satisfactory

Figure 13-38   Using the Nozzle Check on an Epson inkjet printer.

For Canon inkjet printers on Windows systems, use the Maintenance tab of the printing preferences sheet (see Figure 13-39) to clean and align print heads, check nozzles for clogs, clean the bottom plate and rollers, and configure ink usage.

If the print colors are close but not exactly what is wanted on a color photograph or a document with colored graphics or text, you need to set up color management on the printer and the display(s) used to edit the document.

Unable to Install Printer

The unable to install printer issue is caused by not having sufficient privileges; you need administrator (elevated) access. If you are installing a printer in Windows, provide the administrator password when prompted by User Account Control. In Linux, get root access with sudo and provide a password when prompted.

1. Click to clean print heads
2. Click to deep clean print heads
3. Click to align printheads
4. Click to run Nozzle Check

Figure 13-39   The Maintenance tab of a Canon inkjet printer driver.

Error Codes

Printers with LCD or LED panels display error codes or error messages for diagnosis of problems such as paper jams, low ink, or low toner. Error codes vary by printer manufacturer. However, to diagnose a printer that has only status lights, use the printer's documentation to determine the codes being displayed. To determine the meaning of a specific error code and the appropriate solution, check the printer manual and printer vendor's website.

HP LaserJet printers use the following error codes to describe printing problems:

- **13 or 13.xx**—Paper jam. (Replace .xx with specific numeric values that indicate exactly where the paper jam has occurred.)

- **20**—Insufficient memory; press Go or Continue to print a partial page.

- **40**—Bad transmission to EIO interface card.

- **41.xx**—Various printer errors involving media or other problems. (Replace .xx with a value indicating the specific error.)

- **49.xx**—Firmware error.

- **50.4**—Line voltage.

- **50.x**—Fuser error.

- **51.x**—Beam detect (.1) or laser error (.2).

- **52.x**—Scanner speed errors; startup error (.1); rotation error (.2).

- **53.xy.zz**—DIMM memory error in specified module (x = DIMM type; y = location; and zz = error number).

- **54.1**—Sealing tape not removed from the toner cartridge.

- **54.4**—Line voltage error.

- **55.xx**—Internal communications error; can be caused by formatter, firmware DIMM, engine controller board, or fuser problems.

- **56.x**—Error in paper input or accessory (.1) or output bin (.2) connection.

- **57.x**—Printer fan (.4), duplex fan (.7), or main motor (older printer models in LaserJet 4, 5 series) failure.

- **58.2**—Environmental thermistor (TH3) failure.

- **59.x**—Main motor error (.0), startup error (.1), or rotation error (.2).

- **62.x**—Printer memory error in internal memory (.0) or DIMM slots (.1–.4).

- **64**—Scan buffer error.

- **66.xx.yy**—External paper-handling device error.

- **68**—NVRAM or permanent storage error.

- **69.x**—Temporary printing error.

- **79**—Printer detected error (can be caused by memory, firmware, EIO, and formatter).

- **8x.yyyy**—EIO device or slot error.

NOTE A good resource for both numerical- and text-based error codes for HP LaserJet printers is the HP LaserJet Error Codes page at PrinterTechs.com: www.printertechs.com/tech/error-codes/error-codes-index.php. Lexmark error codes are available at www.all-laser.com/aerrorlex/.

Printing Blank Pages

If a printer is printing blank pages, check the following:

- If a new toner cartridge has just been installed in a laser printer, make sure the tape was removed from the toner cartridge.

- The printer might be feeding two or more sheets at a time. Remove the paper, fan it to ensure the paper is not sticking together, reinsert the paper into the printer tray, and retry the print job.

- If the printer is networked, check the network print server configuration. Many network printers are configured to eject a blank page between print jobs for privacy.

- With some printers, you start a print job that uses the rear paper slot before you insert paper. Paper placed in the rear paper slot before the print job starts might be ejected.

No Image on Printer Display

If the there is no image on printer display, press a button to "wake up" the display. Make sure the printer is turned on.

If you are printing directly from a memory card and no pictures are visible, the pictures on the memory card might be the wrong file format. Printers cannot print RAW-format files, but can print JPEG files.

If the display is a plug-in type, the display interface cable might be loose. Turn off the printer, unplug and reconnect the cable, and turn on the printer again.

Using Printer Troubleshooting Tools

Use a toner vacuum to clean up spilled toner.

Use **compressed air** to help remove loose toner from a printer.

Use the **print spooler** to maintain print jobs.

Many HP and other laser printers feature components that should be replaced at periodic intervals. These components often include fuser assemblies, air filters, transfer rollers, pickup rollers, other types of rollers, and separation pads. These components wear out over time and can usually be purchased as a **maintenance kit** as well as separately.

A printer that uses a maintenance kit displays a message or an error code with a meaning such as Perform Printer Maintenance or Perform User Maintenance when the printer reaches the recommended page count for maintenance kit replacement. Depending on the printer model and whether it is used for color or monochrome printing, the recommended page count could be as few as 50,000 pages or as much as 300,000 pages or more.

> **NOTE**   Sources for maintenance kits can also provide useful installation instructions. Sources for HP and Lexmark printers include PrinterTechs.com, Inc. (www. printertechs.com/maintenance-kits.php) and Depot International (www.depotintl. com) among others.

Exam Preparation Tasks

Review All the Key Topics

Review the most important topics in the chapter, noted with the Key Topic icon in the outer margin of the page. Table 13-4 lists a reference of these key topics and the page numbers on which each is found.

Table 13-4   Key Topics for Chapter 13

Key Topic Element	Description	Page Number
List	Causes of system overheating	578
Table 13-2	Using a Multimeter	589
List	List of command-line tools and their uses	627
Section	Backed Up Print Queue	650

Complete the Tables and Lists from Memory

Print a copy of Appendix C, "Memory Tables" (found on the CD), or at least the section for this chapter, and complete the tables and lists from memory. Appendix D, "Answers to Memory Tables," also on the CD, includes completed tables and lists to check your work.

Define Key Terms

access denied, APIPA/link local address, artifacts, BIOS, cable tester, CHKDSK, color patterns, continuous reboots, creased paper, crimper, data recovery software, dead pixels, decrypt email, Defragmentation tool, dim image, Diskpart, distended capacitors, distorted geometry, distorted image, drive not recognized, enclosure, faded prints, failure to boot, file recovery software, flickering image, FORMAT, garbled characters, ghost cursor/pointer drift, ghost images, GPS, indicator lights, intermittent connectivity, intermittent device failure, IP conflict, IPCONFIG, IFCONFIG, limited connectivity, local connectivity, lockup, loopback plug, loud clicking noise, loud noise, low memory errors, low RF signal, manufacturer resources, multimeter, NBTSTAT, NET, NETDOM, NETSTAT, no connectivity, no power, NSLOOKUP, Num lock indicator lights, overheating, paper jam, PING, POST card/USB, POST code beeps, power supply tester, print queue, proprietary crash screens (BSOD/pin wheel), punchdown tools, RAID, Read/write failure, S.M.A.R.T. errors, screwdriver, shutdown, streaks, tone generator and probe, toner, TRACERT, vertical lines, VGA mode, wire strippers, wireless locator, print spooler, maintenance kit

Complete Hands-on Labs

Complete the hands-on labs, and then see the answers and explanations at the end of the chapter.

Lab 13-1: Beep Codes, Fans, Multimeter, and Hard Disk Testing

After disconnecting all power from a desktop computer, remove the memory or video card. Does the computer beep? If not, is a speaker connected to the speaker header pins on the front-panel connectors? If you can connect a PC speaker, try the experiment again. Which beep code was produced by removing all RAM? Which beep code was produced by removing the video card (this works only if the computer does not have onboard video)?

Is there an unused front, rear, or top fan bay on the computer? Determine which size(s) of fans would be needed to improve airflow. Are there available fan headers on the motherboard, or will it be necessary to borrow power from a Molex power connector?

Use a multimeter to check the power leads for +5V, +12V, and Power Good.

Determine which brand of hard disk is installed in the computer (use Device Manager). Download the drive vendor's diagnostic program and use it to test the hard disk. If one is not available, run CHKDSK.

Lab 13-2: Network, Mobile Device, and Printer Troubleshooting

Use Tracert to check the route between a computer and a website or IP address of your choice.

If you use a wired network, disconnect the network cable from a computer running Windows, run the Windows network troubleshooter, and see if it finds the problem.

Use Ipconfig (Windows) or Ifconfig (Linux or OS X) to learn more about your network.

Check the amperage (mA or A) rating of the chargers you use for your smartphone or tablet and verify if they are adequate to the job.

Obtain a laser or inkjet printer-cleaning sheet (depending upon the printer you have) and use it to clean the rollers, etc.

If you use inkjet printers, run the nozzle check and clean the heads if necessary.

Answer Review Questions

1. Your system has begun shutting down suddenly and unexpectedly. Which of the following best describes how to determine whether the cause of these shut-downs is due to the CPU overheating?

   A. Check the CPU temperature in the Device Manager

   B. Check the CPU temperature in the System Properties

   C. Check the CPU temperature in Computer Management

   D. Check the CPU temperature in the system BIOS/UEFI firmware

2. Which of the following best describes the usual cause of a checksum error?

   A. A failing CMOS battery

   B. A corrupt BIOS or UEFI

   C. An error within the system's arithmetic calculator

   D. Overheating due to overclocking

3. Which of the following is usually checked by POST? (Choose all that apply.)

   A. Memory

   B. Keyboard

   C. Mouse

   D. Hard drives

4. When the date and time on your computer are running slowly and losing time, which of the following statements best describes the most likely cause and the most effective course of action?

    A. There is a fault in the BIOS settings and you should flash the BIOS.

    B. The CPU is running slowly and you should check the CPU and its fan for dust that might be clogging it and slowing it down.

    C. At least one of the memory modules may be faulty and you should check the memory information in the BIOS and replace any failing modules.

    D. The CMOS battery is failing and you should replace the battery.

5. Which component is indicated in the following figure?

    A. CPU

    B. CMOS battery

    C. Capacitor

    D. BIOS chip

6. If your system is experiencing frequent STOP errors and is automatically re-booting each time, where would you go to change the configuration setting to stop the automatic reboot process?

    A. System Properties, Advanced tab, Startup and Recovery

    B. Drive Properties, Tools tab

    C. Administrative Tools, Disk Management

    D. BIOS, Boot tab, Automatic Reboot

7. Which of the following voltages is used by a computer in North America?

    A. 115 v

    B. 190 v

    C. 230 v

    D. 400 v

8. Identify the motherboard component in the following figure.

    A. CMOS batteries

    B. Resistors

    C. Jumpers

    D. Capacitors

9. Which of the following tools is used to test AC or DC voltage, continuity, re-sistance, and amperage?

    A. Loopback plug

    B. PING

    C. Multimeter

    D. Tone generator

10. Which of the following voltage levels should be produced by a healthy power supply? (Choose all that apply.)

    A. +3.3

    B. –3.3

    C. +5.0

    D. –5.0

    E. +8.3

    F. –8.3

    G. +12.0

    H. –12.0

11. Which of the following best describes the function of a loopback plug?

    A. It tests power supplies.

    B. It tests serial, parallel, and USB ports.

    C. It tests the boot process.

    D. It tests RAID arrays.

12. During startup, the BIOS transmits codes that indicate what is happening during each phase of the boot. Which of the following tools should be used to see these codes?

    A. Multimeter

    B. Checksum

    C. POST card

    D. Tone generator

13. What is the purpose of the jumper in the following figure?

    A. It protects the prongs inside the connector.

    B. It moves the SATA drive to the first position in the boot sequence.

    C. It is used by RAID to configure a mirrored array.

    D. It slows SATA drive performance.

14. Which of the following statements best describes how to change the boot sequence?

  A. Edit the BIOS and save the changes in CMOS.

  B. Change the jumper settings on the SATA drive to make it the bootable drive.

  C. Reconfigure settings for the RAID array to make a RAID drive the bootable drive.

  D. Use the Disk Management utility in Administrative Tools.

15. S.M.A.R.T. detects and reports errors for which of the following?

  A. CPUs

  B. DDR memory

  C. SATA and PATA hard drives

  D. Expansion cards

16. Which of the following statements best describes the result of selecting a file and pressing the Shift and Delete keys simultaneously?

  A. The file will be moved to the Recycle Bin.

  B. The file will be saved.

  C. The file will be saved in a protected folder.

  D. The file will be permanently deleted.

17. In Windows Vista, 7, 8/8.1, and 10, which of the following troubleshooting tools are located in the Drive Properties, Tools tab? (Choose two.)

  A. Diskpart

  B. Defragmentation

  C. Error-checking

  D. System Restore

18. When booting your system in Safe Mode, which of the following statements best describes how the display will load?

  A. The display will load in VGA mode.

  B. The display will load using the Last Known Good Configuration.

  C. The display will load using the resolution selected when entering Safe Mode.

  D. The display will degauss before entering Safe Mode.

19. A flickering image on an LCD display might be caused by the failing of which components? (Choose two.)

    A. Backlight

    B. Cathode ray tube

    C. Reflector

    D. Inverter

20. Burn-in refers to which of the following?

    A. The process of recording a CD or DVD

    B. The process of preparing a hard drive for formatting for a clean installation

    C. A persistent ghost image on the display screen

    D. The damaged areas in a plasma display

21. Your client reports that computers on the network cannot connect to the Internet but can connect to each other. You determine that each of the computers affected has been assigned an APIPA address. Which type of server would you suspect of having a problem?

    A. DNS

    B. DHCP

    C. Proxy

    D. Router

22. Which of the following statements best describes the primary purpose of a crimper?

    A. It checks cables for proper connectivity.

    B. It creates wired connections for a patch panel.

    C. It tests network cables.

    D. It attaches connectors to network cables.

23. You need to diagnose problems with a network. Use the following answer options to correctly match the command with its function.

Command	Function
A. PING	
B. Tracert	
C. NSLookup	
D. IPConfig	
E. IFConfig	
F. Netstat	

Answer Options:

1. Traces data route (hops) between routers

2. Displays information about the default DNS server

3. Linux and OS X command that displays IP configuration information

4. Tests connectivity between hosts on a network

5. Displays IP address and domain name of a remote computer

6. Displays a computer's IP address, subnet mask, and default gateway

24. When your tablet or smartphone does not get a clear cellular signal, which of the following steps could improve the signal? (Choose two.)

   A. Turn off Wi-Fi.

   B. Change the angle of your screen.

   C. Reset your cellular settings to a faster 802.11 specification.

   D. Use the slider switch on an iOS device to fine-tune reception.

25. Which of the following steps could help increase the battery life on your mobile devices? (Choose two.)

   A. Don't overcharge.

   B. On iOS, turn on the background app refresh.

   C. Use the iOS slider switch to shut down weekly.

   D. Wait until almost out of power before recharging a device.

26. Vertical streaks extending down each page printed by a laser printer usually indicates which of the following problems?

   A. Low toner

   B. A dirty print ribbon

   C. Damaged ink nozzles

   D. Damage to the imaging drum

27. Smudged print from an inkjet printer could be caused by which of the following?

   A. Printheads or rollers are dirty

   B. Fuser does not reach a high enough temperature

   C. Photosensitive drum is not properly charged

   D. Toner cartridge needs to be replaced

28. If toner can be brushed off the page after printing, which component of a laser printer is malfunctioning?

    A. Print drum

    B. Fuser

    C. Paper feed rollers

    D. Corona

29. If a document requires the maximum amount of memory that is available to a laser printer, the printer might attempt to compress the document. Which of the following statements best describes the result of this compression on the final print page?

    A. Some text could be lost.

    B. The printed text may be cloudy.

    C. The print process will be slower.

    D. Some pictures could be deleted.

30. Which of the following print tools is used to manage and maintain print jobs?

    A. Print spooler

    B. Fuser

    C. Printheads

    D. XPS Document Writer

Answers and Explanations to Hands-On Labs

Lab 13-1: Beep Codes, Fans, Multimeter, and Hard Disk Testing

Almost all computers will beep when either memory or video is missing. However, if you need to attach a speaker, search for "PC motherboard internal speaker" or "mainboard internal speaker" at major computer parts online stores to find a single piece or bulk pack.

Most fans for current systems are 120mm or larger. Be sure to choose a ball-bearing model; sleeve-bearing fans wear out prematurely.

If you are testing a Dell computer's power supply, keep in mind that many models of Dell computers do not follow the ATX pin out. Look up your model to determine which pinout to use as a voltage guide.

Seagate (SeaTools), Western Digital (Data Lifeguard Diagnostics), and HGTS (WinDFT) all offer downloadable drive testing apps. Samsung and Maxtor drives use Seagate SeaTools.

Lab 13-2: Network, Mobile Device, and Printer Troubleshooting

Tracert may display as many as 20 hops or more to the website (URL) or IP address of a remote computer.

The Windows troubleshooters have improved tremendously in recent years, although they are not infallible.

For the most comprehensive view of your network connections from a Windows computer, use Ipconfig /all.

If you use a computer's USB port to charge your devices, use the special USB charging port if available on your system.

Laser printer cleaning sheets and inkjet printer cleaning sheets are available at most office supply stores.

Make sure all inkjet printer cartridges have plenty of ink before using the head-cleaning feature. Use it only if the nozzle check indicates some nozzles are clogged, as the cleaning process uses up ink.

Answers and Explanations to Review Questions

1. **D.** Reboot the computer and open the BIOS/UEFI menu. Check the BIOS settings for the CPU temperature. As a technician, you should be very familiar with all of the diagnostic information that is available in the BIOS.

2. **A.** A checksum error is generated when the CMOS settings have failed, either because they have been erased or because the CMOS battery has failed. If you see a checksum error message, acknowledge it and allow startup to continue. The system will load using the default BIOS settings.

3. **A, B, D.** POST checks the memory, keyboard, hard drives, and other essential hardware. The mouse is not considered to be essential to the operation of the computer and is not checked by POST. If POST finds any problems it reports those problems as error messages during startup.

4. **D.** When the clock and calendar on your computer are no longer able to keep accurate time, this is an indication of a failing CMOS battery.

5. **B.** This is a CMOS battery, which provides a constant source of electricity to the CMOS chip to maintain the CMOS programming.

6. **A.** The automatic reboot option is configured in System Properties on the Advanced tab under Startup and Recovery.

7. **A.** North America uses 115 volts. Europe and Asia use 230 volts.

8. **D.** These components are capacitors. Capacitors store an electrical charge and can deliver a painful and even dangerous shock if accidentally discharged.

9. **C.** A multimeter is used to test AC or DC voltage, continuity, resistance, and amperage. A loopback plug is used to test ports. PING is a network diagnostics program. A tone generator is used to test network cables.

10. **A, C, D, G, H.** A power supply should produce +3.3, +5.0, -5.0, +12.0, and -12.0 volts.

11. **B.** A loopback plug is used to test ports. You can attach a loopback plug to a port and run diagnostic programs to make sure that the port receives the same characters it sent.

12. **C.** A POST card is a device that detects the hexadecimal code produced by the BIOS during startup. These codes may be used to diagnose problems that are not necessarily reported by POST beep codes or screen messages.

13. **D.** This jumper forces the SATA drive to run at a slower rate to make it compatible with older host adapters.

14. **A.** Reboot the computer and access the BIOS startup program. Reorder the boot sequence and save the changes. Changes made to the BIOS configurations are saved on the CMOS chip.

15. **C.** S.M.A.R.T. refers to Self-Monitoring Analysis and Reporting Technology, which detects problems with and warns of failure of internal magnetic hard drives.

16. **D.** Normally, when you delete a file, it is not really deleted; it is moved to the Recycle Bin and may be recovered if you change your mind. If you press Shift and Delete at the same time, you will permanently delete the file.

17. **B, C.** Both Defragmentation (defrag) and error-checking (CHKDSK) can be accessed through the drive properties or from the command line.

18. **A.** VGA mode uses low resolution (640 x 480 on Windows Vista/7) with minimum colors and basic drivers and is used when troubleshooting display problems. A Windows system starts in VGA mode if Low-resolution mode or Safe mode has been selected at startup or if the correct drivers are not available.

19. **A, D.** If an LCD display is flickering, the most likely cause is a failing backlight or inverter.

20. **C.** Burn-in, the persistent display of a "ghost" image on-screen that was displayed previously, even after the current screen contents have changed, can affect both LCD and plasma displays. On an LCD display, it is frequently caused by stuck pixels.

21. **B.** A DHCP server is responsible for assigning IP addresses on a network. If valid IP addresses are not available, APIPA (169.254.x.x) addresses will be assigned. If your network is using APIPA addresses, you should add additional valid IP addresses to the DHCP server.

22. **D.** A crimper is used to attach coaxial, RJ45, or RJ11 connectors to network cables.

23.

Command	Function
A. PING	4. Tests connectivity between hosts on a network
B. Tracert	1. Traces data route (hops) between routers
C. NSLookup	2. Displays information about the default DNS server
D. IPConfig	6. Displays computer's IP address, subnet mask, and default gateway
E. IFConfig	3. Linux and OS X command that displays IP configuration information
F. Netstat	5. Displays IP address and domain name of a remote computer

24. **A, B.** Some cellular connections do not work well if Wi-Fi is enabled, so if you are having problems getting a clear cellular signal, you should disable your Wi-Fi connection. You should also try rotating your screen because the antenna is located around the periphery of the screen casing. 802.11 is a Wi-Fi specification. The iOS slider switch does not affect reception.

25. **A, C.** You can increase your battery life by not overcharging and by shutting down an iOS device weekly with the slider switch.

26. **D.** Vertical streaks that show up on every page printed by a laser printer usually indicate damage to the imaging drum. Low toner might cause uneven printing. A dirty print ribbon could create problems on a thermal printer or an impact printer. Damaged ink nozzles would be a problem on an inkjet printer.

27. **A.** Clogged or dirty printheads and rollers on an inkjet printer can cause smudging of the printed page. Fusers, photosensitive drums, and toner cartridges are components of a laser printer, not of an inkjet printer.

28. **B.** The fuser is responsible for heating the toner and pressing it into the paper. Brittle or flaking toner is indicative of a failing fuser.

29. **C.** Compressing the data in a print job takes time and that may make the print job slower.

30. **A.** The print spooler stores print jobs in a queue and releases the computer to perform other tasks while the spooler manages the print job.

This chapter covers the following subjects:

- **Differences Between Windows Versions**—Components and features are compared and contrasted in this section.

- **Boot Methods**—Network, optical disc, and USB boot methods are described in this section.

- **Installation Types**—Installation methods from clean install to image deployment are covered in this section.

- **Partitioning Methods**—Partitioning methods are different on drives over 2.1TB. Learn what has changed.

- **Windows File Systems**—Use this section to choose the best file system.

- **Configuring Windows During/After Installation**—Learn how to bring Windows up to date as quickly as possible.

- **Using the Factory Recovery Partition**—The factory recovery partition resets your system to its original state. Here's how to use it safely.

- **Refresh and Reset (Windows 8/8.1/10)**—Refresh and reset have very different effects, so this section helps you figure out when to use each option.

- **Characteristics of a Properly Formatted Boot Drive**—Discover what a properly formatted boot drive looks like in this section.

## CHAPTER 14

Windows Operating Systems Features and Installation

Windows Vista/7/8/8.1 differ widely in features, but use similar installation methods. In this chapter, you are introduced to the differences in appearance and features as well as the many options available for installing Windows on individual systems or for deployment to multiple computers.

220-902: Objective 1.1 Compare and contrast various features and requirements of Microsoft Operating Systems (Windows Vista, Windows 7, Windows 8, Windows 8.1).

220-902: Objective 1.2 Given a scenario, install Windows PC operating systems using appropriate methods.

Foundation Topics

Differences Between Windows Versions

System requirements for different versions of Windows vary widely. Table 14-1 compares the hardware requirements for Windows 8/8.1, Windows 7, and Vista.

Table 14-1   Minimum Hardware Requirements for Windows 8/8.1, Windows 7, and Vista

	Windows Version		
Component	**8/8.1#**	**7**	**Vista**
Processor	1GHz*	1GHz	800MHz
RAM	1GB (32-bit) 2GB (64-bit)	1GB (32-bit) 2GB (64-bit)	512MB
Free disk space	16GB (32-bit) 20GB (64-bit)	20GB	15GB (20GB partition)
Video/Graphics device	DirectX 9 graphics using WDDM v1.0 or higher driver	DirectX 9 graphics using WDDM v1.0 or higher driver	DirectX 9 graphics using WDDM v1.0 or higher driver; 128MB of RAM
Other	*	DVD-ROM drive	DVD-ROM or CD-ROM drive

Windows 10 requirements are similar to those for Windows 8.1. See https://www.microsoft.com/en-us/windows/windows-10-specifications for details

* See http://windows.microsoft.com/en-US/windows-8/system-requirements for additional processor features required and for other requirements for certain Windows features

NOTE   The specifications in Table 14-1 are the minimum requirements.

The terms *x86* and *x64* are important to understand: x86 refers to older CPU names that ended in an "86"—for example, the 80386 (shortened to just 386), 486, and so on. Generally, when people use the term *x86*, they are referring to 32-bit CPUs that allow for 4GB of address space, while x64 (or x86-64) refers to newer 64-bit CPUs that are a superset of the x86 architecture. This technology can run 64-bit software as well as 32-bit software and can address a maximum of 1TB.

32-bit Windows and **64-bit Windows** versions are available for Windows Vista/7/8/8.1/10 so that users from both generations of computers can run the software efficiently. 32-bit versions are primarily used on tablets that use the Intel ATOM or Celeron processors.

Windows Vista, Windows 7, and Windows 8/8.1 Features Compared

These versions of Windows share many features in common, particularly system management features in Control Panel. However, from the standpoint of user features, there are many differences. Table 14-2 summarizes these features, and the following sections describe them in more detail.

Table 14-2   Feature Comparisons for Windows Vista, 7, 8, and 8.1

Feature Category/Feature	Windows Version			
	8.1	8	7	Vista
Desktop				
Windows Aero	No	No	Yes	Yes
Sidebar	No	No	No	Yes
Gadgets	No	No	Yes	No
Start menu	No	No	Yes	Yes
Start screen	Yes	Yes	No	No
Pinning apps and files	Yes*	Yes*	Yes	Yes
Charms	Yes	Yes	No	No
Multi-monitor task bars	Yes	Yes	No	No
Modern UI (Windows Store) apps	Yes	Yes	No	No
Security				
Live sign-in (Microsoft account)	Yes	Yes	No**	No**
Local account	Yes	Yes	Yes	Yes
User Account Control	Yes	Yes	Yes	Yes
Defender antivirus	Yes	Yes	Yes	Yes
BitLocker full disk encryption	Yes	Yes	Yes	Yes
Windows Firewall	Yes	Yes	Yes	Yes
Action Center	Yes	Yes	Yes	No
Security Center	No	No	No	Yes
Management				
Control Panel	Yes	Yes	Yes	Yes

| | Windows Version | | | |
Feature Category/Feature	8.1	8	7	Vista
Administrative Tools	Yes	Yes	Yes	Yes
Settings	Yes	Yes	No	No
PowerShell	Yes	Yes	Yes	Optional download
Event Viewer	Yes	Yes	Yes	Yes
System Recovery				
Image Backup	Yes	Yes	Yes	Yes
File Backup	Yes	Yes	Yes	Yes
Shadow Copy	No***	No***	Yes	Yes
System Restore	Yes	Yes	Yes	Yes
Refresh and Reset	Yes	Yes	No	No
Software and App Support				
OneDrive (formerly SkyDrive)	Integrated	Optional download	Optional download	Optional download
ReadyBoost flash memory disk caching	Yes	Yes	Yes	Yes
Compatibility mode	Yes	Yes	Yes	Yes
Virtual XP mode	No	No	Optional download	No
Side-by-side apps	Yes	Yes	No	No
Windows Easy Transfer	No****	Yes	Yes	Yes
Windows (App) Store	Yes	Yes	No	No

* Apps and files can be pinned to the Start screen or the desktop taskbar

** System login uses a local account, but access to OneDrive requires a Microsoft account (formerly known as Live sign-in)

***Replaced by File History feature

****Laplink's PCMover Express, in cooperation with Microsoft, is available for free file, setting, and user profile transfers from Windows 8.1 to Windows 10. See http://pcmoverfree.azurewebsites.net/ for details.

Windows Desktop (Aero, Aero Glass, Sidebar, Gadgets, Start Screen, Start Menu)

One of the biggest differences between Windows Vista and Windows 7 and their successors, Windows 8/8.1, is the desktop. Introduced with Windows Vista, **Aero** features translucent windows, window animations, three-dimensional viewing of windows, and a modified taskbar. You can make modifications to the look of Aero by right-clicking the desktop and selecting **Personalization**. From here, you can modify things such as the window color and translucency of windows (Aero Glass). To disable Windows Aero, select **Windows Basic** or **Windows 7 Basic** from the Themes menu.

By contrast, Windows 8/8.1 do not use Aero, because these versions of Windows are designed to work on less powerful systems (low-end laptops and tablets) as well as full-featured desktop and laptop computers.

Figure 14-1 shows Aero Glass in the comparison of Windows 7's Start menu to Windows 8.1's **Start screen**.

1. Start button
2. Most frequently used apps
3. Windows Aero translucent menu and title bar
4. Access to all programs (apps)
5. Gadget (calendar)

1. Swipe in to see Charms
2. Swipe down for all apps
3. Live tile

Figure 14-1   The Windows 7 Aero desktop and Start menu with gadgets (top) compared to the Windows 8.1 Start screen (bottom).

Windows Vista also introduced the Windows **Sidebar** and small programs called **gadgets**. Gadgets are small programs such as clocks set for other time zones, slide-shows, RSS newsfeeds, weather updates, and more. Windows Vista and Windows 7 include a number of gadgets.

In Windows Vista, gadgets run only in the Windows Sidebar (see Figure 14-2), but in Windows 7, gadgets can run anywhere on the Windows desktop. In both versions of Windows, gadgets can have different opacities and sometimes are available in different sizes.

NOTE   Although existing gadgets continue to work, Microsoft no longer offers downloadable gadgets for Windows 7 or Vista because the Windows Sidebar platform has serious security vulnerabilities. For details, see http://windows.microsoft.com/en-US/windows/gadgets.

Live tiles in Windows 8/8.1/10 provide much of the functionality of gadgets without the security risks. For example, the Weather tile can display the current weather for your location, and the News tile can display headlines.

Figure 14-2   The Windows Vista Aero desktop and Start menu.

Vista and 7 can be configured to display a desktop and Start menu that emulate older Windows versions.

NOTE   To change only the Start menu to the Classic mode (Windows Vista only), right-click the Start button, select Properties, and choose Classic Start menu. To change the Start menu and the desktop to the Classic mode in Windows 7 or Windows Vista, open the Display properties sheet, select Personalization, select Themes, and select Windows Classic. You can open the Display properties sheet from Control Panel or by right-clicking an empty area of the desktop and selecting Properties.

Control Panel Views

Windows Vista offers two views of the Control Panel: **Category view vs Classic view.** Category view (the default) collects related applets into categories. Classic view displays all Control Panel icons individually. Classic view is known as Small Icons and Large Icons views in Windows 7/8/8.1/10, but Category view works the same as in Vista. For more information about Control Panel, see Chapter 15, "Managing Microsoft Windows."

Shadow Copy

Windows Vista Business, Ultimate, and Enterprise, and Windows 7 Professional and Ultimate include the Windows Shadow Copy feature. **Shadow Copy** stores previous versions of files in Windows restore points or in Windows Backup.

> **NOTE**   By default, Windows creates restore points only for the system drive. To enable restore points for other drives, you must enable **System Restore** for those drives and specify Restore previous versions of files. For more details, see the "Configuring System Restore Options" section on page 803 in Chapter 15.

If you overwrite a file with a newer one but want to return to the previous version of the file, follow this procedure:

Step 1.   Right-click the file in Windows Explorer.

Step 2.   Select **Properties**.

Step 3.   Click the **Previous Versions** tab.

Step 4.   Select the file version to restore. (If none are listed, no shadow copies are available.) If the file location is listed as Backup, insert the last disk in the backup media set, or attach the backup drive that contains the old version of the file.

Step 5.   Click **Restore** (see Figure 14-3).

Step 6.   To confirm the restoration, click **Restore**. The previous version replaces the current version.

Introduced in Windows 8, Windows now uses File History to make versioned backup copies of files. By default, it backs up files in the user's Documents, Pictures, Music, and Videos folders, but can also be configured to back up files in other folders. Just as with Shadow Copy, you can choose the file version to restore.

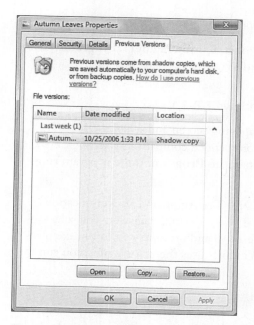

Figure 14-3 Using Shadow Copy to restore an earlier version of a file.

Compatibility Mode

Most commercial business applications should run properly on Windows 8.1/8/7/ Vista as well as on older versions of Windows. However, some commercial and custom applications designed for older versions of Windows and some games might not run properly on Windows 8.1/8/7/Vista.

To enable applications written for older versions of Windows to run properly on your current version of Windows, you can use **compatibility tools** such as the Program Compatibility Wizard built in to Windows or the Compatibility tab located on the executable file's properties sheet to run the program in a selected **compatibility mode**.

Starting Program Compatibility Wizard in Windows 8/8.1

To start the program in Windows 8/8.1, search for **Run Programs Made for Previous Versions of Windows** and click the matching app. You can also start it by opening Control Panel from the Windows desktop, pressing **Windows key+X** and then selecting **Control Panel, Programs, Run Programs Made for Previous Versions of Windows**.

Starting Program Compatibility Wizard in Windows 7

To start the program in Windows 7, click **Start, Control Panel > Programs > Run Programs Made for Previous Versions of Windows**.

Using Program Compatibility Wizard in Windows 7/8/8.1

After the wizard starts, click **Next** on the opening screen and select the program that doesn't work properly. To try the recommended compatibility settings, click **Try Recommended Settings** and click **Start the Program**. If the program runs properly, click **Next** and then click **Yes**.

If the program doesn't run properly, click **No, Try Again** and answer questions about the problems you noticed (see Figure 14-4). From the answers you select, Windows selects settings to try (see Figure 14-5) and prompts you to run the program. After you find settings that work, Windows uses them every time you run the program.

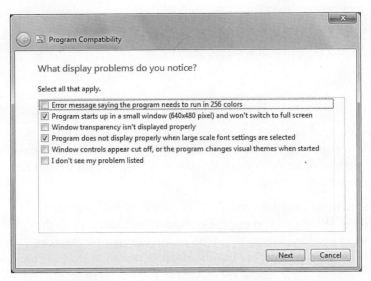

Figure 14-4   Answering questions about problems with an older program with Windows 7's Program Compatibility Wizard.

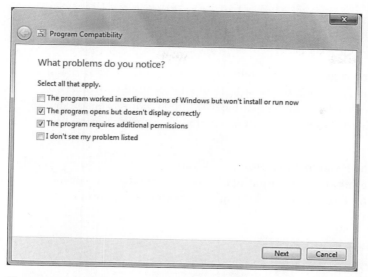

Figure 14-5 Based on your answers, Windows 7's Program Compatibility Wizard selects settings to help your older program run properly.

Program Compatibility Wizard in Windows Vista

To start the wizard in Windows Vista, click **Start, Control Panel > Programs > Use an Older Program with This Version of Windows**.

After the wizard starts, you can select from programs already installed on your computer, select the current program disc in the optical drive, or browse to the program manually. After you select a program, you can select the version of Windows the program worked best under.

On the next screen, you can select one or more of the following options to aid compatibility:

- **256 Colors**—Many older Windows programs can't run under 16-bit or higher color depths.

- **640 × 480 Screen Resolution**—Many older Windows programs use a fixed screen size and can't run properly on a high-resolution screen.

- **Disable Visual Themes**—Many older Windows programs were created before visual themes were common.

After selecting the options, test the program (which applies the settings you selected and runs the program). After you close the program, Windows switches back to its normal screen settings if necessary, and you can decide whether to use these settings for your software or try others. You can choose whether to inform Microsoft of your settings, and the settings you chose for the program are used automatically every time you run the program.

Keep in mind that the Program Compatibility Wizard won't work with all old Windows programs; in particular, the wizard should not be used with antivirus, disk, or system utilities that are not compatible with the Windows version in use. Instead, replace outdated applications with updated versions made for the version of Windows in use.

As an alternative to the Program Compatibility Wizard in Windows, you can apply the same settings by using the Compatibility tab on an executable file's properties sheet (see Figure 14-6). Use this method if you already know the appropriate settings to use.

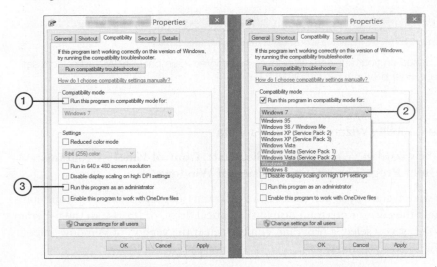

1. Click or tap to choose a Windows version to use for compatibility mode
2. Select the Windows version the program was designed for
3. Click or tap if the program must be run with elevated privileges

Figure 14-6   Using the Compatibility tab to specify compatibility settings in Windows 8.1. Older versions of Windows lack the OneDrive options checkbox.

TIP   To access the properties sheet for an app running Windows 8/8.1, right-click or press and hold the app's icon in the Apps or All Apps dialog, click or tap Open file location, right-click or press and hold the app in File Manager, and click or tap Properties.

Virtual XP Mode

Windows 7 Professional, Ultimate, and Enterprise support a virtualization environment called Windows XP Mode or **Virtual XP Mode**. This mode enables users of these versions of Windows 7 to use a virtualization-ready edition of Windows XP Professional within a virtualization program called Windows Virtual PC. Programs installed in Windows XP Mode can be run from the Windows 7 Start menu as well as from Windows XP Mode. To download **Windows Virtual PC,** go to https://www.microsoft.com/en-us/download/details.aspx?id=3702. To download Windows XP Mode (also known as Virtual XP Mode), go to https://www.microsoft.com/en-us/download/details.aspx?id=8002.

CAUTION   Windows XP is no longer supported by Microsoft, so no new security updates are available for Virtual XP Mode. Use this as a short-term workaround until apps can be updated for use with Windows 7, 8/8.1, or newer Windows versions.

To learn more about virtualization, see the "Client-Side Virtualization Overview" section on page 958 in Chapter 19.

Administrative Tools

Vista/7/8/8.1/10 all include a Control Panel folder called **Administrative Tools**. This folder provides shortcuts to a variety of management, configuration, and troubleshooting tools:

- Component Services—Used by developers and administrators to configure and administer Component Object Model (COM) components

- Computer Management—Manages local and remote computers, including viewing system events, managing services, configuring hard drive storage, and others

- Data Sources (ODBC)—Moves data between different types of databases using Open Database Connectivity (ODBC)

- **Event Viewer**—Displays the contents of system logs for errors, program start and stop, and other significant events

- iSCSI Initiator—Configures devices on storage networks that use Internet Small Computer System Interface (iSCSI) connections

- Local Security Policy—Views and edits Group Policy security settings

- Performance Monitor—Monitors performance of CPU, memory, hard drive, and network

- Print Management—Manages and administers network printers and print servers

- Services—Manages background services (print spooler, search, others)

- System Configuration—Starts MSConfig, which helps troubleshoot problems with Windows

- Task Scheduler—Schedules programs and tasks

- **Windows Firewall** with Advanced Security—Creates rules and other advanced firewall settings for local and remote computers on the network

- Windows Memory Diagnostic—Tests computer RAM to verify proper functioning before the Windows desktop appears

- Windows PowerShell Modules—Runs Windows **PowerShell**, a powerful scripting language

NOTE See Chapter 15 for more information about Computer Management, Device Manager, Event Viewer, local security policy, Windows Firewall with Advanced Security, Performance Monitor, Print Management, Services, Msconfig (System Configuration), Windows Memory Diagnostics, Component Services, Disk Management, and Task Scheduler.

Modern UI

Windows 8/8.1 introduced **Modern UI** (previously known as Metro UI), which runs apps in full-screen. The tiles on the Start screen and the All Apps screen are used to launch programs, and some of these tiles can be live (Weather, Photos, News, Sports, and others), displaying updated information.

Figure 14-7 shows a Modern UI app, Internet Explorer.

TIP Starting with Windows 8.1 Update 1, Modern UI apps can also be closed by moving the mouse to the top-right corner of the screen. The app's title bar appears. Click the X to close the app, or the – to minimize the app, just as with Win32 desktop apps.

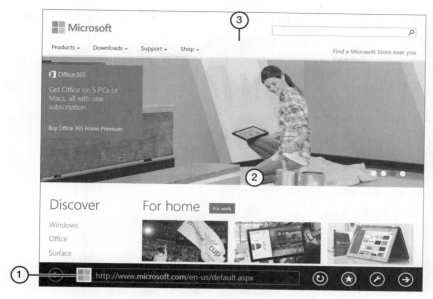

1. Hover mouse at bottom of app to display URL
2. App runs full-screen
3. Click or tap and drag top of window down to the bottom of the display to close app

Figure 14-7   Using a Modern UI app in Windows 8.1, Internet Explorer.

Side-by-Side Apps

Windows 8/8.1 support **side-by-side apps**: when at least two apps are running (the desktop and all the apps running in the desktop count as one app), the apps can share the screen.

After starting the apps, drag one app from the upper-left side of the display into the screen. The screen splits to make room (see Figure 14-8).

1. Active app
2. Running app dragged in from upper-left corner
3. Drag border to adjust screen split

Figure 14-8   Running apps side by side in Windows 8.1

Pinning Programs to the Taskbar

Pinning programs to the taskbar is supported in Windows 7 and newer releases. If the program is already running, right-click or press and hold the program icon on the taskbar and select **Pin this program to taskbar** (with Windows 8/8.1, the taskbar is only available on the Windows desktop).

To pin a program that is not running, drag the program shortcut from the Start menu or desktop to the taskbar. You can also right-click the program shortcut and select **Pin to Taskbar** (see Figure 14-9).

OneDrive Cloud Storage

OneDrive (formerly known as SkyDrive) cloud storage is a free service available to any user with a Microsoft (formerly Windows Live) account. Higher-capacity storage plans are available free to users of Office 365.

NOTE   In late 2015, Microsoft introduced a subscription version known as OneDrive for Business.

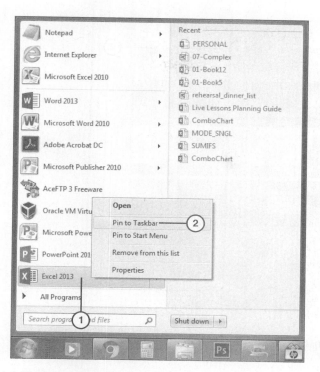

1. Right-click or press and hold the app
2. Select Pin to Taskbar

Figure 14-9 Pinning a program to the Taskbar.

In Windows Vista, 7, and 8, OneDrive can be used by logging into the Microsoft OneDrive Live website and using a browser interface. Windows 7 and 8 can also install the OneDrive client available at https://onedrive.live.com/about/en-us/download/. Windows 8.1 and Windows 10 have an integrated OneDrive app (see Figure 14-10).

Whether OneDrive is used with a browser or the integrated client, it provides file synchronization between the cloud and the selected device.

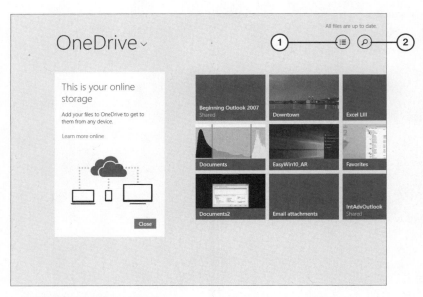

1. Click or tap to change view
2. Click or tap to search for a file

Figure 14-10   The Windows 8.1 OneDrive app.

Windows Store

Windows 8 introduced the **Windows Store** (see Figure 14-11) for free and paid apps. Apps installed through the Windows Store can be easily updated and will be reinstalled when the computer is refreshed. By contrast, apps installed from disc or downloads are removed and must be reinstalled.

The update from Windows 8 to Windows 8.1 must be acquired through the Windows Store.

Multi-monitor Task Bars

In Windows 8.1/10, when you use multiple displays, you can enable the taskbar to be displayed across all screens (**multi-monitor task bars**) with a setting in the taskbar properties sheet.

Charms

Windows 8/8.1 introduced **Charms** (see Figure 14-12), which are displayed when the user swipes in from the right or moves the mouse to the lower-right corner of the screen. The charms in Windows 8/8.1 are Search, Share, Start, Devices, and Settings.

NOTE   Charms have been discontinued in Windows 10. Their replacements are available in the left side of the Start menu.

Figure 14-11   The Windows Store offers free and paid apps and media.

1a. Hover mouse over lower-right corner
1b. Swipe in from the right (touchscreen)

Figure 14-12   Use Charms to access major features of Windows 8.1.

Live Sign In

Starting with Windows 8, the preferred way to sign into your computer is with a Microsoft account, also known as a **Live sign in**. Although you can continue to use a local account (the only kind of account used in Windows Vista and 7), using a local account in Windows 8/8.1/10 prevents use of the Windows Store or synchronization of desktops and settings between computers used by the same account. Also, users with a local account must sign in manually with their Microsoft account before using OneDrive or other services that use a Microsoft account.

Action Center

The Windows **Action Center** is available from the taskbar in Windows 7/8/8.1/10. It replaces the **Security Center** in Windows Vista. Click the flag icon to display messages about your computer. When the flag is white, there are no issues. When the flag is marked with a yellow or red sign, action is recommended or urgent. Click or tap the flag for a digest of needed actions (see Figure 14-13a). Click or tap **Open Action Center** for more information (see Figure 14-13b).

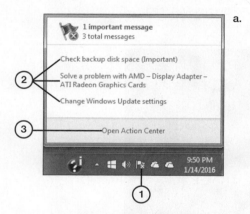

a.

1. Action Center flag indicates problems
2. Click or tap to deal with a specific issue
3. Click or tap to open Action Center

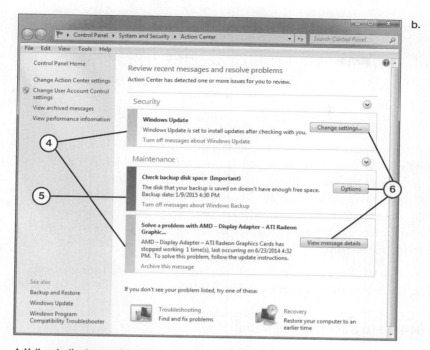

4. Yellow indicates moderate issues
5. Red indicates serious issues
6. Click or tap to deal with the specific issue listed

Figure 14-13   Using the Action Center.

File Structure and Paths

Windows Vista, Windows 7, and Windows 8/8.1/10 **file structure and paths** vary both by operating system version and by whether a 32-bit or 64-bit version of Windows is in use.

In all of these versions of Windows, user folders are stored in the path

  C:\Users*UserName*\

Libraries (Documents, Music, Pictures, and Videos) as well as folders such as Desktop, Download, Favorites, Saved Games, and so on are stored as subfolders of \ UserName\.

NOTE On some systems, particularly those upgraded from older versions of Windows, Documents might be identified as My Documents, Pictures as My Pictures, and so on.

Libraries

Libraries are a folder structure introduced in Windows 7 that permit multiple folders containing related material to be viewed as a single logical folder. For example, by default, the user's Documents library includes the user's My Documents or Documents folder and the shared Public Documents folder. Libraries can be modified by adding other folders, such as a folder on an external drive or a network folder. All local folders in a library are backed up by Windows Backup when the library is selected for backup.

In Windows 8/8.1/10, libraries are still available, but are not created automatically. You can specify whether to use libraries in File Explorer.

32-Bit Versus 64-Bit File Structure and Paths

In 32-bit versions of Windows Vista/7/8/8.1/10, all program files are stored in a subfolder of C:\Program Files\. However, in 64-bit editions C:\Program Files\ is used for 64-bit programs and drivers. 32-bit programs are stored in C:\Program Files (x86)\.

Windows Upgrade Paths

You can use various types of system analysis programs and tools to verify that a system's hardware will be compatible with Windows 8/8.1, Windows 7, or Windows Vista. If you are checking a computer that already has an operating system installed, use the tools discussed next.

If you are upgrading a system to Windows 7, run the Windows 7 Upgrade Advisor, available from https://www.microsoft.com/en-us/download/details.aspx?id=20. It will determine if your system is ready for Windows 7, and what changes might need to be made. Figure 14-14 shows a typical report.

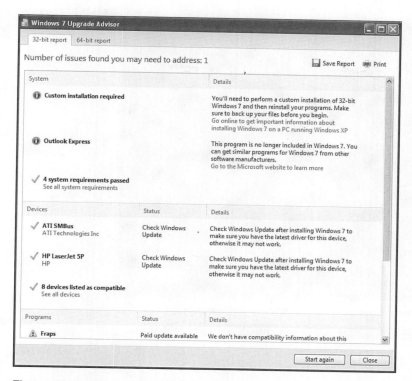

Figure 14-14   The Windows 7 Upgrade Advisor report on this system finds only one minor problem.

If you are upgrading to Windows 8.1, download and run the Windows 8.1 Upgrade Assistant, available from http://windows.microsoft.com/en-us/windows-8/upgrade-from-windows-7-tutorial. It will determine if your system is ready for Windows 8.1, and what changes might need to be made. Figure 14-15 shows a typical report.

On the 220-902 exam, these utilities are referred to as **Windows OS upgrade advisor**.

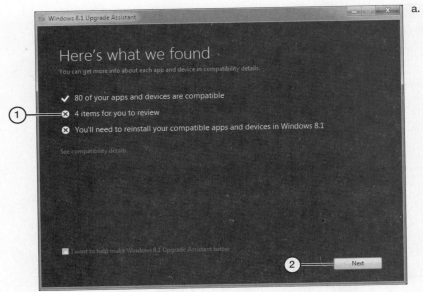

a.

1. Click to see items to review   2. Click to continue with upgrade

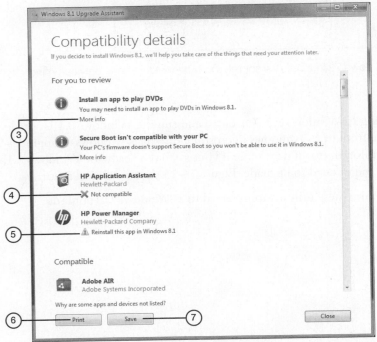

b.

3. Click or tap for more information about the issue   6. Click to print compatibility
4. Listed app will not work in Windows 8.1 (get a replacement if available)   report
5. Reinstall this app after updating to Windows 8.1   7. Click to save report

Figure 14-15   The Windows 8.1 Upgrade Assistant report on this system finds four issues (a). Click to see details (b).

If you want more details about your system's hardware and software, use one of these tools:

- **System Information**—You can access the Windows System Information tool by opening the Run/Search prompt and typing msinfo32.exe. See Figure 14-16.

- **Belarc Advisor**—Currently a free download, you can find this program at www.belarc.com/free_download.html. It's extremely quick and painless; all you need to do is double-click it after the download is complete. It automatically installs, looks for updates, and creates a profile of your computer that runs in a browser window. Here you can find all the hardware-related (and software-related) information on one screen. It also lists system security status.

- **SiSoftware Sandra**—Powerful, flexible system reporting, benchmarking, and evaluation program. Available in limited-feature free and various commercial versions from www.sisoftware.co.uk (current versions support Windows 7 and newer versions).

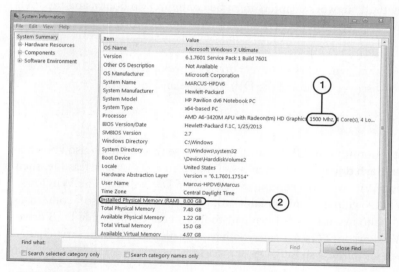

1. CPU speed
2. Memory size

Figure 14-16   System Information shows that this computer has enough RAM and a fast enough processor to run Windows 8.1.

For computers without an installed operating system, use self-booting diagnostic programs such as

- #1-TuffTEST (available from www.tufftest.com)
- PC Check (available from www.eurosoft-uk.com)
- Ultimate Boot CD (available from www.ultimatebootcd.com/index.html)

Boot Methods

You can use many methods to boot a system during the installation process:

- **CD-ROM boot** or **DVD boot** (booting from the distribution DVD or CD)— Use this method to install Windows to an individual PC and to create a master PC from which disk images can be created.

- **PXE boot** (Preboot eXecution Environment) —Use this method to install Windows to one or more systems that have working network connections. To use this method, network adapters must be configured to boot using the PXE boot ROM to a network location that contains an operating system image.

NOTE   **Netboot** is a similar network boot technology developed by Apple. Netboot uses the boot server discovery protocol (BSDP) to locate and install operating system files.

- **USB boot** (booting from USB thumb drive)—Use this method (also known as **solid state/flash drives boot**) when installing from a DVD isn't feasible, such as installing Windows to a computer that lacks a DVD drive. The Windows USB/DVD Download Tool available from https://www.microsoft.com/en-us/download/windows-usb-dvd-download-tool can create a bootable USB drive from a Windows ISO (.iso) image you have downloaded. If necessary, change the boot order in the system BIOS or UEFI firmware to permit booting from USB.

Other sources for Windows installation files include:

- **Internal hard drive (partition)**
- **External/hot-swappable drive**

With each of these types of drives, the Windows installation files could be extracted or, with Windows 7 or later, the ISO file could be used as an installation source.

Installation Types

You can install Windows in a variety of ways. The most common methods include:

- As an upgrade to an existing version
- As a clean install to an empty hard drive or to the same partition as the current version
- To unused disk space (new partition) to multiboot the current or new version as needed
- As a repair installation to fix problems with the current installation
- With the **recovery partition** (resets the system to its original installed state)
- Refresh/reset (Windows 8/8.1/10)

> **NOTE**   Refresh/reset may be listed as "Refresh/restore" on the 220-902 exam.

The preceding installation options typically use the original distribution media or preinstalled recovery files.

Large-scale or customized installations might use the following methods:

- Unattended installation
- Remote network installation
- Image deployment

This second group of installation options typically require the creation of an image file.

Upgrade Installation

To perform an **upgrade** installation of Windows, start the installation process from within your existing version of Windows. You can upgrade directly from Windows Vista to Windows 7, and from Windows 7 to Windows 8, from Windows 8 to 8.1, and from Windows 8/8.1 to Windows 10. These upgrade paths enable the user to retain apps and settings as well as personal files. Other upgrade paths, such as from Windows 7 to Windows 8.1, enable the user to keep personal files but not apps or settings.

The exact upgrade paths between Windows versions vary according to the Windows edition currently in use. You can upgrade to the equivalent or better edition of Windows but not a lower edition. For example, Windows 7 Professional or Ultimate to Windows 8 Pro but not to Windows 8 Home; Windows 8 Pro to Windows 8.1 Pro, but not Home. The 32-bit versions can upgrade to 32-bit versions only; 64-bit versions can upgrade to 64-bit versions only.

> **NOTE**   To learn more about Windows 8/8.1 upgrade paths, see https://technet.microsoft.com/en-us/library/jj203353.aspx. To learn more about Windows 10 upgrades, see www.microsoft.com/en-us/windows/windows-10-upgrade.

Clean Install

Before starting a **clean install** process, check the following:

- Make sure the drive for installation is placed before the hard drive in the boot sequence. The system needs to boot from the Windows distribution media if you are installing to an empty hard drive. You can perform a clean install of Windows 7 from within an older version of Windows if you want to replace the older installation.

- If you will be installing to a drive that might require additional drivers (SATA, RAID, or third-party host adapters on the motherboard or in an expansion slot), have the drivers available on any type of removable media supported by the system. To learn more, see "Loading Alternative Drivers," later in this chapter.

If you are installing from optical media, a disk image (ISO or VXD), or within a virtual machine (VM), after restarting the system with the CD or DVD media or image file in place, press a key when prompted to boot.

During the installation process, be prepared to confirm, enter, select, or provide the following settings, information, media, or options when prompted:

- **Custom installation**—Choose this option if you are performing a "clean boot" installation to an unused portion of the hard drive or if you want to wipe out the existing installation rather than upgrade it.

- **Edition of Windows you are installing**—If you specify the incorrect version, the installation cannot be activated.

- **Location (home, work/office, or public**—The location information is used to configure Windows Firewall.

- **Network settings**—These are normally detected automatically for a wired connection. If your connection is wireless, make sure you have the SSID and password (encryption key) available, or you will need to skip this part of the process.

- **Partition location, partition type, and file system**—See "Partitioning Overview" and "Windows File Systems" in this chapter for details.

- **Password and password hint**—Windows prompts for a password, but only Windows 7 and newer versions also prompt for a password hint.

- **Product key**—Some installation processes enable you to skip this temporarily, but you must provide it before you can activate Windows.

- **Time, date, language, and region**—See "Time/Date/Language/Region Settings" in this chapter for details.

- **Time zone, time, and date**—U.S. editions of Windows default to Pacific time.

- **Username and company name**—The company name is optional.

- **Workgroup or domain name**—See "Workgroup Vs. Domain Setup," later in this chapter, for details.

NOTE   The settings in the previous list are in alphabetical order. Operating systems prompt for this information at different points in the installation process.

At the end of the process, remove the distribution media. Windows is ready to download the latest updates and service packs.

Multiboot Installation

A **multiboot** installation of Windows enables you to choose from two or more operating systems when you start your computer. Windows Vista, Windows 7, and Windows 8/8.1 all support multiboot installations. If you want to use the multiboot support built in to Windows, follow these rules:

- **Install the oldest version of Windows first**—For example, if you want to multiboot Windows 7 and Windows 8.1, install Windows 7 first.

- **You must install Windows into a separate disk partition than the previous operating systems, and the partition must be prepared as a primary partition**—For example, say you want to install Windows 7 and Windows 8.1 to multiboot on a 2TB hard drive. First, install Windows 7 to a primary partition that uses only a portion of the disk, and leave the rest of the drive unassigned. When you install Windows 8.1, you would create a new primary partition on the remainder of the drive and install to that partition.

- **If you want to install multiple editions of Windows as a multiboot, each installation must be to its own primary partition**—You can have up to four primary partitions on a hard drive. However, you can create primary partitions on more than one hard drive, so if you have two bootable hard drives, you could (theoretically) install up to eight different Windows editions.

- **Windows' multiboot support does not cover non-Windows operating systems such as Linux**—Use a third-part boot manager if you want to multiboot Windows and non-Windows operating systems, or if you need to install an older version of Windows to multiboot on a system that already has a newer Windows version installed.

TIP If you need access to older Windows versions or non-Windows operating systems and don't want to reboot your system to switch between operating systems, use virtualization. Virtualization enables you to run operating systems in their own windows inside your primary operating system. To learn more, see the "Virtualization" section in Chapter 19, "Virtualization, Cloud Computing, and Network Services."

Repair Installation

If a Windows operating system installation becomes corrupt, you can use a **repair installation** to restore working files and Registry entries without losing existing programs or information. Repair installations are available in Windows Vista/7/8/8.1. You should make a backup copy of your data files (stored in *User**Username* for each user of your PC) before performing a repair installation in case of problems.

NOTE The repair installation process is also known as an **in-place upgrade**.

To perform a **repair installation** of Windows Vista or Windows 7:

Step 1. Boot your computer normally (that is, to the Windows desktop).

Step 2. Insert your Windows disc.

Step 3. Start the setup program when prompted.

Step 4. Specify or accept the language, time and currency format, and keyboard layout, and click **Next** (see Figure 14-17).

Step 5. Click **Repair your computer**.

Step 6.   Accept the end-user licensing agreement.

Step 7.   Select **Upgrade** as the installation option.

The remainder of the installation proceeds as with a normal installation.

At the end of the installation, be sure to install the latest service pack and updates available for your version of Windows.

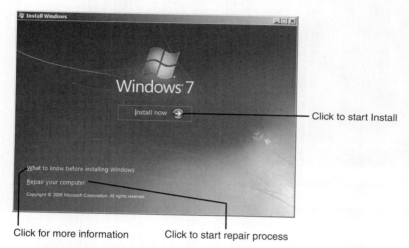

Click to start Install

Click for more information   Click to start repair process

Figure 14-17   Starting the Windows 7 installation from within Windows.

To perform a repair installation on Windows 8/8.1 (see Figure 14-18):

Step 1.   Boot your computer normally (that is, to the Windows Start screen).

Step 2.   Insert your Windows disc.

Step 3.   Start the setup program when prompted.

Step 4.   Confirm language and other settings. Click **Next**.

Step 5.   Click **Repair your computer**.

The remainder of the installation proceeds as with a normal installation.

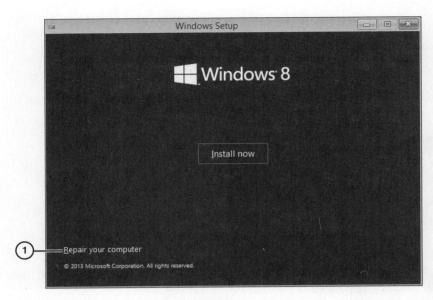

1. Click or tap to run a repair installation

Figure 14-18 Starting a repair installation of Windows 8.1.

At the end of the installation, be sure to install the latest service pack or updates available for your version of Windows.

CAUTION If you run a repair installation on a system that was upgraded from Windows 8 to Windows 8.1, your system will revert to Windows 8. Install necessary updates via Windows Update until you can install Windows 8.1 from the Windows Store. Then update your Windows 8.1 installation via Windows Update.

Unattended Installation

In an attended installation, you must provide information at various points during the process. To perform an **unattended installation**, you must create the appropriate type of answer file for the installation type. Microsoft currently offers the Microsoft Deployment Toolkit (MDT) 2013 Update 2 for automated installation of Windows 7, Windows 8.1, Windows 10, and Windows Server 2008 R2 and newer versions. The MDT creates and updates the Unattend.xml file (used to provide answers during the process) automatically during the deployment. Download the MDT from the Microsoft website (https://technet.microsoft.com/en-us/windows/dn475741.aspx).

Windows 7 and Vista use the Windows System Image Manager to create the Unattend.xml file.

NOTE   The Windows System Image Manager (SIM) for Vista and Windows 7 is part of the Windows Automated Installation Kit (AIK), which can be downloaded from Microsoft's website—search for Windows Automated Installation Kit (AIK).

Remote Network Installation

A **remote network installation** (installing Windows from a network drive) begins by starting the computer with a network client and logging on to the server to start the process. If you want to automate the process, Windows 8/8.1, and 7, and Vista can all be installed from a network drive automatically using **Windows Deployment Services**. Windows Deployment Services is included in Windows Server 2008 and newer server operating systems.

Server-based programs work along with the Microsoft Development Toolkit or Windows System Image Manager program. These programs are used to create an answer file. The answer file provides the responses needed for the installation.

Image Deployment

An **image deployment** is the process of installing Windows from a disk image of another installation. This process is also called disk cloning. You can create a disk image with a variety of tools, including Acronis True Image (www.acronis.com), Seagate DiscWizard (based in part on Acronis True Image, available from www.seagate.com), Acronis True Image WD Edition (available from www.wdc.com), Daemon Tools (www.daemon-tools.cc/eng/downloads), Macrium Reflect (www.macrium.com), and others.

NOTE   You can burn a disc image file, which often has either an .iso or .img filename extension, to a recordable CD or DVD by using Windows Disc Image Burner in Windows 7/8/8.1/10.

However, if you plan to deploy a disk image to multiple computers, rather than as a backup of a single computer, you must consider special issues:

- **Hardware differences**—Traditional image cloning methods, such as those using Acronis True Image, were designed for restoration to identical hardware (same motherboard, mass storage host adapters, same BIOS configuration, same Hardware Abstraction Layer [HAL] and same Ntoskrnl.exe [NT kernel] file). For organizations that have different types and models of computers, this poses a problem.

- **Same Security Identifier**—A cloned system is identical in every way to the original, including having the same Security Identifier (SID). This can cause conflicts in a network.

To overcome these problems, use cloning programs designed to capture an image that can be deployed to different types of computers (laptops, desktops, and tablets) with different hardware and software.

To create an image of Windows 7 or Windows Vista for installation, use the free Microsoft ImageX utility (ImageX.exe) that is part of the Windows Automated Installation Kit. For Windows 8/8.1 (as well as Windows 7), use the Deployment Imaging Servicing and Management (DISM) tool included in the Windows Assessment and Deployment Kit (ADK). DISM is also installed on some Windows 10 editions.

Third-party tools, such as Symantec Ghost Solution Suite (www.symantec.com) and Acronis Snap Deploy (www.acronis.com), are also designed to create images that can be deployed to dissimilar hardware.

To fix problems with the SID and network settings, use the Sysprep utility from Microsoft to enable a system image created with ImageX, DISM, or other imaging tools to make needed changes in SID and network settings after it has been transferred to a destination system. (Ghost Solution Suite and Snap Deploy include similar features.)

The Sysprep utility for Windows is installed with the operating system and can be found by navigating to C:\Windows\System32\Sysprep. Sysprep is installed on a system that will be used for cloning before it is cloned.

When Sysprep for Windows is run as a GUI (see Figure 14-19), the following options are available: System Audit Mode, enabling additional apps and drivers to be added; Generalize, which clears away unique system identification information, such as security ID, restore points, and event logs (this option must be selected for any system that will be used for cloning); and System-Out-of-Box Experience (OOBE), which prompts the user to customize, set up user accounts, name the computer, and perform other first-time startup tasks. Sysprep can be run with additional options from the command line, including the option to use an answer file (Unattend.xml). If the answer file does not have the answer needed by the setup program, the user setting up the system is prompted to provide this information, such as the Windows license number (Product key).

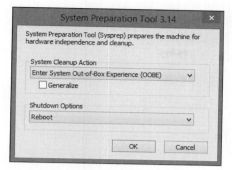

Figure 14-19 Starting the Sysprep tool on a Windows 8.1 system.

All cloning tools can work with a target drive that is the same size or larger than the original cloned system drive. Some can also work with a smaller drive; check documentation for details.

CAUTION Do not use disk cloning to make illegal copies of Windows. You can use disk-cloning software legally to make a backup copy of your installation, but if you want to duplicate the installation on another PC, make sure you clone a system created with a volume license for Windows and make sure that you do not exceed the number of systems covered by that license, or make sure you have the correct license number (Product key) for each duplicate system. You can clone standalone computers or those connected to a workgroup (but not those that are members of a domain). For more information about licensing, see https://www.microsoft.com/en-us/licensing/default.aspx.

Partitioning Methods

Whether Windows is being installed to an empty hard drive or to a hard drive that has unassigned space (for multibooting), at least one new hard drive partition must be created. To do this successfully, you need to understand the differences between

- Master boot record (MBR) and GUID Partition Table (GPT) partition tables
- Primary and extended partitions
- Extended partitions and logical disk drives
- Dynamic and Basic disks

Partitioning Overview

A hard drive cannot be used until it is prepared for use. There are two steps involved in preparing a hard drive:

- Creating partitions
- Formatting partitions (which assigns drive letters)

A disk partition is a logical structure on a hard drive that specifies the following:

- Whether the drive can be bootable
- How many drive letters (one, two, or more) the hard drive will contain
- Whether any of the hard drive's capacity will be reserved for a future operating system or other use

Although the name "disk partition" suggests the drive will be divided into two or more logical sections, every hard drive must go through a partitioning process, even if you want to use the entire hard drive as a single drive letter. All versions of Windows support two major types of disk partitions:

- **Primary**—A **primary** partition can contain only a single drive letter and can be made active (bootable). Only one primary partition can be active. Although a single physical drive using MBR can hold up to four primary partitions, you need only one primary partition on a drive that contains a single operating system. If you install a new operating system in a multiboot configuration with your current operating system, you must install the new operating system to a different disk partition than the previous Windows version. If you want to use a non-Windows operating system along with your current operating system, it should be installed into its own primary partition. A drive partitioned using GPT can have up to 128 primary partitions.

NOTE   Depending on the layout and contents of your current disk partitions, you might be able to shrink the size of existing partitions with Windows Disk Management to make room for a new primary partition, or you might need to use third-party software such as Acronis Disk Director or EaseUS Partition Master.

- **Extended**—An **extended** partition differs from a primary partition in two important ways:
  - An extended partition doesn't become a drive letter but can contain one or more logical drives, each of which is assigned a drive letter.
  - Neither an extended partition nor any drive it contains can be bootable.

Only one extended partition can be stored on each physical drive. Extended partitions are used only with MBR drives.

MBR Versus GPT Partition Types

Master boot record (MBR) partitions are supported by classic ROM BIOS as well as UEFI firmware. MBR supports a maximum drive size of 2TB and up to four primary partitions.

GPT (GUID partition table) supports drives up to 256TB and up to 128 primary partitions. GPT is also more reliable than MBR because it protects the partition table with replication and cyclic redundancy check (CRC) of the partition table's contents. GPT also provides a standard way for system vendors to create additional partitions. GPT partition tables are supported by UEFI firmware.

To boot from a GPT drive, the system must have a 64-bit version of Windows Vista/7/8/8.1 or later (Windows Server 2003 SP1 and newer also support GPT). 32-bit versions of Windows can use GPT drives for data.

Disk Preparation Using MBR

If the drive will be used by a single operating system using an MBR partition table, one of these three ways of partitioning the drive will be used:

- **Primary partition occupies 100% of the physical drive's capacity**—This is typically the way the hard drive on a system sold at retail is used and is also the default for disk preparation with Windows. This is suitable for the only drive in a system or an additional drive that can be used to boot a system but should not be used for additional drives in a system that will be used for data storage.

- **Primary partition occupies a portion of the physical drive's capacity, and the remainder of the drive is occupied by an extended partition**—This enables the operating system to be stored on the primary partition and the applications and data to be stored on one or more separate logical drives (drive letters created inside the extended partition). This is a common setup for laptops but requires the partitioning process to be performed with different settings than the defaults. This configuration is suitable for the only drive or first drive in a multiple-drive system.

- **Extended partition occupies 100% of the physical drive's capacity**—The drive letters on the extended partition can be used to store applications or data but not for the operating system. An extended partition cannot be made active (bootable). This configuration is suitable for additional hard drives in a system (not the first drive); an extended partition can contain only one logical drive or multiple logical drives.

You can also leave some unpartitioned space on the hard drive for use later, either for another operating system or another drive letter.

After a disk is partitioned, the drive letters must be formatted using a supported file system.

- **Extended**—An extended partition differs from a primary partition in two important ways:

  - An extended partition doesn't become a drive letter but can contain one or more logical drives, each of which is assigned a drive letter.

  - Neither an extended partition nor any drive it contains can be bootable.

Only one extended partition can be stored on each physical drive.

After local drives are created in an extended partition, the drive letters must be formatted using a supported file system.

Partitioning Using GPT

GPT partitioning creates one or more primary partitions. There are no extended partitions or logical drives on a GPT drive; each partition can be assigned a drive letter. However, only one can be active.

Dynamic and Basic Disks

Windows supports two types of disks: **basic** and **dynamic**. A dynamic disk is more versatile than a basic disk because you can span two physical drives into a single logical drive, create striped or mirrored arrays, and adjust the size of a partition. However, during installation, Windows creates only basic disks. Only basic disks can be bootable.

> **NOTE**   To learn more about working with disk drives in Windows after installation, see "Disk Management" in Chapter 15.

Creating Partitions During Windows Vista/7/8/8.1/10 Installation

If you install Windows Vista/7/8/8.1 to an empty hard drive, you will be prompted for a location:

- To use all the space in the disk, make sure that the disk and partition you want is highlighted, and click **Next** (see Figure 14-20).

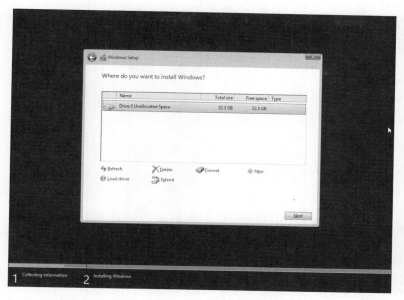

Figure 14-20   Example of using an entire disk for the Windows 8.1 Installation.

- To use only part of the space, click **Drive Options (Advanced),** click **New,** specify the partition size, and click **Apply**. Windows displays a message that it is creating an additional partition. Click **OK** to clear the message. A system-reserved partition is created, followed by the partition size you selected, which will be used by Windows, and the unused (unallocated) space. See Figure 14-21.

- To use an existing partition, highlight the wanted partition, and click **Next**. Be careful; whatever partition you select for the installation will be formatted, and all data on that partition will be erased.

You can also format partitions from here; they are automatically formatted as NTFS. In addition, you can extend existing partitions to increase the size of the partition but without losing any data.

NOTE   When you use the entire drive for Windows, a system-reserved partition is also created. You can see it after starting Windows by using the Disk Management administrative tool.

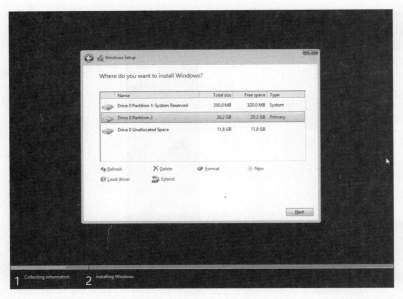

Figure 14-21   The installation dialog after specifying only part of the partition size.

Windows File Systems

What exactly is a **file system**, anyway? A file system describes how data and drives are organized. In Windows, the file system you choose for a hard drive affects the following:

- The rules for how large a logical drive (drive letter) can be and whether the hard drive can be used as one big drive letter, several smaller drive letters, or must be multiple drive letters.

- How efficiently a system stores data; the less wasted space, the better.

- How secure a system is against tampering.

- Whether a drive can be accessed by more than one operating system.

The term *file system* is a general term for how an operating system stores various types of files. Windows supports three different file systems for hard drives and USB flash drives: FAT32, NTFS, and exFAT, and CDFS for CD drives.

> **NOTE**   **CDFS** is the file system used for CD media. Some external drives used for hard drive backup, such as Clickfree Automatic Backup drives, use a small CDFS partition for utility software.

FAT32

FAT32 was introduced in 1995 and has the following characteristics:

- The 32-bit file allocation table, which allows for 268,435,456 entries (2^{32}) per drive. Remember, an entry can be a folder or an allocation unit used by a file.

- The root directory can be located anywhere on the drive and can have an unlimited number of entries, which is a big improvement over FAT.

- FAT32 uses an 8KB allocation unit size for drives as large as 16GB.

- The maximum logical partition size allowed is 2TB (more than 2 trillion bytes).

NOTE Windows can't create a FAT32 partition larger than 32GB. However, if the partition already exists, Windows can use it.

You can use FAT32 to format hard drives, flash memory, and removable media drives. However, it is primarily used today for flash memory cards and USB flash drives.

NOTE If you want to store scheduled backups on a hard drive with Windows, you must use a backup hard drive that uses the NTFS file system.

exFAT (FAT64)

exFAT (also known as FAT64) is a file system designed to enable mobile personal storage media to be used seamlessly on mobile and desktop computers. ExFAT is designed to be as simple as FAT32, but with many improvements in capacity and scalability.

exFAT is also called FAT64 because it supports 64-bit addressing. exFAT's main features include

- Support for volumes (drive letters) larger than 32GB. 512TB is the recommended maximum volume size, but the theoretical volume size is 64ZB (zettabytes; 1ZB = 1 billion TB).

- Recommended and maximum file sizes also increase to 512TB and 64ZB, respectively.

- Improvements in file system structure for better performance with flash media and for movie recording.

- Support for Universal Time Coordinate (UTC) date stamps.

exFAT support is included in Windows Vista SP1, 7, 8/8.1, and 10. To find information about non-Microsoft operating systems that support exFAT, see http://en.wikipedia.org/wiki/ExFAT.

Figure 14-22 illustrates exFAT as a formatting option for a USB thumb drive in Windows 8.1.

Figure 14-22   File system formatting options for a 16GB USB thumb drive in Windows 8.1 include FAT32, NTFS, and exFAT.

NTFS

The New Technology File System (**NTFS**) is the native file system of Windows Vista/7/8/8.1. NTFS has many differences from FAT32, including:

- **Access Control**—Different levels of access control by group or user can be configured for both folders and individual files.

- **Built-in compression**—Individual files, folders, or an entire drive can be compressed without the use of third-party software.

- **Individual Recycle Bins**—Unlike FAT32, NTFS includes a separate recycle bin for each user.

- **Support for the Encrypting File System (EFS)**—EFS enables data to be stored in an encrypted form. No password and no access to files!

- **Support for mounting a drive**—Drive mounting enables you to address a removable-media drive's contents; for example, as if its contents are stored on your hard drive. The hard drive's drive letter is used to access data on both the hard drive and the removable media drive.

- **Disk quota support**—The administrator of a system can enforce rules about how much disk space each user is allowed to use for storage.

- **Hot-swapping**—Removable-media drives that have been formatted with NTFS (such as USB) can be connected or removed while the operating system is running.

- **Indexing**—The Indexing service helps users locate information more quickly when the Search tool is used.

NOTE   If you want to boot from a 3TB or larger hard drive, you must use a 64-bit version of Windows 7 or later on a system that has an EFI or UEFI (Extensible Firmware Interface or Unified Extensible Firmware Interface) BIOS. EFI and UEFI support the GPT partition table. 3TB drives can be used on older systems by splitting the drive into partitions no larger than 2TB each.

3TB and larger hard drives also use a new low-level format scheme known as Advanced Format (4KB sectors rather than 512-byte sectors). If you are planning to move legacy partitions to these drives, you will want to use an alignment tool to re-align the drive for maximum performance. See www.pcworld.com/article/235088/everything_you_need_to_know_about_3tb_hard_drives.html and http://msdn.micro-soft.com/en-us/windows/hardware/gg463524 for more information.

Follow these steps to determine what file system was used to prepare a Windows hard drive:

Step 1.   Open Windows Explorer or File Explorer.

Step 2.   Right-click the drive letter in the Explorer Window and select **Properties**.

The Properties sheet for the drive lists FAT32 for a drive prepared with FAT32 and NTFS for a drive prepared with NTFS (see Figure 14-23).

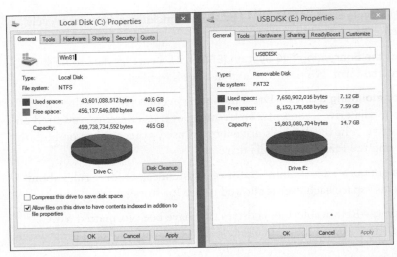

Figure 14-23 A hard drive formatted with NTFS version 5 (left) and a flash memory drive formatted with FAT32 (right).

Converting a Drive's File System with CONVERT.EXT

Windows includes the command-line program **CONVERT.EXE**, which is designed to help you convert a drive from a FAT file system to NTFS.

To convert a drive's file system using CONVERT.EXE, follow these steps:

Step 1. Open a command-prompt window in elevated mode (Run as Administrator).

Step 2. Type **Convert x: /fs:ntfs** and press **Enter**. For example, to convert f:, type **Convert f: /fs:ntfs**.

To see advanced options for Convert, type **convert /?**. To learn more, see https://support.microsoft.com/en-us/kb/214579.

NOTE Other file systems you need to understand for the CompTIA A+ Certification exam include NFS, ext3, and ext4. **Ext3** and **ext4** file systems are used by Linux. **NFS** (network file system) is used in networks that have a mixture of Linux, Windows, and other operating systems.

For more information, see Chapter 18, "OS X and Linux."

During installation, Windows Vista/7/8/8.1/10 automatically format the partitions created by the partition process with NTFS.

Quick Formatting versus Full Formatting

Quick formatting is an option with all versions of Windows discussed here. With new hard drives or existing drives known to be error-free, use **quick format** to quickly clear the areas of the hard drive that store data location records. If you choose the **full format** option, Windows must rewrite the disk structures across the entire disk surface. This can take many minutes with today's large hard drives.

NOTE If you are concerned about the condition of a used hard drive you plan to re-use with Windows, use Windows CHKDSK if the drive has been formatted to check its state. You can also use the drive vendor's disk diagnostic utility program to verify the condition of a drive.

Configuring Windows During/After Installation

Some configuration settings for Windows are made during installation, and others afterwards. Here are the major issues to keep in mind.

Loading Alternative Drivers

If Windows does not detect your hard drives during installation, you must provide **alternate third-party drivers**. The most likely situations in which this could occur include when third-party SATA or RAID onboard or add-on card host adapters are used in Windows Vista/7/8/8.1.

In Windows Vista/7/8/8.1, device drivers are added within the same screen where partitioning was done by clicking **Load Driver** (refer to Figures 14-20 and 14-21). These drivers can be installed from CD, DVD, or USB flash drive.

If you click **Load Driver** and cannot supply a proper driver for Windows or if the computer cannot read the media where the driver is stored, you must exit the installation program.

Workgroup vs Domain Setup

During the installation process, Windows can connect to either a **workgroup** (the default setting) or to a network managed by a **domain** controller. Domain controllers are typically used in large networks at workplaces or schools. Home networks and small-office networks use workgroups, and computers running Windows 7 or newer might also belong to a homegroup. During a manual installation, the user is prompted to supply network information as prompted. The appropriate network login information should be inserted into automatic setup scripts.

To learn more about these network types, see Chapter 16, "Networking Microsoft Windows."

Time/Date/Language/Region Settings

On a new installation, Windows prompts for **time, date, language, and region settings** early in the installation process. However, in the case of a repair ("upgrade in place") installation, the previous Windows installation's settings are used.

Installing Drivers, Software, Updates

After Windows is installed, it should be updated with the latest drivers, hotfixes, and service packs. For individual PCs, the easiest way to perform these steps is to set up Windows Update for automatic updates.

However, if you are installing Windows for the first time and your system or motherboard was supplied with a driver disc, perform **driver installation** first before running Windows Update. **Windows updates** can also be performed manually in some cases.

Using Windows Update and Microsoft Update

To install additional updates for Windows through Windows Update, follow these steps in Windows Vista/7:

Step 1.   Click **Start > All Programs > Windows Update**.

Step 2.   When the Windows Update window appears, click the **Install Updates** button. With Windows 7 only, click **Show all available updates**.

> **NOTE**   Do not select Express or let Microsoft automatically install all updates if you do not want to use newer applications.

Step 3.   Windows Update automatically scans for updates. Updates are divided into the following categories

- **Important**—Critical updates and service packs
- **Optional**—Driver updates and updates to Windows features

Step 4. If you have selected an Express install or if you selected wanted updates, they are downloaded to your system and installed. You might need to restart your computer to complete the update process.

To install additional updates for Windows through Windows Update using the Start screen, follow these steps in Windows 8.1:

Step 1. Open the Charms menu and select **Settings**.

Step 2. Select **Change PC Settings**.

Step 3. Select **Update and Recovery**.

Step 4. Select **Check now**.

Step 5. Select **View details**. Windows Update displays Important, Recommended, and Optional updates. Updates already selected for you are checked (see Figure 14-24).

Step 6. Check any additional updates desired, then click **Install**. Your updates are downloaded and installed.

Step 7. You might need to restart your computer to complete the update process.

NOTE Windows 8/8.1 automatically installs selected updates over the next day or so if you don't choose Install in step 6.

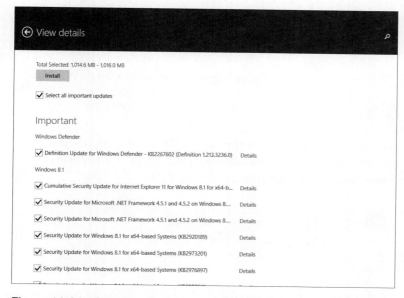

Figure 14-24   Selecting updates to install with Windows Update for Windows 8.1

If you prefer to work from the Windows desktop in Windows 8/8.1, follow this procedure:

Step 1.   Press the **Windows key+X**.

Step 2.   Select **Control Panel** from the menu.

Step 3.   Select **System and Security** from the menu.

Step 4.   Select **Windows Update** from the menu.

Step 5.   Select **Check for updates** from the menu.

To continue, see step 3 for Windows Vista/7.

If you use Microsoft Office or other Microsoft applications as well as Microsoft Windows, Windows Update offers to install Microsoft Update, which provides **software updates** for Microsoft apps as well as for Windows. After you install Microsoft Update, it runs automatically whenever you run Windows Update. Keep in mind that Microsoft Office uses service packs as well.

Installing Service Packs Manually

Microsoft recommends using Windows Update to receive updates (including service packs). However, service packs for Windows Vista/7 are also available for manual download. Service packs for Windows and other Microsoft programs can include hundreds of updates, which means that they can be several hundred megabytes in size. If you need to install service packs on several computers, it can be faster and put less stress on the network's Internet connection to download and install them manually.

NOTE   Updates for Windows 8/8.1/10 are normally received only through Windows Update.

To download service packs manually, go to the Service Pack and Update Center at http://windows.microsoft.com/en-US/windows/service-packs-download. Select your operating system, and choose from the updates available.

NOTE   Before downloading and installing a service pack, determine whether the service pack includes all previous service packs or if you need to install a service pack or other updates first.

To download and install a service pack for Windows manually, follow these steps:

Step 1. Determine whether the system has any service packs installed. You should perform this check even if you have just installed Windows because you can install Windows with service packs included and newer Windows DVDs contain a service pack. Right-click **Computer** and select **Properties** to determine the current service pack. You can also use the command **winver.exe** in the Command Prompt to discern this information. Figure 14-25 illustrates a Windows 7 system with Service Pack 1 installed.

Step 2. Go to http://windows.microsoft.com/en-us/windows/service-packs-download, select your operating system, and follow the links provided for downloads for the version of Windows you need to update.

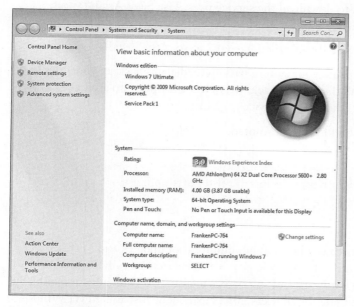

Figure 14-25 This Windows 7 Ultimate system has Service Pack 1 installed.

Step 3. Review the release notes for the service pack to see whether it will cause any problems for your particular configuration, such as problems with networking, peripherals, CD/DVD mastering software, and so forth. Take the necessary actions as noted. (Some might require changes before you perform the service pack installation; others might take place afterward.)

TIP   To save the specific document referenced in the release notes so that you can follow up on the problem, use the File > Save as Web Archive option in Internet Explorer. This saves the entire web page (including graphics) as a single file with an .htm or .html extension. You can then view the file offline with Internet Explorer if necessary.

Step 4.   Select the correct language, and click the link.

Step 5.   Shut down real-time virus checkers.

Step 6.   Select the Manually Installing option to download the service pack from the Download Center.

Step 7.   Click the link to download the service pack. Use **Save As** and when prompted, select a location to store the file with Network Installation.

Step 8.   Open the file you downloaded in step 7 to start the installation process.

Step 9.   You should update your system backup media and back up your files before you install the service pack, and select the option to archive existing Windows files during the service pack installation.

Step 10.   Restart the system when prompted.

TIP   In some cases, you might need to reinstall third-party applications or utilities after you install a service pack.

Service packs are large because they contain hundreds of updates and hotfixes. Hotfixes, which are solutions for specific problems experienced only by users with certain combinations of hardware and software, can also be downloaded individually. When a hotfix is deemed safe for all users, it will usually be distributed via Windows Update or Microsoft Update. However, it can also be downloaded manually or requested by the user. Hotfixes are listed as part of Help and Support (formerly Knowledge Base) articles about specific problems. See http://support.microsoft.com for Help and Support articles.

At one time, it was necessary to call Microsoft to request hotfixes that were not available for automatic downloading. Now, Microsoft provides a link on the Help and Support pages where you can make the request. Enter the wanted information and your email address, and a link to the requested hotfix will be emailed to you.

Using the Factory Recovery Partition

Most vendors no longer provide a full installation DVD/CD of Windows for computers with preinstalled Windows. Instead, the **factory recovery partition** (a disk partition containing a special recovery image of the Windows installation) is provided. Typically, you are prompted to burn the restore image to one or more DVDs or CDs or a USB thumb drive.

NOTE   A recovery disc is also known as a system restoration disc. These special versions of Windows aren't standalone copies of Windows, meaning you can't use them to install Windows on another PC (unless the PC is identical to the one for which the disc was made).

Typically, you have limited choices when you want to restore a damaged installation with a recovery disc or recovery files on a disk partition. Typical options include

- Reformatting your hard drive and restoring it to just-shipped condition (causing the loss of all data and programs installed after the system was first used)
- Reinstalling Windows only
- Reinstalling support files or additional software

After you run the recovery disc to restore your system to its original factory condition, you need to activate your Windows installation again.

CAUTION   You might need the Windows Product key or your system's serial number to run the recovery disc program. Keep this information handy. Most systems with preinstalled Windows have a sticker with the Windows license key (Product key) somewhere on the system case.

If you want to restore your system, not to its original-out-of-the-box condition but to its most recent status, create an image and file backup of the system and update it frequently. See Chapter 15.

Refresh and Reset (Windows 8/8.1/10)

As an alternative to performing a repair installation, you can use the **Refresh or Reset** options in Windows 8/8.1/10 to restore a system to proper operation. These options are available from the Update and Recovery dialog in PC Settings

in Windows 8/8.1 (see Figure 14-26). In Windows 10, a single Get Started button opens a menu with separate choices for Keep my files (equivalent to Windows
8/8.1's Refresh) or Remove everything (equivalent to Windows 8/8.1's Restore).

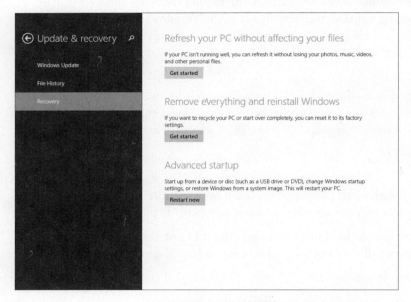

Figure 14-26   Refresh and Reset options in Windows 8.1.

Use Refresh to remove apps that were not obtained from the Windows Store
(downloaded or installed from disc). This includes the installed apps as well as
downloaded apps in the Downloads folder. Windows Store apps are reinstalled.
However, user files are not affected.

TIP   To keep downloaded files, copy them to the Documents folder before running
Refresh.

Use Reset to return the system to its originally installed (out of box) condition. All
apps, including apps from the Windows Store, and all user files are removed.

Characteristics of a Properly Formatted Boot Drive

A properly formatted boot drive with the correct partitions/format has these characteristics:

A boot drive for Windows Vista uses a primary partition (preferably NTFS) occupying all or a portion of the disk.

A boot drive for Windows 7 has a reserved area formatted with NTFS of about 200MB at the beginning of the physical disk, followed by a bootable NTFS partition. On drives that were prepared in a system sold at retail, there might be a FAT32 partition used for OEM-specific tools after the bootable partition. Any unallocated space is located at the end of the physical disk.

A boot drive for Windows 8/8.1 has a reserved area formatted with NTFS of less than 500MB at the beginning of the physical disk, followed by a bootable NTFS partition. Any unallocated space is located at the end of the physical disk. A Windows 10 boot drive typically has a 5GB recovery partition, a 200MB EFI system partition (for use with UEFI firmware), and the Windows partition. As with Windows 8/8.1, any unallocated space is left at the end of the drive. If Windows 8/8.1/10 were upgraded from earlier versions of Windows, additional recovery partitions of 500MB or less each might also be present.

Exam Preparation Tasks

Review All the Key Topics

Review the most important topics in the chapter, noted with the key topics icon in the outer margin of the page. Table 14-3 lists a reference of these key topics and the page numbers on which each is found.

Table 14-3   Key Topics for Chapter 14

Key Topic Element	Description	Page Number
Table 14-2	Feature Comparison Windows Vista, 7, 8, and 8.1	675
Section	File Structure and Paths	694
Section	Creating Partitions During Windows Vista/7/8/8.1/10 Installation	710
Section	NTFS	714

Define Key Terms

Define the following key terms from this chapter, and check your answers in the glossary.

32-bit Windows, 64-bit Windows, Aero, gadgets, user account control, BitLocker, Shadow Copy, System Restore, ReadyBoost, Sidebar, compatibility mode, Virtual XP mode, Windows Easy Transfer, Administrative Tools, Defender, Windows Firewall, Security Center, Event Viewer, file structure and paths, category view vs. classic view, side-by-side apps, Modern UI, pinning, One Drive, Windows Store, multi-monitor task bars, charms, Start Screen, PowerShell, Live sign in, Action Center, in-place upgrades, compatibility tools, Windows OS upgrade advisor, USB boot, CD-ROM boot, DVD boot, PXE boot, solid state/flash drives boot, Netboot, external/hot swappable drive, internal hard drive (partition), unattended installation, upgrade, clean install, repair installation, multiboot installation, remote network installation, image deployment, recovery partition, Refresh/Restore, dynamic (partition), basic (partition), primary (partition), extended (partition), file system, GPT (partition), exFAT, FAT32, NTFS, CDFS, NFS, ext3, ext4, quick format, full format, alternate third-party drivers, workgroup, domain, time/date/region/language settings, driver installation, Windows updates, software updates, factory recovery partition.

Complete the Tables and Lists from Memory

Print a copy of Appendix C, "Memory Tables" (found on the companion website), or at least the section for this chapter, and complete the tables and lists from memory. Appendix D, "Answers to Memory Tables," also on the companion website, includes completed tables and lists to check your work.

Complete Hands-On Lab

Complete the hands-on lab, and then see the answers and explanations at the end of the chapter.

Lab 14-1: Using Windows Features

Perform as many of these tasks as you can:

- Restore a file from a Shadow Copy (Windows Vista or 7).

- Install a program made for an older version of Windows and use the Compatibility Wizard to see if it needs any compatibility settings to work. For old games (Windows 95/98), see www.old-games.com.

- Download and run Windows Virtual PC and Virtual XP mode (Windows 7 Professional, Ultimate, Enterprise editions).

- Use two Modern UI or a Win32 (classic Windows) and Modern UI apps side-by-side (Windows 8/8.1).

- Pin a program to the taskbar (Windows 7/8/8.1/10).

- Open the Action Center (Windows 7/8/8.1/10).

- Run the appropriate Windows upgrade advisor/assistant to see if a Vista, 7, or 8 system is ready for an upgrade.

- Download Windows 8.1 and save it to an .iso file. Get it from http://windows.microsoft.com/en-us/windows-8/upgrade-prod-uct-key-only and also follow the tips at www.cnet.com/how-to/how-to-download-the-official-microsoft-windows-8-1-iso/.

- Install Windows 8.1 to an empty hard disk. Do not activate it unless you have a spare license key.

- During installation, create a partition that uses only about half the hard disk.

TIP   If you don't have a spare system or hard disk, download VirtualBox (www.virtu-albox.org) and use it to set up a VM. Install Windows 8.1 in the VM. Enable AMD-V or Intel VT-x (hardware virtualization) in the BIOS/UEFI firmware.

Answer Review Questions

1. Which of the following statements best describes the term *x86*?

    A. x86 is a type of architecture that supports 86-bit CPUs.

    B. x86 is a system that supports 86GB or more of address space.

    C. x86 is a system that requires a minimum of 8.6GB of RAM for installation.

    D. x86 is old nomenclature referring to the 80386 or 80486 CPU family.

2. Which of the following statements best describes why the gadgets utility in Windows Vista and Windows 7 was discontinued in Windows 8/8.1?

    A. The gadgets utility included serious security vulnerabilities.

    B. Many of the real-time streaming gadgets did not work.

    C. There was very little interest in using these gadgets.

    D. Gadgets have been replaced by Charms in Windows 8/8.1.

3. Which of the following restore options is used by Windows 8/8.1 instead of Shadow Copy to restore earlier versions of a file?

   A. System Restore

   B. Image Backup

   C. File History

   D. File Backup

4. Which utility is used to ensure that older applications or games run properly on newer versions of an operating system?

   A. Compatibility Mode

   B. Virtual XP Mode

   C. Easy Transfer

   D. Ready Boost

5. Which of the following is Window's cloud storage program?

   A. FirstUp

   B. OneDrive

   C. Cloud Drive

   D. Easy Transfer

6. Which of the following statements are true? (Choose three.)

   A. Apps from the Windows Store are free to anyone with a Microsoft account.

   B. Apps from the Windows Store can be easily updated.

   C. Apps from the Windows Store will automatically be reinstalled when the computer is refreshed.

   D. Files created using apps from the Windows Store will automatically be synced each time you access the Windows Store online.

   E. Use of the Windows Store requires a Microsoft account using a Live sign in.

7. In Windows 7/8/8.1/10, the Action Center performs which of the following functions?

   A. It allows you to easily apply updates and service packs to your system.

   B. It is a quick resource for updating drivers.

   C. It warns you about potential security and maintenance problems.

   D. It allows you to change the computer name or join a workgroup.

8. In Windows 7 or 8/8.1/10, libraries do which of the following?

   A. They allow multiple folders stored in different locations to be viewed as a single logical folder.

   B. They allow users to borrow apps for a specified length of time from the Microsoft Store.

   C. They are critical files used in troubleshooting system problems.

   D. They contain updates and service packs.

9. When installing a multi-boot system, which of the following steps should be completed? (Choose all that apply.)

   A. Install the oldest operating system first.

   B. Install the newest operating system first.

   C. Install a Windows operating system and a Linux system on separate primary partitions.

   D. Install all Windows systems on the same primary partition.

   E. Create up to four primary partitions on an MBR drive.

   F. Use a virtual machine if you want to switch between operating systems without rebooting.

10. Which of the following statements best describes how to boot a new computer using the PXE (Preboot eXecution Environment) method?

    A. Use a CD or DVD to boot the computer.

    B. Boot the computer through a network connection.

    C. Use a thumb drive or some other portable media to boot the computer prior to inserting the installation CD or DVD.

    D. Create an ISO image with which to boot the computer.

11. A Windows repair installation allows you to do which of the following?

    A. It allows you to reinstall only selected files, such as corrupt registry files.

    B. It allows you to easily repair corrupt data files without changing the system files.

    C. It allows you to repair the partition on which the operating system is installed.

    D. It allows you to reinstall the operating system without having to reinstall your existing applications and files.

12. Which of the following allows you to create an image of a perfect installation and then deploy that image on one or more computers across a network?

    A. An unattended installation

    B. A repair installation

    C. An image deployment or disk cloning

    D. A multiboot installation

13. Which of the following statements best describes advantages that the exFAT file system offers over FAT32?

    A. exFAT provides support for 64-bit addressing.

    B. exFAT provides increased security with group- and user-level access control.

    C. exFAT supports the use of compression and encryption.

    D. exFAT supports the use of disk quotas.

14. Which of the following statements best describes advantages that the NTFS file system offers over FAT32? (Choose all that apply.)

    A. NTFS provides support for 64-bit addressing.

    B. NTFS provides increased security with group and user level access control.

    C. NTFS supports the use of compression and encryption.

    D. NTFS supports the use of disk quotas.

15. After installing the operating system, which of the following should be performed next?

    A. You should update the latest service packs, hotfixes, and drivers.

    B. You should format the drive before beginning any updates.

    C. You should partition the drive containing the operating system.

    D. You should create the file system you plan to use.

16. Which of the following best describes how to determine whether a service pack has already been installed on your computer?

    A. In the Control Panel, open Administrative Tools and select System Configuration.

    B. In the Control Panel, open the Device Manager and select Disk Drives.

    C. In Windows Explorer or File Explorer, right-click Computer and select Properties.

    D. In Windows Explorer or File Explorer, right-click Computer, select Manage, then select Disk Management.

Answers and Explanations to Hands-On Labs

Using Windows Features

To be able to restore a file from a Shadow Copy, do the following:

Step 1. Make sure System Restore is enabled on a system running Business/ Professional/Ultimate/Enterprise editions.

Step 2. Create a file on C: drive (such as a text file, photo, document). If you decide to use an existing file, make a backup copy first.

Step 3. Create a restore point on C: drive.

Step 4. Edit the file and save the changes.

Step 5. Open Windows Explorer, right-click the file, select Versions, and choose the old version.

Use the Compatibility Wizard or the compatibility tab as you prefer. A common requirement for old games is to run them as Administrator.

If the Windows upgrade advisor or assistant indicates problems with your system, follow the links to get updates or advice.

Even if you aren't currently using hardware virtualization, enabling AMD-V or Intel VT-x (hardware virtualization) in the BIOS/UEFI firmware helps get your system ready for virtualization in the future.

Answers and Explanations to Review Questions

1. **D.** x86 refers to older computers called 80386 or 80486 (or just simply 386 or 486 or x86). These computers used 32-bit CPUs, which provided 4GB of address space. Newer systems, known as x86-64, can run 64-bit CPUs, address up to 1TB of RAM, and support both 32- and 64-bit software.

2. **A.** Gadgets represented a serious flaw in security. Attackers could gain access to your computer's system files or your document files or could even use remote access to take over complete control of your computer.

3. **C.** Shadow Copy was removed from the Windows 8/8.1 operating systems and was replaced with File History.

4. **A.** Compatibility Mode is used to ensure that older programs will run on newer operating systems.

5. **B.** OneDrive is Window's cloud storage program. It ships with Windows 8/8.1/10 but it can also be downloaded as an app for earlier Windows systems, OS X, Android, iOS, and others. It can also be used from a web browser.

6. **B, C, E.** Apps installed using the Windows Store are easy to update and they will be reinstalled automatically if the computer is refreshed. Apps that are downloaded from the Internet or installed from discs will be removed when the computer is refreshed and they must be manually reinstalled. Windows 8/8.1/10 recommendations include using a Microsoft Account and a Live sign in. If you log on using a local account, you will not be able to access the Windows Store. Apps from the Windows Store may either be free or paid. Files are synced in the OneDrive cloud storage system, not when accessing the Windows Store.

7. **C.** The Action Center displays messages warning you about potential security and maintenance problems in your system. The Action Center may be accessed from the taskbar at the bottom-right of the screen or from the Control Panel inside System and Security. A white flag means that no issues have been detected. A yellow flag is an alert meaning that you have an issue of moderate importance. A red flag warns you about more serious issues.

8. **A.** A library is a group of files that are stored in a variety of physical locations but that appear to reside in a single logical folder. When a file in the library folder is opened and changes to that file are saved, the original file in the original location will automatically be saved as well.

9. **A, C, E, F.** When creating a multi-boot system, each operating system must be installed on its own separate primary partition with the oldest operating system being installed first. You may create up to four primary partitions on a single MBR hard drive. You will need third-party software if you want to install a Windows system and a non-Windows system and you will need to create a virtual machine if you want to avoid rebooting each time you switch operating systems. You should never install a second operating system on a single partition unless you are doing an upgrade installation because you will lose the original system when the new one overwrites it.

10. **B.** PXE allows you to boot through a network connection prior to installing an operating system. The advantage of using a network connection is that you can first boot and then install operating systems on multiple computers simultaneously by accessing an image located on the network. To use this method, each computer must be connected to the network.

11. D. A repair installation (also known as an in-place upgrade) allows you to re-install the operating system without reinstalling your applications and files. In a repair installation, you are simply upgrading from one operating system to the same operating system. This will replace any corrupt system files without changing your data files.

12. C. Image deployment or disk cloning allows you to create a perfect installation, make an image of that installation and then deploy the image on multiple computers on the network. Problems may arise if the hardware on every computer is not identical. Also, each computer must have a different computer name and SID, which can create network conflicts. Both of these problems (and other problems) can be solved depending on what type of software you use to make the image.

13. A. exFAT is designed for use with mobile devices and has many improvements over FAT32. It uses 64-bit addressing, but it does not support increased security, compression, encryption, or disk quotas.

14. A, B, C, D. NTFS has many advantages over FAT32. It supports 64-bit addressing, increased security, compression, encryption, and disk quotas. exFAT also supports 64-bit addressing, but only NTFS supports the other features listed above.

15. A. After installing the operating system, you should update the system with any service packs, hot fixes, or drivers that might be needed. Never format a drive on which an active operating system is installed. Formatting will overwrite the drive and you will lose everything that had been written to that drive. Partitioning is done prior to formatting and installing, and while you might be able to add additional partitions after installation, the drive containing the operating system must be partitioned before installation. The file system is created during the installation of the operating system.

16. C. Open Windows Explorer in Vista and Windows 7. Right-click Computer, select Properties, and look under Windows Edition at the top of the page.

This chapter covers the following subjects:

- **Command-Line Tools**—From TASKKILL to DIR, learn how to use Windows command-line tools.

- **Microsoft Administrative Tools**—Discover computer and device management, troubleshooting, scheduling, and security policy settings in Windows.

- **Task Manager**—Learn how to view and shut down apps and processes.

- **MSCONFIG**—Use this tool to configure boot and startup processes.

- **Disk Management**—Learn how to add and manage hard drives.

- **Storage Spaces**—Discover a new, more versatile way to work with hard drives in Windows 8/8.1/10.

- **Windows Upgrade Tools**—Discover how to move data from old to new Windows installations.

- **System Utilities**—From Notepad to Explorer and Dxdiag to MMC, discover even more tools for managing Windows.

- **Control Panel Utilities**—Learn how to switch between category and icon views, find and change display settings, tweak folder options and virtual memory, adjust power settings, adjust audio playback, and locate troubleshooters in this section.

## CHAPTER 15

Managing Microsoft Windows

Microsoft Windows includes a wide variety of management tools, including command-line utilities, components in Control Panel and Accessories, and others. Some can be run from an object's properties sheet. Understanding how to use them is a big challenge (and a large part of the 220-902 exam), and that's exactly what this chapter is intended to help you do.

220-902: Objective 1.3 Given a scenario, apply appropriate Microsoft command line tools.

220-902: Objective 1.4 Given a scenario, use appropriate Microsoft operating system features and tools.

220-902: Objective 1.5 Given a scenario, use Windows Control Panel utilities.

Foundation Topics

Command-Line Tools

Windows contains a number of command-line tools for systems operation and management. These commands and their uses are listed in Table 15-1. Commands are listed in all caps, but can be run in either lowercase or uppercase.

For more information about these commands, see the following sections.

Table 15-1   Microsoft Windows Command-Line Tools

Command	Use
TASKKILL	Stops specified task(s) on a local or remote computer
BOOTREC	Repairs boot configuration (must be run from command line in repair mode)
SHUTDOWN	Shuts down or restarts a computer
TASKLIST	Lists current running tasks on a local or remote computer
MD (MKDIR)	Makes a new folder (subdirectory)
CD (CHDIR)	Changes your current location to the specified folder (subdirectory)
RD (RMDIR)	Removes an empty folder
DEL*	Deletes one or more files on current or specified folder or drive
FORMAT	Creates or recreates the specified file system on recordable or rewriteable storage (magnetic, flash, or optical). In the process, the contents of the drive are overwritten.
COPY	Copies one or more files to another folder or drive
XCOPY	Copies one or more files and folders to another folder or drive
ROBOCOPY	Highly-configurable file/folder copy and move app. Can be configured via various optional GUIs
DISKPART**	Creates, removes, and manages disk partition
SFC**	Scans system files and replaces damaged or missing files
CHKDSK**	Scans specified drive for errors and repairs them
GPUPDATE	Refreshes group policy on local or Active Directory managed systems
GPRESULT	Displays the Resultant Set of Policy for the specified computer and user
DIR	Lists files on current or specified folder or drive
EXIT	Closes command prompt window
HELP	Displays help for command line utilities

Command	Use
EXPAND	Expands a specified file in a specified archive to full size or displays contents of archive
Command/?	Displays help for the specified command

* ERASE works in the same way and with the same syntax as DEL.

** This command must be run in elevated mode (administrative mode or run as administrator).

> **NOTE**   In this chapter and throughout this book, "Windows" refers to Windows Vista, 7, 8/8.1. Specific Windows versions will be listed only if a command is not available or has different syntax in different versions of Windows.

Commands Available with Standard Privileges vs. Administrative Privileges

Most of the commands shown in Table 15-1 can be run with **standard privileges** (in other words, by any user). However, some commands listed can only be run with **administrative privileges** (also known as **elevated mode** or administrative mode). See the table footnotes for details.

Starting a Command Prompt Session with CMD.EXE

Although most computer users won't use the command prompt often, technicians use it frequently because it enables you to

- Recover data from systems that can't boot normally

- Reinstall lost or corrupted system files

- Print file listings (believe it or not, you can't do this in Windows Explorer, File Explorer, This PC, or Computer)

- Copy, move, or delete data

- Display or configure certain operating system settings

You can start a command prompt session in Windows by clicking the Command Prompt option in the Start menu. However, other methods can be faster:

- **In Windows 7/Vista**—Click **Start**, type **cmd** in the Search box, and then press **Enter** or press **Ctrl+Shift+Enter** to run in elevated mode. (It might be necessary for some commands.) You can also right-click **cmd** and select **Run as Administrator** to run in elevated mode.

■ **In Windows 8/8.1 (also works in 10)**—Press the **Windows key+X** and then click or tap **Command Prompt** to run in standard mode. Click or tap **Command Prompt (Admin)** to run in elevated mode (equivalent to Run as Administrator). See Figure 15-1.

1. Windows key+X

2. Select the command prompt mode desired

Figure 15-1   Starting command prompt from the Windows key+X menu in Windows 8/8.1.

NOTE What is elevated mode? Some commands shown in Table 15-1 cannot be run unless they are run with administrative privileges (also known as elevated mode, run as administrator): SFC, CHKDSK, and DISKPART.

Figure 15-2 shows a typical command prompt session in Windows 7.

TIP To get help for any command prompt function or program, type the command name followed by /?. For example, DIR /? displays help for the DIR command.

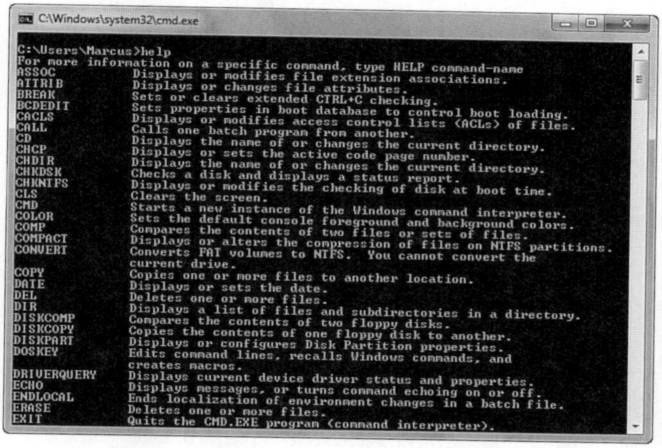

Figure 15-2 Using the Help command to view a list of command prompt commands in Windows 7.

Using Wildcards to Specify a Range of Files

Command-prompt functions and utilities can be used to operate on a group of files with similar names by using one of the following wildcard symbols:

- ? replaces a single character.
- * replaces a group of characters.

For example, DIR *.EXE displays files with the .EXE extension in the current folder (directory). DEL MYNOVEL??.BAK removes the following files: MYNOVEL00. BAK, and MYNOVEL01.BAK, but not MYNOVEL.BAK.

TASKKILL

TASKKILL is a command-line utility for Windows used to shut down a task on a local or remote system. It is a companion utility to Tasklist and shares some of its syntax:

```
TASKKILL [/S system [/U username [/P [password]]]]
         { [/FI filter] [/PID processid | /IM imagename] } [/T] [/F]
```

TASKKILL is used to terminate tasks by process id (PID) or image name.

> **NOTE**   These rules apply when running TASKKILL:
>
> - Wildcard * for /IM switch is accepted only when a filter is applied.
>
> - Termination of remote processes will always be done forcefully (/F).
>
> - "WINDOWTITLE" and "STATUS" filters are not considered when a remote machine is specified.

The following task kills the notepad.exe app (to try this yourself, be sure to start notepad.exe first):

```
TASKKILL /IM notepad.exe
```

The task is killed as soon as the command is issued. When a command is successful, TASKKILL reports that the task has been terminated:

```
SUCCESS: Sent termination signal to the process "notepad.exe" with
PID 4692.
```

This command kills apps with the PID values listed:

```
TASKKILL /PID 1299 /PID 11440 /PID 6784
```

> **NOTE**   To determine the PID values for running apps, use Task Manager.

For a list of all options, use `taskkill /?`.

BOOTREC

The **BOOTREC** command is available only from the command prompt available when using startup repair options.

NOTE To learn how to start Windows to repair your system, see the "System Recovery Options (Windows)" section and the "Safe Mode (Windows)" section in Chapter 22.

BOOTREC is used to repair the boot record or boot configuration database (BCD). Command syntax is `bootrec /option`, using one of the options from Table 15-2.

Table 15-2 BOOTREC Repair Options

OPTION	PURPOSE
/fixmbr	Writes a Windows -compatible MBR to the system partition. It does not overwrite the existing partition table. Use this option when you must resolve MBR corruption issues, or when you have to remove nonstandard code from the MBR.
/fixboot	Writes a new boot sector to the system partition by using a boot sector that's compatible with Windows. Use this option if one of the following conditions is true: The boot sector was replaced with a nonstandard Windows boot sector. The boot sector is damaged. An earlier Windows operating system was installed after Windows Vista or later was installed. In this situation, the computer starts by using Windows NT Loader (NTLDR) instead of Windows Boot Manager (Bootmgr.exe).
/ScanOs	Scans all disks for installations that are compatible with Windows. It also displays the entries that are currently not in the BCD store. Use this option when there are Windows Vista or Windows 7 installations that the Boot Manager menu does not list.
/rebuildbcd	Scans all disks for installations that are compatible with Windows. Additionally, it lets you select the installations that you want to add to the BCD store. Use this option when you must completely rebuild the BCD store.

NOTE For more information about using Bootrec, see "Windows Boot Errors," p.1082, Chapter 22 or visit https://support.microsoft.com/en-us/kb/927392.

SHUTDOWN

The **SHUTDOWN** command is used to shut down Windows and power down the specified local or remote computer(s) from the command prompt:

```
shutdown [/i | /l | /s | /r | /g | /a | /p | /h | /e] [/f]
    [/m \\computer] [/t xxx] [/d [p|u:]xx:yy [/c "comment"]]
```

When SHUTDOWN is run without any options, it also displays a list of reasons for the shutdown. Use the numbers displayed when you use the /d option.

The remote shutdown dialog displayed with the SHUTDOWN /I option is shown in Figure 15-3.

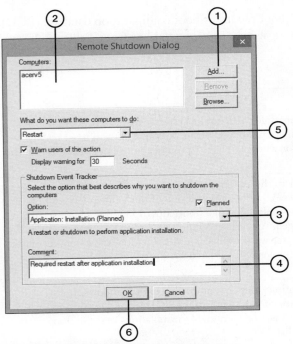

1. Click or tap to add name(s) of computers
2. List of computer(s) to be affected
3. Select option
4. Add comment (required when Other is selected option
5. Click or tap to start process
6. Select action to perform

Figure 15-3 SHUTDOWN's graphical user interface is configured to restart one computer for planned application restart with a 30-second delay.

The remote shutdown banner displayed on all systems being shut down is shown in Figure 15-4.

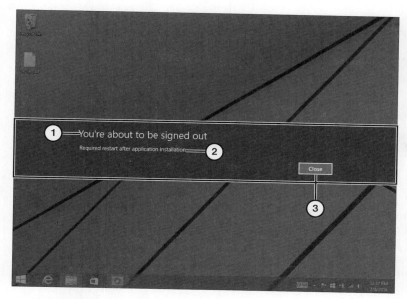

1. User notification of event from Shutdown
2. Comment
3. Click or tap to close notification

Figure 15-4   SHUTDOWN displays a banner on all systems being shut down.

TASKLIST

Use **TASKLIST** to learn about tasks running on the current system or on a remote system. When you use the simple command TASKLIST, it displays a list of all running tasks on the current system. However, TASKLIST supports many option switches:

```
TASKLIST [/S system [/U username [/P [password]]]]
         [/M [module] | /SVC | /V] [/FI filter] [/FO format] [/NH]
```

TASKLIST displays a list of currently running processes on either a local or remote machine.

Here are some examples to try:

Figure 15-5 shows TASKLIST used to displays programs that use the kernel32.dll module.

Figure 15-5   Using TASKLIST /m kernel32.dll to see the programs that use the kernel32.dll file.

TASKLIST can create a .CSV (comma separated value) list of tasks (as well as a table or list). A CSV file can be opened with Microsoft Excel or other spreadsheet programs, and can be imported into most database programs.

For all program options, use tasklist /?.

MKDIR, CHDIR, and RMDIR (MD, CD, and RD)

You can make, change to, or remove folders (directories) with the following commands, as shown in Table 15-3.

Table 15-3   Folder Management Commands

Command	Abbreviation	Use	Example
MKDIR	**MD**	Creates a folder (directory)	MKDIR \Backups
			MD \Backups
			Makes the folder \Backups one level below the root folder of the current drive
CHDIR	**CD**	Changes to a new folder	CHDIR \Backups
			CD \Backups
			Changes to the \Backups folder
RMDIR	**RD**	Removes a folder (if empty)	RMDIR \Backups
			RD \Backups
			Removes the \Backups folder (if empty)

Folders (directories) can be referred to in two ways:

- **Absolute**— An absolute path provides the full path to the **directory** (folder). For example, to change to the folder \Backups\Word from the folder \My Documents on the same drive, you would use the command CD \Backups\Word\.

■ **Relative**—A relative path can be used to change to a folder one level below your location. For example, to change to the folder \Backups\Word from the folder \Backups, you would use the command CHDIR Word (or just CD Word). No backslash is necessary.

NOTE   You can't use the CHDIR (CD) command to change to a different drive and folder. It works only on the current drive.

To change to the root folder from any folder, use CHDIR\ (or just CD\). To change to the folder one level higher than your current location, use CHDIR .. (or just CD ..).

DEL

The **DEL** command is an internal command (that is, a command built in to CMD. EXE) used to delete files. The syntax for DEL (or ERASE, which can be used interchangeably with DEL) is

```
DEL [/P] [/F] [/S] [/Q] [/A[[:]attributes]] names
ERASE [/P] [/F] [/S] [/Q] [/A[[:]attributes]] names
```

For example, the following deletes all *.bak files in the current folder:

```
del *.bak
```

The following deletes all temp files in the C:\Temp\ folder and its subfolders:

```
del c:\temp\*.tmp /s
```

NOTE   File deletions at the command prompt bypass the Windows Recycle Bin. However, files deleted with DEL (ERASE) can be retrieved with third-party disk data recovery tools.

FORMAT

In Windows, the **FORMAT** command is used primarily to create or recreate the specified file system on recordable or rewriteable storage (magnetic, flash, or optical). In the process, the contents of the drive are overwritten.

FORMAT appears to "destroy" the previous contents of magnetic storage (such as a hard disk), but if you use FORMAT on a hard disk by mistake, third-party data recovery programs can be used to retrieve data from the drive. This is possible because most of the disk surface is not changed by FORMAT when a quick format option is selected.

Windows overwrites the entire surface of a disk with zeros if the quick format option is not selected. If the Quick Format or Safe Format option is used, the contents of the disk are marked for deletion but can be retrieved with third-party data recovery software.

NOTE   The hard-disk format process performed by the FORMAT command (which creates the file system) is sometimes referred to as a **standard format** to distinguish it from the **low-level format** used by hard drive manufacturers to set up magnetic structures on the hard drive.

Using FORMAT with USB Flash and Removable-Media Drives

Although USB flash memory drives and removable-media drives are preformatted at the factory, FORMAT is still useful as a means to:

- Erase the contents of a disk quickly, especially if it contains many files or folders.
- Place new sector markings across the disk.

Formatting Drives with Windows Explorer and File Explorer

You can use Windows Explorer/Computer (Vista/7) or File Explorer/This PC (8/8.1) to format all types of drives. Right-click the drive you want to format and select Format. The Format options for Windows display, as shown in Figure 15-6.

Windows also offers the exFAT (FAT64) file system option for hard disks and high-capacity flash drives. Windows Vista and 7 do not offer the compression option on the Format menu, but if you want to compress the drive after formatting it, you can do so from the General tab of the drive's properties sheet.

NOTE   Writeable optical media must also be formatted before it can be used. To learn more about the format options used with these types of media, see Chapter 6, "Storage Devices."

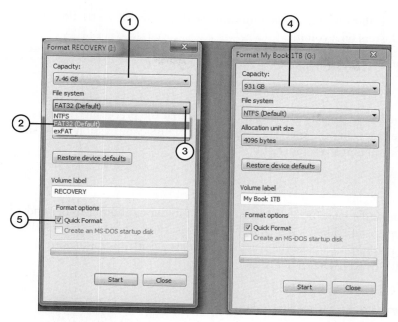

1. Flash drive capacity
2. FAT32 is default file system
3. Click or tap to see other file system options (NTFS, exFAT)
4. Hard disk capacity
5. Click or tap to clear checkbox for full format

Figure 15-6   The Windows 7 Explorer Format menu for a flash drive (left) and hard disk (right).

Using FORMAT from the Command Prompt

The FORMAT command overwrites the current contents of the target drive unless the **/Q** (Quick Format) option is used. When **/Q** is used, only the file allocation table and root folder are overwritten. To retrieve data from a drive that has been formatted, you must use third-party data-recovery software.

FORMAT includes a variety of options for use with hard disks, removable-media and optical drives, and USB flash memory drives. The most useful examples include:

FORMAT F: /FS:exFAT Formats drive F: using the exFAT file system.

FORMAT F: /Q Performs a quick format on drive F:

For additional options for Format, use Format /?.

Note that the FAT and FAT32 files systems impose the following restrictions on the number of clusters on a volume:

- **FAT**—Number of clusters <= 65526

- **FAT32**—65526 < Number of clusters < 4177918

FORMAT immediately stops processing if it decides that the preceding requirements cannot be met using the specified cluster size. NTFS compression is not supported for allocation unit sizes above 4096.

COPY

The **COPY** command copies files from one drive and folder to another folder and drive. The folder specified by COPY must already exist on the target drive. COPY does not work with files that have the system or hidden file attributes; to copy these files, use XCOPY or ROBOCOPY instead.

The syntax for COPY in Windows is

```
COPY [/D] [/V] [/N] [/Y | /-Y] [/Z] [/L] [/A | /B ] source [/A | /B]
     [+ source [/A | /B] [+ ...]] [destination [/A | /B]]
```

Examples include:

- `COPY *.* F:`—Copies all files in the current folder to the current folder on the F: drive

- `COPY *.TXT C:\Users\Username`—Copies all .txt files in the current folder to the *Username* folder on the C: drive

- `COPY C:\WINDOWS\TEMP\*.BAK`—Copies all *.bak files in the \Windows\Temp folder on drive C: to the current folder

- `COPY C:\WINDOWS\*.BMP D:`—Copies all .bmp files in the \Windows folder on drive C: to the current folder on drive D:

For all options for Copy, use `Copy /?`.

XCOPY

The **XCOPY** command can be used in place of COPY in most cases and has the following advantages:

- **Faster operation on a group of files**—XCOPY reads the specified files into conventional RAM before copying them to their destination.

- **Creates folders as needed**—Specify the destination folder name in the XCOPY command line, and the destination folder will be created if needed.

- **Operates as backup utility**—Can be used to change the archive bit from on to off on files if wanted to allow XCOPY to be used in place of commercial backup programs.

- **Copies files changed or created on or after a specified date**—Also useful when using XCOPY as a substitute for commercial backup programs.

XCOPY can be used to "clone" an entire drive's contents to another drive. For example, the following copies the entire contents of the D: drive to the H: drive:

```
XCOPY D:\   H:\   /H /S /E /K /C /R
```

This command copies all files from drive D:'s root folder (root directory) and subfolders to drive H:'s root folder and subfolder, including system and hidden files, empty folders and subfolders, and file attributes. This will continue even if errors are detected and will overwrite read-only files.

For all options for XCOPY.EXE, use `xcopy /?`.

ROBOCOPY

ROBOCOPY is a robust file-copying utility included in Windows that can be used in place of XCOPY. ROBOCOPY has several advantages over XCOPY, including the capability to tolerate pauses in network connections, to mirror the contents of the sources and destination folders by removing files as well as copying files, to perform multithreaded copies for faster copying on multicore PCs, to log copy processes, list or copy files matching specified criteria including minimum file size, and others.

The syntax for ROBOCOPY for Windows is available from https://technet.microsoft.com/en-us/library/cc733145.aspx. Here are two examples of what you can do with ROBOCOPY:

To copy files in *sourcefolder* that are at least 16MB (16,777,216 bytes) in size to *targetfolder*:

```
ROBOCOPY C:\SOURCEFOLDER D:\TARGETFOLDER /MIN:16777216
```

Add the /L option to the end of this command to list the files that would be copied.

To mirror a local folder to a network folder with tweaks for more reliable operation (/FFT uses the two-second rule for comparing files, which can prevent files that are unchanged but have a time stamp that's off by a second or two from the destination's version from being copied again; /W:5 changes the wait time between retries from the default of 30 seconds to 5 seconds) and omit hidden files (/XA:H), use:

```
ROBOCOPY \\SOURCESERVER\SHARE \\DESTINATIONSERVER\SHARE /MIR /FFT /Z
/XA:H /W:5
```

These examples were adapted from the excellent TechNet Wiki posting "Robocopy and a Few Examples" available at http://social.technet.microsoft.com/wiki/contents/articles/1073.robocopy-and-a-few-examples.aspx.

As you can see from these examples, ROBOCOPY uses much different syntax than XCOPY and, for those who used ROBOCOPY in Windows XP or older versions, keep in mind that ROBOCOPY has had syntax changes over its different editions. For these reasons, you might prefer to run it by means of a GUI, such as the ROBOCOPY GUI available at http://technet.microsoft.com/en-us/magazine/2006.11.utilityspotlight.aspx (see Figure 15-7) or third-party GUIs available online.

NOTE   Microsoft TechNet has also introduced RichCopy as an alternative to the ROBOCOPY GUI. To learn more, see http://technet.microsoft.com/en-us/magazine/2009.04.utilityspotlight.aspx.

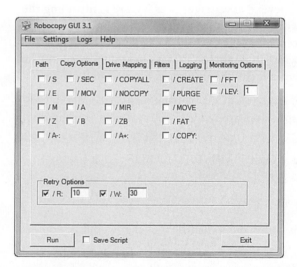

Figure 15-7   The ROBOCOPY GUI available from Microsoft TechNet provides a convenient click-to-select interface for setting ROBOCOPY's many option switches.

Diskpart

DISKPART is a disk management program included in Windows. It can be used to perform disk partitioning and management commands that are not included in Computer Management's Disk Management module.

When you run DISKPART, a new window opens with a DISKPART> prompt. Only DISKPART commands can be entered in the window. For a full list of DISKPART commands, use `DISKPART /?`.

Figure 15-8 demonstrates two DISKPART commands:

```
Select disk x
Detail disk
```

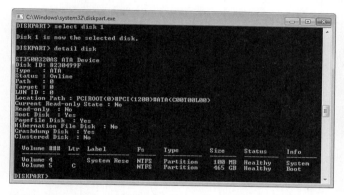

Figure 15-8   Using DISKPART to determine details about the selected disk.

DISKPART shows that the selected disk drive is the boot drive, contains the page-file, and is used to store crashdump information.

TIP   To learn more about using DISKPART, see http://support.microsoft.com/kb/300415 and http://technet.microsoft.com/en-us/library/cc766465(v=ws.10).aspx. DISKPART commands can be included in scripts.

NOTE   A script is a series of commands for one or more supported languages stored in a text file. Windows Script Host, which is included in Windows, is used to interpret and run scripts. A good introduction to Windows scripting is available at www.brighthub.com/computing/windows-platform/articles/83172.aspx. Windows PowerShell, which is included in Windows, is a popular choice for creating and running scripts, and contains many built-in commands. To learn more about PowerShell, see https://msdn.microsoft.com/powershell.

SFC

System File Checker (**SFC**) is a Windows utility that checks protected system files (files such as .DLL, .SYS, .OCX, and .EXE, as well as some font files used by the Windows desktop) and replaces incorrect versions or missing files with the correct files.

Use SFC to fix problems with Internet Explorer or other built-in Windows programs caused by the installation of obsolete Windows system files, user error, deliberate erasure, virus or Trojan horse infections, and similar problems.

To run SFC, open the command prompt in elevated mode (Run as Administrator) and type SFC with the appropriate switch. A typical option is SFC /scannow, which scans all protected files immediately (see Figure 15-9).

```
Administrator: C:\Windows\System32\cmd.exe

C:\Windows\system32>sfc /scannow

Beginning system scan.  This process will take some time.

Beginning verification phase of system scan.
Verification 100% complete.

Windows Resource Protection found corrupt files and successfully repaired
them. Details are included in the CBS.Log windir\Logs\CBS\CBS.log. For
example C:\Windows\Logs\CBS\CBS.log

C:\Windows\system32>_
```

Figure 15-9 SFC /scannow reports that corrupt files were repaired (Windows 7).

Another option is SFC /scanonce, which scans all protected files at the next boot. If SFC finds that some files are missing and replacement files are not available on your system, you will be prompted to reinsert your Windows distribution disc so that the files can be copied to the DLL cache. Other options include /scanboot, which scans all protected files every time the system starts; /revert, which returns the scan setting to the default; and /purgecache and /cachesize=x, which enable a user to delete the file cache and modify its size.

If errors are detected, they are logged in the CBS.log file found in %WinDir%\Logs\CBS\.

To read the contents of CBS.log, you can use the findstr command, which sends the details to a separate file called sfcdetails.txt.

For more information about using SFC and findstr, and to learn how to replace corrupted system files manually if SFC is not able to do it, see https://support.microsoft.com/en-us/kb/929833.

CHKDSK

CHKDSK is a command-line tool for checking disk drives (other than optical) for errors and optionally repairing those errors. It must be run in elevated mode (open cmd.exe as administrator). Note that some commands differ according to the file system (FAT/FAT32 or NTFS) of the target drive.

```
CHKDSK [volume[[path]filename]]] [/F] [/V] [/R] [/X] [/I] [/C]
[/L[:size]] [/B]
```

For a complete list of CHKDSK options, use CHKDSK /?.

Example:

- CHKDSK /F—Scans for and fixes errors on the current drive.

- CHKDSK F: /F—Scans for and fixes errors on drive F:.

If CHKDSK /F is run on the system drive, the following message appears:

```
The type of the file system is NTFS.
Cannot lock current drive.
Chkdsk cannot run because the volume is in use by another
process.  Would you like to schedule this volume to be
checked the next time the system restarts? (Y/N)
```

Answer Y, and CHKDSK runs before the Windows desktop appears, and displays a message in the notification area about the condition of your drive. If CHKDSK /F is run on a non-system drive, it runs immediately.

GPUPDATE

GPUPDATE is used to update the group policy on a local or remote computer:

```
Syntax:  GPUPDATE [/Target:{Computer | User}] [/Force] [/
Wait:<value>]
     [/Logoff] [/Boot] [/Sync]
```

Use this command to refresh the group policy on a specified computer called *AccountingPC* and reboot that computer after the processing is complete:

```
GPUPDATE /target:accountingpc /boot
```

For a complete list of options, use GPUPDATE /?.

GPRESULT

Use **GPRESULT** to display the current policy for a specified user and computer.

```
GPRESULT [/S system [/U username [/P [password]]]] [/SCOPE scope]
         [/USER targetusername] [/R | /V | /Z] [(/X | /H) <file-
name> [/F]]
```

For a complete list of options, use GPRESULT /?. Examples:

- GPRESULT /R —Displays summary data

- GPRESULT /H GPReport.html —Saves report as GPReport.html

- GPRESULT /USER *targetusername* /V—Verbose information for specified username

- GPRESULT /S system /USER *targetusername* /SCOPE COMPUTER /Z—Super-verbose information for specified remote system and user name, limited to computer in scope

- GPRESULT /S system /U *username* /P *password* /SCOPE USER /V —Verbose information for specified system and user, includes password to avoid being prompted for it, and limited to user in scope

DIR

Use **DIR** to display a list of files and subfolders (subdiretories) in a folder (directory). DIR provides many more options for listing files and folders than Windows Explorer or File Explorer.

Use DIR /? for a complete list of options.

```
DIR [drive:] [path] [filename] [/A[[:]attributes]] [/B] [/C] [/D] [/L]
[/N]
   [/O[[:]sortorder]] [/P] [/Q] [/R] [/S] [/T[[:]timefield]] [/W] [/X]
[/4]

   [drive:] [path] [filename]
              Specifies drive, directory, and/or files to list.
```

Examples:

- DIR /Q/P—Displays owner of file and filename and pauses after each screen

- DIR /AH —Displays hidden files/folders in current location

EXIT

Use **EXIT** to close an app that has its own command prompt. For example, to close DISKPART, type `EXIT` at the DISKPART> prompt to close it and return to the command prompt.

When run from the command-line, this command closes the command prompt window and returns you to the Windows GUI. For additional options, use `EXIT /?`.

HELP

The **HELP** executable in Windows can be used to get help for most command-line utilities:

- `HELP`—Displays a list of commands with brief descriptions.

- `HELP /command`—Displays detailed help for the specified command.

EXPAND

The **EXPAND** executable is used to view compressed files in a .CAB (cabinet) archive and uncompress them to the current or specified folder. .CAB files are used by some versions of Windows for installation or update files. Windows XP Recovery Console also uses Expand for system repair. For command syntax for a particular version of Windows, use `EXPAND /?`. Examples:

- `EXPAND -d filename.cab`—Displays files stored in specified archive

- `EXPAND filename.cab -f:FilesInCAB`—Specifies files to extract to current location. To extract files to a different location, specify it at the end of this command.

Command /?

Command /? is used to display help for the specified command.

For example, `CHKDSK /?` displays help for CHKDSK. If the /? option is not supported for a command, use `HELP Command` or search for help online.

Microsoft Administrative Tools

Windows contains a number of administrative tools and features designed to help you manage operations and users. The following sections discuss many of these components, including:

- Computer Management
- Device Manager
- Performance Monitor
- Services
- System Configuration
- Task Scheduler
- Component Services
- Data Sources
- Print Management
- Local Security Policy
- Windows Memory Diagnostic

> **NOTE**   The following Administrative Tools are covered in other chapters:
> - **Local users and groups**; see "Users and Groups," p.1039, Chapter 21.
> - **Windows Firewall and advanced settings**, "Firewall Settings," p.862, Chapter 16.

To start any of the Administrative Tools:

Step 1.   Open **Control Panel**.

Step 2.   Open the **System and Security** category.

Step 3.   Click or tap **Administrative Tools**.

Step 4.   Click or tap the tool you want to use.

Computer Management (MMC)

Instead of hunting around for different utilities in different places in Windows, it's simpler to use the **Computer Management** console window because it has most of the tools you need in one organized window system. Here are the ways to open Computer Management:

In Windows Vista and 7, use one of the following:

- Click **Start**; then right-click **Computer/My Computer** and select **Manage**.

- Navigate to **Start > All Programs > Administrative Tools > Computer Management**.

- Open the Run prompt (**Windows key+R**) and type **compmgmt.msc** (a personal favorite).

In Windows 8/8.1/10:

Press the **Windows key+X** and select **Computer Management** from the menu. In Computer Management, you find the **Event Viewer > Device Manager > Local Users and Groups > Services > Disk Management**.

Using the Microsoft Management Console

Computer Management is an example of the Microsoft Management Console (MMC). This is a blank console that uses various snap-in console windows. MMC saves the consoles you snap in and remembers the last place you were working, and this becomes a valuable and time-saving tool.

To open it, click the Search box (Windows 7, Vista) or press Windows key+R, select Run (Windows 8/8.1/10) and type MMC. This opens a new blank MMC. Then, to add console windows, go to File and then Add/Remove Snap-in (or press Ctrl+M). From there, click the Add button to select the consoles you want, such as Computer Management, Performance Logs and Alerts, or ActiveX Controls. When you are finished, save the MMC and consider adding it as a shortcut within the desktop or in the Quick Launch area and maybe add a keyboard shortcut to open it. The next time you open it, it remembers all the console windows you added and starts you at the location you were in when you closed the program. MMC version 3.0 is used with Windows 7/8/8.1/10. Windows Vista uses MMC version 2.0.

Using Device Manager

Windows **Device Manager** is used to display installed device categories and specific installed devices, and to troubleshoot problems with devices.

You can also start Device Manager using these steps.

To start Device Manager in Windows 7/Vista, follow these steps:

Step 1. Click **Start**, right-click **Computer**, and select **Properties**. This displays the System window.

Step 2. Click the **Device Manager** link on the left side under Tasks.

To start Device Manager in Windows 8/8.1/10:

Step 1.   Open the Charms menu and click **Search** (8/8.1) or click the Search window (10).

Step 2.   Search for **Device Manager**.

Step 3.   Click or tap the **Device Manager** link.

Alternatively:

Step 1.   Press the **Windows key+X**.

Step 2.   Click or tap **Device Manager**.

NOTE   You can also start Device Manager from the Computer Management console window: click Device Manager in the left window pane.

To view the devices in a specific category, click the plus (+) sign next to the category name, as shown in Figure 15-10. If a particular category contains a device with problems, the category automatically opens when you start Device Manager.

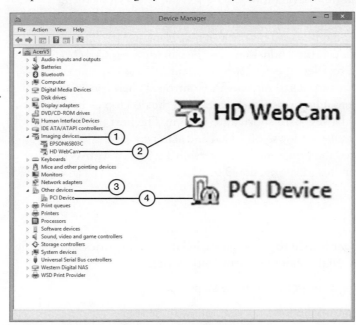

1. Imaging devices category has a device with a problem
2. The HD webcam has been disabled
3. Other devices category is used for unidentified devices
4. An unidentified device

Figure 15-10   Device Manager with selected categories expanded.

NOTE   Different systems will have different categories listed in Device Manager because Device Manager lists only categories for installed hardware. For example, the system shown in Figure 15-10 is a laptop, so it has a Batteries category.

If your computer has devices that are malfunctioning in a way that Device Manager can detect, or has devices that are disabled, they will be displayed as soon as you open Device Manager. For example, in Figure 15-10 the Imaging devices category lists a disabled device, indicated by a down-arrow icon. The Other devices category lists a device that cannot run, indicated by an exclamation mark [!] in a yellow triangle.

If the malfunctioning or disabled device is an I/O port, such as a serial, parallel, or USB port, any device attached to that port cannot work until the device is working properly.

To see more information about a specific device, double-click the device to open its properties sheet. Device properties sheets have a General tab and some combination of other tabs:

- **General**—Displays device type, manufacturer, location, status, troubleshoot button, and usage. Applies to all devices.
- **Properties**—Device-specific settings. Applies to multimedia devices.
- **Driver**—Driver details and version information. Applies to all devices.
- **Details**—Technical details about the device. Applies to all devices.
- **Policies**—Optimizes external drives for quick removal or performance. Applies to USB, FireWire (IEEE 1394), and eSATA drives.
- **Resources**—Hardware resources such as IRQ, DMA, Memory, and I/O port address. Applies to I/O devices.
- **Volumes**—Drive information such as status, type, capacity, and so on. Click Populate to retrieve information. Applies to hard disk drives.
- **Power**—Power available per port. Applies to USB root hubs and generic hubs.
- **Power Management**—Specifies device-specific power management settings. Applies to USB, network, keyboard, and mouse devices.

Figure 15-11 illustrates some of these tabs.

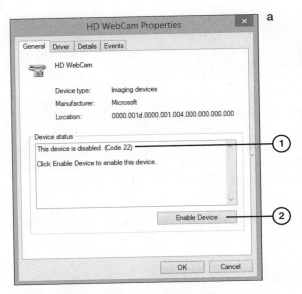

1. Device status – disabled device (Code 22)
2. Troubleshoot button – click or tap to enable device

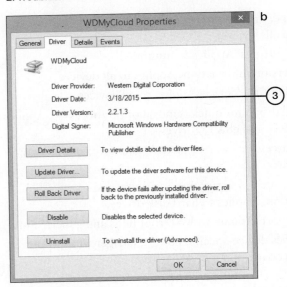

3. Driver overview

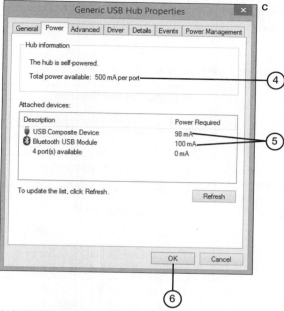

4. Available power per USB port on this hub
5. Power required for connected devices
6. Click or tap to close properties sheet

Figure 15-11 Selected Device Manager tabs: The General tab for a disabled device (A); the Driver tab for a network storage device (B); and the Power tab for a USB hub (C).

To troubleshoot problems with a device in Device Manager, open its Properties sheet by double-clicking the device. Use the General tab shown in Figure 15-11a to display the device's status and to troubleshoot a disabled or malfunctioning device.

When you have a malfunctioning device such as the one in Figure 15-11a, you have several options for resolving the problem:

- Look up the Device Manager code to determine the problem and its solution (see Table 15-4 for a few examples).

- Click the Troubleshoot button (if any) shown on the device's General Properties tab; the button's name and usage depends on the problem. Table 15-4 lists a few examples, their meanings, and the solution button (if any).

- Manually change resources (applies primarily to older systems that don't use ACPI power management). If the nature of the problem is a resource conflict, you can click the Resources tab, change the settings, and eliminate the conflict if possible.

- Manually update drivers. If the problem is a driver issue but an Update Driver button isn't available, open the Driver tab and install a new driver for the device.

Table 15-4   Examples of Some Device Manager Codes and Solutions

Device Manager Code Number	Problem	Recommended Solution
Code 1	This device is not configured correctly.	Update the driver.
Code 3	The driver for this device might be corrupted, or your system might be running low on memory or other resources.	Close some open applications. Uninstall and reinstall the driver. Install additional RAM.
Code 10	Device cannot start.	Update the driver. View Microsoft Help and Support article 943104 for more information.
Code 12	This device cannot find enough free resources that it can use. If you want to use this device, you need to disable one of the other devices on this system.	You can use the Troubleshooting Wizard in Device Manager to determine where the conflict is, and then disable the conflicting device. Disable the device.
Code 22	The device is disabled.	Enable the device.

NOTE   For a comprehensive discussion of Device Manager error codes in Windows, see https://support.microsoft.com/en-us/kb/310123.

You can also use the Device Manager to disable a device that is conflicting with another device. To disable a device, follow these steps:

Step 1.   Click the plus (+) sign next to the device category containing the device.

Step 2.   Double-click the device, click the **Driver** tab, and select **Disable**.

Depending on the device, you might need to physically remove it from the system to resolve a conflict. To use the Device Manager to remove a device, follow these steps:

Step 1.   Click the plus (+) sign next to the device category containing the device.

Step 2.   Double-click the device and select **Uninstall**.

Step 3.   Shut down the system and remove the physical device.

or

Step 1.   Double-click the device and select **Properties**.

Step 2.   Click the **Driver** tab and click the **Uninstall** button.

Step 3.   Shut down the system and remove the physical device.

If a device malfunctions after a driver update, roll back the driver. Use the Roll Back Driver button on the Driver tab to return to the preceding driver version.

Performance Monitor

The Windows **Performance Monitor** can be used for real-time performance monitoring or to record performance over time.

To access Performance Monitor, open the Run prompt, type `perfmon.exe`, and press Enter. Windows 7/8/8.1/10 opens the Performance Monitor window. In Windows Vista, the Reliability and Performance Monitor window opens. In either case, you must then click the Performance Monitor node.

Many different types of performance factors can be measured with these programs. This is done by measuring objects. Objects include physical devices, such as the processor and memory, and software, such as protocols and services. The objects are measured with counters. For example, a common counter for the processor is % Processor Time.

To see whether additional RAM is needed in a system, select the object called Paging File; then select the counters % Usage and Pages/Sec, as shown in the following steps:

Step 1.   Click the **+** sign or right-click in the table beneath the graph and select **Add Counters**.

Step 2.   Select **Paging File** as the Performance Object and then choose **% Usage**.

Step 3.   Click **Add**.

Step 4.   Select **Memory** as the Performance Object and then choose **Pages/Sec** from the drop-down menu.

Step 5.   Click **Add**.

Step 6.   Click **OK** and then run normal applications for this computer.

If the Performance Monitor/System Monitor indicates that the Paging File % Usage is consistently near 100 percent or the Memory Pages/Sec counter is consistently higher than 5, add RAM to improve performance. Figure 15-12 shows an example of inadequate memory within Windows 7's Performance monitor.

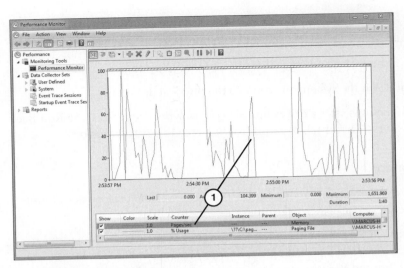

1. High memory pages/sec levels

Figure 15-12   This Windows 7 system needs more RAM for the programs it is running, as indicated by the high levels of the Memory Pages/Sec counters.

Services (Services.msc)

Many of Windows' core functions are implemented as services, including features such as the print spooler, wireless network configuration, DHCP client service, and many more. **Services.msc** can be run automatically or manually and are controlled through the Services node of the Computer Management Console. To open the Computer Management Console, right-click Computer/This PC and select Manage. Then expand the Services and Applications node and click Services.

You can also access the Services dialog from the Services applet in Control Panel's Administrative Tools folder or by running `Services.msc` from the Run line dialog; opening Services in these ways displays the dialog shown in Figure 15-13. The Services dialog lists each service by name, and provides a description, status message, and startup type, and whether the service is for a local system or network service.

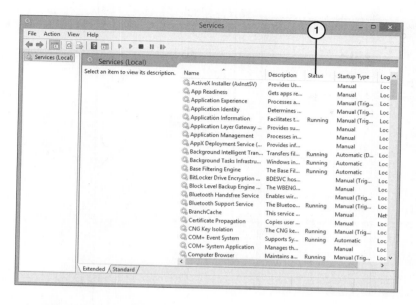

1. Use the Status column to determine if a service is running

Figure 15-13   The Services dialog in Windows 8.1.

To view the properties for a particular service, double-click the service listing. The General tab of the properties sheet, as shown in Figure 15-14, displays the service name, description, path to executable file, startup type, and status. You can also stop, pause, or resume a service from this dialog, as well as from the Services dialog.

Use the Log On tab if you need to configure the service to run for a specific user, the Recovery tab to specify what to do if the service fails, and the Dependencies tab to see what other services work with the specified service.

If a system cannot perform a task that uses a service, go to the Services dialog and restart the service. If a service prevents another task from running (for example, a third-party wireless network client might not run if the Windows WLAN Autoconfig service is running), go to the Services dialog and stop the service.

Figure 15-14   Viewing the General tab for the Print Spooler service.

NOTE   For more information about specific Windows services, I recommend The Elder Geek's Windows Services Guide (Windows 7 version at www.theeldergeek. com/windows_7/windows_7_services.htm), Black Viper's Windows 8 and 8.1 Services Configuration (http://www.blackviper.com/service-configurations/black-vipers-windows-8-service-configurations/ and http://www.blackviper.com/service-configurations/black-vipers-windows-8-1-service-configurations/), or the Answers That Work list of "Task List Programs" at www.answersthatwork.com.

Task Scheduler

Windows uses **Task Scheduler** to run a task on a specified schedule.

Create a Task in Windows

To create a basic task in Windows, follow this procedure:

Step 1.   Open **Control Panel** in Small Icons or Large Icons mode.

Step 2.   Open the **Administrative Tools** folder.

Step 3.   Double-click **Task Scheduler**.

NOTE   You can also run Task Scheduler from the Run or Search box as `taskschd.msc /s`.

Step 4.   Click **Create Basic Task** in the Actions menu.

Step 5.   Enter a name for the task and a description and click **Next**.

Step 6.   Select an interval (daily, weekly, monthly, one-time only, when my computer starts, when I log on, or when a specific event is logged) and click **Next**.

Step 7.   Specify when to start the task and recurrence and whether to synchronize across time zones, and then click **Next**.

Step 8.   Specify what to do (start a program, send an e-mail, or display a message) and click **Next**. The following steps assume that Start a Program has been selected.

Step 9.   Select a program or script to run, add options (arguments), and specify where to start the program or script. Click **Next**.

Step 10.   Review the settings for the task (see Figure 15-15) and click **Finish**.

The task is saved in the Task Scheduler library (see Figure 15-16). You can edit or delete tasks in this folder as needed.

NOTE   Some tasks need to be configured for Windows 7 or Windows Vista. To see this option and other settings you might need to adjust, click the Open the Properties dialog for this Task When I Click Finish checkbox in Step 10 before clicking Finish.

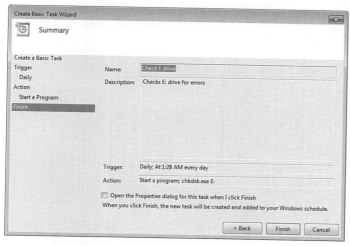

Figure 15-15   Reviewing a Disk Check task created with the Windows 7 Task Scheduler.

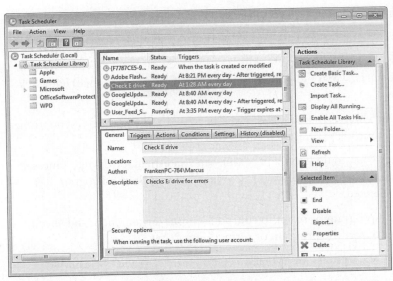

Figure 15-16 The Windows 7 Task Scheduler Library after adding a new task.

Print Management

Print Management is a utility for managing printers connected to the computer or on a network.

To start print management, open the Administrative Tools folder in Control Panel, and double-click Print Management. The Print Management console opens (see Figure 15-17). From it, you can view print servers and connected printers, manage jobs, manage printer ports and forms, and perform other tasks.

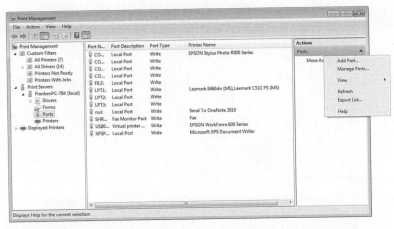

Figure 15-17 The Windows 7 Print Management console.

Component Services

Developers and administrators use the **Component Services** MMC snap-in to manage Component Object Model (COM), COM+ applications, and the Distributed Transaction Coordinator (DTC).

Data Sources (ODBC)

The ODBC Data Source Administrator is used to list and manage **data sources** and drivers. 64-bit versions of Windows include both 64-bit and 32-bit versions. Data sources are listed by user, system, and file, and the administrator also lists drivers and provides options for tracing and pooling data sources.

Local Security Policy

Local Security Policy is a Microsoft Management Console snap-in. Use it to view and set security policies for the local system or a system on a workgroup network. To select a setting for a policy, open the category in the left pane, scroll to the policy in the right pane, and select the setting desired.

For example, to set up an account lockout policy, expand Account policies and click Account Lockout Policy in the left pane. In the right pane, select a value for Account lockout threshold (number of invalid login attempts). Then, specify a lockout duration and other settings as desired.

Windows Memory Diagnostics

The **Windows Memory Diagnostics** tool tests system and cache memory before the Windows desktop is loaded. When it loads, the user can select the type of test and number of test repetitions to perform (see Figure 15-18). The results are displayed in a pop-up message from the taskbar after the Windows desktop reloads.

Windows Memory Diagnostics is also available from the System Recovery Options menu. To learn how to launch System Recovery or repair options, see "System Recovery Options (Windows)," p.1107, Chapter 22.

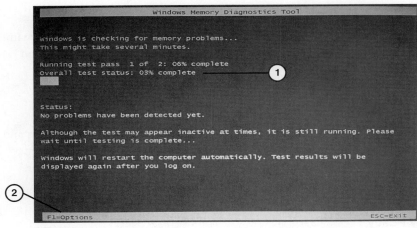

1. Test status
2. Press the F1 key to change test options

Figure 15-18   Windows Memory Diagnostics testing a system running Windows 8.1.

Task Manager

The **Task Manager** utility provides a useful real-time look into the inner workings of Windows and the programs that are running. There are several ways to display Task Manager including:

- Right-click the taskbar and select **Task Manager**.
- Press **Ctrl+Shift+Esc**.
- Open the **Run** or **Search** box and type **taskmgr**.
- Press **Ctrl+Alt+Del** and select **Task Manager** from the Windows Security dialog.

In Windows Vista/7, Task Manager opens to the Applications window shown in Figure 15-19.

The Task Manager tabs include:

- **Applications**—Shows running applications
- **Processes**—Program components in memory
- **Performance**—CPU, memory, pagefile, and caching stats
- **Networking**—Lists network utilization by adapter in use

- **Users**—Lists current users

- **Services**—Lists services and their status

Use the **Applications** tab to determine whether a program has stopped responding; you can shut down these programs by using the **End Task** button.

Use the **Processes** tab to see which processes are consuming the most memory. Use this dialog along with the System Configuration Utility (MSCONFIG) to help determine whether you are loading unnecessary startup applications; MSCONFIG can disable them to free up memory. If you are unable to shut down a program with the Applications tab, you can also shut down its processes with the Processes tab, but this is not recommended unless the program cannot be shut down in any other way.

Use the **Performance** tab to determine whether you need to install more RAM memory or need to increase the computer's paging file size. Use the **Networking** tab to monitor the performance of the computer's connection to the network. Use the Services tab to see the services currently running on a system.

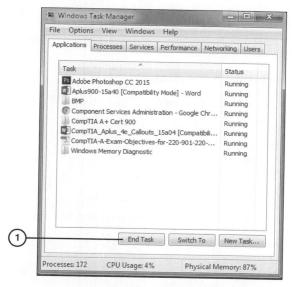

1. To kill a task that is not responding, select it and then click or tap the End Task button.

Figure 15-19   The Windows Task Manager's General tab in Windows 7.

In Windows 8/8.1/10, Task Manager uses a new design that lists only running programs when you start it (see Figure 15-20). Click or tap More details to see details about those programs and additional tabs (see Figure 15-21).

1. Click or tap to see more information and tabs.

Figure 15-20   The Windows Task Manager's opening dialog in Windows 8.1.

The Task Manager tabs in the Windows 8/8.1 version include

- **Processes**—Apps and background processes in memory
- **Performance**—CPU, memory, disk drives, Bluetooth, Ethernet, and Wi-Fi stats
- **App history**—App resource usage in current system session
- **Startup**—Startup programs and their impact on system performance
- **Users**—Lists current users
- **Details**—PID, status, user name, CPU, and memory usage by app or service
- **Services**—Lists services and their status

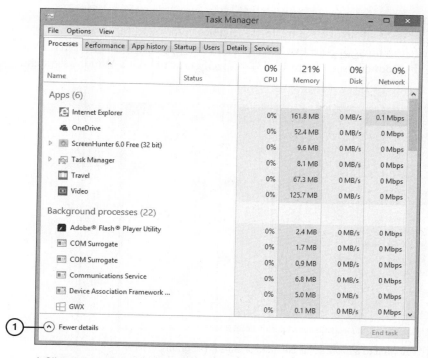

1. Click or tap to return to simplified dialog

Figure 15-21   The More details view of the Windows 8.1 version of Task Manager.

MSCONFIG

The Microsoft System Configuration utility, **MSCONFIG**, enables you to selectively disable programs and services that run at startup. If your computer is unstable, runs more slowly than usual, or has problems starting up or shutting down, using MSCONFIG can help you determine whether a program or service running when the system starts is at fault. To start MSCONFIG with Windows Vista/7:

Step 1.   Click **Start** to open the Windows Desktop Search pane.

Step 2.   Type MSCONFIG and press **Enter**.

To start MSCONFIG with Windows 8/8.1:

Step 1.   Press the **Windows key+X**.

Step 2.   Click or tap **Run**.

Step 3.   Type MSCONFIG and press **Enter**.

All versions of MSCONFIG have a multitabbed interface used to control startup options. The **General** tab (see Figure 15-22) enables you to select from Normal, Diagnostic (clean boot) or Selective Startup. (You choose which items and services to load.) Use the **Boot** tab (see Figure 15-23) to specify how to boot a Windows system.

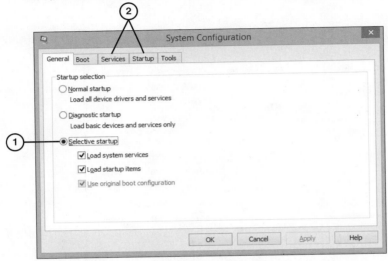

1. Select if you want to disable some services or startup programs.
2. Configure startup services and programs with these tabs.

Figure 15-22   MSCONFIG's General tab (Windows 8.1).

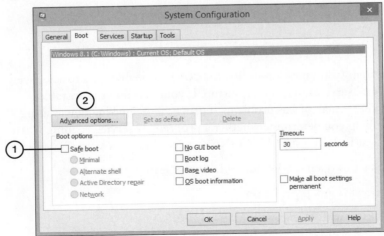

1. Click or tap and select options if you want to start in Safe Mode or use other special startup options
2. Installed operating systems. If you are using the Windows boot loader, the additional operating systems installed are shown here.

Figure 15-23   MSCONFIG's Boot tab (Windows 8.1).

Use the **Services** tab to disable or reenable system services. Use the **Startup** tab to disable or reenable startup programs. Use the **Tools** tab to launch System Restore, Computer Management, and other management tasks.

> **TIP**   When you select a tool from the Tools tab, MSCONFIG displays the command line needed to run it. Add any options desired before starting the tool.

 ## Disk Management

The **Disk Management** snap-in of the Computer Management Console is the GUI-based application for analyzing and configuring hard drives. You can do a lot from here. Try some of the configurations listed on a test computer. All you need is one or two drives with unpartitioned space.

> **CAUTION**   Some operations wipe out all drive contents. Make sure you back up any data you want to keep before trying any of these tasks.

Drive Status

Disk Management displays the status of connected drives with **Drive Status**.

In Figure 15-24, you also can see the disks at the top of the window and their status. For example, the C: partition is healthy. It also shows the percentage of the disk used and other information, such as whether the disk is currently formatting, whether it's Basic or Dynamic, or whether it has failed.

In some cases, you might see "foreign" status. This means that a dynamic disk has been moved from another computer (with another Windows operating system) to the local computer, and it cannot be accessed properly. To fix this and be able to access the disk, add the disk to your computer's system configuration.

To add a disk to your computer's system configuration, right-click the disk and then click Import Foreign Disks. Any existing volumes on the foreign disk become visible and accessible when you import the disk.

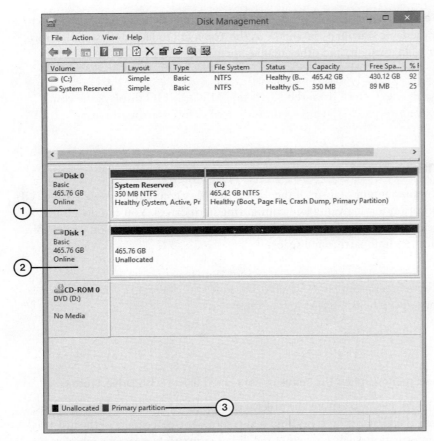

1. A disk with two primary partitions
2. A disk with no partitions
3. Disk status color key (changes as other disk types are added or created)

Figure 15-24   Using Disk Management (Windows 8.1)

NOTE   For more information on the plethora of disk statuses, see the Microsoft TechNet article, "Disk Status Descriptions," at http://technet.microsoft.com/en-us/library/cc738101(WS.10).aspx. Although Windows Vista/7/8/8.1/10 are not mentioned in this document, the terminology is still accurate.

Initializing a Disk

When you connect a new drive, you might be prompted to **initialize** it. If prompted by the Initialize Disk dialog, select the disk and choose the partition style to use (MBR for drives under 2.1TB, and GPT for larger drives). After this, an unformatted drive will appear as **Unallocated** in Disk Management.

NOTE An MBR drive can have up to four primary partitions. A GPT drive can have more than four primary partitions. A GPT partition must be used for drives more than 2.1TB in size.

Creating a New Simple Volume

Adding a drive happens when you create a new simple volume. A new simple volume can occupy a portion or all of the space on an unallocated disk.

Step 1.   Right-click unallocated space on a drive. (With a new drive, the entire drive will be listed as unallocated.)

Step 2.   Select **New Simple Volume**.

Step 3.   Click **Next**.

Step 4.   To use the entire space for a volume (drive letter), click **Next**. To use only part of the space, specify the amount of space to use (in MB) and then click **Next**.

Step 5.   Select the drive letter to install and click **Next**. (You can also select the option to not assign a drive letter or to mount the drive in an empty NTFS folder on an existing drive.)

Step 6.   Specify the file system (NTFS is default), the volume name, and whether to use a quick format or prepare the drive as compressed. Click **Next**.

Step 7.   Review all options and click **Finish** (see Figure 15-25).

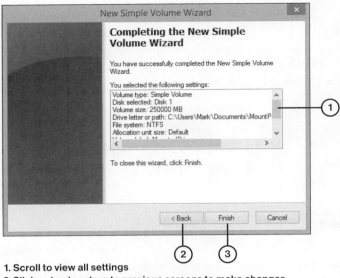

1. Scroll to view all settings
2. Click or tap to return to previous screens to make changes
3. Click or tap to prepare drive with listed settings

Figure 15-25   Creating a new simple volume (Windows 8.1).

Extending Partitions

Windows enables you to **extend** the size of a partition (volume) with the Disk Management utility. It's highly recommended that you back up your data before attempting this operation.

Step 1.   Right-click the volume to be extended.

Step 2.   Select **Extend Volume**. (Remember that a volume is any section of the hard drive with a drive letter.)

Step 3.   Click **Next** for the wizard and select how much space you'd like to add to the partition.

Step 4.   Click **Finish** at the summary screen.

A reboot is not required, and this process should finish fairly quickly. This process can also be done using the Diskpart command.

Shrink Partitions

If you need to free up space on a drive so you can install another operating system, you can **shrink** a partition. As with extending a volume, we recommend you back up your data before starting.

Step 1.   Right-click the volume to be shrunk.

Step 2.   Select **Shrink Volume**.

Step 3.   Select how much space you'd like to shrink the partition.

Step 4.   Click **Shrink**.

The free space created by the Shrink Volume process is listed as unallocated.

Splitting Partitions

If you need to **split** a single partition into two or more partitions using Disk Management, follow this procedure:

Step 1.   Shrink the existing partition to make room for an additional partition.

Step 2.   If you are unable to shrink the partition sufficiently, back up some of the information in the partition and try step 1 again.

Step 3.   Create one or more new partition(s) in the unallocated space you created in step 1.

Mounting a Drive

You can also **mount** drives in Disk Management. A **mounted drive** is a drive mapped to an empty folder within a volume that has been formatted as NTFS. Instead of using drive letters, mounted drives use drive paths. This is a good solution for when you need more than 26 drives in your computer because you are not limited to the letters in the alphabet. Mounted drives can also provide more space for temporary files and can enable you to move folders to different drives if space runs low on the current drive. To mount a drive, follow these steps:

Step 1.   Right-click the partition or volume you want to mount and select **Change Drive Letters and Paths**.

Step 2.   In the displayed window, click **Add**.

Step 3.   Click **Mount** in the following empty NTFS folder.

Step 4.   Browse to the empty folder you want to mount the volume to and click **OK**.

Step 5.   Click **Next** (see Figure 15-26).

Step 6.   Choose drive partitioning settings, then click **Next**.

Step 7.   Review the settings, then click **Finish**.

As shown in Figure 15-26, the hard disk partition has been mounted within a folder on the system hard drive called MountPoint. To remove the **mount point**, go back to Disk Management, right-click the mounted volume, select Change Drive Letters and Paths, and then select Remove. Remember that the folder you want to use as a mount point must be empty and must be within an NTFS volume.

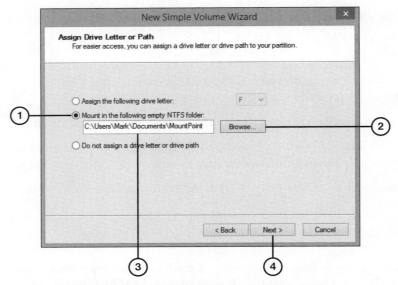

1. The selected drive will be mounted in an empty NTFS folder
2. Click or tap to browse for the folder
3. After selecting the folder, it appears here
4. Click or tap to continue

Figure 15-26   Assigning a partition as a mounted drive.

Assigning/Changing Drive Letters

If you created a volume without assigning a drive letter, you also use Change Drive Letters and Paths. Here's how:

Step 1.   Right-click the partition or volume and select **Change Drive Letters and Paths**.

Step 2.   In the displayed window, click **Add**.

Step 3.   Make sure **Assign the following drive letter** is selected. The next available drive letter is listed. To keep the default, skip to step 5.

Step 4.   If you prefer a different drive letter, use the pull-down menu to choose the drive letter desired.

Step 5.   Click **OK**. The drive is now referred to by the drive letter you selected.

If you want to change the drive letter of a connected drive (for example, so that a USB drive can use the same drive letter on different computers), follow this procedure:

Step 1.   Right-click the partition or volume you want to change and select **Change Drive Letters and Paths**.

Step 2.   The current drive letter assignment is shown. Click **Change**.

Step 3.   To change the drive letter, use the pull-down menu to choose the preferred drive letter.

Step 4.   Click **OK**.

Step 5.   Click **Yes** to change the drive letter. The drive is now referred to by the drive letter you selected.

Adding Arrays

Disk Management supports basic disks, which can be bootable, and dynamic disks. Although dynamic disks can't be used as boot disks, they can be used in the following types of drive arrays:

- **Spanned**—The capacity of all disks is added together. Equivalent to just a bunch of disks (JBOD) hardware array. Requires at least two disks.

- **Striped**—Data is written across all drives to enhance speed. Equivalent to RAID 0 hardware array. Requires two disks.

- **Mirrored**—Copies of data are written to all disks at the same time to enhance data security. If one drive fails, data is still safe and the array can be rebuilt. Equivalent to a RAID 1 hardware array. Requires two disks.

- **RAID 5**—Data and recovery information is written across all disks to enable recovery if one disk in the array fails. Equivalent to RAID 5 hardware array. Requires at least three disks.

To create any of these arrays, follow these steps:

Step 1.   Make sure the disks you are going to use in the **drive array** have been backed up. Any disk in an array has its previous information overwritten.

Step 2.   Right-click the first drive to add to your array and select the array type.

Step 3.   Click **Next** to continue.

Step 4.   Select the next drive to add to your array and click **Add**.

Step 5.   If you are creating a RAID 5 array, repeat step 3 until you have added all of the disks you want to add to the array.

Step 6. Click **Next** to continue.

Step 7. Assign a drive letter or mount point. Click **Next**.

Step 8. Select the option to format the volume and name it. Click **Next**.

Step 9. Review your settings. Click **Finish**.

Step 10. Click **Yes** to convert the drives to dynamic disks (required for arrays). The array is created.

Figure 15-27 shows how two 500GB drives appear in a mirrored, spanned, or striped array.

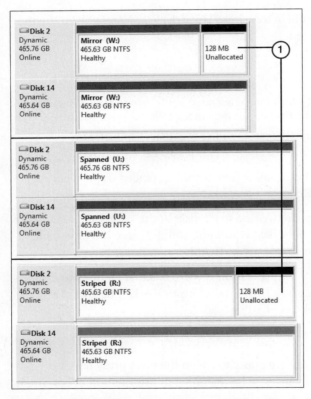

1. The first drive selected in an array has a small unallocated portion of the disk.

Figure 15-27 Mirrored, spanned, and striped disk arrays.

NOTE Windows Disk Management's disk arrays are slower than some hardware RAID arrays (the difference in performance depends on the hardware RAID host adapter in the comparison) but can be set up with standard non-RAID SATA host adapters.

Storage Spaces

Windows 8/8.1/10 include a new way to use multiple hard disk or SSDs to increase available storage: **Storage Spaces**.

Storage Spaces enables the user to combine the capacity of drives together into a storage pool that is used to create storage spaces. Storage spaces can be expanded in size by adding additional drives. Table 15-5 provides an overview of the options available.

Table 15-5 Storage Spaces Overview

Configuration	Use
Simple	Requires at least one drive. Capacity of all drives is grouped together and used as a single logical drive. If any drive fails, all data is lost.
Two-way mirror	Requires at least two drives. Each drive has a copy of the information. If one drive fails, the mirror can be rebuilt from the surviving drive after a new drive is attached.
Three-way mirror	Requires at least five drives. The drive pool includes three copies of your data. If one or two drives fail, the mirror can be rebuilt from the surviving drive after new drives are attached.
Parity	Requires at least three drives. The pool is written with data and parity information. If a single drive fails, the surviving drives can rebuild the pool.

Here's how to use Storage Spaces:

Step 1.   Open Search and search for **Storage Spaces**.

Step 2.   Click or tap **Storage Spaces**.

Step 3.   Click or tap **Create a new pool and storage space**.

Step 4.   Select the drive(s) you want to use.

CAUTION   When you use a drive for a storage pool, all existing files on the drive are deleted, bypassing the Recycle Bin. Make sure you have backups of any files you want to keep before you assign a drive to a storage pool!

Step 5.   Click **Create pool**.

Step 6.   Storage Spaces displays a recommended layout. Make any changes desired and click or tap **Create storage space** (see Figure 15-28).

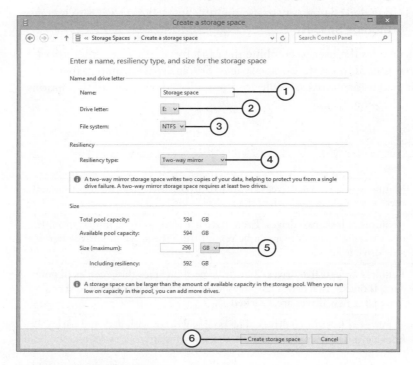

1. Enter name for logical drive
2. Select drive letter desired
3. Select NTFS (default) or ReFS file system
4. Select resiliency type
5. Maximum size; can be reduced
6. Click or tap to create storage space

Figure 15-28   Creating a two-way mirror in Storage Spaces.

After the storage space is created, the Manage Storage Spaces dialog displays the new storage space.

NOTE   In Windows 8.1/10, you can select from two file systems, NTFS and ReFS (resilient file system). ReFS is designed for larger amounts of data and is self-healing. To learn more, see "Resilient File System Overview" at https://technet.microsoft.com/en-us/library/hh831724.aspx.

The Storage Spaces storage pool is assigned a drive letter and shows up in File Explorer and Disk Management as a normal drive. If a drive fails, warnings are displayed in Action Center. Click the link to open Storage Spaces. Take the recommended action to bring your pool back to health.

You must use Storage Spaces to manage the drives in a drive pool. As far as Disk Management is concerned, a drive pool is recognized as only a single drive.

Windows Upgrade Tools

There are different considerations involved when a user upgrades an existing computer to a new operating system or switches to a different computer:

- With an upgrade to an existing system, we need to find out the readiness of the existing computer and apps for a new operating system.

- With a move to a new system, we need to transfer data files and settings to the new computer.

Microsoft offers the following utilities to help with these upgrade challenges:

- **Windows Upgrade Advisor**—Determines whether a computer can run Windows 7. The Windows 8/8.1 versions are known as Windows 8 Upgrade Assistant and Windows 8.1 Upgrade Assistant. To learn more, see "Windows Upgrade Paths," p.694, Chapter 14.

- **Windows Easy Transfer**—Copies files, photos, music, e-mail, and settings (collectively known as the *user state*) to a Windows 8.1, 8, 7, or Windows Vista computer from a Windows Vista, Windows 7, or Windows 8 computer.

- **User State Migration Tool (USMT)**—A command-line tool used to migrate user files and settings for one or more computers. The program can be downloaded from www.microsoft.com/downloads.

The following sections discuss Windows Easy Transfer and USMT and their use.

Windows Easy Transfer (WET)

The **Windows Easy Transfer** (WET) feature included in Windows Vista, Windows 7, and Windows 8 copies files, photos, music, e-mail, and settings (collectively known as the user state) to a Windows 8.1, 8, 7 or Windows Vista computer. To run WET in Windows 7 or Windows Vista:

Step 1.   Click **Start** to open the Windows Desktop Search pane.

Step 2.   Type **Windows Easy Transfer** and press **Enter**.

To run WET in Windows 8/8.1:

Step 1.   **Sweep** in from the right or move the mouse to the lower-right corner to open the Charms menu.

Step 2.   Click **Search**.

Step 3.   Type **Windows Easy Transfer** and press **Enter**.

To learn more, see http://windows.microsoft.com/en-us/windows/transfer-files-settings-from-another-computer#1TC=windows-7.

With Windows Easy Transfer for Windows Vista, 7, or 8, files and settings can be migrated over the network or by a specially designed Easy Transfer cable. The data can also be stored on media like a CD, DVD, or USB flash drive or hard disk until the destination computer is ready (see Figure 15-29).

CAUTION   Windows 8.1 can receive data from Windows 7 or Windows 8 computers via Windows Easy Transfer, but only via a USB flash drive or hard disk (network or USB Easy Transfer cable methods are no longer supported). Windows 8.1's version of Windows Easy Transfer cannot send data to another computer, but is used only to receive data from another computer.

First, run Windows Easy Transfer on the computer that has the files and settings that you want to transfer (the source computer). You can transfer the files and settings for one user account or all the accounts on the computer. All the files and settings will be saved as a single .MIG file (Migration Store).

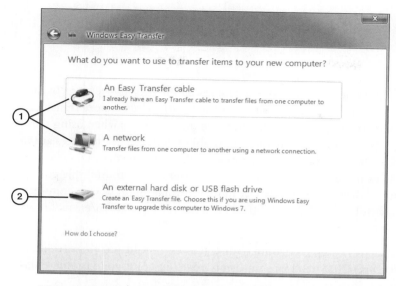

1.Options not supported by Windows Easy Transfer in Windows 8.1
2. Supported by Windows 8.1 and earlier versions of Windows Easy Transfer

Figure 15-29   Selecting a transfer method with Windows Easy Transfer.

Then, move to the computer to which you want to transfer the files (destination computer), start Windows Easy Transfer on that computer, and load the .MIG file from the network, USB cable, optical media, USB flash drive, or USB hard disk source where it is stored. With Windows 8.1, you can choose only from USB hard disk or flash drive.

TIP   Windows 10 does not include Windows Easy Transfer. As a replacement, Microsoft has teamed up with Laplink Software to offer PCmover Express free for personal use. PCmover Express can transfer files and settings from a PC running Windows XP or later to one running Windows 8.1 or Windows 10. Learn more at http://pcmover10.laplink.com/.

User State Migration Tool (USMT)

The **User State Migration Tool** (USMT) is a command-line tool that you can use to migrate user files and settings for one or more computers. USMT 5.0, which is designed for Windows Vista, 7, 8, and 8.1, is part of the Windows Assessment and Deployment Kit (Windows ADK) for Windows 8.1, which is available from http://go.microsoft.com/fwlink/p/?LinkId=393005.

NOTE   The Windows ADK for Windows 10, which contains a version of USMT, is available from http://go.microsoft.com/fwlink/p/?LinkId=526740.

USMT uses two different tools: Scanstate.exe saves all the files and settings of the user (or users) on a computer, known as the user state; and loadstate.exe transfers that data to the destination computer(s). There are many options when using the scanstate and loadstate commands, including the ability to select which users are migrated and whether the store of data is uncompressed, compressed, or compressed and encrypted. By using scripting programs, the transfer of files to multiple computers can be automated over the network. For more information on how to transfer files and settings with USMT 5.0, visit https://technet.microsoft.com/en-us/library/hh825256.aspx.

For an illustrated step-by-step procedure with examples, visit http://blogs.technet.com/b/nepapfe/archive/2013/04/15/using-usmt-v-5-to-migrate-your-profile-data-apps-amp-profile-settings.aspx.

System Utilities

Windows contains a variety of command-line utilities known as **system utilities** that are used for system management. A command-line utility is a program you can start by using the Run dialog. You can also start these utilities by using Windows Desktop Search in Windows Vista and 7 or by opening the program's icon from Windows Explorer (My Computer). In Windows 8/8.1, open the Charms menu and use Search, or open the program's icon in This PC or File Explorer. In Windows 10, use the Search window or open the program's icon in This PC or File Explorer. The most significant ones for the purposes of the A+ exams include:

- **SERVICES.MSC**—Views Windows Services
- **MMC**—Starts Microsoft Management Console
- **NOTEPAD**—Opens Notepad text editor/viewer
- **EXPLORER**—Starts Windows Explorer (Vista/7) or File Explorer (8/8.1/10)
- **MSINFO32**—Starts Windows System Information
- **DXDIAG**—Starts DirectX Diagnostic
- **MSCONFIG**—Starts System Configuration utility
- **REGEDIT**—Launches Registry Editor
- **CMD**—Opens the command prompt

Utilities not otherwise covered are discussed in the following sections.

NOTE   SERVICES.MSC is discussed earlier in this chapter, in the "Services (Services.MSC)" section. MMC is discussed earlier in this chapter, in the "Computer Management Console (MMC)" section.

Using REGEDIT

Under most normal circumstances, the **Registry** will not need to be edited or viewed. However, Registry editing might be necessary under the following circumstances:

- To view a system setting that cannot be viewed through normal interfaces.

- To add, modify (by changing values or data), or remove a Registry key that cannot be changed through normal Windows menus or application settings. This might be necessary to remove traces of a program or hardware device that was not uninstalled properly or to allow a new device or program to be installed.

- To back up the Registry to a file.

To start **REGEDIT**, open the Run or Windows Desktop Search window, type **REGEDIT**, and press **Enter**. Changes made in REGEDIT are automatically saved when you exit; however, you might have to log off and log back on or restart the system for those changes to take effect.

CAUTION   The Registry should never be edited unless a backup copy has been made first because there is no Undo option for individual edits and no way to discard all changes when exiting REGEDIT.

Editing the Windows Registry is even more difficult because Registry keys can be expressed in decimal, hexadecimal, or text. When editing the Registry, be sure to carefully follow the instructions provided by a vendor.

Figure 15-30 shows the Registry in Windows 7 with a modification being made to the MenuShowDelay registry key, which isn't accessible within normal Windows display menus.

Making Changes to the Registry by Importing a Text File

Some changes to the Registry are performed by importing a text file into the Registry. See the "Let Me Fix It Myself" section at http://support.microsoft.com/ kb/950505 for an example of importing a Registry key into the Registry. Some support websites also offer downloadable text files containing registry keys.

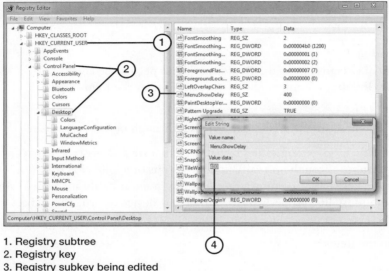

1. Registry subtree
2. Registry key
3. Registry subkey being edited
4. Enter new value here

Figure 15-30   Using REGEDIT (Windows 7).

Backing Up the Registry Before Editing

Always back up the Registry before editing it. Follow these steps to back up part or all of the Registry to a text file:

Step 1.   Start REGEDIT.

Step 2.   To make a partial backup, highlight the section of the Registry you want to back up.

Step 3.   Click **File**.

Step 4.   Select **Export**.

Step 5.   Select a location to store the Registry backup.

Step 6.   Enter a name for the backup.

Step 7.   Click **All** to back up the entire Registry. Click **Selected Branch** to back up only the Registry branch you selected in step 2.

Step 8.   Click **Save**.

COMMAND

In old versions of Windows, command.com was the 16-bit command interpreter, and CMD.EXE was a 32-bit or 64-bit command interpreter. However, in Windows Vista and later, running **Command** actually runs CMD.EXE.

MSTSC (Remote Desktop Connection)

To facilitate connections to remote computers and allow full remote control, Microsoft uses **MSTSC**, better known as the Remote Desktop Connection program (see Figure 15-31), which is based off the Remote Desktop Protocol (RDP). MSTSC works in three ways. First, users can be given limited access to a remote computer's applications such as Word or Excel. Second, administrators can be given full access to a computer so that they can troubleshoot problems from another location. Third, another part of the program known as Remote Assistance allows users to invite a technician to come and view their desktop in the hopes that the technician can fix any encountered problems. These invitations can be made via e-mail or by Windows Messenger or other instant-messaging programs. A remote user needs to have an account on the host computer.

Compatibility with MSTSC Connections

You can use a PC running Windows 8, Windows RT, Windows 8.1, Windows 10, or Windows RT 8.1 to initiate a connection. But you can only connect to PCs that are running these Windows operating systems: Windows 10 Pro or Enterprise; Windows 8.1 Pro or Enterprise; Windows 8 Enterprise or Pro; Windows 7 Enterprise, Professional, or Ultimate; Windows Vista Enterprise, Ultimate, or Professional; Windows XP Professional.

NOTE   Home editions of Windows Vista/7/8/8.1/10 can use Remote Assistance. The checkbox for Remote Assistance is on the same Remote tab used to configure Remote Desktop.

See http://windows.microsoft.com/en-us/windows/remote-desktop-app-faq#1TC=windows-8 for details.

Configuring Remote Settings on the Host Computer

To set up a computer's **remote settings** options to receive remote connections:

Step 1. Open the System properties sheet in Control Panel.

Step 2. Click or tap **Remote**.

Step 3. Click or tap the empty **Allow remote connections to this computer** checkbox.

Step 4. Specify which users can connect, and whether the connection must use Network Level Authentication (NLA). Use NLA unless you need to support connections from Windows XP SP2 or earlier versions.

Step 5. Click **OK** when done.

Starting MSTSC and Connecting to a Remote Computer

To run MSTSC in Windows 7 or Windows Vista:

Step 1. Click **Start** to open the Windows Desktop Search pane.

Step 2. Type **MSTSC** and press **Enter**.

To run MSTSC in Windows 8/8.1:

Step 1. Press **Windows key+X**.

Step 2. Click **Run**.

Step 3. Type **MSTSC** and press **Enter**.

To connect to the remote computer:

Step 1. Enter its name or IP address.

Step 2. Click **Connect**.

Step 3. Select or enter the account name and enter the account password.

The connection starts.

To see options for saving the connection or using a saved connection, click Show options. These options are shown in Figure 15-31.

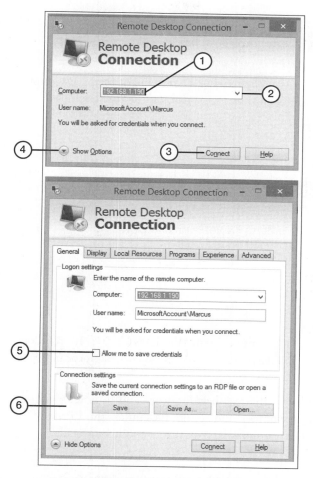

1. Enter IP address of remote computer
2. Open menu to look up a previously added remote computer
3. Click or tap to connect
4. Click or tap to show options
5. Click or tap to save credentials
6. Use these buttons to save or open connection settings

Figure 15-31 Making a remote desktop connection with Windows 8.1.

NOTE If you are having trouble connecting to a system remotely using a remote program such as Remote Desktop Connection or helping someone with using Remote Assistance, RDP port 3389 may be blocked at the firewall and need to be allowed/open for you to connect. The A+ exam may ask you what to do in this scenario.

NOTEPAD

NOTEPAD is a simple plain-text editor; however, it has several uses in system management:

- Creating batch files and scripts. When saving a batch file or script, use quotes around the filename and extension thus: "myscript.scr" or "mybatch.bat".

- Viewing text-based reports.

- Editing HTML files.

NOTEPAD is the default program for opening up .txt (plain-text) files.

To open a text file with a different extension in NOTEPAD:

Step 1.   Right-click the file in Windows Explorer or File Explorer.

Step 2.   Select **Open With**.

Step 3.   Choose **NOTEPAD**.

EXPLORER

Windows Explorer is the file management utility in Windows Vista/7. In Windows 8/8.1/10, it has been renamed as File Explorer. This section uses **Explorer** to discuss common features.

Windows can use Explorer to view both local drive/network and Internet content. By default, Explorer doesn't display hidden and system files unless the View options are changed; see the section Folder Options, later in this chapter, for details.

> **TIP**   To view the contents of a particular drive with Explorer, type Explorer x: into the Run prompt or Search box (replace x with the actual drive letter) and press Enter.

Windows Explorer (Windows Vista/7)

Explorer can be started in any of the following ways in Windows Vista/7:

- From the Start menu, click **Start > All Programs > Accessories > Windows Explorer**.

- Open the **Search** box, type **Explorer**, and press **Enter**.

- Open **Computer** from the Start menu to start Explorer.

Figure 15-32 shows Windows Explorer in Windows 7.

Windows 7 groups shortcuts to a wide variety of locations in its left pane. The Favorites section includes shortcuts to the current user's desktop, downloads folder, and recently visited objects (folders and libraries). The Libraries section includes shortcuts to the current user's Documents, Music, Pictures, and Videos libraries. If the computer is part of a homegroup network (a network type introduced in Windows 7 and supported in Windows 8/8.1/10), the Homegroup section lists other computers in the homegroup. The Computer section lists all connected drives (see Figure 15-32). The Network section lists all computers on the network. The right pane lists the contents of the current location. Common tasks are in a menu strip above the panes.

Windows Vista uses the Favorite Links view, as shown in Figure 15-33. Favorite Links provides shortcuts to the current user's Documents, Pictures, and Music folders, and searches for recently changed files, saved searches, and the system's Public folder. Click the up or down pointer below Favorite Links to toggle Folders on/off. The right pane lists the contents of the current location. Common tasks are in a menu strip above the panes.

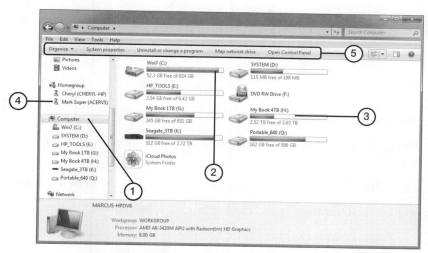

1. Selected object (Computer)
2. Red capacity indicator = 10% or less free space
3. Blue capacity indicator = more than 10% free space
4. Computers/users in homegroup
5. Common tasks

Figure 15-32 Windows Explorer in Windows 7 provides a scrolling pane with access to libraries, local and network locations, and homegroup computers. The Computer view using Tiles is shown here.

Common tasks

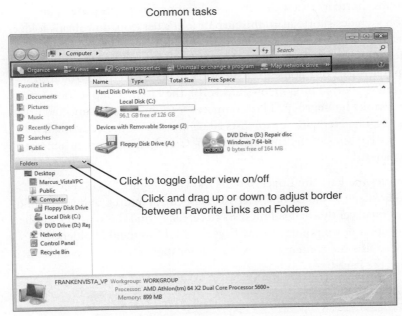

Click to toggle folder view on/off

Click and drag up or down to adjust border
between Favorite Links and Folders

Figure 15-33   The Favorite Links view in Windows Vista provides shortcuts to the most common locations.

File Explorer (Windows 8/8.1/10)

File Explorer (see Figure 15-34) can be started in any of the following ways in Windows 8/8.1:

- Open the **Charms** menu, search for **Explorer,** and tap or click **File Explorer.**

- Tap or click the **Desktop** tile and click or tap the **File Explorer** icon on the taskbar.

- Press the **Windows key+X** and click or tap **File Explorer.**

NOTE   In Windows 10, you can use Windows key+X or open the Start menu and click the File Explorer icon to start File Explorer.

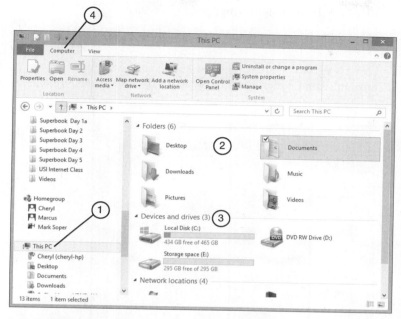

1. Default object selected when File Explorer opens
2. Folders view
3. Drives and devices view
4. Computer tab

Figure 15-34   Windows 8.1 File Explorer's This PC (default) view.

Windows 8/8.1/10's File Explorer opens to the This PC view, which combines the Computer and Libraries views from Windows 7. It uses a multi-tabbed ribbon menu for working with files, computer settings (default tab), and view options.

Displaying Drives, Files, and Folders

Explorer offers the following viewing options:

- **Small icons, List**—Small icons in rows across the Explorer window; List arranges objects in columns

- **Medium, Large, and Extra Large icons**—Different-sized thumbnails of supported file types

- **Details**—File or folder name, date modified, type, size. Right-click or press and hold the header to select additional details to display.

- **Tiles**—Displays capacity of USB, hard disk drives, and SSDs.

Windows 7/8/8.1/10 also include the following:

- **Content**—Lists medium icons (thumbnails) along with the file's last-modified date and size.

Figure 15-35 illustrates the same folder using Large icons, Details, and Content views.

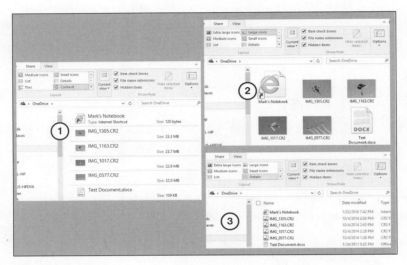

1. Content view
2. Large icons view
3. Details view

Figure 15-35   Content, Large icons, and Details views in File Explorer (Windows 8.1).

Windows Vista also incorporates the Stacks view, which groups files according to what is specified by the user. You can click the stacks to filter the files shown in Windows Explorer.

Libraries (Windows 7/8/8.1/10)

When you open Windows Explorer in Windows 7, the default view shows your libraries. A **library** includes the contents of the current user's documents, music, pictures, or videos folder, but also includes the contents of the corresponding public folder and can display the contents of any other local or network folder the user adds to the library. In Figure 15-36, the Pictures library has been expanded in the left pane to reveal two additional folders that have been added. In any Windows Explorer view in Windows 7, click **Organize** to display file, folder, and layout options and to view properties for the currently selected object.

Windows 8/8.1/10 also include library support. To display libraries in Windows 8/8.1/10, click or tap the **View** tab, click or tap **Options**, and check the **Show libraries** checkbox.

To learn more about libraries, see "File Structure and Paths," p.693, Chapter 14.

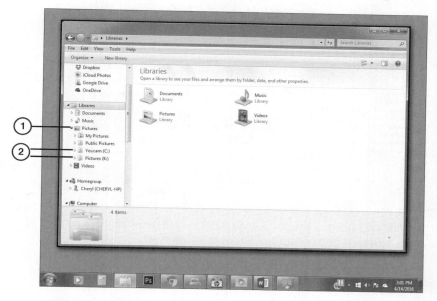

1. Click to expand view
2. Additional folders added to Pictures library by user

Figure 15-36   Windows Explorer in Windows 7 provides a scrolling pane with access to libraries, local and network locations, and homegroup computers. The Libraries view is the default view.

MSINFO32 (System Information)

MSINFO32, also known as System Information, displays a great deal of information about the computer hardware and Windows installation in a system. The System Summary (see Figure 15-37) provides basic information about the Windows installation and hardware configuration. To dig deeper, open the nodes in the left pane. Figure 15-38 lists loaded program modules.

Use the Find window to locate specific information. Use the File menu to save the report or to export it as a text file.

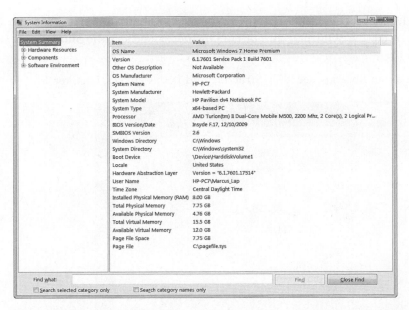

Figure 15-37   MSINFO32 system summary. Click a subnode (left pane) for more detailed information about system hardware, components, or software environment.

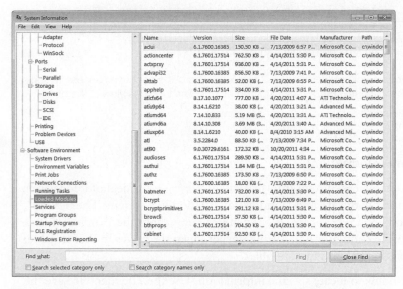

Figure 15-38   MSINFO32 loaded program modules display (right pane).

DXDIAG (DirectX Diagnostics)

DXDIAG displays and troubleshoots DirectX components in Windows. Use it to determine the version of DirectX on your system and to test DirectX components (see Figure 15-39).

NOTE DirectX is Microsoft Windows's 3D gaming application programming interface (API).

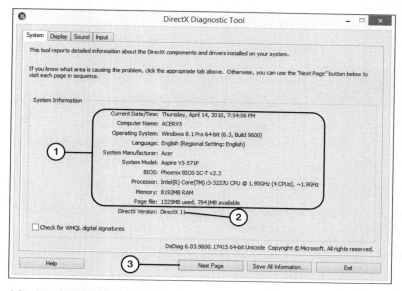

1. Device and Windows information
2. DirectX major version installed
3. Click to view next tab

Figure 15-39 DXDIAG's System tab displays the DirectX version installed, Windows version, and computer hardware features.

NOTE If DXDIAG finds problems with your system, download updated drivers for any problem devices. If you need to download replacement DirectX files for version 9.0x or earlier, use the link in DXDIAG's Help menu. To repair problems with DirectX, see https://support.microsoft.com/en-us/kb/179113. Depending upon your version of Windows, you might need to download and install DirectX manually or use Windows Update.

System Restore

System Restore enables you to fix problems caused by a defective hardware or software installation by resetting your computer's configuration to the way it was at a specified earlier time. The configuration is stored in a file called a **restore point**. The driver or software files installed stay on the system, and so does the data you created, but Registry changes made by the hardware or software are reversed, so your system works the way it did before the installation. Restore points can be created by the user with System Restore and are also created automatically by the system before new hardware or software is installed. Restore points in Windows Vista and Windows 7 also store older versions of data files created by the Windows Shadow Copy service. Windows 8/8.1/10 use File History to store older versions of data files.

> **TIP** Before you make changes to your system configuration, create a restore point so that you can easily reverse the changes if they are not satisfactory.

Creating a Restore Point

To create a restore point in Windows Vista, 7, or 10, follow these steps:

Step 1. Open the Start menu, right-click **Computer** and select **Properties**. This opens the System Properties window.

Step 2. Click the **System Protection** task, which opens the System Protection tab on the System properties sheet.

Step 3. Click the **Create** button. This opens the System Protection window.

Step 4. Type a name for the restore point and click **Create**. The computer's current hardware and software configuration is stored as a restore point.

To create a restore point in Windows 8/8.1, follow these steps:

Step 1. Swipe in from the right to open the Charms menu.

Step 2. Click or tap **Search** and enter **System Restore**.

Step 3. Click or tap **Create a restore point**.

Step 4. Click the **Create** button. This opens the System Protection window.

Step 5. Type a name for the restore point and click **Create**. The computer's current hardware and software configuration is stored as a restore point.

Restoring Your System to an Earlier Condition

Follow these steps to restore your system to an earlier condition:

Step 1.   Open the **System Protection** tab again and this time click the **System Restore** button. This opens the Restore system files and settings window.

For Windows Vista:

Step 2.   Click either **Recommended Restore** or **Choose a Different Restore Point**.

Step 3.   The Recommended Restore point dialog asks you to confirm. If you are choosing a different restore point, you will need to select the appropriate one and confirm.

The system initiates the restore and automatically restarts.

For Windows 7/8/8.1/10:

Step 2.   Click **Next**, which displays the Restore your computer to the state it was in before the selected event.

Step 3.   Select a restore point to restore to and click **Next**. (Note: You can also select the box **Show more restore points** to display a list of older created restore points.)

Step 4.   Click **Finish** on the Confirm your restore point page. The system initiates the restore and automatically restarts.

You can also undo a system restore if it did not repair the problem.

If you cannot boot the system, you can also run System Restore from the Windows Recovery Environment.

Configuring System Restore Options

If System Restore is not available, it might be turned off. You can enable or disable System Restore on any volume from the System Properties window/System Protection tab. Click or tap Configure to add or remove a drive from the list of drives protected by System Restore, to change the amount of disk space to reserve for System Restore, or to delete all restore points.

What to Try Before Using System Restore

Be aware that System Restore is not necessarily the first step you should try when troubleshooting a computer. Simply restarting the computer has been known to "fix" all kinds of issues. It's also a good idea to try the Last Known Good

Configuration. You can access this within the Windows Advanced Boot Options menu by pressing F8 (Vista/7) or using the Special Startup Options (Windows 8/8.1/10) when the computer first boots. Also, if System Restore doesn't seem to work in normal mode, attempt to use it in Safe Mode. Safe Mode is another option in the Windows Advanced Boot Options menu. Learn more about these options in Chapter 22.

Be wary of using System Restore if you're fighting a computer virus or malware infection. If you (or the system) create a restore point while the system is infected, you could re-infect the system if you revert the system to that restore point. To prevent re-infection, most antivirus vendors recommend that you disable System Restore (which eliminates stored restore points) before removing computer viruses.

Windows Update

Use **Windows Update** to install security, functionality, and other updates to Windows. By enabling Microsoft Update, Windows Update can also be used to install updates to Microsoft Office or other Microsoft products. To learn more, see "Using Windows Update and Microsoft Update," p.719, Chapter 14.

Control Panel Utilities

The **Control Panel** is the major starting point for adjusting the hardware and user interface settings in Windows. Although Windows 8/8.1/10 include PC Settings (available from the Charms menu in Windows 8/8.1), most configurations in those versions of Windows are performed through the Control Panel.

Items not discussed elsewhere are covered in the following sections of this chapter.

NOTE   Windows Internet options, Network and Sharing Center, and Windows Firewall are discussed in Chapter 16. User accounts are discussed in Chapter 21. Printing options are discussed in Chapter 10. Device Manager is covered in the "Using Device Manager" section of this chapter.

Starting Control Panel

To start Control Panel in Windows Vista/7:

- Click **Start** and select **Control Panel** from the right-most menu.

- If it is not listed in that menu, click **All Programs > Windows Accessories > System Tools > Control Panel**.

To start Control Panel in Windows 8/8.1:

- Press **Windows key+X** and then click or tap **Control Panel**. From a touch screen, open the **Charms** menu (Windows 8/8.1), search for Control Panel, and then tap **Control Panel**.

To start Control Panel in Windows 10:

- Press **Windows key+X**, then click or tap **Control Panel**.

- Click or tap **Start** and then click or tap **Control Panel**.

- Click the Search window, search for Control Panel, and then tap **Control Panel**.

Category and Icon Views

The Control Panel's default view is known as Category view. When you click a category icon, it displays various available tasks.

Figures 15-40, 15-41, and 15-42 show the Windows 8.1, 7, and Vista versions of the Control Panel configured for the default view.

NOTE   Tasks marked with the Windows security shield trigger a User Account Control (UAC) dialog when opened.

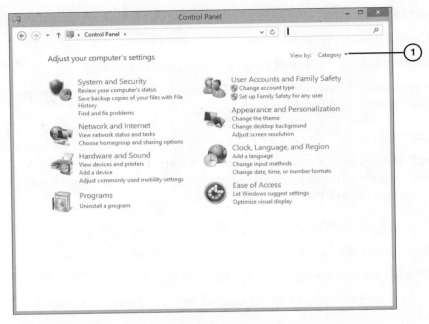

1. Click or tap to change to Large icons or Small icons views

Figure 15-40   The Windows 8.1 Control Panel in its default Category view.

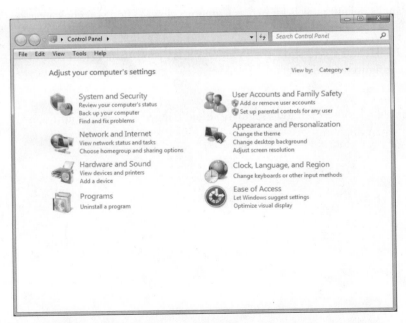

Figure 15-41   The Windows 7 Control Panel in its default Category view.

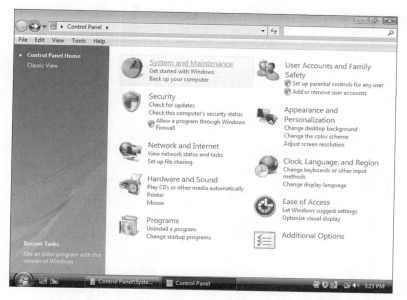

Figure 15-42   The Windows Vista Control Panel in its default Category view.

If you're a Windows newcomer, you might prefer the Category view's task-oriented design. However, if you're already familiar with Control Panel, you'll probably prefer to see each individual applet. This option is known as the Classic view in Vista and the All Control Panel Items view (available in Large or Small Icons variations) in Windows 7/8/8.1/10. Figures 15-43, 15-44, and 15-45 show Windows 8/8.1, 7, and Vista versions of the Control Panel configured to display individual applets.

NOTE   Switching to a view that displays all applets is sometimes necessary to locate applets not part of a category. You can also use the Search tool to locate an applet by name.

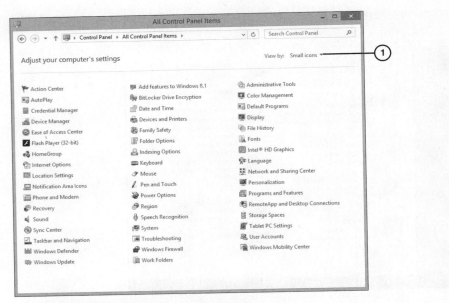

1. Click or tap to change to Large icons or Category views

Figure 15-43 The Windows 8.1 Control Panel in its alternative Small icons view.

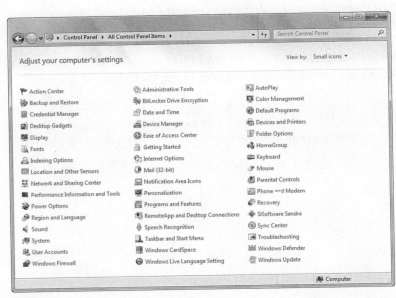

Figure 15-44 The Windows 7 Control Panel in its alternative All Control Panel Icons (small icons) view.

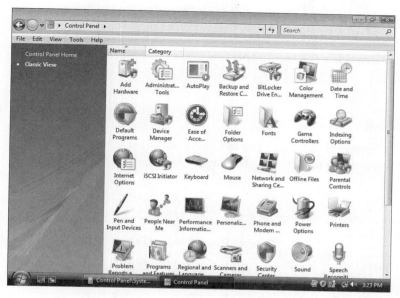

Figure 15-45   The Windows Vista Control Panel in its alternative Classic View.

For the exam, you must know how to open the Control Panel, how to access some of the Control Panel functions by way of Properties sheets, which are located in various areas of Windows, and which Control Panel options to use to configure or solve problems in Windows.

Shortcuts to Control Panel Functions

Some Control Panel functions can be accessed through properties sheets. Here are some examples:

Right-click each of the following to open the listed Control Panel properties sheet:

- Right-click **Computer/This PC** and select **Properties** to open the System properties sheet.

- Right-click **Taskbar** and select **Properties** to open the Taskbar and Start Menu Properties sheet.

- Right-click **Desktop** in Windows Vista and select **Personalize** to configure various display properties.

- Right-click **Desktop** in Windows 7/8/8.1 and choose one of the following: **Personalize**, **Screen Resolution**, or **Gadgets** (Windows 7 only) options.

- Right-click **Network** and select **Properties** to open the Network and Sharing Center dialog.

Display/Display Settings

Depending on the version of Windows you use, there may be several different Control Panel applets to use to configure Display settings. Table 15-6 provides a reference to these.

Table 15-6   Configuring Display Settings in Vista, 7, 8/8.1/10

Display Setting	Control Panel Setting/Tab		
	Vista	**7**	**8/8.1/10**
Resolution	Personalization	Screen Resolution	Screen Resolution
Color depth (number of colors)	Personalization	Display Advanced/List Monitor	N/A (32-bit color used for all modes)
Screen saver	Personalization	Personalization	Personalization* (see Figure 15-46)
Background	Personalization	Personalization	Personalization
Theme	Personalization	Personalization	Personalization
Windows Color	Personalization	Personalization	Personalization
Add additional displays	Personalization	Screen Resolution (see Figure 15-47)	Screen Resolution
Refresh rate	Personalization	Advanced Settings/ Monitor (see Figure 15-48)	Advanced Settings/ Monitor

* Windows 10 menu for this option differs significantly in appearance from Windows 8/8.1

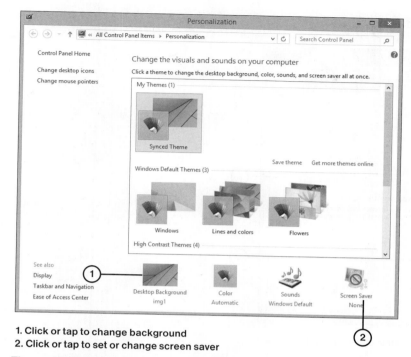

1. Click or tap to change background
2. Click or tap to set or change screen saver

Figure 15-46   The Windows 8.1 Personalization menu.

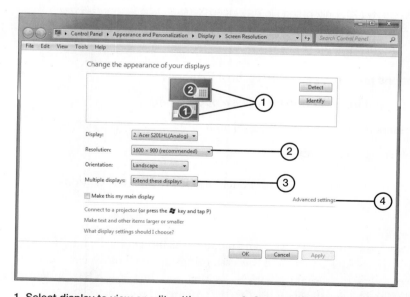

1. Select display to view or edit settings
2. Select resolution
3. Select how to use secondary display
4. Click or tap to view advanced settings

Figure 15-47   The Windows 7 Screen Resolution menu.

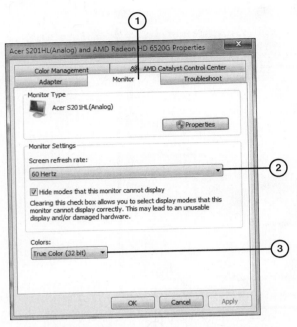

1. Click or tap Monitor tab to change refresh rate and colors
2. Select refresh rate
3. Select 16-bit (high color) or 32-bit (true color)

Figure 15-48   The Windows 7 Monitor menu in Advanced Settings.

Folder Options

The **Folder Options** properties sheet affects how Explorer:

- Displays file and folder information (**View options** tab)

- Selects folders to index for searching (Search tab)

- Opens folders (General options tab)

You can open Folder Options in Control Panel, or open it from the Options menu in Explorer.

NOTE   In Windows Vista and Windows 7, the menu bar is hidden by default. To show it temporarily, press Alt+T (which in this case brings up the Tools menu). To show it permanently, click the Organize button, Layout, and then Menu Bar. In Windows 8/8.1/10, open the View tab to see the Options menu.

By default, Explorer hides the following file information:

- File extensions for registered file types; for example, a file called LETTER. DOCX displays as LETTER because Microsoft Word is associated with .docx files

- The full path to the current folder

- Files or folders with hidden or system attributes, such as the AppData folder

- The Windows folder

Concealing this information is intended to make it harder for users to "break" Windows, but it makes management and troubleshooting more difficult.

As an alternative to using the Folder Options applet in Control Panel, you can use this procedure in Windows Vista/7:

Step 1.   Open **Windows Explorer**.

Step 2.   Click **Tools** on the menu bar, **Folder Options**, and select the **View** tab. If you use the Folder Options applet in Control Panel, select the **View** tab. Continue with step 3.

In Windows 8/8.1/10:

Step 1.   Open **File Explorer**.

Step 2.   Click or tab the **View** tab. Continue with step 3.

Step 3.   Select the options you want (see Figure 15-49). The following changes are recommended for experienced end users:

- Enable the **Display the Full Path in the Title Bar** option. (In Vista and 7, this works only if you are using the Classic theme.)

- To see all file extensions, disable the **Hide Extensions for Known File Types** option.

- If you are maintaining or troubleshooting a system, I also recommend you change the following:

  - To view **hidden files**, enable the **Show Hidden Files, Folders, and Drives** setting.

  - Disable the **Hide Protected Operating System Files** setting.

NOTE   You should probably change these settings back to their defaults before you return the system to normal use.

Step 4.   Click **OK** to close the Folder Options window.

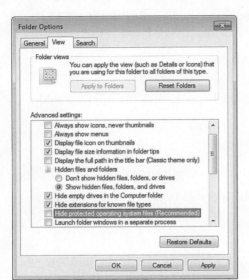

Figure 15-49   The Windows Explorer Folder Options, View tab in Windows 7 after selecting recommended options for use by technicians and experienced end users.

System

Use the System properties sheet to view:

- Windows version

- 32-bit or 64-bit edition

- Processor model number and clock speed

- Windows Experience Index (WEI) (Vista and 7 only)

Figure 15-50 illustrates the System properties sheet for Windows 8.1. Figure 15-51 illustrates the System properties sheet for Windows 7.

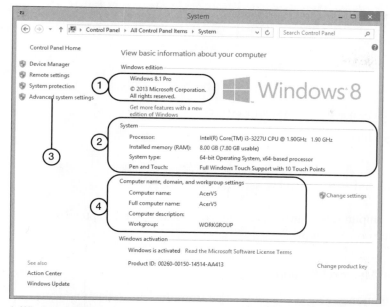

1. Windows edition
2. Processor, RAM, system type, pen/touch support
3. Click to open advanced system settings
4. Network and computer name settings

Figure 15-50 System properties sheet for a Windows 8.1 system with a touch screen.

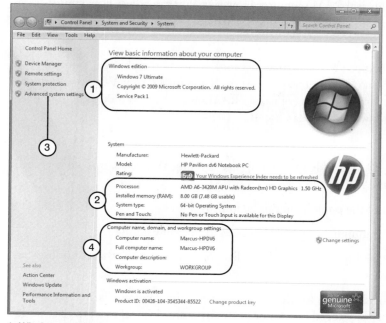

1. Windows edition
2. Processor, RAM, system type, pen/touch support
3. Click to open advanced system settings
4. Network and computer name settings

Figure 15-51 System properties sheet for a Windows 7 system

You can also use the System applet to change

- Computer name
- Workgroup name
- Domain name
- System protection settings (System Restore)
- Hardware profiles
- Remote settings
- Performance and virtual memory settings

For more about computer, workgroup, and domain settings, see Chapter 16, "Networking Microsoft Windows."

Performance (Virtual Memory) Settings

If you run short of money, you can borrow some from the bank (assuming your credit's in decent shape). However, there's a penalty: interest. Similarly, if your system runs short of memory, it can borrow hard disk space and use it as **virtual memory**. The penalty for this type of borrowing is performance: Virtual memory is much slower than real RAM memory. However, you can adjust how your system uses virtual memory to achieve better performance.

> **TIP**   To minimize the need to use virtual memory, increase the physical memory (RAM) in a 32-bit Windows system to at least 3GB and on a 64-bit Windows system to at least 8GB. The largest amount of usable RAM on a 32-bit Windows system is 3.25GB; 64-bit Windows systems can use 4GB or more.

When additional RAM is added to a computer running Windows, it is automatically used first before the paging file.

The performance of the **paging file** can be improved by:

- Setting its minimum and maximum sizes to the same amount.
- Moving the paging file to a physical disk (or disk partition) that is not used as much as others.
- Using a striped volume for the paging file. A striped volume is an identical area of disk space stored on two or more dynamic disks referred to as a single drive letter. Create a striped volume with the Windows Disk Management

tool. If a RAID 0 (striped) disk array is available, use it instead of a striped volume for even better paging file performance.

- Creating multiple paging files on multiple physical disks in the system.
- Moving the paging file away from the boot drive.

To adjust the location and size of the paging file in Windows, follow these steps:

Step 1. From the **System** Properties window, click **Advanced System Settings** under Tasks.

Step 2. Click the **Settings** button in the Performance box.

Step 3. Click the **Advanced** tab and then click the **Change** button.

Step 4. Clear the **Automatically Manage Paging File Size** checkbox.

Step 5. Click or tap the **Custom size** radio button.

Step 6. Specify the initial and maximum sizes you want to use for the paging file and its location (see Figure 15-52). Click **Set** and then click **OK** to finish.

Step 7. If you make any changes to size or location, you must restart the computer for the changes to take effect.

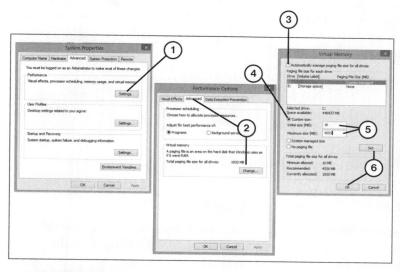

1. Opening the Settings menu
2. Opening the Virtual Memory menu
3. Clear this box to set virtual memory size manually
4. Click or tap to set a custom size
5. Enter the minimum and maximum sizes
6. Click or tap Set, then OK

Figure 15-52 Changing virtual memory settings (Windows 8.1).

Power Options

You can manage **power options** from an applet in the Control Panel. If a Power options icon is available in the notification area of the Windows taskbar, you can use it to view the current power option setting and select a different one.

Hibernate

You can select **Hibernate** as an option from the shutdown menu in Windows Vista/7. Hibernate creates a special disk file (hiberfil.sys) that records open apps, memory contents, and the apps' positions on-screen. In effect, it "pauses" your system so you can return to right where you left off.

In Windows 8/8.1, Hibernate is not a listed option for the shutdown menu. However, it can be added by modifying a power plan.

To awaken a system from hibernation, press the power button on the computer. If the system uses a password for access, you are prompted to enter the password to restart the system.

Sleep/Suspend/Standby

In Windows Vista, what looks like a power button on the Start menu actually puts the computer into sleep/**standby** mode. In this mode, the computer uses very little power and can be awakened much more quickly than from Hibernate. This mode is also known as suspend to RAM (STR).

NOTE   To shut down or hibernate a system running Windows Vista, click the right arrow after the sleep/standby button.

For sleep/standby mode to work correctly, the system needs to support the S3 power setting in the system BIOS.

Sleep/suspend mode is also supported in Windows 7/8/8.1/10.

If the system does not sleep/standby correctly, there might be a problem with startup programs interfering with sleep/standby. Use MSCONFIG to disable startup programs selectively until you discover the offending app.

With most laptops and many desktops, you can put the computer into sleep mode by pressing a special sleep key or by pressing the power key and releasing it right away. To change how the sleep or power key works, modify your power plan.

Power Plans

Windows offers three standard **power plans** (see Figure 15-53):

- **Balanced**—Default plan
- **High performance**—Fastest CPU performance, brightest screen, and shortest battery life
- **Power saver**—Reduces CPU performance and screen brightness more than with Balanced plan for longest battery life

Desktop computers hide Power Saver by default; laptop computers hide High Performance by default. To see these and other plans, click Show Additional Plans.

NOTE Some portable vendors might offer additional plans in systems with pre-installed Windows. Tablets offer only one power plan, Balanced.

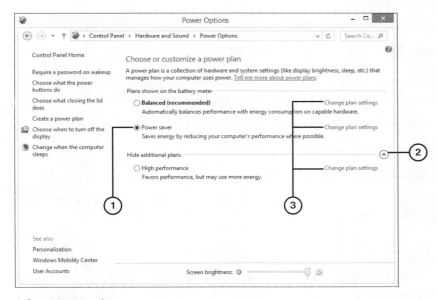

1. Current power plan
2. Click or tap to display/hide additional power plans
3. Click or tap to change plan settings

Figure 15-53   Standard power plans in Windows 8.1.

To change a plan, click **Change Plan Settings**. You can change the display of and sleep settings for each plan, and to change additional settings, click Change Advanced Power Settings. You can change power settings for

- Hard-disk shutoff timing
- Desktop backgrounds
- Wireless adapters
- Sleep timings
- Hibernation options
- USB ports and devices
- Power buttons and lid
- PCI Express devices
- CPU performance and cooling
- Display shutoff timings
- Multimedia idle time and screen quality
- Internet Explorer JavaScript timing frequency

To create a new power plan, click **Create a Power Plan** from the Power Options dialog. From the Create a Power Plan dialog, follow these steps:

Step 1.   Select a plan to use as the basis for your plan.

Step 2.   Enter a plan name and click **Next**.

Step 3.   Specify timings for the display and sleep and click **Create**.

To change additional settings, click **Change Plan Settings**, select the custom plan, and change other settings. See Figure 15-54.

NOTE   To learn more about a system's power management features, use the command-line POWERCFG.EXE program to control additional power settings. To learn more, see http://support.microsoft.com/kb/980869.

Figure 15-54   Editing a custom power plan in Windows 7.

Programs and Features

Programs and Features is used to uninstall or change a program (see Figure 15-55), to turn Windows features on and off (see Figure 15-56), and to view installed updates.

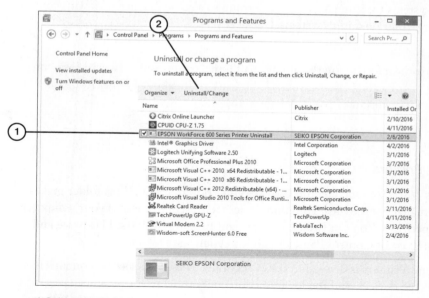

1. Selected program
2. Click or tap to uninstall or change selected program

Figure 15-55   Preparing to uninstall or change a program (Windows 8.1).

Figure 15-56   Turning Windows 7 features on and off.

HomeGroup (Windows 7/8/8.1/10)

Windows 7 introduced the **HomeGroup** feature as part of its network functionality. HomeGroup enables the creation of an easy-to-manage but secure home or home office network, provided it contains only Windows 7 or Windows 8 PCs. HomeGroup can coexist with traditional wired or wireless workgroup networking, enabling systems that are part of a homegroup to also be in a network with computers running other operating systems.

NOTE   Microsoft refers to the technology as HomeGroup, and networks based on that technology are called "homegroups." To learn more about HomeGroup, see "HomeGroup Networking," p.842, Chapter 16.

Devices and Printers

Windows 7/8/8.1/10 include the **Devices and Printers** folder. This folder makes access to managing the most common devices in (or connected to) your computer easier to perform. You can launch Devices and Printers from the Hardware and Sound category of Control Panel or add it to your Start menu.

Devices and Printers is divided into two sections. The upper section contains icons for connected devices, and the lower section contains icons for printers, faxes, and all-in-one units. To manage a device, right-click it, and choose from the options listed. The options available for each device vary with the device selected.

For example, if you right-click the computer icon, you can AutoPlay removable-media drives; browse files; eject drives; configure network, sound, mouse, keyboard, and region and language settings; and view and configure system properties, power options, device installation settings, and Windows Update (see Figure 15-57). Right-click a display and you can access the Display settings dialog. Right-click a mouse and you can access the Mouse properties dialog.

To learn more about managing printers, faxes, and multifunction devices with Devices and Printers, see Chapter 10.

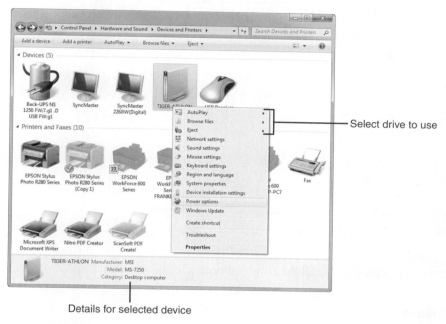

Details for selected device

Figure 15-57   Using Devices and Printers to manage a computer's components.

Sound

To manage audio recording, playback, system sounds, and how to handle calls when media is already playing, open the Sound icon in Control Panel. Use the Playback tab to select which device to use for playback (for example, whether to use analog or digital speakers or HDMI output to a home theater system or HDTV). Use the Recording tab to select a built-in or headset microphone and adjust its volume. Use the Sounds tab to choose which sounds to play during system events; select a sound theme or choose your own. Use the Communications tab to specify what to do with phone calls to/from your PC while audio is already playing. The Sound icon is located in the Hardware and Sound category.

Troubleshooting

Windows Control Panel offers a variety of troubleshooters that can find and fix problems with specific Windows features. Figure 15-58 displays the troubleshooting categories available in Windows 8.1.

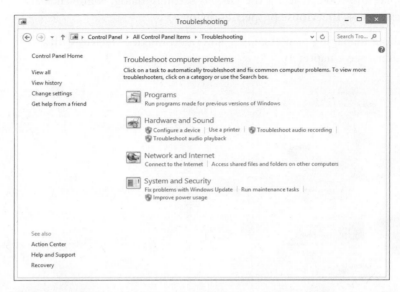

Figure 15-58 Troubleshooters are available in four categories.

Click or tap a category to see all the troubleshooters in the category.

Internet Options

The Internet Options icon in Control Panel has seven tabs. The tabs and their uses are listed in Table 15-7.

Table 15-7 Internet Options

Tab	Function
General	Set home page; tabs settings; delete browsing history, cookies, temporary files, and saved passwords; change appearance, and configure accessibility settings
Security	Configure security zones
Privacy	Select privacy settings for the current zone; location settings; pop-up blocker; InPrivate browsing settings
Content	Family Safety; SSL certificate management; AutoComplete; feeds

Tab	Function
Connections	VPN, dial-up, LAN connections, and proxy server settings
Programs	Select default web browser, manage add-ons, select default HTML editor and default apps for email and other Internet services
Advanced	Enable/disable accelerated graphics; configure Accessibility settings, Browsing settings, HTTP settings, International settings, Multimedia settings, and Security settings; and reset Internet Explorer to default settings

Exam Preparation Tasks

Review All the Key Topics

Review the most important topics in the chapter, noted with the key topics icon in the outer margin of the page. Table 15-8 lists a reference of these key topics and the page numbers on which each is found.

Table 15-8   Key Topics for Chapter 15

Key Topic Element	Description	Page Number
Table 15-1	Microsoft Windows Command-Line Tools	736
Figure 15-9	SFC /scannow reports that corrupt files were repaired (Windows 7)	752
Section	Microsoft Administrative Tools	756
Section	Disk Management	775
Section	Windows Upgrade Tools	785
Section	System Utilities	788
Section	Category and Icon Views	805
Table 15-7	Internet Options	824

Define Key Terms

Define the following key terms from this chapter, and check your answers in the glossary.

standard privileges, standard mode, administrative privileges, elevated mode, TASKKILL, BOOTREC, SHUTDOWN, TASKLIST, MD, RD, CD, DEL, FORMAT, COPY, XCOPY, ROBOCOPY, DISKPART, SFC, CHKDSK, GPUPDATE, GPRESULT, DIR, EXIT, HELP, EXPAND, [*command name*] /?, Computer Management (MMC), Device Manager, Local Users and Groups, Local Security Policy, Performance Monitor, Services, System Configuration, Task Scheduler, Component Services, data sources, Print Management, Windows Memory Diagnostics, Windows Firewall and Advanced Settings, MSCONFIG, General, Boot, Startup, Tools, Task Manager, Applications tab, Processes tab, Performance tab, Networking tab, Disk Management, drive status, mount (drive), mounted drive, initialize (drive), extend (partition), split (partition), shrink (partition), assign (drive letter), change (drive letter), drive array, Storage Spaces, User State Migration tool (USMT), Windows Easy Transfer, Windows Upgrade Advisor, system utilities, REGEDIT, Command, SERVICES.MSC, MSTSC, NOTEPAD, EXPLORER, MSINFO32, DXDIAG, System Restore, Windows Update, resolution, color depth, refresh rate, folder options, hidden files, hide extensions, virtual memory, remote settings, system protection, Power options, hibernate, power plans, sleep/suspend, standby, Programs and Features, HomeGroup, Devices and Printers.

Complete the Tables and Lists from Memory

Print a copy of Appendix C, "Memory Tables" (found on the CD), or at least the section for this chapter, and complete the tables and lists from memory. Appendix D, "Memory Tables Answer Key," also on the CD, includes completed tables and lists to check your work.

Complete Hands-On Labs

Complete the hands-on labs, and then see the answers and explanations at the end of the chapter.

Lab 15-1: Determining System Components

Use these Windows tools (System properties sheet, Msinfo32, and Dxdiag) to determine the following information for a particular system. Be sure to indicate which menu or tab contains the information you are looking for.

Feature	System properties sheet	Msinfo32 / (menu)	Dxdiag / (tab)
Windows version			
CPU brand, model, and clock speed			
Total RAM installed			
Amount of RAM available (current/ maximum) for the video card/CPU-integrated video			
Version of DirectX installed			
Available disk space on C: drive			
Computer name			
Workgroup name			

Lab 15-2: Checking Power and Display Settings

A client reports that his system does not appear to be optimized for fastest performance and best display resolution. The client recently switched to a larger display. Use the following Control Panel utilities to check on possible optimization issues.

- Power (plan)
- Display (resolution)

Answer Review Questions

1. In the following table, match the command used to execute the respective tasks.

Task	Command
A. Open a command prompt	
B. View all the directories in a specified location	
C. Create a new folder	
D. Remove an empty folder	
E. Remove one or more files	
F. Stop running a specified task	
G. Copy single or multiple files	

H. Scan for errors and repair hard drive

I. Close command prompt

J. Create new partitions

K. Display the help files for a specific command

1.	CHKDSK	**7.**	EXIT
2.	CMD or COMMAND	**8.**	MD or MKDIR
3.	COMMAND/?	**9.**	RD or RMDIR
4.	DEL	**10.**	TASKKILL
5.	DIR	**11.**	XCOPY, ROBOCOPY
6.	DISKPART		

2. When using a command prompt, what does it mean to run in elevated mode?

    A. The CPU runs at faster speed.

    B. You are running disk maintenance utilities, such as check disk, scandisk, and defrag.

    C. You have access to the help files.

    D. You are executing commands as an administrator.

3. Which of the following are wildcard symbols that can be used with command-prompt commands? (Choose two.)

    A. *

    B. ?

    C. !

    D. $

4. Which of the following statements best describes the MMC? (Choose two.)

    A. The MMC is a collection of frequently used utilities stored in a single console for easy access.

    B. The MMC is a collection of music and multimedia devices.

    C. The MMC is a utility for troubleshooting your computer's hardware.

    D. The MMC is a console for managing the services currently running on your computer.

5. Which of the following utilities should be used to begin troubleshooting your hardware or updating your drivers on a Windows system?

   A. Device Manager

   B. System Utility

   C. System Configuration

   D. Component Services

6. Your network adapter is failing. How will this be indicated in the Windows Device Manager?

   A. The device will not be listed.

   B. An "!" will be displayed over the device icon.

   C. A down-arrow icon will be displayed over the device icon.

   D. A "?" will be displayed over the device icon.

7. As part of the troubleshooting process, you want to temporarily disable a device. How will this device be displayed in the Device Manager after you disable it?

   A. An "!" will be displayed over the device icon.

   B. The device icon is crossed out.

   C. A down-arrow icon will be displayed over the device icon.

   D. The device is moved to the Unknown Device category.

8. Based on the information in the Performance Monitor shown here, which of the following statements describes the most effective course of action?

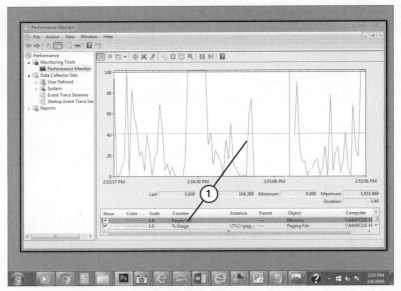

A. You should add more RAM.

B. The page file is working well and the usage is at 40%, so no action is required.

C. You are trying to print too many pages per second, so you should slow your print speed.

D. Click on the green "+" in the menu bar to gather more information.

9. Which of the following utilities would you use to see the items that are set to run automatically at a particular time?

A. Task Scheduler

B. Services

C. Device Manager

D. Performance

10. Which keys are pressed simultaneously to open Task Manager? (Choose all that apply.)

A. Esc   E. Ctrl

B. F1   F. Del

C. Alt   G. Windows

D. Tab   H. Fn

11. Which of the following utilities displays all the programs currently running on your computer?

    A. Disk Management

    B. Task Manager

    C. System Configuration

    D. Device Manager

12. A client reports that the system is starting up very slowly. Which of the following utilities is best for determining what's going on?

    A. Devices and Printers

    B. Programs and Features

    C. System Protection

    D. System Configuration

13. The client wants a RAID array installed but the system doesn't have hardware RAID onboard. Which of the following Windows utilities is used to create a RAID array?

    A. Disk Management

    B. RAID BIOS utility

    C. CHKDSK

    D. MSCONFIG

14. Which of the following utilities determines the readiness of your Windows 7 computer to upgrade to a new Windows 8.1 operating system?

    A. Windows Easy Transfer

    B. Windows Update

    C. Windows Upgrade Assistant

    D. Windows Upgrade Advisor

15. In the following table, write the command used to open the respective utilities.

A. The registry
B. System Information
C. System Configuration
D. Microsoft Management Console

    1. mmc

    2. MSCONFIG

    3. msinfo32

    4. regedit

16. Which of the following is the file management system used by Windows 8/8.1?

    A. Registry Editor

    B. Windows Explorer

    C. System Information

    D. File Explorer

17. Display settings include which of the following? (Choose all that apply.)

    A. Resolution

    B. Synchronization

    C. Refresh rate

    D. File system

18. Which utility allows you to show file extensions for known file types, show hidden files, and show system files?

    A. Folder Properties

    B. System Configuration

    C. System Properties

    D. Folder Options

19. As a computer technician, you must be able to evaluate a system's health and you must be able to find the information with which to diagnose a problem. A utility that contains a wealth of information and with which you should be familiar is the System properties sheet. Which information will you *not* find in the System utility or System Properties?

    A. Which file system your hard drive uses

    B. Which operating system is installed

    C. Any service packs that have been installed

    D. The amount of installed RAM

    E. Whether you are using a 32- or 64-bit operating system

20. Enter the power option that matches the description listed in the following table.

A. Copies open applications, memory contents, and desktop to disk when selected
B. Runs system at fastest clock speeds
C. Requires S3 setting in system BIOS or UEFI firmware
D. Default power plan setting

Answer options:

   A. Sleep/Suspend/Standby

   B. High Performance

   C. Balanced

   D. Hibernation

Answers and Explanations to Hands-On Labs

The following are examples of what you can expect to find as you work through Labs 15-1 and 15-2 on the systems you have.

Lab 15-1: Determining System Components

Feature	System properties sheet	Msinfo32/(menu)	Dxdiag/(tab)
Windows version	Yes	Yes / System Summary	Yes / System
CPU brand, model, and clock speed	Yes	Yes / System Summary	Yes / System
Total RAM installed	Yes	Yes / System Summary	Yes / System
Amount of RAM available (current/maximum) for the video card/CPU-integrated video	No	No	Yes / Display
Version of DirectX installed	No	No	Yes / System
Available disk space on C: drive	No	Yes / Storage>Drives	No
Computer name	Yes	Yes / System Summary	Yes / System
Workgroup name	Yes	No	No

Lab 15-2: Checking Power and Display Settings

A client reports that his system does not appear to be optimized. The client recently switched to a larger display. Use the following Control Panel utilities to check on possible optimization issues.

- For fastest performance, select the High Performance Power Plan.
- Resolution should be set to the Recommended value (which varies by display size and type).

Answers and Explanations to Review Questions

1.

A. Open a command prompt	2. CMD or COMMAND
B. View all the directories in a specified location	5. DIR
C. Create a new folder	8. MD or MKDIR
D. Remove an empty folder	9. RD or RMDIR
E. Remove one or more files	4. DEL
F. Stop running a specified task	10. TASKKILL
G. Copy single or multiple files	11. XCOPY, ROBOCOPY
H. Scan for errors and repair hard drive	1. CHKDSK
I. Close command prompt	7. EXIT
J. Create new partitions	6. DISKPART
K. Display the help files for a specific command	3. COMMAND/?

2. **A.** Elevated mode is the same as Run as Administrator. Some commands cannot be executed except with administrator privileges.

3. **A, B.** The "*" symbol replaces multiple characters. The "?" symbol replaces a single character.

4. **A, D.** The MMC is a collection of frequently used utilities stored in a single console for easy access, and it is a console for managing the services currently running on your computer. You can customize the MMC with snap-ins.

5. **A.** Device Manager contains a list of hardware devices and reports on their condition. From Device Manager, you can update drives and disable or enable or uninstall devices.

6. **B.** If the problem with the network adapter is detected by Windows Device Manager, an "!" will be displayed over the device icon.

7. **C.** A down-arrow icon will be displayed over the device icon.

8. **A.** Performance Monitor provides real-time monitoring of your system's performance. In the display, memory pages/second is running very high and your system would run more efficiently if you were to add more RAM.

9. **A.** Use the Task Scheduler to schedule the Backup utility to run at regularly scheduled intervals.

10. **C, E, F.** Press Ctrl+Alt+Del and select Task Manager. You can also press Ctrl+Shift+Esc, right-click the taskbar, or type **taskmgr** at the Run line or in the Search box.

11. **B.** Disk Management allows you to analyze and configure your hard drive. Task Manager displays all the applications currently running on your computer and allows you to selectively shut down any programs that have stopped responding. System Configuration (MSCONFIG) allows you to select the programs and services that run automatically at startup. Device Manager allows you to view, manage, and troubleshoot hardware.

12. **D.** Devices and Printers provides centralized management of the computer and most of the hardware connected to it. Programs and Features is used to manage programs installed and Windows features available on the computer. System protection is used to configure System Restore. System Configuration allows you to select the programs and services that run automatically at startup.

13. **C.** Disk Management allows you to analyze and configure your hard drives. A RAID BIOS utility is available at startup only on systems with hardware RAID, which is not available on this computer. CHKDSK is used to locate and optionally repair problems with files stored on a drive. MSCONFIG is used to adjust boot options.

14. **C.** Windows Easy Transfer is used to copy files, photos, music, e-mail, and settings from one computer to another. Windows Update is used to download updates, service packs, and fixes for your operating system. Windows Upgrade Assistant is used to determine the readiness of a system to upgrade to Windows 8/8.1. Windows Upgrade Advisor is used to determine the readiness of a system to upgrade to Windows 7 or Vista.

15.

A. The registry	4. regedit
B. System Information	3. msinfo32
C. System Configuration	2. MSCONFIG
D. Microsoft Management Console	1. mmc

16. **D.** Windows Explorer has been renamed File Explorer in Windows 8/8.1.

17. **A, C.** Display settings include resolution, refresh rate, color depth, screen saver, background and theme.

18. **D.** Folder Options allows you to do all of these things and much more.

19. A. You will not find the file system listed in the System utility. The file system is found in the Drive Properties and in Disk Management. The rest of the information is available in System properties and you should be familiar with what is there and how to find it.

20.

A. Copies open applications, memory contents, and desktop to disk when selected	2. Hibernation
B. Runs system at fastest clock speeds	3. High Performance
C. Requires S3 setting in system BIOS or UEFI firmware	4. Sleep/Suspend/ Standby
D. Default power plan setting	1. Balanced

This chapter covers the following subjects:

- **Homegroup vs. Workgroup**—Windows 7/8/8.1/10 support both of these network types. Learn how they vary in this section.

- **Domain Setup**—Discover how to connect a computer to a domain.

- **Network Shares**—Learn how to set up network shares and mapped drives.

- **Administrative Shares**—This section describes these "secret" shares.

- **Printer Sharing versus Network Printer Mapping**—This section discusses connecting to network printers.

- **Establish Networking Connections**—Learn how to create a VPN or other types of network connections.

- **Proxy Settings**—To use the proxy servers used on many organization networks, you must configure the correct settings.

- **Remote Desktop Connection and Remote Assistance**—Learn how these differ and how they are configured.

- **Home vs. Work vs. Public Network Settings**—Discover how the choice of network location affects your options.

- **Firewall Settings**—Discover what the Windows Firewall can do.

- **Configuring an Alternative IP Address in Windows**—When and how to give a Windows PC a second IP address.

- **Network Card Properties**—Discover how to set QoS, speed, duplexing, and other important features.

## CHAPTER 16

Networking Microsoft Windows

Windows networking includes three different types of networks, remote control and assistance options, a built-in firewall, and much more. Use this chapter to master those features.

220-902: Objective 1.6 Given a scenario, install, and configure Windows networking on a client/desktop.

Foundation Topics

Homegroup vs. Workgroup

Windows 7, 8/8.1, and 10 support two different types of SOHO networks: **workgroups** and **homegroups**. Windows Vista supports only workgroups. In the following sections, you learn how these differ from each other.

Workgroup Networking

Windows Vista, 7, 8/8.1, and 10 all support workgroup networks. In a workgroup network:

- All computers can share folders and devices with other computers in a peer-to-peer arrangement—File and Print Sharing (installed by default) is required for any computer that will share resources.

- All computers must be part of the same local network or subnet. For example, computers in the IP address range of 192.168.1.100-120 with a subnet of 255.255.255.0 can share resources with each other, but computers in the IP address range of 192.168.2.100-120 could not share the resources of the devices in the 192.168.1.100-120 range.

- The workgroup itself does not have a password; however, each computer must have a user account for each user who will access that computer (unless password-protected sharing is disabled). For example, a computer can have an account for Mark and for Mary, and another computer could have an account for Mark and for Jerry. Mark can connect to both computers, but Mary and Jerry can connect to only one computer. In this situation, Mark could use one of the computers and log in via the network to another computer.

The workgroup is identified through the Computer Name section of the System properties sheet.

Creating a Workgroup

To create a workgroup with Windows:

Step 1.   Configure all devices in the workgroup to use the same range of IP addresses and the same subnet. If the devices obtain their IP addresses from a router, this step has already been done for you.

Step 2.   Confirm that each device has a unique computer name. The name is generated automatically when Windows is installed on a device. To verify the name, open the System properties sheet from Control Panel or by right-clicking **Computer** (see Figure 16-1). In Windows 8/8.1, you can also open the Charms menu, click or tap **Settings**, and click or tap **PC Info** to see the information.

Step 3.   Confirm that each device is in the same workgroup (the default name is WORKGROUP).

TIP   To add a bit of extra security to your workgroup, use the Change Settings link shown in Figure 16-1 to change the workgroup name for all computers in the workgroup.

In reality, most computers are already in the WORKGROUP workgroup as soon as Windows is installed. However, configuring file and print sharing must be done manually.

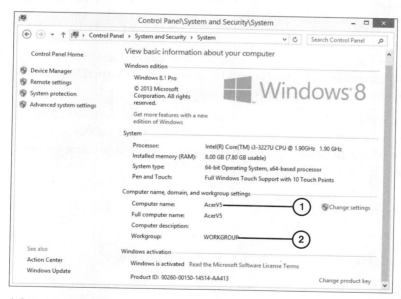

1. Computer name
2. Workgroup name

Figure 16-1   Viewing the computer name and workgroup name with Windows 8.1's System properties sheet.

HomeGroup Networking

Starting with Windows 7, Microsoft introduced a new way to do SOHO networking, the homegroup.

> **NOTE**   Microsoft uses the term "HomeGroup" to refer to the networking technology, and "homegroup" or "homegroups" to refer to networks that use HomeGroup technology.

Homegroup networking coexists with workgroups, but it enables easier security and sharing than workgroup networking does:

- Although one user on one computer creates a homegroup, all computers that join a homegroup can share folders and devices with other homegroup computers in a peer-to-peer arrangement. When a user on a computer joins a homegroup, the user selects what to share using a simple checkbox dialog.

- A single password is used for security for all homegroup shares. The password is generated automatically when a homegroup is created and is used only when a computer/user joins a homegroup.

- If a computer has two or more user accounts, each user can choose whether or not to join a homegroup. For example, Mark on CornerDeskPC can join a homegroup created by Mary on HallwayPC, but Jerry on CornerDeskPC has the option to join the homegroup, or not, as desired.

- When custom file or device shares are created, a single share enables all members of a homegroup to access the device or file share. Contrast this to workgroup networking, in which each computer must have a user account for every remote user or must disable password-protected file sharing, which provides no security.

Creating a Homegroup

To create a homegroup in Windows 7/8/8.1/10, use this procedure:

Step 1.   Open Control Panel.

Step 2.   Click or tap **Network and Internet**.

Step 3.   Click or tap **HomeGroup**.

Step 4.   Click or tap **Create a homegroup**.

Step 5.   Click **Next**.

Step 6. Select the items (folders or libraries, printers) you want to share (see Figure 16-2). In Windows 7, the wizard uses checkboxes.

Step 7. When the homegroup password appears, write it down or print it. Each user who wants to join the homegroup must provide this when prompted.

Step 8. Click or tap Finish.

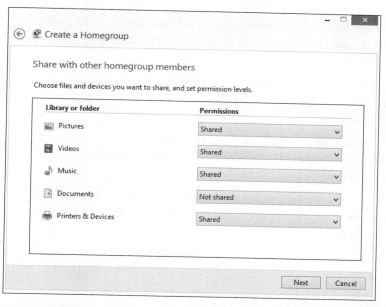

Figure 16-2   Selecting folders and resources to share with the Homegroup wizard in Windows 8.1.

NOTE   Rules for Joining a Homegroup—A computer running Windows 7 can join a homegroup only if its network location is set as Home. To change the network location, use the Network and Sharing Center. A computer running Windows 8/8.1/10 can join a homegroup only if you select the Yes, Turn on Sharing and Connect to Devices option when you connect to the network.

If a network includes only Windows 7, 8/8.1, and Windows 10 computers (in any combination), a homegroup can be created. However, if the network will also be shared with Windows Vista, OS X, or Linux clients, workgroup file and printer sharing settings must also be configured to enable those users to share resources.

One significant limitation to either type of networking is that no more than ten computers can connect at a time to a workgroup or homegroup computer.

Domain Setup

Larger networks, including networks with users in multiple locations, use domain networking. Some of the special features of domain networking include:

- Shared resources (files, folders, printers, devices) and user accounts are stored on servers. An Active Directory server is used to authenticate users, and other servers can be used for print, file, email, or other tasks.

- User accounts are not tied to a particular computer. A user on a domain can use any computer or computers on the domain and have access to their files and shared resources.

- Resources available to a particular user can be limited by Group Policy. For example, Group Policy settings can prevent a user from connecting a USB flash memory drive.

- Group Policy can also be used to limit configuration settings that are available to a user. For example, Group Policy can be used to turn off AutoPlay for removable-media devices.

- Different local networks with hundreds to thousands of users can be part of a single domain.

The **domain setup** for a computer is performed from the Computer Name section of the System properties sheet. To join a domain:

Step 1.   Open the System properties sheet.

Step 2.   Click or tap **Change settings**.

Step 3.   From the Computer Name tab, click or tap **Network ID**.

Step 4.   Confirm that **This computer is part of a business network**… is selected. Click or tap **Next**.

Step 5.   Confirm that **My company uses a network with a domain** is selected. Click or tap **Next**.

Step 6.   Review the information needed to connect to a domain, and click **Next**.

Step 7.   Enter the username, password, and domain name, and click **Next**.

Step 8.   Click **OK** on the Welcome to the…domain message.

Network Shares

A shared folder or drive can be accessed by other computers on the network. Shares can be provided in three ways:

- On a client/server-based network, or a peer-to-peer network with peer servers that support user/group permissions, shares are protected by lists of authorized users or groups. Windows Vista/7/8/8.1/10 support user/group access control.

- A workgroup network can offer unlimited sharing (full control or read-only) for any user who connects to a system if password-protected sharing is disabled (not recommended).

- A homegroup network offers read-only access for any shared resource to any homegroup user. However, individual folders can be configured for read/write (full control) access for any homegroup user.

A **network** share can be accessed by either its mapped drive letters or by its folder names in Windows Explorer (Windows Vista/7) or File Explorer (Windows 8/8.1/10).

When user/group-based permissions are used, only members who belong to a specific group or who are listed separately on the access list for a particular share can access that share. After users log on to the network, they have access to all shares they've been authorized to use without the need to provide additional passwords. Access levels include full and read-only and, on NTFS drives, other access levels, such as write, create, and delete. Let's show the various ways to share data with Windows 7/Vista/8/8.1.

Sharing a Folder

To share a folder with any of these versions of Windows, follow these steps:

Step 1. Ensure that file sharing is enabled. This is done by opening Control Panel and double-clicking the **Network and Sharing Center** icon. In Windows Vista, click the down arrow next to File Sharing and select the **Turn on File Sharing** radio button. (This window is also where you would enable printer sharing.) To access this dialog in Windows 7/8/8.1, click **Change Advanced Sharing Settings** after opening the Network and Sharing Center.

Step 2. Open Windows Explorer/File Explorer. Click **Computer/This PC**.

Step 3. In the Computer/This PC window, navigate to a folder that you want to share.

Step 4. Right-click the folder that you want to share and choose **Share with**.

Step 5.   If you have enabled password-protected sharing, click **Selected People** and select which users will have access to the shared folder and select their permission levels. To allow all users, select the **Everyone** group within the list of users.

Step 6.   When you are done configuring permissions, click **Share** and then click **Done**.

Joining a Homegroup and Custom File Sharing

When you join a homegroup in Windows 7/8/8.1 (and Windows 10), joining the homegroup and configuring default sharing settings is a single process:

Step 1.   From the Network and Internet window, click **HomeGroup**.

Step 2.   Click **Join now**.

Step 3.   Click **Next**.

Step 4.   Select the items you want to share.

Step 5.   Click **Next**.

Step 6.   Type the HomeGroup password.

Step 7.   Click **Next**.

Step 8.   Click **Finish**.

At this point, items shared through the homegroup are shared as read-only. To set up custom access for a particular folder:

Step 1.   In the Computer/This PC window, navigate to a folder that you want to share.

Step 2.   Right-click the folder that you want to share and choose **Share with**. The File Sharing window appears.

Step 3a.   Windows 7: choose from **Homegroup (Read)**, **Homegroup (Read/Write)**, **Nobody** (turns off sharing), or **Specific People** (choose from accounts on your system).

Step 3b.   Windows 8/8.1/10: choose from **Homegroup (View)**, **Homegroup (View/Edit)**, **Stop** Sharing, Specific **People** (choose from accounts on your system).

Step 4.   When you are done configuring permissions, click **Share** and then click **Done**.

TIP   If you use a third-party firewall, consult the documentation or Help files for the appropriate setting to use homegroups.

Mapped Drive Letters

Windows enables shared folders and shared drives to be mapped to drive letters on clients. In Windows Explorer/File Explorer/Computer/This PC, these mapped drive letters show up in the list along with the local drive letters. A shared resource can be accessed either through Network (using the share name) or through a mapped drive letter.

Drive mapping has the following benefits:

- A shared folder mapped as a drive can be referred to by the drive name instead of a long Universal Naming Convention path (see the sidebar "Universal Naming Convention," later in this chapter for details).

- If you still use MS-DOS programs, keep in mind that mapped drives are the only way for those programs to access shared folders.

Mapping drives uses this procedure:

Step 1.   Open the Network view in Windows Explorer/File Explorer.

Step 2.   Right-click the shared folder in Network.

Step 3.   Click **Map Network Drive**.

Step 4.   Select a drive letter from the list of available drive letters; only drive letters not used by local drives are listed. Drive letters already in use for other shared folders display the UNC name of the shared folder.

Step 5.   Click the **Reconnect at Login** box if you want to use the mapped drive every time you connect to the network. This option should be used only if the server will be available at all times; otherwise, the client will receive error messages when it tries to access the shared resource.

Step 6.   Click the **Connect Using Different Credentials** box if you want to use a different username/password to connect to the shared resource. See Figure 16-3.

Step 7.   Click **Finish**.

NOTE   You can browse for any shared folder by its UNC name by starting the Map Network Drive process from the Tools menu in Computer (Windows 7/Vista) or by clicking This PC (Windows 8/8.1) and selecting Map network drive from the Computer ribbon menu.

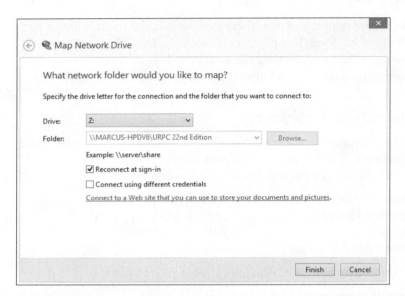

Figure 16-3   The Map Network Drive dialog can be used to create a temporary or permanent drive mapping.

Universal Naming Convention (UNC)

The Universal Naming Convention (UNC) is designed to enable users to access network resources such as folders or printers without mapping drive letters to network drives or specifying the type of device that stores the file or hosts the printer. A UNC name has the following structure in Windows:

\\servername\share name\path\filename

A typical UNC path to a document would resemble

\\Tiger1\O\NetDocuments\this_doc.docx

A typical UNC path to a shared printer on the same system would resemble

\\Tiger1\Printername

What does this mean in plain English?

- **\\Tiger1** is the server.

- **\O** is the share name.

- **\NetDocuments** is the path.

- **\this_doc.docx** is the document.

- **\Printername** is the printer.

UNC enables files and printers to be accessed by the user with 32-bit and 64-bit Windows applications. Because only 23 drive letters (maximum) can be mapped, UNC enables network resources beyond the D–Z limits to still be accessed.

To display the UNC path to a shared folder with Windows, right-click the share and select **Properties**. The Target field in the dialog lists the UNC path.

Administrative Shares

Administrative shares are hidden shares that can be identified by a $ on the end of the share name. These shares cannot be seen by standard users when browsing to the computer over the network; they are meant for administrative use. All the shared folders including administrative shares can be found by navigating to **Computer Management > System Tools > Shared Folders > Shares**. Note that every volume within the hard drive (C: or D:, for example) has an administrative share (for example, C$ is the administrative share for the C: drive). Although it is possible to remove these by editing the Registry, it is not recommended because it might cause other networking issues. You should be aware that only administrators should have access to these shares.

Printer Sharing versus Network Printer Mapping

Printers connected to network computers can be shared or printers can be connected directly to the network with Ethernet or wireless Ethernet (Wi-Fi) connections.

To perform **printer sharing**, follow these steps:

Step 1.   Open the Devices and Printers or Printers and Faxes folder.

Step 2.   Right-click a printer and select **Sharing**.

Step 3.   Select **Share This Printer** and specify a share name. (In Windows Vista, you must click the Sharing tab first.)

Step 4.   Click **Additional Drivers** to select additional drivers to install for other operating systems that will use the printer on the network. Supply driver disks or CDs when prompted.

A printer connected to a computer in a homegroup is shared with other homegroup users through the homegroup wizard.

Whether a printer has its own IP address or is connected to a computer as a shared printer, use this procedure to install it on a system, a process called **network printer mapping**:

Step 1.   Open the Printers and Faxes folder (Windows Vista) or Devices and Printers (Windows 7/8/8.1/10) in Control Panel.

Step 2.   Click or tap **Add a Printer** (or **Add Printer**).

Step 3.   Click or tap **Add a Network**, **Wireless**, or **Bluetooth**. Windows tries to search for a printer automatically. To bypass this, click **The Printer I Want Isn't Listed**.

Step 4.   To find a printer on an Active Directory (domain-based) network, choose **Find a printer in the directory, based on location or features**. To find a printer by name (\\server\printername), choose **Select a shared printer by name**. To find a printer by its URL or IP address, choose **Add a printer using a TCP/IP address or hostname**. Click **Next**.

Step 5.   After the printer is selected, specify whether you want to use the new printer as the default printer. Click **Next**.

Step 6.   Specify whether you want to print a test page. Printing a test page allows you to verify whether the correct print driver has been installed.

Step 7.   Click **Finish** to complete the setup process. Provide the Windows CD or printer setup disc if required to complete the process.

Establish Networking Connections

The Network and Sharing Center includes a Set up a new connection or network wizard for the following connection types:

- Virtual private networking (VPN)
- Dialup networking
- Broadband

NOTE Windows 10 also supports these connection types. To create connections, click or tap Start, Settings, Network & Internet and select the connection type to create.

VPN Connections

A **VPN** connection creates a secure tunnel over the public Internet between two computers. To configure a new VPN connection:

Step 1.   From the Set Up a Connection or Network dialog, click or tap **Connect to a workplace** and click **Next** see Figure 16-4).

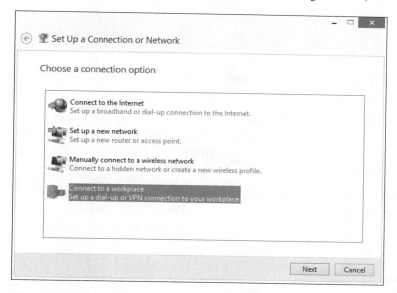

Figure 16-4   Starting the VPN connection creation process in Windows 8.1.

Step 2.   Click or tap **Use my Internet connection** (VPN).

Step 3a.   (Windows 8/8.1) Enter the Internet address (IP address, website) and the destination name, select options such as **Use a smart card** and **Remember my credentials** as desired, and click **Create** (see Figure 16-5).

Step 3b.   (Windows 7) Enter the Internet address (IP address, website) and the destination name, and select options such as **Use a smart card** and **Remember my credentials** as desired. To make the connection later, click **Don't connect now**…. Click **Next** and then click **Close**.

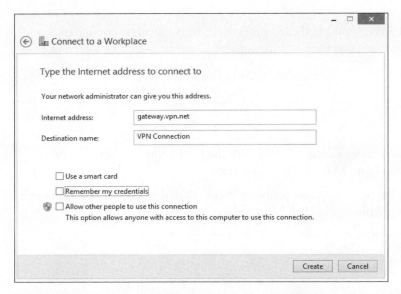

Figure 16-5   Setting up the VPN connection's address and destination in Windows 8.1.

Step 4a.   (Windows 8/8.1) The VPN connection is available from the Networks pane in Windows 8/8.1. To display it, click the network connection icon in the taskbar or from the Charms menu (refer to Figure 16-6). Windows prompts the user for credentials when the connection is started.

Step 4b.   (Windows 7) Enter the username, password, and domain. Click **Create**. The VPN connection is available from the Connections menu that appears when the user clicks the network connection icon in the taskbar.

Dial-Up Connections

A **dial-up** connection is a network connection between two computers via phone lines. Windows can create two types of dial-up connections on systems with analog modems:

- Dial-up networking connections to an ISP
- Direct dial-in connections to a corporate computer

To configure a new dial-up connection to an ISP:

Step 1.   From the Set Up a Connection or Network dialog, click or tap **Connect to the Internet** and click **Next** (refer to Figure 16-4).

Step 2.   Click or tap **Dial-up** and click **Next**.

Step 3.   Enter the ISP's dial-up phone number, username, and password. Check the **Remember this password** box if the user doesn't want to enter the password again. Name the connection, and click **Connect**.

The connection is stored along with other wired and wireless connections.

To configure a new direct dial-in connection to a corporate computer:

Step 1.   From the Set Up a Connection or Network dialog, click or tap **Connect to a workplace** and click **Next**.

Step 2.   Click or tap **Dial directly** and click **Next**.

Step 3.   Enter the remote computer's dial-up phone number and destination name. Select options as desired. To connect now, click **Next**. To set up the connection for later, check the **Don't connect...** box.

Step 4.   Enter username and password. Enter the domain. Check the **Remember this password** box if the user doesn't want to enter the password again. Click **Connect** or **Create**.

The connection is stored along with other network connections (see Figure 16-6).

Figure 16-6   VPN, dial-up ISP, and direct dial-in connections are listed along with wireless connections.

Wireless Connections

A **wireless** connection can be configured when the user clicks on the SSID from the taskbar or Settings menu. However, by using the Wireless Connection option in the Network and Sharing Center, more options can be specified, including WPA2-Personal and WPA2-Enterprise security types:

Step 1. From the Set Up a Connection or Network dialog, click or tap **Connect to a wireless network** and click **Next**.

Step 2. Enter the network name. Select the Security type and enter the security key. To start the connection automatically, check the **Start this connection automatically** box (see Figure 16-7). Click **Next**.

Step 3. Click **Close**. The connection is added to the list of connections.

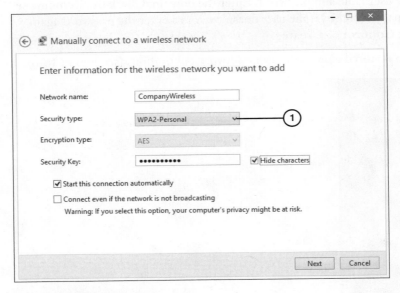

1. Open to select the security type.

Figure 16-7 Creating a wireless connection.

Wired Connections

Use the option to configure a **wired** connection if you need to set up a PPPoE (point-to-point protocol over Ethernet) connection. This type of connection is used by cable or DSL ISPs that require the user to log into the connection:

Step 1. From the Set Up a Connection or Network dialog, click or tap **Connect to the Internet** and click **Next**.

Step 2.   Click or tap **Broadband (PPPoE)** and click **Next**.

Step 3.   Enter the username and password. Enter Domain. Check the **Remember this password** box if the user doesn't want to enter the password again. Click **Connect**.

The connection is stored along with other network connections.

WWAN (Cellular) Connections

A **WWAN (cellular)** connection shows up in the list of Network connections after the SIM card is installed and activated by your mobile provider. To use the connection, select it from the list of Network connections displayed when you click your network icon in the taskbar or Settings.

If the access point name (APN), username, password, or other information has not yet been stored for the WWAN, the user must provide this information during the first use of the connection.

Proxy Settings

Many corporate networks use proxy servers as an intermediary between a network client and the destination of the request (web page, etc.) from the network client.

If a proxy server is used for Internet access and a configuration script or automatic detection are not available, it must be specified by server name and port number To configure manual **proxy settings** for a LAN connection in Windows:

Step 1.   Open the Internet properties (Internet options) dialog from Control Panel.

Step 2.   From the Connections tab, click **LAN settings**.

Step 3.   From the Local Area Network (LAN) Settings window, you have two options underneath Proxy Server. If a single proxy server address and port number is used for all types of traffic, click the **Use a Proxy Server** checkbox and enter the address and port number provided by the network administrator. However, if different proxy servers or ports will be used, click the **Use a Proxy Server** checkbox and click the **Advanced** button.

Step 4.   Specify the correct server and port number to use (see Figure 16-8).

Step 5.   Click **OK** to save changes at each menu level until you return to the browser display.

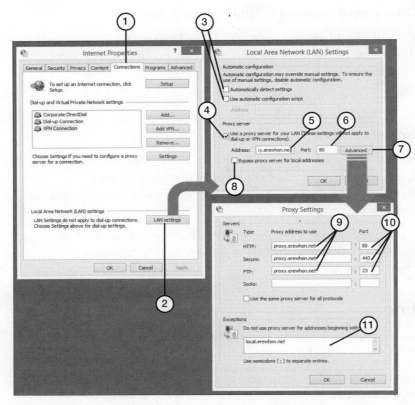

1. The Connections tab of Internet properties
2. Click or tap **LAN settings** to continue
3. If automatic detection or proxy scripts are not used, clear these checkboxes
4. Click this checkbox to add manual proxy server information
5. Proxy server address
6. Proxy server port number
7. To specify different proxy servers or port numbers, click or tap **Advanced**
8. To exclude all local addresses from proxy filtering, check the **Bypass Proxy server...** box.
9. Enter the name for each proxy server by traffic type
10. Enter the port number for each proxy server
11. Enter any exceptions here

Figure 16-8 Setting up manual proxy servers.

Remote Desktop Connection and Remote Assistance

To facilitate connections to remote computers and allow full remote control, Microsoft uses the **Remote Desktop Connection** program, which is based off the

Remote Desktop Protocol (RDP). For more information, see "MSTSC (Remote Desktop Connection)," in Chapter 15, "Managing Microsoft Windows."

Remote Desktop also includes **Remote Assistance**. Remote Assistance allows users to invite a technician to come and view their desktop in the hopes that the technician can fix any encountered problems. These invitations can be made via email or by Easy Connect.

To enable Remote Desktop or Remote Assistance, open the Remote tab of the System properties sheet. Figure 16-9 shows the Remote tab with both remote features enabled.

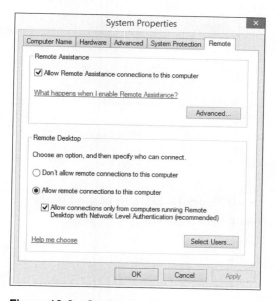

Figure 16-9   Configuring a Windows 8.1 system for Remote Assistance and Remote Desktop.

Click or tap the **Advanced** button to specify how long an invitation remains valid and whether to accept connections only from Windows Vista or newer versions (recommended for improved security).

The msra.exe program is used to send and receive Remote Assistance invitations (see Figure 16-10). To run msra, open it from the command line or search for it.

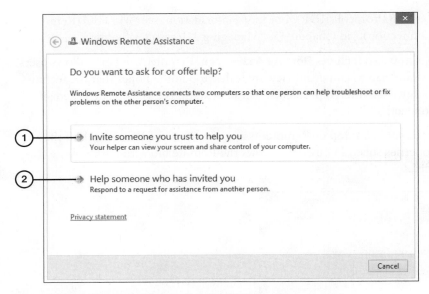

1. Click or tap to send an invitation to get help
2. Click or tap to help someone who sent an invitation

Figure 16-10   Starting msra.exe brings up this dialog.

An invitation file and a separate password (see Figure 16-11) must be used by the helper to gain access to the system requesting Remote Access.

Figure 16-11   Provide this password along with the invitation to get help.

Home vs. Work vs. Public Network Settings

Home, Work, Public, Private—these terms refer to network locations. Selecting the right network location affects how the Windows Firewall configures protection and the networking features available to a particular PC.

Windows 7 Network Locations

When a computer running Windows Vista or 7 is connected to a network for the first time, Windows prompts the user to select a location (see Figure 16-12):

- Home
- Work (7) / Office (Vista)
- Public

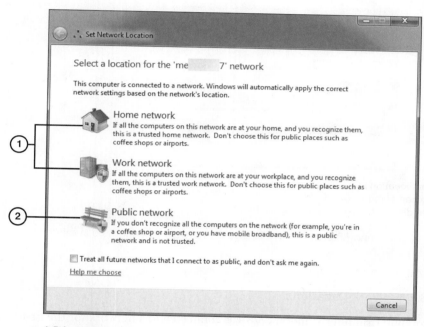

1. Private networks
2. Public network

Figure 16-12   Network location dialog (Windows 7).

Choosing Home or Work (Office) configures the network connection as Private. If this computer is connected to a secure wireless network or a wired network, it is visible only to devices connected to the network. The computer is discoverable, so file and printer sharing and media streaming works.

Choose Home to make Windows homegroup networking available.

Choose Public for non-secured networks (such as in a hotel, coffee shop, library, or other public location). Public turns off network discovery, so the computer is not visible to other computers using the network.

If the location is set incorrectly, click the link below the current network location setting in the Network and Sharing Center (see Figure 16-13) and choose the correct location. Click Close to complete the process.

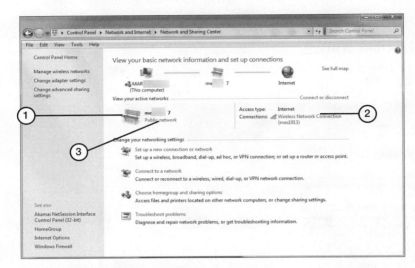

1. Public network location is incorrect
2. No access to homegroup
3. Click or tap to display dialog shown in Figure 16-12

Figure 16-13 Network and Sharing Center displays the network type for the current connection.

Windows 8/8.1 Network Locations

When a computer running Windows 8/8.1 is connected to a network for the first time, Windows prompts the user to select a location. In Windows 8, the dialog has two options:

- Yes, turn on sharing and connect to devices (for home or work networks).

- No, don't turn on sharing or connect to devices (for networks in public places).

The Windows 8.1 version of this dialog looks like Figure 16-14.

As in Windows 7, the Network and Sharing Center displays the current network connection and location. However, if the network location needs to be changed, the user must open the Network dialog in PC Settings:

Step 1.   Sweep in from the right to open the Charms menu.

Step 2.   Click or tap **Settings**.

Step 3.   Click or tap the active network connection icon in the Settings pane. If no network connection is active, click or tap **Change PC Settings, Network**.

Step 4.   Click or tap the connection to change.

Step 5.   Use the **Find devices and content** slider to change the location. Turn it on for a private network. Turn it off for a public network (see Figure 16-15).

Step 6.   Close the menu (drag it down until it disappears).

When you open the Network and Sharing Center, the new location is shown.

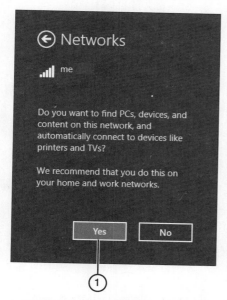

1. Click or tap to enable private networking and support for homegroup networks

Figure 16-14   Selecting a network type for a new network connection in Windows 8.1.

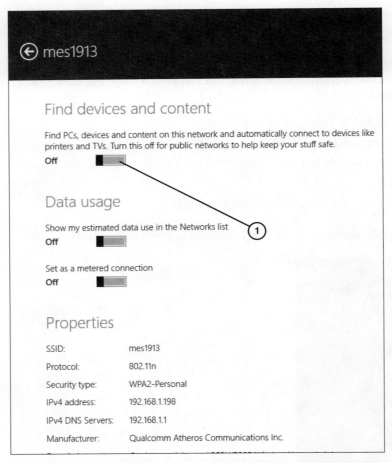

1. Correct setting for a public network; drag right to turn On for a private network

Figure 16-15   Changing the network settings for the current connection in Windows 8.1.

Firewall Settings

Windows Firewall provides protection against unwanted inbound connections and can also be configured to filter outbound connections. To open Windows Firewall, choose one of the following:

- Click or tap the Windows Firewall link in the Network and Sharing Center.
- Search for Windows Firewall and start it.

When Windows Firewall starts, it displays **Firewall settings** for the current connection (see Figure 16-16).

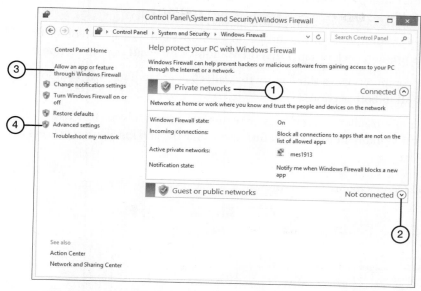

1. Connected network type
2. Click or tap to view settings
3. Click or tap to set up a firewall exception
4. Click or tap to set up an outbound rule or to open a UDP or TCP port

Figure 16-16 Viewing the firewall settings for the current connection (private networks) in Windows 8.1.

To change notification settings or turn the firewall on or off, click or tap the **Change notification settings** or **Turn Windows Firewall on or off** links in the left pane. Either selection opens the Customize dialog (see Figure 16-17). In this dialog, the default settings are the same:

- The Windows Firewall is turned on.
- The user is notified when the Firewall blocks a new app.

To block all incoming connections on a Public network, click or tap the checkbox in the Public network settings section.

Enabling/Disabling Windows Firewall

The Customize dialog can also be used to turn off or turn on Windows Firewall (refer to Figure 16-17):

- If malware or user error has turned off Windows Firewall and no other firewall is present, click or tap **Turn on Windows Firewall** in both sections.

- If the computer uses a third-party firewall, click or tap **Turn off Windows Firewall** in both sections.

- If an app's installer recommends or requires that firewalls be turned off, turn off Windows Firewall and turn it on after the app installation process is complete.

The Action Center reports which firewall is in use on a particular computer.

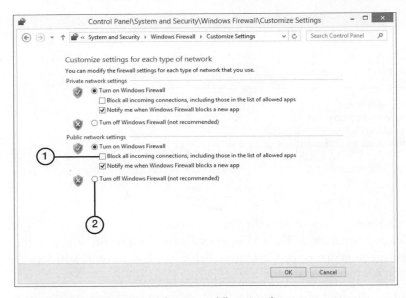

1. Blocks all incoming connections on public networks
2. Turns off Windows Firewall

Figure 16-17   Customizing firewall settings in Windows 8.1.

Exceptions

Windows Firewall can be configured to permit specified applications to pass through the firewall, to open specific ports needed by applications, or to block all traffic. Whenever possible, it's easier to permit traffic by application rather than by UDP or TCP port numbers. Each application or port that is opened is called an **exception**.

Windows Firewall sets up exceptions automatically when an app is blocked and the user allows the app to access the network or Internet.

Configuration

Windows Firewall includes several **configuration** settings. To change firewall settings for an app or feature, click or tap the **Allow an app or feature through Windows Firewall** link (refer to Figure 16-16).

To change the setting for a listed app or feature, click or tap the **Change Settings** button. Click or tap an empty checkbox to permit the app through the firewall; click a filled checkbox to block the app. Click or tap Details to learn more about the app. To remove an app from the list, click Remove. Note that separate settings are available for Private and Public networks (see Figure 16-18).

To browse for another app to add to the list, click the **Allow another app** button and then click Browse. After the app and network type are selected, Windows Firewall puts the app on the list of Allowed apps and features.

In Windows 7/8/8.1, click or tap **Advanced Settings** (refer to Figure 16-16) to open Windows Firewall with Advanced Security. Use this mode to set up rules for inbound or outbound traffic, to block or permit specific UDP or TCP port numbers (see Figure 16-19), and configure monitoring.

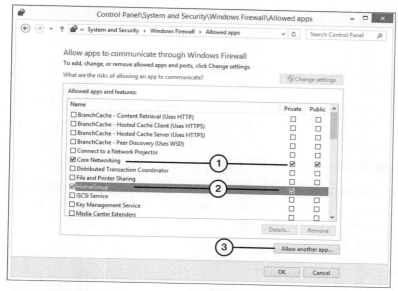

1. Works on both public and private networks
2. Works on private networks only
3. Click or tap to add another app to this list

Figure 16-18   Setting up new exceptions in Windows 8.1's Firewall.

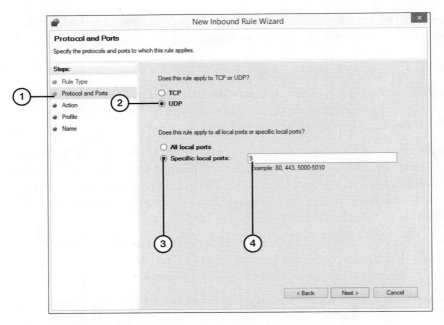

1. Adding a new rule for inbound ports and protocols
2. Specifying the port type
3. Specifying specific ports
4. The port number(s) to use

Figure 16-19   Creating a new rule with Windows Firewall with Advanced Security.

To access the tabbed Windows Firewall interface in Windows Vista, click the **Change Settings** link. You can then click the **Exceptions** tab to see checked programs. With Windows Vista, click **Add Program** to add a program or **Add Port** to add a TCP or UDP port number to the list of exceptions.

Configuring an Alternative IP Address in Windows

An **alternative IP address** enables a system to stay on the network if the DHCP server fails or if the system is sometimes on a different network than normal. To view or change the settings on the Alternate Configuration tab for a network adapter (see Figure 16-20), follow these steps:

Step 1.   Open the Network and Sharing Center.

Step 2.   Click or tap **Change adapter settings**.

Step 3.   Click or tap the connection to change.

Step 4.   Click or tap **Change settings of this connection**.

Step 5.   Click or tap **Internet Protocol Version 4 (TCP/IPv4)**.

Step 6.   Click or tap **Properties**.

Step 7.   Click or tap **Alternate Configuration**.

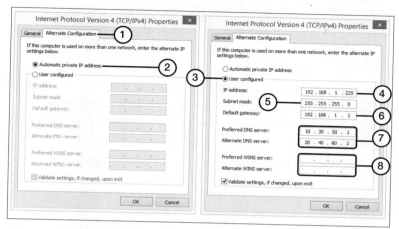

1. Click or tap Alternate Configuration
2. Default setting assigns an APIPA if a DHCP server is not available
3. Click or tap to set up manual IP configuration
4. Enter a unique IP address on the network
5. Enter the same subnet mask as other computers on the network
6. Enter the default gateway for your network
7. Enter the DNS servers you prefer
8. Leave these blank unless your network has WINS servers

Figure 16-20   The Alternate Configuration tab is used to set up a different IP configuration for use on another network or when no DHCP server is available.

The Alternate Configuration tab is used to set up a different TCP/IPv4 configuration for use when a DHCP server is not available or when a different set of user-configured settings is needed, as when a laptop is being used at a secondary location. By default, automatic private IP addressing (APIPA) is used when no DHCP server is in use. APIPA assigns each system a unique IP address in the 169.254.x.x range. APIPA enables a network to perform LAN connections when the DHCP server is not available, but systems using APIPA cannot connect to the Internet. Linux and OS X use the term *IPv4 Link-local*.

You can also use the Alternate Configuration tab to specify the IP address, subnet mask, default gateway, DNS servers, and WINS servers (see Chapter 11, "Networking," to learn more about these settings). This option is useful if this system is moved to another network that uses different IP addresses for these servers.

When this information is set correctly for the network location, the computer can connect to the specified network.

> **NOTE** In IPv6, all devices are assigned a link-local address using the prefix fe80::/64, even if a DHCP server is running or a manual IPv6 address has been assigned.

Network Card Properties

Although most wired network adapters (network cards or NICs) work well using the default settings, some network configurations and requirements might require changes to default settings. The following sections describe **network card properties** and how to change them.

To access the properties listed in the upcoming sections, follow this procedure:

Step 1. Open the Network and Sharing Center.

Step 2. Click or tap **Change adapter settings**.

Step 3. Click or tap a wired connection.

Step 4. Click or tap **Change settings of this connection**.

Step 5. Click or tap **Configure** (see Figure 16-21).

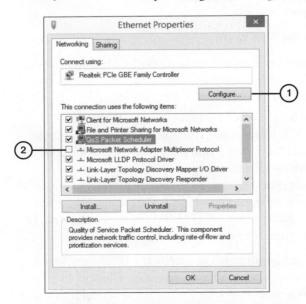

1. Click or tap to configure network adapter settings
2. Checked items are installed and active

Figure 16-21 Configuring a Gigabit Ethernet adapter in Windows 8.1

QoS (Quality of Service)

Quality of Service (**QoS**) enables a computer connected to a wired network to optimize real-time streaming traffic such as VoIP, streaming video, or streaming music services. QoS is installed by default in Windows. To verify that it is installed and enabled, open the properties sheet for the Ethernet or wireless adapter and click the Networking tab. QoS Packet Scheduler should be checked (refer to Figure 16-21).

To enable QoS to perform properly, make sure that Priority & VLAN (also called QoS Packet Tagging) is enabled on the Advanced tab (refer to Figure 16-22).

TIP   Additional QoS optimization can be performed by using Group Policy settings. See http://www.biztechmagazine.com/article/2010/03/boost-network-performance-windows-7-qos for more information.

Half Duplex/Full Duplex/Auto

Half duplex/full duplex/auto are settings that determine how a network card communicates with the rest of the network. If the hardware in use on an Ethernet, Fast Ethernet, or Gigabit Ethernet network permits, you can configure the network to run in full-duplex mode. Full-duplex mode enables the adapter to send and receive data at the same time, which doubles network speed over the default half-duplex mode (where the card sends and receives in separate operations). Thus, a 10BASE-T-based network runs at 20Mbps in full-duplex mode; a 100BASE-T-based network runs at 200Mbps in full-duplex mode; and a 1000BASE-T-based network runs at 2000Mbps in full-duplex mode.

To achieve full-duplex performance on a UTP-based Ethernet network, the network adapters on a network must all support full-duplex mode, and be configured to use full-duplex mode with the device's setup program or properties sheet, and a switch must be used in place of a hub.

The default Auto setting (refer to Figure 16-22 in the next section) allows the adapter to determine the best setting, but it can be overridden if necessary.

Speed

Ethernet adapters can run at more than one **speed**, limited by the slowest network hardware. For example, if network clients have Gigabit Ethernet (10/100/1000Mbps) adapters, but the network switch is a Fast Ethernet (10/100Mbps) device, the network will run at Fast Ethernet speeds.

If network cabling is CAT5e or faster, the network can be upgraded to Gigabit Ethernet speeds by replacing the Fast Ethernet switch with a Gigabit Ethernet switch.

To change duplex and speed settings:

Step 1. Click or tap **Configure** on the adapter properties sheet (refer to Figure 16-21).

Step 2. Click or tap the **Advanced** tab.

Step 3. Click or tap **Speed & Duplex**.

Step 4. Select the value desired (see Figure 16-22).

Step 5. Click **OK** when done.

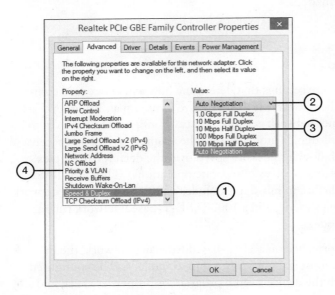

1. Click or tap Speed & Duplex
2. Open menu to view options
3. Select a manual setting if Auto doesn't provide expected performance
4. Click or tap to make sure Priority & VLAN are enabled for use with QoS

Figure 16-22   Viewing Speed & Duplex settings for a Gigabit Ethernet adapter.

Wake-on-LAN

Wake-on-LAN (WOL or WoL) enables a computer connected to a wired network to be awakened from sleep mode via a special "magic packet" signal delivered by the network. Wake-on-LAN can be used to awaken a computer for updates, backup, or other tasks as needed while running in low-power mode when not in use.

The successful configuration of Wake-on-LAN requires changes to the default settings of a computer's BIOS or UEFI firmware, network adapter, Windows services, firewall settings, and router port forwarding.

The changes to a network adapter's default setting include:

- Open the Advanced tab in the properties sheet for the network adapter and enable **Wake on Magic Packet**.

- Open the Power Management tab for the network adapter and check the boxes for **Allow this device to wake the computer** and **Only allow a magic packet to wake the computer**.

Figure 16-23 illustrates these tabs on a system running Windows 8.1.

Other changes in system configuration are needed to make Wake-on-LAN work properly:

- Enable Wake-on-LAN in the system BIOS or UEFI firmware and save changes. Some systems might not have a BIOS/UEFI firmware option for WOL but it might be supported automatically.

- Open Control Panel's Windows Features dialog (in Programs and Features) and turn on Simple TCP/IP Services.

- Open Computer Management's Services dialog, start Simple TCP/IP Services, and configure it to run automatically.

- UDP port 9 (recommended) or port 7 (use if UDP port 9 doesn't work properly) needs to be opened in your firewall. If you use Windows Firewall, start it in Advanced mode and set up a new inbound rule.

- Configure your router to forward UDP port 9 (or UDP 7) to the computers that need WOL services.

See http://windows7-issues.blogspot.com/2011/03/wake-on-lan-wol-for-windows-7-made-easy.html for more information.

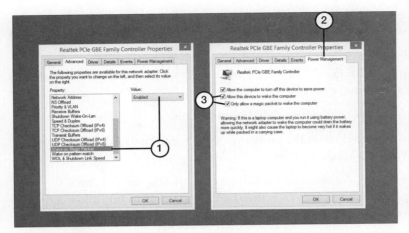

1. Wake on Magic Packet enabled
2. Click or tap Power Management tab
3. Check Allow this device to wake the computer and Only allow a magic
   packet to wake the computer

Figure 16-23   Configuring Wake-on-LAN settings on a typical Ethernet adapter.

BIOS (on-board NIC)

The **BIOS** in an **on-board NIC** can be used to boot the computer if it is configured as a bootable device in the BIOS or UEFI firmware setup. Enable this setting to obtain an installable OS image from the network.

Exam Preparation Tasks

Review All the Key Topics

Review the most important topics in the chapter, noted with the key topics icon in the outer margin of the page. Table 16-1 lists a reference of these key topics and the page numbers on which each is found.

Table 16-1   Key Topics for Chapter 16

Key Topic Element	Description	Page Number
Section	Homegroup vs. Workgroup	840
Section	Network Shares	845
Section	Home vs. Work vs. Public Network Settings	858

Define Key Terms

Define the following key terms from this chapter, and check your answers in the glossary.

Homegroup, Workgroup, Domain setup, Network shares/administrative shares/ mapping drives, Printer sharing, network printer mapping, VPN, Dial-ups, Wireless, Wired, WWAN (Cellular), Proxy settings, Remote Desktop Connection, Remote Assistance, Home vs. work vs. public network settings, Firewall settings, Exceptions, Configuration, Windows firewall, alternative IP address, Network card properties, Half duplex/full duplex/auto, Speed, Wake-on-LAN, QoS, BIOS (on-board NIC).

Complete Hands-On Lab

Complete the hands-on lab, and then see the answers and explanations at the end of the chapter.

Lab 16-1: Windows Networking Tasks

Perform as many of these tasks as you can:

- Create a homegroup (Windows 7/8/8.1/10) or join an existing homegroup.
- Change the sharing settings for a folder in a homegroup or workgroup.
- Map a network folder to a drive letter.
- Share a printer on the network.
- Connect to the shared printer from another computer on the network.
- Review Windows Firewall settings and create a new rule.
- Review the properties for the wired network adapter in a system.

Answer Review Questions

1. Which of the following statements best describes a workgroup? (Choose all that apply.)

    A. Each computer in a workgroup must be on the same subnet.

    B. File and Print Sharing should be enabled on each computer in a workgroup.

    C. The workgroup should have a password.

    D. Each computer in a workgroup must have a user account for each user.

2. Which of the following steps best describes how to change your computer's name?

   A. Open System properties.

   B. Type Msinfo32 at the command line.

   C. Open the System Configuration utility.

   D. Access the drive properties.

3. In which of the following locations are homegroups created?

   A. System Configuration utility.

   B. System properties.

   C. Network and Sharing Center.

   D. Internet Options.

4. Your client wants to create a homegroup, but the homegroup option is not showing up in the Network and Sharing Center. Which of the following statements best describes the most likely cause?

   A. The network location is set to Public.

   B. The network adapter is configured to use half-duplex mode.

   C. A workgroup has already been configured.

   D. An alternative IP configuration is not complete.

5. Active Directory is used to authenticate users on which kind of network?

   A. Peer-to-peer

   B. Workgroup

   C. Homegroup

   D. Domain

6. Which of the following steps is necessary to joining a domain?

   A. Typing Msinfo32 at the command line

   B. Opening System properties

   C. Opening the System Configuration utility

   D. Opening the Network and Sharing Center

7. Which of the following steps is necessary to turning on File Sharing?

   A. Opening the Firewall application

   B. Opening the System properties

   C. Opening the Network and Sharing Center

   D. Opening the System Configuration utility

8. You have created a shared folder on a network server. You have assigned a letter designation to the folder and made it available to all members of the Research department. This folder now appears as a drive letter on each user's computer. Which type of folder have you created?

    A. Administrative share

    B. Homegroup share

    C. Mapped network drive

    D. VPN

9. Which of the following symbols is used to indicate an administrative share?

    A. Asterisk (*)

    B. Dollar sign ($)

    C. Percent sign (%)

    D. Pound sign (#)

10. Which of the following utilities is used to create a VPN?

    A. Network and Sharing Center

    B. Internet Options

    C. System properties

    D. Windows Firewall

11. In which of the following locations are settings for a proxy server configured?

    A. Network and Sharing Center

    B. Internet Options

    C. System properties

    D. Windows Firewall

12. Which of the following utilities is accessed when configuring Remote Assistance?

    A. Network and Sharing Center

    B. Internet Options

    C. System properties

    D. Windows Firewall

13. If you are using your laptop in a public place, such as a restaurant or a hotel, and you have set your network security to Public, which of the following will not be available to you? (Choose all that apply.)

    A. File and printer sharing

    B. Access to the homegroup

    C. Network discovery

    D. Media streaming

14. Which of the following statements best describes a firewall?

    A. A firewall is a specially constructed barrier in the server room to limit the spread of fire.

    B. A firewall is a fire suppression technology that uses plenum grade cabling in ducts and ceiling spaces.

    C. A firewall is a proxy server with a VPN connection.

    D. A firewall is software or hardware that controls the flow of information into a computer from the Internet or from another network.

15. Which of the following can be configured as exceptions in Windows Firewall? (Choose all that apply.)

    A. Applications that are to be allowed through the firewall

    B. Ports and port numbers to be opened

    C. IP address to be used

    D. Subnet mask to be used

16. Setting an Alternate Configuration for the IP address allows you to set up a secondary IP address in case there is no DHCP server available. By default, Automatic Private IP Addressing is used for the alternate configuration. Which of the following addresses might you expect to see if the default alternate address were used?

    A. 10.196.74.12

    B. 192.168.200.24

    C. 169.254.21.3

    D. 172.16.10.5

17. Which of the following statements describes the biggest disadvantage of an APIPA address?

   A. Very few APIPA addresses are available to be assigned across the network.

   B. An APIPA address cannot reach the Internet.

   C. A subnet mask must be manually added to each APIPA address.

   D. Only very large networks can use APIPA.

18. Wake-on-LAN allows a wired network to awaken its client computers from sleep mode for updates, backups, or other tasks. Which of the following statements best describes how it accomplishes this?

   A. The network sends a magic packet signal.

   B. The NIC must have gigabit capability.

   C. QoS must be set for wake-on-LAN.

   D. The network must be configured for full-duplex mode.

Answers and Explanations to Hands-On Labs

Lab 16-1: Windows Networking Tasks

If the computer is running Windows 7 or later and you cannot create or join a homegroup, change the network location to Home (Windows 7), Private (Windows 8), or discoverable (Windows 8.1/10).

To join a homegroup, get the homegroup password from another computer in the homegroup. The link is available in the Network and Sharing Center.

If the wired network adapter is a Gigabit adapter but it is configured for 100Mbps (Fast Ethernet), try changing it to Gigabit. If the connection doesn't work, the switch or router's integrated switch might not support Gigabit speeds.

Answers and Explanations to Review Questions

1. A, B, D. All computers in a workgroup must be part of the same local network or subnet and if they are to share resources, they must use File and Print Sharing. Also, each user must have a local user account on each computer in the workgroup. The workgroup, however, does not have a password.

2. A. Each computer on the network must have a unique name. This is usually done automatically during installation, but if you want to check your computer's name or if you want to change it, you should open the System properties.

There are three ways to do it: Open the Control Panel, access System properties, and select Change Settings. In Vista or Windows 7, open the Start menu, right-click Computer, choose Properties, and then Change Settings. In Windows 8/8.1, press the Windows+X keys, select System, and then Change Settings (or you can open the Charms menu, select Settings, then select PC Info).

3. **C.** To create a Homegroup, open the Control Panel, access the Network and Sharing Center, select Homegroup, and then follow the menu selections.

4. **A.** A network location of Public stops all sharing. Set the network location to Home in Windows 7 and to Private or Allow Network discovery and sharing in Windows 8/8.1/10. Only a Home network will allow you to create or join a homegroup in Windows 7. In Windows 8/8.1/10, use Private as the network (firewall) setting.

5. **D.** Domains use special computers called domain controllers that manage user accounts, file and print sharing, network traffic, and other functions. Active Directory is used by a domain controller running Windows Server software to manage user accounts and shared resources.

6. **B.** When configuring a network, you have two choices: a workgroup or a domain. To join either, open System properties. There are three ways to do it: Open the Control Panel, access the System properties sheet, and select Change Settings. In Vista or Windows 7, open the Start menu, right-click Computer, choose Properties, and then Change Settings. In Windows 8/8.1, press the Windows+X keys, select System, and then Change Settings (or you can also open the Charms menu, select Settings, and then PC Info).

7. **C.** Open the Network and Sharing Center. In Vista, click the down arrow next to File Sharing and select Turn on File Sharing. In Windows 7/8/8.1, click Change Advanced Sharing Settings, select the type of network you want to configure, and then select Turn on file and printer sharing.

8. **C.** You have created a mapped network drive. A mapped network drive is a shared folder or drive on a networked computer that has been assigned a drive letter and mapped to a location on another computer on the network. That share appears to the user as though it is located on the user's own computer.

9. **B.** A dollar sign at the end of a filename indicates an administrative share. For example, C$ is the administrative share for the C: drive.

10. **A.** A VPN is created in the Network and Sharing Center under Set Up a New Connection or Network.

11. **B.** A proxy server is configured in Internet Options. On the Connections tab, choose Settings if you need to configure a proxy server for a connection.

12. **C.** Remote Assistance allows another user at a remote computer to help solve problems on your computer. To configure Remote Assistance, open the Control Panel, access the System utility, Select the Remote settings link, and go to the Remote tab. Or in Vista or Windows 7, open the Start menu, right-click Computer, choose Properties, select the Remote settings link, and go to the Remote tab. In Windows 8/8.1, press the Windows+X keys, select System, and then go to the Remote tab. You can configure both Remote Desktop and Remote Assistance from this location.

13. **A, B, C, D.** All of these features are unavailable when you configure your computer for a public network. When on a public network, you do not want other computers that might be using the network at the same time to be able to see or interact with your computer.

14. **D.** A firewall blocks or allows information to flow into your computer from the Internet or from another network by closing or opening ports. A firewall can prevent hackers and malware from entering your computer, but it can also be used to prevent your computer from sending malware out to other computers.

15. **A, B.** Specific applications that are to be allowed through the firewall and specific ports that are to be opened may be configured as exceptions in Windows Firewall.

16. **C.** 169.254.x.x is an APIPA address. By default an address within this range will be assigned when there is no DHCP server available or when the DHCP server has run out of IP addresses to assign.

17. **B.** A computer with an APIPA address cannot be used to connect to the Internet.

18. **A.** The network sends a magic packet signal out to every computer on the network to awaken them to receive updates, backups, etc. Laptops should not be configured to receive the Wake-on-LAN signal because turning on automatically when on battery power could drain the battery quickly. It also could generate a lot of heat if the laptop comes on while in its case.

This chapter covers the following subjects:

- **Using Appropriate Safety Procedures**—How to make sure electrical outlets are grounded, how to protect components from ESD, how to handle computer-related toxic waste, and how to avoid various workplace hazards.

- **Applying Environmental Controls**—Learn how to use an MSDS, deal with HVAC issues, and protect equipment from power issues (brownouts, blackouts, surges).

- **Addressing Prohibited Content or Activity**—Review the steps needed to respond to an incident, document the incident, and build a chain of custody.

- **Licensing/DRM/EULA**—In this section, learn to deal with DRM data and apps, EULA considerations, the differences between open source and commercial licenses, and personal and enterprise licenses.

- **Personally Identifiable Information**—Learn the considerations needed to protect personally identifiable information on a network or device and how to remove this information from photos or documents.

- **Following Corporate End-User Policies and Security Best Practices**—See tips on how to help your organization build a list of best practices.

- **Communication Methods and Professionalism**—Discover how to relate positively to customers and handle difficult situations.

## CHAPTER 17

Operational Procedures

This chapter is all about safety, the environment, response procedures, and professional behavior. When you build and repair computers and mobile devices, you should carefully consider the safety of your computer components. More important is your own personal safety. Computer and electronic components are expensive, and your well-being is priceless. By employing smart safety precautions you protect your investment and yourself. Thinking bigger, the environment is a factor in the well-being of a computer. Some parts of the environment you can manipulate; others you need to take preventative measures against. However, no matter how much you plan, incidents will occur. By responding quickly and effectively to problems, and documenting everything that happens, you ensure that issues are solved quickly and efficiently. Finally, whenever working with a customer, it's important to be professional and courteous; it's even more important to be able to communicate with the customer successfully.

220-902: Objective 5.1 Given a scenario, use appropriate safety procedures.

220-902: Objective 5.2 Given a scenario with potential environmental impacts, apply the appropriate controls.

220-902: Objective 5.3 Summarize the process of addressing prohibited content/activity, and explain privacy, licensing, and policy concepts.

220-902: Objective 5.4 Demonstrate proper communication techniques and professionalism.

Foundation Topics

Using Appropriate Safety Procedures

Computer safety is about keeping the computer you are working on safe from failure, but it is also about protecting yourself while working with computers and other technology. The four concepts we focus on in this section are how to prevent electrostatic discharge, how to work with electricity safely, how to handle toxic waste, and how to protect your personal and physical safety.

Equipment Grounding

Computers and peripherals such as displays, projectors, printers, scanners, multifunction devices, and surge suppressors are designed to be connected to grounded (earthed) outlets. Grounded outlets have three prongs in almost all world areas. Using an ungrounded outlet can cause this equipment to fail, can represent a shock hazard to users, and a potential fire hazard. Thus, **equipment grounding** is critical to proper operation.

NOTE   For illustrated guides to grounded (earthed) and ungrounded outlets, voltage, and electrical cycles worldwide, see http://electricaloutlet.org/ and https://en.wikipedia.org/wiki/AC_power_plugs_and_sockets.

When a grounded outlet is not available, a grounded to ungrounded adapter (see Figure 17-1) can be used for temporary setups if—and only if—the loop on the adapter can be connected to a working ground (such as a grounding screw or a copper wire wrapped around a metal pipe).

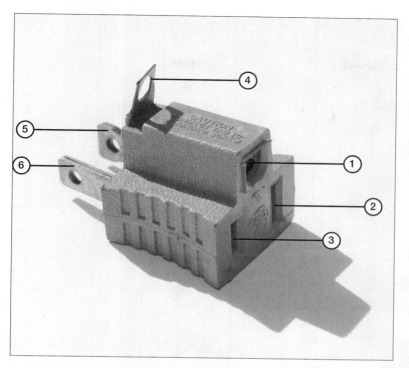

1. Ground connector   4. Ground loop
2. Neutral connector   5. Neutral prong
3. Hot connector   6. Hot prong

Figure 17-1   A three-wire to two-wire adapter must use a ground screw or wire to provide a safe connection for grounded equipment.

In the USA, grounded 120V AC electrical outlets have been required by code since 1962. Thus, a more likely issue in residential and office environments is the possibility of an improperly installed grounded outlet: one in which the ground line doesn't connect to a ground.

The easiest way to determine proper building wiring, including grounding, is to use an electrical outlet tester such as the one shown in Figure 17-2.

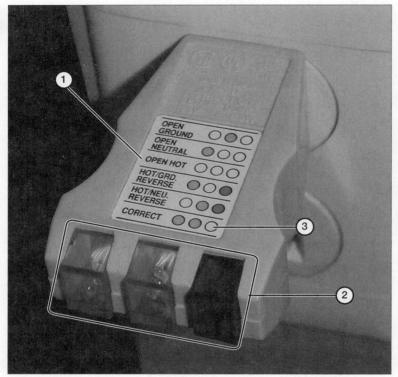

1. Outlet tester legend
2. Test lights
3. Legend indicates wiring is correct

Figure 17-2 An electrical tester can determine whether an outlet is properly wired and grounded (earthed).

Component Handling and Storage

During the building, upgrading, repairing, or teardown of electronic and computer equipment, there are many potential opportunities for equipment to be damaged or destroyed by ESD.

Electrostatic discharge (ESD) is the silent enemy of computer equipment. Because of this it is often disregarded. However, it's real and has been the bane of many a computer component. The human body builds up static electricity all the time, even when you are just sitting at your desk. And the dryer the atmosphere is, the easier static electricity can build. Table 17-1 compares the ESD potential at different humidity levels and activities.

Table 17-1 ESD by Activity and Relative Humidity

Activity	Relative Humidity		
	55%	40%	10%
Normal activities			
Walking on carpet	7,500V	15,000V	35,000V
Walking on vinyl floor	3,000V	5,000V	12,000V
Workbench repair and packing tasks			
Typical worker tasks at an electronics bench	400V	800V	6,000V
Removing DIP** chips from plastic tube	400V	700V	2,000V
Removing DIP chips from vinyl tray	2,000V	4,000V	11,500V
Removing DIP chips from Styrofoam	3,500V	5,000V	14,500V
Removing bubble pack from a printed circuit board (motherboard, video card, etc.)	7,000V	20,000V	26,500V
Packing motherboards, video cards, or other printed circuit boards in a foam-lined box	5,000V	11,000V	21,000V

* Equipment can be damaged by ESD of 700V or higher
**dual inline package

As Table 17-1 demonstrates, even ordinary activities can cause very high levels of ESD, and most of the activities listed in this table can damage or destroy electronic components. As humidity decreases, the voltage released during an ESD climbs.

Without ESD protection, that static electricity will seek to discharge to anything else that has a different electric potential, especially metallic items; or, for example—circuit boards. That's right: if you are sitting at your desk and pick up a $300 PCI Express x16 video card, static will discharge from you to the component, possibly damaging it. This damage could cause a complete failure or it could cause intermittent issues that can be difficult to troubleshoot. Make things easier for yourself by employing antistatic measures at all times. It just might save you or your employer $300—or more.

Four keys to protection include:

- Antistatic bags
- ESD straps
- ESD mats
- Self-grounding

Antistatic Bags

When you remove a component from the computer, immediately place it in an **antistatic bag** and put it off to the side (see Figure 17-3). Parts should never be lying around without their antistatic bag! Normal bubble wrap bags do not constitute antistatic protection, make sure they are proper antistatic bags. Note that some bubble wrap is antistatic, and is so labeled.

After an item is placed in an antistatic bag, place it in a protective box to avoid physical impact damage.

1. Antistatic bag
2. micro PCIe card inside anti-static bag

Figure 17-3 Using an antistatic bag to protect a micro PCIe wireless network adapter.

ESD Straps

ESD straps are sometimes incorrectly referred to as "grounding straps." This is a potentially dangerous misnomer. Instead, an ESD strap is designed to equalize the electric potential of the user and the device the strap is clipped to, such as the interior of a computer. By equalizing the electric potential, ESD is prevented because ESD is the movement of electricity between two objects with different electric potential.

An ESD strap has two pieces:

- An elastic or hook-and-loop strap with a built-in metal snap backed by a metal plate

- A coiled flexible cable with a matching snap at one end and an alligator clip at the other end. The snap contains a 1 Megohm resistor, which can help prevent injury in case of electrical discharge.

Here's how to use an ESD strap:

Step 1. Place the elastic or hook-and-loop strap around one wrist with the flat metal plate against the skin.

Step 2. Adjust the strap until the metal plate stays in place as you move your wrist.

Step 3. Snap the cable to the strap around your wrist.

Step 4. Open the alligator cable and clamp it to unpainted metal on the object you are servicing.

The strap around the wrist with the metal plate, snap, and cable equalizes electrical potential between you and the object you are servicing to prevent ESD.

Figure 17-4 illustrates a typical ESD strap and suitable locations for attaching it to a computer.

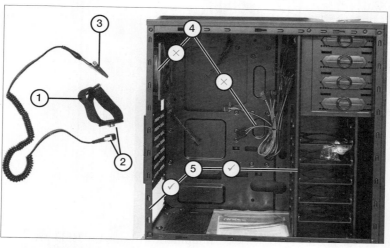

1. Adjustable wrist strap
2. Snap cable to wrist strap
3. Clamp alligator clip to unpainted metal components on the device being serviced
4. Not suitable (plastic fan or coated wires)
5. Suitable (metal chassis frame or drive bay frame)
   Green check (indicates suitable locations for strap)
   Red X (not suitable locations)

Figure 17-4 Using an ESD strap to help prevent damaging ESD when working on electronics.

ESD Mats

The next level of protection for bench repairs and upgrades are **ESD mats**. Mats include one of the following methods for connecting the mat to a device being repaired:

- A cable with alligator clip.
- A cable with a loop designed to be held in place by a case screw, but the cable is snapped to the mat rather than to your wrist.

As with an ESD strap, the end of the cable that snaps to the mat has a 1Megohm resistor built into it.

The ESD mat shown in Figure 17-5 is bundled with an ESD strap, and other versions use anti-fatigue material suitable for floor use.

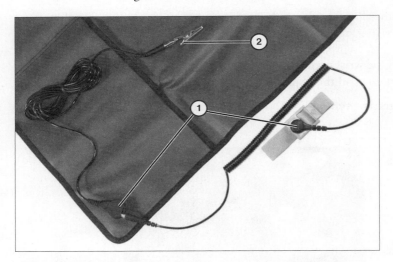

1. Resistors built into cables
2. Attach this clip to equipment being serviced

Figure 17-5   An ESD mat provides additional protection against damaging ESD.

Self-Grounding

Sometimes, it might be necessary to work on equipment without any ESD protection. In such cases, there is still a way to protect the equipment you work on: **self-grounding**.

Self-grounding means that you touch a nearby metal component before you touch the actual device you're servicing. For example, when you are sitting on a chair with metal components, you should touch a metal portion of the chair before picking up or opening the device. Before you open a computer, touch an unpainted portion of the case with both hands before installing or uninstalling a component. Do this every time before you touch a component. If no other antistatic options are available to you, this will be your last resort.

Office workers should also use self-grounding before using keyboards or mice. I have personally administered an ESD to a keyboard that locked it up, requiring the system to be shut down with the power switch and restarted. The files that were open were not saved and had to be reconstructed.

NOTE   Remember to keep the computer unplugged while working inside it. Disconnect the power or hit the power switch on the back of the computer (if there is one) before working on the system. You might not know whether the AC outlet is wired properly. Regardless, by simply disconnecting the power, you eliminate any chance of a shock.

Other ESD and Safety Precautions to Take

When you handle components or cards, hold them by the edge or bracket. Don't touch the chips, contacts, or other circuitry. When you handle components, stay stationary. Don't shuffle your feet or move any more than you must to install or remove the component.

Remove jewelry and wear protective clothing. In some labs you might see technicians wearing antistatic nylon jumpsuits. For the average person, rubber-soled shoes can also help to prevent ESD.

If possible, work in a non-carpeted area when you must work on equipment in the field. Carpet is perhaps the leading cause of high electrical potential that leads to ESD.

Avoid using AC-powered tools near a computer. Use battery-powered devices (such as a multimeter) only when necessary.

Toxic Waste Handling

There are three types of computer-related toxic waste that the CompTIA A+ Certification exam addresses for safe handling:

- Batteries
- Toner
- CRT displays

The following sections provide guidance for **toxic waste handling**.

Recycling Batteries

Nickel-cadmium (Ni-Cad), Nickel-Metal Hydride (NiMH), and Lithium-Ion (Li-Ion) **batteries** for cell phones, computers, and other electronics as well as lead-acid cells used in UPS battery backup units should not be discarded as trash. If not recycled properly, these items will become toxic waste.

There are several ways to recycle these batteries safely to avoid environmental threats:

- For small numbers of rechargeable batteries or devices that contain rechargeable batteries, use a recycling drop-off station located at electronic retailers.

- For large numbers of rechargeable batteries, devices, or UPS devices with batteries, contact an electronics recycler in your area.

- Some batteries can be returned directly to the manufacturer for recycling.

During storage and transport, make sure battery contacts are prevented from touching each other. Check and follow regulations regarding the shipment of Li-Ion batteries, which pose a potentially high fire and explosion hazard in some environments.

Toner

Toner bottles and cartridges for laser printers and copiers should also be recycled instead of discarded. Unlike batteries, users can actually earn money or credits toward additional purchases by recycling these products at local office-supply stores or toner recycling shops.

New toner cartridges can also be returned to the manufacturer by using the pre-paid label packed in the box containing the toner.

Recycling Inkjet Cartridges

Although inkjet cartridges are not recognized as toxic waste, they shouldn't be discarded. They can be turned in for credit at office-supply stores or inkjet cartridge remanufacturers. Some manufacturers include a pre-paid label in the box containing the ink for easy returns.

After removing the old toner cartridge, use a specially designed toner vacuum to remove loose toner from inside the printer before inserting the new cartridge.

CRT Displays

Although cathode ray tube (**CRT**) displays have become much less common in recent years, as long as they exist, they represent a significant environmental and personal safety hazard.

CRT displays contain heavy metals, including lead solder on older models, and a CRT can retain potentially dangerous electric charges long after it has been shut down. To avoid these hazards, use an approved electronics recycler for CRT displays. These organizations can safely discharge the CRT before dismantling it and recycle its components.

NOTE Many electronics recyclers now charge by the pound to recycle CRT monitors and CRT TVs.

LCD-CCFL Displays

Although LCD-CCFL displays are not specifically cited on the CompTIA A+ Certification exam as a potential hazard, the fluorescent backlights in these units contain toxic mercury. Mercury could be released into the environment if panels are crushed or broken when disposed of as ordinary trash.

LCD-CCFL displays as well as all other types of computers, peripherals, and electronics, should be disposed of through an approved electronics recycler.

Personal Safety

In this section, we discuss methods for keeping a bench tech safe while working on computer and electronics equipment.

Disconnect Power First

Electricity is a hazard to computers and to humans. Approach any encounter with electricity with great caution. One snap decision is all it takes to ruin your day, so be sure to **disconnect power before repairing PC**.

Remove Jewelry

Remove jewelry of all kinds (rings, necklaces, earrings, and so on) before working on a computer. You don't want jewelry to come into contact with any components.

Lifting Techniques

Use safe **lifting techniques** to avoid injury. When lifting items, stand close to the item, squat down to the item by bending the knees, grasp the item firmly, keep the back straight and slowly lift with the legs, not the back. Be sure not to twist the body and keep the item close to the body. This helps to prevent back injuries. When moving items, it is best to have them stored at waist level so that minimal lifting is necessary. The Occupational Safety & Health Administration (OSHA) has plenty of guidelines and recommendations for physical safety at the workplace. Their website is http://www.osha.gov/.

Weight Limitations

Know your **weight limitations** to avoid injury. Lifting heavy items incorrectly can cause many types of injuries. As a general rule, if an item is heavier than one quarter of your body weight, you should ask someone else to help. A box doesn't need to be marked "Team lift" to make using two (or more) people to lift it safely a good idea.

Electrical Fire Safety

With **electrical fire safety**, the safest measures are preventative ones. Buildings should be outfitted with smoke detectors and fire extinguishers. The proper type of fire extinguisher for an electrical fire is a Class C extinguisher. CO_2-based BC fire extinguishers are common and relatively safe to humans, but they can cause damage to computers. If equipment needs to be protected more, then an ABC Halotron extinguisher should be used. Server rooms and data centers often are protected by a larger special hazard protection system that uses the FM-200 clean agent system. This clean agent won't cause damage to servers and other expensive equipment and is safe for humans.

If you see an electrical fire, use the proper extinguisher to attempt to put it out. If the fire is too big for you to handle, the first step is to dial your country's emergency number (in the U.S., dial 911). Then evacuate the building. Afterward, you can notify building management, your supervisor, or other facilities people.

Hopefully you will never come near a live electrical wire. But if you do, you want to attempt to shut off the source. Do not attempt to do this with your bare hands, and make sure that your feet are dry and that you are not standing in any water. Use a wooden stick, board, or rope. If this is not possible, contact your supervisor or building management so they can shut down power at another junction. If you find an apparently unconscious person underneath a live wire, do not touch the person! Again, attempt to move the live wire with a wooden stick or similar object. Never use anything metal, and do not touch anything metal while you are doing it. After moving the wire, call 911 and contact your superiors immediately. While waiting, attempt to administer first aid to the person.

Always follow company policy and local government regulations for handling emergencies.

Cable Management

Cable management is even more important outside the computer than it is inside. Routing power cables and data cables inside the PC is important for providing good airflow for cooling. But cables outside the computer can be a trip hazard. Any external USB cables should be routed in a way that they won't interfere with the normal activity of employees. More importantly, network cables should be stationary and routed away from walking areas.

Your municipality will have rules governing how networking and telecommunications wires should be installed. In fact, many municipalities require a license to install any of these cables. When you need to run network cables for new computers, check your local regulations first and see whether you are even allowed to do it yourself. You should always be in compliance with local government regulations. If so, make sure that cables do not pose trip hazards and are not run near any electrical devices or wires if at all possible.

Safety Goggles

Wear **safety goggles** when performing computer repairs, cleaning, or upgrades. Avoid eye injuries from dust, dirt, flyaway screws or bolts, solder, or other activities. The USA standard for protective work eyewear is ANSI Z87.1-2010. Eye protectors that meet this standard can be rated for non-impact or impact (Z87+) applications, so choose according to the risks involved in your specific application.

In other countries, determine the relevant standards for industrial protection when selecting safety goggles.

Air Filter Mask

If you are performing metal machining, buffing, sanding, soldering, waste processing, recycling, or painting as part or all of your technology-related work, an **air filter mask** might be required for safety.

The USA NIOSH (National Institute for Occupational Safety and Health) standards for particulate filtering respirators include the following filter series:

- N (not resistant to oil)
- R (resistant to oil)
- P (oil proof)

The highest ratings available are P100 (99.97 percent efficiency against oil and non-oil particulate aerosols; meetings HEPA standards), R95 (95% efficiency against oil and non-oil particulate aerosols), and N95 (95% efficiency against non-oil particulate aerosols). Some filters can also block ozone.

Check the particulate hazard types associated with a task before selecting an R-series or N-series filter, or choose a P100 filter. Some masks can accept any of these filter types.

Compliance with Local Government Regulations

Compliance with local government regulations is a necessary part of legal and safe electronics and technology work. Check with your local municipality for recommended electronics recyclers. Electronics recyclers should have an ISO 14001 certification. Follow regulations for ventilation and other workplace issues as well.

Applying Environmental Controls

Environmental factors vary greatly from one organization to the next. For the exam you need to know how and why to control temperature and humidity, what an MSDS is and how to use it, and how to deal with dust and debris when it comes to computers.

> **NOTE** For the 220-902 exam, prepare to answer questions on these topics:
> - MSDS documentation for handling and disposal
> - Temperature, humidity level awareness, and proper ventilation
> - Power surges, brownouts, and blackouts
> - **Protection from airborne particles**
> - Compliance with local government regulations

Material Safety Data Sheet (MSDS)

A **material safety data sheet (MSDS)**, also known as a **safety data sheet (SDS)**, is a document that gives information about particular substances, such as the toner in a laser printer's toner cartridge. Products that use chemicals are required to have an MSDS. The MSDS includes the following information:

- Proper treatment if a person comes into contact with the substance or ingests it
- Procedures on how to deal with spills

- Procedures on how to handle and dispose of the substance properly
- How and where to store the substance

TIP   MSDS personal protection ratings are designed to inform the consumer of the safe way to handle the material. The recommendations for ratings A–D are as follows:

Rating A: Safety glasses

Rating B: Safety glasses and gloves

Rating C: Safety glasses, gloves, and apron

Rating D: Face shield, eye protection, gloves, and apron

Most companies have their MSDS documents online. For example, if you were to access www.hp.com/go/ecodata (or do a search for "HP MSDS"), you would find all the MSDS documents for Hewlett-Packard's various inkjet cartridges, toner cartridges, cleaners, digital projector and printer lamps, batteries, and so on. MSDS documents are usually in PDF format so be sure to have Adobe Reader or other PDF reader installed.

Generally, substances that contain chemicals should be stored in a cool, dry place, away from sunlight. "Cool" means the lower end of the OSHA guideline, about 68 degrees F (20 degrees C). Often, this will be in a storage closet away from the general work area and outside the air filtration system. This also allows the items to be stored in a less humid area. As far as disposal, basically, any substance with an MSDS should not be thrown away when it is finished with. It will usually be recycled according to the document's procedures. This could be through the local municipality (in the case of batteries), or by returning items directly to the manufacturer or vendor (in the case of ink/toner cartridges).

It's important to know what to do when someone is adversely affected by a product that contains chemicals. A person might have skin irritation from coming into contact with toner particles or a cleaner that was used on a keyboard or mouse. As a technician, your job is to find out how to help the person. If you do not have direct access to the MSDS, contact your facilities department or building management. Perhaps the cleaning crew uses a particular cleaning agent that you are not familiar with, and only the facilities department has been given the MSDS for this. It's better to review all MSDS documents and be proactive, but in this case, you probably won't have access to the document. Collaborate with the facilities department to get the affected person the proper first aid and, if necessary, take the person to the emergency room. Finally, remove the affected device if it is a keyboard or mouse, for example. Replace it with a similar device until you can get the original device cleaned properly.

Temperature, Humidity, and Air

You should be aware of the temperature and humidity measurements in your building. You also should be thinking about airborne particles and proper ventilation. Collectively, OSHA refers to this as "air treatment," the removal of air contaminants and/or the control of room temperature and humidity. Although there is no specific government policy regarding this, there are recommendations, including a **recommended temperature** range of 68 to 76 degrees Fahrenheit (20 to 24 degrees Celsius) and a **recommended humidity** range of between 20% and 60%. Remember, the higher the humidity, the less chance of ESD, but it might get a bit uncomfortable for your co-workers; they might not want to work in a rainforest, so a compromise will have to be sought. If your organization uses air handlers to heat, cool, and move the air, it will be somewhat difficult to keep the humidity much higher than 25–30 percent anyway.

That brings us to **ventilation**. An organization should employ the use of local exhaust (to remove contaminants generated by the organization's processes) and introduce an adequate supply of fresh outdoor air through natural or mechanical ventilation. As far as air treatment goes, organizations should use filtration devices, electronic cleaners, and possibly chemical treatments activated with charcoal or other sorbents (materials used to absorb unwanted gases). Most filtration systems use charcoal and HEPA filters. These filters should be replaced at regular intervals. Air ducts and dampers should be cleaned regularly, and ductwork insulation should be inspected now and again.

If there still is a considerable amount of airborne particles, portable air filtration **enclosures** can be purchased that also use charcoal and HEPA **air filters**, or possibly utilize ultraviolet light to eliminate particles. These are commonly found in computer repair facilities due to the amount of **dust and debris** sitting in computers that are waiting for repair. Some organizations even foot the bill for **masks** or even respirators for their employees. Many PC workbenches are equipped with a **compressed air** system and **vacuum** system. This way, the PC tech can blow out the dust and dirt from a computer, and vacuum it up at the same time. Otherwise, it is usually best to take the computer outside when cleaning it, unless it is very windy.

Power Surges, Brownouts, and Blackouts

An electrical outlet may be properly wired (see "Equipment Grounding," discussed earlier in this chapter), but there are other threats to the well-being of computers or other devices connected to the outlet. These include:

- Power surges
- Brownouts
- Blackouts

Power Surges and Surge Suppressors

A **surge suppressor** is designed to block power surges from damaging the equipment plugged into it. **Power surges** are defined as overvoltage events that last no more than 50ms, and can reach voltage levels as high as 6000V and 3000A.

Surge suppressors are rated in joules, which measures the amount of energy a surge suppressor can absorb before failing. All other factors being, equal, the higher the joule rating the better. However, keep in mind that a unit with multiple metal oxide varistors (MOVs) on each power lead might provide better protection than a single large MOV.

MOVs absorb power surges, and gradually wear out. Although many (but not all) surge suppressors have lights that indicate when protection has failed, only a few models stop providing power in the event that protection fails.

Watch how many computers you connect to your surge suppressor. Add the combined wattage or volt-amp ratings of the devices you want to plug in to the surge suppressor and compare that to the maximum that the surge suppressor can support. Usually a surge suppressor can handle two basic computers and two monitors. But watch out for high-powered devices. These should get their own surge suppressor; for example, laser printers.

Surge suppressors should be replaced every three to five years, or right after an event that damages the MOVs, such as a nearby lightning strike, frequent power flickers, burn marks, or smoke in any outlet on the unit.

NOTE   For an excellent overview of how surge suppression works, why surge suppressors wear out, and recommendations for current products, see http://thewirecutter.com/reviews/best-surge-protector/.

Blackouts, Brownouts, and Battery Backup Units

Blackouts (total loss of power) and **brownouts** (sustained voltage drops of as much as half of rated output) stop computers and peripherals from working. Unfortunately, if computers and peripherals lose power in the middle of backups, updates, or reports, files can be corrupted. The solution is a **battery backup** (UPS) unit.

NOTE   The term UPS means uninterruptable power supply. Strictly speaking, a true UPS is one in which connected devices are always powered by the battery, which uses an inverter to continually convert AC power into DC power. However, most so-called "UPS" units actually pass AC power through the unit's integrated surge suppressor until the AC power fails. At that point, the battery takes over. This type of unit is most properly known as a standby power supply (SPS) or line-interactive unit. In practice, both types of battery backup units are known as UPS units.

Battery backup units are rated in two ways: volt-amps (VA) or watts (W). Different battery backup units with the same wattage rating can vary by the VA rating. However, the usual calculation for comparing W to VA is to assume that VA*.60=W. Thus, a UPS with a 1000VA will provide about 600W of power.

In addition to providing enough power to run connected devices (computer, display, USB devices, but not a laser printer) the amount of time the devices can run on battery before being shut down by the UPS, run time, is an important consideration.

Some vendors and third party websites (for example, www.easycalculation.com/physics/classical-physics/ups-power-requirement.php) provide calculators that use input watts or amperage draws to calculate the minimum-sized UPS needed. To increase runtime, select a unit with a larger VA or watt rating.

NOTE   Do not use the battery-backed outlets on a UPS for devices such as laser printers. These can drain the battery quickly or damage the unit. Use the surge suppressed outlets that are not connected to the battery.

Table 17-2 provides a quick review of what the exam requires you know for this topic.

Table 17-2   Electrical Conditions and Protective Measures

Type of Electrical Condition	Description	Protective Measure
Power surge	Overvoltage event lasting less than 50ms. Up to 6000V and 3000A.	Surge suppressor
Sag	Momentary voltage drop from 10-90 percent of normal voltage for a few seconds to one minute.	UPS
Brownout	Sustained voltage drop of up to half normal voltage. Can last for minutes to hours.	UPS
Blackout	Total loss of power for an extended period of time	UPS or generator

Addressing Prohibited Content or Activity

Objective: 220-902: 5.3 Summarize the process of addressing prohibited content/activity, and explain privacy, licensing, and policy concepts.

What is **prohibited content**? Any content stored on a company-owned or company-managed computer, mobile device, or network that is contrary to organizational policy.

What is **prohibited activity**? Any activity performed or received by a company-owned or company-managed computer, mobile device, or network that is contrary to organizational policy.

Incident Response

How you follow up on an incident is a good measure of your capability to an organization. **Incident response** is the set of procedures that any investigator follows when examining a technology incident. How you first respond, how you document the situation, and your ability to establish a chain of custody are all important to your investigating skills.

> **NOTE**   Some suggested resources:
>
> - Responding to IT Security Incidents: https://technet.microsoft.com/en-us/library/cc700825.aspx
>
> - CERT's Incident Management website: www.cert.org/incident-management/
>
> - Computer Security Incident Handling Guide—National Institute of Standards and Technology (U.S. Department of Commerce): http://nvlpubs.nist.gov/nistpubs/SpecialPublications/NIST.SP.800-61r2.pdf.

First Response

When you first respond to an incident, your first task is to identify exactly what happened. You must first **identify** whether this is a simple problem that needs troubleshooting or an incident that needs to be escalated.

For example, if you encounter a person who has prohibited content on a computer, this can be considered an incident, and as part of **first response**, you will be expected to escalate the issue to your supervisor, reporting on exactly what you have found. Copyrighted information, malware, inappropriate content, and stolen information could all be considered prohibited. So before you *do* anything as a result of your findings, you should **report through proper channels**, and then take steps to ensure **data/device preservation**. This often means making a backup of the computer's image using special software. However, this will depend on your organization's policies. You might be told to leave everything as is and wait for a computer forensics expert or a security analyst; it depends on the scenario. The idea here is that the scene be preserved for that other person so that he or she can collect evidence.

Documentation

You want to document everything that you find, and anything that happens after that. If your organization doesn't have any other methodology, write it down and/or take pictures! When you leave the scene you will be required to divulge any and all information to your supervisor. If you were able to fix the problem and no other specialists were required, the **documentation** process will continue through to the completion of the task and beyond when you monitor the system. You should also document any processes, procedures, and user training that might be necessary for the future.

Chain of Custody

If you are required to preserve evidence, one way of doing this is to set up a **chain of custody**. This is the chronological documentation or paper trail of evidence. It should be initiated at the start of any investigation, and include **tracking of evidence/documenting process**, who had custody of the evidence all the way up to litigation (if necessary), and verifies that the evidence has not been modified or tampered with.

> **NOTE**   As a PC tech, you will usually not get too involved with investigations. But you should know the basic concepts of first response, documentation, and chain of custody for the exam, and in the case that you find yourself in a situation where you have found prohibited content or illegal activities.

Licensing/DRM/EULA

Software **licensing** issues of all types can complicate your life as a PC tech. It's important to realize that carelessness with licensing could put your company in financial and legal jeopardy.

Some issues to watch out for include:

- The limitations created by Digital Rights Management (DRM)
- End user license agreements
- Open source versus commercial licenses
- Personal license versus enterprise licenses

DRM

Digital rights management (**DRM**) is the general term for software or service mechanisms that limit the end-user's rights to copy, transfer, or use software or digital media. Some examples of DRM include:

- Restrictions on digital music playback when the music has been burned to an audio CD, such as with Apple iTunes
- Limits on the number of systems that can use an application at the same time, such as Adobe Creative Cloud or Microsoft Office 365

When upgrading a system that is running DRM-based apps, it's important to determine in advance how the upgrade might affect DRM issues. In some cases, moving to a new OS might be transparent to the DRM, while in other cases, DRM might require the user to confirm the license.

When removing a system that is running DRM-based apps from service, it's important to determine in advance how to properly move the DRM-based apps or DRM-limited files to another system. It might be necessary to remove authorization from the system before a new system can be authorized to use the app.

EULA

The end-user license agreement (**EULA**) restricts how an app can be used and what the transfer rights might be. If an app was preinstalled on a system, its licensing might not allow for the app to be moved to another system. Be sure to check the EULA for a particular app or for an operating system with bundled apps to determine what can legally be done with the operating system and apps when the original computer is withdrawn from service or upgraded to a new operating system.

Understanding Open Source and Commercial Licenses

According to the Open Source Initiative website:

"Generally, **Open Source** software is software that can be freely accessed, used, changed, and shared (in modified or unmodified form) by anyone. Open source software is made by many people, and distributed under licenses that comply with The Open Source Definition." (https://opensource.org/osd)

Linux operating system distributions (known as "distros") and Linux apps are some of the most well-known examples of open source-licensed software.

Open source software can be used for commercial purposes, and even sold. However, open source licenses do not permit the sellers of open source software from limiting the rights of purchasers to use, change, or share the software. The rights obtained when Company A, for example, starts using Software X must be passed on to Company B when Company A sells any version of Software X, and so on. These rights include source code.

The Open Source Initiative website offers a variety of OSI-approved licenses that can be used as models for licensing at https://opensource.org/licenses.

Most commercial software other than open source, can be called "closed source." For example, Microsoft Windows, Apple OS X, Adobe Creative Cloud, and Microsoft Office are examples of operating systems and apps that use **commercial licenses**. Unlike an open source license, which permits free use, modification, and sharing of source code, commercial licenses do not cover source code (the actual instructions used to make the software) and limit how licensees can use object code (the program).

Here are two examples:

- Windows 10 Pro, Enterprise, and Education include downgrade rights to earlier versions of Windows. This is a useful feature for organizations that must continue to use earlier versions of Windows on some systems and for some tasks. OEM preinstalled versions of Windows 10 Pro can be downgraded to Windows 8.1 Pro or Windows 7 Professional. On the other hand, volume-licensed versions of Windows 10 Pro, Enterprise, or Education offer downgrade rights to versions of Windows back to Windows 95 and Windows 2000 Professional!

- Adobe Creative Cloud subscriptions can be used on two computers (but not at the same time: for example, a work and a home or travel computer). If a third computer has Adobe Creative Cloud installed, Adobe permits Creative Cloud apps to run on the additional device if the other computers' licenses are deactivated by Creative Cloud. The same process allows the original computer to use Creative Cloud when the user is at that system.

When installing software with commercial licenses, be sure to observe the requirements of the software license. If you are asked by an end user to violate the terms when installing an OS or app, escalate the matter to a supervisor who can work with the software vendor to determine a suitable solution.

Personal versus Enterprise Licenses

Personal licenses are the software licenses provided for computers purchased at retail or online stores and downloaded or packaged apps designed for use by individuals. Essentially, these licenses limit the use of the software to one or a very small number of computers in the same household (for example, antivirus utilities designed for up to five Windows, OS X, or mobile devices).

Enterprise licenses can differ from personal software licenses in several ways:

- Software covered by enterprise licenses includes management and security features designed for the enterprise

- Software covered by enterprise licenses have much different rules for software upgrades than personal-licensed software

- Software covered by enterprise licenses may be licensed per seat, per device, per processor, or in other ways.

Some personal software licenses, such as for Microsoft Office Home and Student, are specifically restricted from use in business.

Be sure to follow the licensing terms for the software you are installing for your clients or company. Escalate the issue to a supervisor when you believe you are being asked to violate the terms of a license.

Personally Identifiable Information

Personally Identifiable Information (sometimes abbreviated as PII) such as a person's name, address, driver's license number, credit card numbers, and Social Security number are widely stored in many types of information systems:

- Government databases

- Medical databases

- Employee databases

- Electronic commerce databases (credit and debit cards, bank and credit union records)

Any organization that holds or uses this type of information has responsibility for protecting it from identity thieves. As a computer technician, what is your role in protecting this data? Here are some examples:

- Configure systems to use secure cloud storage rather than locally stored sensitive information on laptops and mobile devices.

- Configure and use strong encryption on wireless networks. Don't overlook point-of-sale (POS) systems.

- Use full-disk encryption such as BitLocker, BitLocker To Go or similar products on laptops and mobile devices that store or access sensitive data.

- Configure hardware and software firewalls to protect sensitive data.

- Educate users on methods to remove personally identifiable information from documents, photos, and other files that might be shared or posted online.

In Microsoft Word, use the Inspect Documents feature (available from the File menu) to inspect a document for personally identifiable information and other metadata (see Figure 17-6).

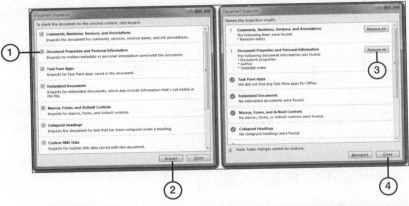

1. By default, document properties and personal information are on the list of items checked by Document Inspector
2. Click or tap to inspect the document
3. Click or tap to remove all document properties and personal information
4. Click or tap to close Document Inspector

Figure 17-6   Using the Inspect Documents feature in Microsoft Word 2013 to look for personally identifiable information.

Figure 17-7 compares the same document's properties before and after using the Remove All button to clear document properties and personal information.

NOTE   Metadata, including geotags and EXIF (exchangeable image file) information about camera settings, is also stored in Adobe Acrobat (PDF) and most types of image files. To learn how to remove this information, see http://www.cnet.com/how-to/remove-metadata-from-office-files-pdfs-and-images/.

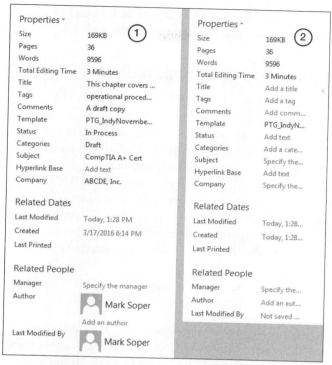

1. Document properties before running Document Inspector
2. Document properties after running Document Inspector and
   using it to clear personal information

Figure 17-7   Document properties (left) are removed (right) by using the Remove All button in Document Inspector.

Following Corporate End-User Policies and Security Best Practices

As have seen in this chapter, computers and networks can pose significant risks to privacy if not properly managed. As you work with computers, mobile devices, and peripherals, be sure to:

- Enforce corporate **end-user policies** (such as prohibited activities, bring-your-own-device issues, password policies, and Group Policy restrictions).

- Follow **security best practices** (such as installing and updating antimalware apps, training users on how to avoid infections from email and websites, and using encryption technologies for sensitive information).

If you work for an organization that has weak or non-existent policies and practices, you might want to encourage your supervisors to develop effective policies.

Communication Methods and Professionalism

Passing the A+ Certification exams isn't an end in itself—it is designed to help start (or advance) your Information Technology (IT) career. In most IT careers, how you deal with customers, whether they're people you see day after day in your company or clients you might see only once or twice, can have as much of an impact on your career progress as your knowledge of hardware, software, firmware, operating systems, and security. According to pop-culture references like the popular TV show *The Big Bang Theory*, the *Dilbert* comic strip, and innumerable others, technology professionals are incapable of relating to "normal" people in either social or professional situations. Unfortunately, these comic stereotypes are based on a lot of real-world data. The following sections help you master the "soft skills" you need to move up in the computing world.

Use Proper Language

What is **proper language**? Language that helps customers understand what is going on. Speak clearly and in a simple, concise manner. Use proper English and no **slang**. Avoid computer **jargon** and **acronyms** such as "WPA2" or "TCP/IP." They often confuse the customer.

Maintain a Positive Attitude/Project Confidence

Customers watch you as you work on their problems, and they can lose confidence in you and your employer when you sound or look worried. Don't be arrogant (in other words, don't reject or brush aside questions and comments), but maintain the attitude that the problem will be solved. After all, you have your personal experience, the resources of your company, and abundant resources are available from software and hardware vendors, and numerous forums and newsgroups to help you solve problems.

Actively Listen to the Customer

Mind your manners! The keys to getting information from your customer include **active listening** (taking notes and encouraging open-ended answers) and not interrupting the customer. Listen carefully to what the person has to say about the problem she is experiencing. This should offer clues as to the reason for the problem. Even when the customer admits to being a nontechnical person or even a technophobe, listen carefully.

Be Culturally Sensitive

Nations, organizations, and departments all have cultures: ways of communicating, rituals to follow, and definitions of good manners. **Cultural sensitivity** helps prevent barriers to good communications. Be sure to use the appropriate honorific titles (Mr., Ms., Mrs., and so on), pick up visual and verbal cues, and use **professional titles** when applicable (doctor, professor, and so on). When a person has an accent and is hard to understand, concentrate harder, and ask the person to repeat anything that you didn't understand.

Be Punctual

Punctuality is probably the most important thing when it comes to customer relationships. If you have to be late, contact the customer. You might also consider contacting your supervisor depending on how late you are.

Avoid Distractions

Don't let your cell phone, the big game on the big-screen TV, or the view out the corner office window get between you and a solution: avoid distractions and/or interruptions when talking with customers. Stay focused on what your customer is telling you, and the solution will be easier to find. Don't talk with other co-workers while interacting with customers. Don't use **social media** sites or use **texting** for non-work related issues; when you send a text to ask for help, make sure your customer knows why you are sending a text. Avoid personal interruptions unless it's an emergency. Save personal calls for breaks or when the job is finished.

Dealing with Difficult Customers or Situations

Solving technology problems is difficult, and customers can make it harder. What makes it easier? Following these tips:

- No matter how tough the problem (or the customer), **avoid arguing with customers and don't be defensive**—Your job is to solve the customer's problem. To do that, you need to work with the customer. Get it? Got it? Good!

- **No matter how many times you've seen the same problem, do not minimize customers' problems**—Sure, you might have seen a couple of dozen instances of drive failure, for example, but keep in mind that every person with a dead drive has lost valuable personal or business data—maybe even enough of a loss to wipe out a business. You wouldn't want your handyman or mechanic acting as if your house or car problems were trivial—don't act as if your customers' problems are trivial, either.

- **No matter how incorrect their actions or poor their judgment, avoid being judgmental of your customers, and while you're at it, drop the insults and name-calling**—Declaring "war" on your customers just adds to everyone's stress level and doesn't get you any closer to a solution. Even if the customer decides to call your ancestry or intelligence into question, avoid responding in kind. "Fight the real enemy"—the computer problem!

- **Clarify customer statements**—Ask the customer **open-ended questions** to further identify what the issue is and narrow the **scope of the problem**. After you think you understand what the problem is, you should always clarify by repeating the problem back to the customer. Restate the issue to verify everyone's understanding of the problem.

- **Don't share your experiences on social media**—No selfies with the IT director or photos of somebody's messy office. No snarky comments about the number of unread e-mail messages on a customer's computer. Your job is to get the customer's problem fixed, not provide Facebook posts or Twitter tweets.

Setting and Meeting Expectations/Timeline and Communicating with the Customer

The process of setting **customer expectations** starts early and continues as the process of solving their problem continues. When you understand what the problem is, state how you plan to fix it and how long it will take. Create a **timeline** of the steps and when you expect to meet them and communicate your status with the customer often.

- If applicable, offer different **repair/replacement** options and allow the customer to select the one that fits his needs best.

- Provide and organize proper **documentation** of any services and products you offer. After the job is complete, document the problem, process, and solution.

- Follow up with the customer at a later date to verify that they are still satisfied.

Dealing Appropriately with Customers' Confidential and Private Materials

Whether you are working in the customer's office or at your workbench, remember that you are a guest and that the customer's computer information, printouts, and other information is the customer's: keep it private, don't snoop, and don't share it!

If possible, ask your customer to move **confidential materials** such as bank statements, accounting information, legal documents, and other top secret company information to another area. **Private materials** belonging to the customer personally should also be moved out of the way.

Exam Preparation Tasks

Review All the Key Topics

Review the most important topics in the chapter, noted with the key topics icon in the outer margin of the page. Table 17-3 provides a reference to these key topics and the page numbers on which each is found.

Table 17-3 Key Topics for Chapter 17

Key Topic Element	Description	Page Number
Figure 17-2	Electrical tester	884
Figure 17-4	Using an ESD strap	887
Section	Addressing Prohibited Content or Activity	899
Paragraph	Communication Methods and Professionalism	906

Complete the Tables and Lists from Memory

Print a copy of Appendix C, "Memory Tables" (found on the CD), or at least the section for this chapter, and complete the tables and lists from memory. Appendix D, "Answers to Memory Tables," also on the CD, includes completed tables and lists to check your work.

Define Key Terms

Define the following key terms from this chapter, and check your answers in the glossary.

antistatic bag, ESD strap, ESD mat, self-grounding, toxic waste handling, battery, toner, CRT, lifting techniques, electrical fire safety, cable management, safety goggles, air filter mask, compliance with local government regulations, material safety data sheet (MSDS), ventilation, power surges, brownout, blackout, battery backup, surge suppressor, protection from airborne particles, enclosures, dust and debris, compressed air, vacuums, incident response, first response, report through proper channels, chain of custody, tracking of evidence/documenting process, licensing, DRM, EULA, open source, commercial license, personal license, enterprise license, Personally Identifiable Information, end-user policies, security best practices, prohibited content, prohibited activity, jargon, acronyms, slang, active listening, cultural sensitivity, professional titles, punctuality, texting, social media, judgmental, open-ended questions, scope of the problem, customer expectations, timeline, re-pair/replacement, documentation, confidential materials, private materials.

Complete Hands-On Labs

Complete the hands-on labs, and then see the answers and explanations at the end of the chapter.

Lab 17-1: Safety and Environmental Policies and Procedures

Evaluate the ESD safeguards in your workplace.

- Are ESD bands and mats available?
- Is antistatic material (bags, foam, bubble wrap) available when needed to protect equipment?
- When these items are not available, determine what would be needed to provide ESD protection. Don't overlook reuse of antistatic bags from new equipment.

Evaluate toxic waste policy in your workplace.

- Are MSDSs available for potentially hazardous materials?

If not, look up the appropriate websites.

- Are obsolete electronics recycled?
- Are worn-out batteries collected for recycling?

If not, research local companies in your area that could perform recycling safely and in accordance with local government regulations.

Evaluate potential hazards:

- Are cables managed safely?
- Are Class C or other electrical/electronic rated fire extinguishers handy?
- Are safety goggles, ventilators, and air filtering equipment available if needed?

Evaluate surge suppressors and UPS systems:

- Do any of these units have indications of failures (burnt outlets, case cracks, warning lights)? If so, request replacements.

- What are the joule ratings of the surge suppressors in your workplace?

Ask your supervisor if it would be acceptable to mark in-service dates on surge suppressor or battery backup hardware if it is not already being done.

Lab 17-2: Prohibited Content, Licensing, Removing Personally Identifiable Content, and Professional Behavior

Does your organization have a policy for addressing prohibited content or activity? If so, have you and your supervisor read and discussed it? If not, consider offering the resources in this chapter as guides to the development of such a policy.

Which type(s) of licensing does your organization use for operating systems and applications?

Create a Microsoft Word document and save it. Turn on Track Changes, make some edits, and save the changes. Copy a picture from a digital camera or smartphone. Look for the personally identifiable information in both files. With a photo, use the Details tab in the file's properties sheet (Windows) to observe camera information, settings, and other material. Follow the guidelines in this chapter to remove that information.

Review your recent customer interactions. Have you been following the best practices recommended, or have you had issues with language, slang or jargon, not actively listening, and so on?

Answer Review Questions

1. Identify the parts of the plug in the following figure.

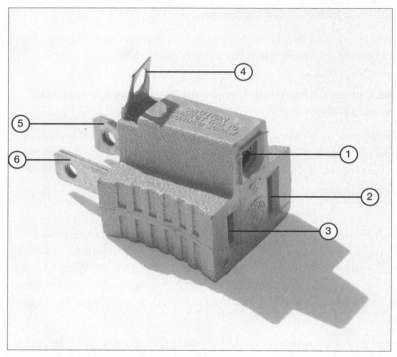

A. Hot prong

B. Hot connector

C. Neutral prong

D. Neutral connector

E. Ground loop

F. Ground connector

2. The object in the following figure is an electrical outlet tester. What does this outlet tester tell you about the outlet into which it is currently plugged?

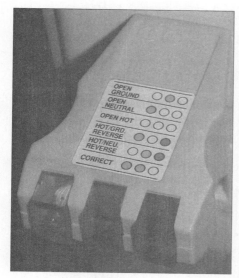

    A. The ground wire is faulty.

    B. The hot wire is faulty.

    C. The neutral wire is faulty.

    D. All of the wires are correct.

3. Which of the following statements best defines ESD?

    A. Electronic shutdown device

    B. Electrostatic discharge

    C. Environmentally sustainable development

    D. Energy sensitive differential

4. Which of the following can be used as protection against ESD? (Choose all that apply.)

    A. An antistatic bag

    B. A three-wire to two-wire adapter

    C. An ESD mat

    D. An ESD strap

5. Which of the following increases the likelihood of ESD?

    A. Carpet on the floor

    B. Increasing the humidity of the room

    C. Increasing the room temperature

    D. Rubber-soled shoes

6. Which of the following best describes how to dispose of used batteries?

   A. Open the battery and very carefully remove the lead core before recycling.

   B. Recycle batteries in the recycling bin.

   C. Recycle NiMH and Li-Ion in the recycling bin; NiCad batteries can be disposed of in the trash.

   D. Return the batteries to an electronics store for recycling.

7. Which of the following is a hazard posed by a CRT monitor?

   A. A CRT presents an electrical shock hazard.

   B. A CRT presents a fire hazard from overheating.

   C. A CRT presents a radiation hazard through the CRT display screen.

   D. A CRT presents toxic chemical hazard.

8. Which class of fire extinguisher should be used on an electrical fire?

   A. Class A

   B. Class B

   C. Class C

   D. Class D

9. When selecting an air filter mask, which category provides you with the highest level of protection?

   A. A

   B. N

   C. P

   D. R

10. Which of the following statements best describes an MSDS?

   A. An MSDS provides simultaneous accessibility to multiple data sources.

   B. An MSDS provides safety information concerning storage, spills, and accidental exposure to dangerous chemicals.

   C. An MSDS helps protect computer components from damage due to ESD.

   D. An MSDS is a legal document used to establish chain of custody in legal cases.

11. A short increase in AC voltage is known as which of the following?

   A. Blackout

   B. Brownout

   C. Whiteout

   D. Power surge

12. Which of the following best describes the function of a UPS in a technology environment?

   A. UPS is a battery backup.

   B. UPS is a rating for system performance.

   C. UPS is a security program.

   D. UPS is a package delivery company.

13. Which of the following best describes chain of custody?

   A. Chain of custody is documentation of the ownership of a computer or of computer components.

   B. Chain of custody is documentation of who was in possession of evidence relative to an investigation.

   C. Chain of custody is documentation of how a computer was repaired, such as what was done and who did it.

   D. Chain of custody is documentation of possession of a computer, not related to ownership.

14. Which of the following best describes open source software? (Choose all that apply.)

   A. Open source software can be used for free.

   B. Open source software can be used for commercial purposes.

   C. Open source software can be sold.

   D. Open source software can be modified.

15. As a computer technician, what can you do to help your clients protect their personal information? (Choose all that apply.)

   A. You can advise them to store their sensitive information using cloud storage instead of local storage.

   B. You can advise them to use BitLocker encryption.

   C. You can advise them to store sensitive information on a PC's hard drive rather than with the backup files.

   D. You can advise them to use firewalls to prevent hacker intrusions.

16. Which of the following statements describes the best way to explain a problem to the customer?

   A. Use as much technical vocabulary as possible because this makes you sound knowledgeable and will impress the customer.

   B. Explain as little as possible because the customer probably would not understand the explanation and it would only confuse him.

   C. Explain the problem in non-technical terms and offer to show him what the problem was and how you fixed it.

   D. Ask the customer to not be concerned about the details and you will take care of the problem.

Answers and Explanations to Hands-On Labs

Lab 17-1: Safety and Environmental Policies and Procedures

ESD bands and mats can wear out over time. When an ESD band cannot fit tightly around a user's wrist or cannot snap reliably to the cable that attaches it to equipment, it should be replaced. When an ESD mat has holes or cuts, it should be replaced.

Antistatic bags can be reused and remain effective as long as they are not torn. Discard torn bags. Bags can be purchased if there are not enough bags for equipment.

All types of material have MSDS, including inkjet cartridges, cleaning supplies, and so on.

Many localities have drop-off points for worn-out rechargeable batteries. Some manufacturers are now producing batteries from recycled alkaline batteries. Contact your local environmental management agency for information on safe recycling of both types of batteries.

Hook and loop straps (Velcro brand and others) provide a low-cost way to temporarily manage cables. Hardware stores and specialty stores sell cable management enclosures.

To determine the joule rating for a particular surge suppressor, look up the model on the manufacturer's website. Keep in mind that the rating listed is for a new, never-in-service unit. The effective rating drops as the unit handles surges.

Lab 17-2: Prohibited Content, Licensing, Removing Personally Identifiable Content, and Professional Behavior

The older a policy on addressing prohibited content or activity is, the more likely it is to have omissions, such as social media comments (Facebook, Twitter, Instagram, and so on). Newer technologies should be considered for coverage when it is time to revise the policy.

When you reviewed the personally identifiable information in a Word document or photo, what surprised you the most about what you saw?

To improve your customer interactions, consider role-playing with another employee.

Answers and Explanations to Review Questions

1.
   - **A.** 6
   - **B.** 3
   - **C.** 5
   - **D.** 2
   - **E.** 4
   - **F.** 1

   The object in this diagram is a three-wire to two-wire (grounded to un-grounded) adapter. You should only use it when the ground loop is to be connected to a metal grounding device such as a water pipe.

2. **C.** In this diagram, the outlet is wired incorrectly. The left light is on and the center and right lights are off. According to the legend, this indicates that the outlet has an open neutral wire.

3. **B.** ESD or electrostatic discharge is the sudden release of static electricity from one object to another. We are not usually aware of the fact that static electricity has built up in our bodies and on the objects around us. When we come in contact with electronic computer components and the static electricity in our bodies discharges into them, those components can be seriously damaged.

4. **A, C, D.** Electronic components come packaged in antistatic bags and should be stored in them when they are not installed in a computer. Electrostatic mats and straps are used by technicians to safely handle computer components.

5. **A.** Carpet on the floor increases the likelihood of ESD, while a linoleum floor decreases it. Low humidity and low room temperature increase the likelihood of ESD, but increasing them will help to lower ESD. Rubber-soled shoes help to insulate the technician against ESD.

6. **D.** You should take all batteries to a recycling center. Many electronics stores will accept batteries for recycling. Never put batteries into the trash or even into a recycling bin.

7. **A.** A CRT monitor case should never be opened because it contains a capacitor that, if touched, can deliver a severe electric shock.

8. **C.** Use a Class C fire extinguisher for an electrical fire.

9. **C.** P = oil proof, R = oil resistant, N = not resistant to oil. A P100 mask is best giving nearly 100 percent protection against oil and non-oil particulate aerosols. An R95 mask is next with 95 percent protection against oil and non-oil particulate aerosols and then an N95 mask with 95 percent protection against non-oil particulate aerosols. There is no class A mask.

10. **B.** MSDS contains information about dangerous chemicals. It describes how to store them, how to clean up spills, and which type of treatment should be used when you are exposed to them.

11. **D.** A short increase in AC voltage is known as a power surge. A brownout is a large drop in voltage. A blackout is a total loss of power. A whiteout occurs in a snowstorm and has nothing to do with computers.

12. **A.** UPS stands for uninterruptable power supply. It is a battery backup that is used to power your system when the main AC power fails. A UPS is not designed to replace the AC power for a long period of time. It is only a backup battery. It is designed to keep your computer running long enough for you to shut down in an orderly manner so that your system does not crash.

13. **B.** A chain of custody documents who had possession of evidence relative to a legal investigation.

14. **A, B, C, D.** All of the options apply to open source software. Open source software may be freely used and it may be modified. It may be sold and it may be used for commercial purposes.

15. **A, B, D.** Storing sensitive information in cloud storage is more secure than storing it locally. BitLocker encryption encrypts the entire hard drive, not just selected files. You should install hardware and software firewalls to prevent intrusion. Files saved to a PC's hard drive, a laptop, or a backup file are all much more vulnerable to hackers than the other methods listed.

16. **C.** Much of the success of your business (and your employer's business) depends on your customer skills. It is one of the most valuable assets that you bring to the job. You should always treat your customer with respect, listen carefully to what he has to say, and explain what you are doing in clear, easy-to-understand terms. Never use a lot of technical jargon that he might not understand and never act aloof.

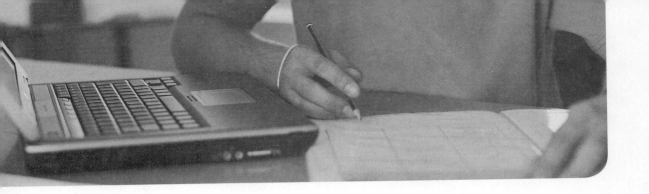

This chapter covers the following subjects:

- **Best Practices**—This section provides an overview of backup features, disk and system maintenance, system updates, patch management, driver and firmware updates, and antivirus and antimalware updates.

- **Tools**—Learn how to configure and use tools common to Linux and OS X: use backup and disk management utilities, restore snapshots and images, use the Terminal utility, use Screen Sharing, and use Force Quit.

- **Features**—Discover OS X features such as Mission Control, multiple desktops, Spotlight search, iCloud backup, Keychain network security, touchpad and Magic Mouse gestures, Finder file manager, Remote Disc access to another computer's CD or DVD drive, Dock app switcher, and Boot Camp OS X and Windows mutiboot utility.

- **Basic Linux Commands**—In this section, learn how to use commands for viewing folder contents (ls), performing plain-text searches (grep), change directory/folder (cd), shutting down shuts down system (shutdown), displaying current working folder (pwd), changing password (passwd), moving files (mv), copying files (cp), removing files (rm), changing permissions (chmod), changing file ownership (chown), viewing wired and wireless network configurations (iwconfig, ifconfig), running command as another user (sudo), switching accounts (su), installing or managing software packages (apt-get), editing files (vi), converting files or block copying files (dd).

## CHAPTER 18

OS X and Linux

Although OS X and Linux operating systems are far less common on organizational desktops than Windows, OS X is very popular in educational markets and Linux runs many of the world's servers. To be a well-rounded computer technician, you need to understand how these operating systems differ from Windows and from each other and be able to perform basic commands and maintenance procedures.

220-902: Objective 2.1 Identify common features and functionality of the Mac OS and Linux operating systems.

Foundation Topics

Best Practices

To maintain any computer system, you should follow these best practices:

- Scheduled backups
- Scheduled disk maintenance
- System updates/App store
- Patch management
- Driver/firmware updates
- Antivirus/antimalware updates

The following sections discuss how to put these best practices in use with OS X and Linux.

NOTE The objectives for the CompTIA A+ Certification exams refer to Mac OS. However, in this book, we use the term OS X, which has been Apple's official name for the operating system since the release of OS X 10.7 "Lion" in 2011.

Scheduled Backups

Scheduled backups help prevent major data loss in case of system failure, accident, or loss. Backups can be used to safeguard:

- Contacts
- Email
- Media files (photos, videos, music)
- Documents

The default backup app in OS X is **Time Machine**. Linux includes several utilities that can be used for backups. These include the command-line `tar` and `rsync` utilities. Others, including the `grsync` (GUI for rsync), `duplicity` (command-line, GUI available as Déjà Dup), and others are available from the repository for a Linux distribution or from the vendors.

> **NOTE** The BackupYourSystem page on Ubuntu Linux help (https://help.ubuntu.com/community/BackupYourSystem) provides a large list of command-line and GUI-based backup tools that also work with other Linux distros.

Scheduled backups should be run at times when the system is idle, such as overnight and on weekends.

Backup Types

A full backup backs up the entire contents of the computer or selected drive to another local or network location. Some backup programs create a compressed file to store backed-up information. With this type of backup, the backup program must run a restore utility to make the files usable again. Another type of backup program simply copies backup files to a different location, where they can be opened by the operating system.

Most backup programs can also run an incremental backup, which backs up only the files that have been created or changed after the last full backup.

Backup features to look for include:

- Compression—Reduces the amount of file space and often the amount of time needed to make a backup.

- Support for incremental as well as full backup—Good backup practice calls for periodic full backups followed by backups of changed files since the last full backup (incremental backups).

- Local and network backup destinations—Some backup utilities might require additional configuration before a network backup can be performed.

For more details about how to perform a backup, see "Backup/Time Machine" later in this chapter.

Scheduled Disk Maintenance

OS X does not require the user to schedule disk maintenance, as routine issues are fixed automatically by the operating system. In Linux, automated tasks of all types, including disk maintenance, can be set up and run by the `cron` utility. The `crontab` utility displays cron scripts by system or user.

Figure 18-1 illustrates a `crontab` that contains a command to back up user accounts at 5:00 AM daily.

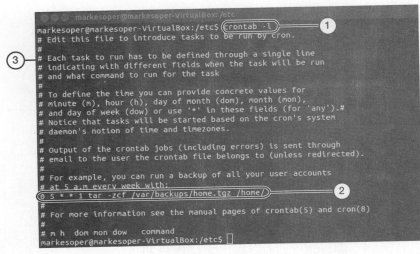

1. Use crontab –l to view and create tasks to be run by cron
2. Backup task to be run by cron
3. Pound sign is equivalent to REM (remark) statement. Remove it from a line that has a command you want to run

Figure 18-1   Crontab with cron script for daily backup.

System Updates/App Store

Linux distributions include a command-line system update tool such as dnf (Red Hat, Fedora) or apt-get (Debian, Ubuntu). Use these tools to update Linux, install apps, and to maintain the list of apps (packages) known to the OS. For more information about using apt-get, see "apt-get" later in this chapter.

If your Linux installation includes GNOME or KDE, it might include an update feature.

OS X has a variety of options for system updates in the App Store section of System Preferences (see Figure 18-2). The App Store can be configured to automatically check for updates for apps and OS X, automatically install updates, and download apps installed on other OS X devices under the same user account.

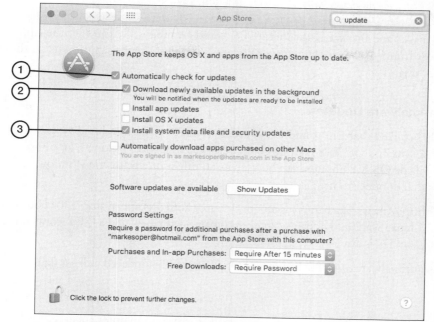

1. Automatic check for updates enabled
2. Automatic download of updates enabled; you decide when to install them
3. System data files and security updates are installed automatically

Figure 18-2   Configuring the OS X App Store to update OS X and apps.

Patch Management

If an organization only has a few Linux systems, running manual system updates with yum or apt-get may be sufficient for patch management. However, as the number of Linux systems increase, or when Linux systems are used for mission-critical functions such as web servers, better patch management methods are desirable.

If you use a script to check for and install updates to Linux or installed apps, the crontab utility can be used to set the task on a schedule that is run by the cron utility.

NOTE   To learn more about using crontab, see http://www.howtogeek.com/101288/how-to-schedule-tasks-on-linux-an-introduction-to-crontab-files/ and http://www.thegeekstuff.com/2009/06/15-practical-crontab-examples/.

Driver/Firmware Updates

In OS X, driver and firmware updates are delivered automatically through the App Store. Most Linux distros include driver updates as part of the distribution using the apt-get command.

Antivirus/Antimalware Updates

It's widely believed that Linux and OS X are immune to viruses and malware. Although Linux and OS X are not targeted nearly as much as Windows, an unprotected Linux or OS X computer can be used as an infection vector for Windows machines that connect to it.

ClamAV (http://www.clamav.net/) is an open-source antivirus app available for both OS X and Linux. Scans and updates can be automated with cron, and a GUI front end known as ClamTK is available.

Antivirus/antimalware apps for Linux and OS X should be updated at least daily.

Tools

Linux and OS X include a variety of applications for system maintenance, referred to here as "tools." The following sections discuss:

- Backup (Time Machine in OS X)
- Restore/Snapshot
- Image (Backup) Recovery
- Disk Maintenance Utilities
- Shell/Terminal
- Screen Sharing
- Force Quit (OS X)

Backup/Time Machine

Some Linux distros already have a backup utility installed, while others might not. OS X includes the Time Machine backup. However, both Linux and OS X must have their backup utilities configured and running to be useful in case of lost data.

Configuring Time Machine

OS X includes Time Machine, an automatic backup utility that creates daily backups and maintains weekly and monthly versions. To enable and configure Time Machine:

Step 1.   Connect a suitable external disk to an OS X system.

Step 2.   When prompted, click Use as Backup Disk. You can also check the Encrypt Backup Disk box to protect the backup (see Figure 18-3).

Step 3.   If you selected the option to encrypt your backup in Step 2, enter a password, confirm it, and enter a password hint. Click Encrypt Disk (see Figure 18-4).

Step 4.   Make sure Time Machine is turned on. After the selected disk is encrypted, the backup starts (see Figure 18-5).

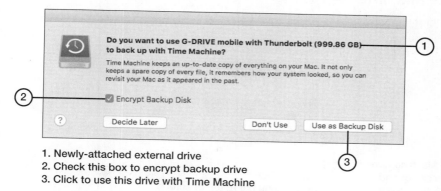

1. Newly-attached external drive
2. Check this box to encrypt backup drive
3. Click to use this drive with Time Machine

Figure 18-3   Selecting an external disk for use with Time Machine.

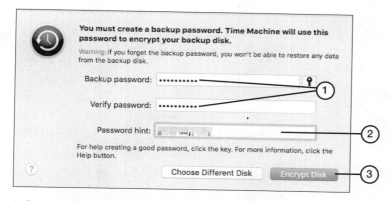

1. Create and confirm password for encrypted Time Machine drive
2. Enter a password hint
3. Click to start encryption of Time Machine drive

Figure 18-4   Encrypting the Time Machine disk.

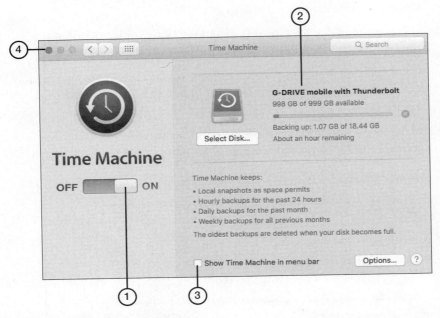

1. Time Machine turned on
2. Progress bar and backup disk information
3. Check box to put Time Machine on menu bar at top of screen
4. Click to close (Red) or minimize (Yellow) Time Machine menu

Figure 18-5   Creating a backup with Time Machine.

Time Machine is designed to back up user files automatically. However, to create a disk image that can be restored in case of disaster, use Disk Utility.

Using Disk Utility in OS X

Disk Utility can be started by pressing the Command+Spacebar keys and searching for Disk Utility, from Launchpad, or from Finder. To start Disk Utility at startup, press and hold Command+R keys until it starts.

Disk Utility (see Figure 18-6) can be used to create blank disk images that can be used as containers for other files, including image backups. It can also be used to erase non-OS X drives and prepare them for use with OS X.

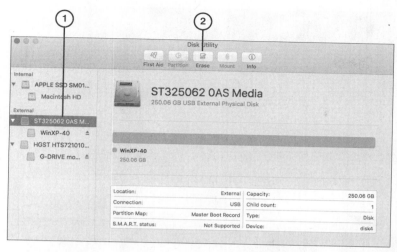

1. Click drive to erase
2. Click Erase to start process

Figure 18-6   Preparing to erase a disk for reuse with Disk Utility.

For details, see https://support.apple.com/kb/PH22247.

Configuring a Backup App in Linux

The Ubuntu 14 distribution has a preinstalled backup application that runs weekly and can also be configured to run daily. Backups can be kept as long as space permits or for at least six months or a year. This backup is designed for new users.

Backup utilities based on `tar`, `rdiff`, and other Linux apps can require a great deal of scripting. One backup utility that helps create backup scripts by filling in the blanks is `backupninja`, which includes `ninjahelper` as a front end (see Figure 18-7).

1. Select a backup job to create
2. Press OK to continue

Figure 18-7   Creating a backup job with backupninja's ninjahelper.

Restore/Snapshot

When a file is deleted from an OS X system, or a different version of an existing file is needed, you can restore a file from a Time Machine backup:

Step 1.   Open a **Finder** window where the restored file belongs (skip this step to restore to the Desktop).

Step 2.   Open **Time Machine** from **Dock**.

Step 3.   Scroll through the backups shown to find the file(s) to restore.

Step 4.   Select the file(s) to restore and click **Restore** (see Figure 18-8).

The file is restored to its original location.

When Time Machine is enabled on an OS X laptop, backups known as **snapshots** are stored on the laptop's system drive as well as on the Time Machine external drive. Backups can also be restored from snapshots.

To restore a file from a Linux backup, see the documentation for the backup app being used.

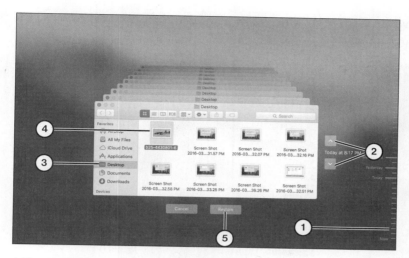

1. Time Machine backup stored locally
2. Select backup to view
3. Select backup location
4. Click file(s) to restore
5. Click to restore selected files

Figure 18-8   Preparing to restore a file with Time Machine.

Image Recovery

OS X offers several types of **image recovery** options:

- After you create an image with Disk Utility, the image can be restored using Edit > Restore. For details, see https://support.apple.com/kb/PH22250.

- Disk Utility can also be used to reinstall OS X. If the Recovery System is available from the Startup drive, the latest edition of OS X is reinstalled. However, if the Recovery System has been deleted or is not available, you must use Internet Recovery. Internet Recovery installs the same edition of OS X originally installed on your system. You can then update it to the latest edition. For details, see https://support.apple.com/en-us/HT201314.

To recover an image with a Linux backup utility, see the utility's documentation for details.

Disk Maintenance Utilities

OS X's Disk Utility app includes options for repairing drives with First Aid. First Aid (see Figure 18-9) can repair problems with the file system, partitions, and other issues. With OS X versions prior to El Capitan, First Aid also repairs file permissions. In El Capitan, file permissions are automatically protected.

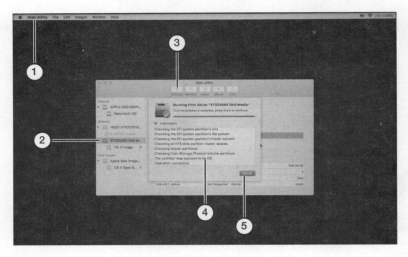

1. Menu bar
2. Selected drive
3. Click First Aid to test drive
4. Results
5. Click Done to complete process

Figure 18-9   OS X's First Aid after a successful disk test.

Some useful disk maintenance commands for the Linux Terminal mode include:

- `df -h` —lists files and free space in a computer

- `>directory path/filename` —removes the contents of the specified file without removing the file itself

- `ls -lsr | tail -5` —Finds the five largest files in the current directory

NOTE   For additional commands, see http://www.azanweb.com/en/linux-most-useful-commands-for-file-system-maintenance/.

Shell/Terminal

OS X and Linux both include **shell/terminal** apps that open a command-line environment. The Linux Terminal utility is used to run commands, scripts, and programs without a GUI (see "Basic Linux Commands," later in this chapter). OS X also has a Terminal utility that supports many of the same commands. Figure 18-10 illustrates the OS X El Capitan Terminal running pmset -g batt to display battery charge percentage in the Terminal command line.

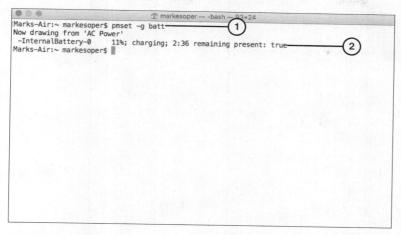

1. Command
2. Result

Figure 18-10   OS X's Terminal in action.

Screen Sharing

OS X includes support for **Screen Sharing**, which enables local users on the network or remote uses running virtual network computing (VNC) to control the screen for training or troubleshooting (see Figure 18-11). Screen Sharing and other types of sharing (file, printer, Internet, Bluetooth, and remote apps) are configured through the Sharing section of System Preferences.

Linux also supports screen sharing, sometimes using the term *VNC* or *Remote Desktop Viewer*. To see if a Linux installation has screen sharing, search for VNC or Remote.

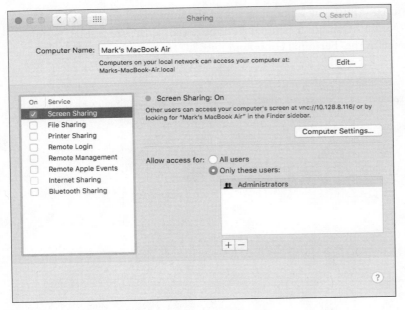

Figure 18-11 Configuring Screen Sharing in OS X.

Force Quit

The **Force Quit** feature in OS X and Linux enables the user to shut down a malfunctioning app.

Force Quit in OS X

To open the Force Quit applications from the keyboard, press Command+Option+Esc keys.

Force Quit can also be started from the menu bar: open the Apple menu and select Force Quit. You can also point at the app's icon in the Dock (bottom of the screen) and right-click or click and hold it to bring up a menu with Quit as an option.

From the Force Quit menu, select the app to stop (see Figure 18-12).

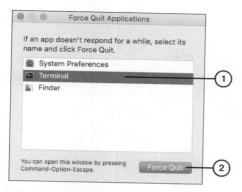

1. Select an app to force quit
2. Click Force Quit to close it

Figure 18-12   Using Force Quit on OS X.

Force Quit in OS X or Linux Terminal

To force quit an app from the Terminal in either OS X or Linux, enter top to see a list of process IDs (PIDs) and the apps they represent. Press q to quit. To kill an app by specifying its PID, enter the command kill *xxx* (where *xxx* is the PID number).

Figure 18-13 illustrates this process.

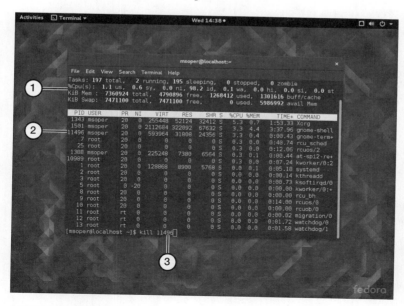

1. General output from top
2. Processes listed by PID
3. Command to kill PID 11496 (terminal)

Figure 18-13   Running kill from a Terminal session in Linux (Fedora 23 Workstation).

Features

Although OS X can run many of the same commands from Terminal as Linux, it isn't Linux, and it has many features that have no Linux counterpart. You can think of the following sections as a "Survivor's guide to OS X." Understand these and you won't be an expert, but you'll be able to work much more comfortably around the OS X laptops and desktops that are often found in the more creative sides of a company's IT infrastructure.

Multiple Desktops/Mission Control

Mission Control (see Figure 18-14) displays all apps open on the desktop so you can copy or move them between different desktops. It is very helpful when working with multiple displays.

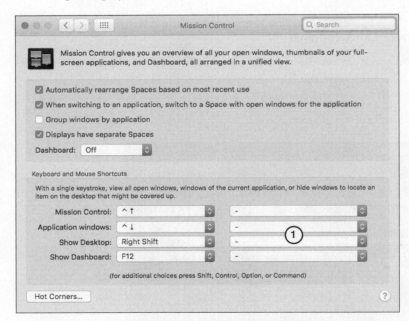

1. Keyboard and mouse shortcuts for viewing Mission Control, Dashboard, application windows, and the Desktop

Figure 18-14   Configuring keyboard and mouse shortcuts in Mission Control.

Spotlight

Spotlight is the OS X search tool for files, apps, photos, web results, movie listings, and more (see Figure 18-15) Open Spotlight by pressing the Command+spacebar keys.

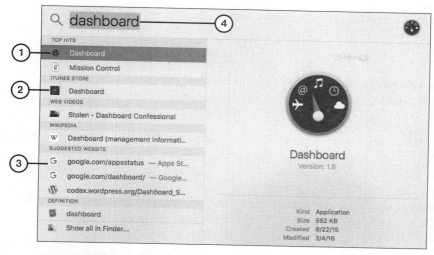

1. Top hits (content on system)
2. iTunes matches
3. Web content matches
4. Search term

Figure 18-15 Searching for "dashboard" finds matches on this computer, iTunes, and the Internet.

iCloud

OS X uses **iCloud** cloud storage for photo sharing, document and data storage, and Find My Mac (see Figure 18-16). When iCloud for Photos is enabled, it enables the user to see a photo stream from other iCloud devices, such as iPads, iPods, and iPhones.

1. Enable Find My Mac when you open iCloud for the first time

Figure 18-16 Use Find My Mac is an optional feature in iCloud. Click the empty checkbox to turn it on.

For more details, see http://www.apple.com/icloud/.

Keychain

Use iCloud **Keychain** to safely store Safari usernames and passwords, credit card information, and Wi-Fi network information (requires iOS 7.0.3 or later, OS X 10.9 or later).

For more details, see https://support.apple.com/en-us/HT204085.

Gestures

OS X supports a wide variety of **gestures** on both touchpads (known as trackpads on OS X) and Apple's Magic Mouse. Here are some of the gestures supported on trackpads:

- Open Launchpad by pinching close with four or five fingers.
- Switch between full-screen apps by left-swiping or right-swiping with three or four fingers.
- Open Mission Control by swiping up with two fingers.

Open Trackpad in the System Preferences folder for more gestures and options.

The Magic Mouse has a touch-sensitive cover, so it can also be used with gestures:

- Hold down the Control key and scroll with one finger to make items on-screen larger.
- Switch between apps by left-swiping or right-swiping with two fingers.

Open Mouse in the System Preferences folder for more gestures and options.

NOTE   More information on trackpad, Magic Trackpad for OS X desktops, and Magic Mouse is available at https://support.apple.com/kb/PH18431.

Finder

Finder is OS X's file manager. In Figure 18-17, Finder displays the contents of the Applications folder and is preparing to perform an operation on the App Store folder.

1. Selected folder.
2. Size of all apps in the selected folder
3. Options for the selected folder

Figure 18-17   Using Finder to work with the Applications folder.

For more details, see https://support.apple.com/en-us/HT201732.

Remote Disc

Remote Disc enables access to files from a CD or DVD on another computer on your OS X computer. However, you cannot burn a disc or delete files from a remote disc. To share a CD or DVD from a Windows system, install DVD or CD Sharing Update 1.0 for Windows from the Apple website.

For more details, see https://support.apple.com/en-us/HT203973.

Dock

OS X uses **Dock** (see Figure 18-18) to display and switch between running apps along the bottom of the display. You can adjust the magnification of the selected app, where Dock is located on screen, and other window controls.

For more details, see https://support.apple.com/en-us/HT201730.

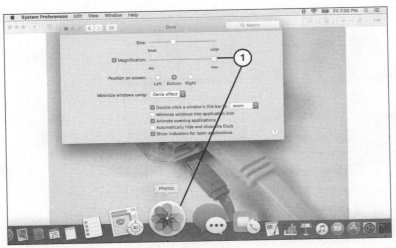

1. Configures the zooming effect as you move your mouse or trackpad pointer along the apps in Dock.

Figure 18-18   Adjusting Dock's settings.

Boot Camp

Boot Camp is the OS X multiboot utility for installing Windows on an OS X computer. For details on how to install Windows on a Mac using Boot Camp, see https://support.apple.com/en-us/HT201468.

Basic Linux Commands

With more and more Linux systems showing up on corporate networks, and with OS X being based in part on Linux, it's important for computer technicians to understand basic Linux commands. The commands in the following sections are the ones you might be tested on.

To use these commands, open a Terminal session. Some commands must be run as root user (log in as root or use sudo to run command as root).

NOTE   There are many additional options for these commands. Linux distributions ("distros") contain a manual (manpages) with options for each command. To view it or print it, use the command man. To learn more, see www.linfo.org/man.html. To view manpages for Ubuntu (one of the most popular distros) online, see http://man-pages.ubuntu.com/.

ls

ls is the OS X and Linux equivalent to the Windows command dir. Use `ls -l` to list the contents of a directory (folder) including permissions and other information (see Figure 18-19).

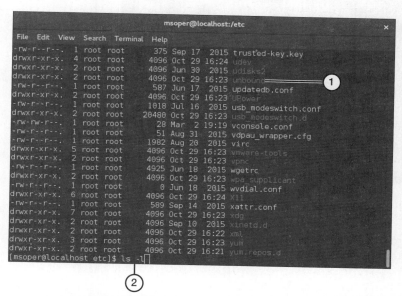

1. Directories are listed in blue
2. Press the up-arrow key to repeat the last command; press it again to repeat the previous one, and so on

Figure 18-19   Using ls -l in Fedora 23 Workstation.

grep

Use **grep** to perform text searches. The grep command line specifies what to search for and where to search.

Grep can be used to find a specified word in one or more specified files. Grep normally searches for exact matches (Linux and OS X are case-sensitive), but can be configured to ignore case with -i.

Grep supports recursive searching (all files in directories [folders] beneath the current directory).

In Figure 18-20, grep is used to search for the word *model* in the /proc/cpuinfo directory (folder).

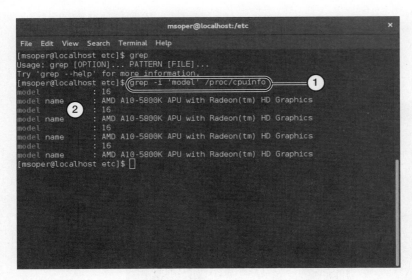

1. Searching for the word *model*
2. Matches

Figure 18-20   Searching for specific text in a folder using `grep`.

cd

Use **cd** to change directories (folders). The syntax is different than in the Windows command-line in that Linux uses this slash: /, while Windows uses this slash: \

- Use `cd /etc` to change to the /etc folder

- Use `cd ..` to move up one level

shutdown

Use **shutdown** to shut down the system. In Figure 18-21, `shutdown` is used along with options to specify when to shut down and to broadcast a warning message. Note that the `sudo` command is part of the command because `shutdown` requires root access.

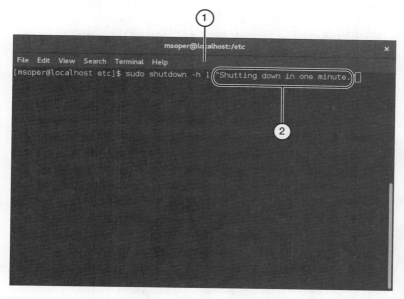

1. One minute (1) to shutdown
2. Message broadcast to all systems logged in to this computer

Figure 18-21   Preparing to shut down the system.

pwd vs. passwd

These two commands can be easily confused. Keep in mind:

- **pwd**—displays name of the current/working directory
- **passwd**—starts the password change process.

mv

Use **mv** to move files to a specified location: `mv thisfile.ext destination-folder`.

cp

Use **cp** to copy files to a specified location (`cp filename /folder/subfolder`) or to a different name in the same folder (`cp -i origfile copiedfile`). Use the `-i` option to be prompted in case the command would overwrite a file.

rm

Use **rm** to remove (delete) files from the system (`rm filename`). Make sure the file is not in use!

chmod

Use **chmod** to change permissions of files and directories using the syntax `chmod permissions filename`. In Figure 18-22, `chmod` is used to change permissions on the file test. The numbers that are used stand for different permissions. To learn more about these values, see the Chmod Calculator at http://chmod-calculator.com/.

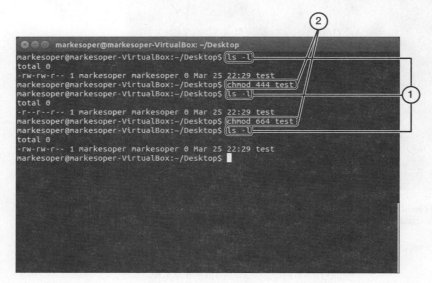

1. Using the `ls -l` command to see the file permissions changes made with `chmod`
2. Changing file permissions with `chmod`

Figure 18-22   Changing permissions for the file test using Ubuntu 14. The command ls –l is used to display file permissions and the filename.

chown

Use **chown** to change file ownership using the syntax `sudo chown newowner filename`. See Figure 18-23.

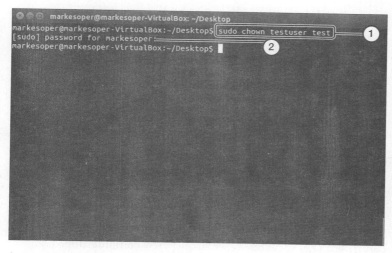

1. `Chown` **command**
2. **Whenever** `sudo` **is used, the user must provide the password as prompted**

Figure 18-23   Changing ownership for the file test using Ubuntu 14.

iwconfig/ifconfig

Use `iwconfig` to display wireless network connections (Linux only).

Use `ifconfig` to display wired network connections (Linux). In OS X, this command also displays wireless network settings.

ps

Use **ps** to list current processes (see Figure 18-24).

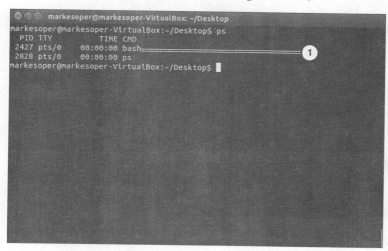

1. **Current processes listed by name and PID.**

Figure 18-24   Listing processes for the current user with `ps`.

su/sudo

Use **sudo** to run a command as another user (refer to Figure 18-23). It is most commonly used by a user to run a command as root.

Use su to switch between accounts. su without specifying options changes to root and prompts for root password.

apt-get

Use **apt-get** to install or manage APT (Advanced Packaging Tool) software packages common in Debian-based distributions such as Ubuntu (see Figure 18-25). Must be used with sudo. Use this syntax: sudo apt-get *function appname*.

vi

Starts the **vi** text editor. For syntax switches, see http://www.computerhope.com/unix/uvi.htm. Note that many Linux distros have easier-to-use text editors installed.

dd

Use **dd** to perform block file copy and to convert between formats. This command must be run as "superuser" (root) and can be used to back up or restore a hard disk or partition. For details, see http://linoxide.com/linux-command/linux-dd-command-create-1gb-file/.

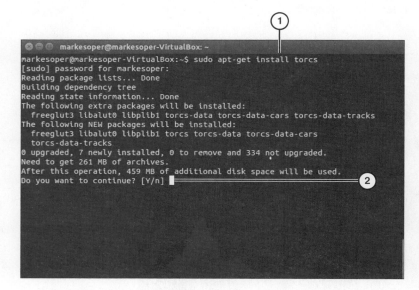

1. The function to perform is install
2. Answer Y to continue

Figure 18-25   Installing torcs (The Open Racing Car Simulator) with apt-get on Ubuntu 14.

Exam Preparation Tasks

Review All the Key Topics

Review the most important topics in the chapter, noted with the Key Topic icon in the outer margin of the page. Table 18-1 lists a reference of these key topics and the page numbers on which each is found.

Table 18-1 Key Topics for Chapter 18

Key Topic Element	Description	Page Number
Section	Configuring Time Machine	926
Section	Force Quit	934
Section	Gestures	938
Note	How to use built-in manuals (manpages) in Linux	940

Complete the Tables and Lists from Memory

Print a copy of Appendix C, "Memory Tables" (found on the companion website), or at least the section for this chapter, and complete the tables and lists from memory. Appendix D, "Answers to Memory Tables," also on the companion website, includes completed tables and lists to check your work.

Define Key Terms

Define the following key terms from this chapter, and check your answers in the glossary.

Time Machine, snapshot, image recovery, Shell/Terminal, Screen sharing, Force Quit, Mission Control, Keychain, Spotlight, iCloud, Gestures, Finder, Remote Disc, Dock, Boot Camp, `ls`, `grep`, `cd`, `shutdown`, `pwd`, `passwd`, `mv`, `cp`, `rm`, `chmod`, `chown`, `iwconfig`, `ifconfig`, `ps`, `su`, `sudo`, `apt-get`, `vi`, `dd`.

Complete Hands-On Lab

Complete the hands-on labs and then see the answers and explanations at the end of the chapter.

Lab 18-1: OS X and Linux Commands

If you have access to an OS X system, use the commands in this chapter to:

- Create a backup
- Delete a file and restore it from a backup
- Prepare an empty drive for use
- Search for a topic that will find both local and online information

If you have access to a Linux system (or can install a virtualized one), use the commands in this chapter to:

- Create a backup
- View the contents of a folder
- Change the permissions of a file
- Copy a file to a different drive

Be sure to view the manpages for the commands you use.

Answer Review Questions

1. Which of the following is the backup utility for the OS X operating system?

   A. Tar

   B. Crontab

   C. Time Machine

   D. File History

2. If you do not want a command to be run in Linux, which of the following should be placed at the beginning of each line that you do not want to activate?

   A. #

   B. *

   C. $

   D. REM

3. What does the `crontab` command do in Linux?

   A. Searches for and downloads updates

   B. Lists commands to be run on a regular schedule

   C. Changes user permissions

   D. Displays the IP address

4. According to the following figure and the key below the figure, when is the backup set to run?

```
markesoper@markesoper-VirtualBox: /etc
markesoper@markesoper-VirtualBox:/etc$ crontab -l
# Edit this file to introduce tasks to be run by cron.
#
# Each task to run has to be defined through a single line
# indicating with different fields when the task will be run
# and what command to run for the task
#
# To define the time you can provide concrete values for
# minute (m), hour (h), day of month (dom), month (mon),
# and day of week (dow) or use '*' in these fields (for 'any').#
# Notice that tasks will be started based on the cron's system
# daemon's notion of time and timezones.
#
# Output of the crontab jobs (including errors) is sent through
# email to the user the crontab file belongs to (unless redirected).
#
# For example, you can run a backup of all your user accounts
#
6 4 * * 2 tar -zcf /var/backups/home.tgz /home/
#
# For more information see the manual pages of crontab(5) and cron(8)
#
# m h  dom mon dow   command
markesoper@markesoper-VirtualBox:/etc$ []
```

Key:

m = minutes

h = hours (24-hour clock)

dom = day (of the month)

mon = month

dow = day (of the week); (0=Sunday, 1=Monday, etc., * = daily)

   A. 2 AM on June 4

   B. 6:04 AM every Monday

   C. 6th day of the week between 2:00 AM and 4:00 AM

   D. 4:06 AM every Tuesday

5. What is the purpose of Disk Utility in OS X?

   A. It prepares a disk to be used for storing image backups and other files.

   B. It manages the network connection to the Internet.

   C. It ejects a disk.

   D. It manages remote storage in the cloud.

6. What is the function of the `tar` command in Linux operating systems?

    A. Compression

    B. IP addressing

    C. Encryption

    D. Backup

7. In OS X, after creating an image with Disk Utility, which menu sequence is used to restore a system image?

    A. Edit > Restore

    B. Backup > Restore

    C. Ubuntu > System > Restore

    D. Déjà New > System Restore

8. Which OS X Disk Utility app can be used to repair hard drive issues, such as file systems and partitions?

    A. Recovery

    B. Partition Wizard

    C. QuickFix

    D. First Aid

9. Screen sharing, file sharing, and printer sharing are configured through which OS X utility?

    A. Control Panel

    B. System Preferences

    C. The Sharing app

    D. Display

10. In the OS X or Linux Terminal, which command is used to force-quit an app by its PID number? ?

    A. `kill`

    B. Ctrl+Alt+Del

    C. `end`

    D. `fq`

11. Which role does Mission Control play in OS X?

    A. It displays all open apps on multiple desktops.

    B. It installs an operating system on a virtual machine.

    C. It manages the flow of incoming and outgoing data across a network.

    D. It manages the flow of data through a firewall.

12. Which of the following OS X apps is used for sharing photos and documents and for data storage?

    A. Time Machine

    B. iCloud

    C. Apple Assist

    D. Spotlight

13. What is the name of the file manager used by OS X?

    A. Explorer

    B. Search

    C. Finder

    D. File Explorer

14. Which of the following refers to the row of icons of currently running apps at the bottom of the display screen in OS X?

    A. Taskbar

    B. Menu bar

    C. Finder

    D. Dock

15. Match the following Linux user commands with their descriptions.

A. `su`		**G.** `rm`	
B. `iwconfig`		**H.** `grep`	
C. `cd`		**I.** `pwd`	
D. `ls`		**J.** `vi`	
E. `chmod`		**K.** `chown`	
F. `ps`			

Answer Options (in alphabetical order):

1. Change file ownership
2. Change folders
3. Change permissions
4. Delete files
5. Display wireless network connections
6. List currently running processes
7. Perform text/word searches
8. Print (display) working directory
9. Run commands as a different user (usually root)
10. Show contents of a directory or folder
11. Start text editor

Answers and Explanations to Hands-On Lab

Lab 18-1: OS X and Linux Commands

Create a backup using Time Machine and use its Restore command to restore a lost file.

Disk Utility is the program to prepare an empty drive for use.

Spotlight is the search tool in OS X.

In Linux, you have a choice of backup commands and GUI backup utilities. Which distro are you using? Which backup utility?

View the contents of a folder with ls.

Chmod is the tool to use to change file permissions.

Use cp or dd to copy a file.

Be sure to view the manpages for the commands you use.

Answers and Explanations to Review Questions

1. **C.** Time Machine is the backup utility for the OS X system. Tar and crontab are commands used to schedule and back up a Linux machine. File History is a file backup program in Windows 8, 8.1, and Windows 10 that can be accessed from the Control Panel.

2. **A.** The # symbol is used to deactivate a command in a file (refer to Figure 18-1). The # symbol is the equivalent of REM (or remark) in a Windows PowerShell script. The * is a wild card in Linux, OS X, and Windows. The $ is used for administrative shares in Windows.

3. **B.** crontab is a text file that lists commands that are to be run on a regular schedule, such as backups or system updates or antimalware protection.

4. **D.** 4:06 AM every Tuesday

   6=minutes (m)

   4=hours (h)

   * = any day of the month (dom)

   * = any month (mon)

   2 = Tuesday (dow)

5. **A.** The Disk Utility can be used to create blank disk images that can be used as containers for other files, including image backups. It can also be used to erase non-OS X drives and prepare them for use with OS X. Use System Preferences > Network to manage the network connection. Drag the disk icon on the desktop to the Trash, wait for it to change into an Eject symbol, and after the symbol disappears, remove the disk. Use iCloud to manage cloud storage.

6. **D.** Linux includes several utilities that can be used for backups. These include the command-line `tar` and `rsync` utilities. `grsync` (GUI for rsync), `duplicity` (command-line, GUI available as Déjà Dup), and others are available from the repository for a Linux distribution or from the vendors. The `compress` command is used to compress files. The `ifconfig` command is used to view IP address information. The `gpg` command is used to encrypt files.

7. **A.** The system image is created using the Disk Utility. System restoration is accomplished using the Edit > Restore commands. The other commands are erroneous.

8. **D.** OS X's Disk Utility app includes options for repairing drives with First Aid. First Aid can repair problems with the file system, partitions, and other issues. With OS X versions prior to El Capitan, First Aid also repairs file permissions. In El Capitan, file permissions are automatically protected. OS X Recovery is used to start Disk Utility. OS X does not include a partition wizard. QuickFix is an implementation of a FIX protocol for multi-asset trading (www.quickfixengine.org).

9. **B.** In OS X-Screen sharing, file sharing, printer sharing, Internet, Bluetooth, and remote apps are configured through Sharing in System Preferences. Control Panel is a Windows configuration utility. OS X does not have a Sharing app. Display is used to configure display resolution and multiple-monitor settings.

10. **A.** To force-quit an app from the Terminal in either OS X or Linux, enter `top` to see a list of process IDs (PIDs) and the apps they represent. Press q to quit. To kill an app by specifying its PID, enter the command `kill xxx` (where *xxx* is the PID number). Ctrl+Alt+Del is used in Windows to display options including the Task Manager. end and fq are not valid terminal commands.

11. **A.** Mission Control allows a user to open and manage applications across multiple displays. Mission Control displays all apps open on the desktop so you can copy or move them between different desktops. This is very helpful when working with multiple displays.

12. **B.** iCloud allows users to store, share, and back up music, video, picture, and document files in a cloud environment. Time Machine is the OS X backup utility. There are many utilities for OS X that contain the word "assist" or "assistant" (for example, Migration Assistant). Spotlight is the OS X search tool.

13. **C.** The file manager and graphical user interface in the OS X operating systems is known as Finder. In Vista and Windows 7, it is Windows Explorer and in Windows 8/8.1/10 it is File Explorer. Search is a Windows search utility.

14. **D.** Dock is the utility that OS X uses to display icons of all the currently running apps. The taskbar and menu bar are used by Windows. Finder is the file manager for OS X.

15. **A.** 10 (su)

    B. 5 (iwconfig)

    C. 1 (cd)

    D. 6 (ls)

    E. 2 (chmod)

    F. 7 (ps)

    G. 9 (rm)

    H. 4 (grep)

    I. 8 (pwd)

    J. 11 (vi)

    K. 3 (chown)

This chapter covers the following subjects:

- **Client-Side Virtualization Overview**—What's a hypervisor? A virtual machine? Read this section to find out what virtualization does, what's required to make it work, and to learn how it can help you prepare for the 220-901 and 220-902 exams while saving you serious money and desk space.

- **Identify Basic Cloud Concepts**—Find out the differences between Software as a Service (SaaS), Platform as a Service, and other types of cloud computing.

- **Properties and Purposes of Network Services—Server Roles**—A typical network has many types of servers, and this section helps you learn what they do.

- **Internet Appliances**—Learn about the different types of devices you can use to protect a network.

- **Legacy and Embedded Systems**—What types of issues can you expect to find when dealing with no-longer supported systems or computers embedded into larger devices, such as ATMs?

## CHAPTER 19

Virtualization, Cloud Computing, and Network Services

In the drive to do more with less, virtualization and cloud computing have become two important tools for organizations of all sizes. With virtualization, a single laptop, desktop, or server can be used to run two or more different operating systems at the same time. Cloud computing can be used for everything from providing "just-in-time" reserve capacity for peaks in Internet traffic and data to a full-time development and deployment environment. However, users also need to be familiar with the many services that network servers and other devices already provide.

220-902: Objective 2.2 Given a scenario, set up and use client-side virtualization.

220-902: Objective 2.3 Identify basic cloud concepts.

220-902: Objective 2.4 Summarize the properties and purpose of services provided by networked hosts.

Foundation Topics

Client-Side Virtualization Overview

Microsoft (Hyper-V) and third-party vendors, such as Oracle (VirtualBox), VMware (VMWare Workstation, VMWare Fusion), and Parallels (Parallels Desktop), have offered **virtualization** solutions for some time. What is virtualization? Virtualization enables a single computer to run two or more operating systems at the same time using the same hardware.

To understand virtualization, make sure you understand these terms:

- Virtual Machine Manager (VMM)
- Virtual machine (VM)
- Hypervisor
- Emulation

A VMM is used to create and manage a **virtual machine (VM)**.

A VM starts out as an empty set-aside memory space that provides access to virtualized storage, ports, video, and other hardware and a set-aside hard disk file known as a virtual hard disk (VHD). When the VM is created, the user specifies the type of operating system that will be installed.

After the VM starts, the user can install the operating system from an .iso image file or from physical media. After the operating system is installed, the virtualized hardware set up by the VMM is detected and used by the VM.

The VMM can start and stop the VM and modify the virtual hardware the VM has access to. For example, the VMM can adjust the amount of RAM used by the VM, change the virtual network adapter used by the VM, specify what type of network access the VM has, or specify the number of virtualized displays the VM can use. If a VM malfunctions, it can be stopped and restarted without affecting the host device.

Type 1 and Type 2 Hypervisors

A hypervisor performs the same type of functions as a VMM. However, sometimes the term **hypervisor** is used to indicate the type of virtualization. So-called **"bare metal" virtualization**, in which the virtual environment runs directly on the physical hardware, uses a **Type 1** or "native" hypervisor. For example, VMware VSphere and Microsoft Hyper-V Server are Type 1 hypervisors.

Type 2 or "hosted" hypervisors run on top of a host operating systems such as Windows, OS X, or Linux. Examples include Windows Virtual PC, VirtualBox, and VMWare Server. Compared to Type 1, guests are one level removed from the hardware and therefore run less efficiently.

CompTIA uses the term *hypervisor* for Type 1 hypervisors only.

There are several categories of virtualization: host/guest, hypervisor, server-hosted, and client-side.

There are two ways that a computer can run a different operating system:

- Virtualization
- Emulation

In virtualization, the physical resources (RAM, disk space, CPU cycles) are divided between VMs that can run independently of each other. An operating system is loaded into each VM.

In **emulation**, on the other hand, a full reproduction of a different OS and different hardware is created by an emulation app, which is then used to run software made for that OS. Many emulators have been created to enable modern PCs to run video game ROMs originally created for systems such as the Atari 2600 (Stella.source-forge.net), Intellivision (http://intellivisionrevolution.com/emulation), and others.

Host/Guest Virtualization

In this type of virtualization, a PC or workstation runs a standard operating system and a VMM that runs inside the operating system; each VM is a guest operating system. Connections to hardware (networking, display, printing, and so on) are passed from the guest operating system to the virtualization program to the host computer's operating system.

Figure 19-1 illustrates Oracle VM VirtualBox, a popular free host virtualizer. Other examples include Windows Virtual PC from Microsoft (for Windows 7), VMware Workstation Player, and others.

Figure 19-1   Oracle VM VirtualBox Manager preparing to start a VM.

This type of virtualization is often used for client-side virtualization. However, client-side virtualization can also be centrally managed from the standpoint of the creation and management of VM images, although the images are being run locally.

Virtualized Hardware

Although a VM must interface with the hardware, it does not do so directly; instead, it uses emulation to communicate with the hardware. The level of emulation varies with the VMM or hypervisor. For example, with Windows Virtual PC (a VMM used with Windows 7), the video card in the virtualized environment is a standard VGA card. It lacks 3D acceleration and support for SLI or CrossFire multi-GPU standards, regardless of the capabilities of the actual video cards used by the host OS. Newer VMMs have better support for some features. For example, current versions of Oracle VM VirtualBox Manager can enable 3D acceleration if the physical video card supports it.

Some VMMs restrict a virtual machine's access to some types of hardware. For example, some older hosted VMMs could not use USB ports for storage devices. With current VMMs, USB storage devices must be specifically configured, and they cannot be used by the VMM and the VM at the same time. Before adopting a particular VMM, make sure you determine whether the hardware you plan to use inside the VM will work.

Hypervisor

CompTIA uses the term *hypervisor* for a VMM that runs directly on the hardware. It does not need to run inside an operating system. Hypervisor-based virtualization (sometimes referred to as bare-metal virtualization) is therefore faster than host/guest virtualization and, because the hypervisor uses few computer resources (memory, CPU), more computer resources can be made available to each VM. Type 1 hypervisors are used for virtual servers and thin client virtualization by web-hosting companies and by companies that offer cloud computing solutions.

Thin-client virtualization, often referred to as virtual desktop infrastructure (**VDI**), runs VMs on the server's own hardware and uses the network to interface with thin clients who interact with the VMs via the network. This type of virtualization, although easy to manage, is not suitable for multimedia-intensive software and requires the client to stay connected to the network at all times.

Examples of hypervisor virtualization include Hyper-V from Microsoft, VMware vSphere, Citrix XenServer, and others.

Purpose of Virtual Machines

The savings over two or more physical workstations can be significant in terms of space, cooling, and peripheral hardware (displays, mice, keyboards, printers, and desks).

Virtual machines enable help desk and support specialists to run older operating systems without changing computers and without rebooting their systems. Virtual machines enable a single PC to run 32-bit and 64-bit versions of the same operating system so that applications that run better in 32-bit mode can be run without the need for a separate computer. For example, in Figure 19-1, a 32-bit version of Windows 8 is virtualized.

Each virtual machine on a computer can perform different tasks at the same time, enabling more work to be done with less hardware investment.

Figure 19-2 illustrates Microsoft Hyper-V Manager after creating a VM running Ubuntu.

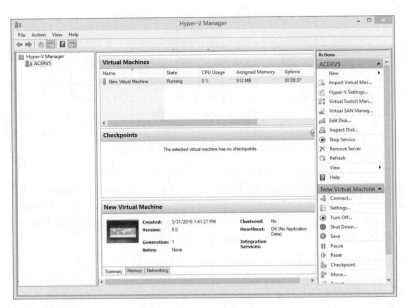

Figure 19-2   Hyper-V Manager.

Preparing for the A+ Certification Exam with Virtual Machines

Many of the operating system screen captures found in the book were created within a virtual machine. VMs make it easy to practice the software skills you need to pass the 220-902 exam.

Windows 8/8.1/10 Pro include Microsoft Hyper-V client VMM; install it by using Add Windows Features in Control Panel. You can download Oracle VM VirtualBox (www. virtualbox.org) or VMware Workstation Player (www.vmware.com/products/player/) VMMs free. Linux distributions such as Ubuntu (http://www.ubuntu.com/download/desktop/try-ubuntu-before-you-install) and Fedora (https://getfedora.org) can be downloaded free as .iso files. You can use these files to create a physical disc for Live CD mode (the OS runs directly from the disc without being installed) or to create a USB drive.

To download free, ready-to-use VirtualBox Linux or Unix VMs, go to www.osboxes. org. To download free, ready-to-use Windows VMs good for 90 days, go to https://developer.microsoft.com/en-us/microsoft-edge/tools/vms/windows/.

Servers running virtual machines enable fewer physical servers to perform the same tasks for continuing cost savings, make scaling to match workload easier, and permit easier disaster recovery.

System images can be centrally created, modified, and managed for easier installation. Because the VMM acts as a translator between the VM and the actual computer hardware, there are fewer problems due to differences in system hardware.

Resource Requirements

A workstation that will be used for virtualization needs to be designed with fast multicore processors and as much RAM as possible given the limitations of the motherboard and VMM (or host operating system). For this reason, it's better to use 64-bit processors and a 64-bit-compatible VMM (and host operating system if hosted virtualization, rather than a hypervisor, is being used). 64-bit operating systems or VMMs avoid the 4GB RAM limit imposed by 32-bit architecture.

Processors selected for a virtualization system should also feature hardware-assisted virtualization. The system BIOS/UEFI firmware must also support this feature and must be enabled in the system BIOS/UEFI firmware. Otherwise, VMs will run much more slowly and some VMMs will not be supported.

If several VMs will be run at the same time on a workstation, the use of two or more displays is highly recommended.

Although VMs are created using an actual operating system rather than a reproduction of one, the physical hardware that will be used for the VMM must meet or exceed the minimum requirements for the VMM. Here are some examples:

- VMware Workstation Player 12 requires a 1.3GHz or faster 64-bit processor; Intel CPU with VT-x support (enabled in BIOS/UEFI firmware) or AMD CPU with segment-limit support in long mode; 2GB or more RAM (recommended); and 3GB or more RAM for Windows 7 Aero graphics on the VM.

- Hyper-V requires a CPU with Data Execution Prevention (DEP) and hardware virtualization (enabled in BIOS/UEFI firmware). Second-level address translation (SLAT) is required on Windows 8/8.1/10 (but not Windows Server 2012 R2).

NOTE SLAT, second-level address translation, is also known as nested paging. It reduces the overhead needed to map virtual to physical addresses. By reducing overhead, more virtual machines can be run at the same time on a server.

Emulator Requirements

Because an emulator must simulate an entire operating system and the hardware originally used with the OS, it requires much more RAM and a faster processor than the original hardware being emulated. For example, the Atari 2600 uses a 1.19MHz 8-bit 6507 processor (a simplified version of the 6502 used by Apple, Atari 400/800/XL, and Commodore 64 home computers) and has 128 bytes of RAM. By contrast, the Windows version of the popular Stella emulator for Atari 2600 requires a 32-bit or 64-bit processor on Windows XP or later (which requires a CPU running at 233MHz or faster).

Checking for BIOS/UEFI and Processor Support for Virtualization

As noted in the previous section, most VMMs or hypervisors require that hardware virtualization be enabled in BIOS/UEFI firmware. To determine whether this feature is already enabled, download and run the Microsoft Hardware Assisted Virtualization tool from http://www.microsoft.com/en-us/download/details.aspx?id=592.

If you prefer, you can use the CPU-Z app (www.cpuid.com), check the Intel list of processors that support Intel VT (virtualization technology) at http://ark.intel.com/VTList.aspx, use the Intel Processor Identification Utility http://www.intel.com/support/processors/tools/piu/, or use the AMD Hardware-Assisted Virtualization Detection tool (http://support.amd.com/us/Processor_TechDownloads/AMD-V_Hyper-V_Compatibility_Check_Utility_V2.zip).

To determine whether a processor has SLAT (also known as rapid virtualization index, Extended Page Tables by Intel, and Nested Page Tables by AMD), run the free Coreinfo utility available from the Microsoft TechNet Sysinternals website (https://technet.microsoft.com/en-us/sysinternals/cc835722.aspx).

Figure 19-3 illustrates Coreinfo's report on a processor that supports SLAT.

1. SVM and NP features are present, so this system can run Hyper-V

Figure 19-3   Coreinfo reports that this AMD FX processor supports SLAT and can be used with Hyper-V.

Security Requirements

Because a single physical computer can house two or more VMs, knowing which computers in an organization are using VMs is a vital first step in securing a virtualized environment. Some of the issues to consider include:

- **Monitoring network traffic**—When multiple VMs running on a single physical workstation or server communicate with each other, the hypervisor must monitor the traffic unless it is routed to the physical network and then back to the other VM. A feature known as extensible switch modules, introduced by Windows Server 2012, enables the OS to monitor network traffic between VMs.

- **Backing up VMs** —Virtualized storage needs to be backed up with tools made especially for VMs. A VM backup needs to back up configuration files and virtual disks to ensure that the VM can be restored wherever needed. Most VMMs and hypervisors include a feature known as virtual machine checkpoints (virtual machine snapshots). A checkpoint saves the state, data, and hardware configuration of a VM while it is running.

- **Security**—A VMM is needed that enables **sandboxing** (isolation) of each VM and provides physical partitioning of resources provides better security against attacks.

- **Best security practices for VMMs and VMs**—Operating systems and apps in VMs must be kept up-to-date and use firewalls and antimalware to protect the VM. VMMs also need to be kept-up-to-date and remote administration should be secured by using a VPN. Connections between the VMs such as clipboards or file sharing should be limited to only those necessary.

> **NOTE**   For more information, see "Guide to Security for Full Virtualization Technologies" at http://csrc.nist.gov/publications/nistpubs/800-125/SP800-125-final.pdf

Network Requirements

Network requirements differ between VMMs.

Microsoft Hyper-V requires the creation of an external virtual network switch for each physical network interface card (NIC) or adapter. It supports up to four legacy NICs and up to eight VMBus NICs. With Oracle VM VirtualBox and with VMware, a physical wired network adapter is connected as a NAT (network address translation) device.

With these VMMs and most others, wireless network adapters on the host must be bridged to the virtualized wired network adapter to permit the virtual machine to use the wireless adapter. In other words, the wireless adapter is visible and works as a wired adapter inside the virtual machine.

 ## Identify Basic Cloud Concepts

The "cloud" is a broad term for any type of computing, including program execution, storage, or services, that takes place remotely. Understanding these basic concepts are important for the 220-902 exam as well as for your clients as you work with them to select the best cloud-based technology solutions for their needs.

SaaS

Software as a Service (**SaaS**) is a term for software that is hosted on servers and accessed through a web browser. Because SaaS processing is performed at the server, a thin client, smartphone, or tablet is sufficient to run the software. A browser-based service that does not require a user to download application code to use the service is an example of SaaS.

Perhaps the best-known SaaS is Google Mail (Gmail). Gmail servers provide the Gmail service to anyone with a web browser. Other examples of SaaS include:

- Google Docs—Word processing, spreadsheets, presentations, forms (www.google.com/intl/en/docs/about/)

- Microsoft Office online—Word processing, spreadsheets, presentations, calendar, collaboration, email (www.office.com)

- Freshbooks—Small business accounting (www.freshbooks.com)

- Salesforce—Customer relationship management (www.salesforce.com)

- Basecamp—Project management (basecamp.com)

- Netsuite—Financial management, customer relationship management, ecommerce, accounting (www.netsuite.com)

SaaS is designed for organizations that need to use a service rather than develop or deploy one. Figure 19-4 illustrates the word processor in Google Docs.

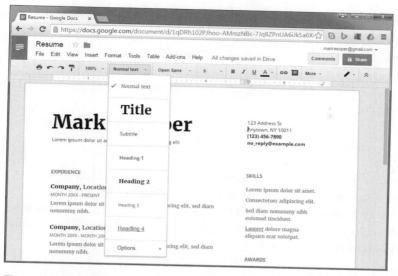

Figure 19-4   Using the Google Docs word processor to create a resume from a template (dummy text shown).

PaaS

Platform as a Service (**PaaS**) enables vendors to develop and deploy software in a cloud environment. A developer using PaaS can concentrate on software features instead of possible issues with server hardware and operating systems.

Some of the major PaaS vendors include:

- OpenShift (Red Hat)—www.openshift.com
- Google App Engine—https://cloud.google.com/appengine/docs
- Microsoft Azure—https://azure.microsoft.com/

NOTE Microsoft Azure is listed in both PaaS and IaaS categories because it can be used in either role, depending on the services purchased by a user.

Some of the considerations in selecting a PaaS vendor include:

- **Language and server-side support**—Make sure the vendor you select supports the languages you develop in and the server-side technologies your apps depend upon. Most major PaaS vendors support languages such as Java, Ruby, PHP, and Python, but server-side technology support varies a great deal.

- **Integration with existing investments**—Some PaaS vendor products can integrate existing apps and data.

- **Costs**—Most PaaS vendors use pricing by the hour, but some price by the month. Be sure your pre-commitment cost estimations take into account the software tools and services you need, as pricing can vary according to the tools or services bundled.

IaaS

Infrastructure as a Service (**IaaS**) enables users to purchase access to data center infrastructure such as storage, network and networking services, virtualization, and servers. Compared to SaaS or PaaS, IaaS puts users in charge of all the software used in a project, from applications and data to the operating system. IaaS vendors supply the hardware and network support tools.

Some major IaaS vendors include:

- Amazon Web Services—http://aws.amazon.com/

- Cisco Metapod—http://www.cisco.com/c/en/us/products/cloud-systems-management/metapod/index.html

- Microsoft Azure—https://azure.microsoft.com/

- Google Compute Engine—https://cloud.google.com/compute/

Public vs. Private vs. Hybrid vs. Community

There are four types of **cloud computing**:

- **Public** cloud computing is public: the service is available to any organization that signs up or pays for it. The connection between services and organizations is the public Internet.

- **Private** cloud computing is available only to dedicated customers (for example, divisions or departments of a single company) and might use a mix of public and private connectivity resources. Private cloud computing is considered to be more secure than public cloud computing.

- **Hybrid** cloud computing combines features of public and private cloud computing. A typical hybrid installation includes dedicated and cloud-based servers and high-speed interconnections with load balancing to move workloads between the environments as needed.

- **Community** cloud computing is a type of hybrid cloud computing that is used by different organizations that are working together.

Rapid Elasticity

Rapid elasticity refers to the ability to rapidly scale up and scale back cloud computing resources as needed.

On-Demand

On-demand is a shortened term for on-demand self-services. On-demand self-services are SaaS providers such as Salesforce.com, Gmail, and others.

Resource Pooling

Resource pooling refers to the dynamic combining of a service provider's resources (servers, storage, network connections, and so on) to meet the needs of multiple organizations as demand increases or decreases.

Measured Service

Measured service refers to how cloud computing services are purchased by organizations. Just as electricity, gas, water, and sewer bills are based on usage, so are cloud computing charges, most typically on a per-hour basis.

Properties and Purposes of Network Services—Server Roles

On a network, a server provides one or more functions to the client devices connected to it called **server roles**. A server might not necessarily be a computer. For example, routers often incorporate one or more of the server functions described in the following sections.

Web Server

A **web server** handles requests that are sent via HTTP or HTTPS, the protocols used by the World Wide Web. When a web browser is used to request a page on the World Wide Web, a web server provides that page.

Built-in web servers are also found in routers and print servers. Web servers built into devices are used to configure the device.

File Server

A **file server** is used to provide shared storage on a network. A file server is typically a computer with a single large drive or a RAID array for storage. Dedicated servers are used only for storage, while a computer that shares storage as well as performing standalone tasks (such as in a Windows workgroup or homegroup) is known as a non-dedicated server.

A network attached storage (**NAS**) device is an increasingly popular supplement to, or replacement for, a traditional file server in small SOHO networks. A NAS is essentially one or more drives fitted with an Ethernet connection; it is assigned its own IP address.

Print Server

A **print server** provides shared printing services on a network. Print servers can be hardware devices or services running on a network server.

Typical hardware print servers are external devices with an Ethernet and/or wireless network connection and one or more USB ports (some print servers support parallel [LPT] ports). Print servers are typically configured through a web interface.

Many printers and multifunction devices now include Ethernet or wireless connections, making a separate print server unnecessary.

DHCP Server

A **DHCP server** supports dynamic host configuration protocol, the protocol that automatically assigns IP addresses to connected devices on a network. DHCP server functions are included in SOHO routers and are a typical role for domain controllers on small to medium business (SMB) networks. On larger networks, DHCP servers are often separate physical or virtualized servers.

DNS Server

A **DNS server** translates domain names used in web page requests into IP addresses. DNS server functions are included in SOHO routers. For larger networks, a separate DNS server can be used. In Windows Server 2012, Server Manager is used to add DNS server services to an existing installation. On Debian-based Linux distributions, the most typical DNS application to run on a server is BIND.

Proxy Server

A **proxy server** is an intermediary between a client and another network, such as the Internet. The proxy server stores web pages that have been requested, and if a client requests a web page, the proxy server checks its cache for the page. If the page exists and is up to date, the proxy server uses its cached copy to supply the client request. If the proxy server does not have the requested page, it downloads the page on behalf of the client, sends the client the page, and retains a copy in its cache.

A proxy server helps reduce traffic between a network and the Internet, and can also be used to block requests for undesirable traffic. Proxy servers can also be used for anonymous surfing. See http://whatis.techtarget.com/definition/proxy-server for more about the licit and illicit uses of proxy servers.

Mail Server

A **mail server** sends or receives email on a network. An SMTP (Simple Mail Transfer Protocol) server is used to send outgoing email and either a POP3 (Post Office Protocol Version 3) or IMAP (Internet Message Access Protocol) server is used to receive mail. Mail server apps are available from many vendors.

Authentication Server

An **authentication server** is used to examine and verify or deny credentials to a user attempting to log into secured networks.

Internet Appliances

Internet appliances are single-purpose devices that are used to perform specific tasks on an IP network.

UTM

Unified threat management (**UTM**) devices provide firewall, remote access, and VPN support, web traffic filtering with antimalware, and network intrusion prevention. UTM devices are located at the connection between the organization's network and the Internet. UTM devices have largely replaced IDS and IPS devices.

Some UTM providers include:

- Barracuda—www.barracuda.com
- Check Point—www.checkpoint.com
- Cisco—www.cisco.com
- Dell SonicWALL—www.sonicwall.com
- Fortinet—www.fortinet.com

- Juniper Networks—www.juniper.net

- Sophos—www.sophos.com

- WatchGuard—www.watchguard.com

IDS

An intrusion detection system (**IDS**) device or program detects network intrusions that might not be detected by a firewall. Typical threats detected by an IDS include attacks against services, malware, data-driven attacks, and host-based attacks. To detect these threats, a typical IDS uses signature-based detection, detection of unusual activities (anomalies), and stateful protocol analysis. An IDS device or program must be updated frequently with new signatures and rules to maintain protection.

A true IDS does not block attacks, but some products and services referred to as IDS actually have characteristics of an IPS (intrusion prevention system).

IPS

An intrusion prevention system (**IPS**) uses methods similar to those used by an IDS, but unlike an IDS, an IPS blocks attacks. Dedicated IDS and IPS devices are not widely used today, but their features are incorporated into UTM devices.

IPS can also be implemented in software with packages such as the open-source Snort for Windows and some Linux distributions (www.snort.org).

Legacy and Embedded Systems

Legacy systems are those that use outdated operating systems, programming languages, applications, or hardware. Maintaining legacy systems is often necessary when newer products are not compatible with legacy applications (for example, applications that can run only under MS-DOS or old versions of Windows).

If a legacy operating system and its applications can be run in a virtualized environment, the problems of maintaining old hardware are eliminated.

Embedded systems, which are dedicated computing devices used for specific tasks such as machine control, point-of-sale systems, or ATMs, often fall into the category of legacy systems. As long as they work, they are maintained. Embedded systems often use older operating systems (for example, it was estimated that 80 percent of worldwide ATMs were still using Windows XP at the time support for XP ended in April 2014).

Perhaps the biggest risk to both legacy and embedded systems is security. If a legacy or embedded system has network or Internet connectivity, it theoretically could be attacked or used as a bot to attack other systems. Although operating systems designed for embedded uses have more security than standard operating systems, the older the OS, the greater the risks.

Because of the potential for security risks, some organizations have paid for extended security updates for otherwise-legacy systems such as Windows XP.

When considering whether and when to update legacy or embedded systems, consider these issues:

- Will the existing data be usable with newer apps?
- Can the existing program run with current operating systems?
- Will changes in network security, wireless, or Internet standards (such as the changeover to IPv6) cause problems with the application?
- Can a proprietary application be licensed to run in a virtual machine?
- Does existing hardware used in the embedded system work with the new operating system?
- Does the embedded application run on current embedded operating systems? If not, is an updated version available?

Evaluation, testing, troubleshooting, and running both systems in parallel are highly advisable when updating legacy or embedded systems.

Exam Preparation Tasks

Review All the Key Topics

Review the most important topics in the chapter, noted with the Key Topic icon in the outer margin of the page. Table 19-1 lists a reference of these key topics and the page numbers on which each is found.

Table 19-1   Key Topics for Chapter 19

Key Topic Element	Description	Page Number
List	Client-side virtualization list of terms	958
Figure 19-1	VirtualBox VMM	960
Section	Checking for BIOS/UEFI and Processor Support for Virtualization	964
Section	Identify Basic Cloud Concepts	966

Define Key Terms

Define the following key terms from this chapter, and check your answers in the glossary.

Virtual machine (VM), hypervisor, Type 1, Type 2, emulation, bare-metal virtualization, thin-client virtualization, VDI, SaaS, IaaS, PaaS, cloud computing (public, private, hybrid, community), rapid elasticity, on-demand, resource pooling, measured service, server roles, web server, file server, print server, DHCP server, DNS server, proxy server, mail server, authentication server, Internet appliance, UTM, IDS, IPS, legacy/embedded systems, virtualization, NAS, sandboxing.

Complete Hands-On Lab

Complete the hands-on labs, and then see the answers and explanations at the end of the chapter.

Lab 19-1: Checking for Virtualization Support

Use the utilities mentioned in this chapter to determine:

- Whether a computer has hardware-assisted virtualization enabled
- Whether a computer's processor has SLAT support

Install a free virtualization utility such as VirtualBox and use it with a pre-made virtualization image. Change settings and note how the system reacts. Use Google Docs or Microsoft Office online. Note the features you normally use with your installed apps that are missing (if any).

Answer Review Questions

1. Which of the following are characteristics of a virtual machine? (Choose all that apply.)

    A. A user can access multiple guest operating systems without rebooting.

    B. 32-bit and 64-bit operating systems may be installed on different virtual machines on a single host machine.

    C. Multiple virtual machines use the same hardware as the host computer.

    D. Running multiple guest operating systems is more expensive than running those same OSs as host systems.

2. What is the name of the program that acts as the translator between the host machine and its virtual machines?

   A. Virtual Machine server

   B. Virtualization Machine Manager

   C. Virtual host manager

   D. Virtualized guest server

3. The Windows 10 VM is selected in the following figure. Assuming the host system has 8GB (8192MB) of RAM, how much RAM is available to the system when the Windows 10 VM is running?

   A. 8192MB

   B. 2048MB

   C. 6144MB

   D. 128MB

4. Which of the following best describes sandboxing as it relates to a virtual machine?

   A. It is a type of hybrid cloud computing.

   B. It is a type of firewall between the host server and the outside world.

   C. It is a backup for virtual machines.

   D. It is the isolating of each VM within the host system for better security.

5. A VMM that runs directly on the hardware rather than inside the operating system is known as which of the following?

   A. Hypervisor

   B. Thin-client virtualization

   C. Client-side host/guest virtualization

   D. DEP (Data Execution Prevention)

6. Match each of the following cloud-based models to its description.

Model	Description
A. SaaS	
B. IaaS	
C. PaaS	

   1. Provides access to storage, network services, virtualization, and servers

   2. Gives application developers the opportunity to develop and deploy software in a cloud environment

   3. Accesses software hosted on remote servers and accessed through web browsers

7. Which of the following is an advantage of cloud computing? (Choose all that apply.)

   A. Rapid elasticity

   B. DHCP services

   C. Resource pooling

   D. Measured service

8. Which type of server acts as an intermediary between a client computer and the Internet?

   A. Web server

   B. DHCP server

   C. DNS server

   D. Proxy server

   E. Authentication server

9. Which type of server automatically assigns IP addresses to computers and printers on a network?

   A. Web server

   B. DHCP server

   C. DNS server

   D. Proxy server

   E. Authentication server

10. Which type of server is responsible for handling HTTP or HTTPS requests?

    A. Web server

    B. DHCP server

    C. DNS server

    D. Proxy server

    E. Authentication server

11. Which type of server receives a domain name request and translates that request into an IP address?

    A. Web server

    B. DHCP server

    C. DNS server

    D. Proxy server

    E. Authentication server

12. Which of the following statements best describes a UTM?

    A. A UTM improves the speed of network address translation.

    B. A UTM integrates legacy software into a modern network.

    C. A UTM provides firewall and network intrusion defenses.

    D. A UTM provides additional memory for file and print servers.

13. Which of the following statements best describes the biggest concern you face when using legacy systems?

    A. The biggest concern is finding applications that will run on these systems.

    B. The biggest concern is maintaining a secure environment.

    C. The biggest concern is finding hardware that can be used by these systems.

    D. The biggest concern is licensing the legacy systems.

Answers and Explanations to Hands-On Labs

Lab 19-1: Checking for Virtualization Support

If you found out that virtualization was not enabled on a system, restart it, enter the BIOS/UEFI firmware setup program, and then see if you can enable virtualization settings. Save your changes and exit.

You might discover that a processor supports virtualization but not SLAT. Some VMM/hypervisor programs, such as Microsoft Hyper-V, require SLAT support.

Some changes to try include changing the amount of RAM available to a VM, changing the number of displays from 1 to 2, and enabling VM access to a USB flash drive or hard disk.

If you decide that Google Docs or Microsoft Office online serves your needs just as well as a locally installed word-processing or spreadsheet program, you might decide to make the cloud-based programs your primary apps.

Answers and Explanations to Review Questions

1. **A, B, C.** Virtualization allows a single machine to act as though it were several machines. A single operating system may host several virtual guest operating systems and may switch between them without rebooting. These virtual machines may be both 32- and 64-bit systems. Each virtual machine uses the same hardware as the host machine, which represents a considerable saving of capital investment.

2. **B.** A VMM or Virtual Machine manager manages the interaction of the virtual environment with the host environment.

3. **C.** 6144MB (6GB) is the amount of RAM available to the system after starting a 2GB VM. 2048MB (2GB) is the size of the VM itself. 4096MB (4GB) is incorrect. 128MB is the size of the video memory assigned to the display.

4. **D.** Sandboxing is a security procedure that isolates a program, separating it from the main system. A VMM that enables sandboxing (isolation) of each VM and provides physical partitioning of resources provides better security against attacks.

5. **A.** A hypervisor VMM runs directly on the hardware. It is faster and uses fewer resources than host/guest virtualization. Because the hypervisor uses few computer resources (memory, CPU), more computer resources can be made available to each VM.

6.

Model	Description
A. SaaS	3. Accesses software hosted on remote servers and accessed through web browsers
B. IaaS	1. Provides access to storage, network services, virtualization, and servers
C. PaaS	2. Gives application developers the opportunity to develop and deploy software in a cloud environment

7. **A, C, D.** Rapid elasticity is the ability of users to quickly increase or decrease the resources they use. Resource pooling allows the cloud provider's resources to be allocated, divided, and used by many clients simultaneously. Measured service means that the user pays only for the resources used. DHCP is a network service that automatically assigns IP addresses to client computers and is not a service provided by cloud computing.

8. **D.** A proxy server stands between an internal network (clients) and an external network (the Internet) and limits the traffic between the two. It can cache web pages for faster access and it can block or allow traffic into or out of the network for better security.

9. **B.** A DHCP server has a list of available IP address on the network and is responsible for automatically assigning those addresses to devices on the network.

10. **A.** A web browser sends an HTTP or HTTPS request to a web server, which then locates and sends the correct web page to the web browser.

11. **C.** To visit a location outside of your network, you must have the IP address of the other location. Most of us know the name of the location we want to visit, but not the IP address. The responsibility of the DNS server is to match the name that we supply to its respective IP address.

12. **C.** UTM devices have replaced IDS and IPS devices for network security. UTMs provide firewall protection, VPN support, antimalware protection, and other forms of network security.

13. **B.** While all of the issues listed might present problems to a modern network, security is the biggest concern when working with a legacy system.

This chapter covers the following subjects:

- **Android vs iOS vs Windows Features**—Whether you use devices from all three brands, or typically use just one, this chapter helps you understand their differences, how to install apps, and how to configure them.

- **Mobile Device Connectivity**—This section shows you how to share or disable cellular data connections and use Bluetooth.

- **Email Configuration**—Learn how to set up corporate or web-based email on your iOS or Android mobile device.

- **PRI Updates/PRL Updates/Baseband Updates**—Learn what these updates to cellular service do to improve connections.

- **Radio Firmware**—Use this section to find out if you can listen to FM radio on any given smartphone.

- **IMEI vs IMSI**—Find out how a smartphone or tablet with cellular data service is identified in case of loss or theft.

- **VPN**—Use this section to learn how to set up a VPN.

- **Data Synchronization**—Discover types and methods of data synchronization in this section.

## CHAPTER 20

Mobile Operating Systems and Devices

Mobile devices are essential to both personal and organizational communications, and that makes understanding how they work a critical factor in being a well-prepared computer tech.

This chapter assumes a basic knowledge of how to operate these devices and moves ahead to building knowledge of advanced features, connectivity, updates, and data synchronization.

220-902: Objective 2.5 Identify basic features of mobile operating systems.

220-902: Objective 2.6 Install and configure basic mobile device network connectivity and email.

220-902: Objective 2.7 Summarize methods and data related to mobile device synchronization

Foundation Topics

Android vs iOS vs Windows Features

Most mobile devices use one of two operating systems made especially for smartphones and tablets: Android and iOS. Windows 10 Mobile is the newcomer used on the latest Windows smartphones and on Windows tablets with screens under 8-inches in size. Its interface resembles the tablet version of Windows 10.

The following sections compare and contrast the features of these operating systems, including how to install apps, configure the device, calibrate the display, and use the devices' GPS features.

NOTE   For the 220-902 exam, you should know the following:

- Android vs. iOS vs. Windows:
- Open source vs. closed source/vendor specific
- App source (play store, app store and store)
- Screen orientation (accelerometer/gyroscope)
- Screen calibration
- GPS and geotracking
- Wi-Fi calling
- Launcher/GUI
- Virtual assistant
- SDK/APK
- Emergency notification
- Mobile payment service

Open-Source vs. Closed-Source/Vendor-Specific

Currently, mobile device software comes in one of two forms: **open-source**, which is effectively free to download and modify, and **closed-source**, otherwise known as **vendor-specific**, which cannot be modified without express permission and licensing. Let's discuss each of these now.

Open-Source: Android

Android is an example of open-source software. It is an operating system based on the Linux kernel and used mostly on smartphones and tablet computers and is developed by the Open Handset Alliance, a group directed by Google. Google releases the Android OS code as open-source, allowing developers to modify it and freely create applications for it. Google also commissioned the Android Open Source Project (AOSP); its mission is to maintain and further develop Android. You know you are dealing with the Android open-source OS and related apps when you see the stylized robot, usually in green. An example of Android running on a smartphone can be seen in Figure 20-1.

1. App Notifications
2. Battery charging level

Figure 20-1   Android v5.1.1 OS Home screen on a Samsung smartphone.

Android OS versions are dubbed with cute names such as Honeycomb (version 3), Ice Cream Sandwich (version 4.0), Jelly Bean (versions 4.1-4.3), KitKat (version 4.4), Lollipop (version 5.0-5.1), and Marshmallow (version 6.0).

To find out the version you are currently running, start at the Home screen; this is the main screen that boots up by default. Tap the **Menu** button and then tap **Settings**. Scroll to the bottom and tap the **About Phone** (or **About**) option. Then tap **Software Information** or similar option. This displays the version of Android. Figure 20-2 shows a smartphone using version 5.1.1 (Lollipop).

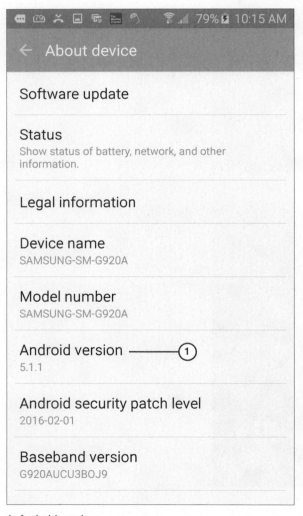

1. Android version

Figure 20-2 Smartphone using Version 5.1.1 of Android.

Unlike other mobile operating systems, Android's licensing agreements allow for a great deal of customization of the finished product. Thus, Android smartphones and tablets from different vendors are likely to have different user interfaces and features.

Closed-Source: iOS and Windows 10 Mobile

Apple's **iOS** is an example of closed-source software. Previously known as the iPhone Operating System, it is now simply referred to as iOS, since it is used on iPod Touches, iPhones, and iPads as well. It is based off of OS X (used on Mac desktops and laptops), and for that reason, it has its roots in Unix. Figure 20-3 shows the Home screen of an iPad mini 2 running iOS version 9.0.1.

1. iOS OS update available
2. App updates available
3. Battery charge level

Figure 20-3 iPad mini 2 Home screen.

To find out the version of iOS you are running, go to the Home screen and tap **Settings > General > About**. You will see the Version number. For example, Figure 20-4 shows an iPad mini 2 running Version 9.01. The build number is 13A404; this was the public release of version 9.0.1.

Unlike Android, iOS is not open-source. Only Apple hardware uses this operating system; this is known as being vendor-specific.

Windows 10 Mobile is a closed-source operating system, like iOS, but unlike iOS, which is used only on Apple devices, Windows 10 Mobile is licensed by Microsoft to a variety of mobile phone manufacturers.

To determine the version of a Windows 10 Mobile phone, open **System > About**.

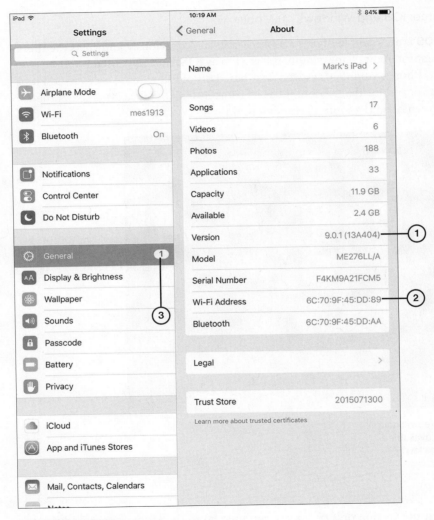

1. iOS version number
2. MAC (physical) address of onboard Wi-Fi adapter
3. Indicates iOS update is available

Figure 20-4   iPad mini 2 using Version 9.0.1 of iOS.

App Source (Apple Store, Google Play Store, and Windows Store)

Mobile devices are nothing without applications. To this end, Android, iOS, and Windows 10 Mobile have application sources where you can download free and/or small-fee applications.

Android users download applications from **Google Play**. This can be done directly from the mobile device through Wi-Fi or a cellular connection. Or, if a mobile device is connected via USB to a computer, the user can browse apps on the Google Play website while working on the computer and download directly from the site to the device, passing through the computer.

iOS users download applications from the **App Store**. This was originally an update to the iTunes store, but on newer iOS mobile devices it is now a separate icon on the Home screen. Apps can also be downloaded from a Mac or other Apple device, or from a PC through the iTunes application.

Windows 10 Mobile users visit the **Windows Store** to download apps for their devices. Some apps also run on Windows 10 for tablets, desktops, or laptops.

Regardless of the OS, a user searches for the name of the application he or she wants, downloads it, starts the installation process, agrees to a license, and then finally uses the app.

Rooting and Jailbreaking

Some applications don't work unless a person hacks the OS and gains superuser privileges. In the Android world this is known as rooting the phone or other mobile device. In the iOS world it is called jailbreaking. This could be a breach of the user license agreement and also void the warranty for a device. It can also be dangerous. These types of hacks often require a person to back up all data on the mobile device, wipe it out completely, and install a special application that may or may not be trustworthy. Many phones or other devices are rendered useless or are compromised when attempting this procedure. Applications that have anything to do with rooting or jailbreaking should generally be avoided.

Screen Orientation and Calibration (Accelerometer/Gyroscope)

The display of a mobile device might need to be configured, oriented, and calibrated properly for efficient usage. Today's mobile devices are usually pretty good out-of-the-box, but a user might need to lock rotation, or could possibly cause the touch screen to behave improperly by misconfiguring it, or by installing applications that modify the display's functionality. Let's discuss display rotation (otherwise known as orientation) and calibration now.

Mobile device displays rotate by default if the user rotates the device, allowing the screen to be viewed vertically or horizontally. This helps when looking at pictures, movies, or viewing websites. But in some cases, a user might want to lock the rotation of the device so that it stays as either vertical or horizontal, without moving.

On an Android device, this can be done by accessing **Settings > Display** and then deselecting the Auto-rotate screen.

On an iOS device (version 7 or later), this can be done by swiping up from the bottom of the Home screen to bring up the Control Center and then tapping the icon that looks like a padlock with an arrow around it; rotation will be locked. Some iPads also have a side switch that can be configured to enable/disable rotation lock: iPad Air, iPad 2, iPad (3rd generation), and iPad (4th generation); iPad mini, iPad mini 2, and iPad mini 3. To select options for the side switch, go to **Settings > General > Use side switch to:** and choose the option desired.

Screen orientation is a pretty simple concept to understand and use. But it can be more complicated when it comes to applications. For example, Apple mobile devices use the **accelerometer**: a combination of hardware and software that measure velocity; they detect rotation, shaking of the device, and so on. The accelerometer enables a mobile device to automatically adjust from portrait (vertical) to landscape (horizontal) mode. It's actually three accelerometers, one for each axis X (left to right), Y (up and down), and Z (back to front). These are manipulated by developers for special applications (such as a compass app) and games so that the program recognizes particular movements of the device and translates to various functions in-game or within the application. Newer Apple devices include a **gyroscope**, which adds the measurements of pitch, roll, and yaw, just like in the concept of flight dynamics. For example, imagine your tablet computer is a model airplane and you are holding it flat in front of you. To change pitch, you would raise or lower the nose of the airplane. To initiate roll, you would turn the airplane right or left so the wings move; the fuselage of the plane rotates but otherwise doesn't move. To start a yaw, you would rotate the airplane left or right while keeping it flat. Now apply this to a tablet computer, as is illustrated in Figure 20-5. You won't need a pilot's license to use an iPad, but this additional measurement of movement has a great impact on the development of newer applications and especially games. Of course, if the accelerometers or gyroscope of the mobile device fail and a reset of the device doesn't fix the problem, it will have to be repaired at an authorized service center.

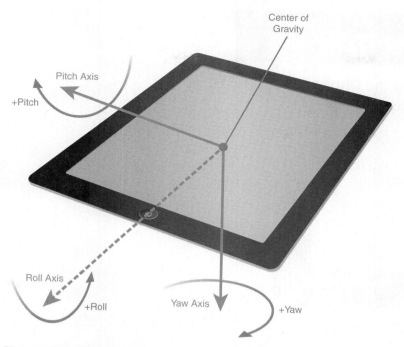

Figure 20-5   Examples of iPad Air 2 gyroscopic pitch, roll, and yaw.

NOTE   iPhones include a calibration utility for the Compass app, but not a screen calibration utility.

Some Android devices include a **screen calibration** utility called G-Sensor calibration. It is found in **Settings > Display.** To make sure that the three axes are calibrated properly, this program is run while the mobile device is laid on a flat surface. You can tell whether the surface is level by the horizontal and vertical leveling bubbles on the display. Then press the Calibrate button to reset the G-Sensor, as shown in Figure 20-6.

Other mobile devices' calibration programs show a crosshair or similar image in the center of the screen. You need to tap with a stylus as close to the center of the display as possible. If a stylus is not available, use the pointed end of a pen cap.

Figure 20-6   G-Sensor calibration on an Android smartphone.

Some vendors include tests for calibration, audio, camera, and video functions by the use of a special dialing code. For Samsung smartphones, use *#0*#. This displays the test screen shown in Figure 20-7.

Sometimes, issues that appear to be calibration problems are actually something else with an easy fix. For example, cheaper screen protectors can bubble and otherwise cause problems when you tap on the screen. Removing the protector and installing a new one properly can fix this problem. When installing a screen protector, use a long flat surface to squeeze all the bubbles out; shims can be purchased for just this purpose. Use a decent screen protector such as Ghost Armor or something similar. Good quality screen protectors not only protect the display, they reduce glare, smudging, and fingerprints, without reducing sensitivity. Dirty screens can also be a culprit when a user is having difficulty tapping on icons or smaller items. Clean the display with a lint-free cloth. If the screen is very dirty, mix 50% isopropyl alcohol and 50% water, apply conservatively to the cloth, then clean the display with the cloth. Make sure all traces of liquid are removed when you are done. If none of these steps work, the device will need to be brought in to an authorized service center for repair.

A reset can also fix problems with calibration (as well as other types of problems). There are two types of resets: soft and hard. A soft reset is usually performed simply by powering the device off and then powering it back on again. This can fix temporary problems quickly and easily. It is similar to rebooting a PC. However, more advanced problems require a hard reset.

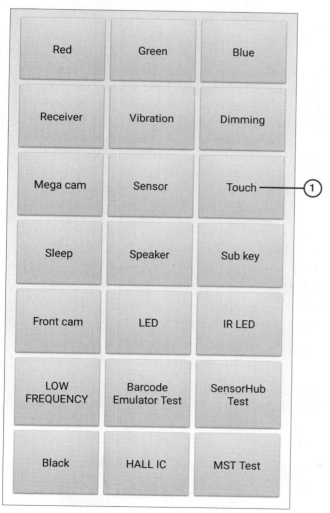

1. Click or tap to test touchscreen

Figure 20-7 Running Samsung's built-in Android smartphone tester.

CAUTION   A hard reset removes all data and applications and returns the device to its original factory state. Do not perform a hard reset without backing up the contents of the memory card in the mobile device and any additional settings you require.

More information on resets can be found in the section "Troubleshoot Mobile OS and Application Issues" in Chapter 22, "Troubleshooting Desktop and Mobile Operating Systems."

GPS and Geotracking

The **Global Positioning System (GPS)**, developed by the United States Department of Defense, is a worldwide system of satellites that provide location information for anything with a GPS receiver. Any mobile device with a GPS receiver can use this system to identify its location and utilize mapping programs and any other applications that rely on GPS. Some mobile devices, mainly tablets that have only Wi-Fi receivers, do not have a GPS receiver, and instead use location services or something with a similar name that uses crowd-sourced Wi-Fi locations to determine the approximate location of the device. This is common in mobile devices that do not have a GSM module. So essentially, if a mobile device cannot be used to make phone calls or connect to cellular data services, it also can't be used with GPS-enabled applications.

To enable/disable location services on an Android-based device, go to **Settings > Location** and use the on/off slider. To specify location methods, tap **Locating method** and select from GPS only; Wi-Fi and mobile networks; or GPS, Wi-Fi, and mobile networks (the most accurate).

To enable/disable location services on an Apple device such as an iPad or iPhone, go to **Settings > Privacy > Location Services**.

To enable/disable location services on a Windows 10 mobile device, tap **Start** and then swipe to **All apps > Settings > Privacy > Location**.

Geotracking is the practice of tracking and recording the location of a mobile device over time. This location tracking is done by Apple and Google as well as other organizations and governments. Privacy issues aside, this practice *is* being done, so if a user doesn't want her location known, simply disable the location services setting.

To locate your phone, iOS, Android, and Windows all offer services to help.

- Apple offers Find My iPhone (which also works with iPad, iPod Touch or Mac computers). To enable it and learn how to use it, see https://support.apple.com/en-us/HT205362.

- Google offers the Android Device Manager; learn more at http://www.an-droidcentral.com/app/android-device-manager.

- To enable the Windows 10 Find My Device feature for laptops and tablets, go to **Start** > **Settings** > **Update & Security** > **Find My Device**. You can also use https://account.microsoft.com/devices to find phones and other devices. Learn more at http://windows.microsoft.com/en-us/windows/find-lost-phone.

Wi-Fi Calling

Wi-Fi connections can be used to make phone calls when this feature is supported by the mobile service provider, phone, or other mobile device and operating system. Almost all U.S. mobile service providers support **Wi-Fi calling** on iPhone 6-series phones, but some also support this feature on some late-model Android phones. Contact your mobile service provider for details.

After the update supporting Wi-Fi calling is released, the user must enable it, typically through the phone menu. Apple also supports making Wi-Fi calls on iPod Touch and iPad models after Wi-Fi calling is enabled on the user's iPhone.

NOTE   For more information about Apple support for Wi-Fi calling, see https://support.apple.com/en-us/HT203032.

Launcher/GUI

Smartphones and tablets based on iOS, Android, and Windows 10 Mobile all support some levels of customization:

- Rearranging app tiles

- Grouping similar apps into folders

- Changing backgrounds or themes

Rearranging Tiles in iOS, Android, or Windows 10 Mobile

To rearrange tiles:

Step 1.   Hold down a tile.

Step 2.   Drag it to another location.

Creating a Folder in iOS

To create a folder for grouping apps in iOS:

Step 1.   Hold down a tile until the tiles begin to jiggle.

Step 2.   Drag the tile to another app's tile.

Step 3.   Release the dragged tile. iOS creates a folder for the apps and names it based on the apps in the folder (see Figure 20-8).

Step 4.   To add more apps to the folder, repeat Step 1, then drag the tile to the folder.

Figure 20-8   Creating a folder to group related apps in iOS 9.0.1.

Creating a Folder in Android

To create a folder for grouping apps in Android:

Step 1.   Hold down a tile until the Create folder icon appears at the top of the screen.

Step 2.   Drag the tile to the Create folder icon.

Step 3.   Name the folder.

Step 4. To add more apps to the folder, hold down an app tile then drag it to the folder. Figure 20-9 illustrates a new folder after adding apps.

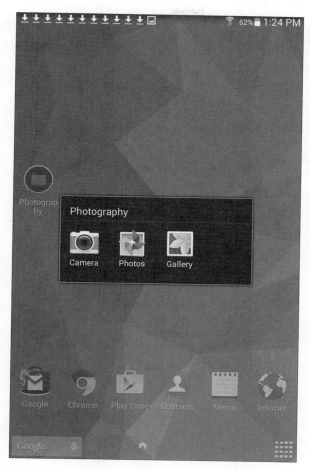

Figure 20-9 Creating a folder to group related apps in Android 5.1.1.

Virtual Assistant

The term **virtual assistant** refers to voice-activated search and action capabilities such as Apple's Siri, Microsoft's Cortana, and Google's OK Google. These apps can be trained to respond to your voice specifically or to respond to any voice (see Figure 20-10).

To configure Siri, go to **Settings** > **General** > **Siri**. To configure OK Google, open **Google (app)** > **Settings** > **Voice**. To configure Cortana, open the Search menu and select the option to configure Cortana.

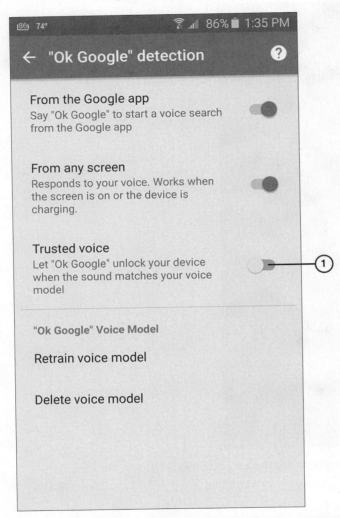

1. Enable "Trusted voice" to have "OK Google" recognize your voice only on this device

Figure 20-10   Configuring OK Google.

SDK/APK

A Software Development Kit (**SDK**) is the combination of programming tools and operating system or emulator used by a developer to create apps for a particular operating system.

If developers want to create an application for iOS, they can download the iOS SDK from https://developer.apple.com.

Developers for Android need Android Studio, SDK, and other resources available from http://developer.android.com/index.html. Android apps are packaged as Android application packages (**APKs**) for distribution and installation.

Developers for Windows 10 Mobile need the Windows 10 SDK and other resources available from https://dev.windows.com/.

See the respective websites for licensing and fee arrangements.

Emergency Notification

Wireless Emergency Alert (WEA) capability (**emergency notification**) is provided by wireless carriers in conjunction with the Federal Emergency Management Agency and the FCC. WEA messages can alert users to storms, AMBER alerts, earthquakes, or other serious threats.

Most smartphones and many feature phones can receive WEA messages, which use a unique vibration and tone pattern to alert the user. Some phones have options to turn off AMBER alerts.

Not all areas support WEA warnings. However, if you install an app for your favorite local news and weather sites, you can receive similar notifications of danger.

Mobile Payment Service

Mobile payment services such as Apple Pay, Samsung Pay, Android Pay, and others use the NFC (near field communication) feature built into many smartphones. Some of these services might be preloaded on your smartphone, while others might need to be downloaded from your phone's app store.

To use these services, a form of payment (usually a credit or debit card) must be linked to the account. Some services can capture the information from the front of your card by using the built-in smartphone camera.

Before enrolling for these services, check with the bank or financial institution to see if the mobile payment service is supported.

Mobile Device Connectivity

Mobile devices offer many ways to connect to other devices, from sharing their Wi-Fi or cellular connections with one or more computers and using Bluetooth for wire-free connections to printers and headsets, and email. The following sections discuss these and other topics.

NOTE   For the 220-902 exam, you should know the following:

- Wireless/cellular data network (enable/disable): hotspot, tethering, airplane mode

- Bluetooth: Enable Bluetooth, enable pairing, find device for pairing, enter appropriate pin code, test connectivity

- Corporate and ISP email configuration: POP3, IMAP, Port and SSL settings, Exchange, S/MIME

- PRI updates/PRL updates/Baseband updates

- Radio firmware

- IMEI vs. IMSI

- VPN

Wireless / Cellular Data Network

Wi-Fi connectivity is performed the same way on a smartphone or tablet as with laptops or other types of computers (see Chapter 11, "Networking," for details). However, smartphones or tablets with cellular radios can also be used to share their connections with others.

To enable mobile device use on airplanes, where electronic communications are usually not permitted, the Airplane mode is used to turn off Wi-Fi, cellular, and Bluetooth signals.

Learn more in the following sections.

Tethering

To use USB **tethering**, follow these steps (which are based on a Samsung phone running Android 5.x):

Step 1.   Connect a USB cable from your computer to the data port on your device.

Step 2.   Select the USB tethering option on your device.

Step 3.   If you are connecting a Windows computer, select the network type (Home) on the computer when prompted.

Step 4.   Use your computer's web browser and other network features normally.

Step 5.   When you're finished, disable USB tethering.

NOTE In Windows Device Manager, the tethered USB connection is listed as Remote NDIS based Internet Sharing Device in the Network Adapters category.

 Hotspot

To use the mobile **hotspot** feature, follow these steps (which are based on a Samsung phone running Android 5.x):

Step 1. Enable the mobile hotspot feature in your device's setup.

Step 2. Select how you want to share your connection wirelessly. Provide the SSID and password listed to any devices that will share your connection.

Step 3. If you decide to permit only allowed devices to connect, you must provide a name for each device and its MAC address. The MAC address is listed on a label attached to an external adapter. To find the MAC (physical) address for an internal network adapter, see the sidebar "Finding the Network Adapter's MAC (Physical) Address."

Step 4. Open the Allowed devices menu (see Figure 20-11), click **Add**, and enter the device name and address in the display provided.

Step 5. Click **OK**.

Finding the Network Adapter's MAC (Physical) Address

If you cannot view the label on an external device, or if your network adapter is internal, use one of these methods to display it. On a Windows device, open a command prompt window and use the command ipconfig /all to see the MAC (physical) address for the device. With OS X 10.4 (Tiger) and newer, the address is located in the Air-Port menu and is labeled as AirPort ID. With most Linux distros, run the command ifconfig –a. MAC addresses can be listed in uppercase or lowercase. The MAC address for an iOS device is called its Wi-Fi address. To see it, open Settings > About. The MAC address for an Android device is called its Wi-Fi MAC address. To see it, open Settings > About > Status.

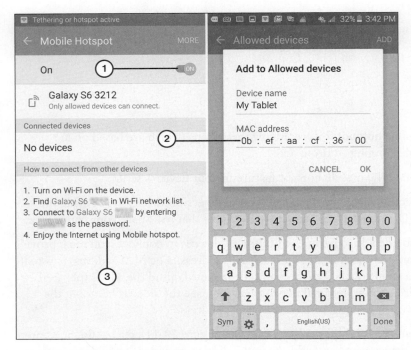

1. Enabling mobile hotspot
2. Entering MAC address of device that will connect to mobile hotspot
3. Instructions for devices that will connect to mobile hotspot

Figure 20-11   Entering the MAC address of the device sharing the hotspot's Internet connection.

Step 6.   Make the connection from your device the same as with any other wireless Internet router or hotspot. Enter the password when prompted.

Step 7.   When your devices are finished using the Internet, you should disable the hotspot setting in your smartphone or tablet.

CAUTION   Some cellular providers charge an additional fee if you turn your cellular device into a hotspot or if you use tethering. Check with your mobile service provider for details. And keep in mind that the data usage of every device connected to a mobile hotspot is counted towards your total data allocation. If you're not careful, using a mobile hotspot could cost you extra money in overages.

If you prefer to use a standalone mobile hotspot for your home, business, or vehicle, check with your wireless provider.

Airplane Mode

Most devices cannot shut off the cellular antenna by itself. However, every device manufactured now is required to have an "**airplane mode**," which turns off any wireless antenna in the device including cellular, Wi-Fi, GPS, and Bluetooth.

On a typical Android device, this can be done by going to **Settings > Connections** and then enabling **Airplane Mode** as shown in Figure 20-12. Note the airplane icon in the upper portion of the figure. You will find that some airlines don't consider this to be acceptable and will still ask you to turn off your device, either for the duration of the flight or at least during takeoff and landing. On Android devices, you can also access airplane mode by pressing and holding the power button.

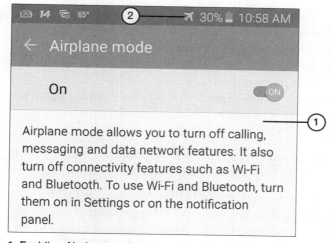

1. Enabling Airplane mode
2. When Airplane mode is enabled, the airplane icon is shown in place of Wi-Fi or cellular connection signal strength

Figure 20-12   Enabling airplane mode on a Samsung smartphone using Android 5.x.

To enable airplane mode on an iOS device, go to **Settings > Airplane Mode** as shown in Figure 20-13. Again, note the icon of an airplane at the top left of the figure.

Airplane Mode Is Enabled

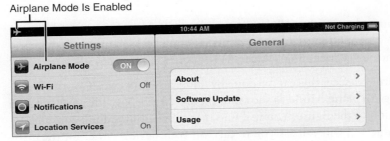

Figure 20-13   Airplane mode on a typical Apple tablet.

Bluetooth

Bluetooth is a short-range, low-speed wireless network primarily designed to operate in peer-to-peer mode (known as ad-hoc) between PCs and other devices such as printers, projectors, smartphones, mice, keyboards, and other devices. Bluetooth runs in virtually the same 2.4GHz frequency used by IEEE 802.11b, 802.11g, and 802.11n wireless networks but uses a spread-spectrum frequency-hopping signaling method to help minimize interference. Bluetooth devices connect to each other to form a personal area network (PAN).

Some systems and devices include integrated Bluetooth adapters, and others need a Bluetooth module connected to the USB port to enable Bluetooth networking.

Bluetooth version 1.2 offers a data transfer rate of 1Mbps. Version 2 is 3Mbps. Bluetooth version 3.0 + HS can reach speeds of up to 24Mbps because it uses Bluetooth only to establish the connection, but the actual data transfer happens over an 802.11 link. This feature is known as alternative MAC/PHY (AMP). Bluetooth 4.0, also known as Bluetooth Smart, is designed for use with very low power applications such as sensors. Bluetooth 4.1, a software update to 4.0, enables Bluetooth to perform multiple roles at the same time and work better with LTE cellular devices. Bluetooth 4.2 adds features to support the Internet of Things (IoT). Most Bluetooth mice, keyboards, and headsets on the market today support version 4.0.

NOTE   The Internet of Things (IoT) refers to the network of physical objects (devices, buildings, vehicles, appliance, and so on) that are connected to each other through embedded electronics, sensors, software, and network connectivity for the collection and exchange of data. For more information, see http://www.cisco.com/c/dam/en_us/solutions/trends/iot/introduction_to_IoT_november.pdf

Bluetooth is divided into classes, each of which has a different range. Table 20-1 shows these classes, their ranges, and the amount of power their corresponding antennae use to generate signal.

Table 20-1   Bluetooth Classes

Class	mW	Range
Class 1	100 mW	100 meters (328 ft.)
Class 2	2.5 mW	10 meters (33 ft.)
Class 3	1 mW	1 meter (3 ft.)

As you can see, Class 1 generates the most powerful signal, and as such has the largest range. The most common Bluetooth devices are Class 2 devices with a range of 10 meters. Examples of this include portable printers, headsets, and computer dongles.

The Bluetooth radio built in to mobile devices and some laptops can be used for many devices, including headsets, printers, and input devices such as mice and keyboards. Before a Bluetooth device can work with your computer or mobile device, it must be paired with the device.

By default, Bluetooth is usually disabled on Android devices but is enabled on iOS devices such as iPads or iPhones. To connect a Bluetooth device to a mobile device, Bluetooth first needs to be enabled; then the Bluetooth device needs to be synchronized to the mobile device. This is known as **pairing** or linking. It sometimes requires a **PIN** code. Once synchronized the device needs to be connected. Finally, the Bluetooth connection should be tested. Let's show the steps involved in connecting a Bluetooth headset to a typical Android-based device and to an iOS device. Before you begin, make sure the Bluetooth headset is charged.

Steps to Configure a Bluetooth Headset on an Android-Based Device

Step 1.   Go to **Settings > Connections** and then enable **Bluetooth**.

Step 2.   Tap **Bluetooth**. This displays the Bluetooth Settings screen.

Step 3.   Prepare the headset. This varies from headset to headset. For example, on a typical Motorola Bluetooth headset, press and hold the button while opening the microphone. If necessary, keep holding the button while completing the next step.

Step 4.   If the Android device is not scanning automatically, tap **Scan**. Keep holding the button on the headset until the Android device finds it.

Step 5.   On the Android device, tap the device to pair with. Most Android devices pair the Bluetooth headset to the mobile device and then complete the connection automatically, allowing full use of the device.

Step 6.   Enter a PIN code if prompted. Many devices come with a default pin of 0000.

When finished, the screen on the Android device looks similar to Figure 20-14. Note the Bluetooth icon at the top of the screen. This icon tells you whether Bluetooth is running on the device. It will remain even if you disconnect the Bluetooth device. For this headset device we would test it simply by making a phone call.

To disconnect the device while retaining pairing, turn it off. To unpair the device, tap the settings (gearbox) icon on the screen and tap **Unpair**. Pair it again to use it again.

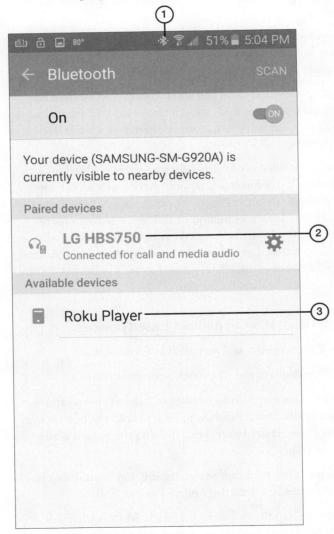

1. Bluetooth device connected
2. Newly connected device
3. Other nearby devices

Figure 20-14 Bluetooth screen on an Android smartphone showing the LG HBS750 headset connected.

Android devices can also connect to other Bluetooth-enabled devices (forming a PAN) or to a computer equipped with a Bluetooth dongle. To do this, you must set the mobile device to discoverable (which generally lasts for only two minutes). In the same fashion that the headset was discovered by the mobile device in the previous procedure, a mobile device can be discovered by a computer or other mobile device.

Steps to Configure a Bluetooth Headset on an iOS-Based Device

Step 1.   Go to **Settings > General** and then tap **Bluetooth**. This displays the Bluetooth screen.

Step 2.   Tap **Bluetooth** to enable it (if it isn't enabled already). This automatically starts searching for devices and will continue to do so.

Step 3.   Prepare the headset. This varies from headset to headset. For example, on a typical Motorola Bluetooth headset, press and hold the button while opening the microphone. Keep holding the button. The iOS device automatically recognizes the device and lists it as discoverable.

Step 4.   Tap the device name; it should automatically connect as shown in Figure 20-15.

Step 5.   Enter a PIN code if prompted.

To remove the device, tap it. On the next screen, tap **Forget This Device**. To stop using it but keep it paired, tap **Disconnect**.

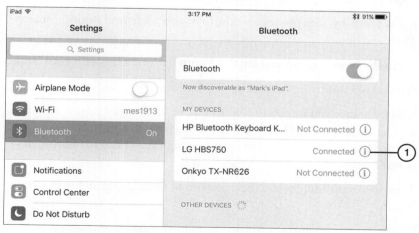

1. Connected device

Figure 20-15   A connected Bluetooth headset on an iOS device.

Note that most Bluetooth devices can only be connected to one mobile device at a time. If you need to switch the Bluetooth device from one mobile device to another, be sure to disconnect it or "forget" it from the current connection before making a new one.

NOTE   To make driving and using a cell phone at the same time safer, take advantage of Bluetooth pairing with your car stereo system. It's the ultimate "hands-free" device.

Email Configuration

Other than making and receiving calls, perhaps the most important function of a smartphone is its ability to send and receive email. Sending and receiving email is also an important function of tablets. In the following sections you learn how to configure email on Android and iOS devices.

Corporate and ISP Email Configuration

There are two different types of email service used by corporations and ISPs: **POP3** (Post Office Protocol 3) and **IMAP4** (Internet Message Access Protocol v4). Depending upon how you receive email, you might need to configure your device to receive either or both types of email services.

To set up a POP3 email account, you must know the server that you want to connect to, the port you need to use, and whether security is being employed.

The following is a step-by-step process of how to connect a typical Android smartphone to a POP3 account.

Step 1.   Go to the Home screen and tap the **Menu** button. Then select **All Apps**.

Step 2.   Scroll down until you see the Email (Mail) app.

Step 3.   Select whether you want a POP3, IMAP, or Exchange account. (For this step-by-step, we select POP3.) If the device already has email accounts set up on it, you might need to open **Settings** and then tap the **Add account** button.

Step 4.   Type the email address and the password of the account and then tap **Next**.

Step 5.   Configure the incoming settings if prompted. Change the username if desired to something different than the email address and then type the POP3 server name. By default, this is the domain name portion of the email address, which is usually correct. If security is being used, select

SSL or TLS. This information should be supplied by the network administrator. Type the port number—for POP3, this is 110 by default. If port numbers are different, they will be supplied to you by the network administrator. Then tap **Next**.

Step 6.   Configure the outgoing settings. Type the SMTP server. Organizations often use the same server name as the POP3 server. However, small office and home office users might have to use their ISP's SMTP server. If security is being used, select SSL or TLS. Type the port number. For SMTP, this is 25. Then tap **Next**.

Step 7.   Configure account options. From here you can tell the mobile device how often to check for mail and whether to notify you when it arrives. Tap **Next**. At this point, new email should start downloading.

Step 8.   Finally, you can give the account an easier name for you to remember it by. Tap **Done**.

Now let's show a step-by-step process on how to connect an iOS device to a POP3 account.

Step 1.   Go to the Home screen and tap the **Settings** button.

Step 2.   Tap **Mail**, **Contacts**, **Calendars**.

Step 3.   Tap **Add Account**.

Step 4.   Tap **Other** at the bottom of the list.

Step 5.   Tap **Add Mail Account**.

Step 6.   Type the name, email address, and password (and an optional description) and tap **Next**.

Step 7.   Tap **Pop**. Then under Incoming Mail Server, type the POP3 server name and the username. Under Outgoing Mail Server, type the SMTP server. Then tap **Save**.

Step 8.   The system verifies the address and password. If successful, the process is finished. If not, check that everything was typed correctly and that the correct parameters, such as the type of server and security, have been configured.

Connecting to IMAP or Exchange Servers

Now, if you instead have to connect an IMAP account, you must enter the IMAP server (for receiving mail), which uses port 143 by default, and the outgoing SMTP server (for sending mail). If you connect to a Microsoft **Exchange** mail server, that server name often takes care of both receiving and sending email. You might need to know the domain that the Exchange server is a member of. Secure email sessions require the use of **SSL** or TLS on port 443. Check with the network administrator to find out which protocol to use. POP3 also has a secure derivative known as APOP, a challenge/response protocol that uses a hashing function to prevent replay attacks during an email session. This protocol can be chosen from the Android platform and is also used by Mozilla Thunderbird, Windows Live Mail, and Apple Mail.

To add **S/MIME** (encryption) support to an email account, turn on the Sign All Outgoing Emails option and create keys for your email accounts.

Integrated Commercial Provider Email Configuration

To set up web-based services such as **Google/Inbox (Gmail)**, **Yahoo! Mail**, or **Outlook.com**, you can use or install the appropriate app from your device's app store.

For example, Android devices come with a Gmail application built in, allowing a user to access Gmail directly without having to use the browser. Apple iOS devices allow connectivity to Gmail, Yahoo!, iCloud Mail, Exchange, Outlook, AOL, and a host of other email providers as well.

Connecting to these services is simple, and works similarly to using a desktop or laptop computer. Choose the type of provider you use, enter a username (the email address) and password (on Apple devices an Apple ID is also required), and the user will have access to web-based email.

When troubleshooting issues with email, make sure that the username and password are typed correctly. Using onscreen keyboards often leads to mistyped passwords. Also make sure that the mobile device is currently connected to the Internet.

PRI Updates/PRL Updates/Baseband Updates

Updates to your smartphone's Preferred Roaming List (**PRL**) and baseband (the portion of the smartphones that makes connections to the cellular network for phone and data) are performed automatically by mobile providers.

When a smartphone or cellular-equipped tablet reports that a system update is available, **PRL** and **baseband** are two of the items that might be updated. For example, in reviewing the AT&T updates to my Samsung Galaxy S6 phone, there were five updates to the baseband out of six total updates between May 2015 and March 2016.

PRI updates (not to be confused with PRL updates) are used to control the speed at which data is sent from a mobile device to a cell tower. PRI updates are also sent automatically and help assure that the cell tower receives data at an acceptable rate.

Radio Firmware

Many of the latest smartphones now include an FM radio chip as part of the **radio firmware**. However, before a smartphone can be used for FM radio, all three of these requirements must be satisfied:

- The phone's FM chips must have a connection to the headphone jack.

- The wireless carrier must permit FM radio apps to access the chip.

- The phone manufacturer must install software controls for the FM chip (volume, tuning, on/off, and so on).

NOTE   To view devices and mobile phone service providers who support NextRadio FM radio, see http://nextradioapp.com/supported-devices/.

IMEI vs IMSI

There are two international standards used to identify cell phones and other devices with cellular service:

- **IMEI**—International Mobile Station Equipment Identity is used to identify phones that support the most common types of cell phones (on the GSM, UMTS, LTE, and iDEN networks). The IMEI can be used to block access to a stolen phone. MEID numbers used by CDMA networks (Sprint, Verizon, and US Cellular) work in the same way as IMEI numbers. Some vendors refer to these numbers as IMEI/MEID numbers.

- **IMSI**—International Mobile Subscriber Identity is used to identify the subscriber using a cell network. It is usually stored in the phone or tablet's SIM card.

In the event that a cell phone is stolen, the owner can contact the cell phone provider and request that the phone be blocked by using its IMEI number. The cell phone provider usually has a record of the IMEI number and can block the phone from being used, even if the SIM card is changed. Support for cell phone blocking by IMEI number varies from provider to provider and from country to country.

If the owner of the stolen cell phone replaces the phone, the new SIM card can be provisioned with the same IMSI code because that code identifies the user of the phone rather than the phone itself.

TIP   To see the IMEI or MEID number for your phone, type *#06# as if you are dialing a phone number. The code is displayed immediately.

VPN

Virtual Private Network (**VPN**) connections aren't just for laptop and desktop computers. VPN connections are also supported by iOS, Android, and Windows 10 Mobile devices.

VPN settings vary by the VPN type, so be sure to know the VPN type and settings needed for the VPN before you create the connection.

To create a VPN with an iOS device, open **Settings > General > VPN > Add VPN Configuration**.

To create a VPN with an Android device, open **Settings > More connection settings > VPN** and then choose **Basic VPN** or **Advanced IPSec VPN**.

To create a VPN with a Windows 10 Mobile device, open **Settings > Network & Internet > VPN > Add a VPN connection**.

Data Synchronization

Synchronization is the matching up of files, email, and other types of data between one computer and another. We use synchronization to bring files in line with each other and to force devices to coordinate their data. When dealing with synchronization, a mobile device can connect to a PC via USB (the most common), other serial connections (much less common), Wi-Fi, and Bluetooth.

The types of files that can be synchronized include:

- **Contacts**
- **Programs**
- **Email**
- **Pictures**
- **Music**
- **Videos**
- **Calendar**
- **Bookmarks**

- **Documents**
- **Location data**
- **Social media data**
- **eBooks**

NOTE For the 220-902 exam, you should know the above list along with:

- Synchronization methods: synchronize to the Cloud, synchronize to the Desktop
- Mutual authentication for multiple services (SSO)
- Software requirements to install the application on the PC
- Connection types to enable synchronization

Synchronization Methods

There are two main methods used for synchronization:

- **Synchronization to the cloud**
- **Synchronization to the desktop**

Cloud-Based Synchronization

With cloud-based synchronization, apps on the mobile device send data to the cloud where it is downloaded by other mobile apps, by web browsers, or by programs running on Windows or OS X computers. Examples of cloud-based synchronization include:

- DropBox (www.dropbox.com)
- Samsung Smart Switch (www.samsung.com)
- Apple iCloud (www.apple.com/icloud)
- Microsoft OneDrive (https://onedrive.live.com)
- Google Drive (www.google.com)

Cloud-based synchronization is encrypted and secured by passwords and user names. Mutual authentication is used by each side of the connection to verify its identity to the other side.

> **Mutual Authentication for Multiple Services (SSO)**
>
> **Mutual authentication** for multiple services (also known as SSO or Single Sign-On) is used by Apple, Microsoft, and Google to enable a single login to provide access to multiple services. For example, a single Microsoft account login provides access to Outlook email, the Windows app store, and OneDrive. A single Apple login provides access to iTunes, iCloud, and other services. A single Google login provides access to Gmail, Android services, and other services.

Desktop-Based Synchronization

With desktop-based synchronization, the user connects the mobile device via a USB cable. With Android-based devices connected to Windows, the mobile device is treated as a drive and data can be dragged and dropped between devices. Third-party options such as Android File Transfer (www.android.com) enable OS X to have simple browse and copy file transfers similar to Windows. On an iOS device, iTunes is used for file transfer and synchronization for music and media files.

Email Synchronization

Email synchronization options are based on the email service in. For example, Microsoft Exchange email uses Exchange ActiveSync. When an email account is configured on a mobile device, synchronization settings are configured as part of the process and can be adjusted, disabled, or re-enabled as needed later.

Software Requirements for Synchronization Software

Most desktop synchronization software for all current versions of Windows requires the PC to have 1GB of RAM or more, USB 2.0 ports minimum, and 300MB of free space on the hard drive. Most desktop synchronization software for OS X requires OS X 10.5 or greater and available USB port, although some require newer versions.

Connection Types for Synchronization Software

For desktop-based synchronization, USB 2.0 ports are the minimum requirement, although some also support Bluetooth connections.

For cloud-based synchronization, the appropriate app or web service must be loaded on the mobile device and the computer used for file synchronization and Internet access must be available.

Exam Preparation Tasks

Review All the Key Topics

Review the most important topics in the chapter, noted with the key topics icon in the outer margin of the page. Table 20-2 lists a reference of these key topics and the page numbers on which each is found.

Table 20-2 Key Topics for Chapter 20

Key Topic Element	Description	Page Number
Section	GPS and Geotracking	992
Section	Tethering	998
Section	Hotspot	999
Paragraph	Setting up email using POP3 or IMAP4 mail servers	1006

Define Key Terms

Define the following key terms from this chapter, and check your answers in the glossary.

Android, iOS, Windows, open-source, closed-source, vendor-specific, Google Play Store, Apple App Store, Windows Store), accelerometer, gyroscope, screen calibration, Global Positioning System (GPS), geotracking, Wi-Fi calling, virtual assistant, SDK/APK, emergency notification, mobile payment service, cellular data network, hotspot, tethering, airplane mode, Bluetooth, pairing, PIN, POP3, IMAP, SSL, Exchange, S/MIME, Google/Inbox, Gmail, Yahoo!, Outlook.com, iCloud, PRI, PRL, baseband (cellular), radio firmware, IMEI, IMSI, VPN, synchronization contacts, programs, email, pictures, music, videos, calendar, bookmarks, documents, location data, social media data, eBooks, synchronize to the cloud, synchronize to the desktop, mutual authentication for multiple services (SSO)

Complete Hands-On Labs

Complete the hands-on labs, and then see the answers and explanations at the end of the chapter.

Lab 20-1: Updating Mobile Devices and Enabling Personal Assistants

Note the brand, model, and operating system of each mobile device you use.

If there are updates available for personally owned devices, check online news sources or with the device vendor for any issues and then update them when it is convenient.

If there are updates available for organization-owned devices, check with your supervisor regarding the update policy.

Set up the personal assistant on your personally owned devices. If personal assistants can be used with organization-owned devices, help other users set theirs up.

Lab 20-2: Tethering, Hot Spots, and Synchronization

Set up tethering on a smart phone and test it.

Set up a hotspot on a smart phone and test it.

Check smart phones you use for the latest PRI, PRL, and baseband update information.

Use cloud-based and desktop-based synchronization to back up at least one of the mobile devices you use. If you have both iOS and Android, use each OS's synchronization app or service.

Answer Review Questions

1. Which of the following best describe the Android operating system? (Choose all that apply.)

   A. Open source

   B. Linux based

   C. Developed by Google

   D. May be modified by user

2. Match the operating system with the application download site for each.

Operating System	Application Download Site
A. Android	
B. Apple iOS	
C. Windows 10 Mobile	

Answer Options:

1. Windows Store
2. Google Play
3. App Store

3. The act of hacking a user's own iOS devices to remove any licensing restrictions is known as which of the following?

    A. Rooting

    B. Jailbreaking

    C. Tethering

    D. Hotspot

4. What is the name of the Android utility that is used to calibrate the screen along the X axis, the Y axis, and the Z axis?

    A. Launcher

    B. Gyroscope

    C. G-Sensor

    D. Accelerometer

5. Which of the following best describes a virtual assistant?

    A. A virtual assistant is a voice-activated search app.

    B. A virtual assistant is a method for organizing files and folders.

    C. A virtual assistant is a feature in a SDK.

    D. A virtual assistant is an online help utility.

6. Which of the following should be downloaded when developing an app for a mobile operating system?

    A. Virtual assistant

    B. SDK

    C. Launcher

    D. APK

7. Which of the following are methods of sharing a wireless connection?

    A. IMAP

    B. Hotspot

    C. Tethering

    D. SSL

8. Which of the following statements best describes airplane mode?

   A. Airplane mode allows mobile devices to communicate safely while in flight.

   B. Airplane mode is an FCC regulation controlling the use of mobile devices on airplanes.

   C. Airplane mode allows mobile devices to communicate only when they are attached to each other by cable.

   D. Airplane mode turns off all wireless antennas so that mobile devices cannot transmit or receive data while in flight.

9. Bluetooth 3.0+HS uses which of the following networking standards?

   A. FireWire

   B. WEP

   C. Ethernet

   D. 802.11

10. Which of the following statements best describes Bluetooth? (Choose all that apply.)

   A. Bluetooth devices form short-range, low-speed wireless networks.

   B. Bluetooth devices connect to form a PAN.

   C. Bluetooth devices create peer-to-peer networks.

   D. Bluetooth devices allow dissimilar devices to communicate on the same network.

11. When setting up a POP3 email account, which type of security protocol might you select for incoming mail? (Choose two.)

   A. HTTP

   B. HTTPS

   C. TLS

   D. SSL

12. Which port is used for POP3?

   A. 25

   B. 53

   C. 80

   D. 110

13. If your phone is stolen, which of the following enables the phone to be blocked so that the thief cannot use it?

   A. SDK

   B. IMEI

   C. S/MIME

   D. IMSI

14. Which of the following are the two basic methods of synchronization? (Choose two.)

   A. Synchronization to the cloud

   B. Synchronization to the app

   C. Synchronization to the drive

   D. Synchronization to the desktop

Answers and Explanations to Hands-On Labs

Lab 20-1: Updating Mobile Devices and Enabling Personal Assistants

If you have two or more devices that use iOS, were they all running the same version of iOS? Keep in mind that some recent iOS versions are not necessarily recommended for the oldest devices they support.

Did you discover any issues with updates you can make for a personally owned or organization-owned device? Sources such as The Register (www.register.co.uk), Neowin (www.neowin.net), and MaximumPC (www.maximumpc.com) are some of the sources I check for issues with bad updates.

Lab 20-2: Tethering, Hot Spots, and Synchronization

Tethering and hot spots can use up a smartphone battery more quickly, so be sure to keep your devices charged or use a portable battery charger.

If you have problems with tethering or charging, make sure your USB sync/charging cable is in good working order.

If you had any problems with synchronization, check to see if you followed all the requirements. These might include locking your device, having enough battery power, and making the computer a trusted device.

Answers and Explanations to Review Questions

1. **A, B, C, D.** All of these answers describe the Android operating system. Android is open source; iOS and Windows 10 Mobile are closed source.

2.

Operating System	Application Download Site
A. Android	2. Google Play
B. Apple iOS	3. App Store
C. Windows 10 Mobile	1. Windows Store

3. **B.** Jailbreaking is the removal of restrictions imposed by the iOS licensing agreement. In the Android operating system, this process is known as rooting.

4. **C.** G-Sensor is Android's screen orientation utility. The accelerometer and gyroscope control screen orientation in iOS apps. Launcher allows users to organize and customize their apps on smartphones and tablets.

5. **A.** A virtual assistant is a voice-activated search app that can be programmed to respond to any voice or only to a specific voice. Examples are Google's OK Google, Apple's Siri, and Microsoft's Cortana.

6. **B, D.** An SDK is a collection of programming tools used in the development of apps. You should download the SDK for the specific operating system for which you want to create an app. An APK is the file format used to package Android apps for distribution. Virtual assistant is a voice-activated search program. Launcher is used to organize and customize apps on a mobile device. G-Sensor is Android's screen orientation utility.

7. **B, C.** Tethering allows two devices to share an Internet connection via a USB cable. A hotspot sets up the smartphone as a temporary SSID that other devices can connect to. IMAP is a protocol for receiving email and SSL is a method for encrypting email.

8. **D.** Airplane mode turns off the antennas in mobile devices so that they cannot transmit or receive data while in flight.

9. **D.** Bluetooth 3.0+HS uses an 802.11 wireless network for data transmission. FireWire is not a networking standard. WEP is an obsolete wireless encryption standard, not a network standard as such. Ethernet is a wired networking standard.

10. **A, B, C, D.** Bluetooth creates a short-range, low-speed, peer-to-peer network populated by dissimilar devices. This type of network is called a PAN (personal area network).

11. **C, D.** SSL and the more advanced TLS provide encryption for secure communication between the email server and the web browser.

12. **D.** POP3 uses port 110 for incoming mail, IMAP uses port 143 for incoming mail, and SMTP uses port 25 for outgoing mail. Port 53 is used for DNS. Port 80 is used for HTTP.

13. **B.** IMEI identifies a mobile device by assigning it a unique security code that allows the network provider or cell phone company to identify and then disable the device when it is reported lost or stolen. You can view this unique identifier by entering *#06# on the device's keypad. IMSI identifies the owner of the device. SDK assists programmers to develop apps for mobile devices. S/MIME provides encryption support for email.

14. **A, D.** Synchronization to the cloud or to the desktop are the two methods that the A+ exam expects you to know. Synchronization to the cloud makes use of secure user ID and password and uses mutual authentication. With synchronization to the desktop, the user must have access to both the mobile device and the computer and the two devices must be physically connected by a cable.

This chapter covers the following subjects:

- **Common Security Threats and Vulnerabilities**—Discover the wide variety of electronic, physical, and human vulnerabilities that can be targeted by data thieves, both human and virtual.

- **Common Prevention Methods**—Discover how to implement protection at a physical and digital level as well as safeguarding the human element.

- **Windows Basic Security Settings**—Learn the basic security features built into Windows and how they work.

- **Best Security Practices for Workstations**—From data encryption to password best practices, discover the policies that help keep workstations on a network safe.

- **Securing Mobile Devices**—Smartphones and tablets can be exploited by malware and human data thieves. This section discusses how to stop them.

- **Data Destruction and Disposal Methods**—In this section, you learn how to destroy data and, when necessary, the devices that store the data to prevent it from being exploited when storage devices and media are retired.

- **SOHO Network Security**—A small office/home office network could be the pathway to a large-scale attack if it isn't secured. Discover the methods needed to help lock down both wired and wireless networks.

## CHAPTER 21

Security

Server rooms, networks, desktops, laptops, and mobile devices provide access to financial data and personal information for businesses, governments, organizations, and individuals all over the world. And, thanks to the interconnected nature of the Internet, a security breach of a single device or network can lead to identity theft, electronic embezzlement, and other threats to the financial and personal lives of millions.

In this chapter, you learn about the multi-faceted threats to security in the modern computing environment and how to deal with them.

220-902: Objective 3.1 Identify common security threats and vulnerabilities.

220-902: Objective 3.2 Compare and contrast common prevention methods.

220-902: Objective 3.3 Compare and contrast differences of basic Windows OS security settings.

220-902: Objective 3.4 Given a scenario, deploy and enforce security best practices to secure a workstation.

220-902: Objective 3.5 Compare and contrast various methods for securing mobile devices.

220-902: Objective 3.6 Given a scenario, use appropriate data destruction and disposal methods.

220-902: Objective 3.7 Given a scenario, secure SOHO wireless and wired networks.

Foundation Topics

Common Security Threats and Vulnerabilities

Security threats and vulnerabilities can come from software or network attacks, but they also target users themselves and their perceptions of who and what can be trusted. In the following sections, we take a closer look at these threats.

> **NOTE**   The 220-902 exam expects you to understand the following security threats:
>
> - Malware, including:
>   - Spyware
>   - Viruses
>   - Worms
>   - Trojans
>   - Rootkits
>   - Ransomware
> - Phishing
> - Spear phishing
> - Spoofing
> - Social engineering
> - Shoulder surfing
> - Zero day attack
> - Zombie/botnet
> - Brute forcing
> - Dictionary attacks
> - Non-compliant systems
> - Violations of security best practices
> - Tailgating
> - Man-in-the-middle

Malware

Malware is a combination of the words *malicious* and *software*. It is any type of software that is used to disrupt computers and gain unauthorized access to systems, networks, and data. The following sections discuss the malware types and infection methods you should understand for the 220-902 exam.

Spyware

Spyware is software that spies on system activities and transmits details of web searches or other activities to remote computers. If you get multiple unwanted pop-up windows when browsing the Internet, it's a good indicator of spyware. Some pop-up windows will show fake security alerts in the hopes that you will click on something that will lead to a purchase such as rogue or fake antivirus software (or perhaps will lead to more malware). Spyware can possibly cause slow system performance. Figure 21-1 illustrates a fake security alert.

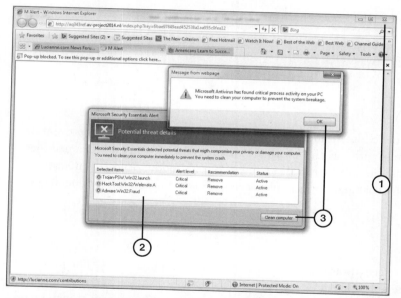

1. The only safe place to click is the close browser button.
2. Fictitious threats.
3. Clicking either of these buttons might launch malware or spyware.

Figure 21-1   This dialog purports to be from Microsoft Antivirus.

CAUTION   Some free apps are advertiser-supported. Many of these apps track your web searches and use the information to display targeted ads.

Viruses

A **virus** is a program that infects files in an operating system; it wreaks havoc on the system by rewriting those files so that they do what the programmer of the virus wants. Viruses can replicate but usually only if the user executes them (unknowingly). Both of these are commonly sent to the unsuspecting user through e-mail or might be found on removable media such as a USB flash drive. Viruses can also hijack a browser and cause it to be redirected to undesirable websites. If your browser suddenly accesses strange sites, a full virus scan will be necessary. Viruses can also cause slow system performance. Viruses might also be the culprit for Internet connectivity issues if they modify the DNS server or gateway address. Computer lockups can also be attributed to viruses and can cause Windows updates to fail.

Worms

Worms are similar to viruses but can self-replicate; no user intervention is required.

Trojan Horse

Trojan horses are malware programs disguised as popular videos or website links that trap keystrokes or transmit sensitive information.

Rootkits

Rootkits are a concealment method used by many types of malware to prevent detection by normal antivirus and anti-malware programs. If you find renamed files, especially system files, this could be an indicator of a rootkit. Another indicator is file permission changes (for example, access denied) and files that suddenly go missing.

Ransomware

Ransomware uses malware to encrypt the targeted computer's files. The ransom demand might be presented after you call a bogus technical support number displayed by a fake error message coming from the ransomware, or the ransom demand might be displayed on-screen. The ransom must be paid within a specified amount of time or the files will not be decrypted.

Phishing

Phishing involves the creation of bogus websites or sending fraudulent e-mails that trick users into providing personal, bank, or credit card information. A variation, phone phishing, uses an interactive voice response (IVR) system that the user has been tricked into calling to dupe the user into revealing information.

Figure 21-2 illustrates a typical phishing e-mail.

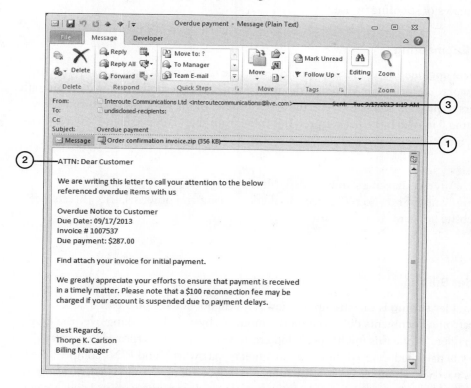

1. Zip archive files are frequently used by malware; open the file and your system is infected
2. Genuine emails from a company you work with will be addressed to a person or account number
3. Live.com is typically used by personal email, not company email

Figure 21-2   This message purports to be about an overdue payment, but shows classic signs of a phishing attack.

Spear Phishing

Spear phishing involves the sending of spoof messages that appear to come from an internal source requesting confidential information, such as payroll or tax information. These attacks typically target a specific person, organization, or business.

Spoofing

Spoofing is a general term for malware attacks that purport to come from a trustworthy source. Phishing, spear phishing, and rogue antivirus programs are three examples of spoofing in use.

Social Engineering

Social engineering is a term popularized by the career of successful computer and network hacker Kevin Mitnick, who used a variety of methods to convince computer users to provide access to restricted systems. One of his favorites is known as "pretexting," in which the hacker pretends to be from the IT department, an investigator, a co-worker from another department, and so on.

NOTE   After his hacking career ended, Mitnick became a security consultant. To learn more about how to recognize social engineering and other security threats, see his website at www.mitnicksecurity.com.

Shoulder Surfing

Shoulder surfing is the attempt to view physical documents on a user's desk or electronic documents displayed on the monitor, by actually looking over the user's shoulder. While this might sound ludicrous, you would be surprised how many people have had their confidential documents, passwords, and PINs compromised in this manner. Shoulder surfers either act covertly, looking around corners, using mirrors or binoculars, or they might introduce themselves to the user and make conversation in the hopes that the user will let his or her guard down.

Zero-Day Attack

A **zero-day attack** (zero-day exploit) takes advantage of a not-yet-patched security flaw in an operating system or app, frequently on the same day the vulnerability has become known. For information about current threats, see Trend Micro's http://www.zerodayinitiative.com/ website.

Zombie/Botnet

A **zombie/botnet** is a computer on the Internet that has been taken over by a hostile program so it can be used for malware distribution, distributed denial of service (DDoS) or other attacks without notification to the normal users of the computer.

Many malware attacks attempt to turn targeted computers into zombies on a hostile botnet.

Brute Forcing

Brute forcing (brute-force attack) is a method of cracking passwords by calculating and using every possible combination of characters until the correct password is discovered. The longer the password used and the greater the number of possible characters in a password, the longer brute forcing will take. Brute forcing can be blocked by locking systems after a specified number of incorrect passwords are offered.

Dictionary Attacks

Dictionary attacks attempt to crack passwords by trying all the words in a list, such as a dictionary. A simple list might include commonly used passwords such as "12345678" and "password." Dictionary attacks can be blocked by locking systems after a specified number of incorrect passwords are offered.

Non-Compliant Systems

Non-compliant systems are systems that are tagged by a configuration manager application (for example, Microsoft's System Center Configuration Manager) because they do not have the most up-to-date security patches installed. Systems that don't have the most up-to-date security patches are especially vulnerable to attacks.

NOTE To see if your own system is missing security updates, download and run Belarc Advisor (http://www.belarc.com/free_download.html), and select the option to update security information.

Violations of Security Best Practices

The specifics of a particular organization's security practices might vary, but in general, systems with the following problems can be said to violate **security best practices:**

- Not updated with the latest security patches for the operating system and apps
- No password or have weak, easily guessed passwords
- Outdated or no antivirus or anti-malware app
- No use of encryption to protect data storage or file transfers
- No use of digital certificates to sign websites
- No limitations on removable media such as USB or rewriteable optical drives

- No use of SSL or other security measures on websites
- No e-mail spam filters
- No network-based security
- No wireless security or weak WEP encryption
- No user training in how to implement security best practices

For more details on many of the items in this list, see www.zdnet.com/article/10-security-best-practice-guidelines-for-businesses/.

Tailgating

Tailgating occurs when an unauthorized person attempts to accompany an authorized person into a secure area by following them closely and grabbing the door before it shuts. This is usually done without the authorized person's consent. If the authorized person is knowingly involved it is known as *piggybacking*.

Man-in-the-Middle

A **man-in-the-middle (MiTM)** attack involves the attacker intercepting a connection while fooling the endpoints into thinking they are communicating directly with each other. Essentially, the attacker becomes an unauthorized and undetected proxy or relay point, using this position to capture confidential data or transmit altered information to one or both ends of the original connection.

Bluetooth Threats

Bluetooth isn't just for convenient wireless connection to devices—it's a network, and any network has vulnerabilities. Three security threats Bluetooth users need to watch out for include:

- Bluejacking—The sending of unauthorized messages over a Bluetooth connection to a device.

- Bluesnarfing—Provides unauthorized access from a wireless device through a Bluetooth connection.

- Bluebugging—Creates unauthorized backdoor access to connect a Bluetooth device back to the attacker.

Common Prevention Methods

Preventing security breaches includes four factors:

- Physical security
- Digital security

- User education/acceptable use policy (AUP)
- Principle of least privilege

The following sections explain these concepts in greater detail.

> **NOTE** For the 220-902 exam, be familiar with these factors in general and in detail.

Physical Security

In some ways, nothing beats physical security. For example, no matter how great the computer hacker, a computer simply cannot open a physical keyed lock. So having locking doors is the first step in protecting an investment, whatever it might be. The door locking system might also incorporate proximity-based access cards, or smart cards. Some organizations combine these types of door security with a biometrics system that, for example, analyzes a person's thumbprint. Finally, documents and passwords should be physically protected. This is generally accomplished by locking the documents in a secure area and by implementing a clean-desk policy.

Lock doors

The easiest way to secure an area is to lock doors! Some organizations have written policies explaining how, when, and where to lock doors. Aside from main entrances, you should also always lock server rooms, wiring closets, labs, and other technical rooms when not in use.

Physical door locks might seem low-tech, but they can't be hacked or taken over by hackers. Other precautions to take include: documenting who has keys to server rooms and wiring closets, and periodically changing locks and keys. Cipher locks that use punch codes also enhance security. Combine these methods with electronic security for greater protection.

Mantrap

Some secure areas include what is known as a **mantrap**: an area with two locking doors. A person might get past a first door by way of tailgating, but might have difficulty getting past the second door, especially if there is a guard in between the two doors. If the person doesn't have proper authentication, he will be stranded in the mantrap until authorities arrive.

Cable Locks

Cable locks can be used to secure laptops and other equipment that include the Kensington security lock port. See "Laptop and Cable Locks," p.547, Chapter 12 for details.

Securing Physical documents/Passwords/Shredding

Securing physical documents, passwords, and shredding are three methods of protecting information in an office.

Confidential documents should never be left sitting out in the open. They should either be properly filed in a locking cabinet or shredded and disposed of if they are no longer needed.

Passwords should not be written down and definitely not left on a desk or taped to a monitor where they can be seen. Many organizations implement a clean desk policy that states users must remove all papers from their desk before leaving for lunch, breaks, or at the end of the day.

Also, the user should lock the computer whenever he leaves the workstation. Desktop and mobile operating systems can also be automatically set to lock after a certain amount of time, even if the user forgets to do so manually.

Biometrics

Biometrics refers to the use of biological information, such as human body characteristics, to authenticate a potential user of a secure area. The most common type of biometric security system for PCs is fingerprint-based, but other methods include voice measurements, face recognition, and scans of the eye's retina or iris.

NOTE Windows Hello (a feature of Windows 10) is an example of biometrics built into an operating system. Windows Hello uses fingerprint readers and high-resolution cameras built into some computers and mobile devices for facial recognition. Learn more about Windows Hello at http://windows.microsoft.com/en-us/windows-10/getstarted-what-is-hello.

ID Badges

ID badges can use a variety of physical security methods:

- Photos—If the bearer of the card doesn't look like the person on the card, the bearer might be using someone else's card and should be detained.

- Barcodes—A barcode enables the card to carry a range of information about the bearer, including levels of access, and can be read quickly by a barcode scanner.

- RFID technology—Cards with RFID chips can be used to open only doors that are matched to the RFID chip.

To prevent undetected tampering, ID badges should be coated with a tamper-evident outer layer.

RFID Badge

An ID badge can include radio-frequency identification (RFID) technology, making it an **RFID badge**. RFID badges typically are passive, receiving power from the radio waves of the RFID receiver. The RFID chip can also store information about the user.

Key Fobs

Key fobs can be used with a variety of security devices. They can contain RFID chips, but many key fobs are used as part of a two-phase authentication protocol:

Phase 1. The user logs into the key fob with a PIN.

Phase 2. The user logs into the system or restricted area using a randomly generated access code displayed on the key fob's LCD display. The code changes every 30 to 60 seconds.

A key fob used in this way is often referred to as a token.

Smart Card

A **smart card** is a credit-card–sized card that contains stored information and might also contain a simple microprocessor or a radio-frequency identification (RFID) chip. Smart cards can be used to store identification information for use in security applications, stored values for use in prepaid telephone or debit card services, hotel guest room access, and many other functions. Smart cards are available in contact, contactless, or proximity form factors.

A smart card–based security system includes smart cards, card readers that are designed to work with smart cards, and a back-end system that contains a database that stores a list of approved smart cards for each secured location. Smart card–based security systems can also be used to secure individual personal computers.

To further enhance security, smart card security systems can also require the user to input a PIN or security password as well as provide the smart card at secured checkpoints, such as the entrance to a computer room.

Tokens

Any physical device that a user must carry to gain access to a specific system can be called a **token**, such as a smart card, an RFID card, or a key fob.

Privacy Filters

Anything that shows on the computer screen can be protected in a variety of ways. To protect data while the person is working, you can install a **privacy filter**, which is a transparent cover for PC monitors and laptop displays. It reduces the cone of vision, usually to about 30 degrees, so that only the person in front of the screen can see the content. Many of these are also antiglare, helping to reduce eye stress of the user.

Entry Control Roster

An **entry control roster**, which is a list of those individuals or representatives who are authorized to enter a secured area, can be used with a variety of security systems. Potential entrants can be looked up on an entry control roster and will be granted access if their credentials match those listed. A keypad lock on an entrance into a secure area can store a list of authorized PINs. Only users with a recognized PIN can enter the secure area.

Digital Security

Physical security helps stop physical threats, such as stolen paper files, hard disks, or other confidential information. However, for many organizations, a far bigger threat is digital thievery and destruction. **Digital security** is designed to stop online, network, and e-mail–based threats.

Antivirus/Anti-malware

Protection against viruses and malware is necessary for every type of computing device, from mobile devices to servers. Computer protection suites that include **antivirus, anti-malware**, anti-adware, and antiphishing protection are available from many vendors, but some users prefer a "best of breed" approach that uses the best available products in each category.

These programs can use some or all of the following techniques to protect users and systems:

- Real-time protection to block infection
- Periodic scans for known and suspected threats
- Automatic updating on a frequent (usually daily) basis
- Renewable subscriptions to obtain updated threat signatures
- Links to virus and threat encyclopedias
- Inoculation of system files
- Permissions-based access to the Internet
- Scanning of downloaded files and sent/received e-mails

When attempting to protect against viruses and malware, the most important thing to remember is to keep your anti-malware application up to date. The second most important item is to watch out for unknown data, whether it comes via e-mail, USB flash drive, mobile device, or elsewhere.

Firewalls

A software firewall is a program that examines data packets on a network to determine whether to forward them to their destination or block them. **Firewalls** can be used to protect against inbound threats only (one-way firewall) or against both unauthorized inbound and outbound traffic; this type of firewall is often referred to as a *two-way* firewall.

As initially configured, the standard firewall in Windows is a one-way firewall. However, it can be configured to work as a two-way firewall. For more information about how it works, see "Firewall Settings," p.862, Chapter 16. Most third-party firewall programs, such as ZoneAlarm, are two-way firewalls.

OS X 10.5 includes an application firewall. In OS X 10.6 and newer, the application firewall offers additional customization options. For details, see https://support.apple.com/en-us/HT201642.

Linux, starting with distros based on kernel 2.4.x and above, includes `iptables` to configure its packet-filtering framework, netfilter. To learn more, see www.netfilter.org. Many distros and third-party Linux apps are available to help make `iptables` and netfilter easier to configure.

A software firewall can be configured to permit traffic between specified IP addresses and to block traffic to and from the Internet except when permitted on a per-program basis.

Corporate networks sometimes use a proxy server with a firewall as the sole direct connection between the Internet and the corporate network and use the firewall in the proxy server to protect the corporate network against threats.

Geofencing

A geofence is a virtual barrier (www.makeuseof.com/tag/can-use-geofencing-improve-privacy-security/). Programs that incorporate geofencing allow an administrator to set up triggers so when a device enters (or exits) the boundaries defined by the administrator, a text message or e-mail alert is sent. Geofencing is also used for location-based marketing (http://www.cio.com/article/2383123/mobile/5-things-you-need-to-know-about-geofencing.html).

User Authentication/Strong Passwords

Requiring passwords for **user authentication** can make systems more secure, but if there is no attempt to enforce the creation of strong passwords, all that is being created is an illusion.

Strong passwords have the following characteristics:

- At least 8 characters long—and the longer, the better
- A variety of uppercase and lowercase letters, numbers, and symbols
- Avoid real names and words

NOTE For more about creating strong passwords, see www.businessinsider.com/how-to-create-strong-password-heartbleed-2014-4.

Multifactor Authentication

The best type of authentication system is one that uses two or more authentication methods. This is known as **multifactor authentication**. An example of this would be a person using a smart card and typing a username and password to gain access to a system. The combination of the password and the physical token makes it very difficult for imposters to gain access to a system.

Directory Permissions

Directory permissions is the term used in OS X and Linux for configuring the access levels a user has to a directory (folder) and individual files. In Windows, the equivalent term is *file and folder permissions*.

In Linux and OS X, directory permissions include:

- Read (opens file)
- Write (changes file)
- Execute (runs executable file or opens directory)

The `chmod` command is used in Linux to change directory permissions. In OS X, the Get Info menu's Sharing & Permissions submenu is used to change directory permissions.

In Windows, file and folder permissions on an NTFS drive include:

- Full control
- Modify
- Read & Execute
- List folder contents (applies to folders only)
- Read
- Write

These settings are configured through the Security tab of the file or folder's properties sheet.

VPN

A Virtual Private Network (**VPN**) is a private (secure) network connection that is carried by an insecure public network, such as the Internet. A VPN connection requires a VPN server at the remote site and a VPN client at the client site. VPN traffic between client and server is encrypted and encapsulated into packets suitable for transmission over the network. VPNs can be used in place of leased lines for connections between locations and for telecommuting workers.

The most common types of VPNs include PPTP and L2TP/IPsec. PPTP uses 128-bit encryption, while L2TP combined with IPsec (L2TP/IPsec) uses 256-bit encryption.

DLP

Data loss/leakage prevention (DLP) refers to the prevention of confidential information from being viewed or stolen by unauthorized parties. DLP goes beyond normal digital security methods such as firewalls and antivirus by observing and analyzing unusual patterns of data access, e-mail, and instant messaging, whether within an organization's network or from the organization's network outwards.

Disabling Ports

Disabling ports refers to preventing specified UDP or TCP ports from being used by a service, application, specific device, or all devices with a firewall appliance or software firewall.

Access Control Lists

Access control lists are the lists of permissions by user and operation for a specific object such as a file or folder. ACLs list which users or groups can perform specific operations on the specified file or folder.

Smart Card

Smart cards can be used to enable logins to a network, encrypt or decrypt drives, and be used for digital signatures when supported by the network server.

E-mail Filtering

E-mail filtering can be used to organize e-mail into folders automatically, but from a security standpoint, its most important function is the blocking of spam and potentially dangerous messages.

E-mail filtering can be performed at the point of entry to a network with a specialized e-mail filtering server or appliance as well as by enabling spam and threat detection features built into e-mail clients or added by security software.

Spam or suspicious e-mails can be discarded or quarantined by the user, and false positives that are actually legitimate messages can be retrieved from the spam folder and placed back into the normal Inbox.

Trusted/Untrusted Software Sources

App stores for iOS, Android, Windows 8 and later, OS X, and many Linux distros are examples of **trusted sources** of software. Apps installed from these sources have been approved by the operating system vendor.

However, not all software for an operating system comes from an app store. Digital certificates included in software are used to identify the publisher, and most operating systems display warning messages when an app without a digital certificate is being installed. Some block the installation of apps that do not have a digital certificate.

> **NOTE** Group policy settings available in Windows 7/8/8.1 can be used to create a Trusted Publishers policy setting to restrict which certificates can be accepted.

User Education/AUP (Acceptable Use Policy)

Regardless of the sophistication of physical or digital security measures, the lack of user education and an **AUP (acceptable use policy)** can lead to security issues. Some elements of a good AUP could include:

- Ask for an ID when approached in person by somebody claiming to be from the help desk, the phone company, or the service company.

- Ask for a name and supervisor name when contacted by phone by someone claiming to be from the help desk, the phone company, or the service company.

- Provide contact information for the help desk, phone company, or authorized service companies and ask users to call the authorized contact person to verify that the service call or phone request for information is legitimate.

- Log in to systems themselves and then provide the tech the computer, rather than giving the tech login information.

- Change passwords immediately after service calls.

- Report any potential social engineering calls or in-person contacts, even if no information was exchanged. Social engineering experts can gather innocuous-sounding information from several users and use it to create a convincing story to gain access to restricted systems.

Users should be educated in how to do the following:

- Keep antivirus, antispyware, and anti-malware programs updated.

- Scan systems for viruses, spyware, and malware.

- Understand major malware types and techniques.

- Scan removable-media drives (optical disks, USB drives) for viruses and malware.

- Disable autorun (the steps for this are shown later).

- Configure scanning programs for scheduled operation.

- Respond to notifications when viruses, spyware, or malware have been detected.

- Quarantine suspect files.

- Report suspect files to the help desk and to the software vendor.

- Remove malware.

- Disable antivirus when needed (such as during software installations) and to know when to reenable antivirus.

- Don't open attachments from unknown senders

- Use antiphishing features in web browsers and e-mail clients.

Principle of Least Permission

The **principle of least privilege** basically says that a user should only have access to what is required. If a person needs to update Excel files and browse the Internet, that person should not be given administrative access. You might think of this as common sense, but it should not be taken lightly. When user accounts are created locally on a computer and especially on a domain, great care should be taken when assigning users to groups. Also, many programs when installed ask who can use and make modifications to the program; often the default is "all users." Some technicians just click Next when hastily installing programs without realizing that the user now has full control of the program, something you might not want. Just remember, keep users on a need-to-know basis; give them access only to what they specifically need and no more.

Windows Basic Security Settings

Controlling access to files, folders, printers, and physical locations is essential for system and network security. The following sections discuss the purposes and principles of access control.

NOTE For the 220-902 exam, be familiar with:

- Users and groups
- NTFS vs share permissions
- Shared files and folders
- System files and folders
- User authentication
- Run as administrator vs. standard user
- BitLocker
- BitLocker To Go
- EFS

Users and Groups

Users in Windows can be assigned to different groups, each with different permissions. The Local Policy (local PCs) and Group Policy (networked PCs connected to a domain controller) settings can restrict PC features by group or by PC. For the 220-902 exam, you need to know the differences between the following accounts:

- Administrator
- Power user
- Guest
- Standard user

There are three standard account levels in Windows:

- **Standard user** —Standard accounts have permission to perform routine tasks. However, these accounts are blocked from performing tasks that involve system-wide changes, such as installing hardware or software unless they can provide an administrator password when prompted by User Account Control (UAC).

- **Administrator**—Users with an administrator account can perform any and all tasks.

- **Guest**—The guest account level is the most limited. A guest account cannot install software or hardware or run already-existing applications and cannot access files in shared document folders or the Guest profile. The Guest account is disabled by default. If it is enabled for a user to gain access to the computer, that access should be temporary and the account should be disabled again when the user no longer requires access.

When a user is created using the Users applet in Windows, the user must be assigned a Standard or Administrator account. Guest accounts are used for visitors.

The **Power users** account was a specific account type in earlier versions of Windows, having more permissions than standard users, but fewer than administrators. In Windows Vista and later versions, power users have the same rights and permissions as standard users. A custom security template can be created if the Power Users group needs specific permissions, such as for the operation of legacy programs.

NTFS vs Share Permissions

NTFS permissions control both local and network access, and can be set for individual users or groups, while **share permissions** affect only network shares. Each permission has two settings: Allow or Deny. Generally, if you want a user to have access to a folder, you would add them to the list and select Allow for the appropriate permission. If you don't want to allow them access, normally you simply wouldn't add them. But in some cases, an explicit Deny is necessary. This could be because the user is part of a larger group that already has access to a parent folder, but you don't want the specific user to have access to this particular subfolder. To learn how permissions are inherited and propagated, see the "Permission Inheritance and Propagation" section on p.1041, this chapter.

Moving and Copying Folders and Files

Moving and copying folders and files will have different results when it comes to permissions. Basically, it breaks down like this:

- When you *copy* a folder or file on the same, or to a different volume, the folder or file inherits the permissions of the parent folder it was copied to (target directory).

- When you *move* a folder or file to a different location on the same volume, the folder or file retains its original permissions.

File Attributes

File attributes are used in Windows to indicate how files can be treated. They can be used to specify which files should be backed up, which should be hidden from normal GUI or command-line file listings, whether a file is compressed or encrypted, and others, depending upon the operating system.

To view file attributes in Windows, right-click a file in File Explorer or Windows Explorer and select Properties. To view file attributes from the Windows command line, use the Attrib command.

Shared Files and Folders

Shared files and folders have their permissions assigned via the Security tab of the object's properties sheet. Folder and file permissions vary by user type or group and can include the following:

- **Full control**—Complete access to contents of file or folder. When Full Control is selected, all of the following are selected automatically.

- **Modify**—Change file or folder contents.

- **Read & Execute**—Access file or folder contents and run programs.

- **List Folder Contents**—Display folder contents.

- **Read**—Access a file or folder.

- **Write**—Add a new file or folder.

Administrative Shares vs Local Shares

Local shares are normally configured on a folder or library basis in Windows. However, Windows sets up special **administrative shares** available across a network for each local drive. For example, the administrative share for the C drive on a system called MARK-PC is \\MARK-PC\C$.

To connect to the administrative share, the user must provide a user name and password for an account on that system.

Permission Inheritance and Propagation

Permission propagation and inheritance describes how files and folders receive permissions.

If you create a folder, the default action it takes is to inherit permissions from the parent folder. So any permissions that you set in the parent will be inherited by the subfolder. To view an example of this, locate any folder within an NTFS volume (besides the root folder), right-click it and select Properties, access the Security tab, and then click the **Advanced** button.

In Windows 7, a checkbox named **Inherit from Parent the Permission Entries that apply to Child Objects** is visible toward the bottom of the window. This means that any permissions added or removed in the parent folder will also be added or removed in the current folder. In addition, those permissions that are being inherited cannot be modified in the current folder. The box is already checked and it is grayed out, so it cannot be cleared. If you want to make modifications to the permissions, you must click the **Change Permissions** button, clear the **Include inheritable permissions from this object's parents** checkbox, and select **Add** (converts and adds inherited parent permissions as explicit permissions on this object), **Remove** (removes inherited permissions), or **Cancel**.

In Windows 8/8.1/10, the Advanced Security Settings dialog offers these buttons: **Add, Remove, View,** and **Disable Inheritance**.

You can also propagate permission changes to subfolders that are not inheriting from the current folder. To do so, select **Replace all child object permissions with inheritable permissions from this object**. Remember that folders automatically inherit from the parent unless you turn inheriting off—and you can propagate permission entries to subfolders at any time by selecting the Replace option.

System Files and Folders

System files and folders are files and folders with the system (s) attribute. They are normally not displayed in File Explorer or Windows Explorer to help protect them from deletion.

To make these files and folders visible:

Step 1.   Click or tap **Tools**.

Step 2.   Click or tap **Folder options**.

Step 3.   Click or tap the **View** tab.

Step 4.   Click the **Show hidden files, folders, and drives** radio button.

Step 5.   Clear the **Hide protected operating system files** checkbox.

User Authentication

Windows includes a variety of authentication protocols that can be used on a corporate network. These include Kerberos, TLS/SSL, PKU2U, NTLM, and others.

BitLocker and BitLocker to Go

To encrypt an entire drive, you need some kind of full disk encryption software. Several currently are available on the market; one developed for business-oriented versions of Windows by Microsoft is called **BitLocker**. This software can encrypt the entire disk, which, after completed, is transparent to the user. However, there are some requirements for this including

- A Trusted Platform Module (TPM), which is a chip residing on the motherboard that actually stores the encrypted keys.

   or

- An external USB key to store the encrypted keys. Using BitLocker without a TPM requires changes to Group Policy settings.

   and

- A hard drive with two volumes, preferably created during the installation of Windows. One volume is for the operating system (most likely C:), which will be encrypted; the other is the active volume that remains unencrypted so that the computer can boot. If a second volume needs to be created, the BitLocker Drive Preparation Tool can be of assistance and can be downloaded from the Microsoft Download Center at:

   http://www.microsoft.com/en-us/download/details.aspx?id=7806

BitLocker software is based on the Advanced Encryption Standard (AES) and uses a 128-bit encryption key.

Starting with Windows Vista SP1, BitLocker can be used to encrypt internal hard disk volumes other than the system drive. For example, if a hard disk is partitioned as C: and D: drives, BitLocker could encrypt both drives.

In Windows 7 and later versions, BitLocker functionality is extended to external USB drives (including flash drives) with **BitLocker To Go**. Windows 7 also simplifies BitLocker and BitLocker To Go configuration: Simply right-click a drive and select **Enable BitLocker** to start the encryption process. During the process, you are prompted to specify a password or a smart card for credentials to access the drive's contents.

To enable access to the contents of BitLocker To Go USB drives on Windows Vista and Windows XP, Microsoft now offers the BitLocker To Go Reader. Download it from the Microsoft website.

EFS

Business-oriented editions of Windows include support for EFS (Encrypting File System). **EFS** can be used to protect sensitive data files and temporary files and can be applied to individual files or folders. (When applied to folders, all files in an encrypted folder are also encrypted.)

EFS files can be opened only by the user who encrypted them, by an administrator, or by EFS keyholders (users who have been provided with the EFS certificate key for another user's account). Thus, they are protected against access by hackers.

Files encrypted with EFS are listed with green filenames when viewed in Windows Explorer or File Explorer. Only files stored on a drive that uses the NTFS file system can be encrypted.

To encrypt a file, follow this process:

Step 1.   Right-click the file in Windows Explorer or File Explorer or Computer and select **Properties**.

Step 2.   Click the **Advanced** button on the General tab.

Step 3.   Click the empty **Encrypt Contents to Secure Data** checkbox.

Step 4.   Click **OK**.

Step 5.   Click **Apply**. When prompted, select the option to encrypt the file and parent folder or only the file as desired and click **OK**.

Step 6.   Click **OK** to close the properties sheet.

To decrypt the file, follow the same procedure, but clear the Encrypt Contents to Secure Data checkbox in Step 3.

NOTE   To enable the recovery of EFS encrypted files in the event that Windows cannot start, you should export the user's EFS certificate key. For details, see the Microsoft TechNet article "Data Recovery and Encrypting File System (EFS)" at http://technet.microsoft.com/en-us/library/cc512680.aspx.

Best Security Practices for Workstations

Keeping a network secure starts with securing the workstations that are used to connect to the network. In the following sections, you learn how to use password best practices, account management, and other methods to make workstations secure.

NOTE   For the CompTIA A+ Exam 220-902, be familiar with:

- Password best practices
- Account management
- How to disable autorun
- Data encryption
- Patch/update management

Password Best Practices

Every user account on a workstation needs a password, but password policies shouldn't end with that requirement. The guidelines in the following sections reflect **password best practices**.

> **NOTE** Many of these requirements can be enforced through security policy settings made with Group Policy.

Setting Strong Passwords

Setting **strong passwords** should include requirements for minimum length and a mixture of alphanumeric and symbol characters. Using a password generator can make the creation of strong passwords easier. As an example, the Norton Identity Safe Password Generator (https://identitysafe.norton.com/password-generator) offers highly customizable random passwords and can generate multiple passwords at the same time.

Password Expiration

No matter how strong a password is, the longer it is used, the less secure it is from social engineering, brute forcing, or other attacks. By using a password expiration policy that passwords expire after a particular length of time and must be reset with different characters, the risk of password discovery by unauthorized users is minimized.

Changing Default User Names/Passwords

Default user names and passwords for SOHO router administration or any other device or service with default passwords should be changed. Default user names and passwords are available in documentation for these devices, making it easy for an attacker to take over a router or other device.

Screensaver Required Password

To help protect computers from unauthorized use, users can be required to enter their password to return to the desktop after the screensaver start. Users should also be required to lock their workstations, which also requires a logon to return to the desktop (see "Timeout/Screen Lock," p.1048, this chapter, for details).

In Windows, the **screensaver required password** settings (**On Resume, Display Logon Screen** checkbox) is located in the Screen Saver Settings window, which can be accessed from Control Panel, Personalization. In OS X, use the Desktop & Screen Saver menu to choose a screen saver, and Security & Privacy to require a password to unlock your system. Linux distributions that use the X11 Window System use the XScreenSaver (https://www.jwz.org/xscreensaver/).

BIOS/UEFI Passwords

BIOS/UEFI passwords prevent unauthorized users from changing settings. Note that they can be removed by resetting the CMOS. Most motherboards feature a jumper block or a pushbutton to reset the CMOS. If this feature is not present, the CMOS can be reset by removing the CMOS battery for several minutes.

NOTE   On a semi-related note, many laptops come equipped with drive lock technology: an HDD password. When enabled, it prompts the user to enter a password for the hard drive when the computer is first booted. If the user of the computer doesn't know the password for the hard drive, the drive will lock and the OS will not boot. An eight-digit or similar hard drive ID usually associates the laptop with the hard drive that is installed. On most systems this password is clear by default, but if the password is set and forgotten, it can usually be reset within the BIOS. Some laptops come with documentation clearly stating the BIOS and drive lock passwords.

CAUTION   Some laptops use the password to permanently restrict access to only the password holder. In such cases, the password cannot be bypassed. See the documentation for your laptop or portable system before applying a BIOS password to determine whether this is the case.

Requiring Passwords

PC users should use passwords to secure their user accounts. Through the Local Security Policy and Group Policy in Windows, you can set up password policies that require users to do the following:

- Change passwords periodically (**Local Policies > Security Options**)
- Be informed in advance that passwords are about to expire (**Account Policies > Password Policy**)
- Enforce a minimum password length (**Account Policies > Password Policy**)

- Require complex passwords (**Account Policies > Password Policy**)

- Prevent old passwords from being reused continually (**Account Policies > Password Policy**)

- Wait a certain number of minutes after a specified number of unsuccessful log-ins has taken place before they can log in again (**Account Policies > Account Lockout Policy**)

To make these settings in Local Security Settings, open the Security Settings node and navigate to the appropriate subnodes (shown in parentheses in the preceding list). In Group Policy (gpedit.msc), navigate to

- **Computer Configuration > Windows Settings > Security Settings > Account Policies > Password Policy**

- **Computer Configuration > Windows Settings > Security Settings > Account Policies > Account Lockout Policy**

- **Computer Configuration > Windows Settings > Security Settings > Local Policies > Security Options** as appropriate

Account Management

User account settings, when combined with workstation security settings, help prevent unauthorized access to the network. The following **account management** settings can enhance security:

Restricting User Permissions

User permissions for Standard users prevent system-wide changes, but additional restrictions can be done with Group Policy or Local Security Policy.

Login Time Restrictions

To prevent a user account from being used after hours or before the start of business, login time restrictions can be used to specify when an account can be used.

Disabling Guest Account

The Guest account in Windows is a potential security risk, so it should be disabled. If visitors need Internet access, a guest wireless network that doesn't connect to the business network is a good replacement.

Failed Attempts Lockout

Password policy should lock out a user after a specified number of failed attempts to log into an account. A **lockout** policy can also incorporate a **timeout** policy, which specifies how long the user must wait after an unsuccessful login before attempting to login again.

Timeout/Screen Lock

Automatic screen locking can be configured to take effect after a specified amount of idle time, helping safeguard systems if a user forgets to lock the system manually. Before screen locking can be used, accounts must have the **screen lock** feature enabled.

In Windows, users can lock their screens manually by pressing Windows key+L on the keyboard or pressing Ctrl+Alt+Del and select Lock Computer. In Linux, the keys to use vary by desktop environment. In OS X, use Control+Shift+Eject or Control+Shift+Power (for keyboards without the Eject key).

Disabling Autorun

When you disable **autorun**, an optical disc or USB drive won't automatically start its autorun application (if it has one) and any embedded malware won't have a chance to infect the system before you scan the media. AutoPlay is a similar feature that pops up a menu of apps to use for the media on an optical drive or USB flash drive.

The easiest way to turn off AutoRun and AutoPlay in Windows Vista/7/8/8.1/10 is to open the AutoPlay applet in Control Panel, clear the Use AutoPlay for all media and devices, and then click Save. From Windows 8/8.1's Start screen, search for "AutoPlay settings" and click or tap it. In the PC and Devices menu, move the **Use AutoPlay for all media and devices** slider to Off.

To disable autorun in Windows using Local Group Policy, complete the following steps:

Step 1.   Click **Start** and in the search field type **gpedit.msc**. This opens the Local Group Policy Editor.

Step 2.   Navigate to **Computer Configuration > Administrative Templates > Windows Components > AutoPlay Policies**.

Step 3. Double-click the **Turn Off Autoplay** setting. This displays the Turn Off AutoPlay configuration window.

Step 4. Click the **Enabled** radio button and then click **OK**. You are actually enabling the policy named Turn off Autoplay.

Use this sparingly on laptops that do presentations, as these computers might require AutoPlay.

OS X does not support autorun/autoplay features.

In Linux, autoplay/autorun can be disabled on systems that use the nautilus file manager by changing the properties on the Media tab to enable **Never prompt or start programs on media insertion** and disable **Browse media when inserted**. See https://scottlinux.com/2011/02/09/ubuntu-linux-disable-autorun/ for details.

Using Data Encryption

Data encryption should be used on laptops and other systems that might be used outside of the more secure corporate network environment. Laptops that contain unencrypted sensitive data have led to many data breaches.

Patch/Update Management

Patches and updates to operating systems and applications should be managed centrally to avoid systems falling out of compliance. Microsoft's Windows Server Update Services (WSUS) can be used for patch/update management of OS and application patches and updates for Microsoft products. OS X Server's Software Update service provides the same role for OS X. Linux distributions use various programs to manage updates. A popular choice is Yellowdog Updater Modified, better known as yum (http://yum.baseurl.org/).

Securing Mobile Devices

Because mobile devices are small, expensive, easy to conceal, and could contain confidential data, they become a target for thieves. But there are some things we can do to protect our data and attempt to get the mobile device back.

NOTE   For the 220-902 exam, be familiar with:

- Screen locks
- Remote wipes
- Remote backup applications
- Failed login attempt restrictions
- Antivirus/anti-malware
- Patching/OS updates
- Biometric authentication
- Full device encryption
- Multifactor authentication
- Authenticator applications
- Trusted sources vs. untrusted sources
- Firewalls
- Policies and procedures

Screen Locks

The first thing a user should do when receiving a mobile device is to set a *passcode*, which is a set of numbers. This one of several types of screen locks. These lock the device making it inaccessible to everyone except experienced hackers. The **screen lock** can be a pattern that is drawn on the display, a PIN (**passcode lock**), or a password. A very strong password is usually the strongest form of screen lock.

This can be accessed on an Android device by going to **Settings > Security**.

You can also select how long the phone waits after inactivity to lock. Generally this is set to 3 or 5 minutes or so, but in a confidential environment you might set this to "immediate." **Swipe lock** apps immediately lock the device when the user swipes the display to one side.

The next option on the Security screen is Visible Passwords. If check marked, this shows the current letter of the password being typed by the user. This type of setting is vulnerable to shoulder surfers (people looking over your shoulder to find out your password) and should be deselected. When deselected, only asterisks (*) are shown when the user types a password.

There is also a Credential Storage option. By default, secure credentials are dropped after a session is over. (an exception to this rule is a Gmail or other similar login). But, if Use Secure Credentials is check marked, and a user accesses a website or application that requires a secure certificate, the credentials are stored on the device. A user can set a password here so that only he or she can view or clear credentials, or install credentials from a memory card. The use of secure credentials is usually only configured if a user needs access to confidential company information on the Internet.

Passcode locking can be accessed on iPad and iPhone devices by going to **Settings > Passcode>** and tapping **Passcode Lock**. This displays the Passcode Lock screen. Tap **Turn Passcode On** to set a passcode.

To enable Auto-Lock, go to **Settings > General > Auto-Lock** and select an amount of minutes. If it is set to "never" then the device will never sleep, negating the security of the passcode, and using valuable battery power. The default setting is two minutes.

Aside from the default timeout, devices can also be locked by pressing the power button quickly. If configured, the passcode must be supplied whenever a mobile device comes out of a sleep or lock state and whenever it is first booted.

Some devices support other types of screen locking, including **fingerprint lock** (the user's fingerprint is matched against a list of authorized users) and **face lock** (the user's face is matched against a list of authorized users). Windows Hello, a Windows 10 feature supported on some devices, is an example of a face lock.

Locator Applications

By installing or enabling a **locator application** or service such as Android Device Manager, Lookout for iOS or Android, or Find My iPhone, a user can track down a lost device.

Remote Wipes

Even if you track your mobile device and find it, it might be too late. A hacker can get past passcodes and other screen locks. It's just a matter of time before the hacker has access to the data. So, an organization with confidential information should consider a **remote wipe** program. As long as the mobile device still has access to the Internet, the remote wipe program can be initiated from a desktop computer, which deletes all the contents of the remote mobile device.

Some devices (such as the iPhone) have a setting where the device will be erased after a certain amount of incorrect password attempts (10 in the case of the iPhone). There are also third-party apps available for download for most mobile devices that will wipe the data after x amount of attempts. Some apps configure the device to automatically take a picture after three failed attempts and e-mail the picture to the owner.

Examples of software that can accomplish this include Google Sync, Google Apps Device Policy, Apple's Data Protection, and third-party apps such as Mobile Defense. In some cases, such as Apple's Data Protection, the command that starts the remote wipe must be issued from an Exchange server or Mobile Device Management server. Of course, you should have a backup plan in place as well so that data on the mobile device is backed up to a secure location at regular intervals. This way, if the data needs to be wiped, you are secure in the fact that most of the data can be recovered. The type of remote wipe program, backup program, and policies regarding how these are implemented vary from one organization to the next. Be sure to read up on your organization's policies to see exactly what is allowed from a mobile security standpoint.

Remote Backup Applications

There are two ways to back up a mobile device: via a USB connection to a desktop or laptop computer, or to the cloud by using a **remote backup** application.

Apple's iCloud offers free cloud backup service for a limited amount of data (currently 5GB), with more space available by subscription. iTunes can be used for USB-based backup, which enables the entire device to be backed up at no additional cost.

Android users have free backup for e-mail, contacts, and other information via Google Cloud. However, backing up photos, music, contents, and other documents must either be performed manually via USB or file sync to the cloud using a service such as Dropbox or with a third-party app.

Both iOS and Android users can use popular third-party cloud-based backups also supported for OS X and Windows such as Mozy (mozy.com), iDrive (www.idrive.com), and others.

Failed Login Attempts Restrictions

Most mobile devices include failed login attempts restrictions. If a person fails to enter the correct passcode after a certain amount of attempts, the device will lock temporarily and the person will have to wait a certain amount of time before attempting the passcode again. If the person fails to enter the correct passcode again, the timeout will increase on most devices.

Antivirus/Anti-malware

Just like there is antivirus software for PCs, there is also **antivirus anti-malware** software for mobile devices. These are third-party applications that need to be paid for, downloaded, and installed to the mobile device. Some common examples for Android include McAfee's VirusScan Mobile, AVG, Lookout, Dr. Web, and NetQin.

iOS works a bit differently. iOS is a tightly controlled operating system. One of the benefits of being a closed-source OS is that it can be more difficult to write viruses for it, making it somewhat more difficult to compromise. But there is no OS that can't be compromised. For the longest time there was no antivirus software for iOS. However, starting in 2011, jailbreaking software began to make iOS devices more vulnerable. As a result, Apple allowed antivirus and anti-malware vendors onto its App Store.

NOTE   iOS jailbreaking is the process of removing the limitations that Apple imposes on its devices that run iOS. This enables users to gain root access to the system and allows the download of previously unavailable applications and software not authorized by Apple.

Patching/OS Updates

Patching/OS updates help protect mobile devices from. By default, you are notified automatically about available updates on Android and iOS-based devices. However, you should know where to go to manually update these devices as well. For Android go to **Settings > General > About device > Software update** or **Settings > System > About device > Software update > check for updates**.

Updates for iOS can be located at **Settings > General > Software Update**.

When it comes to large organizations that have many mobile devices, a Mobile Device Management (MDM) suite should be used. McAfee (and many other companies from AirWatch to LANDESK Mobility Manager to Sybase) have Mobile Device Management software suites that can take care of pushing updates and configuring many mobile devices from a central location. Decent quality MDM software will secure, monitor, manage, and support multiple different mobile devices across the enterprise.

NOTE   Mobile Device Management (MDM) and Mobile Application Management (MAM) solutions are available to assist large enterprises with over the air device management and distribution of mobile applications.

Biometric Authentication

Both current and older Android and iOS devices can use **biometric authentication** through the use of add-on fingerprint readers or iris readers.

Recent and current iOS devices have built-in support for fingerprint reading with the Touch ID feature for iPhone 5s or later, iPad Pro, iPad Air 2, or iPad mini 3 or later. Learn more at https://support.apple.com/en-us/HT201371.

Full Device Encryption

Apple's iOS devices feature **full device encryption** that is activated when a passcode is assigned to the device. To learn more about this and other iOS security, see https://www.apple.com/business/docs/iOS_Security_Guide.pdf.

With Android devices running version 5.x or earlier, you must assign a passcode first before you can encrypt the device. Then, go to **Settings > Lock screen and security > Other security settings > Encrypt device**. You must have at least an 80% charge in your device and plug the device into AC power during the process. Encryption can take an hour or longer. You must also assign a new passcode of six characters or longer including at least one letter and one number. Once you encrypt your Android device, you must enter the passcode every time you turn on or awaken your device from sleep.

With full device encryption, your data is not accessible to would-be thieves unless they know the passkey.

Multifactor Authentication

Any authentication method for e-mail, ebanking, or other tasks that requires two forms of authentication uses **multifactor authentication**. For example, websites and apps might require you to authenticate not only the account information (name and password) but the device being used to access the account. Typically, this is done by sending an SMS text message or making a robocall to the pre-registered mobile phone of the account holder. The account holder must enter the code received when prompted by the website or app before the app can run or the website opens. Unless the app is deleted or cookies are deleted from the browser, the device is now an approved device for that account.

Authenticator Applications

An **authenticator application** is used to receive or generate authentication codes for one or more apps or services.

The Google Authenticator from the Google Play app store enables the user to receive or generate multifactor codes with Android, iOS, and BlackBerry devices. It supports options to add or remove trusted computers and devices and works with the Security Key USB device.

Other authenticator apps for mobile devices include LastPass Authenticator, Authy, FreeOTP, and Toopher.

Before selecting an authenticator app, be sure to determine which websites and services it supports.

Trusted Sources vs. Untrusted Sources

The app stores for iOS (Apple App Store), Android (Google Play), and Windows Store (Windows 10 Mobile) are **trusted sources** for apps for the respective mobile devices. App downloaded from other locations are considered **untrusted sources**, and should not be used.

Firewalls

Android does not include a **firewall**, so third-party apps must be used to provide protection against unwanted Internet traffic. Google Play offers many free firewall apps.

Apple does not include a firewall because the design of iOS uses a feature called "sandboxing" that runs apps in separate protected space.

Policies and Procedures

Many individually owned mobile devices are now being used on corporate networks. Because these devices were not configured by the corporation, they could potentially represent a security threat. To prevent security threats, organizations need to address these issues in their **policies and procedures**.

BYOD versus Corporate Owned Devices

Benefits of bring your own device (**BYOD**) devices include:

- No hardware cost to organization
- Higher usage due to employee satisfaction with their selected device
- Greater productivity

Potential drawbacks include:

- Hidden costs of management and security
- Possibility that some employees will not want to buy their own devices

NOTE   For more background, see www.ibm.com/mobilefirst/us/en/bring-your-own-device/byod.html.

Profile Security Requirements

Whether an organization uses corporate-owned mobile devices, BYOD, or a mixture, setting and following **profile security requirements** are very important to achieving increased productivity without incurring significant risks.

These can include specifying approved devices and operating system versions, requiring passwords and lock screens, device encryption, support issues, and when and how to remove company information when an employee leaves the organization.

NOTE   For more information, see www.cio.com/article/2395944/consumer-technology/7-tips-for-establishing-a-successful-byod-policy.html and http://www.techrepublic.com/blog/it-consultant/learn-byod-policy-best-practices-from-templates/.

Data Destruction and Disposal Methods

Even after a computer has reached the end of its useful life, the hard disk it contains represents a potential security risk. To prevent confidential company or client information from being accessed from a computer that is being disposed of for resale, recycling, or deconstruction for parts, you can use one of the methods discussed in the following sections.

NOTE   For the 220-902 exam, be familiar with:

- Physical destruction methods
- Recycling or repurposing best practices

Physical Destruction Methods

Physical destruction methods render a mass storage device into small pieces that cannot be reconstructed, making the data inside unrecoverable. Methods include:

Shredder

Some office-grade shredders can be used to destroy optical media. Heavy-duty shredders made for hard disk and mass storage devices are used by electronics recyclers to reduce storage devices, tape, or other types of media into small bits of material.

Drill / Hammer

Remove the hard disks and destroy their platters with a **drill**, **hammer**, or other device; then recycle the scrap.

Electromagnetic (Degaussing)

Other tools such as electromagnetic degaussers and permanent magnet degaussers can also be used to permanently purge information from a disk. The drive is physically intact, but all data, formatting, and control track data is missing. Use this if you want to use a drive for display purposes.

Incineration

Incineration of tape, floppy, and other types of magnetic and optical media is available from some firms.

Certificate of Destruction

Data-recycling companies that destroy hard disks or other storage devices can provide a **certificate of destruction**.

Recycling or Repurposing Best Practices

As long as the data on a hard disk or other mass storage device can be rendered unrecoverable, it is not necessary to destroy the media itself. The following sections discuss this approach.

Low-Level Format vs. Standard Format

The **standard format** used in operating systems is a quick format. This type of format only clears the root folder. The remainder of the data on the disk can be recovered until it is overwritten.

A long format rewrites the disk surface. However, data recovery programs available from many third-party firms can recover data from a formatted drive. A **low-level format** is performed by the drive manufacturer before the drive is shipped and cannot be performed in the field.

Overwrite

Some disk maintenance programs from mass storage vendors include options to **overwrite** a hard disk or SSD's data area with zeros. Once again, however, data recovery programs can often recover data that has been overwritten in this fashion.

Drive Wipe

To assure the complete destruction of retrievable data on a storage device, it must be overwritten with a program that meets or exceeds recognized data-destruction standards such as the U.S. Department of Defense 5220.22-M (7 passes) or Peter Gutman's 35-pass maximum-security method. These programs destroy existing data and partition information in such a way as to prevent data recovery or drive forensics analysis. Use this method when maintaining the storage device as a working device is important for **repurposing** (such as for donation or resale). A variety of commercial and freeware programs can be used for this task, which is variously known as disk scrubbing, disk wiping, or drive wiping.

External hard disks should also be handled in one of these ways when being disposed of. USB flash drives that contain sensitive information can be physically destroyed or can be bulk-erased to prevent information from being recovered. To protect information on optical media, shredding is recommended.

SOHO Network Security

Wireless networks have become important to businesses of all sizes as well as individual users. However, they also represent a significant potential vulnerability if they are not properly secured. The following sections help you understand how the different encryption methods work and the additional steps that must be taken to completely secure a wireless network.

NOTE   For the 220-902 exam, be familiar with:

- Wireless specific security settings
- Change default usernames and passwords
- Enable MAC filtering
- Assign static IP addresses
- Firewall settings
- Port forwarding/mapping
- Disabling ports
- Content filtering/parental controls
- Update firmware
- Physical security

Wireless-Specific Security

The default settings for a wireless network should be changed to provide security. The following sections discuss these issues.

Changing Default SSID

The Service Set Identifier (**SSID**) can provide a great deal of useful information to a potential hacker of a wireless network. All wireless networks must have an SSID, and by default, WAPs and wireless routers typically use the manufacturer's name or the device's model number as the default SSID. If a **default SSID** is broadcast by a wireless network, a hacker can look up the documentation for a specific router or the most common models of a particular brand and determine the default IP address range, the default administrator username and password, and other information that would make it easy to attack the network.

To help "hide" the details of your network and location, a replacement SSID for a secure wireless network should not include any of the following:

- Your name
- Your company name
- Your location
- Any other easily identifiable information

An SSID that includes a sports team popular in the area or obscure information (such as the name of your first pet) would be a suitable replacement.

Setting Encryption

An encrypted wireless network relies on the exchange of a passphrase between the client and the wireless access point (WAP) or router before the client can connect to the network. There are three standards for encryption: WEP, WPA, and WPA2.

Wireless equivalent privacy (**WEP**) was the original encryption standard for wireless Ethernet (Wi-Fi) networks. It is the only encryption standard supported by most IEEE 802.11b-compliant hardware. Unfortunately, WEP encryption is not strong enough to resist attacks from a determined hacker. There are several reasons this is true, including key length (64-bit WEP uses a 10-character hex key, and 128-bit WEP uses a 26-character hex key) and the use of unencrypted transmissions for some parts of the handshaking process. Because WEP encryption is not secure, it should not be used to "secure" a wireless network.

As a replacement to WEP, Wi-Fi Protected Access (**WPA**) was developed a few years ago. It is available in two strengths: WPA (which uses TKIP encryption) and the newer, stronger **WPA2** (which uses AES encryption). WPA and WPA2's encryption is much stronger than WEP, supports a key length from 8 up to 63 alphanumeric characters (enabling the use of punctuation marks and other characters not permitted with WEP) or 64 hex characters, and supports the use of a RADIUS authentication server in corporate environments.

NOTE   In some environments, WPA and WPA2 are both referred to as WPA, so the encryption method selected during wireless security configuration determines whether WPA or WPA2 has been chosen.

Because all clients and WAPs or wireless routers on a wireless network must use the same encryption standard, use the strongest standard supported by all hardware.

Ideally, all wireless networks should be secured with WPA2 (WPA has been cracked, although cracking WPA is much harder than cracking WEP). However, the use of WPA2 encryption might require upgraded drivers for older network adapters and upgraded firmware for older WAPs or wireless routers. All currently manufactured Wi-Fi Certified adapters and WAPs or wireless routers must support WPA2.

TIP   There are various ways to create a strong passphrase for use with a WPA or WPA2 network. Some vendors of WAPs and wireless routers include a feature sold under various brand names that is compliant with the Wi-Fi Protected Setup standard (also known as Easy Config). If this cannot be used on some hardware, you can obtain a dynamically generated strong passphrase at Gibson Research Corporation's Perfect Passwords website: https://www.grc.com/passwords.htm.

Copy and paste the passphrase provided into Notepad or another plain-text editor and then copy or paste it into the configuration dialog for a WAP, wireless router, and wireless client as needed.

Disabling SSID Broadcast

Disabling **SSID broadcast** is widely believed to be an effective way to prevent your wireless network from being detected and is so regarded by the A+ Certification exams.

CAUTION   Although disabling SSID broadcast prevents casual bandwidth snoopers from finding your wireless network, Microsoft does not recommend disabling SSID broadcasting as a security measure. According to a TechNet white paper, "Non-broadcast Wireless Networks with Microsoft Windows," available at http://technet.microsoft.com, wireless client systems running Windows transmit ("advertise") the names of non-broadcast (also known as hidden) wireless networks they are configured to connect to. This information can be used by wireless network hacking programs to help launch an attack against the network.

Figure 21-3 illustrates a Linksys router configuration dialog in which several of these security recommendations have been implemented.

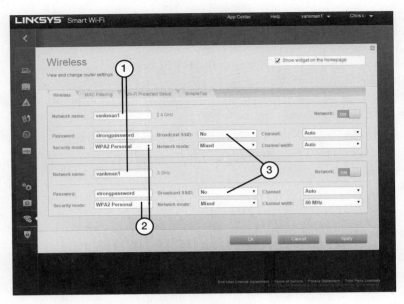

1. User-assigned SSID in place of factory default
2. WPA2 Personal security mode selected
3. SSID broadcast disabled

Figure 21-3   Configuring a router with alternative SSIDs, WPA2 encryption enabled, and SSID broadcast diabled.

Antenna and Access Point Placement

When configuring and/or troubleshooting wireless connections, think about WAP location. The placement of the access point plays a big part in a strong signal. Generally, it should be placed in the middle of an office to offer greatest coverage while reducing the chance of outsiders being able to connect to the device. The antennas on the access point should also be set at a 90-degree angle to each other. Keep the device away from any forms of electrical interference such as other wireless devices, speakers, and any devices that use a lot of electricity.

Radio Power Levels

Another thing to watch out for is radio power levels. Some wireless routers and access points have adjustable radio power levels. When set too low, clients at the perimeter of the building will not be able to gain access. When set too high, computers located in neighboring businesses will be able to attempt access.

TIP   If the wireless signal is too weak regardless of the router location and radio power levels, and the router is a 150Mbps Wireless-N or older technology (Wireless-G, Wireless-B, or Wireless-A), consider replacing it with a Wireless-AC (802.11ac) router.

Wi-Fi Protected Setup (WPS)

Wi-Fi Protected Setup (**WPS**) is an easy way to configure a secure wireless network with a SOHO router, provided that all devices on the network support WPS. There are several ways that WPS can be configured. The most common ways include:

- PIN—A PIN marked on the router is entered into each new device added to the network. This is the only mandatory WPS method and is the default method.

- Push button—The router or WAP has a push button, and each new device has a physical push button or (more often) a software push button in the setup program. Both buttons must be pushed within a short period of time to make the connection.

A security flaw with the PIN method was discovered in late 2011, so the push-button method is recommended if WPS is to be used.

Change Default Usernames and Passwords

As mentioned previously, the documentation for almost all WAPs and wireless routers lists the default administrator password, and the documentation can be readily downloaded in PDF or HTML form from the vendors' websites. Because an attacker could use this information to "take over" the device, it's a good idea to change the default.

Most routers use the Administration or Management dialog for the password and other security settings.

TIP   To further secure the router or WAP, configure the device so it can be managed only with a wired Ethernet connection.

Enable MAC Filtering

Every network adapter—whether it's built in to a PC, an add-on card, or built in to a specialized device such as a media adapter or a networked printer—has a unique identification known as the media access control address or MAC address. The MAC address (sometimes known as the physical address) is a list of six two-digit hexadecimal numbers (0–9, A–F). The MAC address is usually found on a label on the side of the network adapter. Depending on the device, the MAC address might be labeled MAC, MAC address, or ID No. Many devices that have integrated network adapters also list their MAC address on a label. Note that MAC addresses are sometimes listed as 12 digits rather than in six groups of 2 digits.

With most wireless routers and WAPs, you can specify the MAC addresses of devices on your network. Only these devices can access your network; some routers can also be configured to block a list of specified MAC addresses from accessing the network.

MAC filtering can be a useful way to block casual hackers from gaining access to a wireless (or wired) network. However, keep in mind that it is possible to use software to change the MAC address of a network device (a feature sometimes referred to as *MAC address cloning*), and that MAC addresses are not encrypted and can be detected by software used to hack networks. Thus, MAC address filtering alone should not be relied on to stop serious attacks.

Assign Static IP Addresses

The DHCP server built into a router hands out IP addresses to all computers they're connected to. This is a convenience, but if you want to limit access to the Internet for certain computers or log activity for computers by IP address, this setting should be disabled and a **static IP address** should be assigned to each computer instead, using each client's IP configuration dialog. Make sure you assign an IP address range supported by the router. For details, see "Dynamic versus Static IP Addresses," p.444, Chapter 11.

Firewall Settings

By default, most WAPs and wireless routers use a feature called Network Address Translation (NAT) to act as a simple firewall. NAT prevents traffic from the Internet from determining the private IP addresses used by computers on the network. However, many WAPs and wireless routers offer additional firewall features that can be enabled, including

- Access logs
- Filtering of specific types of traffic
- Enhanced support for VPNs

See the router documentation for more information about advanced security features.

Port Forwarding/Mapping

Use **port forwarding** (also known as **port mapping**) to allow inbound traffic on a particular TCP or UDP port or range to go to a particular IP address rather than to all devices on a network. To learn more, see the "Port Forwarding, Port Triggering, and DNAT" section in Chapter 11.

Disabling Ports

Blocking TCP and UDP ports, also known as disabling ports, is performed with a firewall app such as the Windows Firewall with Advanced Security. For details, see "Configuration," p.865, Chapter 16.

Content Filtering / Parental Controls

Microsoft provides optional **content filtering parental controls** in Microsoft Windows 7 with Windows Family Safety, available from http://windows.microsoft.com/en-us/windows/download-windows-essentials. Windows Family Safety is built into Windows 8/8.1/10. Family Safety monitors accounts' web surfing, app usage, and social network usage. To learn more, see http://windows.microsoft.com/en-us/windows/set-up-family#set-up-family and select your versions of Windows.

Parental controls are built into recent versions of OS X. Enable this feature through the Parental Controls menu. To learn more, see https://support.apple.com/kb/PH18571?locale=en_US.

Although Linux distros do not include parental controls, many third-party apps are available. To learn more, see https://help.ubuntu.com/community/ParentalControls for details.

Some wireless routers made for SOHO use also include content filtering and parental controls.

Update Firmware

Most vendors issue at least one firmware update during the lifespan of each model of WAP and wireless router. Updates can solve operational problems and might add features that enhance Wi-Fi interoperability, security, and ease of use. To determine whether a WAP or wireless router has a firmware update available, follow these steps:

Step 1.   View the device's configuration dialogs to see the current firmware version.

Step 2.   Visit the device vendor's website to see whether a newer version of the firmware is available. Note that you must know the model number and revision of the device. To find this information, look on the rear or bottom of the device.

Step 3.   Download the firmware update to a PC that can be connected to the device with an Ethernet cable.

Step 4.   Connect the PC to the device with an Ethernet cable.

Step 5.   Navigate to the device's firmware update dialog.

Step 6.   Follow instructions to update firmware.

Physical Security

In a SOHO network environment, physical security refers to preventing unauthorized use of the network. Copper-based cabling is susceptible to eavesdropping, wiretapping, crosstalk, EMI, and RFI. One way to defend against these is to use shielded twisted pair (STP) cable. Another is to use fiber-optic cable, which is the most resistant to all of these because it uses light instead of electricity to send data.

Also watch out for visible network wires and unused network jacks. Network cables should be routed in the walls and ceiling out of sight. If they are not visible, it cuts down on the chances of someone tapping into the network. RJ-45 jacks that currently don't have a computer connected to them should be noted. In the wiring closet, disconnect those network drops at the patch panel by removing the patch cable that leads to the switch. This way, a person can't just sit down, plug in to a network jack, and attempt to hack the network. On some switches you can also disable ports within the firmware.

Exam Preparation Tasks

Review All the Key Topics

Review the most important topics in the chapter, noted with the Key Topic icon in the outer margin of the page. Table 21-1 lists a reference of these key topics and the page numbers on which each is found.

Table 21-1   Key Topics for Chapter 21

Key Topic Element	Description	Page Number
Section	Malware	1023
List	List of how to update antivirus, scan systems, etc.	1037
List	Account levels in Windows	1039
Section	Wireless Specific Security	1059

Complete the Tables and Lists from Memory

Print a copy of Appendix C, "Memory Tables" (found on the companion website), or at least the section for this chapter, and complete the tables and lists from memory. Appendix D, "Answers to Memory Tables," also on the companion website, includes completed tables and lists to check your work.

Define Key Terms

Define the following key terms from this chapter, and check your answers in the glossary.

malware, spyware, viruses, worms, Trojan horses, rootkits, ransomware, phishing, spear phishing, social engineering, shoulder surfing, zero-day attack, zombie/botnet, brute forcing, dictionary attacks, non-compliant systems, violations of security best practices, tailgating, man-in-the-middle, mantrap, cable locks, biometrics, ID badges, key fob, RFID badge, tokens, privacy filters, entry control roster, digital security, strong password, multifactor authentication, directory permissions, VPN, access control lists, smart card, e-mail filtering, trusted/untrusted software sources, acceptable use policy (AUP), principle of least privilege, administrator, power user, guest, standard user, NTFS permissions, share permissions, file attributes, administrative shares, local shares, permission propagation, inheritance, system files and folders, user authentication, administrator, standard user, BitLocker, BitLocker-To-Go, EFS, password best practices, account management, guest, lockout, time-out, screen lock, autorun, data encryption, patch/update management, fingerprint lock, face lock, swipe lock, passcode lock, remote wipe, locator applications, remote backup, failed login attempt restrictions, antivirus/anti-malware, patching/OS updates, biometric authentication, full device encryption, multifactor authentication, authenticator applications, firewalls, policies and procedures, BYOD, profile security requirements, shredder, drill/hammer, incineration, certificate of destruction, repurposing, security best practices, low level format, standard format, overwrite, drive wipe, SSID, default SSID, SSID broadcast, WPS, MAC filtering, static IP address, radio power levels, firewall, port forwarding/mapping, content filtering, permission propagation, inheritance, remote backup, antivirus, anti-malware, content filtering, parental controls, WEP, WPA, WPA2, parental controls.

Complete Hands-On Labs

Complete the hands-on labs, and then see the answers and explanations at the end of the chapter.

Lab 21-1: Physical, Operating System, Email, and Password Security

- Run Belarc Advisor on a Windows computer to determine if it has all security updates installed.

- Check your junk or spam e-mail folders for phishing messages. Note patterns such as misspelled words, poor grammar, lack of personalization, and unnecessary attachments.

- Look over the laptops, external hard disks, displays, and other equipment for security lock slots. How many of these items are actually locked? Create a sample budget for locking these items to prevent theft or loss.

- Evaluate your own passwords. Do they qualify as strong? If not, visit a website such as the Norton Identity Safe Password Generator (https://identitysafe.norton.com/password-generator) to generate replacements.

Lab 21-2: Protecting Against Autorun, Wiping Disks, and Securing a SOHO Network

- Use one of the methods listed in this chapter to disable autorun/autoplay. Does disabling this feature cause any problems for you in your day-to-day work?

- Use a disk-wiping program to wipe a hard disk that is no longer in use (make sure any useful data is backed up first!). If you don't have a utility, you can choose one from the list at http://www.techrepublic.com/blog/five-apps/five-hard-disk-cleaning-and-erasing-tools/.

- Review the configuration for a SOHO router at your home or place of employment. Implement some of the changes advocated in this chapter. Be sure to record the new settings!

Answer Review Questions

1. Match the type malware to its description.

Description	Type of Malware
A. Infects and rewrites files. Replicates automatically with no user intervention.	
B. A method of hiding malware from detection programs.	
C. Tracks web browsing; uses pop-ups to attract user's attention.	
D. Encrypts target files and then demands payment to unencrypt files.	
E. Infects and rewrites files. Replicates itself if user executes the file.	

Answer Options:

1. Spyware
2. Virus
3. Worm
4. Rootkit
5. Ransomware

2. Which of the following statements best describes phishing?

A. A hacker pretends to be a co-worker or IT professional to gain network access

B. A bogus website that tricks user into revealing personal or financial information.

C. An attempt to physically view information such as passwords or PINs.

D. A computer that has been taken over for the purpose of distributing malware.

3. A brute-force attack can be thwarted by implementing which security policy?

A. Account lockout at logon

B. Digital passwords

C. Physically locking doors to server room

D. Strong encryption

4. As an IT professional, you should be sure to employ best security practices. Which of the following is *not* a best practice?

   A. Strong passwords for user accounts

   B. Antivirus/malware protection

   C. SSL for websites

   D. WEP encryption

5. Which of the following is generally the most difficult form of security for an intruder to overcome?

   A. Firewall

   B. Encryption

   C. Biometrics

   D. Physical lock and key

6. Biometrics includes the use of which of the following? (Choose all that apply.)

   A. Fingerprint scan

   B. RFID

   C. Retinal scan

   D. Token

7. Which of the following is *not* a type of token?

   A. Key fob

   B. Cable lock

   C. RFID card

   D. Smart card

8. Which of the following is a program that either blocks or allows data packets to be delivered to network addresses?

   A. DHCP server

   B. Key fob

   C. Firewall

   D. Network server

9. Which of the following is a characteristic of a strong password? (Choose all that apply.)

   A. No more than six characters

   B. Lowercase only

C. Use of symbols

D. Use of numbers

10. In OS X and Linux, which of the following are directory permissions that are available? (Choose three.)

   A. Full control

   B. Modify

   C. Read

   D. Read and Execute

   E. Write

   F. List folder contents

   G. Execute

11. Which of the following is a private secure network that is used to communicate over an unsecured public network?

   A. Proxy server

   B. VPN

   C. Firewall

   D. ACL

12. When you copy a folder to a different volume, which of the following statements best describes what happens to the folder's permissions?

   A. The folder retains its original permissions.

   B. The folder inherits permissions from the new location's parent folder.

   C. The user selects the permissions option during the file copy process.

   D. The user must manually set up permissions after the file copy process.

13. Which of the following statements best describes how to view and change the attributes of a file? (Choose two.)

   A. Right-click the file, select Properties, and then click the General tab.

   B. Right-click the file and select Sharing.

   C. Type attrib at the command line.

   D. In Administrative Tools, open the Shares folder and select Attributes.

14. Which of the following statements best describes how to turn on or off file inheritance?

    A. Right-click the file, select Properties, and then click the Security tab.

    B. Right-click the file, select Properties, and then click the General tab.

    C. Right-click the file and select Sharing.

    D. In Administrative Tools, open the Shares folder.

15. The computer's system files are not normally displayed. Which of the following statements best describes how to make them visible?

    A. Open Administrative Tools and select Computer Management.

    B. Right-click Computer or This PC and select Properties.

    C. Open Device Manager and select Disk Drives.

    D. Open Control Panel > Folder Options > View > Show hidden files, folders, and drives.

Answers and Explanations to Hands-On Labs

Lab 21-1: Physical, Operating System, Email, and Password Security

If Belarc Advisor detects missing security updates, run Windows Update to update your system. In some cases, you might need to install some updates manually.

In addition to the patterns mentioned in the lab as telltale signs of phishing e-mails, did you see any other clues? Share these with your supervisor.

How many cable locks would be needed to lock all lockable equipment in your office? Consider proposing a phased method for adding locks, starting with the most vulnerable equipment.

Lab 21-2: Protecting Against Autorun, Wiping Disks, and Securing a SOHO Network

If disabling autorun/autoplay doesn't cause any problems, consider suggesting this as a standard configuration option.

How long did it take the utility to overwrite the drive? Were you able to find any data on the drive? Were you able to use the drive as new (repartition, reformat, etc.)? If you used more than one, consider recommending your favorite to be the standard repurposing program in your organization.

Answers and Explanations to Review Questions

1.

Description	Type of Malware
A. Infects and rewrites files. Replicates automatically with no user intervention.	3. Worm
B. A method of hiding malware from detection programs.	4. Rootkit
C. Tracks web browsing; uses pop-ups to attract user's attention.	1. Spyware
D. Encrypts target files and then demands payment to unencrypt files.	5. Ransomware
E. Infects and rewrites files. Replicates itself if user executes the file.	2. Virus

2. **B.** Phishing is a technique that involves tricking a user into revealing confidential information, such as a Social Security Number or credit card information. The technique might involve a bogus security alert in the form of an e-mail or a telephone warning that includes an offer of assistance. In social engineering, the hacker pretends to be a co-worker or IT professional in order to gain network access. Shoulder surfing is an attempt to physically view confidential information (such as passwords or PINs) by looking over a user's shoulder. A zombie or botnet is a program that takes over a computer for the purpose of distributing malware, such as a denial of service attack.

3. **A.** A brute-force attack tries to guess the password by trying combinations of letters, numbers, and symbols until it comes upon the correct combination. This type of attack can be stopped by using an account-lockout policy to lock the computer after a specified number of incorrect attempts to log on.

4. **D.** WEP encryption is a weak type of encryption. Use WPA (better) or WPA2 (best) instead.

5. **D.** A physical lock and key might be the most difficult form of security to overcome because it cannot be bypassed electronically and cannot be done remotely. An intruder must be in possession of a physical key and he must be physically present at the site.

6. **A, C.** Fingerprint scan, retinal or iris scan, facial recognition, and voice recognition are all types of biometric security methods.

7. **B.** A cable lock is used to secure a laptop to an immovable object, such as a post. A token is any physical object used to gain access to a secure system. Key fobs, RFID cards, and smart cards are all types of tokens.

8. **C.** A firewall examines data packets being received by a network to determine whether they should be delivered to a network location or whether delivery should be blocked. Data packets can be allowed or blocked depending upon the threat level that is determined by the firewall programming.

9. **C, D.** A strong password should consist of eight or more characters, a combination of upper- and lowercase letters, symbols, and numbers. In addition, a strong password should not use real names or real words.

10. **C, E, G.** Read, Write and Execute are the directory permissions for both OS X and Linux. The Windows version of file and folder permissions on an NTFS drive includes Full Control, Modify, Read and Execute, List, Read, and Write.

11. **B.** The Internet is an insecure communication network. A Virtual Private Network (VPN) is a private network that provides a secure method for sending and receiving data across the Internet.

12. **B.** When you copy a folder to a different folder on either the same or a different volume, the folder inherits the permissions of the current location's parent folder.

13. **A, C.** To change the attributes of a file, right-click the file and select Properties. File attributes can be changed on the General tab. Alternately, use the **attrib** command on the command line.

14. **A.** To turn the file inheritance on or off, right-click the file and select Properties. Go to the Security tab, click the Advanced button, and follow the procedures for the version of Windows in use.

15. **D.** Open Control Panel > Folder Options > View > Show hidden files, folders, and drives.

This chapter covers the following subjects:

- **Troubleshooting Common Symptoms**—Learn the symptoms of problems with Windows, Linux, and OS and discover their solutions in this section.

- **Tools for Troubleshooting Software**—Discover additional Windows tools and OS X and Linux repair techniques.

- **Troubleshoot Mobile OS and Application Issues**—Find out how to deal with system lockout, issues, when and how to perform soft and hard resets, and uninstall/reinstall apps to solve problems.

- **Troubleshooting PC Security Issues**—Learn the symptoms of malware infection, tools you can use to fight back, and a systematic approach to removing infections.

## CHAPTER 22

Troubleshooting Desktop and Mobile Operating Systems

With the widespread use of mobile devices, troubleshooting is now more than just solving problems with computers. However, many of the same principles apply whether solving problems with computers, peripherals, or mobile devices: knowledge of products and operating system functions, understanding of the tools needed to diagnose and repair problems, and a determination to avoid data loss except when unavoidable. This chapter helps you apply these principles.

220-902: Objective 4.1 Given a scenario, troubleshoot PC operating system problems with appropriate tools.

220-902: Objective 4.2 Given a scenario, troubleshoot common PC security issues with appropriate tools and best practices.

220-902: Objective 4.3 Given a scenario, troubleshoot common mobile OS and application issues with appropriate tools.

220-902: Objective 4.4 Given a scenario, troubleshoot common mobile OS and application security issues with appropriate tools.

Foundation Topics

Troubleshooting Common Symptoms

Windows, OS X, and Linux differ in many ways, and in the following sections, you learn how to use each operating system's features to solve common problems.

Proprietary Crash Screens

The Windows STOP error and the OS X pin wheel are examples of proprietary crash screens. These can be caused by operating system, application, or hardware errors.

Troubleshooting Windows STOP Errors (BSOD)

STOP errors (also known as Blue Screen Of Death or **BSOD** errors) can occur either during startup or after the system is running. The BSOD nickname is used because the background is normally blue (or sometimes black) with the error message in white text. STOP errors in Windows Vista and Windows 7 resemble the example shown in Figure 22-1. The STOP error is listed by name and number.

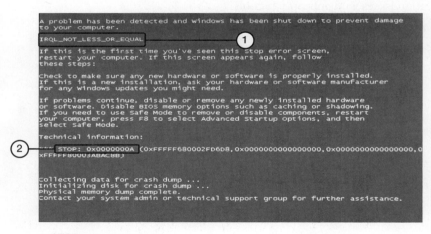

1. STOP error message
2. STOP error number

Figure 22-1   A Windows 7 STOP error.

In Windows 8/8.1/10, STOP errors now look like the example shown in Figure 22-2. In these versions of Windows, the STOP error is listed by name.

NOTE Regardless of when a STOP/BSOD error occurs, your system is halted by default. If the computer does not restart on its own, you must turn off the system and turn it back on. But before you do that, record the error message text and other information so that you can research the problem if it reoccurs. For more information, see the next section, "Causes of BSOD Errors."

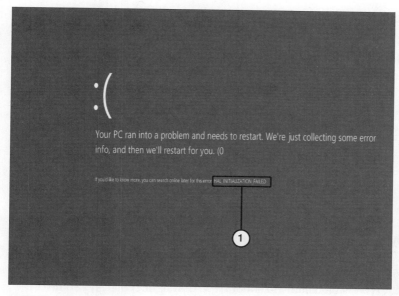

1. STOP error message

Figure 22-2 A Windows 8 STOP error.

Causes of BSOD Errors

BSOD errors can be caused by any of the following:

- **Incompatible or defective hardware or software**—Start the system in Safe Mode and uninstall the last hardware or software installed. Acquire updates before you reinstall the hardware or software. Exchange or test memory. Run SFC/scannow to check for problems with system files.

- **Registry problems**—Select **Last Known Good Configuration** (Windows Vista/7) as described later in this chapter and see whether the system will start. Using System Restore can also be used to revert the system and Registry to an earlier state; see the "System Recovery Options (Windows)" section later in this chapter for details.

- **Viruses**—Scan for viruses and remove them if discovered.

- **Miscellaneous causes**—Check the Windows Event Viewer and check the System log. Research the BSOD with the Microsoft Support website.

To learn how to start Windows in Safe Mode, see "Safe Mode (Windows)," p.1111, this chapter.

Researching Causes and Solutions

To determine the exact cause of a STOP error, note the number or name of the error (for example, STOP 0x0000007B, or HAL INITIALIZATION FAILED) and look it up at the Microsoft support website: http://support.microsoft.com. When you search for the error, be sure to specify the version of Windows in use.

NOTE STOP errors are often referred to with a shortened version of the error code or by name. For example, the short version of a 0x0000007B error is 0x7B.

TIP Unfortunately, you can't take a screen capture of a BSOD for printing because a BSOD completely shuts down Windows. However, if you have a digital camera or smartphone handy, it makes a great tool for recording the exact error message. Just be sure to use the correct range setting to get the sharpest picture possible (normal or close-up, often symbolized with a flower icon). Turn off the flash, and use ISO 400 or higher, or Hi ISO to enable handheld shooting in dim light. You can also install NirSoft's BlueScreenView utility and use it to view any BSOD that already occurred if your system is configured to save a minidump file. Learn more at http://nirsoft.net/utils/blue_screen_view.html.

The solution might involve one or more of the following changes to your system:

- Changing the system registry. Sometimes, an automated registry repair tool can be downloaded to perform these changes for you. Whether you make the changes manually or automatically, back up the registry first!

- Removing a newly added component. For example, to solve the error shown in Figure 22-1, I removed a memory module I had just added to my computer.

- Replacing components such as memory.

- Upgrading an application.

- Downloading and installing a hotfix for your operating system.

On some systems, auto restart is enabled for STOP/BSOD errors, so the error message shown in the previous figures appear for only a moment before the computer restarts. For solutions, see the "Spontaneous Shutdown/Restart" section later in this chapter.

NOTE   Microsoft offers automated registry repair tools sometimes known collectively as "Fix it" to solve various Windows problems. If a registry repair tool is available for a particular problem, the link to it shows up when you search for the problem at the Windows Support website. For example, the results of searching for "problems with Windows security settings" brings up a link to https://support.microsoft.com/mats/malware_prevention. Click the button on the page to fix the problems listed.

OS X Pin Wheel

The official name for the OS X **pin wheel** is the spinning wait cursor (see Figure 22-3).

1. OS X spinning wait cursor (pin wheel)

Figure 22-3   The OS X pin wheel in OS X El Capitan.

It appears most often when an application or OS X itself has become unresponsive. For this reason, it is sometimes referred to as the "pin wheel of death."

Some causes of OS X unresponsiveness include:

- **Lack of system RAM**—If your OS X device frequently displays the pin wheel and the device's RAM can be upgraded, do so.

- **Less than 10 percent free space on the OS X system drive**—Free space is used as a swapfile to substitute for RAM. Remove unwanted apps and save data to external or cloud storage to free up space. Some experts suggest keeping at least 20 percent of the OS X system drive free.

- **Damaged application**—Run Disk Utility using the Verify Disk Permissions option (in OS X versions prior to El Capitan).

Some solutions include:

- If a particular application causes unresponsiveness, open the ~Library/ Preferences folder, find the .plist file for the app, and drag it to the trash. The .plist file will be rebuilt.

- Use Activity Monitor to view CPU, memory, energy, disk, and networking performance stats. For OS X 10.9 and later, see https://support.apple.com/ en-us/HT201464. For OS X 10.8 and earlier, see https://support.apple.com/ en-us/HT201538.

- Upgrade to the latest OS X version and keep it updated.

- Use the Force Quit command to terminate an application that won't respond. It's available from the Apple menu or by pressing Command-Option-Esc. Select the app and click Force Quit.

Failure to Boot

Boot failures (**failure to boot**) can be caused by incorrect boot configuration in the BIOS, corrupt or missing boot files, and missing driver files. The solutions for these problems vary with the operating system version in use.

Windows Boot Errors

Windows uses the bootmgr and BCD files during the startup process. If these files are corrupted or missing, you will see corresponding error messages:

- **BOOTMGR is missing**—This message displays if the bootmgr file is missing or corrupt. This black screen will probably also say Press Ctrl+Alt+Del to Restart; however, doing so will probably have the same results.

- **The Windows Boot Configuration Data file is missing required information—**
  This message means that either the Windows Boot Manager (Bootmgr) entry
  is not present in the Boot Configuration Data (BCD) store or that the Boot\
  BCD file on the active partition is damaged or missing. Additional information you might see on the screen includes File: \Boot\BCD, and Status:
  0xc0000034.

There are two ways to repair a missing BOOTMGR file:

- Boot to the System Recovery Options and select the Startup Repair option.
  This should automatically repair the system and require you to reboot.

- Boot to the System Recovery Options and select the Command Prompt option. Type the bootrec /fixboot command, as shown in Figure 22-4.

> **NOTE** A hard drive's lifespan is not infinite. In some cases, it is not possible to repair
> this file and unfortunately the hard drive will need to be replaced and the operating
> system reinstalled.

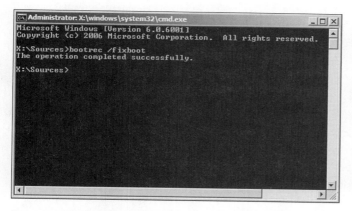

Figure 22-4 Repairing BOOTMGR.exe from the Windows Recovery Environment's command
prompt.

For more about these steps, see https://support.microsoft.com/en-us/kb/2622803.

To repair the BCD store, use this 3-step process:

Step 1. Boot to the System Recovery Options and select the Startup Repair option. This should automatically repair the system and require you to reboot. If not, move on to the second method.

Step 2.   Boot to the System Recovery Options and select the Command Prompt option. Type **bootrec /rebuildbcd**. If the Bootrec.exe tool runs successfully, it presents you with an installation path of a Windows directory. To add the entry to the BCD store, type **Yes**. A confirmation message appears that indicates the entry was added successfully. Restart the system.

Step 2b.   If the Bootrec.exe tool can't locate any missing Windows installations, you must remove the BCD store and then re-create it. To do this, type the following commands in the order in which they are presented. Press Enter after each command.

```
Bcdedit /export C:\BCD_Backup
ren c:\boot\bcd bcd.old
Bootrec /rebuildbcd
```

You can find more information on this process at the following link:

- **Windows Vista, 7**—http://support.microsoft.com/kb/927391 (also works with Windows 8/8.1/10)

- **Windows 7**—http://support.microsoft.com/kb/2004518

NOTE   If you want to install two versions of Windows in a multiboot configuration, install the older version first. For example, install Windows 7 first, followed by Windows 8.1 or Windows 10.

Various issues can happen if you attempt to dual boot an older operating system that you installed after a newer version was installed. For example, the first operating system may cease to boot after the second operating system is installed. This could mean that the master boot record was overwritten, along with other issues. Several steps are involved to repair this problem. The initial command in this process, which will restore the MBR and the boot code that transfers control to the Windows Boot Manager program, is X:\ boot\Bootsect.exe /NT60 All. X is the drive where the installation media exists. See the following Microsoft Help and Support link for more information on how to manually create an entry into the BCD store for the new operating system and how to troubleshoot this further: http://support.microsoft.com/kb/919529.

If Windows boots to Safe Mode or displays an Advanced Boot Options menu, see the "Safe Mode (Windows)" section later in this chapter for more information.

Can't Boot Linux

If Linux won't start normally, hold down the Shift key while starting the system. If the GRUB or GRUB2 boot loader appears, select the entry marked "Rescue" or "Recovery" to load a minimal version of Linux. With some distributions, such as Ubuntu, you might need to select Advanced (see Figure 22-5) before you can select a recovery option (see Figure 22-6).

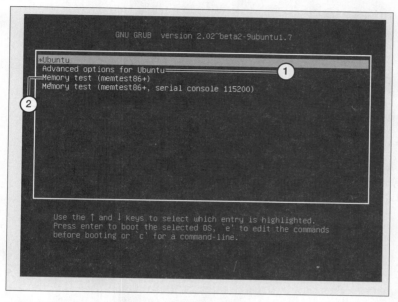

1. Select to see recovery options
2. Select to test RAM

Figure 22-5   GRUB2 bootloader for Ubuntu offers memory diagnostics as well as access to advanced boot options.

When Linux is run in Recovery mode, the screen is full of commands (most distros hide startup commands by default). From the Recovery menu (see Figure 22-7), you might be offered a variety of options to fix your system (varies by distribution). If a Linux distribution doesn't have a menu offering these options, most can be run from the command prompt (might require su or sudo to run).

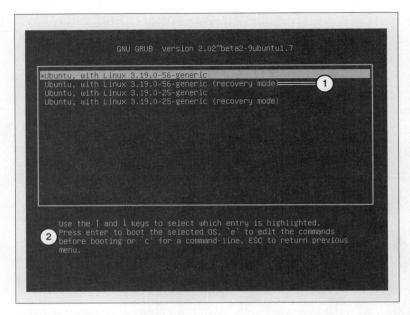

1. **Select to start Linux in recovery mode**
2. **Other options**

Figure 22-6   Select a Recovery mode.

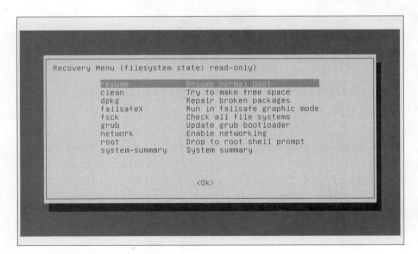

Figure 22-7   Recovery options in Ubuntu.

Here is more information about the Recovery Menu options in Figure 22-7.

- **resume**—Continues normal boot process
- **clean**—Frees up space on your file system (use if disk is about full)
- **dpkg**—Repairs broken software (use if software installation failed); be sure to enable networking first with network
- **failsafex**—Enables system to boot to GUI
- **fsck**—Repairs file system errors
- **grub**—Updates grub boot loader
- **network**—Enables networking, which is turned off in recovery mode
- **root**—Opens system in read/write root shell mode (for experts only)
- **system-summary**—Displays information about the system

Other startup problems:

- Some BIOS will not boot to Linux because Linux partitions don't use the MS-DOS boot flag. To fix the problem, start the system from a Live CD or Live USB drive and open a terminal session. Use the command `sudo fdisk /dev/sda` and view partition table settings by giving the `p` (print) command. A bootable partition is marked as a (active). If no partition is marked as active, use the `a` command to mark this partition as active, save changes with `w` (write), and re-start the system after removing the live CD.

- If Linux is being installed in a separate disk partition on a system running Windows 8/8.1/10, it is usually necessary to disable the BIOS setting for Secure Boot (also known as Windows 8/10 mode) to enable booting from a Linux USB drive or optical disc. After installation, to boot either Windows 8/8.1/10 or Linux, a new version of the grub bootloader must be installed that adds support for EFI/UEFI with the command `sudo apt-get install grub-efi`. For more details, see http://askubuntu.com/questions/459979/operating-system-not-found-error-when-booting-from-usb-in-windows-8.

NOTE   For more help with dealing with boot issues, see www.codecoffee.com/tips-forlinux/articles/8.html and www.howtogeek.com/196740/how-to-fix-an-ubuntu-system-when-it-wont-boot/.

Can't Boot OS X

To start OS X Lion or later in special startup modes, press Command + R keys as soon as the startup sound plays and hold them down until you are prompted to select a language. Select your language, and the OS X Utilities menu (see Figure 22-8) appears. It includes options to:

- **Restore from Time Machine Backup**—Restores the system from a Time Machine backup

- **Reinstall OS X**—Reinstalls OS X

- **Get Help Online**—Opens online help and remote diagnostics options

- **Disk Utility**—Repairs problems with hard drives

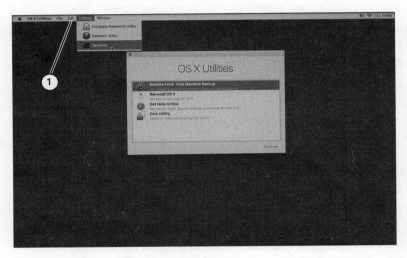

1. Menu bar offers additional options

Figure 22-8   OS X Utilities Menu.

To boot from a different partition than usual, such as a Boot Camp partition, start up your OS X system and hold down the Alt/Option key until a list of bootable drives appears. Select the drive to use.

NOTE   Boot Camp is OS X's multiboot support for Windows.

Improper Shutdown (Windows)

Some startup programs or services might prevent Windows from shutting down properly. To solve **improper shutdown** problems, use msconfig to perform a clean boot to see whether Windows can shut down correctly. If so, reenable services and programs with msconfig until you determine which service or program is causing a problem.

For details, see http://support.microsoft.com/kb/929135. See "MSCONFIG (Windows)" later in this chapter for more.

Spontaneous Shutdown/Restart

A **spontaneous shutdown/restart** event usually happens because of a serious problem with the operating system or with hardware. The following sections cover what to do.

Windows STOP (BSOD) Error Automatic Restart

Windows can be configured to automatically restart if a STOP error occurs. When a STOP (BSOD) error happens on a system configured to restart automatically, the system will seem to spontaneously shut down and restart. This problem is sometimes referred to as an Auto Restart Error.

If a system needs to be available at all times and STOP/BSOD errors are rare, it might be preferable to configure the system to restart automatically. (Different versions of Windows enable or disable this option by default.) To change this option, follow these steps:

Step 1. Open the System Properties window. Click or tap **Advanced System Settings**.

Step 2. Click the **Advanced** tab.

Step 3. Click **Settings** under the Startup and Recovery section.

Step 4. To enable auto restart, select the checkbox for **Automatically Restart** under the System Failure section (see Figure 22-9). To disable auto restart if it is already enabled, clear this checkbox.

TIP Spontaneous shutdown/restart can also be caused by a failing power supply. If you disable automatic restart and the system restarts spontaneously anyway, test the power supply. If the voltage on the Power Good line is too high or too low, the system will shut down and restart. For details, see "Multimeter," p.588, Chapter 13.

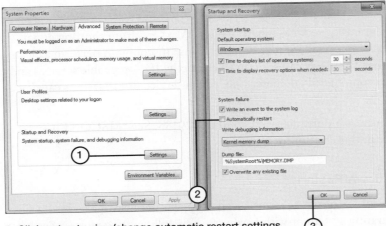

1. Click or tap to view/change automatic restart settings
2. If filled in, click to clear Automatically restart checkbox;
   STOP errors will stay onscreen until user restarts system
3. Click OK when finished

Figure 22-9   The Automatically Restart checkbox on the Startup and Recovery dialog determines whether a STOP error halts or restarts the system.

OS X Kernel Panic Automatic Restart

In the event of a **kernel panic** (a Linux and OS X term for the operating system shutting down after a fatal error), OS X reboots to the screen shown in Figure 22-10.

Figure 22-10   A restart after an OS X El Capitan kernel panic.

Press a key to restart. To learn more about reporting a kernel panic, see the "Kernel Panic (OS X/Linux)" section later in this chapter.

To test your system after a kernel panic or any other issue, restart your system and run Apple Diagnostics (systems built in 2013 or later), or Apple Hardware Test (older systems).

On systems with Apple Diagnostics or Apple Hardware Test built in, disconnect external drives, docking stations, and network adapters, open the Apple menu and select Restart. To launch the diagnostics test, hold down the D key while the system restarts. Follow the onscreen prompts to test your system. For more information, see https://support.apple.com/kb/PH21879. For more about kernel panics, see https://support.apple.com/en-us/HT200553.

Device Fails to Start/Detected (Windows)

A **device fails to start/detected** issue is shown in Device Manager by the device being listed with an error icon, typically a black exclamation mark on a yellow field. When you view the properties sheet for the device, it displays This Device Cannot Start. (Code 10). See Figure 22-11.

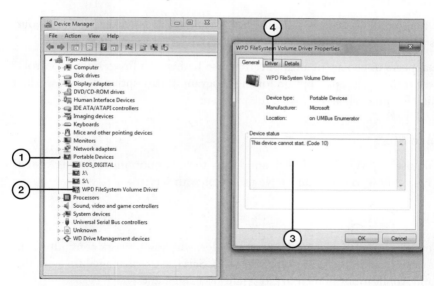

1. Category with problem device expands automatically
2. Problem device (! marking)
3. Problem message
4. Click Driver tab to try an updated driver

Figure 22-11   A Code 10 error for a device in Windows 7 Device Manager.

In most cases, updating the drivers with the Drivers tab solves the problem. If this does not resolve the problem, see http://support.microsoft.com/kb/943104 or search for information about the specific device with an error to learn what to do next.

A device that is detected as an Unknown device has no driver installed. Install the driver, then open Device Manager to see if the device is now working. In some cases, it might be necessary to remove the device before installing the driver, then reconnecting/reinstalling the device after the driver is present.

Missing DLL Message (Windows)

A dynamic link library (**DLL**) file is a binary file used by Windows or a program. An error message indicating a **missing DLL** might indicate one of the following problems:

- File deletion or renaming
- Damage from virus or malware

Before attempting to fix the problem, check your system for viruses and malware and resolve any detected infections.

If the file is a Windows system DLL, use SFC (System File Checker) to check your Windows files and reinstall a replacement.

If the file appears to be part of an application, use Uninstall a Program in Control Panel to see if there's a repair option for the program. If this option doesn't work or is not available, uninstall and reinstall the program.

Services Fail to Start

Services are used by Windows, OS X, and Linux to run important operating system features. Here's how to detect and solve problems with services.

Windows

Many Windows features, such as the print spooler, wireless network configuration, Windows Search, and others, are run as services. Services are managed through the Services and Applications branch of Computer Management.

A service might not start for the following reasons:

- Hardware used for the service is not present. For example, wireless network configuration will not run automatically if a wireless adapter is not installed.
- Other services that are used by the service are not running. In this case, an error such as "The Dependency Service or Group Failed to Start" appears.

- The service requires login information that has not been provided.

- The service has stopped due to previous errors and is not configured to restart automatically.

To learn how to manage services, see "Services (Services.msc)," p.764, Chapter 15.

Linux

Linux services that run at startup are referenced in the /etc/rc.conf DAEMONS array. Services that started correctly are shown in the /var/run/daemons/ directory. Compare these to see if any services failed to start.

To troubleshoot a service that didn't start, open a Terminal session as root and run the service's command to see if there's an error message.

OS X

OS X uses a variety of startup settings to configure system processes. For a list, see http://www.dgkapps.com/blog/osx-tips/OSX-Tips-System-Startup-launchd-launch-daemons-startup-items-launch-agents-and-login-items.

To disable loading all of these items for troubleshooting, start OS X in **Safe Mode** (press the power button while holding down Shift). For more troubleshooting in Safe Mode, see https://support.apple.com/en-us/HT201262.

Compatibility Error (Windows)

Programs written for older versions of Windows might trigger a **compatibility error**, displaying the This Program Has Known Compatibility Issues dialog when you try to run them. The dialog box lists the program name and location and the program developer and provides you with three choices:

- **Check for Solutions Online**—Choose this option to see whether an updated program or a patch is available.

- **Run Program**—Windows will run the program, but it is not likely to work.

- **Cancel**—Windows will not run the program.

Get an updated version of the program, either by selecting the Check for solutions... option or by manually searching for and downloading an update.

For more solutions, see "Compatibility Mode," p.681, Chapter 14.

Slow System Performance

Slow system performance can be caused by many issues in Windows, OS X, or Linux. Here are solutions to try.

Windows

Look at the following possible causes and solutions:

- **System not configured for maximum performance**—To solve this problem, set the Power setting to High Performance using the Power options icon in the notification area or the Power options in Control Panel. This option is not available on tablets.

- **Drive containing paging file and temporary files is nearly full or badly fragmented**—The paging file and temporary files are normally stored on C: (system) drive. If this drive has less than 15 percent free space, performance can suffer. Use Disk Cleanup in drive properties to remove unwanted files, check the drive for errors, and defragment it. If you have more available space on a different drive, use the Advanced tab in System properties to change the location of the paging file and temp files.

- **System is overheating and CPU is running at reduced speed**—Remove dust and dirt on the CPU and system fans. Check for adequate airflow through the system. Change back to Balanced power setting.

- **Add RAM**—Exceed the minimums recommended for the version of Windows in use for better performance.

- **Check for viruses and malware**—Especially important if performance has suddenly plunged.

- **Check for Registry errors**—The Piriform CCleaner is widely used for this task.

- **Use the performance troubleshooters in your version of Windows**—Search for "performance troubleshooter."

Linux

To improve system performance, follow these general guidelines:

- **Remove unneeded startup programs**—With recent versions of Ubuntu, use the Startup Application manager. With Fedora or other distributions, install GNOME-TWEAK and use its startup application manager.

- **Install more RAM**— Exceed the minimums recommended for the version of Linux in use for better performance.

- **Disable unneeded system services**—System services are typically located in the /etc/init.d directory (folder). Depending on your distribution, you might have a control center that can be used to disable system services, or you might need to use the Nautilus file manager, right-click a service, go to Properties > Permissions, and unclick the Execute: Allow Executing File as Program. To determine what a particular service does, look it up in the manpages for your distribution.

NOTE   For many other suggestions, see www.techradar.com/us/news/computing/pc/how-to-speed-up-your-linux-machine-1078475 and www.howtogeek.com/115797/6-ways-to-speed-up-ubuntu/. Using a VM to experiment with speedup strategies is a good idea, as some changes could cause problems if they are used incorrectly. Create a snapshot with your VM manager before trying a speedup tip.

OS X

In addition to following the suggestions in the "OS X Pin Wheel" section of this chapter, try these additional strategies to improve system responsiveness:

- If your MacBook Pro was built in 2012 or earlier and uses a hard disk, replace it with an SSD. Step-by-step instructions are available at www.cnet.com/how-to/upgrade-your-macbook-install-ssd-hard-drive/.

- Add more RAM.

- Use Disk Utility to remove apps you no longer need.

- Use System Preferences to disable unneeded startup apps.

- Be sure to install OS X updates as they become available.

- Remove unwanted Dashboard programs (widgets).

NOTE   For more information, see www.cnet.com/how-to/five-tips-to-speed-up-your-mac/, www.techrepublic.com/blog/apple-in-the-enterprise/five-tips-for-improving-mac-performance/, and www.zdnet.com/article/how-to-boost-your-macbook-pro-performance/.

Boots to Safe Mode (Windows)

If Windows Vista/7 does not shut down properly (such as because of a crash, lockup, or power failure), it displays the option to start in Safe Mode the next time the computer starts. You can accept this option or elect to start the system in Normal mode.

Even if you don't believe there are serious problems with the system, it is usually best to start the system in Safe Mode and then perform the shutdown/restart procedure from the Windows desktop. If there are no serious problems with the system, it usually restarts correctly.

Windows 8/8.1/10 recover from an improper shutdown without user intervention.

File Fails to Open

If a file can be opened from the File, Open menu in an application but not from Windows Explorer/File Explorer, the **file extension** is not associated with a program. A **file association** is used by Windows to determine the default file types that will be opened by an app. In this situation, you might not see an error message, or you might see an error message such as

> This File Does Not Have a Program Associated with It for Performing This Action. Please Install a Program, or if One Is Already Installed, Create an Association in the Default Programs Control Panel.

In Windows Vista/7, open Default Programs in Control Panel and select **Associate a file type or protocol with a program**.

In Windows 8/8.1/10, open the Charms menu, and select **PC Settings > Search and apps > Defaults > Choose default apps by file type**.

Missing GRUB/LILO (Linux)

GRUB or the improved GRUB2 is the most common boot loader in current Linux distributions, while older Linux distributions used **LILO**. In either case, the loss of the boot loader prevents Linux from starting. Frequently, Linux bootloaders are overwritten because of a Windows installation.

Although missing bootloaders can be restored with manual processes, bootable repair programs are recommended. Some of these include:

- Boot-repair (https://sourceforge.net/p/boot-repair/home/Home/)
- Rescatux (www.supergrubdisk.org/rescatux/)
- SystemRescueCd (www.system-rescue-cd.org/SystemRescueCd_Homepage)

These programs can be installed to a bootable CD or USB flash drive. They work by scanning the drive for operating systems and use that information to recreate GRUB or LILO and its entries, including Windows.

Kernel Panic (OS X/Linux)

In OS X and Linux, a kernel panic is the result of a fatal error that prevents the operating system from continuing. With OS X, when a system restarts after a kernel panic, OS X displays "Your computer was restarted because of a problem." To continue, click Ignore. To view a report first, click Report. On the next dialog, you have three options: Show Details, Don't Send, or Send to Apple (default). Click Show Details to see what happened (see Figure 22-12). After reviewing it, you can add a comment, and then click Send to Apple.

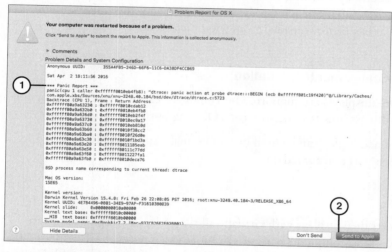

1. Panic report is the report title
2. Click to send report to Apple

Figure 22-12   Reviewing a problem report before sending it to Apple.

With Linux, depending on the distribution and the cause of the kernel panic, you might see a Kernel Panic error message on-screen, or the clues might simply be the Num Lock and Caps Lock indicator lights flashing on the keyboard and a completely unresponsive Linux installation.

Unlike normal shutdowns, which are logged by Linux, a kernel panic itself isn't logged. By examining Linux log files and viewing the times, you might be able to get some clues about what happened, but this can be frustrating and time-consuming.

Check the following:

- **Was new hardware installed shortly before the kernel panic?**—Remove the hardware or update its drivers. Some hardware vendors now provide Linux drivers, so try them instead of open-source versions.

- **Was the system overheating?**—Install Psensor (http://www.tecmint.com/psensor-monitors-hardware-temperature-in-linux/) to provide real-time monitoring of system temperature. If a kernel panic occurs again, you will have information about overheating.

- **Was new software installed?**—Uninstall it and check for updated versions.

- **Is a stable update to the Linux distribution available?**—Install it.

- **Is system memory working properly?**—Run a memory test. Some distributions, such as Ubuntu, include Memtest86+ as an advanced boot option. Otherwise, it can be downloaded from www.memtest.org.

Multiple Monitor Misalignment/Orientation

Multiple monitors (displays) are supported by Windows, Linux, and OS X. The following sections discuss how to configure each OS's support for multiple displays.

Before an additional display can be used by an OS, make sure it is plugged into AC power and a video port and turned on.

Windows

Windows supports dual displays with virtually all recent laptop display hardware as well as with desktop computers with two or more video ports. A USB 2.0 or 3.0 HDMI video dongle can also be added to provide support for an additional display. The additional display can be used as a mirror of the primary display or as an extended desktop running different apps.

To use an additional display with Windows Vista:

Step 1.   Right-click an empty area of the desktop and select **Personalize**.

Step 1a.   From the Vista Personalize menu, click **Display Settings**.

Step 2.   If the additional display is not visible, click **Detect**.

Step 3.   To enable the additional display, click it.

Step 4.   Click **Apply** and then click **OK**; it mirrors the contents of the primary display. One or both displays might change resolution.

Step 5.   To use it as a mirror, click the **Extend My Windows Desktop onto This Monitor**.

Step 6.   Adjust the screen resolution as needed for the second display. To determine usable resolutions, check the documentation for the display.

Step 7.   Click **Apply** and then click **OK** to use the settings.

To use an additional display on Windows 7/8/8.1/10 using the Display properties sheet:

Step 1.   Before turning on the computer, plug in the appropriate video cable to the video port.

Step 2.   Turn on the external monitor, TV, or projector.

Step 3.   Turn on the computer.

Step 4.   Right-click an empty area on the desktop and select **Screen Resolution**.

Step 5.   If the secondary screen is not detected, click **Detect**.

Step 6.   Multiple displays are initially configured as mirrored, and resolutions might be adjusted automatically to enable both displays to run at the same resolution (see Figure 22-13).

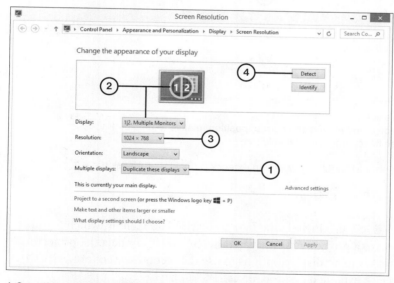

1. Open this menu to select only one display or to use an extended desktop
2. Mirrored displays
3. Resolution menu
4. Click to detect additional display if necessary

Figure 22-13   Additional displays are configured as mirrors of the first display in Windows.

Step 7.   To use extended desktop, open the Multiple Displays menu and select **Extend These Displays**.

Step 8.   Click **Apply**.

Step 9.   Select the second display and adjust the screen resolution as needed. To determine usable resolutions, check the documentation for the display.

Step 10.   Drag the display to match its location relative to the original display (see Figure 22-14).

Step 11.   Click Apply and then click OK to use the settings.

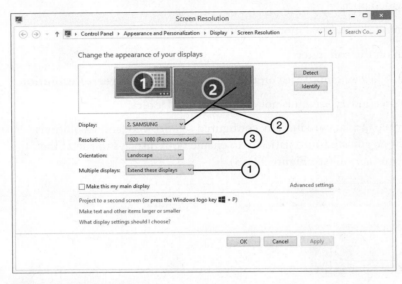

1. Extended desktop selected
2. Second display selected and moved into correct position relative to display 1
3. Each display can use its recommended resolution

Figure 22-14   Using an additional display as an extended desktop in Windows 8.1.

NOTE   Windows Vista/7 also include the Windows Mobility Center, which features an option to connect to a projector. With Windows 8/8.1/10, connect the projector, then press Windows key+P to display options to use the second screen (projector) only, duplicate screens, extended desktop, or use PC screen only.

OS X

Using an additional display with OS X:

Step 1. Connect the additional display and turn it on.

Step 2. Open **System Preferences > Displays**.

Step 3. A window opens for each display. In the Optimize window, you can optimize for the new display, or choose a scaled display from a choice of resolutions (see Figure 22-15).

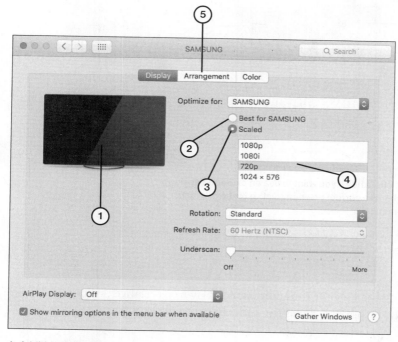

1. Additional display
2. Select if extended desktop to be used
3. Select if displays will be mirrored
4. Select resolution for both displays
5. Click to change arrangement of displays

Figure 22-15 Configuring the display resolutions in OS X.

Step 4. Click the **Arrangement** tab.

Step 5. By default, the displays are mirrored.

Step 6. Drag the new display to the correct position relative to the original display (which is marked with a menu bar across the top of the icon (see Figure 22-16). The menu bar can be dragged to the additional display if desired.

Step 7.   To use the additional display as an extended desktop, clear the **Mirror Displays** checkbox.

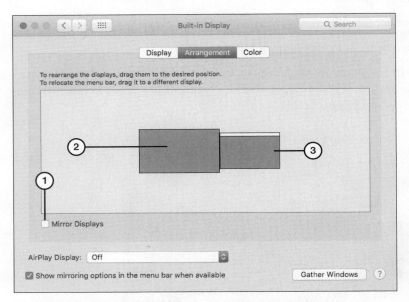

1. Clear Mirror Displays checkbox if you want to use an extended desktop
2. Drag additional display into correct position relative to the original
3. Original display has menu bar

Figure 22-16   The additional display is now at the left of the original display.

NOTE   By dragging the icon for the additional display to its relative position vis-à-vis the original display, the mouse moves smoothly between displays when you drag an app, and so on.

For more information, see https://support.apple.com/en-us/HT202351 and https://support.apple.com/en-us/HT202780.

Linux

To configure multiple displays in Ubuntu Linux:

Step 1.   Open the Settings app and click **Display**.

Step 2.   If only one display is visible, and other displays are plugged in and turned on, click **Detect Displays**.

Step 3.   If a mirrored display is desired, make sure the Mirror box is checked. For an extended desktop, make sure it is not checked.

Step 4.   Select each display and adjust its resolution. When running Linux in a VM (as shown in Figure 22-17), displays are listed as "Unknown display." When running Linux on physical hardware, displays are listed by brand and size.

Step 5.   Drag displays into position and click **Apply**.

Some Linux distributions will not retain multiple monitor alignment positions after restarting. To solve this problem, a startup script that will provide the monitor alignments needs to be created.

A good example for Ubuntu is available from: http://bernaerts.dyndns.org/linux/74-ubuntu/309-ubuntu-dual-display-monitor-position-lost.

For Fedora (and other distributions using KDE or GNOME GUIs), see http://tech.isatya.in/post/9090316930/setting-forcing-changing-fedora-15-screen.

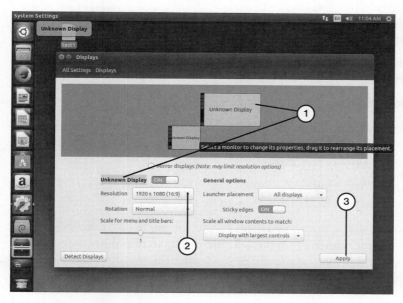

1. Selected display (light green)
2. Resolution for selected display
3. Click to apply changes

Figure 22-17   The additional display is at the upper right of the original display.

Missing Boot Configuration Data

See the "Windows Boot Errors" section in the "Failure to Boot" section later in this chapter.

Missing Operating System / Missing NTLDR

An Operating System Not Found or **Missing Operating System** error can be caused by incorrect or missing hard disk settings in the system BIOS/UEFI firmware or by problems with the hard disk's master boot record (MBR) or GUI partition table (GPT).

Before attempting to repair the MBR or GPT, restart the computer, enter the BIOS setup program, and check the following:

- Make sure the system drive is correctly identified in the system BIOS.
- Make sure the system drive is listed before other bootable drives in the boot sequence or boot order menu.

Save any changes needed, and restart the computer. If the same error is displayed, restart the computer with the Windows installation media.

With Windows, start the Windows Recovery Environment and use Startup Repair.

Missing Graphical Interface

Windows can be started without a graphical user interface (**GUI**) by selecting the Command Prompt Only option from the Advanced Startup menu. To restore the GUI, simply restart Windows normally.

To learn more, see "Safe Mode (Windows)" and "To learn more, see the "Safe Mode (Windows)" section later in this chapter.

If Linux is normally started with a GUI, but fails to launch the GUI, hold down the Shift key when starting Linux. From the GRUB2 menu, boot into Recovery mode. Use a startup option that loads `failsafeX`, or run it after the startup process is complete from the terminal command prompt.

GUI Fails to Load (Windows)

If the display's vertical refresh setting in Windows is out of range, you can see BIOS boot information, such as the splash screen or the summary of onboard components, but you will not see the Windows GUI. Your display might provide a warning of an incorrect vertical refresh rate setting when it's time to load the Windows desktop.

To solve this problem, restart Windows in limited resolution (VGA) mode, open the Advanced Display properties sheet, and select the correct refresh rate (typically 60Hz for LCD or LED panels or integrated LCD or LED displays).

Tools for Troubleshooting Software

Several of the tools for troubleshooting an operating system have already been discussed in this chapter. In the following sections, we discuss additional tools you might need.

BIOS/UEFI

As you learned in Chapter 2, the **BIOS** (traditional or **UEFI** firmware) is the first issue to consider if a system will not start. Make sure the following settings are correct:

- RAID array (if used for boot) is properly configured

- Drives are properly identified and configured (AHCI, SATA 6Gbps, and so on)

- Secure Boot on for running Windows 8/8.1/10 only, or disabled if dual-booting with Linux or older Windows versions

- Memory recognized correctly

- Boot sequence

SFC (Windows)

System File Checker (**SFC**) is a Windows utility that checks protected system files (files such as .DLL, .SYS, .OCX, and .EXE, as well as some font files used by the Windows desktop) and replaces incorrect versions or missing files with the correct files. For more information, see "SFC," p.752, Chapter 15.

Logs

Windows stores system events, warnings, and errors in various event **logs**. Although these events can be viewed from Computer Management Console, it is easier to view them with **Event Viewer**. Event Viewer can be run from the Tools tab in Msconfig or from Administrative Tools in the System folder of Control Panel.

Use the Overview and Summary window or the branches of the Event Viewer or Computer Management Console to locate the log message you need to read. Look for Critical errors (marked with a white X on a red circle) first and then Warnings (yellow triangle). Frequent errors or warnings that point to the same program or device can indicate a serious problem (see Figure 22-18 and Figure 22-19). You might need to update drivers for a problem device, obtain a software update for a problem program, or remove the device or program and replace it with a different one to resolve the problems.

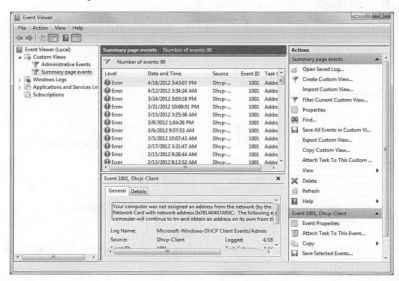

Figure 22-18   Viewing a series of errors involving the DHCP-client with the Windows 7 Event Viewer.

Figure 22-19   Viewing a series of errors involving kernel-power issues with the Windows 8.1 Event Viewer.

System Recovery Options (Windows)

Windows includes **System Recovery Options** that can be started automatically when a Windows system has problems, or by using the Windows distribution media to restart the system.

To start System Recovery Options manually with Windows Vista/7, see "Repair Discs," this chapter, p. 1108.

To restart the system and use System Recovery Options in Windows 8/8.1/10:

Step 1.   Hold down the **Shift** key and click the onscreen power button at the Windows login screen.

Step 2.   Select **Restart**.

Step 3.   Select **Troubleshoot**.

Troubleshooting options:

- Refresh your PC to remove apps not from the Windows Store, reinstall apps from the Windows store, and keep the user's files and settings.

- Reset your PC to return it to its factory condition. All users' files, settings, and programs will be lost.

Select Advanced options for other repair choices:

- System Restore to return the system to its condition as of a **restore point** (System Restore must be enabled for this to be possible)

- System Image Recovery to restore a system image (create the image with the System Image Backup link in File History)

- Startup Repair to repair a system that won't start

- Command prompt to run a command-line program such as bootrec

- UEFI firmware settings to enter the UEFI firmware (BIOS)

- Startup settings to get access to the special startup options (also known as the F8 menu startup options).

Figure 22-20 illustrates these three dialogs.

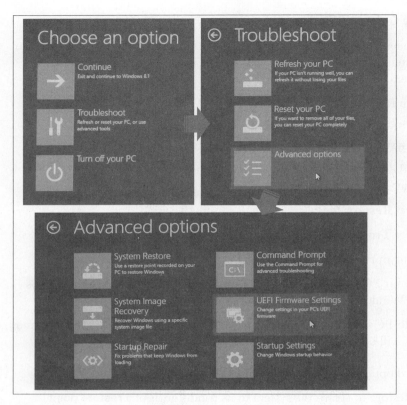

Figure 22-20   The Windows 8/8.1/10 advanced startup menu for repair and troubleshooting.

NOTE   For more information about recovery options in Windows 8/8.1/10, see: http://windows.microsoft.com/en-us/windows-8/restore-refresh-reset-pc, http://windows.microsoft.com/en-us/windows-10/windows-10-recovery-options, and http://www.online-tech-tips.com/windows-8/how-to-boot-to-windows-8-system-recovery-options/.

Repair Discs

Windows Recovery Environment (WinRE) provides access to Startup Repair, System Restore, full-featured command prompt and run-line utilities, Windows memory diagnostics, and Complete PC restore (restores image backup). WinRE can be run from a hidden recovery partition, from the Windows distribution media, or from a repair disc. WinRE is an example of a preinstallation environment.

Windows Repair Disc enables the user to run WinRE from a bootable CD or DVD. Repair discs (also known as **repair disks**) can be created with Windows Vista SP1 or higher and with any release of Windows 7. Windows Repair Disc can be used to re-start the system to run the Windows Recovery Environment (see Figure 22-21).

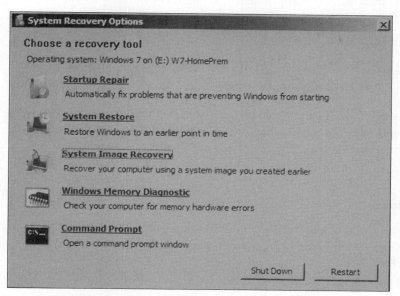

Figure 22-21   The Windows Vista/7 Recovery Environment.

To restart the computer with a repair disc, insert it, turn on or restart the system and, if prompted, press a key to boot from the disc.

Pre-installation Environments

Windows PE is a special version of Windows that can be used to prepare a system for deployment or for other troubleshooting or repair purposes. Windows PE is included with Windows deployment kits. To learn more about Windows PE 5.0 for Windows 7/8/8.1, see https://technet.microsoft.com/en-us/library/hh825110.aspx. Older versions of Windows PE work with Windows Vista.

Windows PE for Windows 10 is described at https://msdn.microsoft.com/en-us/library/windows/hardware/dn938389(v=vs.85).aspx. It can be downloaded as part of the Windows Assessment and Deployment Kit for Windows 10.

NOTE   Many third-party recovery tools are based on Windows PE. To learn more about these, see https://www.raymond.cc/blog/5-system-rescue-boot-disc-based-on-windows-pe/.

MSCONFIG (Windows)

The Microsoft System Configuration Utility, MSCONFIG, enables you to selectively disable programs and services that run at startup. If your computer is unstable, runs more slowly than usual, or has problems starting up or shutting down, using MSCONFIG can help you determine whether a program or service running when the system starts is at fault. See "**MSCONFIG**," p.773, Chapter 15, for more information.

DEFRAG

Defragging a hard disk drive can help improve system performance, especially if the drive has frequent changes. Windows includes **DEFRAG**. For information about using defragmentation tools, see "Defragmentation," p.607, Chapter 13, for more information.

REGSVR32 (Windows)

If a program stops working after another program was installed or removed, some program components might have been replaced or disabled. The Microsoft command-line tool **REGSVR32** (sometimes misspelled as regsrv32) is used to reregister .dll or .ocx files used by applications.

To use Regsvr32.exe, open a command prompt as administrator. Go to the folder containing the file(s) you need to reregister.

The basic syntax to register a program file with Regsvr32 is:

```
Regsvr32 filename.ext
```

For example, to reregister a file called jscript.dll in the current folder, use the following:

```
Regsvr32 jscript.dll
```

> **NOTE**   On a 64-bit version of Windows operating system, there are two versions of the Regsvr32.exe file:
>
> - The 64-bit version is %systemroot%\System32\regsvr32.exe.
> - The 32-bit version is %systemroot%\SysWoW64\regsvr32.exe.
>
> To learn more about Regsvr32, see http://support.microsoft.com/kb/249873.

REGEDIT (Windows)

The Windows Registry Editor, **REGEDIT**, can be used to fix issues with software, drivers, and Windows configuration settings if they cannot be resolved in any other way. To learn more about using Regedit, see "Using REGEDIT," p.789, Chapter 15.

Safe Mode (Windows)

Safe Mode and other advanced boot options can be used when the system won't boot normally; press F8 repeatedly in Windows Vista and Windows 7 when starting the system until you see the Advanced Boot Options menu. Figure 22-22 illustrates the Windows 7 version.

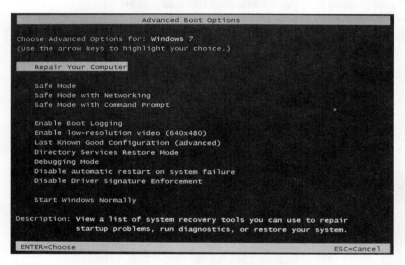

Figure 22-22   The Windows 7 Advanced Boot Options menu featuring Safe Mode and other special startup options. The Repair Your Computer option runs the Windows Recovery Environment.

With Windows 8/8.1/10, getting to the Advanced Boot Options menu takes more steps. Press the Power button on the login screen, hold down the Shift key, and click/tap **Restart**. Select **Troubleshoot > Advanced Options > Startup Settings > Restart**. The Windows 8/8.1 startup settings menu (see Figure 22-23) adds a couple of new features but looks similar to that of Windows 7.

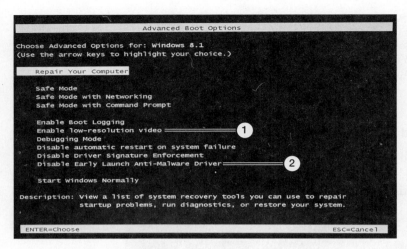

1. Uses lowest resolution of primary display instead of 640×480
2. New in Windows 8/8.1

Figure 22-23   The Windows 8.1 Advanced Boot Options menu featuring Safe Mode and other special startup options.

The Windows 10 Startup Settings menu has similar options to the Windows 8.1 version, but is more graphical (see Figure 22-24).

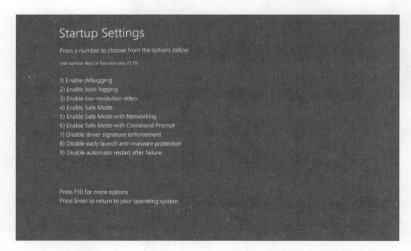

Figure 22-24   The Windows 10 Startup Settings menu has the same options as the Windows 8.1 version, but in a different order and selectable by number.

TIP To return the F8 function key method for accessing the Windows 8.1 Advanced Boot Options menu, follow these steps.

From an administrative command prompt enter:

```
bcdedit /set {default} bootmenupolicy legacy
```

Exit the command prompt and reboot. Press F8 and the Advanced Boot Options menu appears.

To undo and return to standard settings, from an administrative command prompt enter:

```
bcdedit /set {default} bootmenupolicy standard
```

Exit the command prompt and reboot. You are back to standard boot settings and F8 will not work.

Here's what the options do:

- **Safe Mode**—Starts the system with a minimal set of drivers; can be used to start System Restore or to load Windows GUI for diagnostics.

- **Safe Mode with Networking**—Starts the system with a minimal set of drivers and enables network support.

- **Safe Mode with Command Prompt**—Starts the system with a minimal set of drivers but loads command prompt instead of Windows GUI.

- **Enable Boot Logging**—Creates an ntbtlog.txt file.

- **Enable low-resolution video**—Uses a standard VGA driver in place of a GPU-specific display driver, but uses all other drivers as normal.

- **Last Known Good Configuration**—Starts the system with the last configuration known to work; useful for solving problems caused by newly installed hardware or software.

- **Debugging Mode**—An advanced diagnostics tool that enables the use of a debug program to examine the system kernel for troubleshooting.

- **Disable automatic restart on system failure**—Prevents Windows from automatically restarting if a STOP (BSOD) error causes Windows to fail. Choose this option only if Windows is stuck in a loop where Windows fails, attempts to restart, and fails again.

- **Disable driver signature enforcement**—Allows drivers containing improper signatures to be installed.

- **Disable early launch anti-malware protection**—Use this when a legitimate driver is mistaken for malware by Windows 8/8.1/10's Early Launch Anti-Malware Protection feature.

- **Start Windows Normally**—Can be used to boot to regular Windows. This option is listed in case a user inadvertently presses F8 but does not want to use any of the Advanced Boot Options.

If Windows 7 or Vista fails to start properly and then restarts automatically, they normally display the Windows Error Recovery screen and give you the following options: Safe Mode, Safe Mode with Networking, Safe Mode with Command Prompt, Last Known Good Configuration, and Start Windows Normally. This means that Windows has acknowledged some sort of error or improper shutdown and offers a truncated version of the Advanced Boot Options menu.

Table 22-1 lists typical problems and helps you select the correct startup option to use to solve the problem.

Table 22-1   Using the Windows Advanced Boot Options and Startup Settings Menus

Problem	Startup Option to Select	Notes
Windows Vista/7 won't start after you install new hardware or software.	Last Known Good Configuration	Resets Windows to its last-known working configuration; you need to reinstall hardware or software installed after that time. See Note following this table for cautions regarding this option.
Windows won't start after you upgrade a device driver.	Safe Mode	After starting the computer in this mode, open the Device Manager, select the device, and use the Rollback feature to restore the previously used device driver. Restart your system.
Windows won't start after you install a different video card or monitor.	Enable low-resolution video (VGA Mode)	Most video cards should be installed when your system is running in VGA Mode. If a video error occurs, use this option, and then the Display Properties window to select a working video mode before you restart.
Windows can't start normally, but you need access to the Internet to research the problem or download updates.	Safe Mode with Networking	You can use Windows Update and the Internet, but some devices won't work in this mode. This mode also uses low resolution but retains the color settings normally used.

Problem	Startup Option to Select	Notes
Windows doesn't finish starting normally, and you want to know what device driver or process is preventing it from working.	Enable Boot Logging	This option starts the computer with all its normal drivers and settings and also creates a file called ntbtlog.txt in the default Windows folder (usually C:\Windows). Restart the computer in Safe Mode, and open this file with Notepad or WordPad to determine the last driver file that loaded. You can update the driver or remove the hardware device using that driver to restore your system to working condition.
Windows is loading programs you don't need during its startup process.	Boot computer in Normal Mode (or Safe Mode if the computer won't start in Normal Mode); click Start, Run or Start Search; and then type msconfig	Use this program to disable one or more startup programs, and then restart your computer. You can also use it to restore damaged files or to start System Restore to reset your computer to an earlier condition.
Windows prevents you from running an unsigned device driver, so a device doesn't work	Disable driver signature enforcement	Obtain signed device driver from vendor as soon as possible.
Windows reboots as soon as a STOP (BSOD) error occurs	Disable automatic restart after failure	If the STOP (BSOD) error recurs, the system will not restart automatically, enabling you to see the error message and start the diagnostic process.
Windows prevents a driver or program from running because it has incorrectly identified it as malware	Disable early launch anti-malware protection	As soon as you restart the computer, be sure to update anti-malware apps and scan the computer for threats.

NOTE   The Last Known Good Configuration option (Windows Vista/7) will be helpful only before a successful logon occurs. After a user logs on, that becomes the Last Known Good logon. It is recommended that you attempt to repair a computer with Advanced Boot Options before using Windows 7 or Vista's System Recovery Options.

Command Prompt (Windows)

The Windows **command prompt** can be used from recovery modes and special startup options to perform repairs on the boot configuration data store, to run system file checker (SFC) and perform other repair and recovery tasks.

If you need to perform tasks that might change computer configuration from the normal Windows desktop, be sure to run command prompt as elevated (administrative mode):

- Search for CMD, right-click it, and select **Run as Administrator** (Windows Vista/7).

- With Windows 8/8.1/10, press **Windows key+X** and select **Command Prompt (Administrative)**.

Uninstall/Reinstall/Repair

You can run a Windows repair install by restarting a system with the Windows distribution media and selecting **Repair Installation** when prompted.

Windows 8/8.1/10 provide **Refresh** and **Reset** as additional alternatives.

For OS X Recovery (Lion release and later), see https://support.apple.com/en-us/HT201314.

Use Recovery System on your startup drive to reinstall the most recent OS X release installation on that computer; Internet Recovery installs the OS X version the computer was originally shipped with.

A Linux repair installation is destructive, so the system should be backed up first. Use a repair disc (discussed earlier in this chapter) to repair the system if possible first.

Troubleshoot Mobile OS and Application Issues

Some common mobile OS and Application issues you might encounter include:

- System Lockout
- Hard reset
- Soft reset
- Adjust configurations/settings
- Uninstall/reinstall apps

The following sections discuss these issues and the solutions.

NOTE For other mobile device issues, including:

- Dim display
- Intermittent wireless
- No wireless connectivity
- No Bluetooth connectivity
- Touchscreen non-responsive
- Apps not loading
- Slow performance
- Unable to decrypt e-mail
- Extremely short battery life
- Overheating
- Frozen system
- No sound from speakers
- Inaccurate touch-screen response

See "Mobile Device Troubleshooting," p.633, Chapter 13.

System Lockout

A **system lockout** takes place if you have forgotten your password, PIN code, or pattern code (drawing a shape on the screen) and because of too many attempts to log in, login attempts are blocked.

If it's an Android phone, make sure you know your Google (Android) login information. You are prompted to provide this if you are blocked. If you can provide this when prompted, you are logged back into your device. Be sure to change the password, PIN code, or pattern code. If you don't have this information, you might need to perform a hard reset on the phone. This wipes out all apps and data.

On an iPhone, if it has locked you out, you can use iTunes to back up your device before restoring it if you have previously used iTunes for this task. See https://support.apple.com/en-us/HT204306 for more information and how to erase your device.

> **NOTE**   Before you perform a hard reset on an Android device, try the tips provided at https://www.matthewhollander.com/locked-out-of-your-android-phone/.

Soft Reset

A **soft reset**, also known as a "soft restart," restarts an Android device to help fix problems with the phone or its apps without deleting user data. Depending upon the device, you can use one or more of the following methods:

- Press and hold the power button until you are prompted to turn off the device, then tap Power Off. To turn the device back on, press and hold the power button until the device restarts.

- Remove the battery. After a minute or two, reinstall the battery and restart the device.

- Press and hold the power button and volume down button until the device restarts.

On an iOS device, some people use the term "hard reset" to refer to a reset that clears the iOS firmware and can help solve problems with unresponsive hardware, botched updates, and other issues, but does not erase any data or apps. Apple prefers to use the term "restart" or "forced restart" instead. Here's how to do a restart.

Step 1.   Press and hold **Sleep/Wake** until the Slide to power off slider appears.

Step 2.   Drag the slider to off and then wait a few seconds.

Step 3.   Press and **hold Sleep/Wake** until the device displays the Apple logo.

If this doesn't work, try a forced restart:

Step 1.   Hold down the **Sleep/Wake** and **Home** buttons for about 10 seconds until the Apple logo is displayed.

See https://support.apple.com/en-us/HT201559 for more information.

Hard Reset

The term **hard reset** refers to deleting all the information from your mobile device to reset it to factory condition (**reset to factory default**). Apple prefers to use the term *Erase*.

If you decide that you need to erase your iOS device so it can be given away or sold, this can be done with **Settings > General > Reset > Erase All Content and Settings**. See https://support.apple.com/en-us/HT204686 for more information.

Before doing a hard reset on an Android device:

Step 1. Back up the device if possible.

Step 2. Try a soft reset.

Step 3. If you must perform a hard reset, make sure the device is charged.

Step 4. Unplug the device from power.

Step 5. Turn it off.

Step 6. Use the keystroke(s) for your smartphone or tablet and version of Android.

As an example of step 6, with recent Samsung Galaxy smartphones:

Step 1. Press and hold Volume Up, Home, and Power at the same time.

Step 2. Release the Power key only when the Galaxy logo is displayed or the phone vibrates.

Step 3. From the Android system recovery screen, select wipe data/factory reset (use the volume keys to scroll and Power to choose this option).

Step 4. After the factory reset is over, select Reboot system now to restart a phone empty of user data with factory settings only.

NOTE   For more about this process including keystrokes for other popular smartphones and Android versions, see www.smartmobilephonesolutions.com/content/how-to-hard-reset-an-android-phone.

Adjust Configurations/Settings

The Settings menus in iOS and Android provide options for removing unwanted apps, checking for updates, and other troubleshooting features. Table 22-2 lists typical settings for Android and where to make them.

Table 22-2   Android Mobile Configuration Settings

Setting Menu	Option
Connections	Configure Wi-Fi, Bluetooth, Airplane Mode, Mobile Hotspot and Tethering, NFC, Tap & Pay, Printing, MirrorLink (connect to car), VPN, set default messaging app, network operators
	Check data usage
Device > Sounds and Notifications	Configure sounds, vibration, volume, ringtones, sound quality, Do Not Disturb
Device > Display	Change brightness, font, screen timeout, screen mode, others
Device > Motions and Gestures	Change direct call, mute, others
Device > Applications	Change settings for each application, select default apps, uninstall, force stop, or disable apps
Personal	Configure wallpaper, themes, lock screen, security, privacy and safety, accessibility, accounts, backup and reset, easy mode
System	Access language and input, battery and power savings modes, storage usage, date & time, help, developer options, and About device (software updates)

Table 22-3 lists typical settings for iOS and where to make them.

Table 22-3   iOS Mobile Configuration Settings

Setting Menu	Option
General	Siri, software updates, search, multitasking, lock rotation/mute, auto lock, date & time, keyboard
Main Menu	Airplane mode, Wi-Fi, Bluetooth, Notifications, Control Center, Do Not Disturb, settings for individual apps
Display & Brightness	Brightness, text size, bold text
Wallpaper	Choose new wallpaper
Sounds	Volume, event sounds (ringtones, etc.), lock sounds, keyboard click
Passcode	Create or change
Battery	Battery usage, percentage display
Privacy	Location services, contacts, calendars, reminders, photos, Bluetooth sharing, microphone, cameras, HomeKit, motion and fitness, third-party apps (Twitter, Facebook, others), diagnostics and usage data sharing, advertising (limit ad tracking)

Windows 10 Mobile uses the Settings menu for configuration. It is similar to the Windows 10/Windows 10 Pro versions for desktop and laptop computers.

Mobile Devices and Application Security Issues

Mobile devices can have many issues, most caused by their limited storage and memory and their reliance on wireless and cellular networking. The following issues may appear on the exam and reflect the challenges of day-to-day mobile use.

Signal Drop/Weak Signal

With a Wi-Fi connection, scan for other available wireless networks.

With a cellular data connection, move to a different location, preferably near a window or outside the building, or adjust how you hold the phone.

To determine the cellular signal strength in dB for a smartphone, use the Field Test Mode. For more information for iOS and Android phones, see https://www. repeaterstore.com/pages/field-test-mode. Note that a stronger signal is indicated by a lower value.

Check connection speeds with the case on and off to see if it is affecting performance. Ookla Speedtest is available from Google Play and the App Store to test performance over cellular data and Wi-Fi connections.

> **NOTE**   If cellular connections are good outside your office or home but poor inside your home, a cellular repeater can help improve performance. See www.repeaterstore. com and www.ubersignal.com among others.

Power Drain

Power drain is caused by having too many apps running at the same time. Closing apps properly will help, but force closing apps that run continuously saves more power.

See the "Force Stop" section later in this chapter.

Slow Data Speeds

Slow data speeds can be caused by:

- **No connection to a 4G network**—Check the network indicator at the top of your smartphone or cellular-equipped tablet to determine the network connection type.

- **A weak 4G or Wi-Fi signal**—With Wi-Fi, switch to a stronger SSID signal if possible. With 4G, use a cell tower scanner to locate a stronger cell tower.

- **"Unlimited" Data Plan speed caps after reaching 4G speed limit per billing period**—Some of the providers who offer "unlimited" data plans drastically reduce speed after a certain level of data is transferred during a billing period. Check data usage and set up a warning to be displayed before you reach this goal or consider switching users to a different plan.

Unintended Wi-Fi Connection

Some smartphones connect automatically to available Wi-Fi hotspots (for example, AT&T smartphones can connect automatically to AT&T hotspots). These hotspots are not secure connections and are thus not desirable for secure communications.

To disable this feature, check the Wi-Fi settings on your smartphone. On an AT&T Android phone, for example, go to **Settings > Connections > Wi-Fi > More > Advanced > Disable Auto Connect**.

On an iPhone, go to **Settings > Wi-Fi** and then turn off **Ask to Join Networks**.

To prevent reconnections to a previously used network, select the network and tap **Forget**.

Unintended Bluetooth Pairing

To prevent your device from **pairing** with unknown devices:

- Turn off Bluetooth when you do not use Bluetooth devices.

- When you use Bluetooth devices, make sure your mobile device requests a code from a device attempting to pair with it. You can do this by attempting to pair a Bluetooth-enabled device in your possession with another Bluetooth-enabled device.

Leaked Personal Files/Data

To prevent personal files or data from being discovered in the event your mobile device is lost:

Step 1.   Enable encryption.

Step 2.   Enable options to wipe your device in case of loss.

Step 3.   Avoid open Wi-Fi networks.

Step 4.   Use VPN for secure connections if you must use an open Wi-Fi network.

Step 5.   Disable Wi-Fi tethering or connection sharing services if not in use.

Data Transmission Overlimit

Exceeding the amount of data included in your cellular plan (**overlimit**) could be expensive.
To avoid unexpected bills, periodically check data usage. On Android, go to **Settings > Connections > Data usage**. Scroll down to see which apps are using the most data. **Set data limit** should be turned on to set a limit, warning, and to prevent exceeding the limit.

On iOS, go to **Settings > Cellular > Cellular Data Usage**. Use sliders to disable any apps that should not be using cellular connections. Turn off Cellular Data if there is no data allowance left in the current period.

If you see unusual amounts of data usage, it could be a sign of malware.

Unauthorized Account Access

Set up security on your banking or other accounts so that attempts to access it must be authorized by you first. Typically, this is done by specifying an e-mail or messaging number that must be responded to before a new device can be added as an authorized device.

Unauthorized Root Access

Android devices are relatively easy to root (to gain root access to) so that users can install different operating systems and continue to use their cellular and data connections. On the other hand, iOS devices must be "jailbroken" and run the risk that their devices might be blocked for updates.

However, unauthorized **root access** is a different story. Unauthorized root access on an Android device is a risk when users download apps that are not from Google Play. These apps do not properly follow the permissions rules and may elevate permissions without the user's knowledge or consent. Running a device in Developer mode (used for software and service development and testing) disables most safeguards. On current versions of Android, it takes several steps to enable Developer mode so it's difficult to do it accidentally.

Jailbreaking an iOS device or rooting an Android device puts the device and its information at much higher risk than with a normally functioning device.

Unauthorized Location Tracking

Location tracking features are found in both iOS and Android smartphones.

To prevent iOS from tracking your location by Wi-Fi connections:

- Go to **Settings > Privacy > Location Services > System Services** and then turn off **Frequent Locations** and clear history.

To prevent Android from tracking your location by Wi-Fi connections:

- Go to **Settings > Personal > Privacy and Safety > Location > Locating Method > GPS only**.

Third-party apps can be used to perform location tracking without the authorization of the device user. These apps are marketed to parents and organizations who want to keep track of individuals.

Malicious apps with this feature could be installed by a user who does not use Google Play or the App Store to install apps.

Unauthorized Camera/Microphone Activation

Third-party apps can use the device's camera or microphone without the authorization of the device user. These apps are marketed to parents and organizations who want to keep track of individuals.

Some apps can be installed on iOS without physical access to the device: just the Apple ID and password are needed.

Malicious apps with this feature could be installed by a user who does not use Google Play or the App Store.

High Resource Utilization

High resource utilization (cellular data, CPU, memory, storage) can have many causes. To check cellular data use by app, see the "Data Transmission Overlimit" section earlier in this chapter.

To reduce CPU, memory, and storage usage:

- Uninstall apps that are not needed.
- Configure apps to receive updates only via Wi-Fi.
- Turn off background updates.

To see real-time resource usage by app for iOS, download the latest version of Xcode from the Apple Developer website and use its Instruments app. Learn more at http://apple.stackexchange.com/questions/71237/how-to-identify-cpu-and-memory-usage-per-process-on-iphone.

To see real-time resource usage by app for Android, use System Monitor from AndroidPit.com. For additional resource monitoring, see https://www.androidpit.com/best-apps-for-monitoring-system-performance-on-your-android-device.

See the next section, "Tools," for methods for detecting and blocking malware and hostile apps and processes.

Tools

Mobile users and techs have a wide variety of software tools available to help boost performance and security. They're covered in the following sections.

Anti-Malware

Both Android and iOS devices can be protected with **anti-malware** apps, some free, and some paid, from the same vendors who protect desktop and laptop systems. Every mobile device should be protected, if for no other reason than that a mobile device can be used as an infection vector for any other device it connects to. Check Google Play and the App Store for anti-malware apps from AVAST, AVG, Kaspersky Labs, Norton, McAfee, Bitdefender, AVIRA, ESET, and many others.

App Scanner

During the installation process for an app, the user sees a long list of permissions the app is being granted. Reading this list carefully is a bit like listening closely to the side effects for a medicine: you wonder if the app is worth the side effects of potential threats to privacy. An **app scanner** can help determine whether an app is safe to use. Here are two examples:

- The Zscaler Application Profile (http://zap.zscaler.com/) is a well-regarded tool for evaluating iOS and Android apps. Search for the name of an app and the operating system, and Zscaler checks its database for matches. For example, searching for flashlight iOS came up with five matching apps, four of which had security/privacy risks of 50 or greater (100 being greatest risk, 0 being no risk). Zscaler can also check an app you specify on the App Store or Google Play for risks.

- Bitdefender anti-malware offers a free Android app called the Clueful Privacy Advisor through Google Play. Clueful lists apps by potential threat and enables the user to see the permissions for any app.

Factory Reset/Clean Install

Before retiring a device, or as a way to eliminate apps that may risk privacy, perform a **factory reset** on the device. This can be followed by a **clean install** of desired apps.

If the device is not encrypted yet, set up a PIN first. This automatically encrypts the device.

For Android:

Step 1. Make sure **Back up my data** and **Automatic restore** are enabled. See the "Backup/Restore" section in this chapter, for additional backup processes.

Step 2. Go to **Settings > Personal > Backup and reset > Factory Data Reset**.

Step 3. After reviewing the warnings, click **Reset Device**.

The device will be returned to its factory configuration. All data and device updates will be removed from the device.

To restore data to this device or to a different device, see the "Backup/Restore" section later in this chapter.

For iOS:

Step 1. Install the latest version of iTunes on your host PC or OS X computer.

Step 2. Start iTunes.

Step 3. Connect your device to the computer via the 30-pin or Lightning charge/sync cable. Trust the device or enter a passcode if prompted.

Step 4. Select your device.

Step 5. Back up its contents. See https://support.apple.com/en-us/ht203977 "Make a backup using iTunes." Be sure to use Transfer Purchases for content purchased from iTunes, the Health & Activity data stored on your device (backup must be encrypted), and start your backup. To learn more about the iOS Health app, see https://support.apple.com/en-us/HT203037.

Step 6. To erase the device, go to **Summary > Restore**.

Step 7. Click **Restore** again to erase your device and reload it to its original factory condition.

Use iTunes to restore data afterwards. See https://support.apple.com/en-us/ht2041844.

Uninstall/Reinstall Apps

To solve problems with corrupt or outdated apps, you can uninstall them and then reinstall them. For Android:

Step 1. Go to **Settings > Device > Applications > Application Manager**.

Step 2. Select an app and tap **Uninstall**.

Step 3. To reinstall the app, go to Google Play and reinstall it.

Repairing an Android App

Before you uninstall an Android app, try these options first:

- If an update is available, update the app. To change update options, open **Google Play > Menu > Settings > Auto-Update Settings**.

- If the app ran well until the latest update, you might be able to roll back the updates. Click the Uninstall Updates button (when available) to revert to an earlier version.

- All apps offer the Clear Cache button. Use it to discard information that is retained for reuse, which might improve the app's performance and stability.

- The final alternative to uninstalling an app is to use the Clear Data button. This option removes all app settings; it will run as if you have just installed it. However, keep in mind that game progress, social media passwords, and other app data is lost when you use this option.

For iOS:

Step 1. From the apps dialog (home screen), press and hold any app icon until they wriggle.

Step 2. Click the X to remove the app. Click **Delete** to confirm.

Apps can also be deleted by going to **Settings > General > Storage & iCloud Usage > Manage Storage**, selecting an app, and then tapping Delete.

To uninstall an iOS app, press the app's icon, click the **X**, and confirm deletion. You can reinstall it from the Apple App Store.

Updating an iOS App

Before you uninstall an iOS app, try updating it:

- Open the App Store icon from the Start menu and click the Update button for each app to update.

- Tap the app icon and then scroll down to What's New to see what has been changed.

To uninstall an app with Windows 10 Mobile, press and hold the app icon, and select Uninstall. You can reinstall the apps with the Windows Store.

Wi-Fi Analyzer

Use a **Wi-Fi analyzer** app to see which channels are in use and by which SSIDs. If you are using public Wi-Fi, this is useful to locate the best signal. If you are working on setting up or maintaining a home or office wireless network, use this information to choose the best channel.

The Wifi Analyzer from Farpoint is available from Google Play. It provides monitoring in real time, showing SSID, signal strength, and channel (see Figure 22-25).

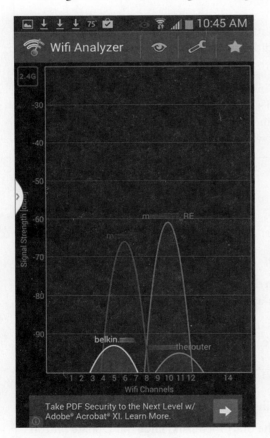

Figure 22-25   Using Wifi Analyzer to view 2.4GHz networks in use.

Force Stop

Even when you close a mobile app, it might restart right away. Use **Force Stop** to close an app that doesn't want to close or won't stay closed.

For Android:

- Go to **Settings > Device > Applications > Application manager**, select an app, tap **Force Stop**, and then tap **OK**.

For iOS:

- Press the **Home** button twice, swipe left to find the preview of the app, and then swipe up on the preview to close it.

Cell Tower Analyzer

Cell tower analyzer apps can detect signal strength for the various 3G and 4G data network services in use. There are numerous third-party apps for Android (Google Play) and iOS (App Store).

Backup/Restore

Backup and restore is an often-neglected part of mobile device maintenance. iOS devices offer two ways to back up:

- iCloud (automatic)
- iTunes (requires connection to the host PC or OS X computer)

iCloud is easier, but free iCloud storage is limited to 5GB. To back up an entire device, use iTunes.

Android Cloud backup can back up most features of your smartphone or tablet to Google Drive (the first 15GB of storage is free).

To back up e-mails, contacts, calendar, and apps:

Step 1.   Go to Settings.

Step 2.   Go to Backup and reset.

Step 3.   Turn on Back up my data.

Step 4.   Turn on Automatic restore.

Step 5.   Select Google account for Backup Account.

Step 6.   Go to Settings.

Step 7.   Go to Accounts.

Step 8.   Select Google.

Step 9.   Select Gmail and select the services to back up.

To back up photos and videos to Android Cloud:

Step 1.   Start Google Photos (download from Google Play if not installed).

Step 2.   Open the menu (it's the three-line icon at the upper left corner of the app).

Step 3.   Sign in if prompted.

Step 4.   Go to **Settings > Back up & sync > Backup (On)**.

Step 5.   Select whether to back up while charging, back up all photos/videos now, or whether to back up while roaming on cellular.

> **NOTE**   For a visual tour of these options, see http://www.techbout.com/backup-android-phone-6081/.

Use third-party apps to back up SMS messages. To back up all phone contents, use backup services provided by some smartphone vendors or download third-party apps from Google Play.

With Windows Mobile, enable automatic cloud-based backup for settings and app data, enable message sync, and turn on camera upload to **OneDrive** for photos and videos. For details, see http://windows.microsoft.com/en-us/windows-10/getstarted-back-up-mobile.

Apple Configurator

The **Apple Configurator** (https://www.apple.com/support/business-education/apple-configurator/) is designed to mass configure and deploy iPhone, iPad, iPod Touch, and Apple TV (second generation or later) devices for schools and organizations. Apple Configurator runs on OS X computers running El Capitan or later with iTunes 12.3 or later.

A *blueprint* is the term for actions that will be applied to devices, such as configuration profiles and app installation.

Configuration profiles specify device settings for networks, e-mail servers, and other options.

After these steps are complete, devices can be prepared for use.

To prepare multiple devices at the same time, connect them to USB 2.0 or 3.0 ports on the device, or use hubs or iPad charge/sync carts that are MFi certified (MFi is Apple's Made for iPhone, Made for iPod, Made for iPad, and AirPlay certification program).

A single device can be prepared and backed up; the backup can be restored to other devices.

The processes can be automated if desired.

Google Sync

Google Sync enables Google Services such as Gmail, Contacts, Calendar, and Chrome search to be synchronized to your computer or mobile device.

Technically speaking, the Google Sync app itself is now restricted to paid users of Google Apps for Work, Education, and Government. Google is now using CardDAV to perform sync for its users of free Gmail, Contacts, Google Calendar, and Chrome services.

When these accounts are set up, CardDAV is configured as part of the setup process.

Sunset for Google Sync?

Google Sync, which uses the Microsoft Exchange ActiveSync protocol to synchronize with Gmail, Google Calendar, and Contacts, is being phased out. It continues to be available to customers using it as of January 30, 2013 but no new devices can be added by customers using free services.

Customers who are paid users of Google Apps for Work, Education, and Government can sign up for new Google Sync accounts.

Troubleshooting PC Security Issues

The following sections help you deal with PC security issues, including common symptoms of malware infections, software tools to help battle malware, and best practices for removing malware.

Common Symptoms of Malware Infections

There are many common symptoms of malware infections. In Table 22-4, you learn what to look for. Be sure to know these for the 220-902 exam.

Table 22-4   Common Symptoms of Malware Infection

Symptom	Possible Causes
Pop-ups	If your browser has pop-up blocking enabled, but pop-ups are showing up anyway, your system might be infected with malware. If many pop-ups are displayed on-screen rapidly and they keep showing up as you close them, your system is almost certainly infected and needs to be scanned immediately.
Browser redirection	Browser redirection takes place when the home page for your browser is changed without your permission. Some "free" apps offer to change your browser home page during installation, but you can opt-in or opt-out of the change. If an app changes your browser home page without notifying you, it could be malware. Scan the system.
Security alerts	Security alerts from Windows Action Center or from your OS might indicate malware infection or other problems. Alleged alerts that pop up without any notification in Action Center are attempts to infect your system by tricking you into clicking a phishing link in the pop-up. Scan the system.
Slow performance	Slow performance that isn't caused by running a lot of apps or using very resource-intensive software could be caused by a malware infection. Use Task Manager or the equivalent to see which programs are running. Unfamiliar programs could be malware. Scan the system.
Internet connectivity issues	Internet connectivity problems that do not affect all computers and devices on the network could be caused by malware. Run troubleshooters to repair the problem. If it continues to occur, scan the system.
PC/OS Lockups	Lockups can be caused by many problems. If you have already checked hardware and OS issues without finding a cause, scan the system.
Application crashes	Application crashes could be caused by malware, but first repair the app or reinstall it. If it continues to crash, update it. If it continues to crash, scan the system.
OS updates failures	If you are unable to install updates for the OS, make sure the computer has enough free disk space and that the antivirus or anti-malware app is not blocking updates. If the problem continues, scan the system.
Rogue antivirus	These programs look like legitimate antivirus programs, but actually are designed to infect your system or phish users for personal information. Follow the links at http://support.kaspersky.com/us/viruses/rogue for more information.
Spam	Unsolicited e-mail can carry malware through attachments or could contain purported links to e-commerce or e-banking websites that are actually phishing sites.

Symptom	Possible Causes
Renamed system files	Malware infections might rename system files that can help block it, such as msconfig, regedit, and taskmgr.
Files disappearing	Some malware infections change file attributes to hidden and might also create file shortcuts that are visible.
File permission changes	Some malware infections change **file permissions** to make the malware harder to remove or to prevent users from running anti-malware apps.
Hijacked e-mail and responses from users regarding e-mail	Hijacked e-mail is almost certainly caused by a malware infection. Receivers of hijacked e-mail might reply to complain about inappropriate content, links, or messages that seem out of character.
Automated replies from unknown sent e-mail	Hijacked e-mail can also trigger automated replies indicating that messages were being rejected. If a user who has previously been able to send messages to a recipient notices that the messages are being rejected ("bouncing"), there could be a malware infection at either end of the connection.
Access denied	If a user sees this message when trying to start anti-malware tools, it indicates that file permissions changes are blocking access to the tools. See https://tinyapps.org/blog/windows/200908160730_access_is_denied_malware.html for a way to fix the problem.
Invalid certificate (trusted root CA)	Digital certificates are used by operating systems and browsers to determine the source of apps and drivers. Certificates that have been obtained fraudulently from a certification authority can be used to launch malware attacks. For an example that also discusses how PDF files can be used to launch malware attacks, see https://blog.malwarebytes.org/threat-analysis/2013/02/digital-certificates-and-malware-a-dangerous-mix/.

Tools

Windows, OS X, and Linux all include tools that can be used to prevent malware attacks or clean up damage, and third-party tools are available to help plug any holes in built-in protection. Table 22-5 discusses these tools. Be aware of these tools and how they help for the 220-902 exam. For more information, follow the links or see the appropriate sections in Chapter 14, Chapter 15, Chapter 18, or Chapter 21.

Table 22-5 OS and Third-Party Tools to Prevent and Fight Malware Infections

Tool	How Used and Where to Find More Information
Antivirus software	Antivirus software provides real-time protection against threats from local files, websites, and e-mail. It should also be configured to perform scans at least weekly. Most recent versions of Windows include antivirus software but OS X and Linux do not. Follow this link for third-party providers for Windows, many of whom also support OS X and Linux: http://windows.microsoft.com/en-US/windows/antivirus-partners.
Anti-malware software	Anti-malware software is normally used to scan for infections that might have been missed by antivirus software. These programs typically do not conflict with antivirus software. Examples include Malware Bytes (www.malwarebytes.org), Sophos HitmanPro (http://www.surfright.nl/en/hitmanpro/intronew), and others.
Recovery Console	The Windows XP Recovery Console can be started from the Windows XP distribution media or can be preinstalled so it is available from the boot menu. Recovery Console includes a special command-prompt mode that can enable and disable services, format drives, read and write data on a local drive, and perform many other administrative tasks. For more, see www.microsoft.com/resources/documentation/windows/xp/all/proddocs/en-us/recovery_console_overview.mspx?mfr=true.
Bootable antivirus programs	Bootable USB flash drives or optical discs (based on WinPE, Live CD, or Live USB) can be used to launch antivirus and anti-malware scans without starting the normal OS. For a list of free bootable antivirus programs, see http://pcsupport.about.com/od/system-security/tp/free-bootable-antivirus-software.htm.
Terminal	Terminal (OS X and Linux) can be used to change file attributes, delete files, and run backup and repair utilities.
Pre-installation environments	WinPE is the basis for many USB- or disc-based repair tools. It can also be used by itself to run programs on a Windows system from its command-line.
Event Viewer	Use the event viewer to see what events have taken place in the system, including app crashes, security changes, and much more.
Refresh/Reset	Windows 8/8.1/10 include **Refresh** (reinstalls Windows and Windows Store apps, removes other apps, leaves user data in place) and **Reset** (returns system to its as-shipped condition, deletes user data).
MSCONFIG/Safe boot	Msconfig can be used to turn off selected startup programs and non-essential system services. The Safe Boot option turns off all startup programs and non-essential system services.

Best Practice Procedure for Malware Removal

Follow this seven-step procedure to remove **malware**:

Step 1.   Identify malware symptoms. Use Table 22-4 to identify symptoms.

Step 2.   **Quarantine** infected system. Disconnect the system from wired and wireless networks and suspect any media that has touched the system as being possibly infected.

Step 3.   Disable System Restore (in Windows). System Restore has been used by some malware programs to reinfect the system. System Restore is designed to help recover from user error or system crashes, not malware.

Step 4.   **Remediate** infected systems. Use a different system to change passwords for network access, e-commerce, and social media. Back up data in case the system must be reformatted. Check backup for malware before reinstalling it.

    a.   Update anti-malware software. To update anti-malware on a quarantined system, download offline update files on a different system, burn them to an optical disc and close the disc so it cannot be written to again, or copy them to a USB flash drive and install the updates on the quarantined system.

    b.   **Scan** and removal techniques (safe mode, pre-installation environment). If a quarantined system's antivirus/antimalware cannot be updated, the apps might be themselves infected or blocked by malware. Download the files needed to create a Live CD or USB bootable anti-malware disc or USB drive on a different system.

Step 5.   Schedule scans and run updates. If the infection source is unknown, run full scans with both antivirus and anti-malware. If the infection source is known by name, first use a specific removal tool (if available) and follow it up with full scans. Scan with more than one tool to assure the infection is removed.

Step 6.   After the system is cleaned, reenable **System Restore** (the source of the infection, such as email, flash drives, downloaded app, and so on) and create a restore point manually.

Step 7.   Educate **end users**. Discuss principles of avoiding malware infections with end users. If the infection vector (the source of the infection, such as email, flash drives, downloaded app, etc.) is known, discuss it specifically as well as provide general guidance for safe computing (avoiding the use of "orphan" USB flash drives, not opening attachments from unknown sources, using real-time antivirus software, scanning systems weekly, etc.).

Exam Preparation Tasks

Review All the Key Topics

Review the most important topics in the chapter, noted with the Key Topic icon in the outer margin of the page. Table 22-6 lists a reference of these key topics and the page numbers on which each is found.

Table 22-6   Key Topics for Chapter 22

Key Topic Element	Description	Page Number
List	How to identify the causes of BSODs	1079
List	How to identify the causes of unresponsive OS X computers	1082
List	Repairing boot problems with Windows, OS X, and Linux	1083
Table 22-1	Using the Windows Advanced Boot Options and Startup Settings Menus	1114
Section	Factory Reset/Clean Install	1125
Table 22-4	Common symptoms of malware infection	1132

Complete the Tables and Lists from Memory

Print a copy of Appendix C, "Memory Tables" (found on the companion website), or at least the section for this chapter, and complete the tables and lists from memory. Appendix D, "Memory Tables Answer Key," also on the companion website, includes completed tables and lists to check your work.

Define Key Terms

Define the following key terms from this chapter, and check your answers in the glossary.

Stop errors, BSOD, pin wheel, failure to boot, improper shutdown, spontaneous shutdown/restart, device fails to start/detected, missing DLL, compatibility error, file extension, file association, boot configuration data, DLL, missing operating system, GUI, GRUB, LILO, kernel panic, multiple monitor, BIOS, UEFI, SFC, logs, system recovery options, repair disks, pre-installation environments, MSCONFIG,

DEFRAG, REGSVR32, REGEDIT, Safe Mode, command prompt, pop-ups, browser redirection, security alerts, rogue antivirus, spam, file permissions, hijacked e-mail, access denied, invalid certificate (trusted root CA), antivirus software, anti-malware software, Recovery Console, terminal, Refresh, Reset, malware, System Restore, quarantine, remediate, restore point, scan, end user, system lockout, hard reset, soft reset, factory default, overlimit, pairing, root access, app scanner, factory reset, clean install, Wi-Fi analyzer, Force Stop, cell tower analyzer, iTunes, iCloud, Apple Configurator, Google Sync, OneDrive.

Complete Hands-On Lab

Complete the hands-on lab, and then see the answers and explanations at the end of the chapter.

Lab 22-1: Troubleshooting Windows, OS X, Linux, iOS, and Android

- Look up Windows STOP errors and causes for the Windows versions you work with.

- Use Activity Monitor on an OS X system to see how it is using resources.

- Start Linux in Recovery or Rescue mode.

- Start Windows in Safe mode.

- Start OS X using Command+R.

- Use Device Manager to see if any devices are unknown, disabled, or can't start.

- Use two displays with Linux, OS X, and Windows and set them up as mirrored or extended desktops.

- Use a soft reset/soft restart with an iOS and an Android device.

- Install a new app on an iOS and/or Android device. Update it and then delete it.

- Check data usage on an iOS and/or Android smartphone.

Answer Review Questions

1. Which operating system is displaying this message?

   A. OS X

   B. Windows 7

   C. Linux

   D. Windows 8.1

   How would go go about researching this problem?

   1. Search online for "A problem has been detected"

   2. Go to Linux.org and search for IRQ_NOT_LESS_OR_EQUAL

   3. Go to Apple.com and search for IRQ_NOT_LESS_OR_EQUAL

   4. Go to Microsoft.com and search for IRQ_NOT_LESS_OR_EQUAL

   Which of the following is the most likely solution to the problem?

   a. Install an update to OS X

   b. Open Device Manager and update a driver

   c. Use apt-get to install a Linux update

   d. Reinstall the operating system

2. In the following figure, the screen is displaying a spinning wait cursor or pin wheel that indicates that the system is unresponsive. One possible cause for this pin wheel could be that there is less than 10 percent free space left on the system drive. Why would a lack of free space be causing a problem for the system?

A. You are running out of space on the drive and cannot store any more files

B. At least 10 percent free space is needed for a swap file.

C. You do not have enough free space on the drive to upgrade to the latest version of the operating system.

D. Your applications need more space in which to run.

3. How would you try to repair a missing or corrupt BOOTMGR file on a Windows system?

A. Use the System Recovery Options.

B. Use the Advanced Boot Options.

C. Reboot the computer and edit the BIOS startup program.

D. Go to the Internet and download a new BOOTMGR file.

4. Which of the following procedures best describes how to create a dual boot system using Windows 7 and Windows 8.1?

A. Install Windows 7 first, then install Windows 8.1 into a separate partition.

B. Install Windows 8.1 first, then install Windows 7 into a separate partition.

C. It does not matter which you install first.

D. You cannot dual boot these two operating systems.

1140 CompTIA A+ 220-901 and 220-902 Cert Guide

5. Which of the following is the most common boot loader in current Linux distributions?

   A. CRON

   B. LILO

   C. BCD

   D. GRUB

6. Which of the following procedures best describes how to access the special startup modes in OS X?

   A. Press Ctrl+R.

   B. Press Command+R.

   C. Press Ctrl+Alt+Del.

   D. Press Alt+F1.

7. If a program that loads automatically during startup is causing problems during startup or shutdown, which Windows utility should be used to diagnose and resolve the problem?

   A. BIOS

   B. SFC

   C. MSCONFIG

   D. REGEDIT

8. Your Windows computer has been configured to automatically restart after a system shutdown due to a STOP error. Which of the following menu options best describes how to disable the automatic restart feature?

   A. MSCONFIG > Boot > No GUI boot

   B. System Properties > Advanced > Startup and Recovery > clear Automatically restart checkbox

   C. Drive Properties > General > Disk Cleanup

   D. System Properties > System Protection > Create

9. In Windows, how will a non-working device be displayed?

   A. In MSCONFIG on the Startup tab, an error message is displayed next to the device.

   B. Action Center displays an error message.

   C. An error message will be displayed in the System Restore utility.

   D. In the Device Manager, the device will be displayed with an exclamation mark inside a yellow triangle.

10. Which of the following statements best describes why a device is listed as Unknown in the Device Manager?

    A. There is no installed driver.

    B. The device is not functioning.

    C. The device has been disabled and is no longer listed.

    D. The device has been removed.

11. If a Windows system file is missing or damaged, which utility is used to recover it?

    A. Device Manager

    B. SFC

    C. MSCONFIG

    D. Safe Mode

12. Which of the following could be causes of poor system performance on a Windows computer? (Choose all that apply.)

    A. The drive containing paging and temporary files is nearly full.

    B. Dust and dirt are restricting airflow and the CPU is overheating.

    C. Too many services are configured to start automatically during startup.

    D. Minimum memory requirements have been met but not exceeded.

13. In Windows, when a file extension is not associated with a program, which of the following occurs?

    A. The file will not open.

    B. The file will open in Notepad with no formatting.

    C. The file will open in Notepad with minimum formatting.

    D. The file will open in either Windows Explorer or File Explorer.

14. When a Linux or OS X system crashes as a result of a fatal error in the operating system, it is known as which of the following?

    A. A STOP error

    B. A fatal error

    C. A kernel panic

    D. A kernel wipe

15. Match the method for configuring multiple displays with the operating system.

Operating System	Method
a. OS X	
b. Linux	
c. Windows	

1. System Preferences > Displays

2. Display > Screen Resolution

3. Settings > Display

16. In which of the following locations would you find the log files that Windows creates describing information, warnings, and errors on your system?

A. Device Manager

B. Event Viewer

C. Finder

D. Recovery Environment

17. System Restore is used to do which of the following?

A. Restore the system to its original configuration

B. Remove apps not from Windows Store and reinstall apps that are from Windows Store

C. Use a system image to restore the computer to its original condition

D. Create a restore point with which to restore the computer to an earlier point in time

18. Which Windows utility is used to disable any programs and services that run when the computer boots?

A. REGEDIT

B. MSCONFIG

C. SFC

D. MSINFO32

19. In Windows, if one program stops working after you install or remove another program, you might need to register the .dll or .ocx files for the first program. Which utility should be used to do this?

A. REGSVR32

B. SFC

C. Recovery System

D. Safe Mode

20. In Windows 8/8.1/10, which of the following procedures is used to open Safe Mode? (Choose two.)

   A. Press F8 during startup.

   B. Press Alt + F1 during startup.

   C. Use MSCONFIG, Boot tab.

   D. Reboot, hold down the Shift key, and select Restart.

21. Match the following Advanced Boot Options or Startup Settings with the phrase that describes their functions.

Boot Options	When would you use this boot option?
A. Safe Mode	
B. Boot Logging	
C. Low Resolution	
D. Last Known Good Configuration	
E. Disable Automatic Restart	

Answer Options:

   1. You want to determine which device or process is stopping startup.

   2. You have just installed new hardware or software and Windows won't start.

   3. You have just upgraded a device driver and Windows won't start.

   4. Configure this setting if you have frequent STOP errors.

   5. You have just installed a new video card and Windows won't start.

22. On an OS X computer, when you reboot and select Internet Recovery from the recovery options, which of the following occurs?

   A. The computer's original operating system reinstalls.

   B. The most recent OS X release installs.

   C. System fixes and updates are installed.

   D. Nothing. You cannot reboot to Internet Recovery.

23. Which of the following procedures best describes how to stop mobile devices from pairing with unknown Bluetooth devices?

   A. Use encryption on your mobile devices.

   B. Require a device to have the correct code before pairing.

   C. Use a VPN whenever possible.

   D. Disable Wi-Fi tethering.

24. Which of the following problems might occur when you install third-party apps on a mobile device? (Choose all that apply.)

    A. Unexpectedly high resource utilization

    B. Unauthorized root access

    C. Unauthorized location tracking

    D. Unauthorized camera or microphone activation

25. You need to back up 14.5GB of information from an iOS device. Which of the following is the best choice?

    A. iCloud

    B. iTunes

    C. Android Cloud

    D. OneDrive

26. You want to prevent an Android smartphone from tracking the user by Wi-Fi connections. Which of the following is the correct command sequence?

    A. Settings > Privacy > Location Services > System Services

    B. Settings > Network > Wi-Fi > Disabled

    C. Settings > Personal > Privacy and Safety > Location > Locating Method > GPS only

    D. Settings > Network > Airplane Mode

Answers and Explanations to Hands-On Lab

Lab 22-1: Troubleshooting Windows, OS X, Linux, iOS, and Android

If you see a STOP (BSOD) error, take a digital photo of it and show it to co-workers for reference. Did you find solutions to problems you have previously seen?

On a Linux system, which boot options are available when starting in Recovery or Rescue mode?

On an OS X system, did you discover any performance problems when using Activity Monitor?

Did you discover any problem devices with Device Manager? Were you able to resolve the problem? If you discovered problems with unknown devices or devices that can't start on a laptop that is running a version of Windows that is newer than the version that was originally loaded on the laptop, you might need to download specific driver packs for the laptop and Windows version.

When you installed the app, were you offered an update automatically? If not, check for an update after a week or two.

When you checked data usage, were you near the device's data plan limit per billing cycle? If so, make sure the user knows when to use Wi-Fi and when to use cellular connections.

Answers and Explanations to Review Questions

1. **B.** This is an error message from Windows 7. 4 To find the answer, search for the error message at the Microsoft website. b Uninstalling the most recent app or hardware device, followed by installing an updated app or a hardware device with an updated driver is the most likely solution. Reinstalling the operating system is the last solution to try, only after all other measures have been tried.

2. **B.** Free space on the system partition is used as a swap file when sufficient RAM is not available. If this is the reason that your system has become unresponsive, you should clear space from the system partition by rebooting the computer to free up temporary files, emptying the Trash, or removing files and storing them on another drive or in the cloud. Upgrading to a newer OS X version can also help to improve responsiveness.

3. **A.** Use the System Recovery Options and select either the Startup Repair option or open a command prompt and enter bootrec /fixboot. Advanced Boot Options are used to start windows in Safe Mode or other troubleshooting modes. Although a change in the BIOS startup settings to a different startup drive could cause this problem, it isn't likely. BOOTMGR cannot be downloaded from the Internet.

4. **A.** You should always install the older operating system first. Thus, you should install Windows 7 first, then install Windows 8.1 into a separate partition.

5. **D.** GRUB is the most common boot loader in current Linux distributions, while older Linux distributions used LILO. To load Grub, press the Shift key while restarting the system. If you need to repair the system, choose Rescue or Recovery when Grub loads. Cron is a time-based job scheduling utility in Linux computer operating systems. BCD is the boot configuration database used by Windows Vista/7/8/8.1/10.

6. **B.** Press Command+R as soon as you hear the startup sound. After choosing your language, you will have the option to restore, reinstall, get help, or open the Disk Utility. OS X uses the Command key in place of the Control key used in Windows. Ctrl+Alt+Del displays a menu that includes Task Manager and other options. Alt+F1 opens the Applications menu in Ubuntu or the Start menu in KDE's K-menu.

7. **C.** MSCONFIG is a Windows diagnostic tool that allows you to disable and reenable programs and services that automatically load and run during startup. The BIOS (also applies to UEFI firmware) is used to configure basic hardware settings before the OS starts. SFC is the Windows System File Checker. REGEDIT is the Windows Registry editor.

8. **B** From the Start menu, right-click Computer and select **Properties** (Windows Vista/7). Press Windows key+X, **System** (Windows 8/8.1/10). Then click **Advanced System Settings**. Under Startup and Recovery, select **Settings**. Under System Failure, clear the **Automatically Restart** checkbox. The MSCONFIG Boot tab is used to specify startup options such as Safe Boot, boot log, and others (equivalent to selecting options from the Advanced Boot Options menu at startup). The General tab in a drive's properties shows the file system, drive letter and name, and free/used space. The System Protection tab in System Properties is used for System Restore functions.

9. **D.** Device Manager reports on the status of all hardware devices on the system. A non-working device will be displayed with a black exclamation mark inside a yellow triangle. Also, when you open the properties of the device, you will see a brief description of the problem on the General tab. MSCONFIG does not list device information. Action Center displays warnings about maintenance and security issues, but not about device drivers. System Restore displays information about device drivers that will be removed or reloaded when a restore point is chosen but it does not display error messages.

10. **A.** An unknown device does not have a driver installed. Try installing the driver and then reconnecting the device. The device cannot function without a driver. A disabled device is still listed, but it's displayed with an icon indicating it is disabled. A removed device is also removed from Device Manager.

11. **B.** SFC checks your system files, locates damaged/corrupted files, and reinstalls replacement files. Device Manager is used to view, manage, and install devices and drivers. MSCONFIG is used to configure Windows startup options. Safe Mode is used to start Windows for troubleshooting.

12. **A, B, C, D.** The drive containing the paging and temporary files must have at least 10 percent free space; 20 percent free space would be better. If dust and dirt build up around internal components, the CPU and system fans might not be able to adequately circulate the air and dissipate the heat that builds up, so the CPU might overheat. If your system is performing at a low level, you might try increasing the amount of RAM. Generally speaking, more RAM equals better performance. Too many programs and services at start up will slow the startup process and slow down system performance afterward.

13. **A.** When a file extension is not associated with the file, Windows will not know which application to use to open it. For example, a file with the .docx extension must be opened with Word; it cannot be opened with Excel.

14. **C.** Kernel panic is when a Linux or OS X system crashes as a result of a fatal error. It is similar to a STOP error in a Windows system. Kernel wipe is not a valid issue with these operating systems.

15. **A—1. B—3. C—2.**

16. **B.** The Event Viewer contains the log files that Windows creates to record problems within the system. Device Manager stores information regarding hardware devices and their drivers. Recovery Environment is used in Windows Vista/7/8/8.1/10 to diagnose and repair system failures. Finder is the file manager program in OS X.

17. **D.** Use the System Restore utility to create restore points before making major changes to your system. Then, if your system has a problem, you can revert to a restore point and your computer will be configured as it was when the restore point was created.

18. **B.** MSCONFIG is a troubleshooting tool that is used to configure your system startup. You may use it to disable or enable any programs or services that run automatically when the system boots. You may also use it to configure a Normal, Diagnostic, or Selective startup and to configure the order in which multiple operating systems boot. REGEDIT can be used to change all Windows settings, but it is not the preferred tool. SFC is used to replace damaged Windows system files. MSInfo32 is used to display Windows and hardware configuration.

19. **A.** Use REGSVR32 to register file types. SFC is used to replace damaged Windows system files. Recovery System is not a valid Windows feature. Safe Mode starts Windows with minimal drivers for troubleshooting.

20. **C, D.** Safe Mode is one of the selections in the Startup Settings menu. In Windows 8/8.1, you should reboot the system, hold down the Shift key, and then select Restart. You can also enter Safe Mode from the MSCOFIG utility on the Boot tab. In previous versions of Windows, you could press F8 when rebooting, but that will not work in Windows 8/8.1.

21.

Boot Options	When would you use this boot option?
A. Safe Mode	3. You have just upgraded a device driver and Windows won't start.
B. Boot Logging	1. You want to determine which device or process is stopping startup.
C. Low Resolution	5. You have just installed a new video card and Windows won't start.
D. Last Known Good Configuration	2. You have just installed new hardware or software and Windows won't start.
E. Disable Automatic Restart	4. Configure this setting if you have frequent STOP errors.

22. **A.** Rebooting the computer and selecting Internet Recovery will reinstall the operating system to the state the computer was in when it was new. If you were to select the Recovery System option, you would install the most recent release of the operating system.

23. **B.** If your mobile devices use Bluetooth, you should configure those devices to request a code from any devices that attempt to pair with them. Encryption, VPN, and disabling tethering are all good security measures but they do not prevent pairing with unknown devices.

24. **A, B, C, D.** All of these problems could be caused by malicious software that was not downloaded from Google Play or the App Store.

25. **B.** iTunes is the best choice because it is limited only by available disk space on the iTunes host. iCloud has only 5GB of capacity unless the user has subscribed to a paid data plan. Android Cloud backs up Android devices. OneDrive is a Microsoft product that can be used by OS X and Android devices but requires a free Microsoft account.

26. **C.** Settings > Personal > Privacy and Safety > Location > Locating Method > GPS only. Settings > Network > Wi-Fi > disabled turns off Wi-Fi. Settings > Privacy > Location Services > System Services > is the correct answer for iOS. Settings > Network > Airplane Mode turns off all radio services.

Glossary

Terms marked with a * are CompTIA acronyms

10000 rpm   Spin rate of a high-performance SATA hard disk.

104-key keyboard   Keyboard layout with Windows and right-click keys added to the old 101-key layout.

1.8-in drive   Form factor for an SSD or hard disk drive suitable for use in a tablet or thin laptop.

20-pin ATX   Power supply connector used by version 1.x of the ATX motherboard form factor standard.

24-pin ATX   Power supply connector used by current version 2.x of the ATX motherboard form factor standard.

2.5-in drive   Form factor for an SSD, hybrid drive, or hard disk drive suitable for use in a laptop or desktop computer.

32-bit architecture   Architecture used by x86 processors.

32-bit Windows   Versions of Windows optimized for x86 processors; also compatible with x64 processors.

3.5-in drive   Form factor for a hybrid drive or hard disk suitable for use in a desktop computer.

5400 rpm hard disk drive   Spin rate for a "green" energy-saving hard disk.

64-bit architecture   Architecture used by x64 processors.

64-bit Windows   Versions of Windows designed for use with x64 processors.

7200rpm hard disk drive   Spin rate of a medium performance desktop (3.5-inch) hard disk drive or a high-performance laptop (2.5-inch) hard disk drive.

802.11a   A wireless Ethernet standard that uses 5GHz radio signals and provides performance at rates from 6Mbps to 54Mbps. It is not compatible with other 802.11-based wireless networks unless dual-band access points are used.

802.11b   A wireless Ethernet standard that uses 2.4GHz radio signaling for performance from 2Mbps to 11Mbps. It is compatible with 802.11g-based wireless networks but not with 802.11a-based networks unless dual-band access points are used.

802.11g   A wireless Ethernet standard that uses 2.4GHz radio signaling for performance up to 54Mbps. It is compatible with 802.11b-based wireless networks but not with 802.11a-based networks unless dual-band access points are used.

802.11n   A wireless Ethernet standard that uses 2.4GHz and 5GHz radio signaling for performance up to 600Mbps. Uses MIMO antenna technology.

802.11ac   A wireless Ethernet standard that uses 5GHz radio signaling for performance up to 1300Mbps. Uses MU-MIMO antenna technology.

A

AC *   Alternating current; the type of electrical current used to run homes and businesses.

AC'97 version 2.3 audio   An analog audio codec standard that supports 96kHz sampling and 20-bit stereo playback. Most implementations support jack sensing.

accelerometer   A combination of hardware and software that measures velocity in mobile devices; accelerometers detect rotation, shaking of the device, etc.

access control lists   *See* ACL.

access denied   Message appears when user doesn't have permissions needed to perform an action on a file.

access point   Also known as wireless access point. Enables wireless (Wi-Fi) devices to connect to a network.

Accessories   Windows Start menu folder containing small apps such as Calculator, Paint, WordPad, Notepad, and others.

ACL *   Access Control List

ACPI *   Advanced Configuration Power Interface

Acronyms   Word created from initial letters in a phrase, such as LAN (local area network).

ACT *   Activity or Application Compatibility Toolkit

Action Center   Windows Control Panel utility that provides one-stop access for security, maintenance, troubleshooting, and recovery options.

active heat sink   Heat sink with attached fan.

active listening   Listening to a customer while asking questions to draw out more information about a problem or need.

ad-hoc   Something that is performed to meet a specific need. An ad-hoc wireless network is created to share printers or information. Implies lack of permanency.

ADSL *   Asymmetric Digital Subscriber Line. A form of DSL that enables faster downloads than uploads. Can be provided over high-quality existing phone lines and is well suited for residential and small business use.

administrative privileges   Privileges necessary to perform system-wide changes in Windows. For example, to run tasks marked with the Windows Security shield in Control Panel.

administrative shares   Hidden shares of the root folder (and all subfolders) of a drive in Windows that are available only to administrators. Listed as C$ (C drive), etc. These shares may be blocked on some Windows installations.

administrative tools   A Control Panel folder in Windows that contains shortcuts to tools such as Event Viewer, Local Security Policy, System Configuration, Services, Windows Memory Diagnostic, and others.

administrator   User account that can perform system-wide changes on a computer in Windows. Can click through UAC prompts.

Advanced RISC Machine (ARM)   In mobile devices, a 32-bit reduced instruction set computing architecture designed for low-power consumption and simplicity.

Aero   Short for Windows Aero or Aero Glass, the default desktop appearance in Windows Vista and 7, featuring translucent window edges, live thumbnails of running apps on the taskbar, and Flip 3D app switching. Windows 8/8.1 do not support Aero, but Windows 10 offers some Aero features as optional settings.

AES encryption   Advanced encryption standard, encryption used by WPA2 wireless networking.

AFP   Apple filing protocol, proprietary network protocol for OS X and original MacOS.

AGP (Accelerated Graphics Port)   A 32-bit I/O bus used for video; provides for a direct connection between the video card and memory.

AHCI *   Advanced Host Controller Interface; SATA setup option in BIOS that supports native command queuing (NCQ) and all other advanced features.

Air filter mask   Protective gear that might be required for computer techs.

Airplane mode   Mobile device setting that turns off cellular, Wi-Fi, and Bluetooth radios.

AirPrint   Apple print technology for OS X and iOS devices to print without installing specific drivers. Most current printers have AirPrint support built in.

alternate third-party drivers   Drivers for Windows that support third-party storage features such as RAID host adapters.

alternative IP address   An IP address used if the DHCP server used to assign IP addresses can't be contacted.

AMR (Audio Modem Riser)   A riser card and slot designed to support surround audio and soft modem on some motherboards.

Analog (audio)   Continuous vibrations at different pitches and frequencies—not sampled.

Android   Mobile operating system for tablets and smartphones. Developed by Google.

anti-malware software   Software that blocks or scans and quarantines malware.

antistatic bag   Protective bag for electronic parts. Prevents ESD.

antivirus software   Software that blocks or scans and quarantines computer viruses.

AP *   Access Point

APIPA *   Automatic Private Internet Protocol Addressing (IPv4).

APIPA/link local address   A self-assigned IP address that cannot be used for Internet access. Link-local is the IPv6 version.

APM *   Advanced Power Management

app scanner   Software or service that scans apps for privacy and security issues.

app store   General name for the trusted software repositories used by iOS (Apple App Store), Android (Google Play), and Windows Mobile (Windows Store).

Apple Configurator   App used for mass configuring and deployment of iOS devices for organizations and schools.

application   Software, program, app.

application crash   App stops responding

apt-get   Linux command for installing and managing apps (packages).

ARP *   Address Resolution Protocol

array   Two or more hard drives addressed as a logical unit, such as RAID or JBOD array.

artifact   A visible problem with video display, such as visual noise, blockiness due to over compression of a photo or video source, and others.

ASR *   Automated System Recovery; special backup option in NTBackup (Windows XP) that enables a bootable Windows installation to be restored from a backup.

assign   In Windows Disk Management, providing a drive letter to a volume that did not have one previously.

assigning/changing drive letters   A feature of Windows Disk Management that enables new drives to receive a user-assigned drive letter and existing drives to switch to a different drive letter. Drive mapping performs the same task for network shares.

ATA *   Advanced Technology Attachment; a family of standards for PATA and (in ATA-7 and above) SATA interfaces.

ATAPI *   Advanced Technology Attachment Packet Interface

ATM *   Asynchronous Transfer Mode

ATX *   Advanced Technology Extended; Motherboard form factor with integrated port cluster at left rear of board, basis for most mid-size to full-size desktop systems.

audio mini-jack   3.5mm (1/8 inch) jacks used for stereo and surround audio, microphones, and line in/line out connections.

AUP *   Acceptable Use Policy

authentication server   A server that checks the credentials of users who log into the network.

authenticator application   An application that validates access to a secured website from a new device or browser by sending a PIN code to the user's mobile phone. The user enters the PIN when prompted.

autorun   Strictly speaking, the ability of an operating system to automatically start an app on an optical disc as soon as the disc is inserted. Also used to refer to automatically starting an app on any removable-media drive as soon as it is inserted or connected.

A/V *   Audio Video

B

Backup/restore   App that creates backup copies of files and restores them when needed. Backup/restore apps are included in Windows, OS X, and Linux, and third-party apps are also available.

barcode reader   Special scanner that reads barcodes for POS, inventory control, security, and other uses.

Baseband   Component in cellular network-enabled device (smartphone, tablet) that translates cell signals to and from the onboard CPU. Baseband firmware is updated by the cellular service provider to handle improvements in cellular service when needed.

basic (disk type)   A basic disk in Windows is bootable and can contain one or more primary partitions.

battery   A rechargeable power source used by laptops, tablets, and smartphones for main power and by a UPS for backup power. A disposable power source used by CMOS batteries on motherboards. Uses NiMH, Li-Ion, Alkaline, or silver oxide chemistry.

battery backup   A device that provides temporary power to connected units until they can be shut down; UPS and SPS devices are two different types of battery backups.

BD-R   Recordable Blu-ray (BD) media.

BD-RE   Rewriteable Blu-ray (BD) media.

Belarc System Advisor   A third-party ActiveX web-based program that identifies the computer's operating system, hardware, Windows version, and security status.

best practices   General term for guidelines that describe the best way to perform a process or achieve a result.

biometrics   Biometrics fall into the category of "something a person is." Examples of bodily characteristics that are measured include fingerprints, retinal patterns, iris patterns, and even bone structure.

biometric authentication   The process of using biometrics to determine whether a potential user can access a secured area or system.

biometric devices   Devices used for biometric authentication, such as fingerprint scanners, iris scanners, etc.

BIOS *   Basic Input Output System. It controls and tests basic computer hardware at the beginning of the boot procedure. *See* also UEFI.

BitLocker   A full disk encryption feature available in the Enterprise and Ultimate editions of Windows Vista and Windows 7, and the Pro and Enterprise editions of Windows 8, 8.1, and Windows 10.

BitLocker-To-Go (BitLocker to Go)   An extension of BitLocker for removable-media and external drives. Introduced in Windows 7 and enhanced in Windows 8 and newer.

blackout   Complete loss of AC power.

Blu-ray   An optical medium originally developed for HD movies; capacity of 25GB single-layer and 50GB in dual-layer; also referred to as BD.

Bluetooth   Short-range wireless network used primarily by mobile devices.

BNC *   Bayonet-Neill-Concelman or British Naval Connector

Bonjour   Apple software for zero-configuration wireless networking. Used by OS X and iOS.

bookmarks   Another name for favorites in a web browser; web pages the user has tagged for easy reloading.

Boot   Starting the computer.

Boot Camp   OS X dual-boot feature that enables Windows to be installed on an OS X system.

Boot Configuration Data   BCD; the configuration information used by Windows Vista/7/8/8.1/10 to determine how to start (boot) the system.

Boot.ini   The configuration information used by Windows XP to determine how to start (boot) the system.

BOOTREC   Windows Recovery Environment (RE) command to fix startup problems in Windows Vista/7/8/8.1/10.

bridge   Device that connects two or more networks together to form a larger aggregate network.

brownout   Reduction in voltage of 10% or more from specifications.

browser redirection   Unauthorized change of the home page, error page, or search page in your web browser to another URL. Can be caused by malware or by apps the user installs that do not allow for opt-outs to these changes when the apps are installed.

brute forcing (brute-force attack)   An attack against a password-secured resource that involves using all possible password combinations until the correct password is found.

BSOD   Blue Screen of Death. So named because the error message is in white text against a blue background. *See* STOP error.

BTX *   Balanced Technology Extended

bus speeds   Speeds of various buses on motherboards (PCI, PCIe, memory, etc.).

bus-powered hub   Receives power from upstream USB port; limits power to 100mA per device.

BYOD   Bring Your Own Device. Acronym for the policy of allowing employees to use their own mobile devices for organization business instead of an organization-provided one.

C

cable   Wire or wire bundle that delivers data or power to a computer or mobile device.

cable lock   Lock that uses a multi-stranded security cable to help prevent the theft of a computer or other technology device. Sometimes called a Kensington lock.

cable management   The act of controlling where cables are installed. They should be kept out of walkways, off the floor, and away from anywhere a person might move about.

cable modem   A device that encodes/decodes cable Internet network signals. Can be connected to a single computer or to a wired or wireless router.

cable select   A PATA jumper setting that enables the 80-wire cable to determine primary and secondary drives.

cable stripper   Tool that strips insulation from coaxial or TP wires during the installation process.

cable tester   Tool that checks the cable's ability to carry data reliably.

CAD/CAM   Computer aided drafting/computer aided manufacturing.

Calendar   Function included in desktop and mobile OS or available from third parties to keep track of dates, appointments, and tasks to complete.

calibration   Adjustments to improve print quality on inkjet or color laser printers.

camcorder   Video camera that records to videotape (DV camcorder) or to flash memory or a hard drive (HD camcorder).

carriage and belt   Components that are part of inkjet or impact printers.

CAPTCHA *   Completely Automated Public Turing Test to tell Computers and Humans Apart

card reader   A single-slot or multislot device for reading from and writing to flash memory cards.

CardBus   32-bit version of PC Card add-on card used in very old laptops.

CAT3   Category 3 TP cable. Supports two-line phones and Ethernet 10Mbps.

CAT5   Category 5 TP cable. Supports Fast Ethernet (10/100Mbps).

CAT5e   Category 5e TP cable. Supports Gigabit Ethernet (10/100/1000Mbps).

CAT6   Category 6 TP cable. Supports 10G Ethernet (10/100/1000/10000Mbps), and reduces crosstalk for more reliable connections at Gigabit speeds.

CAT6a Category 6a TP cable. Supports 10G Ethernet (10/100/1000/10000Mbps), and reduces crosstalk for more reliable connections at 10G speeds.

CAT7 Category 7 TP cable. Supports 10G Ethernet (10/100/1000/10000Mbps) and has faster transmission speeds than CAT6a.

Category view Default Control Panel view in Windows Vista/7/8/8.1/10. Control Panel applets are grouped into categories with the most-frequently used options available from the category menu. Click a category for all options.

Classic view Alternate view of Control Panel that lists each applet separately. Also called Large icons and Small icons views.

CCFL * Cold Cathode Fluorescent Lamp; backlight for conventional LCD displays.

CD * Compact disc; the oldest optical disc format; DVD and BD drives can also use CD media.

CD-ROM * Compact Disc-Read-Only Memory

CD-ROM boot Booting from a CD-ROM disc.

CD-RW * Compact Disc-Rewritable

CDFS * Compact Disc File System

cell tower analyzer Mobile app that displays the signal strength of nearby cell towers.

cellular (data network) Data network that enables smartphones and cellular-equipped tablets to send and receive data via the cellular network.

certificate of destruction Certification from a drive or media-destruction facility that the drive or media has been destroyed.

CFS * Central File System or Common File System or Command File System

chain of custody The chronological documentation or paper trail of evidence that might be used in a court of law.

channels In Wi-Fi, different frequencies available to 2.4GHz and 5GHz signals. In motherboards, the ability of a motherboard to group two or more identical memory modules together as a logical unit for faster data access. In TV, different frequencies that carry programs.

chip creep Socketed chips working their way out of sockets over time due to heating/cooling.

chipset Support chips on a motherboard (North Bridge, northbridge, or memory controller hub; South Bridge, southbridge, or I/O controller hub) that provide interface between onboard components and expansion slots and CPU.

CHKDSK   Windows command for testing and correcting errors on SSDs, flash memory, and hard disk drives.

chmod   Linux command for changing file permissions.

chown   Linux command for changing the owner of a file.

CIFS *   Common Internet File System

clean boot   Starting Windows without startup services or programs.

clean install   Installing an OS on an empty partition rather than as an upgrade to an existing installation.

client   Computer that uses shared resources on network.

client/server   Network using dedicated servers such as Microsoft Windows Server editions.

client-side DHCP   Settings on a network client for DHCP. When enabled, the client receives an IP address from the server. Otherwise, the client must have an IP address manually assigned.

client-side DNS   Settings on a network client for DNS. When enabled, the client uses DNS servers provided by the network. Otherwise, the client must use manually assigned DNS servers.

clock   Clock speed: the speed at which a processor sends and receives information. Same as clock rate.

closed-source   Software/OS/apps developed by a particular vendor and licensed only for use. Object code is not available and modifications are not permitted.

cloud computing   Computing that uses shared Internet-based computers or storage devices.

cloud printing   Printing that uses shared printers that are accessed over the Internet.

CMOS   Complimentary Metal-Oxide Semiconductor. Refers to low-power chip design; it's also a common term for Real-Time-Clock/Non-Volatile RAM chip (RTC/NVRAM).

CNR   Communications Network Riser. Riser slot and card for soft modem and network adapter on some motherboards.

coaxial   A type of cable that consists of a solid center copper core, insulation, a metal braided jacket for grounding, with a vinyl or plastic outer jacket. Commonly used for CATV, cable Internet, and satellite Internet.

collate   Printing multiple copies of a multiple-page document in order, so the document does not need to be assembled later.

color depth   The number of colors in a display. 24-bit color can display over 16 million colors.

color patterns   The patterns visible in a full-color display. A normally functioning display has different patterns than a malfunctioning display.

COMMAND   Old Windows and MS-DOS/PC-DOS command interpreter. Replaced by CMD.EXE.

command prompt   Prompt in Windows where command-line programs can be run. Open a command-prompt session by opening CMD.EXE.

commercial license   Software that is licensed only after the payment of a fee.

community (cloud)   Type of cloud computing in which organizations with common concerns or goals share cloud infrastructure.

Compact Flash   A popular type of flash memory card for professional digital single lens reflex (SLR) cameras.

compatibility error   Programs/apps display this error if they can't run properly under the current operating system.

compatibility mode   Mode in which compatibility settings (changes in resolution, permissions, etc.) are applied to enable a program/app to run under an operating system.

compatibility tools   Tools in the OS to enable a program/app to run under the OS. In Windows, these include the Program Compatibility Wizard and the Compatibility tab.

compliance with local government regulations   Regulations for HVAC, disposal of hazardous chemicals, recycling of old electronics, and others need to be followed to avoid legal penalties.

Computer Management   Windows interface for managing tasks, events, users, performance, storage, and services. Snap-in for the Microsoft Management Console (MMC).

COMx *   Communication Port (x=port number). *See* serial port.

component   Windows features such as COM+, DCOM Config, and Distributed Transaction Coordinator components used by developers.

Component Services   A Microsoft Management Console plug-in for managing COM+, DCOM Config, and Distributed Transaction Coordinator components.

composite   A low-quality video I/O standard that combines all video signals into a single cable. Does not carry audio.

compressed air   Can be used to remove dust, grit, and debris from computers, peripherals, and printers.

confidential materials   Information proprietary to an organization.

content filtering   Feature of some networks, firewalls, and routers that prevents selected content types from reaching the computers or mobile devices that requested the content.

continuous reboots   Symptom of Power Good power supply problem or STOP (BSOD) error if system is configured to restart on BSOD.

Control Panel   A Windows feature that sets Windows hardware options. It can be accessed from the Start or Start, Settings menu in most versions of Windows.

COPY   Windows internal command for copying files between one location and another.

CPU *   Central Processing Unit. An electronic circuit that can process data and execute computer programs (Core i7, FX, etc.).

CPU cache   CPU caches hold the most-recently accessed memory locations. The CPU cache is checked before accessing system RAM in case the information needed is already in cache and can thus be accessed more quickly.

CPU core   Processing unit inside a CPU. Most CPUs produced today have two or more cores.

CPU fan connector   Connection on motherboard to power CPU fan and monitor speed.

CPU socket   Location on motherboard where CPU is placed. A spring-loaded clip or locking plate holds the CPU in place.

CPU-Z   A third-party CPU identification program that provides extensive technical information on a CPU's features and revision level.

creased paper   Paper feed problem that can cause printer jams. Often happens when paper is not aligned before being fed into the printer or the paper guides are not set correctly.

credit card reader   Card reader that plugs into a mobile device's 3.5mm mini-card headset jack for use in accepting credit/debit cards.

crimper   Tool that squeezes a cable connector to the raw cable to create a finished cable assembly. Versions available for RJ-11, RJ-45, and coaxial.

CRT *   Cathode ray tube. A monitor's picture tube, a large vacuum tube that displays information.

cultural sensitivity   Using appropriate language and behavior when dealing with people from a different culture than yours.

custom system configuration   A computer configuration that is not a stock or standard configuration to better fit the computer to a specified task.

customer expectations   What a customer expects during the handling of an installation, repair, or emergency event.

D

DAC *   Discretionary Access Control

daisy-chaining   Connecting multiple devices through a single port; used by EPP and ECP parallel-port modes, SCSI, and FireWire.

DB-25 *   Serial Communications D-Shell Connector, 25 Pins

DB-9 *   9 Pin D-Shell Connector

DC *   Direct current; the type of electrical current supplied by batteries or by a PC's power supply.

DDoS *   Distributed Denial of Service

DDR *   Double Data-Rate Synchronous Dynamic Random-Access Memory. Double Data-Rate SDRAM. A faster form of SDRAM used by many high-performance video cards and motherboards.

DDR RAM *   Double Data Rate Random-Access Memory

DDR SDRAM *   Double Data Rate Synchronous Dynamic Random-Access Memory

DDR2 SDRAM   Double Data-Rate SDRAM (DDR2 SDRAM) is the successor to DDR SDRAM. DDR2 SDRAM runs its external data bus at twice the speed of DDR SDRAM, enabling faster performance.

DDR3 SDRAM   Double Data-Rate Three SDRAM (DDR3 SDRAM) is the successor to DDR2 SDRAM. DDR3 SDRAM runs its external data bus at twice the speed of DDR2 SDRAM, enabling faster performance. DDR3 SDRAM also uses lower voltages than DDR2 and supports higher memory capacities.

DDR4 SDRAM   Double Data-Rate Four SDRAM (DDR4 SDRAM) is the successor to DDR3 SDRAM. DDR4 SDRAM runs its external data bus at twice the speed of DDR3 SDRAM, enabling faster performance. DDR4 SDRAM also uses lower voltages than DDR3 and supports higher memory capacities.

DE15   Video Graphics Array (VGA) connector, using three rows of five pins each.

dead pixels   A pixel on a LCD (CCFL or LED backlight) or OLED display that doesn't light up.

dead short   Short circuit on the motherboard that makes the system appear to be dead.

decrypt   Reverse the encryption of a file or drive so the contents can be viewed.

decrypt e-mail   Reverse the encryption of an e-mail attachment so the contents can be viewed.

default SSID   The SSID assigned to a wireless router or access point by the manufacturer.

Defender   Windows antivirus and anti-malware program.

DEFRAG   A Windows command-line utility for defragmenting a drive.

defragmentation tool   A program/app that can be used to defragment a drive. To launch the defragment tool in Windows, right-click a drive in Windows Explorer or File Explorer, select Properties, select Tools, and select Defragment now.

degaussing   To demagnetize a CRT display. Degaussing removes color fringing and distortions onscreen. Some monitors automatically degauss the CRT when the monitor is turned on, and others offer a degaussing button or menu option to degauss on demand.

DEL   The Windows command-line file deletion tool. The equivalent in Linux or OS X Terminal is rm.

device ID   Method of indicating different devices attached to a SCSI host adapter; each device must use a unique device ID#, which is set on each device.

Device Manager   A Microsoft Windows utility that displays detailed information about the computer hardware in the system, including status and driver information.

Devices and Printers   A Windows 7/8/8.1/10 Control Panel applet that lists devices and printers and management options for each.

DFS *   Distributed File System

DHCP *   Dynamic Host Configuration Protocol. Provides IP addresses as required; allows a limited number of IP addresses to service many devices that are not connected at the same time.

DHCP server   Server on a network that provides IP addresses on demand. Usually incorporated into a SOHO wireless router.

dial-up networking   Network connection that uses an analog (phone line) modem to make a direct connection to a remote computer via phone line.

dictionary attack   An attack on a secure system that uses a dictionary of words and phrases to find the password.

digital camera   A camera that uses a digital image sensor instead of film. Most use flash memory cards for storage.

digital security   Procedures for protecting secure networks, storage, and servers. Includes measures such as network encryption and authentication servers.

digitizer   The touch-sensitive layer of a touchscreen display. The digitizer layer can be damaged without damaging the display on a desktop, laptop, or all-in-one unit and can be replaced.

dim image   Symptom of a possible failing CCFL backlight or may simply indicate the brightness is set too low.

DIMM *   Dual Inline Memory Module. These are available in 168-pin, 184-pin, 240-pin, and 288-pin versions. *Dual* refers to each side of the module having a different pinout.

DIN *   Deutsche Industrie Norm

DIR   Windows command-prompt command for displaying the contents of a folder (directory). Linux and OS X Terminal equivalent is ls.

directory permissions   Permissions assigned to a directory (folder) by the Share command (networking) or by the Advanced properties dialog.

direct thermal   Thermal printing technology in which the printhead heats the paper.

directory   Older term for a folder in Windows.

Disk Management   Windows interface for managing hard drive storage. Can also manage removable-media and tape drives in Vista.

DISKPART   Windows command-line utility for creating and managing disks, partitions, and volumes.

display   General term encompassing monitors, HDTVs, and projectors used with a video card or port.

display settings   Configuration of display resolution, color depth, refresh rate, etc.

DisplayPort   Primarily used to transmit video but can also send audio and USB signals as well. Designed as a replacement for VGA and DVI.

distended capacitors   Bulging, leaking motherboard component that resembles a miniature soft drink can. Replace capacitors or retire motherboard to solve.

distorted geometry   When using a projector, caused by not having the screen/wall and projector lined up properly with each other.

distorted image   Stretched or squeezed images are caused by incorrect resolution settings. Other types of image distortion can be caused by 3D settings, overheating video card, or failing video card.

DLL   Dynamic Link Library. Binary files used by Windows and Windows programs.

DLT *   Digital Linear Tape

DLP *   Digital Light Processing

DMZ *   Demilitarized zone. In network computing it is a subnetwork that provides external services. It is often between the LAN and the Internet but is controlled by the organization that also controls the LAN.

DNAT   Destination network address translation. More often referred to a port forwarding or DMZ.

DNS *   Domain name service or domain name server. Translates domain names into IP addresses.

DNS server   Server that provides DNS server IP addresses to the network. Often incorporated into a wireless router.

Dock   OS X feature for launching and switching applications; displays app icons across the bottom of the desktop.

docking station   Enables laptops and other mobile devices to use devices not built in, such as card slots, high-end audio and video ports, and others; requires a proprietary, dedicated external bus connector.

documentation   Printed or electronic manuals from the vendor explaining how to use an app, OS, or device.

domain   Windows corporate network that uses a domain controller to store routes to network devices (shares, printers, etc.) and authenticate the users of each device.

domain setup   During Windows installation, users are prompted to provide domain information so the computer can be added to the domain immediately.

domain name   Unique alphanumeric identifier for websites.

DoS *   Denial of Service

DRAM *   Dynamic Random Access Memory. Dynamic RAM. The slowest type of RAM, which requires frequent electrical refreshes to keep contents valid.

drill/hammer   Popular data-destruction tools.

drive activity light   Light on the front or top of a computer that lights up when the system drive is being used.

drive array   Two or more drives used as a single logical unit.

Drive not recognized   Error that takes place if misconfiguration, cable error, or other problem prevents the computer from detecting the drive.

Drive status   Feature in Windows Disk Management that displays the condition and partition type of a drive.

drive wipe   Process that overwrites all information on a drive so it cannot be retrieved.

driver   A special file that instructs the OS on how to use a device.

driver installation   Installing a driver for a new or existing device.

DRM *   Digital Rights Management

DSL   Digital Subscriber Line. A type of broadband Internet service that uses telephone lines to carry Internet traffic at speeds up to 1.5Mbps or more while allowing you to use your phone for normal functions at the same time. Two major types of DSL are ADSL and SDSL. *See* those entries for details.

dual rail   A power supply with two +12V DC rails. Using dual rails is typically more reliable than using a single +12V DC rail. Many power supplies feature four or more +12V DC rails.

dual voltage   A power supply that can manually or automatically switch between 115V and 230V DC current.

dual channel   A motherboard feature in which two identical memory modules are treated as a single logical unit for faster access.

duplex   A printing option that automatically prints on both sides of a sheet.

duplexing assembly   The printer options that enables duplex printing.

dust and debris   Common problems after using a thermal printer with a ribbon. Use compressed air or isopropyl alcohol to remove these before printing more.

DVD *   Digital versatile disc; the most common optical disc format.

DVD boot   Starting a computer from a DVD.

DVD-RAM *   Digital Video Disc-Random-Access Memory

DVD-ROM *   Digital Video Disc-Read-Only Memory

DVD-R *   Digital Video Disc-Recordable

DVD-RW *   Digital Video Disc-Rewritable

DVD-RW DL   An optical drive that supports rewriteable DVD and dual-layer recordable DVD media.

DVI *   Digital Visual Interface. Replaced DFP as the standard for support of LCD displays on desktop computers. DVI-D is for digital displays only; DVI-I supports digital and analog displays; DVI-A supports analog displays only. Sometimes this is also referred to as Digital Video Interface.

DXDIAG   DirectX Diagnostics, a Windows utility for identifying the DirectX version in use and testing the computer's DirectX features.

dye sublimation   Thermal printing technology in which dye is released as a gas onto the page.

dynamic partition   Windows disk storage type that permits drive spanning, striping, mirroring, and fault-tolerant volumes.

E–F

eBook   An electronic book. A book in a variety of formats for use with e-reader apps or e-reader devices.

ECC *   Error Correction Code or Error Checking and Correction. Advanced memory that can correct errors and requires special chipsets. It is used primarily in servers.

ECP *   Extended Capabilities Port

ECR   entry control roster

EEPROM *   Electrically Erasable Programmable Read-Only Memory

EFS *   Encrypting File System. The encryption subset of NTFS.

EIDE *   Enhanced Integrated Drive Electronics

electrical fire   A fire caused by an electrical problem. A Class C fire extinguisher is designed for electrical fires.

e-mail   Electronic mail. Messages that can also include attachments that are sent and received with e-mail servers.

e-mail filtering   E-mail server or client feature that blocks sending or receiving of messages with undesirable content.

EMI *   Electromagnetic Interference

eMMC   embedded Multi-Media Controller, a low-cost form of flash memory used in low-cost mobile devices. Slower than SSDs.

EMP *   Electromagnetic Pulse

enclosure   A case that can be used for computer components, usually internal hard disks.

end user The user of a computer or mobile device. Usually assigned standard user privileges.

end-user policies Policies that govern the use of a computer or mobile device by an end user.

enterprise license A software license assigned to an organization rather than an individual computer.

EP Electrophotographic Process. The seven-stage method for printing with a laser printer.

EPROM * Erasable Programmable Read-Only Memory

EPP * Enhanced Parallel Port

e-Reader A device designed for use with eBooks. Some can be converted into tablets by using non-standard firmware.

ERD * Emergency Repair Disk

eSATA External SATA, a version of SATA for use with external drives.

ESD * Electrostatic discharge. The release of static electricity when two objects with varying electrical potentials come into contact with each other.

ESD mat A mat that is connected to unpainted metal on a computer or component to equalize electrical potential.

ESD strap A strap worn by a computer technician and clipped to unpainted metal on a computer or other component to equalize electrical potential.

EULA * End-User License Agreement

EVGA * Extended Video Graphics Adapter/Array

EVDO * Evolution Data Optimized or Evolution Data Only

exFAT (FAT64) File system designed to support high-capacity removable storage media, such as flash drives.

EXIT A Windows command-prompt command to exit a command-line program or to exit the command prompt session.

EXPAND A Windows command-prompt command to expand a .cab archive file containing Windows components.

expansion slots Slots in the motherboard for video, network, mass storage, and other types of cards. Types include PCIe, PCI, and others.

ExpressCard High-performance replacement for CardBus; available in 34mm-wide (/34) and 54mm-wide (/54) versions.

extend (volume)   Disk Management option to increase the size of a disk volume into unallocated space.

extended partition   Windows disk partition that can be divided into one or more logical drives. Cannot be made bootable.

external command   Programs run from the command line, such as XCOPY.

EXPLORER   Runs Windows Explorer (Vista/7) or File Explorer (8/8.1/10) from the command line.

ext3   Popular journaling file system formerly used by most Linux distributions.

ext4   Replacement for ext3 with support for larger drive sizes, more efficient file handling, backward-compatibility, and other improvements. Currently used by most Linux distributions.

face lock   A mobile device security method that uses biometrics to detect your face.

factory recovery partition   Common method used by manufacturers to provide Windows recovery media in compressed form.

factory reset/clean install   The process of resetting a mobile device to its original condition and performing a clean installation of the OS.

faded prints   Common indication of critically low toner level in a laser printer. Can also be caused by using an economy print mode.

failed login attempt restrictions   A security feature that prevents login after a specified number of failed attempts.

failure to boot   System cannot boot, possibly due to BIOS/UEFI boot order, damage to operating system files, or other causes.

fan connector   Connection on the motherboard that powers and monitors a case or CPU fan.

fanless/passive   A heat sink that does not use a fan.

fan   Pulls air through the system past hot components for cooling and then out of the system.

FAT *   File Allocation Table

FAT12 *   12-bit File Allocation Table

FAT16 *   16-bit File Allocation Table

FAT32 *   32-bit File Allocation Table. FAT method is optionally available with Windows. It allows for drive sizes up to 2TB (terabytes).

F-connector   A coaxial cable connector used for CATV, cable Internet, and satellite Internet. Typically used with RG-59 and RG-6 cables.

FDD *   Floppy Disk Drive

feed assembly   Paper feed component on a printer.

feeder   Paper feed component on a printer.

fiber   Short for fiber optic. Network cable that uses glass fibers to transmit photons to carry data.

file attributes   File settings that indicate if a file needs to be backed up, is read-only, hidden, or system.

file permission changes   Changes to the default file permissions setting for a file or folder to prevent or permit certain types of actions to be performed by a user or class of users.

file recovery software   Software that can recover a deleted file if the file bypassed the Recovery Bin or was never sent to the Recovery Bin.

file server   A type of server optimized for sharing files with the network.

file sharing   An OS configuration allowing a file or folder to be used by remote users on a network.

file structure and paths   How the system drive is configured for storing user files.

firewall   A network device or software that blocks unauthorized access to a network from other users. Software firewalls, such as the Windows Firewall, ZoneAlarm, and Norton Internet Security, are sometimes referred to as personal firewalls. Routers can also function as firewalls.

FireWire 400   *See* IEEE 1394.

FireWire 800   *See* IEEE 1394.

firmware   A middle ground between hardware and software, it is a software program that has been written for read-only memory (ROM).

first response   When the first technician arrives at the incident scene and identifies what happened.

fitness monitor   A type of wearable technology that monitors blood pressure, pulse, steps, and other factors. Uses Bluetooth to communicate with the host mobile device.

flash memory   Memory that retains its contents without electricity.

FlexATX   Small version of ATX motherboard designed for low-profile or small form factor systems.

flickering image   Visual problem that can be caused by a failing CCFL backlight or by certain settings on mobile devices.

Fn key *   Function; special key on laptop keyboards that, when pressed, enables other keys to perform an additional task, such as adjusting screen brightness, toggling the Windows desktop to an external display, etc.

Folder options   Windows dialog for setting options such as whether registered file extensions and hidden files are displayed.

Force Quit   Linux and OS X option to shut down an unresponsive app/program.

force stop   Android and iOS option to shut down an unresponsive app.

FPM *   Fast Page Mode

form factor   Physical size and shape of motherboard, power supply. *See* www.formfactors.org for specifications for common motherboard and power supply standards.

FORMAT   Windows command-line tool for preparing a new drive for use or overwriting the drive's contents so the drive can be reused.

front/top panel connectors   Connections on front or side of motherboard for power switch, indicator lights, reset, and other features from the front or top of the computer.

frozen system   A system that is unresponsive to mouse, keyboard, or touch. The power switch must be used to shut down a frozen system.

FRU *   Field Replaceable Unit

FSB *   Front Side Bus

FTP *   File Transfer Protocol. File transfer to or from a special server site on the World Wide Web.

FQDN *   Fully Qualified Domain Name

full device encryption   The contents of the entire device are encrypted. Assign a PIN code to a mobile device to encrypt it.

full format   A disk format that rewrites sector markings over the entire disk rather than simply clearing the root directory (root folder) as with a quick format.

fuser assembly   The laser printer component that heats the toner and paper and bonds them together.

G

Gadget   A Windows 7 feature that allowed the user to place small applets anywhere on the screen. The applets were the same as those used in the Windows Vista sidebar. No longer supported by Microsoft due to security issues.

game pad   Game controller.

garbled characters   Random text and graphic characters produced by a printer. Can indicate damage to the data cable between the printer and computer or the use of an incompatible printer driver.

gateway   The private IP address of a device (such as a router) that connects computers on a LAN to another network.

Gb *   Gigabit

GB *   Gigabyte

GDI *   Graphics Device Interface

general options   The first menu of options displayed when a user opens the Settings menu on an iOS device.

generic hub   USB hub that plugs in to a USB port or USB root hub.

geotracking   The practice of tracking and recording the location of a mobile device over time.

gestures   Finger movements made across an iOS trackpad or Magic Mouse surface or across a touchscreen on other OS that perform specific tasks.

ghost cursor/pointer drift   Symptoms pointing to problems with the touchpad or track pad on a laptop, including accidental thumb swipes, touchpad stuck in the "always clicked" mode, and others.

ghost image   Afterimage of the previous page on a page printed with a laser printer. Usually indicates a problem with the toner subsystem, including incorrect voltage, toner sticking to the rollers, and so on.

GHz *   Gigahertz

Gigabit NIC   A network interface card (or port) that supports 10/100/1000Mbps Ethernet connections.

Glasses and headsets   Two types of wearable technology.

Gmail   Also known as Google Mail.

Google Play Store   The Android app store.

Google Sync   The Android cloud backup service.

Google/Inbox   Google Mail.

GUI *   Graphical user interface. Windows, OS X, GNOME, and KDE (Linux) are examples of GUIs.

GPRESULT   Windows command-line utility that lists the resultant set of policy (RSoP) for a remote user and computer.

GPS *   global positioning system. A worldwide system of satellites that provides information concerning the whereabouts of mobile devices and anything else with a GPS receiver.

GPT   GUID partition table, used for hard drives over 2.1TB in size.

GPUPDATE   Windows command-line utility to refresh group policy settings.

grep   Linux plain-text search command.

GRUB   Linux bootloader.

GRUB2   An improved version of grub that supports booting from Live CD .iso files and scripting support among other changes. Often referred to as GRUB.

GSM *   Global System for Mobile Communications

Guest account   A Windows account with limited permissions.

gyroscope   In addition to the accelerometers, this adds the measurements of pitch, roll, and yaw to mobile devices, just like in the concept of flight dynamics.

H

HAL *   Hardware Abstraction Layer

half duplex/full duplex/auto   Settings for NIC connection speed. Half duplex—port sends, but must wait until sending is over to receive, and vice versa. Full duplex (preferred)—port sends and receives simultaneously, doubling effective throughput. Auto—NIC selects mode according to network defaults.

hard drive   Mass storage device. Can refer to hard disk drive, hybrid drive, or SSD.

hard reset   Also known as factory reset; clears all user information from a mobile device and resets it to as-shipped (factory) condition.

hardware   Objects in a computer that are tangible; can be physically installed or removed.

HAV *   Hardware Assisted Virtualization; features in CPU and BIOS that enable virtualization to perform faster.

HCL *   Hardware Compatibility List

HD15   Another name for the VGA port

HD Audio   An Intel standard for High Definition Audio (also known as HAD or Azalia). It supports 192kHz 32-bit sampling in stereo and 96kHz 32-bit sampling for up to eight channels.

HDD *   Hard Disk Drive

HDMI *   High-Definition Media Interface. A compact audio/video interface for transmitting uncompressed digital data.

header cable   Connects to motherboard header pins connected to integrated I/O ports.

headset   Alternative to speaker or earbuds for listening to audio; when equipped with a microphone, can also be used for hands-free use of a smartphone.

heat sink   Device that draws heat away from a component (CPU, GPU, and memory).

heating element   Thermal printer's equivalent to a printhead. Creates text and graphics on special thermal paper or plain paper with a ribbon.

HELP   Windows command-line utility for displaying help. Use the HELP *command* to see help for a specific command.

Hibernate   Windows power-saving mode that writes the current desktop, open apps, open file information to the hard disk and then shuts down.

hide extensions   The default setting in Windows Explorer/File Explorer; technicians should change this to display all file extensions for troubleshooting.

Hi-Speed USB   USB 2.0 ports and devices.

HID   Human interface device; mouse or keyboard.

hijacked e-mail   When a hacker or malware takes over your e-mail, sends messages without your permission, and similar activities.

Home network setting   Windows Vista/7 network location setting equivalent to selecting Private as the network type in Windows 8/8.1/10. Permits network discovery and supports creating or connecting to a homegroup.

home server   A PC optimized to provide file, print, and backup services on a home or SOHO network.

HomeGroup   Microsoft secure home and SOHO networking technology for Windows 7/8/8.1/10.

homegroup   A secure home and SOHO network created using HomeGroup technology.

hot swappable drive   A SATA or eSATA hard drive configured in AHCI mode. Also applies to drives using USB or FireWire interfaces.

hotspot   Method for sharing a smartphone's Internet access via Wi-Fi.

Hotspot/tethering   Methods for sharing a smartphone's Internet access via Wi-Fi or USB.

HPFS *   High-Performance File System

HTML *   Hypertext Markup Language. A standard for markup symbols that enables hyperlinking, fonts, special text attributes, graphics, and other enhancements to be added to text files for display with web browsers such as Microsoft Internet Explorer and Microsoft Edge, Mozilla Firefox, and Google Chrome. The official source for HTML standards is the World Wide Web Consortium (W3C), but some browsers have added proprietary features to the HTML dialects they understand.

HTPC   Home Theater PC.

HTTP *   Hypertext Transfer Protocol. The basis for hyperlinking and the Internet; it is interpreted by a web browser program.

HTTPS *   Hypertext Transfer Protocol over Secure Sockets Layer. HTTPS connections are often used for payment transactions on the World Wide Web and for sensitive transactions in corporate information systems.

hub   Central connecting point for UTP-based forms of Ethernet. A hub broadcasts messages to all computers connected to it and subdivides the bandwidth of the network among the computers connected to it. *See* switch. Also refers to a device used to enable multiple USB devices to connect to a single USB port.

hybrid   Refers to: cloud computing that shares characteristics of a private and public cloud; a hard disk drive with a small SSD onboard for improving disk access time.

Hyper-Threading (HT Technology)   Intel CPU technology that enables a single processor core to work with two execution threads at the same time.

hypervisor   The program running on a host machine that creates and manages virtual machines. Most often refers to Type 1 virtualization, in which the hypervisor connects directly with the hardware rather than running on top of the host's OS.

I

I/O *   Input/Output; a generic term for ports used for input or output, such as USB, PS/2 mouse and keyboard, and FireWire. Storage device ports (SATA and eSATA) are not categorized as I/O ports.

IaaS   Infrastructure as a service. A type of cloud computing in which users can lease cloud-based network services, servers, storage space, and other resources.

iCloud   iOS cloud backup service.

ICMP *   Internet Control Message Protocol

ICR *   Intelligent Character Recognition

ID badge   Can be used with various types of physical and digital security, including bar code readers and smart card readers.

IDE *   Integrated Drive Electronics

IDS *   Intrusion Detection System

IEEE *   Institute of Electrical and Electronics Engineers

IEEE 1394   A high-speed serial connection. IEEE 1394a (FireWire 400) runs at 400Mbps and IEEE 1394b (FireWire 800) runs at 800Mbps. i.LINK is Sony's name for a four-wire version of IEEE-1394a.

ifconfig   Linux and OS X Terminal command to display and (optionally) change wired network configuration. Similar to Windows' ipconfig command-line utility. In OS X Terminal, also supports wireless networking.

IIS *   Internet Information Services

i.LINK   *See* IEEE 1394.

image deployment   Installing Microsoft Windows from an image.

image recovery   Recreating a working OS from an image backup.

imaging device   How Microsoft Windows identifies devices such as digital cameras or scanners in Computer.

imaging drum   An important component in a laser printer.

IMAP *   Internet Message Access Protocol. Second most common protocol used to download e-mail.

image backup   System backup that stores all information on the system including the operating system, programs, settings, and data. Most recent image backup programs also support restoration of individual files.

IMEI *   International Mobile Equipment Identity

impact paper   Paper designed for impact printers. Typically has holes on both edges for sprocket feeding.

impact printer   Print technology that uses a multipin printhead and an inked ribbon to make an image.

IMSI *   International Mobile Subscriber Identity

inkjet printer   Print technology that sprays fine droplets of ink on the page.

In-place upgrade   Another name for a repair installation in Windows.

incident response   The procedures to follow when unauthorized content or activities are detected.

incineration   A method for destroying tape, optical discs, or flexible magnetic media.

infrastructure   The default Wi-Fi configuration, with wireless clients connecting to each other or to the Internet via an access point rather than directly to each other.

inheritance   How files and folders receive permissions settings from parent folders.

initialize (drive)   Preparing a hard drive for use with Windows Disk Management.

ink cartridge   Ink supply for an inkjet printer. Almost all current products use a separate cartridge for each color.

inkjet printer   A non-impact printer that sprays tiny droplets of ink on plain or glossy paper to create text and images.

integrated GPU   GPU (graphics processing unit) incorporated in the CPU.

integrated I/O ports   Ports built in to the motherboard port cluster or internal headers such as USB, DVI, HDMI, Ethernet, and others.

integrated print server   A printer or all-in-one unit (scan/copy/print or scan/copy/fax/print) that includes a wireless and/or wired print server.

intermittent connectivity   A network problem that is most likely caused by physical problems such as a loose or damaged cable or antenna wire, or network signal strength/interference problems.

intermittent device failure   A hardware problem that is most likely caused by physical problems such as a loose or damaged cable, lack of USB bus power, etc.

internal command   Windows command-line operations built in to the Windows command interpreter, CMD.EXE, such as COPY, DEL, and DIR.

Internet appliance   An Internet-connected device that performs a single task, such as a hardware firewall, e-mail filter, intrusion detection device, etc.

Internet pass-through   When a mobile device connects to a PC to use the PC's Internet connection.

intrusion detection/notification   An IDS device detects and notifies administrators of threats that might not be detected by a firewall.

invalid certificate (trusted root CA)   A trusted root certificate authority (CA) provides digital certificates for use by websites and software developers to authenticate their products and services. An invalid certificate is one that was provided under false pretenses to an attacker. It can be used to take over a system.

inverter   Converts DC current into AC current to power CCFL backlight in LCD displays.

iOS   Apple's mobile OS, used by iPod Touch, iPad, and iPhone devices.

IP *   Internet Protocol

IPv4   IP version 4 is the most common version, using 32-bit addresses.

IPv6   IP version 6 will eventually replace IPv4, offering 128-bit addresses to prevent address exhaustion and easier configuration.

IP addressing   The process of assigning IP addresses to network clients, including standalone devices as well as mobile devices, laptops, and desktops.

IP conflict   Two devices (printers, mobile, computers, etc.) on a network with the same IP address.

IPCONFIG *   Internet Protocol Configuration

IPP *   Internet Printing Protocol

IPS *   In-Plane Switching

IPSec *   Internet Protocol Security

IR *   Infrared

IrDA *   Infrared Data Association. Defines physical specifications and communications protocol standards for the short-range exchange of data over infrared, used in personal area networks (PANs).

IRP *   Incident Response Plan

IRQ *   Interrupt Request

ISDN *   Integrated Services Digital Network

ISO *   International Organization for Standardization/Industry Standards Organization

ISO image   A single file that contains the layout of an optical disc.

ISP *   Internet Service Provider

iTunes   Apple's music and media store. Also used for backing up iOS devices.

ITX   Motherboard form factor designed for small form factor and embedded CPUs. Now obsolete, but was the basis for the smaller mini-ITX form factor and still smaller siblings.

iwconfig   Linux command to display and (optionally) change wireless networks. Not supported in OS X Terminal.

J–K

jailbreaking   The process of removing limitations on Apple devices, giving the user root access and allowing a person to install unauthorized software.

jargon   Technical language that a non-technical user cannot understand; should not be used in discussions with customers.

JBOD *   Just a Bunch Of Disks; also known as spanned; capacity of all drives combined into a single logical volume.

Journaling   File system feature that continually records changes to the drive as they are made, enabling versioning and easier data recovery. Journaling is found in NTFS, ext3, ext4, OS X HFS, Windows NTFS, and most other non-FAT file systems.

joystick   A game controller often used in flight simulators. Plugs into a USB port or might use Bluetooth wireless networking.

judgmental   An undesirable trait in customer service, marked by lack of active listening, jumping to conclusions, and making moral judgements unrelated to the topic at hand.

jumper   Group of two or three pins on a motherboard, storage device, or card; used for configuration.

jumper block   Fits across two jumper pins to enable or disable a feature.

Kb *   Kilobit

KB *   Kilobyte or Knowledge Base

kernel panic   Crash on a computer running OS X or Linux that forces the OS to shut down.

key fob   A device that can be used in various types of security setups: as a digital key for building or room access; as a PIN code/cryptographic code generator; as a USB device for secure access to a computer, among other examples.

keyboard   Alphanumeric data entry device with a typewriter-style keyboard, additional functional, numeric, directional, and text-editing keys. They connect via the USB or PS/2 keyboard port. Laptop keyboards also include Fn keys for special functions.

Keychain   An OS X password management system.

KVM switch   Keyboard-video-mouse; a device that enables a single keyboard, video display, and mouse to work with two or more computers.

L

L1 cache   Level 1 cache memory read by CPU first when new memory information is needed; smallest cache size. *See* cache.

L2 cache   Level 2 cache memory read by CPU if L1 cache does not have wanted information; much larger than L1 cache. *See* cache.

L3 cache   Level 3 cache memory read by CPU if L2 cache does not have wanted information; much larger than L2 cache; used on high-performance CPUs. *See* cache.

LAN *   Local area network. A network in which the components connect through network cables; if a router is used, the network is a WAN.

LGA   Land Grid Array. Intel CPU socket technology that uses small metal lands in the CPU socket instead of pins on the CPU.

laser printer   Type of nonimpact page printer that quickly produces quality text and images. Most use the electrophotographic (EP) printing/imaging process.

LBA *   Logical Block Addressing

LC *   Lucent Connector

LCD *   Liquid crystal display. Type of screen used on portable computers and on flat-panel desktop displays.

LDAP *   Lightweight Directory Access Protocol. Maintains distributed directory information services. Examples include e-mail and Microsoft Active Directory.

LED *   Light Emitting Diode

LED display   LCD display with LED backlighting instead of a cold cathode fluorescent lamp (CCFL).

legacy/embedded systems   Legacy systems are those that rely on outdated, often no-longer-supported, software or hardware—for example, devices that use Windows XP. Embedded systems are computer systems built into larger systems for control or other purposes. For example, a CNC (computer numeric control) router includes a computer that controls the cutting process. Embedded systems sometimes include legacy hardware or software, but not always.

LGA2011   The original LGA 2011 supports high-performance Sandy Bridge E and Ivy Bridge E processors. LGA 2011-v3 supports high-performance Haswell E processors.

LGA1150   LGA socket used by fourth generation (Haswell) and fifth-generation (Broadwell) Intel CPUs. Haswell processors are the first to feature an integrated voltage regulator. Broadwell uses a smaller die size than Haswell for improved power efficiency and allows overclocking of the integrated GPU.

LGA1155   LGA socket used by second- and third-generation Core i-series processors; 1155 lands.

LGA1156   LGA socket used by first-generation Core i-series processors; 1156 lands.

LGA1366   LGA socket used by Extreme Core i7 CPUs; 1366 lands.

LGA775   First LGA socket from Intel; used by late-model Pentium 4, Pentium D, others; 775 lands.

LI-ON *   Lithium-Ion

Library   A Windows feature that enables multiple locations to be viewed in a single Windows Explorer or File Explorer window.

licensing   Legal agreement detailing how computer software, hardware, or firmware can be used by the licensee.

lifting techniques   Methods for safely lifting heavy and bulky equipment, frequently requiring two or more people (team lifting).

lightning   The proprietary, reversible Apple iOS sync/charging connector used on current iOS devices.

LILO   A Linux boot loader used on older Linux distributions. Largely replaced by GRUB and GRUB2.

limited connectivity   Network client can connect to LAN resources, but not to the Internet. Can result from loss of connection to a DHCP server.

line-of-sight wireless   A type of wireless networking in which fixed microwave towers are used to send and receive signals. A popular type of Internet and TV access in rural areas.

Linux   An open-source operating system that is inspired by the commercial Unix operating system. Available in many versions (called distributions or distros).

liquid-based (cooling)   Cooling system for CPU, GPU, and other components that replaces air cooling with heat blocks, a heat exchanger, and liquid-filled hoses; used for extreme overclocking.

Live File System Microsoft's implementation of the Universal Disc Format (UDF) for writing to recordable or rewriteable CD or DVD media in Windows.

Live sign in Signing into a Microsoft (formerly Live) account.

logical drive Drive created inside of an extended partition.

local connectivity *See* limited connectivity.

local security policy Security policy configured on an individual computer using the Local Security Policy MMC snap-in.

local share A share created on a local drive using File and Printer sharing in Windows.

Local Users and Groups A Computer Management node used to manage users and groups that can connect to the Windows computer being managed.

location data Data used for geolocation, such as a device's GPS coordinates or approximate location as determined by cell towers or Wi-Fi access.

locator application Program or service that can be used to locate a lost smartphone, tablet, or computer.

lockout Feature built into encrypted mobile devices and included on many secure websites to block login attempts after a specified number of failures.

lockup A system crash indicated by an unresponsive mouse cursor, keyboard, or touchscreen.

logical In disk partitioning using Windows, a logical drive is all or a specified portion of an extended partition on a drive using the MBR partitioning scheme.

log Event record stored by an OS or app. In Windows, various logs are available in the Event Viewer node of Computer Management.

LoJack for Laptops A locator service that is embedded in the system BIOS/UEFI firmware of most laptops. To activate it, purchase a subscription from LoJack.

loopback plug A plug that routes output to input wires to enable a port to be tested for proper send/receive functions. Widely available for testing Ethernet ports as well as legacy COM and LPT ports. Some BIOS/UEFI and third-party vendors also offer USB loopback plugs.

loud clicking noise A typical symptom of either a hard disk drive or other magnetic drive having read/write problems (the clicking comes from repeated seek movements of the read/write head) or from a failing cooling fan.

loud noise   A loud "bang" or "pop" noise, often accompanied by smoke or a chemical odor, usually indicates the failure of a capacitor on the motherboard or in the power supply. The component must be replaced, and if the power supply is affected, it could have damaged other components as well.

low-level format   The format process used to prepare a hard disk drive or SSD at the factory. Although a true low-level format cannot be performed in the field, overwriting the drive's surface with randomized data prevents existing information from being recovered.

low memory errors   Errors caused by attempting to print a document that will not fit in the laser printer's memory. These include partial page printout, or requiring the page to be ejected manually. Very slow printing due to extreme page compression being used to try to print the document.

low RF signal   Wireless network problem caused variously by obstructions between router and wireless client, use of only one antenna by router or client, excessive distance between router and client.

LPD/LPR *   Line Printer Daemon/Line Printer Remote

LPT *   Line Printer Terminal. *See* parallel port.

ls   Linux, OS X Terminal command to list the contents of the current directory (folder).

LVD *   Low Voltage Differential

M

MAC *   Media Access Control or Mandatory Access Control

MAC filtering   Router configuration that permits network access only to listed MAC addresses. Can be defeated by an attacker spoofing MAC addresses already on the list.

magnetic disk drive   Drive that uses one or more flexible or rigid platters coated in magnetic material. Hard disk drives (but not SSDs) are a current example.

mail server   A server that sends or receives e-mail.

maintenance kit   A kit for laser printers that includes components that are most likely to wear out, such as the fuser, tray, and cassette pickup rollers, tray separation pad, and cassette separation pad. Exact contents vary by model.

malware   Malicious software, or malware, is software designed to infiltrate a computer system and possibly damage it without the user's knowledge or consent. Malware is a broad term used by computer people to include viruses, worms, Trojan horses, spyware, rootkits, adware, and other types of unwanted software.

MAN   Metropolitan area network.

man-in-the-middle   A network attack in which the attacker relays and might alter information passing between two parties, each of which is convinced it is connected directly to the other party.

mantrap   A physical security arrangement in which the first door must close before the second door can open. Door opening can be controlled remotely or by using physical or electronic tokens.

manufacturer resources   General name for instruction manuals, user manuals, service manuals, and other information about a particular computer, mobile device, peripheral, operating system, or app.

MAPI *   Messaging Application Programming Interface

MAU *   Media Access Unit or Media Attachment Unit

Mb *   Megabit

MB *   Megabyte

MBR *   Master Boot Record

MBSA *   Microsoft Baseline Security Analyzer

MD   Abbreviation for MKDIR, a Windows command-prompt command that makes a folder (directory).

measured service   A cloud computing concept for billing for services by one or more of several measures such as by the hour, by data transferred, etc.

Memory/MicroSD   *See* MicroSD.

Metro UI   Windows 8/8.1 UI that is touch-oriented. Windows 10 combines some Metro UI elements (Tablet Mode) with a Start menu similar to Windows 7.

MFD *   Multi-Function Device

MFP *   Multi-Function Product

MDM   Mobile Device Management Software that secures, manages, and monitors multiple mobile devices from a central location.

MicroATX   Reduced-size ATX-family motherboard that supports up to four expansion slots. Usually incorporates video ports and only two memory slots.

MicroDIMM *   Micro Dual Inline Memory Module

microphone   Used for recording audio, live audio, or video chat. Built into laptop displays or can connect via USB or 3.5mm mini-jack.

MicroSD   MicroSD is the most common type of storage expansion used by smartphones and tablets.

MicroUSB   Smallest USB connector. MicroUSB Type B is used for USB-on-the-Go.

MIDI *   Musical Instrument Digital Interface. A standard developed for the storage and playback of music based on digital sampling of actual musical instruments.

MIME *   Multipurpose Internet Mail Extension

MIMO *   Multiple Input Multiple Output

miniDIN-6   Used for PS/2 mouse and keyboard ports.

miniHDMI   Used by high-performance video cards and some tablets.

miniPCI   Used for diagnostics cards and for Wi-Fi networking on older laptops.

miniPCIe   Used for diagnostics cards and for Wi-Fi networking on more recent laptops.

Mini-ITX   VIA Tech-originated ultra-compact motherboard design; used in computing appliances (media servers, etc.).

MiniSD   Smaller than SD, larger than MicroSD. Not in widespread use.

missing boot configuration data   The BCD store file (used for boot configuration in Windows 7/8/8.1/10) is missing. Restart the system with a Windows distribution disc or repair disc and use Startup Repair or BCDEdit to fix the problem.

missing DLL message   A dynamic link library (DLL) file for a program or driver has been deleted or moved. If the file is not in the Recycle Bin, reinstall the app or driver.

missing graphical interface   In Linux, the X Windows server subsystem didn't start or has crashed. Enter startx at the Terminal prompt to load it. In Windows, Safe Mode Command Prompt might have been selected as the startup mode. Restart the system. If the system was started in VGA (low-resolution) mode, the mode selected might be out of the supported range for the video driver. Restart the system.

missing GRUB/LILO   Indicates the Linux boot manager is missing. Can be caused by installing Windows after installing Linux. Use Boot-Repair (https://sourceforge.net/p/boot-repair/home/Home/) to fix.

missing operating system   General error message when OS cannot be located by the system BIOS/UEFI firmware. Check boot order, remove unbootable media, and restart system.

Mission Control   OS X app window manager and app switcher.

MLC   Multi-Level Cell; faster but more expensive than SLC flash memory; used in SSDs.

MMC *   Microsoft Management Console

Mobile payment service   Payment service that uses credentials stored on a smartphone. Usually requires that NFC be enabled.

modem   Short for modulate-demodulate, this device converts digital computer information into analog form and transmits it via telephone system to another computer.

Molex   Four-pin power connector used for desktop PATA drives and some add-on cards. Molex connectors can be adapted to SATA drives, case fans, and Bern connectors (used for floppy drive power).

motherboard   The logical foundation of the computer; all components connect to it.

motion sensor   Feature in Android and iOS devices that can be used for gaming or in conjunction with integrated camera for security or other uses.

mount point   Empty NTFS folder used to mount a drive.

mounted drive   A drive accessed through an empty NTFS folder.

mounting   The process of recognizing a drive so its contents can be viewed.

mouse   A pointing device that connects through the USB port or PS/2 mouse port.

MP3 *   Moving Picture Experts Group Layer 3 Audio

MP4 *   Moving Picture Experts Group Layer 4

MPEG *   Moving Picture Experts Group

MSCONFIG *   Microsoft Configuration

MSDS *   Material Safety Data Sheet. A document that contains information about substances that contain chemicals. It explains how to treat a person who comes in contact with the substance.

MSINFO32   The Microsoft System Information utility displays information about Windows, the computer, peripherals, and installed applications.

MSTSC   Microsoft Remote Desktop Connection app.

MUI *   Multilingual User Interface

multiboot installation   System configuration in which the user's choice of two or more operating systems can be selected when the system starts.

multicore processor   Processor with two or more cores; some desktop processors have as many as eight cores.

multifactor authentication   Use of more than one method for authentication, such as a password and a smart card.

multimeter An electrical testing device that can test amperage, AC and DC voltage, continuity, and other items.

multi-mode fiber Fiber optic cable with a large center core that is designed for short-distance networking.

multi-monitor task bars A feature of Windows 8/8.1/10.

multiple monitor misalignment/orientation OS X, Linux, and Windows all support multiple monitors but use different methods for configuring alignment.

multitouch touchscreens An input device that can sense the presence of two or more contact points. Common in personal computers, game consoles, laptops, tablets, and smartphones.

Music A Windows Vista/7/8/8.1/10 folder/library.

mutual authentication for multiple services (SSO) Access control method in which a user can sign on once to access multiple services. For example, signing in with a Microsoft account provides access to Outlook.com, OneDrive cloud storage, account management, etc.

mv Linux/OS X Terminal command for moving/renaming files.

N–O

NAT Network Address Translation; enables multiple private IP addresses to connect to the Internet through a single public IP address.

NBTSTAT Windows command that troubleshooting NetBIOS name resolution issues on an IP network.

NET Windows command-line utility for managing networks.

NetBEUI * Networked Basic input/output system Extended User Interface

netboot Booting to a network OS image.

NETDOM Windows command-line utility for managing Active Directory domains.

NETSTAT Windows command-line utility for displaying detailed network status.

network card Connects a computer to a network. Term is also used for integrated network adapters and for USB network adapters.

network card properties Connection speed, encryption type (wireless), duplex settings, and other settings.

network printer mapping Connecting to a printer that has its own IP address.

Network shares Folder shares available to users on the network.

NFC   Near Field Communication. Enables wireless sharing between mobile devices and mobile payment systems.

NFS *   Network File System

NIC *   Network Interface Card

NiCd *   Nickel Cadmium

NiMH *   Nickel Metal Hydride

NLX *   New Low profile Extended

NNTP *   Network News Transfer Protocol

no connectivity   Error resulting from loss of network connection due to router, network, or cable failure; Airplane mode being enabled; network adapter disabled.

no power   Problem due to failure of AC current; battery exhaustion or failure; charger malfunction.

non-compliant system   System that does not have all security updates installed.

North Bridge   Chipset component responsible for connection between CPU and high-speed I/O buses such as PCIe and USB 3.0.

Notepad   Windows app for plain-text viewing and editing.

nozzle check   Inkjet printer maintenance option that uses all nozzles to print a pattern that indicates whether some nozzles are clogged.

NSLOOKUP   Displays detailed DNS information.

NTFS *   New Technology File System. Preferred file system for Microsoft Windows operating systems.

NTFS permissions   File and folder permissions assigned with the folder or file's Security tab.

NTLDR *   New Technology Loader

NTP *   Network Time Protocol

null-modem   Serial cable that has transmit and receive wires crossed at one end; used for data transfer.

Num lock indicator lights   When light is on, NumLock is working. Some BIOS/UEFI firmware can configure NumLock to be enabled at startup.

OCR *   Optical Character Recognition

OEM *   Original Equipment Manufacturer

OLED *   OLED displays use organic light-emitting diodes based on organic compounds that emit light.

on-demand   Characteristic of cloud computing, in which users can purchase access to additional resources as needed.

OneDrive   Microsoft cloud storage service.

open-ended questions   Asking questions that receive more than a "yes" or "no" answer; a desirable skill in troubleshooting.

open-source   Software whose object code is freely distributable, enabling third parties to modify it and, in turn, distribute modifications.

optical drive   Drive that uses CD, DVD, or Blu-ray media.

orientation   Mobile device feature that detects device rotation and changes screen orientation to match.

OS *   Operating System

Outlook.com   Microsoft cloud-based e-mail and calendaring service.

overclocking   Running CPU, memory, and other components at faster-than-normal speeds. May require adjustments to component voltage and improved air cooling or a switch to liquid cooling.

overheating   Problem in which CPU, GPU, power supply, or other computer component becomes hotter than its normal design parameters call for; can be caused by inadequate airflow, fan failures, overloaded power supply; can lead to data corruption, system failure, or physical damage to components.

overlimit   Mobile system exceeds its data transfer limit. Could be caused by malware.

P–Q

PaaS   Platform as a Service. Cloud computing category designed for developing and deploying apps.

paging file (virtual memory)   The file stored on the hard drive used by the paging process as virtual memory, also known as a swap file. In Windows it is a file called pagefile.sys.

pairing   The process of connecting two wireless devices together, such as Bluetooth or some wireless mice or keyboards and their receiver.

PAN *   Personal Area Network

paper jam   Printer problem that can be caused by damp paper, not fanning the paper properly before placing in tray, or defective feed rollers.

parallel port   I/O port that enables data-transfer method sending 8 bits or multiples of 8 in a single operation; quite often uses a DB25F port. Also known as LPT port.

parental controls   Program, service, or feature integrated into some routers that provides for filtering of web contents, restrictions on social media use, time restrictions, or game rating restrictions for users based on age and parent/guardian settings.

passcode lock   Mobile device security feature that requires the user to enter a passcode to unlock the device. Must be enabled by the user.

passive heat sink   Heat sink that relies on outside air flow for cooling.

passwd   Linux command for managing passwords.

password best practices   Recommendations for creating strong passwords, such as use of randomized alphanumeric and punctuation characters, using passwords longer than the minimum length, and so on.

PATA *   Parallel Advanced Technology Attachment; term used for drives that use the 40-pin interface formerly known as IDE or ATA-IDE.

patch panel   A panel containing network ports that connects to a router or switch. Users can plug or unplug network cables to enable or disable connections as needed without disturbing the switch or router itself.

patch/update management   Management of OS or app patches and updates. Can be performed by the OS itself or by optional OS-supplied or third-party services.

patching/OS updates   Updates to the OS. In Windows, use Windows Update. In Linux, use apt-get. In OS X, use the Mac App Store.

PC *   Personal Computer

PC Card   16-bit PCMCIA card used in older laptops.

PC2001 system design guide   A series of computer specifications originally developed by Intel and Microsoft in 2001. Most of its recommendations are obsolete, but the port color-coding it contains (carried over from the PC99 design guide) continues to be followed by the industry.

PCI *   Peripheral Component Interconnect; 32-bit I/O bus providing a shared 33-MHz or 66-MHz data path between the CPU and peripheral controllers.

PCI Express   *See* PCIe.

PCIe *   PCI Express; a high-speed set of serial bus communication channels used by adapter cards.

PCIe 6/8-pin   Power leads from the power supply used to power PCIe video cards. Some cards use the six-pin connection; some use the eight-pin connector.

PCI-X *   Workstation/server version of PCI used for network and mass storage cards; provides faster performance than PCI.

PCL *   Printer Control Language

PCMCIA *   Personal Computer Memory Card International Association

PE *   Preinstallation Environment

peer-to-peer   Network in which some or all of the client PCs also act as peer servers.

Performance (virtual memory)   A Windows Control Panel setting that specifies the location and size of the paging file.

Performance monitor   A Windows Computer Management node that enables customized logging of system performance factors including processor performance, memory transfers, network performance, and others.

permission propagation   How NTFS file permissions are propagated to files and folders.

personal license   A software license for personal use.

personal safety   General term for measures to keep computer technicians safe, including ESD prevention, electrical protection, lifting methods, air filtration, and others.

Personally Identifiable Information   Metadata stored in documents and photos that could be used to determine the file's creator or other personal information.

PGA *   Pin Grid Array; CPU socket design in which pins in the rear of the CPU are inserted into holes in sockets and clamped into place.

PGA2 *   Pin Grid Array 2

phablets   Smartphones with screens of 5.5-in or larger.

phishing   The attempt to gain information such as personally identifiable information and credit cards using e-mail or other electronic communications.

physical laptop lock and cable lock   *See* cable lock.

pickup rollers   Printer component that pulls paper from the paper cassette, input tray, or roll feed and moves it into position for printing.

Pictures   A Windows Vista/7/8/8.1/10 folder/library.

PII *   Personally Identifiable Information

PIN *   Personal Identification Number

PING   Windows, Linux, and OS X utility for testing network connectivity.

pinning   Placing shortcuts to apps on the taskbar (Windows)

pinwheel   Slang term for OS X's spinning wait cursor, which appears when an application is busy.

PKI *   Public Key Infrastructure

plasma   Type of display that uses small cells that contain ionized gas.

plastics/frames   Components of laptop computers; they can be easily damaged.

play store   Short for Google Play, the app store for Android devices.

plenum   An air space in a building, such as HVAC ductwork or a suspended ceiling. Plenum cable, which produces very little smoke when burned, is required when a plenum is being used for cabling.

PnP *   Plug and Play

PoE   Power over Ethernet.

pointing device   General term for any mouse-type device.

pointing stick   Generic term for IBM/Lenovo TrackPoint, Toshiba AccuPoint, or other eraser-head pointing devices located in the middle of the keyboard.

policies and procedures   In the CompTIA A+ Certification exam 220-902, refers to mobile device security.

POP3 *   Post Office Protocol 3. E-mail protocol used by client computers to download or receive e-mail.

pop-ups   Ads or other web content that appear in small browser windows. Some websites use pop-ups when a user clicks a link, but most pop-ups are unsolicited advertising, and some might contain links to malware.

port (physical, TCP, UDP)   Physical port: location to attach a cable, especially a data cable. TCP or UDP port: number or range of numbers assigned to a particular connection session or connection type.

port forwarding   Redirection of inbound Internet traffic from a public connection to a particular port on a private connection behind the router. Used when the router would normally block the connection.

port forwarding/mapping   Equivalent terms. *See* port forwarding.

port replicator   Provides a single connection for various types of I/O ports for portable computers; the port replicator is connected to the external devices and is then connected to the portable computer through an external proprietary expansion bus or through a USB port.

port triggering   Similar to port forwarding, but takes place when a private IP address creates an outbound connection and inbound connections for that port are temporarily routed to another port. Unlike port forwarding, inbound connections to the rerouted port are dropped when the outbound trigger port is not being used.

PoS *   Point of Sale

POST *   Power-On Self Test. BIOS test of basic hardware performed during cold boot.

POST card/USB   Device that displays port 80h POST codes. Some are powered by USB cables, but USB does not pass these POST codes. They are transmitted via PCI, PCIe, miniPCI, miniPCIe, or parallel (LPT) ports.

POST code beeps   The POST routine in the BIOS/UEFI firmware might beep in various patterns to indicate errors with video, memory, CPU, or other components. A speaker must be connected to the front-panel speaker header pins on the motherboard to hear POST code beeps.

POTS *   Plain Old Telephone Service

power button   Button that turns on power to the system. Does not connect directly to the power supply, but to the motherboard.

power connections and types   Connections used on the motherboard, add-on cards, and drives to receive power. Types include 20-pin and 24-pin ATX, ATX12V, EPS12V, Molex, Berg, SATA, PCIe 6/8 pin, and others.

power light   Light that indicates power is being received. Might be on top or front of desktop computer, power jack, or AC adapter on laptop or tablet.

power options   OS settings for power usage.

Power over Ethernet injector   Adds power to an Ethernet cable so the cable can provide power as well as data to a PoE device.

power plan   Windows power management setting.

power supply   Converts high-voltage AC to low-voltage DC.

power supply tester   Checks to see if power supply is working or reaching proper voltage levels.

power surges   Short-term overvoltage. Can damage equipment.

power user   Windows user category that has permissions similar to an administrator. Supported for compatibility purposes in Windows Vista/7/8/8.1/10.

PowerShell   Windows command-prompt enhanced command and scripting language.

PPP *   Point-to-Point Protocol

PPTP *   Point-to-Point Tunneling Protocol

pre-installation environment   PE; OS environment that is used before system installation to prepare system for use. Can also be used to troubleshoot existing systems.

PRI *   Primary Rate Interface

primary partition   Disk partition that can be bootable; created with Disk Management in Windows, with DISKPART, or during OS installation.

principle of least privilege   Providing users with just enough permissions to perform ordinary tasks.

print head   Printhead. The printer component that places text or graphics on the paper. Found in impact and inkjet printers.

Print Management   A Windows tool used to manage network printers and print servers.

print queue   List of print jobs waiting to be sent to the printer.

print server   Server optimized for printing. Might be a network server, a self-contained device with its own IP address, or incorporated into a wired or wireless printer.

print sharing   Enabling a local printer to be used by other network clients.

print spooler   Windows service responsible for receiving print jobs and sending them to the printer.

printer   An output device that puts text and graphics on paper, labels, transparency media.

printer calibration   Adjusting the alignment and accuracy of color and monochrome output.

printer preferences   Printer settings such as quality, paper type, monochrome or color; details vary with printer.

printer properties   Printer management options such as sharing, port usage, security, spooling options, and availability.

printer ribbon   Contains ink or other materials that are transferred to the surface being printed. Used by impact, thermal transfer, and dye-sublimation printers.

printer sharing   Configuring a local printer so it can be used by others on a network.

privacy filters   Filter that fits over a screen to prevent anyone other than the user from seeing what is on the screen.

private   Not for public use, display, or knowledge.

private IP address   IP address that is not visible to the Internet.

private materials   Materials belonging to a client.

PRL *   Preferred Roaming List

processes   In Windows Task Manager, activities that are running on a computer, including program modules, program threads, and services.

professional titles   Doctor, Professor, Nurse, etc. These should be used when communicating with or about a client.

profile security requirements   In CompTIA A+ Certification Exam 220-902, refers to determining security settings needed for mobile devices.

programs   Applications, software.

Programs and Features   A Windows Control Panel subcategory used for uninstalling apps, turning Windows features on and off, viewing updates, and using program compatibility tools.

prohibited activity   Any activity that violates an organization's policies and procedures, specifically involving computers and mobile devices.

prohibited content   Any content found on computers or mobile devices that violates an organization's policies and procedures.

PROM *   Programmable Read-Only Memory

proper language   Language that is polite, appropriate, and germane to discussing the client's problems and possible solutions.

properly formatted boot drive with the correct partitions/format   Requirements for Windows OS drive configuration and layout, such as file system, partitioning method, location of user files, etc.

proprietary crash screens (BSOD/pinwheel)   General term for how an OS displays a crash, with an example for Windows (BSOD) and OS X (pinwheel).

protection from airborne particles   A requirement for technicians who will be working on cleaning out computers and peripherals, painting or refinishing chassis, or tearing down equipment.

protective covers/water proofing   Protective accessories for mobile devices.

proxy server   Server that caches Internet page requests, enabling a single page to be viewed by all of the devices requesting it. Reduces outbound traffic to the Internet and can also be used for filtering content.

proxy settings   Specific settings for the types of content using a proxy server and its IP address and port numbers.

ps   Linux and OS X Terminal command to view system processes.

PS/2 *   Personal System/2 Connector. A six-pin Mini-DIN port used for mice or keyboards.

PSTN *   Public Switched Telephone Network

PSU *   Power Supply Unit

public IP address   An IP address visible to the Internet.

public network setting   Windows network location setting that configures the Windows Firewall to protect against unsolicited inbound connections.

punchdown tool   Tool used to punch wire pairs into network connectors such as keystone modules, patch panels, and other receptacles for network cables.

punctuality   Arriving on-time or early for appointments or consultation.

PVC *   Permanent Virtual Circuit or Polyvinyl Chloride

pwd   Linux and OS X Terminal command for displaying the current working directory (folder).

PXE *   Preboot Execution Environment

QoS *   Quality of Service

quick format   Format command that clears the contents of the root folder (directory) on a storage device.

R

radio firmware   Firmware found in some smartphones which, when activated, can receive FM radio signals. Feature must be supported by mobile service provider.

RAID *   Redundant Array of Independent (or Inexpensive) Disks

RAID 0   Striping; data written across both drives; fast, but no protection against drive failure. Uses two drives.

RAID 1   Mirroring; data written simultaneously to both drives; if one drive fails, array can be rebuilt from the contents on the other drives. Uses two drives.

RAID 10   Four drives are set up as two mirrored pairs, with data striped across the pairs. If a drive fails, the array can be rebuilt from the other drives. Can also use additional pairs.

RAID 5   Three or more drives are used with data and parity information striped across all drives. If a drive fails, the array can be rebuilt from the other drives.

RAID array   All of the drives that are used in a particular RAID configuration.

RAM *   Random Access Memory. Volatile memory whose contents can be changed.

RAM slots   Slots (sockets) on a desktop or laptop motherboard for replacement or additional RAM (memory) modules.

ransomware   A type of malware that encrypts your drive(s) and requires you to pay a ransom (usually in a specified time), or the drives' contents will be lost.

rapid elasticity   A characteristic of cloud computing referring to how quickly and easily more or fewer cloud resources can be used or set aside as needed.

RAS *   Remote Access Service

RCA   A type of connector used for stereo audio connectors to a receiver, composite video, or SPDIF coaxial digital audio.

RD   Abbreviation for RMDIR, a Windows, Linux, or OS X Terminal/ command-prompt command for removing a directory (folder).

RDP *   Remote Desktop Protocol

Read/write failure   Storage error that can result from electronics failure, impact damage, cable damage, or other issues.

ReadyBoost   Windows feature that uses flash memory as a disk cache.

Recovery Console   A Windows XP recovery feature that consists of a special command-prompt session. It can be used to repair boot sectors, copy files between local storage devices, and run diagnostic tests. It can be installed as part of a Windows XP boot menu or run from the distribution media.

recovery partition   A common feature of Windows installations on computers sold at retail. It typically contains compressed files that can be used to create recovery media, or might allow recovery to run directly when a system cannot start normally.

refresh rate   Rate at which electron guns in the monitor's CRT repaint the picture onscreen; also called vertical refresh rate. It is measured in hertz (Hz).

Refresh/reset   Features in Windows 8/8.1/10 that are used for fixing systems that won't run properly. Refresh removes apps not obtained from the Windows Store, reinstalls Windows Store apps, but does not delete user files. Reset returns Windows to its as-installed condition, removing all apps installed after initial installation and user files. Reset is also used to prepare a system for repurposing or secure disposal.

REGEDIT   The Windows Registry Editor.

registry   Database of all hardware, software, and system settings in Windows.

REGSRV32   Windows command-line utility to re-register software components.

remediate   The process of restoring an infected computer to health.

Remote Assistance   A Windows feature that allows one user to invite another user to temporarily view the screen and control the first user's computer. Designed for troubleshooting and training.

remote backup   Backing up data to a remote location.

Remote Desktop Connection   Remote control app in Windows.

Remote Disc   OS X feature that enables an OS X computer that lacks an optical disc drive to use another computer's optical disc drive. Drivers available for Windows.

remote network installation   A Windows installation option that allows systems to boot to a network-located OS image and use it for installation.

remote printing   Printing to a printer via a remote connection (typically the Internet)

Remote settings   Windows Control Panel settings for Remote Desktop Connection and Remote Assistance

remote wipe   A mobile device security feature that can wipe a lost or stolen device.

renamed system files   A symptom of a malware infection; renamed files can prevent the system from running properly or from using built-in or third-party security tools.

repair disks   A bootable optical disc or USB drive that can be used to repair an OS.

repair installation   A Windows installation option in which the OS is installed over the same version to fix problems with the previous installation. Also known as an in-place upgrade.

repair/replacement   Options for defective hardware. When discussing these options with a client, be clear about the benefits and drawbacks of each so the client can make an informed decision.

repeater   Amplifies a network signal to enable it to run over longer cable than normal; hubs or switches also act as repeaters.

report through proper channels   Proper initial response to an incident involving prohibited content or activities.

repurposing   Preparing a computer or storage device for another use. Usually involves secure overwriting of existing information.

reset button   Button on front or top of a desktop computer that, when pushed, sends the Reset signal to the power supply for an immediate restart.

reset to factory default   Device has all user data, settings, and optional apps removed. Device works as if it has just been turned on.

resolution   The number of dots per inch (dpi) supported by a scanner or printer, or the number of pixels supported by a display.

resource pooling   Feature of cloud computing in which multiple clients share a pool of hardware, software, and services.

restore point   File that stores configuration information for the system. Created automatically or manually. Used by System Restore. Also stores older versions of data files in Windows Vista/7.

RF *   Radio Frequency

RFI *   Radio Frequency Interference

RFID badge   A device used in electronic security as a token. The badge is swiped past a receiver to permit the bearer access to a secure location.

RG-59   Coaxial cable used to distribute TV signals in a home or office. Replaced by RG-6.

RG-6   Coaxial cable used to distribute HDTV signals in a home or office. RG-6QS uses quad shielding for better signal quality over long runs.

RGB   Red, Green, Blue. Three additive primary colors used in electronic systems, displays, and projectors.

ribbon   Used by thermal transfer and dye-sublimation printers to print text or images onto media.

RIP *   Routing Information Protocol

RIS *   Remote Installation Service

RISC *   Reduced Instruction Set Computer

riser   A card or cable that extends expansion slot connections straight or at a 90-degree angle to make it possible to install cards that would normally not fit into a chassis.

RJ-11 *   Registered Jack Function 11

RJ-45 *   Registered Jack Function 45

rm   Linux and OS X Terminal command for removing files and directories (folders).

RMA *   Returned Materials Authorization

ROBOCOPY   Windows file copying utility with mirroring and logging capabilities. Replaces XCOPY with more options.

rogue antivirus   A malware program that masquerades as a legitimate antivirus program.

roller   A component in a printer that helps move the paper or media through the printer.

ROM *   Read-Only Memory

root access   Provides full access to a device's file system, apps, and other features. Android apps downloaded outside the Google Play store could provide unauthorized root access to the developer.

root hub   Hosts USB ports on a PC.

rootkit   Malware designed to gain administrative-level control of a computer.

rotating/removable screens   A feature of 2-in-1 devices that can be used as tablets or laptops.

router   Device that routes data from one network to another. Often integrated with wireless access points and switches.

RPM   Revolutions per minute.

RS-232   *See* serial port.

RTC *   Real-Time Clock

run as administrator   A requirement for some Windows apps and administrative tools. Also known as run with elevated privileges.

S

S/MIME   A standard for secure e-mail connectivity.

SaaS   Software as a Service. Software programs that can be run from the cloud without downloading an app. Examples include Google Docs and Microsoft Word Online, Excel Online, etc.

SAN *   Storage Area Network

SAS *   Serial Attached SCSI

SATA *   Serial Advanced Technology Attachment; this version of ATA uses thin data and power cables to transmit data serially at rates of 1.5Gbps, 3.0Gbps, 6.0Gbps, and 16Gbps (SATA Express).

SATA1   CompTIA term for first-generation SATA with a 1.5Gbps maximum transfer rate.

SATA2   CompTIA term for second-generation SATA with a 3.0Gbps maximum transfer rate.

SATA3   CompTIA term for second-generation SATA with a 6.0Gbps maximum transfer rate.

SC *   Subscription Channel

scan   In technology, describes the process of looking for threats (spyware, malware, viruses); using a device to read barcodes; using a device to convert a photo or document into a file using a copier-like device.

scanner   A device used to read barcodes; a device used to convert photos or documents into files.

scope of the problem   The goal of open-ended questions is to define this as narrowly as possible to help find the solution.

SCP *   Secure Copy Protection

screen calibration   A program on a mobile device that verifies the three axes (left to right, up and down, and back to front) are calibrated properly.

Screen lock   A pattern drawn on the display, a PIN (passcode), or a password, used to make a mobile device inaccessible to other people.

Screen Sharing   An OS X feature used for remote control.

Screwdriver   A versatile tool that can be used to remove and attach screws and bolts from desktop, laptop, and mobile devices. Multiple removable bits and standard and jeweler's screwdriver sizes are needed to handle the broadest range of jobs.

SCSI *   Small Computer System Interface. A flexible interface usable for hard and optical drives, scanners, and other devices. Narrow SCSI interfaces enables daisy-chaining of 7 devices to a single port. Wide SCSI enables daisy-chaining of up to 15 devices to a single port.

SD Card *   Secure Digital Card

SCSI ID *   Small Computer System Interface Identifier.

SDK/APK   System Development Kit. The software needed to develop an app for an operating system. Android users also need the Android Packaging Kit to package Android apps for distribution. SDKs are available from OS vendors. The APK is available from Google.

SDRAM   Synchronous DRAM. Fast RAM synchronized to the motherboard's clock speed; typical speeds of 66MHz, 100MHz, and 133MHz.

SDSL   Synchronous DSL. A type of DSL connection in which upload and download speeds are the same. SDSL connections are marketed to business rather than to home users and almost always require a newly installed circuit to the location and professional installation. *See also* DSL, ADSL.

SEC *   Single Edge Connector.

Secure Boot   A feature of Windows 8/8.1/10 that uses the UEFI specification to prevent unsigned OS versions from being booted. Must be disabled in UEFI firmware if the user wants to install another OS.

security alert   An alert displayed in the taskbar by Windows when a security issue has been noted. Note that many malware apps display fake security alert dialogs in an attempt to infect a system.

security best practices   General term for desirable security procedures. For example, locking a system keyboard when away, updating anti-malware and antivirus apps, not opening e-mails with attachments from unknown senders, etc.

Security Center   A Control Panel feature in Windows Vista that displayed alerts when potential security threats were detected. Replaced by Action Center starting with Windows 7.

self-grounding   Touching metal on a nearby object to trigger ESD before picking up an electronic component. Used if ESD mats or wristbands are not available.

self-powered hub   Uses AC adapter; provides full power specified for USB port type(s) supported.

separate pad   Separation pad, separator pad. Component found in laser printers as part of the paper feed path and typically included as part of a maintenance kit.

serial port   A serial communication physical interface (also known as COM port) through which information transfers in or out one bit at a time. The RS-232 standard is commonly used to transmit data through DB-9 ports.

server   Computer that shares drives and other resources over a network. Peer servers can also be used as workstations; dedicated servers provide services to other computers such as file, print, e-mail, and so on.

Services   Processes that run in the background on Windows, OS X, and Linux for tasks such as print spooling, wireless networking, and many others.

SERVICES.MSC   Windows CMC snap-in for viewing and managing services.

set-top box   General term for any device used with a TV or HDTV for video, such as a Blu-ray player, cable TV box, or streaming media player.

SFC *   System File Checker

SFF *   Small Form Factor

Shadow Copy   Windows Vista/7 feature that uses restore points to store older versions of files. Replaced by File History in Windows 8/8.1/10.

share permissions   File/folder permissions set through the Share/Share with dialog in Windows/File Explorer.

Shell/Terminal OS X or Linux command-line environment.

shoulder surfing Direct observation techniques used to gain information about a user, document, or computer system.

Shrink (volume) The process of reducing a volume in size to make room for another operating system. Can be performed using Windows Disk Management or command-line DISKPART tools. In OS X, use Disk Utility. In Linux, use the GParted partition editor or other tools.

SHUTDOWN Shuts down the current computer session, logs off all users, and turns off the power. Can be run from the Windows command prompt, with Linux, or OS X Terminal.

SID Security identifier. A unique name assigned to an object such as a user or computer.

sidebar Location for gadgets in Windows Vista. User can select the gadgets to display and their transparency.

side-by-side apps A feature of Windows 8/8.1/10 that permits a mixture of Metro UI and standard Windows apps to run side-by-side on the Windows desktop.

simple volume Windows disk structure similar to a primary partition but resizable. Up to four simple volumes can exist on a drive; the fourth volume will be created as an extended partition containing one or more logical drives.

single sign-on SSO. *See* mutual authentication for multiple services.

single-mode fiber Fiber-optic cable designed to carry a signal for many miles. More difficult to work with than multi-mode fiber.

SiSoftware Sandra A third-party system analysis program that provides extensive technical information on a computer's hardware.

slang Unofficial names for technology, events, people, and locations. Undesirable trait when dealing with clients.

SLC Single level cell; flash memory type most often used in SSDs.

sleep/suspend Low-power settings that turn off most operations in a computer.

SLI * Scalable Link Interface or System Level Integration or Scanline Interleave Mode

slow system performance Can be caused by incorrect configuration of swap files, too many startup programs, too many programs open, not enough RAM, not enough free disk space, too slow a CPU for the apps being used.

S.M.A.R.T. * Self-Monitoring, Analysis, and Reporting Technology

smart cache   Intel term for CPU cache shared among all processor cores.

smart camera   A point-and-shoot camera that uses the Android OS.

smart card   A security token used for access to secure areas, websites, or servers.

smart card reader   Card reader that can be built into a laptop or connected via USB for reading smart cards.

Smart TV   An HDTV with network capabilities and support for streaming content such as Netflix.

smart watches   A watch that connects with a mobile device, typically to act as a relay for notifications, a health monitor, and sometimes as a phone.

smartphones   Phones that have CPUs and RAM, run apps, and support Android or iOS or Windows Mobile OS.

SMB *   Server Message Block or Small to Midsize Business

SMTP *   Simple Mail Transfer Protocol. A common Internet standard for uploading or sending e-mail.

SNMP *   Simple Network Management Protocol

social engineering   The act of obtaining confidential information by manipulating people.

social media   Apps such as Facebook, Twitter, Instagram, and others.

social media data   Usernames, messages, and data from these services are among the user data that is removed from a mobile device during a hard reset (factory reset) operation.

Socket AM3   AMD PGA socket; supports CPUs with dual-channel DDR2 or DDR3 memory controller; 941 pin connectors.

Socket AM3+   AMD PGA socket; supports CPUs with up to eight cores; 942 pin connectors.

Socket FM1   AMD PGA socket; supports first-generation (Llano) AMD APUs with up to four cores. Has 905 pin connectors.

Socket FM2   AMD PGA socket; supports second-generation (Trinity) and third-generation (Richland) AMD APUs with up to four cores. Has 904 pin connectors.

Socket FM2+   AMD PGA socket; supports Kaveri and Godavari APUs with up to four cores; also supports chips used in Socket FM2. Has 906 pin connectors.

SoDIMM *   Small Outline DIMM (Also spelled SODIMM). A compact version of the standard DIMM module, available in various pinouts for use in notebook and laptop computers and laser printers.

soft reset   Shutting down a mobile device and restarting it.

software   Computer instructions (apps, drivers, games) that can be stored locally or in the cloud and run using the CPU and RAM in the computer.

software update   A process that installs patches to the OS or installed applications.

SOHO *   Small Office, Home Office

solid state/flash drives boot   A solid state drive (SSD) looks like a hard disk drive to the BIOS/UEFI firmware and is prepared using the same installation process as a hard disk drive. To enable a USB flash drive as a bootable device, a special process must be used to install an OS image on the drive. Whichever drive is used for booting, it must be placed in the boot sequence before other drives, which could prevent the system from booting.

sound   Can be reproduced on a computer by using a sound card, onboard audio, or a USB adapter.

South Bridge   The chipset component responsible for interfacing with slower devices.

sound card   An add-on card designed for digital sound recording and playback. Plugs into a PCI or PCIe x1 slot.

SP *   Service Pack

spam   Unwanted e-mail.

SPDIF *   Sony/Philips Digital Interface; digital audio standard for interfacing sound cards or onboard sound hardware to a digital amplifier.

speaker   Audio output device. Be sure to select the correct speaker output if both analog (mini-jack) and digital (SPDIF, HDMI, or DisplayPort) outputs are available.

spear phishing   Variation on phishing that involves the use of forged e-mails that appear to request confidential organization information (payroll, ID, etc.) from a member of the organization.

special thermal paper   Heat-sensitive paper used in direct thermal (no ribbon) printing.

SPGA *   Staggered Pin Grid Array

split (volume)   Turning a single volume/partition into two or more. Requires that the volume/partition be shrunk and a new volume (partition) be created in the unallocated space.

spontaneous shutdown/restart   Indicates a serious computer problem. Can result from Windows being configured for automatic restart after a STOP error or from a power supply whose Power Good voltage is not within limits.

spoofing   An e-mail or app pretends to be from a trustworthy source, but is actually coming from an attack on your system.

Spotlight   OS X search tool.

spyware   A type of malware that collects computer and user information without the owner's consent or knowledge.

SRAM *   Static Random Access Memory. Static RAM. RAM based on transistors; requires electricity far less often than DRAM; too expensive and bulky to use as main RAM but popular for use as cache RAM.

SSD   Solid state drive; a hard drive that uses flash memory instead of magnetic storage platters.

SSH *   Secure Shell

SSID *   Service set identifier is a user-friendly name that identifies a wireless network.

SSID broadcast   By default, wireless routers and access points broadcast their SSIDs. This feature can be turned off, which requires users to enter the SSID as well as the encryption key to connect.

SSL *   Secure Sockets Layer. Predecessor of TLS. Used for securing online transactions.

ST *   Straight Tip

standard format   Clears the root folder (directory) of a drive. However, data can still be recovered from the drive.

standard thick client   A computer used to run locally stored and locally processed applications.

standard user   User who has access to information in the personal folder and can run normal apps. Cannot run processes that will affect the system. Lower privileges than an administrator.

Standby   A low-power state that could be selected in older editions of Windows for use when the system was idle. Replaced by sleep mode.

star topology   Network topology in which a central hub or switch is connected to individual workstations with separate cables. This topology is used by Ethernet networks that use TP cables. Wireless networks also use this topology but substitute a wireless access point in place of a hub or switch and radio waves in place of cables.

Start screen   Windows 8/8.1 startup dialog. Uses tiles and is optimized for touch (although it also supports mice). Replaced in Windows 10 by a Start menu with optional tablet mode.

Startup   A tab in Microsoft System Configuration (MSConfig) that enables or disables startup programs.

static IP address   A specific IP address assigned to a device. Not assigned by a DHCP server.

STOP error   Also known as Blue Screen of Death. A Windows error that forces the system to halt until resolved. Systems can be configured to restart automatically after a STOP error or to leave it onscreen.

STP *   Shielded Twisted Pair

streaks   On a laser printer, can be caused by a damaged imaging drum or toner cartridge or by dirty rollers. With other printers, suggests dirty rollers in the paper path.

strong password   A password that has a mixture of alphanumeric characters, punctuation marks, no words, and over-the-minimum length.

su   Linux and OS X Terminal command to switch users.

subnet mask   IP v4 network addressing feature to specify how much of the IP address is the host address and the extended network address.

sudo   Linux and OS X Terminal command to run a command as administrator.

S-Video   Separate Video. An analog video standard used in many VCR and DVD products for input and output of video signals. Some older video cards use S-video for their TV outputs. Can be down-converted to composite video by using an adapter.

SuperSpeed USB   USB 3.0 ports and devices.

SuperSpeed+ USB   USB 3.1 ports and devices.

surround sound audio   Audio that uses more speakers than stereo. Typically 5.1 or 7.1 (five speakers or seven speakers plus subwoofer).

surge suppressor   A device that absorbs overvoltage conditions such as spikes and surges to prevent damage to connected devices.

SVGA   Super Video Graphics Array or Super VGA. May refer to 800x600 VGA resolution or to any VGA display setting that uses more than 16 colors or a higher resolution than 640x480.

swipe lock   Swiping the screen of a mobile device to lock it.

switch   Network device that sets a direct path for data to run from one system to another; can be combined with a router or wireless access point; faster than a hub because it supports the full bandwidth of the network at each port, rather than subdividing the bandwidth among active ports as a hub does.

SXGA *   Super Extended Graphics Array

synchronization   The matching up of files and other data between one computing device and another.

synchronize to the cloud   Matching local files and files in cloud storage. Performed by cloud backup apps such as iCloud.

synchronize to the desktop   Matching local files on a mobile device and on a laptop or desktop. Performed by apps such as iTunes.

System   Can refer to a computer or to the properties sheet in Windows.

system board   Motherboard.

System Configuration   MSConfig utility in Windows; configures startup, boot settings, services, startup apps, and provides access to tools.

system fan connectors   Connectors on the motherboard that provide power and speed monitoring to case fans and sometimes the power supply fan.

system files and folders   Files used by the OS. For example, files in the \Windows folder and subfolders.

System Image Manager   A Windows tool that enables you to create answer files for unattended installations.

System Information   A Microsoft Windows application that displays information about a computer's operating system, hardware, and environment (MSINFO32.exe).

system lockout   When a user is unable to log into a system because the password is forgotten or unknown.

system lockups   System is completely unresponsive; usually caused by overheating leading to corrupted memory contents.

System Protection   System Restore settings in Windows.

system recovery options   Special startup options that can be used to fix a Windows installation that isn't working, including Startup Repair, System Restore, special boot options, and others.

System Restore   Windows feature that enables a system to be returned to a previous condition.

system utilities   Commands in Windows that help manage and troubleshoot the system, such as MSINFO32, DXDIAG, NOTEPAD, and others.

T

T568A   TP wiring standard that uses the following wires from pin 1 to 8: green stripe, green, orange stripe, blue, blue stripe, orange, brown stripe, brown.

T568B   TP wiring standard that uses the following wires from 1 to 8: orange stripe, orange, green stripe, blue, blue stripe, green, brown stripe, brown.

tablets   A mobile device with a larger screen than a smartphone and usually without cellular support. Some can be converted into laptop-like devices by adding keyboards.

tailgating   Also known as piggybacking. When a person tags along behind another person to gain entry to a restricted area.

tape drive   A drive that makes backups of a system or selected files with magnetic tape.

TASKKILL   A Windows command-line utility to shut down a specified process.

TASKLIST   A Windows command-line utility to list processes.

Task Manager   Windows interface for viewing and managing running programs, processes, services, and other information.

TB *   Terabyte

TCP *   Transmission Control Protocol

TCP/IP *   Transmission Control Protocol/Internet Protocol. The Internet's standard network protocol that is now becoming the standard for all networks.

TDR *   Time Domain Reflectometer

Terminal   The primary interface for Linux commands. Also used in OS X.

tethering   The process of sharing a cellular data connection with another device via USB.

texting   Sending or receiving texts while working with a client is unacceptable behavior unless it is intended to help solve the problem and the customer is informed.

TFTP *   Trivial File Transfer Protocol

theme   Windows term for the combination of desktop wallpaper, color scheme, and sound effects.

thermal compound   A material sandwiched between a device and a heat sink to provide the best possible heat transfer from the device to the heat sink.

thermal paste   Material placed between the heat sink and the CPU to draw heat away from the CPU. Might be preapplied or applied by the technician.

thermal printer   A printer that uses heat to print text or graphics.

thermal transfer   Thermal printer technology that uses a heated wax or resin ribbon.

thick client   A computer that is suitable for running locally stored office apps, e-mail, and web browsing; meets or exceeds OS recommendations.

thin client   A computer used to access network stored and processed applications; meets minimum OS requirements.

Thunderbolt   Intel-developed ultra high-speed I/O interface in three versions: 10Gbps (Thunderbolt 1); 20Gbps (Thunderbolt 2); 40Gbps (Thunderbolt 3). Used widely by Apple and by some high-performance PCs.

Time Machine   OS X backup app.

Time/date/region/language settings   Settings that localize an OS and are made during the installation process.

timeline   How long it is expected the service or installation process will take. Keeping the customer informed of changes reflects professional behavior.

timeout   Amount of time after a mobile system is idle until the screen locks.

tokens   A physical object used as part of a security system, such as a smart card, an RFID chip, etc.

Tone generator and probe   A network cable testing device.

toner   What laser printers use for printing.

TN   Twisted Nematic. A fast, low-cost LCD screen design optimized for gaming, but with narrower viewing angles than IPS.

TKIP *   Temporal Key Integrity Protocol

touch screen   Touchscreen. Touch-sensitive display standard on smartphones and tablets. Also widely used on All-in-One PCs, laptops, and convertible (2-in-1) mobile devices.

touchpad   Most common type of pointing device installed in laptops. All emulate mice, but most recent models also support multitouch. Wireless touchpads can also be used in place of a mouse.

toxic waste handling   Obsolete computer hardware can contain lead solder, mercury (CCFL backlights), and other toxins. Use an authorized electronics recycling center to avoid putting this material in landfills.

TLS   Transport Layer Security. Successor of SSL. A cryptographic protocol that provides security and data integrity for communications over networks such as the Internet.

TPM *   Trusted Platform Module

TRACERT   Windows command-line utility for tracing the path from the user location to the IP address or URL specified.

Tracking of evidence/documenting process   Important parts of the chain of custody process.

tractor feed   Paper feed mechanism used on impact printers.

transfer belt   Ink transfer device used in color laser printers.

transfer roller   Part of the transferring mechanism on some laser printers.

triple channel (RAM)   Three identical memory modules addressed as a single logical unit.

Trojan (trojan horse)   A file or program that appears to be legitimate but is used to steal information or gain backdoor access to a computer.

troubleshooting   The process of determining the solution to a problem and documenting the solution.

trusted sources   App stores for Android (Google Play), iOS (Apple App Store), OS X (Apple Mac Store), Windows (Windows Store).

TV tuner   A device that can receive analog or digital TV from over-the-air or cable TV sources for live playback or storage for later viewing.

U–V

UAC *   User Account Control. A security component of Windows that controls how users gain access to resources.

UDF *   User Defined Functions or Universal Disk Format or Universal Data Format

UDP *   User Datagram Protocol

UEFI *   Unified Extensible Firmware Interface

unattended installation   Windows installation process that does not require user intervention to complete.

UNC *   Universal Naming Convention

uninstall/reinstall apps   Process to fix issues with unstable/not working mobile apps.

uninstall/reinstall/repair   Process to fix issues with unstable/not working desktop or laptop apps.

untrusted sources   Software not from the OS app store, from unfamiliar publishers, or not digitally signed.

upgrade Process of installing improved OS, app, or driver files.

UPnP Universal Plug and Play; LAN protocols to allow discovery and use of streaming media sources.

UPS * Uninterruptible Power Supply

URL * Uniform Resource Locator

USB * Universal Serial Bus. High-speed replacement for older I/O ports USB 1.1 has a peak speed of 12Mbps. USB 2.0 has a peak speed of 480Mbps; USB 2.0 ports also support USB 1.1 devices. USB 2.0 devices can be plugged into USB 1.1 devices but run at only USB 1.1 speeds. USB 3.0 runs at 5Gbps; supports older USB devices at the native speeds of those devices. USB 3.1 Gen 2 runs at 10Gbps and is compatible with USB 3.0, 2.0, and 1.1 devices (USB 3.1 Gen 1 is the same as USB 3.0).

USB boot Booting from a USB device such as a flash drive.

USB connector type A Standard connector on a root hub or external hub.

USB connector type B Standard connector on a USB device.

USB connector type micro Smallest USB connector. USB-on-the-Go devices use a Micro B connector.

USB connector type mini Medium-size USB connector. Five-pin Type B version most common.

USB Optical Drive Optical drive that connects to a USB port.

USB tethering When a mobile device shares its Internet connection with other Wi-Fi capable devices via USB.

USB to Bluetooth Bluetooth transceiver that plugs into a USB port.

USB to RJ-45 dongle Adapts Ethernet cable to connect to a USB port.

USB to Wi-Fi dongle Wi-Fi transceiver that plugs into a USB port.

user *See* standard user.

User Account Control UAC. Windows Vista feature that blocks unauthorized system-wide changes. Improved in Windows 7/8/8.1/10.

user accounts Accounts with standard permissions.

user authentication Security procedures to verify the identity of a user.

USMT * User State Migration Tool

UTP * Unshielded Twisted Pair

UXGA * Ultra Extended Graphics Array

vacuum cleaner   Specialized vacuum cleaners are needed to clean up toner spills.

vendor-specific   Ports that are not standard. For example, the charging connections on some tablets.

ventilation   Airflow through a system or workspace.

Vertical lines   In printing, indicates problems with toner cartridge or feed rollers.

VESA *   Video Electronics Standards Association

VFAT *   Virtual File Allocation Table

VGA *   Video Graphics Array. First popular analog video standard; basis for all current video cards.

vi   Linux and OS X Terminal text editor.

video capture   The process of capturing live video from analog or digital sources and storing it as a computer file.

video card   A video card (also known as display adapter or graphics card) is an expansion card that generates video signal and displays it on a monitor.

view hidden files   Setting in Windows File Explorer/Windows Explorer folder options. Recommended option when troubleshooting a system.

view options   Setting in Windows File Explorer/Windows Explorer. Select thumbnail size, file details, and others.

violations of security best practices   Refusing to follow procedures to protect a system, the network, the organization.

virtual assistant   Windows Cortana, iOS Siri, Android Hey Google; voice-activated search tools.

Virtual Machine   VM. A workspace created by a VMM or hypervisor that imitates a computer.

virtual memory   Disk space used as a substitute for RAM.

virtual printer   A program or service that works through the printer menu to create a file.

Virtual XP mode   Virtual Windows XP Mode. A free virtualized copy of Windows XP Professional available to Windows 7 Business and Ultimate to help ease transition from Windows 7.

virtualization   Creating an environment in which operating systems or applications run on a software-created simulation of a computer rather than directly on the computer hardware itself.

virtualization support   Hardware-assisted virtualization. BIOS/UEFI and CPU support for virtualization.

virus   Computer program designed to infect a computer and make unwanted modifications to the operating system. If executed, the virus can replicate itself; in this way it resembles a Trojan horse that can also replicate itself to other computers.

VM *   Virtual Machine

VoIP *   Voice over Internet Protocol. Delivery of voice communications over IP networks such as the Internet.

voltage   Electrical potential measured in volts. Can be measured with multimeters or other test equipment or observed in the PC Health or System Monitor feature in BIOS/UEFI.

VPN *   Virtual Private Network

VRAM *   Video Random-Access Memory

W–Z

Wake-on-LAN   WoL. Network option in which a system in sleep mode is awakened by receiving a "magic packet" from the network.

WAN *   Wide area network. Network that spans multiple cities, countries, or continents. Network sections might be linked by leased line, Internet backbone, or satellite feed; routers connect LANs to WANs and WAN segments to each other.

WAP *   Wireless Access Protocol or Wireless Access Point. A device that enables connectivity between computers with wireless network adapters to create a wireless network.

wattage   Power measurement used to determine the appropriate size of a UPS or a power supply. Also used to measure the thermal design power of a CPU so that an adequate cooling solution can be used.

wearable technology devices   Devices such as watches, wristbands, and goggles that communicate with a host mobile device or computer to measure health, transmit or receive data, or other uses.

web server   A server that distributes web pages.

webcam   A video camera designed for live chat sessions. Resolutions range from sub-VGA to 1080p HD.

WEP *   Wired equivalent privacy. An older wireless network security standard, succeeded by WPA.

Wi-Fi *   Wireless Fidelity. Also spelled WiFi.

Wi-Fi analyzer   Device or app that detects Wi-Fi signals and determines signal strength.

Wi-Fi antenna   Internal or external antennas on a router, access point, laptop, or network adapter that send and receive Wi-Fi signals.

Wi-Fi calling   A feature in iOS that permits telephone calls when a Wi-Fi Internet connection is available.

wildcard   Characters used as variables in command-line operations such as DIR, DEL, or COPY and in searches. * = any characters and ? = any single character.

Windows   Microsoft Windows operating system. Versions covered in the 220-901 and 902 exams include Windows Vista/7/8/8.1 and Windows Mobile. Notes on Windows 10 have been added to this book whenever applicable.

Windows Aero   Windows Vista/7 3D desktop with translucent windows.

Windows Deployment Services   Program run by Windows Server 2012 and 2012 R2 that enables remote installation of operating systems.

Windows Easy Transfer   File transfer app included in Windows Vista/7/8 to help upgrade to a newer version of Windows. Not included in Windows 8.1 or 10.

Windows Explorer   File management interface for Windows desktop. Replaced by File Explorer in Windows 8 and later.

Windows Firewall   Built-in feature to block unwanted inbound traffic. Used in Advanced mode, it can also be used to block unwanted outbound traffic.

Windows Memory Diagnostics   Windows utility to test onboard RAM before loading the desktop. Offers a variety of test options and can be run repeatedly as desired.

Windows Recovery Environment (WinRE)   Windows Vista/7/8/8.1/10 collection of automatic and user-operated repair and diagnostic tools for fixing problems with systems that won't start.

Windows Store   Trusted source for software for Windows 8/8.1/10.

Windows Update   Updates Windows. If updates for other products from Microsoft enabled, it is known as Microsoft Update.

Windows Upgrade Advisor   Tool available in several versions from Microsoft to help users determine if their systems are ready to upgrade to the next version of Windows.

Windows Virtual PC   Virtualization environment supported in Windows 7 Professional, Ultimate, and Enterprise. Required by Windows XP Mode. In Windows 8, Windows 8.1, and Windows 10, Hyper-V replaces Windows Virtual PC.

Windows XP Mode   Virtualized installation of Windows XP Professional; runs under Windows Virtual PC.

WINS *   Windows Internet Name Service. Method sometimes used by Server versions of Windows to dynamically match NetBIOS computer names to their IP addresses (NetBIOS name resolution).

wire stripper   Tool used to prepare raw coaxial or TP cable for assembly into a finished cable.

wired (network)   Ethernet network.

wireless (network)   Usually Wi-Fi, but can also refer to Bluetooth network.

wireless card   Wi-Fi adapter. Can also refer to a USB-based wireless adapter.

wireless locator   App or device that locates wireless networks.

wireless   Synonym for Wi-Fi or Wireless Ethernet network.

WLAN *   Wireless Local Area Network

Work (network setting)   Windows firewall location setting in Windows 7. Configures network as private, discoverable, but does not support Windows homegroup networking.

workgroup   A network that does not use a domain controller. Each computer can share or not share folders or printers with others. Unless password-protected sharing is disabled, anyone wanting to use a different computer's resources must have an account on that system.

worm   A computer worm is a self-replicating type of malware similar to a virus but without the need for a user to execute it. It often uses a network to spread itself.

WOL   *See* Wake-on-LAN.

WPA *   Wi-Fi Protected Access. A security protocol developed by the Wi-Fi Alliance to secure wireless networking. Takes the place of WEP. Uses the TKIP encryption protocol.

WPA2   Wi-Fi Protected Access version 2. A security protocol developed by the Wi-Fi Alliance to secure wireless networking using the AES encryption protocol. Takes the place of WPA.

WPS *   Wi-Fi Protected Setup

WUXGA *   Wide Ultra Extended Graphics Array

WWAN   Wireless Wide Area Network (cellular data network)

WXGA   Wide XGA. A common widescreen graphics resolution for laptops and some displays.

x64   64-bit extension to x86 processor architecture; backward compatible; supports more than 4GB of RAM.

x86   32-bit processor architecture used by AMD and Intel CPUs.

XCOPY   Command-line utility for copying files and folders.

xD   Short for xD-Picture Card, a now-obsolete flash memory card used by Olympus and Fujifilm digital cameras.

XGA   eXtended Graphics Array. 1024 × 768 display standard that is a minimum requirement for most Windows programs.

Yahoo!   A popular search and e-mail provider.

zero-day attack   An attack on a newly discovered computer or device vulnerability.

ZIF *   Zero Insertion Force

ZIP *   Zig-zag Inline Package

zombie/botnet   A zombie is a computer that has been taken over by a hacker or malware. When a group of zombie computers are controlled by a single malware process, the result is a botnet.

Index

Symbols

A

T

X

Y

Z